THE OXFORD HANDBOOK OF

THE
MEROVINGIAN
WORLD

THE OXFORD HANDBOOK OF

THE

MEROVINGIAN

WORLD

Edited by

BONNIE EFFROS

and

ISABEL MOREIRA

OXFORD
UNIVERSITY PRESS

OXFORD
UNIVERSITY PRESS

Oxford University Press is a department of the University of Oxford. It furthers
the University's objective of excellence in research, scholarship, and education
by publishing worldwide. Oxford is a registered trade mark of Oxford University
Press in the UK and certain other countries.

Published in the United States of America by Oxford University Press
198 Madison Avenue, New York, NY 10016, United States of America.

Library of Congress Cataloging-in-Publication Data
Names: Effros, Bonnie, 1965– editor, author. | Moreira, Isabel, editor, author.
Title: The Oxford handbook of the Merovingian world / Bonnie Effros and Isabel Moreira, editors.
Description: New York : Oxford University Press, [2020] | Includes
bibliographical references and index. | Summary: "The Merovingian era is
one of the best studied yet least known periods of European history.
From the fifth to the eighth centuries, the inhabitants of Gaul (what
now comprises France, southern Belgium, Luxembourg, Rhineland Germany
and part of modern Switzerland), a mix of Gallo-Romans and Germanic
arrivals under the political control of the Merovingian dynasty, sought
to preserve, use, and reimagine the political, cultural, and religious
power of ancient Rome while simultaneously forging the beginnings of
what would become medieval European culture and identity"— Provided by publisher.
Identifiers: LCCN 2020021241 (print) | LCCN 2020021242 (ebook) |
ISBN 9780190234188 (hardback) | ISBN 9780197510803 (epub)
Subjects: LCSH: Merovingians—History—Handbooks, manuals, etc. |
Merovingians—Antiquities—Handbooks, manuals, etc. |
Gaul—History—Handbooks, manuals, etc. | Gaul—Antiquities—Handbooks,
manuals, etc. | France—History—To 987—Handbooks, manuals, etc.
Classification: LCC DC65 .O97 2020 (print) | LCC DC65 (ebook) | DDC 944/.013—dc23
LC record available at https://lccn.loc.gov/2020021241
LC ebook record available at https://lccn.loc.gov/2020021242

3 5 7 9 8 6 4 2

Printed by Sheridan Books, Inc., United States of America

TABLE OF CONTENTS

INTRODUCTION

PART I MEROVINGIAN HISTORIOGRAPHY AND THE HISTORY OF ARCHAEOLOGY

PART II EXPRESSING IDENTITY

PART V MEROVINGIAN WRITTEN CULTURE

PART VI MEROVINGIAN LANDSCAPES

PART VII ECONOMIES, EXCHANGE, AND PRODUCTION

PART VIII THE SUPERNATURAL AND THE AFTERLIFE

ACKNOWLEDGMENTS

....

This collection of essays first came into being in spring 2014, when Stefan Vranka suggested that we undertake a handbook on all things Merovingian and we began recruitment for the current volume. We wish to thank Stefan and the staff of OUP in New York and around the globe for their support over the past six years and for giving the two us (Isabel and Bonnie) the opportunity to work together and renew a friendship that first began at a conference in Toronto in 1995. We would also like to offer great thanks to our wonderful contributors who, despite often being not just in different countries but on different continents, have not complained (at least to us) about our regular requests and emails over the past years and have been so supportive when we have needed additional assistance to complete the volume in question. In particular, we would like to thank Jamie Kreiner and Simon Loseby for their help fine-tuning some of our translations and Guy Halsall, who generously offered to provide us with an extra essay (which in the end we did not require). Given the challenges of finishing volume production in the midst of the global Covid-19 pandemic, we are especially grateful to Mike Humphreys who did the heavy lifting to start our index, and to Max Laber who took his first steps into the publishing world and added detail to some of the largest entries. We also thank Justin Sorensen (GIS Services) at the J. Willard Marriott Library, Salt Lake City, Utah, who helped us create the volume's map, and Thulasiraman Venkatesan (SPi Global) for his assistance and patience in the layout of the Merovingian family tree at the front of the volume.

We are grateful to our respective families for their patience, love, and support during the six years of editorial work for this volume. It is to them that we dedicate this book.

List of Abbreviations

AASS	Bollandus, J. et al. (eds.), Acta sanctorum quotquot toto orbe coluntur..., (Brussels, 1643–).
CCSL	Corpus Christianorum Series Latina (Turnhout, 1965–).
CIFM	*Corpus des inscriptions de la France médiévale* (Poitiers/Paris, 1974–).
CIL	*Corpus Inscriptionum Latinarum* (Berlin, 1893–).
CIMAH	*Corpus Inscriptionum Medii Aevi Helvetiae* (Freiburg, 1977–).
DHL	Gregory of Tours, *Decem libri historiarum*.
GC	Gregory of Tours, *Liber in gloria confessorum*.
ICERV	Vives, J. (ed.), *Inscripciones Cristianas de la España Romana y Visigoda* (Barcelona, 1942).
ICG	Le Blant, E. (ed.), *Inscriptions chrétiennes de la Gaule antérieures au VIIIᵉ siècle* (Paris, 1856–1865).
ILCV	Diehl, E. (ed.), *Inscriptiones Latinae Christianae Veteres* (Berlin, 1925–1931).
ILTG	Wuilleumier, P. (ed.), *Inscriptions latines des Trois Gaules* (Paris, 1963).
LHF	*Liber Historiae Francorum.*
MGH	Monumenta Germaniae Historica (Hanover, 1826–).
AA	Scriptores, Auctores antiquissimi
EE	Epistulae
DD	Diplomata regum francorum e stirpe merovingica
LL nat. Germ.	Leges nationum Germanicarum
SRG	Scriptores rerum Germanicarum
SRM	Scriptores rerum Merovingicarum
NR	Le Blant, E. (ed.), *Nouveau Recueil des inscriptions chrétiennes de la Gaule antérieures au VIIIᵉ siècle* (Paris, 1892).
PL	Migne, J.-P. (ed.), *Patrologiae cursus completus: Series Latina.* (Paris, 1844–1864).
PLRE	Jones, A. H. M. et al. (eds.), *Prosopography of the Later Roman Empire* (Cambridge, 1971–1992).
RICG	Gauthier, N. et al. (eds.), *Recueil des inscriptions chrétiennes de la Gaule antérieures à la Renaissance carolingienne* (1975–).
VP	Gregory of Tours, *Liber vitae patrum.*

List of Contributors

Editors
Bonnie Effros, University of Liverpool
Isabel Moreira, University of Utah

Contributors
Jonathan J. Arnold, University of Tulsa
Lisa Kaaren Bailey, University of Auckland
Maude Barme, Centre de recherche archéologique de la Vallée de l'Oise (CRAVO)
Michel Bonifay, Aix Marseille Univ, CNRS, CCJ, Aix-en-Provence, France
Luc Bourgeois, Université de Caen Normandie/ UMR 6273 - CRAHAM
Thomas Calligaro, Centre de recherche et de restauration des musées de France, C2RMF, Palais du Louvre/ PSL Research University, Chimie ParisTech-CNRS, Institut de Recherche Chimie Paris, UMR8247
Alexandra Chavarría Arnau, Università degli Studi di Padova
Pascale Chevalier, Université Clermont Auvergne—UMR 6298-ARTEHIS Dijon
Lynda Coon, University of Arkansas
Magali Coumert, Université de Bretagne Occidentale
Andrea Czermak, University of Oxford
Albrecht Diem, Syracuse University
Wolfram Drews, Westfälische Wilhelms-Universität Münster
Bonnie Effros, University of Liverpool
Stefan Esders, Freie Universität Berlin
Robin Fleming, Boston College
Paul Fouracre, University of Manchester (emeritus)
Andrew Gillett, independent scholar
Agnès Graceffa, Université Libre de Bruxelles
Bernard Gratuze, Centre Ernest-Babelon, IRAMAT, UMR 5060, CNRS–Université d'Orléans
Gregory Halfond, Framingham State University
Guy Halsall, University of York
Mark A. Handley, independent scholar
Matthias Hardt, Leibniz-Institut für Geschichte und Kultur des östlichen Europa (GWZO), Leipzig
Yitzhak Hen, Hebrew University of Jerusalem
Peregrine Horden, Royal Holloway University of London
Edward James, University College Dublin (emeritus)

William E. Klingshirn, Catholic University of America

Genevra Kornbluth, independent scholar

Jamie Kreiner, University of Georgia

S. T. Loseby, University of Sheffield

Ralph W. Mathisen, University of Illinois, Urbana-Champaign

Isabel Moreira, University of Utah

Ralph J. Patrello, independent scholar

Émilie Perez, Université de la Polynésie française

Patrick Périn, Musée d'archéologie nationale (emeritus)

Edith Peytremann, Institut national de recherches archéologiques préventives (Inrap)

Jean-Michel Picard, University College Dublin (emeritus)

Dominique Pieri, Université Paris 1 Panthéon-Sorbonne, Collège de France-CNRS UMR 8167-Orient et Méditerranée

Constantin Pion, Institut royal du Patrimoine artistique (IRPA-KIK), Brussels/ Centre de Recherches en Archéologie et Patrimoine, Université libre de Bruxelles

Helmut Reimitz, Princeton University

Alice Rio, Kings College London

Els Rose, Universiteit Utrecht

Laury Sarti, Albert-Ludwigs-Universität Freiburg

Paolo Squatriti, University of Michigan

Jürgen Strothmann, Universität Siegen

Frans Theuws, Universiteit Leiden

Dries Tys, Vrije Universiteit Brussel

Kevin Uhalde, Ohio University

Jean-Hervé Yvinec, Institut national de recherches archéologiques préventives (Inrap)/ UMR 7209 du CNRS

List of Maps

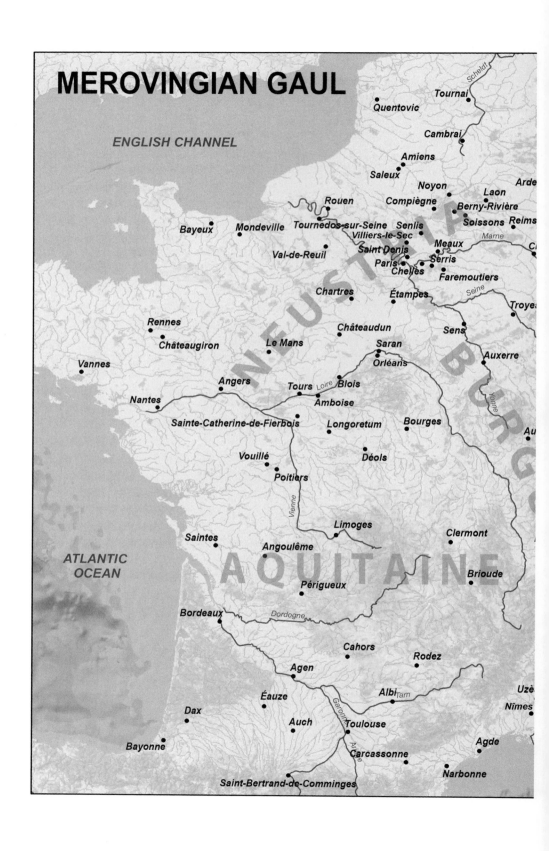

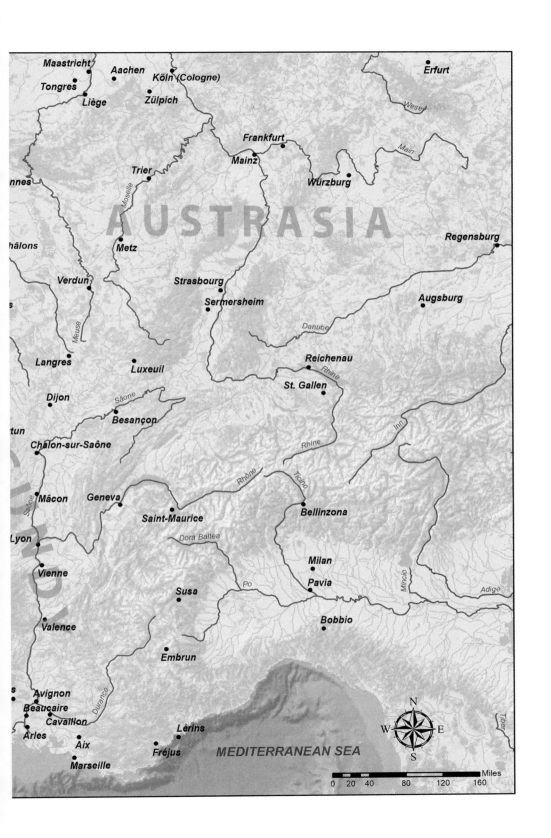

Maastricht
Tongres
Aachen
Köln (Cologne)
Erfurt
Liège
Zülpich
Weser
nnes
Frankfurt
Mainz
Main
Trier
Würzburg
Moselle
AUSTRASIA
Regensburg
hâlons
Metz
Verdun
Strasbourg
Augsburg
Sermersheim
Danube
Meuse
Langres
Luxeuil
Reichenau
Rhine
St. Gallen
Dijon
Saône
Besançon
Inn
tun
Rhine
Chalon-sur-Saône
Rhône
Mâcon
Geneva
Bellinzona
Saône
Saint-Maurice
Ticino
Lyon
Dora Baltea
Milan
Vienne
Pavia
Mincio
Po
Adige
Susa
Bobbio
Valence
Embrun
Durance
Avignon
Beaucaire
Cavaillon
Lérins
Tiber
Arles
Aix
Fréjus
N
Marseille
MEDITERRANEAN SEA
W · E
S
Miles
0   20   40   80   120   160

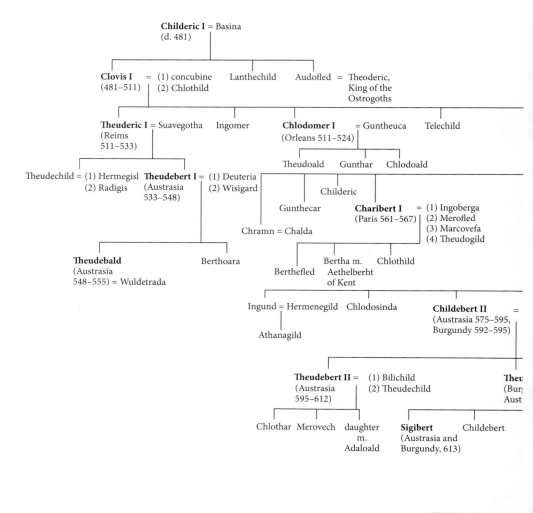

MEROVINGIAN FAMILY TREE

Modified from: Ian Wood, *The Merovingian Kingdoms, 450–751* (London: Longman, 1994), pp. 344–349; Suzanne F. Wemple, *Women in Frankish Society: Marriage and the Cloister, 500–900* (Philadelphia: University of Pennsylvania Press, 1981) pp. viii–ix; Richard Gerberding, *The Rise of the Carolingians and the Liber Historiae Francorum* (Oxford: Clarendon Press, 1987). Note: Regnal dates are provided but some are debated. The listed order of the wives and partners of Merovingian kings is speculative in places.

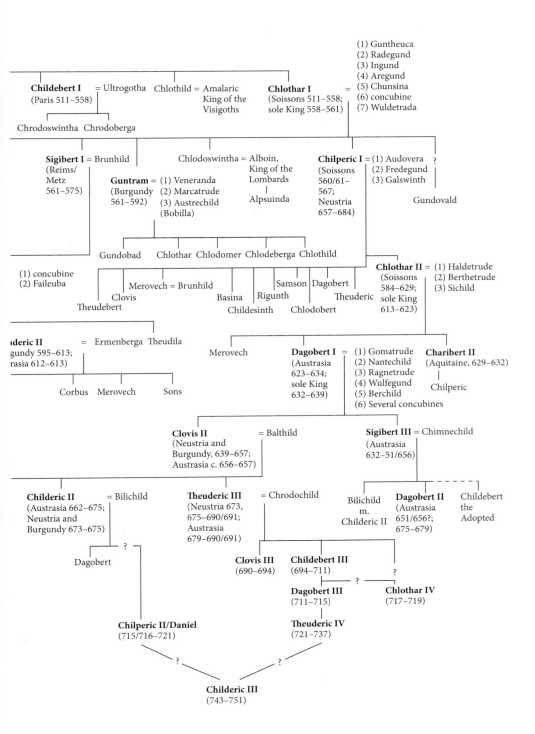

INTRODUCTION

CHAPTER 1

··

PUSHING THE BOUNDARIES OF THE MEROVINGIAN WORLD

··

BONNIE EFFROS AND ISABEL MOREIRA

ALTHOUGH the Merovingians did not escape Edward Gibbon's scrutiny in his *History of the Decline and Fall of the Roman Empire* (1776–1789), the reader was not encouraged to expect much of them: "The Franks, or French, are the only people of Europe, who can deduce a perpetual succession from the conquerors of the Western Empire. But their conquest of Gaul was followed by ten centuries of anarchy, and ignorance" (*DFRE* II. 38, p. 471). The Merovingians thereby also escaped the notice and interest of many Anglophone readers of history brought up on Gibbon's version of Late Antiquity. This blind spot notwithstanding, the Merovingian world (481–751) has become more visible in Anglophone historical scholarship in the past two decades, and, for better or for worse, it has become more firmly rooted in the narrative of a long Late Antiquity. Modern interest in the social and economic networks of empires and modes of communication has begun to change older frameworks that viewed these centuries in terms of decline and characterized them as the "Dark Ages" (see Graceffa, Chapter 3, this volume). Rather than being viewed as an era of stagnation, as was the case in the nineteenth century, recent studies have highlighted the vitality and importance of Western Christendom from the fifth through the eighth centuries, not only in Europe but also in other parts of the late Roman world.

Indeed, studies of the Merovingians and their world have come to play a critical role in the generation of new insights into the transitional period between Antiquity and the Middle Ages. Once overlooked as a chaotic and obscure interlude between the fall of the Roman Empire and the beginnings of the medieval world, and named for a dynasty with a reputation for few accomplishments and even fewer memorable kings (in nineteenth-century France, they were long known as *les rois fainéants*, or the "do-nothing kings"), the Merovingian era is now a field that is growing in its own right. In part, new interest in this period has arisen as scholars of cultural and religious history in Late Antiquity have demonstrated greater flexibility in working horizontally in a decentralized world and in seeing beyond the political developments that until recently were the bread and butter of most historians. Another source of renewed interest in the Merovingian world is the rise of new and more comprehensive archaeological approaches to the period; rather than echoing the historical sources, scholars of material culture are showing that it is possible to question the written sources and shed new light on subjects that previously were inaccessible. Above all, in digging into the local, regional, and contingent nature of the lived environment in these centuries, the Merovingian period has become something more than a simple or hasty response to an older paradigm of decline, emerging as a period in its own right and with its own peculiarities. In casting our view over recent developments in a wide array of disciplines and perspectives, we can attempt to slow the rush to the Middle Ages and assess the evidence without recourse to the discursive imperatives of stagnation, decline, transition, transformation, or rise.

In gathering essays for this handbook on the Merovingian world (rather than Gaul or Francia; see Fouracre, Chapter 2, this volume), we have built around the modern understanding of the Merovingian territories as being at once a coalescence of regional interests and the center of a far-flung network of interconnected political and economic interests. With Ian Wood's *The Merovingian North Sea* (1983) and the work that followed, the Merovingian era can no longer be confined to activities that transpired among Gallo-Romans and Franks and to the dynastic history of the Merovingians. Far from being isolated from the world around it, the Merovingian elite, through the exchange of goods and ideas, their letters, laws, culture, and religion, as well as through military actions and familial alliances, sat at the center of an intensely connected world. From the Byzantine-controlled territories to the south and east, to the politically fragmented lands to the north (including the British Isles and Ireland), the Merovingian kings and their peoples touched the peoples and cultures around them—sometimes in bonds of amity and exchange, sometimes (as in the case of the Byzantine emperors) as wary allies, and sometimes as hegemonic overlords. Their place in the post-Roman world was not always secure, as may be seen in the case of Clovis's competition with Theoderic for Byzantine titles and accolades in the early sixth century (see Arnold, Chapter 21, this volume). However, their footprint was large, and they interacted with political entities on every side. We are now learning that trade, even if indirect, extended the reach of the inhabitants of the Merovingian kingdoms even further, as far afield as Sri Lanka, the Indian Ocean, and the Red Sea (see Pion et al., Chapter 36, this volume). The world of the Merovingians was intrinsically connected to contemporary developments not just among the Burgundians, the Visigoths, and the Alamanni with whom they shared and contested borders (see Mathisen, Chapter 19; Patrello, Chapter 39, this volume), but also among the Byzantines, Ostrogoths, Lombards, Thuringians, Avars, Bavarians, Anglo-Saxons, Frisians, and the Irish (see Arnold, Chapter 21; Esders, Chapter 16;

Fleming, Chapter 17; Hardt, Chapter 20; and Picard, Chapter 18, this volume), peoples who, like the Merovingians, were once viewed in isolation.

It is this highly connected world that we present in this collection of forty-six essays from both junior innovators and leading scholars of the Merovingian world. In striving to achieve a panoramic view of this networked entity of intersecting and (and sometimes conflicting) identities, political interests, religions, economies, patronage, and cultures, and how these have changed our understanding of this complex period, it has been necessary to bring together many disciplines of study. Nonetheless, space constraints and unanticipated obstacles to achieving our original vision of the volume in 2014 have made it impossible to include every possible topic, and we are all too aware of lacunae with reference to important fields like Merovingian manuscript studies, biblical studies, onomastics, and the emerging and contested ground of DNA research (for the first, see Coulson and Babcock 2020). Similarly, areas of rich possibility such as the eighth-century transition to the Carolingian period, are not addressed in full (but see Fouracre, Chapter 2; Hardt, Chapter 20; Picard, Chapter 18, this volume). Although many of these topics are touched upon in related essays, each could easily have been the subject of an independent examination.

Pushing back against myths of Frankish barbarism and cultural decline, the essays presented here on the history and archaeology of the Merovingian era explore a world that was complex, changing, but mostly stable: bureaucratic, innovative, and adaptive in some arenas, yet disrupted, conservative, and limited in others. Our knowledge of the Merovingians is growing rapidly from evidence gleaned from an assortment of texts, coins, architectural remains, inscriptions, cemeteries, skeletal matter, and refuse pits. Indeed, the resilience of Merovingian rule over two and a half centuries is particularly impressive in light of the challenges of climate and disease that prevailed across Europe in the sixth and seventh centuries and that we have only begun to fully appreciate. The arrival in Europe of the "Justinianic Plague," one of the most well documented instances of bubonic plague caused by the bacterium *Yersinia pestis*, is described in Merovingian sources but its impact is debated (Haldon et al. 2018c; Mordechai et al. 2019; Yvinec and Barme, this volume). Furthermore, from the fifth to the late seventh centuries, Europe experienced climate changes as the result of what is now termed the "late-antique little ice age" (Harper 2017; contra, see: Haldon et al. 2018a, 2018b; see Horden, Chapter 14; Squatriti, Chapter 32, this volume). Catastrophic events on such a scale would challenge most regimes, yet the Merovingian dynasty endured. Therefore, it has been important for the organization of this volume to recognize that, whereas our view of the Merovingians was once dominated by the perspectives of the extant written sources and their focus on kingship, migration, and war, new evidence is offering original perspectives and allowing us to ask questions about climate, disease, environment, and the trading decisions of distant polities. The more we learn about the cultural and economic contributions of the Merovingians and the challenges they presented and overcame, the more nuanced our view of early medieval history becomes. These important developments are generating new audiences for the study of the Merovingian period.

PROBLEMATIC LABELS AND
TEMPORAL CHALLENGES

The Merovingian era has a name recognition problem for nonacademic Anglophone readers, some of whom are more apt to associate it with Lambert Wilson's character in the popular science fiction cult film, *The Matrix* (1999), or with the alleged royal descendants of Mary Magdalene and Jesus in Michael Baigent, Richard Leigh and Henry Lincoln's *The Holy Blood and the Holy Grail* (1982) and Dan Brown's conspiracy novel, *The Da Vinci Code* (2003). For German-speakers, Heimito von Doderer's novel *Die Merowinger oder die Totale Familie* (1962) is not likely to leave the reader better informed about the dynasty. Even the name "Merovingian" seems difficult and obscure. Named for a quasi-mythical leader, Merovech, of a Frankish tribal family, the term *Merovingian* has come to describe a dynasty, a time frame, a people, a culture, and a land mass. But the challenges go deeper than that. Scholars disagree about where to place the Merovingian era in the wider arc of Western history. Does the Merovingian era mark the final phase of a Roman "Late Antiquity"? Or is it the early beginning of the "Middle Ages"? A pragmatic answer is that it depends on the historical perspective of the researcher. A Merovingian scholar looking back in time to emphasize continuities with the former western Roman Empire will likely view the sixth and seventh centuries as Late Antiquity or, in the apt phrasing of Peter Brown, as the "end of a very ancient world" (Brown 2000, p. 59). A scholar emphasizing the Merovingian Frankish kingdoms as a break with the Roman Empire in the fifth century will likely view the Merovingian period as being early medieval. Sometimes these viewpoints are not mutually exclusive. These differences in perspective can often make the field of Merovingian studies seem divided.

This chronological challenge is exacerbated by the fact that the Merovingian period was not a monolithic era but rather witnessed notable changes between the sixth and seventh centuries (in religious culture, court life, legal traditions, and Frankish identity), and again from the 680s onward (in terms of coinage, exchange, and the economy). The resulting Janus-like impression of the field is not merely an impression but a reflection of a certain reality. Yet, at the same time, there was coherence to this period that went beyond its dynastic kings in that it was regulated by a religious culture and political, legal, and administrative systems that were to change fairly dramatically under the Carolingians. It is important to see the Merovingian period as a cultural entity in its own right, and not merely as an era that was "transitioning" between Antiquity and the age of Charlemagne.

Layered over these problematic distinctions is the way that curricula, and the departments of history that produce them, sometimes engineer a break between the ancient and medieval fields. Typically, in the United Kingdom, the Merovingians are viewed as part of early medieval history and are taught in history and archaeology departments by medievalists. This makes sense from a British perspective because the Merovingians were contemporary with England's earliest post-Roman authors like Gildas and because of the national primacy traditionally accorded to the Northumbrian historian, Bede (672/673–735). The national story of the conversion of the Anglo-Saxons to Christianity by Pope Gregory the Great was played out against the background of Merovingian politics and, it has been argued, Merovingian intervention. The Merovingians are thus part of England's medieval story. In France, the Middle Ages are typically thought to have begun with Charlemagne's coronation in 800. Although the Merovingians received the designation of the "première race" in the nineteenth century, they were largely characterized as non-French due to their arrival during the "grandes invasions" (see Graceffa, Chapter 3, this volume). This schema relegated the Merovingians to being only proto-medieval, as was the case in Belgium, where the Carolingian epoch was favored over the Merovingian period. German academic understanding of this period conflicts with English and French historiography in that it sees the Merovingian era as one of Germanic migration, the *Völkerwanderungszeit*, yielding a more positive interpretation of the influx of Germanic peoples and culture in the sphere of the Roman Empire (see Coumert, Chapter 5, this volume). In the United States, where the Merovingians are usually first encountered in university courses, it is only since the 1980s that the Merovingian period has been seen as anything more than the Dark Ages, given the lack of interest in this period among classicists and the longstanding preference for the twelfth century and afterward among American medievalists. This change has been deeply informed by the work of Peter Brown, a progenitor of the field of late-antique studies, whose work has addressed the religious and cultural environment of Merovingian authors such as Gregory of Tours in new and meaningful ways.

The anachronistic and inaccurate characterization of Merovingian studies as part of the Dark Ages primarily reflects historical gaps in our knowledge of the immediate post-Roman period. British historians were apt to use this terminology, which was also handily adopted in the United States, to refer to the Europe that existed after the "fall" of the Roman Empire. Although there are certainly challenges faced by those who work to reconstruct Merovingian history and society, this period of history in Gaul is no longer understood to be particularly "dark," and certainly not as "dark" as were some other parts of Europe in the same period (on the Avars, see Hardt, Chapter 20, this volume). As Chris Wickham (2005) observed, the Merovingians preserved much of the late Roman systems of administration, including the use of papyrus for official documents, so that the denigration and loss of much of the evidence for their bureaucratic industry and quotidian activity from as early as the Carolingian period are certainly tragic. However, we can postulate much of what may have existed in the way of correspondence, for instance, through comparison with other parts of the Mediterranean such as Egypt (see Gillett, Chapter 25, this volume). And many other kinds of written sources have survived. The Merovingian era saw the flowering of hagiography, which was a great literary moment, in terms not solely of the number of extant examples, but also its influence on hagiographic writing in other parts of Europe (see Kreiner, Chapter 24, this volume). Church councils produced and preserved conversations about the religious life (see Halfond, Chapter 13, this volume); monastic rules were generated and copied to organize religious houses (see Diem, Chapter 15, this volume); histories, letter collections, and poems narrated and promoted stories about the recent and more distant past (see Gillett, Chapter 25; Horden, Chapter 14; Reimitz, Chapter 22, this volume); wills, laws, and formularies sought to regulate transactions (see Rio, Chapter 23, this volume); coinage reveals a lot about the generation of wealth and the payment of taxes (see Strothmann, Chapter 35, this volume); sermons, liturgical works, penitentials, and bibles testify to the spiritual life and condemned practices that were seen as contrary to them (see Bailey, Chapter 44; Rose, Chapter 43; Uhalde, Chapter 45, this volume); visionary texts and burial inscriptions give insight into the mapping of the Merovingian otherworld and its connection to the living (see Moreira, Chapter 42; Handley, Chapter 26, this volume); and collections of divinatory texts speak to the significance of magic and the supernatural to early medieval Christians (see Klingshirn, Chapter 41, this volume).

Surviving architectural and art historical evidence also attests to the vitality of the Merovingian epoch, whether in reference to innovations in religious architecture (see Chevalier, Chapter 30, this volume), sculptural innovation encouraging personal religious experience (see Coon, Chapter 46, this volume), or the changes wrought to fortified centers, villas, and cities (see Bourgeois, Chapter 28; Chavarría Arnau, Chapter 29; Loseby, Chapter 27, this volume). Archaeological excavations, whose methods and objectives have changed since the members of antiquarian societies began plying their hobby in earnest in the 1830s (see Effros, Chapter 4, this volume), have produced myriad kinds of data that allow modern scholars to view the Merovingian epoch from a variety of perspectives. Whether we examine the rich evidence for the period produced from graves (see Czermak, Chapter 7; Halsall, Chapter 8; Patrello, Chapter 39; Perez, Chapter 9; Pion et al., Chapter 36; Theuws, Chapter 38, this volume), trading centers (see Bonifay and Pieri, Chapter 37; Fleming, Chapter 17; Tys, Chapter 34, this volume) or rural landscapes (see Peytremann, Chapter 31; Squatriti, Chapter 32; Yvinec and Barme, Chapter 33, this volume), it is impossible to suggest that life in early medieval Gaul had come to a standstill. In short, the Merovingian period is anything but a "Dark Age" following the end of the Roman administration of Gaul.

Instead, what the essays in this volume demonstrate is that the Merovingian world was a connected world even if it was not centralized: it was linked with the Mediterranean as well as northern Europe, central Europe, and the Byzantine world through diplomacy, culture, religion, war, and trade (on connections with Byzantium, see Esders, Fox, Hen, and Sarti 2019). The Merovingian orbit was a very functional center, not just of saints' cults, but also religious and military administration, local, regional, and international trade, learned culture and communication, Christian charity and theological innovation, and religious and secular law and custom. Through it, despite great change over the course of the more than three centuries we associate with the Merovingian dynasty, much of Rome still survived, something that the Carolingians were able subsequently to put to practical and symbolic use.

New Research and Alternative Visions of the Merovingian Past

Overlooked by Henri Pirenne as an uneventful period of slow decline before the rise of the Carolingians and the eventual rebirth of cities (1937), the Merovingian era is now a field growing in its own right. As noted earlier, new interest in this period has arisen in part from the cultural and religious focus of scholars of Late Antiquity, who have demonstrated significant flexibility in working horizontally in a decentralized world. They have refined discussion of the political developments that were once the core focus of many historians, and they have begun to ask questions about communication, climate, diet, settlement, and trade. This volume has sought to present the field in a way that overcomes some of the earlier disciplinary divides, setting material evidence alongside the written sources, in order to ask important questions about the disciplinary obstacles that still hamper a fully integrated view of the Merovingian period. Indeed, new and multidisciplinary approaches to the period have generated a revival of interest in this field by a new generation of scholars. Rather than echoing the historical sources, scholars of material culture are showing that it is possible to move beyond the finite number of extant written sources and explore subjects that previously were inaccessible. The shift within Merovingian archaeology from primarily grave sites to settlements, trading centers, and landscapes, which occurred especially from the 1980s, has likewise had a significant impact on the questions that can be asked and answered (see Effros, Chapter 4, this volume). These important developments have created not just new approaches to, but also new audiences for, the study of the Merovingian period.

As seen in this volume, new scientific techniques, many with obscure-sounding names, have been added to the arsenal of early medieval specialists and have allowed them to shed new light on material goods prevalent in Merovingian-era graves and settlements. For instance, fission-track dating has made it possible to date glass and identify the origin of its ingredients on the basis of minute quantities of uranium. These studies have suggested that some of the materials used to make raw glass traveled long distances, in some cases from as far away as Sri Lanka and the Red Sea, before making their way into Merovingian jewelry and tableware in the late fifth and early sixth centuries. Likewise, the noninvasive technique of microspectrometry has made it possible to measure the wavelengths of electromagnetic radiation that gemstones like garnet, which were used in gold cloisonnée brooches, purse clasps, weapon handles, and belt buckles, absorb or reflect. These markers help scientists identify the source of the materials, suggesting in some cases that, at least until the late sixth century, their point of origin lay far beyond the frontiers of the Merovingian kingdom and even the Mediterranean basin (for discussion of both, see Pion et al., Chapter 36, this volume).

Human bones and teeth, and remains of fauna and flora, too, have become important sources of data for scholars of the Merovingian period. Osteological studies of human adults and children tell us about life expectancy and some of the diseases that affected the population (see Perez, Chapter 9, this volume). Archaeozoological research in the north of France, for instance, has made it possible to assess the composition and size of Merovingian flocks and herds (see Yvinec and Barme, Chapter 33, this volume). Although the techniques are still costly, and hence are used more rarely in France than in England and Germany on early medieval human remains, DNA analysis has improved our knowledge of certain genetic traits and given anthropologists an additional tool with which to determine the biological sex of poorly preserved skeletons, even if they cannot tell us about the way in which individuals experienced their gender identity (see Halsall, Chapter 8, this volume). Although new methods of sequencing have made it possible to work with the shorter strands of DNA typically found in ancient skeletal remains, the technology has only recently begun to deliver on geneticists' promises of the possibility of using ancient mitochondrial DNA to suggest migration patterns linked to the historical record (Amorim et al. 2018).

While still relatively new in the field of Merovingian studies, isotopic analysis has begun to produce intriguing results related to determining whether there was extensive mobility in early medieval communities. More specifically, assessment of oxygen and strontium signatures in early medieval tooth enamel has permitted bio-archaeologists to distinguish migrant and more stable individuals within the context of early medieval cemeteries. Carbon and nitrogen stable isotope analysis of bone collagen, by contrast, has shed light on the diets of these same individuals, indicating, for instance, who among them enjoyed diets heavy in seafood or game (Müldner 2009). More specific to Gaul, we learn from skeletal remains in early medieval cemeteries like Niedernai in the upper Rhine area from the mid-fifth to the early sixth century that boys appear to have received diets richer in animal protein than their sisters (see Czermak, Chapter 7, this volume). This finding nuances our understanding of the distribution of the foodstuffs identified by archaeobotanists and archaeozoologists by providing insight into the distribution of the produce of farming and husbandry in early medieval communities in Gaul (see Peytremann, Chapter 31; Squatriti, Chapter 32, this volume).

Not only has technology made us rethink the potential significance of once overlooked or modest materials, such as glass beads, ceramics, garnets, and bone, for understanding trade and diet in the Merovingian period, but also these bountiful objects have begun to change the way we address research problems that have beset Merovingian scholars for generations. An issue, for instance, that has dogged archaeology since its start is how to determine most accurately the relative and absolute chronologies of Merovingian-period sites and artifacts. Among antiquarians and early archaeologists, the approach to this question often relied heavily on the presence of coins that might offer a *terminus post quem*, in other words, the date after which a grave or a settlement was thought to have been used. Numismatic evidence, together with stratigraphic analysis, made it possible, in turn, to establish the relative chronologies of stylistic developments in categories of artifacts such as brooches, buckles, or weaponry in the late nineteenth and early twentieth centuries (Périn 1980). Even in the late twentieth century, improvements to the accuracy of these dating techniques were hampered by the fact that they were affected by distinctions in the regional density of excavations, significant variations in local custom, and bias toward higher-status artifacts. Moreover, alternative means of dating, such as ^{14}C, could not be used on inorganic materials. The introduction of detailed databases for fairly ubiquitous artifacts like ceramics and beads, which are found in a large number of graves but were traditionally not given extensive attention, has now made it possible to propose modifications to existing chronologies (Bonifay 2013; Pion and Vrielyck 2014). A more fully contextual reading of architectural evidence from the Merovingian period has also made it possible to date these structures more accurately (see Chevalier, Chapter 30, this volume).

New conversations are now taking place that bring together unlikely combinations of data that would have been inconceivable even thirty years ago. In environmental studies of the Merovingian period, texts are being used in partnership with climatological and archaeological data to suggest diachronic changes in the early medieval landscape and settlement patterns due to weather and the availability of foodstuffs. Likewise, directions in animal husbandry affected not just diet, clothing, and the availability of manure to fertilize crops, but they also left their mark on contemporary legislation regarding property and religious imagery of the afterlife (Kreiner 2017; see Yvinec and Barme, Chapter 33, this volume). Trade, too, is increasingly being seen holistically, with research aimed at movement not just in the Roman interior and the Mediterranean, but increasingly on the margins like Scandinavia, the Russian steppes, and the heartlands of the Sassanid Empire. The increasing willingness of early medievalists to explore comparisons with regions further afield, whether in the Maghreb, the eastern Mediterranean, along the ancient silk route, or the Red Sea and Indian Ocean trade routes, suggests that there is still much more to learn about Merovingian connections to long-distance trade. These increasingly daring research strategies seem likely to strengthen in future research, especially as large-scale collaborations and comparative research clusters are encouraged by schemes such as the European Research Council and the European Science Foundation in the European Union, and the Arts and Humanities Research Council and the Economic and Social Research Council in the United Kingdom.

DAILY LIFE IN THE MEROVINGIAN ERA

This volume demonstrates how our expanding source base for the Merovingian period allows us to glimpse more aspects of lives lived in the Merovingian era and shows that we can do so with much greater granularity than was previously possible, even if many issues still cannot be resolved with precision. It is clear that many people living in the kingdoms were migrants, whether migration was necessitated by economic demand, religious calling, status as a slave, or the ravages of war. Some of the inhabitants of the Merovingian kingdoms identified as Gallo-Romans, Franks, Goths, Irish or eastern monks, Syrian merchants, Jews, Homoian Christians (often called Arians in older sources to associate them with the heretic Arius, who was condemned at the Council of Nicaea in 325; Dunn 2013), or had other identities (see Drews, Chapter 6, this volume). Although we may not know their names, we increasingly have the opportunity to learn more about the livelihoods and life cycles of women, children, and slaves who rarely found their way into the historical or legal record (see Halsall, Chapter 8, this volume). While many of our sources are biased against the possible contributions of women, for example, or rural inhabitants or non-Christians, blaming them for magic or unholy rituals, scholars today are less willing to accept their characterizations without comment (see Klingshirn, Chapter 41, this volume). They have found other means, such as through law codes, formularies, charters, cemeterial remains, stone structures and sculpture, and hagiography, to render the lives and environment of marginal groups more visible than the clerical constituency that mostly authored early medieval texts wanted them to be.

To understand in more depth the daily lives of the majority of inhabitants in Gaul (with the possible exception of urban-dwelling elites in the south), we must look to the countryside and the roads and rivers that connected them (see Theuws, Chapter 38, this volume). For the agrarian communities of Roman Gaul, significant changes occurred in the third century. The elites who held villas in northern Gaul had largely abandoned them in the third century, but the case was quite different in the south, where such properties continued to be used well after this period. It was only in the fifth century that these complexes underwent significant transformation and in the sixth century that they vanished altogether, never to return (see Chavarría Arnau, Chapter 29, this volume). The third century also saw the abandonment of many older rural settlements in favor of the construction of new ones (see Peytremann, Chapter 31, this volume). We now believe, however, in contrast to older theories about the impermanence of villages in the Merovingian period, that these new settlements had significant staying power. Early medieval villages or hamlets, along with the cemeteries that served them, became larger and more densely populated in the late seventh and eighth centuries (see Bourgeois, Chapter 28, this volume). During the Christianization of Gaul, many villages were the recipients of new or improved religious structures, which provide evidence of the flowering of religious architecture in this period (see Chevalier, Chapter 30, this volume). Such Merovingian implantations laid the seed for Carolingian settlements and indeed some that still exist today.

Such modest population centers were not just the site of agricultural undertakings but often the site of small-scale production of items such as iron, ceramics, glass, marquetry, leather products, and cloth, many of which appeared in the graves of the dead in local cemeteries (see Peytremann, Chapter 31, this volume). Although we do not know a lot about the artisans whose handiwork survives, such as what percentage of them were itinerant, the older Roman infrastructure was critical to their ability to travel and trade. As the population of post-Roman Gaul began to expand from the mid-fifth century, it is clear that inhabitants, many of them of modest means, were able to accumulate wealth, even if we do not know whether these resources passed from generation to generation. Judging from the investment they regularly made in placing valuable items in the burial displays of kin and leaders, Merovingian rural dwellers in northern Gaul left their imprint on the landscape in more lasting ways than once was thought possible (see Theuws, Chapter 38, this volume).

Architectural and archaeological remains also suggest that, under Merovingian rule, some former Roman administrative centers faced demotion and others were created anew. Nonetheless, there appears to have been significant continuity in towns even if their populations temporarily declined and their appearance evolved. Regardless of the change in administration, these population centers, many of which were founded by the Romans, remained important anchoring points for lay and ecclesiastical institutions (see Bourgeois, Chapter 28, this volume). They were often the locations in which health initiatives were organized (see Horden, Chapter 14, this volume). As the centers in which coins were minted, cities and towns experienced some of their most important changes not between the late Roman and early Merovingian period but rather centuries into Frankish rule, from 675, when silver became the standard currency. This change in coinage reduced the number of places in which coins might be minted (see Strothmann, Chapter 35, this volume). The concentration of this important fiscal activity led to new hierarchies of power in the Merovingian landscape.

We have also learned from the work of Michael McCormick how necessary it is to move beyond Pirenne's sweeping but flawed arguments about continuity in the post-Roman economy (2001). Some of the most important studies have come from archaeological ceramics. Namely, although research on the amphorae that were used to transport olive oil, wine, and fish sauce across the Mediterranean has demonstrated their decline from the fifth century associated with the end of the *annona* (tax-in-kind) shipments of grain to Rome, their recovery occurred in the sixth century followed by steady decline until the 730s. Moreover, we now know of the increasing diversity of imports into southern Gaul (and, to a much lesser extent, northern Gaul), which now came not just from the Maghreb but also from Spain and the eastern Mediterranean. These changes suggest significant alteration, but not elimination, of vital Mediterranean trade in foodstuffs following the cessation of grain shipments to Rome. By contrast, the importation of fine ceramics, especially African Red Slipware (ARS), disappeared from ships' cargoes more quickly and dramatically, to be replaced typically by locally made coarser, or in some cases high-end, productions. This trade with Gaul would come to a definitive end only in the third decade of the eighth century (see Bonifay and Pieri, Chapter 37, this volume). Northern Gaul also saw ceramics from England, even though most of the traffic in pots moved in the opposite direction (see Fleming, Chapter 17, this volume).

It is also important to recognize that trade was affected by the fact that the Merovingians broke from the Roman tradition of maintaining standing armies as they existed under imperial rule. Although a large number of men served as soldiers (*milites*) in the early medieval period, their duties were short term, and they were not provisioned as consistently as they had been under Roman rule. Consequently, there was no longer a need for a complex supply system like the *annona*, a change that had a significant impact on the organization of regional and long-distance trade. This alteration also affected the organization of fighting forces under Merovingian leadership, since it made the amassing of armies significantly more fluid and unpredictable than it had been under Roman imperial leadership (see Sarti, Chapter 12, this volume). The organization of trade through markets and fairs likewise became a vector of the spread of disease, something with which Merovingian bishops like Caesarius of Arles and Desiderius of Cahors had to contend in the sixth and seventh centuries (see Horden, Chapter 14, this volume).

With respect to local and regional food production, pollen and environmental studies now give us greater insight into early medieval cereal cultivation and dietary trends (see Squatriti, Chapter 32, this volume). In addition, archaeobiology allows us to see what kinds of livestock and fish early medieval agriculturalists preferred, which wild animals were hunted and butchered for food, and how these practices varied by region (see Yvinec and Barme, Chapter 33, this volume). Whereas the results of isotope analysis hint at inequities in the diets of the population based presumably on available resources and their accessibility to those of differing means and biological sex in childhood (see Czermak, Chapter 7, this volume), bone and tooth analysis also tells us about levels of malnutrition and child mortality in early medieval populations (see Perez, Chapter 9, this volume). Historical accounts, too, offer information about human health and efforts to quell disease in a variety of ways. Gregory of Tours, for instance, complained that Christians in Gaul continued to use amulets to protect their health or that of their families, despite more effective methods such as the cult of saints. We cannot assume from his writings, however, that the symbolism and function of these rites remained a constant from the late Roman period to the early Middle Ages (see Klingshirn, Chapter 41; Kornbluth, Chapter 40, this volume).

MOVEMENT OF PEOPLE AND OBJECTS: IDENTITY IN THE MEROVINGIAN PERIOD

In seventh-century sources (the *Chronicle of Fredegar* II. 4–8, III. 2, and the *Liber Historiae Francorum* [*LHF*] 1–4), a myth was propagated in the Merovingian kingdom that the Franks were descended from the Trojans. Although in the centuries since then many ideas have been proposed with respect to Merovingian and Frankish origins, these discussions have also required scholars to rethink the functions and motivations of the historical and hagiographical sources of the Merovingian period (see Coumert, Chapter 5; Graceffa, Chapter 3, this volume). Our view of this evidence, along with that derived from early medieval graves and cemeteries, has in recent years become increasingly nuanced; it is no longer possible to see historical narratives and grave site evidence as a faithful reflection of the events they recounted (see Kreiner, Chapter 24; Reimitz, Chapter 22, this volume) or understand ethnicity as something either biological or fixed (see Coumert, Chapter 5, this volume). No historical works of the period, for instance, were written to reflect Merovingian dynastic aims (see Reimitz, Chapter 22, this volume). As constructed, genres, biographies, histories, and grave assemblages were all positioned by their authors and makers to make a case for or against particular individuals or groups, whether Franks or otherwise. They offered competing visions of practical or spiritual aspirations to the communities to which they were addressed (see Patrello, Chapter 39, this volume).

Because of the outsize influence of polemical debates about ethnicity on historical and archaeological debates about the Merovingian period, this volume has been intentionally organized to decenter the discussion in favor of topics that highlight the existence of a mosaic of early medieval identities. The Merovingian kingdoms were not characterized by the simple binary of Franks and Gallo-Romans but were at their core a multiethnic community. Migrants of every stripe played a major role in religious life, and economic, intellectual, and military undertakings in Merovingian Gaul (see Drews, Chapter 6, this volume). While this is not to say that one's place of origin did not matter, too much dependence on historical narratives like that of Gregory of Tours may skew our understanding of the period (see Coumert, Chapter 5; Reimitz, Chapter 22, this volume). In recent studies, isotope analysis, just as artifactual studies, suggests that adaptation to dominant mores could occur quite quickly: incoming individuals adapted to local customs either soon after arrival or at most within a generation (see Czermak, Chapter 7; Patrello, Chapter 39, this volume). Over time, a steady erosion of Gallo-Roman names occurred in favor of Frankish ones, suggesting that general points of reference for identity were shifting and unity was increasing (see Fouracre, Chapter 2, this volume).

When read closely, written sources allow us to see inconsistencies in earlier interpretations. Surviving texts push us to question the speed of the expansion of Merovingian territory under Clovis (see Mathisen, Chapter 19, this volume), and the kingdom's relations with the Byzantine Empire and peoples like the Thuringians and Avars (see Esders, Chapter 16; Hardt, Chapter 20, this volume). They also underpin how much the Merovingian aristocracy depended on Roman notions of a court, which made allusions to older civic and military political ideology and provided a support network for royal ambitions both at the center and throughout the kingdoms (see Hen, Chapter 10, this volume). Moreover, it was cooperation with Irish monastics and participation in overseas military conflicts that helped the Merovingian kings expand their authority to more distant territories (see Picard, Chapter 18, this volume). They also provide crucial evidence of alliances brokered within the Merovingian kingdoms and with allies further abroad through military intervention, marriage, and gift exchange (see Arnold, Chapter 21; Hardt, Chapter 20; James, Chapter 11; Picard, Chapter 18, this volume). Closer reading of our sources allows us to draw up a more refined understanding of lay and religious elites, as well as the factions that often pitted them against one another.

On a more intimate scale, new readings of the historical and archaeological evidence also lead us to question simple binaries between what it meant to be male or female in the early Middle Ages (see Halsall, Chapter 8, this volume). Isotope analysis suggests that biological sex mattered, too, since it might be reflected in access to foods rich in animal protein (see Czermak, Chapter 7, this volume). Additionally, extant evidence allows us to reexamine the subtle vicissitudes in the divide between pagans and Christians, Homoian and Nicene Christians, and Jews and Christians, especially in regions controlled first by the Visigoths until the early sixth century and then by the Franks (see Drews, Chapter 6, this volume). Moreover, a range of legal options existed for conflict resolution, depending on the parties involved and the details of the case (see Rio, Chapter 23, this volume).

While our historical and hagiographical sources give limited attention to the integration of recent arrivals of different origins into the existing population of Merovingian Gaul, archaeological evidence from emporia, graves, and settlement sites allow us to see far more. For one, there were close ties between Britain, Gaul, and Germany in the late Roman period, based in some part on trade, especially bulk trade in low-value commodities. Although these exchanges drew to a halt by the first quarter of the fifth century, new contacts were initiated in the sixth century through two networks: one tying together Kent, Flanders, and the Rhine delta, and the second bringing together Frankish regions like Poitou-Charentes with western Britain. They allow us to see contacts as circular migration rather than as movement in a single direction, and they also permit us to see the objectives of such movement as primarily commercial rather than military (see Fleming, Chapter 17; Tys, Chapter 34, this volume). While the scale of exchange in this later period may have been muted compared to the late Roman era, such newer studies shift emphasis away from discussions based primarily on ethnic conflict.

Religion in Merovingian Gaul

The story of religion in Merovingian Gaul was once told primarily through written texts. Today, our view of the religious cultures of Merovingian Gaul's inhabitants has benefited from some of the same discoveries and new technologies that have transformed our view of other aspects of Merovingian society. Increasingly, archaeological findings are used to confirm, or challenge, written sources, allowing historians to reconsider traditional narratives that, in the past, were founded largely on sources generated by monks, nuns, and the clergy. Archaeological investigations of graves and cemeteries yield insights into regional religious practices, although, in the absence of robust documentary sources on burial objectives, it is unclear how this evidence relates to religious belief. New scientific methods enabling investigation of the fabric of religious buildings and monastic complexes are proving particularly fruitful, as they allow us to perceive the scale, organizational layout, and ornamental elements of the religious spaces that formed the environment in which Christians worshipped (see Chevalier, Chapter 30, this volume). As we learn more about the religious material environment, we can ask fresh questions about how Christians conducted and experienced their religion in Merovingian Gaul.

At the same time, and as the essays in this collection show, the peoples of Merovingian Gaul were not isolated from their neighbors. Indeed, trade, communication, and the constant movement of people ensured that they were aware of religious trends arising from outside their borders, even if they did not always actively engage with them. So, whereas there is much yet to be learned about how religion was practiced within Gaul, it is also important to consider that Merovingian religious ideas and practices were situated within the broader frames of religious expression. Christianity was a Mediterranean religion, and representatives of the Merovingian church actively sought to maintain contacts with Christian authorities and communities further afield, especially those in Byzantium and Rome. At the same time, its geopolitical position meant that contacts with northern European missionaries and reformist movements were important to the future direction of religious practices in Gaul (see Picard, Chapter 18, this volume).

The national story of King Clovis's conversion to Christianity, largely shaped by Gregory of Tours' narrative in his *Histories*, has had a formative role in situating the Merovingians within the history of European Christianity (see Graceffa, Chapter 3; Mathisen, Chapter 19, this volume). And yet almost every element in the traditional story has been challenged by modern scholars. For centuries, the Merovingian dynasty was indelibly associated with the iconic moment when Clovis stepped out of the baptismal pool, having washed away the "leprosy" of pagan belief, his locks anointed with oil, to receive the sign of the cross. According to the account of this moment, provided three quarters of a century later by Bishop Gregory of Tours, more than 3,000 Frankish warriors were then baptized, as was one of Clovis's sisters (*Decem Libri Historiarum* [*DLH*] 2.31). As a result of this act, Clovis, his followers, and his dynasty were no longer barbarian— they were Christian, in contrast to his father Childeric (Theuws 2019, pp. 140–147). Thereafter, historians and annalists celebrated and excoriated individual members of the dynasty, but above all, they integrated them into the universal history of the Christian Church. If the scions of the dynasty did not always live up to the elevated destiny Gregory of Tours hopefully imagined for them, their Christianity rendered them manageable, and when they failed, their misfortunes could be attributed to divine punishment. Of the various origin myths that came to be associated with the Merovingian dynasty—that they descended from a sea monster or from Trojan warriors—the myth of the miraculous transformation of a whole people from paganism to Christianity had the longest staying power as an iconic, transformative moment long celebrated in French history. In part, this story was so successful because church leaders in Gaul wanted it to be so. If Clovis was a "new Constantine" as Gregory of Tours proposed, then the security and religious future of his corner of the world were assured (Geary 2002, pp. 116–118).

Although Gregory is not the only source to attest to the importance of Clovis's conversion and baptism (others include Avitus of Vienne [MGH AA 4.2, pp. 75–76], Remigius of Reims [Gundlach (ed.), CCSL 117, pp. 409–410], and Nicetius of Trier [Gundlach (ed.), CCSL 117, pp. 419–423]), it is Gregory's description of that day that has provided the iconic elements that inspired future literary and artistic representations. It is also Gregory's account that wove the Franks into the history of the church, lauding Clovis as the Frankish defender of the faith alongside Gregory's own hero, the ascetic bishop, Martin of Tours. Christianity "took" as a Merovingian dynastic value, in contrast to the fate of some royal converts in other regions of Europe. Clovis's successes on the battlefield and his elimination of rival leaders ensured the dynasty's adherence to a Christian future. As Avitus predicted to Clovis, he and his descendants would "reign in heaven" (Avitus of Vienne, *Epistularum ad diversos libri tres, Ep.* 46 [41]). Indeed, despite the obvious personal failings of some individual Merovingian kings, the centuries of Merovingian rule saw the church benefit from prodigious support from the Merovingian dynasty and from the Frankish aristocracy in what amounted to a dynastic declaration of religious identity.

Gregory of Tours's focus on Clovis as an iconic figure can also be seen in the account of Clovis's conquest of Aquitaine. Clovis's campaign against the Visigothic kingdom in

Aquitaine may have been a longer-term project than previously recognized (see Mathisen, Chapter 19, this volume), but it resulted in conquest in 507. Gregory of Tours cast the conquest in religious terms, with the Christian Clovis prevailing over the "Arian" Alaric II, ignoring the support Alaric received from Catholics both within and outside his kingdom. Clovis's success was rewarded with imperial recognition and the visible symbols of his authority to rule. Some scholars identify this moment, in 507 or 508, as the date of Clovis' conversion, departing from the traditional date of 496 (Wood 1985). As a result, the Franks were brought firmly into the orbit of Mediterranean Christianity and Christian politics (see Esders, Chapter 16, this volume). Thenceforth, church leaders were drawn into the theological, doctrinal, and political upheavals that roiled in Italy and distant Byzantium. However, as it often lacked political and religious unity at home, the Merovingian church rarely achieved a monolithic stance toward such disputes, nor did it often strive to intervene directly in religious contests that were generated outside their borders.

The spectacle of Clovis's baptism has impressed modern historians, too. Drawing on the mythic grandeur of Gregory's narrative, Napoleon I's construction and decoration of the Pantheon in Paris elevated the baptism of Clovis to a national story (Wood 2013, pp. 79–81). From this perspective, a murky and inchoate period of migrations gave way to a vision of Christian kingship that would eventually dominate a unified Frankish empire, placing the people of Merovingian Gaul early, and securely, on a path of religious orthodoxy. Although its significance was disputed between Catholics and Republicans in the nineteenth and early twentieth centuries, Clovis's baptismal ceremony was an important symbolic event for French nationhood (see Coumert, Chapter 5, this volume). In 1996, the 1,500-year anniversary of 496, the traditional date, was duly celebrated across France. However, whereas Clovis's baptism once prompted scholars to debate the quality of his conversion to Christianity, today we are readier to question the quality of Clovis's original 'paganism.' Christianity of one sort or another was probably already far advanced in some circles, at least before the Franks converted "as a whole." Modern scholars can point to the imperatives of political expediency and the influence of family alliances to render Clovis's baptism a "symbolic concession to Constantinople" (see Esders, Chapter 16, this volume).

Although critical analyses of the written sources that address religion, including accounts of Clovis's baptism, continue to yield insights into the religious and political aspirations of the Franks on an international scale, historians interested in religion are no longer dependent on them. More challenging to eradicate, perhaps, is the fact that modern historical assessments of Merovingian religion have been susceptible to some of the same polarized characterizations and comparisons with what came before and what came after that haunt the period generally. Viewed from the perspective of the late-antique Mediterranean world, and especially in comparison with the intense theological activity of the fourth and early fifth centuries, Merovingian Christianity has sometimes appeared to be theologically unsophisticated, naïve, static, retrograde. The era's theologians, Gregory the Great, Julian of Toledo, Isidore of Seville, and the Venerable Bede, to name a few, wrote from centers of learning outside Gaul's borders, creating an impression, undoubtedly incorrect, of a theological void (see Moreira, Chapter 42; Coon,

Chapter 46, this volume). Furthermore, the energy that Merovingian Christians devoted to cataloguing and marveling at the miraculous power of the saints—sometimes seen as a lower form of religious practice—has encouraged the notion of religious decline in these centuries. The potential for distortion is also present when the Merovingian dynasty and the Merovingian church are seen from a reversed chronological perspective. In contrast to the ambition of the Carolingian church to impose unity and uniformity on religious practice, and especially the elevated aspirations of Charlemagne to yoke religion and empire, the Merovingian dynasty's approach to religious patronage can appear ad hoc. However, Merovingian kings did not require the church to legitimate their right to rule, and by contrast with the destructive imposition of unity by the Carolingians, the mosaic of local traditions that flourished under the Merovingians, especially with regard to the liturgy and the cult of the saints, favored the claims of regions and peoples to their own history. In an era when such claims are given greater voice in contemporary Europe, the survival of local variations under the Merovingians, even if only as a by-product of the fragmented nature of Merovingian rule, has a measure of worth. Similarly, Merovingian generosity to the church in terms of land donations and immunities might appear profligate (as it was viewed by the Carolingians) when it did not result in a stronger bond between the church and the dynasty in the long term. Scholars today have moved decisively beyond the easy storylines of Merovingian decay touted by their Carolingian successors, recognizing that such teleology masks thornier and more tantalizing questions about religion in Merovingian Gaul. The essays in this volume allow us to evaluate religion in the Merovingian centuries on its own terms: as a Christian culture that was remarkably functional, connected, engaged in wider religious affairs, and capable of religious expression that was meaningful and sometimes open to new ideas.

CHURCH ORGANIZATION

Whereas the Frankish elite was seemingly learning its new religion, the Gallo-Roman population had long been exposed to Christianity, and by the time of Clovis's conversion, they were likely predominantly Christians of one sort or another. In the sixth century, the Gallo-Roman church was guided by religious leaders who were, at the higher echelons at least, highly educated, connected, and organized. Notwithstanding the challenges they faced in maintaining contact with one another, especially when dioceses were cut through by secular political boundaries—a situation that could place some bishops and their communities in territories under the control of more than one king— bishops of the fifth and sixth centuries maintained a schedule of church councils, both major and regional, that sought to regulate practices and occasionally attempted to arrive at theological consensus (on councils and solidarity, see Halfond, Chapter 13, this volume). Some of these councils were better attended than others, as was always the case, and there were more of them than have left a written record. In the fifth and sixth centuries at least, church officials strove to discuss issues of common interest and to communicate conciliar deliberations and agreements to those who could not attend. Religious consensus was the ideal, and disagreement was often the reality, yet contact and communication fostered sufficient episcopal solidarity to allow clerics to speak for the church's interests when confronted by threats arising from the secular sphere. Even when councils were less regularly called in the seventh century and ceased to leave a record after about 680, bishops continued to communicate by letter on church matters, with each other, with kings and queens, and with popes. We know that early on, bishops and other members of the religious elite communicated often by letter, on papyrus, which could be easily transported by couriers along roads and waterways. Under the Merovingians, clerics continued the administrative practices of the late Roman state. As Andrew Gillett explains, the remarkable survival of over 500 letters from Gaul points to a level of bureaucratic activity that can be compared usefully with that of Coptic Egypt (see Gillett, Chapter 25, this volume). Populated by seasoned administrators, the Gallo-Roman church continued the documentary practices that helped shape legal practices under the Merovingians, including the Frankish "Salic" Law, property rights and property transfer, dispute resolution, inheritance and testamentary models, labor, gender, and slave status (see Rio, Chapter 23, this volume). A robust commitment to protecting a post-Roman legal culture in southern Gaul and the construction of Frankish law in the north helped define and protect the status and aspirations of religious communities, and monastic and clerical leaders.

THE BUILT ENVIRONMENT

Archaeological excavations of religious sites such as churches, cathedral complexes, and monasteries continue to shed light on religious life under the Merovingians. Since virtually nothing of the religious superstructure of Gaul remains, the investigation of structures below ground is crucial. From the descriptions of building programs and of interior spaces in hagiography and poetry, historians knew that Gaul's church interiors were highly decorated and colorful, furnished with paintings and mosaics analogous to those visible in the surviving structures of the late-antique jeweled style in Ravenna and Rome. Recent archaeological findings confirm that interior design continued to develop under the Merovingians, so that not only were mosaics used, as in Italy, but new elements were added so that "what is new and original is the interaction of architectural glass, mosaics and stained glass windows, which contributed to the luminosity of the interior church space" (see Chevalier, Chapter 30, this volume). Pascale Chevalier's essay discusses the vigorous "spatial conquest by the new faith" in which renovation, adaptation, and appropriation of ancient remains (*spolia*) were so extensive as to amount to "a definition" of Merovingian architectural style. Most churches in this era were on a smaller scale than those in former imperial cities, and timber roofs were common, but they reveal continued adherence to the Roman basilica model (central nave, aisles, domed apse) and the continued use of traditional construction methods. Meanwhile, excavations of modest religious structures in rural areas are furnishing materials for ongoing debates about the emergence of the parish system in Gaul. Crypts built under churches to accommodate the pious dead *ad sanctos*, such as the necropolis under the abbey church at Luxeuil, are also being examined, expanding our view of the world of the dead and the role of secular and religious patronage in shaping it. A push to identify and excavate monastic complexes promises that this will be an area of expanding knowledge in the future (see Chevalier, Chapter 30, this volume). In many cases for the first time, archaeology is allowing us to see the ritual spaces in which Christians practiced their religion.

Scale matters. Knowing that the structures within which Christians worshipped were smaller than the population they ostensibly served prompts reflection on the definition of the Christian "community" to which written sources so regularly appealed. As new evidence emerges that churches were highly compartmentalized by the use of arches, transepts, elevated platforms and seating, and that they were provided with spaces such as niches for relics and processional stations, we can begin to see how discrete spaces for sacred activities allowed for different spheres of cultic action within churches (see Chevalier, Chapter 30, this volume).

How was this population served, and how were the requirements of eucharistic ritual, in particular, managed? New studies of the liturgy help us to imagine how Christians participated in the daily, weekly, and yearly round of religious practices that defined their religious lives. The degree to which Christians participated in the religious rites of their religion is contested, however. Lisa Kaaren Bailey (Chapter 44, this volume) sees evidence, even from the fragmentary liturgical texts that have survived, that Christians had opportunities to participate in church ritual, in song, prayer, and responses, in processions, and in the eucharistic mass. At the same time, fewer laypeople took communion than before, and, increasingly clerical ritual was screened from their view. Ultimately, Bailey argues, both clerics and the laity shaped the Merovingian liturgy. Liturgical texts help us see another Merovingian practice—the naming of the dead for the purpose of remembrance. As Els Rose explains (Chapter 43, this volume), this practice fostered a sense of community and civic identity between the living and the dead, and between celebrants and the people. All members of the Christian community had the potential to fulfill their baptismal promise to be citizens of heaven. The distinctive feature of the Merovingian version of the naming rite, associated with the offertory, underscored the connection between the faithful who offered intercession and the dead who received it.

The religious activities of women are by no means hidden from view. Women were important members of the Merovingian religious community. However, they were not equal participants with men in the public performance of the Christian religion. Women could not be consecrated as priests, although the rarely referenced status of "deaconess" and the honorific title of *episcopa* for the wife of a bishop were gestures to the pastoral work that some women undertook. Infamously, in some communities at least, women were prohibited from touching either liturgical cloths or the communion host with bare hands (Council of Auxerre (561–605), canons 36, 37, and 42), and by virtue of their nonclerical status, certain spaces of sacred activity were denied them. Social and marital status determined the religious options open to women and the degree to which church authorities accepted and respected their choices. Women could become nuns if their families permitted it and if their families had the requisite resources to support them in a lifetime of prayer. Some rose to prominence within the monastic hierarchy (see James, Chapter 11, this volume). However, convents were also home to lower-status women whose service roles likely confined them permanently to a lower place in the religious hierarchy. Laywomen, especially those in a position to become benefactors and patrons, were important members of church communities in Late Antiquity. As congregants, they offered gifts, including bread for use in the eucharistic celebration. It is likely, too, that women had a role in making and laundering vestments and cloths used in churches, although the evidence for this comes mostly in the form of prohibitions (Caesarius of Arles, *Rule for Nuns*).

From the start, women connected to the Merovingian dynasty were recorded as public supporters of the church, and it was expected that queens in particular would foster religious and cultic activity within their spheres of influence (see Moreira, Chapter 42, this volume). Queens could command resources of land and precious objects that were desirable to the church; throughout the period, they feature as patrons and founders of monasteries and churches, in some cases co-signing royal donation charters for under-age sons. Furthermore, the church sought to protect wills in which women left property to the church against other claimants (see James, Chapter 11, this volume). Clerics were not reticent to acknowledge the support of high-profile women for the advancement of Christianity. Clovis's wife, Chlothild, was credited by Gregory of Tours as having been instrumental in the conversion of her husband to Christianity. The ambitiously ascetic Queen Radegund, the Thuringian wife of Clovis's son Chlothar I, acquired a fragment of the True Cross for her convent in Poitiers, which allowed her to be compared to St. Helena, mother of Constantine (Moreira 1993). Radegund was an especially important figure for the Merovingians. Not only did her relic acquisition bring to Gaul a symbol of Christian empire, but it showed her power to touch the wider Christian world through her connections in Constantinople (Moreira 1993; see Esders, Chapter 16, this volume). In fact, Radegund was not the first woman in Gaul to possess a piece of this prestigious relic, but her foundation of the Sainte-Croix convent in Poitiers, together with her reputation for personal sanctity, made her a model for subsequent queens and their aristocratic daughters (see James, Chapter 11, this volume). Indeed, queens and aristocrats who honored the church had a pathway to sanctity. But pride in their elevated status was the way they were most likely to fail. Hagiographers described queens undertaking the most menial of household tasks at court and in the convent, thereby reflecting how religious humility was gendered. However, monastic founders were under no illusion that cleaning held parity with prayer as a path to respect and status. Despite her reputation for cleaning latrines, Radegund adopted a rule for her nuns from St. Caesaria's convent in Arles that expressly forbade nuns from taking in laundry.

The elite are more visible in the sources than their humbler counterparts because they often controlled resources that could be put to the direct support of the church (see James, Chapter 11, this volume). In their secular lives, queens were encouraged to exert their domestic influence with the king and with their sons to promote the religion and to promote clerical careers. Like kings and bishops, queens had households in which they could shape religious learning and culture. Although we have evidence for this only later, the role of elite women in the religious and moral education of their sons and daughters may have been significant in this period, although their influence once their sons reached majority was variable. Widows with young sons could achieve considerable political influence, aided, as in Queen Balthild's case, by allies in the church. Hagiographies of queens and aristocrats dominate the written sources on women, but humble serving women sometimes appear on the periphery of the texts, living parallel lives of asceticism and service without literary recognition (Bailey 2012).

Those who escaped the notice of the authors of texts were by far the largest segment of the population. Because burial was for most a family responsibility, mortuary archaeology sheds important light on the practices and rituals of "ordinary" Christians, even accepting the challenges of identifying religious practice and personal agency in burial contexts. While burial with objects was a Christian practice in this area (see Kornbluth, Chapter 40, this volume), and such burials have been long documented, discussions of religious practice can be moved into new areas by asking how communities were able to access items they deposited. Frans Theuws's analysis of the rural population of northern Gaul in the sixth and first half of the seventh centuries reveals a population that was able to "satisfy their ritual demands" through trade (Chapter 38, this volume). This trade, even if not direct, brought rural inhabitants items whose component parts were sourced from both local and distant lands, including cowrie shells from the Red Sea and Indian Ocean, and garnets from India and Sri Lanka (see Pion et al., Chapter 36, this volume). This rural population that buried its dead with "immense" numbers of objects used these artifacts to express the religious ideas of their communities and community connections with the supernatural. Eventually, the exuberance of this form of religious expression changed, possibly for economic and structural reasons (see Theuws, Chapter 38, this volume), but this reflected a change in religious expression rather than religious affiliation. The presence of a wide variety of goods in the graves of populations that likely identified as Christian shows that religious identity could be expressed variously, and that amulets and other items whose function is not always known but that may have been intended to ward off evil (apotropaic), fell within acceptable parameters of Christian burial practice (on amulets, see Kornbluth, Chapter 40, this volume).

IDEAS FROM ABROAD

An aspect of Merovingian religious culture that we can appreciate today more than in the past is the role of human mobility. The connections that recent studies of trade and traded items are beginning to expose likewise supported the movement of clerical personnel, religious goods, manuscripts, and religious ideas. Early medieval written sources describe how kings and bishops, along with their extensive retinues, traveled long distances across Europe for the purposes of education, pilgrimage, dispute of cases in Rome, and (in the case of select bishops) acceptance of the *pallium* (a liturgical scarf) from the pope. Merovingian Gaul's geographic position at the center of land and sea routes to and from Rome from northern Europe meant that outsiders crossed through its borders, used its transportation systems, visited shrines, and took up residence in its towns for months or even years.

Merovingian episcopal culture was evidently worthy of admiration in some quarters. Viewed from outside its borders, Wilfrid of York, for example, had an admiration and affinity for Merovingian episcopal culture. Besides reportedly receiving the tonsure from the bishop of Lyon, he lived for years in Gaul as well as Rome. While the journeys of Irish monks to Britain and Gaul are preserved in written sources, and we know of a few named individuals who traveled between England, Gaul, and Ireland for education to take up clerical positions, or because they were in exile, archaeology reveals that such journeys followed long-established trade routes that conveyed ceramics, glass, and other wares such as wine (used for the celebration of the mass), and coins (see Fleming, Chapter 17; Picard, Chapter 18; Tys, Chapter 34, this volume). As Jean-Michel Picard notes, better knowledge of trade activity in the Loire estuary "confirms that both Columbanus in Co. Down and Fursey in Co. Louth left Ireland from regions that had direct commercial contacts with the Merovingian world" (Chapter 18, this volume). These routes carried not only people, but also books, letters, diplomatic gifts, religious items, paintings, religious craftsmen (and perhaps their families), and musicians. Written sources reveal that Merovingian Gaul, just as much as Italy and beyond, provisioned goods and personnel for the advancement of Christian life in remote areas of northern Europe. Nor was the traffic one way. Franks traveled to England and to Ireland even if they are not as visible in the written sources as the Irish who traveled to the continent. Merovingian Gaul was a hub for religious activity.

Outsiders had long been important to the practice of religion in Gaul, and this continued under the Merovingians. The rise of monasticism in Gaul, patterned after eastern Mediterranean models from the late fourth to the sixth century, shaped by the influence of Irish monks and their monastic values in the seventh century, and the activity of Anglo-Saxon missionaries on its eastern frontiers in the eighth are indicative of the ways that the population of Merovingian Gaul could be influenced by religious movements from outside its borders. Nor were Merovingian royal courts deaf to papal appeals for support when missionary campaigns to other regions were underway. Pope Gregory's plan to Christianize Kent was supported by Queen Brunhild and her court (Wood 1994). Augustine and his monks lingered in Merovingian Gaul as they collected liturgical texts and other items that would enable them to succeed in Canterbury. Merovingian Gaul, alongside Italy, could satisfy the shopping sprees and gifted acquisitions by which Benedict Biscop provisioned the monasteries of Wearmouth and Jarrow (Bede, *Lives of the Abbots*, 4, 6). This is not to say that there was no pushback against outsiders or their persecution. But overall, and compared with Spain under the Visigoths, the fact that Jewish communities maintained a presence in Gaul at the Merovingian court and in southern cities where they had long been resident, and that Irish monks were able to take up residence in Merovingian Francia, points to the "cultural diversity and vitality of the Merovingian world" (Drews, Chapter 6, this volume). Systems of political and spiritual patronage played their part in the success of these foreigners and their ideas in Gaul (see Picard, Chapter 18, this volume). This was particularly the case with the settlement of Irish monks in northern Gaul alongside the more "mixed crowd" at Agaune (see Diem, Chapter 15, this volume). Merovingian Gaul was geographically situated to be a point of convergence for people and ideas from outside their borders. Merovingian church leaders were kept busy assessing, absorbing, and adapting to the religious ideas and practices of newcomers, and placed a premium on maintaining theological orthodoxy at home (see Moreira, Chapter 42, this volume).

Merovingian churches, alongside other churches of Europe, were on the sidelines of the Mediterranean religious powerhouses of Rome and Constantinople, but this did not mean that they were not invested or involved in what was going on there. High-status clerics, in particular, were as informed as they could be about disputes rumbling around the Christian world, and individually they could develop a stance, debate the issues, and disagree. Stefan Esders points to three major disputes in the sixth and seventh centuries to which Merovingian clerics demonstrably reacted: the Three Chapter controversy (548–553), the Lateran Synod (or Council) of 649, and the Sixth Ecumenical Council (680–681). As noted earlier, the Merovingian church was not a monolithic entity in its religious stance, with kingdoms reacting differently to events abroad—as they did in the case of the Lateran Council of 649 (see Esders, Chapter 16, this volume). Even if our sources reveal this only occasionally, Merovingian religious leaders cared about theology and the disputes emanating from the Mediterranean basin.

At home, Merovingian churchmen set their religious agendas according to their resources. For many bishops, attention to local concerns meant promoting the cult of local saints. This was a religious agenda that did not ignore the laity, for in providing for the needs of the populace in their localities, high-ranking clerics sometimes promoted their own. Gregory of Tours is a vital resource for this world. If, however, we rely only on Gregory for our information on the cult of the saints, we are presented with a world of competition dominated by personal squabbles and community shenanigans. The political stakes of the cult of saints dominates this view, with towns and monasteries vying with each other for the acquisition of relics, and with stories of how the supernatural "protection" offered by powerful saints could debase the ambitions of nobles and kings. Saints were patrons, protectors, and big business (Brown 1981). The theological implications of this veneration does not often surface in Merovingian texts. Yet communities made choices about the saints they revered, even the homegrown saints they supposedly inherited. Over time, some cult allegiances blossomed while others faded into the background. Churches and monasteries that adopted universal cults, such as those of St. Peter, the Virgin Mary, and the True Cross, or foreign cults such as St. Mamas and St. Vincent, broadcast their values and allegiances, and signaled their aspirations to be part of a wider Christendom. Such choices were not devoid of theological understanding or intent. By the seventh century, St. Martin had serious competition among the Franks in the figure of St. Peter. The promise of the saints to provide salvation and protection, and to generally navigate the afterlife became increasingly acute as time went on. It was a shift in theological perception that closed off hell to the plunder of saints like Martin. Increasingly, the dying expected to see St. Peter waiting for them at the gates of heaven (see Moreira, Chapter 42, this volume).

In the salvific scope of penance and in the views of the afterlife, we see critical theological choices being made. Informed by the penitential theologies of John Cassian and Augustine of Hippo in the early fifth century, the sermons of Caesarius in the sixth century, and the afterlife visions of Pope Gregory the Great's *Dialogues* in the late sixth century, church authorities were primed to encounter new penitential ideas from Irish missionaries at the turn of the seventh century and new views of the afterlife as preached by Anglo-Saxon missionaries at its easternmost borders in the eighth (see Uhalde, Chapter 45, this volume). But whereas penitential revivalism touched a spiritual chord among many Christians, and was embraced by monastic communities in many places, Merovingian texts about the afterlife reveal a notable degree of caution about innovations, and in particular ideas about postmortem purgation that were circulating contemporaneously in Italy, England, and Ireland (see Moreira, Chapter 42, this volume). The position of Merovingian religious authorities on theological innovation needs to be understood on its own terms. What appears in hindsight as an inherent conservatism in the Merovingian theological worldview could be equally understood as a reasonable reaction to some very strange ideas. And we must recall the loss of so many works from Merovingian libraries and other manuscript deposits (papyrus and parchment) that informed them. In their approach to eastern religious disputes (see Esders, Chapter 16, this volume), their divided reaction to Irish newcomers (see Diem, Chapter 15, this volume), and their conservative views about the afterlife (see Moreira, Chapter 42, this volume), we can see how Merovingian religious authorities were more than capable of having theological opinions, debating theological interpretations, and dampening rash and possibly dangerous theological novelties.

It is important to emphasize that Christians in the Merovingian period had, at different times and places, opportunities to hear about, observe, and join those living a spiritual life. On an individual level, access to religious opportunities would be highly moderated—the institution of religion was a hierarchy above all, dominated by economics, family, gender, and ritual—but in general, the Merovingian Christian found diverse ways to express love for God and his saints. At the altar of their local church or on pilgrimage to a cultic hotspot, Christians could ask for divine protection in time of ill health or other need, and they were often provided with other forms of support at these locations in the form of alms or medical attention. Church services, monasteries, and saints' cults provided most people with a path through which to express a religious appetite. In the seventh and eighth centuries, an era of "religious revivalism," penitential remedies for sin continued to evolve. (see Uhalde, Chapter 45, this volume). By their very nature, reform movements encouraged new groups to participate in religious thinking and to challenge the status quo. In this great age of hagiographic literature, the image of Christian saint and martyr, proclaiming a life of faith, spoke to the desire for a richly imagined life of the soul, and the companionship of all of the saints who offered healing and solace in the present life and protection in the next (see Kreiner, Chapter 24, this volume). Our sources reveal expressions of love for the word of God, a reverence for the scriptures, a devotion to the saints, and a passion for the mystical figure of Christ, whether expressed in liturgical prayers, in hagiography, in stone, or in other creative modes of artistic expression (see Coon, Chapter 46, this volume). Yet, any attempt to judge the "quality" of Christianity from the written sources, using a modern religious perspective, is irremediably flawed and inevitably teleological; to do so from physical remains is no less problematic. The presence of grave goods in burials, even those in churches, that led earlier generations to question the commitment of this population to Christianity, is roundly dismissed today as providing evidence for pagan burial (Effros 2002). And practices at the edges of religion, such as devotion to amulets or interest in divinatory magic, are today less likely to be labeled pagan, primitive, or deviant than was the case in the past (see Kornbluth, Chapter 40; Klingshirn, Chapter 41, this volume).

That said, there is much that we do not know about the daily experiences of the population of Gaul. The presence of priests, the activity of councils, and the local provisions of pastoral and substantive care for the community that was a feature of Merovingian Gaul (see Horden, Chapter 14, this volume) meant that religion mattered in this society. As for the elite, its investment in religion reaped enormous political dividends. The fate of those who felt trapped into the religious life, and the social realities that made any kind of personal choice a privilege, meant that the spiritually lukewarm had a harder journey. Nuns trying to escape from convents and monastic rules designed to imprison unhappy monks hint at individual horrors. But there is no doubt that Merovingian Gaul was a society that, while it may have offered its best face to only a few, had no doubt about its identity as a Christian region when facing those around them.

Conclusion

The Merovingian Franks we have encountered in this volume are not Gibbon's Franks. The cultural vitality of the diverse inhabitants of Gaul in these centuries, their embeddedness in the Mediterranean and European worlds, and their historical importance to the history of Europe give the lie to Gibbon's extraordinarily reductive assessment of them. But whereas the inhabitants of Merovingian Gaul are not Gibbon's Franks, neither are they an obscure historical interlude of even a generation ago. The scope of Merovingian studies continues to expand as new lines of inquiry emerge from multiple disciplinary directions. This is true not only of our expanding knowledge base gleaned from new archaeological work and the application of new scientific methods, but also in terms of the accessibility of Merovingian-era written and material sources to scholars and even to the interested public. Editions of Merovingian texts can be found in the publications of the *Monumenta Germaniae Historica,* especially the dedicated series on Merovingian writings, the *Scriptores rerum Merovingicarum,* which has been available since 2004 in digital format, free, searchable, and online, and in the *Corpus Christianorum, series Latina* published by Brepols. Most Merovingian written works are known from later copies, so projects that make medieval manuscripts available through digitization, especially those of the Carolingian era, advance our knowledge of works composed in the Merovingian period also. The digitization of early medieval manuscripts held in collections across the globe is providing access to sources that were once available only to a few privileged researchers, or else through expensive facsimiles. For example, the virtual manuscript library of Switzerland (https://www.e-codices.unifr.ch/en), an ongoing project that includes, to date, over 600 digitized manuscripts from the St. Gall Monastery library (Codices Electronici Sangallensis http://www.cesg.unifr.ch/de/index.htm), is both a codicological gem and a model for other repositories. Furthermore, digitization is allowing for imaginative projects of library reconstruction, such as the virtual reassembly of the now dispersed contents of the Carolingian library and the scriptorium of Lorsch (Bibliotheca Laureshamensis), which includes manuscripts from as early as the fourth century (http://bibliotheca-laureshamensis-digital.de/en/kloster/bibliothek_skriptorium.html). Another recent virtual library reconstruction, the Bibliotheca Palatina (http://digi.ub.uni-heidelberg.de/bpd), combines over 3,500 manuscripts in the collection of Heidelberg University and the Vatican Library, including early medieval copies of the work of Gregory of Tours and Fredegar. Most national libraries provide electronic access to digitized documents, and some also provide images and/or databases for objects in their collection. Some sleuthing is required to keep on top of ever-expanding electronic resources, but the following offer a starting point. For scholarship on the Merovingian era generally, Gallica, the digitized collection of the Bibliothèque nationale de France (BnF) (https://gallica.bnf.fr), provides access to written works as well as to images of early medieval artifacts and links to the collections of regional museums. Merovingian items in European collections are found on their websites, although these may not represent entire holdings. Places to start include the electronic resources of the British Museum (London), the Musée d'archéologie nationale (Saint-Germain-en-Laye), the Römisch-Germanisches Museum (Köln), the Römisch-Germanisches Zentralmuseum (Mainz), the Rijksmuseum van Oudheden (Leiden), and the Metropolitan Museum of Art (New York). New ways of thinking about manuscripts, libraries, and historical library collections promise to advance our knowledge of the Merovingian period.

We are grateful to the *Oxford Handbook* series for giving us this opportunity to bring together some of the exciting scholarship being done on the Merovingian world and on a scale hitherto not available in English. It is not our intention to be comprehensive—that is impossible in any case—but to bring together studies and disciplinary voices that do not often share the same publication space. We hope that this volume, with its diverse perspectives and approaches, conveys something of the dynamism of the field, providing a snapshot and an entry point into research currently underway in the field of Merovingian studies. By providing English-language essays on areas of research activity that are sometimes hidden from view in Anglophone scholarship, and in some cases presented here in English for the first time, we hope to make the Merovingian world more accessible to students and scholars of Late Antiquity and the Middle Ages.

Works Cited

Ancient Sources

Avitus of Vienne, *Epistularum ad diversos libri tres, Ep.* 46(41). R. Peiper (ed.). (1883). AA 6.2, pp. 75–76. Berlin: Weidmann.

Bede, *Lives of the Abbots of Wearmouth and Jarrow.* C. Plummer (ed.). (1946). *Baedae Opera Historica* (Vol. 1, pp. 364–387). Oxford, UK: Clarendon Press.

Bede, *Lives of the Abbots of Wearmouth and Jarrow.* C. Grocock and I. N. Wood (eds. and trans.). (2013). *Abbots of Wearmouth and Jarrow*, pp. 21–75. Oxford, UK: Oxford University Press.

Caesarius of Arles, *Rule for Nuns.* A. de Vogüé and J. Courreau (eds.). (1988). *Césaire d'Arles: Oeuvres monastiques.* SC 345. Paris: Editions du Cerf.

Caesarius of Arles, *Rule for Nuns.* M. C. McCarthy (trans.). (1960). *The Rule for Nuns of St. Caesarius of Arles.* Washington, DC: Catholic University of America Press.

Council of Auxerre (561–605). J. Gaudemet and B. Basdevant (eds.). (1989). *Les canons Mérovingiens (VIe-VIIe siècles.* (t. 2). SC 354. Paris: Editions du Cerf.

Fredegar, *Chronicle.* J. M. Wallace-Hadrill (ed. and trans.). (1960). *The Fourth Book of the Chronicle of Fredegar with Its Continuations.* Oxford, UK: Oxford University Press.

Gregory of Tours. *Histories.* B. Krusch (ed.). (1951). *Decem libri historiarum.* MGH SRM 1.1. Hanover: Hahn.

Liber Historiae Francorum. B. Krusch (ed.). (1984). MGH SRM 2. Hanover, Germany: Hahn.

Nicetius of Trier, *Epistula* 3. W. Gundlach (ed.). (1957). *Epistulae Austrasicae.* CCSL 117, pp. 419–423. Turnhout, Belgium: Brepols.

Remigius of Reims, *Epistula* 3. W. Gundlach (ed.). (1957). *Epistulae Austrasicae.* CCSL 117, pp. 409–411. Turnhout, Belgium: Brepols.

Modern Sources

Amorim, C. E. G., Vai, S., Posth, C., Modi, A., et al. (2018). "Understanding 6th-Century Barbarian Social Organization and Migration through Paleogenomics." *bioRxiv preprint.* doi:10.1101/268250

Bailey, L. K. (2012). "Within and Without: Lay People and the Church in Gregory of Tours' Miracle Stories." *Journal of Late Antiquity* 5(1): 119–144.

Bonifay, M. (2013). "Africa: Patterns of Consumption in Coastal Regions versus Inland Regions. The Ceramic Evidence (300–700 AD)." In L. Lavan (ed.), *Local Economies? Production and Exchange of Inland Regions in Late Antiquity* (pp. 529–566). Leiden: Brill.

Brown, D. (2003). *The Da Vinci Code.* New York: Doubleday.

Brown, P. (1981). *The Cult of the Saints: Its Rise and Function in Late Antiquity.* Chicago: University of Chicago Press.

Brown, P. (2000). "The Decline of the Empire of God. Amnesty, Penance, and the Afterlife from Late Antiquity to the Middle Ages." In C. W. Bynum and P. Freedman (eds.), *Last Things. Death and the Apocalypse in the Middle Ages* (pp. 40–59). Philadelphia: University of Pennsylvania Press.

Coulson, F. and Babcock, R. (eds.) (2020). *The Oxford Handbook of Latin Palaeography.* Oxford: Oxford University Press.

Dunn, M. (2013). *Belief and Religion in Barbarian Europe c. 350–700* London: Bloomsbury.

Effros, B. (2002). *Caring for Body and Soul: Burial and the Afterlife in the Merovingian World.* University Park: Pennsylvania State University Press.

Esders, S., Fox, Y., Hen, Y., and Sarti, L. (eds.). (2019). *East and West in the Early Middle Ages: The Merovingian Kingdoms in Mediterranean.* Cambridge: Cambridge University Press.

Geary, P. J. (2002). *The Myth of Nations: The Medieval Origins of Europe.* Princeton: Princeton University Press.

Gibbon, E. (1995). *History of the Decline and Fall of the Roman Empire,* vol. 2. Edited by D. Womersley. London: Penguin Classics.

Haldon, J., Elton, H., Huebner, S. R., Izdebski, A., Mordechai, L., and Newfield, T. P. (2018a). "Plagues, climate change, and the end of an empire: A response to Kyle Harper's *The Fate of Rome* (1): Climate." *History Compass* 16: e12508. doi:10.1111/hic3.12508

Haldon, J., Elton, H., Huebner, S. R., Izdebski, A., Mordechai, L., and Newfield T. P. (2018b). "Plagues, climate change, and the end of an empire. A response to Kyle Harper's *The Fate of Rome* (2): Plagues and a crisis of empire." *History Compass* 16: e12506. doi:10.1111/hic3.12506

Haldon, J., Elton, H., Huebner, S. R., Izdebski, A., Mordechai, L., Newfield, T. P. (2018c). "Plagues, climate change, and the end of an empire: A response to Kyle Harper's *The Fate of Rome* (3): Disease, agency, and collapse." *History Compass* 16: e12507. doi:10.1111/hic3.12507

Harper, K. (2017). *The Fate of Rome: Climate, Disease, and the End of an Empire.* Princeton, NJ: Princeton University Press.

Kreiner, J. (2017). "Pigs in the Flesh and the Fisc: An Early Medieval Ecology." *Past and Present* 236: 4–42.

McCormick, M. (2001). *Origins of the European economy. Communications and commerce, AD 300-900.* Cambridge, UK: Cambridge University Press.

Mordechai, L., Eisenberg, M., Newfield, T. P., Izdebski, A., Kay, J. E., and Poinard, H. (2019). "The Justinianic plague: An inconsequential pandemic?" *Proceedings of the National Academy of Sciences* December 116 (51): 25546–25554. doi:10.1073/pnas.1903797116

Moreira, I. (1993). "Provisatrix optima: St. Radegund of Poitiers' Relic Petitions to the East." *Journal of Medieval History* 19: 285–305.

Müldner, G. (2009). "Investigating Medieval Diet and Society by Stable Isotope Analysis of Human Bone." In R. Gilchrist and A. Reynolds (eds.), *Reflections: Fifty Years of Medieval Archaeology, 1957-2007* (327–346). Society for Medieval Archaeology Monographs 30. London: Routledge.

Périn, P. (1980). *La datation des tombes mérovingiennes: Historique-Méthodes-Applications.* Centre de recherches d'histoire et de philologie de la IVe section de l'École pratique des hautes études 5. Hautes études médiévales et modernes 39. Geneva: Librairie Droz.

Pion, C., and Vrielyck, O. (2014). "Le cimetière de Bossut-Gottechain (Belgique) et son implication dans l'établissement d'une nouvelle chronologie normalisée des perles en Gaule mérovingienne." *Bulletin de Liaison de l'Association française d'archéologie mérovingien* 38: 87–91.

Pirenne, H. (1937). *Mahomet et Charlemagne.* Paris: F. Alcan.

von Doderer, Heimito. (1962). *Die Merowinger oder Die totale Familie.* Munich: Biederstein Verlag.

Theuws, F. (2019). "Burial Archaeology and the Transformation of the Roman World in Northern Gaul (4th to 6th Centuries)." In S. Brather-Walter (ed.), *Archaeology, History and Biosciences: Interdisciplinary Perspectives* (pp. 125–150). Berlin: De Gruyter.

Wickham, C. (2005). *Framing the Early Middle Ages. Europe and the Mediterranean 400-800.* Oxford, UK: Oxford University Press.

Wood, I. N. (1983). *The Merovingian North Sea*. Occasional Papers on Medieval Topics 1. Alingsås, Sweden: Viktoria Bokförlag.

Wood, I. N. (1985). "Gregory of Tours and Clovis." *Revue Belge de Philologie et d'Histoire* 63: 249–272.

Wood, I. N. (1994). "The Mission of Augustine of Canterbury to the English." *Speculum* 69: 1–17.

Wood, I. N. (2013). *The Modern Origins of the Early Middle Ages*. Oxford, UK: Oxford University Press.

PART I

MEROVINGIAN
HISTORIOGRAPHY
AND THE HISTORY
OF ARCHAEOLOGY

CHAPTER 2

FROM GAUL TO FRANCIA
The Impact of the Merovingians

PAUL FOURACRE

THE Merovingian dynasty ruled for 270 years (481–751), and during this period it can be said that "Gaul" became "Francia." This transition has had enormous impact on thinking about how European society developed in the early Middle Ages. In the early modern period, historians looked to the way in which the Franks created a long-lasting kingdom in order to understand the nature of the political institutions and social structures of their own day. Political thinkers with very different agendas saw in the establishment of the Frankish kingdom the origins of both "good" and "bad" elements in their world. Of primary concern were the transfer of power from the Romans to the barbarians and the role Christianity played in the formation of European culture, for better or worse, according to their personal stance over religion (Wood 2013). This discussion began with the Carolingians, was developed in the later Middle Ages, and continued through to the Enlightenment, the Age of Revolution, and beyond. Each European nation that grew up on soil once ruled by the Romans had its own set of questions about how it had come into being and how the seeds of the present (good or bad) had been sown. It was in France, however, that the history of post-Roman development was most strongly contested and that the debate had the strongest political resonance. It was indeed the experience of working through the long-term ramifications of the transfer of power from the Romans to the barbarians that gave French scholarship the leading edge in early medieval history. This in turn meant that interpretations of development in France became models for Europe as a whole (Fouracre 2014). Such a long-established Francocentric view of early medieval history has had the effect of throwing the spotlight onto the Merovingians and making the fact that Gaul turned into Francia a salient point in European development.

French thinkers were uniquely well placed to speak to the present through the medium of "their" early medieval history because they had clear access to it via an unbroken chain of narrative sources. That narrative began with Gregory of Tours's *Ten Books of Histories*, a work that was usually read in a shortened six-book version that came to be known as the "History of the Franks" (Krusch 1951; Thorpe 1971). Gregory took the history of the Merovingians from the beginning up to the end of the sixth century. His history was embellished in the *Chronicles of Fredegar* and continued into the 640s (Wallace-Hadrill 1960). The story up to the 720s was then taken up in the *Book of the History of the Franks* (*Liber Historiae Francorum*, henceforth *LHF*; Fouracre and Gerberding 1996) and, finally, the *Continuations of the Fourth Book of Fredegar* (Wallace-Hadrill 1960) completed Merovingian history with an account of the decline and replacement of the dynasty and the rise to power of their successors, the Carolingians (on historiography, see Reimitz, Chapter 22, this volume). The narrative then continued first with the annals of the Carolingian period and then with the recording of history in a host of local annals and chronicles that copied the earlier works. What could now be regarded as a national past was, finally, standardized in the widely circulated *Chroniques de France* of the fourteenth century (Viard 1920–1953). Alongside the narrative there were charters from the Merovingian period available as originals or, later, as cartulary copies (Kölzer 2001; Pardessus 1843–1849), as well as the law code *Lex Salica* (Fischer Drew 1991) and further legislation, as well as the largest corpus of hagiography in Europe. Great continuities could be traced through these sources, not the least of which was that the Franks had given their name to France (Francia) which imbued the French with a sense of direct descent from the inhabitants of the Merovingian world, albeit from the Gallo-Roman inhabitants of that world (see Graceffa, Chapter 3, this volume). It was important, too, that many of the religious institutions first appearing in the Merovingian period survived up to 1789, and the proximity to Paris of two of them, the monasteries of Saint-Germain-des-Prés and Saint-Denis, reinforced the capital city's sense of continuity with the distant past (Fouracre 2014).

On the one hand, unbroken narrative, the survival and recording of institutions over more than a millennium, and an unparalleled effort to edit and publish the sources produced by those same institutions offer the historian an unrivaled opportunity to study one society in one region as it developed over an extraordinarily long term: hence the way in which west European developments have tended to be modeled on Frankish history. On the other hand, we must be aware of the distortions produced by this particular national focus. First, it should be noted that emphasis on continuities in a specifically French past has had the effect of dragging Merovingian history westward. Southern and central Germany, which could equally lay claim to the Merovingian past, did not do so, if for no other reason than that there was no state of Germany to do so before the later nineteenth century (see Hardt, Chapter 20, this volume). We must therefore be careful not to overprivilege the history of the Franks in the west, as opposed to the east. Second, canonizing these particular narratives has had the effect of producing history that focuses on kings, queens, and a very few named members of a social elite (see Hen, Chapter 10, this volume). In this history, the personality of rulers looms very large. Much aided by the Carolingian denigration of their predecessors, Merovingian history has often been written in terms of the progressive decline of the dynasty as manifested in the personal failings of its members, to the point that one wonders how the dynasty possibly could have survived longer than any other in Europe (Fouracre 2005). Third, we know so much more about the Merovingians than about other regimes in the same period that comparison is difficult and perspective hard to establish.

From the works of Gregory of Tours, much can be learned about events in sixth-century Gaul. His narrative is indeed consistently thick enough for historians to analyze Merovingian family politics in some detail, even when they recognize that Gregory's account is socially one dimensional and constructed according to a religious agenda. At the heart of this picture are the Merovingian family itself and the affairs of the Catholic Church. Kings are judged very much in terms of their relations with the church, others in terms of how power and wealth affected their behavior. A range of peoples is mentioned: Franks, Gallo-Romans, Burgundians, Saxons, Thuringians, Goths, and the inhabitants of various regions and towns, but these names do little more than tell of where people were and of what happened to them as a group. So flat is this picture that historians can say very little about ethnicity or social structure in Gregory's world. One of the main debates about the Franks among historians of the later twentieth century was over whether or not they had had an aristocracy of birth from the beginning. If not, where did the aristocracy, so visible in the seventh century, come from? Was it, in other words, an aristocracy of blood (*Geburtsadel*), or was it one of service (*Dienstadel*) (Irsigler 1969; Grahn-Hoek 1971)? The works of Gregory of Tours offer little help in answering these questions. The same is true of the earliest Frankish law code, the *Pactus Legis Salicae, or Lex Salica,* composed before the death of King Clovis in 511, which made a strong distinction between free and unfree people in society but did not differentiate among groups within the free. Documentary sources, which can be traced back into the sixth century through formularies (models for drawing up various kinds of document) (Rio 2008; see Rio, Chapter 23, this volume), likewise distinguish between free and unfree people but say virtually nothing about other forms of social distinction. What these sources do show, however, is a surprising degree of social and legal pragmatism. Women's inheritance, for instance, was postponed behind that of male relatives, but according to the evidence of the formularies, parents could decide to make daughters equal co-heirs if they wished (Fouracre 2000a; see James, Chapter 11, this volume). Free and unfree people could not marry according to *Lex Salica,* but if they did do so, arrangements could be made for them to live together without hindrance (Rio 2006). *Lex Salica* itself largely consists of a tariff of compensations for various injuries. These set out in public the amount that an injured party might receive in lieu of taking direct action to avenge loss or injury. An agreed tariff was a way of making the acceptance of compensation honorable, but the unspoken alternative of violent self-help was always on the cards. Each "people" in the territories dominated by the Franks had their own laws; Roman law continued to be cited, and churchmen lived according to their own rules. Court cases, records for which survive from the later seventh century onward, could take all of these factors into account (Fouracre 1986).

As already noted, the Merovingian family itself dominates the sixth-century narrative, but their followers and underlings came from a variety of backgrounds and had different ethnic origins. Gallo-Romans are especially prominent in Gregory's *Histories,* though their background is often indicated only by their names. From the end of the sixth century, people with Frankish names begin to predominate. Intermarriage, and a growing preference for Frankish naming practices and for Frankish ways, would seem to be the explanation for this. It is also the key to how Gaul became Francia as a degree of cultural solidarity coalesced around a landholding elite drawn from a variety of backgrounds but who shared in the legitimation of power and privilege that came from support for the Catholic Church and from association with one or other Merovingian regime (Fouracre 2004). The result was the development of a polity based on a highly integrated elite. Frankish identity, which rested ultimately on success in warfare against other peoples, was sufficiently flexible to accommodate local custom, and there was a common interest in being part of a successful polity that could reward adherents (Reimitz 2015). Over the course of the Merovingian period, that polity grew to a massive size despite having what can only be characterized as weak governing institutions. This was "Francia" as the Carolingians inherited it in the mid-eighth century, by which time it was a polity set for further expansion. Let us now look more closely at its making.

In *Mahomet et Charlemagne* (1937), Henri Pirenne famously argued that the Roman world came to an end not with the so-called Germanic invasions but with the rise of Arab power that severed trading connections across the Mediterranean. His thesis was based on a reading of narrative sources, prominent among them being the works of Gregory of Tours. In these sources, Pirenne found references to Mediterranean merchants visiting Gaul and the continuing importation of "typical" Mediterranean products: wine, olive oil, papyrus, and spices from further east. Fed by Mediterranean trade as it had been at the height of the Roman Empire, Gaul, according to Pirenne, remained a basically Roman society until the later seventh century, when the Mediterranean lifeline was cut (for recent research on ceramics and trade, see Bonifay and Pieri, Chapter 37, this volume). Thereafter the nature of society changed as land became the most significant source of wealth and power, and power migrated northward to the agrarian heartlands of west continental Europe. It was in this area that a new dynasty, the Carolingians, arose, and their power was based on landholding. In one unforgettable phrase, Pirenne summed up his entire thesis: "Without Mahomet [i.e., the rise of Islam and Arab power] there could have been no Charlemagne."

Despite being published over eighty years ago and being challenged on almost every point, Pirenne's ideas remain an excellent entry point into the question of how Gaul became Francia. After decades of archaeological research, unavailable to Pirenne of course, it is now generally accepted that exchange networks in the Mediterranean had declined long before the rise of Arab power. References in Gregory to long-distance trade proved to be the exception rather than the rule, and one can question the very assumption that cross-Mediterranean trade had ever determined the state of economic relations in Gaul, even at the height of Roman power. Today's historians place much greater emphasis on the disintegration of the late-Roman taxation system as a factor in the transformation of Gaul, for this meant that rulers had progressively weaker resources to draw upon and that the monetary economy lost a key driver (Wickham 2005). Decline in taxation was thus combined with a long-term recession in trading activity.

To this may be added the disruption brought by frequent bouts of warfare. From the fifth century onward, there was also demographic change as populations shrank as a result of the wetter and cooler conditions brought about by a shift in the Atlantic jet stream (Cheyette 2008). Then, in the sixth century, the population declined further in the face of recurrent outbreaks of plague (see Horden, Chapter 14, and Yvinec and Barme, Chapter 33, this volume). Not surprisingly, towns continued to shrink as they had been doing since the fourth century, and with the disappearance of civic life, society came to be structured around a landholding elite and a mass of peasants (on cities, see Loseby, Chapter 27, this volume). Power came to have a largely military basis, resting in the hands of those who had the most land and the largest number of armed followers (see Sarti, Chapter 12, this volume). This end result, "Carolingian Francia," is very much as Pirenne envisaged it, but rather than his monocausal explanation (the severing of links across the Mediterranean), we can now identify a complex combination of factors that are impossible to disentangle in terms of cause and effect.

What Pirenne and present-day historians would have agreed on, however, are the notions that the transition from Gaul to Francia was not simply brought about by the conquest of Roman Gaul by the Merovingian Franks (the "Germanic barbarians") and that the traditional questions about the "good" or "bad" effects of any such conquest are, to say the least, not helpful. Nevertheless, Pirenne and some later historians (notably his pupil François-Louis Ganshof) still built on the late-nineteenth-century view of post-Roman development in thinking that when the structures of Roman government (whether based on trade or tax) disappeared, they must have been replaced by something else. Otherwise, the existence of a large Frankish state would not have been possible. That "something else" was "feudalism," a way of organizing society in order to channel power through land (Ganshof 1960). In this view, under the Merovingians, there was a rather unstructured relationship between land and power. Lack of structure and accountability allegedly meant that the Merovingians squandered their wealth in land (as they had their resources in taxation) for little return, hence their "weakness." The Carolingians, by contrast, gave out land to followers only on strict terms of service, and out of that service they built up a nearly invincible army and, as a consequence, a "superstate." In this scenario, Gaul effectively fell apart under the Merovingians. In the process of picking up the pieces and fashioning them into a dynamic polity, the Carolingians created Francia. It is a scenario that follows a cursory reading of the narrative sources rather nicely, but it is also one formed with hindsight and informed by writings of the supporters of the Carolingians themselves. It is more constructive to think about why Gaul/Francia did not disintegrate at various points in the Merovingian period. Rather than simply concentrating on the supposed weakness of its kings, it is more useful to note that here, and only here, there was a regime that could survive when there were no adult heirs available to take the throne. Where else in early medieval Europe might one see rule by children and queen regents? The answers to these questions lie in the underlying stability of the seventh-century Merovingian kingdom. But we also have to reckon with the fact that this stability could be disturbed by periodic conflict within a ruling elite.

The Franks appeared in Gaul in the mid-fifth century as troops allied themselves to the Roman military (Halsall 2007). As Roman political organization fell apart after the death of Emperor Majorian in 461, the Franks began to occupy the political and military space that opened up as a result. Thanks to the chance find of his lavishly furnished grave, we know that the Frankish leader Childeric was styled "king" at his death in 481 (Halsall 2001). His son Clovis was also a king and recognized as such by the Gallo-Roman church, which championed him in the cause of Catholicism since Clovis was not an Arian Christian as were the Goths in the south of Gaul. Clovis duly converted to Catholic Christianity (from what is not entirely clear) (Wood 1994, pp. 42–46). With his patronage of the cult of Gaul's premiere saint, St. Martin, his dynasty, the Merovingians, was firmly established as the Catholic rulers of Gaul and completed their takeover with the expulsion of the Arian Visigoths from Aquitaine in 507 (see Mathisen, Chapter 19, this volume). The Merovingians were also rulers of lands east of the Rhine, and their heartlands straddled the old Roman frontier. By the year 540, the Franks had driven out rivals in the east and were at least partly in control of Burgundy, Thuringia, Alemannia, and Bavaria, each of which received Frankish rulers (Wood, 1994: 33–70).

There is some disagreement about what Gaul, especially northern Gaul, was actually like in the early sixth century (Halsall 2014, pp. 221–238). We can cut through the debate by noting that even if there had been social collapse and transformation in the early sixth century, northern Gaul had recovered within a century. Thereafter, we can see political institutions and social and religious organization that are common both to the north and to the more obviously Romanized south. It is also an oversimplification to imagine that *Romanitas* thinned out from south to north because the old Roman capital of Trier was in the north and powerful people with Roman-sounding names appear in this area well into the seventh century.

We can see the pull of common factors against different regional and local back-grounds by looking at two towns with which Gregory was associated: Clermont (now Clermont-Ferrand) in the Auvergne and Tours on the Loire. Clermont and the Auvergne had been a center of Roman power and culture, even producing an emperor, Avitus, in the mid-fifth century. One of the last great letter collections of Antiquity comes from the Auvergne and was the work of Avitus's son-in-law, Sidonius Apollinaris, which shows the vibrancy of Roman culture in the later fifth century. The Franks took control of Clermont after the defeat of the Visigoths. Gregory of Tours, whose family connections with the region were strong, reported how it was attacked and plundered by the Franks in the year 532. However, we can track families of Roman origins who continued to exercise influence there right up to the beginning of the eighth century (Wood 1983a). According to hagiographical evidence (*Passio Praejecti* ca. 31, Fouracre and Gerberding, p. 294), the leaders of the region continued to be termed "senators" into the later seventh century, and one of them, again called Avitus, became bishop in 676. Nevertheless, Clermont was tightly bound into the Merovingian Frankish kingdom: Avitus himself became bishop with Frankish help. His predecessor, Praeiectus, had fallen victim to fac-tional struggles in the Frankish court, and in the struggles over this bishopric in the later seventh century, we can see a town riven by disputes between its leading families.

Gregory had written about disputes in the town that took place over a century earlier (Gregory, *Decem libri* II, cc. 13, 22; Krusch and Thorpe, 1971, pp. 129, 134–137) and again, names suggest that the same families were involved. In one sense, there is remarkable continuity here, but by the later seventh century, those same leaders were members of an elite that was of mixed origin and fully involved in kingdom-wide politics. When Gallo-Roman names largely disappear from the region in the eighth century, we could say that these people had now become Frankish. In the later seventh-century account of the rise and fall of its bishop, Praeiectus, we see an urban focus: the action mostly takes place in urban space, and the bishop can only be killed once he steps outside the town (*Passio Praejecti* c. 29, Fouracre and Gerberding, pp. 292–293). But thereafter Clermont itself fades in importance, or at least it is mentioned less and less in our sources. Civic life seems to have dwindled to the point that the town no longer supported important families and no longer visibly suffered from factional dispute.

Tours declined even more rapidly as a town, although one might not think so from the works of Gregory of Tours that read as if the town had streets thronged with citizens. Archaeological evidence, however, shows that over the course of the sixth century the town contracted to an area around the cathedral, with a new focus on the suburban monastery of Saint-Martin (Galinié 2007). Gregory was in effect an outsider imposed on the town as bishop, and he faced opposition from the town's count. The struggle between the two can be seen as part of the rivalry between different Merovingian kings and their supporters, and control of Tours was important because each king and royal faction identified with the cult of St. Martin. The cult was already strongly established in the later fifth century, by which time it was attracting substantial wealth in land. Gregory wrote up at great length the miracles performed at Martin's shrine, and, by the mid-seventh century, the monastery of St. Martin's was a wealthy and powerful institution (Van Dam 1993). In relative terms, it was far more important than the town of Tours itself had ever been. The first accounting documents to survive in the post-Roman West come from Saint-Martin at Tours. They are from the later seventh century (probably from the 660s), and they show in some detail how the monastery took dues in kind from the peasants living on its lands (Sato 2000). If we follow the "fiscalist" line on how and why tax-based Roman systems of government broke down as taxation metamorphosed into rent, then these documents become key evidence that this process had occurred in the region of Tours by the mid-seventh century. The emergence of powerful monasteries, which collected rents from substantial landholdings and were supported by, and in their turn supported, kings, is another way of characterizing the transition from Gaul to Francia.

By the end of the Merovingian period, Clermont and Tours belonged to a common culture that comprehended and complemented regional differences. The same is true of Cologne, Mainz, or, at a later date, Regensburg or Salzburg in the south of the German-speaking part of the Merovingian kingdom. Patrick Geary notably demonstrated how, by the end of the seventh century, leading families in the Rhône basin were bound into and related to families in Neustria, in the northwest of Francia (Geary 1985). Families like the Agilolfings, who ruled in Bavaria, also had kindred in the Rhineland

(Zöllner 1951). The massive territory of the Frankish polity was thus to some extent held together by intermarriage at the aristocratic level, a knitting together that preceded (and actually facilitated) the Carolingian policy of creating an "imperial aristocracy" over a century later.

For the sixth century, the family of Gregory of Tours itself shows ties across Gaul, from Lyons in the south, through Clermont in the Auvergne, up through Dijon in the east, and over to Tours in the west (Wood 1994, p. 28). This Gallo-Roman family exercised influence through the church, at a time when the church was largely in the hands of Gallo-Romans. Things look rather different in the seventh century when we see people with Frankish names, though not exclusively so, linked through the Frankish court and exercising power and influence as counts and dukes as well as bishops. There is a problem here that lies at the heart of any account of the transition from Gaul to Francia: namely, the extent to which the appearance of change over the sixth and seventh centuries should be put down to the fact that Gregory's narrative is our main source for the earlier period, whereas for the seventh century we have a much bigger palette of works from a considerably wider range of places. In other words, does a change from a single witness to multiple authors mask a more continuous line of development? One can never be sure that this is not the case, but there are good reasons to think that the change in the nature of the sources across the sixth and seventh centuries also reflects change in the cultural, religious, and political configuration of what was becoming a distinctly Frankish polity.

In the seventh century, we have a much thinner political narrative from our two chronicle sources (*Fredegar* and the *LHF*), but this is complemented by a growing corpus of hagiography, the records of church councils that come from a greater variety of regions than the sixth-century councils (see Halfond, Chapter 13, this volume). In addition, from midcentury onward, there is the evidence of charters, which are rich in names and relationships, and, importantly, also reveal patterns of landholding and land use. All of this evidence takes us out of the cathedral towns and into the countryside, and it is here that we meet the Frankish aristocracy.

This is the case with new monasteries in rural spaces that were founded and backed by members of the Frankish elite (see Diem, Chapter 15, this volume). The new monasteries were part of the so-called Columbanian movement, which was inspired by the Irish missionary, Columbanus, his most famous foundation being that of Luxeuil on the western edge of the Vosges Mountains (Clarke and Brennan, 1981). How much this wave of monastic foundations was a coherent "movement," and how "Irish" it ever was, is a matter of debate, but the foundations did spread (see Picard, Chapter 18, this volume). The *Life of Columbanus*, composed by the monk Jonas around the year 640, tells of how Columbanus was driven out of Luxeuil in the year 609 (*Vita Columbani*, I, c. 20). He then traveled across Francia on his way to exile in Italy. On his travels, he met leading Frankish families (a veritable "Who's who of the Frankish aristocracy" as Edward James (1982) described his contacts). Excited by Columbanus's holiness, they founded monasteries after the fashion of Luxeuil, endowing them from their landed wealth. These new kinds of monasteries were in principle to be independent from the local bishop, and, although Columbanus actually intended them to be free of interference from the found-ers' families too, they quickly became centers of family influence and prestige (Tatum 2007). One can therefore see why these magnate families took so rapidly to the "new" monasticism and why it spread across the network of aristocratic landholdings. Monasteries that were linked to particular families would continue to be founded long after the death of Columbanus. Founders were inspired by other Irish holy men, and foundation became something of a religious fashion. Sometimes referred to as "Iro-Frankish," this monastic culture was instrumental in the formation of an aristocratic identity in which power and privilege were in part legitimated through spiritual pres-tige. It has even been suggested that it led to a process of "aristocratic self-sanctification" (*Adelsselbstheiligung*): members of the founders' families were interred in the new mon-asteries and might be hailed as saints, for each foundation required a patron saint, and in regions that were not known to have suffered from the persecutions of the early Christian period, new saints were needed (Prinz 1965). This process was neither deliber-ate nor planned, but it did spread a shared monastic culture northward and eastward. It was another strand that knitted the aristocracy together. It is from the hagiography pro-duced in the process of sanctification that we learn more about the leading families (see Kreiner, Chapter 24, this volume).

All of the main characters who figure in the often dramatic narratives of later seventh-century politics (*LHF, Fredegar* IV, *Continuations of Fredegar, Passio Leudegarii, Passio Praejecti, Vita Balthildis*) have strong connections with the monastic movement we have just been describing. They, or their parents, had founded monasteries or had been great donors to established monasteries, and many families had members who were bishops too. For example, the family that would eventually replace the Merovingians as kings, the so-called Pippinids, expanded their power through a great arc of monasteries that stretched from the Rhineland across the Moselle and down into the Seine Valley. They counted (or claimed) a saint-bishop and a saint-abbess among their ancestors, they used their landed wealth to build up a large military following, and they served as the highest officials to the Merovingian kings. The office of "mayor of the palace" was not just a source of wealth, but also another means of legitimating power (see Hen, Chapter 10, this volume). In this family, spiritual and worldly prestige and power were united with abundant riches. One could say this for the heads of perhaps a dozen families—for instance, the saintly Audoin of Rouen (d. 684) or, earlier, Erchinoald who was "mayor of the palace" in Neustria up to 657.

Remarkably, in this later Merovingian period (i.e., from the mid-seventh century onward), the same people often appear in hagiography, in the chronicle sources, and in charters. This small circle includes the Merovingian family itself alongside their mag-nates. It is testimony to the closeness and dominance of the ruling elite that they should appear in different genres of writing. That these different genres of writing were so thor-oughly interconnected is witness to the strength and cohesiveness of elite culture. A fig-ure such as Leudegar, bishop of Autun, who was put to death in about 678, was a martyr and a hero saint in one source (in the *Passio Leudegarii*, Fouracre and Gerberding), a scandalous interfering bishop in another (the *Passio Praejecti* c. 23, Fouracre and

Gerberding, p. 288), and a key political leader, with a brother who held the important position of count of Paris and with whom he led a palace coup in the year 673 (*LHF* c. 45, Fouracre and Gerberding, pp. 89–91). His family was connected with that of Ansoald of Poitiers whom we see in an early charter donating great amounts of land to one of the "new" monasteries—that of Noirmoutier. Leudegar's nemesis, the "mayor of the palace," Ebroin (killed ca. 680), was cast as a villain in the *Passio Leudgarii*, treated quite favorably as an effective leader in a few other hagiographic sources, and described as a clever but ruthless operator in league with the saintly Audoin of Rouen in the *LHF*. Charters show him as supportive of the new monasticism and as the founder and generous patron of a convent in Soissons. The elite was made up of warriors, their wives, churchmen, and (increasingly) church women. What united the laypeople and church people was the family. The members of a single family could be active in all spheres of elite culture.

So great is the crossover between the sacred and the secular in Merovingian-period sources that historians have often characterized the later Merovingian church as having been effectively secularized: its saints were not convincing as holy men or women, its bishops were likely to be warriors with blood on their hands, and greedy magnates treated churches like their own property. Reform could only come from the outside, first from Irish and then from Anglo-Saxon missionaries (Wallace-Hadrill 1983). By contrast, one could argue that the sacred had actually advanced into the secular world to the extent that it had become a normal attribute of power, a situation that Gregory of Tours might well have longed for. Reform, at least as we see it under the Carolingians, was an act of political will as much as it was a drive for spiritual renewal. One aim of reform was to cut the claws of the great families of the later Merovingian period who controlled the most important churches and who were in danger of populating the ranks of the saints with people who opposed the new dynasty (Fouracre 1999).

Apart from chronicles, hagiography, and charters, we also have evidence of letters that show how members of the leading families were schooled together at the royal palaces (see Gillett, Chapter 25, this volume). These alumni remained in contact even when they went on to reside in different kingdoms (Desiderius of Cahors, *Epistulae*). The letters confirm the impression from our other sources that many of the leading families knew each other well. They would have met at annual assemblies held at the palaces, and as we have seen, there was significant intermarriage between groups. However, although the elite in the later Merovingian period were strongly integrated as a group, they were also highly fractious, and a significant number of them, including bishops, met violent ends at the hands of their peers (Fouracre 2003). The violence that transpired between magnates is hard to understand, and one must be wary of forcing an explanation. As it appears in *Fredegar*, the *LHF*, and in hagiography, the unrest was linked to competition for power. We could read it as a struggle for the resources that power brought, against a background of diminishing wealth and opportunity for enrichment. Perhaps one could contrast their behavior with that of the magnates a century later under Charlemagne when foreign wars brought in plunder, tribute, and opportunity. At that time, there seems to have been very little violent conflict between magnate groups; it is hard even to identify different groups in the time of Charlemagne.

For the later Merovingian period, one can see something of a pattern in the narrative sources as one group of magnates (*factio* is the term used) became dominant at the royal court and began to exclude others from power. Those excluded then eventually attacked the ruling faction in the hope of replacing it. This happened at a local or regional level too, for counts and bishops often seem to have had local rivals, and ruling groups at the center stoked that rivalry as a means of building up their influence in the provinces (Fouracre 2004). In hagiography, one can see this in the way in which bishops were said to have been brought down by rivals driven by diabolical envy, this being one way that authors could address violent conflict between Christians (Fouracre 1999). What seems to have sparked this pattern of behavior was the formation of larger kingdoms after the rise of King Clothar II in 613. The larger kingdom, mostly at peace but riven by periodic faction fighting, was what replaced the warring kingdoms of the earlier period. Gregory of Tours had written of the many civil wars, *bella civilia*, between the rulers of these kingdoms. That situation may have been even more violent than the one we see in the seventh and early eighth centuries. We have no way of telling how many people were killed below the level of magnates in either period, and we cannot estimate overall, or relative, levels of violence.

Factional violence on a large scale erupted on four occasions in the later Merovingian period. First, in the aftermath of the death of King Dagobert I (638), there was fighting among the magnates of Austrasia who were competing to dominate the court of Dagobert's young son, Sigebert. The Pippinid family emerged dominant from that struggle but at the expense of conceding what amounted to an independent lordship to one Duke Radulf on the border with the Wendish Slavs, and they still faced rivals in their heartlands around the Ardennes. When King Sigebert died in 656, the Pippinid mayor, Grimoald, exiled Sigebert's young son, Dagobert, to Ireland and had his own son, Childebert, made king in his place, since Childebert apparently had been adopted by Sigebert (Fouracre 2008). After a few years, and presumably on the death of this Childebert "the adopted" (probably in 662), there was a rising against Grimoald. He was brought to Paris, where he was put in chains, tortured, and executed, as, according to the *LHF,* "one worthy of death because he had acted against his lord" (*LHF* c. 43, Fouracre and Gerberding, pp. 87–88). A rival faction then took power in Austrasia. In the west, one Flaochad was dominant in the palace of Clovis II, Dagobert's second son. His faction was challenged by a group of southern magnates, and the *Fourth Book of the Chronicle of Fredegar* closes with a powerful description of a pitched battle between the two factions (*Fredegar IV,* c. 90; Wallace-Hadrill, pp. 76–79). This struggle took place ca. 642 after the death of Queen Nantechild, who had apparently been keeping the peace between the rivals.

The second major eruption came in 673 with the death of King Clothar III in the west, and it lasted into 676. The discord that followed is recorded in contemporary hagiography, in the *LHF,* and finds an echo in charters and possibly even in coinage: it was at this time that the coinage switched from gold to silver (Blackburn, 2005; see Strothmann, Chapter 35, this volume). The switch could be connected with the need to pay troops in the fighting, or it might also have been the result of ending direct taxation in the previous decade, which might in turn explain why conflict broke out at this time as the elite fought over diminishing resources Our main source for the crisis is the *Passio Leudegarii*, for Bishop Leudegar lost his life as a result of the conflict, as did Bishop Praeiectus. It was said that the "mayor of the palace," Ebroin, had been excluding magnates from Burgundy (Leudegar's power base) from the palace. When Clothar III died, Ebroin could not prevent all the magnates assembling to raise the new king, Theuderic. According the *Passio Leudegarii*, the leaders were frightened that if Ebroin were able to keep the new king "in the background and just use his name . . . he would be able to do harm to whomsoever he wished with impunity" (*Passio Leudegarii* cc. 4–6; Fouracre and Gerberding, pp. 220–223). This passage is a telling indication of the power that came from the palace, and of how the palace could be manipulated if a king were too young or too inexperienced to handle his officers. During the event, Ebroin was deposed along with Theuderic, and Leudegar took his place alongside Theuderic's brother Childeric, king of Austrasia (the king who had been sent to rule in Austrasia in 662 when Grimoald had been ousted). At this point, a single king ruled over all of Francia. But the Neustrian magnates then began to feel excluded by Childeric's Austrasian supporters and, above all, by the "mayor of the palace," Wulfoald, who drove Leudegar out. Childeric was killed by the Neustrians and Wulfoald and the Austrasians fled. Yet, Ebroin, Leudegar, and Theuderic then came back, and their factions fought to the death, with Ebroin emerging in complete control. In this dramatic sequence, factions in areas south of the River Loire seem to have turned their backs on the Neustrian establishment, as may have those in areas east of the Rhine.

The third outburst came when the leaders of Austrasia were excluded from the Neustrian palace, much as the Burgundians had been in 673. Famously, the fight for inclusion came to a head in 687, when the Austrasians and Neustrians met in battle at Tertry. The outcome was that the Austrasians became ascendant, with the family of Pippin, which had recovered power in Austrasia after Childeric's assassination, becoming "mayors of the palace" again in a single Frankish kingdom. Carolingian sources would mark this as the moment at which the Pippinids took the kingdom from the powerless and "useless" Merovingian kings, but analysis of charter material would suggest that the kings still enjoyed support that limited the power of any one magnate group (Fouracre 1984). As the author of the *LHF* saw it, this was how things should always have been: a kingdom in which *consilium* was a brake on factionalism. Peace should have been the norm, conflict an aberration. We might judge this system to have been one that "worked," with a periodic redistribution of power through conflict. It had a palace administration that was issuing an increasing number of charters. It settled disputes between the powerful, and oversaw a countryside that seemed, despite the occasional conflict between magnate factions, to have been relatively peaceful. Lords do not seem to have lived in fortified residences, and the labor force on the great estates was so much under control that in land transactions, it would be treated as a mere appurtenance of the land in question (Fouracre 2000a, pp. 19–22). This condition explains how estates could be divided at will and land could be held on a temporary basis, for what was at stake here was the income from the land that could be assigned with immediate effect as long as the workforce stayed in place.

The fourth, and last, bout of Merovingian conflict may not have disturbed the way in which the elite drew resources from the peasantry, but it did sweep away the political configuration that had been in place since the time of Clothar II. It began in 714 with the murder of Grimoald, the Pippinid "mayor of the palace," an event that was followed not long after by the death of his father, Pippin. An alliance of Neustrians, Frisians, and Aquitanians, took advantage of the family's disarray to drive it out of Neustria and attempted to destroy it in Austrasia too. The result was conflict that lasted an entire generation, at the end of which the old families that had ruled alongside and in conjunction with the Merovingian kings had either been destroyed or subjugated. As a result, the kings themselves became just what the author of the *Passio Leudegarii* had feared, that is, mere mouthpieces of the "mayor of the palace." The "mayor" in question here was Charles Martel, who rose to power in 716 and was so powerful by the time of his death in 741 that he had ruled for the previous four years without a king (Fouracre 2000b). It is not the place here to speculate why Charles Martel was so successful: suffice it to say that he went to war in almost every year between 716 and 740, and he never lost a battle. Besides hunting down adherents of the old regime throughout Francia, he also fought Frisians, Saxons, Alemans, and, to his great glory in the west, Muslim forces that had driven up from Spain as far as Tours itself.

Charles Martel and his allies defeated the Muslims at the Battle of Poitiers in 732 or 733. The so-called *Chronicle of 754*, a Spanish source, described the Austrasian Franks at this battle as "immobile as a wall, holding together as glacier in the cold region" (*Chronicle of 754*, c. 80; Wolf 1990, p. 145), Later, the text terms them "the Europeans." We can take this event to mark the final phase in the transition from Gaul to Francia: by the time of Charles Martel's triumph, Gaul and the areas east of the Rhine had taken on a Frankish identity that was associated with success in war and defense of the Christian Church. Their "immobile wall" protected it throughout "Europe." A generation later, the Prologue to a revised version of the *Lex Salica* would put it thus: "In battle [the Franks] shook off the powerful and very harsh yoke of the Romans. And, after the knowledge of baptism, the Franks adorned with gold and precious stones the bodies of the blessed martyrs whom the Romans had mutilated with fire and sword" (Fischer Drew, p. 171). This iteration of Frankish identity is the first time we see the drive to judge the consequences of the fall of Rome with which we began: here it was the Franks who saved the church, and thus saved civilization, from the oppression of the Romans.

This claim owes much to the fact that Carolingians expressed themselves as holding a new religious mandate to rule that justified their taking the throne from the Merovingians. However, the form of justification—that power was to be used to protect the weak and to defend the faith (something which, in the Carolingian view, the Merovingians were no longer able to do)—reveals just how much the Carolingians built on the convergence of the secular and the sacred that marked the transition from Gaul to Francia. What was different after Charles Martel was, as we have seen, that there were no longer different factions vying for control of the palace, and no longer any need for a "mayor of the palace" to mediate between king and aristocracy. The demise of the factions may be put down to the overwhelming superiority of the Carolingian kings.

It may also be because the Carolingian line could supply adult males to rule in every generation up to the year 888, thus avoiding the periods of minority rule that were breeding grounds for factional politics. What is remarkable about the Merovingian regime, as suggested earlier, is that despite the growth of factionalism, it could survive repeated royal minorities. Even when there were child kings and infighting among the magnates, the polity did not break up. Radulf, who defeated the Austrasians under Sigibert III, "rated himself 'King of Thuringia,'" said *Fredegar,* but "he did not in so many words deny Sigibert's overlordship" (Wallace-Hadrill, p. 74). That is to say, Radulf may have become effectively independent, but he did not actually found a new kingdom, preferring to remain within the Frankish polity (see Hardt, Chapter 20, this volume). The survival of Francia is the strongest testimony to the stability of its political and religious culture, and it was this stability that was the bedrock of Carolingian power. Let us close by reviewing the emergence of that culture.

Gaul became Francia as the area of Europe north of the Alps and Pyrenees, and west of the rivers Danube and Saale, adjusted to the decline and disappearance of Roman power. In this area, the Merovingian kings were never challenged from the outside. Although members of the Merovingian family fought each other, there was no challenge from within to the family's right to rule until the mid-eighth century. Fighting between Merovingians in the sixth century did not seem to weaken the hold of the Franks over Gaul. Indeed, Frankish power expanded over the course of the sixth century, and it has been suggested that at this time the Merovingians even had influence in southern England (Wood 1983b). Expansion and civil war went hand in hand with the militarization of aristocratic life, and the growth of an identity based on war (see Sarti, Chapter 12, this volume).

At the same time, there were evident continuities in the way in which the richest in society drew their wealth from a tied labor force on the land, and this was against a background of vanishing taxation, declining trade, and falling population. It can be said that despite the shrinkage in economic activity, there was relative social stability. Violence between kingdoms can be seen as a means of distributing and redistributing power and resources, fueled by the likelihood that the total amount of resources available to the powerful was declining. Service to the kings was becoming the gateway to what power and wealth remained. Across the course of the seventh century, this arrangement was run on a larger scale as after the year 613, there were only two kingdoms (and often only one) in Francia. The seventh century saw less warfare between kingdoms, but the ruling elite was periodically riven by factional violence. The aristocracy remained militarized, but there were long periods of peace in the seventh century.

The aristocracy's growing involvement in religion, increasing religious discourse in government, intermarriage among the ruling elite, the shuffling of landed estates between families and between families and monasteries (all with the proviso that there was a stable labor force) were elements that combined in a common culture in which the kings continued to play a role as facilitators, mediators, and arbiters. Periods of rule by children were possible because the king's functions could be carried out through palace government (on children, see Perez, Chapter 9, this volume).

Against the background of what can only be described as a very "light touch" government, there were strong regional differences with different "peoples," each with their own laws and customs. Francia was a polity shared by two different language groups with a host of dialect subgroups between them. Nevertheless, a common Frankish identity was beginning to overlay regional differences. This was Francia as it would be developed by its Carolingian rulers, who strengthened a common culture by articulating it around religious norms. Through their victories, they demonstrated the divinely ordered succession of the Franks.

WORKS CITED

Ancient Sources

Crónica mózarabe de 754. E. López Pereira (ed. and trans.). (1980). *Crónica mózarabe de 754: edición crítica y traduccióni*. Zaragoza: Anurar Ed.

The Chronicle of 754. K. Wolf (ed.). (1999). *Conquerors and Chroniclers of Early Medieval Spain* (2nd ed., pp. 111–160). Liverpool: Liverpool University Press.

Desiderius of Cahors, *Letters*. D. Norberg (ed.). (1961). *Epistulae Sancti Desiderii*. Studia Latina Stockholmiensis 6. Uppsala: Acta Universitatis Stockholmiensis.

Diplomata, Chartae, Epistolae, Leges ad res Gallo-Francicas spectantia, 2 vols. J. M. Pardessus (ed.). (1843–1849). Paris: Lutetiae Parisiorum.

Fischer Drew, K. (trans.). (1991). *The Laws of the Salian Franks*. Philadelphia: University of Pennsylvania Press.

Fredegarii Chronicorum Liber Quartus cum Continuationibus (*The Fourth Book of the Chronicle of Fredegar with Its Continuations*). J.-M. Wallace-Hadrill (ed. and trans.). (1960). Oxford: Oxford University Press.

Gregory of Tours, *Decem libri historiarum*. B. Krusch (ed.). (1951). MGH SRM 1.1. Hanover: Hahn.

Gregory of Tours, *Decem libri historiarum*. L. Thorpe (trans.). (1971). *Gregory of Tours, History of the Franks*. Harmondsworth: Penguin.

Liber Historiae Francorum. B. Krusch (ed.) (1888). MGH SRM 2. Hanover: Hahn.

Liber Historiae Francorum. P. Fouracre and R. Gerberding (eds. and trans.). (1996). *Late Merovingian France. History and Hagiography 640–720* (pp. 79–96). Manchester: Manchester University Press.

Marculfi Formularum Libri Duo. A. Uddholm (ed.) (1962). *Marculfi Formularum Libri Duo*. Uppsala: Acta Universitatis Stockholmiensis.

Pactus Legis Salicae and *Lex Salica*. K. Eckhardt (ed.) (1961/1969). MGH Legum sectio 1.4, parts 1 and 2. Hanover: Hahn.

Passio Leudegarii. B. Krusch (ed.). (1910). MGH SRM 5. Hanover: Hahn.

Passio Leudegarii. P. Fouracre and R. Gerberding (ed. and trans.). (1996). *Late Merovingian France. History and Hagiography 640–720* (pp. 191–253). Manchester: Manchester University Press.

Passio Praejecti. B. Krusch (ed.). (1910). MGH SRM 5 (pp. 223–248). Hanover: Hahn.

Passio Praejecti. P. Fouracre and R. Gerberding (ed. and trans.). (1996). *Late Merovingian France. History and Hagiography 640–720* (pp. 254–300). Manchester: Manchester University Press.

Rio, A. (trans.). (2008). *The Formularies of Angers and Marculf: Two Merovingian Legal Handbooks*. Translated texts for historians 45. Liverpool: Liverpool University Press.

Die Urkunden der Merowinger. T. Kölzer (ed.). (2001). *Die Urkunden der Merowinger* (2 vols.). MGH DD Die Urkunden der Merowinger I. Hanover: Hahn.

Viard, J. (ed.). (1920–1953). *Les grands chroniques de France*. Société de l'histoire de France, 10 vols. Paris: Société de l'histoire de France.

Modern Sources

Blackburn, M. (2005). "Money and Coinage." In P. Fouracre (ed.), *The New Cambridge Medieval History I* (pp. 660–674). Cambridge: Cambridge University Press.

Cheyette, F. (2008). "The Disappearance of the Ancient Landscape and the Climatic Anomaly of the Early Middle Ages: A Question to Be Pursued." *Early Medieval Europe* 16(2): 127–165.

Clarke, H., and Brennan, M. (eds.). (1981). *Columbanus and Merovingian Monasticism*. BAR International Series 113. Oxford: British Archaeological Reports.

Fouracre, P. (1984). "Observations on the Outgrowth of Pippinid Influence in the 'Regnum Francorum' after the Battle of Tertry (687–725)." *Medieval Prosopography* 5: 1–31.

Fouracre, P. (1986). "*Placita* and the Settlement of Disputes in Later Merovingian Francia." In W. Davies and P. Fourace (eds.), *The Settlement of Disputes in Early Medieval Europe* (pp. 23–43). Cambridge: Cambridge University Press.

Fouracre, P. (1999). "The Origins of the Carolingian Attempt to Regulate the Cult of Saints." In J. Howard Johnston and P. Hayward (eds.), *The Cult of Saints in Late Antiquity and the Early Middle Ages* (pp. 143–165). Oxford: Oxford University Press.

Fouracre, P. (2000a). "The Origins of the Nobility in Francia." In A. Duggan (ed.), *Nobles and Nobility* (pp. 17–24). Woodbridge: Boydell Press.

Fouracre, P. (2000b). *The Age of Charles Martel*. Harlow: Pearson.

Fouracre, P. (2003). "Why Were So Many Bishops Killed in Merovingian Francia?" In N. Fryde and D. Reitz (eds.), *Bischofsmord im Mittelalter* (pp. 13–35). Göttingen: Vandenhoeck & Ruprecht.

Fouracre, P. (2004). "Conflict, Power and Legitimation in Francia in the Late Seventh and Eighth Centuries." In I. Alfonso, H. Kennedy, and J. Escalona (eds.), *Building Legitimacy. Political Discourses and Forms of Legitimation in Medieval Societies* (pp. 3–26). Leiden: Brill.

Fouracre, P. (2005). "The Long Shadow of the Merovingians." In J. Story (ed.), *Charlemagne. Empire and Society* (pp. 5–21). Manchester: Manchester University Press.

Fouracre, P. (2008). "Forgetting and Remembering Dagobert II: The English Connection." In P. Fouracre and D. Ganz (eds.), *Frankland: The Franks and the World of the Early Middle Ages* (pp. 70–89). Manchester: Manchester University Press.

Fouracre, P. (2014). "*Francia* and the History of Medieval Europe." *Haskins Society Journal* 23: 1–22.

Galinié, H. (ed.). (2007). "Tours antique et medieval: lieux de vie, temps de la ville." *Revue de Centre de la France* (Suppl. 30). Tours: Revue de Centre de la France.

Ganshof, F. (1960). *Feudalism*. P. Grierson (trans). London: Longmans.

Geary, P. (1985). *Aristocracy in Provence. The Rhône Basin at the Dawn of the Carolingian Age*. Stuttgart: Beiheft der Francia.

Grahn-Hoek, H. (1971). "Die fränkische Oberschicht im 6. Jahrhundert. Studien zu ihrer rechtlichen und politischen Stellung." *Vorträge und Forschungen* 21. Sigmaringen: Thorbecke.

Halsall, G. (2001). "Childeric's Grave, Clovis' Succession and the Origins of the Merovingian Kingdom." In R. Mathisen and D. Shanzer (eds.), *Society and Culture in Late Roman Gaul: Revisiting the Sources* (pp. 116–133). Aldershot: Ashgate.

Halsall, G. (2007). *Barbarian Migrations and the Roman West, 376–568.* Cambridge: Cambridge University Press.

Halsall, G. (2014). *Worlds of Arthur.* Oxford: Oxford University Press.

Irsigler, F. (1969). *Untersuchungen zur Geschichte des frühfränkischen Adels.* Rheinisches Archiv 69. Bonn: Oldenbourg.

James, E. (1982). *The Origins of France: From Clovis to the Capetians, 500–1000.* London: Macmillan.

Pirenne, H. (1937). *Mahomet et Charlemagne.* Paris: F. Alcan.

Prinz, F. (1965). *Frühes Mönchtum im Frankenreich: Kultur und Gesellschaft in Gallien, den Rheinlanden und Bayern am Beispiel der monastischen Entwicklung (4. bis 8. Jahrhundert).* Munich: Oldenbourg.

Reimitz, H. (2015). *History, Frankish Identity and the Framing of Western Ethnicity, 550–850.* Cambridge: Cambridge University Press.

Rio, A. (2006). "Freedom and Unfreedom In Early Medieval Francia: The Evidence of the Legal Formularies." *Past and Present* 193: 7–40.

Sato, S. (2000). "The Merovingian Accounting Documents of Tours." *Early Medieval Europe* 9(2): 143–161.

Tatum, S. (2007). "Hagiography, Family and Columbanan Monasticism in Seventh-Century Francia." Unpublished PhD thesis, University of Manchester.

Van Dam, R. (1993). *Saints and Their Miracles in Late Antique Gaul.* Princeton, NJ: Princeton University Press.

Wallace-Hadrill, J.-M. (1983). *The Frankish Church.* Oxford: Oxford University Press.

Wickham, C. (2005). *Framing the Early Middle Ages. Europe and the Mediterranean 400–800.* Oxford: Oxford University Press.

Wood, I. (1983a). "The Ecclesiastical Politics of Merovingian Clermont." In P. Wormald, D. Bullough, and R. Collins (eds.), *Ideal and Reality in Frankish and Anglo-Saxon Society: Studies Presented to J.-M. Wallace-Hadrill* (pp. 34–57). Oxford: Blackwell.

Wood, I. (1983b). *The Merovingian North Sea.* Occasional Papers on Medieval Topics 1. Alingsås: Viktoria Bokförlag.

Wood, I. (1994). *The Merovingian Kingdoms 450–751.* Harlow: Longman.

Wood, I. (2013). *The Modern Origins of the Early Middle Ages.* Oxford: Oxford University Press.

Zöllner, E. (1951). "Die Herkunft der Agilolfinger." *Mitteilungen des Instituts für österreichische Geschichtsforschung* 59: 245–264.

CHAPTER 3

....

WRITING THE HISTORY
OF MEROVINGIAN GAUL
An Historiographical Survey

....

AGNÈS GRACEFFA

THE history of Merovingian Gaul is closely bound up with the history of the breakup of the Roman Empire. As with the Visigothic kingdom in Spain and the Anglo-Saxon kingdoms in England, the Merovingian period is often referred to as the Dark Ages: a troubled and opaque period of transition between the end of classical Antiquity and the start of the Middle Ages. The epoch is often characterized as a time of barbarian destruction of high Roman civilization (Wood 2013, pp. 8–10). The challenge of Merovingian history is thus twofold: the period suffers from a paucity of written sources, and this fact makes it particularly difficult for scholars to assess the enormous political changes that transpired during this time.

Indeed, surviving historical information about the fifth, sixth, and seventh centuries is limited for Gaul and even scarcer for the Germanic past of its ruling dynasty. Extant texts are few in number, a consequence of the loss of written Roman culture and the resurgence of oral culture. Most written documents that do survive were composed by Roman authors or ecclesiastics, who provided an account of events specific to their particular worldview (Kaiser-Scholz 2014, pp. 19–35). Moreover, besides the scarcity of documentary sources, for many centuries, historians had few artifacts or architectural remnants at their disposal, in part due to the small number of early medieval stone structures in comparison to those constructed from wood (but see Chevalier, Chapter 30; Chavarría Arnau, Chapter 29, this volume). All of the extant sources give the impression of a great modification of the civilization inherited from Antiquity, especially in the areas of administration, architecture, material culture, and literacy, a process that has usually been understood as regressive. These lacunae have left a lot to interpretation.

From an ideological perspective, the paradox of a Roman Empire supplanted by the politically weaker system of Frankish government has been exacerbated further by the fact that Merovingian Gaul is recognized as the source of the future nations of France,

Switzerland, Belgium, and Germany. These nations all emerged from the Frankish kingdoms, and this legacy helps explain the enormous political and ideological investment that has been made in writing Merovingian history in each country (Graceffa 2009, pp. 7–28). Finally, the Merovingian period has been seen as unique in that it saw the political triumph of Christianity in western Europe. The memory of this fact survives thanks to the baptism of Clovis, which was an iconic moment in Merovingian history and made it possible for monarchists in the 1830s to call France "the first eldest daughter of the Church" (Venayre 2013).

From the period of the Ancien Regime until the French Revolution, the importance of Merovingian Gaul as the birthplace of the French monarchy and French Catholicism was particularly entrenched. The geographical and political connections between the Merovingian kingdoms and modern France further explain their importance to French historiography. Nevertheless, the meaning of Merovingian history has been much debated in modern French discourse, and approaches to this period have reflected contemporary political trends. Post-Revolutionary republican and secular France, for instance, renounced the concept of monarchy as a divinely ordered institution. At the same time, the spread of nationalism in nineteenth-century Europe gave Merovingian history—as a place of the nation's origins—a prominent role in French historiography and the construction of modern national identity. However, in time, another myth of origins, that of the ancient Gauls, soon overshadowed the ideological and commemorative importance of the Merovingian period for republican historians and politicians of the Third Republic (1870–1940). The popularization of this narrative took root especially in the schools of the Third Republic—given that the politics of teaching were contentious during this period. Consequently, the Merovingian past partly lost its place of prominence inside of the "national fiction" promoted by the historical curriculum (Nicolet 2006, pp. 227–343). Three successive conflicts between France and Germany (1870, 1914–1918, and 1939–1945) led to increased mistrust of contemporary Germans, a reaction magnified by the conflation of the ancient Franks with modern Germans in French popular thought (Rouche 1997, vol. 2, pp. 709–727).

The historiography of the Merovingian period has been important in multiple national traditions. In addition to the French approach to the Merovingian past, German historians, then Swiss and Belgian historians, and most recently North American scholars, have contributed substantial and decisive works to this literature. For German scholars, interest in Merovingian history has existed since as far back as the late Middle Ages with the birth of German national consciousness. Based on their reading of ancient ethnographic and historical texts, these historians proposed German descent from Frankish tribes (Garber 1989). Moreover, at the end of the eighteenth century, philological scholars tried to define scientifically the relationship between European languages. They gave an influential place to the family of Germanic languages.

With the triumph of nationalism in Europe during the nineteenth and twentieth centuries, interest in Merovingian history increased especially in Germany, Belgium, and Switzerland. For most German scholars, the period of the barbarian migrations

(*Volkerwanderungszeit*) was fulfilled by the rise of the Frankish nation, the creation of the Merovingian kingdoms, and the reign of Charlemagne; each of these developments symbolized the power and the triumph of the Germanic people. The strong connection between language, nation, and culture advocated by some scholars allowed ethnophilological theories to proliferate. Moreover, the rise of biological theories of evolution at the end of the nineteenth century bred a racial conception of Germanic peoples that portrayed the Merovingians as racially pure. This approach reached a terrible apogee during World War II under National Socialism (Dietz, Gabel, and Tiedau 2003, pp. 225–237). Consequently, after the war, the political investment of German scholars in Merovingian history progressively declined.

By contrast, the localization of the geographic reality of the Merovingian kingdoms largely explained Swiss and Belgian interest in this history. Territories in what is now Switzerland were located in the center of the future Carolingian Empire and were identified as the historical land of the Alamanni, a so-called Germanic nation that was beaten by Clovis at the Battle of Tolbiac/Zülpich circa 496, and subsequently integrated into the Merovingian kingdoms (Geuenich 1998). The confusion between modern languages and ancient territories led nationalist politicians to claim that the Swiss had a "Sonderweg" (a special path of historical development) and, during the National Socialist period, even a claim to German membership (Geuenich 1997, pp. 10–12). Swiss historians could thus claim linear descent from the Merovingian period to the present, as was also the case with Belgium, which was founded in 1830. In the case of Belgium, the Merovingian past was overshadowed by nationalist movements that claimed affinity to the pre-Roman and Celtic origins of the Belgae (the name given by the Romans to the peoples who inhabited the regions that are now part of modern Belgium). In the nineteenth century, for this reason, historians did not mobilize the Merovingian period in a positive manner: they viewed the Franks as invaders. Although King Childeric, father of Clovis and founder of the Merovingian dynasty, was buried in Tournai circa 481 and had the potential to be seen as an ancestor of the Belgians, scholars focused instead on the Pippinids, the eighth-century predecessors of the Carolingians (Tollebeeck 2011). The debate about Germanic-Frankish origins in Belgium was reinvigorated at the end of the nineteenth century with racial and linguistic controversies over the linguistic frontier between French and Flemish. This division occurred again under German occupation during World War I and II (Federinov, Docquier, and Cauchies 2015; Simmer 2015).

The trauma of World War II made historians question the nationalist dimension of their discourse. With the development of a new European consciousness in the 1990s, there was a progressive move away from nationalist scholarly discourse. However, the danger of turning back to nationalism in historical analysis has always remained (Geary 2002). The study of historiography is thus imperative if we are to understand how scholarly knowledge was established and developed over the course of the nineteenth and twentieth centuries.

Merovingian History until the French Revolution

The myths of Frankish origins and of Clovis as a descendant of Trojans were born in the seventh century (Coumert 2007, pp. 267–379; see also Coumert, Chapter 5, this volume). In the eighth century and beyond, the Pippinids and Carolingians developed a paradoxical approach to the stories that constituted Merovingian "memory." On the one hand, this new dynasty encouraged the development of the myth of the Franks, as described in the writings of Pseudo-Fredegar and encouraged the legend that the Franks were descended from the Trojans (Fredegar III, 2–9). On the other hand, they consciously condemned the Merovingian kings to *damnatio memoriae*, so that their own empowerment as the monarchs of France could be seen as legitimate. This paradoxical policy combined belief in the Merovingian tradition (and thus the authority of the past) with significant innovations in that tradition (which was necessary to justify the change of dynasties). On this basis, the Frankish-Trojan myth thrived and grew throughout the Middle Ages until the Renaissance (Beaune 1985; Führer 2016, pp. 37–43).

During the European Renaissance, two main changes modified existing historical approaches: the rediscovery of Antiquity and the discovery of the New World. Both changes had a significant impact on contemporary approaches to national origins. On the one hand, an admiration of the Greek and Roman past transformed the traditional view of barbarians: Huns, Goths, and other tribes were now held responsible for the destruction of classical civilization (Joye 2016, pp. 89–93). On the other hand, the rediscovery of ancient texts like those of Jordanes, Tacitus, and others, emphasized in part the positive qualities of the Germanic past and supported national feeling. The first modern edition of Tacitus's *Germania* appeared in 1425 and that of Jordanes's *History of the Goths* appeared in 1431–1449 (Wood 2013, pp. 10–11). Tacitus described the ancient Germanic peoples in favorable terms and held up their society as a model for ancient Roman readers. He characterized them as being endowed with numerous admirable qualities: courage, military talent, virtue, honesty, loyalty, and love of freedom. Jordanes's history revealed that the Goths, whom he claimed had originated in Sweden, were the oldest nation in Europe, and thereby opened up a very political debate about the origins of each nation (Ridé 1976, p. 1206; Wolfram 2001, p. 12). At the same time, the discovery of the New World compelled historians to revisit biblical cosmogony and question the scheme of the unity of human race. Thanks to these changing paradigms, new definitions of barbarians, or savages, were proposed that led to the development by Jean-Baptiste Dubos of the notion of human stages of development, and to theories of the connection of barbarism to climate proposed by Montesquieu: just as the savage became the opposite of civilized people, the positive qualities of northern countries were contrasted favorably with those located further south (Bourdieu 1980, pp. 21–25).

To reinforce the legitimacy and nobility of the ancient Franks as the founders of the French monarchy, scholars introduced two new hypotheses regarding the Franks' origins and the foundation of the Merovingian dynasty. They claimed first that the Franks and Gauls belonged to the same ancient nation, and second, that the Frankish conquest of Roman Gaul was not a usurpation of Roman power but a liberation of the ancient Gauls (Hotman 1573). These approaches largely agreed with the contemporary German-Scandinavian thesis of the Nordic origin of the Franks, whether or not they were pure Germanic (Leibniz 1715). The popularity of the Merovingian kings was signaled by the attempt to canonize Clovis during the reign of Louis XIII (Savaron 1622); its failure demonstrated the limits of efforts to highlight a positive memory of the first Christian monarch of the Frankish kingdoms. In addition, another key development relating to Merovingian royal history was the discovery in 1653 of the grave of the Frankish king Childeric at Tournai (Belgium): the archduke Leopold William gave Louis XIV the treasure found in the tumulus, including the golden bee ornaments with which the monarch was buried, which thereafter became a royal symbol (Chifflet 1655). Contemporary representations of Clovis with the Sun King's facial features suggested his significance to that monarch, especially since the Franks' activities justified Louis XIV's claims beyond the Rhine (Grell 1996, pp. 173–218). A quite positive view of Clovis's accession to the throne and the start of the Merovingian dynasty still characterized the two main strands of French historiography at this time: Catholic historians underscored the meaning of Clovis's baptism for the future nation of France and for Christianity's success. By contrast, the Gallican historical tradition (which upheld the monarch's authority over the Catholic Church) presented Clovis as conqueror and precursor of France's political power. For both parties, the first mythic ancestor of Clovis, Pharamond, remained an important part of French history due to his role as the founder of the French monarchy, "the oldest and noblest of all people in the world" (Bossuet 1681, p. 131). His historical existence was not questioned.

In the late seventeenth and early eighteenth centuries, French historiography consisted mostly of a brief catalog of Merovingian kings that mentioned their religious foundations and territorial conquests. New editions of Gregory of Tours's *Histories* and Fredegar's *Chronicle* (Ruinart 1699) brought scholars the opportunity to engage in more complex approaches to the Merovingian period. The work of the historian Gabriel Daniel (1696) focused positively on the Frankish army and military talent, for example. If Clovis himself remained safe from criticism, the dark portrait of his heirs given by the two early medieval authors made an impression on classical scholars.

The discussion took a new turn at the beginning of the eighteenth century. Partly based on former argumentation, Henri de Boulainvilliers proposed a new interpretation of early Frankish history, and his arguments laid the foundation for the Germanist or "aristocratic" tradition of historical thought (Boulainvilliers 1727, 1732). According to his hypothesis, the Franks did not originate from Troy, but rather came from Germania. They were not wild people but warriors, and they conquered the Gallo-Romans, who became subjects (slaves) of the Frankish state. This conquest explained the origin of feudalism and justified aristocratic privileges: the French nobility comprised the descendants of the Franks, whereas the descendants of the enslaved Gallo-Romans formed the Third Estate. The word "Frank" in this sense meant free, and Boulainvilliers portrayed their society as an aristocratic republic. This approach emphasized the role of the early Germanic peoples and Scandinavia, with whom liberty and democracy were to be associated.

By contrast, Jean Baptiste Dubos gave a critical response to Boulainvilliers's view and proposed an alternative thesis. The object of his *Histoire critique de l'établissement de la monarchie française dans les Gaules* (1734) was to prove that the Franks had entered Gaul not as conquerors, but at the request of the nation, which had called upon them to govern. In Dubos's view, theirs was a lawful settlement. Clovis gained his power legally from the Roman Empire and instituted an absolute monarchy in which there was no difference in status between Franks, Romans, Gauls, and other barbarians. Moreover, aristocracy did not exist in the ancient Frankish society; for Dubos, the name "Frank" meant ferocity. According to him, the Germanic people had given up their tribal affiliation in favor of Roman wealth.

These debates laid the groundwork for two long-term trends in historiography: the first one, called "Germanist," considered the deposition of Romulus Augustus and the reign of Clovis as the true end of Antiquity and the start of the Middle Ages in the West. The barbarians brought a new civilization and, with it, the birth of Europe. By contrast, the second trend, the so-called Romanist perspective, asserted that the Merovingian period belonged to the Roman Christian epoch. Medieval culture was shaped more by its Roman inheritance and Christianity than by barbaric Germanic culture about which little was known. Twentieth-century advocates of Late Antiquity reused these arguments in defense of a modified periodization of the transition between Antiquity and the Middle Ages.

In the eighteenth century, the debate over Frankish origins attracted many responses. One of them was the magisterial work of Montesquieu in *De l'Esprit des lois* (1748, book 31) and his more focused *Considérations sur les causes de la grandeur des Romains et de leur décadence* (1734). In these works, the Franks were invaders, but they did not reduce Gallo-Romans to slavery. On the contrary, they tried to maintain Roman institutions and laws in Merovingian society. However, they also brought many innovations to early French society: these included the concepts of liberty and democracy that were specifically developed among the ancient Germanic peoples (an argument that applied neatly to Montesquieu's climatic theory). Another was the specific tradition of fiefs and the function of offices that resulted in the feudal system. The rise of the office of the *maior domus* (mayor of the palace), starting with the Edict of Chlothar II (613), explained the weakening of Merovingian kings' power, the ascent of the Pippinids, and the further development of the vassals in the feudal system. Montesquieu thus markedly increased the Germanic contribution to Merovingian society. More moderate was the work of Gabriel Bonnot de Mably, author of *Observations sur l'histoire de France* (1765), who underlined the complexity of Gallo-Roman and Frankish interactions and the process of creation of a new society. He documented the slow evolution of the status of different categories of people and proposed the adaptation of the Frankish aristocracy and monarchy to alternate traditions.

Breaking with these pluralistic approaches, Voltaire provided a very dark vision of the era without making any concession to the positive contribution of the Merovingian kings. He denied them recognition for any talent or political concept, and he described them as pure barbarians (Voltaire 1756, 1764). In his view, the Franks' name came from the Latin *ferocitas*, which he believed was the nature of this nation. He reduced the whole Merovingian period to one of significant regression in terms of culture and civilization: "they have no city, no law, no literature, and no police" (Voltaire 1764, 1878, p. 174). His harsh criticism of Catholicism and absolutism made his approach converge with that of Edward Gibbon in the *Decline and Fall of the Roman Empire* (1776). Voltaire's reading of this period nonetheless remained marginal during the Ancien Regime.

Liberalism, Nationalism, and the Emergence of Progressive Scholarly Historiography (1789–1870)

Because of their questioning of absolute monarchy, revolutionary discourses largely broke with classical approaches. Both Romanist and Germanist approaches to the Merovingian past were profoundly impacted by this historiographical turn, and aristocratic theory was the biggest victim of the new paradigm of equality. Nobles' privileges were abolished, and the historical legitimacy of their status was denied. Moreover, revolutionaries asserted that the heirs of the Gallo-Romans, because of their ancient subjection, gained special rights over the aristocracy. The well-known discourses pronounced by Joseph Emmanuel Sieyès to the Third Estate in 1789 to justify the abolition of aristocratic privileges summarized this new point of view: Sieyès asked the nobles, whose prerogatives were supposed to have derived from the conquest of Gaul by their ancestors, the Franks, to go back to the Germanic forests from whence they came (Sieyès 1820). He interpreted Clovis's ascent to power as usurpation, and thus condemned the Merovingian dynasty, as well as its successors, as illegitimate and illegal. Instead, Gallo-Romans formed the true substrate of the French nation. In Sieyès's view, French history needed to be the story of the progressive recovery of the rights of the Third Estate. This polemical discourse dominated contemporary historiography, especially the writings of the young liberal historian Augustin Thierry, who employed it quite literally during the Restoration (1827). For Thierry, Merovingian history symbolized the illegal origin story of the monarchy and its alliance with the Catholic Church. Now that the Revolution had brought this situation to an end, it was necessary to engineer a completely different approach to the early Middle Ages. From this perspective, Gallic times were the true beginning of the French nation (Martin 1833; Amédée Thierry 1828).

Historiography in the first half of the nineteenth century was characterized by historians' ideological investment in nationalism. The political context of the French Revolution, the Napoleonic Wars, and the Treaty of Versailles encouraged the development of national consciousness in Europe, and history was a foundational pillar of romantic nationalism. Historical discourse was also strongly impacted by the rise of history as an academic discipline, its incorporation into university curricula, and its continuing professionalization. The École des Chartes was established in Paris in 1821, and the first historical seminar in medieval history in German territory opened at Konigsberg University in 1832 (Poulle 1987, pp. 26–39; Weber 1984, p. 110).

In France, especially before 1840, historians were mostly polemicists. In this specific context, following the trauma of the Revolution, historiographical trends followed one another in short succession. First, aristocratic historians took advantage of the opportunities provided by the Restoration and Charles X's coronation to take Boulainvilliers's stance on the status of the Frankish monarchy (Montlosier 1814). Part of this current, albeit more moderate, was the historical work of Mademoiselle de Lézardière, who presented a strong analysis of the political and legal system of Merovingian kingship and underlined the role and power of the Frankish aristocracy (1844). One of the merits of her approach was her use of legal texts (both Roman and barbarian codes) to add to scholarly knowledge. The issues raised by this approach also encouraged the exploration of ancient municipalities and "clientèle" (the personal relationship between a powerful figure and his entourage), or, in other words the function of ancient communities and their connection to the development of feudality (Mignet 1822). Breaking with a negative vision of the impact of Christianity (Gibbon 1776), historians of a more Catholic bent pointed out the importance of Clovis's conversion in the formation of Merovingian society. They proposed new periodization between Antiquity and the Middle Ages from the third century (Chateaubriand 1831). Clovis's baptism brought a symbolic message insofar as it renewed the model of Constantine. Historians also underlined the tribute of Gregory of Tours's *Histories* to Greco-Roman culture. This approach suggested the importance of Christianity in binding together the Gallo-Romans and barbarians in Gaul. Chateaubriand's approach was taken up by and underlined by Frédéric Ozanam in his relatively positive description of the ancient Germanic peoples (1847–1849).

The major French historiographical trend in the mid-nineteenth century was the liberal one. Progressively liberated from Revolutionary radicalism, liberal historians, including Jules Michelet, François Guizot, and Augustin Thierry, mostly joined the moderate party of the July Monarchy. In accordance with the ideological project of this party, the aim of their historical approach was to reduce political and social tension and restore national unity. They tried to offer the French population a form of French history that was no longer exclusively the history of the king but the nation as a whole from its origins to the French Revolution (Guizot 1828; Michelet 1833). Another characteristic of this liberal current was its romantic leanings: historians combined colorful style with a careful reading of sources. With regard to the Middle Ages, this work was achieved thanks to an exceptional synthetic effort by Constant Leber that made the scientific findings of the historiography of the Ancien Regime accessible to the next generation: a collection of twenty volumes of historical writings organized by themes and periods (1826–1838). Liberal historians became progressively aware of the importance of editing historical texts, especially literary but also legal and administrative works. In order to make it possible for people to consult all the extant texts from the Middle Ages, they (re)started ambitious publishing enterprises like the *Receuil des historiens de la Gaule et de la France* or the *Collection des documents inédits sur l'histoire de France*. Some of these editions also influenced the next scholarly generation (Guerard 1844; Pardessus 1853), even if the whole project revealed itself to be unrealistic with regard to the number of texts and the means available to publish them (Graceffa 2009, pp. 35–37).

The writings of these liberal scholars presented different approaches to the monarchy at the same time as they sought to reintegrate the Merovingian past into a global national narrative. The works of Augustin Thierry, in particular, suggested the barbarization of the Merovingian period down to its very vocabulary. The *Récits des temps mérovingiens*, for example, reinvented the names of the Frankish kings so that they seemed more "Germanic": Clotaire (as Chlothar is known in French) became *Chlother*, Chilpéric (Chilperic) became *Hilpéric* (Thierry 1840, pp. 363, 379). Thierry's description of French historiography and his knowledge of literary and legal sources distanced Merovingian history from its classical themes (1828). Nevertheless, his vision of race and class war as a driving force in history made his narrative the prisoner of two opposing forces: a race of conquerors (the Franks) and a race of the conquered (the Gallo-Romans). He described Merovingian kingship as pure tyranny. The historians François Guizot and Jules Michelet supported this perspective, but they chose not to portray the French people as pitted against one another. It was more important for them to write a national history in which everyone mattered and had a place. Even if they kept describing Franks as real barbarians—in other words, savages—they tried to integrate Merovingian history into a larger history of France starting with prehistoric times (Michelet 1833). Gaul was described as a predestined territory, a melting pot in which Gauls, Romans, Franks, and other barbarians mixed together to create the future French people. Thanks to Michelet's anthropomorphic metaphor of France as a person, the Frankish period became the childhood of the nation and its barbarity was compared to the innocent barbarity of a small child (Petitier 1997; Graceffa 2009, pp. 49–52).

For liberal historians, the main objective was to understand how Merovingian society functioned and whether the Merovingian kingdoms managed to become a real nation. On this subject, Guizot agreed with Thierry's perspective and underlined the lack of unity by any criterion (ethnicity, language, law, culture, and religion) and the Merovingian king's inability to create it (Guizot 1828; Thierry 1840). The impact of Gregory of Tours's writings was evident here, especially his description of the beginning of civil war in the late sixth century that directly inspired the *Récits* (Thierry 1840). The book provided a really dark vision of Merovingian society and the Merovingian kingdoms. At the same time, however, it offered a window into the Merovingian period, and his lively style allowed his readership to discover the complexity of Merovingian society (including Christian and pagan practices, religious and civil architecture, customs, dress, arms, and material culture). Moreover, other contemporary studies tried to improve understanding of fifth-century political events (Fauriel 1836) and social structures, especially kinship ties (Lehuërou 1841–1842), involved in the long conquest of southern Gaul. Such works described the importance of Germanic kinship bonds for medieval society in detail.

Only a few studies of this era, and authored mostly by minor scholars (e.g., Martin 1833, vol. 1), continued with the former theory of Gallo-Frankish unity. Although the Germanic identity of the Franks and their northern origins (generally thought to have been in Schleswig-Holstein) were no longer denied even in France, German scholars increasingly emphasized the importance of a distinct Germanic character to the promotion of the Germanic past and culture. Driven by their desire for German national unity, German-speaking historians underlined the physical and moral qualities of the ancient Germanic peoples. Germans were favorably portrayed in this manner: "Tall, strong and beautiful, so were the Germans in ancient times. Their skin was white and pure in color, their golden curly hair fell onto their shoulders like a lion's mane, men and women both, and from their big blue eyes shone courage and noble pride in their freedom" (Duller 1840, p. 6). The German language was seen as the most perfect heir of Sanskrit (Schlegel 1808), and the development of Indo-Germanic philology resulted in an improved understanding of the relationships among European languages, especially the Germanic branch.

One particularity of German approaches was the popularity of the genealogical model (von See 1970; Fehr 2010, pp. 70–76). This philological approach was progressively expanded to include ethnicity (Schleicher 1860). The ancient Germanic peoples were described as a *Volk* (nation), endowed with an original territory (between the Elbe and Oder rivers), unity of origins, and historically divided into several *Stammen* (branches or tribes) (Gaupp 1844). Their historical fate was to reunite one day. Frankish tribes were seen as one group of numerous Germanic tribes, and the Merovingian kingdoms were interpreted as a successful Germanic nation that prefigured the empire of Charlemagne (Bethmann Hollweg 1850). Clovis's capacity to federate the different nations (Salic and Rhenish Franks, Alamanni, Burgundians, Visigoths, and so on) prefigured the Carolingian Empire. One of the decisive features of the ancient Germanic peoples was their military talent (Bethmann-Hollweg 1850): this interpretive trope soon became a commonplace among scholars. To improve this approach, the aim of German historians consisted of four main, intimately connected projects: first, to collect systematically all traces of the Germanic past (languages, literature, law, material culture, and popular culture as songs or tales) to prove the reality of a common Germanic culture. An emblematic example of this scheme was the work of Jakob Grimm on fairy tales (1828). The second project involved drawing a genealogical connection between German tribes and their relations with other European nations (Zeuss 1837; Gaupp 1844). In the third project, scholars sought to edit all of the historical texts regarding the history of the Germanic nation, especially the oldest (Graceffa 2009, pp. 35–38). Early publication projects were supported by German scholars like Grimm, Karl-Friedrich von Savigny, and Georg Heinrich Pertz in the case of *Geschichtsschreiber der deutschen Vorzeit in deutscher Bearbeitung*, or by French scholars like François Lelong and François Guizot in the *Histoire littéraire de la France*. In accordance with the Lutheran tradition of providing popular access to seminal texts, the nationalist dynamic was expressed clearly in the motto of the MGH: *Sanctus amor patriae dat animum/Holy love for the fatherland gives the spirit* (Fuhrmann 1994, p. 175).

The fourth project consisted of analyzing the ancient Germanic law codes; this legal material attested to the strong specificity of German societies and demonstrated the existence of Germanic culture that was just as important as Roman civilization. Moreover, the existence of barbarian law attested to the existence of a Germanic political and moral sense, in addition to evidence of an organized society. Such evidence argued against French assumptions about the savage nature of barbarians and suggested that ancient German society was ruled by laws, not anarchy. Even the vengeance system of feud (*faide*) could be explained rationally, and its existence demonstrated a specific system of regulation (Rogge 1820). The role and place of monarchy became a real historiographical challenge. Georg Waitz's studies proved the existence of Germanic kingship as a legal system, and the successive versions of his *Verfassungsgeschichte Deutschland* showed the evolution of his ideas (1844; 1865). In parallel, attention to the age of invasions allowed Ernst Gaupp to demonstrate that a period of military billeting preceded the settlement of the barbarians in the Roman Empire (1844). At the same time, decisive works allowed historical knowledge to develop regarding early medieval political events and the chronology of Merovingian kings (Pertz 1828), using more culturally based approaches to Merovingian society (Loebell 1839).

Modern conceptions of ethnicity promoted by nationalism, including those linked to biology that might more accurately be identified as race, also had an impact on historical writing in the nineteenth century. In examining questions related to language, culture, biology, and history, historians sought to prove the existence of the nation as far as possible into the past and define its original territory. Based on linguistic evidence of the Indo-Germanic tradition, historians sought to obtain a better understanding of the connections between different cultural groups and their origins. These studies were especially prominent in the German states where, before 1870, the lack of a unified nation stimulated inquiries into Germanic origins. Quite different from the French tradition, intellectual concern about the disappearance or contamination of German culture led to scholarly attachment to the idea of ethnic purity. The former opposition between "active" and "passive" race, pronounced by Montesquieu, was thus reinterpreted and connected to the idea of Germanic nobility: "the Ancient Germans are proud and free and never submitted or mixed, they sway their own destiny" (Wietersheim 1862, vol. 4, p. 486). Closely connected were the promotion and valorization of the warlike character, military talent, and dominating power of the ancient Germanic peoples (Arndt 1854).

The notion of purity also reflected the way in which German scholars staked intellectual positions opposed to those of French scholars. They defied French conceptions of identity based on ethnic diversity; the success of these ideas may be seen in the popularity of a new definition of race promoted by Arthur de Gobineau (1853). Race was no longer a synonym of people or tribe understood genealogically, as had been the case earlier, but was now supposed to be a classification of humans into groups based on physical, biological, and psychological traits. Racial theory had a substantial impact on historical discourse related to the early Middle Ages. Indeed, Gobineau and his followers denied the reality of a single humanity and established a hierarchical classification of the races.

XENOPHOBIA, CONTROVERSIES, AND NEW SOCIOECONOMIC APPROACHES (1870–1950)

In 1871, after the Prussian War, the German historian Theodor Mommsen argued that the German annexation of the French departments of Alsace and Moselle was legitimate (Leterrier 1997, pp. 60–61; Hartog 2001, pp. 397–419). Mommsen's major argument was based on the historical identity of these regions. By contrast, the French historian Fustel de Coulanges denied these allegations: from his perspective, membership in a state should not be defined by history or biology but by the desire to live together (Fustel de Coulanges in Hartog 2001, pp. 398–404). The fact that certain territories had affinity with broader German culture did not justify their inclusion into the German Empire. This debate reveals how French and German traditions were divided by conceptions of ethnicity and how medieval history was used as evidence in historians' arguments. The use and abuse of the past by politicians was exaggerated by the circumstances brought on by three successive wars between France and Germany. Thus, the rise of xenophobia and racism deeply affected historical discourse.

In Germany, unification was an important source of renewed German nationalism from 1871 onward. It was further heightened during World War I and its aftermath. Felix Dahn's best-selling novel, *Die Könige der Germanen*, illustrated the success of the pan-Germanic approach based on a variety of primary sources, including the *Niebelungenlied*, *Beowulf*, and the Germanic law codes (Dahn 1861–1909). The model of the Nibelungen inspired faith in an "eternal return" of German glory. Gobineau's conception of a racial hierarchy was popular among German historians, who saw the Germanic race at the top. Its superiority was based on both physical and moral characteristics. The question of the history of settlement (*Siedlungsgeschichte*) was also thought to substantiate scientifically the existence of an original German territory, attested to by language, customs, culture, and place names. The structure of settlements in the landscape and the shape of traditional dwellings were thought to demonstrate the reality of a common Germanic culture, especially in the region of Alsace (Arnold 1875; Schiber 1894).

French and Belgian scholars likewise became invested in the quest for ethnically identifiable settlements. Toponymical research on the origins of place names in France were aimed at mapping each of the ancient Germanic tribes and evaluating their former demographic importance (Longnon 1878). In a scholarly conflict that divided Belgium, the French-speaking historian Godefroid Kurth proposed that a linguistic frontier delimited two historically attested territories, one occupied by Franks and the other by

Gallo-Romans. He believed that the Charbonnière Forest may have played the role of a natural frontier and explained the historical stopping point of Germanic settlement in the territory of modern Belgium (Kurth 1898). This presumption was revisited after World War I (Vanderlinden 1923).

In the meantime, historians mobilized not only linguistic and cultural data, but also archaeological and anthropological information furnished by a growing number of excavations (Effros 2012; see Effros, Chapter 4, this volume). These archaeological undertakings provided archaeological artifacts and racial historical types that strengthened the mapping of Germanic settlements in ancient Gaul. They also bolstered the idea of Germanic unity and Germanic soil dating back to Antiquity: Schleswig-Holstein was understood to have been the birthplace of the ancient Germanic peoples. Most prominently, the philologist and archaeologist Gustav Kossinna argued in favor of the indigenous character and racial unity of the population of northern Germany (Kossinna 1926). Most of these studies focused on two main territories, Belgium and Alsace-Moselle, because of the sensitive political issues they raised. Similarly, after World War I, German historians assessed the French-occupied Rhineland in order to identify the parameters of its inherent German character. A group of young German historians from Bonn University thus defined the notion of *Kulturströmungen* (cultural currents) to underline the maintenance of Germanic patterns in the subsequent Frankish kingdoms (Aubin, Frings, and Hansen 1922).

If some scholars were affected by racial prejudice, others argued in favor of a cultural and historical definition of the German nation (Levison 1948). The long-term study of the Rhineland shows the particularity of its development: this region appeared in studies as a place of contact, first inhabited by Germanic tribes, before it was profoundly Romanized during the Roman Empire, and then later re-Germanized by the Frankish conquest. While some scholars sought to offer a global view of the barbarian invasions (Schmidt 1910–1918; Lot 1927), a specific group of German historians focused on the highly fraught question of a German living space (*Lebensraum*) and its historical justification, both to the west (Steinbach 1926; Petri 1937) and to the east (Aubin, Brunner 1942). Their argumentation and maps were used by the National Socialists to justify the colonization of a great part of Europe, especially Belgium and the Loire Valley in France (Schöttler 1997, 1999, pp. 89–113).

At the same time in France, republican nationalism placed great emphasis on historical knowledge, especially in the schools, due to the trauma of the 1871 defeat and the loss of Alsace-Moselle to Germany (Digeon 1959). Medievalists like Gabriel Monod and Ernest Lavisse, who had been partly educated in Germany and were influential in shaping educational policy in France, were especially impressed by German historical science and nationalist pride. They decided to follow the same model in France and used the new republican primary and secondary school curriculum, particularly education in history, to stimulate a renewal of national consciousness. They drew heavily from the works of Michelet and Thierry, and thus famous episodes in Merovingian history were chosen for study among French students. These included the accounts from the works of Gregory of Tours, including reference to the incident of the "vase of Soissons" (Clovis's murder in cold blood of an insubordinate soldier who had stolen a vase as booty from the church of Soissons and smashed it rather than returning it as demanded by the king), Clovis's baptism, Dagobert's achievements, and the Merovingian civil wars, which now became well known to all French pupils (Effros 2012).

Textbooks of the Third Republic depicted Clovis as either an ancient Gaul or a barbarian, in other words, a savage (Graceffa 2010, pp. 21–42). In the first case, textbooks reduced the Frankish character of the Merovingian king significantly: he only carried the *umbo* (the shield of the Franks) and the *francisque* (a double-bladed axe). His long hair and winged helmet made him look like the contemporary figure of the Gallic leader Vercingetorix, and he was often portrayed being carried on the *pavois* (large shield), as were Gallic leaders. In the second case, school textbooks insisted on the supposed anarchy of these dark times: beleaguered towns and destroyed monuments were shown to give pupils the impression of despair and decadence. These images were intended to remind French students of the fate of contemporary besieged towns, the destruction of Strasbourg and Reims cathedrals, and the devastation of Ypres. The similarities between these Merovingian representations and the crimes committed by the German armies during the Franco-Prussian War and World War I were, without any doubt, intended to leave an impression of the connectedness of the two eras on contemporary students. Medievalists and historians such as Lavisse, Monod, Joseph Bédier, Louis Bréhier, Camille Enlart, Auguste Geffroy, Louis Halphen, Ferdinand Lot, and Charles Petit-Dutaillis condemned German barbarity in wartime (Graceffa 2014, pp. 159–180).

For the French, the historical term *barbarian* took on new meaning with respect to ancient and contemporary Germans. This approach was seen as legitimate given the barbaric acts performed by German armies in wars on French and Belgian soil. German war crimes were seen as a sign of the constitutive behavior of this nation. Whether ancient or modern, Germans were portrayed as barbarians and the destroyers of civilization. The lexical proximity of the French words "Allemand" (German) and "Alamans" (the Germanic tribe of the Alamanni) strengthened this view. The prominence of Germanophobia in this era reinforced a dark vision of Merovingian society, and even more so because of its historical place as the first Catholic monarchy, which displeased secularists and antiroyalists in France. In their eyes, Clovis was a cruel and cynical plotter who accepted Christianity only to win over episcopal authorities to his cause and secure his future conquest of Gaul. However, the fourteen hundredth commemoration of Clovis's baptism in 1896 provided Catholic historians an opportunity to restore a more positive interpretation of Christianity and underline the role of bishops and saints as pacifists (Kurth 1896). No longer was the community of Catholic historians disrupted by controversies that questioned the historical use of sacred texts (Duchesne 1925; Mores 2015). Moreover, a positive approach to Christianization became compulsory during World War I. In the context of the belated canonization of Joan of Arc, the conflict was seen as a divine consequence of the recent laicization of French society, and re-Christianization was urged. A clear sign of this change was revealed by the popular success of holy figures in literature, painting, and the iconography of late nineteenth-century churches, including Martin, bishop of Tours, Vaast, bishop of Arras (who helped convert Clovis), Genovefa, the Gallo-Roman savior of Paris during the Hunnic invasions, and the goldsmith Eligius, bishop of Noyon (Blin 2002).

Besides these political tensions, the turn of the twentieth century was characterized by the professionalization of history, and even medieval studies, as well as the influence of the social sciences on the scholarly community of historians. First, these changes meant more effective control of the methods and ethics of the profession, and greater self-consciousness concerning historians' activities. The European community of scholars' critical review of Karl August Pertz's publication of *Diplomata Regnum Francorum e stirpe Merowingica* (1872), for instance, led to the author's suicide (Brühl 1990). Despite the perils of military conflicts, scholars continued to engage in critical reviews. There were also joint international scholarly ventures among medievalists, such as the emblematic French and Belgian periodical *Le Moyen Âge* created in 1888. Similarly, international meetings and research travel stimulated scholarly discussions, including the International Historical Congress held in London 1913, which created an international working board to update Charles du Fresne, sieur du Cange's seventeenth-century *Glossarium ad scriptores mediae et infimae latinitatis* (1678). The project, undertaken jointly by European historians and philologists, resulted in the analysis of Merovingian and Carolingian written sources and the cataloguing of each term to identify the meaning and evolution of Latin vocabulary.

The process was not without historical controversy, however, especially regarding the sources and their interpretation: these discussions mostly concerned administrative and hagiographic sources. For one, there was great division among those conducting research on administrative sources that offered alternative interpretations of Merovingian kingship and its function. Scholars like Julien Havet contributed to the debates regarding preservation of a Roman-type administration in Gaul (1896). The traditional constitutional approach, once reinterpreted (Sohm 1871; Brunner 1887), progressively abandoned the study of kingship in favor of the place and role of aristocracies (Tellenbach 1939; Schlesinger 1941). By contrast, special attention was given to hagiographical texts, an original and rich source for the early Middle Ages. Following efforts to edit many of these texts and include them in the publications of the MGH, the community of medievalists had greater access to these important resources (Krusch and Levison 1888–1920). This edition was nevertheless marred by its hypercritical approach based on Karl Lachman's method of publishing sources, which led to the exclusion of texts or manuscripts from consideration as unauthentic or delayed. Differences in opinion led to controversies over Merovingian chronology, over matters such as the date of Clovis's baptism and his subsequent conquest of the Visigoths (Rouche 1997; Levillain 1935, pp. 161–192). Likewise, some German historians considered the *vita* of Genovefa apocryphal, whereas others accepted its historical authenticity (Kurth 1919; Heinzelmann and Poulin 1986). The revised publication of Gregory of Tours's works in the MGH challenged his objectivity as a historian (Krusch and Levison 1937–1951).

The birth of the social sciences had an impact on medieval studies; German law historians, for instance, began to study the ancient Germanic family, where the influence of Marxist approaches was felt (Engels 1884). They also addressed the egalitarian functioning of *Marke* (the common tenure and cultivation of land) in ancient Germanic communities (von Maurer 1856; Gierke 1868–1913) and discussed whether these were preserved or transformed into feudalism (Lamprecht 1885–1886). After World War I, historians developed new approaches to understanding the roots of feudalism by focusing on the socioeconomic transformation of the countryside (Bloch 1939–1940; Ganshof 1947) and towns (Dopsch 1918–1920; Pirenne 1937). This brought new perspectives for understanding the chronology of the transition between Antiquity and the Middle Ages and its interpretation: this evolution was connected with a more global cultural evolution (Riegl 1901). In this interpretation, the mutations seen in the social structures of the Merovingian period were less a regression than a transformation (Lot 1946–1950) and signaled the origin of the Carolingian renaissance (Halphen 1926; Ennen 1953).

THE "EUROPEAN TURN" AND THE DENATIONALIZATION OF HISTORICAL DISCOURSE (1950–2015)

The trauma of World War II and the Holocaust forced early medieval historians to rethink scholarly discourse and encouraged a progressive denationalization of the history of the early Middle Ages (Pfeil 2008). The previously restrictive definitions of nation and tribe were abandoned in favor of a more comprehensive approach that underlined exchanges between different cultures. The invention of the notion of Late Antiquity and the establishment of a community of specialists made possible significant advances in knowledge of this transitional period, especially the socio economic problems that confronted it. In discussions about the modalities of Germanic or barbarian settlement (Musset 1965; Demougeot 1969), the traditional vision of a clash of civilizations was progressively replaced by a model that underlined the cohabitation of Romans and barbarians (Brown 1971; Marrou 1975). The Merovingian world now appeared to be the consequence of the mixture of three cultures during the fourth and fifth centuries: Roman, barbarian, and Christian.

Eugen Ewig's studies, for instance, proposed a new rational approach to the division of Frankish kingdoms and demonstrated the unreliability of the presumed existence of the Ripuarian Franks (Ewig 1979). The first point had significant influence on new research regarding the unity of the *res publica* during the Merovingian period, which was maintained among the royal family despite existing divisions. The successive distributions of territories no longer appeared to be an individualistic conception of the power and the state, but rather as the adaptation of a Frankish tradition that promoted equal heritage over primogeniture to preserve the unity of the kingdom (Werner 1984). Indeed, research on royal names and Germanic anthroponomy supported this view. People's names were no longer considered an ethnic marker that determined beyond doubt the nationality of a person. Instead, name-giving appears to have been a cultural practice of integration, whether Roman, German, or Christian (Ewig 1991; Lebecq 1996). This practice also had a political dimension, especially for the royal family and elites. Germanic names were composed of a combination of several ethnic or family markers, and could be used to stress the power of relatives and dynastic power (Le Jan 1995). The second point, the lack of an actual Ripuarian tribe, had a substantial impact on studies on Germanic tribes and the formalization of these communities: historians wondered whether these tribes shared a common origin (*gens*) or whether they were just aggregate groups. In this last case, Frankish tribes, made up of members of a variety of origins, decided to join and accept the leader's name. This model helped explain the relative historical disappearance of the Alamanni after their defeat by Clovis at Tolbiac/Zülpich: rather than being eliminated, they were integrated into the Frankish nation and took up its name (Geuenich 1998).

These evolutions benefited from a new approach to ethnic identity, especially in Germany (see Coumert, Chapter 5, this volume). Related to this challenge was the work of Reinhard Wenskus on the concept of ethnogenesis, which attracted considerable attention. He proposed a cultural conception of early medieval tribes that were formed around a small nucleus, the *Traditionskern*, which was not ethnic but cultural; this nucleus was preserved and transmitted by the elite over the course of centuries. The principal source of cohesion in early medieval peoples was thus not biological but cultural, and a central element of Wenskus's hypothesis was belief in a common, heroic past (Wenskus 1961). The constitution of a nation through crystallization around a nucleus and the promotion of legendary history, or myth, allowed for a restoration of Germanic continuity reconfigured as imagined national identity rather than racial identity (Anderson 1991). Historians further explored the idea of a fiction of common origin and how ancient texts helped relay and spread it. Forged in the 1980s and 1990s, the notion of ethnogenesis gave rise to the concept of Germanic identity (Wolfram 1979, 1999). From the same perspective, the systematical collection of Germanic names and their study provided insight into the process of constituting and preserving memory (Geuenich, Haubrichs, and Jarnut 1997). For other historians, however, the myth of origins relied on nothing. They denied the possibility of ever reconstructing the Germanic past and evaluating its contribution to Merovingian society (Coumert 2007; Bauduin, Gazeau, and Modéran 2008).

In the 1970s, interest in Merovingian history declined because the small number of sources made it impossible to apply new quantitative methods. Most French medievalists instead specialized in the central Middle Ages: Georges Duby turned to feudal structure, Robert Fossier examined the evolution of the countryside, and Jacques Le Goff addressed the history of the mentalities. This lack of interest explains the persistence of stereotypes regarding the Merovingian period as a time of decadence.

The development of a relationship between historians and other late antique and early medieval specialists across Europe offered the impulse for creation of a truly European community of scholars, favored by the postwar reconciliation between Germans and French led by German medievalists such as Karl Ferdinand Werner and

Carl-Richard Brühl (Werner 1984; Brühl 1992). The small group of French historians who carry on work on the early Middle Ages have mostly developed a fiscal approach that dates back to the traditional Romanist trend and especially the observations of Fustel of Coulanges (1891). They have focused on preservation of the late Roman Empire's direct system of taxation during the early Middle Ages. According to this approach, the transition between the Roman Empire and the barbarian kingdoms was relatively smooth, amounting to no more than a change of regimes. Contrary to the idea of barbaric decline and the disappearance of the state, Merovingian kings were now seen as having protected the Roman tax system and its administrative organization. This approach proposed some major changes to existing understanding of the Merovingian economy and supported prosopographical research of the royal administration. Several Latin terms received new fiscal definitions: *possessor/dominus,* "eminent/fiscal owners" of public lands or holders of a dominion and *description,* which became similar to a cadastral statement, described tax bases (*fundi*), and was divided into *villae* and *mansi* (Magnou-Nortier 1993–1997). From this perspective, the barbarian invasions amounted to an appropriation of taxes (i.e., eminent or fiscal property) without direct appropriation. Far from destroying the Roman system, Clovis and other barbarian leaders tried to protect it (Goffart 1980). The Merovingian aristocracy, whether civil or religious, took charge of public duties, especially the collection of the fisc (public taxes) (Werner 1998).

This fiscal approach appears to have been too systematic for most historians (Wickham 1993; Devroey 2003), and so many historians progressively promoted another position influenced by the anthropology and theory of Germanic ethnogenesis. Focusing on the elite, they sought to understand the complex relationship inside Merovingian society between aristocratic families and territorial and sacral power, just between identity and memory (Le Jan 2006). These new perspectives were well represented in the European Science Foundation project "Transformation of the Roman World" in the 1990s, which brought together specialists from around the world to revise scholarly understanding of this period. This interdisciplinary project gathered not only European historians and archaeologists but also specialists from America and Russia. All managed to speak and think together beyond traditional national historical boundaries. In addition to fostering historical knowledge, this approach raised awareness about the use and misuse of the past by contemporary Europe (Geary 2002; Wood 2013, pp. 327–329; Evans and Marchal 2015). The thoroughly interdisciplinary approach to each aspect of the momentous changes during this period contributed to the project's important and often unexpected findings. An important result of the program was the discussion of identities and communities, and how they were constructed through integration and accommodation. The proceedings of the "Transformation of the Roman World" demonstrated how much of a cliché modern approaches to ethnicity were and how this approach was completely anachronistic with regard to early medieval realities. Contrary to the certitude with which former views were held, it could now be said that a single Germanic people probably never existed (Pohl 2003). This revised vision of Germanic and Merovingian history has encouraged historians to go back to primary texts and reconnect with history removed from nationalist impulses. In opposing the revival of the paradigm of clash of civilizations, the study of late-antique and Merovingian history now has to meet the challenge of genetic history (Lee, Nelson, and Wailoo 2012; Pohl 2015, pp. 201–208).

The recent return to the texts—especially literature and hagiographical works—has been bolstered since the 1970s by the extensive development of medieval archaeology. Concerning written sources, Martin Heinzelmann has demonstrated how the eschatological dimension of Gregory of Tours's thinking affected his writing (Heinzelmann 1994). In the same way, the reevaluation of hagiographical material has led to a better understanding of social reality (see Kreiner, Chapter 24, this volume). Archaeological research has similarly brought new data to bear on urban and rural settlements and has improved our knowledge of material culture (see Bourgeois, Chapter 28; Chevalier, Chapter 30; Peytremann, Chapter 31, this volume). The role and location of Christian bishops, in particular, have shown continuity with the ancient Roman administration of cities (Durliat 1990; Werner 1998; see Loseby, Chapter 27, this volume). The rise of monasteries during the Merovingian period has similarly been understood to have promoted economic development and social organization (see Diem, Chapter 15, this volume). Rural archaeology has likewise offered key insights into these developments (Peytremann 2003; Guillaume-Peytremann 2005; Verslype 2007; Gaillard 2014), and scholars have initiated a new rural history, including animals, nature, and the environment (Guizard-Duchamp 2009). New fields of study, including poverty and power, the place of children, gender history, and the history of the emotions have shaped the field (Pancer 2001; Rosenwein 1999, 2006). Cultural history allows better understanding of the function and structure of Merovingian society, especially its political elites and their competition (Bougard, Bührer-Thierry, and Le Jan 2013; Patzold and Ubl 2014). Historians have now proved that Christianization was not a linear development and that rivalry existed among a plurality of religious forms, including the resurgence of paganism (Rouche 1979; Pietri 1983; Dumézil 2005; Mériaux 2006). New connections between anthropological and economic history thus allow Merovingian history to be reconsidered through many more prisms than ethnicity.

Works Cited

Ancient Sources

Krusch, B., and Levison, W. (eds.). (1888–1920). *Passiones vitaeque sanctorum aevi Merovingici.* MGH SRM. 4 vols. Hanover: Hahn.

Krusch, B., and Levison, W. (eds.). (1937–1951). *Gregorii episcopi Turonensis Libri Historiarum X.* MGH SRM 1, 1. Hanover: Hahn.

Ruinart, T. (1699). *Sancti Georgi Florenti Gregori episcopi Turonensis opera omnia.* Paris: Muguet.

Wallace-Hadrill, J. M. (ed. and trans.). (1960). *The Four Books of the Chronicle of Fredegar with Its Continuations = Fredegarii Chronicorum liber quartus (Fredegarii Chronica) cum continuationibus.* London: Thomas Nelson & Sons.

Modern Sources

Anderson, B. (1991). *Imagined Communities. Reflections on the Origin and Spread of Nationalism.* London: Verso.

Arndt, M. (1854). *Pro populo Germanico.* Berlin: Reimer.

Aubin, H., Frings, T., and Hansen, J. (eds.). (1922). *Geschichte des Rheinlandes von der ältesten Zeit bis zur Gegenwart.* Essen: Baedeker.

Aubin, H., and Brunner, O. (eds.). (1942). *Deutsche Ostforschung: Ergebnisse und Aufgaben seit dem ersten Weltkrieg.* Leipzig: Hirzel.

Arnold, W. (1875). *Ansiedlungen und Wanderungen Deutscher Stämme.* Stuttgart: Elwert.

Bauduin, P., Gazeau, V., and Modéran, Y. (2008). *Identité et ethnicité. Concepts, débats historiographiques, exemples (IIIe-XIIe siècles).* Caen: Editions du CRAHM.

Beaune, C. (1985). *Naissance de la Nation France.* Paris: Gallimard.

Bethmann-Hollweg, M. A. (1850). *Über die Germanen von der Völkerwanderung.* Bonn: A. Marcus.

Blin, J.-P. (2002). "Les églises de la reconstruction entre éclectisme et modernité." In E. Bussière, P. Marcilloux, and D. Varaschin (eds.), *La Grande reconstruction. Reconstruire le Pas-de-Calais après la Grande Guerre* (pp. 323–337). Arras: Archives départementales du Pas-de-Calais.

Bloch, M. (1939–1940). *La société féodale.* Paris: Albin Michel.

Bougard, F., Bührer-Thierry, G., and Le Jan, R. (2013). "Les élites du Haut Moyen Age. Identités, stratégies, mobilité." *Annales. Histoire, sciences sociales* 4: 1079–1112.

Bossuet, J.-B. (1681). *Discours sur l'Histoire universelle depuis le commencement du monde jusqu'à l'Empire de Charlemagne.* Paris: Sebastien Marbre-Cramoisy, Imprimeur du Roi.

Boulainvilliers, H. de. (1727). *Histoire de l'ancien gouvernement de la France.* La Haye-Amsterdam: Aux dépens de la Compagnie.

Boulainvilliers, H. de. (1732). *Essai sur la noblesse de France.* Amsterdam: Tabary.

Bourdieu, P. (1980). "Le Nord et le Midi: Contribution à une analyse de l'effet Montesquieu." *Actes de la recherche en sciences sociales* 35: 21–25.

Brown, P. (1971). *The World of Late Antiquity.* London: Harcourt Brace Jovanovich.

Brühl, C. (1990). *Deutschland-Frankreich. Die Geburt zweier Völker.* Cologne: Böhlau.

Brühl, C. (1992). "Splendeur et misère de la diplomatique: le cas de l'édition des Diplômes royaux mérovingiens de Bréquigny à Pertz." *Comptes rendus des séances de l'Académie des Inscriptions et Belles-Lettres* 136(1): 251–259.

Brunner, H. (1887–1889). *Deutsche Rechtsgeschichte.* Leipzig: Duncker & Humblot.

Chateaubriand, F. R. de. (1831). *Études ou discours historique sur la chute de l'Empire romain, la naissance et les progrès du christianisme et l'invasion des Barbares, suivi d'une étude raisonnée de l'histoire de France.* Paris: Lefevre.

Chifflet, J.-J. (1655). *Anastasis Childerici I Francorum regis, siue thesaurus sepulchralis tornaci neruiorum effossus, & commentario illustratus.* Antwerp: Officina Plantiniana Balthasaris Moreti.

Coumert, M. (2007). *Origines des peuples (550–850).* Paris: Institut d'études augustiniennes.

Daniel, G. (1696). *Deux dissertations pour une nouvelle histoire de France depuis l'établissement de la monarchie dans les Gaules.* Paris: S. Bernard.

Dahn, F. (1861–1909). *Die Könige der Germanen.* 11 vols. Leipzig: Breitkopf and Hartel.

Demougeot, E. (1969). *La formation de l'Europe et les invasions barbares.* Paris: Aubier.

Devroey, J. P. (2003). *Économie rurale et société dans l'Europe franque (VIe-IXe siècles).* Paris: Belin.

Dietz, B., Gabel, H., and Tiedau, U. (2003). *Griff nach dem Westen. Die Westforschung der völkisch-nationalen Wissenschaften zum nordwesteuropäischen Raum (1919–1960)*. New York: Waxmann Verlag.

Digeon, C. (1959). *La crise allemande de la pensée française (1870–1914)*. Paris: Presses universitaires de France.

Dopsch, A. (1918–1920). *Wirtschaftliche und soziale Grundlagen der europäischen Kulturentwicklung*. Vienna: Seiden and Sohn.

Dubos, J. B. (1734). *Histoire critique de l'établissement de la monarchie française dans les Gaules*. Paris: Osmont.

Du Cange, C. D. F. (1678). *Glossarium ad scriptores mediae et infimae Latinitatis*. 3 vols. Paris: G. Martini.

Duchesne, L. (1925). *L'Église au VIᵉ siècle*. Paris: E. de Boccard.

Duller, E. (1840). *Geschichte des deutschen Volkes*. Leipzig: Wigang.

Dumézil, B. (2005). *Les racines chrétiennes de l'Europe. Conversion et liberté dans les royaumes barbares, Vᵉ–VIIᵉ siècle*. Paris: Fayard.

Durliat, J. (1990). *Les Finances publiques. De Dioclétien aux Carolingiens (284–888)*. Sigmaringen: J. Thorbecke.

Effros, B. (2012). *Uncovering the Germanic Past. Merovingian Archaeology in France, 1830–1914*. Oxford: Oxford University Press.

Engels, F. (1975 [1884]). *L'origine de la famille, de la propriété privée et de l'État*. Paris: Éditions sociales.

Ennen, E. (1953). *Frühgeschichte der europäischen Stadt*. Bonn: Röhrscheid.

Evans, R., and Marchal, G. P. (eds.). (2015). *The Uses of the Middle Ages in Modern European States. History, Nationhood and the Search for Origins*. New York: Palgrave Macmillan.

Ewig, E. (1979). *Spätantike und fränkische Gallien. Gesammelte Schriften (1952–1973)*. Zürich-Munich: Artemis Verlag.

Ewig, E. (1991). "Die Namengebung bei den ältesten Frankenkönigen und im merowingischen Königshaus." *Francia* 18(1): 21–69.

Fauriel, C. (1836). *Histoire de la Gaule méridionale sous la domination des conquérants germains*. Paris: Paulin.

Federinov, B., Docquier, G., and Cauchies, J. M. (2015). *A l'aune de "Nos Gloires". Edifier, narrer et embellir par l'image*. Musée de Mariemont. Brussels: Presses de l'Université Saint-Louis.

Fehr, H. (2010). *Germanen und Romanen im Merowingerreich: frühgeschichtliche Archäologie zwischen Wissenschaft und Zeitgeschehen*. Berlin: Walter de Gruyter.

Fuhrmann, H. (1994). "Les premières décennies des MGH." *Francia* 21(1): 175–180.

Führer, J. (2016). "Du monstre sacré à la mémoire rationnelle ? Les récits génétiques des Mérovingiens et des Capétiens." In I. Luciani and V. Piétri (eds.), *L'Incorporation des ancêtres. Généalogie, construction du présent* (pp. 37–53). Aix-en-Provence: Presses universitaires de Provence.

Fustel de Coulanges, N.-D. (1891). *Histoire des institutions politiques de l'ancienne France*. Paris: Hachette.

Gaillard, M. (ed.). (2014). *L'empreinte chrétienne en Gaule du IVᵉ au IXᵉ siècle*. Turnhout: Brepols.

Ganshof, F. (1947). *Qu'est ce que la féodalité?* Brussels: Editions de la Baconnière.

Garber, J. (1989). "Trojaner-Römer-Franken-Deutsche. Nationale Abstammungstheorien im Vorfeld der Nationalstaatsbildung." In. K. Garber (ed.), *Nation und Literatur im Europa der Frühen Neuzeit. Akten des I. Internationalen Osnabrücker Kongresses des zur Kulturgeschichte der frühen Neuzeit* (pp. 108–163). Tübingen: M. Niemeyer Verlag.

Gaupp, E. T. (1844). *Die germanischen Ansiedlungen und Landtheilungen in den Provinzen des römischen Westreiches*. Breslau: J. Max.

Geary, P. (2002). *The Myth of Nations: The Medieval Origins of Europe*. Princeton, NJ: Princeton University Press.

Geuenich, D. (1997). *Geschichte der Alemannen*. Stuttgart: Kohlhammer.

Geuenich, D. (ed.). (1998). *Die Franken und die Alemannen bis zur "Schlacht bei Zülpich," 496–97*. Berlin: Walter de Gruyter.

Geuenich, D., Haubrichs, W., and Jarnut, J. (eds.). (1997). *Nomen et gens. Zur historischen Aussagekraft frühmittelalterlicher Personennamen*. Berlin: Walter de Gruyter.

Gibbon, E. (1776–1788). *The Decline and Fall of the Roman Empire*. London: Strahan & Cadell.

Gierke, O. (1868–1913). *Das deutsche Genossenschaftsrecht*. Berlin: Walter de Gruyter.

Gobineau, A. (1853). *Essai sur l'inégalité des races humaines*. Paris: Firmin Didot.

Goffart, W. (1980). *Barbarians and Romans, A.D. 418–583. The Techniques of Accommodation*. Princeton, NJ: Princeton University Press.

Graceffa, A. (2009). *Les historiens et la question franque. Le peuplement franc et les Mérovingiens dans l'historiographie française et allemande des XIXᵉ et XXᵉ siècles*. Turnhout: Brepols.

Graceffa, A. (2010). "Simplifier et édifier. Les Mérovingiens à l'école de la République" In P. Hummel (ed.), *Mésavoirs: études sur la (dé)formation par la transmission* (pp. 21–42). Paris: Philologicum.

Graceffa, A. (2014). "Médiévistes en guerre, entre engagement et regard critique, 1870/1918." In J.-F. Condette (ed.), *Les Écoles dans la guerre* (pp. 159–180). Villeneuve d'Ascq: Septentrion.

Grell, C. (1996). "Clovis du grand siècle aux lumières." *Bibliothèque de l'École des chartes* 154(1): 173–218.

Grimm, J. (1828). *Deutsche Rechtsalterthümer*. Göttingen: Dietrich.

Guérard, B. (1844). *Polyptique de l'abbé Irminon*. Paris: Imprimerie royale.

Guillaume, J., and Peytremann, E. (2005). *L'Austrasie. Sociétés, économies, territoires, christianisation*. Nancy: Presses universitaires de Nancy.

Guizard-Duchamp, F. (2009). *Les terres du sauvage dans le monde franc (IVᵉ–IXᵉ siècles)*. Rennes: Presses universitaires de Rennes.

Guizot, F. (1828). *Histoire de la civilisation en Europe*. Paris: Didier.

Halphen, L. (1926). *Les Barbares*. Paris: Alcan.

Hartog, F. (2001). *Le XIXᵉ siècle et l'histoire. Le cas Fustel de Coulanges*. Paris: Seuil.

Havet, J. (1896). *Questions mérovingiennes*. Paris: Champion.

Heinzelmann, M. (1994). *Gregor von Tours (538–594). Zehn Bücher Geschichte: Historiographie und Gesellschaftskonzept im 6. Jahrhundert*. Darmstadt. Wissenschaftliche Buchgesellschaft.

Heinzelmann, M., and Poulin, J.-C. (1986). *Les anciennes vies de sainte Geneviève de Paris. Études critiques*. Paris: Champion.

Hotman, F. (1573). *Franco-Gallia*. Geneva: J. Stoer.

Joye, S. (2016). "Représentations modernes et contemporaines: barbares redécouverts, barbarie réinventée." In B. Dumézil (ed.). *Les Barbares* (pp. 89–116). Paris: PUF.

Kaiser, R., and Scholz, S. (2014). *Quellen zur geschichte der Franken und der Merowinger. Vom 3. Jahrhundert bis 751*. Stuttgart: Kohlhammer.

Kossinna, G. von. (1926). *Ursprung und Verbreitung der Germanen in vor- und frühgeschichtlicher Zeit*. Berlin-Lichterfelde: Germanen Verlag.

Kurth, G. (1896). *Clovis*. Paris: Mame.

Kurth, G. (1898). *La frontière linguistique en Belgique et dans le nord de la France*. Brussels: F. Hayez.

Kurth, G. (1919). *Études franques*. Paris: Champion.

Lamprecht, K. (1885–1886). *Deutsches Wirtschaftsleben im Mittelalter*. Leipzig: A. Dürr.

Lebecq, S. (1996). *Les origines franques*. Paris: Seuil.

Leber, C. (1826–1838). *Collection des meilleures dissertations, notices et traités particuliers relatifs à l'histoire de France, composée en grande partie de pièces rares, ou qui n'ont jamais été publiées séparément*. XX. Paris: A. Dentu.

Lee, C., Nelson, A., and Wailoo, K. (eds.). (2012). *Genetics and the Unsettled Past: The Collision of DNA, Race, and History*. New Brunswick, NJ: Rutgers University Press.

Leibniz, G. W. (1715). *De origine Francorum*. Hanover: Foerster.

Le Jan, R. (1995). *Famille et pouvoir dans le monde franc (v^e–xe siècles)*. Paris: Publications de la Sorbonne.

Le Jan, R. (2006). *Les Mérovingiens*. Paris: PUF.

Lehuërou, J.-M. (1841–1842). *Histoire des institutions mérovingiennes et du gouvernement des Mérovingiens jusqu'à l'Édit de 615*. Paris: Joubert.

Leterrier, S.-A. (1997). *Le XIXe siècle historien: anthologie raisonnée*. Paris: Belin.

Levillain, L. (1935). "La conversion et le baptème de Clovis." *Revue d'histoire de l'église de France* 21(91): 161–192.

Levison, W. (1948). *Aus rheinischer und fränkischer Frühzeit. Ausgewählte Aufsätze*. Düsseldorf: L. Schwann.

Lézardière, P. de. (1844). *Théorie des lois politiques de la monarchie française*. Revised ed. Paris: Au comptoir des imprimeurs unis.

Loebell, J. W. (1839). *Gregor von Tours und seine Zeit*. Bonn: Brockhaus.

Longnon, A. (1878). *Géographie de la Gaule au vi^e siècle*. Paris: Hachette.

Lot, F. (1927). *La fin du monde antique et le début du Moyen Âge*. Paris: La Renaissance du livre.

Lot, F. (1946–1950). *Recherches sur la population et la superficie des cités remontant à la période gallo-romaine*. Paris: Champion.

Mably, G. (1788[1765]). *Observations sur l'histoire de France*. Paris: Khell.

Magnou-Nortier, E. (ed.). (1993–1997). *Aux sources de la gestion publique*. Villeneuve d'Ascq: Presses Universitaires de Lille.

Martin, H. (1833). *Histoire de France* 1. Paris: Furne.

Marrou, H.-I. (1975). *Décadence romaine ou Antiquité tardive*. Paris: Seuil.

Mériaux, C. (2006). *Gallia irradiata. Saints et sanctuaires dans le nord de la Gaule du haut Moyen Âge*. Stuttgart: F. Steiner.

Michelet, J. (1833). *Histoire de France*, vol. 1. Paris: Hetzel.

Mignet, F. (1822). *De la féodalité*. Paris: L'Huillier.

Montesquieu, Ch. S. de. (1734). *Considérations sur les causes de la grandeur des Romains et de leur décadence*. Amsterdam: J. Desbordes.

Montesquieu, Ch. S. de. (1748). *De l'esprit des lois*. Geneva: Barillot.

Montlosier, F. D. de. (1814). *De la monarchie française depuis son établissement jusqu'à nos jours*. Paris: Nicolle.

Mores, F. (2015). *Louis Duchesne: alle origini del modernismo*. Brescia: Morcelliana.

Musset, L. (1965). *Les Invasions: les vagues germaniques*. Paris: Presses universitaires de France.

Nicolet, C. (2006). *La Fabrique d'une nation: la France entre Rome et les Germains*. Paris: Perrin.

Ozanam, F. (1847–1849). *Études germaniques*. Paris: Lecoffre.

Pancer, N. (2001). *Sans peur et sans vergogne. De l'honneur des femmes aux premiers temps mérovingiens*. Paris: Albin Michel.

Pardessus, J. (1853). *Loi salique*. Paris: Imprimerie royale.

Patzold, S., and Ubl, K. (2014). *Verwandtschaft, Name und soziale Ordnung (300–1000)*. Ergänzungsbände zum Reallexikon der Germanischen Altertumskunde 90. Berlin: De Gruyter.

Pertz, G. H. (1828). *Histoire des maires du Palais*. Paris: Tenon.

Petitier, P. (1997). *La Géographie de Michelet. Territoire et modèles naturels dans les premières œuvres de Michelet*. Paris: L'Harmattan.

Petri, F. (1937). *Germanisches Volkserbe in Wallonien und Nordfrankreich*. Bonn: Röhrscheid.

Peytremann, E. (2003). *Archéologie de l'habitat rural dans le nord de la France du IVe au XIIe siècle*. Saint-Germain-en-Laye: Association française d'archéologie mérovingienne.

Pfeil, U. (2008). *Die Rückkehr der deutschen Geschichtswissenschaft in die "Ökumene der Historiker": ein wissenschaftsgeschichtlicher Ansatz*. Munich: Oldenbourg.

Pietri, L. (1983). *La ville de Tours du IVe au VIe siècle. Naissance d'une cité chrétienne*. Rome: Ecole française de Rome.

Pirenne, H. (1937). *Mahomet et Charlemagne*. Paris: Alcan.

Pohl, W. (2003). "Die Anfänge des Mittelalters. Alte Probleme, neue Perspektiven." In H.-W. Goetz and J. Jarnut (eds.), *Mediävistik im 21. Jahrhundert* (pp. 361–378). Munich: Fink.

Pohl, W. (2015). "Political Uses of Ethnicity in Early Medieval Europe." In University of Cologne forum (ed.), *Ethnicity as political resource. Conceptualizations across Disciplines, Regions, and Periods* (pp. 201–208). Bielefeld: Transcript Verlag.

Poulle, E. (1987). "Historiens ou fonctionnaires de la conservation?" In *Ecole nationale des Chartes. Histoire de l'école depuis 1821* (pp. 26–39). Thionville: Gérard Klopp.

Ridé, J. (1976). *L'image du Germain dans la pensée et la littérature allemandes de la redécouverte de Tacite à la fin du xvie siècle*. Paris: Champion.

Riegl, A. (1901). *Die Spätrömische Kunstindustrie nach den Funden in Österreich-Ungarn*. Vienna: Kaiserliche königliche Hof- und Staatsdrückerei.

Rogge, K. A. (1820). *Über das Gerichtswesen der Germanen*. Halle: Gebauer.

Rosenwein, B. (1999). *Negotiating Space. Power, Restraint and Privileges of Immunity in Early Medieval Europe*. Ithaca, NY: Cornell University Press.

Rosenwein, B. (2006). *Emotional Communities in the Early Middle Ages*. Ithaca, NY: Cornell University Press.

Rouche, M. (1979). *L'Aquitaine, des Wisigoths aux Arabes*. Paris: Thouzot.

Rouche, M. (ed.). (1997). *Clovis. Histoire et mémoire*. Paris: Presses de l'Université de Paris-Sorbonne.

Savaron. (1622). *De la saincteté du roy Louys, dict Clovis, avec les preuves et autorites et un abregé de sa vie et de ses miracles*. Paris: P. Chevalier.

Schiber, A. (1894). *Die fränkischen und alemannischen Siedlungen in Gallien, besonders in Elsass und Lothringen*. Strasbourg: Trübner.

Schlegel, F. (1808). *Über die Sprache und Weisheit der Indier*. Heidelberg: Mohr und Zimmer.

Schleicher, A. (1860). *Die deutsche Sprache*. Stuttgart: Cotta.

Schlesinger, W. (1941). *Die Entstehung der Landesherrschaft*. Darmstadt: Wissenschaftliche Buchgesellschaft.

Schmidt, L. (1910–1918). *Geschichte der deutschen Stämme bis zum Ausgang der Völkerwanderung*. Berlin: Weidmann.

Schöttler, P. (ed.). (1997). *Geschichtsschreibung als Legitimations-Wissenschaft 1918–1945*. Frankfurt-am-Main: Suhrkamp.

Schöttler, P. (ed.). (1999). "Von der rheinischen Landesgeschichte zur nazistischen Volksgeschichte." In W. Schulze and O. G. Oexle (eds.), *Deutsche Historiker im Nationalsozialismus* (pp. 89–113). Frankfurt-am-Main: Fischer.

Sieyès, E. (1820). *Qu'est-ce que le Tiers État ?* Paris: Correard.

Simmer, A. (2015). *Aux sources du germanisme mosellan.* Metz: Editions des Paraiges.

Steinbach, F. (1926). *Studien zur westdeutschen Stammes- und Volksgeschichte.* Jena: Wissenschaftliche Buchgesellschaft.

Sohm, R. (1871). *Die Fränkische Reichs und Gerichtsverfassung.* Weimar: Böhlau.

Tellenbach, G. (1939). *Königtum und Stämme in der Werdezeit des Deutschen Reiches.* Weimar: Böhlau.

Thierry, A. [Amédée] (1828–1845). *Histoire des Gaulois depuis les temps les plus reculés jusqu'à l'entière soumission de la Gaule à la domination romaine.* Paris: Hachette.

Thierry, A. [Augustin]. (1827). *Lettres sur l'histoire de France.* Paris: Garnier.

Thierry, A. [Augustin]. (1840–1842). *Récits des Temps mérovingiens précédés des Considérations sur l'histoire de France.* Paris: Dentu.

Tollebeeck, J. (2011). "An Era of Grandeur. The Middle Ages in Belgian National historiography, 1830–1914." In R. J. W. Evans and G. P. Marchal (eds.), *The Uses of Middle Ages in Modern European States. History, Nationhood and the Search for Origins* (pp. 113–135). New York: Palgrave Macmillan.

Vanderlinden, H. (1923). "La foret Charbonnière." *Revue belge de philologie et d'histoire* 2: 203–214.

Venayre, S. (2013). *Les origines de la France. Quand les historiens racontaient la nation.* Paris: Seuil.

Verslype, L. (2007). *Villes et campagnes en Neustrie (IVe–Xe s.). Sociétés, économies, territoires, christianisation.* Montagnac: Édition Mergoil.

Voltaire, F. M. A. (1880 [1764]). *Dictionnaire philosophique.* Paris: Hachette.

Voltaire, F. M. A. (1880 [1756]). *Essai sur les mœurs et l'esprit des nations et sur les principaux faits de l'histoire depuis Charlemagne jusqu'à Louis XIII.* Paris: Hachette.

von Maurer, G. L. (1856). *Geschichte der Markenverfassung in Deutschland.* Erlangen: F. Enke.

von See, K. (1970). *Deutsche Germanenideologie vom Humanismus bis zur Gegenwart.* Frankfurt-am-Main: Athenäum Verlag.

Waitz, G. (1844–1847, 1865–1884). *Deutsche Verfassungsgeschichte.* 2 vols. Kiel: Weidmann.

Weber, W. (1984). *Priester der Klio. Historisch-sozialwissenschaftliche Studien zur Herkunft und Karriere deutscher Historiker und zur Geschichte der Geschichtswissenschaft 1800–1970.* Frankfurt: P. Lang.

Wenskus, R. (1961). *Stammesbildung und Verfassung. Das Werden der frühmittelalterlichen gentes.* Cologne: Böhlau.

Werner, K. F. (1984). *Les Origines.* Paris: Fayard.

Werner, K. F. (1998). *Naissance de la noblesse. L'essor des élites politiques en Occident.* Paris: Fayard.

Wickham, C. (1993). "La chute de Rome n'aura pas lieu." *Le Moyen Âge* 99: 107–126.

Wietersheim, E. von (1862). *Geschichte der Völkerwanderung.* 4 vols. Leipzig: Weigel.

Wolfram, H. (1979). *Geschichte der Goten.* Munich: C. H. Beck.

Wolfram, H. (1999). *Die Germanen.* Munich: C. H. Beck.

Wolfram, H. (2001). *Die Goten und ihre Geschichte.* Munich: C. H. Beck.

Wood, I. (2013). *The Modern Origins of the Early Middle Ages.* Oxford: Oxford University Press.

Zeuss, K. (1837). *Die Deutschen und ihre Nachbarstämme.* Munich: W. Reichel.

CHAPTER 4

TWO CENTURIES OF EXCAVATING MEROVINGIAN-ERA CEMETERIES IN FRANCE

BONNIE EFFROS

HAD it not been for the industrial revolution, the early decades of the history of Merovingian archaeology might have transpired in a very different manner. Indeed, given the paucity of monumental stone structures dating from the Merovingian period known in the nineteenth century, only a few were the object of early archaeological excavations (Barral I Altet 1991; Gran-Aymerich 1998; on Merovingian religious architecture today, see Chevalier, Chapter 30, this volume). Consequently, it was typically chance discoveries of early medieval material beneath the earth that drove exploration. Without the impetus of the laying of rail lines, urbanization, and more intensive agricultural exploitation (Weber 1976), there is no doubt that early medieval exploration would have developed significantly later than it did.

Merovingian archaeology, unlike classical studies that were focused on the excavation and, in some cases, reconstruction of impressive military, civic, and religious structures (Effros 2018b), was driven initially by the serendipitous discoveries of previously unknown cemeteries. They delivered significant quantities of metalwork in the form of weaponry and buckles, ceramics, human bone, and glass vessels (or their fragments). The furnished graves uncovered on the property or in the towns of bourgeois and noble landowners, many of whom were members of local antiquarian societies, encouraged them, in turn, to discuss the significance of these finds and look for additional artifacts with which to embellish their collections and burnish their scholarly reputations. Without these factors, it is unlikely that many Merovingian-era cemeteries would have been uncovered before the 1950s. There is no small irony in the fact that the modernization and growth of France's industrial, agricultural, and urban infrastructure led to the discovery (and, in many instances, the destruction) of evidence of its late and post-Roman past (on the excesses of nineteenth-century archaeological practice, see Vallet 2000).

Despite its precocious start, the emergence of the discipline of what was known as national archaeology in France was stymied by a number of structural restraints on provincial initiatives. Consequently, French archaeology remained largely decentralized and inconsistently funded well into the 1980s (Talon and Bellan 2009). Up until this time, the process of formalizing the institutions and laws that regulated oversight of training in and practice of archaeology in France was gradual. Moreover, recognition of the importance of the contributions of what had been for a century and a half largely a discipline of amateur excavators affiliated with local archaeological societies was late in coming (Perrin-Saminadayar 2001). There were numerous reasons for this delay, and the consequences were significant. First, most archaeological sites were not protected by French law, nor was formal training required of archaeologists until the mid-twentieth century, when the Loi Carcopino of September 27, 1941, was validated following the liberation of France in 1945 (Choay 2001). This law required formal prefectural authorization for the initiation of archaeological excavations or exploration of ancient monuments. Second, the work of archaeologists, who were decentralized in local antiquarian and archaeological societies rather than being centrally based (Chaline 1998), was rarely valued as highly as work produced by academic scholars and architects in Paris (Gerson 2003). Third, substantial methodological challenges dogged the research of archaeological practitioners. Namely, nineteenth-century excavators had significant difficulties in developing approaches by which to standardize even approximate dating of artifactual and human remains. The development of reliable methodologies rested in large part on numismatic, typological (mainly stylistic), and stratigraphical features. Also, ^{14}C dating of organic matter was first applied on material derived from archaeological sites in the 1940s. Consequently, it took more than a century from the time in which amateurs first excavated Merovingian-era cemeteries to establish more accurate relative and absolute chronologies for these sites (Périn 1980).

Of note, too, was the fact that the discipline of archaeology (outside of the field of prehistory) was heavily dependent on historical narratives (Gran-Aymerich 2001). Particularly influential for the Merovingian period was the work of the liberal historian Augustin Thierry, such as his *Récits des temps mérovingiens*, first serialized in the late 1820s and 1830s (1880 [1840]). His emphasis was on the perpetual struggle between Gallo-Romans and Franks derived from Gregory of Tours' *Histories* (Graceffa 2009; Wood 2013; see also Graceffa, Chapter 3, this volume). This myopic or blinkered vision, in which nationalist questions prevailed over nearly all other facets of the French past, profoundly shaped the exploration and vision of early French archaeologists as they researched the early medieval past (Young 1992). Indeed, few dared to challenge the constraints imposed by the historical narrative and suggest conclusions that challenged the written record (Halsall 1997). Despite the quality of the publications of some of the most forward-thinking archaeological practitioners, the voices of archaeologists working on the Merovingian period were muted or even ignored in late nineteenth- and early twentieth-century academic and public debates about the origins of France, which remained largely dependent on historical sources (Effros 2012c).

As a consequence of these factors, and particularly the influence of Thierry's popular narrative, the interpretation of the growing number of weapon burials discovered in Merovingian-era cemeteries in France from the 1830s was surprisingly uniform and largely uncontested. Amateur archaeological practitioners, most of whom belonged to the learned societies established in their local towns and cities, were afforded access through these organizations to the archaeological journals and monographs of other regional societies as well as to the collections of scores of small museums that were frequently founded by these same societies. Archaeological enthusiasts confidently identified graves that were replete with armament and their respective cemeteries as Frankish, first in Normandy and Lorraine, and subsequently in heavily industrialized and research-intensive regions of France like Picardy (Dugas de Beaulieu 1843; Rigollot 1849; Périn 1980, pp. 16–22). From the 1860s and 1870s, local archaeologists similarly began to refer to furnished necropoleis in the southeast and southwest of France as Burgundian and Visigothic, respectively (Baudot 1857–1860; Gosse 1859; Dusan 1867; Delamain 1892). This tradition culminated in, and was codified by, Casimir Barrière-Flavy's unparalleled and personally funded survey of 2,315 known Merovingian-era cemeteries in France (1901), which alleged the possibility of distinguishing Frankish, Burgundian, and Visigothic regions on the basis of the unique qualities of furnished burials found in those areas (Effros 2012a; see Patrello, Chapter 39, this volume), conclusions that were challenged even in his own lifetime.

Mutually reaffirming one another, the conclusions of nineteenth-century archaeologists interested in the early Middle Ages challenged the dominant and historic French claim of descent exclusively from Gallic forebears (Dietler 1994). These cultural-historical claims were bolstered by the research of French craniologists writing in the late nineteenth century, who identified the alleged physiological characteristics of ancient Germanic inhabitants, most prominently their dolichocephalic (long-skulled) attributes, which they believed could be distinguished from their brachycephalic (round-skulled) Gallo-Roman contemporaries (Lagneau 1874; 1875; Trigger 1995, pp. 268–270). Although the approaches developed by physical anthropologists were ultimately discredited due to their small sample sizes and overstated conclusions (Effros 2010), they nonetheless buoyed an abiding popular and, in some instances, academic acceptance of racial distinctions between Gallo-Romans and Franks. However, because the allegation that the French were the product of racial mixing was rarely welcomed or included in contentious national discussions of French origins and identity, the fruits of Frankish archaeology were largely ignored in France despite their acceptance elsewhere in Europe.[1] Both during the reign of Napoleon III and the Third Republic, French scholars and public intellectuals generally favored the perspective that the Franks were the progenitors exclusively of the Frankish royal house and aristocracy, whereas the Gallo-Romans were the ancestors of the French (Thiesse 1999; Geary 2002). This outlook laid the groundwork for Merovingian archaeology in the twentieth century (both before and in the decades that followed World War II), during which the binary of Gallo-Roman versus Germanic graves remained the most common trope of archaeological exploration (Halsall 1995; Fehr 2010; see Coumert, Chapter 5, this volume).

Although the annual meetings of Arcisse de Caumont's Société française pour la conservation des monuments nationaux (1834) and the meetings of what would ultimately be called the Comité des travaux historiques et scientifiques (from 1861) helped coordinate the findings of the growing number of archaeological societies in the nineteenth century, their impact was relatively limited (Landes 2009). Far more central to the integration of Merovingian cemeteries and the grave goods they contained into a narrative that reached beyond the local provinces in which archaeology was practiced, however, was the foundation in 1862 (and inauguration in 1867) of the national antiquities museum in Napoleon III's château at Saint-Germain-en-Laye, to the west of Paris. Although the emperor originally conceived of the collection as focusing on the Gallo-Roman period, before its inauguration (timed to match the well-attended Exposition universelle of 1867), it expanded to include all periods of France's past prior to Charlemagne (Larrouy 1998; Effros 2012b). Prominent among the museum's vitrines dedicated to the history of France before 800 CE were displays of the products of late nineteenth- and early twentieth-century cemeterial excavations, including the collections of Frédéric Moreau and Baron Joseph de Baye (Effros 2012c, pp. 264–288).

For the most part, however, governmental funding tended to favor periods other than the Merovingian period, most prominently with large-scale national projects such as Napoleon III's Gallo-Roman excavations at Alésia in the early 1860s (Le Gall 1980). Significant funding also went to archaeological sites abroad, such as those overseen by the École française d'Athènes and the École française de Rome (Gran-Aymerich 1998) in locations as far-flung as Greece, Syria, Tunisia, Mespotomia, and Algeria (Díaz-Andreu 2007; Effros, 2018a, 2018b). In contrast, no regional archaeological undertakings of the Merovingian period were accorded similar resources on this scale at any point in the nineteenth century; they lacked the monumental prominence and potential for a national narrative of their prehistoric and ancient competition. Although in the early years of the Third Republic development of a nationalist agenda for indigenous archaeology was spurred by rivalry with German archaeological investment and advances in "big scholarship" intended to replace the fragmented system of learned societies (Marchand 1996, pp. 171–178),[2] political sensitivity toward allegedly ancient Germanic sites did not bring about a significant change in the French national agenda for archaeology. Whereas the French established the Service des monuments historiques for its Algerian colony in 1880, policies regulating archaeological research (rather than solely historic monuments) in metropolitan France were not promulgated until the early 1940s (Oulebsir 2004, pp. 180–181; Gran-Aymerich 2009; Effros 2018a). New approaches to archaeological research of the early medieval period in metropolitan France bore fruit at last after World War II in Édouard Salin's landmark publication of a four-volume assessment of Merovingian civilization, which offered a synthesis of the period's known historical and archaeological evidence (Salin 1952–1959).

Interpretive Approaches to Merovingian-Era Cemeteries in France Prior to World War II

Most archaeological discoveries in the nineteenth century were unplanned since they were brought to light in the course of agricultural work, quarrying, the laying of railway track, or construction. Consequently, few excavations of early medieval cemeteries were well planned or executed, and even fewer were recorded. Although some artifacts recovered during such activities entered into private collections, the vast majority were no doubt destroyed or dispersed by those who had little use for the detritus of ancient cemeteries (Provost et al. 1996, p. 40) However, once local amateurs learned of finds from local farmers or laborers, they often sought permission to revisit these sites so that they might dig exploratory trenches or otherwise investigate the graves in which these artifacts had been deposited (Beauchet-Filleau 1864, p. 261). Typically, local agricultural laborers were hired and paid by the hour or day to do much or all of the actual digging in the off-season from planting and harvesting (Colney 2000, p. 105).

From the period of the Second Empire, however, discoveries of serendipitously found archaeological sites began to be reported more regularly, often to local antiquarian societies. A small minority of such undertakings resulted in publication of the sites in question, typically in a local archaeological journal and more rarely, in the case of a particularly noteworthy site, in a self-financed monograph (Pilloy 1886, pp. 19–20). However, market forces impeded this process as the number of eager collectors grew. By the end of the nineteenth century, an entrepreneurial excavator could unearth thousands of graves and expect to earn a profit in exchange for the sale of the more aesthetically pleasing or unique finds (Goury 1908, p. 1). Although some private collections, like that of the retired banker Frédéric Moreau (Effros 2012c, pp. 246–248), survived relatively intact after being donated to or purchased by major museums, this kind of rapid excavation, which in some cases might be described more accurately as pillage, discouraged the appropriate documentation of many Merovingian-period sites (Reinach 1911, p. 287; Vallet 2000).

As mentioned earlier, one of the most vexing challenges related to early medieval cemeteries was how to date them accurately. Archaeologists depended on numismatic finds to establish rough absolute chronologies of finds in their cemeteries, and over time they were able to document the relative chronologies of specific artifact types (Terninck 1876, p. 227). Also important to these developments was the refinement of the study of layers or *couches*, which were first proposed in the context of early medieval cemeteries by Frédéric Troyon in his exploration of a cemetery at Bel-Air (Switzerland). He suggested that such sites did not date from a single battle or massacre but were occupied over decades or even centuries that led to the accretion of debris (Troyon 1841, p. 8). The work of prehistorians like Jacques Boucher de Perthes, which profited from advances in geography and paleontology, incorporated more stratigraphical approaches to archaeological exploration (Olivier 1998, p. 191) and prompted historical archaeologists to make more of the physical evidence from the cemeteries at their disposal (Déchelette 1908, pp. 2–3; Laming-Emperaire 1964, pp. 159–166). Archaeologists also benefited from architectural practices such as surveying, rendering architectural-style drawings, and understanding the construction techniques used in successive developmental phases of early medieval funerary structures (Leclercq 1907, pp. 458–459). In the 1880s, these techniques were directed effectively at early medieval cemeteries by Jules Pilloy in the Aisne, who employed a combination of stratigraphic, spatial, and typological analyses to establish a more accurate chronology of these burial sites than had been achieved in the past, and which allowed him to dispute the conclusions of Barrière-Flavy and others (Pilloy 1886; Périn 1980, pp. 23, 32–33).

The most advanced publications in the second half of the nineteenth century included maps of cemeteries with numbered graves, along with a list of artifacts found in each burial. (Seillier 1974, pp. 45–46). By the century's end, this practice evolved in the best documented cases to recording the positions of artifacts in individual graves, so that readers of these reports might gain some understanding of how these items had been laid to rest with the dead at the time of burial or during subsequent reopenings of the tombs (De Loë 1890, pp. 35–36). Yet, these best-case scenarios were far from common, and even leading archaeologists did not always meet the standards they proposed. The Abbé Jean-Benoît-Désiré Cochet (d. 1875), who is often considered the "father" of Merovingian archaeology, did keep excavation diaries during his digs, but he often omitted site maps and artifact inventories from his publications since he felt that they were not essential to his central narrative (Périn 1980, pp. 28–29; Flavigny 1992, p. 245). Most typically, archaeologists of this era published lists and in some instances highly skilled drawings of the most interesting artifacts; few archaeologists, by contrast, gave attention to skeletal matter or less noteworthy material such as ceramic sherds and glass fragments.

The general state of archaeology as described here is not meant to suggest that no contemporaries attempted to encourage more systematic documentation of early medieval cemeteries. In 1893, for instance, two Belgian scholars, L.-F. de Pauw and Émile Hublard, proposed the means by which contemporary archaeologists might catalogue their excavations more consistently. They created a system of preprinted cards or *tablettes* that could be filled in by excavators with grave numbers, data on the age and gender of the deceased, and the dimensions and orientation of each burial. The cards also included a schematic diagram onto which excavators could map the type and position of artifacts laid to rest with the dead. The *tablettes* were ingenious in not only simplifying the task of recordkeeping but also signaling what kind of data contemporary archaeologists were expected to keep. The cards thus enabled even the most inexperienced excavator to meet minimum standards for recordkeeping (De Pauw and Hubbard 1893–1894). It does not appear, however, that this system was employed by many contemporary archaeologists conducting cemeterial fieldwork in France.

It was only in the course of the early decades of the twentieth century that contemporaries began to lay out concrete expectations as to the minimum amount of data to be kept and published following the excavation of an early-medieval necropolis, potentially in the form of detailed excavation journals, inventories of objects, and site mapping. Clodomir-Tancrède Boulanger, who by profession was a notary of the city of Péronne but whose passion was archaeology, offered advice for contemporary amateurs (Neumayer 2002, pp. 50, 75–78). He advised those interested in excavating early medieval graves to lay exploratory trenches in the soil; once graves were identified, he recommended digging to a depth of roughly 25 to 40 centimeters from the bottom of the sepulcher before beginning the more painstaking and delicate task of extricating grave goods:

> [O]ne begins by lifting the vessel resting at the feet [of the deceased] and throwing the remaining soil out [of the sepulcher], then one continues by working towards the knees and head, always finely and carefully sifting through the soil before placing it behind oneself. One should be doubly cautious near the hands and the neck due to the rings and beads which may easily escape notice. It is always necessary to free each artifact completely before lifting it with a trowel; one risks breaking it by pulling upon it when it is still buried. It is critical to excavate the trench fully and not leave any object at the bottom, no matter how small it may be, under the pretext that it has no value; it is only when the object is cleaned and studied that one may appreciate it.   (Boulanger 1902–1905, p. 199)

Boulanger also encouraged his readers to number and map the graves, as well as label artifacts (or the sacks in which they were deposited) with these numbers.

One of the few cemeteries excavated in the early twentieth century to have been documented to this standard was located at Bourogne, south of Belfort. Two local amateurs, Anatole Lablotier and Ferdinand Scheurer, the latter a chemist, who dug the site between 1907 and 1909, noted that they carefully laid parallel trenches at the start of their exploration of the burial ground. Their 1914 publication of the Merovingian-period cemetery included site maps, detailed object inventories, and drawings of the artifacts uncovered (Lablotier and Scheurer 1914; Colney 2000, p. 107). Indeed, with Scheurer's guidance, Édouard Salin, an engineer by training, began his famous excavation of the early medieval cemetery of Lezéville (Haute-Marne) in 1922. Over the course of the 1930s, Salin expanded his research to include a number of recently excavated cemeteries in Lorraine, where he believed that improved absolute and relative chronologies made it possible to identify the blending of Gallo-Roman and Frankish populations over the course of generations (Salin and France-Lanord 1943). This research clearly contradicted contemporary German claims that the populations in the east of France were descended primarily from Germanic ancestors (Legendre 1999). Although Salin's work helped popularize in France the importance of dating methods in the analysis of cemeterial evidence, its heavy emphasis on ethnic identity as opposed to other facets of these cemeterial sites (which was not surprising for the epoch of its composition) set the tone for subsequent French debates about how to interpret early medieval necropoleis.

Many other cemeteries found in this era were excavated but left undocumented, or were published only decades later. Such is the case of the early medieval necropolis of 367 sepulchers at Lavoye (Meuse), occupied between the late fifth and late seventh centuries, which was first discovered in 1902 and subsequently excavated by Dr. Meunier between 1905 and 1914 (Joffroy 1974, pp. 5–11). However, nearly seven decades later, René Joffroy undertook the challenging task of publishing a full site report based on Meunier's notes. Although these conditions limited what could be known about the cemetery to type and quality of data collected at the start of the century, present understanding of the chronology and organization of the cemetery has continued to be refined (Halsall 1995, pp. 118–121). The cemetery of Ennery (Moselle), which saw more than 100 of its original sepulchers destroyed in the 1930s by a local landowner, Jules Barbé, likewise waited decades for full publication. In 1941, Emile Delort conducted a three-month excavation of the remaining graves during the German occupation (Reusch 1941/1942), but only published a more complete report of the site, including a study by the anthropologist Marcel Heuertz, a decade after the conclusion of World War II (Delort 1947; Heuertz 1957; Simmer 1993).

One of the most significant archaeological developments in France during the interwar period was the creation of territorial archaeological services aimed at preserving local archaeological sites. These organizations complemented regional federations of archaeological societies such as the Association bourguignonne des sociétés savantes (1914) and the Fédération historique du Languedoc méditerranéen et du Rousillon (1926), which sought to alleviate some of the isolation felt by individual researchers (Landes 2009). Despite the important impact of improved regional coordination of archaeological undertakings, in addition to the fruitful bibliographic efforts initiated by Robert de Lasteyrie in the late nineteenth century to catalog French archaeological publications,[3] the high standard of research and publication of early medieval cemeterial sites established by the likes of Lablotier, Scheurer, and Salin remained rare since they depended almost exclusively on individual initiative.

Close to the outbreak of World War II, among the improvements in the status of archaeological undertakings within metropolitan France was the creation of the Centre national de la recherche scientifique (CNRS) in 1939 under the authority of the minister of National Education and, soon afterward, the inaugural issues of the archaeological journal *Gallia* (Gran-Aymerich 1998, pp. 444–445; 455–468). Of great significance during the Vichy regime was the promulgation of the first portion of the Loi Carcopino on September 27, 1941 (Aeberhardt 1993, pp. 34–35; Reboul 2009).[4] Although not formally promulgated in occupied France, Nazi authorities did allow the law to be applied there as well (Corcy-Debary 2003, p. 331; Fehr 2018). The measures enacted in this legislation included the establishment of a mechanism for state regulation of archaeological digs. However, these laws were never intended to bring about systematic disciplinary professionalization, and amateurs remained a very important part of French metropolitan archaeology for at least another three decades. Even so, the parts of the Loi Carcopino that were reconfirmed in 1945 after the liberation of France succeeded in creating at least theoretical safeguards for exploring archaeological sites and establishing mechanisms penalizing those who flouted its conventions.

THE CHALLENGES OF POSTWAR ARCHAEOLOGY FOR MEROVINGIAN-PERIOD CEMETERIES IN FRANCE

Over the past half century, structural changes with regard to the practice of archaeology and the identification and protection of the French patrimony have been significant. To start, unlike in the period before World War II, cemeteries no longer constitute the primary focus of early medieval archaeological research in France. As is evident from the essays in this volume, archaeologists in France and elsewhere in western Europe engage in questions related to the early medieval landscape (see Bourgeois, Chapter 28; Chavarría Arnau, Chapter 29; Petyremann, Chapter 31, this volume), the early medieval economy and trade (see Bonifay and Pieri, Chapter 37; Pion et al., Chapter 36; Tys, Chapter 34, this volume), early medieval church architecture (see Chevalier, Chapter 30, this volume), and a host of other issues. Data collected from early medieval cemeteries nonetheless continue to play an important role in fulfilling these kinds of research agendas.

In the reconstruction efforts that followed World War II, the impact on archaeological sites of the construction of the modern network of French highways and high-speed rail, the intensification of urban development, and the expansion of suburban housing that occurred after decolonization cannot be underestimated. While the Loi Carcopino offered some continued protection to early medieval archaeological sites, its regulations proved difficult to enforce in metropolitan France in the face of the widespread development of the postwar period. Although the Ministry of Culture became responsible for archaeology and archaeological conservation upon its creation in 1959, the lack of agreement over national standards and resources for conservation in France represented a significant obstacle given the considerable latitude of prefects in dictating conditions in their departments. In the absence of appropriate administrative infrastructure, a legal framework that afforded sufficient protections, and essential funding to safeguard ancient remains, the destruction of historically significant sites remained commonplace. Local and regional organizations were some of the sole obstacles to their obliteration, and they were not always successful in safeguarding ancient monuments from demolition or badly planned modifications. Some of the most publicized casualities of this period included damage to archaeological vestiges beneath the Place Bellecour in Lyons during the construction of a subway (1974–1975), at the ancient curia of Avignon (a parking lot until 1970), at the site of the Forum des Halles in central Paris with construction of the RER station and shopping center (1971–1972), and at the Parvis Notre-Dame (1965–1972) in Paris, where a parking lot was built at what is now the site of an archaeological crypt and museum (Garmy 1999).

Destruction of early medieval cemeteries may not have received as much press as monuments of other periods, but there is no doubt that the impact of modernization on these sites was similarly consequential when local organizations were not in place or created for this purpose (on the importance of local intervention during the extension of the Paris metro line 13 to the station Basilique de Saint-Denis in the 1970s, see Rodrigues 2009).[5] Nonetheless, important excavations transpired in this period despite the challenges of funding, and the determination of individual archaeologists to excavate and publish important sites meant that some early medieval necropoleis discovered by chance fared better than others. Unearthed by a farmer in 1970, for instance, the row grave cemetery of Frénouville (Calvados) in Normandy, which was in use between the late third and late seventh century and occupying a space of more than 4,000 m², was excavated over the course of eighteen months. Directed by Christian Pilet, the excavation revealed a total of 650 graves with the remains of at least 801 individuals; there is some uncertainty as to the actual numbers because many of the skeletons had deteriorated significantly in the chalky soil (Pilet 1980, pp. 1–7). Published within a decade, Pilet's study was thorough: it carefully documented individual graves and associated skeletal remains and artifacts; it established the chronology of the cemetery's employment over the course of four centuries on the basis of grave depth, orientation, and contents; and it included an osteological examination of the bone matter conducted by the physical anthropologist Luc Buchet (Buchet 1978, pp. 6–27; Pilet 1980).

Importantly, however, the weaknesses of the publication of Frénouville lay not in the documentation of the cemeterial report, the standard of which was quite good for its time, but in its interpretation, which flew in the face of findings elsewhere in western Europe and reflected the unique, and somewhat insular, circumstances of conducting an excavation in northwestern France in this period. For example, on the basis of the continued use of grave goods, Pilet alleged that the interred had only undergone superficial conversion to Christianity in the fifth century (1980, pp. 153–157), despite the fact that high-status Christians in this period, and even two centuries later, continued to employ grave-goods with little hesitation (Dierkens 1981, pp. 56–59; Effros 1996). With regard to the allegedly unique identity of Normandy, one may point to the insistence by both Pilet and Buchet, based on a combination of artifactual and skeletal data, that the composition of the population buried at Frénouville consisted exclusively of indigenous inhabitants as opposed to Frankish invaders. These conclusions were reached on the basis of the supposed continuity of skull shapes and the relative paucity of weapon burials at the cemetery (Buchet 1978; Pilet 1980). But these conclusions contradicted contemporary understanding, however problematic, that weapon burials were a sign of Germanic presence (Steuer 1968). Moreover, Buchet's conclusions that ethnic identity in the early medieval period was biologically determined contradicted the growing consensus following World War II as to the constructed nature of such affiliations (Wenskus 1961; Geary 1983; Effros 2003; see Coumert, Chapter 5, this volume). In such circumstances, one may suggest that the publication of Frénouville, like other cemeteries studied in this period, reflected the framework in which archaeology was conducted in France in the 1970s. Research was often self-edited (released in series such as the international series of British Archaeological Reports), was regional in its intellectual scope and bibliographic citations, and did not engage with discussions occurring beyond the borders of France. The potential contribution of such a publication to larger debates about the Merovingian period was thereby significantly constrained.

The isolation faced by regional archaeologists in this period was alleviated somewhat by the foundation of the privately organized Association pour les fouilles archéologiques nationales (Afan) in 1973, which helped draw attention to the need for conservation measures for threatened archaeological sites and also created a forum for the exchange of ideas. Unfortunately, however, although the Afan received state funding for the purpose of rescue excavations, its resources were far from sufficient to achieve these goals. Moreover, the contractual nature of the work undertaken by agents of Afan discouraged sustained research at individual sites. By contrast, local associations that might have contributed to these undertakings likewise did not often have the necessary funding to engage in large-scale or long-term excavation projects. And, significantly, the archaeologists employed by the CNRS and French state universities were not at this time generally involved in the field of rescue archaeology (Garmy 1999).

In response to the public outcry over the loss of important archaeological sites in the 1960s and 1970s, the French prime minister Jacques Chirac appointed Jacques Soustelle, former governor-general of Algeria and member of the Académie française, to study the existing challenges for ancient monuments and archaeology. In April 1975, with the completion of the Soustelle report, the French state acknowledged the need not just for centralized infrastructure dedicated to archaeological conservation but also a more complete inventory of the French patrimonial heritage that included both historical monuments (protected by a law of December 31, 1913) and archaeological sites (protected from 1941) (Talon and Bellan 2009). In 1979, an important development for early medieval archaeology complementary to the Afan was the founding of the Association française d'archéologie mérovingienne (AFAM), with Michel Fleury as its first president (1979–1981), followed by Gilbert Delehaye (1981–1982), Patrick Périn (1981–2014), and Edith Peytremann and Laurent Verslype (2014–present). Although it does not conduct its own excavations, the organization's objectives are to promote exploration of the Merovingian period through annual conferences, publication of both an annual bulletin and conference proceedings, and creation of a stronger network of like-minded practitioners.[6] From the 1980s, the resources of the AFAM have also provided a venue for, and supported the publication of, reports on a number of Merovingian-period cemeteries, some of which, like Ennery (discussed above) were long unpublished, and others that were more recently excavated, like that of La Grande Oye (Doubs) in Burgundy (Urlacher, Passard, and Manfredi-Gizard 1998), which otherwise might have had difficulty finding a press for dissemination.

Efforts within France in the late twentieth century to create stricter legal protections for metropolitan antiquities and ancient archaeological sites were also reinforced by international and European discussions that occurred in this period. A landmark undertaking for the protection of ancient remains was the 1970 UNESCO Convention on the Means of Prohibiting and Preventing the Illicit Import, Export and Transfer of Ownership of Cultural Property, to which France was a signatory and which went into effect in 1972.[7] Of great significance, too, was the series of European-wide patrimonial negotiations over the course of the 1970s and 1980s that culminated in the Malta Convention of 1992 and became law in France in 1995.[8] The nations that were party to this gathering delineated the tenets and financing of conservation archaeology, acknowledged the importance of the diffusion of rescue archaeology as a scientific undertaking, and pledged measures to prevent the illict circulation of archaeological artifacts (Gauthier 2009). Finally, in November 1998, the Demoule, Pêcheur, and Poignant (1999) report made increasingly clear the shortcomings of archaeological conservation in France after two and a half decades of dependence on the independent agents of the poorly funded and significantly decentralized Afan. Consequently, leading French archaeologists who were committed to stronger conservation measures pressured the French state to meet its patrimonial obligations to European law. In 2001, the result was the establishment of the Institut national de recherches archéologiques préventives (Inrap) (Baruch 2009).

EXCAVATING CEMETERIES IN THE AGE OF INRAP (2001 TO THE PRESENT)

Since the rapid inception and implementation of Inrap, the organization has faced many challenges. Undergoing a series of modifications and reforms between 2001 and 2004, Inrap's administrators have made adjustments that emphasize the continued importance of collaborating with the existing Service régional de l'archéologie (SRA) in each territory. Changes in the funding structure have meant that investment in archaeological undertakings now comes largely from the private sector; businesses, just as governmental entities, must apply for permits for construction or modifications to existing land use (Pot 2009). In each region, the SRA has the authority to examine building permits and determine the necessity of performing diagnostic exploration of affected archaeological sites, a duty that can also be performed by Inrap and accredited local archaeological entities. For the purpose of excavations, private companies may also be hired. Although this system is an improvement over the era of Afan, this protocol has resulted in significant restrictions on archaeologists' ability to respond quickly and effectively to conservation challenges and research questions when they are not linked directly to discrete projects. With the increased regionalization of its functions, which has made departmental prefects more powerful in this process, and the opposite pull of improved and formalized collaboration between the CNRS and university-based laboratories, known as Unités mixtes de recherche (UMR), Inrap's long-term effectiveness and viability remain unclear at this time (Demoule 2009).

Overall, the foundation of Inrap has had a positive effect by shifting the focus of state-sponsored archaeological activities from "spectacular sites" to a more global and territorial approach to documenting archaeological remains. At the same time, however, Inrap has become an organization driven largely by the locations in which construction is projected and the economy and speed with which such efforts can be undertaken. Thus, while the reform of archaeological conservation has resulted in an overall increase in the number of sites, including cemeteries, that have been excavated due to imminent development, too many of those that have been addressed have not been studied in their entirety. Indeed, many of these reports remain unpublished, housed in the archives of the Directions régionales des affaires culturelles (DRAC) or Inrap itself (Demoule 2009), though some are now accessible on Dolia (https://dolia.inrap.fr).

Because there have been fewer resources available (sometimes as little as 7 percent of the total project time spent on an excavation) for the publication of scientific research, the imbalance has led to a surfeit of unpublished archaeological reports and dissertations. In addition, the utilitarian focus of Inrap has left many archaeologists with little time to undertake syntheses of regional or comparative data with respect to specific research questions (see Yvinec and Barme, Chapter 33, this volume). In addition, budgetary constraints have limited the kinds of technology and laboratory techniques available to French archaeologists (for recent exceptions, see Pion et al., Chapter 36, this volume). With greater emphasis on mechanical excavation and less investment in costly diagnostic tools like isotopic analysis (see Czermak, Chapter 7, this volume) and DNA sequencing that are more commonly used in the United Kingdom, Germany, and elsewhere on the continent (Effros 2000; Effros 2017, pp. 197–199), the kinds of data collected at French archaeological sites have often not seen the same pace of scientific innovation in the past fifteen years that have occurred outside of France (Demoule 2009).

How, specifically, have these developments affected early medieval cemeterial excavations? It is still too early to reach a final judgment on the impact of Inrap, since, as has been made clear in this chapter, full archaeological excavations of necropoleis have traditionally had a long gestational period. In recent years, exploration of Merovingian-period cemeteries continues to bear fruit. These excavations have not only produced data specific to particular sites but have supported archaeologists' and historians' ability to address larger research questions (see Patrello, Chapter 39; Perez, Chapter 9; Theuws, Chapter 38, this volume). This is true even when the sites addressed have been modest in size or comprise incomplete accumulations of graves rather than the large necropoleis that saw the light of day in earlier decades. It thus seems safe to say that individual Merovingian-era necropoleis will continue to be published in their entirety on an occasional basis, such as Florence Carré's publication on the cemetery of Louviers (Eure) (2008); that of Jean-Pierre Urlacher, Françoise Passard-Urlacher, and Sophie Gizard on the cemetery of Saint-Vite (Doubs) (2008); and René Legoux's ambitious two-volume report on the mid-fifth to late seventh-century cemetery of Bulles (Oise) (2011). However, these projects often owe more to the temerity and persistence of their authors in publishing the fruit of decades of research rather than to infrastructural investment from the state. There is no doubt that the data presented in such publications continues to improve, with larger numbers of color photographs, drawings, maps, and charts; these publications provide a wealth of information about artifactual typologies, osteological signs of disease among the deceased, and relative and absolute chronologies of individual cemeteries. In this sense, they continue to yield critical data about early medieval life and death in Gaul. Nonetheless, given the fact that the number of burial sites yet to be excavated is necessarily finite and that there appears to be no end in sight to current archaeological organizational and financial constraints, early medieval cemeteries are unlikely any time in the foreseeable future to occupy again their once privileged place in early medieval archaeological exploration in France.

Notes

1. In Germany from the 1870s, French craniological research (and research on the Franks more generally) received significant attention in early medieval research (Effros 2012b, pp. 351–366).
2. Ministère de l'Instruction publique et des Beaux-Arts, Commission de la Topographie des Gaules, Circulaire de Mai 1871. Archives Nationales F¹⁷13308.
3. Seventeen volumes of the *Bibliographie générale des travaux historiques et archéologiques par les sociétés savantes de la France des origines à 1940* were published between 1888 and 1961.
4. For the complete text of the 1941 Loi Carcopino, see http://www.archeodroit.net/Textes/Terrain/loi1941.html (consulted on December 21, 2016).
5. For the purpose of full disclosure, this author was a volunteer in May 1988 at the early medieval excavations organized by the Unité d'archéologie de la ville de Saint-Denis.
6. For the statutes of the AFAM, see http://www.afamassociation.fr/?q=pages/statuts-et-objectifs (consulted on December 23, 2016).
7. For more on the UNESCO Convention on the Means of Prohibiting and Preventing the Illicit Import, Export and Transfer of Ownership of Cultural Property, see: http://www.unesco.org/new/en/culture/themes/illicit-trafficking-of-cultural-property/1970-convention (consulted December 23, 2016).
8. For the full text of the Malta treaty, see https://www.coe.int/en/web/conventions/full-list/-/conventions/treaty/143 (consulted December 23, 2016).

Works Cited

Modern Sources

Aeberhardt, A. (1993). "Trois figures d'archéologues du centre-ouest de la France, au XIXᵉ siècle." In *Les archéologues et l'archéologie. Colloque de Bourg-en-Bresse (Archives). 25, 26 et 27 septembre 1992* (pp. 30–37). Université de Tours, Caesarodunum 27. Tours: Centre de recherches A. Piganiol.

Barral I., Altet, X. (1991). "Les étapes de la recherche au XIXᵉ siècle et les personnalités." In *Naissance des arts chrétiens: Atlas des monuments paléochrétiens de la France* (pp. 348–367). Paris: Imprimerie nationale.

Barrière-Flavy, C. (1901). *Les arts industriels des peuples barbares de la Gaule du Vᵉ au VIIIᵉ siècle* 1. Toulouse: Édouard Privat.

Baruch, M. O. (2009). "Fabrique de l'archéologie ou fabrique de rapports sur l'archéologie? Du rapport Soustelle au rapport Demoule-Pêcheur-Poignant." In J.-P. Demoule and C. Landes (eds.), *La fabrique de l'archéologie en France* (pp. 239–246). Paris: La Découverte.

Baudot, H. (1857–1860). "Mémoire sur les sépultures des barbares de l'époque mérovingienne découvertes en Bourgogne et particulièrement à Charnay." *Mémoires de la Commission des antiquités du département de la Côte-d'Or* série 2.5: 127–204.

Beauchet-Filleau, M. (1864). "Notice sur des sépultures antiques et mérovingiennes." *Mémoires de la Société des antiquaires de l'Ouest* 29: 255–274.

Boulanger, C.-T. (1902–1905). *Le mobilier funéraire gallo-romain et franc en Picardie et en Artois.* Paris: Charles Foulard Libraire.

Buchet, L. (1978). "La nécropole gallo-romaine et mérovingienne de Frénouville (Calvados): Étude anthropologique." *Archéologie Médiévale* 8: 5–53.

Carré, F., Jimenez, F., et al. (2008). *Louviers (Eure) au haut Moyen Âge: Découvertes anciennes et fouilles récentes du cimetière de la rue du Mûrier.* Saint-Germain-en-Laye: Association française d'archéologie mérovingienne.

Chaline, J.-P. (1998). *Sociabilité et érudition: les sociétés savantes en France.* Paris: Éditions du Comité des travaux historiques.

Choay, F. (2001). *The Invention of the Historic Monument*, trans. L. M. O'Connell. Cambridge: Cambridge University Press.

Colney, M. (2000). "Une fouille exemplaire au début du XXe siècle: la nécropole mérovingienne de Bourogne." *Bulletin de la Société belfortaine d'émulation* 91: 85–122.

Corcy-Debray, S. (2003). "Jérôme Carcopino et le patrimoine: une protection ambiguë." In P. Poirrier and L. Vadelorge (eds.), *Pour une histoire des politiques du patrimoine* (pp. 321–334). Paris: Comité d'histoire du Ministère de la culture.

Déchelette, J. (1908). *Manuel d'archéologie préhistorique, celtique et gallo-romaine* 1. Paris: Librairie Alphonse Picard et Fils.

Delamain, P. (1892). *Le cimetière d'Herpes.* Angoulême: Chez L. Coquemard.

De Loë, A. (1890). *L'archéologie préhistorique gauloise, gallo-romaine et franque à l'Exposition universelle de Paris.* Brussels: Imprimerie de Ve Julien Baertsoen.

Delort, E. (1947). "Le cimetière franc d'Ennery." *Gallia* 5: 351–403.

Demoule, J.-P. (2009). "Perspectives pour l'archéologie en France." In J.-P. Demoule and C. Landes (eds.), *La fabrique de l'archéologie en France* (pp. 281–298). Paris: La Découverte.

Demoule, J.-P., Pêcheur, B., and Poignant, B. (1999). *L'organisation de l'archéologie préventive en France.* Paris: Documentation française.

De Pauw, L.-F., and Hublard, É. (1893–1894). "Tablettes du fouilleur de cimetières francs." *Bulletin de la Société d'anthropologie de Bruxelles* 12: 87–88.

Díaz-Andreu, M. (2007). *A World History of Nineteenth-Century Archaeology: Nationalism, Colonialism, and the Past.* Oxford: Oxford University Press.

Dierkens, A. (1981). "Cimetières mérovingiens et histoire du haut moyen âge. Chronologie-société-religion." In *Acta Historica Bruxellensia IV: Histoire et méthode* (pp. 15–70). Brussels: Éditions de l'Université de Bruxelles.

Dietler, M. (1994). "'Our Ancestors the Gauls': Archaeology, Ethnic Nationalism, and the Manipulation of Celtic Identity in Modern Europe." *American Anthropologist* new series 96(3): 584–605.

Dugas de Beaulieu, J.-L. (1843). "De diverses sépultures antiques trouvées en Lorraine." In *Archéologie de la Lorraine* 2 (pp. 72–94). Paris: Librairie le Normant.

Dusan, B. (1867). "Boucles mérovingiennes (visigothiques?) trouvées à Gibel (Haute-Garonne)." *Revue archéologique du Midi de la France* 2: 46–48.

Effros, B. (1996). "Symbolic Expressions of Sanctity: Gertrude of Nivelles in the Context of Merovingian Mortuary Custom." *Viator* 27: 1–10.

Effros, B. (2000). "Skeletal Sex and Gender in Merovingian Mortuary Archaeology." *Antiquity* 74: 632–639.

Effros, B. (2003). *Merovingian Mortuary Archaeology and the Making of the Early Middle Ages.* Berkeley: University of California Press.

Effros, B. (2010). "Anthropology and Ancestry in Nineteenth-Century France: Craniometric Profiles of Merovingian-Period Populations." In W. Pohl and M. Mehofer (eds.), *Archäologie der Identität* (pp. 233–244). Forschungen zur Geschichte des Mittelalters 17. Vienna: Österreichische Akademie der Wissenschaften.

Effros, B. (2012a). "Casimir Barrière-Flavy and the (Re)Discovery of Visigoths in Southwestern France." In S. Patzold, A. Rathmann-Lutz, and V. Scior (eds.), *Geschichtsvorstellungen. Bilder, Texte und Begriffe aus dem Mittelalter. Festschrift für Hans-Werner Goetz* (pp. 559–576). Cologne: Böhlau.

Effros, B. (2012b). "'Elle pensait comme un homme et sentait comme une femme': Hortense Lacroix Cornu (1809–1875) and the Musée des antiquités nationales de Saint-Germain-en-Laye." *Journal of the History of Collections* 24: 25–43.

Effros, B. (2012c). *Uncovering the Germanic Past: Merovingian Archaeology in France, 1830–1912.* Oxford: Oxford University Press.

Effros, B. (2017). "The Enduring Attraction of the Pirenne Thesis," *Speculum* 92.1: 184–208.

Effros, B. (2018a). *Incidental Archaeologists: French Officers and the Rediscovery of Roman North Africa.* Ithaca, NY: Cornell University Press.

Effros, B. (2018b). "Indigenous Voices at the Margins: Nuancing the History of French Colonial Archaeology in Nineteenth-Century Algeria." In Bonnie Effros and Guolong Lai (eds.), *Unmasking Ideology in Imperial and Colonial Archaeology: Vocabulary, Symbols, and Legacy* (pp. 201–225). Los Angeles: Cotsen Institute of Archaeology Press.

Fehr, H. (2010). *Germanen und Romanen im Merowingerreich. Frühgeschichtliche Archäologie zwischen Wissenschaft und Zeitgeschehen.* Berlin: Walter de Gruyter.

Fehr, H. (2018). "German Archaeology in Occupied Eastern Europe during World War II: A Case of Colonial Archaeology?" In B. Effros and G. Lai (eds.), *Unmasking Ideology in Imperial and Colonial Archaeology: Vocabulary, Symbols, and Legacy* (pp. 29–58). Los Angeles: Cotsen Institute of Archaeology Press.

Flavigny, L. (1992). "L'abbé Cochet, un champion de l'archéologie nationale, 1812–1875." In A.-F. Laurens and K. Pomian (eds.), *L'anticomanie: la collection d'antiquités aux 18ᵉ et 19ᵉ siècles* (pp. 241–249). Paris: Éditions de l'École des hautes études en sciences sociales.

Garmy, P. (1999). "France." *Report on the Situation of Urban Archaeology in Europe* (pp. 91–102). Strasbourg: Council of Europe Publishing.

Gauthier, M. (2009). "L'élaboration de la convention de Malte." In J.-P. Demoule and C. Landes (eds.), *La fabrique de l'archéologie en France* (pp. 227–238). Paris: La Découverte.

Geary, P. J. (1983). "Ethnic Identity as a Situational Construct in the Early Middle Ages." *Mitteilungen der Anthropologischen Gesellschaft in Wien* 113: 15–26.

Geary, P. J. (2002). *The Myth of Nations: The Medieval Origins of Europe.* Princeton, NJ: Princeton University Press.

Gerson, S. (2003). *The Pride of Place: Local Memories and Political Culture in Nineteenth-Century France.* Ithaca, NY: Cornell University Press.

Gosse, H.-J. (1859). "Suite à la notice sur d'anciens cimetières trouvés soit en Savoie, soit dans le canton de Genève et principalement sur celui de la Balme près la Roche, en Faucigny." *Mémoires et documents publiés par la Société d'histoire et d'archéologie de Genève* 11: 81–100.

Goury, G. (1908). *Essai sur l'époque barbare dans la Marne.* Les étapes de l'humanité 1.3. Nancy: Imprimerie J. Coubé.

Graceffa, A. (2009). *Les historiens et la question franque. Le peuplement franc et les Mérovingiens dans l'historiographie française et allemande des XIXᵉ et XXᵉ siècles.* Turnhout: Brepols.

Gran-Aymerich, È. (1998). *Naissance de l'archéologie moderne, 1798–1945.* Paris: CNRS Editions.

Gran-Aymerich, È. (2001). "Archéologie et préhistoire: les effets d'une révolution." In É. Perrin-Saminadayar (ed.), *Rêver l'archéologie au XIXe siècle: de la science à l'imaginaire* (pp. 17–46). Centre Jean-Palerne, Mémoires 23. Saint-Étienne: Publications de l'Université de Saint-Étienne.

Gran-Aymerich, È. (2009). "La réorganisation de l'archéologie française entre 1939 et 1969: les conséquences de la décolonisation." In J.-P. Demoule and C. Landes (eds.), *La fabrique de l'archéologie en France* (pp. 134–144). Paris: La Découverte.

Halsall, G. (1995). *Settlement and Social Organization. The Merovingian Region of Metz.* Cambridge: Cambridge University Press.

Halsall, G. (1997). "Archaeology and Historiography." In M. Bentley (ed.), *The Routledge Companion to Historiography* (pp. 805–827). London: Routledge.

Heuertz, M. (1957). "Étude des squelettes du cimetière franc d'Ennery." *Bulletin et Mémoire de la Société d'Anthropologie de Paris* 8: 81–141.

Joffroy, R. (1974). *Le cimetière de Lavoye (Meuse): Nécropole mérovingienne.* Paris: A. & J. Picard.

Lagneau, G. (1874). "Ethnogénie des populations du Nord de la France." *Revue d'anthropologie* 3: 577–612.

Lagneau, G. (1875). "Ethnogénie des populations du Nord-Ouest de la France." *Revue d'anthropologie* 4: 620–649.

Laming-Emperaire, A. (1964). *Origines de l'archéologie préhistorique en France: des superstitions médiévales à la découverte de l'homme fossile.* Paris: Édition A. et J. Picard.

Landes, C. (2009). "Amateurs et sociétés savantes." In J.-P. Demoule and C. Landes (eds.), *La fabrique de l'archéologie en France* (pp. 54–66). Paris: La Découverte.

Larrouy, P. (1998). "Les premières années du Musée des antiquités nationales." *Antiquités nationales* 30: 197–206.

Leclercq, H. (1907). *Manuel d'archéologie chrétienne depuis les origines jusqu'au VIIIe siècle* 1. Paris: Letouzey et Ané, Éditeurs.

Le Gall, Joël. (1980). *Alésia. Archéologie et histoire*, new edition. Paris: Fayard.

Legendre, J.-P. (1999). "Archaeology and Ideological Propaganda in Annexed Alsace (1940–1944)." *Antiquity* 73(279): 184–190.

Legoux, R. (2011). *La nécropole mérovingienne de Bulles (Oise).* 2 vols. Mémoires de l'Association française d'archéologie mérovingienne 24. Saint-Germain-en-Laye: Association française d'archéologie mérovingienne.

Marchand, S. L. (1996). *Down from Olympus: Archaeology and Philhellenism in Germany, 1750–1970.* Princeton, NJ: Princeton University Press.

Neumayer, H. (2002). *Die merowingerzeitlichen Funde aus Frankreich.* Museum für Vor- und Frühgeschichtliche Bestandskataloge 8. Berlin: Staatliche Museen zu Berlin.

Olivier, L. (1998). "Aux origines de l'archéologie française," *Antiquités nationales* 30: 189–195.

Oulebsir, N. (2004). *Les usages du patrimoine: monuments, musées et politique coloniale en Algérie (1830–1930).* Paris: Éditions de la Maison des sciences de l'homme.

Périn, P. (1980). *La datation des tombes mérovingiennes: Historique-Méthodes-Applications.* Centre de recherches d'histoire et de philologie de la IVe section de l'École pratique des hautes études 5. Hautes études médiévales et modernes 39. Geneva: Librairie Droz.

Perrin-Saminadayar, É. (2001). "Les résistances des institutions scientifiques et universitaires à l'émergence de l'archéologie comme science." In É. Perrin-Saminadayar (ed.), *Rêver l'archéologie au XIXe siècle: de la science à l'imaginaire* (pp. 47–64). Centre Jean-Palerne, Mémoires 23. Saint-Étienne: Publications de l'Université de Saint-Étienne.

Pilet, C. (1980). *La nécropole de Frénouville: Étude d'une population de la fin du IIIe à la fin du VIIe siècle* 1. BAR International Series 83(i). Oxford: British Archaeological Reports.

Pilloy, J. (1886). *Études sur d'anciens lieux de sépultures dans l'Aisne* 1. Saint-Quentin: Chez M. Triqueneaux-Devienne, Libraire.

Pot, N. (2009). "L'Inrap, une construction difficile et mouvementée." In J.-P. Demoule and C. Landes (eds.), *La fabrique de l'archéologie en France* (pp. 266–280). Paris: La Découverte.

Provost, M., Hiernard, J., Pascal, J., Bernard, É., and Simon-Hiernard, D. (1996). "La recherche archéologique en Vendée." In Provost et al., *La Vendée* (85) (pp. 37–41). Carte Archéologique de la Gaule 85. Paris: Académie des inscriptions et belles-lettres.

Reboul, J.-P. (2009). "Genèse et postérité des lois Carcopino." In J.-P. Demoule and C. Landes (eds.), *La fabrique de l'archéologie en France* (pp. 120–133). Paris: La Découverte.

Reinach, S. (1911). "La méthode en archéologie." *La revue du mois* 11: 279–292.

Reusch, W. (1941/1942). "Fränkische Funde aus lothringischem Boden: Bericht über den gegenwärtigen Stand der frühgeschichtlichen Spatenforschung in Lothringen." *Westmärkische Abhandlungen zur Landes- und Volksforschung* 5: 39–58.

Rigollot, M.-J. (1849). "Recherches historiques sur les peuples de la race teutonique qui envahirent les Gaules au Ve siècle, et sur le caractère des armes, des boucles et des ornements recueillis dans leurs tombeaux, particulièrement en Picardie." *Mémoires de la Société des antiquaires de Picardie* 10 (1849): 121–127.

Rodrigues, N. (2009). "La création de l'Unité d'archéologie de la ville de Saint-Denis." In J.-P. Demoule and C. Landes (eds.), *La fabrique de l'archéologie en France* (pp. 210–217). Paris: La Découverte.

Salin, É. (1922). *La cimetière barbare de Lezéville*. Nancy: Berger-Levrault.

Salin, É. (1952–1959). *La civilisation mérovingienne d'après les sépultures, les textes et le laboratoire*. 4 vols. Paris: A. et J. Picard.

Salin, É., and France-Lanord, A. (1943). *Rhin et Orient: Le fer à l'époque mérovingienne*. 2: *Étude technique et archéologique*. Paris: P. Geuthner.

Scheurer, F., and Lablotiers, A. (1914). *Fouilles du cimetière barbare de Bourogne*. Paris: Berger-Levrault, Éditeurs.

Seillier, C. (1974). "Daniel Haigneré (1824–1893): L'archéologue et son temps." *Septentrion* 4 (1974): 45–60.

Simmer, A. (1993). *La nécropole mérovingienne d'Ennery (Moselle). Fouilles d'Emile Delort (1941)*. Mémoires de l'Association française d'archéologie mérovingienne 4. Woippy: Imprimerie Gérard Klopp.

Soustelle, J. (1975). *Rapport sur le recherche française en archéologie et anthropologie*. Paris: Documentation française.

Steuer, H. (1968). "Zur Bewaffnung und Sozialstruktur der Merowinger." *Nachrichten aus Niedersachsens Urgeschichte* 37: 18–87.

Talon, M., and Bellan, G. (2009). "Développement et professionnalisation de l'archéologie préventive en France: l'Afan (1973–2001)." In J.-P. Demoule and C. Landes (eds.), *La fabrique de l'archéologie en France* (pp. 251–265). Paris: La Découverte.

Terninck, A. (1876). "Cimetière mérovingien de Maroeuil près d'Arras." *Bulletin de la Commission des antiquités départementales* 4(3): 212–229.

Thierry, A. (1880[1840]). *Récits des temps mérovingiens*. New ed. Paris: Calmann Lévy, Éditeur.

Thiesse, A.-M. (1999). *La création des identités nationales: Europe XVIIIe–XXe siècle*. Paris: Éditions du Seuil.

Trigger, B. G. (1995). "Romanticism, Nationalism, and Archaeology." In P. L. Kohl and C. Fawcett (eds.), *Nationalism, Politics, and the Practice of Archaeology* (pp. 263–279). Cambridge: Cambridge University Press.

Troyon, F. (1841). *Description des tombeaux de Bel-Air.* Lausanne: Imprimerie-Librairie de Marc Ducloux, Éditeur.

Urlacher, J.-P., Passard, F., and Manfredi-Gizard, S. (1998). *La nécropole mérovingienne de la Grande Oye à Doubs (département du Doubs), VIᵉ–VIIᵉ siècles après J.-C.* Mémoires de l'Association française d'archéologie mérovingienne 10. Saint-Germain-en-Laye: Association française d'archéologie mérovingienne et la Revue archéologique de l'Est.

Urlacher, J.-P., Passard-Urlacher, F., and Gizard, S. (2008). *Saint-Vit, les Champs traversains (Doubs): nécropole mérovingienne, VIᵉ–VIIᵉ siècle après J.-C., et enclos protohistorique, IXᵉ–Vᵉ siècle avant. J.-C.* Besançon: Presses universitaires de Franche-Comté.

Vallet, F. (2000). "The Golden Age of Merovingian Archaeology." In K. R. Brown, D. Kidd, and C. T. Little (eds.), *From Attila to Charlemagne: Arts of the Early Medieval Period in The Metropolitan Museum of Art* (pp. 12–27). New York: Metropolitan Museum of Art.

Weber, E. (1976). *Peasants into Frenchmen: The Modernization of Rural France, 1870–1914.* Stanford, CA: Stanford University Press, 1976.

Wenskus, R. (1961). *Stammesbildung und Verfassung: Das Werden der frühmittelalterlichen Gentes.* Cologne/Graz: Böhlau Verlag.

Wood, I. N. (2013). *The Modern Origins of the Early Middle Ages.* Oxford: Oxford University Press.

Young, B. K. (1992). "Text Aided or Text Misled? Reflections on the Uses of Archaeology in Medieval History." In B. J. Little (ed.), *Text-Aided Archaeology* (pp. 135–147). Ann Arbor, MI: CKC Press.

PART II

EXPRESSING IDENTITY

CHAPTER 5

TRANSFORMATIONS OF IDENTITIES

Barbarians and Romans in the Merovingian Realm

MAGALI COUMERT

THE issue of identity has served as a catalyst for research in a number of different academic disciplines and has brought about a general shift in perspectives concerning the rise of Merovingian kingdoms. Traditional interpretations of this transitional period portrayed the Gallo-Roman world upended by destructive barbarian invasions. Walter Pohl has characterized this traditional perspective as "the ideology-packed Roman narrative of the civilizing missions of the Empire in defence against the brute forces of human nature" (Pohl 2013, p. 2). In this scenario from 407, the Gallo-Romans, defeated by the invaders, had no choice but to try to save a few remnants of knowledge. With the help of the Catholic Church, they pacified their conquerors by converting them to Christianity. Lucien Musset (1965) conceived of the period as one of "invasions" of Christian Europe by "Germanic hordes." From this perspective, conflicting Roman and Germanic identities, created by centuries of separate existence, were brutally thrown together, and their convergence led to the fall of the western Roman Empire in 476. On the one hand, there were the Gallo-Romans, who had been using Latin for centuries. Their large, rich, educated families of senatorial rank actively participated in the political life of the empire and had converted to Christianity without sacrificing their love of literature. On the other hand, there were savage barbarians, including Franks, Goths, and Burgundians, who upheld Germanic traditions unchanged since they left Scandinavia. They imposed their authority on unarmed and impoverished populations that were forced to live by the law of the dominant powers.

Although this understanding of a "civilization shock" between closed and hostile groups still has its proponents (Heather 2009), a new way of thinking about the formation of barbarian groups and identities has developed on the basis of "ethnogenesis" theory. Such reflections on ethnicity derive from the groundwork laid by

Reinhard Wenskus (1961). This approach moves away from the projection of ethnic identities and anachronisms onto a period that has been actively exploited since the Renaissance as the origin of, and justification for, the construction of various European states (Wood 2013; see Graceffa, Chapter 3, this volume). It accepts that, although objective factors such as genetic ancestry, matrimonial alliances, languages, and religion need to be considered, the determining factor of ethnic belonging is ultimately subjective, that is, its members' sense of belonging. So, how and why did someone come to feel like a Frank or a Goth in the fifth century? Wenskus first tries to construct an alternative to the racial understanding developed over centuries and particularly exalted by the Nazis. In opposition to the representation of Romans and Germans as closed genetic groups with specific traditions, which developed separately from their environment over centuries, he instead proposes a new interpretation of the sources and archaeological findings based on the perpetual remaking of an ethnic group as the product of circumstance. A small group of leaders, upholding core ethnic traditions, the "Traditionskern," were surrounded by individuals who identified as members of the ethnic group and accepted its traditions. The number of these individuals rose and fell over time, for example, depending on cumulative victories or defeats.

This approach, which came to be known as ethnogenesis, became better known after it was further developed in Herwig Wolfram's work (1979). Wolfram's book, *The History of the Goths*, was the first book based on the ethnogenesis theory to be translated into English, followed by that of Walter Pohl (1998). The approach gained further recognition from the European Science Foundation-funded project, "The Transformation of the Roman World" (1993–1997), and its publication of fourteen edited volumes in a series, "The Transformation of the Roman World," published by E. J. Brill between 1997 and 2004.

This major shift in research orientation met with some reluctance (Heather 2008). Was this image of flexible and open barbarian identities, subsidized by European funds, simply intended as an effort to support the contemporary politics of the European Union by camouflaging the reality of the fall of the Roman Empire and the catastrophic consequences for its inhabitants (Ward-Perkins 2006)? Moreover, even when referring to ethnogenesis theory, revised accounts of the period have maintained many facets of the older interpretations, which some researchers have critiqued. Ethnogenesis theory, for instance, did not challenge concepts of migration and orally transmitted ancient ethnic traditions. Instead, these core ethnic traditions were limited to a small, decisive group that upheld and maintained them and tended not to leave any archaeological traces (Gillett 2002a; Goffart 2006). Moreover, ethnogenesis theories still gave a determining role to the barbarians and contributing factors outside of the empire, without taking into account the internal transformation of the Roman world during Late Antiquity (Halsall 2007a). Ethnogenesis theory also attributed a determining role to ethnic identities within the political maneuvering of the fifth and sixth centuries. However, did a close reading of the texts mean that the type of source studied influenced the level of importance attributed to ethnic categories (Gillett 2002b)?

Finally, an understanding of ethnic communities as open and changing social groupings contradicts the traditional interpretation of the "Reihengräberfelden" (row grave cemeteries), which systematically divided Romans and barbarians (Fehr 2010; see Effros, Chapter 4, this volume). In grave deposits, specific objects have been associated with the expression of ethnic identities. From this perspective, any grave containing such objects has been interpreted as belonging to a member of the ethnic group linked to those artifacts (Halsall 2011). For example, specific fibulae or pieces of female clothing have been thought to enable researchers to identify the graves of Goths (Kazanski and Périn 2011). This method of interpreting graves has been the object of radical theoretical critique (Effros 2004; Brather 2004, 2010; Fehr 2010). Other approaches have thus been used to explore alternative explanations for changes in burial practices, including elements related to the social identity of the buried individual beyond ethnicity (Pohl 2010). This method suggested that new practices of clothed burial, which appeared in Gaul in the fifth century, had social meaning "linking this ritual display with the instability of local social hierarchies and competition for authority" (Halsall 2010, p. 9; see also Czermak, Chapter 7; Patrello, Chapter 39, this volume).

The debate on these different points, sometimes contentious, rages on (Gillett 2002a; Brather 2011; Halsall 2011; Périn and Kazanski 2017). Yet ethnogenesis theory has won out, insofar as it has eliminated the idea of dichotomous or unchanging ethnic identities in Antiquity and the Middle Ages and has explored how these identities were transformed and instrumentalized. Following on these developments, this chapter reflects on the nature of ethnic identity and its dynamic construction in the Merovingian period. Ethnicity is only one element of social identity, which might be based on gender, rank, age, family, legal status, and religion, and also reflected a situational construct. Ethnic identities underwent numerous transformations between the fifth and eighth century in the Frankish kingdom and played an important role in the justification of new political structures. As Walter Pohl has written, "the decisive change after the end of Roman rule in the West is not so much the emergence of single peoples whose names were bound to remain on the map. It was the gradual development of a system in which ethnic rule was considered legitimate" (2013, p. 12).

THE CONSTRUCTION OF THE MEROVINGIAN REALM IN THE FIFTH AND SIXTH CENTURIES AND THE FLUIDITY OF FRANKISH IDENTITY

When Clovis inherited the kingdom from his father, Childeric, in 481 or 482, the Franks had only recently begun to play an important role in the western Roman Empire. Roman writers only recognized the existence of a group called *Franci* in the second half of the third century. It is likely that the Franks first came to the empire's territories during the imperial crisis circa 260, under Gallienus (Wood 1995; Coumert 2007, pp. 282ff.). Thereafter, despite the Franks' lack of unity, Latin authors considered them a threat in coastal areas along the Channel, and then in Germania and Belgium in the fifth century.

With respect to the Franks prior to their arrival in the imperial territories, scholars have questioned the very existence of specific Frankish ethnic traditions.

Some Franks made a career for themselves by serving the Roman Empire; among them were Merobaudes, Richomeres, and Arbogast, who were *magistri militum*, in the second half of the fourth century (Goetz 2003). An inscription in Pannonia states *Francus ego, cives Romanus, miles in armis*, meaning "I, a Frank, a Roman citizen, a soldier in arms, with exemplary courage brought to war." (CIL III 3576 Aquincum (Budapest); Rigsby 1999). This inscription, though difficult to date, shows that this individual blended his ethnic origin, personal status, and professional identity (see Sarti, Chapter 12, this volume). When precisely the Franks settled in the territories of the Western Roman Empire is not known; whereas the *Alani, Suebi,* and *Alamani* crossed the Rhine in winter 406/407, and it must be assumed that Franks came with or after them but were not important enough to be mentioned.

The Franks' names demonstrate that they were using a Germanic language, but a specific Frankish language cannot yet be identified for that period of time (Goetz 2003). Their relatively late interaction with the Roman Empire, notably in comparison to the Goths, likely explains why the Franks largely remained pagan at the end of the fifth century. However, the lack of an official position did not stop conversions on an individual level. For example, Clovis's own sister, Lanthechild, converted to Arianism before the Catholic baptism of her brother (Gregory of Tours, *Libri historiorarum decem* I, 31).

Nonetheless, whatever the ethnic traditions of the Franks in the fifth century, they were open to innovation: Childeric's grave in Tournai, discovered by chance in the mid-seventeenth century, revealed an unprecedented combination of prestigious burial practices, including over twenty-one sacrificed horses and a tumulus somewhere between 20 and 40 meters in height. The grave also contained a collection of symbols of authority demonstrating "the ambivalence of his power, as a barbarian king and an officer of the Roman Empire" (Lebecq 2002). The sophistication and inventiveness of the burial rite is impressive, in particular, if we accept the recent hypothesis related to the coins found in the grave that claims that "the solidus hoard together with the other coins is a meaningful composition that has been manipulated for ideological purposes by Clovis himself" (Fischer Lind 2015).

In general, living on Roman-held soil profoundly changed the barbarian monarchy, which was subsequently modified (Dick 2008; Pohl 2009; see also Hen, Chapter 10, this volume). Despite the prestigious display associated with the burial of his father, Clovis was not the only king of the Franks at the beginning of his reign; Gregory of Tours refers to numerous maneuvers in which Clovis engaged in an effort to remove the rival kings of the Franks and their heirs (Gregory of Tours, *Libri historiarum decem* II,9; Fanning 2011). As a result of the extraordinary political and military success of his reign, Clovis was able to unite all Franks under his rule. He also succeeded in reserving the throne for his descendants, a new and decisive factor for the Franks.

Catholicism was another new facet of Frankish identity. When Clovis chose Catholicism over Arianism, he was baptized and, in Orléans in 511, met with the Catholic bishops of the regions he had conquered. Gregory, bishop of Tours, who wrote his

Histories between 572 and 594, states that Clovis's choice of a Catholic baptism led to the concurrent baptism of more than 3,000 Frankish warriors (*Libri historiarum decem*, II, 31). Although this is a retrospective and reconstructed account of the Franks' conversion, it shows how, in less than a century, Catholicism had become inseparable from Frankish identity, as opposed to the form of Arian Christianity supported by other barbarian elites (Dumézil 2005).

THE ROMANS IN GAUL

French historiography describes the inhabitants of Gaul under Roman imperial rule as "Gallo-Romans" to emphasize an image of a territory that had a specific identity and destiny from the beginning (Graceffa 2009, and Chapter 3, this volume). Without supporting this teleological argument, according to which France exists because it has always existed, it is important to underline the local choices of the elite Romans in Gaul after 400, that is, after the last time a Roman emperor went north of the Alps.

For some time, the description of graves thought to have belonged to the barbarian invaders hindered reflections on changes in the practices and representations of native populations. However, civil Roman society gradually transformed into a world "where the military had once more become crucial to most aspects of everyday life" (Sarti 2013, p. 4, and Sarti, Chapter 12, this volume). Roman legions in Gaul played a decisive role for the last time in 451, when they joined forces with the armies of the barbarian kings to defeat the Huns. In this context, the Romans gradually changed their clothing and funeral practices (von Rummel 2007, 2013), as well as how they asserted their power. The relationships between different groups can only be understood at a local level, from graves as well as from texts, and the anachronistic application of a dichotomy between Romans and barbarians does not allow the diversity and flexibility of the time to be taken into account (Fehr 2010; Pohl 2013). Instead, questioning the nature of the relationships between civilians and soldiers allows us to underline changes the elites in Gaul underwent. Whereas during the fifth century there were no familial ties between the Roman civil aristocracy and the Roman military leaders, this dissociation ended later in the century. Thereafter, local civil and military powers were jointly exercised by a prominent individual, whether a civilian, such as Sidonius Appolinaris, bishop of Clermont, or a soldier, such as *magister militum* Aegidius (Sarti 2013). Members of the Roman Christian elite abandoned the idea of central Roman rule to concentrate on employing their power locally. Their collaboration was decisive in the formation of new political and military structures (Wood 2009).

Moreover, Clovis's choice of Catholicism provided an advantageous negotiating framework since local elites enjoyed a monopoly over the role of the bishops and acted in their interest (Patzold 2014; see also Halfond, Chapter 13, this volume). These new frameworks for asserting power were familiar to Clovis, whose family had inhabited northern Gaul for more than three generations. Bernhard Jussen thus speaks of "Clovis the Gaul," and a division of power between the civil and military elites of Gaul, regardless of their ethnic identity (2014). Between 511 and 549, four other ecclesiastical councils were assembled in Orléans under the authority of Clovis's sons. The frequent collaboration between the bishops and the development of liturgical unity in the Frankish kingdoms played a major role in spreading a sense of Frankish identity and asserting the territorial authority of their kings (Pontal 1989; on liturgy, see also Rose, Chapter 43, and Bailey, Chapter 44, this volume).

To be certain, Gregory of Tours acknowledged that he lived in the Frankish kingdom, but he did not identify himself as a member of the Frankish people, as implied in his fifth volume: "It tires me to record the diverse civil wars which afflicted the people and kingdom of the Franks." (*Libri historiarum decem*, V, preface). He nonetheless played an active role in the Merovingian court (Halsall 2007b). According to Helmut Reimitz's interpretation, Gregory of Tours's goal, as a historian, "was to study the reality and the potency of pastoral power in the past, present and future of Gaul" (Reimitz 2015, pp. 51–73). Consequently, he made a strenuous effort to challenge alternative visions of the community. From this perspective, his writings underline the lack of importance of being of a Frank or a Roman, and highlight the diversity of identities that existed at this time. Nonetheless, this vision quickly became obsolete, and the writers who elaborated on his description of the events of the Frankish kingdom chose to transform his work into a Frankish point of view (Coumert 2007; Reimitz 2008, Reimitz 2015, pp. 166–239, and Reimitz, Chapter 22, this volume).

The King's Territorial Authority

Prosper of Aquitaine (d. 455) described the formation of a Gothic kingdom south of the Loire, which he dated to 419, as a voluntary action on the part of the Roman state: "The *patricius* Constantius made peace with Wallia by giving him *Aquitania secunda* and some other *civitates* of the neighboring provinces" (Prosper, *Chronicon*, 1271, p. 469). The Roman Empire thus granted territorial authority over some of its territories south of the Loire to a barbarian king.

In the Gothic kingdom itself, the follow-up to this account appears in the prologue to the collection of Roman law compiled in 506 during Alaric II's reign. Therein, the king is referred to as "*rex Alaricus*" and is concerned with the "profits of our people," without distinguishing between the Goths and the Romans (*Commonitorium Alarici regis*). No reference is made to an ethnic basis for his authority, and the publication of his laws aligns with the tradition of the emperor and his imperial rulings, as well as the edicts issued by the prefects of the praetor. The king claimed to supplement, and not replace, older legislation for the entire population, regardless of their ethnic identity (Barnwell 2000; Wormald 2003). Although no official recognition was mentioned relative to Childeric's kingdom, it seems that he was also quickly convinced of the necessity of a territorial, rather than ethnic, basis for royal authority. Evidence for this is seen on the seal ring found in Childeric's grave, which simply bears the words "*Childirici regis*," thus employing the title "*rex*" without the addition of an ethnonym. There is no indication that this king ruled only the Franks. Furthermore, when Clovis inherited his throne in 481, Bishop Remigius of Reims sent him a letter of congratulations, which was kept in a letter collection, the *Epistulae Austrasicae*, dating back to the reign of Childebert II. In this letter, the bishop congratulates Clovis for inheriting the governance of the entire *Belgica secunda* province: the Frankish king's authority is thus considered to be governing a territory rather than an ethnic group (*Epistulae Austrasicae* 2, p. 113, but see Barrett Woudhuysen 2016).

Although Clovis's conquests during his reign enlarged this territory (see Mathisen, Chapter 19, this volume), they do not seem to have changed its nature: the honorary title of consul that the king received from Anastasius, the eastern Roman emperor, and celebrated in Tours in 508 (Gregory of Tours, *Libri historiarum decem*, II, 38), shows that Clovis claimed to exercise his authority over the conquered territories of the Visigoth kingdom and all their inhabitants. Furthermore, when addressing the council of bishops assembled at his request in Orléans in 511, Clovis described himself as "*gloriosissimus rex*" (*Concilium Aurelianense* a. 511, p. 2). The construction of the Merovingian kingdom therefore seems to have depended on recognition of the king's personal authority over a territory, not on his dominion over an ethnic group.

Rulers contemporary to the sixth-century king of the Franks in Gaul also relied on territorial jurisdiction and drew on Roman titles to emphasize their power. In the Burgundian kingdom, for instance, King Gundioc, his son Gundobad, and his own son Sigismund, who succeeded him in 516, most frequently referred to themselves as *magister militum* (Wood 2014, 2016). By contrast, two-thirds of a century later, when Gregory of Tours wrote of Syagrius, son of *magister militum* Aegidius, who ruled the area of Gaul around Soissons, he referred to him as "Syagrius, king of the Romans, son of Aegidius" (Gregory of Tours, *Libri historiarum decem*, II, 27). Although these terms had already been used to refer to Roman emperors (Fanning 1992), this shift demonstrates how, by the last third of the sixth century, the perception of Roman identity and authority had evolved. It now foregrounded the transmission of power from father to son, over a specific ethnic group, and outside any central authority.

The Salic Law

The earliest surviving versions of the Salic Law were copied after the deposition of the last Merovingian king in 751. Nonetheless, these versions, A and C (which were called *Pactus legis salicae* by the editor K. A. Eckhardt) may date back to Clovis's time, before 507 (Wood 1994, pp. 108–113; Renard 2009; Ubl 2014).[1] This legislation does not appear to have been linked with a particular king, as it does not contain an official prologue. Nor does it seem to have been linked with a particular ethnic identity, insofar as it concerns all inhabitants of the land under the king's authority. It nonetheless refers to ethnic differences, and it occasionally grants varying access to the law on this basis. Rather than looking for the origin of the *Lex Salica* in military law established under Roman authority or in vulgar Roman law, the existence of which remains unsubstantiated, Karl Ubl underlines the innovative nature of this law, which accounts for violations of the public order in its prescribed punishments (2014). He interprets it as the foundation of a new, elaborate system, which includes a public penal system within a private system functioning on the basis of compensation equivalent to damages suffered (on law, see Rio, Chapter 23, this volume).

Some provisions are explicitly addressed to Romans (*Pactus legis salicae*, XVI, 5; XXXIX, 5; and XLII 4). Others provide for differing fines depending on the ethnic identity and status of the individual concerned (Wood 1986). For example, the guilty party must pay 12,000 denarii for murdering a Roman in royal service. Should the victim be a Roman landowner, with no link to the king, the amount drops to 4,000 denarii. Last, for the murder of a Roman tributary, the fine is divided by two and drops to 2,000 denarii (*Pactus legis Salicae*, XLI, 8–10). The *Lex Salica* is thus based on a hierarchy that takes ethnic identity, as well as the social status of the individual, into account.

The law not only referred to ethnic identities, but it also probably played a role in creating them. For example, Matthias Springer demonstrates that there was no "Salian" ethnic group before the Salic Law (Springer 1997). By contrast, the *Lex Salica* created a new legal category, that of the barbarian who lived by Salic Law: "He who kills a free Frank or other barbarian who lives by Salic law, and it is proved against him (called *leodi* in the Malberg gloss), shall be liable to pay 8000 *denarii* (i. e. 200 *solidi*)" (*Pactus legis salicae*, XLI, 1). Moreover, there is an indication not only that the Salic Law was applicable to both Franks and Romans, but that it also may have been an integrating factor among the ruling elite: the fine of 8,000 denarii for the murder of an individual protected by the Salic Law is extremely high, despite the fact that it is lower than the amount due for the murder of a man "in the service of the king," *in truste dominica*, for which 24,000 denarii had to be paid (*Pactus legis salicae*, XLI, 5).

Various edicts were issued by the Merovingian kings alongside the Salic Law in its different versions. The earliest surviving edicts were addressed to the people as a whole and contained a title similar to "*rex*" as well as provisions that distinguished among different statuses, but not among ethnic identities (*Diplomata regum Francorum e stirpe merovingica* 22, p. 63; 25, p. 69; and 28 p. 76).[2] Such distinctions only appear in the edict of Guntram in 585, in which the king is called "*rex Francorum*." This title also appears in the decree of Childebert II, in 596, in which the provisions again distinguish between *Francus* and *Romanus*. Among the *Epistulae Austrasicae*, a letter written by Childebert II, probably between 584 and 590, is the first to use the title "*rex Francorum*" (*Epistolae austrasicae* 32, p. 141). In documentary culture, the title of "*rex Francorum*" appears to have been used first in a copy of a charter issued by Theudebert II in 596 and in two original charters issued by Chlothar II, who reigned from 584 to 629 (Reimitz 2015, pp. 98–103).

It therefore seems that, after 580, royal power only gradually chose to be linked with the Franks as a specific group in its kingdom. This new positioning could have been related to both the heightened competition between different allegiances during the civil wars between the Merovingian kings (572–613), and the expansion of the sense of Frankish identity, after a century under Merovingian authority.

THE TRANSFORMATION OF FRANKISH IDENTITY UNDER MEROVINGIAN RULE (SEVENTH AND EIGHTH CENTURIES): THE ROLE OF THE MEROVINGIANS

The territories acquired by Clovis (*Aquitania* and *Alamannia*) and his sons (Burgundy, Thuringia, Bavaria, and Provence) came with different ethnic groups that were integrated into the Frankish kingdom (Esders 2016). The dynasty became one of the central reference points for Frankish identity, as its unity and continuity created the kingdom's symbolic unity. This unity arose despite the fact that the kingdom was rarely ruled by a single sovereign (the exceptions occurred during 558–561, 613–623, 631–639, and possibly 673–675), before coming under the authority of the mayor of the palace of Austrasia, a member of the Pippinid family, beginning in 687.

In the seventh century, the kings who descended from Clovis following the paternal line were called Merovingians in reference to Merovech, Clovis's supposed ancestor (Fredegar, *Chronicle*, III, 9; Coumert 2007, pp. 320–323). The Merovingians monopolized political power and "sanctified" themselves by way of sacred customs (as "long-haired kings") and through attitudes and myths, such as their alleged descent from a sea beast (Diesenberger 2003). Loyalty to the king and the assertion of power through the titles appointed by the sovereign structured the social life of the elite.

Elite groups were united through matrimonial practices, which blended different ruling families, and through the choice of names. In Gregory of Tours's time, different naming customs appeared that partly corresponded to different social identities: for example, in the *Histories*, there are twenty-seven *comites* (counts) and eleven *duces* (dukes) with Roman names as opposed to twelve *comites* and twelve *duces* with Germanic names, demonstrating that higher military responsibility was more often associated with Germanic names (Goetz 2003, p. 328). During the following generations, Germanic forenames were increasingly chosen by the elites in the kingdom, and they took a programmatic approach (Le Jan 1995). For example, Lupus, a member of the Roman family of Aquitaine, who was *dux* of Champagne and was a contemporary of Gregory of Tours, had sons named Johannes and Romulf. The latter became bishop of Reims. Lupus had a grandson named Romaric (Reimitz 2015, p. 211).

The description of the ruling elite and their king as Franks appears in the *Chronicle of Fredegar*, written in the 660s at the earliest. It presents the Franks as descendants of Trojans, led from Troy to Gaul by Priam's successors (Coumert 2007, pp. 295–324). In line with this vision of the past, the king speaks of "his Franks." In the case of Clovis, he was portrayed as wishing that he could have avenged the Passion of the Christ *cum Francis meis*, or "with my Franks" (Fredegar, *Chronicle*, III, 21, p. 101). The past and the future of the elite seem to have been limited to the *Franci*, united behind their king.

New Laws and New Ethnic Identities in the Frankish Kingdom

Various origins of the law coexisted within the Frankish kingdom. Roman law was maintained by the Breviary of Alaric, a compilation of the legislation issued by a Visigoth king, and the law of the Burgundian kings was also copied. Salic Law was added to them alongside various edicts issued by the Merovingian monarchs. The apparent goal was to use different legal codes to complement one another. It is clear that the diversity of the law was recognized within the Merovingian kingdom from the formula for appointing the title of duke, *patricius*, or count by royal order, based on acts relating to this practice principally dating from the seventh century (on such collections, see Rio 2008, 2009, and Chapter 23, this volume): "so that all the peoples that inhabit it, the Franks as well as the Romans, the Burgundians and the other nations live and are disciplined by your rule and your government, and that you discipline them with rectitude according to their law and their customs" (Formulary of Marculf, I, 8).

Here, the geographical or ethnic basis for the diversity of the law is not specified (Guillot 1995). Yet this legal diversity, the by-product of conquests, is likely at the origin of the political practices of the Merovingian sovereigns. From the seventh century, these monarchs—if the prologues sometimes linked with them are to be believed—drew up laws for groups deprived of their own royal authority: the Alemanni, the Bavarians, as well as those to whom the Ripuarian Law applied.

The drawing up of the *Lex Ribuaria* (and not the law of the Ripuarians; see the introduction to F. Beyerle, *Lex Ribuaria*, MGH, p. 9) in the seventh or eighth century, which was modeled on Salic Law and royal Merovingian edicts, was probably intended for the members of the Frankish kingdom of Austrasia. It shows that sovereigns used the law, intended for a particular group, for political ends due to the unfolding power dynamics within the kingdom. It is nonetheless impossible to determine how the group which this law applies to was defined, as there is no mention of a "Ripuarian" before this code (Springer 1998). However, the Ripuarian law states:

> we decreed that within the Ripuarian territory (*pagus Riboarius*) whether Franks, Burgundians or Alamanni or whatever nation one belongs to, let one respond when summoned to the court according to the law of place in which one was born.
> (*Lex Ribuaria* XXXV, 3, p. 87)

Here, the idea of laws characterized by their place of origin seems to be established, facilitating the decision of whether to apply the Ripuarian Law, the law of the Burgundians, or the law of the Alamanni. The *Lex Ribuaria* nonetheless establishes a hierarchy between the different ethnic groups by imposing higher fines for a Ripuarian who kills a Frank, 200 solidi (gold coins), than for a Ripuarian who kills a Burgundian, an Alamanni, a Frisian, a Bavarian, or a Saxon, 80 solidi, or a Roman, 50 solidi

(*Lex Ribuaria*, XL, p. 92). Helmut Reimitz understands this as "an ethnic reinterpretation of the Merovingian royal politics of the sixth century, placing the kings in an equidistant relation to all the different groups and nations whose members had to respond to and obey their judicium" (2015, p. 234).

In the Merovingian kingdoms, such political use of the law, in relation to particular ethnic identities, goes hand in hand with the new political importance placed on ethnic belonging. Frankish historiography shows the growing interest in the *gens Francorum* (the people or nation of the Franks). Reimitz demonstrates that this was systematically foregrounded in the *Chronicle of Fredegar*, written in the second half of the seventh century and the *Liber Historiae Francorum* (2008, 2015, and Reimitz, Chapter 22, this volume).

The *Liber Historiae Francorum* was first written in 727 by a Frank from Neustria, yet the Frankish kingdom of Neustria had been under the control of the Frankish kingdom of Austrasia, ruled by the Pippinid mayor of the palace, under the increasingly symbolic authority of a Merovingian king (Gerberding 1987). The author highlights his Neustrian identity: the Neustrian kingdom is called the *regnum Francorum*, its military *exercitus Francorum*, whereas the kingdom in the east is called *Auster* and its king *rex Auster*. The text nonetheless shows the recognition of a broader meaning of *Franci*, by sometimes also using the term to refer to Austrasian and Ripuarian Franks (Wood 1995). In the *Liber Historiae Francorum*, the ethnic group of the *Franci* is depicted as a small group of warriors, close to the king, and descended from Trojan soldiers and Priam (Coumert 2007, pp. 325–339). The history of the Franks cannot be considered separately from the history of their king, as the beginning of the narrative demonstrates: "Let us set forth the beginnings of the kings of the Franci, their own origin, and that of the peoples as well as their deeds" (*Liber Historiae Francorum*, A, § 1). The legitimacy of the Merovingians is reasserted in the text, but it does not oppose the dominion of the mayor of the palace of Austrasia. This demonstrates the emergence of a new unification of the Franks, united behind the Merovingians and Pippinids (Dörler 2013).

Furthermore, the authority of the Frankish kings is mentioned in reference to drawing up the laws intended for ethnic groups that were historically independent prior to their subjugation. A prologue to the law of the Alamanni, only a part of which survives, appears under the following title "here begins the law of the Alamanni [year . . .], in accordance with the Orthodox Lord King Chlothar, when there were 33 dukes, 33 bishops, and 45 earls" (*Pactus legis Alamannorum*, p. 21). The king in question is Chlothar II (584–629), and the text stresses that the application of this law to an ethnic group within the Frankish kingdom was a political choice on the part of the Merovingian king.

This provision of a legal code thus appears to be a mark of royal Frankish authority, but it also recognizes that the Alamanni had a certain level of autonomy within the kingdom. If the very content of the law falls under Frankish influence, this legislation appears to be a sign of bowing to the Merovingian kings, or of asserting independence, depending on the political circumstances. Another legal code for the Alamanni foregrounds the revision of the law instigated by Lantfrid, duke of Alamannia, just before 724, when he had independent authority (Mc Kitterick 1989, p. 65; Reimitz 2015, p. 328). With legal authority challenged in this way, the prologues, as found in the law of the

Bavarians cited below, seem to demonstrate reaction to the Pippinids' expanding power. They thus identify with an increasingly symbolic reigning Merovingian royalty.

This new idea is expressed by the prologue to the law of the Bavarians, probably written between 720 and 740 (Landau 2004; Esders 2016). It reproduces the list of lawmakers, from Moses to Theodosius, from Isidore of Seville's *Etymologies*, and adds:

> Then each people chooses their own law based on custom. Indeed, ancient custom is considered law. The law is a written constitution. . . . Theuderic, King of the Franks, when he came to Châlons, chose four wise men, who, in his kingdom, had been educated in the ancient laws. He declared that he had ordered the laws of the Franks, the Alamanni and the Bavarians, of each people that came under his authority, to be written according to custom; he added what needed to be added and removed what was unfitting and poorly instructed. And he transformed what was aligned with the customs of the pagans in accordance with the law of the Christians. And what King Theuderic could not change, owing to the ancient customs of the pagans, King Childebert then undertook, and King Chlothar completed. The very glorious King Dagobert revised them with the illustrious men, Claudius, Chadoind, Magnus and Agilulf, and he improved what was old about the laws, had [a law] put in writing for each people and they survive to this day."
>
> (*Lex Baiwariorum*, pp. 200–202)

Here, the law is presented as a custom belonging to each ethnic group, put in writing by royal order. It bases its legitimacy on a variety of sources: the oral tradition of the ethnic group, royal, Merovingian authority, the Christian faith, and the advice of four sages: Claudius, Chadoind, Magnus, and Agilulf. The king's authority is presented as being superior to custom, as the king can modify custom. The most groundbreaking point here is the text's reference to a written law for each people, thus corresponding to a new political use for law developed by the Merovingian kings and related to powerful groups in the kingdom associated with different ethnonyms.

This text might accurately be called "Prologue to the Law of the Bavarians" since it appears twenty times in introducing this law. However, this prologue also serves as an introduction to the *Lex Salica* (six times), the *Lex Alamannorum* (three times), and the *Lex Wisigothorum* (once). This text is thus thought to explain the composition of the different collections of laws. Furthermore, its description of the Frankish king as the founding legal authority seems sufficiently important to be referred to systematically in a variety of legal collections.

Conclusion

As we have seen, the claim that ethnic traditions were the basis for the law cannot be seen in the sixth century. The introductions to the legal codes discussed in this chapter illustrate the continued malleability of ethnic identities in the various political discourses developed in the seventh century. According to the cases examined, the Frankish kings appear to have been in a position of superiority over other ethnic groups, establishing laws that applied to all of them, or, on the contrary, using the groups' own customs, which merely had to be made concrete, for the good of all. Depending on the circumstances, the Franks were presented as being loyal to the king, at his side since the fall of Troy; or, on the contrary, they could also be a specific, privileged group, alongside the Alemanni, the Austrasians, or the Romans. These distinctions, arising after the seventh century, probably served competing aristocratic groups.

It therefore seems that the assertion and role of ethnic identity depended on the specific context in which such claims were made. The importance of this factor must be compared with that of other categories of social identity, including gender, clerical or lay status, and membership in the local or supraregional elite. Moreover, it was the establishment of Merovingian authority that allowed the role of ethnic identity in the Frankish kingdom to be transformed by alliances of different elite groups. It is more difficult for scholars today to determine the stages of these transformations than it was for the writers of the Carolingian era. The latter modified and transmitted the majority of the documents of the time, choosing to give new meanings to Frankish identity, selecting the documents that survived, and establishing their authority first over the Merovingian kingdom and then an empire. Carolingian dominion was characterized by both the exaltation of Frankish identity and its expansion on an imperial level (Nelson 2008).

Notes

1. Karl Ubl's (2014) and Wolfgang Haubrichs' (2008) criticisms have convinced me to disregard the hypotheses once again put forward by J.-P. Poly claiming that the Salic Law was compiled from military regulation in the fourth century (Poly 2016).
2. Despite the ideas proposed by Oliver Guillot (2003), the argument developed by Stefan Esders (1997) is more convincing and, in this case, I consider Chlothar's precepts to be associated with Chlothar II. If we go along with Guillot's argument, this text, written between 558 and 561, would have been the first text to use the term *rex Francorum* and distinguish between different ethnic identities within the kingdom as in the Salic Law.

Works Cited

Ancient Sources

Commonitorium Alarici regis. T. Mommsen (ed.). (1902). MGH Leges nationum Germanicarum 1 (pp. 465–467). Hanover: Hahn.
Concilium Aurelianense a. 511. F. Maassen (ed.). (1893). MGH Concilia, Concilia aevi Merowingici 1 (pp. 2–14). Hanover: Hahn.
Diplomata regum Francorum e stirpe Merovingica. T. Kölzer (ed.). (2001). MGH, Diplomata regum Francorum e stirpe Merovingica 1. Hanover: Hahn.
Epistolae Austrasicae. W. Gundlach (ed.). (1892). MGH: Epistolae 3, Epistolae Merowingici et Karolini aevi 1 (pp. 110–153). Berlin: Weidmann.

Fredegar, *Chronicae*. B. Krusch (ed.). (1888). MGH Scriptores rerum Merovingicarum 2 (pp. 1–193). Hanover: Hahn.

Gregory of Tours, *Libri historiarum decem*. B. Krusch and W. Levison (eds.). (1951). MGH SRM 1.1. Hanover: Hahn.

Lex Baiwariorum. E. de Schwind (ed.). (1926). MGH Leges nationum Germanicarum 5.2. Hanover: Hahn.

Lex Ribuaria. F. Beyerle and R. Buchner (eds.). (1954). MGH Leges nationum Germanicarum 3.2. Hanover: Hahn.

Liber Historiae Francorum. B. Krusch (ed.). (1888). MGH Scriptores rerum Merovingicarum 2 (pp. 215–328). Hanover: Hahn.

Marculf, *Formulary*. K. Zeumer (ed.). (1886). MGH Leges, Formulae Merowingici et Karolini aevi (pp. 32–106). Hanover: Hahn.

Marculf, *Formulary*. A. Rio (trans.). (2008). *The Formularies of Angers and Marculf: Two Merowingian Legal Handbooks*. Liverpool: Liverpool University Press.

Pactus Legis Alamannorum. K. Lehmann and K. Eckhardt (eds.). (1888/1966). MGH Leges nationum Germanicarum 5.1 (pp. 21–34). Hanover: Hahn.

Pactus Legis Salicae. K. A. Eckhardt (ed.). (1962). MGH Leges nationum Germanicarum 4.1. Hanover: Hahn.

Pactus Legis Salicae. K. Fisher Drew (trans.). (1991). *The Law of the Salian Franks*. Philadelphia: University of Pennsylvania Press.

Prosper Tiro, *Chronicon*. T. Mommsen (ed.). (1892). MGH AA 9 (pp. 341–399) *Chronica minora* 1. Berlin: Weidmann.

Modern Sources

Barnwell, P. S. (2000). "Emperors, Jurists and Kings: Law and Custom in the Late Roman and Early Medieval West." *Past and Present* 168: 6–29.

Barrett, G., and G. Woudhuysen. (2016). "Remigius and the 'Important News' of Clovis rewritten." *Antiquité Tardive. Revue Internationale d'Histoire et d'Archéologie (IVᵉ–VIIᵉ siècle)* 24: 471–500.

Brather, S. (2004). *Ethnische Interpretationen in der frühgeschichtlichen Archäologie. Geschichte, Grundlagen und Alternativen*. Berlin: Walter de Gruyter.

Brather, S. (2010). "Bestattungen und Identitäten. Gruppierung innerhalb frühmittelalterlicher Gesellschaften." In W. Pohl and M. Mehofer (eds.), *Archaeology of Identity—Archäologie der Identität* (pp. 25–49). Vienna: Verlag der Österreichischen Akademie der Wissenschaften.

Brather, S. (2011). "Ethnizität und Mittelalterarchäologie. Eine Antwort auf Florin Curta." *Zeitschrift für Archäologie des Mittelalters* 39: 161–172.

Coumert, M. (2007). *Origines des peuples. Les récits du haut Moyen Age occidental (550–850)*. Paris: Collection des Études Augustiniennes.

Dick, S. (2008). *Der Mythos vom germanischen Königtum. Studien zur Herrchaftsorganisation bei den germanischsprachigen Barbaren bis zum Beginn der Völkerwanderungszeit*. Berlin: Walter de Gruyter.

Diesenberger, M. (2003). "Hair, Sacrality and Symbolic Capital in the Frankish Kingdoms." In R. Corradini, M. Diesenberger, and H. Reimitz (eds.), *The Construction of Communities in the Early Middle Ages. Texts, Resources and Artefacts* (pp. 173–212). Leiden: Brill.

Dörler, P. (2013). "The *Liber Historiae Francorum*: A Model for a New Frankish Self-Confidence." *Networks and Neighbours* 1: 23–43.

Dumézil, B. (2005). *Les racines chrétiennes de l'Europe. Conversion et liberté dans les royaumes barbares, Vᵉ-VIIIᵉ siècle.* Paris: Fayard.

Effros, B. (2004). "Dressing Conservatively: Women's Brooches as Markers of Ethnic Identity?" In J. Smith and L. Brubaker (eds.), *Gender and the Transformation of the Roman World: Women, Men and Eunuchs in Late Antiquity and After, 300–900 CE* (pp. 165–184). Cambridge: Cambridge University Press.

Esders, S. (2016). "Late Roman Military Law in the Bavarian Code." *Clio@Themis. Revue électronique d'histoire du droit* 10: 1–24.

Fanning, S. (1992). "Emperors and Empires in Fifth-Century Gaul." In J. F. Drinkwater and H. Elton (eds.), *Fifth-Century Gaul. A Crisis of Identity?* (pp. 288–297). Cambridge: Cambridge University Press.

Fanning, S. (2011). "*Reguli* in the Roman Empire, Late Antiquity, and the Early Medieval Germanic Kingdoms." In R. Mathisen and D. Shanzer (eds.), *Romans, Barbarians and the Transformation of the Roman World, Cultural Interaction and the Creation of Identity in Late Antiquity* (pp. 43–53). Farnham: Ashgate.

Fehr, H. (2010). *Germanen und Romanen im Merowingerreich. Frühgeschichtliche Archäologie zwischen Wissenschaft und Zeitgeschehen.* Ergänzungsbände zum Reallexikon der Germanischen Altertumskunde 68. Berlin: Walter de Gruyter.

Fischer, S., and Lind, L. (2015). "The Coins in the Grave of King Childeric." *Journal of Archaeology and Ancient History* 14: 3–36.

Gerberding, R. A. (1987). *The Rise of the Carolingians and the* Liber Historiae Francorum. Oxford: Clarendon Press.

Gillett, A. (2002a). (ed.) *On Barbarian Identity. Critical Approaches to Ethnicity in the Early Middle Ages.* Turnhout: Brepols.

Gillett, A. (2002b). "Was Ethnicity Politicized in the Earliest Medieval Kingdoms?" In A. Gillett (ed.), *On Barbarian Identity. Critical Approaches to Ethnicity in the Early Middle Ages* (pp. 85–121). Turnhout: Brepols.

Goetz, H. W. (2003). "*Gens*, Kings and Kingdoms: The Franks." In H. W. Goetz, J. Jarnut, and W. Pohl (eds.), *Regna and Gentes. The Relationship between Late Antique and Early Medieval Peoples and Kingdoms in the Transformation of the Roman World* (pp. 307–344). Leiden: Brill.

Goffart, W. (2006). *Barbarian Tides: The Migration Age and the Later Roman Empire.* Philadelphia: University of Pennsylvania Press.

Graceffa, A. (2009). *Les historiens et la question franque: le peuplement franc et les Mérovingiens dans l'historiographie française et allemande des XIXᵉ-XXᵉ siècles.* Turnhout: Brepols.

Guillot, O. (1995). "La justice dans le royaume franc à l'époque mérovingienne." In *La giustizia nell'alto medioevo (secoli V–VIII). Settimane di studio del centro italiano di studi sull'alto medioevo* 42 (pp. 653–731). Spoleto: Centro italiano di studi sull'alto medioevo.

Guillot, O. (2003). "Autour du précepte de Clotaire Iᵉʳ (558–561)." In *Le droit par-dessus les frontières. Il diritto sopra le frontiere: Atti delle journées internationales, Torino 2001* (pp. 373–410). Naples: Jovene.

Halsall, G. (2007a). *Barbarian Migrations and the Roman West, 376–568.* Cambridge: Cambridge University Press.

Halsall, G. (2007b). "The Preface to Book V of Gregory of Tours' Histories: Its Form, Context and Significance." *The English Historical Review* 122: 297–317.

Halsall, G. (2010). *Cemeteries and Society in Merovingian Gaul. Selected Studies in History and Archaeology, 1992–2009.* Leiden: Brill.

Halsall, G. (2011). "Ethnicity and Early Medieval Cemeteries." *Arqueología y territorio medieval* 18: 15–27.

Haubrichs, W. (2008). "Namenbrauch und Mythos-Konstruktion. Die Onomastik der Lex-Salica-Prologe." In U. Ludwig and T. Schilp (eds.), *Nomen et Fraternitas. Festchrift für Dieter Geuenich zum 65. Geburstag* (pp. 53–79). Berlin: Walter de Gruyter.

Heather, P. (2008). "Ethnicity, Group Identity, and Social Status in the Migration Period." In I. Garipzanov, P. J. Geary, and P. Urbańczyk (eds.), *Franks, Northmen and Slaves: Identities and State Formation in Early Medieval Europe* (pp. 17–49). Turnhout: Brepols.

Heather, P. (2009). *Empires and Barbarians*. London: Macmillan.

Jussen, B. (2014). "Chlodwig der Gallier. Zur Strukturgeschichte einer historischen Figur." In M. Meier and S. Patzold (eds.), *Chlodwigs Welt. Organisation von Herrschaft um 500* (pp. 27–43). Stuttgart: Steiner.

Kazanski, M., and Périn, P. (2011). "Identity and Ethnicity during the Era of Migrations and Barbarian Kingdoms in the Light of Archaeology in Gaul." In R. Mathisen and D. Shanzer (eds.), *Romans, Barbarians and the Transformation of the Roman World: Cultural Interaction and the Creation of Identity in Late Antiquity* (pp. 299–329). Farnham: Ashgate.

Kazanski, M., and Périn, P. (2017). "Archéologie funéraire et ethnicité en Gaule à l'époque mérovingienne (réponse à Guy Halsall)." In J. López Quiroga, M. Kazanski, and V. Ivanišević (eds.), *Entangled Identities and Otherness in Late Antique and Early Medieval Europe. Historical, Archaeological and Bioarchaeological Approaches* (pp. 199–212). Oxford: BAR Publishing.

Landau, P. (2004). *Die Lex Baiuvariorum. Entstehungszeit, Entstehungsort und Charakter von Bayerns ältester Rechts- und Geschichtsquelle*. Munich: Verlag der bayerischen Akademie der Wissenschaften.

Le Jan, R. (1995). *Famille et pouvoir dans le monde franc (VIIᵉ–Xᵉ siècle). Essai d'anthropologie sociale*. Paris: Publications de la Sorbonne.

Lebecq, S. (2002). "The Two Faces of Childeric. History, Archaeology, Historiography." In W. Pohl and M. Diesenberger (eds.), *Integration und Herrschaft. Ethnische Identitäten und soziale Organisation im Frühmittelalter* (pp. 119–132). Vienna: Verlag der Österreichischen Akademie der Wissenschaften.

McKitterick, R. (1989). *The Carolingians and the Written World*. Cambridge: Cambridge University Press.

Musset, L. (1965). *Les invasions: le second assaut contre l'Europe chrétienne (VIIᵉ–XIᵉ siècle)*. Paris: Presses universitaires de France.

Musset, L. (1965). *Les invasions: les vagues germaniques*. Paris: Presses universitaires de France.

Nelson, J. (2008). "Frankish Identity in Charlemagne's Empire." In I. Garipzanov, P. J. Geary, and P. Urbańczyk (eds.), *Franks, Northmen and Slaves: Identities and State Formation in Early Medieval Europe* (pp. 71–83). Turnhout: Brepols.

Patzold, S. (2014). "Bischöfe, soziale Herkunft und die Organisation lokaler Herrschaft um 500." In M. Meier and S. Patzold (eds.), *Chlodwigs Welt. Organisation von Herrschaft um 500* (pp. 523–543). Stuttgart: Steiner.

Pohl, W. (1998). "Introduction: Strategies of Distinction." In W. Pohl and H. Reimitz (eds.), *Strategies of Distinction. The Construction of Ethnic Communities, 300–800* (pp. 1–15). Leiden: Brill.

Pohl, W. (2009). "*Regnum* und *gens*." In W. Pohl and V. Wieser (eds.), *Der frühmittelalterliche Staat- Europäische Perspektiven* (pp. 435–450). Vienna: Verlag der Österreichischen Akademie der Wissenschaften.

Pohl, W. (2010). "Archaeology of Identity: Introduction." In W. Pohl and M. Mehofer (eds.), *Archaeology of Identity—Archäologie der Identität* (pp. 9–23). Vienna: Verlag der Österreichischen Akademie der Wissenschaften.

Pohl, W. (2013). "Christian and Barbarian Identities in the Early Medieval West: Introduction." In W. Pohl and G. Heydemann (eds.), *Post-Roman Transitions. Christian and Barbarian Identities in the Early Medieval West* (pp. 1–46). Turnhout: Brepols.

Poly, J.-P. (2016). "Freedom, Warriors' Bond, Legal Book. The Lex Salica between Barbarian Custom and Roman Law. Liberté, lien des guerriers, livre de droit. La lex salica entre coutume barbare et loi romaine." *Clio@Themis. Revue électronique d'histoire du droit,* 10: 1–25.

Pontal, O. (1989). *Histoire des conciles mérovingiens.* Paris: Éditions du Cerf.

Reimitz, H. (2008). "*Omnes Franci.* Identifications and Identities of the Early Medieval Franks." In I. Garipzanov, P. J. Geary, and P. Urbańczyk (eds.), *Franks, Northmen and Slaves: Identities and State Formation in Early Medieval Europe* (pp. 51–70). Turnhout: Brepols.

Reimitz, H. (2015). *History, Frankish Identity and the Framing of Western Ethncity, 550–850.* Cambridge: Cambridge University Press.

Renard, E. (2009). "Le *pactus legis salicae,* règlement militaire romain ou code de lois compilé sous Clovis ?" *Bibliothèque de l'École des chartes* 167: 321–352.

Rigsby, K. J. (1999). "Two Danubian Epitaphs." *Zeitschrift für Papyrologie und Epigraphik,* 126: 175–176.

Rio, A. (2008). "Charters, Law Codes and Formulae: the Franks between Theory and Practice." In P. Fouracre and D. Ganz (eds.), *Frankland and the World of the Early Middle Ages. Essays in Honour of Dame Jinty Nelson* (pp. 7–27). Manchester: Manchester University Press.

Rio, A. (2009). *Legal Practice and the Written Word in the Early Middle Ages: Frankish Formulae, c. 500–1000.* Cambridge: Cambridge University Press.

Sarti, L. (2013). *Perceiving War and the Military in Early Christian Gaul (ca. 400–700 A.D.).* Leiden: Brill.

Springer, M. (1997). "Gab es ein Volk der Salier ?" In D. Geuenich and W. Haubrichs (eds.), *Nomen et gens: zur historischen Aussagekraft frühmittelalterlicher Personennamen* (pp. 58–83). Berlin: Walter de Gruyter.

Springer, M. (1998). "Riparii-Ribuarier-Rheinfranken nebst einigen Bemerkungen zum Geographen von Ravenn." In D. Geuenich (ed.), *Die Franken und die Alemannen bis zur Schlacht bei Zülpich* (pp. 200–269). Berlin: Walter de Gruyter.

Ubl, K. (2014). "Im Bann der Traditionen. Zur Charakteristik der *Lex Salica.*" In M. Meier and S. Patzold (eds.), *Chlodwigs Welt. Organisation von Herrschaft um 500* (pp. 423–445). Stuttgart: Steiner.

von Rummel, P. (2007). *Habitus barbarus: Kleidung und Repräsentation spätantiker Eliten im 4. und 5. Jahrhundert.* Berlin: Walter de Gruyter.

von Rummel, P. (2013). "The Fading Power of Images: Romans, Barbarians, and the Uses of a Dichotomy in Early Medieval Archaeology." In W. Pohl and G. Heydemann (eds.), *Post-Roman Transitions. Christian and Barbarian Identities in the Early Medieval West* (pp. 365–406). Turnhout: Brepols.

Ward-Perkins, B. (2006). *The Fall of Rome and the End of Civilization.* Oxford: Oxford University Press.

Wenskus, R. (1961). *Stammesbildung und Verfassung. Das Werden der frühmittelalterlichen Gentes.* Cologne: Böhlau Verlag.

Wolfram, H. (1979). *Geschichte der Goten: Von den Anfängen bis zur Mitte des sechsten Jahrhunderts. Entwurf einer historischen Ethnographie.* Munich: C. H. Beck.

Wolfram, H. (1988). *History of the Goths*, trans. T. J. Dunlap. Berkeley: University of California Press.

Wood, I. (1986). "Disputes in Late Fifth- and Sixth-Century Gaul: Some Problems." In W. Davies and P. Fouracre (eds.), *The Settlement of Disputes in Early Medieval Europe* (pp. 7–22). Cambridge: Cambridge University Press.

Wood, I. (1994). *The Merovingian Kingdoms 450–751*. London: Longman.

Wood, I. (1995). "Defining the Franks : Frankish Origins in Early Medieval Historiography." In S. Forde, L. Johnson, and A. V. Murray (eds.), *Concepts of National Identity in the Middle Ages* (pp. 47–57). Leeds: Leeds Studies in English.

Wood, I. (2009). "The Governing Class of the Gibichungs and Early Merovingian Kingdoms." In W. Pohl and V. Wieser (eds.), *Der frühmittelalterliche Staat—Europäische Perspektiven* (pp. 11–22). Vienna: Verlag der Österreichischen Akademie der Wissenschaften.

Wood, I. (2013). *The Modern Origins of the Early Middle Ages*. Oxford: Oxford University Press.

Wood, I. (2014). "The Political Structure of the Burgundian Kingdom." In M. Meier and S. Patzold (eds.), *Chlodwigs Welt. Organisation von Herrschaft um 500* (pp. 383–396). Stuttgart: Steiner.

Wood, I. (2016). "The Legislation of *Magistri militum*: The Laws of Gundobad and Sigismund." *Clio@Themis. Revue électronique d'histoire du droit* 10: 1–16.

Wormald, P. (2003). "The *leges barbarorum*: Law and Ethnicity in the Post-Roman West." In H. W. Goetz, J. Jarnut, and W. Pohl (eds.), *Regna und gentes. The Relationship between Late Antique and Early Medieval Peoples and Kingdoms in the Transformation of the Roman World* (pp. 21–53). Leiden: Brill.

CHAPTER 6

··

MIGRANTS AND
MINORITIES IN
MEROVINGIAN GAUL

··

WOLFRAM DREWS

THE topic of this chapter relates to numerous issues, including the entanglement of Merovingian Gaul with the wider Mediterranean and northern European world, internal differentiation in the Merovingian world, and the self-perception of individuals and groups forming part of Merovingian society. The author of the main narrative source for this period is a good starting point from which to consider these questions. Interestingly, the historian Gregory of Tours does not use any precise term to refer to the majority of the population living in Gaul, peoples that modern scholarship mostly refers to as Romans or Gallo-Romans. Incidentally, Gregory himself belonged to this very group, and his silence regarding the "Roman" identity of most of the population is puzzling to people accustomed to conceptualizing identities by means of ethnic or "national" markers. Because Gregory fails to define the majority, it is difficult to tell which minorities might be distinguished from it. Significantly, Walter Goffart refers to "the peculiarly limited place that Gregory accords to the various dimensions of foreignness" (Goffart 1982, p. 84). From Gregory's perspective, the identity of a person was defined by his or her city of origin, the *civitas* (Goffart 1982, pp. 86–87). However, we should avoid calling people who moved from one city in Gaul to another "migrants," which would—after all—apply to a considerable number of people, including Gregory himself, who resided in the Auvergne before moving to Tours to accept the bishopric. Calling members of the Gallo-Roman elite migrants hardly enhances scholarly understanding of the period. Nonetheless, Gregory's silence begs the question as to whether any majority living in Gaul should or could be defined on the basis of ethnic, religious, social, linguistic or legal categories.

THE FRANKS—A RULING
MINORITY OF MIGRANTS?

One group that might be called migrants is the Franks, an ethnic agglomeration that dominated northern Gaul from the fifth century onward (see Coumert, Chapter 5, this volume). Scholars have repeatedly pointed out that, unlike other barbarian peoples, the Franks settled on Roman territory while remaining close to their previous areas of settlement in modern Belgium, which means that, unlike most migrants, they did not move to territories geographically separated from their origins. What is more, the Franks probably did not regard themselves as migrants after settling down in Gaul. Not only had they converted to Roman Christianity but they had also taken over what was left of the Roman provincial administration, including collecting tax revenues. Whether Gallo-Romans like Gregory of Tours regarded the Franks as migrants is an open question, but it is doubtful that Franks and Merovingian kings were perceived as migrants after several generations of rulership in Gaul. Hardly any cultural markers, like religion, set them apart from more narrowly defined "Romans."

After several generations, Franks were distinguished from "Romans" more by social than by ethnic markers, like their right to attend spring assemblies still attested in the early Carolingian period. It is important to bear in mind that language was not perceived as identifying a person in the first place. As Walter Goffart observed, "language was a badge of class and education as well as of nationality" (1982, p. 88). The term *Frank* may have had social as well as "ethnic" connotations; Gregory of Tours may have even implied this when he refers to the Merovingian dynasty as the only point of reference for determining who might be an outsider.[1]

RELIGIOUS MIGRATION—*PEREGRINATIO*
RELIGIOSA

However, the term *migrants* may be useful in other cases. Irish or Scottish monks such as Columbanus and Gallus left their respective countries of origin to embark on a path of *peregrinatio religiosa*, which was perceived as an imitation of the example set by the Egyptian desert fathers, who left the "civilized" world for the desert to practice asceticism (Kötting 1950; Angenendt 1982, pp. 52–79; Rekdal 1991, pp. 67–83; Dietz 2005; see Picard, Chapter 18, this volume). Irish ascetics compensated for the lack of deserts on the British Isles by leaving their customary surroundings for foreign lands (Lohse 2015, pp. 237–249). On the continent, they founded monasteries in Merovingian Gaul and Italy, marked by a form of life different from earlier versions of Latin monasticism. As the topic of Merovingian monasticism is treated in another chapter (see Diem,

Chapter 15, this volume), it will not be explored in great detail in the present context. What is important for our purposes is to note that Irish monks coming to Merovingian Gaul wanted to be seen as *peregrini*. On the one hand, they kept their Irish identity by maintaining links to their insular roots (Riché 1981, pp. 59–72; Schäferdiek 1982, pp. 171–201); on the other hand, Christians from Gaul saw them as migrants. This perception is reflected in the traditional names that are still attached to a number of Irish foundations in modern Germany and Austria: monastic churches originally founded by Irish *peregrini* are called *Schottenkirche* in Vienna, Erfurt, Würzburg, and Regensburg (Flachenecker 1995).

The fact that both Christians originating from Merovingian Gaul and Irish monks themselves perceived Irish monasticism as being different from other forms of Frankish monastic life may justify categorizing expressions of Irish *peregrinatio religiosa* as indications that Irish monks lived as a group of migrants in Merovingian Gaul. Although Irish Christians were not perceived as belonging to a different Christian denomination or a "heresy," they were thought to be different from native, Gallic Christians. To maintain their identity as pilgrims who had chosen a kind of desert for ascetic purposes, they needed to keep their Irish identity apart. Any assimilation to Gallic Christianity would have been tantamount to losing their status as pilgrims who had emigrated from their native lands.

Eastern Christians and "Heretics"

Another group we might call migrants was made up of Syrians and other oriental Christians living in Gaul.[2] However, literary and epigraphic references are few and far between, and it is often unclear whether individuals called Greeks or Syrians actually belonged to a group of foreigners or migrants living permanently in Gaul, or whether they were travelers passing through Gaul who sometimes died in the course of their journeys.

In the imperial period, Christianity in Gaul was marked by a strong oriental character. Several early bishops in Gaul came from the east; Irenaeus of Lyons came from Smyrna, as did his predecessor Pothinus (Ewig 1964, pp. 386–387). On some occasions, recalcitrant oriental bishops were banished to places in Gaul. Interestingly, the old Gallic liturgy shows a marked oriental character.[3] In the fifth century, monasticism in the Rhone Valley was marked by strong oriental influence; Gregory of Tours mentions a monk named Abraham from the Euphrates, who settled in the Auvergne around 475/479 (*Liber vitae patrum*, 3. 1; Ewig 1964, p. 388). As late as the early seventh century, the church in the monastery of Abbess Rusticula of Arles was dedicated to the Holy Cross, as well as to Gabriel, Raphael, and Thomas. All four of these *patrocinia* are clear indications of connections with eastern churches (Ewig 1964, p. 390).

We may doubt, however, whether Christians coming from the east were regarded as migrants, let alone religious minorities, in the imperial period. It was only during the early medieval period that separate oriental churches formed in the east, following the ecumenical councils of Ephesus (431) and Chalcedon (451). At both of these councils, certain dogmatic statements regarding the human and divine natures of Christ were branded as heretical; diverging Christians were called Nestorians or Monophysites, by their enemies representing imperial Christianity.

Although Christians living in Syria and Egypt gradually developed an adherence to such "heretical" forms of Christianity, communities of Chalcedonian, imperial Christians also continued to live in both of these territories during the sixth and seventh centuries. Therefore, it is impossible to tell whether Syrian or eastern Christians living in or passing through Gaul in Merovingian times belonged to any "heretical" church, if any such church already existed at the time.[4] Syrians and individuals from the eastern Mediterranean living in the west may even have been unaware of the dogmatic issues tearing apart eastern Christianity, and most Christians in the Latin west had little understanding of the Christological problems discussed at the fifth-century councils (Claude 1985, pp. 181–182).

In any case, we have no indication that eastern Christians living in Gaul ever formed churches of their own different from the Catholic Church around them; after 610, there are no extant references to oriental Christians.[5] If eastern Christians had founded any churches of their own, based on a separate Christian denomination, such churches might have survived longer, but their total disappearance suggests that they had not belonged to different denominations in the previous period.

After around 400, compared to the imperial period, the role of eastern merchants seems to have increased, especially in the fifth and in the first half of the sixth century, when a considerable degree of immigration may be observed.[6] Explanations given for the increase in arrivals from the east are unsatisfactory, the most probable reason being a growing population in Syria itself (Claude 1985, pp. 170–175). After the fifth century, more or less stable groups of Greeks or Syrians are attested only in Arles, Narbonne, and Orléans, and possibly also in Marseille (Devroey 1995, p. 62). In Arles, for instance, the psalms were sung alternatively in Greek and in Latin (*Vita Caesarii* 1, 19; Devroey 1995, p. 59). At the beginning of the sixth century, the Greek doctor Anthimus wrote a book on diet for King Theuderic (d. 534) (*Medicus, De observatione ciborum ad Theodoricum regem Francorum epistula*; Effros 2002); Gregory of Tours mentions a doctor named Reovalis who had studied in Constantinople (Gregory of Tours, *Decem libri historiarum,* 10. 15; Brunner 1992, p. 46). For individual travelers, Bishop Ansoald of Poitiers founded a *xenodochium* at the end of the seventh century (*Fragmentum testamenti Ansoaldi, episcopi Pictavensis*; Ewig 1964, p. 390; see Horden, Chapter 14, this volume).

In the Merovingian period, settlements of eastern colonies are attested in Gallic towns,[7] in contrast to the Carolingian period, when there is only evidence for individuals coming from the east. The name "Syrian" given to these merchants should be understood in a wide sense, as referring to people of different ethnic backgrounds (Devroey 1995, p. 52, n. 11). Only a minority of them can be said to have been wealthy. In Merovingian Gaul, most people of eastern origin lived in the south and in the west. However, there is no indication of their involvement in overseas trade; they confined their mercantile activities to local and regional exchange (Claude 1985, pp. 178–179).[8] There is also evidence for travel activity between Egypt and Gaul; the *Life* of the Alexandrian patriarch John Eleemosynarius, who was in office between 612 and 616, refers to people called *gallodromoi*, whose main activity was to conduct trade with Gaul (*Vita Joh. Eleem.* 36, p. 385; Claude 1985, p. 185). Several sources can be adduced to show the presence of ships and merchants from the orient in the west between the sixth and eighth centuries (Claude 1985, p. 186).

Eastern migrants living in Gaul are certainly an indication for the continuing entanglement of Merovingian Gaul with the wider Mediterranean world, which is also attested to by the horizon opened up by the historian known as Fredegar. However, they cannot be taken as evidence for the settlement of such migrants in Gaul, let alone in groups of foreigners or migrants, as can be said regarding Irish monastic establishments. Nonetheless, there are occasional mentions of oriental migrants together with other groups, such as canon 4 of the Council of Narbonne, meeting under Visigothic rule in 589, which required all Goths, Romans, Syrians, Greeks, and Jews to refrain from work on Sundays (Linder 1997, nr. 827; CCSL 148A, pp. 254–255). In addition, canon 9 forbade Jews from singing psalms at funerals (Linder 1997, nr. 828; CCSL 148A, p. 255).

People from Merovingian Gaul may have referred to people as Syrians because of their accent or geographic origins, but not on account of a separate Christian denomination (Devroey 1995, p. 55; Devroey and Brouwer 2000, p. 341). Such an accent may have been responsible for their being regarded as migrants. By contrast, whereas the oriental background of individuals probably professing the same kind of Christianity may have been sufficient to regard such people as migrants, they could not be seen as members of a minority group. Unlike Irish monks who formed institutionalized groups maintaining their identity over a certain period of time, oriental Christians—as far as we know—probably neither formed groups nor maintained their identity after the seventh century. Such groups did not possess sufficient size, internal cohesion, or autonomy to maintain their cultural and religious profile (Devroey and Brouwer 2000, p. 347).

Moreover, unlike Irish monks, eastern migrants may not have given conscious expression to their identity, if they possessed any such thing setting them apart from the majority. Occasionally we hear of contacts between oriental and Irish Christians; when Columbanus came to Orléans, he stayed with a Syrian woman born in the east (*Nam et ego advena sum ex longiquo Orientis solo*; *Vita Columbani* 1. 21). In general, "Syrians and Jews probably were bi- or trilingual. They were an ordinary part of the local landscape rather than foreigners" (Goffart 1982, p. 88).

Things are different in the case of another group of Christians living in Gaul. The Arians, confined mainly to southern parts of Gaul, also adhered to a different denomination branded as heretical by the Catholic majority. Arian Christianity had come to Gaul mainly as a consequence of the immigration of the Goths who had been adhering to Arianism since the fourth century. Arian Christianity was one of the main markers of a separate Gothic identity setting it apart from the Roman majority. Arianism was a means to give expression to an identity, enabling a minority group to maintain its cohesion in a situation when it tried to establish its rule over a majority. When Clovis conquered southern Gaul after the battle usually associated with the site of Vouillé, the center of the Gothic kingdom moved to the Iberian peninsula; only Narbonne and the region of Septimania remained under Gothic, Arian rule in Gaul (see Mathisen, Chapter 19; Patrello, Chapter 39, this volume).

Although Arians had originally come to Gaul as migrants, in Merovingian times they were no longer regarded as migrants or outsiders. However, they did belong to a minority that did not possess Roman citizenship, while at the same time adhering to a different Christian denomination. Arians in southern Gaul were separated from the majority by both legal and religious markers; unlike oriental Christians, they belonged to a group living permanently in Gaul that managed to maintain several identity markers over a substantial period of time. For Gregory of Tours, Arians were the most important religious outsiders; the distinction between orthodoxy and heresy mattered much more to him than ethnicity (Goffart 1982, p. 90). However, we may doubt that he ever met a significant number of Arians in northern Gaul. It is equally improbable that Arians were in a position to conduct theological disputes with Catholics, let alone to win Catholics over to their form of Christianity. Gregory treats a statement by Sidonius Apollinaris, who describes Catholic bishoprics being vacant following the establishment of Gothic rule under King Euric in the fifth century, as being the normal state of affairs under Gothic rule (Gregory of Tours, *Decem libri historiarum*, 2. 25, referring to Sidonius Apollinaris ep. 7, 6). However, there does not seem to have been any systematic persecution of Catholics by Arian monarchs. As Ian Wood stated, "In fact there is plenty of evidence to suggest that the oppression was merely temporary, being imposed while the king established his grip on the country" (1994, p. 18).

As a rule, there was no religious conflict between Arians and Catholics in the Gothic kingdom of Toulouse; the exile of some Catholic bishops under Alaric II does not seem to have been imposed for religious reasons. Caesarius of Arles, for instance, was accused of treason by one of his own clergy. The Arian king Alaric II even supported a council of the Catholic Church meeting under the presidency of Caesarius at Agde in 506, and he consented to the meeting of another council the following year, which did not convene after the Merovingian victory at Vouillé (Wood 1994, pp. 46–47). References to Arianism become less frequent over time. The more or less tacit demise of Arianism suggests that after the collapse of Gothic rule in southern Gaul, it was not an attractive alternative in the eyes of Catholic Christians.

THE JEWS: A ROMAN MINORITY

The most important minority group in Gaul was certainly the Jews; there were Jewish communities in Marseille, Arles, Orléans, Bourges, Clermont, and perhaps Uzès, as well as in Visigothic Narbonne (Devroey and Brouwer 2000, p. 345; Toch 2013, pp. 65–79). Among the oldest evidence in Gaul are lamps with Jewish symbols (Solin 1983, p. 615). Sources for their presence are more abundant than for Arians or individuals of eastern

Mediterranean origin; in addition to historiography and hagiography, there are also legal (ecclesiastical and royal) as well as epigraphic sources (for the literary evidence, see Juster 1914, pp. 184–186; Noy 1993, no. 189–192, pp. 263–272; Lotter 2003a, p. 89). Jews had originally come to Roman Gaul as migrants, but from 212 onward, free Jewish males had enjoyed Roman citizenship everywhere in the Empire. Jews in Gaul did not speak a different language in everyday life;[9] however, their liturgy may have been celebrated in Greek, and the Bible may also have been read in Greek in the synagogues.

In Antiquity, Jewish communities had spread all over the Mediterranean world; the main centers were close to the coastline or situated on rivers linking them to the seashore (Toch 2013, p. 69). In Gaul, ancient communities were found in Marseille, Narbonne, and Lyon. Most of them were situated south of the Loire and of the Alps, with the significant exception of Cologne, where a Jewish community is attested in a decree of Constantine the Great from 321 preserved in the Theodosian Code. However, there is no evidence for the continued presence of Jews in Cologne after the late Roman period. The Jewish community in Cologne was probably founded anew in Carolingian times, and recent attempts to postulate an ongoing presence of Jews there since the fourth century have found little acceptance outside of Cologne itself (Schieffer 2015).

Jewish communities in the Merovingian world were confined to territories south of the Loire, and it is even doubtful whether there was a community in the city of Paris; individual Jews mentioned in the context of the royal court need not have belonged to a local community. Merovingian Judaism was mainly a continuation of late Roman Judaism, both in terms of areas of settlement and of its social, cultural and religious profile. However, there may have been a nascent trend of Rabbinic influence entailing a gradual replacement of Greek by Hebrew and Aramaic in the Jewish liturgy. Rabbinic influence was felt in the western Mediterranean only from the early medieval period onward, most strongly at first in North Africa (Carthage) and Rome, and less so in Spain and Gaul.[10] Growing Rabbinic influence meant the gradual replacement of Greek by Hebrew and Aramaic in liturgy and biblical study.[11] As regards everyday life, Jews stuck to the form of vulgar Latin also spoken by their non-Jewish Roman neighbors.

The freedom of the Jews to practice their religion was guaranteed by Roman law (*Codex Theodosianus* 2, 8, 26 = *Lex Romana Visigothorum* 2, 8, 3).[12] The Jewish minority was even given a certain degree of autonomy to regulate internal affairs:

> The Jews who live under the Roman and common law should address the courts in the usual way in those cases that do not concern so much their superstition as court, laws, and rights, and all of them shall bring actions and defend themselves under the Roman laws; in conclusion, they shall be under our laws. Certainly, if some shall deem it necessary to litigate before the Jews or the patriarchs through mutual agreement, in the manner of arbitration, with the consent of both parties and in civil matters only, they should not be prohibited by public law from accepting their verdict; the governors of the provinces should even execute their sentences as if they were appointed arbiters through a judge's award.
>
> (Codex Theodosianus 2, 1, 10 = Lex Romana Visigothorum 2, 1, 10;
> Linder 1997, no. 435)

Continuity regarding the position of the Jews is also illustrated by the *Life* of Caesarius of Arles, which relates that when the city was besieged by Franks and Burgundians in 508, local Jews were entrusted with defending a part of the walls allotted to them by casting lots. The Jews took their charge very seriously, even reporting their suspicion that the bishop might have committed treason (Lotter 2004, p. 320).

As did other Romans, Jews kept Roman citizenship, according to the *Lex Romana Visigothorum*.[13] Unlike Visigothic Spain, where Roman citizenship was finally abolished in 654 with the promulgation of a new law code, the *Liber Iudiciorum*, no such official replacement ever took place in Merovingian Gaul. This meant that the Christian and the Jewish part of the provincial Roman population were never legally separated. As a consequence, Jews remained a self-confident part of the population.[14] They did not bow to Christian clerics, as indicated by a complaint uttered in canon 14 by the fathers meeting for a council in Mâcon in 581/583 (Mikat 1995, pp. 41–42; Linder 1997, no. 823). Canon 2 of the same council complained about Jews entering the monastic precinct of a nunnery to have conversations with consecrated virgins (Linder 1997, no. 821). This may be an indication of business transactions, but it is also testimony to the close integration of Jews in Merovingian society (Mikat 1995, p. 42). It is plausible that Jews fleeing from oppression in Visigothic Spain sought refuge in Merovingian Gaul. An inscription difficult to decipher, coming from Auch in the Armagnac region close to the border, tentatively dated to the seventh or the eighth century, may provide evidence for a donation made by a man called Jona for the benefit of pilgrims or foreigners, who might be regarded as refugees (Noy 1993, nr. 191, pp. 268–269; *Corpus Inscriptionum Iudaicarum*, nr. 671).

MEROVINGIAN POLICIES

Merovingian kings never pursued any coherent policy regarding the Jews. In contrast to Visigothic Spain, where several kings tried repeatedly to convert Jews to Catholic Christianity in the seventh century, no such attempt was ever made by a Merovingian king, at least regarding the entire Jewish community of the kingdom. Chilperic I is an exception. According to Gregory of Tours, Chilperic tried to convert several Jews close to his court but without lasting success. As a rule, Merovingian Jews kept the status they had enjoyed in the late Roman period. Interestingly, kings even gave public offices to Jews (Lotter 1997, pp. 872–873), probably on account of their good education. This practice nonetheless met with severe criticism in canon 6 of the Council of Clermont in 535 (Linder 1997, no. 815), the Council of Paris in 614 (Linder 1997, no. 830; Mikat 1995, p. 36), and canon 13 of the Council of Clichy in 626/627 (Mikat 1995, p. 26; Linder 1997, no. 832; Lotter 2003b, p. 355). King Chlothar II made this prohibition part of general legislation with his decree of 614 that "Jews are not allowed to exercise public function over Christians" (Linder 1997, no. 578).

The *Lex Romana Visigothorum*, an abbreviation of the Theodosian Code issued by the Gothic king, Alaric II, remained in force, which also contributed to the preservation of the Roman status of Merovingian Jews. The barbarian law codes, the *Lex Salica* and the *Lex Burgundionum*, contain much less material relating to the Jews, which is no surprise given the fact that Gallic Jews formed part of the Roman provincial population (Lotter 1997, p. 852). As regards the barbarian abbreviations of Roman law, the *Lex Romana Visigothorum* takes up thirteen regulations from the Theodosian Code, whereas the *Lex Romana Burgundionum* confines itself to a single one, related to mixed marriages (Linder 1997, no. 405–408).

In general, the legal position of the Jews in Merovingian Gaul was not worse than it was under Roman rule (Mikat 1995, p. 95). In addition, public authorities were often unable or unwilling to enforce coercive measures against Jews; severe measures of secular legislation were often replaced by ecclesiastical sanctions, not directly applicable to Jews (Lotter 1997, p. 878). That Jews were mostly accepted as fellow citizens by their Christian neighbors is also shown by hagiographical accounts in which Jews occasionally perform the function of mourners (among others) after the death of a bishop or some other Christian dignitary. As Friedrich Lotter has shown, saints' lives have a certain claim of truthfulness: the story told and read out has to be believed by the hearers. There would be no point in inventing Jews if in reality there were none (2004, pp. 318, 322). Thus, we may assume that there is some truth to the story of Jews mourning the death of Bishop Gallus of Clermont.[15] Mentioning the Jews may be an indication of their belonging to and their inclusion in the civic community, which in Merovingian Gaul as a rule also contained some Jews.

ECCLESIASTICAL LEGISLATION AND THE PROBLEM OF "PROSELYTISM"

In the sixth and seventh centuries, church councils were held on a number of occasions, the last of which was the Council of Chalon-sur-Saône in 647/653 (*Concilia Galliae*; see also Halfond, Chapter 13, this volume); most of the topics discussed at these councils had also been treated by late Roman synods (Mikat 1995; Lotter 2000, pp. 527–528). Nine out of the total of more than sixty Merovingian councils passed legislation regarding the Jews; the councils dealt with the possession of Christian slaves by Jews, they forbade mixed marriages,[16] and they restricted the access of Jews to public office giving them authority over Christians. Furthermore, these measures were directed against common meals of Christian clerics and laypeople with Jews.

Finally, the public behavior of Jews on certain Christian holidays, mainly during Holy Week, was regulated. This last aspect was first adopted in canon 33 (30) at Orléans in 538; it was not present in Roman conciliar legislation (Mikat 1995, p. 37; Linder 1997, no. 818; Lotter 1997, p. 874). Merovingian conciliar legislation against mixed marriages was less severe than that in the late Roman Empire (Lotter 1997, p. 855). More than half of all the councils dealing with Jews addressed the issue of Christian slaves in Jewish ownership.

As a rule, the church did not question the right of Jews to possess such slaves. However, the clerics tried to prevent "Jewish proselytism," which may not have been due to active missionary activity, but rather to the attractiveness of Judaism. The principal aim of the church was to protect the Christian faith of the slaves who were serving Jewish masters.

Jews were active in a number of professions: Some of them, for example, probably owned agricultural properties (Devroey and Brouwer 2000, p. 351; Lotter 2000, p. 528; Toch 2013, pp. 77–79), as was the case of elite Jews (*honorati, domini*) around Narbonne in Gothic Septimania (Lotter 2003b, p. 341). Most of them, however, lived in towns predominantly in the south of Gaul (Devroey and Brouwer 2000, p. 346). The range of their commercial activities was similar to the scope of action of Syrians and Greeks: they were mostly active in regional trade, but much less so in overseas exchange, although there were some exceptions (Claude 1985, p. 188; Devroey and Brouwer 2000, p. 361; Lotter 2003b, p. 345; Toch 2013, p. 193). Some of them were active in the slave trade, which Christians also practiced (Toch 2013, pp. 178–190). A bishop, criticized by Gregory of Tours, used to conduct business with Jews.[17]

The principal interest of ecclesiastical legislation with regard to Jews was to prevent Jewish owners from converting Christian slaves to Judaism. Jewish proselytism, the alleged missionary activity of Jews among Christians, has been hotly debated; scholars usually assume that Jews, like Christians, were driven to convert others to their religion (Blumenkranz 1961; see, however, the cautionary remarks by Toch 2001, p. 22). There are some passages in the Babylonian Talmud relating to this issue (Mikat 1995, p. 92, following Blumenkranz; Linder 1978, pp. 432–433; Heil 1998, p. 50), but it is doubtful whether the Talmud was already studied in Merovingian Gaul. Moreover, outside of ecclesiastical legislation, there is little evidence that Jews attempted to circumcise Christians. Epigraphic sources are meager (Lotter 2003a, p. 133). In the Amoraic period, which broadly overlapped with Late Antiquity, any missionary impulse that had been expressed earlier had decreased considerably (Hoenig 1965, pp. 43, 49).[18] It is unclear whether the concept of the Noahidic commandments, by which non-Jews are only required to observe the commandments given to Noah after the Flood, was already known by Jews in Merovingian Gaul. These commandments were considered far easier to observe than the duties the Jews were obliged to fulfill (which are later even described as the "yoke" of the Torah). If non-Jews could attain salvation by observing the less severe commandments given to Noah, then there was no incentive or need to convert them to Judaism.

Converting household slaves was regarded as a "practical measure to enable the slave to function in the household without violating dietary and other ritual laws" (Toch 2003, p. 180). We may also recall the early modern phenomenon of the "Shabbes goy," known from eastern European Jewry: Christian servants were used to perform household chores that were forbidden to Jews on the Sabbath. It is precisely non-Jewish identity that turned the "Shabbes goy" into such a useful figure, a utility that would be lost if he or she were converted to Judaism.

These remarks suggest that we should not assume that Jews consistently pursued missionary activities among non-Jews. There may have been cases when Jews did convert non-Jews, but this was certainly not a general phenomenon, as may be seen in the aforementioned examples of the Noahidic commandments and the "Shabbes goy." We do not know to what extent these issues were relevant to Jews living in Merovingian Gaul. However, the reality behind alleged Jewish proselytism may be a different one: Judaism always held a certain attraction for some people living around it.[19] In Antiquity, its attractiveness may have been due to the monotheistic belief or to the communal organization, including welfare for members in need (Wasserstein 1996, p. 316). Even if this pull may have declined after the spread of Christianity, which possessed similar traits without requiring circumcision, Judaism may have continued to appeal to some non-Jews because of its peoples' high degree of literacy and education, or because of the "literal" observance of some biblical commandments that medieval Christians practically ignored.[20]

Cases of alleged Jewish proselytism may therefore sometimes have to be interpreted as instances pointing to the attractiveness of Judaism rather than necessarily involving any positive intention by Jews to win over non-Jews to their religion. The Jewish population may have increased slightly, following wars in Italy in the sixth century or the waves of persecution in Visigothic Spain in the seventh century (Lotter 1984, p. 48).

The Jewish slave trade is attested by ecclesiastical legislation and by letters sent by Pope Gregory the Great. There was no Jewish monopoly of this trade, which, as mentioned earlier, was also practiced by Christians (Claude 1985, pp. 95–99; Devroey and Brouwer 2000, pp. 356–357). Most sources referring to slaves owned by Jews "can be more convincingly read as evidence for the purchase, employment and selling of household slaves" (Toch 2013, p. 189). In addition, most Jews were active in other professions; evidence from outside Gaul points to Jewish doctors (Gregory of Tours, *Libri historiarum*, 5. 6), butchers, merchants, painters, tax collectors, actors, and soldiers (Lotter 2003a, 134–135). Gregory of Tours mentions a Jew named Armentarius who had formed a guild with another Jew and two Christians dealing with tax farming. Interestingly, this is the only passage in which Gregory associates Jews with money, in this case lending money with interest (*cum usuris*), and significantly, in this case, they were assisted by an equal number of Christians (Gregory of Tours, *Decem libri historiarum,* 7. 23; Brunner 1992, p. 48; Geisel 1998, pp. 310–315; Lotter 2003b, p. 343).

FORCED CONVERSIONS

The case of King Chilperic, who in 582 wanted to convert some Jews in his entourage and act as godfather, is reported by Gregory of Tours, who strikes a critical note when indicating that some newly baptized Jews reverted to their ancestral religion (*Decem libri historiarum*, 6. 17). This futile attempt by a king whom Gregory constantly portrays as an incapable ruler is just another indication of Chilperic's lack of theological knowledge (Goffart 1985, pp. 482–486). In addition, one year earlier, Chilperic had tried to convince the Jew Priscus, a merchant close to the court, to accept baptism in the course of a theological disputation (Gregory of Tours, *Decem libri historiarum*, 6. 5; Parente 1980, pp. 543–552; Geisel 1998, pp. 283–297). However, neither the king nor Gregory of Tours, who was called to assist in the matter, was able to achieve this objective. The implications of Gregory's description are that a royal policy of conversion was not likely to achieve any positive result; not only were such measures not required by Christian tradition, but also a king who tried to act in this manner revealed his ignorance. Moreover, the alleged conversion of all Frankish Jews by order of Dagobert I is probably a legend. If it had taken place, one would have expected subsequent complaints about "relapsing" Jews, such as in Visigothic Spain. No such complaints can be found in Merovingian sources.[21]

Neither were bishops required to pursue such policies. Pope Gregory the Great reprimanded the bishops of Marseille and Arles in 591 for having forced the Jews of their cities to accept baptism (Gregory the Great, *Registrarum epistolarum*, 1. 45; Stemberger 1993, p. 95). The most well-known case of forced conversion occurred when Bishop Avitus of Clermont baptized a large part of the Jewish population of his city in 576. Indeed, he is praised for this by Gregory of Tours. It is important to note that Gregory originated from the region of Clermont, which was his native *civitas* defining his personal identity; what is more, Avitus was his former tutor. Gregory's positive view of the whole affair is further highlighted by the fact that we not only possess his narrative (*Decem libri historiarum*, 5. 11), but there also exists a poem composed by Venantius Fortunatus, who had received news of the events from Gregory himself. Gregory had commissioned the poet to write a poem at short notice, which was probably meant to be read aloud to praise the achievements of the bishop of his own native city one year following the event (Venantius Fortunatus, *Carmina*, 5, 5; Brennan 1985, p. 327). Venantius Fortunatus points out that the civic community of Clermont was rent by strife.[22] This internal division was finally overcome by the bishop, who converted some of the Jews to Christianity, while the others left town. In Gregory's language, they "returned" to Marseille, the main center of Gallic Jewry.

The Jews of Clermont lived in a suburb close to the baptistery and a Christian basilica situated on a riverbank (Goffart 1985, p. 491). This topographical location was different from that in later centuries, when German Jews often lived in quarters next to the center of town, close to the town hall or the bishop's palace–that is, close to authorities that might offer protection in times of crisis. The Jews of Clermont evidently did not feel any such threat, being content to live outside of town. Their residence in a suburb did not, however, preclude the obligation they felt to their hometown, since at the end of the affair a considerable part of them preferred to accept baptism so that they could stay. They evidently did not regard themselves as strangers or outsiders, and they gave up their religion rather than forego their livelihoods and familiar surroundings.

The Clermont affair was sparked by a Jew baptized at Easter at the shrine close to the river. When the procession leading back to the cathedral passed the city walls, a Jew poured rancid oil on the recently converted man, mocking his baptism (which had included a ceremony of ritual anointment). According to Gregory, the Christian crowd tried to kill the culprit, an act that was prevented by the intervention of the bishop. After a period of time, the Christian mob attacked the synagogue, destroying it on Ascension Day. The Jews, besieged by a hostile Christian crowd, called for the bishop to protect them, promising to accept baptism. Baptism was finally administered at Pentecost to more than 500 Jews, while other members of the community left for (or "returned to") Marseille. Remarkably, while Venantius Fortunatus does mention the episode of the Jews being besieged by a hostile Christian crowd in their house(s), Walter Goffart notes that Gregory omits any reference to the armed crowd: "His omission is the one case of *suppressio veri* in the *Histories* that may be documented" (Goffart 1985, p. 488). Furthermore, Venantius (who got all his information from Gregory) mentions a sermon delivered by the bishop urging the Jews to convert; Gregory, by contrast, does not mention this in his account, but instead narrates that Avitus sent envoys with an ultimatum, giving the Jews some time for deliberation before deciding to convert (Claude 1991, pp. 141–142). This portrayal is in line with Gregory's tendency to present conversions not as an outcome of human preaching, but as divinely ordained, miraculous interventions (Blumenkranz 1960, p. 89; Reydellet 1992, p. 374 n. 16).[23] It is in this light that Gregory wanted the "miracle" of Jewish conversion in Clermont to be perceived; therefore, he explicitly denied that any force had been employed.[24]

The Clermont affair has been analyzed by various scholars (Brennan 1985; Goffart 1985; Claude 1991, pp. 137–147; Reydellet 1992, pp. 371–379; Stemberger 1993, pp. 92–94; Geisel 1998, pp. 261–278),[25] some of whom have highlighted that the events are presented as having taken place on three important Christian festivals (Brennan 1985, p. 329). The role of the bishop is somewhat unclear. At least according to Gregory, he did not take the initiative but instead reacted to situations of crisis provoked by others. However, in view of the strong ecclesiastical factionalism present in Clermont, Brian Brennan remarks that "Avitus, through his missionary fervour, may have shattered the fragile *modus vivendi* that had existed in the peaceful days of Bishop Cautinus and unleashed, if not actively fuelled, religious animosities" (Brennan 1985, p. 329).

Gregory is well aware that forced baptisms were not in accordance with ecclesiastical tradition; therefore, the actual role of the bishop may have been downplayed, even though he still received praise for finally "overcoming" the internal division of the city. This last point may have been the most important one for Gregory, who always focused his prime attention on the leading role of a bishop in his *civitas*, propagating a role model adopted by the historian himself.[26] If interpreted from this perspective, the episode is first of all not a story praising the conversion of the Jews—luckily enough, it was not imitated by other bishops of Merovingian Gaul—but rather an illustration of the episcopal office as the focal point of civic identity.

EXPRESSIONS OF JEWISH IDENTITY

In general, Jews were able to keep their status from Roman times through the Merovingian period. Bernard Bachrach comments:

> The Jews of Gaul . . . seem to have been too important and to have had too many influential friends and supporters to have been victimized successfully and in a

sustained manner by barbarian monarchs who lacked the administrative resources sufficient to the task. When a powerful royal presence developed in Gaul with the Carolingian dynasty, the Jews of the *regnum Francorum* . . . were not a shattered remnant that had been battered by Merovingian persecution but rather an important element in a new Europe.   (1977, p. 65)

A change in Jewish life only occurred in the Carolingian era: the area of Jewish settlement, which in Merovingian times was confined to the south, gradually extended to northern Gaul and the Rhineland. In the East Frankish kingdom, Jewish communities were founded only in Ottonian times, from the tenth century onward. However, growing restrictions on slave ownership made it difficult for Jews to maintain their rural possessions. According to Lotter, the Jewish upper class, still present in Merovingian times, gradually disappeared, but perhaps only after the end of the Carolingian period (2003b, pp. 357–358). Northern France and northeastern Germany were the core regions in which a distinct kind of Jewish life, Ashkenazic Judaism, developed in the eleventh century and gave birth to the school of the Tosafists who focused on the study of the Bible and Rabbinic literature. The Tosafists may be regarded as a cultural and religious expression of Ashkenazic Jewish identity at the beginning of high medieval Judaism in central Europe. Slightly later, the Hassidei Ashkenaz, a mystical and ethical movement, was another expression of the religious vitality of a distinct kind of European Judaism.

By contrast, no such movement can be found in Merovingian Gaul. "Merovingian" Jewry was basically late Roman Jewry that did not develop a cultural profile of its own. In general, there is no reason to assume that Jews living in the Merovingian kingdoms felt a need to express a distinct Jewish identity, if they had one.[27] Such expressions can be found only in exceptional cases. When Gregory of Tours describes the solemn entry of king Guntram at Orléans, he mentions the Jews as a group of their own. They sang praises in their own language (*hinc lingua Syrorum, hinc Latinorum, hinc etiam ipsorum Iudaeorum*), which must be regarded as an expression of their distinct identity (Devroey 1995, p. 61; *Decem libri historiarum*, 8, 1; Geisel 1998, pp. 279–282). However, it was a very special occasion, and it was also in the very best interest of the historian—and of the king—to count on the presence of the Jews to add to the solemn character of the event. In this context, Jews appear as a minority group whose presence testified to the diversity and magnitude of Guntram's kingdom; it can be compared to other kinds of rulership described as imperial, where embassies from various peripheral regions, from subjected peoples and foreign lands, greeted the ruler in the center of his vast empire. Guntram was certainly not an imperial ruler, but Gregory makes an effort to highlight the magnitude of his royal authority. He includes in his description various royal subjects who added color to the diversity of Guntram's kingdom, a kingdom that should be imagined as consisting of a conglomerate of "peripheries," regions, and groups, all of which pay homage to the "great" king.

Gregory gives another reason for the presence of Jews at the Orléans *adventus*: they wanted to impress the king, hoping that he might grant them funds to rebuild their synagogue which had been destroyed by a Christian mob. Guntram, however, rejected this claim, which is interpreted by Gregory as evidence for his good qualities as a Christian ruler. He knew the theological difference between the "New" and the "Old" Israel.

The Jews fulfilled a twofold purpose in Gregory's narrative: they were a living testimony to the vastness of Guntram's royal—possibly imperial—rule,[28] and they offered a convenient occasion for Guntram to show his theological expertise. Needless to say, the twofold purpose is perfectly in line with Gregory's overall tendency to describe Guntram as a model king embodying the ideal of a perfect Christian, Merovingian rule. Therefore, we need not interpret the singing of praises in "their" language as a genuine expression of Jewish identity that would have been motivated by a wish felt by the Jews themselves to highlight publicly their own, distinct self-image; the occasion was motivated first by the predicament of the Jews who had lost their synagogue, and by the wish of the historiographer—and of those responsible for organizing Guntram's solemn entry—to stage a grandiose entry faintly reminiscent of imperial triumphs of Antiquity.

Another exceptional case in which Jewish "identity" is given public expression is at the beginning of the Clermont conversion narrative. A Jew who has converted to Christianity was mocked by another Jew, pouring rancid oil on him. It is important to note that it was an individual Jew taking action in this case; he does not seem to have acted as the representative of his community. At the end of the affair, the Jewish community split, some Jews converting to Christianity while others emigrated to Marseille. Significantly, according to Gregory, they "returned" (*redditi sunt*) to Marseille, which may imply that some Jews living in Clermont originated from there. May we speculate that the Jew mocking the recent convert belonged to the second group (Goffart 1985, p. 493)? He clearly resented the conversion of his fellow Jew, and those emigrating ("returning") to Marseille also adopted a negative attitude to Jewish conversion, which could give rise to the hypothesis that the person mocking the convert may have belonged to a group of (recent?) Jewish migrants having come north to Clermont. As already mentioned, a considerable part of the community of Clermont declined to leave their city of origin; they chose, rather, to change their religion than to leave their hometown. Goffart comments, "If the effect of the newcomers was to arrest and reverse the tendency of the long-settled majority toward assimilation, then the crisis of 576 came to a point when the two elements could be detached from each other by Avitus's action" (1985, p. 493f.).

The episode clearly shows that "Merovingian" Jewry was not a uniform community; it consisted of various groups with a differing degree of attachment both to their respective cities of origin and their ancestral religion. Those Jews who chose to stay on in Clermont probably did not feel a need to give expression to their distinct identity; they chose rather to remain citizens of Clermont. The principal obligation they felt was toward their *civitas*, perhaps not unlike Gregory's own conviction. The Jews migrating between Marseille and Clermont were of a different orientation, with their prime obligation being geared towards their ancestral religion.

CONCLUSION

Jews living in the Merovingian kingdoms were the most important minority. They were perceived as such, but not as outsiders, and they also regarded themselves as a distinct group within Merovingian society. However, they were regarded neither as migrants nor as foreigners or strangers. Being part of the Roman provincial population, they kept their traditional Roman identity, which their Christian neighbors mostly accepted. From a social and cultural perspective, the Jews were an element of Merovingian society that we might call conservative: they preserved Roman, Mediterranean traditions. At the same time, they transmitted Judaism to later, Carolingian times, when Frankish Judaism entered a new period of its existence, marked by a gradual territorial shift to the north and a slow reception of Rabbinic traditions.

By contrast, the most important group of migrants can probably be found among Irish ascetics coming to and living in Merovingian Gaul. Unlike the Jews, they did not continue a tradition started in late-Roman times, nor did they keep their separate identity into the high medieval period. However, the presence of both Jews and Irish monks in Francia testifies to the cultural diversity and vitality of the Merovingian world.

NOTES

1. As Goffart observed, "Typically, the word 'outsider,' *extraneus*, occurs only in reference, not to a foreigner, but to someone whose claims to belonging to the Frankish royal family were disputed (6.24; 7.27)" (1982, p. 92).
2. For the imperial period, see the comprehensive treatment by Solin 1983, pp. 598–789 and specifically for Gaul (pp. 753–760). In Gaul, there are few hints at contact with Egypt, compared to numerous ones referring to Syria, probably including Asia Minor.
3. Ewig 1964, p. 388; Demougeot 1972, p. 924: The old Gallic liturgy shows stronger eastern influences than the Roman one. It is also remarkable that oriental saints were venerated much earlier in Gaul than in Rome, where only Pope Symmachus (498–415) allowed the spread of oriental saints' cults, which did, however, include cults from Egypt, which were almost entirely absent in Gaul (Ewig 1964, p. 398).
4. A Monophysite priest from Syria, traveling in Gaul in 560, made contact with Nicetius of Lyon (Ewig 1964, p. 387). According to Gregory of Tours, in 591 an Armenian bishop visited Tours in order to ask for help rebuilding his church, which had been devastated by the Persians (Greg. Tur. *Hist.* 10. 24). For his *Liber vitae patrum*, Gregory relied on the assistance of a Syrian translator of the legend of the Seven Sleepers (Ewig 1964, p. 387). Interestingly, "out of the several hundred miracle stories that he composed or recorded, only four involve Jews, and of these, a single one takes place in Gaul; the three other stories came to him at second or third hand from the eastern Mediterranean" (Goffart 1985, pp. 474–475).
5. The last evidence is in the *Vita Columbani* 1. 21 (Devroey and Brouwer 2000, p. 340).

6. On the increase of the number of Syrian merchants and clerics in the West, see Solin 1983, p. 603. For the role of oriental merchants in Merovingian trade, see Devroey and Brouwer 2000, p. 339.

7. As in Orléans in 585, attested by Gregory of Tours, *Decem libri historiarum*, 8. 1. The interpretation of a passage in Salvian of Marseille (*De gubernatione dei*, 4, p. 69) is contested; some have taken it to mean that Syrians in fifth-century Gaul were to some extent merchants and "bankers"; according to Solin, this latter meaning was even restricted to Gaul (1983, p. 647). For Devroey and Brouwer (2000, p. 343), however, Salvian's statement refers to his memories of his earlier life in the imperial capital of Trier; for problems associated with the term *colonies*, see Devroey and Brouwer (2000, p. 340).

8. In Merovingian Gaul, only two Syrians have been identified as merchants (Devroey 1995, p. 54).

9. The inscription on a bronze seal (Noy 1993, nr. 190; *Corpus Inscriptionum Iudaicarum*, 667) possibly from Avignon, shows a menorah and two etrogs, typical Jewish symbols, next to the name Ianu(arius). As noted by David Noy, "The use of Latin rather than Hebrew on a private seal provides some support for a relatively early date" (1993, p. 267). The inscription from Vienne (Noy 1993, p. 200; *Corpus Inscriptionum Iudaicarum*, nr. 666), reads "Shmuel bar Justu" in Hebrew characters. The dating proposed by former scholars—on palaeographical grounds—to the sixth or seventh century is rejected by Noy (following Blumenkranz); the latter dates it to the tenth century, as does Toch 2013, p. 70. In either case, the inscription provides evidence for the use of Hebrew to express Jewish identity in the early medieval period (as distinct from late Roman practice). In general, Jewish communities in the western Mediterranean were marked by parallel processes of an increasing use of Latin and Hebrew, with Greek receding from the seventh century onward (Lotter 2003a, p. 94).

10. There is epigraphic evidence for the presence of rabbis in early medieval Africa, Italy, and Spain, but not in Gaul (Lotter 2003a, p. 131).

11. See the inscription in Noy 1993, nr. 189, *Corpus Inscriptionum Iudaicarum,* nr. 670, from Narbonne, dated to 688/689, written in Latin and Hebrew; on the overall tendency, see Lotter 2003a, pp. 98, 108–110.

12. For text, translation, and commentary, see Linder 1997, no. 436: "We order, that no one shall be obliged to do anything or be summoned in any way whatsoever, on the Sabbath day or on the other days on which the Jews keep the reverence of their cult, for it is clear that the remaining days should suffice for the fiscal revenues and for private litigation."

13. There is no reason to assume that, as postulated by Katz 1937, Jews lost their civic or legal status, being considered as foreigners (Brennan 1985, pp. 333–334). What is more, Jews were not subject to ecclesiastical law as claimed by Brennan (1985, p. 335). For the issues concerning Jews included in the *Lex Romana Visigothorum*, see Lotter 1997, no. 435–447, p. 851.

14. "Gregory does not in any way single out the Jews as outsiders" (Goffart 1985, p. 476).

15. *Iudaei, accensis lampadibus, plangendo prosequebantur* (Gregory of Tours, *Liber vitae patrum*, 6. 7).

16. Remarkably, the first Merovingian council forbidding mixed marriages, meeting in Orléans in 533, does not take up formulations from earlier church councils but from Roman secular legislation (the *Lex Romana Visigothorum*). This practice indicates the authority given to Roman law under Merovingian rule (Mikat 1995, p. 95). For text, translation, and commentary of canon 19 of the council of Orléans II, see Linder 1997, nr. 814.

The problem of mixed marriages is the only one that disappeared after the middle of the sixth century (Lotter 2000, p. 527).

17. *Iudaeis valde carus et subditus erat, non pro salute, ut pastoris cura debet esse sollicita, sed pro comparandis speciebus, quas cum hic blandiretur, et illi se adulatores manifestissime declararent, maiori quam constabant pretio venundabant* (Gregory of Tours, *Decem libri historiarum*, 4. 12). Significantly, this bishop, Cautinus, was the predecessor of Avitus, who was in turn very much cherished by Gregory (Brennan 1985, p. 323).

18. Cautions introduced during this period can be found in a baraitha (a traditional, oral law not included in the Mishnah) of the Babylonian Talmud (Yebamoth 47b; p. 52). See also Goodman 1989, 1994; Cohen 1992.

19. See the Talmudic story about Rabbi Jochanan in which a gentile woman exclaims: "A religion which teaches such concern for the public welfare is worthy to adopt as one's own," after which she converts to Judaism (Hoenig 1965, p. 54). The atractiveness of Judaism is also attested by *Codex Theodosianus* 19.9.4, hinting at forced as well as voluntary converts: . . . *ut eos nec invitos nec volentes caeno propriae sectae confundat* (Mikat 1995, pp. 75–77). See also Lotter 1997, p. 876: "les Juifs se presentent à nous comme un groupe de population ayant encore un sentiment de sa propre valeur, et qui a développé dans son mode de vie imprégné de religiosité une force d'attraction."

20. On the prohibition of "Judaizing" practices, adopted in imitation of Jewish customs, by the Synod of Orléans of 538, canon 31, see Lotter 1997, p. 871.

21. Lotter 2000, p. 529. However, there may have been a local conversion at Bourges, an event that is related in the *Vita Sulpicii Episcopi Biturigi* (Linder 1978, p. 415; Lotter 1984, p. 50; see also Bachrach 1977, pp. 60–62).

22. *Plebs Arverna etenim, bifido discissa tumultu, urbe manens una non erat una fide* (Venantius Fortunatus, *Carmina*, 5. 5, l. 17–18). Remarkably, the Clermont incident took place after the murder of King Sigibert in 575, with his successor being a minor (Goffart 1985, pp. 488; 492). Clerical factionalism in the sixth century may have involved the charge of Judaizing; Avitus had only gained the bishopric after factional dispute, and due to strong opposition, his consecration was performed in Metz instead of Clermont (Brennan 1985, pp. 322–323).

23. See also Lotter 1997, p. 877, on a certain resignation felt by ecclesiastics whose missionary efforts always proved vain. As a case in point, one might mention Gregory of Tours describing the discussion between King Chilperic, the Jew Priscus, and himself.

24. *Vi ego vos confiteri Dei filium non impello* (Gregory of Tours, *Decem libri historiarum*, 5.11; Claude 1991, p. 142). The use of force is also denied by Venantius Fortunatus.

25. By contrast, Rouche 1979, pp. 105–124, is highly speculative and generalizing, proposing that both Visigothic and Merovingian rulers followed the example set by Byzantine emperors when they took measures against Jews of their realm. In this instance, Mezei 2005 should be used with caution, due to several mistakes.

26. This point is further highlighted by Gregory's very first sentence, serving as introduction to the whole episode: *Et quia semper Deus noster sacerdotes suos glorificare dignatur, quid Arverno de Iudaeis hoc anno contigerit pandam* (hist. 8. 1).

27. According to Lotter, the growing use of Hebrew can be taken as evidence not so much for a Hebrew "revival" or "renaissance," but for a gradual process of identity formation, which was fostered by the Palestinian patriarchate (which finally disappeared in 429) and by the spread of rabbinic teaching (2003a, p. 135).

28. Significantly, the Jews are said to have acclaimed Guntram as follows: *Omnes gentes te adorent tibique genu flectant adque tibi sint subditae* (hist. 8. 1); the words are adapted from a Jewish prayer (Goffart 1985, p. 478 n. 17).

WORKS CITED

Ancient Sources

Anthimus, *Medicus*. E. Liechtenhan (ed.). (1928). *De observatione ciborum ad Theodoricum regem Francorum epistula*. Corpus medicorum Latinorum 8.1. Leipzig: Teubner.

Concilia Galliae, a. 511–a. 695. C. De Clercq (ed.). (1963). CCSL 148A. Turnhout: Brepols.

Fragmentum testamenti Ansoaldi, episcopi Pictavensis. E.-J. Tardif (ed.). (1899). *Les chartes Mérovingiennes de l'abbaye de Noirmoutier. Avec une étude sur la chronologie du règne de Dagobert II* (pp. 30–31). Paris: Larose.

Frey, J.-B. (1936). *Corpus Inscriptionum Iudaicarum. Recueil des Inscriptions Juives qui vont du IIIᵉ siècle avant Jésus-Christ au VIIᵉ siècle de notre ère 1*. Vatican City: PIAC.

Gregory the Great, *Registrarum epistolarum*. D. L. Norberg (ed.). (1982). CCSL 140–140A. Turnhout: Brepols.

Gregory of Tours, *Decem libri historiarum*. W. Arndt and B. Krusch (eds.). (1885). MGH SRM 1.1. Hanover: Hahn.

Gregory of Tours, *Liber vitae patrum*. W. Arndt and B. Krusch (eds.). (1885). MGH SRM 1.2 (pp. 211–293). Hanover: Hahn.

Jonas of Bobbio, *Vitae Columbani*. B. Krusch (ed.). (1902). MGH SRM 4 (pp. 1–156). Hanover: Hahn.

Noy, D. (1993). *Jewish Inscriptions in Western Europe* (vol. 1). Cambridge: Cambridge University Press.

Salvian of Marseille, *De gubernatione dei: Du gouvernement de Dieu*. G. Lagarrigue (ed.). (1975). Sources Chrétiennes 220. Paris: Editions du Cerf.

Sidonius Apollinaris, *Epistulae*. C. Lütjohann (ed.). (1887). MGH AA 8. Hanover: Hahn.

Venantius Fortunatus, *Carmina*. F. Leo (ed.). (1881). MGH AA 4. Hanover: Hahn.

Vita Caesarii. B. Krusch (ed.). (1896). MGH SRM 3 (pp. 433–499). Hanover: Hahn.

Modern Sources

Angenendt, A. (1982). "Die irische *peregrinatio* und ihre Auswirkungen auf dem Kontinent vor dem Jahre 800." In H. Löwe (ed.), *Veröffentlichungen des Europa-Zentrums Tübingen. Kulturwissenschaftliche Reihe*. vol. 1 (pp. 52–79). Stuttgart: Klett-Cotta.

Bachrach, B. S. (1977). *Early Medieval Jewish Policy in Western Europe*. Minneapolis: University of Minnesota Press.

Blumenkranz, B. (1960). *Juifs et Chrétiens dans le Monde Occidental 430–1096*. Études Juives 2. Paris/La Haye: Mouton.

Blumenkranz, B. (1961). "Die christlich-jüdische Missionskonkurrenz (3.–6. Jhd.)." *Klio* 39: 227–233.

Brennan, B. (1985). "The Conversion of the Jews of Clermont in AD 576." *Journal of Theological Studies* 36: 321–337.

Brunner, K. (1992). "Juden und Christen im Frühmittelalter." In H. Birkham (ed.), *Die Juden in ihrer mittelalterlichen Umwelt* (pp. 37–56). Bern: Lang.

Claude, D. (1985). *Der Handel im westlichen Mittelmeer während des Frühmittelalters. Bericht über ein Kolloquium der Kommission für die Altertumskunde Mittel- und Nordeuropas im Jahre 1980*. Göttingen: Vandenhoeck & Ruprecht.

Claude, D. (1991). "Gregor von Tours und die Juden: Die Zwangsbekehrungen von Clermont." *Historisches Jahrbuch* 111: 137–147.

Cohen, S. J. D. (1992). "Was Judaism in Antiquity a Missionary Religion?" In M. Mor (ed.), *Jewish Assimilation, Acculturation, and Accommodation. Past Traditions, Current Issues, and Future Prospects* (pp. 14–23). Creighton University Studies in Jewish Civilization 2. Lanham, MD: University Press of America.

Demougeot, É. (1972). "Gallia I." In *Reallexikon für Antike und Christentum* 8 (pp. 822–827). Stuttgart: Hiersemann.

Devroey, J.-P. (1995). "Juifs et Syriens. À propos de la géographie économique de la Gaule au Haut Moyen Âge." In J.-M. Duvosquel and E. Thoen (eds.), *Peasants and Townsmen in Medieval Europe. Studia in honorem Adriaan Verhulst* (pp. 51–72). Ghent: Snoeck-Ducaju & Zoon.

Devroey, J.-P., and Brouwer, C. (2000). "La participation des Juifs au commerce dans le mode franc. VIᵉ–Xᵉ siècles." In A. Dierkens and J.-M. Sansterre (eds.), *Voyages et voyageurs à Byzance et en Occident du VIᵉ au XIᵉ siècle; actes du colloque international organisé par la Section d'Histoire de l'Université Libre de Bruxelles en collaboration avec le Département des Sciences Historiques de l'Université de Liège (5–7 Mai 1994)* (pp. 343–354). Brussels: Université Libre de Bruxelles, Section d'Histoire.

Dietz, M. (2005). *Wandering Monks, Virgins, and Pilgrims. Ascetic Travel in the Mediterranean World, A.D. 300–800.* University Park: Pennsylvania State University Press.

Effros, B. (2002). *Creating Community with Food and Drink in Merovingian Gaul.* New York: Palgrave Macmillan.

Ewig, E. (1964). "Die Verehrung orientalischer Heiliger im spätrömischen Gallien und im Merowingerreich." In H. Atsma (ed.), *Spätantikes und Fränkisches Gallien. Gesammelte Schriften (1952–1973)* (pp. 393–310). Munich: Artemis.

Flachenecker, H. (1995). *Schottenklöster. Irische Benediktinerkonvente im hochmittelalterlichen Deutschland.* Quellen und Forschungen aus dem Gebiet der Geschichte NF 18. Paderborn: Schöningh.

Geisel, C. (1998). *Die Juden im Frankenreich. Von den Merowingern bis zum Tode Ludwigs des Frommen.* Freiburger Beiträge zur Mittelalterlichen Geschichte 10. Frankfurt-am-Main: Lang.

Goffart, W. (1982). "Foreigners in the Histories of Gregory of Tours." *Florilegium* 4: 80–99.

Goffart, W. (1985). "The Conversions of Avitus of Clermont, and Similar Passages in Gregory of Tours." In J. Neusner and E. S. Frerichs (eds.), *"To See Ourselves As Others See Us". Christians, Jews, "Others" in Late Antiquity* (pp. 473–497). Chico, CA: Scholars Press.

Goodman, M. (1989). "Proselytizing in Rabbinic Judaism" *Journal of Jewish Studies* 40: 175–185.

Goodman, M. (1994). *Mission and Conversion. Proselytizing in the Religious History of the Roman Empire.* Oxford: Clarendon Press.

Heil, J. (1998). "Agobard, Amolo, das Kirchengut und die Juden von Lyon" *Francia* 25: 39–76.

Hoenig, S. B. (1965). "Conversion during the Talmudic Period." In D. M. Eichhorn (ed.), *Conversion to Judaism. A History and Analysis* (pp. 33–66). New York: KTAV Publishing House.

Juster, J. (1914). *Les Juifs dans l'Empire romain* 1. *Leur condition juridique, économique et sociale.* Paris: P. Geuthner.

Katz, S. (1937). *The Jews in the Visigothic and Frankish Kingdoms of Spain and Gaul.* Monographs of the Mediaeval Academy of America 12. Cambridge, MA: Indiana University Press.

Kötting, B. (1950). *Peregrinatio religiosa. Wallfahrten in der Antike und das Pilgerwesen in der alten Kirche.* Forschungen zur Volkskunde 33/35. Münster: Regensberg.

Linder, A. (1978). "Christliche—jüdische Konfrontation im kirchlichen Frühmittelalter." In H. Frohnes, H.-W. Gensichen, and G. Kretschmar (eds.), *Kirchengeschichte als Missionsgeschichte* 2(1), pp. 397–341. Munich: Kaiser.

Linder, A. (1997). *The Jews in the Legal Sources of the Early Middle Ages*. Detroit: Wayne State University Press.

Lohse, T. (2015). "Heimat und Heimatlosigkeit bei Columban von Luxeuil." *Zeitschrift für Geschichtswissenschaft* 63: 237–249.

Lotter, F. (1997). "La crainte du prosélytisme et la peur du contact: les Juifs dans les actes des synodes mérovingiens." In M. Rouche (ed.), *Clovis* (pp. 850–879). Paris: Presses de l'Université de Paris-Sorbonne.

Lotter, F. (1984). "Zur Entwicklung des Judenrechts im christlichen Abendland bis zu den Kreuzzügen." In T. Klein, V. Losemann, and G. Mai (eds.), *Judentum und Antisemitismus von der Antike bis zur Gegenwart* (pp. 41–63). Düsseldorf: Droste Verlag.

Lotter, F. (2000). "Zur Stellung der Juden im Frankenreich der Merowinger und Karolinger." *Aschkenas* 10: 525–533.

Lotter, F. (2003a). "Die Grabinschriften des lateinischen Westens als Zeugnisse jüdischen Lebens im Übergang von der Antike zum Mittelalter (4.-9. Jahrhundert)." In C. Cluse, A. Haverkamp, and I. J. Yuval (eds.), *Jüdische Gemeinden und ihr christlicher Kontext in kulturräumlich vergleichender Betrachtung* (pp. 87–150). Hanover: Hahn.

Lotter, F. (2003b). "Zur sozialen Hierarchie der Judenheit in Spätantike und Frühmittelalter." *Aschkenas* 13: 333–359.

Lotter, F. (2004). "Sind christliche Quellen zur Erforschung der Geschichte der Juden im Frühmittelalter weitgehend unbrauchbar?" *Historische Zeitschrift* 278: 311–328.

Mezei, M. (2005). "Jewish Communities in the Merovingian Towns in the Second Half of the Sixth Century As Described by Gregory of Tours." *Chronica* 5: 19–29.

Mikat, P. (1995). *Die Judengesetzgebung der merowingisch-fränkischen Konzilien*. Nordrhein-Westfälische Akademie der Wissenschaften und der Künste, Geisteswissenschaften, Vorträge G 335. Opladen: VS Verlag für Sozialwissenschaften.

Parente, F. (1980). "La controversia fra Ebrei e Cristiani in Francia e in Spagna dal VI al IX secolo." In *Gli Ebrei nell'alto medioevo (XXVI Settimane di Studio del Centro italiano di studi sull'alto medioevo* 2 (pp. 529–539). Spoleto: Centro Italiano di Studi sull'Alto Medioevo.

Rekdal, J. E. (1991). "The Irish Ideal of Pilgrimage as Reflected in the Tradition of Colum Cille (Columba)." In *Proceedings of the Third Symposium of Societas Celtologica Nordica Held in Oslo 1–2 November 1991* (pp. 67–83). Uppsala: AUU.

Reydellet, M. (1992). "La conversion des juifs de Clermont en 576." In L. Holtz and J. C. Fredouille (eds.), *De Tertullien aux Mozarabes, I: Antiquité Tardive et Christianisme Ancien (IIIe–VIe siècles). Mélanges offerts à Jacques Fontaine à l'occasion de son 70e anniversaire* (pp. 371–329). Collection des Études Augustiniennes, Série Moyen-âge et Temps Moderne 26. Paris: Institut d'Études Augustiniennes.

Riché, P. (1981). "Columbanus, his Followers and the Merovingian Church." In H. B. Clark and M. Brennan (eds.), *Columbanus and Merovingian Monasticism* (pp. 59–72). BAR International series 113. Oxford: B. A. R. Reprinted in P. Riché (1993). *Education et culture dans l'occident medieval*. Variorum Collected Studies Series 420, nr. 5. Aldershot: Ashgate.

Rouche, M. (1979). "Les baptêmes forcés de Juifs en Gaule mérovingienne et dans l'Empire d'Orient." In V. Nikiprowetzky (ed.), *De l'antijudaïsme antique à l'antisémitisme contemporain*, (pp. 105–124). Lille: Presses Universitaires.

Schäferdiek, K. (1982). "Columbans Wirken im Frankenreich (591–612)." In H. Löwe (ed.), *Die Iren und Europa im früheren Mittelalter. Veröffentlichungen des Europa-Zentrums Tübingen. Kulturwissenschaftliche Reihe* (pp. 171–201). Stuttgart: Klett-Cotta.

Schieffer, R. (2015). *Die ältesten Judengemeinden in Deutschland*. Nordrhein-Westfälische Akademie der Wissenschaften und der Künste, Geisteswissenschaften, Vorträge G 450. Paderborn: Schöningh.

Solin, H. (1983). "Juden und Syrer im westlichen Teil der römischen Welt. Eine ethnisch-demographische Studie mit besonderer Berücksichtigung der sprachlichen Zustände." *Aufstieg und Niedergang der Römischen Welt* 2, 29 (pp. 598–589). Berlin: Walter de Gruyter.

Stemberger, G. (1993). "Zwangstaufen von Juden im 4. bis 7. Jahrhundert—Mythos oder Wirklichkeit?" In C. Thoma, G. Stermberger, and J. Maier (eds.), *Judentum—Ausblicke und Einsichten. Festgabe für Kurt Schubert zum 70. Geburtstag* (pp. 81–114). Judentum und Umwelt 43. Frankfurt-am-Main: Lang.

Toch, M. (2001). *"Dunkle Jahrhunderte." Gab es ein jüdisches Frühmittelalter?* Kleine Schriften des Arye-Maimon-Instituts 4. Trier: Arye-Maimon-Institut für Geschichte der Juden.

Toch, M. (2013). *The Economic History of European Jews. Late Antiquity and Early Middle Ages*. Études sur le Judaïsme Médiéval 66. Leiden: Brill.

Wasserstein, A. (1996). "The Number and Provenance of Jews in Graeco-Roman Antiquity: A Note on Population Statistics." In R. Katzoff, Y. Petroff, and D. M. Schaps (eds.), *Classical Studies in Honour of David Sohlberg* (pp. 307–317). Ramat Gan: Bar-Ilan University Press.

Wood, I. (1994). *The Merovingian Kingdoms 450–751*. London: Longman.

CHAPTER 7

···

HUMAN REMAINS AND WHAT THEY CAN TELL US ABOUT STATUS AND IDENTITY IN THE MEROVINGIAN PERIOD

···

ANDREA CZERMAK

OSTEOLOGICAL examinations of excavated human remains are a central component of anthropological studies. They provide the required basic information for demographic reconstructions such as age at death or biologically manifested sexual characteristics (see Perez, Chapter 9, this volume). They also pay attention to pathologies, for instance, such as signs of wear and tear on joints and teeth, diseases, or signs of violence visible on the skeletal remains (e.g., White and Folkens 2005). These data provide information about general health and living conditions, physical workload, and exposure to substantial danger and violence, which, in turn, allow researchers, with certain limitations of course, to posit conclusions about social structures and relations within a population.

In the last two decades, human remains have found their way more frequently from physical anthropologists' study collections into modern laboratories, and isotope analyses have increasingly become a "must-have" in archaeological studies (although for the case of France, see Effros, Chapter 4, this volume). Whereas oxygen and strontium isotopes are used to gain information about mobility and migration, such as to identify "nonlocal" individuals (Bentley and Knipper 2005; Bentley 2006), stable isotope analyses of carbon and nitrogen ratios are a useful tool for the general characterization of individuals' diets (Ambrose and Norr 1993; Lee-Thorp 2008).

Nowadays, large-scale studies of burial sites employ quantitative methods aiming to describe the "average" individual. In contrast, new microhistorical approaches put emphasis on individuals and small populations. Studies focusing on an individual's life history can offer insight into the everyday experiences of people and, when used comparatively, can shed light on social differences within a society. By asking "large questions in small places" (Joyner 1999, p. 1), individuals stand in as representative "agents" of history to reveal the details and differentiation of social change within a population (LeRoy Ladurie 1975, 1979; Ginzburg 1980; van Dülmen 2001). Social and cultural changes are often reflected in individuals' life histories. Diet does reflect residence and subsistence, and thus can potentially display cultural changes, as well as social differences within a population.

The period between the fourth and seventh centuries was marked not only by far-reaching economic and political changes, but also significant social and cultural developments in Europe (e.g., Martin 1995; Whittaker 1997; Jussen 1998; Demandt 2007; Becher 2011). The process of transformation continued over several decades and led to new social structures and cultural identities. Stable isotope analysis on human remains can provide important clues into this transitional period. It can, for instance, detect potential changes in subsistence levels sustained during an individual's life history, in addition to suggesting at which period of life the change took place. An interpretation of individuals' biological data in a broader archaeological and historical context can help answer questions about social status and identities in the Merovingian period.

Stable Isotope Analysis

Isotopes are variants of a particular chemical element, which have the same number of protons but differ in neutron numbers in the atom's nucleus. The atomic number of an element is equal to the number of its electrons (or protons, respectively) and identifies the specific element. The number of nucleons, the sum of protons and neutrons in the atomic nucleus, provide the mass number. For example, the atomic number of carbon is 6, representing six protons in the nucleus. The most common form of carbon (^{12}C) in the atmosphere is composed of six neutrons in the nucleus added to the six protons there, leading to a mass number of twelve. However, two additional stable isotopes naturally occur in carbon, including (^{13}C) with one additional neutron and (^{14}C) with two additional neutrons. Those isotopes of an element that do not undergo radioactive decay are called stable isotopes. Ratios of stable isotopes are quantified with an isotope rationing mass spectrometer; the abundances are typically expressed relative to a standard and as ratios of the rare to common isotope in delta (δ) notation in per mill (δ^xE: $[(R_{sample}/R_{standard}-1] \times 1000$); for example, nitrogen as ^{15}N/^{14}N = δ^{15}N and carbon as ^{13}C/^{12}C = δ^{13}C. As the data gives the ratio heavier to lighter isotopes of the sample relative to the ratio of a standard, negative δ values mean less heavy isotopes in the sample compared to the standard (for a review of stable isotopes, see West et al. 2006; Lee-Thorp 2008).

Stable isotope analysis is widely used in food chemistry, ecology, archaeology, and related sciences (e.g., Aggarwal, Habicht-Mauche, and Juarez 2008). Meanwhile, isotope analyses of bone and teeth from archaeological sites have become a routine addition to archaeological research to reconstruct life parameters, addressing questions relating to diet, dietary differentiation, life history, and other topics of interest. While earlier research focused primarily on human subsistence, economy, and interaction of systems, more recent approaches have also considered how social rules are a dynamic force of cultural change. They have highlighted, for instance, the contributions of acting individuals, social practice, and identity to shaping social worlds and political structures. Stable isotope analysis in archaeology thus considers both subsistence and social reasons that cause human dietary and mobility decisions. It addresses questions related to social dynamics, including the collective social and political motivations for human mobility, socially constructed food acquisition, and its distribution within communities.

Stable isotope analyses draw on the larger and longer-established field of isotope geochemistry in earth and plant sciences (e.g., Craig 1953, 1954; Park and Epstein 1960). The method was then adapted in ecology to reconstruct the complex dietary behavior of animals in their specific habitats, as well as to scale trophic structures (e.g., DeNiro and Epstein 1978, 1981; Schoeninger, DeNiro and Tauber 1983; Schoeninger and DeNiro 1983, 1984; Minagawa and Wada 1984).

Eventually, stable isotope analysis found its way to archaeology. Early applications focused mostly on analysis of human skeletal tissues as a way to reconstruct major shifts in human diet such as during the Neolithic transition. Current stable isotope approaches include high-resolution analyses, which are helping to define changes in the human diet more accurately. Hence, we are able to address questions such as socially mediated food access and diet choices, mortuary practices, and social identity (see review of Makarewicz and Sealy 2015).

Isotope ratios in body tissues, predominantly carbon, nitrogen, oxygen, and strontium,[1] are used as proxies for measuring dietary strategies, ecological change, and mobility patterns (e.g., Lee-Thorp 2008; Nehlich et al 2009; West, Bowen, Dawson, and Tu 2010). The approach is based on the assumption that the isotopic composition of human tissue reflects the isotopic composition of the food and water ingested by that individual (Ambrose and Norr 1993; Jim, Ambrose, and Evershed 2004). As people live in different habitats and under different environmental conditions, their consumed food is also expected to be different. Carbon and nitrogen isotopes are the main indicator for dietary analysis, providing important hints on food sources, such as the predominant consumption of C_3 (e.g., wheat) or C_4 (e.g., millet) plants, marine or terrestrial food, and the amount of animal protein. Collagen, the organic, protein-rich part of bone and tooth remains, by contrast, is used for C/N-isotope analyses, as carbon and nitrogen in collagen originate from the protein component of the human diet (Ambrose and Norr 1994; Jim, Ambrose and Evershed 2004).

More specifically, nitrogen isotopes provide insight into dietary behaviors related to protein intake. Nitrogen isotope ratios fractionate during physiological processes within an organism, resulting in increasing values with each step in the food chain (e.g., Hedges and Reynard 2007; Caut, Angulo, and Courchamp 2009). The stepwise enrichment of ^{15}N with each upward shift in trophic level is used to investigate the role of animal protein, such as meat or dairy products in the human diet (on animal husbandry, see Yvinec and Baume, Chapter 33, this volume). Generally, the trophic level of consumers and the relative contributions of plant and animal foods in omnivores are determined by comparing the $\delta^{15}N$ values of humans, with the values of herbivores and carnivores in the same ecosystem. However, this underestimates the complexity of the distribution of nitrogen isotopes in ecosystems and how dietary ^{15}N is incorporated into body tissues and then expressed in collagen $\delta^{15}N$ values. For example, it does not account for the distribution of the isotopes in the plant portion of the food, the incorporation and fractionation into body tissues, and its actual enrichment in consumers' tissues that, according to different studies, can be between 3 and 6‰ (per mill). Thus, to interpret the $\delta^{15}N$ values of the higher trophic level of consumers in order to "reconstruct" diet, we first need to understand isotope structuring in the flora and fauna of the same ecosystem (Makarewicz and Sealy 2015).

Carbon isotopes instead provide information about the photosynthetic pathway of food plants—that is to say, they tell us about which biochemical mechanisms these organisms use to fix carbon from the atmosphere. So-called C4 plants are able to fix carbon more efficiently in dry areas with high temperatures. In temperate Europe, the C3 pathway is dominant, and millet is the only relevant C4 plant that has been introduced since the Neolithic period (e.g., Rösch 1998; Le Huray and Schutkowski 2005). The differences in the $\delta^{13}C$ values of plants that use different types of photosynthesis are passed on to the body tissues of the consumer (e.g., Tieszen et al. 1983; Farquhar et al. 1989). Carbon values can also reflect the so-called canopy effect. Namely, leaves incorporate CO_2 for photosynthesis. The presence of ^{13}C-isotope is thus lower under a canopy of leaves than in the atmosphere because most of the heavier, naturally lower, abundant version of the carbon isotope is already bound in plants. Therefore, plants growing under a dense ceiling of leaves have less access to the fresh, balanced isotope composition from the atmosphere. Thus, $\delta^{13}C$ is lower in plants growing in woodland areas, providing the potential to detect differences between species feeding in open versus forested environments (e.g., Drucker and Bocherens 2009). Similarly, we can determine whether the carbon originated from an oceanic or a terrestrial carbon cycle (Fry and Sherr 1989). The combination of $\delta^{13}C$ and $\delta^{15}N$ is used in differentiating between terrestrial, freshwater, and marine diets (e.g., Schoeninger et al. 1983; Schoeninger and DeNiro 1983, 1984).

In summary, we can distinguish between broad food categories in animal and human diets like meat versus plants, terrestrial versus aquatic protein sources, and C3 fruits and vegetables versus C4 grasses/cereals (Fig. 7.1). Stable C/N isotope ratios, however, do not reproduce exact menus. To characterize the contribution of the potential dietary sources, human isotope data are generally compared with faunal samples. Hence, the potential human data range is calculated by adding a "trophic level" to the mean value of the animal data (one trophic level = $\delta^{13}C$: 0.8–1.3‰; $\delta^{15}N$: 3–5‰).

Occasionally, a human-faunal spacing occurs in carbon data where the human data plot is less than expected for a trophic level shift along a food chain as presumed from the herbivore collagen data (e.g., Knipper et al. 2013). Such exceptions reveal that human data is not directly deducible from faunal collagen data. To get more reliable results, it is

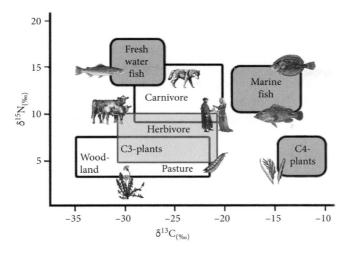

FIGURE 7.1. Schematic representation of a central European food web in the early Middle Ages, including main food sources and their isotopic position.

absolutely necessary to have access to floral data as well (on the latter, see Squatriti, Chapter 32, this volume).

Nitrogen isotope ratios in different species of wild or domestic herbivores depend on their dietary preferences, seasonality, and availability of food sources. There is no nitrogen isotope homogeneity to plant eaters. Numerous environmental, anthropogenic, and metabolic factors contribute to nitrogen isotope shifts in herbivores (Makarewicz and Sealy 2015). While most of these factors remain poorly understood, they can all have consequences, with an impact on our data, which has to be considered for interpreting the $\delta^{15}N$ values of consumers at higher trophic levels. Thus, the makeup of the human diet is not directly deducible from faunal collagen data. "Mixing models" are used as a means of estimating source contributions in human diet, in an effort to try to detangle different dietary components. They consider food sources with clearly separated isotope values. If the isotope values of the consumer, the foods, and the extent of fractionation in the consumer tissue are known, it is possible to calculate the proportion of each food in the total diet (e.g., Caut, Angulo, and Courchamp 2010; Phillips et al. 2014). The main problem with mixing models is that complex metabolisms and other factors, discussed above, cannot be incorporated. Therefore, mixing models may give all too simplistic answers to complex questions. In general, the more food sources there are in an animal's diet, the less meaningful are estimates of their importance, particularly for dietary generalists such as humans (on animals, see Yvinec and Barme, Chapter 33, this volume).

Due to the lack of settlement remains in direct association with the investigated cemeteries, faunal samples are most often not directly related to the humans, and sometimes they are not even contemporary. In addition, the number of plant and animal samples available from archaeological contexts is often too small to characterize adequately the extent of isotopic variation in food sources. Moreover, diet available in early medieval central Europe offers little variation regarding isotope composition. With no sea-fish available and millet known, but nonetheless uncommon, the possibility of differentiation is therefore extremely limited. Thus, only a small-scale variation in diet can be expected.

A comparison of bulk bone isotope composition from various early medieval cemeteries located in different environments and ecosystems in central Europe is shown in Figure 7.2. Riverside sites along the Danube in central Bavaria such as Kelheim (Strott 2006), Grossmehring (Czermak 2012), and Straubing (Hakenbeck et al. 2010), as well as Volders (McGlynn 2007), situated in an Alpine region near the River Inn in Tyrol (Austria), tend to have higher δ^{15}N isotope ratios. By contrast, sites located in the Alpine foothills such as Bruckmühl (Czermak 2012), Altenerding, Klettham (Hakenbeck et al. 2010), and Unterigling (Strott 2006) in Upper Bavaria show lower δ^{15}N. However, the sites of Obermoellern and Rathewitz (Knipper et al. 2013) in Thuringia, though situated in an entirely different environment, blend well into the isotope distribution of the previous sites. In contrast, the mean δ^{15}N ratio in Weingarten (Schutkowski et al. 1999), also located in the Alpine foothill region near Lake Constance in Baden-Wuerttemberg, is almost 2‰ (per mill) less than that in Altenerding (Upper Bavaria). This lower value corresponds to at least half a trophic level, indicating a smaller proportion of animal protein in the diet. The mean isotope ratios of the individuals buried at the Niedernai cemetery, located the Upper Rhine area, also shows slightly lower δ^{15}N, but particularly slightly less negative δ^{13}C isotope ratios. These findings, may indicate a diet containing a small amount of C4 plants like millet (Czermak et al. 2018).

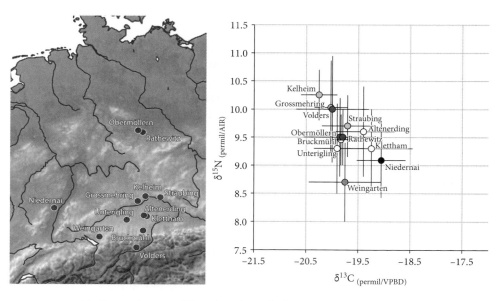

FIGURE 7.2. Median and range of data from bone-bulk isotope analysis of various early medieval sites from different environments and ecosystems in central Europe (data from Schutkowski et al. 1999; Strott 2006; McGlynn 2007; Hakenbeck et al. 2010; Czermak 2012; Knipper et al. 2013).

Isotope ratios of the early medieval cemeteries listed above display typical variation within every site. Those variations are most likely caused by local small-scale differences in diet. A relatively large distribution of isotope values within a population can be an indication, however, that the diets of some individuals could have been substantially different from the diet of the majority.

Overall, the differences between sites are far smaller than variations within each site. Generally, individuals' bone remains show the typical diet of a preindustrialized population, using common food resources in central Europe (e.g., Willerding 2003). Comparisons between individuals often show no statistically significant differences, rendering the approach of little use in providing evidence of social or cultural differentiation and changes within a community and over a specific time period.

Bones and Teeth

Carbon and nitrogen isotope ratios are usually gained from bone material, which represents an "isotope blend" of dietary intake of roughly ten years preceding an individual's death: they reflect an individual's diet during the last years of life. Bone has a relatively high turnover rate, depending on the bone type and age of the individual. Isotope signals obtained from bone bulk collagen represent an average of several years. Thus, this approach is not useful for detecting changes in diet over the course of an individual's entire lifetime.

In contrast to bone, teeth have almost no material turnover and do not remodel during lifetime. Once formed during childhood and adolescence, their element and isotope composition do not change, and so they reflect nutrition over this time span. Hence, teeth are a lifelong storage for isotopes and provide a chronology of dietary intake during childhood and youth. Teeth also offer a much higher temporal resolution than bone because the isotopic consequences of dietary changes are "averaged out" through bone remodeling (Hedges et al. 2007). Sample material from teeth is also suspected to suffer less from postdepositional chemical alterations (Lee-Thorp et al. 2003), and their appositional growth, reflected in incremental structures, provides us with a time-related, comprehensive archive of isotopes ingested during growth (Fig. 7.3).

Calcified tissue in teeth emerges periodically. The timing of the development of human teeth, the direction and rate of growth, and mineralization are all well established (e.g., Dean et al. 1993, 2014; Dean and Scandrett 1995). Tooth growth starts at the cusp of the crown, with the enamel growing upward and dentine growing downward to the apex of the root. Whereas enamel consists mainly of mineral and little organic matter, dentine is rich in collagen. Predentine, containing collagen fibers, is secreted by odontoblasts and is then mineralized by carbonate-hydroxyapatite crystal secreted from the odontoblast extensions along the collagen fibers (Beniash 2011). The daily secretion rate of dentine in human teeth ranges from 2 to 6 μm per day, resulting in short-period lines ("von Ebner's lines"). Long period lines ("Andresen lines") are formed every

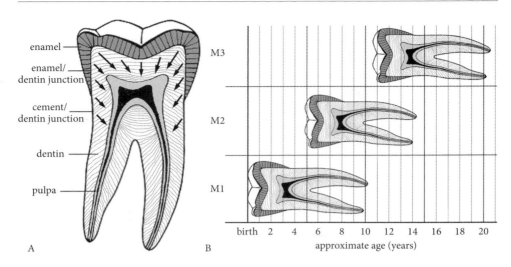

FIGURE 7.3. Tooth structure and development. Teeth grow in layers from crown to root (**A**). Molars provide a chronology of dietary intake during childhood and youth (**B**).

8 to 10 days, with a distance ranging from 20 to 30 μm (e.g., Kawasaki, Tanaks, and Ishikawa 1980; Dean and Scandrett 1995; Dean 1998; Smith 2006, 2008). Incremental manifestations are revealed as a contrasting linear pattern, which is visible in transmission of light microscope images (Smith 2006). Counts and measurements of the incremental lines have been used to determine the rate and duration of tooth formation (e.g., Dean and Scandrett 1995) and age at death for juveniles (e.g., Huda and Bowman 1995).

As dentine provides sufficient organic material, namely, collagen, we focused on this hard tissue in our study of the cemetery of Niedernai to reconstruct individuals' dietary intake. The methodology takes advantage of the fact that dentine grows sequentially from the crown to the root tip, forming incremental features with consistent periodic repeat intervals (e.g., Kawasaki, Tanaka, and Ishikawa 1980; Dean 1998; Smith 2006) (Fig. 7.3A). The deposited tissues are neither remodeled nor altered during lifetime. Thus, an individual's dentine incremental structure preserves a permanent record of his or her ingestion during the period of formation, producing an "archive of life history." Serial sampling that follows the pattern of dentine incremental structures provides a high-resolution isotope record of dietary changes and can give information about changing environmental conditions during an individual's early lifetime.

A number of recent studies have focused on analysis of teeth to reconstruct diet or migration (e.g., Fuller et al. 2003; Pollard et al. 2012; Whitmore, 2016; Eriksson et al. 2018). Serial sampling of teeth has been used recently to address various aspects of individuals' life histories (e.g., Eerkens et al. 2011, 2013, 2016; Beaumont et al. 2012, 2014, 2016; Henderson, Lee-Thorp, and Loe 2014; Sandberg et al. 2014; Burt 2015).

To reconstruct individuals' early life histories and to detect potential changes, our study used molars of permanent teeth as the basis for analysis. First molars start growing around birth, with the root tips completing growth between the ages of nine and

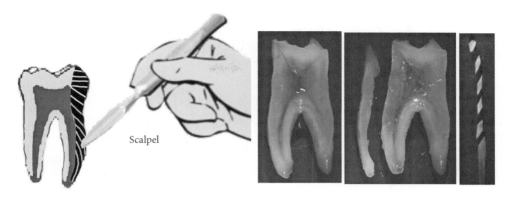

FIGURE 7.4. Schematic illustration of taking microsamples of a demineralized tooth half.

eleven years; crown mineralization of second molars starts at the age of two, and the root is complete at around fifteen years of age. The third molar, showing a wider growth range, starts growing between the ages of twelve and fourteen, and the average of root completion occurs between the ages of nineteen and twenty-two. By sampling the first, second, and third molars, it is possible to reconstruct the dietary pattern over the first twenty to twenty-two years of an individual's life (Fig. 7.3B).

In order to take microsamples from tooth dentine, teeth are first cut longitudinally into two halves with a Buehler saw (for details, see Beaumont et al. 2012). One tooth-half is then demineralized, and serial microsamples are cut off the complete root with a scalpel (Fig. 7.4), before isotope ratios of carbon and nitrogen stable isotopes are measured using a mass spectrometer. To assign samples to an approximate age, we developed a scheme for molars, based on the "London Atlas of Human Tooth Development and Eruption" (Al Qahtani et al. 2010). The atlas uses developmental stages of dentition to estimate the age of an individual (Moorrees et al. 1963; Demirjian et al. 1973; Liversidge and Molleson 2004); the atlas is generally used in forensic age determination. This scheme allows for a relatively precise age-related mapping of dietary intake (Czermak et al. 2018). The tooth data are then compared to the isotope ratio from bone collagen, which reflects an average of dietary intake before death.

TRACING INDIVIDUALS' LIFE HISTORIES

The burial site of Niedernai provides ideal conditions for investigation of individuals' life histories during the transition from Late Antiquity to the early Merovingian period. The small cemetery in the upper Rhine Valley (France), located at the (former) Roman Rhine frontier (Fig. 7.5), dates from the mid-fifth to the early sixth century. The cemetery was used for a relatively short period of time, representing about two generations. Individuals from the earliest graves were likely born in the last decades of the Roman

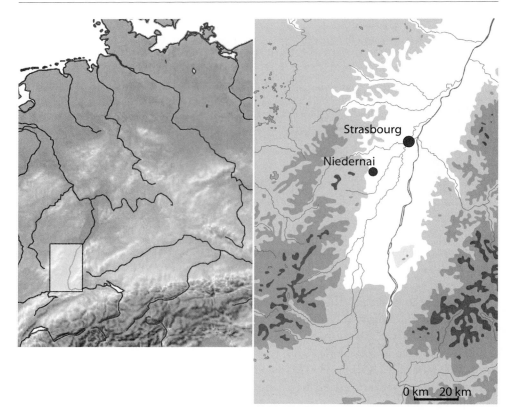

FIGURE 7.5. Location of the cemetery Niedernai. The site is located in the upper Rhine area in Alsace.

Empire, and those who were interred last witnessed the start of Merovingian rule. As a region at the outskirt of "Roman civilization," next to the border of the "barbarian world" during Roman times, the upper Rhine Valley took center stage in a newly established cultural and political zone ruled by Frankish monarchs in the mid-sixth century (see Hen, Chapter 10, this volume).

The upheaval associated with this transition from the Roman Empire to the Frankish kingdoms is assumed to have had profound effects on the population's culture, identity, and daily life. The collapse of the Roman social order may have led to new forms of "representation" and "consensus-rituals" (Jussen 1998). For instance, a profound shift in burial assemblages occurred during the fifth century: in the mid-fifth century, grave furnishing was reintroduced, showing burials of lavish ostentation (for a discussion of how we should interpret grave assemblages, see Theuws, Chapter 38, this volume; on southwestern Gaul, see Patrello, Chapter 39, this volume). We can see one of the earliest manifestations of this new form of burials in Niedernai.[2]

There is an ongoing controversy that relates to understanding the dimensions and timing of a possible migration of Alamannic population groups into Alsace. In the context of discussions of the comprehensive transformation of the Roman world, Sebastian Brather and Hubert Fehr have suggested that the furnished burial sites in this region established in the mid-fifth century should not be seen as a direct expression of barbarian migration, but rather as an expression of a cultural realignment of the societies in the former Roman frontier area (Brather 2008; Fehr 2008). If we view this realignment as a dynamic process, specifically, as a transformation of society characterized by cultural exchange, migration, integration, and acculturation, we might expect, as a consequence thereof, to see changes in the life histories of the individuals buried in Niedernai.

In our study, we thus focused on the question of whether the radical cultural changes, which are evident in the archaeological material culture, indicated a possible migration of populations from eastern Europe or whether they reflected cultural alterations of the former Roman population. Distinct deviations from locally expected nutrition patterns can be indicators of either a (local) crisis in subsistence or a change of location of residence that was accompanied by changes in subsistence. Using C/N-isotope analysis on tooth serial microsamples, our bioarchaeological aim was to obtain a "timeline" of individuals' early life histories. On the basis of a detailed chronology of individuals' isotope data, and thus their dietary intake, as well as supporting strontium stable isotope data from the same teeth, we addressed the following questions: (1) Is it possible to detect any changes in individuals' life history? (2) In which period of life did the change take place? (3) Which individuals were affected by these changes? (4) How did changes in individuals' isotope data reflect the wider archaeological and historical context? (5) What conclusions can be drawn in terms of migration, acculturation, and cultural exchange? Here, we present the initial results of our effort to apply a novel tooth dentine microsampling method for the first time on individuals from the small cemetery of Niedernai.

When possible, all three molars were analyzed from each individual to obtain a chronology of the dietary intake during the first twenty years of his or her life. Additionally, strontium isotopes from the same tooth samples were analyzed to compare the dietary markers with a location marker. Further, conventional carbon and nitrogen isotope ratios from bone bulk collagen were analyzed to establish an average isotopic profile of the individuals' last years of life.

In all, we were able to analyze the bone bulk collagen of twenty-one individuals at the site. The median $\delta^{15}N$ was 9.1‰ ($1\sigma = 0.67$; $2\sigma = 1.34$) and $\delta^{13}C$ was −19.2‰ ($1\sigma = 0.47$; $2\sigma = 0.94$). Compared to other early medieval sites, the Niedernai cemetery was on a slightly lower nitrogen level and a higher carbon level than average (Fig. 7.2). Conventional carbon and nitrogen plots (Fig. 7.6) show that the values for almost the entire population (except for five outliers) were within the second standard deviation. Those individuals with elevated nitrogen ratios were small children, indicative of breastfeeding and weaning signals (Figs. 7.6A and 7.6C). Elevated carbon ratios were visible in three individuals, slightly higher in one man and one woman, and noticeably higher in the woman, with a $\delta^{13}C$ value of less than −17.5 [3] (Fig. 7.6B). Although mature individuals showed a slightly higher likelihood of an animal protein diet, the bone data showed no significant differences between age groups (Fig. 7.6C). In addition, there were no

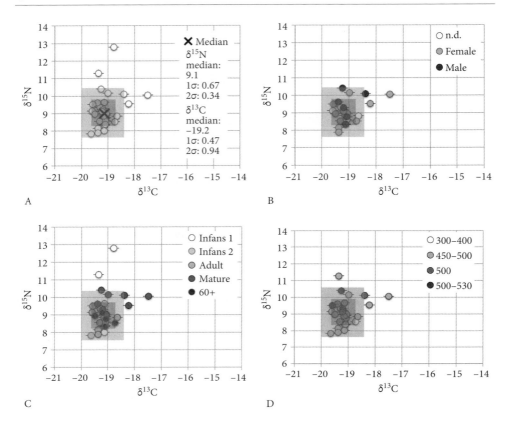

FIGURE 7.6. Conventional carbon and nitrogen isotope ratio plots of bone-bulk collagen analysis of individuals (n = 21) from the Niedernai cemetery. Median: δ^{15}N = 9.1‰, δ^{13}C = −19.2‰; gray (1σ) and dark gray (2σ) areas: δ^{15}N 1σ = 0.67, 2σ = 1.34 and δ^{13}C 1σ = 0.47, 2σ = 0.94. (A) Median of data from adult individuals (B) Female—Male. (C) Age groups. (D): Radiocarbon results.

observable dietary differences between female and male bone remains (Fig. 7.6B) or as a reflection of the grave chronology (Fig. 7.6D).

The analysis of tooth dentine serial samples from the first, second, and third molars over the first twenty years of two female individuals (Fig. 7.7) illustrates the potential of reconstructing the chronology of an individual's dietary intake. The elevated nitrogen values at the beginning of life reflect breast milk consumption. As breast milk provides nutrition from the mother, the δ^{15}N of the nursling's trophic level is expected to be one above its mother's (Fig. 7.7B). The decline in ^{15}N from approximately six months onward is the result of the weaning process, that is, the transition from breast milk to regular food. This process is typically observable in every individual and has been the subject of many studies focusing on weaning practices (e.g., Schurr 1998; Richards et al. 2002; Fuller et al. 2003, 2006; Reynard and Tuross 2015).

We can detect distinct dietary changes in the course of individual #1's first twenty years of life. During the phase from late childhood to adolescence, δ^{15}N values were

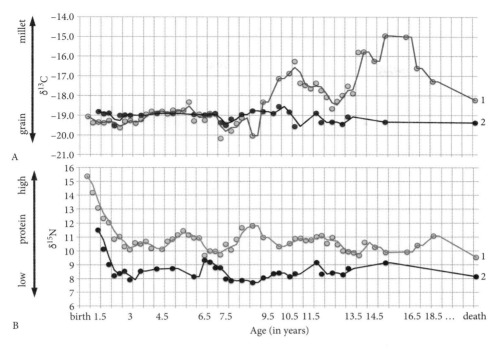

FIGURE 7.7. Chronology of two individuals' dietary intake as an example of an almost steady diet throughout life (individual #2) and large-scale changes in dietary intake (individual #1). Timeline of nitrogen (**A**) and carbon (**B**) isotope ratios of multiple microsamples from tooth dentine of first (M1), second (M2), and third (M3) molars. Individual #1's elevated $\delta^{15}N$ values indicate higher amounts of animal protein in her diet. The $\delta^{13}C$-data show distinct alterations during adolescence (**A**). Increasing $\delta^{13}C$-data reveal a change from a C3-plant-based diet (e.g., grain) to a C4-plant diet (millet).

staggered within 1–1.5‰, indicating alternating amounts of animal protein in her diet during that particular period of life. Complementary to this, the $\delta^{13}C$-data also showed distinct alterations during adolescence. While remaining largely stable during the first six years of her life, we can see a large increase of 3‰, followed by a decrease of 2‰ and another rise to about 3‰ before declining in early adulthood. The carbon isotope ratio at the end of her life reached close to the level of her early childhood, which was also in the range of the average bone collagen data of all of the individuals buried at the site (Fig. 7.7A). As the ^{13}C-data reveals a C3 or C4-plant diet, the higher values are evidence for a C4-plant diet, most likely millet. Accordingly, over a period of at least twelve years (within the timescale we are able to track), individual #1 had a diet that can be considered "nonlocal." Accompanying strontium isotope analysis also shows signals that can be considered "nonlocal," thus backing this finding.

In contrast, isotope serial data measured from individual #2 show few (detectable) changes, thus indicating a very stable diet in comparison to individual #1. Minor variations in $\delta^{15}N$ values in the range of 1–1.5‰ may have been related to seasonal changes in access to animal protein (Fig. 7.7B). Corroborating this, $\delta^{13}C$ values also show less than

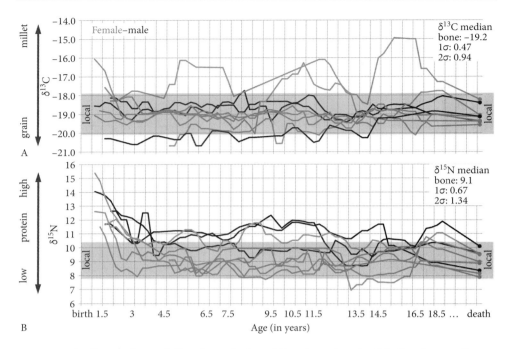

FIGURE 7.8. Comparison of diet chronologies of female and male. (Median bone collagen: $\delta^{15}N$ = 9.1‰; 1σ = 0.67, 2σ = 1.34, and $\delta^{13}C$ = –19.2‰; 1σ = 0.47, 2σ = 0.94). The second standard deviation (2σ) of the isotope results from bone samples indicates the local isotope range, as they represent the dietary intake of the last years of life. (**A**) $\delta^{13}C$: Individuals with elevated $\delta^{13}C$ ratios, indicating a millet-based diet, are female. (**B**) $\delta^{15}N$: Male (*n* = 3) tend to have a higher animal protein proportion in their diet compared to female (*n* = 6) throughout their first 20 years of life.

1‰ variation throughout the first twenty years of this individual's life. Even during the last years of life, as represented by the bone isotope data, this person's diet did not change (Fig. 7.7A).

In total, we were able to collect tooth dentine microsamples from seventeen out of the twenty-one individuals buried at the cemetery of Niedernai. All three molars were available in seven adults, two molars could be sampled in three, and at least one molar in five. Additionally, we were able to collect data from two small children. The chronologies of dietary intake from all individuals are shown in Figures 7.8 and 7.9. By comparing differences in the various parameters expressed by individuals, we were able to address the question as to which individuals were affected by dietary changes and thus were "different" from the others. To achieve this goal, we used standard deviations of the isotope results from bone samples as "local markers." They represented the dietary intake of the last years of life, hence indicating the local isotope range (Median $\delta^{15}N$ = 9.1‰; 1σ = 0.67, 2σ = 1.34, and $\delta^{13}C$ = –19.2‰; 1σ = 0.47, 2σ = 0.94).

When comparing female and male diet chronologies, we observed a significant difference between male and female children (Fig. 7.8B): young males tended to have a higher proportion of animal protein in their diets throughout the first twenty years of

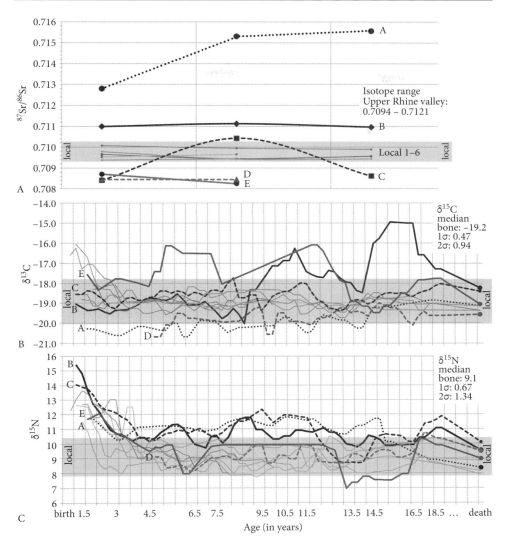

FIGURE 7.9. Comparison of diet chronologies of all individuals and strontium isotope data from the same teeth (only individuals with at least two available molars are shown). (A) Strontium isotope data reflect their geographical origin. By comparing the data with local reference data (local isotope range for the upper Rhine Valley after Schuh & Makarewicz 2016), we are able to detect individuals who changed their residence. (B) Chronology of δ ^{13}C and (C) of δ ^{15}N data. The "local range" is defined by using the second standard deviation (2σ) of the isotope results from bone samples, which represent the dietary intake of the last years of life. (Median bone collagen: δ^{15}N = 9.1‰; 1σ = 0.67, 2σ = 1.34 and δ^{13}C = −19.2‰; 1σ = 0.47, 2σ = 0.94). Although the majority stays within the local strontium range during the first twenty years of life (gray areas), we can detect at least five individuals who were not born in Niedernai (A). Some of them also changed their location in the course of childhood and youth (individual A and C). Individuals with other than local strontium isotope signatures (A) also show an offset in their diet and different dietary pattern (B and C) during their early lifetime than "local" individuals (staying within gray areas).

their lives, whereas young females, with one exception (see also Fig. 7.7), consumed less protein, or protein resources of a lower trophic level, than their male counterparts. By contrast, these differences did not exist during the last years of their lives.

There are several records of sex-based differences in isotope signatures in adults, in which researchers reported markedly lower nitrogen values in women than in men (e.g., Richards et al. 2006; Kjellström et al. 2009; Reitsema et al. 2010, Reitsema and Vercellotti 2012; Nitsch 2012; Whitmore 2016). These differences were related to physiological factors such as pregnancy or disease (Fuller et al. 2004, 2006), or were seen as a result of labor characteristics particular to each sex (Reitsema et al. 2010). Differential $\delta^{15}N$ values in sons and daughters might indicate high-quality foods such as meat made available to boys and withheld from girls. Further, elevated $\delta^{15}N$ results of boys from an early age indicated that their breastfeeding mother was consuming a higher amount of animal protein. Hence, this may reflect a special appreciation for women delivering sons—or at least of those whom we could examine in this study.

Notably, the two individuals with elevated $\delta^{13}C$ values were female. These women clearly had a different diet than most of the other individuals buried in the Niedernai cemetery. Elevated ^{13}C-ratios indicated a potentially millet-based, or at least millet-inclusive, diet. Additionally, the respective curves alternated, likely caused by a change from C3- to C4-plants and back again (Fig. 7.8A). Due to the small number of individuals, however, these findings should not be taken as definitive since they are not statistically significant.

On the basis of the known dietary chronologies of the people buried in Niedernai, we can state that some individuals very likely changed their diet significantly during their first twenty years of life (Figs. 7.9 B and C). Higher $\delta^{15}N$ values, indicating a diet enriched in animal protein, occurred mainly in males. Access to animal protein might have been determined by gender or status and thus can be seen as the "diet" of the wealthy and "important" members of society (e.g., Richards et al. 1998; Schutkowski et al. 1999; Privat et al. 2002; Knipper et al. 2015). Elevated $\delta^{15}N$ values may be attributed to status-related meat consumption. However, without a more nuanced understanding of food distribution during this time, it is impossible to say how differential protein intake was related to this community's social organization. Alternatively, differences in diet may have been caused by a variety of environmental conditions rather than social distinctions in food distribution and intake (e.g., Montgomery et al. 2005; Hakenbeck et al. 2010).

A higher $\delta^{13}C$ indicates a millet-based or millet-including diet. Millet is not unknown but nonetheless is uncommon in early medieval western and central Europe (Rösch, Jacomet, and Karg,1992; Hunt et al. 2008; Lightfoot, Lin, and Jones 2013; Murphy 2015). C4-plants like millet are adapted to warm, arid climates, and hence are more common in the southern and eastern parts of Europe. The evidence of a C4-plant-based diet of at least two individuals (maybe five, according to their very early life data) thus suggests that they originated from regions in which a C4 diet was more common. There is no question that we would not have been able to trace these changes in diet or even detect the diverging diet incorporated in the early lifetime on the basis of simple bone bulk analysis.

To back up the results from carbon and nitrogen isotope analyses, we compared the tooth dentine serial data with strontium data from the same teeth, using this as a second marker to identify potential newcomers (Fig. 7.9). Our strontium analyses revealed the presence of at least seven out of seventeen individuals who ingested childhood diets from areas outside the upper Rhine Valley. While ten individuals solely exhibited local signals, the teeth of seven individuals who were analyzed exhibited $^{87}Sr/^{86}Sr$ values outside the biologically available strontium range for the upper Rhine Valley ($^{87}Sr/^{86}Sr$: 0.7094–0.7121, after Schuh and Makarewicz 2016). Hence, these seven individuals should be regarded as newcomers to the region.

The most striking result of this aspect of the study, however, is the fact that those individuals who showed an offset in their diet and different dietary pattern during their early lifetime also exhibited a "nonlocal" strontium isotope signature. This evidence demonstrates that some people buried in Niedernai had a distinctly different diet than the majority. Moreover, the same individuals who ate different food were also the ones who did not spend their childhood, youth, and early adulthood in the upper Rhine area.

What Can Stable Isotope Analysis tell us about Status and Identity?

Stable isotope analysis can contribute to our understanding of the impact of larger structural changes in the early medieval period. We can capture isotope signatures from different life stages, which allow us in turn to reconstruct the chronology of an individual's diet. Serial microsampling of dentine from different teeth allows for detection of dietary changes within brief time spans that would not have been possible to trace by means of simple bone isotope analysis. Bone, with its time-averaged isotope signatures, does not reveal episodic nutritional changes but gives us information about dietary intake during the last period of an individual's life.

We were able to measure clear isotope signature changes over time in some individuals. These finds indicated that some did change their diet, possibly in response to altered environmental factors within their detectable time span. Moreover, individuals of extra-local childhood origin were scattered throughout the entire burial area. They included adult females and males of all chronological periods. Most individuals, however, showed no significant changes in isotope ratio during their early life, indicating that these individuals neither altered their diets nor changed their environment within the detectable time spans.

Our findings strongly support the coexistence of an indigenous burial community with some newcomers. Some individuals were clearly different according to their early life histories. They joined the community later or near the end of their lives; their bone data does not allow us to distinguish them from those who spent their lifetime in the upper Rhine area. The presence of newcomers, literally integrated with the cemeterial community, likely resulted from cultural exchange and the expression of sociopolitical interaction rather than direct evidence of residential origin. Even if it is most improbable that scholars will be able to pinpoint the residential origins of those individuals with "nonlocal" strontium signals, it will still be possible to demonstrate that residential mobility took place.

Stable isotope analysis can also help answer questions on status and identity. Based on the assumption of a status-based distribution of food, diet has been used in numerous studies on social stratification as a marker for individuals' status and identity. Certain types of food may be linked to the richer, upper strata of society and others to the poorer people who belonged to the lower strata (e.g., Schutkowski et al. 1999; Hakenbeck et al. 2010; Killgrove, Robert, and Tykot 2013; Knipper et al. 2015). Some foods were also tied to ethnic groups (Lightfoot et al. 2016). Isotope studies of medieval Europe have provided data as to how food may have been distributed within populations, including differences in diet based on sex (Richards et al. 2006), age (Richards et al. 2002), status, and religious profession (e.g., Polet and Katzenberg 2003; Czermak et al. 2006; Reitsema et al. 2010; van der Sluis et al. 2015). These results suggest that some foods, such as meat and animal products, were considered more prestigious than others, and their distribution thus reflected these priorities.

General subsistence practices in society such as the acquisition, preparation, distribution, and consumption of food, are strongly linked to social organization. Variation between individuals can reflect the social hierarchy and the relationship between diet and social identity. Food encodes social and cultural values and has an important role in defining identities (Douglas 1972; Harris 1998). On the one hand, diet can be a means of social integration. Immigrants might change their diet habits to that of the indigenous population in order to assimilate or in response to the availability of food resources. On the other hand, relatively small numbers of newcomers may have occasionally caused social and cultural change related to food-based customs and diet, particularly if they attained high social status (Anthony 1997).

The examination of individuals' life histories has numerous implications beyond the mere determination of geographic residence. The identification of nonlocals in local cemeteries has clear implications for how ancient communities viewed themselves as well as their relationship with outsiders. If we consider "cemetery membership" or persons included in a mortuary setting as an expression of social identity, the presence of nonlocals suggests that definitions of kinship and social identity may have been flexible between members of the local community and newcomers. Permitting nonlocals to be included in mortuary rituals and cemeteries may have played a socioeconomic or even a political role as nonlocals became integrated in the community. This practice also suggests the malleable or flexible nature of social identity in a heterogenic society.

In our study, we have demonstrated that, at least with respect to their diet, newcomers were fully integrated at Niedernai in the mid-fifth to early sixth century. Incoming people, who may be identified by traces left by their distinct diet during early lifetime, as well as their unique strontium isotope signal, had the same isotope composition at the end of their lives as those who were identified as "locals." Furthermore, we have shown that the newcomers were also a heterogenic group with different places of origin. This conclusion supports the assumption that only small groups or even single individuals were migrating into the community laid to rest at Niedernai, a situation that resulted in a diverse population. New arrivals contributed to the dynamic settlement patterns of the upper Rhine Valley after this former Roman frontier region was incorporated into the realm of the Merovingian kingdom.

The isotope data presented here provide evidence of the coexistence of an indigenous community and some newcomers. It is important to note, however, that these results still need to be discussed in light of associated archaeological findings for a more conclusive assessment of the social status of the individuals in question. Moreover, it is necessary still to affirm whether a pattern between burial evidence and geographical origin existed, and whether factors other than residential provenance played an important role in burial practices exhibited at this cemetery. Nevertheless, the presence of immigrants, who were literally absorbed into the cemeterial community and adopted diets similar to those of the indigenous residents following their arrival, can be interpreted as an expression of social integration and acculturation. People sharing their lives, their food, and their final resting place might have also shared their identity.

NOTES

1. Usually, strontium isotopes are used for the reconstruction of origin and migration. Their composition in tissues can provide an indication for geographical origin. By comparing the data with local isotopic ratios or reference data, it is possible to detect an individual's potential change of residence. See Bentley and Knipper (2005), Bentley (2006), and Tütken (2008, 2010) for detailed descriptions of the strontium isotopic method. An adequate interpretation of Sr-isotope data depends on the ability to distinguish "local" and "nonlocal" isotopic signatures.
2. For further archaeological information on the cemetery of Niedernai, see the forthcoming publication by Susanne Brather-Walter.
3. Unfortunately, no teeth from this individual were available.

WORKS CITED

Modern Sources

Aggarwal, J., Habicht-Mauche, J., and Juarez, C. (2008). "Application of Heavy Stable Isotopes in Forensic Isotope Geochemistry." *Applied Geochemistry* 23(9): 2658–2666.

Al Qahtani, S. J., Hector, M. P., and Liversidge, H. M. (2010). "Brief Communication: The London Atlas of Human Tooth Development and Eruption." *American Journal of Physical Anthropology* 142: 481–490.

Ambrose, S. H., and Norr, L. (1993). "Experimental Evidence for the Relationship of the Carbon Isotope Ratios of Whole Diet and Dietary Protein to Those of Bone Collagen and Carbonate." In J. B. Lambert and G. Grupe (eds.), *Prehistoric Human Bone: Archaeology at the Molecular Level* (pp. 1–37). Berlin: Springer-Verlag.

Anthony, D. W. (1997). "Prehistoric Migration as a Social Process." In J. C. Chapman and H. Hamerow (eds.), *Migrations and Invasions in Archaeological Explanation* (pp. 21–32). BAR International Series 664. Oxford: Archaeopress.

Beaumont, J., Gledhill, A., Lee-Thorp, J., and Montgomery, J. (2012). "Childhood Diet: A Closer Examination of the Evidence from Dental Tissues Using Stable Isotope Analysis of Incremental Human Dentine." *Archaeometry* 55(2): 277–295.

Beaumont, J., Gledhill, A., and Montgomery, J. (2014). "Isotope Analysis of Incremental Human Dentine: Towards Higher Temporal Resolution." *Bulletin of the International Association of Paleodontology* 8(2): 212–223.

Beaumont, J., and Montgomery, J. (2016). "The Great Irish Famine: Identifying Starvation in the Tissues of Victims Using Stable Isotope Analysis of Bone and Incremental Dentine Collagen." *PLoS One* 11.8, e0160065.

Becher, M. (2011). *Chlodwig I. Der Aufstieg der Merowinger und das Ende der antiken Welt.* Munich: C. H. Beck.

Beniash, E. (2011). "Biominerals—Hierarchical Nanocomposites: The Example of Bone." *Nanomedicine and Nanobiotechnology* 3(1): 47–69.

Bentley, R. A. (2006). "Strontium Isotopes from the Earth to the Archaeological Skeleton: A Review." *Journal of Archaeological Method and Theory* 13: 135–187.

Bentley, R. A., and Knipper, C. (2005). "Geographical Patterns in Biologically Available Strontium, Carbon and Oxygen Isotope Signatures in Prehistoric SW Germany." *Archaeometry* 47: 629–644.

Brather, S. (2008). "Zwischen Spätantike und Frühmittelalter. Einführung." In S. Brather (ed.), *Zwischen Spätantike und Frühmittelalter. Archäologie des 4. bis 7. Jahrhunderts im Westen.* (pp. 1–12). Reallexikon der Germanischen Altertumskunde, Ergänzungsband 57 Berlin: Walter de Gruyter.

Burt, N. (2015). "Individual Dietary Patterns during Childhood: An Archaeological Application of a Stable Isotope Microsampling Method for Tooth Dentine." *Journal of Archaeological Science* 53: 277–290.

Caut, S., Angulo, E., and Courchamp, F. (2009). "Variation in Discrimination Factors ($\Delta^{15}N$ and $\Delta^{13}C$): The Effect of Diet Isotopic Values and Applications for Diet Reconstruction." *Journal of Applied Ecology* 46: 443–453.

Craig, H. (1953). "The Geochemistry of the Stable Carbon Isotopes." *Geochimica Cosmochimica Acta* 3: 53–92.

Craig, H. (1954). "Carbon 13 in Plants and the Relationships between Carbon 13 and Carbon 14 Variations in Nature." *Journal of Geology* 62: 115–149.

Czermak, A. (2012). "Soziale Stratifizierung im frühen Mittelalter. Aussage- und Nachweismöglichkeiten anhand von biologischen Indikatoren." Doctoral dissertation, Ludwig-Maximilians-Universität Munich.

Czermak, A., Ledderose, A., Strott, N., Meier, T., and Grupe, G. (2006). "Social Structures and Social Relations—An Archaeological and Anthropological Examination of Three Early Medieval Separate Burial Sites in Bavaria." *Anthropologischer Anzeiger* 64(3): 297–310.

Czermak, A., Schermelleh, L., and Lee-Thorp, J.-A. (2018). "Imaging-Assisted Time-Resolved Dentine Sampling to Track Weaning Histories." *International Journal of Osteoarchaeology* 28(5): 535–541.

Dean, M. C. (1998). "Comparative Observations on the Spacing of Short-Period (Von Ebner's) Lines in Dentine." *Archives of Oral Biology* 43: 1009–1021.

Dean, M. C., Beynon, A. D., Reid, D. J., and Whittaker, D. K. (1993). "A Longitudinal Study of Tooth Growth in a Single Individual Based on Long- and Short-Period Incremental Markings in Dentine and Enamel." *International Journal of Osteoarchaeology* 3: 249–264.

Dean, M. C., and Scandrett, A. E. (1995). "Rates of Dentine Mineralization in Permanent Human Teeth." *International Journal of Osteoarchaeology* 5: 349–358.

Dean, M. C., Liversidge, H. M., and Elamin, F. (2014). "Combining Radiographic and Histological Data for Dental Development to Compare Growth in the Past and the Present." *Annals of Human Biology* 41(4): 336–347.

Demandt, A. (2007). *Die Spätantike. Römische Geschichte von Diocletian bis Justinian 284–565 n. Chr.* Munich: C. H. Beck.

Demirjian, A., Goldstein, H., and Tanner, J. M. (1973). "A New System of Dental Age Assessment." *Human Biology* 45(2): 211–227.

DeNiro, M. J., and Epstein, S. (1978). "Influence of Diet on the Distribution of Carbon Isotopes in Animals." *Geochimica Cosmochimica Acta* 42: 495–506.

DeNiro, M. J., and Epstein, S. (1981). "Influence of Diet on the Distribution of Nitrogen Isotopes in Animals." *Geochimica Cosmochimica Acta* 45: 341–351.

Douglas, M. (1972). "Deciphering a Meal." In *Myth, Symbol, and Culture. Daedalus: Proceedings of the American Academy of Arts and Sciences* 101(1): 61–81.

Drucker, D. G., and Bocherens, H. (2009). "Carbon Stable Isotopes of Mammal Bones As Tracers of Canopy Development and Habitat Use in Temperate and Boreal Contexts." In J. D. Creighton and P. J. Roney (eds.), *Forest Canopies: Forest Production, Ecosystem Health, and Climate Conditions* (pp. 103–109). New York: Nova Science Publishers.

Eerkens, J. W., Berget, A. G., and Bartelink, E. J. (2011). "Estimating Weaning and Early Childhood Diet from Serial Micro-Samples of Dentine Collagen." *Journal of Archaeological Science* 38: 3101–3111.

Eerkens, J. W., and Bartelink, E. J. (2013). "Sex-Biased Weaning and Early Childhood Diet among Middle Holocene Hunter-Gatherers in Central California." *American Journal of Physical Anthropology* 152(4): 471–483.

Eerkens, J. W., Sullivan, K., and Greenwald, A. M. (2016). "Stable Isotope Analysis of Serial Samples of Third Molars As Insight into Inter- and Intra-Individual Variation in Ancient Diet." *Journal of Archaeological Science* 53: 277–290.

Eriksson, G., Frei, K. M., Howcroft, R., Gummesson, S., Molin, F., Lidéna, K., Frei, R., and Hallgren, F. (2018). "Diet and Mobility among Mesolithic Hunter-Gatherers in Motala (Sweden)—The Isotope Perspective." *Journal of Archaeological Science: Reports* 17: 904-918.

Farquhar, G. D., Ehleringer, J. R., and Hubick, K. T. (1989). "Carbon Isotope Discrimination and Photosynthesis." *Annual Reviews of Plant Physiology and Plant Molecular Biology* 40: 503–537.

Fehr, H. (2008). "Germanische Einwanderung oder kulturelle Neuorientierung? Zu den Anfängen des Reihengräberhorizontes." In S. Brather (ed.), *Zwischen Spätantike und Frühmittelalter. Archaeologie des 4. bis 7. Jahrhunderts im Westen.* (pp. 67–102). Reallexikon der Germanischen Altertumskunde, Ergänzungsband 57. Berlin: Walter de Gruyter.

Fry, B., and Sherr, E. B. (1989). "$\delta^{13}C$ Measurements as Indicators of Carbon Flow in Marine and Freshwater Ecosystems." *Stable Isotopes in Ecological Research, Series Ecological Studies* 68: 196–229. (Reprinted from [1984]. *Contributions in Marine Science* 27: 13–47.)

Fuller, B. T., Fuller, J., Sage, N., Harris, D., O'Connell, T., and Hedges, R. E. M. (2004). "Nitrogen Balance and $\Delta^{15}N$: Why You're Not What You Eat during Pregnancy." *Rapid Communication in Mass Spectrometry* 18: 2889–2896.

Fuller, B. T, Fuller, J. L., Harris, D.A., and Hedges, R. E. M. (2006). "Detection of Breastfeeding and Weaning in Modern Human Infants with Carbon and Nitrogen Stable Isotope Ratios." *American Journal of Physical Anthropology* 129: 279–293.

Fuller, B. T, Richards, M. P., and Mays, S. A. (2003). "Stable Carbon and Nitrogen Isotope Variations in Tooth Dentine Serial Sections from Wharram Percy." *Journal of Archaeological Science* 30: 1673–1684.

Ginzburg, C. (1980). *The Cheese and the Worms: The Cosmos of a Sixteenth-Century Miller.* Trans. J. and A. Tedeschi. Baltimore: Johns Hopkins University Press.

Hakenbeck, S., McManus, E., Geisler, H., Grupe, G., and O'Connell, T. (2010). "Diet and Mobility in Early Medieval Bavaria: A Study of Carbon and Nitrogen Stable Isotopes." *American Journal of Physical Anthropology* 143(2): 235–249.

Harris, M. (1998). *Good to Eat: Riddles of Food and Culture.* Long Grove, IL: Waveland Press.

Hedges, R. E. M., Clement, J. G., Thomas, C. D. L., and O'Connell, T. C. (2007). "Collagen Turnover in the Adult Femoral Mid-Shaft: Modeled from Anthropogenic Radiocarbon Tracer Measurements." *American Journal of Physical Anthropology* 133: 808–816.

Hedges, R. E. M., and Reynard, L. M. (2007). "Nitrogen Isotopes and the Trophic Level of Humans in archaeology." *Journal of Archaeological Science* 34: 1240–1251.

Henderson, R. C., Lee-Thorp, J., and Loe, L. (2014). "Early Life Histories of the London Poor Using $\delta^{13}C$ and $\delta^{15}N$ Stable Isotope Incremental Dentine Sampling." *American Journal of Physical Anthropology* 154: 585–593.

Huda, T. F., and Bowman, J. E. (1995). "Age Determination from Dental Microstructure in Juveniles." *American Journal of Physical Anthropology* 97: 135–150.

Hunt, H. V., Linden, M. V., Liu, X., Motuzaite-Matuzeviciute, G., Colledge, S., and Jones, M. K. (2008). "Millets across Eurasia: Chronology and Context of Early Records of the Genera Panicum and Setaria from Archaeological Sites in the Old World." *Vegetation History and Archaeobotany* 17 (Suppl. 1): S5–18.

Jim, S., Ambrose, S. H., and Evershed, R. P. (2004). "Stable Carbon Isotopic Evidence for Differences in the Dietary Origin of Bone Cholesterol, Collagen and Apatite: Implications for Their Use in Palaeodietary Reconstruction." *Geochimica Cosmochimica Acta* 68: 61–72.

Joyner, C. W. (1999). *Shared Traditions: Southern History and Folk Culture.* Urbana: University of Illinois Press.

Jussen, B. (1998). "Liturgie und Legitimation, oder: Wie die Gallo-Romanen das Römische Reich beendeten." In R. Blänkner and B. Jussen (eds.), *Institutionen und Ereignis. Über historische Praktiken und Vorstellungen gesellschaftlichen Ordnens.* (pp. 75–136). Veröffentlichungen des Max-Planck-Instituts für Geschichte 138. Göttingen: Vandenhoeck & Ruprecht.

Kawasaki, K., Tanaka, S., and Ishikawa, T. (1980). "On the Daily Incremental Lines in Human Dentine." *Archives of Oral Biology* 24: 939–943.

Killgrove, K., Robert, H., and Tykot, R. H. (2013). "Food for Rome: A Stable Isotope Investigation of Diet in the Imperial Period (1st–3rd Centuries AD)." *Journal of Anthropological Archaeology* 32(1): 28–38.

Kjellström, A., Storå, J., Possnert, G., and Linderholm, A. (2009). "Dietary Patterns and Social Structures in Medieval Sigtuna, Sweden, as Reflected in Stable Isotope Values in Human Skeletal Remains." *Journal of Archaeological Science* 36: 2689–2699.

Knipper, C., Peters, D., Meyer, C., Maurer, A.-F., Muhl, A., Schöne, B., and Alt, K.W. (2013). "Dietary Reconstruction in Migration Period Central Germany: A Carbon and Nitrogen Isotope Study." *Archaeological and Anthropological Science* 5: 17–35.

Knipper, C., Held, P., Fecher, M., Nicklisch, N., Meyer, C., Schreiber, H., Zich, B., Metzner-Nebelsick, C., Hubensack, V., Hansen, L., Nieveler, E., and Alt, K. W. (2015). "Superior in Life – Superior in Death." *Current Anthropology* 56(4): 579–589.

Lee-Thorp, J. A. (2008). "On Isotopes and Old Bones." *Archaeometry* 50: 925–950.

Lee-Thorp, J. A., Sponheimer, M., and Van der Merwe, N. J. (2003). "What Do Stable Isotopes Tell Us about Hominid Dietary and Ecological Niches in the Pliocene?" *International Journal of Osteoarchaeology* 13: 104–113.

Le Huray, J. D., and Schutkowski, H. (2005). "Diet and Social Status during the La Tène Period in Bohemia: Carbon and Nitrogen Stable Isotope Analysis of Bone Collagen from Kutnà Hora-Karlov and Radovesice." *Journal of Anthropological Archaeology* 24: 135–147.

LeRoy Ladurie, E. (1975). *Montaillou, village occitan de 1294 à 1324*. Paris: Gallimard.

LeRoy Ladurie, E. (1979). *Le carnaval de Romans. De la chandeleur au mercredi des cendres, 1579–1580*. Paris: Gallimard.

Lightfoot, E., Liu, X., and Jones, M. K. (2013). "Why Move Starchy Cereals? A Review of the Isotopic Evidence for Prehistoric Millet Consumption across Eurasia." *World Archaeology* 45(4): 574–523.

Lightfoot, E., Naum, M., Kadakas, V., and Russow, E. (2016). "The Influence of Social Status and Ethnicity on Diet in Medieval Tallinn As Seen Through Stable Isotope Analysis." *Estonian Journal of Archaeology* 20(1): 81–107.

Liversidge, H. M., and Molleson, T. (2004). "Variation in Crown and Root Formation and Eruption of Human Deciduous Teeth." *American Journal of Physical Anthropology* 123: 172–180.

Makarewicz, C. A. and Sealy, J. (2015). "Dietary Reconstruction, Mobility, and the Analysis of Ancient Skeletal Tissues: Expanding the Prospects of Stable Isotope Research in Archaeology." *Journal of Archaeological Science* 56: 146–158.

Martin, J. (1995). *Spätantike und Völkerwanderung*. Oldenbourg Grundriß der Geschichte 4. Munich: Walter de Gruyter.

McGlynn, G. (2007). "Using ^{13}C-, ^{15}N-, and ^{18}O Stable Isotope Analysis of Human Bone Tissue to Identify Transhumance, High Altitude Habitation and Reconstruct Palaeodiet for the Early Medieval Alpine Population at Volders, Austria." Doctoral dissertation, Ludwig-Maximilians-Universität München.

Minagawa, M., and Wada, E. (1984). "Stepwise Enrichment of ^{15}N along Food Chains: Further Evidence and the Relation Between D15n and Animal Age." *Geochimica Cosmochimica Acta* 48: 1135–1140.

Montgomery, J., Evans, J. A., Powlesland, D., and Roberts, C. A. (2005). "Continuity or Colonization in Anglo-Saxon England? Isotopic Evidence for Mobility, Subsistence Practice, and Status at West Heslerton." *American Journal of Physical Anthropology* 126: 123–138.

Moorrees, C. F., Fanning, E. A., and Hunt, E. E. Jr. (1963). "Age Variation of Formation Stages for Ten Permanent Teeth." *Journal of Dental Research* 42: 490–502.

Murphy, C. (2015). "Finding Millet in the Roman World." *Archaeological and Anthropological Science* 8(1): 65–78.

Nehlich, O., Montgomery, J., Evans, J., Schade-Lindig, S., Pichler, S., Richards, M. P., and Alt, K. W. (2009). "Mobility or Migration. A Case Study from the Neolithic Settlement of Nieder-Mörlen (Hessen, Germany)." *Journal of Archaeological Science* 36: 1791–1799.

Nitsch, E. K. (2012). "Stable Isotope Evidence for Diet Change in Roman and Medieval Italy: Local, Regional and Continental Perspectives." Doctoral dissertation, University of Oxford.

Park, R., and Epstein, S. (1960). "Carbon Isotope Fractionation during Photosynthesis." *Geochimica Cosmochimica Acta* 21: 110–126.

Phillips, D. L., Inger, R., Bearhop, S., Jackson, A. L., Moore, J. W., Parnell, A. C., Semmens, B. X., and Ward, E. J. (2014). "Best Practices for Use of Stable Isotope Mixing Models in Food-Web Studies." *Canadian Journal of Zoology* 92: 823–835.

Polet, C., and Katzenberg, M. A. (2003). "Reconstruction of the Diet in a Mediaeval Monastic Community from the Coast of Belgium." *Journal of Archaeological Science* 30: 525–533.

Pollard, A. M., Ditchfield, P., Piva, E., Wallis, S., Falys, C., and Ford, S. (2012). "'Sprouting like a Cockle Amongst the Wheat': The St. Brice's Day Massacre and the Isotope Analysis of Human Bones from St. John's College, Oxford." *Oxford Journal of Archaeology* 31(1): 83–102.

Privat, K. L., O'Connell, T. C., and Richards, M. P. (2002). "Stable Isotope Analysis of Human and Faunal Remains from the Anglo-Saxon Cemetery at Berinsfield, Oxfordshire: Dietary and Social Implications." *Journal of Archaeological Science* 29: 779–790.

Reitsema, L. J., Crews, D. E., and Polcyn, M. (2010). "Preliminary Evidence for Medieval Polish Diet from Carbon and Nitrogen Stable Isotopes." *Journal of Archaeological Science* 37: 1413–1423.

Reitsema, L. J. and Vercellotti, G. (2012). "Stable Isotope Evidence for Sex- and Status-Based Variations in Diet and Life History at Medieval Trino Vercellese, Italy." *American Journal of Physical Anthropology* 14(4): 589–600.

Reynard, L. M., and Tuross, N. (2015). "The Known, the Unknown and the Unknowable: Weaning Times from Archaeological Bones Using Nitrogen Isotope Ratios." *Journal of Archaeological Science* 53: 618–625.

Richards, M. P., Fuller, B. T., and Molleson, T. I. (2006). "Stable Isotope Paleodietary Study of Humans and Fauna from the Multi-Period (Iron Age, Viking, and Late Medieval) site of Newark Bay, Orkney." *Journal of Archaeological Science* 33: 122–131.

Richards, M. P., Hedges, R. E. M., Molleson, T. I., and Vogel, J. C. (1998). "Stable Isotope Analysis Reveals Variations in Human Diet at Poundbury Camp Cemetery Site." *Journal of Archaeological Science* 25: 1247–1252.

Richards, M. P., Mays, S., Fuller, B. T. (2002). "Stable Carbon and Nitrogen Isotope Values of Bone and Teeth Reflect Weaning Age at the Medieval Wharram Percy Site, Yorkshire, UK." *American Journal of Physical Anthropology* 19: 205–210.

Rösch, M. (1998). "The History of Crops and Crop Weeds in South-Western Germany from the Neolithic Period to Modern Times, As Shown by Archaeobotanical Evidence." *Vegetation History and Archaeobotany* 7: 109–125.

Rösch, M., Jacomet, S., and Karg, S. (1992). "The History of Cereals in the Region of the Former Duchy of Swabia (Herzogtum Schwaben) from the Roman to the Post-Medieval Period: Results of Archaeobotanical Research." *Vegetation History and Archaeobotany* 1: 193–231.

Sandberg, P. A., Sponheimer, M., Lee-Thorp, J., and van Gerven, D. (2014). "Intra-tooth Stable Isotope Analysis of Dentine: A Step toward Addressing Selective Mortality in the Reconstruction of Life History in the Archaeological Record." *American Journal of Physical Anthropology* 155: 281–293.

Schoeninger, M. J., and DeNiro, M. J. (1983). "Carbon Isotope Ratios of Bone Apatite and Animal Diet Reconstruction." *Nature* 301: 178.

Schoeninger, M. J., and DeNiro, M. J. (1984). "Nitrogen and Carbon Isotopic Composition of Bone Collagen from Marine and Terrestrial Animals." *Geochimica Cosmochimica Acta* 48: 625–639.

Schoeninger, M. J., DeNiro, M. J., and Tauber, H. (1983). "Stable Nitrogen Isotope Ratios of Bone Collagen Reflect Marine and Terrestrial Components of Prehistoric Human Diet." *Science* 220: 1381–1383.

Schuh, C., and Makarewicz, C. A. (2016). "Tracing Residential Mobility during the Merovingian Period: An Isotopic Analysis of Human Remains from the Upper Rhine Valley, Germany." *American Journal of Physical Anthropology* 161(1): 155–169.

Schurr, M. R. (1998). "Using Stable Nitrogen-Isotopes to Study Weaning Behavior in Past Populations." *World Archaeology* 30: 327–342.

Schutkowski, H., Herrmann, B., Wiedemann, F., Bocherens, H., and Grupe, G. (1999). "Diet, Status and Decomposition at Weingarten: Trace Element and Isotope Analyses on Early Mediaeval Skeletal Material." *Journal of Archaeological Science* 26: 675–685.

Smith, T. (2006). "Experimental Determination of the Periodicity of Incremental Features in Enamel." *Journal of Anatomy* 208: 99–113.

Smith, T. (2008). "Incremental Dental Development: Methods and Applications in Hominoid Evolutionary Studies." *Journal of Human Evolution* 54(2): 205–524.

Strott, N. (2006). "Paläodemographie frühmittelalterlicher Bevölkerungen Altbaierns—Diachrone und allopatrische Trends." Doctoral dissertation, Ludwig-Maximilians-Universität München.

Tieszen, L. L., Boutton, T. W., Tesdahl, K. G., and Slade, N. A. (1983). "Fractionation and Turnover of Stable Carbon Isotopes in Animal Tissues: Implications for Δ^{13}C Analysis of Diet." *Oecologia* 57: 32–37.

Tütken, T. (2010). "Die Isotopenanalyse fossiler Skelettreste—Bestimmung der Herkunft und Mobilität von Menschen und Tieren." *Tagungen des Landesmuseums für Vorgeschichte Halle* 3: 33–51.

Tütken, T., Knipper, C., and Alt, K. W. (2008). "Mobilität und Migration im archäologischen Kontext. Informationspotential von Multi-Element-Isotopenanalysen (Sr, Pb, O)." In J. Bemmann and M. Schmauder (eds.), *Kulturwandel in Mitteleuropa. Langobarden—Awaren—Slawen (Akten der Internationalen Tagung in Bonn vom 25. – 28. Februar 2008)* (pp. 13–42). Kolloquien zur Vor- und Frühgeschichte Band 11. Römisch-Germanische Kommission des Deutschen Archäologischen Instituts Frankfurt a. M. Bonn: Dr. Rudolf Habelt GmbH.

van der Sluis, L., Reimer, P., and Lynnerup, N. (2015). "Investigating Intra-individual Dietary Changes and ^{14}C Ages Using High-Resolution δ^{13}C and δ^{15}N Isotope Ratios and ^{14}C Ages Obtained from Dentine Increments." *Radiocarbon* 57(4): 665–677.

van Dülmen, R. (2001). *Historische Anthropologie. Entwicklungen, Probleme, Aufgaben.* 2nd ed. Cologne: Böhlau.

West, J. B., Bowen, G. J., Cerling, T. E., and Ehleringer, J. R. (2006). "Stable Isotopes as One of Nature's Ecological Recorders." *Trends in Ecology and Evolution* 7(21): 408–414.

West, J. B., Bowen, G. J., Dawson, T. E., and Tu, K. P. (2010). *Understanding Movement, Pattern, and Pprocess on Earth through Isotope Mapping.* New York: Springer.

White, T. D., and Folkens, P. A. (2005). *The Human Bone Manual.* Amsterdam: Elsevier Academic Press.

Whitmore, K. (2016). "Diet at Medieval Alytus, Lithuania: Stable Carbon and Nitrogen Isotope Analysis of Bone and Dentine Collagen." Master's Thesis, University of Central Florida.

Whittaker, Ch. R. (1997). *Frontiers of the Roman Empire. A Social and Economic Study.* Baltimore: Johns Hopkins University Press.

Willerding, U. (2003). "Die Landwirtschaft im frühen Mittelalter (6.–10. Jh.). Ackerbau." In N. Benecke, P. Donat, E. Gringmuth-Dallmer, and U. Willerding (eds), *Frühgeschichte der Landwirtschaft in Deutschland* (pp. 151–172). Beiträge zur Ur- und Frühgeschichte Mitteleuropas 14. Langenweißbach: Beier & Beran.

CHAPTER 8

GENDER IN MEROVINGIAN GAUL

GUY HALSALL

In Tours, the holy woman Monegund had a little garden next to her cell where she could go to be alone (Gregory of Tours, *VP* 19.1). One day while she was there, a woman was able to watch her from a neighboring rooftop: "she gazed upon her importunely, filled with worldly desires" and consequently went blind until Monegund healed her. This is not the easiest passage to unravel. Who was filled with worldly cares—Monegund or the importunely watching woman—is not entirely clear; what exactly the worldly cares were and what the transgression was that robbed the woman of her sight are likewise fairly obscure. These ambiguities, however, have surely been present to any readers of, or listeners to, this text and, as Jacques Derrida (1967/1997) showed, no text has a stable, originary meaning present to itself. This—decidedly queer—tale raises interesting and important aspects of gender in the Merovingian world.

Gender remains an understudied area of early Frankish social history and, indeed, of early medieval history in general. Thirty years after Joan Scott's (1986) classic paper on gender as a useful category of historical analysis, which set out so clearly the difference between women's history and gender history, early medieval historians remain—in relation to students of other disciplines and periods within the broad church of medieval studies—comparatively unsubtle investigators of the topic. "Gender" is frequently still employed as a simple placeholder, signaling token comments about women.[1] It is hard not to paraphrase Scott: my understanding of, for example, aristocratic patronage is not changed by the knowledge that women participated in it. Analytical confusion remains about whether one is studying women's history or gender history (e.g., Smith 2001; Nelson 2004; Hen 2004). Many articles putatively dealing with "gender" treat women as a transhistorical or ahistorical category (the continuing wide citation of Nelson 1996 is indicative of the general conceptual malaise). Although now examining masculinity as well as femininity (e.g., Hadley 1999), early medieval historians have not moved on sufficiently from the idea that gender is the social construction placed on the biological category of sex. Man and woman are timeless categories; only the way people write about or envisage them changes (e.g., Halsall 1996, 2010a).

But, as Judith Butler (1993; 1999) showed, it is not so simple to separate biological sex from gender. The way we inhabit our bodies and social space and live our lives is something that is negotiated, discursively, with society, however unconsciously, from the moment we enter the world of the symbolic (on which see, e.g., Lacan 1978, pp. 238–375; Evans 1996, pp. 201–203). The relationships between gender, biological sex, and sexuality are not straightforward, and there is no meaningful point in our lives at which we experience sex separately from gender. The fundamentally bipolar scale of biological sex (genitalia, chromosomes, etc.) and the processes of human sexual reproduction do not and cannot *in themselves* determine sexuality or marital or family structures, not least because their perception and representations are as enmeshed in language as are the notions of sex, marriage, family, or idealized woman- or manhood. Butler's famous concept of performativity came not just from the idea of *performance* but also from the speech–act category of *the performative*: phrases (e.g., "I pronounce you man and wife"), which create the thing they describe (Butler 1999, p. 185, is quite clear on this). It is thus not the case that a somehow natural ungendered or pregendered body performs gender as something that is extrinsic to itself, something that, unlike that notionally sexed but pregendered body, is contingent upon social and linguistic structures. Gender is constituted *in* its performance; behind the mask is nothing or—rather—only another mask (Deleuze 1994, pp. 27–30). Philosophically, this is old news and has not gone unchallenged (Copjec 1994), but it is indicative of early medieval history's resistance to "theory" that this has yet to make much impact on our subject. Julia Smith, for example, mentions Butler's notion of performativity once (2004, p. 17) but seems to have misunderstood it to mean performance.

Identification is an "enacted fantasy" (Butler 1999, p. 185). All identities are structured ultimately by fantasy and desire: a mental image of what the identity ideal might mean in terms of its relations with people of other identities, and a desire to occupy that space. That means behaving toward people of other identities in a particular fashion, in the manner that (one thinks) people expect, as well as in ways that might be thought best to achieve one's own ends. The motion toward this ideal can never be complete; however close one comes, one can never simply *be* the identity-ideal: thus the enactment of fantasy.

Consider another story from Gregory of Tours's gallery of the unexpected: the case of the cross-dressing Poitevin at the tribunal of the rebellious nuns of Sainte-Croix (*Histories* 10.15). Nancy Partner (1993, pp. 418, 439) noted that Gregory describes this person as a man in woman's clothing, not as a woman, but are we authorized to take that as any sort of basis for discussion, any more than we should take modern Republicans' insistence that a transgendered person is a man "dressed up as a woman" (Badash 2016)? Are we permitted to refer to the Poitevin as "he" rather than "she" on Gregory's say-so? Whether the Poitevin lived her life as a woman or lived *his* life *dressed as* a woman is impossible to say. Gregory reports that, when questioned, the Poitevin said that s/he had made the decision to dress as a woman because s/he was incapable of manly work (*opus virile*), but we cannot know what to make of this because the whole text, above all its evident distinction between biological sex and material cultural gender, is soaked in a gendered discourse of power. One of the story's attractions is that it is so undecidable at so many levels that trying to claim what Gregory, or the Poitevin, "really meant" by any of the crucial phrases is quite pointless. In noting the story's separation of the "man" from the "clothing," we are, however, presented with a difficult course to chart between the Scylla of essentialism and the Charybdis of endless, disabling relativism. How do we investigate agency or resistance to normative views? How might we identify the difference between a man who dressed as a woman and a biological male who lived as a woman?

If this person was born anatomically male, that clearly did not determine the construction of his/her gender. We do not know what was meant by the claimed incapacity to perform *opus virile*, or whether or how this related to her/his sexuality (Dailey 2015, pp. 56–57; Halsall 2018). Lewis Thorpe's somewhat misleading translation, which Partner (1993) relies on too heavily, suggests that (*qua* man) the Poitevin was impotent. If so, his gendering did not relate to his sexuality. Perhaps he was married; perhaps his sexuality had little bearing on his decision to marry and try to raise a family. Other sixth-century options visible in the story include gendering oneself as male but refraining from all sexuality (as a monk or secular ecclesiastic), or as a married woman and similarly abstaining from sex (as a nun—married to Christ).[2] Even what we might suppose was the normative Frankish family unit, with a mother, father, and children, was not the sole vehicle for socialization. The masculine child could leave his natal family and spend a long period of time in another family household or in the overwhelmingly masculine society of a retinue (Halsall 2010a, 2010b).

The rebellious nuns' accusation that the Poitevin dressed to conceal his masculinity and thus work in a house of religious women (with no implications for his sexuality) adds yet a further dimension. If we accept the bishops' decision that the accusation was groundless and trust the Poitevin's own account of the reasons for his/her costume, another unanswerable question arises: if identity is an "enacted fantasy," what was the mental image or ego-ideal in question? This story illustrates how anatomical sex, sexuality, gender, living arrangements, marriage, and so on, combine in a galaxy of historically contingent ways.

One advantage of studying the social history of northern Gaul is, however, that while documentary sources are comparatively scarce, a vast archive of material cultural data exists in hundreds of cemeteries and thousands of sixth- and seventh-century burials. These have much to tell us, not least because the dead were commonly interred in an archaeologically visible funerary costume, alongside various other artifacts—the whole (elements of clothing and the other items) referred to by the shorthand term gravegoods.[3] Most serious scholars have moved away from interpretations of this practice as either "Germanic," "pagan," or both (for critique, see Effros 2003; Brather 2004a). Where skeletal data survive, intact burials allow us to compare a range of treatments of the body with their biological age and sex and to separate (from our perspective) the Merovingian social treatment and experience of the body from its anatomical sex, physiological development (whether or not ever experienced separately from sociolinguistic categories), and so on. This does not undermine Butler's point but rather provides a way of further interrogating it in a past context. It does not solve the problems identified earlier, but it adds another critical perspective and an additional dataset.

As a further example, let us take Grave 32 at the cemetery of Ennery, in which a body sexed anthropologically as male was interred with objects—most notably a necklace—which otherwise was only found with biologically female skeletons (Simmer 1993, pp. 46–47; Halsall 1995, pp. 78–94; 2010b). We cannot say whether the person known as "Ennery 32" thought of himself as a man who dressed as a woman, or of herself as a woman, or was thought of as a woman by the community or as a man who dressed, or lived life as a woman, or what their preference was (if any) for sexual partners (if any), or whether any link existed between that and the funerary costume. The grave evidence does not allow us to identify dominant and subversive readings (and say which was which) or by whom such opinions were held. This case, and others like it, do, however, demonstrate that, while necessary to correct many fundamental errors at the time, the 1990s debate over whether the reading of skeletal or the material evidence was "correct" (e.g., Lucy 1997; Effros 2000) was theoretically misconceived. Equally, Halsall's (2010c) attempt to read "discrepancies" between the two forms of data in terms of transgression is too unsubtle.

The sixth-century furnished burial ritual was a public event (Halsall 2010d, pp. 203–260). Communal norms were important in determining the appropriate numbers and forms of goods deposited with the dead of different genders at particular stages of the life cycle. Thus, if the physical anthropology of Ennery Grave 32 is correct (and there seems no good reason to doubt it), the implication is seemingly that someone born with male physical attributes was interred publicly in a way that permitted his/her identity and lifestyle to be reflected in how s/he was laid to rest before an audience. That leaves many questions unanswerable but challenges modern ideas about what is "natural," "traditional," or "normal," or ideas that ground their references to the "natural" and the "normal" in claims about long-term European history, and do so without idealizing the medieval past. The funerary data also permit the exploration of change through time; the quantity of material recovered allows the dating of burials to roughly a twenty-five-year period (Périn 1980; Legoux, Périn, and Vallet 2009).

THE CONSTRUCTION OF SEX AND GENDER: FROM ROMAN TO MEROVINGIAN

The construction of gender had changed since the late Roman period. Classical Roman gender construction had largely revolved around the notion of the civic Roman male, a single set of model behaviors concerned with moderation, self-control, and so on. Not only the female but also the barbarian and the animal revolved around this central focus, praised for closeness to it, derided for distance from it (see Foxhall 2013 for an excellent, recent overview). While a barbarian might be able to perform masculine Romanness so effectively that his non-Roman origins were effaced, a woman (by which I mean anyone living a life as a woman) was apparently prevented by her sex from ever fully occupying that central position. It would be wrong, however, to suppose that that central position was fixed or attainable even by men. Classical civic masculinity concerned the citation of an always unreachable ideal. The fact that the single-gendered ideal was masculine and performative implies that its enactment distinguished the social actor from a set of characteristics that were gendered feminine. In an inversion of Simone de Beauvoir's (2011, p. 293) famous dictum, one was not born a man but only "became" one. Implicit in Roman thought is the idea that (in modern terms) the default, "pre-social" gender was feminine or, in terms more easily assimilable with Roman concepts, that outside this performance, while not everyone was a woman, everyone was "womanly."

The implications of cemetery archaeology are that this situation had changed by the early Merovingian period (see discussion in next section below). The roots of this transformation should be sought in later fourth- and fifth-century shifts. After the formal separation of the different branches of imperial service during the Tetrarchic period, a new, martial form of Roman masculinity seems to have emerged. Late imperial military culture strongly suggests that the army began to develop new identities, stressing the opposite of the traditional model Roman male: barbarian and even animal (Halsall 2007, pp. 102–110). However, in order to round out its symbolic context, this new masculinity required the older one to exist. In the final analysis, both forms were based on Roman imperial legitimation. The "martial model" inverted civic masculine ideals, but the efficaciousness of that strategy depended squarely on the authority and prestige of those traditional ideals. This "barbarizing" identity, and the legitimacy of military and civil titles, also relied on a link to the emperor who embodied military and civil office and both models of masculinity. While, in a late Roman context, some could emphasize martial masculinity's wild, fierce, animal, barbarian traits to imply a weakness in civic manhood, it always had to be remembered that anyone with an education would view such characteristics as lesser, uncivilized, and womanly. The traditional or orthodox concepts thus remained in place even as an alternative "reading" of its symbols and bases (its citations, in Butler's terms) emerged, which flagged up their implicit blind spots.

Employing Simon Critchley's (2014) insights into Derridian philosophy, I have called this a deconstruction of classical gender (Halsall 2018). As stated, identity is a constant movement toward an ideal, so these renegotiations, oscillations, and redefinitions of what such an unattainable object of identification was were crucially important in the lived gender of late and postimperial people. The situation I have described endured for a couple of generations beyond the deposition of Romulus "Augustulus" because the postimperial western kings continued to occupy, however notionally, positions within the imperial hierarchy and, like the emperor, to embody points at which civic and martial masculinities came together.

I would suggest that, by playing with and valorizing the traditional civic male ideal's "constitutive other," this "oscillation" within the masculine ideal enabled more actively idealized feminine traits to emerge, based more strongly on sex, the body, and reproduction, and thus not simply dependent on emulation of the male. This, I suggest, is visible in the furnished inhumations, where two distinct artifact sets were employed to denote masculinity and femininity (Halsall 1995, pp. 79–83; Effros 2003, pp. 99–100, 154–163, for notes of caution; Halsall 2010b for response).

It is immediately clear that the feminine cluster of artifacts is composed, overwhelmingly, of costume or bodily adornments: brooches, earrings, hairpins, dress-pins, bracelets, and necklaces. Items that might be representative of female work—breadcutters, weaving batons, spindle-whorls—are quite rare in a Frankish context and occur in what seem to be quite prestigious contexts. It is also important to note that—with the important exception of weaponry—most earlier Merovingian technical and decorative expertise (especially in metalwork) was invested in items of female adornment. Archaeologically visible elements of sixth-century masculine costume are usually relatively plain. Written sources allude to jeweled or otherwise decorated belts in elite contexts, but we rarely find archaeological examples; the belt evidently did not need decoration for its symbolic weight (on belt sets, see Patrello, Chapter 39, this volume).

GENDER AND THE LIFE CYCLE

The ontology of gender can be investigated through the material construction of the life cycle, as revealed through the deposition of grave-goods, and the written sources' sparse information read in the light of these more plentiful data. The basic account can be fairly brief and relates primarily to burial in sixth-century northern Gaul.[4] In early childhood, the furnishing of burials made little recognition of the child's sex. The lack of stress on communal relations produced by a small child's death (which should emphatically not be understood as equating with a lack of grief) meant that these burials were rarely the occasions for the expenditure of resources (see Perez, Chapter 9, this volume). It is not unusual to find feminine artifacts in the burials of slightly older children, possibly reflecting the betrothal of the deceased child (betrothal as young as eight is attested in written sources: Venantius, *Carmina* 4.26). The gendering (and indeed sexing) of the female child could then be brought about by the demands for marriage alliances that lay at the core of communal politics. (In line with the foregoing discussion, use of the terms *male* and *female* throughout the remainder of this chapter implies nothing about the anatomy of the person in question.) What has been called interpellation into the gendered world (Butler 1993, p. xvii) may not have been decisive in the child's earliest years. It is worth noting that masculine items remain scarce in burials of subjects who died before puberty. The exceptions invariably concern unusual and lavish burials of members of the elite (e.g., Werner 1964). It might appear, on that basis, that aristocratic male children could be seen as sexed/gendered earlier than those of other levels of society (regarding Merovingian military practice, see Sarti, Chapter 12, this volume). This would have meant a very real difference in the experience of gender at different social levels. It might, however, equally be that different demands of burial ritual, a need to mark a distinction from other social strata, and different stresses caused by the death of a male heir caused a young boy's body to be gendered in his funeral in a way that was not necessarily reflected during his life.

The first major change in the construction of masculine and feminine identity occurred at puberty, when adolescent women were frequently interred with a wide range of feminine objects, most notably the jewelry mentioned earlier. The *Pactus Legis Salicae* (*PLS*) notes that the *wergeld* (compensation owed to a family for a killing) of a woman of childbearing age was three times that of a typical free, Frankish *ingenuus* (cp. *PLS* 24.8, 41.1). Two clauses imply that this increase in legal value was triggered by the woman's having begun to bear (or breastfeed) children (*PLS* 24.8: *postquam coeperit infantes habere*; 41.16: *postquam ceperit nutrire*), whereas another clause appears to see the woman's value in terms of the victim being of an age where there was *potential* childbearing, which it regards as beginning at the age of twelve (*PLS* 65e). This evidence, alongside written references (including inscriptions), suggests that the onset of the menarche brought the immediate sexualization of the female body, marriage, and potential childbearing. The interpellation of a child into a fully sexed/gendered female role was sudden and brutal. The comparatively high investment in the funeral display for women of this age presumably related to the tension within community relations that their deaths might cause, undoing fairly recently made marriage alliances when any children produced would have been very young.

The funerary record suggests that the masculine body remained ungendered at this age. Weaponry is rarely found with the bodies of anatomical males in their teens, although other masculine items are occasionally present. The difference from the feminine teenager is underlined by the fact that the *Pactus* marks a point of transition for males at twelve years of age. It is the boy *under* twelve years who has the higher, 600-*solidus wergeld* but who is also considered legally incapable (*PLS* 24.7). Clearly, the law dealt with a young boy's murder in terms of his potential to become a man. The superficial discrepancy between the legal and archaeological evidence is probably explained by the fact that the *wergeld* relates to compensation for the damage done to a family by a killing, whereas the burial data are explained by the rift in social relationships between families caused by a death. The transition to legal responsibility, seemingly at the age of twelve, was marked by the first cutting of the boy's hair—apparently making the male body visibly different from the female for the first time (*PLS* 24.2). It is important to note, nonetheless, that the acquisition of legal responsibility and a nonfeminine hairstyle does not, according to the archaeologically visible data at least, appear to have resulted in the full recognition of a masculine identity. Even in the context of public ritual display, when we might expect gender distinctions and attendant costumes to have been made more visible, the deceased male was not strongly gendered. Yet, young men's sexual desires were well recognized by contemporaries. Cassian (*Institutes* 6.1) said that the spirit of fornication, against which a monk must strive, commenced its attacks with puberty. It is noteworthy, however, that young male sexuality was less clear-cut. Before twenty, sexual explorations between "boys" could be treated as "games" (*ludi*) and treated less severely than sexual relations between older men (Cummean, *Penitential* 10; see also *Penitential of Theodore* 1.2.4). The funerary record is suggestive here too. Double interments from the sixth-century cemetery of Ennery (graves 6 and 8: Simmer 1993, pp. 33, 37) and the seventh-century necropolis of Audun-le-Tiche (grave 103: Simmer 1988, pp. 50–53, 55), contain two males with their arms laid deliberately on top of each other (whether interlocked is difficult to say). The subjects were all younger than about twenty. Perhaps the somewhat ambivalent semiotics of the burial display (Halsall 2010c, pp. 347–349) were considered acceptable among men of this age group.

Having reached his twenties, a male could expect to be buried with masculine items, including weaponry. A more clearly gendered masculine identity could now be ascribed to the dead. A male might by now have been serving in another household for some time, creating bonds between his family and the head of that household (Halsall 2010b). It is likely, too, that he was betrothed. As with younger women, his death could threaten a range of interfamilial relationships requiring their maintenance through the burial ritual. Women dying at this stage of the life cycle might, however, be buried with a larger overall number of grave-goods but with a less lavish display of bodily and costume adornments (see also Stauch 2008). This stage of the female life cycle appears to have lasted until about the age of forty. Again, the investment of resources in their burials should be seen in terms of the stress placed on interfamilial alliances brought about by their deaths. Even at forty, a woman's eldest male children, and younger daughters, might still be unmarried, raising complicated questions about inheritance between the families involved (*PLS* 101, 110; *Decretio Childeberti* 1.1).

From about thirty, some males were buried with the full panoply of weaponry. Evidence for male age of marriage is vague, but on balance it seems that it was typically in the late twenties (Halsall 2010a). Males dying between about thirty and sixty were typically the members of the early Merovingian community who received the most lavish interments, with numerous masculine items and other grave goods.[5] Explanation should again be sought in communal politics and in the synchronicity of the different generations' life cycles. A man dying in his thirties or forties was probably married, but his children, especially sons, would still be minors. Even in his late forties, his eldest daughters would likely only recently have married and his eldest sons would be unlikely to be much older than twenty, well short of male marital age. Given that marriage and fictive kin alliances around his daughters and sons were doubtless intended to secure his support or allegiance, his death questioned such ties. Perhaps more importantly, his death left open the problem of succession, as his eldest sons would not have established themselves sufficiently to inherit his communal standing. The issues of his widow's property and remarriage (*PLS* 44, 100) also pertained. Therefore, not surprisingly, the deaths of men in this age group could necessitate the fullest ritual attention in feasting, gift-giving, and display of the family's ability to lay their dead to rest in the most appropriate fashion. Importantly, the distinctions in the lavishness of male grave-furnishing become sharpest at this stage in the life cycle.

Women older than about forty and men above sixty received far less attention in their grave-furnishing, mostly receiving interments that, like children's, were "neutral" in gendered terms. While the burials of women above age forty were sparsely furnished and rarely contained jewelry, male graves, though poorly furnished overall, occasionally included a weapon or other masculine items. One should, however, hesitate before assuming a low esteem for old people on this basis. The lack of investment in the archaeologically visible elements of burials, as explained earlier, relates primarily to the relative lack of tension caused by deaths at this age, when children had reached maturity and had established households and communal standing. It is significant, nonetheless, that gender was more frequently marked in masculine than in female burials.

Gendered Time

It is immediately apparent from this account that the experience of time itself was gendered. Masculine and feminine life cycles were constructed differently, with socialization and sexualization running at significantly different speeds. It is noteworthy, too, how much more sexualized the feminine life course was and how much more violently it was punctuated by gendered social expectations or by interpellation into the sex/gender system (classically, see Rubin 1975). Feminine socialization and the sexualization of the female body were apparently simultaneous and rapid processes, supposedly occurring at the onset of the menarche. This apparently physiological rule is immediately destabilized, however, by the *Pactus's* displacement of the grounds for higher female legal status from the *actuality* of childbirth or breastfeeding into the *potential* for childbearing, determined according to age group (*PLS* 65.e). The bearing of this upon female sexuality is unclear. Same-sex relations posed no threat to the legitimacy of children, and a marriage was possibly considered to remain valid even if the woman ceased to cohabit with her husband. Gregory of Tours (*Histories* 5.32) makes it clear that it was the rumor of a wife's sexual relations with another man that brought about the violent dispute between two Parisian families; the wife's leaving her husband is relegated to an ablative absolute subclause.

The female's bodily adornment suggested by the grave-goods merits further reflection. The indications are that the forms of clothing not normally visible archaeologically could also be highly decorated. Interestingly, these items are mostly associated with the hand and arms, the breast, and the hair (especially if tied up or covered, signifying marriage), the female bodily areas that Frankish law penalized touching (*PLS* 20.1–4, 104). The unavailable female body is not concealed but highlighted. Significantly, too, the costume that most emphasized these aspects began to be worn at puberty and was mostly set aside after forty: during the life cycle stage wherein a woman's *wergeld* was three times higher than a freeman's. The law saw this as the age of the (legitimately) sexually active woman. The costume in which women were interred might be interpreted as symbolizing feminine ideals: the beautiful, chaste, good wife and mother. Merovingian female status and identity were based solidly on reproductive sex and marriage.

Male socialization took much longer, between puberty and about thirty (Halsall 2010b), and appears to have established a man's right to marry and start a household.

It seems likely, too, that in the sixth century it was closely related to the acquisition of an ethnic identity, Roman or Frankish. The *Pactus* (e.g., *PLS* 41) only assigns ethnicity to adult males. Before about age twenty, it might also be that, as noted, male sexuality was given some latitude. Although, by the sixth century, the martial, Frankish model was generally considered more dominant, various ideals of identity still existed. The variation between burials with weapons and those without possibly relates to this, and the divergence between lavishly and poorly furnished graves among males at this stage of the life cycle could reflect the varying success with which the male managed to achieve a fully gendered identity as the head of a household. It is even possible that Gregory of Tours's Poitevin chose his/her particular lifestyle as a result of the demands of that earlier phase of the life cycle. Furthermore, the crucial "citational" points in the masculine life cycle were much less (notionally) dependent on physiological development and reproductive sexual practice. Again, these physiological or bodily developments should not be seen as neutral or pre-social canvases on which society inscribed gendered identities (Butler 1993).

Significantly, before marriage, males were referred to as *pueri* (boys), regardless of physiological age (Halsall 2010b). That this phase of the life cycle could produce various models of masculinity is important. As noted, the difference between mature adult males buried with weapons and those buried without might relate to ethnicity: Frankish identity was closely related to military service (Halsall 2003, pp. 46–48; see Sarti, Chapter 12, this volume). If the martial (Frankish) model of masculinity increasingly dominated, it nevertheless continued to relate primarily to the civic ideal represented by the free Roman male. Traditionally, as described earlier, civic masculinity had been differentiated from a backdrop of "womanly" characteristics, which the martial forms had in turn played upon and valorized. Consequently, the two gendered "poles" most visible in the archaeological record, the martial masculine and the feminine, were constructed not as binary oppositions but in relation to the civic masculine ideal, now weakening in its social importance. This seemingly more "bipolar" construction of gender, I suggest, opened up the space within which the anonymous Poitevin/e of Gregory's *Histories* or Ennery Grave 28 operated (Halsall 2018). The feminine was no longer necessarily the constitutive outside of the masculine. Young males' performance and citation of gender seem to have been much less "teleological" than was the case for females (see Freeman 2010, pp. 4, 8, for teleological time).

CHRISTIANITY AND GENDER IN THE SIXTH CENTURY

Fifth-century developments in Christian attitudes to gender have been well discussed (e.g., Cooper and Leyser 2001). The debate over the absolute repudiation of sex and the trend toward it was perhaps as yet less resolved in Gaul than elsewhere, and the emphasis on chastity and abstinence produced a convergence of masculine and feminine ideals that resembled classical gender construction. The church might have been a repository for many of the old ideals of civic masculinity, and classical gender as the martial model became more dominant in secular life. Many sixth-century bishops entered the church after a secular career, marriage, and children. A good example is Gregory of Langres who entered the church after a long career as a *comes* (count) (*VP* 7.1; see Wemple 1985, pp. 132–136 for a useful survey of the earlier Merovingian church's ambivalent attitude toward married clergy). Unsurprisingly, the principal virtues in claiming ecclesiastical and religious authority were moderation and continence rather than asceticism. Gregory of Langres only had sexual relations with his wife for the purpose of procreation, according to his great-grandson, biographer, and namesake (*VP* 7.1). Out of 293 recorded sixth-century saints, 148 were bishops (James 1982, p. 55). Although asceticism was well known, the trend toward extreme, competitive, public renunciation noted elsewhere was far from dominant in early Merovingian religious life. Seclusion, secrecy, modesty, and an especial worry about the vainglory that might beset ascetic virtuosi seems to have been more heavily emphasized. Gregory of Langres again furnishes an example. After his ordination, he performed his asceticism in secret (*VP* 7.2). The punishment of vainglorious (or potentially vainglorious) holy men is recorded (*VP* 15.2; *Histories* 4.34), and, famously, Vulfolaic's attempt to emulate Syrian stylites in the Ardennes was quickly stifled by the local episcopate (*Histories* 8.15). The flaws of those condemned as "false" holy men doubtless included "showy" asceticism (*Histories*, 9.6; 10.25). Even the recluse Lupicinus's excessive and ultimately fatal self-mortification was performed beyond public view, while walled up in a cave (*VP* 13.1). Some male holy men only decided to abandon the worldly possibilities of marriage and family during the long phase of *pueritia* (loosely 'boyhood'). Bracchio, Venantius, Patroclus and Leobardus all, according to Gregory, chose the religious life when faced with the social expectation that they would marry, during or at the end of this phase of the life cycle, sometimes on their father's death (*VP* 9.1, 12.2, 16.1, 20.1). This further underlines the variety of gender and sexuality models that were seemingly available to males at this age.

Many of the known sixth-century religious women (most of whom had royal connections) similarly had family lives before entering their religious vocation: Chlothild, Radegund (see Coon, Chapter 46, this volume), Ingitrude, and Monegund (on elite women, see James, Chapter 11, this volume). Female monasticism was in its infancy and it was uncommon for young people to enter or be given to monasteries (de Jong 1996). Many holy women, like Ingitrude and Monegund, lived as individual religious or formed small communities of like-minded women near the great urban shrines, like that of St. Martin of Tours. Many such communities, like Ingitrude's, did not survive their founder's death, and even large and prestigious houses like St John, Arles, or Sainte-Croix, Poitiers, could have chequered histories. This was not, however, so different from contemporaneous male monasticism. Early Merovingian models for female religious life were rarely provided by cloistered virgins. The author of Saint Genovefa's *life*, it has been pointed out (Wood 1988, p. 378; *Vita Genovefae*), had difficulty finding an exemplar for a female *vita*, so that Genovefa appears rather episcopal (the bishop of Paris is a figure significantly absent from the text). Over half of Venantius's *Vita Radegundis* concerns her life before she secluded herself in her nunnery of Sainte-Croix. Even the cult of the Virgin Mary seems not to have flourished in sixth-century Gaul. Gregory's *Glory of the Martyrs*, for instance, contains few miracles associated with her veneration (*GM* 8–10, 18–19). Something like the single, masculine-gendered ideal known in classical thought might have persisted in this sphere. In the prologue to his life of Monegund (*VP* 19), Gregory tells us that the Lord provides holy examples of how to live: not just men but also women, who struggle "not feebly but manfully" (*non segniter sed viriliter*), presumably accounting for Monegund's inclusion among the "Fathers."

Doing Unto Others?

Let us return to the secular sphere. Sixth-century masculine objects, apart from the largely undecorated belt (see Patrello, Chapter 39, this volume), symbolized things that men did to, or with, things or other people: weapons, tools, flints, strike-a-lights, knives. These have many implications for identity and personhood (see Cohen 2003). By comparison, the highlighting of the female body suggested by feminine grave-goods implies that woman was the *object* of the gaze. Female identification was performed bodily, publicly, in the gaze of the community. The "barbarian" term Venantius used to describe the bejeweled costume that the saint laid aside when she renounced the world (and adequately describing that revealed by sixth-century grave-goods: *composita sermone ut loquar barbaro stapione, Vita Radegundis* 13.30) seems to mean "stepping-out" costume (McNamara, Halborg, and Whatley (trans.) 1992, p. 76 n. 55). Such visibility was doubtless not purely feminine; especially in northern Gaul, sixth-century society was very *visible* or "optic," where resources were heavily invested in public display and in which public ritual was crucial to the operation of society. The local community, its politics and its "structures," were performed in front of an audience. The big cemeteries, the foci for the burial ritual discussed earlier, are one part of this. The *Pactus Legis Salicae* stresses public performance as a strong component of legal procedure (*PLS* 46, 58, 60). The investment of wealth in costume and display must go some way toward explaining the ephemeral traces of earlier Merovingian rural settlement.[6] Although the sixth-century northern Gallic rural *community* might have been quite large, comprising several small settlements, it was nevertheless a very *local* arena (Halsall 2012).

This argument does not imply female passivity or a lack of status. Although institutions or formal codes might be established by and for a masculine social elite, the everyday inhabitation of social spaces could create, in the interstices of the boundaries set out on such a "social map," social standing and power (Halsall 1996, pp. 22–23). Nevertheless, the evidence suggests that the motion of feminine identification in particular required performance in the gaze of others. Ontologically, to be a woman was inseparable from that *visible* occupation of a point in public space, in the communal gaze. The implication might be that the female gaze differed subtly from the male gaze, with the woman, instead of just looking, "seeing herself being seen." This would result in a form of biopolitical control that could easily be imposed by women on other women. In comparative perspective, none of this is surprising, but it applied particularly in sixth-century Gaul. It is interesting to compare that conclusion with the invisibility of women in so many of our documents.

Here we may return to Monegund, the Poitevin/e of the nuns' tribunal, and "Ennery 32". Whatever is going on in the story of Monegund and her neighbor, part of the problem is that the woman is *looking*. Whatever lay behind Gregory's text, it is also clear that looking at a woman was almost impossible without some sort of thinking about sex or "worldly desires" taking place. This only underlines why female religious had to be taken out of the normal public arenas and be enclosed (Dailey 2014). This is in some ways underscored by cases like the Poitevin/e and the person buried at Ennery. Both instances, as they are known to us, come from very public contexts: a tribunal in a *civitas* capital (the Poitevin/e stepped forward *coram omnibus*: "in front of everyone") and a burial ritual. Lacking the overt references to the sexual body, Ennery 32's costume would possibly be appropriate for a man who lived life dressed as a woman (Halsall 2010c, pp. 342–343). Perhaps. But by concentrating too heavily on a "transgressive" interpretation, that reading ignores the important, if seemingly obvious, point that follows from Butler's philosophy of gender: whatever the biological sex of the deceased's bodily remains, someone who lived life as a woman and died between the ages of forty and sixty was, simply enough, buried in a costume appropriate for a woman aged between forty and sixty. However, the deceased did not dress themselves for their funerals. Ennery 32's family (I assume) prepared and clothed the body for its burial, which must have meant that—assuming the anthropological sexing is correct—they were well enough aware of the disjunction between the physical body and its social skin and were prepared to represent the latter in public display. What does the expenditure of resources on this funeral display have to say to the thesis that the lavishness of burial is related to the stress in society (discussed earlier, pp. 169–171)? All we can do is throw out a series of questions and possibilities, and mistrust any attempt to close down or (hetero-) normalize them.

CHANGE AROUND 600

Important changes occurred around 600, including very significant transformations of the burial ritual (Halsall 1995, pp. 262–269). Grave-goods declined, and the relative investment in more permanent, above-ground commemoration increased; cemeteries became more numerous as earlier large sites ceased to be used by multiple settlements; the audience present at funerals probably declined commensurately. These changes, surely related to the social hierarchy's increased stability and the local elite's security, affect our evidence's ability to answer questions about gender in the same way as before. Nonetheless, several issues deserve our attention.

The first is the shift in grave-goods to the masculine. There is usually relative decline in the number of burials marked by feminine grave-goods and in the number of types of grave-goods used to signify feminine identity (Halsall 1995, pp. 110–1163). Those that remain are often rather less ornate than before (Legoux, Périn, and Vallet 2009). By contrast, although the number and variety of weapons—the objects employed to signify at least one, probably dominant, form of masculinity in the sixth century, decline, the percentage of adult male burials with at least a token weapon increases (e.g., Halsall 1995, p. 134). These aspects are surely interlinked. More importantly for current purposes, at least some males began to be buried in a more archaeologically visible costume—notably the great decorated plate-buckles that dominate the seventh-century artifactual record of Gaul (Lorren 2001; Legoux, Périn, and Vallet 2009, pp. 32–35). Further, the most elaborate brooch forms of the century, disc brooches with cabochons and filigree, can be found in masculine as well as feminine graves (e.g., Liéger, Marguet, and Guillaume 1984). Did seventh-century feminine attire really become as plain as the cemetery data suggest? Perhaps not. Embroidered clothing, for instance, is rarely archaeologically visible (Vierck 1978; Effros 1996). Women were possibly no longer buried in a costume that bore much relationship to their formal attire in life. This would nonetheless be significant, and the change is not easy to explain away, even if it is yet more difficult to explain or describe with certainty.

Some points can nevertheless be made. The greater solidification of the social hierarchy and, compared with the sixth century, the consequent rise in the relative importance of descent and of male family or lineage heads seem to lie at the heart of the issue. Nevertheless, we might again focus on the issues of visibility and performance. The later phase of the cemetery of Lavoye (Meuse) suggests that, in the seventh century, only one of the three different groups that had earlier used the site continued to do so for all of its burials (Halsall 1995, pp. 138–139, 141–142). The others apparently interred mainly adult males at the site. This might imply that, as the everyday social arena contracted to the still more local level of the individual settlement, political gatherings, whether at the level of the old community or higher, became more exclusively masculine affairs. A possible development in seventh-century northern Gaul is the fragmentation of the former *civitates* into smaller *pagus* communities at a level between the old *villae* and the *civitas* (Halsall 2012). Furthermore, politics may have been played out to a greater extent away from the old public spaces of the cities and more in the private, or privatized, spaces of royal or aristocratic palaces or villas/estate centers, or rural monasteries. This might have increased the political invisibility of most women. Perhaps the masculine body now became something more crucially in the political gaze, and masculinity became something performed rather differently than before. We might consider the location of the greatest foci of display in masculine costume, the ever-larger, often lavishly adorned plate buckles and counterplates, across the lower stomach. Like the high, narrow-waisted doublets and full breeches of the late sixteenth and earlier seventeenth centuries, they might be read as highlighting virility.

Gender and Costume in
the Seventh Century

Plate buckles are not common in sixth-century graves and are found overwhelmingly in masculine burials (Lorren 2001, p. 197). When women began to wear these objects, they were initially small and plain. Masculine versions then gradually became larger and more ornate as women began to wear decorated plate buckles. This is an interesting dynamic. One might suggest that as a hitherto masculine symbol was adopted by women, men redefined it, and so on. Such a dynamic has many parallels. One is the way in which, as women began to be depicted in Roman funerary art with symbols of learning, symbols that earlier were only used to depict the model of a good father and husband, male sarcophagi began to show such things less and to stress pastimes like hunting instead (Huskinson 1999).

Why did women start wearing hitherto masculine objects? Perhaps this is another indication of the shift suggested earlier: the return to a more "monopolar" construction of gender. The good wife, the good woman, has virtue demonstrated partly through masculine artifacts. One might be able to move from there to consider the most lavish disc brooches in a similar light. Rather than simply being a feminine accessory, these objects possibly transcend the normal plainness of female dress adjuncts to be as decorated as masculine brooches. Grave 147 at Audun-le-Tiche, buried in a clearly prestigious location and possibly even a founder-burial, might take on a different aspect (Simmer 1988, pp. 65–66, 68). This is one of the most lavish female graves of the cemetery, with unusual displays of jewelry. What is surprising, after a study of sixth-century burials, is that the occupant of the grave was an old woman. If, however, the postulated redefinition of gender around 600 is correct, it might be that the display here is not fundamentally related to sex, reproduction, and the family, as would have been the case earlier, and *perhaps* it is not an example either of how distinction in seventh-century funerary display was made by consciously breaking communal rules about the correct grave-goods or of the more straightforward display of familial wealth and standing (as argued by Halsall 1995, pp. 264–265). The grave's dimensions are exceptional, requiring more effort than usual for their construction. Perhaps the recognition of female status had come to be based on issues other than marriage, sex, and childbearing.

Conclusion: Seventh-Century Gender
in Secular and Religious Spheres

Have we returned to something more like the Roman construction of gender? The clearest difference between the fourth- and seventh-century situations is that the martial model of masculinity was now dominant. Various factors, including the spread of Frankish ethnicity had led to a shift in the ways of raising the army away from the "ethnically based" force of the sixth century to an army based more on aristocratic retinues in the seventh (Halsall 2003, pp. 53–56). This model was now, in important regards, more socially restricted, its performance confined to more select political gatherings of men. Few, if any, women—and indeed only a minority of men—could approach *this* ideal. In this connection, it is noteworthy that the distinctly "virile" figure of the Neustrian Queen Fredegund, leading her army to battle, belongs not to the sixth century, when she lived, but to the early eighth (*Liber Historiae Francorum* [LHF] 36). That was profoundly different from the classical situation.

However, another model, religious and consciously asexual, stood outside reproduction and the family. The shifts that occurred in this area of Merovingian Gaul were subtle, but, at the risk of overschematization, some suggestions are possible. One aspect of the greater entrenchment of local aristocratic power around 600 was, as is well known, the increased focus on more organized rural monasticism, which often, and too simplistically, was associated with the Irish holy man Columbanus (Fox 2014). Away from towns and frequently less subject to effective episcopal domination, these houses became the foci for much of seventh-century Gaul's secular as well as religious politics (see Diem, Chapter 15; Picard, Chapter 18, this volume). With grants of immunity, abbots could become almost as significant religious and political figures as bishops (Rosenwein 1999, pp. 59–96), while the estates with which their houses were endowed sometimes put them on a course toward equal landowning importance. Female rural monasteries often had a male house attached, not least to provide the nuns with officiants at mass. Consequently, these "double-houses" were often governed by women.

This flourishing and comparatively more stable monasticism may have led to a greater level of entry into religious life during childhood or adolescence. Some saints of traditional, sixth-century type are nevertheless recorded. Saint Arnulf is unusual for having led a successful life as a warrior as well as a politician before becoming bishop of Metz (*Vita Arnulfi* 4–5) and eventually retiring to be a recluse in the Vosges. Nonetheless, many bishops, as before, entered the church after secular service: Eligius, Audoin, and Desiderius of Cahors are famous examples. Yet, marriage is rarely mentioned, and, as with some sixth-century holy men, the crucial point seems to have come at the end of their period of unmarried apprenticeship: their *pueritia*. Most of the famous abbots seem to have entered the church quite early. If the period of *pueritia* had become more teleological in its gendered outcome, as the nonmartial form of masculinity now dominated, sexual renunciation and the ecclesiastical life was perhaps the only alternative for those who could choose. This limitation of gendered models was probably yet more acute for females, if the suggested shift toward a more monopolar construction of gender is correct. Chaste widows entering the religious life are attested in the seventh century (most famously with St. Balthild) but the saints' lives of the period are dominated by women who dedicated themselves to a virginal life early on, so that the struggles that occurred when their families demanded that they marry become a common feature of the *vitae*.[7] Obviously, as more successful female houses were established and as many emerging Frankish noble families listed nuns and abbesses among their number, the availability of this gendered model increased exponentially. It would be interesting to examine whether this was accompanied by a change in the significance of the cult of the Virgin or whether the *vitae* of Roman virgin martyrs circulated more than before. Crucially, then, while the idealized "center" of the gendered secular world could never truly be occupied other than by a male, in the religious sphere, such a central role could be occupied effectively by a woman as well as a man. It is small surprise that the seventh century was an age of great abbesses.

The roles and possibilities opened up by the performance of an identity can never remain fixed. The impossibility of stasis stems not only from the demands of, in Pierre Bourdieu's terms, the *habitus*, of everyday coexistence, or the constant renegotiation of roles and statuses in Anthony Giddens's theory of structuration, although this is clearly a major element. It stems similarly from the fact that identities are not entities, but idealized, unattainable objects, and so they can never have a fixed, stable, authentic meaning. As Derrida said in his classic (1988) discussion of performatives, the communication of such signifieds in daily performance always, through their iterability, risks miscommunication and slippage (see also Butler 1993). There was no such single thing as medieval gender or a finite number of genders, and there was always scope for change, active renegotiation, play, transgression, and, yes, repression (in all senses). The everyday lived existence of the people of Merovingian northern Gaul between, say, 500 and 650 was constituted by gender and its performance. Reciprocally, gender delineated performance and went far beyond the simple construction of men and women.

More than that, close analysis of Merovingian gender, in all its surprising malleability, changeability through time, and stubborn refusal to conform to the patterns that modern readers expect of "the medieval" is a valuable political resource in the present, when so many politicians appeal to a mythical past "normality" and "naturalness" in order to attempt to fix modern sexuality and gender relations in a particular mode. The Merovingian case study tells us that there is nothing timeless and "natural" about past gender and sexuality, other than the impossibility of keeping them in their place.

Notes

1. For example, recently, see Fox 2014, p. 13: "The question of gender is another component of the same question.... [A]fter [Columbanus's] death women came to occupy an increasingly important place in the leadership of Columbanian communities."
2. This example illustrates the profound error committed by those who wish to label the chaste clergy a "third gender," as though there are otherwise only two (McNamara, 2002).
3. For introductions in English to Merovingian cemeteries and their study, see Dierkens and Périn (1997); Périn (2002); and Effros (2003).
4. For fuller accounts, see Halsall (1995, 1996, 2010b); Brather (2004b, 2005, 2008); Lohrke (2004); and Stauch (2008).
5. Many of the famous early Merovingian "tombes de chef" are of males of this age group such as the occupant of the famous grave 319 at Lavoye (Meuse) and the two "chefs"

(graves 11 and 13) recently excavated at Saint-Dizier: see Joffroy (1974, pp. 95–101); Truc and Paresys (2008).

6. See, above all, van Ossel (1992) and Peytremann (2003). Excellent overviews can be found in Burnouf et al. (2009), pp. 95–153, and Catteddu (2009), especially pp. 25–87. In English, see Périn (2002, 2004) and Zadora-Rio (2003).

7. The lives of the saints mentioned in this paragraph: *Vita Eligii*; *Vita Audoini Episcopi Rotomagensis*; *Vita Desiderii Cadurcae Urbis Episcopi*; *Vita Sanctae Balthildis*,

Works Cited

Ancient Sources

Cassian, *Institutes*. J.-P. Migne (ed.). (1874). *Patrologia Latina* 49. Paris: Thibaud.

Cassian, *Institutes*. B. Ramsay (trans.). (2000). *John Cassian: The Institutes*. Ancient Christian Writers 58. New York: Paulist Press.

Cummean, *Penitential*. L. Bieler with D. A. Binchy (eds.). (1963). *The Irish Penitentials* (pp. 108–135). Dublin: Dublin Institute for Advanced Studies.

Decretio Childeberti. K.-A. Eckhardt (ed.). (1962). *Pactus Legis Salicae* (pp. 267–269). In *MGH Legum*, Section 1, 4.1. Hanover: Hahn.

Decretio Childeberti. K. Fischer Drew (trans.). (1991). *Laws of the Salian Franks* (pp. 156–159). Philadelphia: University of Pennsylvania Press.

Gregory of Tours, *GM*. B. Krusch and W. Levison (eds.). (1969). MGH SRM 1.2 (pp. 34–111). Hanover: Hahn.

Gregory of Tours, *GM*. R. Van Dam (trans.). (1988). *Gregory of Tours, Glory of the Martyrs*. Liverpool: Liverpool University Press.

Gregory of Tours, *Histories*. B. Krusch and W. Levison (eds.). (1951). *Gregory of Tours, Historiae Libri Decem*. MGH SRM 1.1. Hanover: Hahn.

Gregory of Tours, *Histories*. L. Thorpe (trans.). (1974). *Gregory of Tours, History of the Franks*. Harmondsworth: Penguin.

Gregory of Tours, *VP*. B. Krusch and W. Levison (eds.). (1969). MGH SRM 1.2 (pp. 211–294). Hanover: Hahn.

Gregory of Tours, *VP*. E. James (trans.). (1991). *Gregory of Tours, Life of the Fathers*. 2nd ed. Liverpool: Liverpool University Press.

Gregory of Tours, *VP*. G. de Nie (ed. and trans.). (2015). *Gregory of Tours, Lives and Miracles* (pp. 1–297). Dumbarton Oaks Medieval Library 39. Cambridge, MA: Harvard University Press.

Liber Historiae Francorum. B. Krusch (ed.). (2015). *La Geste des Rois des Francs. Liber Historiae Francorum*, trans. S. Lebecq. Paris: Les Belles Lettres.

McNeill, J. T., and Gamer, H. M. (trans.). (1990[1938]). *Medieval Handbooks of Penance. A Translation of the Principal Libri Poenitentiales* (pp. 179–215). New York: Columbia University Press.

PLS. K.-A. Eckhardt (ed.). (1962). *Pactus Legis Salicae*. MGH Legum, Section 1, 4, 1. Hanover: Hahn.

PLS. K. Fischer Drew (trans.). (1991). *The Laws of the Salian Franks*. Philadelphia: University of Pennsylvania Press.

Penitential of Theodore. F. W. H. Wasserschleben (ed.). (1851). *Die Bussordnungen der abendländischen Kirche nebst einer rechtsgeschichtlichen Einleitung* (pp. 182–119). Halle: Graeger.

Venantius Fortunatus, *Carmina*. M. Reydellet (ed. and trans.). (2002–2004). *Venance Fortunat, Poèmes*. 3 vols. Paris: Les Belles Lettres.

Venantius Fortunatus, *Vita Radegundis*. B. Krusch (ed.). (1888). MGH SRM 2 (pp. 358–77). Hanover: Hahn.

Venantius Fortunatus, *Vita Radegundis*. J.-A. McNamara, J. E. Halborg, and E. G. Whatley (trans.). (1992). *Sainted Women of the Dark Ages* (pp. 70–86). Durham, NC: Duke University Press.

Vita Arnulfi. B. Krusch (ed.). (1888). MGH SRM 2 (pp. 426–446). Hanover: Hahn.

Vita Audoini Episcopi Rotomagensis. B. Krusch (ed.). (1910). MGH SRM 5 (pp. 536–567). Hanover: Hahn.

Vita Desiderii Cadurcae Urbis Episcopi. B. Krusch (ed.). (1902). MGH SRM 4 (pp. 547–602). Hanover: Hahn.

Vita Eligii Episcopi Noviomagensis. B. Krusch (ed.). (1902). MGH SRM 4 (pp. 634–661). Hanover: Hahn.

Vita Genovefae. B. Krusch (ed.). (1896). MGH SRM 3 (pp. 204–238). Hanover: Hahn.

Vita Genovefae. J.-A. McNamara, J. E. Halborg, and E. G. Whatley (trans.). (1992). *Sainted Women of the Dark Ages* (pp. 19–37). Durham, NC: Duke University Press.

Vita Sanctae Balthildis. B. Krusch (ed.). (1888). MGH SRM 2 (pp. 475–508). Hanover: Hahn

Modern Sources

Badash, D. (2016). "Ted Cruz tells transgender women to only use the bathroom at home." http://www.thenewcivilrightsmovement.com/davidbadash/watch_ted_cruz_tells_transgender_women_to_only_use_the_bathroom_at_home [accessed August 2, 2016].

Beauvoir, S. de (2011). *The Second Sex*, trans. C. Borde and S. Malovany-Chevallier. London: Random House.

Brather, S. (2004a). *Ethnische Interpretationen in der frühgeschichtlichen Archäologie: Geschichte, Grundlagen und Alternativen*. Ergänzungsbände zum Reallexikon der Germanischen Altertumskunde 42. Berlin: Walter de Gruyter.

Brather, S. (2004b). "Kleidung und Identität im Grab: Gruppierungen innerhalb der Bevölkerung Pleidelsheims zur Merowingerzeit." *Zeitschrift für Archäologie des Mittelalters* 32: 1–58.

Brather, S. (2005). "Alter und Geschlecht zur Merowingerzeit. Soziale Strukturen und frühmittelalterlichen Reihengräberfelder." In J. Müller (ed.), *Alter und Geschlecht in ur- und frühgeschichtlichen Gesellschaften* (pp.157–178). Bonn: Habelt.

Brather, S. (2008). "Kleidung, Bestattung, Identität: die Präsentation sozialer Rollen im frühen Mittelalter." In S. Brather (ed.), *Zwischen Spätantike und Frühmittelalter: Archäologie des 4. bis 7. Jahrhunderts im Westen* (pp. 237–273). Erganzungsbände zum Reallexikon der germanischen Altertumskunde 57. Berlin: Walter de Gruyter.

Brubaker, L., and Smith, J. M. H. (eds.). (2004). *Gender in the Early Medieval World: East and West, 300–900*. Cambridge: Cambridge University Press.

Burnouf, J., Arribet-Deroin, D., Desachy, B., Journot, F., and Nissen-Jaubert, A. (2009). *Manuel d'archéologie médiévale et moderne*. Paris: Colin.

Butler, J. (1993). *Bodies that Matter. On the Discursive Limits of "Sex."* London: Routledge.

Butler, J. (1999). *Gender Trouble. Feminism and the Subversion of Identity*, 2nd ed. London: Routledge.

Catteddu, I. (2009). *Archéologie médiévale en France: Le premier Moyen Âge (Vᵉ–XIᵉ siècle)*. Paris: La Découverte.

Cohen, J. J. (2003). *Medieval Identity Machines*. Minneapolis: University of Minnesota Press.

Cooper, K., and Leyser, C. (2001). "The Gender of Grace: Impotence, Servitude and Manliness in the Fifth-Century West." In Pauline Stafford and Anneke B. Mulder-Bakker (eds.), *Gendering the Middle Ages* (pp. 6–21). Oxford: Blackwells.

Copjec, J. (1994). *Read My Desire. Lacan against the Historicists.* London: Verso.

Critchley, S. (2014). *The Ethics of Deconstruction. Derrida and Levinas.* 3rd ed. Edinburgh: Edinburgh University Press.

Dailey, E. T. (2014). "Confinement and Exclusion in the Monasteries of Sixth-Century Gaul." *Early Medieval Europe* 22(3): 304–335.

Dailey, E. T. (2015). *Queens, Consorts, Concubines: Gregory of Tours and Women of the Merovingian Elite.* Leiden: Brill.

de Jong, M. (1996). *In Samuel's Image: Child Oblation in the Early Medieval West.* Leiden: Brill.

Deleuze, G. (1994). *Difference and Repetition,* trans. P. Patton. London: Bloomsbury.

Derrida, J. (1967). *De la Grammatologie.* Paris: Minuit.

Derrida, J. (1988). *Limited Inc,* trans. A. Bass and S. Weber. Evanston, IL: Northwestern University Press.

Derrida, J. (1997). *Of Grammatology,* trans. G. Chakravorty Spivak. 2nd ed. Baltimore: Johns Hopkins University Press.

Dierkens, A., and Périn, P. (1997). "Death and Burial in Gaul and Germania, 4th–8th century." In L. Webster and M. Brown (eds.), *The Transformation of the Roman World, AD 400–900* (pp. 79–95). London: British Museum.

Effros, B. (1996). "Symbolic Expressions of Sanctity: Gertrude of Nivelles in the Context of Merovingian Mortuary Custom." *Viator* 27: 1–10.

Effros, B. (2000). "Skeletal Sex and Gender in Merovingian Mortuary Archaeology." *Antiquity* 74: 632–639.

Effros, B. (2003). *Merovingian Mortuary Archaeology and the Making of the Early Middle Ages.* Berkeley: University of California Press.

Evans, D. (1996). *An Introductory Dictionary of Lacanian Psychoanalysis.* Hove: Routledge.

Fox, Y. (2014). *Power and Religion in Merovingian Gaul: Columbian Monasticism and the Frankish Elites.* Cambridge: Cambridge University Press.

Foxhall, L. (2013). *Studying Gender in Classical Antiquity.* Cambridge: Cambridge University Press.

Freeman, E. (2010). *Time Binds. Queer Temporalities, Queer Histories.* Durham, NC: Duke University Press.

Hadley, D. M. (ed.). (1999). *Masculinity in Medieval Europe.* London: Longman.

Halsall, G. (1995). *Settlement and Social Organization. The Merovingian Region of Metz.* Cambridge: Cambridge University Press.

Halsall, G. (1996). "Female Status and Power in Early Merovingian Central Austrasia: The Burial Evidence." *Early Medieval Europe,* 5(1): 1–24. Repr. in Halsall (2010d), pp. 289–314.

Halsall, G. (2003). *Warfare and Society in the Barbarian West, 450–900.* London: Routledge.

Halsall, G. (2007). *Barbarian Migrations and the Roman West, 376–568.* Cambridge: Cambridge University Press.

Halsall, G. (2010a). "Merovingian Masculinities." In G. Halsall (ed.), *Cemeteries and Society in Merovingian Gaul: Selected Studies in History and Archaeology, 1992–2009.* Leiden: Brill, pp. 357–381.

Halsall, G. (2010b). "Growing Up in Merovingian Gaul." In G. Halsall (ed.), *Cemeteries and Society in Merovingian Gaul: Selected Studies in History and Archaeology, 1992–2009,* pp. 383–312.

Halsall, G. (2010c). "Material Culture, Sex, Gender, Sexuality and Transgression in Sixth-Century Gaul." In G. Halsall (ed.), *Cemeteries and Society in Merovingian Gaul: Selected Studies in History and Archaeology, 1992–2009,* pp. 323–355.

Halsall, G. (2010d). *Cemeteries and Society in Merovingian Gaul: Selected Studies in History and Archaeology, 1992–2009.* Leiden: Brill.

Halsall, G. (2012). "From Roman *fundus* to Carolingian Grand Domaine: Crucial Ruptures between Late Antiquity and the Middle Ages." *Revue Belge de Philologie et d'Histoire* 90, 273–298.

Halsall, G. (2018). "Classical gender in deconstruction." In S. Joye and R. Le Jan (eds.), *Genre et compétition dans les sociétés Occidentales du haut moyen-âge (IVe-XIe Siècle)* (pp. 27–42). Collection Haut Moyen Âge 29. Turnhout: Brepols.

Hen, Y. (2004). "Gender and Patronage of Culture in Merovingian Gaul." In L. Brubaker and J. M. H. Smith (eds.), *Gender in the Early Medieval World: East and West, 300–900* (pp. 217–233). Cambridge: Cambridge University Press.

Huskinson, J. (1999). "Women and Learning: Gender and Identity in Scenes of Intellectual Life on Late Roman Sarcophagi." In R. Miles (ed.), *Constructing Identities in Late Antiquity* (pp. 190–213). London: Routledge.

James, E. (1982). *The Origins of France. From Clovis to the Capetians, 500–1000.* London: Macmillan.

Joffroy, R. (1974). *Le Cimetière de Lavoye. Nécropole mérovingienne.* Paris: Picard.

Lacan, J. (1978). *Le Séminaire, Livre II. Le Moi dans la théorie de Freud et dans la technique de la psychanalyse*, ed. J.-A. Miller. Paris: Seuil.

Legoux, R., Périn, P., and Vallet, F. (2009). *Chronologie normalisée du mobilier funéraire mérovingien entre Manche et Lorraine.* 3rd ed. Condé-sur-Noireau: Association française d'archéologie mérovingienne.

Liéger, A., Marguet, R., and Guillaume, J. (1984). "Sépultures mérovingiens de l'abbaye de Saint-Evre à Toul (Meurthe-et-Moselle)." *Revue Archéologique de l'Est et de Centre-Est* 35, 301–317.

Lohrke, B. (2004). *Kinder in der Merowingerzeit. Gräber von Mädchen und Jungen in der Alemannia.* Freiburger Beiträge zur Archäologie und Geschichte des ersten Jahrtausends 9. Rahden: Leidorf.

Lorren, C. (2001). *Fibules et plaques-boucles à l'époque mérovingienne en Normandie: Contribution à l'étude du peuplement, des échanges et des influences, de la fin du Ve au début du VIIIe siècle.* Condé-sur-Noireau: Association française d'archéologie mérovingienne.

Lucy, S. J. (1997). "Housewives, Warriors and Slaves? Sex and Gender in Anglo-Saxon Burials." In E. Scott and J. Moore (eds.), *Invisible People and Processes: Writing Gender and Sexuality into European Archaeology* (pp. 150–168). London: Leicester University Press.

McNamara, J.-A. (2002). "Chastity as a Third Gender in the History and Hagiography of Gregory of Tours." In K. Mitchell and I. N. Wood (eds.), *The World of Gregory of Tours* (pp. 199–209). Leiden: Brill.

McNamara, J.-A., Halborg, J. E., and Whatley, E. G. (trans.). (1992). *Sainted Women of the Dark Ages.* Durham, NC: Duke University Press.

Mitchell, K., and Wood, I. N. (eds.). (2002). *The World of Gregory of Tours.* Leiden: Brill.

Nelson, J. L., (1996). "Gender and Genre in Women Historians of the Early Middle Ages." In J. L. Nelson, *The Frankish World, 750–900* (pp. 183–197). London: Hambledon.

Nelson, J. L. (2004). "Gendering Courts in the Early Medieval West." In L. Brubaker and J. M. H. Smith (eds.), *Gender in the Early Medieval World: East and West, 300–900* (pp. 185–197). Cambridge: Cambridge University Press.

Partner, N. F. (1993). "No Sex, No Gender." *Speculum* 68, 419–443.

Périn, P. (with contribution by R. Legoux), (1980). *La Datation des tombes mérovingiennes. Historique—Méthodes- Applications.* Paris: Droz.

Périn, P. (2002). "Settlements and Cemeteries in Merovingian Gaul." In K. Mitchell and I. N. Wood (eds.), *The World of Gregory of Tours* (pp. 67–99). Leiden: Brill.

Périn, P. (2004). "The Origin of the Village in Early Medieval Gaul." In N. Christie (ed.), *Landscapes of Change: Rural Evolutions in Late Antiquity and the Early Middle Ages* (pp. 255–278). Aldershot: Ashgate.

Peytremann, E. (2003). *Archéologie de l'habitat rural dans le Nord de la France du IVe au XIIe Siécle.* 2 vols. Condé sur Noireau: Association française d'archéologie mérovingienne

Rosenwein, B. (1999). *Negotiating Space: Power, Restraint and Privileges of Immunity in Early Medieval Europe.* Manchester: Manchester University Press.

Rubin, G. (1975). "The Traffic in Women: Notes on the 'Political Economy' of Sex." In R. R. Reiter (ed.), *Toward an Anthropology of Women* (pp. 157–210). New York: Monthly Review Press.

Scott, J. Wallach (1986). "Gender: A Useful Category of Historical Analysis." *American Historical Review* 91, 1053–1075.

Simmer, A. (1988). *Le Cimetière mérovingien d'Audun-le-Tiche: Archéologie d'aujourd'hui 1.* Paris: Association française d'archéologie mérovingienne.

Simmer, A. (1993). *La Nécropole mérovingienne d'Ennery (Moselle). Fouilles d'Emile Delort (1941)* Woippy: Association française d'archéologie mérovingienne.

Smith, J. M. H. (2001). "Did Women Have a Transformation of the Roman World?" In P. Stafford and A. B. Mulder-Bakker (eds.), *Gendering the Middle Ages*, pp. 22–41.

Smith, J. M. H. (2004). "Introduction: Gendering the Early Medieval World." In L. Brubaker and J. M. H. Smith (eds.), *Gender in the Early Medieval World: East and West, 300–900* (pp. 1–19). Cambridge: Cambridge University Press.

Stafford, P., and Mulder-Bakker, A. B. (eds.). (2001). *Gendering the Middle Ages.* Oxford: Blackwells (= *Gender and History* 12.3 [2000]).

Stauch, E. (2008). "Alter ist Silber, Jugend ist Gold! Zur altersdifferenzierten Analyse frühge-schichtlicher Bestattungen." In S. Brather (ed.), *Zwischen Spätantike und Frühmittelalter: Archäologie des 4. bis 7. Jahrhunderts im Westen* (pp. 275–295). Erganzungsbände zum Reallexikon der germanischen Altertumskunde 57. Berlin: Walter de Gruyter.

Truc, M.-C., and Peresys, P. (2008). "Trois tombes d'exception a Saint-Dizier." In C. Varéon (ed.), *Nos ancêtres les barbares. Voyage autour de trois tombes de chefs francs* (pp. 50–69). Saint-Dizier: Somogy.

van Ossel, P. (1992). *Établissements ruraux de l'antiquité tardive dans le Nord de la Gaule (51e Supplément à Gallia).* Paris: Éditions du CNRS

Vierck, H.E.F. (1978). "La 'Chemise de Sainte-Bathilde' à Chelles et l'influence byzantine sur l'art de cour merovingien au VIIe siècle." In *Actes du Colloque international d'archéologie: centenaire de l'abbé Cochet* (pp. 521–570). Rouen: Musée départemental des Antiquités de Seine-Maritime

Wemple, S. F. (1985). *Women in Frankish Society. Marriage and the Cloister.* Philadelphia: University of Pennsylvania Press.

Werner, J. (1964). "Frankish Royal Tombs in the Cathedrals of Cologne and Saint-Denis." *Antiquity* 38, 201–216.

Wood, I. N., (1988). "Forgery in Merovingian Hagiography." In *Fälschungen im Mittelalter. Internationaler Kongress der MGH, München 16–19 September 1986, 5: Fingierte Briefe. Frömmigkeit und Fälschung. Realienfälschung* (pp. 369–384). MGH Schriften 33. Hanover: Hahn.

Zadora-Rio, E. (2003). "The Making of Churchyards and Parish Territories in the Early-Medieval Landscape of France and England in the 7th–12th Centuries: A Reconsideration." *Medieval Archaeology* 47: 1–19.

CHAPTER 9

··

CHILDREN'S LIVES AND DEATHS IN MEROVINGIAN GAUL

··

ÉMILIE PEREZ

UNTIL recently, childhood in Merovingian Gaul has been little studied. Children are poorly represented in contemporary texts and pictures, and they are underrepresented in archaeological remains. Consequently, historians and archaeologists have paid little attention to this important segment of the early medieval population in Gaul. However, the relative invisibility of children in the sources has been countered in recent years by the work of researchers of many nationalities. The beautiful book edited by Güner Coşkunsu, *The Archaeology of Childhood* (2015), with its focus on Antiquity, is a welcome sign of progress. It reflects new interdisciplinary approaches in present archaeological debates that make use of a combination of texts, material remains, and bones from early medieval graves.

Unlike the written sources from the early Middle Ages, archaeological remains are rapidly growing in number: excavations continue to bring new data to bear on this period, especially in France, where preventive archaeology (that which is conducted in advance of construction—once called salvage archaeology) is a very dynamic sector (Chapelot 2010). Although fifth- to seventh-century cemeteries dominated the archaeological literature of the nineteenth and early twentieth century (see Effros, Chapter 4, this volume), this imbalance is no longer the case. Many excavations now address sites such as monasteries, churches, rural and urban dwellings, and landscapes (Peytremann 2003). Recent research has greatly improved our understanding of the Merovingian period through fields like archaeobotany, including palynology (the study of ancient pollen, spores, and plankton), carpology (the study of fruit and seeds), and anthracology (the study of charcoal or carbonized wood). Advances have also been made in ceramology (the study of ceramics), archaeozoology, and biological anthropology (Verslype and Périn 2007). Despite this expansion of perspectives on the early Middle Ages, it appears that only the patient study of hundreds of graves and thousands of skeletons is likely to improve our understanding of early medieval children (Crawford 2000; Gilchrist 2012; Lally and Moore 2011; Stoodley 2011).

Indeed, biological anthropology provides a multifaceted approach to the funerary treatment of children, linking biological features (e.g., sex, age, height, and pathology) with archaeological data (e.g., burial mode, location, and grave goods). Improved osteological methods, and especially their full integration with historical data, have shown that age and gender have an important influence on burial rites (Halsall 1996; Stoodley 2000; Effros 2003; Lucy 2005; Gowland 2006; see also Halsall, Chapter 8, this volume).

Research on children in Merovingian Gaul is considerably more rare than that for other periods and regions (Halsall 1996, 2010b; Alduc-Le Bagousse 1997), despite the rich archaeological documentation that has been published in recent years on funerary assemblages and human remains.[1] In this context, the recent analysis of 315 children from four burial grounds in northern Gaul dating from the sixth to the eighth century allows us to discuss the role of age, as well as gender, in the construction and expression of their social identity (Perez 2013).

CHILDREN FROM GRAVES AND BONES: PROBLEMS AND PERSPECTIVES

Between the fifth and the late seventh centuries, men, women, and children were buried with an assortment of grave-goods, including weapons, brooches, beads in necklaces or bracelets, belt fittings, buckles, knives, ceramic pots, and glass vessels. Considered as evidence for pagan practice in the nineteenth century, the deposition of objects in graves is today understood as a social practice (Halsall 1996; Périn 1998; Effros 2002; Verslype 2005; Young 2006). The large variation in the quality and quantity of the grave goods appears indicative of social hierarchy in early medieval communities (see Theuws, Chapter 38, and Patrello, Chapter 39, this volume). In addition, many modern assessments of these graves have focused on the ethnicity of the deceased (Périn and Kazanski 2011), and on the significance of the extant high-status graves as evidence for the ostentatious funerals of the elite (Young 2006; Alduc-Le Bagousse 2009).

Children's graves have been the subject of growing interest among archaeologists since the 1990s, following the publication of a number of collective projects on medieval childhood (Shahar 1990; Lett 1997; Orme 2003). However, many problems continue to challenge these studies. For example, it is often the case that Merovingian cemeteries are only partially excavated, which means that we do not have a complete and representative view of the spaces occupied by the dead and indeed all of the buried population (such as those who might have been relegated to the margins or beyond the boundaries of cemeteries). Furthermore, many early medieval cemeteries were disturbed by reburials or looted by treasure hunters, meaning that bones and grave-goods were removed or scattered on the ground in the process. Consequently, archaeologists regularly observe a lack of infant and young children in Merovingian cemeteries, a phenomenon known as underrepresentation. This conflicts with what we know about high infant mortality rates among preindustrial populations (Gilchrist 2012; Séguy and Buchet 2013). A failure to identify relevant bones as those of children, the greater fragility of the bones of infants and young children, and disruptions due to successive burials in these cemeteries, do not completely explain this phenomenon (Treffort 1997; Buckberry 2000; Kamp 2001; Lewis 2007). "Underrepresentation" suggests, in fact, that a different process was at work: it is likely that not all children were buried in the collective cemetery for any of a number of reasons. Indeed, we do not know whether there were rules for access to burial in Merovingian cemeteries: they do not survive in written sources and are not evident from excavations. Baptism, the first ritual of integration into the Christian community, cannot be invoked as having been a condition of burial: between the fifth and the seventh centuries, baptizing children at birth or shortly thereafter does not seem to have become a widespread ritual habit in Gaul (Cramer 1993, Treffort 1997). Rules determining access to medieval cemeteries seem to have developed only by the tenth century, when rites of consecration for burial grounds seem to have been implemented. It was even later that discourses concerning the exclusion of certain people from sacred space multiplied, for instance, in the case of twelfth- and thirteenth-century legislation condemning the inclusion of unbaptized children in Christian cemeteries (Treffort 1996, pp. 137–143; Lauwers 2005, pp. 166–167; Perez 2015), though examples as early as the Merovingian period exist (Effros 1997). Before this decisive stage in the medieval funerary process, these children were buried in cemeteries but perhaps without the benefit of liturgical rites or a complete funeral (Riché and Alexandre-Bidon 1994, p. 85; Lett 1997, p. 211).

Because of these many challenges, the study of children's graves has long been neglected. Since children were considered as passive and secondary agents of ancient and medieval societies, their socioeconomic, familial, religious, and domestic roles have been minimized (Coşkunsu 2015, p. 4–6), as was the case for women before them. For the last decade, however, multidisciplinary research has integrated the contributions of osteology to our understanding of some aspects of living conditions, health, and child mortality during the early Middle Ages. This research has helped restore children to narratives of this period (Lewis 2002, 2007; Halcrow and Tayles 2011).

AGE FROM A SOCIAL PERSPECTIVE

Understanding the modalities of burial ritual is a major challenge in addressing Merovingian society. Age and sex are part of social identity and are visible in the deposition of grave goods at death. Although there is considerable research on these rituals for adults, even if they do not always agree (Halsall 1996; Périn 1998; Lucy 2005), far less research has been conducted on children, especially in France (Perez 2013).

Physical anthropologists determine the sex of ancient skeletons from the hipbone or cranium (Séguy and Buchet 2013), but the accuracy of the results depends primarily on the preservation of the bones, which is not always optimal in large and long-used cemeteries. Because of these difficulties, archaeologists have often used grave-goods to sex individuals, thus creating inevitable contradictions between "archaeological" and "biological" sex. Some, like women wearing presumably male buckles with counterbuckle plates, have not caused too much confusion, but women with weapons have been disputed to a greater degree (Effros 2000). Still, double-blind osteological analysis provides the accuracy and reliability that is necessary for a methodological discussion of the sex and gender features of these graves. Based on recent studies, it appears that grave goods are generally specific to sex, but that their choice varies by cemetery: the division of goods by sex is generally characterized by the deposit of weaponry for men and jewelry (brooches, beads, bracelets, pins, earrings, and rings) for women (Halsall 1995; Riché and Périn 2013 on amulets for women and children, see Kornbluth, Chapter 40, this volume).

However, anthropological assessments of age at death for adults are more difficult to render accurately; the margin of error ranges between ten and thirty years, depending on the methods employed. Certain biological indicators, including the auricular surface of the ilium (hip bone), the synostosis of cranial sutures, and multifactorial methods, help improve the accuracy of results (Séguy and Buchet 2013). Because these difficulties are inherent in the use of biological parameters in the analysis of grave sites, they must be taken into account in the social interpretation of the burial ritual, especially when adults are grouped within ranges of ten- or twenty-five-year clusters on the basis of old, and therefore questionable, data (Halsall 1996; Stoodley 2000).

Unlike the case of adults, the age of children can be estimated quite precisely because of their progressive dental development and rapid bone growth. In addition, in the last few years, studies have addressed the reliability of the indicators used, including tooth mineralization and the length of the long bones (Lewis 2007). For fetuses and perinatal infants (those under two months of age), for whom death came very early, anthropologists use the length of long bones: genetic and environmental factors did not yet have time to impact their bone growth (Scheuer, Black, and Schaefer 2009). For children up to 12 years, tooth mineralization is considered the most reliable indicator of age (e.g., Ubelaker 1989; Al Qahtani, Hector, and Liversidge 2010; for isotope studies of teeth, see Czermak, Chapter 7, this volume). For adolescents over 12 years of age, the accuracy of the age estimated from dental development decreases (e.g., 15 years +/– 36 months in Ubelaker 1989). However, anthropologists can observe the fusion of the epiphysis (the end of the long bone of a subadult, which fuses with the diaphysis only between the ages of fifteen and twenty) (Lewis 2007; Scheuer et al. 2009). For these reasons, the results presented in this study are based on dental mineralization (Ubelaker 1989), complemented by data on the fusion of the epiphysis during adolescence. Despite a number of attempts, it has not been possible to determine the sex of prepubescent children except by means of DNA analysis.

Biological and Social Age

Compared to gender, it is only recently that the study of age as a marker of social identity has been addressed from a broader perspective (Gowland 2006, pp. 143–144). Because any assessment of the implications of age in burial requires the involvement of history, archaeology, and osteology, such a study requires a multidisciplinary approach. Indeed, age at death is estimated using *biological* indicators (bones, teeth), whereas *social* age, a nonuniversal construction, is linked to the social and cultural system of a particular society (Buchet and Séguy 2008). There is significant variation in the way different societies understand and divide the life cycle, with some stages (majority, marriage, childbearing) playing a greater role in some communities than in others (Gowland 2006). Hagiographical and historical sources demonstrate the evolution of the adults' attitude toward children in the Middle Ages according to gender and age (Lett 1997; Réal 2001). In the late Middle Ages, childhood was theorized and divided into more distinct stages following a tradition dating back to Antiquity (Alexandre-Bidon 2003; Cochelin and Smyth 2013). At that time, real and symbolic ages marked the stages of childhood, and the ages of seven, twelve, and fourteen were frequently cited in contemporary texts (Lett 1997).

Absent the more plentiful texts of the later Middle Ages, archaeologists of Merovingian sites study the age distribution at individual cemetery sites by dividing children into distinct age groups: with the variations and differences evident among these groups, it is possible to point to their differential treatment in burial organization, in addition to the level of infant and child mortality, and so they can discuss their representation in cemeteries. Whereas studies in the context of Anglo-Saxon England use age groups of different lengths (Stoodley 2000; Gowland 2006; Lewis 2007), French studies employ age groups of roughly five years in length for children with the exception of a group dedicated exclusively to infancy (0–1, 1–4, 5–9, 10–14, and 15–19 years). Because these groups are fairly standardized, they are especially well suited to historical demography, for which age is a precise input, allowing for a measure of the time between two demographic events, for example, between birth and marriage. For archaeological populations, however, age estimates are almost never accurate. They represent a probable estimate derived from biological indicators that are by nature subject to variability. Unlike later periods of history, early medieval demographics cannot be determined from historical sources such as parish records (Séguy and Buchet 2013).

For all of these reasons, the choice of the parameters of age groups remains extremely important. The research presented here suggests a new division of childhood into "social age groups," adapted to medieval society, following the method developed by Isabelle Séguy and Luc Buchet (Buchet and Séguy 2008; Séguy and Buchet 2013). Children from birth to seventeen years of age are distributed into four groups of five years each, except the first group, which consists of just three years. When a subject is estimated to be on the margin between two age groups (for instance, 5 years +/– 16 months), we calculate the statistical probability that he or she belongs to one or the other group.[2] The groups, then, are as follows:

- 0–2 years: This group reveals the risk of infant and toddler mortality, which was particularly high in preindustrial populations.
- 3–7 years: The age of seven years was regularly considered an important stage in childhood in medieval society. Children under seven years of age were regarded as irresponsible, fragile, and dependent on adults.
- 8–12 years: The child started a new stage of life that brought him or her closer to puberty and adulthood.
- 13–17 years: According to his or her sex, the child became an adult between twelve and fifteen years, depending on the relevant law codes,[3] while sharing the same rights (marriage, inheritance) and the same risks (childbirth, fighting) as adults.

I have applied this approach to four rural cemeteries of northern Gaul used between the sixth and eighth centuries, which were excavated thoroughly (except the cemetery at Saint-Sauveur, 80 percent of which was excavated) and their results published (Table 9.1). These sites are Cutry (Meurthe et Moselle; Legoux et al. 2005), Saint-Sauveur (Oise; Ben Redjeb 2007), Goudelancourt-lès-Pierrepont (Aisne; Nice et al. 2008), and Saint-Martin-de-Fontenay (Calvados; Pilet et al. 1994) (Fig. 9.1). Only children and adults buried individually in their graves or only cases where two skeletons were buried at the same time (multiple graves: see Duday 2005) are taken into account in this study. Collective graves, which contain several skeletons buried on successive occasions, were not included because of the difficulty of linking the grave-goods to the skeletons. The study counts 315 children, 256 of which can be identified with an estimated known age of death (Table 9.2). Children under three years of age are significantly underrepresented, as is the case in other Merovingian-period cemeteries. On the basis of these data, it is possible to identify some trends in the custom of interring grave-goods and understand the contribution of children's age to the construction of their social identity in a mortuary context.

Table 9.1. Sites Studied

Sites	Centuries in Use	Number of Children	Number of Individuals	Percentage of Children
Goudelancourt-lès-Pierrepont	6th–8th	69	402	17%
Cutry	6th–7th	46	223	21%
Saint-Sauveur	6th–8th	70	332	21%
Saint-Martin-de-Fontenay	6th–7th	130	425	31%

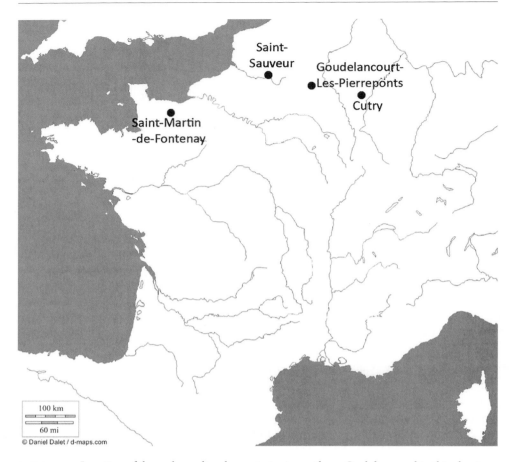

FIGURE 9.1. Location of the early medieval cemeteries in northern Gaul discussed in this chapter.

GROWING UP AND CHANGING STYLE:
GRAVE-GOODS AND SOCIAL IDENTITY

There were important differences between the burial customs employed for adults and those for children. The bodies of men, women, and children were deposited mainly in wooden coffins, but sometimes also in stone coffins, sarcophagi, or simple earthen pits. Although hagiographical texts highlight the use of shrouds,[4] it is difficult to demonstrate their presence by means of excavation (but sometimes pins or the arrangement of the bones of the deceased suggest that their use: see Duday 2005). Because the sites used in this study were excavated between 1981 and 1991, the lack of sufficient taphonomic observations (the rate of organic decay, but also the shift of grave contents over time) makes additional observations difficult. For instance, we cannot easily distinguish a

Table 9.2. Distribution of Children in Cemeteries by Age Group

	Cutry	Saint-Sauveur	Goudelancourt-lès-Pierrepont	Saint-Martin-de-Fontenay
0–2 years	7	18	4	21
3–7 years	10	14	17	34
8–12 years	10	12	18	47
13–17 years	5	10	5	24
Unknown	14	16	25	4
Total	46	70	69	130

plain-earth burial from that with a decomposed wooden coffin. Recent excavations suggest that simple pits were not as common as once thought during the early Middle Ages in Gaul (Gleize and Maurel 2009). However, prestigious grave containers like coffins carved from a single log, or stone and plaster sarcophagi, were reserved for adults, except at the cemetery of Saint-Sauveur, where sixth-century sarcophagi contained 42 percent of children of all ages (Perez 2013, pp. 400–410).

The dead were most frequently buried on their backs, with their arms placed along the length of their body or with their hands resting on their pelvis. In exceptional cases, however, arms were laid crossed on the stomach or chest, or the body was buried lying on its side or facing down. Finally, between 5 and 18 percent of the graves, usually sarcophagi and stone coffins, were reused for adults and for children over seven years of age. This practice increased in the seventh century (Perez 2013, pp. 392–394), as was the case at other Merovingian sites (Gleize and Maurel 2009; Raynaud et al. 2010).

THE DEPOSITION OF GRAVE-GOODS DURING THE MEROVINGIAN PERIOD

As scholars have already observed, from the seventh century, grave-goods became scarce and their choice standardized among children and adults (Table 9.3). Before this period, however, there was significant variation in the frequency of grave-goods deposition, depending on the cemetery in question. These statistics are also affected by later disturbances of burial sites, including the looting of graves (Fig. 9.2). The cemetery of Cutry is exceptionally well preserved, which explains why over 80 percent of the individual graves excavated at the site were furnished with grave-goods (Legoux et al. 2005). At Goudelancourt-lès-Pierrepont, the graves present rich assemblages of goods despite later erosion and disruption of the site (Nice et al. 2008). By contrast, a third of the burials uncovered were looted or reused at Saint-Sauveur (Ben Redjeb 2007), and in Saint-Martin-de-Fontenay, the cemetery was likewise heavily disturbed: around half of the graves were robbed (Pilet et al. 1994).

Table 9.3. Frequency of Children's Graves with Grave-Goods, by Site

	6th	7th	8th
Cutry	100%	63%	
Saint-Sauveur	75%	64%	13%
Goudelancourt-lès-Pierrepont	100%	83%	
Saint-Martin-de-Fontenay	62%	30%	

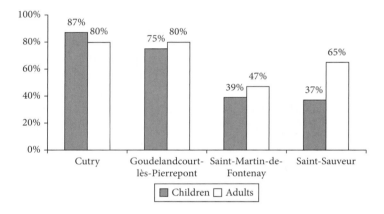

FIGURE 9.2. Frequency of grave goods in each of the cemeteries.

Indeed, looting is a serious challenge for mortuary archaeology, since in some cases it was practiced contemporary to the burial, while in others it occurred several centuries after the cemetery was abandoned (Klevnäs 2015). We may thus assume that, in most cases, the graves under study have already been disturbed, a factor that complicates their use in studies of material culture. However, children's graves were less seriously affected by pillage, no doubt because of their small size: they likely went unnoticed when grave robbers dug trenches to access the graves. As a whole, the wealth of grave-good depositions was typically higher immediately after the funeral than it was centuries later.

On average, at the cemeteries in question, 58 percent of adults and 52 percent of children were buried with grave-goods whatever their age. However, when the dead were between eight and twelve years of age, deposits increased (Fig. 9.3), but the assortment of objects in adult graves was always more numerous and diverse. In the sixth century, the average number of objects per adult was still higher than for children: 3.5 versus 2.8, respectively. The most frequent deposits consisted of jewelry,[5] ceramics, and belts (buckles and plate-buckles), these categories together representing at least half of all grave deposits. In all, 2,498 items were distributed in the graves under study, including 392 associated with children (Fig. 9.4). Jewelry represented a third of the deposits made in the graves of children and consisted mainly of beads,[6] usually of glass, sometimes of

FIGURE 9.3. Frequency of grave goods in children's graves, by age.

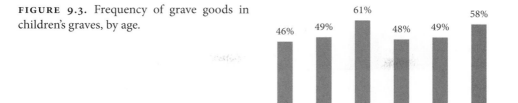

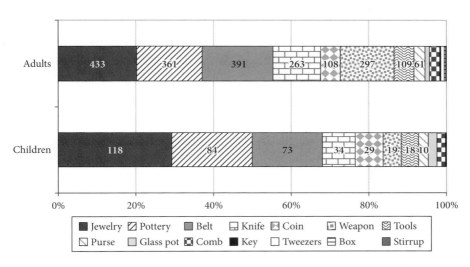

FIGURE 9.4. Distribution of grave-goods among adults and children, all sites.

amber or bone, which were strung on necklaces or bracelets (Fig. 9.5, see Pion et al., Chapter 36, this volume). Pendants of pierced shells and teeth, antler, and rock crystal, were frequently associated with children (Fig. 9.6), while brooches, earrings, rings, and pins were less commonly deposited. Bracelets (gold, silver, or bronze), chatelaines, and cord belts (signaled in graves by large beads found around the knees: *cordelières*) were used too infrequently to be significant.

Weapons and knives were associated with both war and utilitarian functions strongly linked to adulthood: only 6 percent of weapons and 11 percent of knives have been found deposited in the graves of children (Fig. 9.6). Tools were common, with 24 percent of scissors and 18 percent of needles found with children, but iron pins (*fiches à bélière*) were rarer. Prestige objects such as glass vessels, coins, and keys remained exceptional. Coins were not discovered as frequently as our figures suggest since one grave of a child buried at an age between ten and fourteen years old was found at Cutry with a purse containing fifteen coins: this abundance contrasted with the fact that only eight other children over the age of six were buried with any coins at all (on coinage, see Strothmann, Chapter 35, this volume).

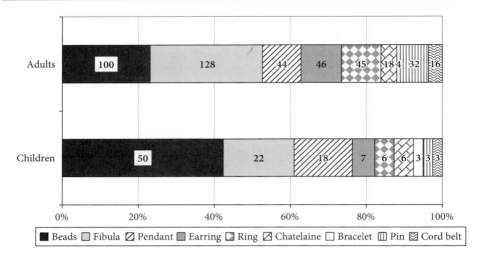

FIGURE 9.5. Distribution of jewelry among adults and children, all sites.

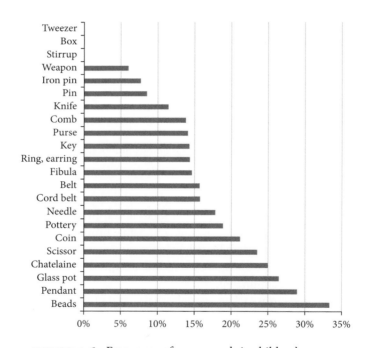

FIGURE 9.6. Frequency of grave-goods in children's graves.

Whereas the deposit of jewelry in graves decreased beginning in the seventh century, biconical pottery increased and became a major element in burial ritual, especially for children. Finally, although there were no goods exclusive to children's graves, certain items, like tweezers, spurs, and pyxides (small containers), were never placed in their graves (Fig. 9.6).

FROM BIRTH TO ADULTHOOD

While the frequency of grave-goods deposited in the graves of the deceased, whether overall or at specific cemeteries, does not correlate precisely with age, the average number of objects found in children's graves is always less than in those of adults. However, it is important to bear in mind that the four sites studied here represent a relatively small sample size. For this reason, the data have been amalgamated. Overall, they show a steady increase in the number of grave-goods laid to rest with deceased children up to the age of twelve years, when the average number nearly reached the level deposited in the graves of adults (Fig. 9.7).

Cemeterial sites reveal that variation in the number of grave-goods reflected the age of the deceased, but the results are difficult to interpret with greater granularity because of the limited number of children at each cemetery. At Cutry, Goudelancourt-lès-Pierrepont, and Saint-Martin-de-Fontenay, some objects were used in the graves of children ranging from three to eight years of age, at which point the assemblage of objects increased and diversified. The distribution of the 307 objects belonging to 134 children of known age of death (grouped by social age group) is therefore shown in Fig. 9.8.

First, the graves of infants and toddlers under three years of age at the time of death were less well furnished than the graves of older children. The grave-goods deposited with them at burial consisted mainly of pottery, belt buckles, and jewelry such as bead necklaces, pairs of brooches, and antler pendants. From three years of age, the grave-goods children received became more diversified, the quantity of jewelry increased, and some objects appeared for the first time in modest quantities, including a few pendants, a glass vessel, a coin, two purses, and, in Cutry, the first adult weapons from the age of four: axe, spear, and arrow (Fig. 9.9). Knives then became a typical deposit.

Children buried between the ages of eight and twelve years received more diverse kinds of jewelry, including pins, bronze bracelets, and earrings. In addition, weapons

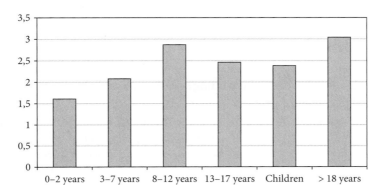

FIGURE 9.7. Average number of grave deposits by age group.

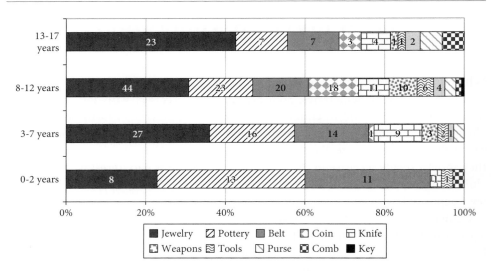

FIGURE 9.8. Distribution of grave goods by age group.

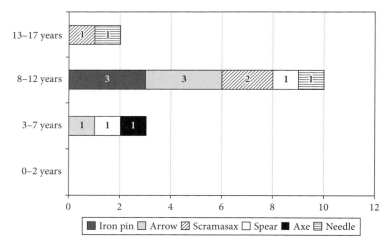

FIGURE 9.9. Distribution of weapons and tools by age group.

were more varied and frequent, including scramasaxes, spears, axes, and arrows; some were adapted to the size of children.

Finally, the graves of adolescents buried between the ages of thirteen and seventeen were typically characterized by the deposition of jewelry (42 percent of grave-goods) and by a decrease in the inclusion of weapons, tools, and especially ceramics, which regularly decreased with age category. Adolescent girls were laid to rest with fewer bead necklaces but more rings, pendants, pins, and earrings. All of the elements of the standard adult female grave assemblage were now present (Fig. 9.10).

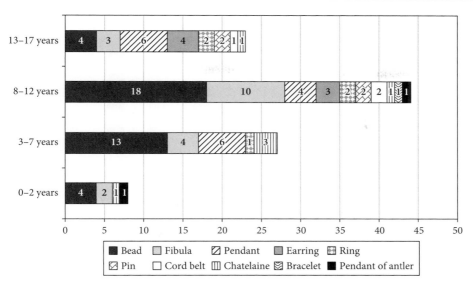

FIGURE 9.10. Distribution of jewelry by age group.

PROPHYLACTIC PENDANTS AND AMULETS

Some objects likely had a prophylactic or symbolic character, by their nature, rarity, or the manner in which they were deposited in a particular grave (Crawford 2004; Gilchrist 2008; see Kornbluth, Chapter 40, this volume). Indeed, all elements of burial dress may have had a symbolic function in addition to their utility or social role (Effros 2002). Some texts testify to the perceived powers of antler, amber, or animal teeth (Perez 2013, pp. 513–524). But nails contained in a purse or placed in the mouth or the hand, and objects that had been "killed" or rendered ineffective by fire or otherwise (including knives and other weapons) referred to a world of symbols and beliefs that have left little or no trace in contemporary texts.

Amber, a valuable material originating from the shores of the Baltic Sea, was considered a prestigious and an effective social marker. It is found in the richest female graves from the sixth to the seventh century (Curta 2007). In the sites studied here, 543 amber beads were found in only 7 percent of women and children's graves, suggesting that these were rare and precious (Fig. 9.11). Their presence and their number increased with the age of the deceased. Adolescents, in particular, had an average number of seven amber beads per necklace. Children under the age of seven possessed only one or two amber beads, highlighting the specificity of this material, with girls approaching or exceeding the age of majority, which was twelve years according to Frankish law.

Indeed, amber was not only a luxury good, but it was often said to have protective and apotropaic qualities (Gilchrist 2008, p. 139), which was also the case for some ornaments or items of women's clothing in traditional societies (Effros 2002; Périn and

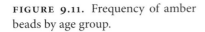

FIGURE 9.11. Frequency of amber beads by age group.

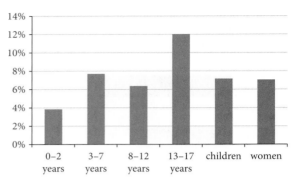

Kazanski 2011). In the sixth and seventh centuries, bishops condemned the use of amber as an amulet. Caesarius of Arles, at the turn of the sixth century, included in his *Sermons to the People* evidence of the use of amber as a means of fighting against infertility: "My dearest brethren, some men and women have the custom, when they see that their marriage is childless, of grieving excessively and, what is worse, sometimes they succumb to the temptation and rely not on God but all manner of sacrilegious remedies, for example, amber (literally the resin of trees), in order to have children" (Réal 2001, p. 393). Bishop Eligius of Noyon, whose *Life* was written in the seventh century, discussed the use of amber by women, which might include wearing it in necklaces as an amulet, stitching it into clothing, or crushing and mixing it with dye (for clothing or hair?). However, it was not amber itself that was condemned, but its use as an amulet: "Let no woman suspend amber on her neck, use it in cloth or in dye, or in another manner, invoking Minerva, or the name of any other evil being. Instead, she should seek the grace of Christ in all of her works and trust her heart to the power of his name" (Krusch 1902, II, 16, p. 706).

The discovery of amber ornaments in early medieval burial contexts confirms the attraction of this exotic material, the value and cost of which were highlighted by ancient authors (Perez 2013, pp. 513–515). Its association with the richest female assemblages, in the form of necklaces with as many as ten amber beads, reveals the prestige of the material.

At the cemeteries of Cutry, Saint-Martin-de-Fontenay and Goudelancourt-lès-Pierrepont, the dead were also laid to rest with small pierced objects hanging from belts or necklaces, including shells, fossils, animal teeth, and rock crystal. Fabricated from various materials, pendants were typically made of metal (pierced coins, bells, medallions, bronze cones, or cylinders), bone (teeth, bone pyramids, plates, or discs), antler, shell, or ammonite. They were found in the graves of female adults in small quantities: one or two objects per person.

However, when correlated with age, amulets were more commonly used in children's graves than in those of adults (Fig. 9.12). They grew more varied in selection in the graves of children from the age of eight, and most especially in the graves of adolescents. In the cemetery of Cutry, two of four antler pendants were deposited with children aged eight to ten years old. Jewelry incorporating animal teeth is rarely uncovered in these

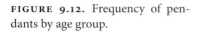

FIGURE 9.12. Frequency of pendants by age group.

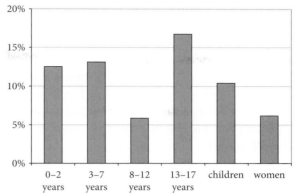

cemeteries. Teeth were typically reserved for adults and adolescents: including about five bear and horse teeth, and a boar's tusk that was worn by an adolescent of about thirteen to fifteen years of age. Similarly, small pierced objects made of metal, bones, fossils, and shells were placed in the graves of women and children over the age of three. However, these deposits are exceptional: they made up only 4 percent of the burials studied here.

It is possible that the pendants were female symbols invested with magical or prophylactic powers (on magic, see Klingshirn, Chapter 41, this volume). However, in the absence of sexual identification based on biological criteria, we cannot determine that all of the children were girls, especially in the case of newborns. In many societies, as in Merovingian Gaul, gender was not necessarily acquired at birth (Sofaer Derevenski 1997; see Halsall, Chapter 8, this volume).

Age and Gender: A Reflection of Social Identity

Childhood was a special stage in the lifecycle, as was manifested in early medieval burial customs. Analysis of grave-goods suggests that their type, quality, quantity, and diversity were directly correlated with the age of the deceased, and they represented an essential factor in the construction of social identity in childhood (Lucy 2005; Halsall 2010b). However, the use of social age groups allows us to go beyond the binary opposition of adult versus child (Gowland 2006, p. 146; Sofaer Derevenski 1997, p. 193). We can highlight the problem of methods that place individuals in opposing pairs like man/woman, rich/poor, free/nonfree, since these individuals formed a spectrum of participants in groups that we seek to identify and analyze (Halsall 2010b, p. 16). Although it is problematic to apply status categories (married or single; free, nonfree, or freed) from historical sources to archaeological remains, status and the social prestige of individuals based on factors such as birth, wealth, political and religious affiliation, or military function may be perceptible in the burial process (Stoodley 2000; Halsall 2010a).

It is thus clear that age is only one factor defining social identity, which is also affected by gender, status, religious beliefs, kinship, and ethnic group. Each individual in the early Middle Ages moved in different groups and hierarchies (Effros, 2002, p. 17). How, then, did age interact with other factors of social identity in early medieval Gaul? Was it the predominant factor, or was it only one element among many which together contributed to the construction of social identity (Lucy 2005; Gowland 2006; Halsall 2010a)?

As we saw earlier, it is still impossible to reliably determine the sex of prepubescent children on the basis of their bones. To discuss the concept of gender construction in childhood, we have relied largely on the gender associations of these objects in adult graves. In recent studies, jewelry has been determined to be typically female, a category that includes beads, brooches, bracelets, rings, earrings, pins, chatelaines, cords, and pendants. By contrast, weapons and accessories linked to horses have been considered typically male. The remaining categories of objects have been identified as neutral since they are commonly found with individuals of both sexes (Halsall 1995; Stoodley 1999). Yet, because many Merovingian-period skeletons are too decayed to provide sufficient skeletal remains to determine the sex of adults based on osteological indicators, it has been and remains common practice to sex skeletons based on accompanying grave-goods. As highlighted by Bonnie Effros (2000), this approach has masked possible exceptions to the above categories of strongly male- and female-associated grave-goods since the biological and archaeological indicators were not tested independently.

For the cemeteries under study, I compared biological sex (from hip bones) with archaeological sex (from grave-goods) in a sample of 500 adult skeletons from Cutry, Goudelancourt-lès-Pierrepont, and Saint-Martin-de-Fontenay. Although there were a few anomalies, they did not lead to a reconsideration of the association of these objects with the designated sex of the deceased (Fig. 9.13). More specifically, four fibulae (5 percent), three sets of beads (3 percent), a ring, and a pin were deposited with adult males, and one tweezer and two iron pins were buried with adult women. The number of bracelets and pendants was too small to be representative in the sample. At these sites, it was thus determined that masculine objects corresponded to weapons, tweezers, sewing needles, and iron pins. Feminine grave-goods included jewelry, chatelaines, and cord belts. Neutral objects were represented by belt buckles and plates, ceramics, knives, glass vessels, coins, scissors, combs, and purses. In light of these results, the goods found in children's graves were understood to be gendered largely in parallel with those found in the graves of adults, even if the quantity of artifacts was often reduced. Hopefully in the future, if DNA testing of early medieval human remains in France is expanded to include assessment for biological sex, it will be possible to confirm the hypothesis that the gender of children was constructed in a fashion similar to that of adults.

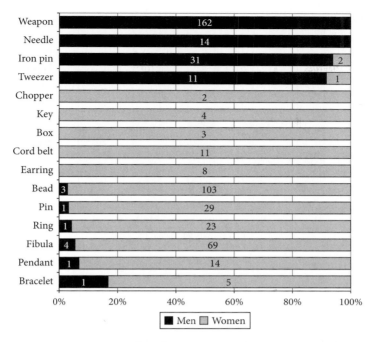

FIGURE 9.13. Frequency of gendered grave-goods among men and women.

SEXUAL IDENTITY AND GENDER CONSTRUCTION DURING CHILDHOOD

In the present study, 2,421 objects were inventoried in adult and children's graves. Of these, 936 (39 percent) found with adults were strongly gendered either masculine or feminine, and 371 found with children also had strong gender associations. However, the majority of grave goods were neutral (Fig. 9.14). The assortment of neutral artifacts decreased gradually with children of an older age favoring feminine grave-goods, which reached their maximum between the ages of thirteen and seventeen (42 percent). Juvenile burials were essentially characterized by neutral (77 percent) and feminine grave-goods (23 percent).

As we have seen, the number of feminine objects found in children's graves increased and diversified significantly once the deceased had reached the age of three (Fig. 9.10). From the age of eight, beads, which had previously been plentiful, decreased substantially in favor of earrings, pins, cord belts, and pendants, worn as a necklace or hung from the belt. For boys, eight seems to have been an important stage as well: they received the first tools (iron pins and needles) and some weapons, some of which were adapted to their smaller size, including spears, scramasaxes, axes, and arrows (Fig. 9.9).

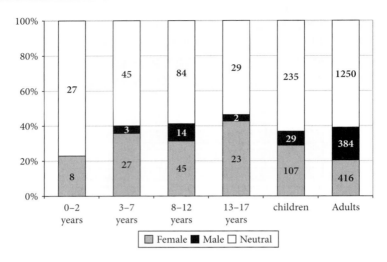

FIGURE 9.14. Frequency of gendered grave-goods by age group.

By contrast, among adolescents, these deposits were scarcer: only two scramasaxes were found. Perhaps rather than commonly being deposited in adolescents' graves, they were redistributed among members of the family or companions.

In addition, weapons were generally deposited alongside the bodies of children, with spears arranged solely to the right of the body and scramasaxes to the left, whereas these had more varied positions among adults, especially at Cutry (Legoux et al., 2005). Arrowheads were usually found at their feet. Equally, the orientation of armament varied, but the archaeological reports do not note the specific disposition of their blades or cutting edges. Nonetheless, the homogeneity of the disposition of weapons in children's graves is still striking, even if the sample is small, since the position of weapons in adult graves shows significant variation (Nice et al. 2008, p. 116).

Adults' weapons must be distinguished from those that were adapted to the size of children. Of nineteen weapons found at the sites studied in this chapter, four have been termed "miniature." This term, however, seems inappropriate because it is frequently linked to the world of play and suggests that these weapons may have been toys.

At the cemetery of Cutry, two scramasaxes with a blade length less than 25 cm were found (Legoux et al., 2005, p. 89), whereas two axes were identified at Goudelancourt-lès-Pierrepont and Saint-Sauveur and four arrows in all the sites (Ben Redjeb 2007, p. 84; Nice et al. 2008, p. 115), were associated with children between the ages of six and eleven. Their burials, despite looting, contained rich grave-goods: arrowheads, belt buckles, lighters, coins, antler combs, and glass. Adapted weapons, an exceptional deposit, may in part be linked to a problem of representation: especially in older publications, archaeologists may have regarded the scramasaxes as knives. And how do we interpret these deposits? Were these weapons given to children as toys so that they could imitate their elders, or did they serve a more formal function, that of fulfilling an apprenticeship in the handling of weapons? Were such grave-goods symbolic?

Such artifacts were deposited with children between six and eleven years old, an age that was compatible with the period when they began training as a warrior.

Written sources suggest that boys of early medieval aristocratic families could start their military apprenticeship at a young age (Devroey 2006, p. 254). Hunting, horsemanship, and the use of weapons were the three pillars of the military education of sons of elites (Le Jan 1993, p. 215). Sent to their uncles or to the royal court late in their childhood, they grew up distant from their families where they were raised or "nourished" by other high-status families. This tradition was part of the military and moral education of the elite in Merovingian Gaul (Le Jan 1993, p. 220; Devroey 2006, p. 70; see Sarti, Chapter 12, this volume). In the ninth century, Gerald of Aurillac said he "had been trained in childhood in secular exercises, as was the tradition for noble children" (Odo of Cluny, PL., 133, col. 645; Le Jan 1993, p. 215). These customs may suggest why children between eight and twelve years of age at death may have been laid to rest with arrows, and presumably also a bow, though the latter are now missing. Bows and arrows served the dual function of weapons and tools for hunting, and the ritualized deposit of two or three arrows may have derived from an ancient Germanic custom (Périn 2006, p. 105). Hunting, practiced frequently in the Frankish court, was mainly a prestige activity; involvement brought social recognition (Le Jan 1993, p. 216) and also provided "physical and mental preparation for war and killing" (Devroey 2006, p. 255). Finally, weaponry in children's graves may have referred to their family's aspirations for their future identity; they were connected with the warriors they would have become had they lived into adulthood (Riché and Périn 2013, p. 374).

The expression of masculine gender in graves seems to have been especially strong when the deceased were between the ages of eight and twelve. The deposit in their graves of gendered and precious objects, such as ornaments and adult or adapted armaments, some of which had ritual connotations or strong warrior or social symbolism, shows that it was an important stage in childhood, probably linked with puberty and majority. By contrast, adolescent boys (between thirteen and seventeen years of age) apparently did not benefit from such visibility: weapon deposits were exceptional, and their graves were not distinguished by either the quality or wealth of objects deposited with them.

Indeed, in most legal codes of the sixth and seventh centuries, majority occurred between twelve and fifteen years (see note 5), following puberty. The study of wergeld, the amount of which varied depending on the crime and status of the victim, permits discussion of the legal value placed on individuals in Visigothic, Frankish, and Burgundian society (Halsall 2010b, p. 388; Herlihy 1978, p. 115). In the Salic Law, the wergeld of a free man was always lower than that of women and children of the same status[7] (Fig. 9.15). The wergeld of a woman, and therefore her value, was as much as three times that of a man, and was connected to her fertility.[8] When she was elderly or proved sterile, the woman's value decreased to that of a free man,[9] whereas a pregnant woman was accorded one of the highest sums of wergeld under Salic Law.[10] In addition, adults and minors, boys and girls were clearly distinguished in legal texts. Wergeld for the murder of a boy under twelve years of age was three times higher than that for the murder of

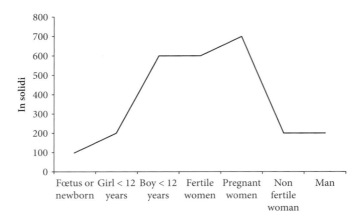

FIGURE 9.15. Amount of wergeld for murder in the Salic Law on the basis of age.

a free man; For girls, it was only from the age of twelve, when they were considered to have reached majority, that they received an equal value in the law codes.[11] Salic Law demonstrates the importance of puberty and majority as major steps in childhood. Sexual maturity is thus accompanied by the valuation of procreation and pregnancy, marked by a higher wergeld for women of childbearing age.

At this time, grave deposits in children's graves could help with the acquisition, enhancement, or support of female sexual identity, especially when the grave-goods associated with a burial were especially rich and similar to the assemblages with which adult women were laid to rest. Emphasis on the expression of female gender was confirmed in adolescence: unlike boys, girls between thirteen and seventeen years of age had considerable visibility. In their graves, jewelry and protective or prophylactic pendants were even more frequent and numerous than in the burials of adult women. They helped in essence to "stage" the adolescent's body, and the customs were accentuated when the deceased had reached childbearing age (Stoodley 2000, p. 461; Gowland 2006, p. 148) Guy Halsall also evokes puberty and sexual maturity as a process of socialization, and he points to the importance of young women in family alliances: "It seems that these young women were public figures, displayed by their families in the hope of making a useful marriage alliance within the community" (Halsall 2010b, p. 402).

Finally, tweezers, pyxides, large chopping knives, and spurs, while admittedly found rarely, are never found with children. These objects seem to have had strong symbolism linked to power, status, or gender: the spurs referred to the cavalry, war, and combat; tweezers were used in male grooming; pyxides and chopping knives were found in the richest female burials. The impetus for avoiding their deposition with children does not seem to have been a result of their gender associations since many masculine and feminine objects were found among children. Nor was the reluctance due to their value, since glass vessels, amber beads, rich jewelry, and belt buckles made of precious materials (gold, silver, gilded bronze, and garnets) were not uncommon in children's graves. The decision not to deposit such artifacts in children's burials was either symbolic or had to do with their function: excess hair removal, for instance, was no doubt more of an adult concern than one associated with children. The distribution of grave-goods also suggests that the acquisition of gender identity and sexual maturity may have occurred at different times, depending on whether the child was a boy or girl.

TO KNOW ONE'S AGE: A MODERN CONCEPT?

The stages of childhood, visible in burial custom and, to some extent, in the written sources as well, corresponded to the rites of passage that punctuated the lives of children. According to Salic Law, the first major stage took place on the ninth day of life, when a newborn received his or her name, and from which time the infant's wergeld increased.[12] Yet, very few children under two years of age have been found in excavations, and there is nothing to distinguish this moment in the funeral process, contrary to the visible changes in the rite that occurred at the age of three, when the infant transitioned into early childhood and received different grave-goods than earlier. Similarly fraught were the ages of eight and twelve years, when more children were buried in prestige graves and were accompanied in this space with grave-goods. This development may have been linked to the approach of puberty and late childhood, very present in the literary or normative sources.

In Merovingian sites, the funeral treatment of boys and girls began to diverge at puberty (Halsall 1996; Stoodley 2000; Perez 2013). The quality, quantity, and diversity of male and female grave-goods valued the boys most highly around eight to twelve years of age and girls between thirteen and seventeen. Puberty was therefore a key stage that preceded or came with civil majority and marked the end of childhood and the start of adulthood, between twelve and fifteen. After this time, even if they were considered young adults by their contemporaries, they nonetheless were members of a particular social group that was set off by particular expectations and rites of passage: for males, the cutting of hair and the receipt of weapons, and for both sexes, marriage. The grave-goods they received shows this gendered distinction and were an important means of expressing social identity in the Merovingian period (Halsall 2010a; Périn and Kazanski 2011). Unfortunately, however, we know little or nothing about their funerals, the possible presence of a clergyman, or the deposit of perishable items (food, drink, wax objects, and plants), which appear to have been an important part of the funeral ritual (Treffort 1996, p. 181; Effros 2002, p. 17). Children must have nonetheless occupied a special place as the future and the offspring of a family: their premature death affected the successful survival of the kin group.

All of these concepts are based on the supposition that early medieval men and women knew their age or at least that of their children. To know one's age should not be assumed to have been a natural act for the people who lived in the Middle Ages, and, indeed, the written sources often suggest that this information was inaccurate (Alexandre-Bidon 2003; Handley 2003). Indeed, some ages had strong symbolic connotations, and the ages of three, seven, and twelve were often mentioned in the writings of clerics or hagiographers, whereas other ages were not (Lett 1997, pp. 35–36). By contrast, in his chronicles and hagiographies, Gregory of Tours, for instance, did not mention children's ages (Alexandre-Bidon 2003; Laes 2011). So, did age really count? And was it more important than visible biological changes like growth, menarch, or physical development? Or was the latter some sort of reference to the former? For instance, the growth of baby teeth ended between the ages of two and three, and the age of six or seven years corresponded to the eruption of the first adult molars (Ubelaker 1989; Lewis 2007). Similarly, puberty often occurred between twelve and fifteen years of age, marked by the first menarche, the deepening of the voice, and the appearance of facial and pubic hair. These visible biological phenomena likely reinforced socially constructed age markers (Gowland 2006), more than is expressed in texts. In the countryside of Merovingian Gaul, it is likely that physiological development and growth, while varying from person to person, played a more important role than chronological age in the medieval conception of childhood.

Conclusion

Burial practices in northern Gaul during the sixth to eighth centuries appear to have been relatively homogeneous, which allows us to compile different archaeological sites to establish a numerically significant and representative sample of funerary custom in the Merovingian world. Burial ritual, body position, and deposited grave goods helped fulfill social norms shared across different regions of northern Gaul. In light of the results of a study of 315 subadults from four Merovingian cemeteries, we can see some trends in the evolution of funeral treatment during childhood. Using a multidisciplinary approach, and comparing different kinds of sources, we can discuss the construction of age and gender in childhood. The use of social age groups highlighted important stages in the life cycle: the approximate ages of one, eight, and twelve years were when children entered new phases in their lives, and these transitions were expressed in contemporary burial rituals.

It appears, on this basis, that children under the age of one were considered marginal beings. If they experienced death before being integrated ritually in the community, with the acquisition of a name, and later, through baptism, they may have received a distinct funerary treatment like burial outside of the collective cemetery, which was not necessarily negative or dishonorable. Indeed, as we saw earlier, the "underrepresentation" of infants and juveniles in the collective cemetery from the fifth to the eighth century seems to correlate with the discovery of their graves in isolated or ruined places, as well as in wells, pits, abandoned houses, or along roads (e.g., Raynaud et al. 2010). From the age of eight, the deposition of grave goods, including those associated with adult males, increased and diversified, and the identity of girls and especially boys seems to have been more strongly asserted. Finally, from thirteen years of age, jewelry assemblages in children's graves were especially rich and varied, marking gender identity and valuing the female body as it entered into adulthood, probably as a result of hopes for procreation. Age and gender thus appear to have been essential to the social construction of identity in childhood at this time.

NOTES

1. For examples, see Legoux et al. 2005; Ben Redjeb 2007.
2. For more details concerning the categorization of social age groups, please refer to my doctoral dissertation, which is available online in French (Perez 2013, pp. 29–36): https://upf-pf.academia.edu/EmiliePerez
3. The age of majority is twelve in the *Pactus Legis Salicae* 24-1 to 24-7; fourteen in the *Lex Visigothorum* II-4-11, II-5-10, IV-3-1; and fifteen in the *Lex Ribuaria* 84, and the *Lex Burgundionum* 87. On law, see also Rio, Chapter 23, this volume.
4. For example "we wrapped her in a clean shroud and we buried her." Gregory of Tours, *Ten Books of the Histories* 6.29 (Latouche 1963).
5. The category of jewelry includes beads, brooches, rings, earrings, pins, chatelaines, cord belts, bracelets, and pendants.
6. These figures refer to discrete bead assemblages rather than individual beads.
7. *Pactus Legis Salicae* 41, 1.
8. *Pactus Legis Salicae* 24, 8.
9. *Pactus Legis Salicae* 24, 9.
10. *Pactus Legis Salicae* 24, 5.
11. *Pactus Legis Salicae* 24, 1–4.
12. *Pactus Legis Salicae* 24, 6.

WORKS CITED

Ancient Sources

Caesarius of Arles, *Sermons to the People*. Delage, M.-J. (ed. and trans.). (1978). *Césaire d'Arles, Sermons au peuple*. Paris: Editions du Cerf.

Gregory of Tours, *Ten Books of the Histories*. Latouche, R. (ed. and trans.). (1963). *Grégoire de Tours, Les Dix livres d'Histoire*. Paris: Les Belles Lettres.

Lex Burgundionum. L. R. De Salis (ed.). (1892). MGH LL nat. Germ. 2.1. Hanover: Hahn.

Lex Ribuaria. F. Beyerle and R. Buchner (eds.). (1954). MGH LL nat. Germ. 3.2. Hanover: Hahn.

Lex Visigothorum. Zeumer, K. (ed.). (1902). MGH LL nat. Germ. 1. Hanover: Hahn.

Odo of Cluny, *Vita Geraldi Auriliacensis comitis*. A.-M. Bultot-Verleysen (ed. and trans.). (2009). *Subsidia hagiographica* 89. Brussels: Société des Bollandistes.

Pactus Legis Salicae. K. A. Eckhardt (ed.). (1962). MGH LL nat. Germ. 4.2. Hanover: Hahn.

Vita Eligii ep. Noviomagensis. B. Krusch (ed.). (1902). MGH SRM 4 (pp. 634–741). Hanover: Hahn.

Modern Sources

Al Qahtani, S. J., Hector, M. P., Liversidge, H. M. (2010). "The London atlas of human tooth development and eruption." *American Journal of Physical Anthropology* 143: 545–554.

Alduc-Le Bagousse, A. (1997). "Comportements à l'égard des nouveau-nés et des petits enfants dans les sociétés de la fin de l'Antiquité et du haut Moyen Âge." In L. Buchet (ed.), *L'enfant, son corps, son histoire. Actes des VIIᵉ journées anthropologiques de Valbonne* (pp. 81–95). Antibes: APDCA.

Alduc-Le Bagousse, A. (ed.). (2009). *Inhumations de prestige ou prestige de l'inhumation? Expressions du pouvoir dans l'au-delà (IVᵉ-XVᵉ siècle)*. Caen: Publications du CRAHAM.

Alexandre-Bidon, D. (2003). "Seconde enfance et jeunesse dans la théorie des 'âges de la vie' et dans le vécu familial à la fin du Moyen Âge, images et théories." In J.-P. Bardet (ed.), *Lorsque l'enfant grandit: entre dépendance et autonomie* (pp. 159–172). Paris: Presses Paris-Sorbonne.

Ben Redjeb, T. (ed.). (2007). "La nécropole mérovingienne de Saint-Sauveur (Somme)." *Revue archéologique de Picardie* 1–2: 31–299.

Berthelot, S. (1995). "Objets de parure en pate de verre et en ambre de la fin du IIIᵉ au VIIᵉ siècle en Basse-Normandie." *Archéologie Médiévale* 25: 1–25.

Buchet, L., & Séguy, I. (2008). "L'âge au décès des enfants: âge civil, âge biologique, âge social?" In F. Gusi Jener, S. Muriel, and C. R. Olaria Puyoles (eds.), *Nasciturus, infans, puerulus vobis mater terra. La muerte en la infanzia* (pp. 25–39). Castelló: Servei d'Investigacions Arqueològiques i Prehistòrique.

Buckberry, J. (2000). "Missing, Presumed Buried? Bone Diagenesis and the Under-Representation of Anglo-Saxon Children." *The Sheffield Graduate Journal of Archaeology—Assemblages* 5. http://www.assemblage.group.shef.ac.uk/5/buckberr.html [last consulted August 29, 2016].

Chapelot, J. (ed.). (2010). *Trente ans d'archéologie médiévale en France. Un bilan pour un avenir*. Caen: Publication du CRAHM.

Cochelin, I., and Smyth, K. E. (eds.). (2013). *Medieval Life Cycles: Continuity and Change*. Turnhout: Brepols.

Coşkunsu, G. (ed.). (2015). *The Archaeology of Childhood. Interdisciplinary Perspectives on an Archaeological Enigma*. Albany: State Universtity of New York Press.

Cramer, P. (1993). *Baptism and Change in the Early Middle Ages, c.200–c.1150*. Cambridge: Cambridge University Press.

Crawford, S. (2000). "Children, Grave Goods and Social Status in Early Anglo-Saxon England." In J. Sofaer Derevenski (ed.), *Children and Material Culture* (pp. 169–179). London: Routledge.

Crawford, S. (2004). "Votive Deposition, Religion and the Anglo-Saxon Furnished Burial Ritual." *World Archaeology* 36(1): 87–102.

Curta, F. (2007). "The Amber Trail in Early Medieval Eastern Europe." In C. Chazelle and F. Lifshitz (eds.), *Paradigms and Methods in Early Medieval Studies. The New Middle Ages* (pp. 61–79). New York: Palgrave Macmillan.

Devroey, J.-P. (2006). *Puissants et misérables. Système social et monde paysan dans l'Europe des Francs (VIᵉ–IXᵉ siècles)*. Brussels: Académie Royale de Belgique.

Duday, H. (2005). "L'archéothanatologie ou l'archéologie de la mort." In O. Dutour, J.-J. Hublin, and B. Vandermeersch (eds.), *Objets et méthodes en paléoanthropologie* (pp. 153–216). Paris: Comité des travaux historiques et scientifiques.

Effros, B. (1997). "Beyond Cemetery Walls: Early Medieval Funerary Topography and Christian Salvation." *Early Medieval Europe* 6(1): 1–23.

Effros, B. (2000). "Skeletal Sex and Gender in Merovingian Mortuary Archaeology." *Antiquity* 74(285): 632–639.

Effros, B. (2002). *Caring for Body and Soul: Burial and the Afterlife in the Merovingian World.* University Park: Pennsylvania State University Press.

Effros, B. (2003). *Merovingian Mortuary Archaeology and the Making of the Early Middle Ages.* Berkeley: University of California Press.

Gilchrist, R. (2008). "Magic for the Dead? The Archaeology of Magic in Later Medieval Burials." *Medieval Archaeology* 52: 119–159.

Gilchrist, R. (2012). *Medieval Life: Archaeology and the Life Course.* Woodbridge: Boydell Press.

Gleize, Y., and Maurel, L. (2009). "Les sépultures du haut Moyen Âge du Champs-des-bosses à Saint-Xandre: organisation et recrutement particulier de tombes dispersées." *Bulletins et mémoires de la Société d'Anthropologie de Paris* 21(1–2): 59–77.

Gowland, R. (2006). "Ageing the Past: Examining Age Identity from Funerary Evidence." In R. Gowland and C. Knüsel (eds.), *Social Archaeology of Funerary Remains* (pp. 143–154). Oxford: Oxbow Books.

Halcrow, S., & Tayles, N. (2011). "The Bioarchaeological Investigation of Children and Childhood." In S. C. Agarwal and B. A. Glencross (eds.), *Social Bioarchaeology* (pp. 333–360). Oxford: Wiley-Blackwell.

Halsall, G. (1995). *Settlement and Social Organization: The Merovingian Region of Metz.* Cambridge: Cambridge University Press.

Halsall, G. (1996). "Female Status and Power in Early Merovingian Central Austrasia: The Burial Evidence." *Early Medieval Europe* 5(1): 1–24.

Halsall, G. (2010a). *Cemeteries and Society in Merovingian Gaul.* Leiden: Brill.

Halsall, G. (2010b). "Growing up in Merovingian Gaul." In *Cemeteries and Society in Merovingian Gaul* (pp. 385–312). Leiden: Brill.

Handley, M. (2003). *Death, Society and Culture. Inscriptions and Epitaphs in Gaul and Spain, AD 300–750.* BAR International Series 1135, Oxford: Archaeopress.

Herlihy, D. (1978). "Medieval Children." In B. Lackner & K. Philip (eds.), *The Walter Prescott Webb Memorial Lectures. Essays on Medieval Civilization.* Austin, TX: University of Austin Press, pp. 109–141.

Kamp, K. A. (2001). "Where Have All the Children Gone? The Archaeology of Childhood." *Journal of Archaeological Method and Theory* 8(1): 1–34.

Klevnäs, A. (2015). "Give and take: grave goods and grave robbery in the Early Middle Ages." In A. Klevnäs and C. Hedenstierna-Jonson, (eds.), *Own and Be Owned: Archaeological Approaches to the Concept of Possession* (pp. 157–188). Stockholm Studies in Archaeology 62. Stockholm: Department of Archaeology and Classical Studies.

Laes, C. (2011). "Disabled Children in Gregory of Tours." In K. Mustakallio and C. Laes (eds.) *The Dark Side of Childhood in Late Antiquity and the Middle Ages* (pp. 39–62). Oxford: Oxbow Books.

Lally, M., and Moore, A. (ed.). (2011). *(Re)thinking the Little Ancestor: New Perspectives on the Archaeology of Infancy and Childhood.* Oxford: Archaeopress.

Lauwers, M. (2005). *Naissance du cimetière. Lieux sacrés et terre des morts dans l'Occident médiéval.* Paris: Aubier-Flammarion.

Legoux, R., Buchet, L., Dhénin, M., Liéger, A., Poirot, J.-P., Rodet-Belarbi, I., and Calligaro, T. (2005). *La nécropole mérovingienne de Cutry (Meurthe-et-Moselle)*. Saint-Germain-en-Laye: Association française d'archéologie mérovingienne.

Le Jan, R. (1993). "Apprentissages militaires, rites de passage et remises d'armes au haut Moyen Age." In P. Sigal (ed.), *Éducation, apprentissages, initiation au Moyen Âge* (p. 211–32). Montpellier: Les Cahiers du Centre de recherche interdisciplinaire sur la société et l'imaginaire au Moyen Âge.

Lett, D. (1997). *L'enfant des miracles : enfance et société au Moyen Âge, XIIᵉ–XIIIᵉ siècle*. Paris: Aubier.

Lewis, M. (2002). "Impact of industrialization: comparative study of child health in four sites from medieval and postmedieval England (A.D. 850–1859)." *American Journal of Physical Anthropology* 119(3): 211–223

Lewis, M. (2007). *The Bioarchaeology of Children : Perspectives from Biological and Forensic Anthropology*. Cambridge: Cambridge University Press.

Lucy, S. (2005). "The Archaeology of Age." In S. Lucy (ed.), *The Archaeology of Identity: Approaches to Gender, Age, Status, Ethnicity and Religion* (pp. 43–66). New York: Routledge.

Nice, A., Fleche, M.-P., Thouvenot, S., Legoux, R., Fedi, L., and Feyeyx, J.-Y. (2008). "La nécropole mérovingienne de Goudelancourt-lès-Pierrepont (Aisne)." *Revue archéologique de Picardie*, (n. spécial 25).

Orme, N. (2003). *Medieval Children*. New Haven, CT: Yale University Press.

Perez, É. (2013). *L'enfant au miroir des sépultures médiévales (Gaule, VIᵉ–XIIᵉ siècle)*. (Thèse en Histoire et Archéologie). Nice: Université de Nice Sophia-Antipolis.

Perez, É. (2015). "Les enfants dans le cimetière médiéval : vers une nouvelle organisation funéraire (VIIᵉ–XIIᵉ siècle)." In *Le cimetière au village dans l'Europe médiévale et moderne* (pp. 173–191). Toulouse: Presses Universitaires du Midi.

Périn, P. (1998). "Possibilités et limites de l'interprétation sociale des cimetières mérovingiens." *Antiquités nationales* 30: 169–183.

Périn, P. (2006). "L'archéologie funéraire reflète-t-elle fidèlement la composition et l'évolution de l'armement mérovingien ?" In A. Erlande-Brandenburg (ed.), *Materiam superabat opus. Hommages à Alain Erlande-Brandenburg* (pp. 95–111). Paris: Réunion des Musées Nationaux.

Périn, P., and Kazanski, M. (2011). "Identity and Ethnicity during the Era of Migrations and Barbarian Kingdoms in the Light of Archaeology in Gaul." In R. Mathisen and D. Shanzer (eds.), *Romans, Barbarians and the Transformation of the Roman World* (pp. 299–230). Farnham: Ashgate.

Peytremann, E. (2003). *Archéologie de l'habitat rural dans le nord de la France du IVᵉ au XIIᵉ siècle*. 2 vols. Saint-Germain-en-Laye: Association française d'Archéologie mérovingienne.

Pilet, C., Alduc-Le Bagousse, A., Buchet, L., Helluin, M., Kasanski, M., and Pilet-Lemière, J. (eds.). (1994). *La nécropole de Saint-Martin-de-Fontenay (Calvados), Recherche sur le peuplement de la plaine de Caen du Vᵉ siècle avant J.C. au VIIᵉ siècle après J.C.* Paris: CNRS édition.

Raynaud, C., Berdeaux, M.-L., Crubézy, É., Duchesne, S., Forest, V., Garnotel, A., and Romon, P. (2010). *Les nécropoles de Lunel-Viel, Hérault, de l'Antiquité au Moyen âge*. Revue archéologique de Narbonnaise, Vol. supplément 40. Montpellier: Editions de l'Association de la Revue archéologique de Narbonnaise.

Réal, I. (2001). *Vies de saints, vie de famille. Représentation et système de la parenté dans le Royaume mérovingien (481–751) d'après les sources hagiographiques*. Turnhout: Brepols.

Riché, P., and Alexandre-Bidon, D. (1994). *L'enfance au Moyen Âge*. Paris: Seuil.

Riché, P., and Périn, P. (2013). *Dictionnaire des Francs. Les Mérovingiens et les Carolingiens.* Paris: Bartillon.

Scheuer, L., Black, S., and Schaefer, M. C. (2009). *Juvenile Osteology: A Laboratory and Field Manual.* Amsterdam: Elsevier Academic Press.

Séguy, I., and Buchet, L. (2013). *Handbook of Palaeodemography.* New York: Springer International Publishing.

Shahar, S. (1990). *Childhood in the Middle Ages.* New York: Routledge.

Sofaer Derevenski, J. (1997). "Engendering Children, Engendering Archaeology." In J. Moore and E. Scott (eds.), *Invisible People and Processes: Writing Gender and Childhood into European Archaeology* (pp. 192–202). London: Leicester University Press.

Stoodley, N. (1999). *The Spindle and the Spear: A Critical Enquiry into the Construction and Meaning of Gender in the Early Anglo-Saxon Burial Rite.* BAR British Series 288. Oxford: BAR.

Stoodley, N. (2000). "From the Cradle to the Grave : Age Organization and the Early Anglo-Saxon Burial Rite." *World Archaeology* 31(3): 456–472.

Stoodley, N. (2011). "Childhood to Old Age." In *The Oxford Handbook of Anglo-Saxon Archaeology* (pp. 641–666). Oxford: Oxford University Press.

Treffort, C. (1996). *L'église carolingienne et la mort : christianisme, rites funéraires et pratiques commémoratives.* Lyon: Centre interuniversitaire d'histoire et d'archéologie médiévales.

Treffort, C. (1997). "Archéologie funéraire et histoire de la petite enfance. Quelques remarques à propos du Haut Moyen Âge." In R. Fossier (ed.), *La petite enfance dans l'Europe médiévale et moderne. Actes des XVIe Journées Internationales d'Histoire de l'Abbaye de Flaran,* (pp. 93–107). Toulouse: Presses universitaires du Mirail.

Ubelaker, D. H. (1989). *Human Skeletal Remains: Excavation, Analysis, Interpretation.* Washington, DC: Taraxacum.

Verslype, L. (2005). "Les tertres funéraires et les sépultures délimitées entre Somme et Rhin. Signal social ou culturel, politique ou religieux, individuel ou communautaire ?" *Bulletin de liaison de l'Association française d'Archéologie mérovingienne* 29: 51–55.

Verslype, L., and Périn, P. (eds.) (2007). *Villes et campagnes en Neustrie: sociétés, économies, territoires, christianisation. Actes des XXVe Journées internationales d'archéologie mérovingienne de l'AFAM.* Montagnac: Éd. M. Mergoil.

Young, B. K. (2006). "Rituel funéraire, structure sociale, choix idéologique et genèse du faciès funéraire mérovingien." In X. Delestre, M. Kazanski, and P. Périn (eds.), *De l'Âge du Fer au haut Moyen Âge, archéologie funéraire, princes et élites guerrières* (pp. 215–229). Longroy: Mémoires de l'Association Française d'Archéologie Mérovingienne.

PART III

STRUCTURES
OF POWER

CHAPTER 10

......

THE MEROVINGIAN POLITY

A Network of Courts and Courtiers

......

YITZHAK HEN

SOON after they had established their kingdoms on Roman soil, the barbarian leaders, following the late Roman imperial practice, settled with their administrative and military retinue in a central strategic town (on cities and towns, see Loseby, Chapter 27, and Bourgeois, Chapter 28, respectively). The Vandals chose Carthage; the Ostrogothic chieftain, Theoderic the Great, opted for Ravenna, the old residence of the western Roman imperial court; the Visigothic kings settled in Toulouse and subsequently in Toledo; and the Burgundians favored Geneva (Ripoll and Gurt 2000). The Merovingians were no different. Childeric, the Roman governor of *Belgica secunda* (Quast 2015), administered his province from Tournai, and his son, Clovis, king of the Franks, established his "seat of government" (*cathedra regni*) in Paris (Gregory of Tours, *Libri historiarum*, II.38; trans. Thorpe 1974, p. 154). After his death, Clovis's kingdom was divided among his four sons—Theuderic, Chlodomer, Childebert, and Chlothar—who established four different independent royal courts in Reims, Orléans, Paris, and Soissons, respectively (Ewig 1952, 1963; Wood 1977; Périn 1989; Rouche 1997; Dierkens and Périn 2000; see also Fouracre, Chapter 2, this volume).

These newly established *sedes regiae* were much more than mere royal residential towns. They almost instantly became administrative centers, from where the kingdoms were ruled and to where aristocrats from all corners of the Merovingian kingdoms flocked in order to serve the king or in hope for honors and promotion. In what follows, I examine the function of the Merovingian royal court as a center of government, as a melting pot for the Frankish provincial elite, and as an intellectual community that set the cultural tone for many a generation to come.

Unfortunately, the sources for such a probe are remarkably limited, fragmentary, and often very difficult to interpret. Unlike the courts of their Roman imperial predecessors or their Carolingian successors, the courts of the Merovingian kings were never described in detail by a former member, nor does the legal corpus that survives from the Merovingian period provide a clear picture of these courts' personnel and inner workings (on law, see Rio, Chapter 23, this volume).[1] However, since royal courts were part and parcel of the Merovingian political, social, and cultural reality, they are mentioned in passing by numerous sources, such the grand historical narratives of the period, that is, Gregory of Tours's *Ten Books of History*, the so-called *Chronicle of Fredegar*, and the *Liber Historiae Francorum*, as well as by a plethora of saints' *Lives* that were composed during the Merovingian period or shortly thereafter (on history and hagiography, see Reimitz, Chapter 22, and Kreiner, Chapter 24, respectively, this volume). To these reports one can add some information from poems and correspondence that were produced at court or for the court (see Gillett, Chapter 25, this volume), and from official documents that were drafted by the royal chancery. Hence, though fragmentary and anecdotal, the various bits and pieces of information that can be gleaned from our sources provide a rather coherent and fascinating picture of the Merovingian court, albeit with some lapses and lacunae. Let us, then, have a closer look at the sources and the image they project.

ROMAN ROOTS

A bustling *palatium* (palace) that inhabited the emperor's entourage (*comitatus*), was an integral part of the late-antique polity. Such a *palatium* was composed of the emperor's military retinue, that is, the praetorian guard (*praetoriani*), his administrative functionaries and secretaries (*scrinia*), his panel of counselors (*consistorium*), as well as his personal household staff (*cubicularii*) (Jones 1964, pp. 42–68, 100–110; Kelly 1998; McCormick 2000). The imperial court was a strategic instrument of power and control, and it enabled the Roman emperor to govern his empire efficiently. It also served as a template for provincial governors, who, in turn, established their own provincial courts as bastions of local government throughout the empire.

The Merovingians, who rose to power within the Roman orbit of the late fifth century, and who established themselves as the governors of the province *Belgica secunda*, inherited much of the Roman imperial tradition of political thought, and with it the late Roman notion of *palatium* (Barnwell 1997, pp. 23–40; Hen 2004b). From a fairly early stage, the Frankish rulers of Gaul surrounded themselves with military troops and various counselors (on the military, see Sarti, Chapter 12, this volume). Consequently, the Merovingian royal court that evolved throughout the late fifth and early sixth centuries, was modeled on both the Roman provincial and the Roman imperial courts of the later empire, with some changes and modifications. It accommodated both the ruler's military retinue and civil council, as well as the kingdom's highest bureaucrats and ecclesiastics; through them the Merovingian kings could reign and rule.

One of the first indications of the formation of a Merovingian court is provided by the famous letter Remigius of Reims addressed to Clovis on the occasion of his accession to the position of provincial governor (ca. 481). After some short formal greetings, Remigius, the aged metropolitan bishop of northern Gaul, wrote to the young Clovis:[2]

> You must summon to your side counsellors who can enhance your reputation.... You should pay respect to your bishops and always have recourse to their advice; and if there is good agreement between you and them, your province will better endure.... Let your court be open to all, so that no one shall depart from there downhearted.   (*Epistulae Austrasicae*, 2; trans. Murray 2000, p. 260)

Remigius's notion of a court, it appears, was deeply imbued with allusions to old Roman notions of civic and military political ideology. According to Remigius, an effective ruler could not act alone but had to rely on trustworthy counselors and act with justice (*iustitia*) and respect (*pietas*) toward his people, his ancestors, and his country. Although one can clearly recognize the paternal tone in Remigius's letter, which is a splendid expression of the earnestness of contemporary Christian sentiments (Hen 1998), this letter uses a kind of rhetoric that owes its effect to the close analogies between the Merovingian ruler and his Roman equivalents. Its effectiveness was made possible through the absorption of Roman civic and martial ideals of rulership by the Christian elite of late antique Gaul (Halsall 2007; Hen 2014). By using Roman models, Remigius (and many of his followers) spoke a social language that their contemporaries could understand, that was familiar to them, and that they recognized as authoritative.

Continuation of Roman traditions is also apparent in the Merovingian adoption of the traditional imperial nomenclature and the reverential language that had customarily been employed to address the emperor. Clovis, according to Gregory of Tours, was called "consul" and "Augustus," and Remigius of Reims called him "leader of the regions, guardian of the homeland, and conqueror of nations" (*regionum praesul, custos patriae, gentium triumphator*) (*LH* II.38; *Epistulae Austrasicae* 3). At the same time, Roman imperial ideals gradually infiltrated into the various statements on the qualities that a good ruler should display, and hence *iustitia*, *aequitas*, and *pietas* bulk large in the writings on kingship from the sixth century onward (Ewig 1956; Anton 1968, pp. 45–79; Wallace-Hadrill 1971, pp. 47–71; Hen 1998, 2004b).

Yet, although based on a Roman model and influenced by Roman imperial traditions, the Merovingian court was never a replica of the imperial one. It was indeed a center of power and government, but, as we shall see, it was less rigid and more adaptable to the changing reality of late antique and early medieval Gaul, and it was closely tied to the local secular as well as ecclesiastic elites. Moreover, in keeping with their nonsacral nature of kingship (Hen 2004b), the early Merovingians made no attempt to usurp the imperial title, nor did they employ the term *sacrum* (sacred) to mark the eminence of their royal palace or their office.[3]

The Royal Palatini

The Merovingian court, like its imperial counterpart, operated mainly as a center of government (on Byzantine relations, see Esders, Chapter 16, this volume). As such, it monopolized the role of royal functionaries, who were all personally nominated by the king himself.[4] Whereas no document from the Merovingian period lists the various royal offices at court, a short passage in Gregory of Tours's *Libri historiarum* gives us a rare glimpse of the categories of royal functionaries at court and the ways in which such a court was established:

> In this same year [i.e., 589] King Childebert went to stay with his wife and mother near a town called Strasbourg. Some of the more important citizens of Soissons and Meaux visited him there and said: "Send us one of your sons, so that we may serve him. If we have a member of your family resident among us as a pledge, we shall resist your enemies with all the greater zeal and have more reason to protect the lands around your city." The king was very pleased with the suggestion. He promised to send his elder son Theudebert to them. He appointed counts (*comites*), personal servants (*domestici*), major-domos (*maior domus*), and tutors (*nutricii*) to serve him, and everyone else necessary for his royal household.
> (Gregory of Tours, *Libri historiarum* IX.36; trans. Thorpe 1974, p. 523)

These counts, personal servants, *maior domus* (chief of the household), and tutors mentioned by Gregory, represent the formal ranks of the royal entourage that turned the Merovingian court into an efficient instrument of royal government. They point at the three missions with which the royal court was preoccupied—the administrative and fiscal management of the kingdom; the welfare of the king and his family; and the formation of a loyal and able local elite. Although no hierarchy among the various officials nominated by King Childebert to the newly founded court of Theudebert is explicitly indicated, it seems that from an early stage the ranks of servants and advisors at the Merovingian royal court were standardized and hierarchically stratified. An excellent case in point is provided by a certain Conda, who slowly paved his way to power in the courts of several Merovingian kings. His friend, the poet Venantius Fortunatus, describes his long, dazzling career with much admiration and panache:

> For long years rich splendour has been glorious in the King's court through your merits, Conda.... What intellect was it and what maturity of feeling, when you were thus the single love of such great kings?... So he who wishes to exalt his name by these deeds, let him speedily think upon your achievement. Starting from humble beginnings, you have always advanced to the heights and through all stages held to the lofty pinnacles. Theuderic, rejoicing, adorned you with the office of tribune, from that point you already had the mark of successful advance. For Theudebert granted you the prize of being a count, and added a belt in recognition of your services. He saw that excellent characters deserve better, and was soon willing to raise the rank you had earned. He saw to it urgently that you then became *domesticus*,

you rose suddenly, and the court rose with you.... Then, whilst Theudebald's young child was yet alive, your great care was for his nurture. Thus by distinguished action you fostered the public order, that you could bring the young king to mature age. You governed yourself, as though you were there as guardian, and the business entrusted to you flourished. Again, you held sway in Lothar's great court, who ordered the household to be ruled with the same love. Kings changed, but you did not change your offices, and as your own successor you were worthy of yourself.... For now through the love of gentle King Sigibert, gifts are lavishly given to reward your services. He has commanded you to establish yourself amongst the noble magnates, appointing you to his table companion, a promoted post.....

(Venantius Fortunatus, *Carmina*, VII.16; trans. George 1992, pp. 65–67)

Starting as a *tribunus* (a tax collector) in the service of Theuderic I, Conda was made *comes* (a high-ranked royal official with some judicial responsibilities). He was then made *domesticus* by King Theudebald,[5] and subsequently the young prince's tutor. After serving under both Chlothar I and Sigibert I, the latter attached Conda to the *convivia regis* (the royal table companions) and made him one of the *potentes*, that is, one of the highest-ranking magnates of the kingdom. Conda's career as related by Venantius Fortunatus is indeed telling, but it must not be taken to imply that all Merovingian courtiers took the same route, nor does it suggest that a clear, stratified, *cursus honorum* ever existed in Merovingian Francia.

As Conda's biography clearly indicates, the king's favor was a vital prerequisite for one's recruitment and advancement at court, and the closer one was to the king, the higher were his chances to be noticed and promoted. Moreover, the administrative role of the various dignitaries at court was never clearly outlined or rigidly defined. We know, for example, that the *referendarius* (chancellor), an administrative post inherited from the Roman imperial court, was in charge of the royal chancery (Classen 1983). But often we also find him active in the royal legal courts and in the treasury, as well as acting in the capacity of a royal delegate for important missions. Hence, our tendency to associate certain titles with specific jobs or assignments is at odds with the fluidity and inconsistency with which our sources use such titles and associate them with particular duties.

What is remarkable in Conda's career is not so much the fact that he climbed the administrative ladder at court, moving readily from one post to another, but the fact that he served successfully under five Merovingian kings—Theuderic I, Theudebert I, Theudebald, Chlothar, and Sigibert I. This suggests that although one's status at court was defined by one's proximity to the king, the Merovingian court as an institution of government had a powerful operational infrastructure that was not entirely dependent on the favor of a specific king. Continuity was the name of the game, and kings had to rely on the trained personnel of their predecessors, even if at times they introduced their own *fideles* (faithful) to the royal household or promoted their favorite reliable courtiers to new posts. That was also the gist of Remigius's letter to the young Clovis, warning him from dismissing his father's counselors and reshuffling his court.

Whereas the *comites* (counts), who were in charge of the administration of justice, the treasury or the royal chancery, were all members of the highest Merovingian elite, the *domestici* (personal servants) were recruited from among lower strata of Frankish society. Patroclus, for example, who came from a free landowning family "not of the highest nobility," as Gregory of Tours puts it, was a shepherd before being recruited by a certain Nunnio to service at the court of Childebert I (Gregory of Tours, *Vitae Patrum*, IX.1). Similarly, the talented goldsmith Eligius, who joined the royal mint at the time of Chlothar II, excelled at his job and gained the favor of the old king. Subsequently, Chlothar II's son and successor, King Dagobert I, made him one of his closest counselors (*Vita Eligii*; Lafaurie 1977; Heinzelmann 2013). These remarkable young men, who attracted the attention of someone at court either because of their exceptional talent or because of their ambition, normally started their careers as the personal servants of the king. Nevertheless, these humble-sounding positions were exceptionally advantageous, and they served as an excellent jumping board to higher posts at court and throughout the kingdom, offering those coming from the lower strata of the Frankish nobility a unique opportunity of social mobility (Jones 2009). Bertharius, for example, the royal *cubicularius* (a servant at the royal bedchamber), was given the title of *comes* and was even chosen by King Theudebert II to command an army (Fredegar, *Chronicon*, VI.36 and 38; Ebling 1974, no. 74, p. 80). Similarly, the educated slave Andarchius was brought to the attention of King Sigibert, who later sent him on some official missions (Gregory of Tours, *Libri historiarum*, IV.46). And the jeweler Eligius, whom we have already mentioned, became one of King Dagobert's most esteemed counselors (*Vita Eligii*, 14). These, however, were the exception that proves the rule: the vast majority of courtiers throughout the Merovingian period were members of the uppermost strata of the Frankish nobility.

As far as the elite is concerned, the *aula regis* (the king's court) was the best starting point for a young nobleman, and many of those who gathered at the courts of the Merovingian kings became powerful and influential magnates later in their careers (Hen 2007, pp. 100–106; Hen, in press). A certain Desiderius, for example, the son of an aristocratic family from Aquitaine, reached the royal court around 614, where he met the young prince Dagobert and was educated with him. He later became Dagobert's treasurer, and in 630 Dagobert himself nominated him to the bishopric of Cahors (*Vita Desiderii*; Durliat 1979). Similarly, Audoinus, the son of a Neustrian aristocratic family, was also sent to be educated at the court of Chlothar II, where he spent his youth with Dagobert and other aristocratic youngsters. He was later appointed *referendarius* by Dagobert, and in 641 he became the bishop of Rouen (*Vita Audoinii*; Fouracre and Gerberding 1996, pp. 132–152).

After several years at the service of the Merovingian kings, these successful courtiers retired from royal service and slipped effortlessly into high ecclesiastical offices (on bishops, see Halfond, Chapter 13, this volume). Eligius, King Dagobert's counselor, became the bishop of Noyon; Desiderius, as we have already noted, was appointed to the see of Cahors; Faro, Dagobert's *referendarius*, was appointed to the see of Meaux; Wandregisilus, another one of Dagobert's counselors, found his way to the abbey that later was named after him—Saint-Wandrille; he was succeeded there by Ansbert, Chlothar III's *referendarius*, who was later nominated to the see of Rouen; Geremer, yet another of Dagobert's counselors, founded the abbey of Saint-Samson-sur-Risle and was its first abbot, while holding at the same time the abbacy of Saint-Germer-de-Fly; and Philibert, another aristocrat who was educated at the court, became the abbot of Rebais, Jumièges, and Noirmoutier.[6] This is by no means an exhaustive list, but it is fairly representative, and it certainly suffices to demonstrate the powerful network that stemmed from the royal court—a network of power and control.

Throughout their lives, these ex-courtiers exchanged letters to ensure support when needed, and these lines of communication ensured that old friendships were never forgotten (see Gillett, Chapter 25, this volume). Years after he left the royal court, "the memory of the camaraderie and the sweetness of a youth passed under a cloudless sky" was recalled by Desiderius of Cahors in a letter addressed to King Dagobert himself (Desiderius of Cahors, *Epistulae*, I.5). In another letter, to Audoinus of Rouen, Desiderius mentions the good old times at the court of Chlothar II, where they met Eligius, future bishop of Noyons, and many others:

> May the old affection we had to each other and, indeed, to our Eligius, remain unchanged just as our close brotherhood used to be. In my silent prayers I beg that we shall be worthy to live together in the palace of the supreme heavenly king, just as we had been friends in the court of an earthly prince. And may we also have [with us] the two brothers from our fraternity [Rusticus and Siagrius], who had already died, the venerable Paul, and the not less laudable Sulpicius.
>
> (Desiderius of Cahors, *Epistulae*, I.10)

These were not mere nostalgic sentiments. Desiderius's correspondence with his old friends Eligius of Noyon, Paul of Verdun, and Sulpicius of Bourges, all mentioned in his letter to Audoinus, illuminates the ways in which this network of amity—which Barbara Rosenwein would define as an "emotional community" (Rosenwein 2006, pp. 135–155)—provided moral as well as political support to its members. (Williard 2014) Moreover, Desiderius's correspondence casts interesting light on the operation of the royal court, and on the ways it functioned as a melting pot for these aristocratic brilliant young men.

There was nothing new or exceptional in the ways Merovingian kings used their courtiers to control local politics or that royal administrators and churchmen used the written word to cultivate their friendship and sense of identity. What is noteworthy is the fact that all those courtiers, who started their careers at the royal court of the Merovingian kings, slowly took control of the highest secular and ecclesiastical ranks in Merovingian Francia. They all owed their promotion and high status to the king himself, and therefore they were bound to protect the king's interests and act on his behalf. The training at court prepared them for the job, and the time spent together with fellow courtiers was an ingenious mechanism for creating a loyal and obedient elite, whose members were closely tied to one another and to the king himself, with sentiments of camaraderie and allegiance (Hen 2007, pp. 94–123; Williard 2014; Hen 2015).

Sedes Regiae

In the later Roman Empire, emperors used to travel with their courts around the territories under their control. The reasons for this custom were mainly strategic. By moving around from one region to another, emperors could monitor the functioning of local administrators, impose some checks and balances, and be closer to the *limes* (border), where military action was needed (Noreña 2011). The Merovingian royal courts that evolved throughout the sixth and seventh centuries were also itinerant, though on a lesser scale. King Chilperic, for example, hardly left the triangle of Paris, Soissons, and Rouen, whereas Chlothar II and Dagobert I preferred their royal *villae* around Paris, most notably Clichy, Compiègne, and Étrépagny. Hence, although considered to be itinerant,[7] the Merovingian royal court did not move often, nor did it travel long distances. Its moves were rather limited and calculated, and they normally did not take the king and his entourage far from the central town that was chosen as the seat of government. We have already noted that Reims, Orléans, Paris, and Soissons were chosen by the sons of Clovis, and these remained the central foci around which royal courts rambled for much of the Merovingian period (Ewig 1952, 1963; Wood 1977; Barbier 1990, 2007a).

Whether in Paris, Clichy, or any other place throughout Merovingian Gaul, the court was, in practice, wherever the king resided. In fact, the king's presence was crucial for the successful function of the court as a whole, since only the king could delegate authority. Einhard's account of the *maior domus* Pippin III dragging the Merovingian king Childeric III to meet ambassadors or to the public assembly is extremely revealing (Einhard, *Vita Karoli*, 1). It appears that even when the king was virtually powerless and the *maior domus* ruled the kingdom, the king's presence still generated authority and legitimation that were necessary for the smooth operation of Merovingian polity.

As the official seat of the king and his entourage, the Merovingian court was the nerve center of the royal administration and the epicenter of political and judicial power, for it housed the royal chancery, the royal treasure, as well as the high court of justice, and it was also where the royal council was convened. These four institutions formed the backbone of the royal administration that enabled the Merovingian kings to rule effectively and to reign firmly over their kingdoms. Although mentioned in our sources more than once, none of these institutions was clearly defined or described in detail by our Merovingian authors. Nevertheless, some observations can be made.

The treasury (*fiscus*), headed by the *thesaurarius* or *camerarius*, was a constitutive element of royal power (Le Jan 1995, pp. 60–71; Barbier 2009), and gaining control of it was of utmost importance for those who sought political power. Fredegar is quite clear about this when he writes that in 613, "the entire Frankish kingdom was united as it has once been under the first Chlothar and it fell with all its treasure to the rule of the second Chlothar" (Fredegar, *Chronicon*, IV.42). For him, Chlothar's control of the royal treasury was a straightforward sign of his supremacy. Subsequently, Fredegar relates, Dagobert's rise to power was marked by endless efforts to secure and increase his treasury. First, shortly after the death of his father in 628, "Dagobert took possession of all Chlothar's kingdom, Neustria as well as Burgundy, and of all the treasure" (Fredegar, *Chronicon*, IV.57).

Then, after settling in Paris in 629, "he longed for ecclesiastical property and for the goods of his subjects and greedily sought by every means to amass fresh treasure" (Fredegar, *Chronicon*, IV.60). After his brother's death in 630, "Dagobert at once took control of the entire kingdom of Charibert, Gascony included; and he ordered Duke Barontus to take Charibert's treasure and bring it to him" (Fredegar, *Chronicon*, IV.67). No wonder that mighty queens, such as Brunhild and Fredegund, made an heroic effort to keep the treasure of their late husbands in order to secure their own position and the position of their children (Gregory of Tours, *Libri historiarum*, V.1 and VII.4, respectively; on queens, see James, Chapter 11, this volume).

The royal treasure, which consisted of coins and precious objects, was stored in wooden chests that were carried to wherever the king and his entourage resided (Gregory of Tours, *Libri historiarum*, IX.34). The royal sources of income were varied, ranging from tax revenues and wealth from the royal estates (Goffart 1982a, 1982b; Durliat 1990; see Strothmann, Chapter 35, this volume) through war booty, plunder, and tribute from neighboring peoples (Fredegar, *Chronicon*, IV.73, 74), all the way up to diplomatic negotiations and agreements, especially with the Byzantines (Zuckerman 1998; Goffart 2012; Drauschke 2019). All these enriched the royal treasury, turning the Merovingian court into an economic center that could mobilize huge resources for various political, cultural, or religious objectives.

The fact that a few powerful and charismatic Merovingian queens had access to the royal treasury led some scholars in the past to speculate on the role of the Merovingian queen as the guardian of the royal *fiscus*. However, opportunities to wield power and influence should not be interpreted as an open access to, and full control of, the royal treasury. Given the paramount importance of the treasury in royal governmental strategy, it is more likely that Merovingian queens, even queens as dominant and obstinate as Brunhild or Fredegund, had limited access to the *fiscus* (Hen 2004a, pp. 227–229; on queens, see James, Chapter 11, this volume).

The second important administrative institution at court was the chancery (*scrinia*), which was overseen by the *referendarius*.[8] It was noted in the past that Merovingian Gaul was, to a certain extent, a bureaucratic society "used to, needing and demanding documents" (Fouracre 1986, p. 26; Wood 1990, p. 63). This documentary feature of Merovingian society was a direct continuation of the late Roman bureaucratic tradition, and consequently the Merovingian royal chancery followed the late Roman imperial model (Classen 1983). It is extremely difficult to gauge how such an office evolved and operated as part of the Merovingian court. Our narrative sources yield little information on the workings of such a bureau, and from the hundreds (if not thousands) of documents that were drafted at Merovingian courts, only thirty-eight survive in their original form, and they are all associated with the monastery of Saint-Denis (Kölzer 2001, pp. xiii–xv).[9] Consequently, the Merovingian chancery is a shadowy institution in the extreme.

This is not the place to relate in detail the arguments for and against the existence of a well-organized office that produced documents on behalf of the king and his executive administrators.[10] For our purpose it will suffice to say that a certain office at court did indeed produce documents for the king, authenticated them, and sent them to their destination. These documents dealt mainly with royal precepts, judgments, donations of land, and the granting of immunities (Fouracre 1986; Rosenwein 1999; Kölzer 2001). They were all authenticated by the *referendarius* and sealed with a wax stamp that was impressed with the royal seal (Tessier 1962; Kölzer 2001, pp. xix–xxvi; Kano 2008) At the stage of sealing, some hair, presumably royal hair, was added to the wax. It is impossible to ascertain whether that practice was meant to consolidate the wax, or whether it was an extra element of authentication (Charlier, Nielen, and Prévost 2012, 2013; Dumézil 2015).

Yet, the most important administrative facet of the Merovingian court was the so-called king's audience. Sitting on his throne "in majesty," the king held regular audiences, which allowed him to maintain close ties with his officials throughout the kingdom. (Barbier 2007b) This is also where he received foreign envoys and ambassadors, and where the *placitum* (general assembly or royal council) was convened. Hence, the king's audience, to judge from the extant sources, was the most significant occurrence in the life of the Merovingian court, where administrative and governmental matters could be discussed and agreed upon, and where political and judicial conflicts at the highest level were managed and resolved.

Many of these audiences were routine procedures of administering the kingdom. In 616, for example, "Chlothar summoned to the villa of Bonneuil his mayor Warnachar and all the bishops and notables of Burgundy. Here he listened to all their just petitions and confirmed his concessions in writing" (Fredegar, *Chronicon*, IV.44). Similarly, in 628, King Dagobert held several audiences around Burgundy, giving "justice to all, rich and poor alike, with such equity as must have appeared pleasing to God. . . . Such was his great goodwill and eagerness that he neither ate nor slept, lest anyone should leave his presence without having obtained justice" (Fredegar, *Chronicon*, IV.58). Other audiences were more dramatic and violent. For example, in an audience that was held in the villa of Clichy in 627, a violent argument erupted between two factions of the Frankish magnates, during which the governor of Charibert's palace was killed and the king had to act firmly to prevent further bloodshed (Fredegar, *Chronicon*, IV.55).

At the pinnacle of the Merovingian administrative ladder stood the *maior domus* (mayor of the palace), who orchestrated the operation of the entire court and acted as vice-king. At first the *maiores* were elected from the most noble and powerful families of the Frankish elite; like all officers at court they were personal nominations of trust and recognition made by the king himself. The power and authority entrusted to the *maior domus* were immense, and they were intensified and consolidated over the years (Heidrich 1989). A rare glimpse of the status and operation of the *maior domus* is provided by a short passage from the so-called *Chronicle of Fredegar*, which describes two successive, but completely different, *maiores*:

> In the tenth year of his reign and at the wish of Brunhild, Theuderic made Protadius mayor of the palace. In every way Protadius was as clever and as capable as a man could be; but in certain cases he was monstrously cruel, extorting the last penny for

the fisc and with ingenuity both filling the fisc and enriching himself at the expense of others. He set himself to undermine all those of noble birth, so that nobody could deprive him of the position he had acquired. In this and other ways his excessive cunning harassed everyone, and not least the Burgudians, every man of whom he made his enemy.... In the eleventh year of Theuderic's reign, after the death of Protadius, Claudius was appointed mayor of the palace. By birth a Roman, Claudius was an intelligent man and a good storyteller, yet a man that got things done, resolute and full of good advice, well-read, absolutely trustworthy and the friend of all. He took of what had happened to his predecessors and behaved quietly and kept his temper while he held this office.   (Fredegar, *Chronicon*, IV.27–28)

Powerful, ambitious and resolute were the *maiores*, who stood at the most important junctions of Merovingian polity. This impression is also corroborated by the sole extant listing of dignitaries from the Merovingian kingdom, which is preserved in a compendium of legal material from mid-ninth-century Francia. According to this list, a rather clear hierarchy existed among the various functionaries at court, and at the top of the pyramid stood the *maior domus*, who was in charge of the *scola regis* and the *domus palatii*, and even had authority over the *duces civitatum* (Conrat 1908, pp. 248–250).[11]

The immense power of the *maiores* and their crucial role as brokers of consensus and collaboration with the local elites are best reflected in the provisions agreed upon in the so-called Edict of Paris, issued by King Chlothar II on October 18, 614, shortly after the unification of the entire Frankish kingdom (Murray 1994; Wood 1994, pp. 140–158; Esders 1997, pp. 88–267).[12] Chlothar clearly realized that in order to rule his kingdom with *pax et disciplina* (peace and order), he had to make some concessions to the local elites of the territories he had just annexed. Hence, he secured the position of all the courtiers who served under previous kings, reconfirmed the grants made to them in the past by himself or his kinsmen, and provided for the reinstitution of their possessions (*Chlotharii II edictum*, cc. 11, 16, 17). In other words, Chlothar maintained the courts of the three Merovingian kingdoms, each of which had its own *maior domus*—Gundoland in Neustria, Rado in Austrasia, and Warnachar in Burgundy (Ebling 1974, nos. 196, 257, 309, pp. 165, 201, 235–238). And so, writes Fredegar, "The entire Frankish kingdom was united as it has once been under the first Chlothar and it fell with all its treasure to the rule of the second Chlothar" (Fredegar, *Chronicon*, IV.36). Only this time there was one Merovingian king, with three distinct courts and three different *maiores*.

Each of the three *maiores* was accountable to the king, and each was responsible for pacifying the local elite and subordinate it to the will of the new monarch. That was not an easy task, but the sources leave little room for doubt that the *maiores* not only exercised real power in their respective regions, but also had open access to the king himself and were able to influence his decisions. No wonder, then, that when the Lombard king sent some envoys to Chlothar II to beg for the annulment of the annual tribute paid to the Franks, "they took the wise precaution of making private gifts, of one thousand solidi each, to Warnachar, Gundeland and Chuc" (Fredegar, *Chronicon*, IV.45). No one would attempt to bribe a useless functionary, who had no influence at court.

By the mid-seventh century the *maiores* were the most powerful men in the kingdom, and their privileged position enabled them to increase their wealth and authority. This, in turn, helped several *maiores* to overshadow their kings and, in some cases, to influence the election of their own successors. The result, as we all know, was fatal to the Merovingian dynasty. A series of ambitious and power-driven *maiores* from the Pippinid family managed to create a strong enough power base, first in Austrasia and subsequently in Neustria and Burgundy, to overthrow the Merovingian kings and establish themselves as the newly enthroned royal family (Fouracre 1984; Gerberding 1987; Costambeys, Innes, and MacLean 2011, pp. 31–65). No one describes this process better than Einhard, Charlemagne's biographer:

> The family of the Merovingians, from which the Franks used to make their kings, is thought to have lasted until king Childeric, who was deposed and tonsured and forced into a monastery on the order of Pope Stephen. Although it might seem to have ended with him, it had in fact been without any strength for a long time and offered nothing of any worth except the empty name of king. For the wealth and power of the kingdom were in the possession of the governors of the palace, who were called mayors of the palace and the highest command in the kingdom belonged to them....when Childeric was deposed Pippin, the father of King Charles, held that office, as if by hereditary right. For his father Charles had brilliantly discharged that same civil office which had been laid down for him by his own father, Pippin.
>
> (Einhard, *Vita Karoli*, 1–2; trans. Ganz 2008, pp. 18–19)

Although biased, derogatory, and acerbic, Einhard's account of the Pippinids' rise to power reflects quite accurately the position of many *maiores* in late Merovingian Francia. Not all Merovingian kings in the seventh and the first half of the eighth centuries were as *fainéant* (lazy/idle) as Childeric III was (Kölzer 2004), but all of them had to deal with ambitious *maiores*, whose rise to power was indeed a bad omen and an enormous challenge to the Merovingian charisma.

Court and Culture

The early Merovingian kings and queens, as far as we can tell, were not particularly interested in cultivating cultural activity, unless it was directly associated with exerting their authority over their kingdoms (Hen 2007, pp. 97–100). This situation had changed toward the middle of the sixth century. It was King Theudebert I who first sought to turn his royal court into an intellectual center by surrounding himself with learned aristocrats, among them Asteriolus and Secundinus, who, according to Gregory of Tours, were both *sapiens et retoricis inbutus litteris* (educated and trained in rhetoric; Gregory of Tours, *Libri historiarum*, III.33), and Parthenius, the grandson of Emperor Avitus and Bishop Ruricius of Limoges, who was educated in Ravenna (Gregory of Tours, *Libri historiarum*, III.36). Whether this was an attempt to imitate the Ostrogothic court of

Theoderic the Great, who had recruited to his service both Boethius and Cassiodorus, is unknown (see Arnold, Chapter 21, this volume). Nevertheless, Theudebert's acts set up a formidable model that was duly followed by future Merovingian kings.

Twenty years later, when King Sigebert I recruited the learned Gogo as his advisor and probably *maior domus*, Theudebert's and Parthenius's legacy was still prominent in the Austrasian court (Gregory of Tours, *Libri historiarum*, V.46). Gogo, who was a student of Parthenius himself, was well versed in the culture of Antiquity, as testified in the four surviving letters he penned (*Epistolae Austrasicae*, 13, 16, 22, 48). But Gogo was not alone. A group of talented young aristocrats associated in one way or another with the Austrasian court began to crystallize around Gogo. Members of this group joined forces in political, diplomatic, and social struggles, and mobilized forces to protect their own personal interests (Dumézil 2007).

The formation of Gogo's intellectual faction had received a further boost with the arrival of the Italian poet, Venantius Honorius Clementianus Fortunatus. Having been cured from an eye infection through the agency of St. Martin, Fortunatus decided to visit the saint's shrine in Tours. Whether this was a true act of devotion or a mere coverup story for a secret mission on behalf of the Byzantine Exarch of Ravenna is unknown. Nevertheless, Fortunatus's journey took him through Francia, and in 566 he arrived at the Austrasian court in Metz just in time for the grand occasion of King Sigebert's marriage to the Visigothic princess Brunhild. A verse panegyric and an *epithalamium* in honor of the royal couple on their wedding night, provided Fortunatus with a grand entry to the Austrasian royal circle, and paved his way for success as a poet in Merovingian Gaul (Godman 1987, pp. 1–37; George 1992; Pietri 1992; Roberts 2009).

This could hardly have been accidental. Wandering poets do not land out of the blue in royal courts, and admitted just like that to a royal wedding without any qualms or reservations. No doubt, Fortunatus's appearance at the wedding of the royal couple was carefully planned well in advance and orchestrated by people from the court, if not by Gogo himself. Many of the Frankish aristocrats whom Fortunatus had met at the royal wedding in Metz, among them Duke Lupus of Champagne, the *maiores* Gogo and Conda, Dynamius and Iovinus of Provence, as well as various bishops and religious women of aristocratic origins, became the dedicatees of numerous poems and epitaphs (Venantius Fortunatus, *Carmina*, VI. 9–10, VII. 1–2, 7-8, 11–12, 16). This could only mean that by the mid-sixth century, the royal court, under the auspices of the Austrasian king, was indeed becoming a cultural center that attracted talented intellectuals from all over Francia, and some from abroad. But the nature of this cultural center is very difficult to gauge.

No doubt during the reign of Sigibert I, a certain group of aristocrats who were associated with the royal court of Austrasia in one way or another, or who passed through the royal court, emerged as a unique intellectual group. They were "the friends of Gogo," as Bruno Dumézil has so nicely called them (Dumézil 2007). The time at court was a formative period for these young members of the Merovingian elite, during which they played a crucial role in the formation of the court's culture, first as an audience, then as producers, and subsequently, as chief disseminators. These young men developed a strong sense of camaraderie (*contubernium*) and friendship (*amicitia*) that was cultivated by the adoption of the insignia and gestures of the late Roman imperial bodyguard and lubricated through exchange of poetry and letters (Riché 1976, pp. 236–246; Wood 1990, pp. 67–71; Wood 1994, pp. 149–152; Hen 2007, pp. 100–106; Williard 2014). At court, these were forms of courtly entertainment and maybe competition; beyond the court, such letters and poetic epistles served as a system of communication of social and political news. As the various letters collected in the so-called *Epistulae Austrasiacae* and the various poems by Venantius Fortunatus testify, even after they left court, these friends exchanged letters to ensure support when needed. These lines of communication ensured that old friendships were never forgotten.

That such poems and letters were written at all is a clear indication, on the one hand, of the strength of literary tradition within the court circle of Merovingian Francia and, on the other hand, of the innovative and widespread use of the written word for creating friendships and forming support groups (see Gillett, Chapter 25, this volume). Needless to say, this practice did no emerge *ex nihilo*. It was deeply rooted in Roman traditions that went back to Cicero and continued well into Late Antiquity and the early Middle Ages, as attested by the letters of Pliny the Younger, Sidonius Apollinaris, Avitus of Viennes, Ruricius of Limoges, and Ferreolus of Uzès, whose letters unfortunately did not survive (Wood 1992, 1993; Ebbler 2009). And yet, the Merovingian courtiers gave this tradition a new twist that, eventually, enabled them to mold themselves as a political and social support group. Against the background of the political turmoil of the late sixth and early seventh centuries, they surely needed such a support.

Whether the Merovingian court with its intellectual circle was also an educational center for the young members of the Frankish elite is not at all clear. We know that Gogo was entrusted with the education of the young prince Childebert II (Gregory of Tours, *Libri historiarum*, V.46). After Gogo's death in 581, the duty was passed on to his successor, Waldelenus, and after Waldelenus's death, Brunhild herself took over and supervised the education of her son (Gregory of Tours, *Libri historiarum*, VI.1, VIII.22). This is, in fact, the first evidence we have for the education of a young prince in Merovingian Gaul, and from Praetextatus's harsh criticism of Fredegund for neglecting the education of her son, we may assume that whatever was going on in Austrasia was only the beginning of something that would become widespread (Gregory of Tours, *Libri historiarum*, VIII.31). However, the fact that Sigibert and Brunhild took care of the education of their son must not be taken to imply that a school for the education of young aristocrats was founded at the court, nor is there any evidence to suggest that other young members of the Austrasian elite joined the young Childebert.

The first vague sign of the formation of some sort of a court school for the education of young aristocrats began to appear only in the next phase of Merovingian rule. Pierre Riché lamented that King Chlothar II did not received proper education at court, even though his father, King Chilperic was by far the most intellectually ambitious monarch of Merovingian Francia (Riché 1976, pp. 226–227). Yet, Chlothar was determined to provide a good education for his son, and for that purpose he had to rely on the Austrasian court and its tradition. When he appointed his eleven-year-old son, Dagobert I, as king of Austrasia, he placed him under the close supervision of the Austrasian *maior domus* Pippin I and Bishop Arnulf of Metz, two of the most prominent members of the Austrasian elite (Fredegar, *Chronicon*, IV.58). If we are to believe the seventh-century *Vita Arnulfi*, and there is no reason why we should not in this case, Arnulf was also entrusted with the young prince's education (*Vita Arnulfi*, 16).

The increasingly sedentary nature of the royal courts, especially after the unification of Francia in 613, facilitated the development of a certain court "school." The existence of such a school is confirmed not only by the writings of its alumni, whom we have just mentioned, but also by the list of Merovingian dignitaries mentioned above. According to this list, the *praeses* was in charge of the *scola regis*, and this *praeses* was, as I have argued, most probably the *maior domus* himself (Conrat 1908, pp. 248–250). This suggests that a school was part and parcel of the Merovingian royal court, and it accords extremely well with the Austrasian tradition, adduced above, of entrusting the education of the young prince to the *maior domus*, be it Gogo, Waldelenus, or Pippin I.

Aristocrats from all corners of the Merovingian kingdom sent their children to be educated at court with the young princes and under the supervision of the *maior domus*. Such a practice, whose roots can be observed in the late-sixth-century Austrasian tradition of educating the young prince (Gregory of Tours, *Libri historiarum*, V.46), became more prominent and still more widespread during the first decades of the seventh century. Consequently, a flow of talented young aristocrats frequented the Frankish court and turned it into a lively center of cultural activity (Hen 2007, pp. 100–106; Hen 2015). Its fame grew far and wide, so that it even reached the Anglo-Saxon queen Æthelburh, who sent her sons to be educated at Dagobert's court (Bede, *Historia ecclesiasticae*, II.20). What was taught at court, and precisely in what context, we do not really know. Pierre Riché suggested that it was not a school in the modern sense of the word, but more of a staff school that trained officers and bureaucrats to ensure a steady supply of loyal officers (Riché 1976, pp. 239–246). This may well be true, but given the fragmentary nature of our evidence, it is impossible to reconstruct the court school's curriculum with any certainty.

Although the nature of our evidence, and the mobility of the Merovingian elites, especially after 613, make it difficult to discuss Merovingian culture in regional terms, it appears that the emergence of intellectual court circles and networks of courtiers who used the written word as a means to preserve and cultivate their friendship, affection (*dulcedo*), and support, was stronger in Austrasia than elsewhere and survived longest among members of the Austrasian elite, as the evidence from the middle of the seventh century clearly indicates (Hen, in press).

Conclusion

To sum up, the royal court was the major center of political power in Merovingian Gaul. Following the late Roman model, it became an administrative center from whence the kingdom was ruled and to which aristocrats flocked in order to serve the king, or in hope for honors and promotion. As such, the Merovingian court encompassed both the ruler's military retinue and the kingdom's highest bureaucrats. Members of the court monopolized the role of royal functionaries and administrators, and their time at court in the service of the king served for many of them as a springboard to higher governmental and ecclesiastical positions throughout the kingdom. The Merovingian court also housed the meetings of the king's royal council, and this was the highest court in which political and judicial conflicts were managed and resolved. These two functions— as the center of political power and as the stage for the administration of justice and the settlement of disputes—helped to generate a sense of authority and consensus politics that served as a symbolic unifier in an otherwise factional reality. Finally, the Merovingian court was a magnet that drew ambitious and talented young men from all over Francia and beyond, who turned it into a vibrant intellectual and cultural center.

NOTES

1. Modern historians also refrained from providing a comprehensive account of the Merovingian court, to the effect that the fullest treatment of the subject is still Fustel de Coulanges 1930, vol. 3. Some general accounts are given in Geary 1998; Staab 1990; Wood 1994; Van Dam 2005.
2. Clovis was still a young man at the time, probably fourteen or fifteen years old. On Clovis and his reign, see Wallace-Hadrill 1962, pp. 163–185; Wood 1994, pp. 41–50; Rouche 1996; Meier and Pazold 2014.
3. *Sacrum palatium* (the sacred palace) was the name given by Byzantine authors to the great palace of Constantinople (Carile 2012), and it was later adopted by the Carolingians to mark their own palace (de Jong 2003).
4. At a later stage, a few of the honors became hereditary, such as the office of the *maior domus*. See Heidrich 1989.
5. The office of *domesticus* is not mentioned in any other Merovingian source. It is probably an honorary title given to members of the king's inner circle.
6. On all these courtiers and officials, see the relevant entries in Ebling 1974, and in Riché and Périn 1996.
7. Itinerant courts became visible in the sources in the Carolingian period, and more so in the Ottonian period. See Bernhard 1993; McKitterick 2011.
8. The term *cancelaria* (chancery) is much later than the Merovingian period and is only attested in the sources from the twelfth century onward.
9. Altogether, some 200 royal documents from Merovingian Gaul survive in one form or another, from which only 78 (or parts thereof) are considered authentic.
10. On this debate, see Kölzer 2001, pp. xv–xviii; Dumézil 2015.
11. This list of royal officials is traditionally associated with the court of Chlothar II and Dagobert I, but even if one doubts its Merovingian authenticity, it is obvious that by the mid-ninth century (i.e., the date of the manuscript in which it is preserved) someone in Francia thought that a Merovingian court was structured in such a way. On this list, see Conrat 1908; Hen 2015.
12. This edict has been seen in the past as a sign of royal weakness vis-à-vis the demands of the local elites. However, such a view is untenable, given the effectiveness with which Chlothar controlled the local elites throughout his reign. This edict was modeled on a novella by Justinian for Italy. See Pontal 1989, pp. 205–212; Murray 1994; and Halfond 2010.

Works Cited

Ancient Sources

Bede, *Historia ecclesiastica gentis Anglorum*. B. Colgrave and R. A. B. Mynors (eds. and trans). (1969). Oxford: Clarendon Press.

Chlotharii II edictum, in *Capitularia regum Francorum* 1. A. Boretius (ed.). (1883). MGH Legum sectio 2, no. 9 (pp. 20–23). Hanover: Hahn Verlag.

Desiderius of Cahors, *Epistulae*. D. Norberg (ed.). (1961). Studia Latina Stockholmiensia 6. Uppsala: Almqvist & Wiksel.

Einhard, *Vita Karoli Magni*. O. Holder-Egger (ed.). (1911). MGH SRG in usum scholarum 25. Hanover: Hahn Verlag.

Epistolae Austrasicae. E. Malspina (ed. and trans.). (2001). *Il Liber epistolarum della cancellaria austrasica (sec. V–VI)*. Rome: Herder Editrici.

Fredegar, *Chronicorum liber quartus cum continuationibus*. M. Wallace-Hadrill (ed. and trans.). (1960). London: T. Nelson.

Ganz, D. (trans.). (2008). *Two Lives of Charlemagne*. Harmonsdworth: Penguin.

Gregory of Tours, *Decem Libri Historiarum*. B. Krusch and W. Levison (eds.). (1951). MGH SRM 1.1. Hanover: Hahn Verlag.

Gregory of Tours, *Liber Vitae Patrum*, B. Krusch (ed.). (1885). MGH SRM 1.2. (pp. 211–294). Hanover: Hahn Verlag.

Kölzer, T. (2001). *Die Urkunden der Merowinger*. MGH Diplomata regum Francorum e stripe Merovingica. Hanover: Hahn Verlag.

Thorpe, L. (trans.) (1974). *Gregory of Tours: History of the Franks*. Harmondsworth: Penguin.

Venantius Fortunatus, *Carmina*. M. Reydellet (ed. and trans.). (1994–2004). 3 vols. Paris: Les Belles Lettres.

Vita Arnulfi episcopi et confessoris. B. Krusch (ed.). (1888). MGH SRM 2 (pp. 432–446). Hanover: Hahn Verlag.

Vita Audoini episcopi Rotomagensis. W. Levison (ed.). (1910). MGH SRM 5 (pp. 553–567). Hanover: Hahn Verlag.

Vita Desiderii episcopi Cadurcensis. B. Krusch (ed.). (1902). MGH SRM 4 (pp. 563–593). Hanover: Hahn Verlag. [Reprinted (1957) CCSL 117 (pp. 343–401) Turnhout: Brepols.]

Vita Eligii episcopi Noviomensis. B. Krusch (ed.). (1902). MGH SRM 4 (pp. 663–741). Hanover: Hahn Verlag.

Modern Sources

Anton, H. H. (1968), *Fürstenspiegel und Herrscherethos in der Karolingerzeit*. Bonner Historische Forschungen 32. Bonn: L. Röhrscheid.

Barbier, J. (1990), "Le système palatial franc: genèse et fonctionnement dans le Nord-Ouest du regnum." *Bibliothèque de l'École des Chartes* 148: 245–299.

Barbier, J. (2007a). "Les lieux du pouvoire en Gaule franque: l'example des palais." In C. Ehlers (ed.), *Deutsche Königspfalzen*, VIII—*Orte der Herrschaft* (pp. 227–246). Göttingen: Vanderhoek und Ruprecht.

Barbier, J. (2007b). "Un ritual politique à la cour mérovingienne: l'audience royale." In J. P. Callier and M. Sot (eds.), *L'Audience: rituels et cadres spatiaux dans l'Antiquité et haut Moye Âge* (pp. 241–263). Paris: Picard.

Barbier, J. (2009). "Le fisc du royaume franc: quelques jalons pour une reflexion sur l'État au haut Moyen Âge." In W. Pohl and V. Wieser (eds.), *Der frühmittelalterliche Staat: europäische Perspectiven* (pp. 271–285). Vienna: Verlag des Österreichischen Akademie der Wissenschaften.

Barnwell, P. S. (1997). *Kings, Courtiers and Imperium: The Barbarian West, 565–725*. London: Duckworth.

Bernhardt, J. W. (1993). *Itinerant Kingship and Royal Monasteries in Early Medieval Germany, c. 936–1075*. Cambridge: Cambridge University Press.

Carile, M. C. (2012). *The Vision of the Palace of the Byzantine Emperors as a Heavenly Jerusalem*. Spoleto: Centro Italiano di Studi sull'Alto Medioevo.

Charlier, P., Nielen, M.-A., and Prévost, A. (2012). "Les sceaux des 'rois chevelus', une énigme médiévale." *Archéologia* 504: 40–47.

Charlier, P., Nielen, M.-A., and Prévost, A. (2013). "La découverte de poils ou cheveux humains dans les sceaux." In E. Marguin (ed.), *Le Pouvoir en actes: fonder, dire, montrer, contrefaire l'autorité* (pp. 137–139). Paris: Archives nationales.

Classen, P. (1983). "Spätrömische Grundlagen mittelalterlicher Kanzleien." *Vorträge und Forschungen* 28: 67–84.

Conrat, M. (1908). "Ein Traktat über romanisch-fränkisches Ämterwessen." *Zeitschrift der Savigny-Stiftung für Rechtsgeschichte: Germanistische Abteilung* 42: 239–260.

Costambeys, M., Innes, M., and MacLean, S. (2011). *The Carolingian World*. Cambridge: Cambridge University Press.

de Jong, M. (2003). "Sacrum palatium et ecclesia: L'autorité religieuse royale sous les Carolingiens (790–840)." *Annales: Histoire, Sciences Sociales* 58: 1243–1269.

Dierkens, A., and Périn, P. (2000). "Les sedes regiae mérovingiennes entre Seine et Rhin." In G. Ripoll and J. M. Gurt (eds.), *Sedes regiae (ann. 400–800)* (pp. 267–304). Barcelona: Reial Acadèmia de Bones Lettres.

Drauschke, J. (2019). "Archaeological perspectives on communication and exchange between the Merovingians and the Eastern Mediterranean." In S. Esders, Y. Fox, Y. Hen, and L. Sarti (eds.), *East and West in the Early Middle Ages: The Merovingian Kingdoms in Mediterranean Perspective* (pp. 9–31). Cambridge: Cambridge University Press.

Dumézil, B. (2007). "Gogo et ses amis: écriture, échanges et ambitions dans un réseau aristo-cratique de la fin du VIᵉ siècle." *Revue historique* 309: 353–393.

Dumézil, B. (2015). "La chancellerie mérovingienne au VIᵉ siècle." In *Le corti nell'alto medioevo*, Settimane di studi del Centro italiano di studi sull'alto medioevo 62 (pp. 473–499). Spoleto: Centro Italiano di Studi sull'Alto Medioevo.

Durliat, J. (1979). "Les attributions civiles de l'évêques mérovingiens: l'example de Didier, évêque de Cahors (630–655)." *Annales du Midi* 91: 237–254.

Durliat, J. (1990). *Les finances publiques de Dioclétien aux Carolingiens (284–889)*. Sigmaringen: Thorbecke.

Ebbler, J. (2009). "Tradition, Innovation, and Epistolary Mores." In P. Rousseau (ed.), *A Companion to Late Antiquity* (pp. 270–284). Chichester: Wiley-Blackwell.

Ebling, H. (1974). *Prosopographie der Amtsträger des Merowingerreichs von Chlothar II (613) bis Karl Martell (741)*. Beihefte der Francia 2. Munich: Thorbecke.

Esders, S. (1997). *Römische Rechtstradition und merowingisches Königtum. Zum Rechtscharakter politischer Herrschaft in Burgund im 6. und 7. Jahrhundert*. Veröffentlichungen des Max-Planck-Instituts für Geschichte 134. Göttingen: Vandenhoeck & Ruprecht.

Ewig, E. (1952). *Die fränkischen Teilungen und Teilreiche (511–613)*. Wiesbaden: Franz Steiner Verlag [reprinted in Ewig 1976–1979, pp. 114–171].

Ewig, E. (1956). "Zum christlichen Köningsgedanken im Frühmittelalter." In T. Mayer (ed.), *Das Königtum: seine geistigen und rechlichen Grundlagen* (pp. 7–73). Sigmaringen: Thorbecke [reprinted in Ewig 1976–1979, pp. 3–71].

Ewig, E. (1963). "Résidence et capitale pendant le Haut Moyen Age." *Revue historique* 230: 25–72 [reprinted in Ewig 1976–1979, pp. 362–408].

Ewig, E. (1976–1979). *Spätantikes und fränkisches Gallien. Gesammelte Aufzätze zur merowingischn Geschichte (1952–1973)*, ed. H. Atsma. 2 vols. Beihefte der Francia 3. Darmstadt: Thorbecke.

Fouracre, P. (1984). "Observations on the Outgrowth of Pippinid Influence in the 'Regum Francorum' after the Battle of Tertry (687–715)." *Medieval Prosopography* 5: 1–31.

Fouracre, P. (1986), "'Placita' and the Settlement of Disputes in Later Merovingian Francia." In W. Davies and P. Fouracre (eds.), *The Settlement of Disputes in Early Medieval Europe* (pp. 23–43). Cambridge: Cambridge University Press.

Fouracre, P., and Gerberding, R. (1996). *Late Merovingian France: History and Hagiography, 640–720*. Manchester: Manchester University Press.

Fustel de Coulanges, N. D. (1930). *Histoire des institutions politiques de l'ancienne France*, III— *La monarchie franque*. 6th ed. Paris: Hachette.

Geary, P. J. (1988). *Before France and Germany. The Creation and Transformation of the Merovingian World*. New York: Oxford University Press.

George, J. W. (1992). *Venantius Fortunatus: A Poet in Merovingian Gaul*. Oxford: Clarendon Press.

Gerberding, R. (1987). *The Rise of the Carolingians and the Liber Historiae Francorum*. Oxford: Clarendon Press.

Godman, P. (1987). *Poets and Emperors. Frankish Politics and Carolingian Poetry*. Oxford: Clarendon Press.

Goffart, W. (1982a). "Old and New in Merovingian Taxation." *Past and Present* 96: 3–21.

Goffart, W. (1982b). "Merovingian Polyptychs: Reflections on Two Recent Publications." *Francia* 9: 55–77 [reprinted in Goffart 1989, pp. 213–231].

Goffart, W. (1989). *Rome's Fall and After*. London: Hambledon Press.

Goffart, W. (2012). "The Frankish Pretender Gundovald, 582–585. A Crisis of Merovingian Blood." *Francia* 39: 1–27 [reprinted in Goffart 1989, pp. 233–253].

Halfond, G. I. (2010). *The Archaeology of Frankish Church Councils, AD 511–768*. Leiden: Brill.

Halsall, G. (2007). *Barbarian Migration and the Roman West, 376–568*. Cambridge: Cambridge University Press.

Heidrich, I. (1989). "Les maires du palais neustriens du milieu du VIIᵉ au milieu du VIIIᵉ siècle." In H. Atsma (ed.), *La Neustrie: les pays au nord de la Loire de 650 à 850*, (vol. 1: 217–229). Beihefte der Francia 16. Sigmaringen: Thorbecke.

Heinzelmann, M. (2013). "Eligius monetarius: Norm onder Sonderfall?" In J. Jarnut and J. Strothmann (eds.), *Die Merowingischen Monetarmünzen als Quellen zum Verständnis des 7. Jahrhunderts in Gallien* (pp. 243–291). Paderborn: Wilhelm Fink.

Hen, Y. (1998). "The Uses of the Bible and the Perception of Kingship in Merovingian Gaul." *Early Medieval Europe* 7: 277–290.

Hen, Y. (2004a). "Gender and the Patronage of Culture in Merovingian Gaul." In L. Brubaker and J. M. H. Smith (eds.), *Gender in the Early Medieval World: East and West, 300–900* (pp. 217–233). Cambridge: Cambridge University Press.

Hen, Y. (2004b). "The Christianisation of Kingship." In M. Becher and J. Jarnut (eds.), *Der Dynastiewechsel von 751: Vorgeschichte, Legitimationsstrategien und Erinnerung* (pp. 163–77). Münster: Scriptorium.

Hen, Y. (2007). *Roman Barbarians: The Royal Court and Culture in the Early Medieval West.* Basingstoke: Palgrave-Macmillan.

Hen, Y. (2014). "Conversion and Masculinity in the Early Medieval West." In I. Katznelson and M. Rubin (eds.), *Religious Conversions: History, Experience and Meaning* (pp. 151–67). Farnham: Ashgate.

Hen, Y. (2015). "Court and Culture in the Barbarian West: A Prelude to the Carolingian Renaissance." In *Le corti nell'alto medioevo*, Settimane di studi del Centro italiano di studi sull'alto medioevo 62 (pp. 627–651). Spoleto: Centro Italiano di Studi sull'Alto Medioevo.

Hen, Y. (in press). "Les élites culturelles." In A. Bayard, B. Dumézil, and S. Joye (eds.), *L'Austrasie: pouvoirs, espaces et identités à la charnière de l'Antiquité et du Moyen Âge*. Turnhout: Brepols.

Jones, A. E. (2009). *Social Mobility in Late Antiquity: Strategies and Opportunities for the Non-Elite.* Cambridge: Cambridge University Press.

Jones, A. H. M. (1964). *The Later Roman Empire, 284–602.* 2 vols. Oxford: Blackwell.

Kano, O. (2008). "Quelques notes sur la représentativité des actes transmis des Mérovingiens." *Hersetec* 2: 33–42.

Kelley, C. (1998). "Emperors, Government and Bureaucracy." In A. Cameron and P. Garnsey (eds.), *Cambridge Ancient History*, XIII—*The Later Empire, A.D. 337–425* (pp. 138–183). Cambridge: Cambridge University Press.

Kölzer, T. (2004). "Die letzten Merowinger: rois fainéants?" In M. Becher and J. Jarnut (eds.), *Der Dynastiewechsel von 751: Vorgeschichte, Legitimationsstrategien und Erinnerung* (pp. 33–60). Münster: Scriptorium.

Lafaurie, J. (1977). "Eligius monetarius." *Revue numismatique* 19: 111–151.

Le Jan, R. (1995). *Famille et pouvoire dans le monde franc (VIIᵉ-Xᵉ siècle): Essai d'anthropologie sociale.* Paris: Publications de la Sorbonne.

McCormick, M. (2000). "Emperor and Court." In A. Cameron, B. Ward-Perkins, and M. Whitby (eds.), *Cambridge Ancient History*, XIV—*Late Antiquity: Empire and Successors, A.D. 425–600* (pp. 135–163). Cambridge: Cambridge University Press.

McKitterick, R. (2011). "A King on the Move: The Place of an Itinerant Court in Charlemagne's Government." In J. Duindam, T. Artan, and M. Kunt (eds.), *Royal Courts in Dynastic States and Empires: A Global Perspective* (vol. 1, pp. 145–169). Leiden: Brill.

Meier, M., and Patzold, S. (eds.) (2014). *Chlodwigs Welt: Organisation von Herrschaft um 500.* Stuttgart: Franz Steiner Verlag.

Murray, A. C. (1994). "Immunity, Nobility, and the Edict of Paris." *Speculum* 69: 18–39.

Murray, A. C. (ed.). (2000). *From Roman to Merovingian Gaul: A Reader.* Peterborough, Ontario: Broadview Press.

Noreña, C. F. (2011). *Imperial Ideals in the Roman West: Representation, Circulation, Power.* Cambridge: Cambridge University Press.

Périn, P. (1989). "Paris mérovingien, *sedes regiae.*" *Klio* 71: 487–502.

Pietri, L. (1992). "Venance Fortunat et ses commanditaires: un poète italien dans la société gallo-franque." In *Committenti et produzione artistico-letteraria nell'alto medioevo occidentale*, Settimane di studio del Centro italiano di studi sull'alto medioevo 39 (pp. 729–754). Spoleto: Centro Italiano di Studi sull'Alto Medioevo.

Pontal, O. (1989). *Histoire des conciles mérovingiens.* Paris: Cerf.

Quast, D. (ed.) (2015). *Das Grab des fränkischen Königs Childerich in Tournai und die Anastasis Childerici von Jean-Jacques Chifflet aus dem Jahre 1655.* Mainz: Verlag des Römisch-Germanischen Zentralmuseums.

Riché, P. (1976). *Education and Culture in the Barbarian West from the Sixth through the Eighth Century*, trans. J. J. Contreni. Columbia: University of South Carolina Press.

Riché, P., and Périn, P. (eds.). (1996), *Dictionaire des Francs: les temps mérovingiens*. Paris: Éditions Bartillat.

Ripoll, G., and Gurt, J. M. (eds.). (2000). *Sedes regiae (ann. 400–800)*. Barcelona: Reial Acadèmia de Bones Lettres.

Roberts, M. (2009). *The Humblest Sparrow: The Poetry of Venantius Fortunatus*, Ann Arbor: University of Michigan Press.

Rosenwein, B. H. (1999). *Negotiating Space. Power, Restraint, and Privileges of Immunity in Early Medieval Europe*. Ithaca, NY: Cornell University Press.

Rosenwein, B. H. (2006). *Emotional Communities in the Early Middle Ages*. Ithaca, NY: Cornell University Press.

Rouche, M. (1996). *Clovis*. Paris: Fayard.

Rouche, M. (1997). "Entre *civitas* et *sedes regni*: Grégoire de Tours et les espaces politiques de son temps." In N. Gauthier and H. H. Galinié (eds.), *Grégoire de Tours et l'espace gaulois. Actes du congrès international, Tours, 3–5 Novembre 1994* (pp. 179–184) Tours: Association Grégoire.

Staab, F. (1990). "Palatium in der Merowingerzeit: Tradition und Entwicklung." In F. Staab (ed.), *Die Pfalz: Probleme einer Begriffsgeschichte vom Kaiserpalast auf dem Palatin bis zum heitigen Regierungsbezirk* (pp. 49–67). Speyer: Pfälzische Gesellschaft zur Förderung der Wissenschaften.

Tessier, G. (1962). *Diplomatique royale française*. Paris: Picard.

Van Dam, R. (2005). "Merovingian Gaul and the Frankish conquest." In P. Fouracre (ed.), *The New Cambridge Medieval History, I—c. 500–c. 700* (pp. 193–231). Cambridge: Cambridge University Press.

Wallace-Hadrill, J. M. (1962). *The Long-Haired Kings*. London: Methuen.

Wallace-Hadrill, J. M. (1971). *Early Germanic Kingship in England and on the Continent*. Oxford: Blackwell.

Williard, H. D. (2014). "Letter-Writing and Literary Culture in Merovingian Gaul." *European Review of History* 21: 691–710.

Wood, I. N. (1977). "Kings, Kingdoms and Consent." In P. Sawyer and I. N. Wood (eds.), *Early Medieval Kingship* (pp. 6–29). Leeds: Leeds University Press.

Wood, I. N. (1990). "Administration, Law and Culture in Merovingian Gaul." In R. McKitterick (ed.), *The Uses of Literacy in the Early Middle Ages* (pp. 63–81). Cambridge: Cambridge University Press.

Wood, I. N. (1992). "Continuity or Calamity? The Constraints of Literary Models." In J. Drinkwater and H. Elton (eds.), *Fifth-Century Gaul: A Crisis of Identity?* (pp. 9–18). Cambridge: Cambridge University Press.

Wood, I. N. (1993). "Letters and Letter-Collections from Antiquity to the Early Middle Ages: The Prose Work of Avitus of Vienne." In M. A. Meyer (ed.), *The Culture of Christendom: Essays in Medieval History in Commemoration of Denis Bethell* (pp. 29–43). London: Hambledon Press.

Wood, I. N. (1994). *The Merovingian Kingdoms, 450–751*. London: Longman.

Zuckerman, C. (1998). "Qui a rappelé en Gaule le Ballomer Gundovald?" *Francia* 25: 1–18.

CHAPTER 11

....

ELITE WOMEN IN THE
MEROVINGIAN PERIOD

....

EDWARD JAMES

In the early Middle Ages, women normally acquired status either through their father or husband, or through their choice to live a monastic life. There are thus two different kinds of elite, one secular and the other spiritual: the elite and the elect, to use different words derived from the same Latin original. In practice, however, the spiritual elect seem to come mostly from the secular elite. Most women of whom we know anything at all from Merovingian sources can probably be described as elite women: others appear either anonymously or are merely incidental to stories of miracles or other events.

Elite women mostly appear in the sources in ways that make them difficult to understand or evaluate in their own terms. They are found generally in texts written by men and in works that tend to offer a picture dictated by the genre within which the text was composed. And they simply do not appear in texts as often as men: Gregory of Tours's *Histories* mentions 1,346 individuals, and only 197 of those are women (Harrison 1998, p. 75). Individuals seldom appear in more than one text, so it is difficult to obtain a nuanced view. One notable exception is that of Radegund: not only do we learn about her from Gregory's *Histories*, but we also have two *Lives* of her, one by the Italian poet Venantius Fortunatus and the other by Baudonivia, a nun in her convent—the only significant Merovingian text known to have been written by a woman. Another exception is Balthild, a benefactor of the church and a saint in Frankish texts, but, in Stephen's *Life of Wilfrid of York*, she is an evil Jezebel who slew nine bishops. In the case of Balthild, we can reconcile the problem by suggesting that Stephen was simply inventing, in order to dramatize the early years of his hero, Wilfrid. But in many cases we have no means of checking; we simply have to remember, when faced by descriptions of wicked women, that our clerical writers had many late-antique texts that led them to think of women as being inferior, weak, and potentially evil (Richlin 2014). There were some female role models in the Christian tradition—bold martyrs or determined ascetics—but a wealth of contrary traditions. It is significant that great female saints could be praised for behaving *viriliter*; that is, they attained greatness only by abandoning their femininity and embracing the male values of the world around them (on gender, see Halsall, Chapter 8, this volume).

Until the 1970s, little work was done on women in the late Roman and Frankish worlds. Much research on women has appeared since then (Wemple 1981; Affeldt 1990; Goetz 1995); the limited material has been examined from all angles, and much of it has been translated to make it more widely known (McNamara and Halborg 1992; Amt 2010). One of the frequently asserted propositions, championed by scholars such as Suzanne Fonay Wemple, Jane T. Schulenberg, and Jo Ann McNamara, has been that elite women in the Merovingian period had more power and independence than later, in the Carolingian period, and perhaps than before, at the time of the Roman Empire (McNamara 1976; Wemple 1981; Schulenburg 1998). A key to their status was their ability to control property; before we look at women in the elite and among the elect, we need to examine property.

WOMEN AND PROPERTY

We will start this discussion by looking in detail at one female religious figure, for reasons that will become clear. Burgundofara—also known as Fara, or, in modern French, Sainte Fare—first appears as a small child in Jonas's *Life of Columbanus*, a text completed while she was still alive. The Irish holy man Columbanus came to the house of King Theuderic II's friend, Chagneric, at Meaux; he blessed the house and consecrated Chagneric's daughter, Burgundofara, still a child, to Christ (Jonas, *VC* 1.26). Some time later, after Columbanus had gone to Italy to found the monastery of Bobbio (in 612), his follower Eustasius (the first abbot of Columbanus's foundation Luxeuil) visited Chagneric too (Jonas, VC 2.7). He discovered that Burgundofara was ill, with a fever and an eye problem. This illness had come about, says Columbanus's hagiographer, because Burgundofara's father had organized her betrothal against the wishes of Columbanus and the girl herself. Eustasius cured Burgundofara and discovered that her fervent wish was to dedicate herself to God, as Columbanus had intended. Eustasius promised to receive her as a nun on his return, but Chagneric still insisted that she be married. She fled to sanctuary in the cathedral at Meaux, and her father sent armed men after her, to kill her if necessary. Eustasius rescued her and she received her vows as a nun.

Burgundofara did not enter a preexisting convent. She built her own monastery on her own land, at Eboriacum, about 15 kilometers from Meaux. It soon took the name of Farae Monasterium (from which is derived the current name of Faremoûtiers-en-Brie). Jonas says that Eustasius appointed Chagnoald, her brother, and Waldebert (his successor as abbot of Luxeuil) to train her in the rule (Jonas, VC 2.7). Chagnoald later became bishop of Laon; another of her brothers, Burgundofaro, after a military career and a marriage, became bishop of Meaux.

Faremoûtiers was one of the first monasteries for women founded under the direct influence of Columbanus, and it became one of the more distinguished (on Merovingian monasticism, see Diem, Chapter 15, this volume). It was the destination of a number of members of newly converted English royal families: Eorcengota, the daughter of the Kentish king, and two members of the East Anglian royal family, Sæthryth and Æthelburh, both of whom ended up as its abbesses (Bede, HE 3.8).

Fara was clearly a member of a secular Frankish elite, but she became a member of the clerical elite as well. Fara's historical significance from our point of view stems from the fact that we can add another documentary dimension to what we learn about her from Jonas of Bobbio and from a ninth-century *vita*: her last will and testament, edited by Jean Guérout (1965). It seems that she had it drawn up by the notary Waldo in the mid- to late 630s, after an illness (mentioned by Jonas, VC 2.12) which she barely survived. It is slightly odd, as a will, in that it is largely concerned with confirming the gifts of property to Eboriacum that had already been made: presumably she wanted to make it difficult for her family to recover what they might have believed was "their land" after she died. But it gives us a fascinating glimpse, and the only one that survives, into the sources of a Frankish woman's wealth in the seventh century.

The elements of Fara's property are clearly distinguished. She and her brothers had each received from their father a portion of two estates, "with lands, houses, slaves, vines, woods, meadows, pasturage, and water and water-courses." Half of another estate had been assigned to her by her father's written testament. In the territory of Meaux, she and her brothers had divided up another estate "by legal partition"; presumably, this was a family holding divided up between the surviving heirs, following Frankish legal tradi- tion. She also mentions her portion of houses and lands, both inside and outside the walls of Meaux and two water-mills. She had acquired two vineyards by exchange with her brother Chagnulfus. All but one of her holdings on these properties went to her monastery. As if to buy the goodwill of her siblings (named here as brothers Chagnulfus and Burgundofaro and sister Chagnetradis, who is not otherwise known), she quotes the Theodosian Code as allowing her to give them her portion of an estate near Paris. Before the final standard clauses calling down the wrath of God on anyone who ignores her decisions, she adds: "may all those male and female slaves whom I have freed by tab- let or by letter live free in possession of those goods that have been given to them."[1]

We shall look at the implications of joining a monastery for family property in the final section. But it is worth pointing out here that Burgundofara's independence in dealing with her own portfolio of landed property was already prefigured at the very beginning of the Merovingian period in the *Rule for Nuns* written by Caesarius (bishop of Arles, ca. 502–542): "Those who do not control their own wealth, because their par- ents are still living, or who are still minors, shall be required to draw up charters when they gain control over their parents' property, or when they reach the age of majority" (ca. 6; Amt 184). Caesarius assumed that, although women did not have control of their property while underage or while their parents were alive, they did when they were adults, and in the absence of other heirs they did control their parents' property after their deaths. The nuns were being required to "draw up charters," enabling them to transfer all their wealth to their monastery.

Our best evidence otherwise for the independent resources of elite women comes from the example of queens. When King Chilperic and his Franks were upset to see fifty cartloads of gold, silver, and other precious things disappearing in 584 in the direction of Spain, when his daughter Rigunth left to marry a Visigothic prince in 584, Rigunth's mother, Fredegund, said: "Everything you see belongs to me. Your most illustrious king has been very generous to me, and I have put aside quite a bit from my own resources, from the manors granted to me, and from revenues and taxes. You, too, have often given me gifts. From such sources come all the treasures which you see in front of you. None of it has been taken from the public treasury" (*Decem Libri Historiarum*; henceforth *DLH* 6.45; Thorpe 1974, p. 378). The story not only tells us that Fredegund had considerable resources, but that the Franks feared that she was raiding the royal treasury itself, which suggests that she had access to it. The text of the Treaty of Andelot in 587, which Gregory of Tours preserves in his *Histories* (*DLH* 9.20; Thorpe 1974, pp. 503–507), gives some precious details of the resources that the most elite of women could control. It mentions that when Galswinth came from Spain to marry Chilperic, he gave her the city-territories of Bordeaux, Limoges, Cahors, Lescar, and Cieutat as her *Morgengabe* or wedding gift. The revenues of Lescar and Cieutat may not have amounted to much, but Bordeaux in particular was a major city, and Limoges and Cahors were not far behind. Interestingly, when Galswinth died (strangled soon after her marriage, sometime around 567), her sister Brunhild—married to Chilperic's brother Sigibert—inherited these cities, "by the decree of King Guntram and with the agreement of the Franks." The same treaty specified that Brunhild, Brunhild's daughter Chlodosinda, and Brunhild's daughter-in-law Faileuba should hold "in all security and peace, and in all honor and dignity, such men and such goods, such cities, lands, revenues, rights of all sorts and wealth of all kinds, as at this present time they are seen to hold, or as, in the future, with Christ to guide them, they are able lawfully to acquire." Guntram's daughter Chlothild (not mentioned by Gregory of Tours elsewhere) is given similar assurances about her "men, cities, lands, or revenues": these should "remain in her power and under her control," and "if she shall decide of her own free will to dispose of any part of the lands or revenues or monies, or to donate them to any person, by God's grace they shall be held by that person in perpetuity, and they shall not be taken from him at any time or by any other person."

We have few details from other sources about women's property. But Gregory tells us an intriguing anecdote about Duke Rauching's wife. When Rauching conspired against King Childebert II, the king had him killed. The news was taken to the duke's wife.

> At that moment she was on horseback and being carried along a street in the city of Soissons, bedecked with fine jewels and precious gems, bedizened with flashing gold, having a troop of servants in front of her and another one behind, for she was hurrying off to the church of Saint Crispin and Saint Crispian.... As soon as she saw the messenger, she turned down another street, flung all her ornaments on the ground and sought sanctuary in the church of St Medard the Bishop.
>
> (*DLH* 9.9; Thorpe 1974, p. 490)

We do not know what happened to her; but it would seem unlikely that any of her fine jewels and precious gems ended up in her grave, as happened to various women whose graves have been excavated, like Arnegund, buried at the church of St. Denis, or the anonymous woman under Cologne Cathedral (Wamers and Périn 2013).

Elite women could clearly inherit and dispose of property (Nelson and Rio 2013). This right was undisputed among the Franks. The collection of legal formulas known as *Marculf's Formulary* describes a remarkable formula that illustrates this problem and that deserves to be quoted in full:

> To my sweetest daughter A.B. An ancient but impious custom is held among us, that sisters may not have a share of their father's land along with their brothers. But I, carefully considering this impiety [say]: just as you were equally given to me by God as children, you should also be loved by me equally, and enjoy my property equally after my death. Therefore, by this letter, I name you, my sweetest daughter, the equal and legitimate heir of my entire inheritance, along with your brothers, my sons C-D, so that you should divide and share whatever we may leave when we die, whether from my father's inheritance or from a purchase, unfree servants or moveable property, in equal parts with my sons, your brothers; and in no way are you to receive a portion smaller than theirs, but you must divide and share everything equally between you in every way.   (Marculf 2.12, p. 196)

Most commentators have assumed that the "ancient and impious custom" refers to Title 59.6 of the earliest Frankish law, the *Pactus Legis Salicae*: "But concerning Salic land, no portion of the inheritance shall pass to a woman but all the land belongs to members of the male sex who are brothers" (Drew, p. 192). But *Marculf's Formulary* would seem to preserve a seventh-century misunderstanding of the early sixth-century law. Title 59 of the *Pactus* is headed *De alodis*, "Concerning Allodial Land," that is, family land that is not held as a benefice from anyone else. The first five clauses of Title 59 make it fairly certain that women can inherit allodial land; indeed, women are actually given precedence in the hierarchy of inheritance. The misunderstanding arises partly because although clause 1 says that children (*liberi*) inherit, it does not specify daughters as well as sons. But it goes on to say that if there are no children, the father or mother inherit; if there are no parents, the heirs are the brother or sister; if there are no siblings, then the sister of the mother inherits; and after that, the sisters of the father. Title 59.6 gives the exception to the norm of female inheritance, and although *terra Salica* is not defined, it can be assumed that this is land that is not allodial land, but probably land held of the king specifically in return for military service. The distinction between allodial and Salic land may have already been ignored in the sixth century, however, since the edict of King Chilperic I (561–584) says that only if there are no sons should women inherit (Title CVIII; Drew 1991, p. 148). Perhaps this was Marculf's "ancient but impious custom," and not Title 59.6.

The origins of a propertied class of elite women are as obscure as the origins of the secular elite itself. Obviously, the Gallo-Roman aristocracy had centuries-old traditions, but notoriously, no Frankish aristocratic class is to be found in the *Pactus Legis Salicae*.

This distinguishes that law code from other barbarian law codes of the sixth and seventh centuries. It has been suggested that if it dates from the later years of Clovis's reign (specifically between 507 and 511), as many scholars have thought, it may reflect a time when Clovis had gotten rid of most members of the aristocracies of other kingdoms and was busy establishing one loyal to himself. Nevertheless (and again unusually in terms of barbarian law codes), there were wergeld differentiations relating to childbearing: between puberty and the menopause, a woman's wergeld was 600 solidi, triple the norm. Killing a pregnant woman required the payment of 600 solidi for the woman and 100 for the fetus (although one version specifies 600 solidi for the woman and an additional 600 for the fetus; Ganshof 1962). The only other category of person to warrant a 600-solidi wergeld was a boy under the age of twelve: the implication is that after the age of twelve the boy should be considered capable of defending himself (see Perez, Chapter 9, this volume). But in both the case of a young boy and a childbearing woman, the emphasis is on the importance of ensuring the survival of the people. And what little we know about infant mortality suggests that this was a sensible strategy. Queen Fredegund, about whose pregnancies we know more than any other Frankish woman, had at least five children: four of them—Samson, Chlodobert, Theuderic, and an unnamed son—died in infancy, and only Chlothar II survived into adulthood.

QUEENS AND REGENTS

Fredegund, we are told, was a royal servant before she married King Chilperic. While it was a long-standing literary tradition to denigrate enemies by emphasizing or inventing their low status, if we are to take our sources literally there are plenty of examples of kings marrying servants or other lowborn women. While Clovis and his grandsons Sigibert and Chilperic married foreign princesses, that was very much the exception, and Gregory says that Sigibert did so precisely because his brothers "were so far degrading themselves as to marry their own servants" (*DLH* 4.27; Thorpe 1974, p. 221). Charibert married Merofled, a servant of his former wife and the daughter of a wool-worker, and later had a child by the daughter of a shepherd (Gregory, *DLH* 4.25). When he then decided to marry Merofled's sister Marcovefa, he was excommunicated—not, probably, because he had married two sisters, perhaps simultaneously, but rather because Marcovefa was a nun. His brother Chilperic had married a servant, Fredegund, but followed his brother Sigibert's example, bringing Galswinth from Spain and putting Fredegund away; shortly afterward, Galswinth was found strangled in her bed, and he remarried Fredegund (Gregory, *DLH* 4.28). Venantius Fortunatus was given his most difficult commission: to write a poem lamenting the queen's death (6.5, trans. in George, 1995, pp. 40–50).

In the seventh century, Balthild would seem the most obvious example of a lowborn wife. She was Saxon and came from over the seas into the household of Erchinoald, the mayor of the Neustrian palace. She apparently refused marriage to Erchinoald but did marry King Clovis II around 648; when Clovis died, around 658, she became regent for his eldest son. She then retired to a convent at Chelles in 663/664, where she lived as a nun until her death around 680. Her *Life*, written at Chelles by one of the monks or nuns (see the discussion in Wemple, 1981, p. 182), states that she was sold cheaply to Erchinoald as a slave, and most historians have taken this at face value. However, Fouracre and Gerberding note that the *Liber Historiae Francorum* (c. 43) described her as "a girl from the Saxon nobility" and suggested that her early career might have been more complicated than is apparent from the *Life* (Fouracre and Gerberding 1996, pp. 97–104). Erchinoald had close connections with England, making it more than likely that Balthild was Anglo-Saxon and not a Saxon from Saxony. It is possible that Erchinoald was the father of Emma, who married King Eadbald of Kent; if so, he was the great-grandfather of Eorcengota, who later came to Faremoûtiers as a nun, and perhaps also of Bishop Eorcenwald of London (675–693): Eorcenwald was the English version of the name Erchinoald (see the discussion in Fouracre and Gerberding 1996, p. 104). So Balthild might have been from English royalty, exiled to Francia (perhaps in some palace coup), and fostered by Erchinoald. Her ability to move from mayor's "slave" to regent of Francia would thus be easier to explain. We could compare her to Radegund, a Thuringian princess captured by the Franks as booty of war around 530, who moved from being captive to wife of Chlothar I and then, as we will later explain, to being founder of the nunnery in Poitiers.

By and large, we have little information about the role that queens played while their husbands were still alive. Gregory of Tours shows us Chlothild's influence over her husband Clovis in matters of religion (*DLH* 2.29) and gives us several instances of how Fredegund influenced the political and financial choices made by her husband, Chilperic (*DLH* 5.34, 5.39, 6.35). There is some evidence that queens looked after or at least had access to the king's treasure. Kings kept some of their gold and silver in the form of lavish table plate, which could be displayed at the banquets that were such an important part of royal ritual (Gregory, *DLH* 6.3); queens presided at such occasions. Perhaps Frankish queens, as queens elsewhere, had the significant social duty of offering drink to those at the feast. Michael J. Enright explores this idea in *Lady with a Mead Cup* (1996), where he takes Wealhtheow, Hrothgar's queen in *Beowulf*, as an exemplar of the queen as peaceweaver in the king's hall (on Merovingian women and food, see Effros 2002).

We have much more evidence about what queens might be able to do as widows or, more specifically, as queen mothers. Chlothild, Brunhild, Fredegund, and Balthild all provide us with images of women with power and influence. As Janet Nelson has shown in a famous article on "Queens as Jezebels" (1978), the power and influence they wielded was not necessarily going to endear them to those who thought of political power as the prerogative of men.

Chlothild appears in Gregory of Tours's account as an oddly enigmatic person. Gregory presumably got the story of her eventually successful campaign to persuade Clovis to convert to Catholicism from the lost *Life of St. Remigius* (which Gregory mentions, *DLH* 2.31). And he may well have acquired some knowledge of her later life from people in Tours, even though she died there in 544 and he did not arrive until 573.

> After the death of her husband Queen Chlothild came to live in Tours. She served as a religious in the church of St Martin. She lived all the rest of her days in this place, apart from an occasional visit to Paris. She was remarkable for her great modesty and her loving kindness.   (*DLH* II.43; Thorpe 158)

Her "loving kindness" (*benignitas*), in Gregory's account, presumably included her strong urge to protect her family's interests, which took the form of persuading her three sons to declare war on the Burgundians to avenge the death of her family. After the death of Chlodomer in battle, she told her two surviving sons to kill Chlodomer's three sons rather than tonsure them in order to prevent them from becoming kings. But it is interesting that Gregory felt it necessary to conclude the story of her involvement in the murder of Chlodomer's little boys with a single lengthy sentence that eulogized her piety, charity, and chastity, concluding oddly: "neither the royal status of her sons, nor earthly ambition, nor her riches could bring her to ruin, but her humility led her to heavenly grace" (*DLH* III.18; my translation). Chlothild's "humility" also did not prevent her from interfering in ecclesiastical politics: Gregory tells us that she ordered that Theodorus and Proculus, who had been expelled from their sees in Burgundy, should be appointed joint bishops of Tours in 520, and their successor Dinifius (another Burgundian) was her candidate too (*DLH* 3.17, 10.31).

If Chlothild as royal widow could still involve herself in the affairs of the kingdom, all the more could women who were both widows and regents of their young children do so. Two women who can be considered together in this respect are Brunhild, the Spanish princess who was widowed when Sigibert was assassinated in 575, and Fredegund, the former servant whose husband, Chilperic, was assassinated in 584. When they were widowed, Brunhild had a five-year-old son, Childebert II, to protect, and Fredegund had the four-month-old Chlothar II (*DLH* 4.51, 7.5). The politics of the period from 575 onward used to be seen in terms of the feud, or at least rivalry, between Fredegund and Brunhild. But for much of this time their main business was survival, and they had very different experiences. It was undoubtedly hard for Brunhild, who had her main asset— her son Childebert—taken from her early in her widowhood. Childebert was looked after by a group of aristocrats, who seem to have set up a council of regency. When her late husband's enemy, King Chilperic, took Paris, she was seized and sent into exile in Chilperic's kingdom and her two daughters were imprisoned. Her fight back to independence and power was a long one. It started with a move that must have startled everyone, perhaps even the participants: she married Chilperic's son Merovech. Chilperic moved against them, and Merovech became a hunted man. Nevertheless, Brunhild was able to take advantage of the situation; she moved back to her husband's former kingdom and began to make alliances and exert authority. In 581, we see her intervening—*viriliter* (in a manly fashion), says Gregory—to quell a potential battle between her ally and two of Childebert's regents. One of those tellingly says (according to Gregory): "Stand back, woman! It should be enough that you held regal power when your husband was alive. Now your son is on the throne and his kingdom is under our control" (*DLH* 6.4; Thorpe 1974, p. 329). It may have been technically true that she no longer "held the kingdom" (as the Latin phrases it), but her position as queen mother did allow her access to royal courts, and she was able to exert considerable influence. Once Childebert came of age in 585 and began exerting himself (Gregory, *DLH* 7.33), he picked off one of his former counselors after another, apparently regarding them as his mother's enemies as well as his own.

From 585 until her death in 613, Brunhild was a major power in the kingdom, above all after her son's death in 596, when she became regent for his young sons, Theudebert II and Theuderic II, who ruled in Austrasia and Burgundy, respectively. Brunhild was chased out of her base in Austrasia in 597 and struggled for years to regain her position there, finally succeeding in 612. She made many enemies along the way, and our understanding of her last years is confused since we have to rely on sources written after her ignominious death at the hands of Fredegund's son Chlothar II, which are mostly hostile: Fredegar's *Chronicle*, Jonas's *Life of Columbanus*, and the *Life of Desiderius of Vienne*, by the Visigothic King Sisebut (see the discussion in Nelson 1978, reprint pp. 27–31).

Fredegund, perhaps learning from Brunhild's error, was better prepared for survival when she heard of her husband's assassination. She did not make the mistake that Charibert's widow, Theudechild, had made in 567, which was to offer herself and her treasure to Charibert's brother Guntram. (Guntram took the treasure and sent Theudechild off to a convent, where she was beaten and imprisoned by the abbess when she tried to escape: *DLH* 4.26). Fredegund took both herself and the treasure into the cathedral of Paris, so that with the help of Bishop Ragnemod she could negotiate for her future (Gregory, *DLH* 7.4). Guntram became her protector, thus keeping Brunhild's son Childebert out of the picture. Chilperic's main subjects recognized Chlothar as their king, and Fredegund retired north to the area of Rouen, to a portion of her late husband's kingdom, there to plot her survival and that of her son. If we are to believe Gregory (and I am not sure I do), she did so through tireless plotting and assassination attempts (most of which failed). Childebert and Guntram were the targets of some of her attempts, but Gregory is sure that she was responsible for the most blasphemous attack: the stabbing of Bishop Praetextatus of Rouen during Mass in 586 (*DLH* 8.31). Praetextatus was an old supporter of Brunhild, in charge of the most important bishopric in Chlothar II's kingdom, so his death certainly benefited Fredegund. Nor was she averse to hiring armies to gain her ends: Gregory tells how Saxons settled in northern Gaul intervened in a war between Franks and Bretons, on the side of the Bretons so that she could get rid of a Frankish aristocrat she detested (*DLH* 10.9).

Of the three "reigning royal widows"—this is Dick Harrison's phrase (1998, p. 31), getting around the fact that they are less than kings but much more than most queens—Balthild is in some ways the most interesting. This Anglo-Saxon woman married the young King Clovis II, probably around the time he came of age in 648. She embarked on her career of charity and ecclesiastical endowment, which she was to pursue after her husband's death. Janet Nelson noted that her "hagiographer paints the picture of a *palatium* in which all revolves around the queen" (1978, p. 18). When Clovis II died in 657 (followed shortly afterward by the death of his chief minister and Balthild's former owner, Erchinoald), Balthild continued to run the three kingdoms (Neustria, Austrasia, and

Burgundy) as one kingdom, in the name of the oldest of her three sons, Chlothar III (later sending the seven-year-old Childeric II to Austrasia). Balthild's *Life* (McNamara and Halborg 1992) listed her achievements, all of which, as far as the clerical author was concerned, were related to the church: she acted to eliminate simony and infanticide; she founded the monastery of Chelles, and installed Bertilla as abbess; she founded the monastery of Corbie and filled it with monks from Luxeuil; she gave land to Jumièges, Jouarre, Faremoûtiers, and the churches of Paris; she reformed and enriched the great churches of the kingdom—those of the saints Denis (St-Denis), Germanus (Paris), Medard (Soissons), Peter (Sens), Anianus (Orléans), and Martin (Tours); she forbade the sale of Christian slaves both inside and outside the kingdom; "and even to Rome, to the basilicas of Peter and Paul, and the Roman poor, she directed many and large gifts" (McNamara and Halborg 1992, p. 273).

According to the *Life*, the Franks eventually allowed her to retire to Chelles, as she had always wanted to. The nuns, however, suspected her motives and were not happy to receive her. We might well imagine that the brutal political fact was that she was forced into the monastery by the ambitious Ebroin, her own choice as replacement for Erchinoald as mayor of the palace. Nonetheless (according to the *Life*), she became a model nun, even willingly performing chores like cleaning out the latrines. "Who would believe that one so sublime in power would take care of things so vile?" (McNamara and Halborg 1992, p. 274).

In the medieval world, the political careers enjoyed by some women were quite extraordinary. Even in the early medieval world they were unusual. They stemmed ultimately from the rare Frankish loyalty to the dynasty. Over the rest of Europe, subjects seem mostly to have preferred a competent adult from a new dynasty rather than suffer a child king. The first child king we see in Anglo-Saxon history was Osred, who became king in Northumbria in 705; this is sometimes seen as the beginning of the decline of the Northumbrian kingdom, but in reality it suggests the strength and vitality of the kingdom, indicating that it was able to survive with a child king for eleven years (he died shortly after gaining his majority). But Osred was very much the exception; and what little we know of his reign suggests that it was Bishop Wilfrid who controlled his kingdom at the beginning, and not a queen mother. Reigning royal widows who, in the words of the *Life of Balthild*, were "sublime in power," seem to have been very much a Merovingian phenomenon.

Nuns and Abbesses

Opportunities for women to play a role in the Merovingian church were rare. Early Merovingian councils abandoned the early Christian practice of consecrating deaconesses "because of the fragility of the female sex."[2] *Episcopae*—the sometimes influential wives of bishops—likewise do not appear to have survived beyond the sixth century (Brennan 1985). Gregory seemed ambivalent about the institution: he describes the learned wife of the bishop of Clermont who instructed artists about the sacred scenes they were painting of church walls, but also the monstrously cruel wife of the bishop of Le Mans (*DLH* 2.16 and 8.39). But the Merovingian period did see considerable extension of the idea of communities of nuns living under the rule of an abbess. In the sixth century, those communities that we do have some knowledge of lived in or close to towns and relied on the episcopal clergy for their liturgical needs. In the seventh century, we begin to see rural nunneries (like the one founded by Burgundofara, described at the beginning of this chapter), which (again for liturgical reasons) had communities of monks attached. These so-called double monasteries were always under the rule of an abbess. These foundations often had considerable estates, with all their resources, including free peasants and slaves, donated by their founders and by later benefactors. Like queens, abbesses could be wealthy and had control over men as well as land. Numerous abbesses came to be regarded as saints; almost all new saints' cults in the Merovingian world centered around bishops, abbots, or abbesses.

There were occasional female saints whose monastic career was spent as simple nuns rather than as abbesses. Their lowly monastic status was the consequence of their extreme humility, not lack of opportunity. Two Merovingian queens, both of whom started as slaves or captives, ended up as renowned saints thanks to their postreginal career as humble nuns. We have just looked at Balthild; it is worth also considering Radegund. She was the daughter of a king of the Thuringians, who had been killed in battle in a civil war with his brother Hermanfred. Theuderic and his half-brother, Chlothar I, attacked Thuringia and massacred so many of the Thuringian army at the River Unstrut that they were able to cross the river by walking on the corpses. Radegund was part of Chlothar's booty. He married her, which, as Gregory noted, did not stop him from having her brother assassinated (*DLH* 3.7). As already mentioned, for Radegund we have a *Life* written by her longtime friend Venantius Fortunatus, and another *Life* written by a nun called Baudonivia, which deliberately filled in the gaps left in Venantius's account. The two Lives interestingly offer different facets of the saint (Gäbe 1989). Venantius (who was probably bishop of Poitiers by the time he wrote the *Life*) emphasizes her humble and domestic role within the convent; Baudonivia "portrays a Radegund who is an astute politician, a destroyer of pagan shrines, an active participant in the cult of the dead" (Coon 1997, p. 127). In other words, the male writer looks at her as a passive woman, whereas the female writer sees her as an active member of the church.

Chlothar died in 561, but at some point before this event Radegund had left him and had gone to live as a nun. All our sources (the two *Lives* and Gregory of Tours) rather skip over the scandal of a wife leaving her husband (even though Chlothar's brutality and lustfulness seem to have been without parallel among the Merovingians). Venantius stresses that she lived as chaste and prayerful a life as she could, as a married woman (Venantius Fortunatus, c. 3). He also says that she went to Medard, bishop of Soissons, begging him to receive her as a nun, but he ordained her as a deaconess instead: this position required neither celibacy nor the leaving of her husband. When Radegund did finally leave Chlothar, she went to Saix, one of her own estates (just south of the River

Loire), and there she began to live the life of a religious. Somewhat before the time of her husband's death (in 561), and apparently with his blessing and a gift of land, she moved to Poitiers. There she remained until her death in 587. Although she insisted that she would not be the abbess (she appointed a woman named Agnes to undertake that role), it seems to have been under her guidance and control that it became one of the most important monasteries in sixth-century Gaul. In her letter of foundation, quoted in full by Gregory of Tours (*DLH* 9.42), she announced her intention to adopt the *Rule for Nuns,* which Caesarius of Arles (d. 542) had written for his sister Caesaria as her Rule in Poitiers. She led the campaign to accumulate relics, most conspicuously the relics of the Holy Cross, which she acquired from the emperor in Constantinople. Before she died, she wrote a lengthy letter to the bishops (also quoted in full by Gregory at *DLH* 9.42), calling on them to protect her nunnery.

The fears Radegund expressed in that letter seem to have been in part fulfilled just two years after her death. What happened illustrates some of the problems of introducing monastic ideals of poverty and humility to communities of women raised within the secular elite (Scheibelreiter 1979; Hartmann 2005).

The abbess Agnes had died a year earlier than Radegund and had been replaced by Leubovera. In 589, a number of the nuns began a revolt against the new abbess. The leader was Chlothild, who maintained that she was the daughter of King Charibert. Although Gregory of Tours doubted that she was actually of royal blood (*DLH* 9.38), enough of the women believed her to give her considerable authority. Among the forty nuns who walked out of the nunnery with her was Basina.

Basina is an interesting example of the type of nun who does not often get mentioned in the sources. She was the daughter of King Chilperic and his first wife Audovera. When her brother Clovis was put to death after his revolt against Chilperic, Basina was persuaded to enter the nunnery at Poitiers; all her property was then confiscated by Fredegund, according to Gregory (*DLH* 5.39). Later, in 584, Chilperic thought to send her to Spain to marry Reccared, the son of King Leuvigild. However, he gave up the idea when both Basina and Radegund objected (Gregory, *DLH* 6.34).

In Gregory's narrative, we slowly learn about the progress of the revolt. Chlothild and her nuns established themselves in the church of St. Hilary in Poitiers and gathered a band of male supporters. They took over the estates of the nunnery. When winter came, there was no fuel, and so some drifted back to their former homes or to other monasteries; Chlothild and Basina were left largely on their own, quarreling and trying to establish dominance over each other. But the revolt continued. Just before Easter, Chlothild sent men into the nunnery to drag out the prioress Justina, Gregory of Tours's niece, and then the abbess. They looted the building; men were killed by Radegund's tomb, and outside Holy Cross (*DLH* 10.15). Finally, the kings Childebert and Guntram ordered a committee of bishops to settle the matter, including Gundegisel of Bordeaux and Gregory of Tours. Gregory refused to go to Poitiers at all until Count Macco had suppressed the rebellion properly. Macco did indeed take over the nunnery by force, despite Chlothild's attempts to keep them out by threats: "I warn you! Do not lay a finger on me! I am a queen, the daughter of one king and the niece of another! If you touch me you can be quite sure that the day will come when I shall have my revenge!" (*DLH* 10.15; Thorpe 1974, p. 570).

The complaints of these elite women, whose spokeswomen were Chlothild and Basina, make odd reading, partly because of the self-contradictions they contain. They complained about the poor food and clothing and their harsh treatment (*DLH* 10.15). At the same time, they complained about the abbess not being sufficiently punctilious about the Rule: the abbess allowed people to share their bathroom; she played gambling games; she allowed parties to be held in the nunnery; she made dresses for her niece out of a silken altar cloth; she allowed a man in the nunnery, dressed as a woman, whose job was to sleep with the abbess; she kept eunuchs in the monastery, just like the imperial court.

The text of the committee's judgment, which Gregory presents in full (*DLH* 10.15), refutes all of Chlothild's accusations—but in a way that is rather revealing of monastic life there. The food was not bad, considering the times; if one examined their *arcellulae* (little chests or boxes) one would see that they had more clothes than were necessary; the bathroom was only being shared while the plaster dried properly; the Rule did not prohibit the playing of board games; the party was not in the nunnery itself, and the bishop and other clergy had attended; the piece of silk which the abbess cut off was not needed for the altar cloth; the man who dressed as a woman did it because he was impotent, and anyway he lived a long way from Poitiers (on this episode, see Halsall, Chapter 8, this volume); the eunuch had been castrated for medical reasons, by a doctor who had seen the operation performed in Constantinople. The judgment inevitably went against the rebels Chlothild and Basina, and they were excommunicated and the abbess was restored. Chlothild and Basina immediately went to King Childebert and gave him the names of those men who were having sex with the abbess and also carried messages to Childebert's enemy, Queen Fredegund. These charges were investigated and found to be baseless: yet, they must have come at an opportune time for the two nuns, since, according to Gregory, the meeting took place only days after Childebert's men had discovered that Fredegund had sent twelve assassins to kill the king. In the end, Basina begged for forgiveness and was returned to the nunnery; Chlothild refused to return, and the king gave her an estate on which to live.

Although there are hints of tensions in other male and female monasteries in the Merovingian world, the tensions never reached this pitch anywhere else, nor does any source cover them in so much detail. We can grasp some of the significance of these events, even while suspecting that Gregory is not telling us the whole story. The actual accusations Chlothild and Basina made in public against Abbess Leubovera were so relatively minor that we are surely justified in imagining that something lay behind them. Dick Harrison has suggested that the revolt was all Leubovara's fault: she contravened the unwritten rule that royal nuns should retain their superior status in the nunnery, regardless of what the written rule said (1998, pp. 168–169). Chlothild made her position clear at the outset: "I am going to my royal relations to tell them about the insults which we have to suffer, for we are humiliated here as if we were the off-spring of low-born serving women, instead of being the daughters of kings!" (*DLH* 9.39; Thorpe 1974, p. 526). The dispute was openly about the Rule; but actually it was about the difficulty of removing the social status of those who entered the monastic life. We are at least certain that clause 33 of Caesarius's Rule was being disregarded: "You should have no quarrels.... and if they happen, let them be ended as soon as possible, lest anger grow into hatred" (Amt 2010, p. 188).

One of our problems in understanding the role of elite women within monasteries is that, apart from Gregory's account of the nuns of Poitiers, most of our evidence comes from the lives of female saints, the great majority of whom were abbesses: Caesaria of Arles, Rusticula of Arles, Glodesind of Metz, Burgundofara, Sadalberga of Laon, Rictrude of Marchiennes, Gertrude of Nivelles, Aldegund of Maubeuge, Waldetrude of Mons, Bertilla of Chelles, Anstrude of Laon and Austreberta of Pavilly. (All of these lives have been translated by Jo Ann McNamara and John E. Halborg; for Merovingian hagiography, see Kreiner, Chapter 24, this volume.) Stories of conflict tend to describe conflicts between the world and the nunnery, and specifically between the would-be nun and her aristocratic family. Joining a monastery in order to avoid a forced marriage was probably enough of a reality that its occurrence in the hagiography is rather more than just a topos. We have already seen how Burgundofara's father tried twice to force her into marriage.

The most vivid hagiographical account of the refusal of marriage occurs in the *Life* of St. Gertrude, the first abbess of the abbey of Nivelles and an early patron saint of the family that came to be known as the Carolingians. Her father was Pippin, who had invited King Dagobert I to his house. The son of the Duke of Austrasia was there, and he asked Dagobert whether he could marry Gertrude, without having asked her parents first. Dagobert and Pippin both agreed to this suggestion, and Gertrude and her mother Ida were summoned into the royal presence. "Then, between the courses, her father asked if she would like to have that boy, dressed in silk trimmed with gold, for her husband. She lost her temper and flatly rejected him with an oath, saying that she would have neither him nor any earthly spouse but Christ the Lord" (McNamara and Halborg 1992, p. 223). The author of the *Life*, who wrote after the death of Gertrude's sister Begga in 693, claims that he had this account from someone who had been present. "Lost her temper" is a rather flat translation of *quasi furore repleta*: "as if filled with rage" is more literal and is emphasized by the author's comment immediately afterward, that the king and his nobles marveled that this little girl (*parva puella*) had said these words "under God's command" (see Peyroux 1998).

Dagobert died in 639 and Pippin in 640. It was some time after Pippin's death, after considerable political opposition according to the *Life*, before Gertrude was able to become a bride of Christ. So afraid was her mother (Ida) that Gertrude would be taken away from her by a would-be husband that she herself cut a tonsure into her daughter's hair to prevent any marriage from happening (*Vita Geretrudis*, 2). This event seems to be the only mention of a woman being tonsured, following the model of a male cleric, as well as the only mention of a tonsure performed by a woman (Wade 2013). The two women entered a monastery together (the *Life* does not talk about the financial details), and Ida appointed Gertrude as abbess.

This was not the only time, in hagiography at least, that Dagobert tried to promote the marriage of wealthy young women. Sadalberga, whose *Life* was written not too long after her death, was another young woman in whom Eustasius of Luxeuil had discerned sanctity (according to Jonas, *VC* 2.8). She was widowed and wanted to become a nun. But "in obedience to her parents, by order of the King, and for procreation of children," she unwillingly married one of Dagobert's men (McNamara and Halborg 1992, pp. 183–184) and prayed for children. She had three girls and two boys; determined that all of them would join the church, she enlisted the help of Eustasius's successor, Waldebert. With his help (and with the agreement of her husband), she first founded a monastery near Langres and then moved to a more secure site within the walls of the city of Laon. It is unclear what happened to her family, but it is significant that it was only on her deathbed that her brother agreed to release to the monastery the estates that she had bestowed on the monastery by a series of charters, but that he had retained until then (*Vita Sadalbergae* c. 29). The decision of an elite woman to found a monastery had profound effects on her family and their property holdings; we can normally only guess at the consequent resentment of parents and relations.

Looking at Merovingian nuns, with the inadequate sources at our disposal, we can understand something of the problems of Merovingian women, even though largely viewed through a male lens. We learn about forced marriage and about the strategies that some women adopted to avoid marriage altogether or to leave brutal husbands (e.g., Radegund's Chlothar). We see the relative freedom of action that the possession of property gave women, both inside and outside the monastery. What we do not see is the extent to which removing themselves from the marriage market simply engaged women in other family strategies, involving the creation of family monasteries or the establishment of saints' cults, over which they had little control. Moreover, our sources only show us a small proportion of elite women (who themselves, of course, constitute a small minority of the population). Queens are hardly normal members of society, and nuns and abbesses, whose way of life is (or should be) a rejection of all the norms of secular society, even less so. The proper history of elite women in the Merovingian world can probably never be written.

NOTES

1. I am translating from the edition of Guérout 1965, pp. 817–821.
2. Council of Orléans, 533, c. 17, quoted and discussed by Wemple 1981, p. 140. For the text, see Gaudemet and Basdevant 1989, pp. 202–203.

WORKS CITED

Ancient Sources

Baudonivia, *Vita S. Radegundis*. B. Krusch (ed.). (1888). MGH SRM 2 (pp. 377–395). Hanover: Hahn.
Bede, *Historia Ecclesiastica Gentis Anglorum*. In B. Colgrave and R. A. B. Mynors (eds.), (1969). *Bede's Ecclesiastical History of the English People*. Oxford: Oxford University Press.

Caesarius of Arles. A. de Vogüé and J. Courreau (eds. and trans.). (1988). *Césaire d'Arles. Oeuvres monastiques I. Oeuvres pour les moniales*. SC 345 (pp. 35–273). Paris: Éditions du Cerf.

Councils. J. Gaudemet and B. Basdevant (eds. and trans.). (1989). *Les Canons des conciles mérovingiens (VIe–VIIe siècles)*. SC 353–4. Paris: Éditions du Cerf.

George, J. (1995). *Venantius Fortunatus: Personal and Political Poems*. Translated Texts for Historians 23. Liverpool: Liverpool University Press.

Gregory of Tours, *DLH*. B. Krusch and W. Levison (eds.).(1937–1951). *Decem Libri Historiarum*. MGH SRM 1.1. Hanover: Hahn.

Gregory of Tours, *DLH*. L. Thorpe (trans.). (1974). *Gregory of Tours: The History of the Franks*. Harmondsworth: Penguin.

Jonas of Bobbio, *Vita Columbani (VC)*. B. Krusch (ed.). (1902). MGH SRM 4 (pp. 1–156). Hanover: Hahn.

Marculf's Formulary. A. Rio (ed.). (2008). *The Formularies of Angers and Marculf: Two Merovingian Legal Handbooks*. Translated Texts for Historians 46. Liverpool: Liverpool University Press.

McNamara, J. A., and Halborg, J. E., with E. G. Whatley (eds. and trans.). (1992). *Sainted Women of the Dark Ages*. Durham NC: Duke University Press.

Pactus Legis Salicae. K. F. Drew (trans.). (1991). *The Laws of the Salian Franks*. Philadelphia: University of Pennsylvania Press.

Venantius Fortunatus. B. Krusch (ed.). (1885). *Vita S. Radegundis*. MGH SRM 2 (pp. 364–377). Hanover: Hahn.

Vita Sadalbergae abbatissae Laudunensis. B. Krusch (ed.). (1910). MGH SRM 5 (pp. 40–66). Hanover: Hahn.

Vita Sanctae Balthildis. B. Krusch (ed.). (1885). MGH SRM 2 (pp. 477–508). Hanover: Hahn.

Vita Sanctae Geretrudis. B. Krusch (ed.). (1885). MGH SRM 2 (pp. 447–464). Hanover: Hahn.

Modern Sources

Affeldt, W. (ed.). (1990). *Frauen in Spätantike, Lebensbedingen—Lebensnormen—Lebensformen*. Thorbecke: Sigmaringen.

Amt, E. (ed.). (2010). *Women's Lives in Medieval Europe: A Sourcebook*. 2nd ed. Abingdon, Oxfordshire: Routledge.

Brennan, B. (1985). "'Episcopae': Bishops' Wives Viewed in Sixth-Century Gaul." *Church History* 54: 311–323.

Coon, L. L. (1997). *Sacred Fictions: Holy Women and Hagiography in Late Antiquity* Philadelphia: University of Pennsylvania Press.

Effros, B. (2002). *Creating Community with Food and Drink in Merovingian Gaul*. New York: Palgrave Macmillan.

Enright, Michael J. (1996). *Lady with a Mead Cup: Ritual, Prophecy and Lordship in the European Warband from La Tène to the Viking Age*. Dublin: Four Courts.

Fouracre, P., and Gerberding, R. (eds.). (1996). *Late Merovingian France: History and Hagiography, 640–720*. Manchester, NY: Manchester University Press.

Gäbe, S. (1989). "Radegundis: Sancta, Regina, Ancilla. Zum Heiligkeitsideal der Radegundisviten von Fortunat und Baudonivia." *Francia* 16: 1–30.

Ganshof, F. L. (1962). "Le statut de la femme dans la monarchie franque." *Recueil de la Société Jean Bodin* 12: 5–58.

Goetz, H. W. (1995). *Frauen im frühen Mittelalter. Frauenbild und Frauenleben im Frankenreich.* Weimar: Böhlau.

Guérout, J. (1965). "Le testament de sainte Fare. Matériaux pour l'étude et l'édition critique de ce document." *Revue d'histoire ecclésiastique* 60: 761–821.

Harrison, D. (1998). *The Age of Abbesses and Queens: Gender and Political Culture in Early Medieval Europe.* Lund: Nordic Academic Press.

Hartmann, M. (2005). "*Reginae sumus.* Merowingische Königstöchter und die Frauenklöster im 6. Jahrhundert." *Mitteilungen des Instituts für österreichische Geschichtsforschung* 113: 1–19.

McNamara, J. A. (1976). "The Ordeal of Community: Hagiography and Discipline in Merovingian Convents." *Vox Benedictina* 3: 293–326.

Nelson, J. L. (1978). "Queens as Jezebels: Brunhild and Balthild in Merovingian History." In D. Baker (ed.), *Medieval Women: Essays Dedicated and Presented to Professor Rosalind M.T. Hill* (pp. 31–77). Oxford: Blackwell. Reprinted in J. L. Nelson (1986). *Politics and Ritual in Early Medieval Europe* (pp. 1–48). London: Hambledon.

Nelson, J. L., and Rio, A. (2013). "Women and Laws in Early Medieval Europe." In J. M. Bennett and R. M. Karras (eds.), *The Oxford Handbook of Women and Gender in Medieval Europe* (pp. 103–117). Oxford: Oxford University Press.

Peyroux, C. (1998). "Gertrude's *furor*: Reading Anger in an Early Medieval Saint's *Life.*" In B. H. Rosenwein (ed.), *Anger's Past: The Social Uses of an Emotion in the Middle Ages* (pp. 36–55). Ithaca, NY: Cornell University Press.

Richlin, A. (2014). *Arguments with Silence: Writing the History of Roman Women.* Ann Arbor: University of Michigan Press.

Scheibelreiter, G. (1979). "Königstöchter im Kloster. Radegund († 587) und der Nonnenaufstand von Poitiers (589)." *Mitteilungen des Instituts für österreichische Geschichtsforschung* 87: 1–37.

Schulenburg, J. T. (1998). *Forgetful of Their Sex: Female Sanctity and Society, ca. 500–1100.* Chicago: University of Chicago Press.

Wade, S. W. (2013). "Gertrude's Tonsure: An Examination of Hair as a Symbol of Gender, Family and Authority in the Seventh-Century Vita of Gertrude of Nivelles." *Journal of Medieval History* 39: 129–145.

Wamers, E., and Périn, P. (eds.). (2013). *Königinnen der Merowinger. Adelsgräber aus den Kirchen von Köln, SaintDenis, Chelles und Frankfurt am Main.* Regensburg: Schnell and Steiner.

Wemple, S. F. (1981). *Women in Frankish Society: Marriage and the Cloister, 500 to 900.* Philadelphia: University of Pennsylvania Press.

CHAPTER 12

THE MILITARY AND ITS ROLE IN MEROVINGIAN SOCIETY

LAURY SARTI

In the year 451, Attila crossed the Rhine with the Huns to threaten the cities of Gaul. A contemporary chronicle reports that "both our people and the Goths soon agreed to oppose with allied forces the fury of their proud enemies." The resulting combat in the vicinity of Chalons, with Goths and Romans fighting on one side of the battle line, was a short-term constellation triggered by the immanent Hunnic menace. The chronicle testified to the great haste with which the local army was gathered by explaining that their general Aëtius "had such great foresight that, when fighting men were hurriedly collected from everywhere, a not unequal force met the opposing multitude" (Prosp., *Chron.* a. 451, p. 481; trans. Murray 2000, p. 73). Although this chronicle's author was uncertain about the battle's outcome, the Hunnic retreat is generally assumed to have initiated the breakup of Attila's rule.[1] The Battle of Chalons was the last major military victory under Roman leadership fought north of the Alps. Concurrently, it might have marked the rise of the Franks in the north as a new power in Gaul, if later authors mentioning their participation may be trusted (Jordanes, *Get.* 36.191; Greg., *Hist.* 2.7. See also Dixon and Southern 2000; Whitby 2000; Southern 2007). This chapter discusses the manner in which the Frankish army emerged from this fifth-century situation and the role the military adopted in post-Roman Gaul.

LATE ROMAN TRANSITIONS

The Merovingian army has not been the subject of elaborate monographic study in recent years. Besides the very short treatment by Philippe Contamine in 1992 (1997, pp. 5–19), the standard reference remains the now significantly outdated but still useful

Merovingian Military Organization (1972) by Bernard S. Bachrach. This work traces the development of the Frankish army from the late fifth century to argue that the Roman military structures had widely survived, including a reduced standing force and garrisons. In subsequent works, Bachrach has sustained this general thesis, while he has reworked many of his earlier findings. Only in the early twenty-first century has the Frankish military again attracted more attention, with detailed treatments included in works by Guy Halsall (2003) and Leif Inge Ree Petersen (2013).

When exactly the Roman army system was abandoned, and to what extent it actually did collapse, is difficult to determine. The few glimpses we do have into the obscurity that surrounds this question suggest that this was a gradual process. Eugippius's *Life of Saint Severinus,* covering the late 460s or earlier 470s, contains the most elaborate testimony. It reports that soldiers (*milites*) in Batavis (modern Passau) and the *civitas Favianis* (a city-state near the Danube, possibly Mautern), who had been maintained at public expense until payments ceased, set out for Italy to fetch their *stipendium* (pay).[2] Subsequently, the remaining soldiers had to fend for themselves. Although the *Life* refers to Noricum (located in modern-day Austria), a similar evolution probably took place in Gaul. This assumption is backed by the testimony of Sidonius Apollinaris of Clermont, a contemporary to the events in Noricum. In a letter addressed to his friend, Eucherius, he covertly criticized the interruption of the payment of military wages.[3]

The gradual breakdown of the professional Roman army is also attested in a regulation in the Theodosian Code dated to the year 409 and addressed to the vicar of Africa. It decreed that groups occupying land or strongholds that previously had been assigned to barbarians in return for safeguarding the frontiers should either take on the same responsibility or cede it to barbarians or other veterans (*CTh* 7.15.1). Once more, although this decree did not refer to Gaul, it is very likely that similar procedures were in place there as well. A famous excursus contained in Procopius's *Wars* mentions Roman soldiers stationed at the Roman frontier who, subsequent to the Visigothic expansion in Gaul, had been cut off from Italy and thus found themselves on their own. They consequently decided to give themselves and the land they had been guarding to the neighboring "Arborychi and Germanic peoples" (i.e., the Franks) in order to become their allies (Procop., *Wars* 5.12.16–17).

ARMY LEADERSHIP AND COMPOSITION

Although warfare is a major subject in historiographical narratives, the available source material is mostly incomplete and varies in quality and detail throughout the three Merovingian centuries. The most abundant references are contained in the *Histories* of Gregory of Tours and the *Chronicle of Fredegar,* but neither work deals with the military systematically. Their testimony tends to be more precise the closer an event took place—both in time and space—to the respective author. These and other historiographical narratives are complemented by a large variety of sources, including laws, letters, poems, and lives (see France 2005). Although they become more elaborate and explicit in the Carolingian era, these sources must be used with caution, if at all, since it is difficult to assess to what extent their contents may be assumed to have operated in preceding centuries.

The evidence suggests that Merovingian military forces were recruited ad hoc, straight from the local population, and this only for the time of a specific purpose or campaign (Bachrach 1972a; Weidemann 1982, pp. 243–248; cf. Petersen 2013, pp. 53–55). Clovis and his sons generally convened and commanded these armies themselves (e.g., Greg., *Hist.* 2.27, 3.6, 4.17), whereas by the third generation, this function was progressively delegated to local royal representatives: the patricians (*patricii*), dukes (*duces*), and counts (*comites*).[4] Among those kings belonging to the following generations, only Childebert II, Chlothar II, Dagobert I, and Sigibert III commanded their own armies in the field more systematically (Halsall 2003, p. 28). Comital levies were most frequently mentioned in connection to small-scale conflicts or where a specific local region was concerned (e.g., Greg., *Hist.* 3.13, 7.24, 10.5; Bachrach 1972a, p. 68; Reuter 1997, pp. 34–35), while long-distance campaigns, which involved large armies composed of comital, ducal, and patrician levies (e.g., Greg., *Hist.* 4.49, 8.30, 10.3), required foregoing travel and collection of men over large distances. Besides these temporal levies, there is also evidence of some kind of garrison services under the authority of local *comites* to secure settlements, bridges, and border crossings (e.g., Greg., *Hist.* 6.19, 7.29, 9.32). It nonetheless remains unclear who could be recruited for these duties and on what (legal) basis.

Military organization revealed some regional differences: armies from Burgundy and Provence were headed by a *patricius* (e.g., Greg., *Hist.* 4.30, 4.42, 5.13), whereas those from the less Romanized regions in the north and the east, including Champagne, Aquitaine, and the territories east of Rhine, were commanded by *duces*. In western and southwestern Gaul, they were generally superordinate to local *comites*.[5] The troops levied from these regions also differed in size. Comital levies were recruited on the basis of a *civitas* and thus were comparably small. Margarete Weidemann (1982, pp. 245–246; cf. Bachrach 1972a, p. 33; 1999; Petersen 2013, pp. 211–214) has estimated that the size of these levies averaged 2,000 men. The area of responsibility of *duces*, by contrast, encompassed two or more comital levies (e.g., Greg., *Hist.* 8.18). *Duces* were also mentioned regularly as sole army leaders of campaigns fought outside Gaul (e.g., Greg., *Hist.* 10.3). In the northern and eastern territories, on the other hand, hardly any *comites* are known. The only exceptions are the *comites* located in the *pagus Ultraioranus* and mentioned in the *Chronicle of Fredegar* (4.37). Apart from this, the evidence suggests that in these regions *duces* levied armies on a regional scale (e.g., Greg., *Hist.* 7.30; Bachrach 1972a, pp. 66–68; Weidemann 1982, pp. 243–245). The same is true for Burgundy and Provence, where one *patricius* was in place at a time.[6]

How things changed subsequently is difficult to tell, as the source material is increasingly fragmentary, particularly after the time of redaction of the *Chronicle of Fredegar* around 660. Extant evidence suggests that things altered perceptibly. The *civitas* was now mentioned only rarely in connection with military levies, which makes it more difficult to establish which groups could be requested to join a military host. Moreover, fragmentary evidence makes it more difficult to assess the size of armies with sufficient reliability, as local authorities with armed followings and dependents became increasingly preponderant as constitutive elements of the military and as independent actors (Halsall 2003, pp. 54–56), while the sources fail to provide more details as to the composition and size of these followings. The keeping of large personal retinues by military commanders, as known in Late Antiquity (Diesner 1972; Schmitt 1994), was pursued by the Merovingian elite on a large scale.[7] Concurrently, fields of responsibility related to different titles and offices became increasingly blurred (e.g., *Fred.* 4.90; Sprandel 1957). For the following decades, our main sources are the sparsely detailed *Liber Historiae Francorum,* the *Continuations of Fredegar,* and several saints' lives. They testify to the increased importance of the mayor of the palace (*maior domus*) to the detriment of Merovingian kings, while other royal representatives continued to act as local and regional authorities (e.g., *LHF*, 45–49).

MILITARY RECRUITMENT

Like the late Roman army, the Merovingian military was multiethnic. Alongside Franks and Romans, it included Alamanni, Armoricans, Bretons, Burgundians, Goths, Saxons, Taïfals, and Thuringians (Sarti 2013a, p. 25). The large majority of the individuals participating in royal campaigns remain anonymous. Where the sources allude to entire armies, they mostly use the term *exercitus.* Sometimes, they also refer more specifically to *inferiores, iuniores, pauperes,* or the *populus minor* (e.g., Greg., *Hist.* 5.26, 7.35, 10.9). Whether these appellations allude to common fighters in general or to more specific groups inside a military host is difficult to tell given the inconsistent use of these terms. If Bachrach (1972a, p. 71; 1993, p. 57; similarly, Petersen 2013, p. 217; cf. Schneider 1967, p. 245) is right, the *minor populus* represented the rank and file of the city levies, ranging above the *inferiores* and *pauperes,* which according to Weidemann (1982, pp. 248, 251), were responsible for baggage. In contrast, the *rubustiores viri* or *robustiores* (Greg., *Hist.* 7.35; 10.9) and the *viri fortissimi, forti,* or *fortiores* (Greg., *Hist.* 7.9, 7.38, 9.36) most likely ranked above the two first groups and might have represented groups of older and more experienced fighters (Halsall 2003, p. 50) or cavalry (Schneider 1967, p. 245; Bachrach 1994, p. 129). A distinction between infantry and cavalry was recorded in the context of King Guntram's campaign against Septimania, where it was noted that those with horses could escape, while those without could not (Greg., *Hist.* 9.31). However, the sources prevent us from making any further deductions as to the internal organization of Merovingian armies.

Historians commonly assume that every (free) man was expected to follow a royal call.[8] However, once again, the evidence is incomplete, so it is impossible to determine to what extent this was the case. Most significant are two references contained in Gregory's *Histories* stating that members or affiliates of the church were asked to pay a fine ([*here*]*bannum*) for failing to participate in a royal campaign (Greg., *Hist.* 5.26, 7.42; cf. 6.12). This evidence, which is backed by mention of the ban (*bannum*) as a royal service (with reference to military obligation) in the *Ribuarian Law* (68.1–2 cf. *Fred.* 4.73, 4.87), supports the idea that every man of a certain age and physical constitution was expected (at least under certain circumstances) to act as part of a military host. Apparently, this also applied to the clergy (see Esders 2009b, p. 220; cf. Goffart 1982), although their duties probably focused on tasks related to pastoral care. Moreover, a revised diploma dated to the time of Childeric II (662–675) granting immunity to the church in Speyer (*Dipl.* 99), and a *placitum* of 694 mentioning a certain Ibbo being fined 600 *solidi* for having failed to join the host of his king Theuderic III (*Dipl.* 143), both attest to the continuous enforcement of the *herebannum*. Although these documents are insufficient to confirm Bachrach's conclusion that "the Roman model prevailed and the recruitment burden still fell on the land,"[9] there are manifest parallels between late Roman and Carolingian legislation in this regard (see Esders 2009b, pp. 206–234).

Because of the largely inconclusive source material, the legal basis for the Merovingian levy of troops remains an issue for debate. Referring to Bachrach's thesis that military obligation goes back to late Roman regulations applied to military land (1997b–c; cf. Halsall 2003, pp. 46–47; similarly, Goffart 2008, pp. 184–185), and postulating that the same obligations applied to the *terra Salica* (*Lex Sal.* 59.5[6]), historians such as Walter Goffart (1982, 2008, 178–179 n. 39) and Stefan Esders (2009b) have suggested that military service was based on continued unpaid obligations (*munera/servitia*). Halsall (2003, pp. 53, 69), by contrast, has proposed a more identity-based liability to the king. Any positioning in favor of one of these or any other conceivable option largely depends on the weight historians are disposed to attribute to the extant fragmentary pieces of evidence.

Considering the predominantly agricultural character of Merovingian society and the risks linked with leaving a settlement bereft of potential fighters, it appears most unlikely that all men were requested to serve at the same time (Bachrach 1972a, pp. 68, 71; Halsall 2003, pp. 55; 132–133; Esders 2009b, pp. 209, 233). This assumption is backed by a document contained in the *Formularies of Angers,* which mentions a father who thanked his son for having "serve[d] us faithfully in all things and in every way, and hav[ing] endured on our account many hardships and injuries in various places, and [having gone] . . . in my place to fight the Bretons and Gascons in the service of [our] lords" (*Form. And.* 37, p. 16; trans. Rio, 2008, p. 78; see also Goffart 2008, p. 182). Unfortunately, there is no other comparable testimony, and the piece of evidence just quoted does not contain any further information regarding the reasons why the father was obliged to serve, while his son was not. The *Formulary* proves, however, that further regulations must have been in place, even if they can no longer be reconstructed (on law, see Rio, Chapter 23, this volume). Perhaps lists of men liable to military service were still kept in the Merovingian kingdoms, as Halsall (2003, p. 60) has suggested. They would have been a useful tool to organize a fair distribution of military duties among the inhabitants of a *civitas*. Another option would have been distribution by lot, a method that is mentioned in other contemporary contexts (Greg., *Hist.* 2.27, 4.22; Greg., *Jul.* 7, 13; *Fred.* 4.16). There is no conclusive evidence, however, supporting one or the other of these two possibilities.

PROFESSIONAL STANDING ARMIES IN POST-ROMAN GAUL?

Given the scattered indications of a continuation of late Roman practices in the Merovingian era, Petersen's (2013) assumption that the early Frankish army was "dominated by professional troops settled between the Rhine and the Loire, who were the direct descendants of Roman legions" (p. 214; similarly, p. 226) does not seem to be farfetched. However, besides what was said earlier, the sources contain hardly any evidence for such a thorough continuity and the existence of a state-run standing army.[10] Petersen's assumption goes back to Bachrach's argument for a permanent and professional force composed of Saxons, *laeti*, *milites*, *antrustiones*, and perhaps custodians (*custodes*) as part of the *centenarii*.[11] None of these groups can be identified as members of a standing army. Moreover, the text passages used to suggest that those labeled "Saxon" were mercenaries are not sufficiently specific to serve as evidence. They include diverse references, for example, to armed *pueri* accompanying a merchant, a few Saxons from Bayeux in the private service of Queen Fredegund, and Saxon *duces* (Greg., *Hist.* 7.3, 7.46, 8.18, 10.9, 10.22; *Fred.* 4.78; cf. *Fred.* 2.18; *Vita Eligii* 1.10), alongside mentions of *Saxones* as a people (e.g., Greg., *Hist.* 4.42, 5.26; *Fred.* 4.38).

Considering the multiethnic character of the Merovingian realm and the scattered use of the term *saxo*, it appears much more likely that the term was used in an ethnic sense. *Laeti*, in contrast, a term used in late Roman times to refer to auxiliary forces (Günther 1977), was subsequently only mentioned in the Salic Law (26.1, 13.7, 35.5, 42.4, 50.1), which never explicitly associates the term with the use of arms. As the terminology could change significantly over the space of a century, use of the term *laeti* does not suffice on its own to postulate a military function. The *centenarii*, who are also mainly known from legal evidence,[12] represented local authorities with judicial and police functions. However, there is no evidence suggesting that they represented anything more than a small local force. The term *custos* was used to refer to different types of guards supervising bridges, public buildings like churches, or town entrances, and caring for the safety of kings.[13] The *antrustiones*, who were also referred to as *qui in truste dominica fuerit* ("who have been part of the lord's following"), represented an incomparably higher-ranking group. Although the evidence that mentions this term did not provide any information beyond the particularly high *wergeld* attributed to this group (*Lex Sal.* 41.5, 42.1–2, 63.2; *Cap.* 7, praef.), the word's meaning suggests that they were high-ranking men in the closest surrounding of the kings. This assumption is supported by a seventh-century formulary mentioning an oath of fealty and fidelity (*trustem et fidelitatem*), which was offered to the king by members of this same group by holding their own weapons in their hands (*Form. Marc.* 1.18).

These groups, which Bachrach identified as potential members of a standing army, were thus quite heterogeneous. Although the evidence is inconclusive, it is not unlikely that the *custodes, centenarii,* or *antrustiones* received food and lodging, or that they were remunerated at the king's expense, be it at specific times or even in the long term. However, the sources do not prove that they represented anything more than small groups of local functionaries or an impressive royal retinue, respectively. Nor do they confirm that the *antrustiones,* together with the retinues of other magnates, made up very large groups of professional, full-time soldiers, as Petersen suggests (2013, pp. 218–219; cf. Halsall 2003, p. 49).

The term *miles* still requires discussion. Bachrach (1972a, pp. 24–25) postulates that the Merovingian sources used this term just as previous ones did, that is, in its classical sense to refer to regular soldiers. However, in sixth- to early eighth-century Gaul, contemporary authors only used it to refer to men in charge of the supervision and execution of prisoners when speaking of the Merovingian kingdoms.[14] Moreover, they consistently used *miles* to refer to individuals involved in activities taking place inside a *civitas,* never to men on a military campaign. Thus, in Merovingian Gaul, *milites* must have represented local functionaries, more specifically custodians of prisoners, not soldiers.

Similarly, the Merovingian sources do not have an alternative word to label its military with any specificity. This is all the more noteworthy, as several convenient terms such as *armatus, bellator,* or *pugnator* obviously were available, given that they were used in the same source material. However, although the designation *armatus* could refer to any armed man, it was only used infrequently and in most diverse contexts, including in reference to individual armed men (*Fred.* 4.51), municipal fighting men (Greg., *Hist.* 5.18, 6.11), armed followings of men of high standing (Greg., *Hist.* 7.47, 9.12), royal fighting men (Greg., *Hist.* 3.7, 7.18), and the custodians of bishops (Greg., *Hist.* 5.20). Clearly, *armatus* alluded to an individual's use of armament at a particular moment, and it was not used as a more common term to refer to the military in general. The same was the case for terms like *belliger* (Fort., *Carm.* 9.1, l. 102), *bellator* (*Fred.* 2.57; *Cont.* 14), *armiger* (*LHF* 41), *pugnator* (Greg., *Hist.* 2.12; *Fred.* 3.12, 4.55, 4.87; *LHF* 7, 10), or *proeliator* (Greg., *Hist* 2.27). They were used even more infrequently and almost exclusively in reference to men belonging to higher social strata, including kings. The only term that was used a little more frequently, and with a clearer focus on common army members as well, at least in the legal evidence and the majority of examples in the *Chronicle of Fredegar,* was *leudes.*[15] Like the *antrustiones,* they were tied to the king via *sacramentum* (Greg., *Hist.* 9.20), although both bonds probably differed in nature. As the remaining narratives largely used the term *leudes* to refer to smaller groups of potentially high-standing military men (Greg., *Hist.* 2.42, 3.23, 8.9; *Fred.* 4.27, 4.41, 4.56, 4.76), it is rather unlikely that *leudes* commonly referred to the military in general. Obviously, neither was it considered as an alternative designation for ordinary army men. Given the large number of instances in which Merovingian chroniclers did refer to the military but did not choose to use available terminology to refer to an army's members, one may conclude that contemporaries believed there was no obvious need for such a general designation.

Used in its classical sense, the term *miles* distinguished the military from the noncombatant part of society. This designation contained the notion of service (*militia*), a connotation that might explain why contemporaries did not consider it appropriate to allude to temporary Merovingian military men. Moreover, the necessity of distinguishing between army members and noncombatants had likely become superfluous once every man could be considered as a potential fighter, and royal calls to arms basically determined who belonged to the military and who was to be considered a civilian (Sarti 2013b). The situation was even more confused as high-ranking men were generally accompanied by an armed retinue, whose members were not necessarily military men in the sense of belonging to an army. As the distinction between civilians and the military was only possible if one referred to a man's current function, an alternative designation for a long-term identity as fighter had become superfluous as well. It thus became more appropriate to refer to a man's membership in an army (*exercitus*), his current armament (*armatus*), or his function (*bellator, custos, antrustio, dux*). Consequently, the sources typically use much less specific terms such as *vir* to refer to a man who could also have been designated as a fighter (e.g., Greg., *Hist.* 5.14, 7.29; *Fred.* 4.38, 4.87). This change in the terminology is remarkable, as it fits with the previous findings that the Merovingians did not maintain a professional standing army and that the common model on which they relied was the use of short-term fighters.

The general impression left by the narrative sources is that the Merovingian army had a deficient organization and was not a professional standing army. On campaign, Merovingian armies seem to have lived on local resources, which included raids committed on their own domestic population by armies heading toward destinations further away (e.g., Greg., *Hist.* 6.31). According to Gregory of Tours, Childebert II's army returning from fighting the Lombards in Italy was too weak to loot due to shortages in their food supply and thus had to exchange their weapons for nourishment (Greg., *Hist.* 10.3). One account in his *Histories* points to more elaborate methods of local provisioning: in preparation for Princess Rigunth's nuptial travel to Spain, the locals were requested to stockpile provisions along the road (Greg., *Hist.* 6.45). The sources, however, do not contain any indication that a comparable procedure was used in the context of military campaigns. It is probable that army members were expected to provision themselves individually with food, clothes, and weapons, as was later the case under Carolingian rule (Contamine 1997, p. 15; Bachrach 1997a, p. 28, 1997b, p. 699; Goffart 2008, p. 180;). With the exception of Procopius's excursus mentioned at the beginning (Procop., *Wars* 5.12), there is no indication in either the archaeological (e.g., Steuer 1968, pp. 56–58) or the written source material that Merovingian army members used recognizably standardized clothing or armament to facilitate the differentiation between friend and foe, as in Roman times (against Bachrach 2008, p. 182). This view is backed by Gregory's suggestion that members of a same army were not necessarily able to recognize themselves: he explains that some Burgundians had pretended to be among the Frankish troops simply by imitating King Chlodomer's rallying cry (Greg., *Hist.* 3.6).

Historians generally agree that post-Roman military service was unpaid and that the primary expected types of remuneration were royal thanks, renown, and a share of the booty. The last is particularly well documented in Gregory of Tours's *Histories*, which on several occasions underlines the significance of loot as a motivational force. Remuneration could include prisoners, cattle, precious metal, food, or clothing.[16] One method of distributing loot was to draw lots (see Greg., *Jul.* 7, 13; Greg., *Mart.* 65. Fort., *Rad.* 4–5), although this method certainly was not suitable for organizing distribution of plunder among the members of larger armies. Scattered manuscript notes show that one should not exclude the possibility that some type of payment or financing was still in force. Two diplomas dated to the time of Childebert III and Dagobert III, respectively, grant immunity to the monastery of Saint Serge in Angers and the church of Le Mans. They mention a tax called *aurum pagense*, which might have referred to the late-antique *aurum tironicum* that had been levied to compensate for those who did not provide military service (*Dipl.* 145; 163; Esders 2009b, pp. 227–230). Moreover, the narrative sources on several occasions mention taxes levied in the name of the kings but without providing any further information about their nature and purpose.[17] This evidence, however, is not sufficiently conclusive to either prove or disprove Goffart's thesis (2008, p. 181) that taxes were used to finance the military or, more specifically, that an army tax (*hostilicium*) was raised for this purpose from tributary manses.

THE MILITARIZATION OF SOCIETY

In Merovingian Gaul, military men were largely integrated into society. Unlike the Roman period, the military was not stationed in camps or other areas specifically conceived for this purpose. As men were only temporarily levied, fighting was not their prime or only occupation (Gutsmiedl-Schümann 2012)—a situation that in Late Antiquity might have already applied to a large percentage of soldier–farmers settled mainly in the frontier regions of the Roman Empire (Bachrach 1993, pp. 56–57; Sarti 2016a). These men, who were recruited straight from their family homes, shared their military experience with those friends and relatives joining them as well as with their native communities when they returned from campaign. Moreover, the local population was much more strongly involved in the protection of its home settlement and territory, as threats were frequently the reason they had been called to arms.[18] As every man was a potential army member, learning how to fight must have been part of any boy's education. Early training and extensive practice were vital to a man's survival in battle (cf. Bachrach 1995; Halsall 2003, pp. 35–36).

Familiarity with the use of weapons is indicated by several contemporary references to locals who resisted military troops threatening their home settlements and livelihood (Greg., *Hist.* 7.35, 10.5, 10.9). The sources mention in several instances that the bearing of weapons had become common in a civil setting. Gregory of Tours, for example, recounts how a local resident of the *civitas* of Tours refused two fighters a drink and was almost killed at his doorstep. He saved his life by defeating both of them with his sword (Greg., *Hist.* 7.21). It thus appears that Merovingian society was quite militarized, a phenomenon that had been perceptible in the frontier regions since Late Antiquity. Militarization was not limited to the merging of the civil and the military population but also had significant repercussions on contemporary behavior and thinking (Halsall 2009; Esders 2014; Sarti 2016a).

The amalgamation of the military with the male population as such meant that weapons were common outside of a military context. They played an important role in rituals, as in the above-mentioned oath by prospective *antrustiones* to their king. Gregory of Tours mentions a ritual comparable to this oath when he describes how the *patricius* Mummolus and the usurper Gundovald mutually exchanged a sword and golden baldric as symbols of friendship (Greg., *Hist.* 7.38). The same author also recounts that the young king Childeric II was adopted by his uncle Guntramn, who inaugurated his successor by placing a spear in his hand to symbolize the transfer of *regnum* (Greg., *Hist.* 7.33; cf. 5.17). Such rituals were not limited to the elite. *Salic Law* (44.1, 46.1) mentions a shield used as a ritual tool in the context of rites taking place during judicial assemblies (*thing*), and Ripuarian Law stipulates that an accusation of theft could be disclaimed either by putting down one's sword in front of the church door (62.4) or by hanging it on the door jamb of the accuser's home (36.4). Subsequently, the opposing parties had to settle the dispute in single combat. The same law also specifies that, in the case of disputed property, an oath should be given with the right hand armed (*cum dexteras armatas*; 37.1). This provision probably refers to a sword, as suggested by the burial evidence, in which this weapon was usually placed to the right side of a body (Böhme 1974, p. 100; cf. Hüppe-Dröge 1981, p. 126).

The sources also document an altered concept of peace. In opposition to late Roman expectations (Sid., *Epist* 7.7.1–3, 9.5.2), *pax* was progressively understood as a repose from armed conflict. While this term was used until the late fifth century to refer to long-lasting absence from military activity (cf. *pax Romana*; e.g. *Cap.* 1), in the seventh century it mainly alluded to a short time lacking violence (e.g., Baud., *Vita Rad.* 10; *Fred.* 3.58). Both concepts are contained in a letter of Avitus of Vienne urging the recipient to see a current "brief period of peace" as "a respite from the crises that we suffer rather than an end to them" and to "stop believing that there is an end to troubles" (Avit., *Epist.* 37, p. 66; trans. Shanzer and Wood 2002, p. 325). Although Avitus obviously did hope for a longer peace, his letter also testifies to the awareness that this was not to be expected. The idea of war as the normative condition is attested in Gregory's account of a man from his *civitas* asking that vigils should be kept, as he was hoping that this would help "pass this year in peace" (Greg., *Patr.* 8.11). The sources also leave the impression of an ongoing situation of violence and general brutality,[19] which was not limited to war-related experiences such as killing, looting, burning, or taking prisoners and/or slaves.[20] Gregory, for example, mentions bands of armed men in Tours (Greg., *Hist.* 5.47–49, 6.32, 7.22, 8.40, 10.5), Poitiers (Greg., *Hist.* 7.3, 10.21), Clermont (Greg., *Hist.* 3.16; *Mart.* 65), and Toulouse (Greg., *Mart.* 88), most of whom were high-ranking military who terrorized the local population. Although he mainly records these activities in his own vicinity, it appears likely that this phenomenon was not restricted to these *civitates*.

The potential military function of a majority of the male community and the extensive exposure of the local population to armed violence are likely reasons why military activity, competence, and exploits were valued in Merovingian society. That physical abilities and military skills were admired in secular men is suggested by characterizations such as *strenuous* (e.g., Greg., *Hist.* 5.3; *Fred.* 4.85; *LHF* 16, 41; *Form., Marc.* 1.8), *fortis*, or *fortissimus* (e.g., Greg., *Hist.* 4.29, 9.36; Fort., *Carm.* 9.1; *Fred.* 2.53, 4.87; *LHF* 1, 42; cf. *Fred.* 3.12) used in the sources to praise outstanding fighters. The appreciation of warlike qualities is documented best in the term *utilis*, a word that did not normally refer to military skills or virtues but was used to extol individuals who particularly exhibited those skills or had given proof of these as "being useful." The meaning of *utilitas* employed in this context emerges, for example, from Gregory's report of how Chilperic's troops prevailed in 575 over those of Sigibert. The bishop of Tours laments that strenuous and useful men (*strenuos atque utilis viros*) perished during this battle (Greg., *Hist.* 5.3). Likewise, in the *Chronicle of Fredegar,* the author specifies that when the *maiores domi* Bertoald and Landeric fought a duel, their aim was to establish whose *utilitas* was superior (*Fred.* 4.25). The sources further attest to the significance of this set of qualities relating that Basina had decided to become Childeric's wife due to his outstanding *utilitas* (Greg., *Hist.* 2.12; cf. *Fred.* 3.9), and that the merchant Samo had become king of the Wends as he had proven his *utilitas* in battle (*Fred.* 4.48). Finally, *utilitas* was a prime criterion for being invested as a royal officer (*Form. Marc.* 1.8).

THE MILITARY ELITE

The most militarized part of Merovingian society was the secular elite. Although the evidence is incomplete, it appears that a higher social status was strongly associated with the conduct of war. The sources do not mention any faction inside this group without military functions. They include royal offices, membership in the *antrustiones*, as well as other less well-documented functions like leaders of armed retinues or followers of high standing.

The functions associated with the offices of *patricius, dux,* and *comes*—titles that referred to continuously altered fields of responsibility but that went back to antiquity— were not limited to the leading of armies. These men acted as the representatives of royal power on a local or regional basis, and, as such, they administered their respective districts, supervised tax collection, and presided over procedures of law enforcement and jurisdiction.[21] The *duces* and *patricii* were also regularly mentioned at royal courts, be it to attend important festivities or advise their respective king (e.g. Greg., *Hist.* 10.28; Fort., *Carm* 6.1, 7.7, 7.14). It is noteworthy that these officers were identical to the group of military leaders, attesting to the significance of this function and the ongoing process of militarization of the post-Roman elite.[22] The same conclusion may be drawn from the fact that, alongside the *duces* with a regional affiliation, there are almost as many without such an assignment.[23] As these *duces* were obviously of the same rank and regard, their

elevated status must have emanated mainly from military command. As royal representatives, these army leaders had the right to claim the oath of allegiance from a conquered
population, which they received in the name of the king (Greg., *Hist.* 4.30, 4.45, 7.13, 10.3;
Esders 2009a). This honor is likely one reason for rivalries among ambitious leaders,
like those recorded in the sources (Greg., *Hist.* 8.18, 9.31, 10.9; *Fred.* 3.4, 4.26, 4.77).
Besides these officers, the *maior domus* rose in importance from the late sixth century,
and soon the task of military leader was also assigned to this functionary (e.g., *Fred.* 4.25,
4.40, 4.90; *LHF* 46, 48, 49; Heidrich 1989; Nonn 2002; Goetz 2004).

The aforementioned elite represented the group that identified itself most strongly
with its military activity and functions—alongside isolated potential full-time bearers of
arms such as the *custodes*. Their belligerent identity is well attested in terms such as *bellator, pugnator,* or *proeliator,* which we have seen were mainly used by contemporary
authors as a reference. The military character of the elite is also well attested in burial
evidence. Lavish male sepulchers not only contained precious clothing and adornment,
like decorated belt sets or brooches, but also impressive sets of weaponry (e.g., Steuer
1987; Halsall 2003, p. 31; cf. Hüppe-Dröge 1981, pp. 111–112).

One reason for the strong linkage between warfare and a higher secular standing was
that military campaigns could be highly profitable with regard to both reputation and
wealth. These campaigns offered the opportunity to attract royal attention through the
demonstration of military assertiveness, which could be rewarded with promotion
(*Fred.* 4.78), and to gather important riches through pillage. Material wealth, again, was
an important tool for an individual to enhance his standing, be it by its display
(Effros 2002, p. 14; Halsall 1992, p. 205; 2003, p. 162; 2008) or by making gifts to establish
or maintain friendship (*amicitia*) or dependence (Sarti 2013a, pp. 213–232). The secular
elite thus relied on participation in military activities as the opportunity to amass riches
and give proof of their own abilities.

Unsurprisingly, the military activity of bishops is recorded from the fifth century,
when many Gallo-Roman aristocrats took high office to maintain their privileged position. This process resulted in the election of local episcopal authorities who also adopted
functions related to secular jurisdiction and the conduct of local defense.[24] Such responsibilities included the gathering of armed followings, as in the case of Hilary of Arles,
who, according to legal evidence, was accused by Pope Leo I of using his retinue to interfere with the selection of candidates for vacant episcopal sees.[25] Bishop Nicetius of Trier
is known to have erected a fortified *castrum* near the River Mosel (Fort., *Carm.* 3.12),
while other bishops like Magnulf of Toulouse conducted the defense of their episcopal
city (Greg., *Hist.* 7.27; see also Bourgeois, Chapter 28, this volume). The brothers Salonius
and Sagittarius are the most prominent examples. In the early 570s, they fought against
the Lombards, an engagement that subsequently resulted in their condemnation (Greg.,
Hist. 4.42, 5.27; Mar., *Chron.* an. 579). Although bishops fighting worldly battles never
represented the normative case, a continuous rapprochement of the holders of religious
and secular offices may be perceived until the eighth century. One reason is that from the
seventh century, many bishops emerged from the royal entourage, having been recruited
from the same families that also held secular offices. Many among these bishops had

themselves been in the position of *dux* or *comes* before ordination (e.g., Greg., *Hist.* 10.19; cf. *Pass. Leud.* 20). Bishops thus increasingly could act like secular authorities.[26]

The sources mention a large variety of high-ranking men in the entourages of the Merovingian kings (see Hen, Chapter 10, this volume). Besides officers, *antrustiones*, and, increasingly, bishops, there were less well-defined groups labeled *proceres, primates,* and *optimates,* alongside *leudes* and *franci.* Given the largely inconsistent use of these and related designations (see Irsigler 1969, pp. 82–116; Grahn-Hoek 1976, pp. 55–79), it is difficult to assess more specifically their respective status and functions. Apart from embracing those groups of highest status discussed above, these terms might have referred to any other local authority or high-ranking landowner. The sources attest that all those labeled with these and related designations were strongly involved in royal decision making, including questions related to law and the designation of a new *maior domus* or even a king (e.g., *Fred.* 4.54, 4.79; *LHF* 40, 48, 51). They also imply regular, perhaps even yearly meetings, as was the case for those testified in the context of consecutive laws dated between the years 596 and 598 and those enacted with the consent of *optimates* and *leudes* under the authority of Childebert II.[27] Although some of these gatherings are dated to the month of March, they did not necessarily all take place at this specific time of the year (Bachrach 1972b). These meetings often have been interpreted as musters of the entire military body (e.g., Halsall 2003, p. 43). However, as Matthias Springer (1995) has noted, it is most unlikely that every potential fighter was invited or requested to appear at these meetings. Rather, it seems that these were conventions of the military elite participating in their king's annual consultation. If this interpretation is correct, the political weight of the military elite was not limited to the functions as royal representatives and military leaders performed by *patricii, duces* and *comites.* Instead, the advisory role of the upper social stratum would imply that the military elite was involved to a significant extent in the core functionalities of Merovingian governance.

Conclusion

The evidence discussed here confirms the thesis by Bachrach and subsequent historians that Merovingian military organization went back to late Roman army structures (Bachrach 1972a, p. 17, 1993, 1997a; Contamine 1997, pp. 14–15; Halsall 2003, p. 45). The trend toward general military obligation by means of short-term recruitments from the local population, which marked the end of a professional standing army, can be traced back to the earlier fifth century. This evolution was perceptible concurrently in late Roman frontier regions. There was also an increasing tendency toward consideration of land as a criterion for otherwise unpaid military obligation, which might still have been in force in Merovingian Gaul. Answers to questions as to the potential one-to-one adoption of Roman army features, like the legal basis of military obligation or remuneration, are largely dependent on the subjective approach that one adopts to the sources. Argumentation in favor of the strong continuity of Roman military structures and procedures lasting until the Merovingian era requires a high degree of attributed importance to mostly scattered legal evidence, especially if one considers that it may be difficult to assess to what extent the wording and content of these documents depended on late Roman precedents or whether they described a different contemporary reality. By contrast, speaking in favor of a stronger caesura between the two eras presumes that more weight should be attributed to narrative sources, despite their tendency to offer a most incomplete and negative impression of the military (e.g., Goffart 1988, pp. 219–220; Sarti 2013a, 103–129).

Although the degree of continuity in military tradition can be debated, the sources disprove the existence of a professional standing army. The Merovingian military consisted of temporary levies recruited and led by local officers, while more permanent services were much smaller and restricted to the *civitates* and the royal courts. As such, the military consisted of two groups that differed in social status and political significance: the large majority were common part-time fighters, who could be called to arms at any time but mainly had other occupations, and a less numerous group comprising officers and members of the royal and other high-ranking retinues who must have identified themselves more strongly with their military activity and functions. This second group not only served as army commanders but was also involved in governance of the kingdom.

The changes in the military structure occurred as a gradual process. Nonetheless, Merovingian military practices eventually represented a significant caesura from earlier Roman practice. The same is true with respect to militarization, a phenomenon that characterized a significantly altered society. The Frankish army thus showed important differences from the standard Roman military organization, even though it reflected the incorporation of preexisting late-fifth-century structures and procedures.

Notes

1. See, however, Fischer 2009, pp. 187–196; Kim 2013, pp. 73–83; Kelley 2014, pp. 193–208. This work has been written in the framework of the project "Militarisierung frühmittelalterlicher Gesellschaften" supported by the Fritz Thyssen Foundation. I would like to thank François Benduhn and the editors for their suggestions to improve the original draft.

2. Eug., *Vita Sev.* 4, 20; cf. 44. See also Mierow 1915, pp. 180–182; Alfoldy 1974, pp. 213–228; Thompson 1982, pp. 88–133; Bachrach 1993, p. 55.

3. Sid., *Epist.*3.8. That he is referring to the military is backed by his subsequent mention of *viri militari.* See also Halsall 2007, pp. 445–447.

4. See Freiherr von Guttenberg 1952; Sprandel 1957; Claude 1964; Ebling 1974, pp. 10–26; Lewis 1976; Claude 1997; Sarti 2016b.

5. For example, Greg., *Hist.* 4.50, 6.19, 8.30, 9.7; Greg., *Patr.* 4.2; Bachrach 1972a; Weidemann 1982, pp. 246–248. See, however, *Fred.* 4.78: *comitebus plurimis, qui docem super se non habebant.*

6. On the Burgundian-Neustrian *patricius*, see, for example, Greg., *Hist.* 4.24, 5.13; *Fred.* 4.2, 4.78; *Pass. Leud.* 23; *Vita Eligii* 2.28, the provincial *patricius,* for example, Greg., *Hist.* 4.437.15, 9.22; Fort., *Carm.* 7.12; *Fred.* 4.5; *Pass. Leud.* 9, 26; *Pass. Praei.* 23. See also Bachrach 1972a; Weidemann 1982, pp. 238–239. *Fred.* 4.25 also mentions a *patricius* in the *pagus Ultraiorano et Scotingorum.*

7. For example, Greg., *Hist.* 3.35, 6.17, 7.46; *Fred.* 4.54; *Pass. Leud.* 16; Dippe, 1889; Halsall 2003, pp. 66–70; Nicholson 2004, p. 46; Althoff 2004, pp. 102–135; Steuer 2009; Petersen 2013, pp. 218–219. Slightly opposed Petersen 2013, pp. 224–230.

8. Fehr 1914; Bachrach 1972a, p. 71; Goetz 1995, p. 479; Contamine 1997, pp. 15–16; cf. Halsall 2003, pp. 47–48, 55; Goffart 2008, p. 184.

9. Bachrach 1993, p. 60; similar Goffart 2008, pp. 167, 179–181; cf. Halsall 2003, pp. 47, 53–55, 60, 77; 2007, pp. 446–447. On the *bannus*, see also Bayerle 2008. Cf. Goffart 1982.

10. Whitby 2000, pp. 288, 299; Halsall 2003, pp. 41, 109, 112. Against Bachrach 1972a, followed by Durliat 1990, pp. 126–128; Harrison 2002, p. 293; Nicholson 2004, p. 40; cf. Hendy 1988, pp. 59–70.

11. Bachrach 1972a, pp. 17, 71–72; see also Halsall 2003, pp. 111–112; Bachrach 1997a, p. 28; 2008, pp. 178–180.

12. *Lex Sal.* 44.1, 44.2; *Capit.* 2.9, 2.16, 7.9, 7.11, 7.12; *Vita Eligii* 2.61. See also Dannenbauer 1949; Murray 1986, pp. 790–798; 1988; Weidemann 1993, pp. 547–549.

13. See, for example, Greg., *Hist.* 3.32, 5.3, 8.30, 10.15. In the latter sense, they probably were comparable or identical to the *armati*; see Greg., *Hist.*7.8, 7.18.

14. Greg., *Hist.* 5.48; Greg., *Patr.* 4.3, 7.4; Greg., *Virt. Mart.* 1.21; Greg., *Conf.* 99; Fort., *Germ.* 180–81; Fort., *Alb.* 12; Jon., *Vita Col.*, 1.19, 1.20; *Vita Eligii* 2.15. See also Weidemann 1982, p. 269 n. 58; Sarti 2013b, 323–325, and the full discussion in Sarti 2018. Most noteworthy, the classical sense of this term is still used in reference to the Roman era, the Byzantine world, or where the sources refer to soldiers in general, see Sarti 2013a, pp. 153–161. It is also used in *Cap.* 5.117, § 2.

15. Greg., *Hist.* 9.20; *Cap.* 4.2, 7.2, 9.17; *Fred.* 4.1, 4.42, 4.46, 4.53, 4.54, 4.58, 4.60, 4.78, 4.79, 4.87. See also Dopsch 1926; von Olberg 1981, 1987, p. 102, 1991, pp. 60–74; Sarti 2016b.

16. Most explicitly in Greg., *Hist.* 7.28. On reputation and royal thankfulness as a motive for force, see Greg., *Hist.* 9.31, 10.9; Fort., *Carm.* 3.30, ll. 15–16; *Fred.* 4.9, 4.77, 4.87. See also Reuter 1985, pp. 78–89; Gerberding 1987, 165; Scheibelreiter 1999, pp. 340–356; Halsall 2003, pp. 135–136.

17. For example, Greg., *Hist.* 3.36, 6.28, 10.7; *Fred.* 4.24, 4.27; see also *Conc. Arvern.* an. 535. epist., p. 71; *Form. Marc.* 1.3.

18. For example, Greg., *Hist.* 4.45, 6.31, 7.13; *Fred.* 4.37, 4.78; Bachrach 1997a, p. 28; see also *Form. Marc.* 1.33, 1.34.

19. For example, *Vita Chroth.* 2; Greg., *Hist.* 3.26, 4.20; Mar., *Chron.* an. 560, an. 576; *Fred.* 4.38, 4.67; *Form. Marc.* 2.28.

20. For example, Greg., *Hist.* 2.37, 5.29, 6.45, 9.24; Greg., *Jul.* 7, 23; Greg., *Mart.* 65; Greg., *Conf.* 22; *Fred.* 3.87, 4.54; *LHF* 37, 38, 46; *Cont.* 3.

21. On tax collection, see Greg., *Hist.* 3.36, 5.28, 6.22, 9.30, 10.21, on judicial tasks, see Greg., *Hist.* 4.43, 6.8, 7.47; Greg., *Patr.* 7.1, 8.3; Fort., *Carm.* 4.2, 7.5, 7.7; *Lex Rib.* 51[50].1; on law enforcement, see Greg., *Hist.* 5.14, 7.2, 8.29, 8.43, 10.15; *Pass. Leud.* 26. See also Sprandel 1957; Claude 1964, 1966, p. 279; Lewis 1976; Sarti 2016b.

22. See van Ossel 1995; James 1997; Harrison 2002; Halsall 2007, 494–497; 2009; Esders 2014; Dick 2014; Sarti 2016a.

23. For example, Greg., *Hist.* 3.32, 6.26, 7.13, 9.31, 10.3; Greg., *Patr.* 4.2; Mar., *Chron.* an. 548, an. 565, an. 573; *Fred* 4.14; Sprandel 1957, pp. 50–52; Selle-Hosbach 1974, pp. 25–27.

24. For example, Stroheker 1948; Prinz 1973; Heinzelmann 1976; Scheibelreiter 1983; Brennan 1985; Barnish 1988; Mathisen 1993, pp. 89–104; Jussen 1995; Patzold 2010; Diefenbach 2013.

25. *Nov. Val.* 17.1. See also Greg., *Hist* 3.35, 8.31; *Pass. Leud.* 2–3; Prinz 1973, pp. 14–15; Whittaker 1993, p. 291.

26. See *Fred.* 4.41, 4.58, 4.90; *Pass. Leud.* 23; *Vita Eligii* 1.14, 2.1; *Act. Aun.* 2, 3; *Cap.* 6. Cf. Petersen 2013, pp. 230–232.

27. *Cap.* 7. praef., 2, 4, 8. Comparable meetings in Greg., *Hist.* 2.27; *Ann. Mett.* an. 692; *Cap.* 10. praef., 11.1; *Cont.* 48. See also *Cap.* 4.2, 5, 6. *Cap.* 4.1, p. 8, mentions *viris magnificentissimis obtimatibus vel antrustionibus et omni populi nostro. Cap.* 10. praef. dates a meeting to *XI. Kalendas Maias.* Cf. *Cont.* 48.

Works Cited

Ancient Sources

Act. Aun. P. Perrier (ed.). (1760). *Acta Sancti Aunemundi alias Dalfini episcopi.* AASS, Sept. VII (pp. 744–746). Antwerp: Société des Bollandistes.

Ann. Mett. B. De Simson (ed.). (1905). *Annales Mettenses priores. Accedunt additamenta annalium Mettensium posteriorum.* MGH SRM 10. Hanover: Hahn.

Avit, *Epist.* R. Peiper (ed.). (1883). *Alcmi ecdicii Avtiti. Opera quae supersunt.* MGH EE 6.2 (pp. 29–103). Berlin: Weidmann.

Baud., *Vita Rad.* B. Krusch (ed.). (1888). "Vita sanctae Radegundis." In *Fredegarii et aliorum Chronica. Vitae Sanctorum.* MGH SRM 2 (pp. 358–395). Hanover: Hahn.

Cap. A. Boretius (ed.). (1883). "Capitularia Merowingici." In *Capitularia Regum Francorum.* MGH LL 2.1 (pp. 1–23). Hanover: Hahn.

Conc. F. Maassen (ed.). (1893). *Concilia aevi Merovingici.* MGH LL 3.1. Hanover: Hahn.

Cont. B. Krusch (ed.). (1888). "Continuationes." In *Fredegarii et aliorum Chronica. Vitae Sanctorum.* MGH SRM 2 (pp. 168–193). Hanover: Hahn.

CTh. T. Mommsen and P. M. Meyer (eds.). (1995). *Theodosiani libri XVI cum constitutionibus Sirmondianis et leges novellae ad Theodosianum pertinentes* 1.2. Berlin: Deutsche Akademie der Wissenschaften.

Dipl. T. Kölzer (ed.). (2001). *Die Urkunden der Merowinger. Nach Vorarbeiten von Carlrichard Brühl (†).* MGH DD Mer 1. Hanover: Hahn.

Eug., Vita Sev. H. Sauppe (ed.). (1877). *Eugippii vita Sancti Severini.* MGH AA 1.2 (pp. 7–30). Berlin: Weidmann.

Form. And. K. Zeumer (ed.). (1886). "Formulae Andecavense." In *Formulae Merowingici et Karolini aevi.* MGH LL 5 (pp. 4–25). Hanover: Hahn.

Form. Marc. K. Zeumer (ed.). (1886). "Marculi Formulae." In *Formulae Merowingici et Karolini aevi accedunt Ordines iudiciorum dei.* MGH LL 5 (pp. 36–106). Hanover: Hahn.

Fort., *Alb.* B. Krusch (ed.). (1885). "Vita sancti Albini." In *Venanti Honori Clementiani Fortunati presbyteri Itallica opera pedestria.* MGH AA 4.2 (pp. 27–33). Berlin: Weidmann.

Fort., *Carm.* F. Leo (ed.). (1881). *Venanti Honori Clementiani Fortunati presbyteri Italici opera poetica.* MGH AA 4.1. Berlin: Weidmann.

Fort., *Germ.* B. Krusch (ed.). (1885). "Vita sancti Germani." In *Venanti Honori Clementiani Fortunati presbyteri Itallica opera pede*stria. MGH AA 4.2 (pp. 11–27). Berlin: Weidmann.

Fort., *Rad.* B. Krusch (ed.). (1885). "Vita sanctae Radegundis." In *Venanti Honori Clementiani Fortunati presbyteri Itallica opera pedestria.* MGH AA 4.2 (pp. 38–49). Berlin: Weidmann.

Fred. B. Krusch (ed.). (1888). *Chronicarum quae dictuntur Fredegarii Scholastici Libri IV.* In *Fredegarii et aliorum Chronica. Vitae Sanctorum.* MGH SRM 2 (pp. 19–168). Hanover: Hahn.

Greg., *Conf.* B. Krusch and W. Levison (eds.). (1885). "Libri in gloria confessorum." In *Gregorii Turonensis Opera. Miracula et opera omnia.* MGH SRM 1.2 (pp. 744–820). Hanover: Hahn.

Greg., *Hist.* B. Krusch and W. Levison (eds.). (1951). *Gregorii Episcopi Turonensis historiarum libri X.* MGH SRM 1.1. Hanover: Hahn.

Greg., *Jul.* B. Krusch and W. Levison (eds.). (1885). "De passione et virtutibus sancti Iuliani Martyris." In *Gregorii Turonensis Opera. Miracula et opera omnia.* MGH SRM 1.2 (pp. 562–584). Hanover: Hahn.

Greg., *Mart.* B. Krusch and W. Levison (eds.). (1885). "Liber in gloria martyrum." In *Gregorii Turonensis Opera. Miracula et opera omnia.* MGH SRM 1.2 (pp. 484–561). Hanover: Hahn.

Greg., *Patr.* B. Krusch and W. Levison (eds.). (1885). "Liber vitae patrum opere Georgi Florenti Gregori Toronici." In *Gregorii Turonensis Opera. Miracula et opera omnia.* MGH SRM 1.2 (pp. 661–744). Hanover: Hahn.

Greg., *Virt. Mart.* B. Krusch and W. Levison (eds.). (1885). "De passione et virtutibus sancti Martini episcopi." In *Gregorii Turonensis Opera. Miracula et opera omnia.* MGH SRM 1.2 (pp. 584–661). Hanover: Hahn.

Jon., *Vita Col.* B. Krusch (ed.). (1902). "Vita Columbani Abbatis Discipulorumque eius." In *Passiones vitaeque sanctorum aevi Merovingici aevi.* MGH SRM 4 (pp. 64–108). Hanover: Hahn.

Jordanes, *Get.* T. Mommsen (ed.). (1882). *Iordanis Romana et Getica.* MGH AA 5.1. Berlin: Weidmann.

Lex Rib. F. Beyerle and R. Buchner (eds.). (1954). "Lex Ribuaria." In *Leges nationum germanicarum.* MGH LL 3.2. Hanover: Hahn.

Lex Sal. K. A. Eckhardt (ed.). (1962). *Pactus legis Salicae.* MGH LL 4.1. Hanover: Hahn.

LHF. B. Krusch (ed.). (1888). "Liber Historiae Francorum." In *Fredegarii et aliorum Chronica. Vitae Sanctorum.* MGH SRM 2 (pp. 215–328). Hanover: Hahn.

Mar., *Chron.* T. Mommsen (ed.). (1894). "Marii episcopi Aventicensis chronic a. CCCCLV-DLXXXI." In *Chronica Minora Saec. IV, V, VI, VII.* MGH AA 11.2 (pp. 232–239). Berlin: Weidmann.

Nov. Val. T. Mommsen and P. Krüger (eds.). (1905). "Novellae Valentiniani." In *Theodosiani libri XVI cum constitutionibus Sirmondianis* 1.2 (pp. 69–154). Berlin: Weidmann.

Pass. Leud. B. Krusch (ed.). (1910). "Passiones Leudegarii prima." In *Passiones vitaeque sactorum aevi merovingici.* MGH SRM 5 (pp. 282–322). Hanover: Hahn.

Pass. Praei. B. Krusch (ed.). (1910). "Passio Praeiecti episcopi et martyris Arverni." In *Passiones vitaeque sactorum aevi merovingici.* MGH SRM 5 (pp. 225–48). Hanover: Hahn.

Procop., *Got.* H. B. Dewing (ed.). (1919). "Gothic War." In *History of the Wars* 3, The Loeb Classical Library 107. Cambridge, MA: William Heinemann.

Prosp., *Chron.* T. Mommsen (ed.). (1892). "Prosperi Tironi epitoma chronicon." In *Chronica Minora Saec. IV, V, VI, VII.* MGH AA 9.1 (pp. 385–499). Berlin: Weidmann.

Sid., *Epist.* C. Luetjohann (ed.). (1887). "Gai Sollii Apollinaris Sidonii epistularum libri." In *Gai Sollii Apollinaris Sidonii. Epistulae et Carmina.* MGH AA 8 (pp. 1–172). Berlin: Weidmann.

Vita Chroth. B. Krusch (ed.). (1888). "Vita S. Chrothildis." In *Fredegarii et aliorum Chronica. Vitae Sanctorum.* MGH SRM 2 (pp. 342–348). Hanover: Hahn.

Vita Eligii. B. Krusch (ed.). (1902). "Dadonis Rothomagensis Episcopi, Vita Eligii episcopi Noviomagensis." In *Passiones vitaeque sanctorum aevi Merovingici aevi.* MGH SRM 4 (pp. 663–742). Hanover: Hahn.

Modern Sources

Alfoldy, G. (1974). *Noricum*. New York: Routledge.

Althoff, G. (2004). *Family, Friends and Followers. Political and Social Bonds in Medieval Europe*. Cambridge: Cambridge University Press.

Bachrach, B. S. (1972a). *Merovingian Military Organization, 481–751*. Minneapolis: University of Minnesota Press.

Bachrach, B. S. (1972b). "Was the Marchfield Part of the Frankish Constitution?" *Medieval Studies* 36: 178–185.

Bachrach, B. S. (1993). "Grand Strategy in the Germanic Kingdoms. Recruitment of the Rank and File." In F. Vallet and M. Kazanski (eds.), *L'armée romaine et les barbares du IIIe au VIIe siècle* (pp. 55–63). Paris: Association française d'archéologie mérovingienne.

Bachrach, B. S. (1994). *The Anatomy of a Little War. A Diplomatic and Military History of the Gundovald Affair (568–586)*. Boulder, CO: Westview Press.

Bachrach, B. S. (1995). "The Education of the 'Officer Corps' in the Fifth and Sixth Centuries." In F. Vallet and M. Kazanski (eds.), *La noblesse romaine et les chefs barbares. Actes du colloque international du Musée des Antiquités nationales* (pp. 7–13). Paris: Musée des antiquites nationales.

Bachrach, B. S. (1997a). "The Imperial Roots of Merovingian Military Organization." In A. N. Jørgensen and B. L. Clausen (eds.), *Military Aspects of Scandinavian Society in a European Perspective AD 1–1300* (pp. 25–31). Copenhagen: Publications from the National Museum.

Bachrach, B. S. (1997b). "Quelques observations sur la composition et les caractéristiques des armées de Clovis." In M. Rouche (ed.), *Histoire et mémoire. Clovis et son temps, l'évènement* (pp. 689–703). Paris: Presses de l'Université de Paris-Sorbonne.

Bachrach, B. S. (1997c). "Military Lands in Historical Perspective." *Haskins Society Journal* 9: 95–122.

Bachrach, B. S. (1999). "Early Medieval Military Demography. Some Observations on the Methods of Hans Delbrück." In D. J. Kagay (ed.), *The Circle of War in the Middle Ages. Essays on Medieval Military and Naval History* (pp. 3–20). Woodbridge: Boydell Press.

Bachrach, B. S. (2008). "Merovingian Mercenaries and Paid Soldiers in Imperial Perspective. In J. France (ed.), *Mercenaries and Paid Men. The Mercenary Identity in the Middle Ages. Proceedings of a Conference Held at University of Wales* (pp. 167–192). Leiden: Brill.

Barnish, S. J. B. (1988). "Transformation and Survival in the Western Senatorial Aristocracy, c. A.D. 400–700." *Papers of the British School at Rome* 56: 120–155.

Bayerle, K. (2008). "Einsatzfelder des weltlichen Bannes im Frühmittelalter." In H. Hermann, T. Gutmann, et al. (eds.), *Von den Leges barbarorum bis zum Ius barbarum des Nationalsozialismus. Festschrift für Hermann Nehlsen zum 70. Geburtstag* (pp. 13–34). Cologne: Böhlau Verlag.

Böhme, H. W. (1974). *Germanische Grabfunde des 4. bis 5. Jahrhunderts zwischen unterer Elbe und Loire. Studien zur Chronologie und Bevölkerungsgeschichte*. Munich: C. H. Beck Verlag.

Brennan, B. (1985). "Senators and Social Mobility in Sixth-Century Gaul." *Journal of Medieval History* 11: 145–161.

Claude, D. (1964). "Untersuchungen zum frühfränkischen Comitat." *Zeitschrift der Savigny-Stiftung für Rechtsgeschichte, GA* 81: 1–69.

Claude, D. (1966). "Zu Fragen frühfränkischer Verfassungsgeschichte." *Zeitschrift der Savigny-Stiftung für Rechtsgeschichte, GA* 83: 273–280.

Claude, D. (1997). "Niedergang, Renaissance und Ende der Präfekturverwaltung im Westen des römischen Reiches (5.–8. Jh.)." *Zeitschrift der Savigny-Stiftung für Rechtsgeschichte, GA* 114: 352–379.

Contamine, P. (1997). *Histoire militaire de la France.* Vol. 1: *Des origines à 1715.* Paris: Presses universitaires de France.

Dannenbauer, H. (1949). "Hundertschaft, Centena und Huntari." *Historisches Jahrbuch* 63–69: 155–219.

Diefenbach, S. (2013). "'Bischofsherrschaft'. Zur Transformation der politischen Kultur im spätantiken und frühmittelalterlichen Gallien." In S. Diefenbach and G. M. Müller (eds.), *Gallien in Spätantike und Frühmittelalter—Kulturgeschichte einer Region* (pp. 91–152). Berlin: Walter de Gruyter.

Diesner, H. (1972). "Das Buccellariertum von Stilicho und Sarus bis auf Aëtius (454/455)." *Klio* 54(1): 321–350.

Dippe, O. (1889). *Gefolgschaft und Huldigung im Reiche der Merowinger. Ein Beitrag zur Frage über die Entstehung des Lehnswesen.* Unpublished doctoral dissertation. Kiel.

Dixon, K. R., and Southern, P. (2000). *The Late Roman Army.* London: Routledge.

Dopsch, A. (1926). "Die *leudes* und das Lehenswesen." *Mitteilungen des Instituts für österreichische Geschichtsforschung* 41: 35–43.

Durliat, J. (1990). *Les finances publiques de Dioclétien aux Carolingiens (284–889).* Sigmaringen: Jan Thorbecke Verlag.

Ebling, H. (1974). *Prosopographie der Amtsträger des Merowingerreiches. Von Chlothar II. (613) bis Karl Martell (741).* Munich: Thorbecke Verlag.

Effros, B. (2002). *Caring for Body and Soul: Burial and the Afterlife in the Merovingian World.* University Park, PA: Pennsylvania State University Press.

Esders, S. (2009a). "Rechtliche Grundlagen frühmittelalterlicher Staatlichkeit. Der allgemeine Treueid." In W. Pohl (ed.), *Der frühmittelalterliche Staat. Europäische Perspektiven* (pp. 423–434). Vienna: Verlag der österreichischen Akademie der Wissenschaften.

Esders, S. (2009b). "'Öffentliche' Abgaben und Leistungen im Übergang von der Spätantike zum Frühmittelalter. Konzeptionen und Befunde." In T. Kölzer and R. Schieffer (eds.), *Von der Spätantike zum frühen Mittelalter. Kontinuitäten und Brüche, Konzeptionen und Befunde* (pp. 189–244). Ostfildern: Jan Thorbecke Verlag.

Esders, S. (2014). "Nordwestgallien um 500. Von der militarisierten spätrömischen Provinzgesellschaft zur erweiterten Militäradministration des merowingischen Königtums." In M. Meier and S. Patzold (eds.), *Chlodwigs Welt. Organisation von Herrschaft um 500* (pp. 339–361). Stuttgart: Franz Steiner Verlag.

Fehr, H. (1914). "Das Waffenrecht der Bauern im Mittelalter." *Zeitschrift der Savigny-Stiftung für Rechtsgeschichte, GA* 35: 111–211.

Fischer, A. (2009). "Attila, die Franken und die Schlacht auf den Katalaunischen Feldern." In Historisches Museum der Pfalz Speyer (ed.), *Hunnen zwischen Asien und Europa. Aktuelle Forschungen zur Geschichte und Kultur der Hunnen* (pp. 187–196). Langenweissbach: Beier & Beran.

France, J. (2005). "War and Sanctity. Saints' Lives as Sources for Early Medieval Warfare." *Journal of Medieval Military History* 3: 14–22.

Freiherr von Guttenberg, E. (1952). "*Iudex h. e. comes aut grafio.* Ein Beitrag zum Problem der fränkischen 'Grafschaftsverfassung'." In *Festschrift Edmund E. Stengel zum 70. Geburtstag* (pp. 93–129). Münster: Böhlau Verlag.

Gerberding, R. A. (1987). *The Rise of the Carolingians and the "Liber Historiae Francorum."* Oxford: Clarendon Press.

Goetz, H.-W. (1995). "Social and Military Institutions." In R. McKitterick (ed.), *The Cambridge Medieval History* vol. 2 (pp. 451–480). Cambridge: Cambridge University Press.

Goetz, H.-W. (2004). "Der fränkische *maior domus* in der Sicht erzählender Quellen." In S. Happ (ed.), *Vielfalt der Geschichte. Lernen, Lehren und Erforschen vergangener Zeiten. Festgabe für Ingrid Heidrich zum 65. Geburtstag* (pp. 11–24). Berlin: Wissenschaftlicher Verlag Berlin.

Goffart, W. A. (1982). "Old and New in Merovingian Taxation." *Past and Present* 96: 3–21.

Goffart, W. A. (1988). *The Narrators of Barbarian History (A.D. 550–800). Jordanes, Gregory of Tours, Bede, and Paul the Deacon.* Princeton, NJ: Princeton University Press.

Goffart, W. A. (2008). "Frankish Military Duty and the Fate of Roman Taxation." *Early Medieval Europe* 16(2): 166–190.

Grahn-Hoek, H. (1976). *Die fränkische Oberschicht im 6. Jahrhundert. Studien zu ihrer rechtlichen und politischen Stellung.* Sigmaringen: Thorbecke Verlag.

Günther, R. (1977). "Einige Untersuchungen zu den Laeten und Gentilen in Gallien im 4. Jahrhundert und ihre historische Bedeutung." *Klio* 59: 313–321.

Gutsmiedl-Schümann, D. (2012). "Merovingian Men—Fulltime Warriors? Weapon Graves of the Continental Merovingian Period of the Munich Gravel Plain and the Social and Age Structure of the Contemporary Society. A Case Study." In R. Berge, M. E. Jasinski, and K. Sognnes (eds.), *Proceedings of the 10th Nordic TAG conference at Stiklestad, Norway 2009* (pp. 251–261). BAR International Series vol. 2399. Oxford: Archaeopress.

Halsall, G. (1992). "The Origin of the Reihengräberzivilisation. Forty Years On." In J. Drinkwater and H. Elton (eds.), *Fifth-Century Gaul. A Crisis of Identity?* (pp. 196–207). Cambridge: Cambridge University Press.

Halsall, G. (2003). *Warfare and Society in the Barbarian West, 450–900.* London: Routledge.

Halsall, G. (2007). *Barbarian Migrations and the Roman West, 376–568.* Cambridge: Cambridge University Press.

Halsall, G. (2008). "Gräberfelduntersuchungen und das Ende des römischen Reiches." In S. Brather (ed.), *Zwischen Spätantike und Frühmittelalter. Archäologie des 4. bis 7. Jahrhunderts im Westen* (pp. 103–117). Berlin: Walter de Gruyter.

Halsall, G. (2009). "Die Militarisierung Nordgalliens. Föderaten und 'Föderatengräber.'" In S. Burmeister (ed.), *2000 Jahre Varusschlacht. Imperium, Konflikt, Mythos* (pp. 270–277). Stuttgart: Konrad Theiss.

Harrison, D. (2002). "The Development of Elites. From Roman Bureaucrats to Medieval Warlords." In W. Pohl and M. Diesenberger (eds.), *Integration und Herrschaft. Ethnische Identitäten und soziale Organisation im Frühmittelalter* (pp. 289–300). Vienna: Verlag der Österreichischen Akademie der Wissenschaften.

Heidrich, I. (1989). "Les maires du palais neustriens du milieu du VIIe au milieu du VIIIe siècle." In H. Atsma (ed.), *La Neustrie. Les pays du nord de la Loire de 650 à 850. Colloque international.* Vol. 1 (pp. 217–229). Sigmaringen: Jan Thorbecke Verlag.

Heinzelmann, M. (1976). *Bischofsherrschaft in Gallien. Zur Kontinuität römischer Führungsschichten vom 4. bis zum 7. Jahrhundert. Soziale, prosopographische und bildungsgeschichtliche Aspekte.* Zürich: Artemis-Verlag.

Hendy, M. E. (1988). "From Public to Private. The Western Barbarian Coinages as a Mirror of the Disintegration of Late Roman Structures." *Viator* 19: 29–78.

Hüppe-Dröge, D. (1981). "Schutz- und Angriffswaffen nach den Leges und verwandten fränkischen Rechtsquellen." In R. Schmidt-Wiegand (ed.), *Wörter und Sachen im Lichte der Bezeichungsforschung.* Berlin: Walter de Gruyter.

Irsigler, F. (1969). *Untersuchungen zur Geschichte des frühfränkischen Adels*. Bonn: Ludwig Röhrscheid Verlag.

James, E. (1997). "The Militarization of Roman Society, 400–700." In A. N. Jørgensen and B. L. Clausen (eds.), *Military Aspects of Scandinavian Society in a European Perspective AD 1–1300* (pp. 19–24). Copenhagen: Publications from the National Museum.

Jussen, B. (1995). "Über 'Bischofsherrschaften' und die Prozeduren politisch-sozialer Umordnung in Gallien zwischen 'Antike' und 'Mittelalter'." *Historische Zeitschrift* 260: 673–718.

Kelley, C. (2014). "Neither Conquest nor Settlement. Attila's Empire and Its Impact." In M. Maas (ed.), *The Cambridge Companion to the Age of Attila* (pp. 193–208). Cambridge: Cambridge University Press.

Kim, H. J. (2013). *The Huns, Rome and the Birth of Europe*. Cambridge: Cambridge University Press.

Lewis, A. R. (1976). "The Dukes in the *Regnum francorum*, A.D. 550–751." *Speculum* 51(3): 381–410.

Mathisen, R. W. (1993). *Roman Aristocrats in Barbarian Gaul. Strategies for Survival in an Age of Transition*. Austin: University of Texas Press.

Mierow, C. C. (1915). "Eugippius and the Closing Years of the Province of Noricum Ripense." *Classical Philology* 10(2): 166–187.

Murray, A. C. (1986). "The Position of the *grafio* in the Constitutional History of Merovingian Gaul." *Speculum* 61(4): 787–805.

Murray, A. C. (1988). "From Roman to Frankish Gaul. 'Centenarii' and 'Centenae' in the Administration of the Frankish Kingdom." *Traditio* 44: 59–100.

Murray, A. C. (2000). *From Roman to Merovingian Gaul. A Reader*. Peterborough: Broadview Press.

Nicholson, H. J. (2004). *Medieval Warfare. Theory and Practice of War in Europe, 300–1500*. New York: Palgrave Macmillan.

Nonn, U. (2002). "Beobachtungen zur 'Herrschaft' der fränkischen Hausmeier." In F. Erkens and E. Boshof (eds.), *Von Sacerdotium und Regnum. Geistliche und weltliche Gewalt im frühen und hohen Mittelalter. Festschrift für Egon Boshof zum 65. Geburtstag*. Vol. 12 (pp. 27–46). Cologne: Böhlau Verlag.

Patzold, S. (2010). "Zur Sozialstruktur des Episkopats und zur Ausbildung bischöflicher Herrschaft in Gallien zwischen Spätantike und Frühmittelalter." In M. Becher and S. Dick (eds.), *Völker, Reiche und Namen im frühen Mittelalter* (pp. 121–140). Munich: Wilhelm Fink Verlag.

Petersen, L. I. R. (2013). *Siege Warfare and Military Organization in the Successor States (400–800 AD). Byzantium, the West and Islam*. Leiden: Brill.

Prinz, F. (1973). "Die bischöfliche Stadtherrschaft im Frankenreich vom 5. bis zum 7. Jahrhundert." *Historische Zeitschrift* 217, 1–35.

Reuter, T. (1985). "Plunder and Tribute in the Carolingian Empire." *Transactions of the Royal Historical Society* 5 (35): 75–94.

Reuter, T. (1997). "The Recruitment of Armies in the Early Middle Ages. What Can We Know?" In A. N. Jørgensen and B. L. Clausen (eds.), *Military Aspects of Scandinavian Society in a European Perspective AD 1–1300* (pp. 32–37). Copenhagen: Publications from the National Museum.

Rio, A. (trans.). (2008). *The Formularies of Angers and Marcul. Two Merovingian Legal Handbooks*. Liverpool: Liverpool University Press.

Sarti, L. (2013a). *Perceiving War and the Military in Early Christian Gaul (ca. 400–700 A. D.)*. Leiden: Brill.

Sarti, L. (2013b). "Die Identität des Kämpfenden nach dem Zusammenbruch des römischen Militärwesens in Gallien." *Archiv für Kulturgeschichte* 95(2): 309–332.

Sarti, L. (2016a). "Die spätantike Militärpräsenz und die Entstehung einer 'Grenzgesellschaft' in der nordwesteuropäischen *limes*-Region." In C. Rass (ed.), *Militärische Migration vom Altertum bis zur Gegenwart* (pp. 43–56). Paderborn: Schöningh.

Sarti, L. (2016b). "Eine Militärelite im merowingischen Gallien? Versuch einer Eingrenzung, Zuordnung und Definition." *Mitteilungen des Instituts für österreichische Geschichtsforschung* 124(2): 271–295.

Sarti, L. (2018). "Der fränkische *miles*: weder Soldat noch Ritter." *Frühmittelalterliche Studien* 52.1: 99–117.

Scheibelreiter, G. (1983). *Der Bischof in merowingischer Zeit*. Vienna: Böhlau Verlag.

Scheibelreiter, G. (1999). *Die barbarische Gesellschaft. Mentalitätsgeschichte der europäischen Achsenzeit 5.–8. Jahrhundert*. Darmstadt: Wissenschaftliche Buchgesellschaft.

Schmitt, O. (1994). "Die Bucellarii. Eine Studie zum militärischen Gefolgschaftswesen in der Spätantike." *Tyche* 9: 147–174.

Schneider, J. (1967). "Bemerkungen zur Differenzierung der gallorömischen Unterschichten im sechsten Jahrhundert." *Klio* 48: 237–249.

Selle-Hosbach, K. (1974). *Prosopographie merowingischer Amtsträger. In der Zeit von 511 bis 613*. Unpublished dissertation. Bonn.

Shanzer, D., and Wood, I. N. (trans.). (2002). *Avitus of Vienne. Letters and Selected Prose*. Liverpool: Liverpool University Press.

Southern, P. (2007). *The Roman Army. A Social and Institutional History*. Oxford: Oxford University Press.

Sprandel, R. (1957). "Dux und comes in der Merovingerzeit." *Zeitschrift der Savigny-Stiftung für Rechtsgeschichte, GA* 74: 41–84.

Springer, M. (1995). "Jährliche Wiederkehr oder ganz anderes. Märzfeld oder Marsfeld?" In P. Dilg, G. Keil, and D. Moser (eds.), *Rhythmus und Saisonalität. Kongreßakten des 5. Symposiums des Mediävistenverbandes in Göttingen 1993* (pp. 297–324). Sigmaringen: Jan Thorbecke Verlag.

Steuer, H. (1968). "Zur Bewaffnung und Sozialstruktur der Merowingerzeit. Ein Beitrag zur Forschungsmethode." *Nachrichten aus Niedersachsens Urgeschichte* 37: 18–87.

Steuer, H. (1987). "Helm und Ringschwert. Prunkbewaffnung und Rangabzeichen germanischer Krieger. Eine Übersicht." In Hans-Jürgen Häßler (ed.), *Studien zur Sachsenforschung* 6 (pp. 189–236). Hildesheim: Isensee Verlag.

Steuer, H. (2009). "Archäologie der Gefolgschaft." In S. Burmeister (ed.), *2000 Jahre Varusschlacht-Konflikt* (pp. 309–419). Stuttgart: Theiss Verlag.

Stroheker, K. F. (1948). *Der senatorische Adel im spätantiken Gallien*. Tübingen: Alma-Mater-Verlag.

Thompson, E. A. (1982). *Romans and Barbarians. The Decline of the Western Empire*. Madison: University of Wisconsin Press.

van Ossel, P. (1995). "Insécurité et militarisation en Gaule du Nord au bas-empire. L'exemple des campagnes." *Revue du Nord* 77: 27–36.

von Olberg, G. (1981). "Leod 'Mann'. Soziale Schichtung im Spiegel volkssprachiger Wörter der Leges." In R. Schmidt-Wiegand (ed.), *Wörter und Sachen im Lichte der Bezeichnungsforschung* (pp. 91–106). Berlin: Walter de Gruyter.

von Olberg, G. (1987). "Zum Freiheitsbegriff im Spiegel volkssprachiger Bezeichnungen in den frühmittelalterlichen Leges." In D. Simon (ed.), *Akten des 26. Deutschen Rechtshistorikertages Frankfurt am Main* (pp. 411–426). Frankfurt-am-Main: Klostermann Verlag.

von Olberg, G. (1991). *Die Bezeichnungen für soziale Stände, Schichten und Gruppen in den Leges Barbarorum*. Berlin: Walter de Gruyter.

Weidemann, M. (1982). *Kulturgeschichte der Merowingerzeit nach den Werken Gregors von Tours*. 2 vols. Mainz: Römisch-Germanisches Zentralmuseum Mainz.

Weidemann, M. (1993). "Adel im Merowingerreich. Untersuchungen zu seiner Rechtsstellung." *Jahrbuch des Römisch-Germanischen Zentralmuseums Mainz* 40: 535–555.

Whitby, M. (2000). "The Army, c. 420–602." In A. Cameron, B. Ward-Perkins, and M. Whitby (eds.), *The Cambridge Ancient History*. Vol. 14: *Late Antiquity. Empire and Successors, A.D. 425–600* (pp. 288–314). Cambridge: Cambridge University Press.

Whittaker, D. (1993). "Landlords and Warlords in the Later Roman Empire. In J. Rich and G. Shipley (eds.), *War and Society in the Roman World* (pp. 277–302). London: Routledge.

CHAPTER 13

CORPORATE SOLIDARITY AND ITS LIMITS WITHIN THE GALLO-FRANKISH EPISCOPATE

GREGORY HALFOND

A recent assessment of the Gallo-Frankish episcopate in the Merovingian era glumly concluded that it was "characterized by an awkward mixture of representatives of faded Roman families and energetic courtiers…the Gallic bishops of the age of Gregory of Tours were a diverse and somewhat drab body of men" (Brown 2015, pp. 169–170). This is a rather far cry from J. M. Wallace-Hadrill's earlier appraisal of these same bishops as "a brotherhood of apostolic successors," whose "corporate flavor" was decidedly Roman (1983, pp. 94, 101). Despite the divergent assumptions of these two assessments, they are not entirely incompatible. The Gallo-Frankish bishops of the Merovingian era were diverse in their social origins, probably more so than traditionally has been assumed (Patzold 2010, 2014a, 2014b; Patzold and Walter 2014). Furthermore, it would be wrong to extrapolate about the entirety of the episcopate from those few exceptional cases—in the areas of sanctity, impiety, or literary productivity—for which we have the most evidence (see Horden, Chapter 14, this volume). If not necessarily dull and dowdy, the average bishop in Merovingian Gaul lacked in sufficient quantity those qualities that attracted the attention of contemporary and near-contemporary hagiographers and historians. Of the several thousand men who held episcopal office in these centuries, we know the names of fewer than half and have biographical information about far fewer still.[1]

Yet, while the average Merovingian-era bishop was destined for historical anonymity, or at least near anonymity, his subscription to a common corporate identity—grounded in apostolic succession, Roman cultural, legal, and administrative norms, and an association with sanctity—significantly augmented his contemporary authority and profile.[2] The primary means by which the Gallo-Frankish episcopal *ordo* demonstrated its corporate solidarity was through expressions of *consensus*.[3] The same adhesive force that bound together in a single body the lay and ecclesiastical members of the Christian community was the principal bonding agent that supported the administrative apparatus of the Gallic episcopate. Its effectiveness can be gauged in part by the surprising durability of the provincial organization of the Gallo-Frankish church, which maintained a good measure of its integrity even through the politically tumultuous decades of the early eighth century (Halfond 2010, pp. 200–208; cf. Pontal 1989, pp. 255–257). The bishops of the Merovingian era thus recognized themselves to be, in Wallace-Hadrill's words, members of a singular brotherhood, with shared spiritual, pastoral, and administrative responsibilities over a united federation of over 100 episcopal sees.[4]

The Limits of Episcopal *Consensus*

None of this is to suggest, however, that *consensus* was an easily or consistently realized goal. As Lisa Bailey (2010, pp. 40–41) has observed, the Gallo-Frankish bishops themselves harbored few illusions regarding the ease of attaining either communal or corporate *consensus*: "Its achievement was so rare, so contrary to human nature, that it was seen not only as a triumph of human virtue, but also as a signal of the working of the Holy Spirit." While as civic administrators, spiritual leaders, and patrons Merovingian bishops could wield considerable influence, this did not shield them from harassment by the royal court, secular officeholders, or even their own clergy (Wood 1983, 1994, pp. 71–87; Coates 2000, pp. 1131–1136; Fouracre 2003; Gradowicz-Pancer 2003; Kreiner 2011, pp. 337–340).[5] Not surprisingly then, within their dioceses, bishops regularly employed the language and rituals of *consensus* to express their authority (Claude 1963, pp. 22–62; MacCormack 1972; Brennan 1992, pp. 131–132; Jussen 1997, pp. 25–26; Jussen 2001, pp. 170–179; Bailey 2010, pp. 18–19).

Similarly, there is no reason to think that *consensus* was any easier to achieve within the corporate body of the episcopate. Interpersonal conflicts between individual bishops seem to have occurred with relative frequency over such issues as ecclesiastical jurisdiction, property claims, theology, and politics. Letter collections from late antique Gaul are particularly valuable records for intraepiscopal communication and conflict (see Gillett, Chapter 25, this volume). While most instances of antagonistic epistolary exchanges are not quite so linguistically colorful as the justly famed (and possibly satirical) correspondence between Bishops Frodebert of Tours and Importunus of Paris—anatomical inferences and all—tense communications could result in passive aggressive or even quite heated language (Walstra 1962; Shanzer 2010; Hen 2012). To cite only a few examples: when Caesarius of Arles wrote Ruricius of Limoges to gently admonish him for failing to attend the Council of Agde (506), Ruricius replied testily to the younger prelate, implying unsubtly that Caesarius's reputation had more to do with his *civitas* than his own merits (Ruricius, *Epistulae* 2.33). When around AD 550 Nicetius of Trier admonished his fellow metropolitan, Mappinus of Reims, for a similar reason,

Mappinus responded defensively that he would have attended the council at Toul had he simply been informed in a timely manner as to its purpose (*Epistolae Austrasicae* 11). In an even more tense exchange ca. 512, when Remigius of Reims received a letter from the bishops of Paris, Sens, and Auxerre, who had rather ungraciously suggested that "it would have been better if you had never been born," he responded with barely suppressed fury that in his fifty-three years as bishop he had never been so rudely addressed (*Epistolae Austrasicae* 3). In contrast to these unpleasant exchanges, when Desiderius of Cahors received an abusive letter from Bishop Felix (of Limoges?) in the mid-seventh century, his response was to seek reconciliation, an effort that proved successful when a contrite Felix sent a sincere letter of apology to Desiderius (*Epistolae* 1.15 and 2.21).

Without minimizing the possible ramifications that such interpersonal conflicts could have on the corporate integrity of the episcopate, far more damaging were those cases in which bishops aligned themselves with secular authorities or factions. In such cases, there was a real danger that bishops could lose their sees or even their lives. As Paul Fouracre (2003, p. 21) has observed in his study of violence against bishops, "Bishops . . . were fair game in politics if they had taken sides." There were, of course, any number of reasons why bishops might take sides in disputes between political factions within the royal court or between separate *regna*. Their actions might be motivated by obligations of kinship, friendship, or political loyalties, by the impact of regnal politics on local communities, by ambition, by coercion, but also (as suggested below) as a response to royal patronage. Typically, when the competition between oppositional parties gave way to violence, bishops served as willing or unwilling participants in the struggle.

For example, following the assassination of King Childeric II in 675, the resurgent Neustrian mayor Ebroin gathered his ecclesiastical and secular supporters, who included such notables as Bishops Audoin of Rouen, Desideratus (Diddo) of Chalon, and Bobo of Valence. With his political and military alliances reassembled, Ebroin captured King Theuderic III along with the royal treasury in a bid to regain control of the Neustrian court (*Liber Historiae Francorum* 45; *Passio Leudegarii I* 20, 23, 25–26).[6] Not surprisingly, those ecclesiastics who opposed Ebroin, most famously Bishop Leudegar of Autun, found themselves deposed or even killed. Despite Ebroin's attacks on individual prelates, there is no reason to think that these attacks were motivated by the mayor's supposed anticlericalism. Ebroin had little difficulty attracting supporters from the Gallo-Frankish episcopate, whose members were willing to do the mayor's bidding even when it meant condemning their fellow prelates. Around 677/679, Ebroin convoked an ecclesiastical synod (in Theuderic's name) at the royal villa of *Masolacus* (Mâlay-le-Roi), ostensibly "for the welfare of the church and the encouragement of peace" ("pro statu aeclisiae vel confirmacione pacis"; *Die Urkunden der Merowinger* no. 122). This council, under the direction of the metropolitan bishops of Lyon, Vienne, Besançon Sens, and Bourges, ordered the deposition of one of Ebroin's episcopal opponents, Chramlinus of Embrun. Whether the metropolitan participants in the council were coerced is uncertain; they may have been motivated by either self-preservation or a genuine willingness to support the mayor's agenda.

Furthermore, the divisive effects of political factionalism on episcopal corporate solidarity could be felt even without any direct mayoral or royal pressure. Florentius's *Vita Rusticulae* (9–12), for instance, describes how Chlothar II summoned the abbess Rusticula to his court around 613 on charges of supporting his Austrasian enemies. The charges were brought by the *patricius* Ricomer "with many bishops," including a certain Bishop Maximus. Rusticula had her own prominent supporters, however, including Bishop Domnolus of Vienne, who, Florentius claims, threatened divine wrath against Chlothar's progeny if he continued to persecute the abbess. This episode reflects clearly how the efforts by local elites, including bishops, to maintain sociable relations with the royal court could have corrosive effects (on court politics, see Hen, Chapter 10, this volume). Not only could the court become a forum in which these elites could play out their own petty disputes, but royal politics had a way of intensifying quarrels between local factions or families.[7]

RESTORING *CONSENSUS*

It is not surprising then, considering the potential damage that could stem from internal disputes or factionalizing, that the Gallo-Frankish bishops were deeply concerned with diffusing, if not necessarily preventing, such breakdowns in corporate solidarity. This was one of their fundamental goals when assembling in council. Following normative procedural rules, councils of bishops were convoked in accordance with the provincial administration of the Gallic church, with the expectation of regular interprovincial, provincial, and diocesan councils (Halfond 2010, pp. 60–61). Following the conclusion of a council's business, if original rules, privileges, or judgments were formulated, it was customary for those decisions to be recorded as acts (*acta*), with the subscriptions of the participating bishops appended in order to illustrate their collective agreement on the contents of the document. The episcopal subscribers insisted as a matter of course that the decisions contained in the *acta* were reached "with the consensus of all" (*cum consenu omnium*). This formula did not imply that discussions began with unanimous agreement or that they were easily reached; rather, it served as a formulaic allusion to one of the fundamental sources of the episcopate's corporate *auctoritas* (Halfond 2010, pp. 87–89). The difficult process of achieving this state of unanimous accord only reinforced the unity of the assembled body. The dissemination of conciliar legislation through the copying, collection, recitation, and consultation of acts strengthened the claim that locally produced *canones*—by virtue of their theological orthodoxy and link to canonical tradition as manifested through the *consensus* of the participants—were contributions to a universal canon law (*ius canonum*) (Halfond 2010, pp. 132–137; 174–179).

Councils were the embodiment of corporate *consensus* not only procedurally, but also legislatively. A number of sixth- and seventh-century Frankish councils attempted to craft practical administrative processes by which the episcopate could repair fractures in its own corporate body. The first such effort was in 541, at the Council of Orléans, which in its twelfth canon dealt specifically with disputes between bishops over movable and immovable property. The canon urges the timely settlement of such conflicts, encouraging the intervention of the disputants' episcopal colleagues. The canon also permits the disputants to bring unresolved cases before chosen judges (*iudices*) (Orléans 541, ca. 12).[8] The terminology here is somewhat surprising. Elsewhere in the *acta* (cc. 13 and 20), and indeed throughout the Merovingian conciliar corpus,[9] the term *iudices* typically refers to secular officeholders, primarily counts (*comites*). However, the Council of Orléans (538) only a few years earlier had employed very similar phrasing, that is, *electi iudices*, in two of its canons (cc. 13 and 25). In the context of these earlier canons, *iudices* seems to be referring more generally to chosen arbiters, either secular or ecclesiastical, rather than to holders of specific offices.[10] So, while the bishops at the Council of Orléans (541) presumably intended the latter use of *iudex*, their phrasing nevertheless was admittedly vague, possibly even too vague in the minds of subsequent conciliar legislators.

Over twenty-five years later, two councils from different Frankish *regna* again took up the issue of intraepiscopal conflict, in both cases abandoning the problematic language of the earlier rule. The Council of Tours (567), representing the dioceses of the kingdom of Paris, then ruled by Charibert I, elaborated upon, and clarified, the procedures for the settlement of disputes without identifying specific issues of contention. The council determined that *presbyteres* should be selected as the mediators in disputes between bishops. Should this mediation fail, it would fall to a full council of bishops to determine the appropriate penalty (Tours 567, c. 2). In contrast, the Council of Lyon (567/570), convoked in Burgundy by Charibert's brother Guntram, differentiated between intraprovincial and interprovincial episcopal conflicts. In the case of the intraprovincial conflicts, the council determined that a provincial synod, under the leadership of the metropolitan bishop, would address the quarrel.[11] In the interprovincial situation, two metropolitans would take on the duty of settling the dispute (Lyon 567/570, c. 1). The final Merovingian council to craft administrative procedures for settling intraepiscopal conflicts was the Council of Paris (614), convoked by Chlothar II, which supported the Lyonnaise canon's insistence on metropolitan adjudication. Additionally, the bishops at Paris stressed that disputants were not to bring their case before the *iudex publicus*, that is, the local *comes* (Paris 614, c. 13), possibly in implicit reference to the earlier ruling of the Council of Orléans (541).

Whether these canonical procedures were ever enforced consistently is unknown. Gregory of Tours does describe a dispute in 584 between the newly elected Innocentius of Rodez and Ursicinus of Cahors over contested parishes, noting that after several years the metropolitan bishop of Bourges intervened by convoking a synod at Clermont, thus following the procedures dictated by the Council of Lyon (*DLH* 6.38). Anecdotes, however, are not strong evidence of procedural uniformity. Furthermore, it is clear that despite the efforts of the Councils of Lyon and Paris (and others) to assert the adjudicating authority of metropolitan bishops, these prelates frequently struggled to exercise supervisory *auctoritas* over independent-minded suffragans.[12]

Regardless of the canons' efficacy, not only are they explicit admissions of the occurrence of intraepiscopal disputes, but also, more importantly, they constitute utilitarian attempts by the episcopate to fashion administrative procedures for the quick and fair settlement of such conflicts. Complicating this normative view of episcopal dispute settlement, however, was the reality of royal involvement, both in fomenting and settling disputes. When rulers directed metropolitan inquiries and convoked conciliar tribunals, not only was the outcome likely preordained, there also was an increased danger of the settlement exacerbating the original conflict, or even fomenting a new one. Probably the two best known examples of royal intrusion into episcopal judicial affairs are Gregory of Tours's accounts of Chilperic I's interventions in the conciliar trials of Praetextatus of Rouen and Gregory himself (*DLH* 5.18 and 5.49), in which the king convoked the councils, participated in their deliberations, presented evidence, and effectively determined the verdicts. In both trials, Chilperic I had the cooperation of episcopal allies, whom Gregory, normally a believer in the virtue of royal–episcopal collaboration, later dismissed as sycophants (*adolatores*) (Heinzelmann 2001, pp. 172–191).

While disputes between bishops could and did occur without the intrusion of the royal court, as suggested earlier, those fractures in the corporate body of the episcopate caused by the intrusion of secular politics were the most difficult to repair. Bishops and sovereigns recognized, in theory, the benefits of collaboration. In return for royal patronage—which ranged from support for episcopal candidacies to financial subsidies to intervention in local conflicts—bishops could unify and direct community support for the benefit of the monarch as well as serve as partners in the promotion of peace and order.[13] But patronage bred factionalism. Even ostensibly pious, seemingly innocuous, support directed by the court toward an episcopal see and its occupant had the effect of aligning a bishop more closely with a royal patron to the detriment of episcopal corporate solidarity. Thus, while a bishop might be motivated by a range of immediate factors in determining whether, and with whom, to align himself politically, underpinning this decision were structural and ideological pressures encouraging ecclesiopolitical collaboration in the governance of the *regnum Francorum*.

Such pressures are clearly visible in the episcopal patronage of the sons of Chlothar I and their wives. Over more than five decades, from 561 to 613, these sovereigns diligently and systematically courted, and competed for, episcopal allies, demonstrating little tolerance for those prelates who refused their overtures (Halfond 2012a, 2012b, 2012c, 2014). Their success is discernible in the resulting factionalizing of the episcopate itself along political lines. This weakening of episcopal corporate solidarity is perhaps most visible in the conspiracy supporting the efforts by the royal pretender Gundovald to secure a *regnum* in Frankish Gaul (582–585). Not only did Gundovald's campaign pressure bishops, particularly in contested *civitates*, to declare their political loyalties, but his ultimate failure further accentuated already deepening divisions within the Gallic episcopate. It is instructive, then, to examine, as a case study, episcopal involvement in the Gundovald affair in conjunction with subsequent efforts by Guntram of Burgundy to dictate an "episcopal" response to the participation of prelates in the conspiracy.

THE GUNDOVALD AFFAIR AND ITS CONCILIAR RESPONSE: A CASE STUDY

Few events in Merovingian history have attracted more scholarly attention than the efforts by Gundovald, a royal pretender claiming to be the son of King Chlothar I, to secure a *regnum* in Frankish Gaul.[14] This prominence is due not simply to Gundovald's pivotal and disruptive role in the civil wars of the late sixth century, but also to the unanswered (and in many cases unanswerable) questions surrounding the details of the plot. Even Gundovald's ultimate territorial aims remain the subject of dispute.[15] Virtually everything we know of Gundovald and his backers comes from Gregory of Tours's *Decem Libri Historiarum*. Despite the many lacunae peppering Gregory's fragmented narrative of the plot, one could never accuse the bishop of attempting to conceal the enormous impact of Gundovald's arrival on the royal, aristocratic, and episcopal elites of Frankish Gaul. Whether or not Gregory himself harbored any sympathy for the pretender remains a matter of conjecture (Weidemann 1982, pp. 57, 213–214; Wood 1993, p. 264; Bachrach 1994, p. 173 n.1; Halsall 2002, p. 346 n. 39), but his narrative is clear that a diverse group of secular and ecclesiastical potentates from throughout the *regnum Francorum* supported Gundovald's claims to royal status (Rouche 1979, p. 75; Goffart 2012, pp. 25–26).

When Gundovald arrived in the port city of Marseille from Constantinople in 582, the bishop of the city, Theodore, was waiting there to receive the self-proclaimed Merovingian. Theodore, a longstanding supporter of Austrasian claims to the contested *civitas* (Bachrach 1994, pp. 52–54; Halfond 2014, pp. 21–22), provided Gundovald with the horses that took the pretender and his entourage to Avignon. Later, the bishop claimed that in welcoming Gundovald to Gaul, he was merely following the orders of the magnates then dominating the Austrasian court (Gregory of Tours, *DLH* 6.24). Gregory of Tours himself appears to have accepted the bishop's defense and makes no effort in his narrative to conceal the bishop's involvement in the plot (Goubert 1955, pp. 2.1.57–28; Wood 1993, p. 263; Wood 1994, pp. 84–86; Bachrach 1994, pp. 65–68). Gregory even goes so far as to "quote" the pretender himself, recalling how Theodore received him "with great courtesy" (*DLH* 7.36).

Theodore is one of no fewer than ten named prelates whose participation in the Gundovald conspiracy Gregory unequivocally acknowledges, along with Antidius of Agen, Bertram of Bordeaux, Epiphanius (of Fréjus?),[16] Faustianus of Dax, Nicasius of Angoulême, Orestes of Bazas, Palladius of Saintes, Sagittarius of Gap, and Ursicinus of Cahors. In addition, Gregory implicates an additional three prelates without stating explicitly their loyalty to the pretender: Egidius of Reims, Ferreolus of Limoges, and Rufinus of Convenae. A collective examination of these thirteen prelates (see Fig. 13.1) provides valuable insight into not only the goals and planning of the conspiracy, but also the inclination of Gallo-Frankish bishops to factionalize along political lines. Excluded from this examination are those bishops, like Aunacharius of Auxerre, whose

Name	Civitas	Province	Regnum (AD 582–585)	Tenure (All Dates PCdBE)	References to Collaboration
Antidius	Agen	Aquitanica Secunda	Chilperic until 584...afterwards Guntram	...585-before 614	DLH 8.2
Bertram	Bordeaux	Aquitanica Secunda	Chilperic until 584...afterwards Guntram	...577–585	DLH 7.31, 8.2, 8.20
Egidius	Reims	Belgica Secunda	Childebert II	before 565–590...	DLH 7.33
Epiphanius	Frejus?	Arelatensis	Childebert II?	...574?–582...	DLH 6.24
Faustianus	Dax	Novempopulana	Chilperic until 584...afterwards Guntram	...584-before Jan. and Oct. 585...	DLH 7.31, 8.2, 8.20
Ferreolus	Limoges	Aquitanica Prima	Chilperic until 584...afterwards Guntram	...579–591...	DLH 7.10
Nicasius	Angouleme	Aquitanica Secunda	Chilperic until 584...afterwards Guntram	After 579/80–585-Before 614	DLH 7.26 and 8.2
Orestes	Bazas	Novempopulana	Chilperic until 584...afterwards Guntram	...584/5–585...	DLH 7.31 and 8.20
Palladius	Saintes	Aquitanica Secunda	Chilperic until 584...afterwards Guntram	...573-596-before 614	DLH 7.31, 8.2, 8.7, 8.20
Rufinus	Convenae	Novempopulana	Chilperic until 584...afterwards Guntram	...585...	DLH 7.34
Sagittarius	Gap	Arelatensis	Guntram	...After 552–566/7-585	DLH 7.28, 7.34, and 7.37–9
Theodore	Marseille	Arelatensis	Guntram and Childebert II; Childebert II after 584	...566-June 591...	DLH 6.24, 7.36, 8.5, and 8.12
Ursicinus	Cahors	Aquitanica Prima	Chilperic until 584...afterwards Guntram	...580–585...	DLH 8.20

FIGURE 13.1. Bishops Implicated in the Gundovald Affair

participation has been speculated upon by modern historians, but for which no sure evidence exists (Bachrach 1994, pp. 41, 43–45, 200 n. 72; Widdowson 2008, pp. 617–618; Zuckerman 1998, p. 10 n. 31).[17]

Also excluded are those two bishops named by the seventh-century Fredegar *Chronica*—but not by Gregory—as participants in the plot: Syagrius of Autun and Flavius of Chalon. There are several reasons for this exclusion. The accusations against both bishops are found in Fredegar's chapter-length synopsis of Gundovald's doomed effort to secure a *regnum* in Frankish Gaul (*Chronica* 3.89). In Fredegar's account, both the pretender's goals and conspiratorial accomplices are explicitly identified. According to the chronicler, Gundovald's return to Gaul from Constantinople was facilitated by three men: the *patricius* Mummolus, Bishop Syagrius of Autun, and Bishop Flavius of Chalon, with the ultimate aim of placing Gundovald on the throne of Burgundy. In contrast, Gregory of Tours never so explicitly identifies the primary objective of the conspiracy, nor does he populate his narrative of the plot with a predominantly Burgundian cast. Not only does Gregory never actually name Syagrius and Flavius as conspirators, he also makes no mention of the royal bodyguard (*spatharius*) Cariatto, whom Fredegar credits with reporting the news of Gundovald's death to Guntram, an act for which he supposedly was awarded the episcopal see of Geneva. Fredegar's pithy narrative of the Gundovald conspiracy seems to represent a deliberate effort to refashion what in reality was an interregnal, even international, series of events into a specifically Burgundian affair. This was in keeping with the chronicler's keen interest in the activities of the Burgundian aristocracy and episcopate.

Furthermore, both Flavius and Syagrius seem to have remained close to Guntram of Burgundy following Gundovald's death, despite the king's fierce enmity toward other episcopal conspirators. Both participated in the Council of Mâcon (585), at which other episcopal conspirators were censured, and both accompanied Guntram to Paris six years later to witness the baptism of Chlothar II (Halfond 2012a, pp. 88–89). We simply do not know where the Fredegar Chronicler heard of the two bishops' involvement; he may very well have been simply repeating popular rumors when he refashioned Gregory's narrative of the conspiracy into a Burgundian affair. But the total absence of corroborating evidence from sources closer in time to actual events is enough to justify the exclusion of Syagrius and Flavius from this discussion (cf. Goubert 1955, pp. 2.1.79–80; Bachrach 1994, pp. 49, 151, 165).

Of the thirteen bishops implicated by Gregory of Tours in the Gundovald affair, ten (approximately 77 percent) had their episcopal sees in just three southern provinces: Arelatensis (three), Novempopulana (three), and Aquitanica Secunda (four).[18] The only northern Gallic bishop implicated by Gregory is Egidius of Reims (Belgica Secunda). This geographical distribution is not in itself surprising, as Gundovald's primary sphere of military and political activity was Aquitaine (Ewig 1976, p. 143; Rouche 1979, p. 72). Rather more unexpected is the political distribution of the conspirators. A sizable majority of implicated bishops (nine or 69 percent) resided in *civitates* that were ruled by King Chilperic I in the years leading up to the king's death in 584 and that subsequently were claimed by his brother, Guntram of Burgundy. Three of these *civitates* (Bordeaux, Limoges, and Cahors) had once been part of the morning gift (*Morgengabe*) of Galswinth, Chilperic's ill-fated Visigothic bride, and remained contested until the Treaty of Andelot (587). Sagittarius, the deposed bishop of Gap and another Gundovald supporter, was a defector from the *regnum Gunthramni*, while Egidius of Reims, often assumed to have been a ringleader in the plot to bring Gundovald to Gaul, enjoyed considerable influence in the Austrasian court of Childebert II (Kurth 1919, p. 283; Goubert 1941, p. 422; Rouche 1979, p. 499 n. 145; Bachrach 1994, p. 151; Dumézil 2008, p. 205; Goffart 2012, p. 25). Marseille, the see of the aforementioned Theodore, was reluctantly shared by Guntram and his nephew, Childebert II, until 584.

How then are we to explain the apparently dominant role played by bishops of the former *regnum Chilperici* in the Gundovald conspiracy? Might it be simply an illusion cast by Gregory in an effort to shield his Austrasian colleagues from blame? Gregory's sympathetic treatment of Theodore already has been noted. Moreover, the bishop of Tours never directly implicates Egidius of Reims in the plot, despite the Egidius's obvious involvement (Wood 1993, pp. 267–68). Instead, Gregory merely relates that Guntram warned his nephew Childebert against Egidius's counsel during a conference called to discuss the Gundovald affair (*DLH* 7.33). It certainly is conceivable that Gregory knew of more guilty parties than he chose to name in his *Histories*, Austrasian or otherwise.

It does not follow, however, that Gregory falsely implicated those among his colleagues who—like himself—once owed allegiance to the Neustrian King of Soissons. Even if Gregory's narrative skews the percentages calculated above, the heavy involvement in the Gundovald conspiracy by these bishops seems indisputable. Furthermore, we know from Gregory that several of the conspirators, that is, Egidius of Rheim, Bertram of Bordeaux, Ferreolus of Limoges, and Palladius of Saintes, had on various occasions demonstrated their loyalty to Chilperic or to his wife, Fredegund (Halfond 2012c). While specific information on the political allegiances of the remainder of implicated bishops is mostly lacking, it nevertheless is striking that roughly one-third of known episcopal conspirators were either loyal subjects or supporters of the recently deceased Neustrian king.

The prominent role of former residents of the *regnum Chilperici* in the Gundovald conspiracy begins to make more sense if we recall the suggestion by Walter Goffart (2012, p. 7) that "the motivation behind Gundovald's usurpation was a succession problem in Neustria." According to Goffart's reconstruction of events, when Gundovald first was summoned to Gaul from Constantinople by the Austrasian *dux* Guntram Boso, it was at a time when Chilperic was without a male blood heir, and the appearance of the baby Theuderic shortly before the pretender's arrival at Marseille led to the abandonment of the operation.[19] When Chilperic died unexpectedly in 584, his lone surviving male heir—the future Chlothar II—had not yet been formally proclaimed, and Gundovald's second attempt to claim royal power in Francia was supported by both Austrasian and Neustrian magnates initially unaware of the baby's existence. So, whereas the pretender accepted oaths (*sacramenta*) in the name of Childebert II from the local landowners (*cives*) of Aquitanian cities formally controlled by Sigibert, he demanded that oaths be sworn directly to himself in those *civitates* previously loyal to Chilperic (Gregory of Tours, *DLH* 7.26).[20] Chlothar's subsequent recognition by Guntram and the bulk of the Neustrian elite, was the major factor, according to Goffart, that doomed Gundovald's second campaign.

Those Aquitanian bishops of the former *regnum Chilperici* who supported Gundovald need not have been motivated by any special affection for the pretender, who actively sought episcopal collaborators. Those who resided in *civitates* whose political allegiances were thrown into question by the death of Chilperic had to make a political calculation in choosing which of several competing royal masters to support. Gundovald's presence in Aquitaine applied extra pressure in an already-tense atmosphere, as the pretender demanded loyalty oaths in exchange for his displays of generosity (Gregory of Tours, *DLH* 6.26). Like Theodore of Marseille, who suffered greatly from the effects of holding episcopal office in a deeply divided *civitas*, these Aquitanian bishops took a genuine risk in supporting any of the royal claimants to their cities.

A closer look at some of the involvement of these Aquitanian bishops in the Gundovald conspiracy is revealing. Some of these prelates probably had given little thought to Gundovald or his claims to royal power prior to his arrival at their city walls. For instance, when the pretender arrived in Angoulême in 585, Chlothar's status as heir to Chilperic had yet to be established (Goffart 2012, p. 11), and Bishop Nicasius chose to recognize the pretender as his new royal master.[21] Conversely, his colleague Charterius of Périgueux, whom Chilperic had once suspected of retaining a secret loyalty to his previous royal master, Guntram, refused and was duly punished (Gregory of Tours, *DLH* 6.22 and 7.26). Besides fear of the sort of punishment inflicted on the unfortunate Charterius, Nicasius's decision no doubt was influenced by Angoulême's uncertain political status since the death of Chilperic a year earlier. Although Guntram had reclaimed the city, Gundovald's arrival raised the legitimate question of whether the king of Burgundy could seriously defend his claim. So, Nicasius took a risk and, after the collapse of Gundovald's campaign, predictably earned a reprimand by Guntram (Gregory of Tours, *DLH* 8.2).

On the same occasion, Guntram also vented his anger toward Bishop Antidius of Agen, whose *civitas* similarly had owed its allegiance to Chilperic until shortly before Gundovald's arrival, as well as toward two other bishops of Aquitanica Secunda, Palladius of Saintes, and his metropolitan Bertram of Bordeaux.[22] In possible contrast to Nicasius and Antidius, the latter of whom probably only recognized Gundovald's authority upon the pretender's arrival, the participation of Palladius and Bertram in the plot likely was prompted more out of free will than coercion (Bachrach 1994, pp. 99, 232–233 n. 49). Palladius, Gregory explicitly states, had proven habitually untrustworthy in his dealings with his royal master Guntram (*DLH* 8.2: "quod ei saepius fallacias intulisset"),[23] while Bertram, who actually was related to Guntram, had been Chilperic's intimate and loyal partisan (Halfond 2012c, pp. 61, 69). After Chilperic's death, Bertram shifted his allegiance to Gundovald, apparently with great enthusiasm if Gregory's account is to be believed: "At this time, while in the city of Bordeaux, Gundovald was highly esteemed by bishop Bertram" (*DLH* 7.31: "Erat tunc temporis Gundovaldus in urbe Burdegalensi a Berthramno episcopo valde dilectus").

Both Palladius and Bertram were implicated in the ordination of the presbyter Faustianus as bishop of Dax, on Gundovald's orders, in 585. The ordination was part of a coordinated effort by Gundovald to assert his *auctoritas* in *civitates* once claimed by Chilperic by invalidating the latter's *decreta*, including one appointing the *comes* Nicetius of Dax as bishop (Gregory of Tours, *DLH* 7.31). The task initially had been assigned to Bertram, who, rather than refusing to recognize the legitimacy of the ordination, conveniently claimed debilitating eye trouble, and reassigned the task to his suffragan Palladius (*DLH* 7.31). Guntram refused to believe that Palladius had been coerced in agreeing to perform the ceremony (Gregory of Tours, *DLH* 8.2).

What is not immediately clear is why Bertram, the metropolitan bishop of Bordeaux, should be assigned a task that under normal circumstances should have been the responsibility of the metropolitan bishop of Eauze. It has been suggested that Eauze temporarily lost its metropolitan status around this time (Longnon 1878, pp. 185–186, 589). However, there is no compelling evidence beyond this single event to suggest that a major ecclesiastical reorganization had taken place in the Aquitanian provinces. A better explanation for the absence of Bishop Laban of Eauze from the consecration of Faustianus was an unwillingness to align himself with Gundovald, who had seized Eauze from Guntram. Not all of his suffragans joined Laban in his boycott, however;

Orestes of Bazas was present at the consecration and quite possibly other former subjects of Chilperic's as well (Bachrach 1994, pp. 99–100).[24] Those bishops who attended had to answer to Guntram later for their tacit recognition of Gunovald's authority (Gregory of Tours, *DLH* 8.2, 8.20).

Among the episcopal collaborators of Aquitaine, Ursicinus of Cahors holds several distinctions. He is the only bishop known to have confessed his guilt in the plot, at least without claiming coercion as Palladius of Saintes had done (Bachrach 1994, p. 151). Additionally, his is the only *civitas* known to have been the residence of multiple ecclesiastics in league with Gundovald.[25] Ursicinus also was a fairly recent episcopal appointee compared to some of his fellow conspirators, having been ordained in the final years of Chilperic's reign (ca. 580), likely with the king's knowledge, if not necessarily on his orders (Gregory of Tours, *DLH* 5.42).[26] Finally, Ursicinus is the only bishop whom Gregory of Tours identifies as being punished specifically for the crime of formally receiving Gundovald into his *civitas*: "...for he confessed publically that he had welcomed Gundovald" (*DLH* 8.20: "... pro eo quod Gundovaldum excipisse publice est confessus").

By one estimate, Gundovald had claimed nearly twenty cities in Gaul (Rouche 1979, p. 72, carte 8); so, why should the bishop of Cahors have been singled out? It is, of course, quite possible that he was not singled out at all and that Gregory of Tours's account of the Council of Mâcon (585) is truncated, a possibility discussed in greater detail later in this chapter. Another possibility, however, is that Guntram intended Ursicinus's excommunication as a statement on the political status of the long-contested *civitas* of Cahors. In a relatively short span of time in the mid-sixth century, Cahors went through a rapid succession of royal masters (Longnon 1878, pp. 522–523; Rouche 1979, p. 497 n. 128). After the death of Chlothar I in 561, the *civitas* became part of the *regnum* of Paris, ruled by Charibert I. Upon Charibert's death, Chilperic claimed the city and included it in Galswinth's *morgengabe* shortly thereafter (on elite women, see James, Chapter 11, this volume). After Galswinth's murder ca. 570/571, her former brother-in-law Sigibert took the city. Chilperic fought to reclaim the *civitas* but only secured his claim following Sigibert's death in 575. Chilperic held Cahors until his own death in 584, after which Guntram claimed the *civitas*, only to lose it almost immediately to Gundovald. Even following Gundovald's death, Cahors's political status remained contentious. At Andelot in 587, Guntram agreed to give up the *civitas* to its "rightful" master, Sigibert's widow Brunhild. But the Treaty of Andelot was still two years away when Ursicinus was judged at the Burgundian Council of Mâcon for the crime of welcoming Gundovald. The royal convoker of the council, Guntram, knew, of course, that both Neustria and Austrasia harbored claims to the *civitas*. Thus, in orchestrating Ursicinus's excommunication, the king effectively accentuated his own right to Ursicinus's city.

In contrast to the aforementioned Aquitanians, Gregory only obliquely implicated Ferreolus of Limoges and Rufinus of Convenae. In the case of Ferreolus, Gregory reports that Limoges was Gundovald's first stop upon leaving his refuge in Avignon and where the royal pretender was declared king at the basilica of a certain "St. Martin" in Brives-la-Gaillarde. Gregory himself harbored some doubts about whether the occupant of the tomb was really a *discipulus* of his own similarly named patron saint. Apparently,

Ferreolus did not share these doubts and later had the basilica housing the tomb rebuilt following its destruction by Guntram's forces (*DLH* 7.10). In highlighting Ferreolus's devotion to a "pretender St. Martin" Gregory draws a parallel with the welcoming reception that Gundovald the royal pretender received at the pseudo-saint's shrine (Van Dam 1993, p. 136 n. 101). Furthermore, Gregory's account suggests that Gundovald did not face any serious local opposition in Limoges, which may explain the pretender's decision to make it his initial destination upon leaving Avignon as well as the site of his acclamation as king (Bachrach 1994, pp. 96; 231 n. 34). As the bishop of Limoges, another of the five *civitates* that once comprised Galswinth's *Morgengabe*, Ferreolus may very well have shared his colleague Ursicinus's Neustrian loyalties and thus have been reluctant to support Guntram's claim to the *civitas*. At the very least, he would have been aware that several monarchs were in competition for his city. Nevertheless, Gundovald's arrival would have pressured him to declare his allegiances.

Dramatic, albeit rather confusing, circumstances similarly compelled Rufinus of Convenae to act on his loyalties. Gregory describes a trick by Gundovald to seize the provisions of the *cives* of Convenae.[27] After advising the people to bring their food and supplies within the walls of the city, ostensibly to protect them from Guntram's army, Gundovald declared that enemy forces were in sight and the time to fight had come. Gundovald then shut the gates behind the departing *populus* with their (unnamed) bishop and seized their property. On the one hand, Gregory's narrative makes the poor bishop out to be a dupe of the wily Gundovald, implying perhaps that the pretender had been looking for a good excuse to rid himself of a local nuisance. But Rufinus does not fit comfortably the role of passive victim; Gregory's account is quite explicit in stating that the *cives* (and presumably their bishop) not only followed Gundovald's advice willingly to bring their provisions within the city walls (*DLH* 7.34: "Haec illis credentibus"), but were also prepared to fight on the pretender's behalf (Bachrach 1994, pp. 125, 130. 243 n. 20, 246 n. 37 and 41). Gundovald's duplicity certainly does not absolve Rufinus from his active participation in the ostensible defense of the *civitas* against Guntram's army.

This brief survey of Aquitanian bishops implicated in the Gundovald conspiracy thus confirms the earlier observation that necessity as much as political affinities motivated their choice to back the pretender. Most resided in occupied cities whose political allegiances were in dispute following Chilperic's death and in some cases had been the subject of decades of diplomatic and military maneuvering between the sons of Chlothar I. Chlothar II, whose very existence was at first unknown, simply was not in a position around 584/585 to defend Aquitanian civic and ecclesiastical interests or property. The position of his mother, Fredegund, during this period, similarly was precarious. Guntram, who had claimed most of these Aquitanian cities following Chilperic's death, had yet to prove his ability to reinforce his claims in the face of a significant military threat. Furthermore, for some of those bishops who had enjoyed congenial relations with the Neustrian monarchy, Guntram may have appeared as much a usurper as his putative brother, Gundovald. Gundovald, in contrast, may have seemed a viable, and possibly even legitimate, alternative. He claimed royal blood, he had the backing of some of the most powerful magnates in the *regnum Francorum*, and he had the military resources to occupy virtually the entirety of Aquitaine. Like his putative half-brothers, he presented himself to the Aquitanian bishops not as a persecutor, but rather as a potential friend and patron. For the bishops of occupied *civitates*, simply ignoring or waiting out Gundovald was not a serious option, and refusing to acknowledge his legitimacy constituted a huge personal and political risk. So, a significant number of Aquitanian bishops chose to cooperate with the pretender for the simple reason that circumstances seemed to require it.

Although necessity may have been a major force compelling these bishops to recognize Gundovald, their decision had serious implications not only for their personal safety, but also for episcopal collegiality and corporate solidarity in the aftermath of the failed conspiracy. Palladius of Saintes and Bertram of Bordeaux, for example, had a serious falling out after Guntram learned of their involvement. Although Palladius initially tried to shield his metropolitan from Guntram's wrath, he and Bertram, under the threat of royal punishment, ultimately resorted to accusing each other of various political and moral transgressions. Bertram even attempted to extract damning testimony from Palladius's own clergy (Gregory of Tours, *DLH* 8.7, 8.22).

Less dramatic, but perhaps even more divisive, was the Council of Mâcon (585), at which some, but possibly not all, of the episcopal collaborators were identified and penalized. Arrangements for the council, which assembled in late October 585, had begun at least as early as July (Gregory of Tours, *DLH* 8.5, 8.7), only a few months after Gundovald's death and the conclusion of the siege of Convenae. Although convoked on royal command, the council's *acta* stress the leadership role played by the provincial metropolitans, particularly Priscus of Lyon, at the meeting (Mâcon 585, *praefatio* and c. 20).[28] Among the fifty-four bishops and twelve clerical delegates in attendance, the bulk came from Provence and the Burgundian heartland. If we exclude the delegates present at the proceedings, the Aquitanian provinces were represented in all by sixteen bishops (including the deposed Faustianus of Dax), thus constituting slightly less than 30 percent of the total number of prelates in attendance. These sixteen bishops included all nine of the Aquitanian bishops implicated in the Gundovald conspiracy, of whom at least five—Faustianus, Bertram, Palladius, Orestes, and Ursicinus—were censured by the council.

It is unknown whether Antidius, Ferreolus, Nicasius, or Rufinus were ever formally censured by their episcopal colleagues at Mâcon or on another occasion. It perhaps is not surprising that Gregory of Tours—our source for the censures, which are not mentioned in the council's *acta*—should fail to mention if the council condemned Ferreolus and Rufinus, since the bishop of Tours had only indirectly alluded to their guilt. While Guntram had publicly questioned the loyalty of Antidius and Nicasius shortly before the council assembled (Gregory of Tours, *DLH* 8.2), he may have lacked the evidence to prove that they willingly had opened their cities to Gundovald, and thus he did not push for the council to penalize them. Despite his ire, Guntram was not reckless in pursuing vengeance. Gregory of Tours (*DLH* 8.20) suggests, in fact, that the king originally had planned to exile more bishops for their support of Guntram but was stricken with illness as divine punishment around the time of the council's assembly. Gregory implies that the king's recovery was due to his decision to forgo his original plan. In addition to the Aquitanians, the council absolved Theodore of Marseille, possibly as Guntram's good-faith gesture toward Childebert, to whom he had ceded his claim to Marseille the previous year and who was angered by Guntram's persecution of the bishop (Gregory of Tours, *DLH* 8.12–8.13).

So, while the council's actual prosecution of episcopal conspirators was selective and surprisingly lenient, the bishops at Mâcon nevertheless had the opportunity to address comprehensively the problem of episcopal involvement in the plot. Among the thirteen prelates implicated in the Gundovald affair by Gregory of Tours, only three were absent from the council: Egidius of Reims, who was not subject to Guntram's authority, and Bishops Epiphanius and Sagittarius of Gap, both of whom already were deceased at the time of the council's assembly. As already has been suggested, there is every reason to think that in prosecuting their colleagues tainted by their involvement in the Gundovald affair, the bishops at the council were carrying out the will of the king. Guntram, in fact, had sent to the council as his representative, the *dux* Leudegisel, who only several months earlier had directed the siege at Convenae (Gregory of Tours, *DLH* 8.20).

But might this have caused any discontent or division among the assembled bishops, the bulk of whom were put in the position of penalizing colleagues for what amounted to crimes against the state? Only Ursicinus, so far as we know, was penalized specifically for committing a treasonous act, possibly for the reasons suggested earlier. In contrast, the four bishops penalized for their involvement in the ordination of Faustianus were censured because they carried out the orders of Gundovald, who ostensibly lacked the royal authority to demand the ordination. In other words, the actions for which they were being punished were not against the state, but in violation of ecclesiastical standards. The fine they were obligated to pay was intended for Faustianus himself, not the royal fisc. Additionally, the assembled prelates may very well have been relieved that Guntram ceded to them the right to adjudicate cases involving their episcopal colleagues. The same council that stressed in several canons (cc. 9–10) the right of bishops to adjudicate cases involving members of their *ordo* or lower clerics was able to carry out the Burgundian king's judicial agenda without compromising (too obviously) its own stated canonical principles. The council's cooperation with the king similarly fulfilled Guntram's own expectation that bishops were to collaborate with royal officials in ensuring proper observance of the *canones et leges*.[29]

At the same time, however, the council subjected its Aquitanian attendees to the judgment of their colleagues, the bulk of whom never had been under any pressure (or even had the opportunity) to choose between royal masters. While maintaining the veneer of intra-ecclesiastical justice, the council effectively divided the assembled bishops based on their recent political affiliations and loyalties. Despite its geographically inclusive attendance, the Council of Mâcon only reemphasized that those bishops with whom Guntram most frequently and sociably collaborated had their sees in relative proximity to the Rhône River and Guntram's residence at Chalon-sur-Saône (Halfond 2012a). Owing to decades of royal partitions and competition in Aquitaine, most of the bishops of that region lacked their colleagues' intimacy with Guntram and his court. Some, as we have seen, may have maintained Neustrian sympathies even after Chilperic's death. Along with the more immediate disruptions caused by the Gundovald affair, one of its lasting effects was the accentuation of existing divisions among the Gallic episcopate along regional and political lines.

CONCLUSION

As the *acta* of the Frankish councils emphasized time and again over the course of the Merovingian period, the natural state of the church was *pax* (Halfond 2015). But the *pax ecclesiae*, which required episcopal *consensus*, was not always an easily achievable goal. Intraepiscopal conflict and factionalism were regular threats to the *unitas* and *tranquilitas* of the Church. *Pax* was often fleeting, and *consensus* less a stable reality than—in Emily Dickinson's words—a "thing with feathers." But both were consistent and integral components of episcopal solidarity and ideology in the Merovingian era, despite—or perhaps even because of—the frequency of conflicts and divisions within the episcopate. Ironically, the perpetual challenge of asserting corporate identity helped provide a real substance to this identity, as the prodigious conciliar activity of the Gallo-Frankish episcopate attests. Diverse and, perhaps on occasion, even somewhat drab as well, the bishops of Merovingian Gaul also were brothers who doggedly asserted their fraternal unity in the face of bitter estrangements, disruptive and sometimes violent conflicts, and the never-ceasing pressures of court and local politics.

NOTES

1. Claude 1963, p. 4, estimates that between 2,000 and 3,000 bishops held office between 507 and 751, citing Duchesne 1907–1915, who names approximately 1,000 bishops for this period. On these estimates, see also Patzold 2010, pp. 126–127; Patzold 2014b, pp. 183–184.
2. Rapp 2005 identifies pragmatic, spiritual, and ascetic authority as the bases for episcopal power over the course of Late Antiquity. On the growing significance of sanctity during the sixth century, see Diefenbach 2013.
3. On the ecclesiastical and political value of *consensus*, see Oehler 1961; Sieben 1979, pp. 103–70; Hannig 1982; Stocking 2000.
4. On the Gallic church as a federation, see Gaudemet 1985, p. 110. On the number of episcopal sees, see Claude 1963, p. 4.
5. German scholars have dominated the debate over the sources of Gallic bishops' civic authority. On *Bischofsherrschaft* or *bischöfliche Stadtherrschaft*, see Anton 1996, and Patzold 2005.
6. In reference to the *Passio Leudegarii I* 25, which claims that Bobo had been deposed from his see, Fouracre and Gerberding 1996, p. 241 n. 130, suggest that both Bobo and Diddo had been exiled by Childeric II, for which reason they despised Leudegar.
7. I would like to thank Dr. Jamie Kreiner for drawing my attention to the significance of this episode.

8. De Clercq 1963 is the standard edition of the Merovingian conciliar *acta*. All canonical references are to this edition.

9. For example, Orléans (538), c. 34; Tours (567), c. 16; Mâcon (581/583), c. 8; Mâcon (585), c. 12; Auxerre (561/605), c. 43; Clichy (626/627), c. 7; Chalon (647/653), c. 11.

10. This usage, however, is not given by Niermeyer et al. 2002, s.v. "Judex."

11. Cf. Orléans (549), c. 17.

12. On the structural weaknesses of the metropolitan hierarchy, see Ewig 1988, p. 105.

13. On the political values of *pax* and *disciplina*, see Murray 2001.

14. The bibliography of studies of the Gundovald affair is enormous. For studies written prior to the 1950s, see the works cited by Goubert 1941 and 1955. A crucial study is Goffart 1957, on which virtually all subsequent analyses, to varying degrees, depend. Subsequently published studies include Lizop 1963; Nonn 1990; Bachrach 1994; Zuckerman 1998; Widdowson 2008; Delaplace 2009; and Goffart 2012.

15. Cf. Kurth 1919, p. 286; Rouche 1979, p. 76; Bachrach 1994, p. 63; Dumezil 2008, pp. 263–264; Goffart 2012, p. 11

16. Cf. Bachrach 1994, p. 214 n. 3, who argues that Epiphanius the bishop should not be identified with the priest of Fréjus who attended the Council of Orléans (549) and that Epiphanius was more likely to be an Italian prelate. The evidence admittedly is inconclusive, although the association with the see of Fréjus still is routinely accepted: Pietri and Heijmans, 2013, p. 639 (Epifanius 4).

17. Additionally, Faustus of Auch is identified as a conspirator by Bachrach 1994, pp. 99, 130, 151, 232 n. 47, and 245 n. 35. While it is certainly possible that Faustus joined other former subjects of Chilperic in recognizing Gundovald's territorial claims in Aquitaine, Bachrach's suggestion (p. 232 n. 47) that Gregory's description of the end of Faustus's tenure in *DLH* 8.22 ("In loco Fausti Auscensis episcopi Saius presbiter subrogatur") implies that deposition is not entirely convincing, as Gregory uses similar language elsewhere in cases where deposition clearly did not occur (e.g., *DLH* 4.4). Bachrach 1994, pp. 99 and 101, also implicates Amelius of Bigorra on the evidence of *DLH* 8.28, which quotes a letter (possibly forged) accusing the bishop of serving as a secret envoy between Leuvigild and Fredegund. Somewhat more skeptical of a Visigothic connection is Goffart 2012, pp. 20–21.

18. In calculating these tallies, I have assumed that Epiphanius was the bishop of Fréjus.

19. Theuderic died prematurely in early 584. See Gregory of Tours, *DLH* 6.34–35.

20. On oaths of fidelity, see Esders 2012.

21. Angoulême originally may have been part of Guntram's share of Charibert's *regnum*; see Ewig, 1976, p. 139. Cf. Longnon, 1878, p. 553. If so, it almost certainly was captured by Chilperic's *dux* Desiderius in 581: Gregory of Tours, *DLH* 6.12. It is uncertain whether Nicasius was already in office at this point, as his predecessor died ca. 579/80; see Pietri and Heijmans 2013, pp. 1364–1365 (Nicasius 6). It is quite possible that he was a Chilperic appointee.

22. Like Angoulême, Agen originally had been part of Guntram's share of Charibert's *regnum*; see Longnon 1878, p. 549; Ewig 1976, p. 137 n. 113. It was captured by Chilperic's armies in 581 (Gregory of Tours, *DLH* 6.12).

23. Saintes had been part of Guntram's kingdom from AD 567 to 576, when it was captured by Chilperic's forces (Gregory of Tours, *DLH* 5.13). Palladius already was in office at this point.

24. On the city's prior allegiance to Chilperic, see Longnon 1878, p. 597.

25. Gregory of Tours, *DLH* 7.30 refers to an anonymous *abba Caturcinae* carrying secret messages on Gundovald's behalf along with another unnamed *clericus*. On this abbot, see Bachrach 1994, pp. 228–229 n. 17.

26. See also Council of Mâcon (585), *subscriptiones*, where Ursicinus's name appears below those of other bishops implicated in the plot.

27. On the city's prior allegiance to Chilperic, see Longnon 1878, p. 591.

28. See also Esders 1997, pp. 314–316. On the council's legislative program, see also Pontal, 1989, pp. 186–191.

29. An ideal expressed by Guntram in his edict: Boretius 1883, pp. 10–12. See also Heinzelmann 2001, pp. 184–189.

Works Cited

Ancient Sources

Capitularia regum Francorum. A. Boretius (ed.). (1883). *Capitularia regum Francorum*. MGH Leges 2.1. Hanover: Hahn.

Concilia Galliae: A.511–A.695. C. De Clercq (ed.). (1963). *Concilia Galliae: A.511–A.695*. CCSL 148A. Turnhout: Brepols.

Desiderius of Cahors, *Epistolae*. W. Gundlach (ed.). (1892). *Desiderii episcopi Cadurcensis epistolae*. MGH Epistolae 3 (pp. 191–214). Berlin: Weidmann.

Epistolae Austrasicae. W. Gundlach (ed.). (1892). *Epistolae Austrasicae*. MGH Epistolae 3 (pp. 110–153). Berlin: Weidmann.

Florentius, *Vita Rusticulae*. B. Krusch (ed.). (1902). *Vita Rusticulae sive Marciae abbatissae Arelatensis*. MGH SRM 4 (pp. 337–351). Hanover: Hahn.

Fredegar, *Chronica*. B. Krusch (ed.). (1888). *Chronica*. MGH SRM 2 (pp. 1–194). Hanover: Hahn.

Gregory of Tours, *Decem Libri Historiarum*. B. Krusch and W. Levison (eds.). (1937–1951). *Decem Libri Historiarum*. MGH SRM 1.1. Hanover: Hahn.

Liber Historiae Francorum. B. Krusch (ed.) (1888). *Liber Historiae Francorum*. MGH SRM 2 (pp. 215–328). Hanover: Hahn.

Passio Leudegarii I. B. Krusch (ed.). (1910). *Passiones Leudegarii episcopi et martyris Augustodunensis*. MGH SRM 5 (pp. 249–362). Hanover: Hahn.

Ruricius of Limoges, *Epistulae*. B. Krusch (ed.). (1887). *Epistulae*. MGH AA 8 (pp. 299–350). Berlin: Weidmann.

Die Urkunden der Merowinger. C. Brühl, T. Kölzer, M. Hartmann, and A. Stieldorf (eds.). *Die Urkunden der Merowinger*. Hanover: Hahn.

Walstra, G. J. J. (ed.). (1962). *Les cinq épîtres rimées dans l'appendice des formules de Sens*. Leiden: Brill.

Modern Sources

Anton, H. H. (1996). "'Bischofsherrschaften' und 'Bischofsstaaten' in Spätantike und Frühmittelalter. Reflexionen zu ihrer Genese, Struktur und Typologie." In F. Burgard (ed.), *Liber amicorum necnon et amicarum für Alfred Heit* (pp. 461–473). Trier: Verlag Trierer Historische Forschungen.

Bachrach, B. (1994). *Anatomy of a Little War: A Diplomatic and Military History of the Gundovald Affair (568–586)*. Boulder, CO: Westview Press.

Bailey, L. K. (2010). *Christianity's Quiet Success: The Eusebius Gallicanus Sermon Collection and the Power of the Church in Late Antique Gaul*. Notre Dame, IN: University of Notre Dame Press.

Brennan, B. (1992). "The Image of the Merovingian Bishop in the Poetry of Venantius Fortunatus." *Journal of Medieval History* 18(2): 115–139.

Brown, P. (2015). *The Ransom of the Soul: Afterlife and Wealth in Early Western Christianity.* Cambridge, MA: Harvard University Press.

Claude, D. (1963). "Die Bestellung der Bischöfe im merowingischen Reich." *Zeitschrift der Savigny-Stiftung für Rechtsgeschichte Kanonistische Abteilung* 49: 1–75.

Coates, S. (2000). "Venantius Fortunatus and the Image of Episcopal Authority in Late Antique and early Merovingian Gaul." *English Historical Review* 115(464): 1109–1137.

Delaplace, C. (2009). "'L'affaire Gundovald' et le dispositif défensif de l'Aquitaine wisigothique et franque." *Aquitania* 25: 199–211.

Diefenbach, S. (2013). "'Bischofsherrschaft.' Zur Transformation der politischen Kultur im spätantiken und frühmittelalterlichen Gallien." In S. Diefenbach and G. M. Müller (eds.), *Gallien in der Spätantike und Frühmittelalter: Kulturgeschichte einer Region* (pp. 91–152). Berlin: Walter de Gruyter.

Duchesne, L. (1907–1915). *Fastes épiscopaux de l'ancienne Gaule.* Paris: Albert Fontemoing.

Dumézil, B. (2008). *Brunehaut.* Paris: Fayard.

Esders, S. (1997). *Römische Rechtstradition und merowingisches Königtum. Zum Rechtscharakter politischer Herrschaft in Burgund im 6. und 7. Jahrhundert.* Göttingen: Vandenhoeck & Ruprecht.

Esders, S. (2012). "'Faithful believers.' Oaths of Allegiance in Post-Roman Societies as Evidence for Eastern and Western 'Visions of Community.'" In W. Pohl, C. Gantner, and R. Payne (eds.), *Visions of Community in the Post-Roman World, the West, Byzantium and the Islamic World, 300–1100* (pp. 357–374). Aldershot: Ashgate.

Ewig, E. (1976). "Die fränkischen Teilungen und Teilreiche (511–613)." In H. Atsma (ed.), *Spätantikes und fränkisches Gallien*, vol. 1 (pp. 114–171). Munich: Artemis.

Ewig, E. (1988). *Die Merowinger und das Frankenreich.* Stuttgart: W. Kohlhammer.

Fouracre, P. (2003). "Why Were So Many Bishops Killed in Merovingian Francia?" In N. Fryde and D. Reitz (eds.), *Bischofsmord im Mittelalter* (pp. 13–35). Göttingen: Vandenhoeck & Ruprecht.

Fouracre, P., and Gerberding, R. (1996). *Late Merovingian France.* Manchester: Manchester University Press.

Gaudemet, J. (1985). *Les sources du droit de l'Eglise en Occident.* Paris: Éditions du Cerf.

Goffart, W. (1957). "Byzantine Policy in the West under Tiberius II and Maurice: The Pretenders Hermenegild and Gundovald (579–585)." *Traditio* 13: 73–118.

Goffart, W. (2012). "The Frankish Pretender Gundovald, 582–585, A Crisis of Merovingian Blood." *Francia* 39: 1–27.

Goubert, P. (1941). "L'aventure de Gondovald et les monnaies franques de l'empereur Maurice." *Échos d'Orient* 39 (199–200): 414–457.

Goubert, P. (1955). *Byzance avant l'Islam, Tome Second: Byzance et l'Occident.* Paris: A. et J. Picard.

Gradowicz-Pancer, N. (2003). "Femmes royales et violences anti-épiscopales à l'époque mérovingienne Frédégonde et la meurtre de l'évêque Pretextat." In N. Fryde & D. Reitz (eds.), *Bischofsmord im Mittelalter* (pp. 37–50). Gottingen: Vandenhoeck & Ruprecht.

Halfond, G. (2010). *The Archaeology of Frankish Church Councils, ad 511–768.* Leiden: Brill.

Halfond, G. (2012a). "All the King's Men: Episcopal Political Loyalties in the Merovingian Kingdoms." *Medieval Prosopography* 27: 76–96.

Halfond, G. (2012b). "Charibert I and the Episcopal Leadership of the Kingdom of Paris (561–567)." *Viator* 43(2): 1–28.

Halfond, G. (2012c). "Sis quoque catholics religionis apex: The Ecclesiastical Patronage of Chilperic I and Fredegund." *Church History* 81(1): 48–76.

Halfond, G. (2014). "Negotiating episcopal support in the Merovingian kingdom of Rheims." *Early Medieval Europe* 22(1): 1–25.

Halfond, G. (2015). "War and Peace in the *acta* of the Merovingian Church Councils." In G. Halfond (ed.), *The Medieval Way of War: Studies in Medieval Military History in Honor of Bernard S. Bachrach* (pp. 29–46). Farnham: Ashgate Publishing.

Halsall, G. (2002). "Nero and Herod? The Death of Chilperic and Gregory's Writing of History." In K. Mitchell and I. Wood (eds.), *The World of Gregory of Tours* (pp. 337–350). Leiden: Brill.

Hannig, J. (1982). *Consensus fidelium*. Stuttgart: Anton Hiersemann.

Heinzelmann, M. (2001). *Gregory of Tours: History and Society in the Sixth Century*. Translated by C. Carroll. Cambridge: Cambridge University Press.

Hen, Y. (2012). "Changing Places: Chrodobert, Boba, and the Wife of Grimoald." *Revue belge de philologie et d'histoire* 89(2): 225–244.

Jussen, B. (1997). "Zwischen Römischem Reich und Merowingern." In P. Segle (ed.), *Mittelalter und Moderne. Entstehung und Rekonstruktion der mittelalterlichen Welt* (pp. 15–29). Sigmaringen: Thorbecke.

Jussen, B. (2001). "Liturgy and Legitimation, or How the Gallo-Romans Ended the Roman Empire." In B. Jussen (ed.), *Ordering Medieval Society: Perspectives on Intellectual and Practical Modes of Shaping Social Relations* (pp. 147–199). Translated by P. Selwyn. Philadelphia: University of Pennsylvania Press.

Kreiner, J. (2011). "About the Bishop: The Episcopal Entourage and the Economy of Government in Post-Roman Gaul." *Speculum* 86(2): 321–360.

Kurth, G. (1919). "La reine Brunehaut." In G. Kurth (ed.), *Études Franques* (pp. 1.265–1.336). Paris: H. Champion.

Lizop, R. (1963). "Herménégilde et Gondovald: Deux épisodes de la politique byzantine en Occident." *Revue de Comminges* 76: 134–140.

Longnon, A. (1878). *Géographie de la Gaule au VIe siècle*. Paris: Hachette.

MacCormack, S. (1972). "Change and Continuity in Late Antiquity: The Ceremony of *adventus*." *Historia* 21: 721–752.

Murray, A. (2001). "*Pax et disciplina*: Roman Public Law and the Merovingian State." In K. Pennington, S. Chodorow, and K. H. Kendall (eds.), *Proceedings of the Tenth International Congress of Medieval Canon Law* (pp. 269–285). Vatican City: Biblioteca Apostolica Vaticana.

Niermeyer, J. F., van de Kieft, C., & Burgers, J. W. J. (2002). *Mediae Latinitatis Lexicon Minus*. 2nd revised ed. Leiden: Brill.

Nonn, U. (1990). " 'Ballomeris Quidam': Ein merowingischer Prätendent des VI. Jahrhunderts." In E. Konsgen (ed.), *Arbor amoena comis* (pp. 35–39). Stuttgart: Franz Steiner Verlag.

Oehler, K. (1961). "Der Consensus Omnium als Kriterium der Wahrheit in der antiken Philosophie und der Patristik." *Antike und Abendland* 10: 103–129.

Patzold, S. (2005). "L'épiscopat du haut Moyen Âge du point de vue de la médiévistique allemande." *Cahiers de civilisation médiévale* 48: 341–358.

Patzold, S. (2010). "Zur Sozialstruktur des Episkopats und zur Ausbildung bischöflicher Herrschaft in Gallien zwischen Spätantike und Frühmittelalter." In M. Becher and S. Dick (eds.), *Völker, Reiche und Namen im frühen Mittelalter* (pp. 121–140). Munich: Wilhelm Fink.

Patzold, S. (2014a). "Bischöfe, soziale Herkunft und die Organisation lokaler Herrschaft um 500." In M. Meier and S. Patzold (eds.), *Chlodwigs Welt. Organisation von Herrschaft um 500* (pp. 523–543). Stuttgart: Steiner.

Patzold, S. (2014b). "Die Bischöfe im Gallien der Transformationszeit. Eine sozial homogene Gruppe von Amtsträgern?" In S. Brather, H. U. Nuber, H. Steuer, and T. Zotz (eds.), *Antike im Mittelalter. Fortleben, Nachwirken, Wahrnehmung* (pp. 179–193). Ostfildern: Thorbecke.

Patzold, S., and Walter, C. (2014). "Der Episkopat im Frankenreich der Merowingerzeit: eine sich durch Verwandtschaft reproduzierende Elite?" In S. Patzold and K. Ubl (eds.), *Verwandtschaft, Name und soziale Ordnung (300–1000)* (pp. 109–139). Berlin: Walter de Gruyter.

Pietri, L., and Heijmans, M. (2013). *Prosopographie de la Gaule chrétienne, 314–614.* Prosopographie chrétienne du Bas-Empire 4. Paris: Association des amis du Centre d'histoire et civilisation de Byzance.

Pontal, O. (1989). *Histoire des conciles mérovingiens.* Paris: Éditions du Cerf.

Rapp, C. (2005). *Holy Bishops in Late Antiquity: The Nature of Christian Leadership in an Age of Transition.* Berkeley: University of California Press.

Rouche, M. (1979). *L'Aquitaine, des Wisigoths aux Arabes, 418–781: Naissance d'une région.* Paris: L'École des hautes études en sciences sociales.

Shanzer, D. (2010). "The Tale of Frodebert's Tail." In E. Dickey and A. Chahoud (eds.), *Colloquial and Literary Latin* (pp. 376–405). Cambridge: Cambridge University Press.

Sieben, H. J. (1979). *Die Konzilsidee in der Alten Kirche.* Paderborn: Ferdinand Schöningh.

Stocking, R. L. (2000). *Bishops, Councils, and Consensus in the Visigothic Kingdom, 589–633.* Ann Arbor: University of Michigan Press.

Van Dam, R. (1993). *Saints and Their Miracles in Late Antique Gaul.* Princeton, NJ: Princeton University Press.

Wallace-Hadrill, J. M. (1983). *The Frankish Church.* Oxford: Clarendon.

Weidemann, M. (1982). *Kulturgeschichte der Merowingerzeit nach den Werken Gregors von Tours.* Mainz: Verlag des Römisch-Germanischen Zentralmuseums.

Widdowson, M. (2008). "Gundovald, 'Ballomer,' and the Problems of Identity." *Revue belge de philologie et d'histoire* 86(3): 607–622.

Wood, I. (1983). "The Ecclesiastical Politics of Merovingian Clermont." In P. Wormald, D. Bullough, and R. Collins (eds.), *Ideal and Reality in Frankish and Anglo-Saxon Society* (pp. 34–57). Oxford: Blackwell.

Wood, I. (1993). "The Secret Histories of Gregory of Tours." *Revue belge de philologie et d'histoire* 71(2): 253–270.

Wood, I. (1994). *The Merovingian Kingdoms: 450–751.* London: Longman.

Zuckerman, C. (1998). "Qui a rappelé en Gaule le ballomer Gundovald?" *Francia* 25: 1–18.

CHAPTER 14

PUBLIC HEALTH, HOSPITALS, AND CHARITY

PEREGRINE HORDEN

To his eternal lord and apostolic father, papa Desiderius, Gallus a sinner [writes]:

> Since such news is coming from Marseille about the plague, that it is ravaging and depopulating almost all of Provence, the lord bishop [Desiderius] should order guards to be sent [to ensure] that no one should presume to go out from the Cahors region to those fairs [coming up] in Rodez or neighboring cities, lest (God forbid), for whatever reason, such an evil should be seen to come into your city. For guards have been placed throughout the regions adjoining those parts so that no one should have any chance of buying or selling. If you will not ask them to make careful provision, the danger of death threatens. Moreover, sending greetings with due veneration, o lord and venerable father, I beg that you may think it worthy to remember our little self in your sacred prayers.   (Desiderius, *Ep.* 2.20)

Here is the entire text of a letter, from around the mid-seventh century, written by one Merovingian bishop to another. Desiderius was bishop of Cahors, Gallus bishop of Clermont. This chapter concerns such figures and their innovations in what we might call public welfare and poor relief (for more on their councils, see Halfond, Chapter 13, this volume). In the second part of the chapter, we meet the hospital as a form of poor relief still new to Europe in the Merovingian period. First, however, we shall examine the evidence for a notable public health initiative.

PUBLIC HEALTH

The letter just quoted *is* the evidence. It has a number of extraordinary features, not least its mere survival. Letters mostly come down to us because they were included in collections usually meant to show off style and to provide models of conduct (Sogno, Storin, and Watts 2017; see Gillett, Chapter 25, this volume). Yet this letter has very little style and no general ethical implications. It is found in the small letter collection of its recipient, Desiderius, bishop of Cahors from 630 to 655, not its writer, Gallus (II), bishop of Clermont (Mathisen 2017, pp. 349–350). Why Desiderius or his admirers included it is a matter to ponder, but its survival raises the question of whether it was typical of countless administrative letters that have been lost. As it is, the contents of the letter now *seem* unique (as are those of another letter, also concerned with movement, in which Desiderius requests safe passage for a priest from all ecclesiastical and public officials—a primitive passport: *Ep.* 2.8).

Gallus, almost 500 kilometers (300 miles) distant in Clermont-Ferrand, is aware of an epidemic (*clades*) widely ravaging Provence. It seems that guards, *custodes*, have already been posted by some authority on the frontiers of adjacent regions to hinder movement (presumably of peasants or merchants) to and from market. Yet there are fairs upcoming at Rodez, just over 100 kilometers (70 miles) from Cahors and elsewhere. Desiderius should see to it (*ordinet*) that similar guards are sent out, apparently not just to the perimeter of the city, but to the frontiers of the province or diocese (the *Cadurcinum*, not merely the city of *Cadurca*: Durliat 1979, pp. 238–239). The purpose is to stop people from making a round trip to Rodez, thus bringing the epidemic disease back with them to Cahors—which they will do if Desiderius does not make adequate provision, joining up his officials with those already stationed and putting them on high alert. Although some details are obscure, the general sense of the request is clear.

When cited by historians, this letter is usually recruited simply as evidence of bubonic plague in the early Middle Ages (Biraben and Le Goff 1969; although see McCormick 2007, p. 311). Its special features have been neglected. Historians view the mortality referred to as belonging to one of the repeated waves of the plague of Justinian. Perhaps it was, but there are no other attestations of serious epidemic in western Europe from the period of Desiderius's episcopacy. The episode falls between widespread epidemics of the 580s and the 660s. Still, the report of this epidemic and the response to it can be interpreted in the light of plague literature of the time. The measures urged by Gallus were intended to prevent the transmission of the disease by the movement of people and goods.

That might be thought surprising. In the medical world of the time, broadly, diseases were held to arise from miasma, corrupt air. Divine dispensation lay behind the original appearance of such miasmata. Then, however, the disease would spread according to very general circumstances (human and natural) on the one hand and the varying susceptibility of individuals at risk on the other. There was seemingly no concept resembling modern notions of infection or contagion (Stearns 1974; Conrad and Wujastyk 2000). Hence, the saying later attributed to Desiderius's near contemporary, the Prophet Muhammad (of whose military impact he may have been aware: Woudhuysen forthcoming). The saying was *lā ʿadwā*, no contagion, even though, as the Bedouin had always known, it was conceded that mange could spread from sick to healthy camels. By apparent contrast, in the mother of all plague descriptions, Thucydides had noted, a millennium earlier, that in the plague of Athens those caring for the sick, especially the doctors, rapidly succumbed. In his version of interpersonal transmission, they died like sheep, having become "filled with disease," *anapimplamenoi*, by the sufferers they were visiting (*History* 2.47, 51). Procopius, chronicling the reign of Justinian, took Thucydides as his literary model. Yet in his vivid account of the plague's ravages in Constantinople in 542, he asserted that neither doctors nor anyone else attending the sick contracted the disease through touch (*Wars* 2.22). Contemporary historians of plague such as Procopius knew that the diseases moved around the world following lines of human contact, and were often evident in ports before spreading inland. Describing the arrival at Marseille in 588 of a wave of the epidemic, Gregory of Tours used the word *contagio* for it, although not in a precise medical sense. He noted that a ship from Spain put in "with the usual kind of cargo, unfortunately bringing with it the tinder [or source: *fomes*] of this disease" (*DLH* 9.22). Many citizens purchased items from the cargo and a whole household of eight people was left empty, all having perished from the "contagion." In this passage in his *Histories*, Gregory goes on to give a strikingly accurate depiction of the stuttering progress of a new outbreak of bubonic plague, *yersinia pestis*. He displays a sound lay understanding of the ways in which a disease could be spread by the movement of goods and people. Such an understanding did not contradict the idea of plagues as diffused miasma. There were micromiasmas, local pockets of corrupt air, in bales or containers or under peoples' clothes and on their breaths.

It would seem to be an obvious measure against the spread of plague to limit that movement of possibly infected goods and people, not least because of the risk that those fleeing an infected city (Gregory of Tours, *DLH* 6.33) were taking the disease with them. But, so far as we can tell, neither in the late Roman world nor in Gregory's time was any such public health measure enacted. The local deployment of guards revealed in the letter of Gallus to Desiderius is the sole surviving example. In the various writings of Gregory of Tours, for example, the collective remedies for plague are religious: fasts, vigils, processions, or calling upon saints who might divide the space of a city up between them in order to achieve blanket protection (Horden 2000, pp. 19–21). Another Gallus, an earlier bishop of Clermont (from 525 to 551) safeguarded his city with the processions called "rogations" when plague first hit Gaul in 543 (Gregory of Tours, *VP* 6.5). As plague approached the region, mysterious signs in the form of a "tau" (T-shaped) cross reportedly appeared on the doors of churches and houses, including the house of Gregory's own mother (Gregory of Tours, *GM* 50; *DLH* 4.5). We should resist the temptation to compare these premonitory marks with the ones made by "searchers" on households known to harbor plague in the early modern period. Yet the measures urged by the second Bishop Gallus do seem to prefigure those introduced in the wake of the Black Death. In Pistoia in 1348, for example, the Council forbade entrance to the city of *materia infirmitatis*, people or goods bearing the sickness. Only authorized communication was to be held with Lucca and Pisa, both of them already in the grip of epidemic. Gatekeepers enforced these rulings (Carmichael 1986, pp. 108–109). It is hard to say why measures that seem obvious in retrospect were not adopted more quickly, and why there are apparently no examples of them from the early medieval pandemic other than that already quoted. Those with power did not see it as part of their remit to confront divine providence. They did not want to second-guess the movements of miasmas or to challenge the household as the proper place of care and healing for the smitten. These generalizations may be part of the explanation (Nutton 2000, p. 161). But they cannot be the whole of it since they would apply with almost as much force in the fourteenth century as in the seventh.

If a unique or at least a very unusual experiment in plague control were to have emerged anywhere in early medieval Europe, Merovingian Gaul would have been a conducive setting. Bishops had become the local leaders of their communities (Prinz 1974; Diefenbach 2013). They represented the interests of the locality in the turbulent politics of the court (Wickham 2005, p. 176). The king normally had a count as his man on the spot (see Hen, Chapter 10, this volume). But the bishop was the magister factotum. The seventh-century Gallus of Clermont is a shadowy figure, even in a diocese so otherwise richly documented (Wood 1983). Desiderius, by contrast, appears to us as the "go-to" bishop for public works as well as public health. Hence, in another letter in his collection, to yet another bishop of Clermont, Gallus II's predecessor Caesarius, Desiderius asks his colleague to send him specialist craftsmen, who can make the wooden pipes necessary for the subterranean water conduit the city so desperately needs and which he is constructing. He does this neither because of authority delegated by or usurped from king or count (Fouracre 2005, pp. 383–384) nor because he has access to church funds as bishop—but because he is wealthy in his own right.

The best evidence for this is the *Life* of him (*Vita Desiderii*) composed a long while later, probably in the ninth century, but from contemporary documents in local archives (Durliat 1979; Mathisen 2013; Woudhuysen, forthcoming). His family may not have been old money but his parents were quite rich, with land in the region of Albi. Born in or around 600, he spent his adolescence at the court of Chlothar II along with his two brothers. One brother took charge of the royal chapel and then left to be bishop of Cahors; the other held regional office in Albi and then Marseille (on cities, see Loseby, Chapter 27, this volume). Desiderius stayed at court as treasurer. Royal patronage flowed through his hands, and he could have enhanced his personal resources considerably. Then came the *annus horribilis* of 629. His brother in Marseille died. The other, after seven or more years as bishop of Cahors, may have been caught in the politicking between the new king, Dagobert, and his half-brother and was murdered—by some of his own flock. Dagobert took revenge on the city and brutally asserted his power there. Desiderius left the dangerous world of the court and succeeded his brother as bishop of Cahors, although he was not yet in holy orders, formally appointed by Dagobert on Easter Day 630. We have to assess Desiderius as bishop against this fraught personal and local background. We also have to bear in mind the repeated devastation to which Cahors had been subject at several points in the preceding century (Gregory of Tours, *DLH* 4.48–50). No forerunner of Thomas Becket, Desiderius remained the king's man on his unplanned installation as bishop. He lived in some style, seemingly not on easy terms with either populace or clergy. Yet he appeased them, if the twenty-two years of his episcopate are any guide, and he thwarted potential opposition with a massive building program (Rey 1953). Apart from establishing a new palace for himself, he saw to the city walls. He founded a monastery. He built or restored a number of basilicas and country churches. He enhanced the property of the Church and left it, thanks to his bequests, as probably the largest landowner in the region: one of the great "manager bishops" of the age (Brown, 2012, p. 496). In all this, he was preparing "eternal rewards" for himself. But he also laid up treasure in heaven, his Carolingian biographer reports, with more usual forms of piety: looking after his household and his clergy, and distributing goods from his table to paupers and pilgrims (*Vita Desiderii* 2. 21, 26, 27, 33).

Desiderius was not unique in his public works. We see bishops of the sixth and seventh centuries bolstering their positions as local leaders by taking thought for aqueducts and fortifications, dams, and flood-prevention measures, as well as by looking to the economy (Prinz 1974; Horden 2000). No one else is known to have tackled plague, however. There, Desiderius and his correspondent Gallus are apparently unique. It was a period of prosperity in Aquitaine, perhaps because epidemic mortality in the sixth century had raised living standards for the survivors on the land (Rouche 1979). The problems Desiderius faced were those of prosperity, of people moving between fairs. These people were more likely traders and consumers, not rootless beggars.

Hospitals

Would those measures have made any difference? It is unlikely, for two reasons. First, there was no apparent extension of the network of control. Second, historians of the early modern period still debate whether such measures helped end the early modern wave of European epidemics in the 1720s (Slack 1981). We are not, on Merovingian evidence, likely to be able to do any better. Still, we might tentatively allow the Merovingian age some credit in the history of public health efforts and especially responses to epidemics. That age has another claim to attention. It marks the beginnings of hospital foundations, in significant numbers, in western Europe. If we take hospitals as institutions providing designated space for the overnight care of the poor and sick—charitable institutions essentially—then the remote ancestors of those hospitals that were regular features of European society into the nineteenth century are predominantly Merovingian.

That is a large claim. I shall try to substantiate it, first by giving some of the background to Merovingian beginnings, and then as a parallel to the discussion of Desiderius, by opening up more general arguments through a single detailed example. Hospitals as just defined originated in the Byzantine world, in Constantinople and parts of Anatolia, in the middle of the fourth century, during the reign of Constantius II (337–361) (Brown 2002, pp. 33–38; Horden 2012). They were no simple reflex response to urban poverty or to epidemic sickness. Nor were they a straightforward outgrowth of Judeo-Christian charity. They originated at a time when the Christian Church was established and growing rich. The enrichment happened increasingly during the second half of the century. It came not only from the benefactions of wealthy converts, but also from the immunities and tax exemptions enjoyed by the clergy. These were intended by Constantine and his son Constantius to give churchmen the time and the resources to devote themselves to praying for the empire—and to serving the poor. The hospital has been attractively interpreted as a visible expression of the latter purpose, a conspicuous expenditure to justify the special treatment (Brown 2002, pp. 29–32; 2012, pp. 43–44; Corbo 2006).

Even if there was more to it than that, the larger point stands. The hospital is not an obvious solution to the problems of the needy. It is an idea, not a reflex; an idea that arises in only specific circumstances and that is reinvented or transmitted in only specific circumstances. Once the hospital idea has been invented in this sense in the Byzantine East, we can trace its transmission both around the Middle East and westward around the Mediterranean and into northern Europe (Horden 2005). But the movement is very slow and does not always follow predictable paths. We know of few such foundations in North Africa. Before the sixth century, there seem to have been only a handful in Italy, mostly in or near Rome, from around the year 400 onward (Stasolla 1998; Arcuri 2006, pp. 223–224). In Gaul, in this respect, even less happens until circa 500. Then one hospital in particular emerges blinking into the light of the evidence.

The hospital founder is Caesarius (b. 469/470). He was bishop of Arles from 502 until his death in 542 when, as it happened, the Justinianic Plague was just beginning to ravage Byzantium. The foundation is reported by some of those who knew him well, in a hagiography written within seven years of his death (Klingshirn 1994a, 1994b, pp. xi–xvi).

> He [Caesarius] had a very great concern for the sick and came to their assistance. He granted them a most spacious house (*spatiosissima domus*) in which they could listen undisturbed to the holy office [being sung] in the basilica (*basilicae opus sanctum*). He set up beds and bedding, provided for their expenses, and supplied a person to take care of them and heal them.
>
> (*Vita Caesarii* 1.20, trans. Klingshirn 1994b, modified)

Assuming its broad veracity, the passage prompts several immediate observations. First, here is a hospital for the sick. We can assume they were the poor sick, not those who could afford the personal administrations of a doctor. This is partly because, second, the bishop supplied someone to care and heal (*obsequi et medere*) but not, or not explicitly, a doctor, a *medicus*, who would presumably have been more expensive. Third, this seems to be a place for overnight accommodation. That is what marks out a hospital as I am defining it here from a charitable distribution center. And good accommodation it is. The comfort of bedding (*lectuaria*) was worth mentioning, not to be taken for granted. Fourth, there is a making over of space, perhaps considerable space. Exactly what it is that has been designated, however, is not quite clear to the bishop's biographers. They have no special word for it. This is at the least a very early Christian hospital in Gaul; quite possibly, it is the first. The biographers have not yet added to their lexicon the Greek loan word *xenodochium*, which will become the usual term for this sort of welfare facility.

Finally, there is the liturgical aspect of the hospital: its position close enough to (presumably) the cathedral church of St. Stephen for the sound of the singing to carry. Before beds and bedding and care and healing comes liturgy. The patients need to be able to listen to this liturgy "undisturbed," to give it the fullest attention that their health permits. It was a conception of hospital priorities with a long future.

But it already had a past as well. Basil of Caesarea's hospital in that city is the first Christian hospital of Late Antiquity that is at all well-documented. Basil both established a place where the sick might receive medical attention, not necessarily from self-styled doctors, and he was alert to the therapeutic effects on the soul of psalmody (Horden 2001). Caesarius stands squarely within the Basilian tradition. Like Basil, too, he was happy to call upon several different kinds of healing.

This pluralism is evident from the course of his career. Caesarius joined the monastery of Lérins. Sacked as cellarer—a position that might bear some resemblance to running a hospital—for withholding customary supplies, he gave himself up to a regime of Egyptian austerity that included eating once a week and singing psalms (*Vita Caesarii* 1.6). The regime induced a periodic (quartan) fever, a symptom of general debilitation. Not surprisingly, there was no doctor on the island. Quite surprisingly, Caesarius was forced by his abbot to leave the monastery and go on a rest cure. He went to Arles, where there were reputable doctors to whom he presumably resorted (Avitus of Vienne *Ep.* 11, 2002, p. 358). (In one of Caesarius's posthumous miracles, quartan fever would be reckoned to fall within the province of secular doctors except in the very worst cases: *Vita Caesarii* 2.41.) The move to Arles set him on the path to his bishopric. Once bishop, he made sure that his clerics sang the full complement of hours in the cathedral church, in Greek or Latin, for the benefit of the laity, who were to join in (1.15, 19). He even expected peasants to learn psalms for recitation or singing in the fields—the way they learned the latest love song, he said, oblivious to protest (Klingshirn 1994a, pp. 93, 184–185). It must have seemed natural to his biographers to place a paragraph on psalmody immediately before their report of the hospital.

Caesarius did not disparage secular medicine. Doctors could be dissolute, expensive, and ineffectual (*Vita Caesarii* 1.50; Caesarius, *Sermon* 5). On the whole, however, in his sermons he endorsed medicine, first, very traditionally, as a model of how the pastor adjusts penances and advice to the needs of the individual sinner (1.17), and second as an "upright art" that could achieve acceptable results, provided it was not mixed with magic (Flint 1989; see also Klingshirn, Chapter 41; Kornbluth, Chapter 40, this volume). This was of course not to place the sources of the medical knowledge of these self-styled doctors on a level with Christ and his saints. The ultimate recourse of the sick should be to the latter. The sick should "run to church," receive the sacraments, be anointed with holy oil, and ask priests and deacons to pray over them (Klingshirn 1994a, p. 162; Caesarius, *Sermon* 19.5). They were not encouraged to get to the hospital, we note, presumably because the hospital was selective in its admissions and wanted exemplary patients who had attended to the needs of their souls first.

The hospital was a place of charity as well as healing. The bishop's biographers placed their report of it immediately in the context of a range of other charitable activity:

He did not deny to captives and the poor the place and opportunity to make requests. He regularly used to tell his attendants, "see whether any of the poor are standing at the door, afraid and ashamed because of their poverty, lest for the sake of my own convenience and as a result of my own sinfulness they suffer any harm while waiting."   (*Vita Caesarii* 1.20)

The implication is that the poor congregated at the entrance to the bishop's house, and some at least were what later ages would call "shamefaced," those of means fallen on hard times and embarrassed to stand around among the regular indigent.

The *Life of Caesarius* sets out for us, in a sequence doubtless too tidy to be accurate, but revealing of essentials, the steps by which he came to found his hospital. First, he met some powerful exemplars of charitable activity. Upon arrival in Arles, Caesarius seems to have entered the circle of two aristocrats who, instead of living a life of luxury, "transferred their resources to paradise for themselves by bringing relief to the poor" (*Vita Caesarii* 1.8). By this stage in the Christian West, it was well established that almsgiving, along with fasting, penance, and above all the offering to God of the Eucharist, atoned for sins (Brown 2015). These two laypeople were followers of the priest Julianus Pomerius, an émigré from Vandal North Africa, now also resident in Arles. He outlined a program for the ideal reforming bishop that combined a similar rejection of the aristocratic lifestyle in favor of a monastic one and that placed great emphasis on pastoral activity as well as on using the wealth of the church to feed the hungry, clothe the naked, protect the poor from their oppressors, and ransom captives (Klingshirn 1994a, pp. 75–82; Brown 2012, p. 485, 2015, p. 130). We can observe Caesarius carrying out much of this program, not least ransoming captives—in plentiful supply thanks to the wars between Franks, Burgundians, and Goths that swirled round Arles (Klingshirn 1985). Captives filled the churches and even clogged the bishop's own house. They were given food and clothing until their freedom could be purchased (*Vita Caesarii* 1.32, 37). This largesse won respect and privileges for his church. In a passage in the Life that immediately follows the first mention of his ransoming, Caesarius is shown as gaining a subvention for the activity from Alaric II of the Visigoths, then master of the region. He also gains from Alaric perpetual immunity of his church from taxation. This passage in the Life is of questionable authenticity (Klingshirn 1994b, p. 19). But that Caesarius really did secure some such immunity is supported by a reference to it in his own will (*Testamentum* 8: Klingshirn 1994b, p. 74). And we might associate the extra revenue accruing from the immunity as having something to do with the hospital as well as with the ransoming: both were forms of conspicuous expenditure. Charity, however, could be highly contentious. Like Desiderius later, Caesarius faced considerable opposition from his clergy, who, among other things, did not like his expenditure of church plate on barbarian "unbelievers" (*Vita Caesarii* 1.32). He clearly stretched church wealth to the limit. Only by a miracle were his granaries refilled so as to meet the competing and seemingly insatiable needs of captives and local poor (*Vita Caesarii* 2.8–9; Brown 2012, p. 512).

To found a hospital for the sick was not, therefore, an obvious or straightforward use of church property or personnel. It required a particular decision, responsive to a variety of competing local priorities and interests. That is why the idea of the hospital spread slowly. We can see how this idea might have occurred to Caesarius in Arles with its mixed population of Latin and Greek speakers and its Mediterranean connections to Italy and the Byzantine world (Klingshirn 1994a, pp. 172–173).

Where did it spread next? The next clearly attested location is, not surprisingly, up the Rhône at Lyon (McCormick 2001, pp. 77–80, 357–359 for pilgrimage routes). What is more striking is that the initiative for the foundation should have been royal, not episcopal. Childebert I of the Franks and his queen Ultrogotha set up, in Lyon, a *xeno-dochium* (the Greek term for hospital, or at least a version of it, has quickly become familiar). They did so around the time of Caesarius's death. We have this on good authority. When the fifty bishops and twenty-one priests and deacons gathered at Orléans for the fifth church council to be held there (*Concilia*), they recorded the hospital in one of their canons (15): "Concerning the *exenodocio* [*sic*] which the most pious King Childebert and his wife and queen Ultrogotha have founded in Lyon through divine inspiration." They went on to confirm its constitution and to guarantee, from an interfering bishop, the security of the endowment and the alms that the hospital could enjoy thanks to its royal benefactors. The king had summoned the council to express and strengthen his hold over this part of his kingdom. He and his queen, unusually prominent in the evidence of this period, had noticed the support for the needy that a hospital could provide as a suitable manifestation of the piety that God had inspired in them. Though of royal origin, the hospital remains an ecclesiastical institution, run by priests, under church law. It is still a new type of entity in Gaul, requiring the weight of collective episcopal oversight to protect its resources from predators: the founders take nothing for granted. Anyone who appropriates its endowment so that it can no longer function is a killer of the poor (*necator pauperum*). This now established formula for lending an aura of untouchability to church wealth had already been deployed in a preceding canon of the council, in which, significantly, the hospital is set alongside church and monastery as a free-standing type of religious house for the "poor" with legal personality (Paxton 2001, pp. 259–261; Brown 2012, p. 508). In canon no. 15, any such murderer will be struck with perpetual anathema. Like the hospital of Caesarius, its task is the care of the sick (*cura aegrotantium*). But it is also for the reception of pilgrims (*exceptio peregrinorum*). How far the two groups overlapped or differed—local sick, poor strangers?—we cannot now say. The only safe generalization is that all were seen as being in some sense poor—and all Christians are on a pilgrimage in this world.

As the chronology moves to the middle of the sixth century, the obvious question is: what about Tours, seat of Gregory, the bishop whose writings on miracles, medicine, and poverty do so much to shape our perception of the earlier Merovingian world? An oblique reference to poor houses of some kind, *hospitiola pauperum*, is our only indication of a hospital in Gregory's or anyone else's writings about Tours in this period (Gregory of Tours, *VM* 2.27). Only once, it seems, does the word *xenodochium* or any variant of it appear in Gregory's history or hagiography, and that is not in this passage. Other forms of charity are of course attested. For example, at her nunnery in Tours, there was the saintly Monegund dispensing "salutaria medicamenta" (effective medication) to the sick, after praying over them (Gregory of Tours, *VP* 19.3). In Gregory's Miracles of St. Martin (*VM*), the context is the depredation of Roccolen, one of the Frankish King Chilperic's men. He besieged Tours laying waste the city and its suburban estates, the revenues of which supported the "houses of the church" (*domus ec[c]lesiae*) (one of which, outside the city his men tore apart) as well as the poor houses (see also Gregory of Tours, *DLH* 5.4), leaving them without any hope of supplies. If that is the correct translation of *hospitiola*, then once again, as in Lyon, a tight connection is being drawn between a hospital and its endowment. There is still the alternative that the *hospitiola pauperum* are individual homes of poor people supplied or fed by the church. Gregory uses *hospitiolum* to mean personal dwelling a number of times in his works. Overall, whatever arrangements he may have made for looking after local poor and pilgrims in need, he did not, in his own city, explicitly adopt the "hospital idea" himself.

Not that he failed to recognize it elsewhere. In two places, Gregory writes of Agricola, bishop of Chalon-sur-Saône from 532 to 580, an ascetic aristocrat responsible for many building projects in his city including a lavishly decorated cathedral (Gregory of Tours, *DLH* 5.45). The first of these occurs in one of Gregory's miracle books. He tells the story of Desideratus, a reclusive monk in a house some 35 kilometers (21 miles) away from Chalon, who had been a priest in the city. He accomplished the healing of "toothaches and other illnesses" through his prayer. When he died, Bishop Agricola wanted to have him interred in a city cemetery, but the monks resisted, not wanting to lose one of their stars and the cult he might inspire. So a compromise was struck. "Having built an *exsinodochium* for lepers in a suburb [of the city], and having gathered the abbots and the entire clergy in its church," he transferred the blessed body there and buried it "with utmost respect" (Gregory of Tours, *GC* 85).

Here, then, is the first clearly recorded instance of a Gallic leper hospital (Sternberg 1991, pp. 167–174; Miller and Nesbitt 2014, pp. 121–123). Leprosy was a relatively new disease in western Europe in the early Middle Ages. And of course, in its most extreme (lepromatous) form, it was very striking. Lepers made good inmates. They were the poorest of the poor, the most visibly afflicted, the clearest sign of the outreach of ecclesiastical charity, the ones whose prayers for the souls of their benefactors would be the most effective. Those who, biblically, should dwell "outside the camp" (Lev. 13.46) now found themselves outside the walls. But perhaps that was for convenience as much as for symbolism—they were in a location where they would be able to solicit alms from passersby. The hospital had its own church, represented as big enough for a gathering of monks and priests. As in the hospital of Caesarius, the lepers could hear the liturgy. How had Agricola come across the "hospital idea"? He was present at the Council of Orléans in 549 and knew all about the royal hospital foundation. Canon 21 of that Council, whose proceedings he subscribed, enjoined all priests and all faithful to look after the poor, especially the leprous: when the bishop found that anyone in his diocese, not just the city, had contracted the disease, he should meet their need for food and clothing from his own household. Agricola took the means of provision a stage further. An additional stimulus might have been that Chalon was the hometown of Caesarius and his family, and they remembered his Arles hospital there.

The connection with Arles may also be important to the vivid, if brief, depiction by the poet–bishop Venantius Fortunatus of the ministrations of the saintly Radegund (d. 587) (*Vita Sanctae Radegundis*). The daughter of a Thuringian king, she was in effect abducted by a Frankish ruler, Chlothar I, and taken to a Merovingian villa at Athies, a few miles south of Péronne in Picardy (see Coon, Chapter 46; James, Chapter 11, this volume). There Radegund built what has been considered the first house we come across specifically for needy women. Beds were elegantly made up for them. "She herself washed them in warm baths, curing the putrescence of their diseases." But she also washed men (the alternative reading in one of the manuscripts of "the living," *vivorum* rather than *virorum*, makes little sense here) and gave them a potion of her own mixing to revive those weak from sweat (men worn out by their labors?). "The mistress of the palace was a servant of the poor" (Venantius Fortunatus, *Vita Sanctae Radegundis* 12). But perhaps the men got outpatient care, not beds. Such care was certainly instanced at other points in her biography. And when Radegund and her abbess Agnes came to regulate their nunnery in Poitiers, they looked to Arles and the house of Caesaria, sister of Caesarius, for an exemplar (Sternberg 1991, p. 221).

Having taken the hospital of Caesarius as a starting point, from near the start of the Merovingian period, I will mention only one further example, from a much later time. This is for the interest of how the report of it is worded. In early 676, Praeiectus, bishop of Clermont-Ferrand for the preceding decade, was murdered on a journey back to his see from the court of Childeric II. The story of his martyrdom, his *passio*, was written up soon after the event. It tells us that he established a *xenodochium* "in propriis rebus," with his own resources (that is, presumably, not the church's) "having followed in the manner of the easterners" (*orientalium more secutus*). He had doctors "or attentive male orderlies" (*medicos vel strenuos viros*) in attendance to provide care to twenty sick men who would each vacate their places once they had recovered (*Passio Praeiecti* 16). This is a rare reference to patient turnover. Yet more remarkable is the reference to eastern, which must mean Byzantine, models (see Esders, Chapter 16, this volume). What was "Byzantine" about this in the late seventh century? The idea of the hospital was no longer new, so that its oriental derivation hardly needed stressing. Was it the use of private property—not in fact an especially Byzantine mode of endowment? Or was it the doctors, although as we have seen that was hardly new either? Perhaps the author of the *Passio* was simply unfamiliar with a project of this kind.

There is no need to pursue the spread of the hospital idea further in this way. We can generalize. First, there is the question of numbers. Sternberg (1991, pp. 287–290) provided ample supporting material for a database of thirty-four places in which Merovingian hospitals may have been founded. That gives a total number of institutions in the forties. I do not think the years since 1991 have added significantly to the tally, whether from online textual evidence or epigraphy or archaeology. Indeed, the total should probably be deflated. Sternberg himself is doubtful about some entries in his own catalogue, which are based on inadequate evidence. If we went further, we might omit from the reckoning those hospitals attested only in much later and probably unreliable texts and those to which the references are ambiguous. Doing so would reduce the number of places by about half. That may be too severe, but on either reckoning the total is small. It is small in both absolute and relative terms. Counting medieval hospitals has been a scholarly pastime since 1680 when Du Cange published his *Constantinopolis Christiana*. A more recent tabulation for the capital finds thirty-one *xenones* and hospitals and twenty-seven old people's homes (Janin 1969, pp. 552–567). A survey for the provinces of the Byzantine Empire, from the fourth to the mid-ninth century, yields a total of over 160 charitable facilities of various kinds, of which the most numerous are *xenodocheia* and *xenones* (seventy-one), *nosokomeia* or houses for the sick (forty-four), and *ptocheia* or poorhouses (twenty-one) (Mentzou-Meimare 1982). Anderson's more general survey of the late and post-Roman world for the fourth to seventh century (2012) includes 282 foundations that can be identified with relative confidence. Compare that with around 300 leper hospitals founded in England between the Norman conquest and about 1350 (Rawcliffe 2006, pp. 106–107) and over 1,000 hospitals and almshouses opened between 1350 and 1600 (McIntosh 2012, p. 69). However we view it, the Merovingian yield of between twenty and forty seems meager.

Of course, while there is a danger of inflating the number of hospitals because some were very shortlived, or the supposed documentation for them is misleading, there is surely a countervailing likelihood that others went unrecorded. There were several hundred monasteries in Merovingian towns, rising from around 220 in about the year 600 to around 550 by circa 700 (Wood 2013, p. 41). A number of monasteries in our documented pool came to have *xenodochia* attached (Sternberg 1991, p. 293). It is implausible that they were the only ones. Similarly, there were some 130 bishoprics in Merovingian Gaul (Wood 2013, p. 41). Bishops form the majority of the founders in the securely evidenced cases, but that is mostly because they were canonized. Only some eighty saints' Lives survive from the Merovingian period, covering at best a tiny proportion of what must have been a total of over 2,000 Merovingian bishops (Wood 2013, p. 44; on hagiography, see Kreiner, Chapter 24, this volume). Some of these could also have run hospitals.

Speculation about unrecorded hospitals could slide into special pleading. Whatever allowances we make for the vagaries of documentation, the numbers were still small. Even so, those vagaries make it hard to generalize. It would be interesting, for example, to see where, if anywhere, hospitals were more prevalent. Sternberg's total pool shows several along the Rhône Valley, as is to be expected if the hospital idea spread from Arles. There may have been a significant clustering between the Seine and the Meuse. Skeptically cutting the number of hospitals by half blurs that distribution.

A more secure general observation is that the hospitals we know about seem to fall within a distinct period. I have not taken the space to review the evidence that has sometimes been adduced for hospitals in Gaul earlier than that of Caesarius. It will suffice to report that the evidence is weak, which is to be expected if we recall that there were apparently very few hospitals anywhere in the West before 500 outside papal Rome and its immediate region. At the other end of the Merovingian age, in the eighth century, hospital foundation seems to have withered. This could have arisen from the dwindling of resources in the age of Charles Martel, whose secularizing of church property may have been extensive and damaging (Wood 2013). Or it might have been a by-product of the deurbanization of the nascent Carolingian world, hospitals being primarily urban institutions. Whatever its causes, there is something of a gap in the history of hospitals from the late Merovingian period until the ninth century and the Carolingian "reform" (Sternberg 1991, pp. 298–301).

Within this distinctive period, of the sixth and seventh centuries, who were the founders? They were royal, including royal women, members of the lay aristocracy, bishops and monks, or nuns. Among the examples that we know most about, the bishops who predominated tended to be those with experience at court (Sternberg 1991, pp. 292, 296). The history of hospitals illustrates the convergence of interests and pious ambitions between bishops, Gallo-Frankish aristocrats, and Merovingian kings that scholars have identified from other vantage points (McKenzie 2012). The hospitals are usually individual foundations. There do not seem to have been more than one or two hospitals in a city at any one time—although seven contemporaneous ones were claimed for Le Mans in older scholarship (Sternberg 1991, pp. 234–243) and twelve hospitals (*bis sena xenodochia*) were attributed to one Attolus in an inscription recorded by Flodoard of Reims in the tenth century (p. 245). Were these in actuality twelve cells within a single hospital? Merovingian hospitals were small, intended for an apostolic twelve, or sixteen (twice the sacred eight) or eighteen patients. They did not display any of the concern to identify particular constituencies such as the aged or the blind that we encounter in the Byzantine world. They were all very much of a piece, although sickness might be privileged more in one hospital than in another.

Before we are too hard on them and characterize these "cottage hospitals" as merely boutique establishments (Brown 2015, p. 173), we need to recall that they represented only one choice among several possibilities for the disbursement of resources. In Gaul, the choice was perhaps not very constrained. The wealth of churches and religious houses, enhanced by tithes and the offerings of the faithful, and further enlarged by bequests, became very substantial indeed in the Merovingian world; one of the richest bishops owned land perhaps as big as half a modern *département* (Wood 2007, p. 228). By the eighth century, some 30 percent of Francia may have been in church hands. Still, there were many calls on this wealth. Even though all of it might be labeled the "patrimony of the poor" as a way of trying to protect it (Brown 2012, pp. 507–508), the poor could not have it all. Resources were needed, after all, for the building and upkeep of churches and monasteries, staging and lighting the liturgy, and the personnel, of course. And the share of "the poor"? According to a ruling of Pope Simplicius in 465 for Italian churches, a quarter of episcopal income was supposed to be devoted to the poor (Sternberg 1991, p. 36; Rapp 2005, pp. 216–217). But was this or any similar ruling observed in Italy and elsewhere? And who were "the poor"? There was a growing tendency to erase the boundary between (on the one hand) clergy and monks, the *voluntary* poor, and (on the other hand) the economically deprived, the *involuntary* poor. Even leaving clerical and monastic ranks out of account, contemporary representations of lay poverty were highly ambiguous, blending social and economic categories. Agreed, the poor in question were Christians and not Jews, the free and not slaves. Yet were these poor the truly destitute, or the larger stratum of those whose livelihoods were at risk (the "laboring poor" as later centuries would call them), or the yet larger one of all who lacked power and the great wealth that made power possible?

Merovingian categories are not our categories. We put founding or funding churches or monasteries in one category, as a work of piety, and doing the same for a hospital in another, as a work of poor relief. But in the sixth or seventh century it was long established that both were good works that would benefit the donor's soul in the hereafter: both were gifts to God (Brown 2012, p. 42). When he was in Paris as a moneyer and goldsmith at the court of Chlothar II and then Dagobert (see Strothmann, Chapter 35, this volume), Eligius, bishop of Noyon and Tournai (d. 660), first engaged in ransoming captives, according to a Life probably written soon after his death by a friend (Audoin, *Vita Eligii* 10). He next founded and endowed a monastery (15). He then "thought to build a *xenodochium* in Paris" (17); but "on taking more excellent advice, and with Divine inspiration, he began to build, in his own house, which he had received in the same city as a gift from the king, a house for virgins of Christ"—a nunnery to match his monastery, not a hospital. We cannot know exactly why. It is not clear that Paris already had a hospital, which might make a second one seem unnecessary (Sternberg 1991, pp. 272–273). We can, on the other hand, be reasonably confident that no one thought the saint was in any way betraying the poor or misusing royal patronage. He was simply, as with the monastery, "raising a ladder" by which he and the king might both climb to heaven (Audoin, *Vita Eligii* 15).

This is a reminder that the chief beneficiary of a hospital was the founder and not the patient. To lament the incapacity of small hospitals to satisfy the very needy poor and sick is in some ways anachronistic. Even so, there were many ways of paying attention to their needs. Bishops had choices to make: along the spectrum of possible gifts to God, and along that of poor relief. Desiderius, with whom we began this chapter, apparently did not run a hospital. Nor did some other yet greater names across the late antique world: neither Augustine nor Ambrose, to look no further. But all bishops owed a duty of hospitality, especially hospitality to the poor, at the front doors of their residences. Unless he has received everyone, Jerome had said in his commentary on Titus 1:8, a bishop is *inhumanus* (*PL* 26, col. 568A). The bishop's house should receive everyone without exception, repeated the bishops of the Council of Macon in 585, tellingly adding that the bishops should not keep dogs that might bite supplicants (c. 13). We saw Caesarius's house thronged by captives. Desiderius had two priests to offer food and drink to strangers.

Perhaps Desiderius's limited, stage-managed provision was nearer the norm. The church preferred its poor in small, carefully vetted groups, not uncontrolled throngs (Brown 2012, p. 512). "That each city feed its poor and indigent inhabitants with suitable food according to its resources, and the priests of each village [*vicani presbyteri*] and all citizens should nourish their poor [*suum pauperem*]. This is to be done so that the poor do not wander off to cities elsewhere" (Tours [567], c. 5; compare Orléans [511], c. 16 in

Concilia Galliae: A.511–A.695). The conciliar decree hints at a role for parish priests in poor relief of which very little other documentation survives, but which might have been growing in the Merovingian period as the number of parishes grew (Brown 2012, p. 520). It also more clearly points to a desire to discourage refugees or economic migrants (presumably as distinct from pilgrims).

The clearest expression of this urge to control is what might be another Merovingian institution to set beside the hospital. That is the *matricula*—except that the *matricula* is best considered not as an institution but simply as what the Latin word means, a "list"— in this case, a list of the approved poor. On it were the worthy local beggars, perhaps of good family but sunken socially, named and registered, able-bodied enough to haunt the church atrium or perhaps even in a hospital-like house of their own—and, since they were unemployed and available, perhaps taking on minor duties at the shrine or elsewhere within the church. Although historians have tended too often to see the *matricula* as a singular institution with a monastic ancestry in Egypt and Italy, it is essentially just a regulated "outdoor relief," performed on a much smaller scale in some Merovingian towns than it had been in the great cities of Byzantium (Sternberg 1991, ch. 3; Brown 2002, pp. 65–66; Finn 2006, pp. 74–75; Dey 2008; Jones 2009; Brown 2012, p. 510). Some might have had a specific endowment; but the *matricula*, unlike the hospital, is not mentioned in Merovingian conciliar decrees as a type of institution. Those on the list could, however, at times develop a sense of corporate identity, in the assertion of which they might be unruly, sometimes brutal:

> As we brothers, in God's name [A–B], who are known to belong to the *matricula* of Saint C, and whom Almighty God is seen to feed there through the donations of Christians, found a new-born child there, who did not yet have a name, and as we were unable to find his parents among all the people, we therefore agreed unanimously, and following the wish of the priest named D, keeper of relics, that we should sell this child to the man named E; which we did. And we received for this, as is the custom among us, one third [of his value] along with a meal.
>
> (*Formulae Andecavenses* no. 49)

They could not keep the child themselves, and the law allowed them to sell it and pocket some of the proceeds—hence the preservation of this model document in the earliest Merovingian collection of legal *formulae* (see Rio, Chapter 23, this volume).

CHARITY AND THE CONTEXT OF POVERTY

The vignette illustrates the limits to Merovingian poor relief. Inmates of a *xenodochium* were perhaps a well-chosen set of paupers comparable to those on the *matricula*. We might guess that they were not physically capable of full-time begging. Their role was to embody the Church's reaching out to the margins: the physically disabled, the sick, the elderly, and the transient—the *xenoi* of the *xenodochium*, strangers of the approved kind in need of a roof over their heads, pilgrims and refugees, not vagabonds. Perhaps they did not stay in the hospital as long as some beggars on the *matricula* who might camp out in the atrium of a church.

Both groups, hospital inmates and *matricularii*, were small, select subgroups of a larger population of those vulnerable to chronic or intermittent hardship. With regard to that larger pool and about the extent to which their needs were met, it is almost impossible to generalize. The two largest sectors of charity to the involuntary poor were private individual almsgiving or acts of kindness and the more egalitarian help of poor friends, neighbors, or relatives. We can gain some ideas of the first through such materials as the sermons of Caesarius, though that is, of course, prescriptive rather than descriptive (Filippov 2010). And we can derive images of both the strengths and the failings of "horizontal" poor relief from vignettes in hagiography, especially, for our period, that of Gregory of Tours (e.g., *VM* 2.24, 4.14). But none of this evidence allows quantification. Assessing the impact on the levels and types of poverty of the wider social and material environment involves yet more conjecture. The Merovingian period was one of climatic deterioration across Europe, a wetter regime unfavorable to agriculture, changing settlement patterns, predatory landlords, and frequent political dislocation (Devroey 2003; Cheyette 2008). To the chronically depressive effect on the population of endemic diseases, malaria foremost among them (Newfield 2017), we must add the deeper impact of waves of plague. On the one hand, it is easy to compile catalogues of wars, floods, and epidemics (human and animal: Newfield 2015), and to imagine the outcome of these for poor families—families probably small and thus vulnerable to what historical demographers have called nuclear hardship (Laslett 1988). On the other hand, if this is a plague-ridden period at all analogous to the later fourteenth and fifteenth centuries in Europe, then those who survived might have found themselves in a world of improved opportunities, with more land available and landlords on the back foot. The cities that form the setting for almost all the hospitals and *matriculae* were very likely small, often with a total population of only a few thousand (Liebeschuetz 2001, pp. 83–88). These will not have witnessed sudden influxes of migrants that they could not absorb. A comparison with another premodern period and place may help. The poor relief measures of early modern England were probably the most comprehensive in Europe. And among small towns the most sophisticated system of relief that we know about belonged to Hadleigh in Suffolk, its population between 2,500 and 3,300. Hadleigh's system supported between 5 and 10 percent of its population; say, on average, 300 people (McIntosh 2013). That is a good measure of poverty in the town. Was such a level of relief *wholly* beyond the various, quite unsystematic, institutions of Merovingian cities?

The Church was good at providing schemes—the *xenodochium*, the *matricula*—for small-scale local relief aimed at carefully selected recipients. And at least sometimes, it was good in a crisis. Recall the throngs of captives in Caesarius's house, or the measures to contain plague that Desiderius and others may have implemented. It was the middle ground between these extremes, inhabited by the "laboring poor," that the church tended to ignore. It did come into contact with such people, but as landlord, not almsgiver (Sarris 2011, pp. 3–8). It was the largest nonroyal landowner in any of the Merovingian kingdoms. The pressure of ecclesiastical or monastic lordship must be factored into any reckoning of Merovingian welfare. A final vignette, then: the peasants tied to some land that an ascetic missionary, Thrutpert (or Trudpert), had been given in the Black Forest at some point in the seventh century were worked so hard by the holy man that one of them, diabolically inspired, murdered him while he was dozing. The Christian landlord as martyr (*Passio Thrutperti* 5). If the story is legendary, it is nonetheless all too plausible.

Works Cited

Ancient Sources

Audoin, *Vita Eligii*. B. Krusch (ed.). (1902). *Vita Eligii episcopi Noviomagensis*. MGH SRM 4 (pp. 663–741). Hanover: Hahn.

Avitus of Vienne. D. Shanzer and I. Wood (trans.). (2002). *Avitus of Vienne: Letters and Selected Prose*. Liverpool: Liverpool University Press.

Caesarius of Arles, *Sermons*. M.-J. Delage (ed. and trans.). (1971–1986). *Césaire d'Arles: Sermons au peuple*. Source chrétiennes 175, 243, and 330. Paris: Éditions du Cerf.

Concilia Galliae: A.511–A.695. C. De Clercq (ed.). (1963). CCSL 148A. Turnhout: Brepols.

Concilia Galliae: A.511–A.695. J. Gaudemet and B. Basdevant-Gaudemet (eds. and trans.). (1989). *Les canons des conciles mérovingiens (VIe-VIIe siècles)*. Sources Chrétiennes, 353–354. Paris: Cerf.

Desiderius, *Ep*. W. Gundlach (ed.). (1892). *Desiderii episcopi Cadurcensis epistolae*. MGH Epistolae 3. Berlin: Weidmann.

Desiderius, *Ep*. D. Norberg (ed.). (1961). *Epistulae S. Desiderii Cadurcensis*. Stockholm: Almqvist and Wiksell.

Desiderius, *Ep*. St. Gallen, Stiftsbibliothek Cod. Sang. 190 (manuscript of *Epistolae*). Retrieved from http://ww:.e-codices.unifr.ch/en/list/one/csg/0190.

Formulae Andecavenses. K. Zeumer (ed.). (1986). MGH Legum 5. Hanover: Hahn.

Formulae Andecavenses. A. Rio (trans.). (2008). *The Formularies of Angers and Marculf: Two Merovingian Legal Handbooks*. Liverpool: Liverpool University Press.

Gregory of Tours, *GC*. B. Krusch (ed.). (1885/1969). *De gloria confessorum*. MGH SRM 1.2 (pp. 294–370). Hanover: Hahn.

Gregory of Tours, *GC*. R. Van Dam (trans.). (1988). *Glory of the Confessors*. Liverpool: Liverpool University Press.

Gregory of Tours, *GM*. B. Krusch (ed.). (1885/1969). *De gloria martyrum*. MGH SRM 1.2 (pp. 34–111). Hanover: Hahn.

Gregory of Tours, *GM*. R. Van Dam (trans.). (1988). *Glory of the Martyrs*. Liverpool: Liverpool University Press.

Gregory of Tours, *DLH*. B. Krusch and W. Levison (eds.). (1951). *Decem libri historiarum*. MGH SRM 1.1. 2nd ed. Hanover: Hahn.

Gregory of Tours, *VM*. B. Krusch (ed.). (1885/1969). *De virtutibus sancti Martini*. MGH SRM 1.2 (pp. 134–211). Hanover: Hahn.

Gregory of Tours, *VM*. R. Van Dam (trans.). (1993). *Saints and Their Miracles in Late Antique Gaul* (pp. 200–303). Princeton, NJ: Princeton University Press.

Gregory of Tours, *VP*. B. Krusch (ed.). (1885/1969). *De vita patrum*. MGH SRM 1.2 (pp. 211–294). Hanover: Hahn.

Gregory of Tours, *VP*. E. James (trans.). (1985). *Gregory of Tours. Life of the Fathers*. Liverpool: Liverpool University Press.

Jerome, *Commentary on the Epistle to Titus*. J.-P. Migne (ed.). (1845). *Commentariorum in Epistolas Paulinas ad Galatas, ad Ephesios, ad Titum, ad Philemonem*. In *PL* 26. cols. 555–600. Paris.

Klingshirn, W. E. (ed.). (1994b). *Caesarius of Arles: Life, Testament, Letters*. Liverpool: Liverpool University Press.

Passio Praeiecti episcopi. B. Krusch (ed.). (1910). MGH SRM 5 (pp. 225–248). Hanover: Hahn.

Passio Thrudperti martyris Brisgoviensis. B. Krusch (ed.). (1902). MGH SRM 4 (pp. 357–363). Hanover: Hahn.

Procopius, *Wars*. H. B. Dewing and G. Downey (eds. and trans.). (2014). *Procopius, History of the Wars*. Loeb Classical Library. Cambridge, MA: Harvard University Press.

Thucydides, *History*. C. F. Smith (ed. and trans.). (2014). *History of the Peloponnesian War*. Loeb Classical Library. Cambridge, MA: Harvard University Press.

Venantius Fortunatus, *Vita Sanctae Radegundis*. B. Krusch (ed.). (1888). MGH SRM 2 (pp. 364–395). Hanover: Hahn.

Venantius Fortunatus, *Vita Sanctae Radegundis*. J. A. McNamara, J. E. Halborg, and E. G. Whatley (trans.). (1992). *Sainted Women of the Dark Ages* (pp. 70–86). Durham, NC: Duke University Press.

Vita Caesarii Arelatensis. G. Morin (ed.) and M. J. Delage (trans.). (2010). *Vie de Césaire d'Arles*. Paris: Éditions du Cerf.

Vita Desiderii Cadurcae urbis episcopi. B. Krusch (ed.). (1902). MGH SRM 4 (pp. 563–602). Hanover: Hahn.

Vita Desiderii Cadurcae urbis episcopi. Bibliothèque nationale de France, MS. Lat. 170002, ff. 207r–217v, digital facsimile retrieved from http://gallica.bnf.fr/ark:/12148/btv1b52500999h

Modern Sources

Anderson, M. (2012). "Hospitals, Hospices and Shelters for the Poor in Late Antiquity." Unpublished doctoral dissertation. New Haven, CT: Yale University, New Haven.

Arcuri, R. (2006). "Modelli di evergetismo regale nella Gallia tardoantica: L'istituzione di xenodochia pauperibus et peregrinis tra V e VII secolo." In R. Marino, C. Molè, and A. Pinzone, with M. Cassia (eds.), *Poveri ammalati e ammalati poveri* (pp. 197–222). Catania: Prisma.

Biraben, J.-N., and Le Goff, J. (1969). "La peste dans le Haut Moyen-Age." *Annales* 24: 1484–1510.

Brown, P. (2002). *Poverty and Leadership in the Later Roman Empire*. Hanover, NH: University Press of New England.

Brown, P. (2012). *Through the Eye of a Needle: Wealth, the Fall of Rome, and the Making of Christianity in the West, 350–550 AD*. Princeton, NJ: Princeton University Press.

Brown, P. (2015). *The Ransom of the Soul: Afterlife and Wealth in Early Western Christianity*. Cambridge, MA: Harvard University Press.

Carmichael, A. G. (1986). *Plague and the Poor in Renaissance Florence*. Cambridge: Cambridge University Press.

Cheyette, F. L. (2008). "The Disappearance of the Ancient Landscape and the Climatic Anomaly of the Early Middle Ages: A Question to Be Pursued." *Early Medieval Europe* 16: 127–165.

Conrad, L., and Wujastyk, D. (eds.). (2000). *Contagion: Perspectives from Pre-Modern Societies.* Aldershot: Ashgate.

Corbo, C. (2006). *Paupertas: La legislazione tardoantica (IV-V sec. d. C.).* Naples: Satura.

Devroey, J.-P. (2003). *Economie rurale et société dans l'Europe franque (VIᵉ-IXᵉ siècles).* Paris: Belin.

Dey, H. W. (2008). "Diaconiae, xenodochia, hospitalia and monasteries: 'Social security' and the meaning of monasticism in early medieval Rome." *Early Medieval Europe* 16: 398–422.

Diefenbach, S. (2013). "'Bischofsherrschaft': Zur Transformation der politische Kultur im spätantiken und frühmittelalterlichen Gallien." In S. Diefenbach and G. M. Müller (eds.), *Gallien in Spätantike und Frühmittelalter: Kulturgeschichte einer Region* (pp. 91–149). Berlin: Walter de Gruyter.

Durliat, J. (1979). "Les attributions civiles des évêques Mérovingiens: L'exemple de Didier, Évêque de Cahors (630–655)." *Annales du Midi* 91: 237–254.

Filippov, I. (2010). "Les élites et la richesse à Arles à l'époque de Saint Césaire." In J.-P. Devroey, L. Feller, and R. Le Jan (eds.), *Les élites et la richesse au Haut Moyen Âge* (pp. 183–220). Turnhout: Brepols.

Finn, R. D. (2006). *Almsgiving in the Later Roman Empire: Christian Promotion and Practice (313–450).* Oxford: Oxford University Press.

Flint, V. (1989). "The Early Medieval 'Medicus', the Saint—and the Enchanter." *Social History of Medicine* 2: 127–145.

Fouracre, P. (2005). "Francia in the Seventh Century." In P. Fouracre (ed.), *The New Cambridge Medieval History, I: c.500–c.700* (pp. 371–396). Cambridge: Cambridge University Press.

Horden, P. (2000). "Ritual and Public Health in the Early Medieval City." In S. Sheard and H. Power (eds.), *Body and City: Histories of Urban Public Health* (pp. 17–40). Aldershot: Ashgate.

Horden, P. (2001). "Religion as Medicine: Music in Medieval Hospitals." In P. Biller and J. Ziegler (eds.), *Religion and Medicine in the Middle Ages* (pp. 135–153). Woodbridge, NY: Boydell and Brewer.

Horden, P. (2005). "The Earliest Hospitals in Byzantium, Western Europe, and Islam." *Journal of Interdisciplinary History* 35: 361–389.

Horden, P. (2012). "Poverty, Charity, and the Invention of the Hospital." In S. F. Johnson (ed.), *The Oxford Handbook of Late Antiquity* (pp. 715–743). Oxford: Oxford University Press.

Janin, R. (1969). *La géographie ecclésiastique de l'empire byzantin* 1.3: *Les églises et les monastères,* 2nd ed. Paris: Institut français d'études byzantines.

Jones, A. E. (2009). *Social Mobility in Late Antique Gaul: Strategies and Opportunities for the Non-Elite.* Cambridge: Cambridge University Press

Klingshirn, W. E. (1985). "Charity and Power: Caesarius of Arles and the Ransoming of Captives in sub-Roman Gaul." *Journal of Roman Studies* 75: 183–203.

Klingshirn, W. E. (1994a). *Caesarius of Arles: The Making of a Christian Community in Late Antique Gaul.* Cambridge: Cambridge University Press.

Laslett, P. (1988). "Family, Kinship and Collectivity as Systems of Support in Pre-Industrial Europe: A Consideration of the 'Nuclear-Hardship' Hypothesis." *Continuity and Change* 3: 153–175.

Liebeschuetz, J. H. W. G. (2001). *Decline and Fall of the Roman City.* Oxford: Oxford University Press.

Mathisen, R. W. (2013). "Desiderius of Cahors: Last of the Romans." In S. Diefenbach and G. M. Müller (eds.), *Gallien in Spätantike und Frühmittelalter: Kulturgeschichte einer Region* (pp. 455–469). Berlin: Walter de Gruyter.

Mathisen, R. W. (2017). "The Letter Collection of Ruricius of Limoges." In C. Sogno, B. K. Storin, and E. J. Watts (eds.), *Late Antique Letter Collections: A Critical Introduction and Reference Guide* (pp. 337–356). Berkeley: University of California Press.

McCormick, M. (2001). *Origins of the European Economy: Communications and Commerce AD 300–900*. Cambridge: Cambridge University Press.

McCormick, M. (2007). "Toward a Molecular History of the Justinianic Pandemic." In L. K. Little (ed.), *Plague and the End of Antiquity: The Pandemic of 541–750* (pp. 290–312). Cambridge: Cambridge University Press.

McIntosh, M. K. (2012). *Poor Relief in England, 1350–1600*. Cambridge: Cambridge University Press.

McIntosh, M. K. (2013). *Poor Relief and Community in Hadleigh, Suffolk 1547–1600*. Hatfield: University of Hertfordshire Press.

McKenzie, A. (2012). "Model Rulers and Royal Misers: Public Morality among the Merovingian Aristocracy." In C. Kosso and A. Scott (eds.), *Poverty and Prosperity in the Middle Ages and Renaissance* (pp. 1–24). Turnhout: Brepols.

Mentzou-Meimare, K. (1982). "Eparchiaka evage idrymata mechri tou telous tes eikonomachias." *Byzantina* 11: 243–308.

Miller, T. S., and Nesbitt, J. W. (2014). *Walking Corpses: Leprosy in Byzantium and the Medieval West*. Ithaca, NY: Cornell University Press.

Newfield, T. P. (2015). "Human-Bovine Plagues in the Early Middle Ages." *Journal of Interdisciplinary History* 46: 1–38.

Newfield, T. P. (2017). "Malaria and Malaria-Like Disease in the Early Middle Ages." *Early Medieval Europe* 25: 251–300.

Nutton, V. (2000). "Did the Greeks Have a Word for it? Contagion and Contagion Theory in Classical Antiquity." In L. Conrad and D. Wujastyk (eds.), *Contagion: Perspectives from Pre-Modern Societies* (pp. 137–162). Aldershot: Ashgate.

Paxton, F. S. (2001). " 'Oblationes Defunctorum': The Poor and the Dead in Late Antiquity and the Early Medieval West." In K. Pennington, S. Chodorow, and K. H. Kendall (eds.), *Proceedings of the Tenth International Congress on Medieval Canon Law* (pp. 245–267). Vatican: Biblioteca Apostolica Vaticana.

Prinz, F. (1974). "Die Bischöfliche Stadtherrschaft im Frankenreich vom 5. bis zum 7. Jahrhundert." *Historische Zeitschrift* 217: 1–35.

Rapp, C. (2005). *Holy Bishops in Late Antiquity: The Nature of Christian Leadership in an Age of Transition*. Berkeley: University of California Press.

Rawcliffe, C. (2006). *Leprosy in Medieval England*. Woodbridge: Boydell.

Rey, R. (1953). "Un grand bâtisseur au temps du roi Dagobert: S. Didier, évêque de Cahors." *Annales du Midi* 65: 287–294.

Rouche, M. (1979). *L'Aquitaine des Wisigoths aux Arabes, 418–781: Naissance d'une région*. Paris: Editions de l'Ecole des hautes études en sciences sociales.

Sarris, P. (2011). "Restless Peasants and Scornful Lords: Lay Hostility to Holy Men and the Church in Late Antiquity and the Early Middle Ages." In P. Sarris, M. Dal Santo, and P. Booth (eds.), *An Age of Saints? Power, Conflict and Dissent in Early Medieval Christianity* (pp. 1–10). Leiden: Brill.

Slack, P. (1981). "The Disappearance of Plague: An Alternative View." *Economic History Review* 34: 469–476.

Sogno, C., Storin, B. K., and Watts, E. J. (eds.). (2017). *Late Antique Letter Collections: A Critical Introduction and Reference Guide.* Berkeley: University of California Press.

Stasolla, F. R. (1998). "A proposito delle strutture assitenziali ecclesiastiche: gli xenodochi." *Archivio della Società Romana di Storia Patria* 121: 5–45.

Stearns, J. K. (1974). *Infectious Ideas: Contagion in Premodern Islamic and Christian Thought in the Western Mediterranean.* Baltimore: Johns Hopkins University Press.

Sternberg, T. (1991). *Orientalium more secutus: Räume und Institutionen der Caritas des 5. bis 7. Jahrhunderts in Gallien.* Münster: Aschendorff.

Wickham. C. (2005). *Framing the Early Middle Ages: Europe and the Mediterranean 400–800.* Oxford: Oxford University Press.

Wood, I. (1983). "The Ecclesiastical Politics of Merovingian Clermont." In P. Wormald, with D. Bullough and R. Collins (eds.), *Ideal and Reality in Frankish and Anglo-Saxon England: Studies Presented to J. M. Wallace-Hadrill* (pp. 34–57). Oxford: Blackwell.

Wood, I. (2007). "Review Article: Landscapes Compared." *Early Medieval Europe* 15: 223–237.

Wood, I. (2013). "Entrusting Western Europe to the Church, 400–750." *Transactions of the Royal Historical Society* 23: 37–73.

Woudhuysen, G. (forthcoming). "The First Western View of Islam?"

CHAPTER 15

MEROVINGIAN MONASTICISM
Voices of Dissent

ALBRECHT DIEM

A first encounter with Theo Kölzer's monumental *Merowingerurkunden*—an edition that includes all the extant royal charters dated to the Merovingian period—might cause alarm for anyone interested in learning more about Merovingian royal monastic foundations.[1] Among the first seventy-nine documents, there are just six originals (all for the monastery of Saint-Denis) and two interpolated charters. The rest are forgeries. And, with the exception of the charters of Saint-Denis, not one of the royal privileges, legal transactions, or donations for monastic communities issued in the first six generations of Merovingian rule is genuine. King Sigibert III (d. 656) issued the first possibly authentic foundation charters between 643 and 648 for the monasteries of Cugnon and Stavelot-Malmedy, followed by a donation of King Chlothar III (d. 673) to Montier-la-Celle (658/659) and an exemption for Corbie (661) (Kölzer 2001, vol. 1, nos. 80–81, 92, 96). Only after the mid-seventh century do we see a slowly growing stream of genuine royal immunities and confirmations of immunities, but, even then, the majority of Merovingian charters purportedly granted to monasteries are still regarded as forged.

Forgeries are nevertheless not at all worthless. Much like works of hagiography and historiography, they are documents that describe a created and imagined past that may have been more powerful and influential than any "real" story (Goffart 1966; Koziol 2012, pp. 315–357).[2] Although the determination of authenticity or falsification of charters marks the beginning of the modern profession of the historian, many of the narratives regarding early medieval monastic foundations—or the history of monasticism in general—still live on, remarkably unharmed by rigorous source criticism.[3]

Our set of forged Merovingian charters, which was produced between the Carolingian period and the late Middle Ages, documents the pronounced interest of monastic communities in extending their history, legal status, and property ownership into the past as far as possible—ideally into the period when the Frankish people first converted to Christianity. Consequently, Clovis and his sons were retroactively turned into avid supporters of well-endowed monastic institutions where monks and nuns lived according to a rule (*regula*) and prayed for the well-being of their patrons and the stability of the kingdom.

These forged charters looked plausible because they could easily fit into a broader narrative that described monasticism as a stable entity—a way of life lived according to a model that was refined and adjusted but never fundamentally changed. Monasteries always played an important role in history, but monasticism itself did not have much of a history after the alleged founders of eremitic and communal monastic life, Anthony (d. 366) and Pachomius (d. 348), had created its basic manifestations that "spread" like an oil slick over the Roman and post-Roman world. Hagiographers praised monastic founders not because they were pioneers in shaping new forms of Christian life, but because they embodied, established, or—in some cases—restored a model that had already been shaped in a distant past. Monastic founders were meant to be recognized as new Anthonys or new Martins.[4] Those monastic founders who wrote guidelines—*regulae*—codified well-proven practices and resolved misunderstandings about how to adjust to new circumstances. We still tend to imagine and tell the history of monasticism as it was told by medieval authors.

This chapter makes some suggestions for moving beyond this paradigm of stability, challenging a narrative in which monasticism made history without having much of a history of its own. The assumption of the fundamental stability of the monastic model has had a profound effect on much previous research—specifically, both survey studies on the history of monasticism and studies of Merovingian history have paid little attention to the first four centuries of the history of Western monasticism. Surveys of monastic history such as Clifford Hugh Lawrence's *History of Monasticism* (2015, pp. 10–49) and, more recently, Gert Melville's *Medieval Monasticism* (2016, pp. 13–49), jump from the fourth to the eighth century with seven-league boots, showing little awareness of how the disintegration of the Roman Empire and the rise of post-Roman barbarian kingdoms affected monasticism. After having paid due attention to Anthony and Pachomius (as founding fathers), most surveys briefly mention Martin of Tours (as one of the first Western monastic founders), the monastery of Lérins (as the first regular monastery), Cassian (who brought the wisdom of the desert fathers to the West), Caesarius of Arles (as author of the first rule for nuns and inventor of monastic enclosure), and Columbanus (who allegedly brought "Irish" monasticism to the Continent). These surveys suggest that the only achievement of the early medieval monastic world that deserves attention is the creation and spread of the Rule of Benedict (*Regula Benedicti*), which became the guideline and legal basis of monastic life forever afterward. This disinterest is somewhat puzzling since much of what we could call "medieval monasticism" emerged during the period addressed in this volume, and the Rule of Benedict played but a minor role in this process (for a thorough re-assessment of this narrative, see now Beach and Cochelin 2020).

Consensus

I would like to begin with a short summary of the accepted narrative of the history of monasticism in late antique Gaul and the Frankish world under Merovingian rule, indicating some places where it might be worthwhile to ask new questions and move beyond the established story. (For a much more detailed overview, see Prinz 1988 and Dunn 2000.) Monasticism in Gaul begins, as is generally assumed, with Martin of Tours, who in the 360s founded the first ascetic communities of Ligugé and Marmoutiers. It is probable that neither monastery survived for long and that both were refounded later, after Martin had become a cult figure—a saintly bishop rather than monastic founder. We know of Martin through the work of the Roman aristocrat Sulpicius Severus, who had turned his own villa into a monastic community (Stancliffe 1983). A generation after Martin, around 400, another Roman aristocrat, Honoratus, founded the island monastery of Lérins in order to transplant the monastic ideal of the desert fathers into Gaul (on Lérins, see Codou and Lauwers 2009). Lérins became the model of numerous monastic foundations in southern Gaul, particularly in the Rhône Valley, and the monks of Lérins may have produced the very first monastic rules written in Gaul. A great number of ascetically inclined bishops received their training on the island. Its learned monks, in interaction with the monastic theologian John Cassian (d. 430), shaped a theological response to Augustine's teachings on predestination that gave the individual at least some agency in the pursuit of his or her salvation. Modern historians have given this theology the name "semi-Pelagianism" (Markus 1990; Leyser 2000; Codou and Lauwers 2009, pp. 35–227; Rousseau 2010).

The most influential Lérinsian monk-bishop was Caesarius (d. 542). As bishop of Arles, he lived through the expansion of the Frankish kingdom and the incorporation of Arles into the realm of King Childebert I (d. 558). At the Council of Orange in 529, Caesarius shaped a theological compromise between "semi-Pelagianism" and Augustine's theology. He also receives acknowledgment for developing the first female variant of Lérinsian monasticism by establishing a strictly enclosed convent in Arles. The *regula* he wrote for this monastery became one of the foundational texts for medieval female monasticism (on Caesarius, see Klingshirn 1994).

The sixth century witnessed not only the creation of female monasticism but also the inception of close cooperation between barbarian rulers and monastic founders. Aurelianus (d. 555), Caesarius's successor to the episcopal see of Arles, founded a monastery in collaboration with King Childebert I and his wife Ultrogotha. This may have been among the earliest specifically Merovingian royal foundations, though this type of collaborative project had already been invented by the Burgundians a generation earlier when King Sigismund (d. 524), together with the bishop of Geneva, founded a monastery at the shrine of the martyr Maurice and his Theban legion at Agaune in 515. Other pioneering royal monasteries include King Guntram's (d. 592) basilica of Saint-Marcellus in Châlons, Queen Radegund's (d. 587) monastery, which started out as a "monasticized" royal villa and later moved to the city of Poitiers, and, possibly, Saint-Calais (Anisola) in Le Mans. Bishops participated in the establishment of monastic life in Gaul either by founding their own monasteries or by organizing their episcopal households in a monastic manner (for an overview of Merovingian monastic foundations, see Ueding 1935). Three of these sixth-century monastic foundations, Lérins, Saint-Maurice d'Agaune, and Saint-Marcellus, appear a century later as *Musterklöster* (model monasteries) in a number of episcopal privileges for monasteries—an attempt to root this new legal status in a venerable past (Diem 2002, pp. 77–84).

There are two ways of looking at the extremely fragmentary evidence pertaining to monastic life in fifth- and sixth-century Gaul. One can characterize the remarkable diversity of monastic foundations (colonies of hermits and their followers, island settlements striving to emulate the desert fathers, "monasticized" Roman or royal villas, houses of praying virgins and widows, enclosed convents, hospitals and pilgrims' homes, monastic-episcopal households, and suburban relic shrines administered by monastic communities) simply as variations of a model created in the Egyptian desert and assess them on the basis of their similarity to Anthony's and Pachomius's models. One can also approach them as "monasticisms"—as an analogy to Peter Brown's "micro-Christendoms" (Brown 2013, pp. 355–379). That is, they can be viewed as highly diverse experimental and entrepreneurial attempts to form an ideal Christian life, loosely held together by an overlapping semantic repertoire (*monachus, monasteria, abbas, coenobium,* etc.) and a common claim of embodying an imagined ideal of the desert fathers. Working with the notions of "monasticisms," as Hendrik Dey has suggested (2011, pp. 19–40), seems to be more productive, even if it makes studying the phenomenon itself infinitely more complicated, as it restrains us from directly transferring any insight from one context—one monasticism—to another. We would have to reevaluate prevailing assumptions about topics such as normative observance, poverty, prayer, space and boundaries, monastic theology, ascetic standards, hierarchies and discipline, legal circumstances, interactions with the outside world, accessibility, patterns of recruitment, and even the role of chastity and sexuality, if we stop assuming that there was a general consensus on these aspects of "monastic" life.

Monasticism in the sixth century ended with a metaphoric bang—one that showed that monastic experiments could just as easily fail as succeed. Shortly after Queen Radegund's death in 587, her monastery in Poitiers exploded in a violent uprising that included allegations of employing cross-dressing toy-boys, backgammon tournaments, and fugitive nuns joining marauding bandits, and ended with the near murder of an abbess and the excommunication of several members of the royal family. Gregory of Tours devotes large parts of the last two of his *Ten Books of History* to these events. He presents himself as a skillful episcopal crisis manager who eventually ensured that what was left of the enflamed monastery came under firm episcopal control (*Histories* IX, 39–43; X, 15–17, pp. 460–475; 501–509). His picture of this failed experiment did not find its way into the triumphant grand narrative of early medieval monasticism.

The seventh century began with another bang: the dramatic showdown between the Irish wandering monk Columbanus and the Merovingian queen Brunhild (d. 613), along with her ill-mannered grandson, King Theuderic II (d. 613). According to Jonas of Bobbio, Columbanus's undoubtedly biased hagiographer, the Irish saint had come to Gaul to restore the *medicamenta paenitentiae* (the remedies of penance) in a world that, due to the negligence of the bishops, had barely remained Christian. With strong royal support, Columbanus had founded the monasteries of Luxeuil and Annegray as eremitical hideouts in a supposedly uninhabited and remote wilderness—a true Frankish "desert" in the border region between Austrasia and Burgundy, which, as recent archaeological excavations show, was actually densely populated and of great strategic importance for the kings who sponsored Columbanus's foundations (Bully et al. 2015; O'Hara 2015; see also Picard, Chapter 18, this volume).

Columbanus's attempt to impose his moral standards on Merovingian rulers led to a major fallout with Theuderic II and his grandmother Brunhild. Columbanus was forced to leave Luxeuil and was sent into exile, but instead of returning to Ireland, he traveled to neighboring Merovingian kingdoms, where he sought the support of Theuderic's competitors. He died in Bobbio, his third foundation, in the year 615. On his journey, according to another hagiographic legend, he left the monk Gallus behind at Lake Constance, whose hermitage later became the Carolingian mega-monastery St. Gallen. This story, possibly a Carolingian invention, provided St. Gallen with a convenient origin myth of Irish roots and a Columbanian past (Diem 2015a). Luxeuil became the center of a ramified monastic network that moved the gravitational point of Frankish monasticism to the north and marginalized the grand old monasteries of the south such as Lérins and Caesarius's foundation at Arles. This "Columbanian" monastic movement led to the foundation of more than a hundred new male and female monastic houses operating under a remarkably stable and successful model (Fox 2014). Many of these new monasteries lasted throughout the Middle Ages and would probably still exist were it not for the French Revolution. Measured by continuity and endurance, Columbanian monasticism could be regarded as one of the most important social experiments in Western history.

The Columbanian success depended on a number of innovations (or ingenuous appropriations of already existing models). Most Columbanian and post-Columbanian monasteries were collaborative endeavors with rulers, aristocrats, local bishops, and existing monasteries rather than the initiative of a single charismatic individual gathering followers around him. The founding of a monastery became a carefully calibrated legal transaction that included land grants, property rights, and privileges (hence the production of charters), but also the responsibility to live a life according to the *regula* and pray for those who supported the monastery. Another crucial contribution to the longevity of these communities was the practice of laypeople "investing" a portion of their offspring in monastic communities in the form of child oblation (de Jong 1995).

The monastic world of the seventh century increasingly allowed outsiders to participate in the monastic endeavor as founders, patrons, and benefactors but it also induced them to follow ethical standards and develop ascetic practices analogous to those within monastic communities. Monastic fasting, chastity, purity, and liturgical discipline found their equivalents in lay piety. Private penance and confession, in particular, crossed monastic boundaries and transformed from an ascetic practice into a pastoral prerogative, though we still do not know precisely how this and other crossovers from ascetic practice to pastoral tool actually happened (Meens 2014).

The function of monasteries within society became diversified. Monastic foundations inspired by the Columbanian model, for example, became economic centers, bases of military recruitment, places of confinement for political or dynastic competitors, strongholds of literacy, and centers of education and learning—to mention just a few functions. Monasteries turned from places of withdrawal from the world to major support pillars of Merovingian society (Riché 1962; Rosenwein 1999; de Jong 2001).

Friedrich Prinz coined the term *Iro-Fränkisches Mönchtum* (Hiberno-Frankish monasticism) in his *Frühes Mönchtum im Frankenreich*, assuming that many of the innovations that emerged in the world of Jonas of Bobbio had their roots in the Irish monastic world whence his hero Columbanus came.[5] This may hold true for some aspects of monasticism such as the practice of penance according to a fixed tariff, though we will probably never know how much of what is now considered typical for Irish monasticism was in fact a Frankish re-import. The wind could blow either way across the Irish Sea (Wood 2015; Wycherley 2015). In the course of the second half of the seventh century, the name of Columbanus dropped out of the equation, but the model that emerged out of his foundations was already sufficiently well-established to survive the transition from Merovingian to Carolingian rule. It is unlikely that monasticism in the late Merovingian period fell prey to decline. New monasteries were founded; others, for example, Chelles and Luxeuil, became centers of book production. Bishop Chrodegang of Metz (d. 766) adapted the monastic model for his communities of clerics, and alleged do-nothing kings like Dagobert III (d. 715), Chilperic II (d. 721), Theuderic IV (d. 737), and Childeric III (d. 753) issued more immunities and exemptions than most of their predecessors.

From the late seventh century onward, monastic life in the Frankish kingdoms received new impulses from Anglo-Saxon monks and nuns who exported their monastic form of life and missionary zeal into the Frankish kingdoms. It is important to keep in mind that the Anglo-Saxon church was not determined by a dichotomy of monasteries and episcopal church structures—a dichotomy that may have still played a role in the Frankish world (on late Merovingian monastic life, see Wood 2001; Claussen 2004; Lifshitz 2014). Anglo-Saxon monks and monasteries associated themselves more strongly than other monasteries with the Pippinid mayors of the palace and facilitated the transition toward Carolingian rule and political expansion, along with, eventually, the projects of monastic reform and revival of learning that took off under Charlemagne and Louis the Pious (de Jong 1995).

COMPLICATIONS

I will place some obstacles into this organic monastic narrative that comfortably carries us from the Thebaid over Lérins and Luxeuil to St. Gallen. Attention to these obstacles allows us to identify turning points and moments of contention and conflict that are less visible under the assumption that monasticism remained static in its essence. These obstacles are constructed around a number of short source fragments, most of them from texts that do not form part of the canon used to establish the greater lines of the monastic story. The purpose is to suggest new themes and approaches but not to create an entirely alternative narrative out of a prohibitively limited number of examples.

HYMNOMODUS, THE SINGING BARBARIAN

The *Vita abbatum Acaunensium* (*Life of the Abbots of Agaune*), a hagiographic collection probably written around 525, begins with ambivalent praise of the Burgundian courtier Hymnemodus who established a monastic community at the martyr shrine of the Roman general Maurice and his legion at Agaune in the year 515. The text describes Hymnemodus as "mild and gentle of manner though a barbarian by birth" (*Vita abbatum Acaunensium*, c. 1, p. 330). In a fervent desire to embrace monastic life, he left the court of King Gundobad and traveled to the monastery of Grigny close to the city of Vienne. When he knocked at the door of the monastery, the monks were not amused:

> When the venerable abbot Caelestius, who at that time was leading this monastery, and the entire community saw him, they were thunderstruck and Caelestius did not dare to admit him to the community of the monastery because of the function that at that moment had been bestowed upon Hymnemodus by the king. When Saint Hymnemodus was not able to overcome the resistance of the abbot through begging, he withdrew to a certain cave for a while. After having cut off the hair of his head at this place and having devoted every thought to God, he returned to the monastery for which he had longed. After he was admitted and joined the community in such a way, he advanced in stages of piety with all charity and the virtue of humility.   (*Vita abbatum Acaunensium*, c. 1, p. 330)

The new monk, whose musical name might have been programmatic, eventually succeeded Caelestius as abbot and was later commissioned to establish a community that eventually became the spiritual center of the Burgundian kingdom and served as the prototype of a "royal monastery."

The monks of Grigny were understandably astonished that a *barbarus* and member of a royal court would want to enter their community. Hymnemodus may have been among the first *barbari* who chose to join an institution that was in every regard a product of the Roman world, but he was, remarkably enough, also one of the last monks whose ethnicity is explicitly labeled as "barbarian." Encapsulated in this short passage we see the otherwise rarely visible transition during which institutions that were deeply rooted in Roman traditions and institutions (the *villa*, the *domus*, the slave household, the army, episcopal households) began to provide opportunities to live a more perfect Christian life that were accessible to Romans and barbarians alike. This transformation may have largely contributed to a process of integration that caused the distinctions between Romans and barbarians to disappear slowly in the course of the sixth century. It certainly marked a turning point in the history of monasticism and a major factor allowing monastic life to survive into the Middle Ages. This transformation must have taken place in one way or another in all barbarian kingdoms, but it rarely became as tangible as in the foundation story of Saint-Maurice d'Agaune (Diem 2013a; Helvétius 2015).

One detail in Hymnemodus's conversion adds a remarkable dimension to the "barbarization" of monasticism: Hymnemodus's transitory state as a self-tonsured hermit. Hymnemodus is by no means the only hermit in the sixth century with a distinctly non-Roman name. Venantius Fortunatus mentions three of them in his *Life of Radegund*: Iumero, Dato, and Gundulf (*Vita Radegundis*, c. 13, p. 369). Similarly, four of the five hermits described in Gregory of Tours's *Liber Vitae Patrum* (*Life of the Fathers*) have names that do not sound Roman: Friardus, Caluppa, Senoch, and Leobardus (plus an abbot named Brachio). The names of bishops mentioned in Gregory's work indicate a different background: Illidius, Gallus, Gregorius, and Nicetius (*Liber Vitae Patrum*, pp. 211–294). It is possible that, at least for some period of time, becoming a hermit, as opposed to joining a monastic community, was the most obvious option for a non-Roman pursuing an ascetic life.

The "Mixed Crowd" at Agaune

The next source fragment also relates to the monastery of Saint-Maurice d'Agaune, albeit from a different perspective. It comes from another early sixth-century hagiographic collection, the *Life of the Jura Fathers*. This work, one of the richest sources on fifth- and sixth-century monastic life in Gaul, was written at the request of the monk Johannes and the hermit Armentarius, both of whom belonged to the martyr shrine of Agaune. In the dedicatory letter of the work, we find the following words:

> This "Acaunus" of yours is in the ancient Gallic language recognized to be a "rock" (*petra*) in truthful prefiguration of Peter, both originally through nature and now also through the Church. Nevertheless, Your Charity may now acknowledge that also among the woods of pines and furs of the Jura, this rock has once been *discovered* by the psalmist in an allegorical sense *in the woods of the forests* (cfr Ps. 131, 6)—a rock on which the holy brothers today walk with firm stability, which has now revealed the secret of this prefiguration.
>
> (*Vita Patrum Iurensium*, prologue.3, p. 240)[6]

The depiction of Agaune as a "rock" turned out to be no more than wishful thinking. Johannes and Armentarius were probably among the monks who fell prey to a rigorous cleansing of the holy place of Agaune that took place in the year 515. According to the *Vita abbatum Acaunensiusm*, Hymnemodus did not find any proper monks at Agaune, instead he encountered a mixed crowd of people (*vulgus promiscuum*) with their families—a crowd that had defiled the holy space and needed to be replaced by a proper *familia Dei*. This *familia Dei* consisted of clerics recruited from the neighboring episcopal sees who, thanks to lavish material support from the Burgundian king, would be able to establish a continuous liturgy—the *laus perennis* (everlasting praise), as it is called by modern historians—for the benefit of this same Burgundian ruler (Rosenwein, 2000).

The *Life of the Jura Fathers* can be read as a strong voice of dissent proposing an alternative trajectory for Agaune, one that would avoid turning the institution into a "factory" of intercessory prayer. The text is a chronicle of a group of monasteries in the remote valleys of the Jura that emerged out of a hermit colony founded by two Roman aristocrats, Romanus and Lupicinus. With the gradual disintegration of Roman power serving as a backdrop, its author describes how a community of hermits transformed their dwellings into a thriving and stable network of monastic communities. Their inhabitants were able to sustain themselves through the work of their own hands, independent of the aid of kings and bishops. They also managed to establish practical ascetic standards without compromising the founders' original zeal. The text emphasizes that the Jura monasteries avoided becoming monastic communities of clerics who served those in power through their intercessory prayer. In fact, everyone was welcome to join, except for priests. Romanus, the first abbot of the Jura Fathers, was ordained explicitly against his will, and Eugendus, its third abbot, flat-out refused to be ordained. In these ways, the Jura monasteries could not have been more different from Saint-Maurice d'Agaune in their organizational structure, social composition, economy, and ascetic goals.

For Johannes and Armentarius, the Jura monasteries may indeed have been a "different kind of rock," but emulating them was probably a much more desirable option than removing everyone and allowing the place to be resettled by liturgical professionals. The commission of the *Life of the Jura Fathers* may have been part of a desperate attempt to change Agaune's course of transformation, but the Jura monasteries were a model of the past. The future belonged to royally and episcopally sponsored places of prolific prayer, and Saint-Maurice d'Agaune became their prototype (Diem 2013).

Comparing the *Life of the Jura Fathers* with the *Life of the Abbots of Agaune* shows that different monastic models—the hermit colony, the monastic network, the martyr shrine, the royal foundation—competed with one another, and that transformations never occurred without conflicts. The issues that divided the Jura monasteries and Saint-Maurice d'Agaune, particularly the question of monastic economy and the balance between manual labor and liturgy, continued to play a crucial role in the development of monasticism.

It is worthwhile to read our sources on early medieval monasticism with a keen eye for such markers of conflict, while resisting the temptation to side with the author. The depraved "mixed crowd" at Agaune may have consisted of monks and hermits like Johannes and Armentarius. Or, to use another example, monks of the kind that were vilified as *gyrovagi* (wandering, freeloading monks) and *sarabaites* (monks without rule and discipline) in the *Regula Benedicti* might appear as truly holy men and monastic pioneers in hagiographic sources.

The most effective way of suppressing voices of dissent is to monopolize the memory of events. The winner is whoever's version of the story is remembered. In the opening sentence of his work, the author of the *Life of the Abbots of Agaune* thus expresses the desire to defend *his* version of the story against *fabulae confusae* (inflated stories) that other people might tell (and most certainly did):

> The reputation that is affirmed by merits always enjoins succeeding generations to imitate the memory of the holy way of life of blessed men. Nevertheless, lest I seem to omit a certain line of the narration on account of the long passage of time and inflated stories, it is necessary for the truth to be set down in writing. We do this in order that those who, while they are burning with the heat of faith and the love of sanctity, desire that their hearts be filled with words, do as they are thirsty, swallow true water instead of empty air from a dark cloud.
>
> (*Vita abbatum Acaunensium*, prologue, p. 329)

Although written in the convoluted Latin typical of hagiographic prologues, his words could be applied to almost every monastic narrative text.

A ROMAN MATRON ADDRESSES A MEROVINGIAN QUEEN

At some point in the 560s, the Merovingian queen Radegund (d. 587) received a letter from Abbess Caesaria, the niece of Bishop Caesarius and head of the monastery he had founded in Arles. Radegund had requested a copy of Caesarius's *Rule for Virgins*, which the abbess sent her, along with some remarkably condescending pieces of advice (on elite women, see James, Chapter 11, this volume). This is how a proper Roman matron addressed a former Thuringian hostage who became a Merovingian queen:

> I have done what you asked me. I have sent you a copy of the rule which our lord, Bishop Caesarius of blessed and holy memory has created for us. See in which ways you might follow it.   (Caesaria, *Letter to Richildis and Radegund*, v. 63–64, p. 486)

Caesaria evidently doubted that a rule designed for a strictly enclosed community of Roman ladies would be suitable for Radegund's monastic endeavor—and she was probably right. Radegund's foundation did not emerge under auspicious circumstances. Inspired by unaccredited holy men, Radegund left her husband and established a community at the royal villa of Saix near Poitiers, where she lived partly as recluse and partly as a member of a community of nuns of mixed backgrounds. Under constant threat of being forced to return to her royal husband, she moved her community to the city of Poitiers. Around that time she must have requested a copy of the Rule of Caesarius in an attempt to give her community a well-respected institutional shape and protect it from external interference. She also obtained a splinter of the Holy Cross from Constantinople, which was installed in her monastery against the fierce resistance of

Maroveus, the bishop of Poitiers, who later went so far as to refuse to attend Radegund's funeral (Baudonivia, *Vita Radegundis* c. 16; Gregory of Tours, *Histories* 9.40; Dailey 2015).

Caesaria must have looked with a combination of amusement and horror at this rather clumsy and, as became evident later, flawed attempt of a barbarian queen to establish a hybrid of a monastic villa, enclosed urban community, relic shrine, place of intercessory prayer, and retreat for members of the royal clan. Perhaps to make up for her shortcomings, Venantius Fortunatus commemorated Radegund as someone who frantically tried to embody all that the Christian ascetic tradition had to offer, like a child in a candy shop who cannot choose a single treat and therefore wants everything. In Venentius's version, she is a martyr, virgin, perfect wife, perfect queen, maidservant, wonderworker, teacher, radical, self-mutilating ascetic, a new Anthony, Martin, Melania, and Simeon the Stylite, a monastic founder, political peacekeeper, caregiver, vigorous leader, monastic officeholder, and humble nun who willingly obeyed the abbess she had installed because she considered herself unworthy of the position.

Radegund, the barbarian amateur Christian, had clearly missed the point, and Caesaria gave her the motherly advice not to overdo it; her excessive asceticism made her incapable of ruling a community:

> It has reached my ears that you are overdoing it in abstinence. Do everything with reason so that you stay alive for my sake and that you are always able (to be abstinent). Because if you start to get sick as a result of this excess, which God may prevent, you will then have to ask for special food and take it outside the designated hour, and you will not be able to rule the blessed girls.
>
> (Caesaria, *Letter to Richildis and Radegund*, v. 74–75, pp. 486–488)

The events that took place soon after Radegund's death show that her experiment of a multifunctional institution, established against royal and episcopal resistance, inhabited by nuns of diverse backgrounds, and led by a radical ascetic who tried to impose her own extreme standards on her followers, was bound to fail. And we must keep in mind that the *Lives* of Radegund were written with knowledge of what happened after her death. Failures like this were certainly part of a phase of experimentation with different monastic forms; they were the rule rather than the exception. Examples are easy to find in other sources if we rub off the thin rhetorical veneer of triumph and divine favor.

NO STYLITE IN MY BACKYARD

We know about the uprising in Radegund's monastery only through the work of Gregory of Tours. Gregory was a bishop with no monastic inclinations. His work describes monastic life from the unusual perspective of an outsider, unconstrained by any desire to provide a glorifying and unifying view of monasticism that we find in most sources produced by monastic insiders. Gregory's agenda was different. He was not necessarily fond of hermits and monastic holy men, but he had to deal with them in his capacity as bishop. One of the most effective means of keeping them under control was by selectively telling their stories and thus determining how they were remembered and what would stand as their legacy. In Gregory's view, the only good saint was a dead saint.

Gregory devoted one of his hagiographic collections to mostly homegrown ascetics and their communities. Its title, *Liber vitae patrum*, refers back to the tradition of the desert fathers. This work is his attempt to create in Francia a figurative desert according to his own liking—inhabited by monks, hermits, and recluses whose full obedience toward the bishop was a crucial attribute of their sanctity (Diem 2015b). The example presented here comes from Gregory's *Ten Books of Histories*, although it could have just as easily appeared in his *Liber vitae patrum*. The author recounts, with some sympathy, the story of a certain Lombard monk named Vulfilaic—another holy man with a distinctly non-Roman name. Vulfilaic moved to a still-active temple of the goddess Diana, built a column next to her statue, and preached ceaselessly against her cult from the top of his column. He endured snow and other effects of cold weather, including icicles growing on his beard. He finally succeeded in converting the worshippers of Diana and convinced them to destroy her sanctuary. Perhaps having incurred the wrath of the goddess, Vulfilaic contracted a nasty skin disease. He stripped naked in front of the altar (*denudavi me coram sancto altario*, as he tells Gregory) and anointed himself with holy oil. Miraculously healed, he returned to his column. The local bishops were not amused and admonished him:

> This way you follow is not the right one, and you, an uneducated person, will not be able to match Simeon of Antioch who had his seat on a column. Moreover, the circumstances of the place do not allow that you endure this torture. It is better that you descend and live with the brothers you have gathered around you.
>
> (Gregory of Tours, *Histories* VIII.15, pp. 382–383)

One of the bishops lured him away from his column by inviting him to a meal and used his absence to have the column torn down. Vulfilaic returned and wept bitterly, but he did not dare to rebuild his column. Instead, he transformed himself from an eccentric man of God (*vir Dei*) to a proper monk. Vulfilaic represents a form of ascetic life that is rarely visible outside of Gregory's work, but it must have played a prominent role in the Frankish world, perhaps even to the extent of forming its own sort of parallel Christianity. He, and possibly countless other holy men, tried to emulate the mode of the desert fathers in their own ways, yet were not authorized by the emerging hierarchy of bishops. From the bishops' perspective, they annoyingly ignored the fact that the desert fathers belonged to a world of the past as well as to a foreign land. They did outrageous things, tonsuring themselves (like Hymnemodus) or, in the case of Vulfilaic, stripping in front of the altar; they rose in popularity and gathered followings that protected them from suppression by their local bishops. Indeed, they may have been more effective and more consistent than these bishops in battling remnants of non-Christian religious practice. Some of the communities that gathered around these holy men became *monasteria*, but few of them endured.

Aside from giving examples of their lives in his *Liber vitae patrum*, Gregory mentions several holy men, such as the already-discussed Vulfilaic, in his *Histories*. He carefully draws a line between genuine ascetic eccentrics who were willing to submit themselves to episcopal power and thereby earned a certain amount of leeway, and those who had crossed the line of acceptability by causing unrest and openly challenging the authority of their bishops.

The world of homegrown ascetic life, of hermits, their followers, and their mostly unsuccessful attempts to establish lasting institutions, is a segment of monastic life that still awaits systematic investigation. It is hard to imagine that Gregory's world of grassroots saints entirely faded away in subsequent centuries, even though their appearance in our sources became scarce. There are still, however, occasional references to notorious and dangerously popular troublemakers, such as the wandering monks Clemens and Aldebert who deeply annoyed Boniface by carrying around an allegedly authentic letter from Christ (Meeder 2011), or maladjusted hermits such as Gallus, who, even in his romanticized hagiography produced in the Carolingian period, comes across as a stubborn naysayer. The fact that our sources carefully separate these subjects into heroes and villains should not prevent us from seeing what they had in common.

THE ROYAL SHOWDOWN

Gregory probably would not have been happy with the transformations of monastic life that took place a generation after his death. Monasteries finally turned from institutions whose power was largely delimited by bishops into self-confident, independent entities operating within the web of power in Merovingian society. This development is closely linked with the arrival of Columbanus and his twelve Irish companions in Gaul in the 580s, although the true turning points may have occurred after Columbanus's death around 615. These turning points were incited by his successors, particularly the abbots Eusthasius (d. 629) and Waldebert (d. 670) of Luxeuil, and by Jonas, the chronicler of the "Columbanian" movement (O'Hara/Wood 2017). It is Jonas who tells us how to understand the *Regula Columbani* (Rule of Columbanus). Columbanus himself, as he emerges in his own work, appears to be remarkably different from Jonas's hagiographical rendition of the Irish saint, and it was Jonas's Columbanus rather than the historical Columbanus who had the largest impact.

The historical Columbanus could to some extent be put in the same box as Vulfilaic and other grassroots saints as they appear in Gregory's work. He was an outsider with unorthodox manners and teachings, much missionary zeal, and a good deal of defiance toward the local episcopacy. Yet, unlike the figures described in the *Liber vitae patrum*, he was *not* a self-made holy man. He had received a profound literary and ascetic training and entered Gaul with superior knowledge of foundational Christian texts and a strong sense of pride in his ascetic lineage (Stancliffe 2011). Moreover, he made the wise move of aligning himself immediately with the other major power players in Frankish society: courtiers (on which, see Hen, Chapter 10, this volume). He gained royal support, was allocated land, and, more successfully than his ascetic predecessors, gathered followers from the local aristocracy, who were attracted by the idea of actively pursuing a path toward their eternal salvation. Columbanus offered the *medicamenta paenitentiae* (on penance, see Uhalde, Chapter 45, this volume).

The initial harmony between Columbanus and Brunhild's grandson, King Theuderic II, came to an end when Brunhild and Theuderic II realized that the holy man was not as appreciative and controllable as they had expected and that the monastic institutions he established seemed to be different from the ones with which the court normally dealt (on Brunhild, see James, Chapter 11, this volume). Brunhild and Theuderic probably thought they had helped establish another Saint-Maurice d'Agaune or a counterpart to the monasteries Brunhild had founded in Autun. The showdown between Columbanus and Theuderic, the dramatic high point of Jonas's *Life of Columbanus*, is supposed to have transpired as follows:

> Blessed Columbanus, since he was courageous and vigorous in spirit, responded to the king who objected, with these words: "that it is not his custom that the dwellings of the servants of God provide access to secular people and those who are strangers to the religious way of life, and that he has prepared places that were adequate and suitable for this purposes, so that the arrival of all guests (can happen there)." The king responded to this: "If you desire to take the gifts of our generosity and the support of our funding, then access to all places will be open for all." The holy man responded: "If you try to violate what until now was entirely bound by regular discipline, you should know that I will no longer be sustained by your gifts or any support. And if you came to this place for the reason that you destroy the houses of the servants of God and defile the regular discipline, your kingdom will soon be destroyed from the ground upwards and will perish with the entire royal offspring".
>
> (Jonas of Bobbio, *Vita Columbani* I, c. 19, p. 190, my translation)

Knowing through hindsight that the entire branch of the Merovingian dynasty descending from Brunhild was extinguished, Jonas stonily states: "Thereafter the outcome of the matter has provided a proof for this" (Jonas of Bobbio, *Vita Columbani* I, c. 19, p. 190). Subsequently, Jonas explains the ascent of Chlothar II as ruler over all Merovingian kingdoms with the king's reverence toward Columbanus and support for his foundations. Columbanian monasticism became an issue of priority for this ruler and his son Dagobert I. The fate of kings and the prosperity of monasteries became closely intertwined, and monasteries gained a spiritual and political power previously unseen.

There are older examples of holy men threatening rulers, but Jonas's definition of the monastery as a sacred space that had to be respected unconditionally, under threat of divine punishment, was a novelty—or at least a radical culmination of spatial concepts that may have existed in some older forms of monasticism. Even Columbanus himself might have been astonished by the words Jonas had put in his mouth—at least, there are no references to monasteries as sacred spaces and no threats of divine punishment in his own writings. In Jonas's *Life of Columbanus*, the fundamental redefinition of the monastery as a sacred space, became a recurring theme; it formed a central aspect of royal immunities and episcopal privileges granted to Columbanian monasteries, and it was certainly one of the keys to the longevity of Columbanian monastic foundations. Yet, as we will see in the next section, not everyone agreed with the way Jonas of Bobbio and Columbanus's successors appropriated and defined the heritage of the Irish troublemaker.

An (Anti-) Columbanian Voice of Dissent

One of the lasting innovations of "Columbanian" monasticism, which tends to be "retrojected" problematically into a monastic past, is the notion of monasticism as a *vita regularis*—a life according to a rule. It may be true that most of the roughly thirty-five extant monastic rules date from the period before Columbanus, but within the variants of monastic life in fifth- and sixth-century Gaul, a text-based *vita regularis* was not more than one variant among many. Gregory's holy men and their communities did not need a written *regula*—neither did, as far as we know, Saint-Maurice d'Agaune or the Jura monasteries. The terms *regula* and *regularis* did not necessarily refer to a written a catalog of norms and regulations. Even the written *regulae* that are preserved may have had different functions at different moments in time (Diem and Rousseau 2020). Caesarius's *Rule for Virgins*, for example, was transformed from a reflection on the theological basis of monastic life and a blueprint for a community capable of overcoming human sinfulness into an instrument used to rein in a group of marauding royals and their entourage. In other words, the same text took on very different functions at different times and in different contexts. The term *Regula Columbani* may, for some, have referred to a short bipartite rule written by Columbanus. However, if Jonas of Bobbio referred to a *Regula Columbani*, he had in mind instead his own understanding of Columbanus's ideal and legacy: a *Regula Columbani* that had little to do with the text transmitted under Columbanus's name.

The following short source fragment is the opening statement of the *Regula cuiusdam patris* (Rule of a certain father), an anonymous monastic treatise preserved only in a manuscript of Benedict of Aniane's *Codex regularum*, a collection dating from the turn of the ninth century:

> A good reader should take heed that he does not submit scriptures to his understanding but that he submits his understanding to the holy scriptures.
> (*Regula cuiusdam patris*, c. 1.1, p. 10)

Based on intertextual relations, we can date this anonymous rule with some precision. Aside from the *Rule of Basil* and John Cassian's work, the text uses the monastic rule written by Columbanus. Since it does not contain any traces of the *Regula Benedicti*, which spread among Columbanian monasteries within a generation of Columbanus's death, we can cautiously assume that it was written shortly after 615, the year in which Columbanus died. As such, it was a product of the world that Jonas of Bobbio described (or rather created) in his *Vita Columbani* (Diem 2017).

The almost Lutheran *"sola scriptura"* opening sentence of the *Regula cuiusdam patris* (which was in fact inspired by Jerome) is followed by an outburst of anger about recalcitrant, disobedient, and socially dysfunctional monks who needed to be either incarcerated or expelled from the community. No other *regula* addresses incarceration and expulsion as often as the *Regula cuiusdam patris*. The author pairs these threats of cleansing the monastery with enflamed remarks about negligent abbots, who are incompetent, corrupt, disobedient to the *mandata Dei* (commands of God), or do not serve as examples for their community. These abbots are to be expelled or, if this is impossible, abandoned—either way, they will most certainly burn in hell. We can assume that this text addressed a deeply divided community and that it was written by someone who may not have been on friendly terms with his superiors. The rule places *oboedientia* to the *mandata Domini* above the slavish *oboedientia* to one's superiors, which the rules of Benedict and Columbanus require.[7]

In his *Vita Columbani*, Jonas of Bobbio does not conceal the fact that Columbanus's succession was anything but smooth and harmonious. Athala, the abbot of Bobbio, had to contend with an uprising and a group of monks leaving the monastery. The monk Agrestius challenged Eusthasius's authority and attacked him and his understanding of Columbanus's rule as heretical. I suggest reading the *Regula cuiusdam patris* in the context of these insurgencies against Columbanus's successors. The text shows disagreement with Jonas's depiction of Columbanian monasticism at various levels. It proclaims a dissenting concept of obedience by making the *mandata Dei* the sole benchmark of a monk's behavior instead of defining obedience as submission to his superiors. It vigorously refutes the accumulation of wealth and emphasizes austerity, the necessity of manual labor, and care for the poor. It rejects any involvement in the world and worldly politics, and it attacks abbots who travel instead of fulfilling their responsibilities in their own community. The monastic community that the *Regula cuiusdam patris* envisions has no sacred space or impenetrable boundaries; it may even be dispersed over different geographical locations.

More importantly, the *Regula cuiusdam patris* expresses dissenting views on the theological core of Columbanian monastic life. For its author, there are no *medicamenta paenitentiae* that might heal the effects of human sinfulness and open the gateway to salvation. Whenever he paraphrased Columbanus's rule, he carefully removed all references to tariffed penance. Also absent are references to the salutary effects of intercessory prayer; in the *Regula cuiusdam patris*, liturgy plays a secondary role. Discussing the monastic hours, the author uses the rather neutral term *conventus* (gathering) and assigns significantly fewer psalms that Columbanus did. For him the only effective remedy against sins and instrument for attaining forgiveness is the eucharist. The rule, which began with a warning against misreading scripture, ends with the words:

> On Sundays one always has to receive the eucharist as a remedy for sins. But we have
> to approach the body and blood of our Lord Jesus Christ with all holiness of the
> heart and the body.   (*Regula cuiusdam patris*, c. 32, p. 35)

The *Regula cuiusdam patris*, which served as a voice of theological dissent, has important historical implications beyond revealing struggles in Columbanian monasticism. It
shows that early medieval monasticism in general was highly diverse—not only in its
organizational models, ascetic requirements, notions of discipline, physical space, place
in the world, and so on, but also in its theological foundations, which, like more practical aspects of monastic life, remained matters of dissent and strife. Every jigsaw piece—
not just the *Regula cuiusdam patris*—that we use to assemble the history of monasticism
in one way or another makes statements about monastic theology. It might be productive to read these statements *against* one another rather than assuming that they all form
part of a doctrinal consensus—even if this makes early medieval monasticism more
complicated and difficult to understand.

Eligius's Rigor Mortis

The last voice of dissent belongs to Bishop Eligius of Noyon (d. 660) who was in many
regards the ideal product of Columbanian monasticism. He started his career as a goldsmith and *monetarius* at the courts of Chlothar II and Dagobert I and had close contact
with the monastery of Luxeuil, which he regularly visited (see Strothmann, Chapter 35,
this volume). Yet, instead of becoming a monk himself, he lived (if we are confident in
the *Life* written by his friend Audoin) a layperson's perfect alternative to a monastic
existence: it was a life of penance, fasting, prayer, tears, vigils, and lavish almsgiving. He
used his secular position to become a founder and benefactor of numerous male and
female monastic communities (on gender, see Halsall, Chapter 8, this volume). After
Dagobert's death, Eligius became the bishop of Noyon. When Eligius died in 660, a
dispute arose as to which institution would profit from the presence of the holy man's
relics, a conflict that Eligius himself, like other saints before him, resolved by making
himself immovable, as Audoin reprots:

> The queen [Balthild] was eager to move the body of the holy man somehow to her
> monastery at Chelles. But another party tried to bring him to Paris. But the citizens
> of Noyon opposed both of them, claiming the limbs of their bishop as [his] legacy
> to themselves....Then the queen decided to be the wisest and, entrusting her case to
> God, declared: "Now let these debates be discarded, and if it is the Lord's will or the
> will of this holy man that he go there where I desire, let him be lifted without any
> delay. But if it [God's will] is different, we will approve of it now." And when she had
> spoken, they went to the bier [of Eligius] and attempted to raise it, but felt so much
> weight pushing it down that they could not move it from that spot. Then in turn

others tried but none prevailed. Finally the queen, wishing to test it by herself, stretched out and turned up her forearm and began to push [to see] whether she could move even a single corner of the bier. And although she was struggled greatly, trying with all her might and pushing it as if it were a huge mountain, she accomplished nothing. Then, turning to the noblemen, she acknowledged: "Behold! We clearly learn now that it is not his [Eligius's] will that we take him away. Let us concede—be it unwillingly—to this people what we still do not wish to accept." The counsel was acceptable and they all decided with one voice that he should be buried in that very same city.   (Audoin, *Vita Eligii* II, c. 37, pp. 721–722)

This conflict about Eligius's body opens yet another door to disputes about Merovingian monasticism and its transformation. In his *Vita Eligii,* Audoin emphasized three main qualities of the saint: he lived like a monk while fulfilling his responsibilities in the world; he founded and supported monasteries while remaining a layman for most of his life; and he was an avid supporter of the cult of relics. He built and rebuilt numerous *basilicae,* discovered the graves of martyrs, and organized the *translatio* of these martyrs. Yet, according to Audoin, Eligius's two main activities, founding monasteries and supporting the cult of relics, had nothing to do with one another. In Eligius's world, monasteries needed their *regula* but no saints, and saints needed their cult but no monasteries. In this regard, Audoin and Eligius were entirely in line with the monastic ideal as expressed by Jonas in his *Vita Columbani* and as we find it in many other texts related to the first generations of Columbanian monasticism. Columbanus's successors attempted to "organize" collective sanctity through strict discipline, penance, separation from the outside world, and adherence to the *regula,* rather than relying on the presence of a saint. Jonas devotes no more than one sentence to Columbanus's death and burial, and the saint's physical remains play no role whatsoever in the second part of the work. The founder lives on in his *regula,* not in his bones. The first Columbanian monasteries were dedicated to Peter or Paul but not to a specific saint or martyr. Most of them were, at least initially, named after a place rather than a specific martyr or saint: Luxeuil, Bobbio, Rebais, Eboriacum (later named *monasterium Farae* = Faremoutiers, after its founder Burgundofara), Habendum (later named *monasterium Romarici* = Remiremont after its founder Romaricus).

Queen Balthild favored the luxury of allowing a saint, a saintly founder, or an imported martyr to serve as the focal point of sanctity instead of putting all the responsibility of establishing a sacred space on the community. Eligius may have won the battle over his own relics, but Columbanus's bone-free monastic experiment was nevertheless largely phased out. The bold idea of organizing sanctity on the basis of discipline and boundaries rather than the presence of a saint may have persisted as a variant, but the future belonged instead to Gallus's St. Gallen, to Boniface's Fulda, or to Montecassino and Fleury, the two monasteries that both claim to have the bones of Benedict, the author of the *sancta regula* (holy rule) that, as we are told, finally established order on the wonderfully chaotic, anarchic, confusing, and subversive playground of early medieval monasticism.

CONCLUSION

There is nothing wrong with master narratives as long as we turn them into *objects* of historical inquiry rather than use them as convenient frameworks. We may treat them as scratching posts to sharpen our claws or as points of departure for a proper *peregrinatio* (pilgrimage without return to hearth and home). In this contribution, I have made some suggestions as to how to depart from a narrative that regards monasticism as a unified stable entity that moves through history without having much of a history of its own. This departure exposes us to the joy of reading against the grain the scattered sources we possess;[8] For repertories of primary sources, see Heinzelmann 2010; De Vogüé 1985; Dekkers and Gaar 1995, especially nos. 427–536. it allows us to stop worrying about the historical "truth" of hagiographic stories, dismiss the idea of a consensus within the diversity of monastic rules, and replace the presumed unity in expressions of monastic theology with a persistent scuffle about the doctrinal grounding of any attempt to live a more perfect Christian life. Studying monasticism means looking for trouble.

I suggest replacing the idea of monasticism by a vast diversity of "monasticisms" that compete with each other and can be wrested from our stubbornly harmonious sources by looking for markers of dissent and conflict underneath the rhetorical veneer of consensus and uniformity—a rhetoric that posits the preferred practice as a transhistorical standard and every variation as deviance. One author's fraud, heretic, or betrayer of monastic ideals might be another author's true saint, role model, or charismatic leader—a consideration that should prevent us from accepting blindly any assessment given by our sources. We should also be aware that monastic communities and institutions might transform beyond recognition within the shortest periods of time. Columbanus's Luxeuil or Bobbio may have been vastly different from Jonas's experience of the same institutions, just as Radegund's monastery differed enormously before and after the uprising that happened shortly after her death, and Agaune was a different place before and after Hymnemodus's cleansing. One turning point that we can anticipate generally brought change was the transition that occurred following the death of the founding generation. The extant success stories conceal the fact that the transition from community to institution may have failed more often than it succeeded—at least in the early phase of experimentation that had not yet produced clear-cut models to follow.

A number of themes might problematize accepted chronologies and turning points, and I reiterate them here without making a claim that this list is in any way exhaustive: the intersection of monasticism and post-Roman ethnicity, the diversity of monastic theologies, different attempts at constituting collective sanctity (using bones or rules), shifting definitions of monastic space and boundaries, the ever-contentious relationship between monastic communities and an emerging ecclesiastical hierarchy, and techniques of shaping an ever-fluid past in a battle for a discursive monopoly.

Additional themes are omitted or addressed peripherally here for the sake of brevity. First, the simple and awe-inspiring fact that monastic experiments created models that were to a large extent not gender specific deserves much more attention—just as the fact that Merovingian monasticisms had stronger roots in late antique female monastic experiments than in an imagined Egyptian desert (Diem 2013b). Second, monastic ritual and liturgy is far too interesting to leave to a handful of specialists. Even the most basic notions of monastic life such as poverty and the prerequisite of chastity and sexual abstinence manifest themselves in a variety of ways and were matters of conflict and dissent (Diem 2005). Third, monastic chastity and virginity have histories of their own, and once we leave the beaten path, the notion of "asceticism" must be abandoned in favor of something much more complicated and exciting. It is clear that each of our "monasticisms" forms its own mirror of society at large, and all those who are willing to look will realize that there is a lot to see in this multitude of mirrors that would otherwise have remained invisible.

NOTES

1. I would like to thank Joshua Campbell, Giles Constable, Eric Goldberg, Patrick Geary, Alex O'Hara, Matthieu van der Meer, and Ian Wood for their comments and suggestions. I would also like to express my deep gratitude to the American Council of Learned Societies and the Institute for Advanced Study in Princeton for allowing me to spend a year in the most inspiring surrounding a scholar could imagine. This chapter is a contribution to the Spezialforschungsbereich F 4202 "Visions of Community," funded by the *Fonds zur Förderung der wissenschaftlichen Forschung* (FWF), the Faculty of History and Cultural Sciences of the University of Vienna, and the Austrian Academy of Science. All translations from primary sources are produced in collaboration with Matthieu van der Meer.
2. Citations are usually limited to the most important and most recent publications, which provide references to the state of research on the respective topics covered here.
3. For example, historians duly take into consideration Athanasius's remark that the desert father Anthony died at the age of 105 by doing the math and noting his life dates as c. 251–356. A critical reading of Athanasius's story does not go beyond cautiously adding "circa."
4. Through Sulpicius Severus's *Life of Martin,* Martin of Tours (d. 397) became one of the most influential models of monastic founder and bishop.
5. Prinz's work is still an invaluable source of detailed information even for those who disagree with his prosopographical and cartographic approach and his factual reading of sources.
6. The translation of this passage is mine. For a complete English translation of the *Vita patrum Iurensium,* see Vivian, Vivian, and Russell 1999.
7. On the expulsion of socially dysfunctional monks: *Regula cuiusdam patris,* c. 4–10, pp. 13–18. On the *mandata Domini* as absolute guideline: c. 14.3, p. 21; c. 19.3, p. 21; c. 24.6, p. 28, c. 27.3, p. 31. On incompetent superiors: c. 20, p. 26; c. 25, p. 29. Diem (2017) provides a detailed analysis and translation of the rule.
8. For repertories of primary sources, see Heinzelmann 2010; De Vogüé 1985; Dekkers and Gaar 1995, especially nos. 427–536.

Works Cited

Ancient Sources

Audoin of Rouen, *Vita Eligii*. B. Krusch (ed.). (1902). MGH SRM 4 (pp. 663–741). Hanover: Hahn.

Audoin of Rouen, *Vita Eligii*. J. A. McNamara (trans.). (2001). In T. Head (ed.), *Medieval Hagiography. An Anthology* (pp. 137–167). New York: Routledge.

Baudonivia, *Vita Radegundis*. B. Krusch (ed.). (1888). MGH SRM 2 (pp. 387–389). Hanover: Hahn.

Caesaria, *Lettre à Richilde et à Radegonde*. A. De Vogüé and J. Courreau (ed. and trans.). (1988). Sources Chrétiennes 345 (pp. 170–272). Paris: Cerf.

Caesarius of Arles, *Regula ad virgines*. A. De Vogüé and J. Courreau (ed. and trans.). (1988). Sources Chrétiennes 345 (pp. 476–494). Paris: Cerf.

Caesarius of Arles, *Regula ad virgines*. M. C. McCarthy (trans.). (1960). *The Rule for Nuns of St. Caesarius of Arles. A Translation with a Critical Introduction*. Washington, DC: Catholic University of America Press.

Columbanus, *Regulae*. G. S. M. Walker (ed. and trans.). (1957). *Columbani Opera* (pp. 122–180). Dublin: Dublin Institute for Advanced Studies.

Gregory of Tours, *Histories*. B. Krusch and W. Levison (eds.). (1951). *Decem Libri Historiarum*. MGH SRM 1.1. Hanover: Hahn.

Gregory of Tours, *Histories*. L. Thorpe (trans.). (1974). *Gregory of Tours, The History of the Franks*. Harmondsworth: Penguin.

Gregory of Tours, *Liber in gloria confessorum*. B. Krusch (ed.). (1885). MGH SRM 1.2 (pp. 744–820). Hanover: Hahn.

Gregory of Tours, *Liber vitae patrum*. B. Krusch (ed.). (1969). MGH SRM 1.2 (pp. 211–294). Hanover: Hahn.

Gregory of Tours, *Liber vitae patrum*. E. James (trans.). (1991). *Gregory of Tours: Life of the Fathers*. Translated Texts for Historians 1. Liverpool: Liverpool University Press.

Jonas of Bobbio, *Vita Columbani*. B. Krusch (ed.). (1905).MGH SRG 37. Hanover: Hahn.

Jonas of Bobbio, *Vita Columbani*. A. O'Hara and I. Wood (trans.). (2017). *Jonas of Bobbio, Life of Columbanus, Life of John of Réomé, and Life of Vedast*. Translated Texts for Historians. Liverpool: Liverpool University Press.

Kölzer, T. (ed.). (2001). *Merowingerurkunden* 1. MGH: Die Urkunden der Merowinger. Hanover: Hahnsche Buchhandlung.

Regula Benedicti. R. Hanslik (ed.). (1977). CSEL 75. Vienna: Hoelder-Pichler-Tempsky.

Regula Benedicti. B. L. Venarde (ed. and trans.). (2011). *The Rule of Saint Benedict*. Dumbarton Oaks Medieval Library 6. Cambridge, MA: Harvard University Press.

Regula cuiusdam patris. F. Villegas (ed.). "La 'Regula cuiusdam Patris ad monachos'. Ses sources littéraires et ses rapports avec la 'Regula monachorum' de Colomban." (1973). *Revue d'Histoire de la Spiritualité* 49: 3–36.

Regula cuiusdam patris. A. Diem (trans.) "Disputing Columbanus' Heritage: The Regula cuiusdam patris ." In A. O'Hara (ed.), *Columbanus and the Peoples of Post-Roman Europe* (pp. 259–306). Oxford: Oxford University Press.

Venantius Fortunatus, *Vita Radegundis*. B. Krusch (ed.). (1888). MGH SRM 2 (pp. 364–377). Hanover: Hahn.

Venantius Fortunatus. *Vita Radegundis*. J. A. McNamara, J. E. Halborg, and E. G. Whatley (trans.). (1992). *Sainted Women of the Dark Ages* (pp. 70–86). Durham, NC: Duke University Press.

Vita abbatum Acaunensium absque Epitaphis. B. Krusch (ed.). (1920). MGH SRM 7 (pp. 329–336). Hanover: Hahn.

Vita patrum Iurensium. F. Martine (trans.). (1968). *Vita patrum Iurensium.* Sources Chrétiennes 142. Paris: Cerf.

Vita patrum Iurensium. T. Vivian, K. Vivian, and J. B. Russell (trans.). (1999). *The Life of the Jura Fathers.* Cistercian Studies Series 178. Kalamazoo, MI: Cistercian Publications.

Modern Sources

Beach, A. and Cochelin I. (eds.). (2020). *The Cambridge History of Medieval Monasticism in the Latin West* 1. Cambridge: Cambridge University Press.

Brown, P. (2013). *The Rise of Western Christendom: Triumph and Diversity, A.D. 200–1000.* 3rd ed. Malden, MA: Wiley-Blackwell.

Bully, S., Bully, A., Čaušević-Bully, M., and Fiocchi, L. (2015). "Die Anfänge des Klosters Luxeuil im Licht der jüngsten archäologischen Untersuchungen (6.–9. Jahrhundert)." In F. Schnoor, K. Schmuki, E. Tremp, P. Erhart, and J. Kuratli Hüeblin (eds.), *Gallus und seine Zeit. Leben, Wirken, Nachleben* (pp. 127–160). St. Gallen: Verlag im Klosterhof.

Claussen, M. A. (2004). *The Reform of the Frankish Church. Chrodegang of Metz and the Regula canonicorum in the Eighth Century.* Cambridge: Cambridge University Press.

Codou, Y., and Lauwers, M. (eds.). (2009). *Lérins, un îsle sainte de l'antiquité au Moyen Âge.* Turnhout: Brepols.

Dailey, E. T. A. (2015). *Queens, Consorts, Concubines: Gregory of Tours and Women of the Merovingian Elite.* Leiden: Brill.

de Jong, M. (1995). "Carolingian Monasticism: The Power of Prayer." In R. McKitterick (ed.), *The New Cambridge Medieval History, vol. 2: c. 700–c. 900* (pp. 622–653, 995–1002). Cambridge: Cambridge University Press.

de Jong, M. (2001), "Monastic Prisoners or Opting Out? Political Coercion and Honour in the Frankish kingdoms." In M. De Jong, C. van Rhijn, and F. Theuws (eds.), *Topographies of Power in the Early Middle Ages* (pp. 291–328). Leiden: Brill.

de Vogüé, A. (1985). *Les règles monastiques anciennes (400–700).* Typologie des sources 46. Turnhout: Brepols.

Dekkers, E., and Gaar, E. (1995). *Clavis Patrum Latinorum.* 3rd edition. Turnhout: Brepols.

Dey, H. (2011). "Bringing Chaos out of Order: New Approaches to the Study of Early Western Monasticism." In H. Dey and E. Fentress (eds.), *Western Monasticism* ante litteram: *The Spaces of Monastic Observance in Late Antiquity and the Early Middle Ages* (pp. 19–40). Disciplina Monastica 8. Turnhout: Brepols.

Diem, A. (2002), "Was bedeutet Regula Columbani?" In M. Diesenberger and W. Pohl (eds.), *Integration und Herrschaft. Ethnische Identitäten und soziale Organisation im Frühmittelalter* (pp. 63–89). Vienna: Verlag der Österreichischen Akademie der Wissenschaften.

Diem, A. (2005). *Das monastische Experiment. Die Rolle der Keuschheit bei der Entstehung des westlichen Klosterwesens.* Münster: LIT-Verlag.

Diem, A. (2013a), "Who Is Allowed to Pray for the King? Saint-Maurice d'Agaune and the Creation of a Burgundian Identity." In G. Heydemann and W. Pohl (eds.), *Post-Roman Transitions. Christian and Barbarian Identities in the Early Medieval West* (pp. 47–88). Cultural Encounters in Late Antiquity and the Middle Ages 14. Turnhout: Brepols.

Diem, A. (2013b), "The Gender of the Religious: Wo/Men and the Invention of Monasticism." In J. Bennett and R. Marzo-Karras (eds.), *The Oxford Companion on Women and Gender in the Middle Ages* (pp. 432–446). Oxford: Oxford University Press.

Diem, A. (2015a), "Die 'Regula Columbani' und die 'Regula Sancti Galli'. Überlegungen zu den Gallusviten in ihrem karolingischen Kontext." In F. Schnoor, K. Schmuki, E. Tremp, P. Erhart, and J. K. Hüeblin (eds.), *Gallus und seine Zeit. Leben, Wirken, Nachleben* (pp. 67–99). St. Gallen: Verlag im Klosterhof.

Diem, A. (2015b), "Gregory's Chess Board: Monastic Conflict and Competition in Early Medieval Gaul." In P. Depreux, F. Bougard, and R. Le Jan (eds.), *Compétition et sacré au haut Moyen Âge: entre médiation et exclusion* (pp. 165–191). Turnhout: Brepols.

Diem, A. (2018), "Disputing Columbanus' Heritage: The *Regula cuiusdam patris*." In A. O'Hara (ed.), *Columbanus and the Peoples of Post-Roman Europe* (pp. 259–306). Oxford: Oxford University Press.

Diem, A., and Rousseau, P. (2020). "Monastic Rules, 4th–9th c.," In A. Beach and I. Cochelin (eds.), *The Cambridge History of Medieval Monasticism in the Latin West* 1 (pp. 162–194). Cambridge: Cambridge University Press.

Dunn, M. (2000). *The Emergence of Monasticism. From the Desert Fathers to the Early Middle Ages*. Oxford: Blackwell.

Fox, Y. (2014). *Power and Religion in Merovingian Gaul. Columbanian Monasticism and the Frankish Elites*. Cambridge: Cambridge University Press.

Goffart, W. (1966). *The Le Mans Forgeries. A Chapter from the History of Church Property in the Ninth Century*. Cambridge, MA: Harvard University Press.

Heinzelmann, M. (2010). "L'hagiographie mérovingienne. Panorama des documents potentiels." In M. Heinzelmann and M. Goullet (eds.), *L'hagiographie mérovingienne à travers les réécritures* (pp. 27–82). Beihefte der Francia 71. Sigmaringen: Jan Thorbecke Verlag.

Helvétius, A.-M. (2015). "L'abbaye d'Agaune, de la fondation de Sigismond au règne de Charlemagne (515–814)." In B. Andenmatten and L. Ripart (eds.), *L'abbaye de Saint-Maurice d'Agaune, 515–2015*, vol. 1: *Histoire et archéologie* (pp. 111–133). Saint-Maurice: Gollion.

Klingshirn, W. E. (1994). *Caesarius of Arles. The Making of a Christian Community in Late Antique Gaul*. Cambridge: Cambridge University Press.

Koziol, G. (2012). *The Politics of Memory and Identity in Carolingian Royal Diplomas: The West Frankish Kingdom (840–987)*. Turnhout: Brepols.

Lawrence, C. H. (1984/2015). *Medieval Monasticism. Forms of Religious Life in Western Europe in the Middle Ages*, 4th edition. London: Routledge.

Leyser, C. (2000). *Authority and Asceticism from Augustine to Gregory the Great*. Oxford: Clarendon Press.

Lifshitz, F. (2014). *Religious Women in Early Carolingian Francia: A Study of Manuscript Transmission and Monastic Culture*. New York: Fordham University Press.

Markus, R. A. (1990). *The End of Ancient Christianity*. Cambridge: Cambridge University Press.

Meeder, S. (2011). "Boniface and the Irish Heresy of Clemens." *Church History* 80(2): 251–280.

Meens, R. (2014). *Penance in Medieval Europe*. Cambridge: Cambridge University Press.

Melville, G. (2016). *The World of Medieval Monasticism. Its History and Forms of Life*. Collegeville, MI: Cistercian Publications, Liturgical Press.

O'Hara, A. (2015). "*Columbanus ad Locum*: The Establishment of the Monastic Foundations." *Peritia* 26: 143–170.

Prinz, F. (1988). *Frühes Mönchtum im Frankenreich. Kultur und Gesellschaft in Gallien, den Rheinlanden und Bayern am Beispiel der monastischen Entwicklung (4. bis 8. Jhd.)*, 2nd edition. Munich, Vienna: Oldenbourg Verlag.

Riché, P. (1962). *Éducation et culture dans l'occident barbare, VIe-VIIIe siècles*. Paris: Éditions du Seuil.

Rosenwein, B. H. (1999). *Negotiating Space: Power, Restraint, and Privileges of Immunity in Early Medieval Europe*. Ithaca, NY: Cornell University Press.

Rosenwein, B. H. (2000). "Perennial Prayer at Agaune." In S. Farmer and B. H. Rosenwein (eds.), *Monks and Nuns. Saints and Outcasts. Religion in Medieval Society. Essays in Honor of Lester K. Little* (pp. 37–56). Ithaca, NY: Cornell University Press.

Rousseau, P. (2010). *Ascetics, Authority, and the Church in the Age of Jerome and Cassian*. 2nd edition. Notre Dame, IN: University of Notre Dame Press.

Stancliffe, C. E. (1983). *St. Martin and His Hagiographer: History and Miracle in Sulpicius Severus*. Oxford: Oxford University Press.

Stancliffe, C. E. (2011). "Columbanus's Monasticism and the Sources of His Inspiration: from Basil to the Master?" In F. Edmonds and P. Russell (eds.), *Tome. Studies in Medieval Celtic History and Law in Honour of Thomas Charles-Edwards* (pp. 17–28). Woodbridge: Boydell Press.

Ueding, L. (1935). *Geschichte der Klostergründungen der frühen Merowingerzeit*. Berlin: Verlag Dr. Emil Ebering.

Wood, I. N. (2001). *The Missionary Life: Saints and the Evangelisation of Europe 400–1050*. Harlow: Longman.

Wood, I. N. (2015). "The Irish in England and on the Continent in the Seventh Century: Part I." *Peritia* 26: 171–198.

Wycherley, N. (2015). *The Cult of Relics in Early Medieval Ireland*. Turnhout: Brepols.

PART IV

MEROVINGIAN GAUL IN A WIDER CONTEXT

CHAPTER 16

··

THE MEROVINGIANS
AND BYZANTIUM

Diplomatic, Military, and Religious Issues,
500–700

··

STEFAN ESDERS

THE Roman Empire cast a long shadow over the barbarian kingdoms established on Roman provincial soil during the fifth, sixth, and seventh centuries. Following the deposition of the last Roman emperor in Ravenna in 476, Constantinople continued to exercise considerable influence on the western kingdoms. But how can the nature of this relationship be described? Despite diplomatic gestures between Byzantium and the Merovingian kingdoms, "international law" or "foreign policy" would be anachronistic categories, as the *regna* in the West were in some respects willing to accept that they were still part of the Roman Empire and, therefore, in modern terminology, under Byzantine rule. To judge such claims as mere lipservice would downplay their importance and simplify the complicated, indeed multilayered, nature of the legitimacy of the Merovingian kingdoms. The Roman Empire had an elephant's memory in regard to its historical size and the regions that once had been under its direct control; this outlook shaped eastern Rome's perspective on the barbarian kingdoms in its former western parts as regards their nature, function, and legitimacy. Moreover, the Roman Empire could provide a source of legitimacy in many different ways: the emperor could bestow legitimacy on the new western kings by recognizing them, just as he could revoke such imperial legitimacy, for instance, by supporting usurpers who were somehow related to one of the ruling dynasties. As a consequence, the formula "kingdoms of the Empire" (Pohl 1997) may point to a common language in which claims and expectations rooted in the history of the Roman Empire could be negotiated.

It would be misleading, however, to treat the relationship between Byzantium and Merovingian Gaul as a bilateral one. For most of Merovingian history, there were at least two Merovingian kingdoms that often did not coordinate their relations with Byzantium as part of a joint policy. Moreover, from the perspective of eastern Rome, what happened in Gaul was only part of a major western constellation that included Spain and, more importantly, Italy, but potentially also North Africa or even Britain. In the eyes of Constantinople, relations with the Franks thus often depended on the nature of eastern Rome's relations with the Ostrogoths, Visigoths, and later the Lombards, as they all were somehow regarded as being part of the "Byzantine commonwealth" (Obolensky 1971; Fowden 1993). Finally, it is important to emphasize that Christianity transcended political frontiers. Thus, when Clovis decided to adopt the empire's Christian religion for his kingdom and people, the churches of Merovingian Gaul were regarded as subordinate to the western patriarchate of the bishop of Rome (Schieffer 1991). Conflicts on large looming dogmatic issues such as the Three Chapters and monothelitism, both of which centered around debates on the relation between the human and divine nature of Christ, shook the Mediterranean world, precisely because they were also political conflicts with an impact on western acceptance of Roman imperial religious policies (Chazelle and Cubitt 2007; Booth 2013).

Relations between Byzantium and Merovingian Gaul must therefore be looked at from a broader perspective, not confined to "diplomacy" (Chrysos 1992; Drauschke 2011, pp. 246–263), but rather exploring the role of several main players. It becomes evident that such relations were multilayered and developed quite dynamically, often depending on, or reacting to, broader changes that occurred outside of Gaul. Owing to the paucity of evidence in our sources, however, a full narrative can hardly be given. Nonetheless, our information on Frankish–Byzantine relations often points to periods of intense contact over several years, when rapid changes in political circumstances meant that closer relations between eastern Rome and the Franks could serve both partners' purposes. The following outline of Frankish–Byzantine relations in the sixth and seventh centuries therefore focuses on such periods of intensification.

EMPEROR ANASTASIUS I RECOGNIZES CLOVIS'S RULE OVER GAUL (CA. 506–511)

Although the establishment of the Frankish kingdom during and after the events in Ravenna in 476 is difficult to assess in its imperial dimensions, it seems clear that eastern Rome did not involve itself in Gallic matters until a somewhat later date. The authority of Constantinople was clearly felt in the Burgundian kingdom of southern Gaul around 500, where laws and inscriptions are dated according to consulate years (Scheibelreiter 1989; Handley 2000). It seems likely that Clovis's victory over the Visigoths in Aquitaine was made possible by an alliance with the Burgundian king and *magister militum* Gundobad, which may also have brought Clovis into contact with the emperor Anastasius (Ewig 1983, pp. 9–10; Wood 2014b, pp. 195–196). It is very likely that Byzantine naval support hindered the Ostrogoths from entering Clovis's fight against the Visigoths

(Marcellinus Comes, *Chron.*, ad. ann. 508). Given that Clovis was initially part of the marriage alliance network established by the Ostrogoth Theoderic, the Franks' conversion to the Catholic faith certainly must also be seen as a symbolic concession to Constantinople, although there is still no consensus on the exact date of Clovis's baptism (Shanzer 1998; Becher 2011). Larger groups of Roman soldiers located in northwestern Gaul more or less independently arranged a settlement with Frankish troops some time after 500 on the basis of sharing the Christian religion with the Franks (Procopius, *Wars* V, 12).

During his famous victory celebration held at Tours in 508 as reported by Gregory of Tours (*Hist.* II, 38), Clovis seems to have received the patriciate, which made him a sort of imperial representative (Faussner 1986), and honorary consulate. The victory ceremony that followed was a military ritual in which Clovis, wearing a purple tunic and Roman cloak (*chlamys*), paraded on horseback while distributing coins in the fashion of a reception ceremony (*adventus*), which was otherwise celebrated by Roman dignitaries of highest imperial rank (Hauck 1967; McCormick 1989; Mathisen 2012). His coronation with a diadem clearly had imperial connotations, legitimizing his status as king. Meanwhile, his acclamation as *augustus* and the purple tunic may have framed him as an imperial agent superior to Gundobad (Guillot 1997; Wood 2014b, p. 196), and Clovis's sons may also have received some sort of imperial recognition (Ewig 1983, p. 11 n. 32). The relevance of this legitimation becomes strikingly visible in Clovis's invitation of the Gallic episcopate to a Gallic council in Orléans in 511 (*Concilia Galliae*, 3–19), undoubtedly a response to the Visigothic council held at Agde only five years before, but apparently also modeled on the example of Emperor Constantine (Guillot 1997, pp. 729–730; Halfond 2012, pp. 151–153, 162). The synod not only served to incorporate the conquered part of Aquitania into the Frankish realm, but on a more general level also sought to integrate bishops and their cities and ecclesiastical provinces into a Frankish church (see also Halfond, Chapter 13; Hen, Chapter 10, this volume). While Roman tradition and support allowed Clovis to consolidate local areas under his dominion, this in turn also provided Byzantium with a modicum of religious and temporal authority.

Justinian Recognizes Frankish Expansion during the Ostrogothic Wars (533–555)

It appears that Byzantium did not become involved in the first phase of Frankish expansion under the sons of Clovis, when expeditions were conducted against the Burgundians, the Visigoths, and the Thuringians in the 520s and early 530s. However, Frankish defeat and absorption of the Burgundian kingdom in 532 changed the western constellation of power, as the Franks became direct partners of Constantinople in regard to imperial policies in Italy. This was most obvious shortly thereafter in Justinian's wars against the Ostrogoths. A Byzantine embassy was dispatched to the three Merovingian kings—Childebert I of Paris, Chlothar I of Soissons, and Theudebert I of Reims in 535—shortly before Roman troops under Belisarius were sent to Sicily (Procopius, *Wars* V, 5, 8–9; see also VIII, 24, 6–30). This event underlines the relevance of Frankish support at this early stage (Ewig 1983, p. 12 n. 33), as it shows a Byzantine awareness that there were three independent Frankish players acting in Gaul with whom it could be necessary to negotiate (on Frankish relations with the Ostrogoths, see Arnold, Chapter 21, this volume).

In the same year, east Roman reorganization of military and provincial structures in the Balkans led to a rearrangement of political and military structures around the Alpine regions. Under intense military pressure, King Witigis of the Ostrogoths surrendered the Ostrogoth-controlled regions of "Northern Italy," once part of the Italian prefecture, to the Franks (Claude 1997, pp. 355–356), thereby effectively making the Franks new rulers of the Alpine region (see Arnold, Chapter 21, this volume). In 536, Justinian's recorded agreement ceded Ostrogothic Provence to the three Frankish kings (Procopius, *Wars* V, 11 and 13; Ewig 1983, pp. 12–13, Beisel 1993, pp. 45–47), suggesting that a complete change of power was the issue at hand. East Roman confirmation was given on the condition that Theudebert I and later Theudebald promised to treat the Romans in Provence properly (*Ep. Austr.* 6; Ewig 1983, pp. 13–14). This could also apply to Burgundy, which was finally annexed by the Franks in 534 (Wood 2014a, pp. 1–2). Immediately prior to this, the Franks had eliminated the kingdom of Thuringia, which led to the formation of a Thuringian duchy (Kaelble 2009, pp. 337–338, 346–358).

Additionally, the Frankish-Lombard marital alliance between King Theudebert I of Reims (533–547) and Princess Wisigard helped secure the new landscape, backing territorial claims over Pannonia and possibly Italy (Beisel 1993, pp. 53–57). The formation of the Bavarian duchy (Hammer 2008, pp. 52–82) and the corresponding establishment of the adjoining Alemannic duchy (Hartung 1983) around the years 537/538 appears to have been part of a new Frankish power structure legitimized by the eastern Roman emperor. We find this most elaborately expressed in a letter of Theudebert I to Justinian apparently written sometime after 533, in which the Frankish king claimed that his kingdom extended from the Danube and the frontiers of Pannonia to the ocean, with Thuringians, northern Swabians and Saxons settled east of the Rhine now subject to his rule (*Ep. Austr.* 20; Kaeble 2009, p. 337). Theudebert is duly criticized by Procopius for arrogating imperial prerogatives by holding circus games and having his image placed on coins (*Wars*, VII, 33). This presumption can be confirmed by extant coinage, of which one coin produced in Metz gives Theudebert the title of Augustus (Jenks 2000). In 537, Justinian introduced a reform of chronology that made calculation after regnal years and the fifteen-years' taxation cycle (*indictio*) obligatory (Justinian, *Novel* 47; Feissel 1993). This sign of Justinian's authority appears to have been adapted by the Merovingian kings very quickly, as Gallic inscriptions continuously date according to the indiction years from 540 onward (Heidrich 1968, p. 172).

According to a Justinianic law from 534 after the reconquest of North Africa (*Cod. Iust.* I, 27), building work at the Straits of Gibraltar (Septem) was intended to exact control not only over Spain, but also over Frankish Gaul (*in partibus Hispaniae vel Galliae seu Francorum*). Despite this strategic orbit, Justinian seems at first to have accepted Frankish expansion as necessary to his plans to drive the Ostrogoths out of Italy. The restitution of the imperial prefecture of Italy shortly after 537 (Claude 1997, pp. 355–356) could be connected to this objective. Measures taken to settle the Heruls in the Balkans were directed primarily against the Ostrogoths (Steinacher 2010). The new order of cooperation between two Catholic powers was eloquently expressed in the letter from Justinian to the Frankish kings (Procopius, *Wars* V, 5, 8–9). However, Procopius criticized the invasion of northern Italy by the eastern Frankish King Theudebert, beginning as early as 539. Procopius stated that the Franks had broken faith and had not fulfilled their military obligations toward Byzantium, and that they were rather trying to gain territory in Italy for their dominion and find an agreement with the Goths (*Wars* VII, 33; VIII, 24, 6–11; Collins 1983; Beisel 1993, pp. 37–64; Cameron 1985, pp. 210–213). Quite clearly, the military plans of Theudebert I and his son Theudebald (547-555) were to extend Frankish rule over large parts of northern Italy (Collins 1983), although Justinian constantly reminded them both of their obligations toward Constantinople (*Ep. Austr.* 18; Ewig 1983, pp. 21–22). As Agathias noted, Theudebert felt insulted by Justinian's use of *Alamannicus, Francicus, Gepidicius,* and *Langobardicus* in his official titulature, by which he presented himself as having subdued these peoples and conquered their territories. To counter such claims and extend Frankish influence as far as Thrace, Theudebert sent envoys to the Gepids and Lombards to gain their military support against eastern Rome, whose general Narses was fighting against Totila in Italy in the 540s (Agathias, fragment 4; Cameron 1968; Collins 1983, p. 12). Frankish control over parts of northern Italy lasted until Theudebald I of Reims died in 555 and was succeeded by Chlothar I of Soissons. After the Ostrogothic War, eastern Rome managed to drive the Franks out of Italy and the southern Alps between 556 and 562 (Ewig 1983, pp. 24–25).

MEROVINGIAN GAUL AND THE THREE CHAPTERS CONTROVERSY (548–553)

It is difficult to connect this series of events to the religious issues that were at stake around the same time. The legitimacy of Frankish rule and the acceptability of the Franks as allies and partners depended to some extent on the Franks' adherence to the Catholic faith. Evidence for this stance may be found in the above-mentioned imperial letter cited by Procopius (Procopius, *Wars* V, 5, 8–9) and also in Frankish legislation— for example, when Childebert I of Paris adopted imperial policies and legislation suppressing pagan practices and restricting the mobility of Jews during Easter time in the late 530s (*Capitularia regum Francorum* 1 n. 2; Mordek 1995, pp. 970–971; see also Drews, Chapter 6, this volume). The earliest collections of Gallic canon law, written around 550, show conciliar legislation under Frankish rule in line with the ecumenical and Gallic councils of the late Roman period, as is also illustrated through lists of popes and the inclusion of papal decretals (Esders 1997, pp. 36–37). By the same token, the papacy sought to spread its influence over the Gallic church through the archbishop of Arles as apostolic vicar for Gaul (Langgaertner 1964), who was usually appointed with imperial consent, as is attested for the 540s (Ewig 1983, pp. 14–15).

The complex nature of relations between the Gallic church, the papacy in Rome, and the emperor in Constantinople first becomes visible in the Three Chapter controversy of the mid-sixth century. This controversy was instigated by the east Roman emperor Justinian's condemnation of three theological treatises on the divine and human nature of Christ in an effort to achieve unanimity with the eastern churches by the use of anathematization. The emperor's intervention in Christological dogma caused a major crisis, with implications for large parts of the Mediterranean (Chazelle and Cubitt 2007). By keeping the pope under arrest in Constantinople from 547 to ensure he would subscribe to Justinian's edict (Caspar 1933, pp. 226–286), Justinian also exerted enormous pressure on western bishops. This policy provoked fierce resistance among the churches of the western provinces of the Roman Empire and beyond, as may be seen in the letter collection of Arles (*Epistolae Arelatenses* nos. 40–56; Wood 2007, pp. 224–230). The fifth Synod of Orléans held under Childebert I in 549, ostensibly condemning the teachings of Nestorius and Eutyches, most likely sought to deal with the Three Chapter controversy (*Concilia Galliae*, pp. 148–149; Stueber 2019). A dossier of three letters written by Pope Vigilius during his detainment in Constantinople in 550 sought to clarify his position and evoke resistance against condemnation of the Three Chapters. Preserved in a Gallic canon law collection (Schwartz 1940), the dossier appears to have been transmitted to Gaul to manipulate opinion among the episcopacy and the Frankish royal courts. It was supplemented by a lengthy report apparently written by the clergy of the archbishopric of Milan addressing the ambassadors of an unknown Frankish king about to depart for Constantinople (Schwartz 1940, pp. 18–25) to report in some detail the maltreatment of the pope and the archbishop of Milan in Constantinople.

In the absence of the pope and archbishop, the letter sent from the Milanese clergy to one of the Merovingian courts describes how imperial agents were gaining ground all over Italy, consecrating bishops "who would assent to novelties." Apparently, some "heretical" envoys had also been sent to Gaul and managed to outmaneuver the apostolic vicar of Arles and, through bribery, "induce the minds of all the Gallic bishops to condemn the chapters over which these scandals have arisen" (transl. Price 2009, 1, pp. 165–170). Mediterranean-wide communication of rumors, texts, censorship, and propaganda framed this attempt to involve the Frankish kingdoms in the inner conflicts among the northern Italian and Gallic clergy (Wood 2007) and exert a certain pressure on Constantinople.

The letter from Milan may have been addressed to the Austrasian king Theudebald (Ewig 1983, 22–23), who was then in conflict with east Roman troops in northern Italy. However, as Procopius recounts, it was around this time that a Frankish embassy had been sent to Constantinople. This embassy included a group of Angles who had settled in Gaul with Frankish consent and who now served to back a Frankish claim of ruling over Britain (*Wars* VIII, 20, 6–10; Thompson 1980, pp. 498–507; Wood 1983, pp. 12–19; 1992). If this is correct, some proponents deliberately sought to combine political, diplomatic, and military issues with the religious controversy over the Three Chapters. It appears that the Austrasian kings were not willing to submit too easily, as Nicetius, archbishop of Trier (who died after 566), criticized the eastern emperor as the "son of the devil" and "enemy of righteousness" in a letter possibly written around 550 (*Epp. Austr.* 7; Pohlsander 2000) that dealt with the Three Chapters; formally addressing the emperor, it could have been destined for circulation in Gaul. After the defeat of the Ostrogothic troops, Pope Vigilius eventually subscribed to the fifth ecumenical council's condemnation of the Three Chapters in 553, causing a lasting alienation from the papacy of many western bishops from Italy, Dalmatia, North Africa, and even Gaul. It took subsequent popes several attempts to mitigate the conflict with the Gallic church (Wood 2007).

FRANKISH–BYZANTINE RELATIONS FOLLOWING THE LOMBARD INVASION OF ITALY (565–590)

From about 552, when the Visigothic King Athanagild called for outside help in an internal struggle for the throne, the authority of eastern Rome was also present in southern Spain. The Austrasian and Neustrian branches of the Merovingian dynasty soon concluded alliances with Athanagild: in 566, Sigibert I of Austrasia married Athanagild's daughter Brunhild, who converted from Arianism to Catholicism, and soon afterward his half-brother Chilperic of Neustria married Brunhild's sister Galswinth (see James, Chapter 11, this volume). Merovingian dynastic policy extended remarkably beyond their political frontiers, although dynastic change in Visigothic Spain, following Athanagild's death most likely played a role in Galswinth's murder around 570, which paved the way for deadly conflicts between the Neustrian and Austrasian branches. Sigibert's Austrasian court at Metz maintained its Visigothic link through Queen Brunhild and concluded a peace treaty with the newly appointed Emperor Justin II (565-578) (Greg., *Hist.* IX, 40; Cameron 1976), which included the transfer of a relic of the True Cross from Constantinople to Queen Radegund's monastic foundation in Poitiers (Moreira 1993). Around the same time, a sworn treaty between Sigibert, Guntram, and Chilperic dividing up the territories of their deceased brother Charibert (561-567/568) was protected by Polyeuctus, a Byzantine saint (Greg., *Hist.* VII, 6), whose relics had been brought to the Austrasian capital of Metz. King Sigibert may thus have used Byzantine support to dominate his brothers in the division of Charibert's kingdom (Esders 2014). Such intensification of Byzantine–Austrasian affairs was undoubtedly facilitated by Radegund's Amal-Thuringian connection to Constantinople through her cousin, Amalafrid, who at that time was *magister militum* in Byzantium (Brandes 2009, pp. 302–305). It was almost certainly motivated by the Lombard invasion of Italy, which caused Justin to reach out to the Austrasian branch of the Merovingians as allies.

To motivate the Austrasian court to intervene in Italy, Emperor Tiberius II (574/578-581) sent money for the recruitment of Frankish soldiers against the Lombards (Greg., *Hist.* VI, 2; Ewig 1983, p. 29; Loseby 2016, p. 470) but, interestingly called for Frankish mercenaries in the Near East (Evagrius, *Hist. eccl.* V, 14; Fourlas 2019). Although the origins of this policy are difficult to trace, Byzantium also played some role in the Merovingian dynastic quarrels that followed. Following the murder of Sigibert I in 575, King Guntram of Burgundy sought peaceful relations with the Lombards, while kings Chilperic and Childebert II sent embassies to Constantinople in 578 (Greg., *Hist.* V, 17 and VI, 2) and promised military support in return for subsidies from Byzantium. The alliance between Austrasia and Neustria, according to a papal letter of 580, possibly encouraged by Constantinople (*Epp. aevi merowingici collectae* 9), led to Childebert II's adoption by King Chilperic in 581 (Greg., *Hist.* V, 17; see also VI, 3, 31, 41). As a consequence, some Austrasian noblemen who opposed Frankish intervention in Italy switched to Guntram's side, while the Austrasian court supported his opponent, the usurper Gundovald in Gaul (Goubert 1955, pp. 19–24; Goffart 1957, pp. 85–94; Zuckerman 1998). Gundovald was most likely a son of King Chlothar I and was at first accepted by kings Charibert I and Sigibert I in the 560s (Bachrach 1994, pp. 3–30), but eventually fled first to Italy and later to the imperial court at Constantinople (Zuckerman 1998; Widdowson 2008), where the envoys of Childebert II and Chilperic most likely met him (Ewig 1983, p. 33). When Gundovald returned to Gaul in 582 with Byzantine financial support and supported by Bishop Theodore of Marseille (Loseby 2016, p. 488), he claimed Guntram's territories for himself and King Childebert II (Goffart 1957, 2012; Bachrach 1994). The Austrasian court in turn renewed its alliance with the new emperor Maurice (582-602), sending an embassy to Constantinople (*Epp. Austr.* 42). It was only in 584, after Chilperic's murder, that Gundovald attempted to create a kingdom for himself (*Hist.* VII, 10; 26–27). He laid claim to Sigibert's former cities in southwestern Gaul, which had come under the control of King Guntram of Burgundy after Chilperic's death (*Hist.* VII, 14), and took over Chilperic's possessions, including the marriage portion given to Chilperic's daughter Rigunth for her Visigothic marriage with King Reccared, co-ruler with his father Leovigild and brother Hermenegild since 573 (*Hist.* VII, 10, 31). However, following a renewal of the Austraso-Burgundian alliance between Childebert II and Guntram (*Hist.* VII, 33–34), Gundovald failed and was murdered in 585.

The fact that Emperor Tiberius II simultaneously supported the insurrection of the Visigothic king Hermenegild against his father Leovigild in Spain from 579 and the usurpation of Gundovald in Francia (Goffart 1957; Collins 2016, pp. 500–515) may have been facilitated by the Austrasian queen Brunhild (Dumézil 2008): her daughter Ingund had married Hermenegild, who was captured by his father in 584 and murdered the following year. Following Hermenegild's death, his wife Ingund and son Athanagild came into Byzantine custody. Emperor Maurice therefore had leverage over Brunhild. The Lombards, after an interregnum of ten years, had appointed Authari as king in 584, in reaction to the threatening Franco-Byzantine alliance and the newly established exarchate of Ravenna. In exchange for support against the Lombards, Brunhild may have pursued the liberation of her grandchild (*Epp. Austr.* 26–39; Goubert 1955, pp. 127–159;

Gillett 2010) as part of a plan to bring him to rule in Spain (Ewig 1983, p. 44). There are also signs of Austrasian collaboration with King Reccared, sole ruler of Visigothic Spain, who had converted to Catholicism in 587 (Greg. *Hist.*, IX, 1; 16, 20, 25) and sought contact with Byzantium shortly thereafter (Schreiner 1985). However, the Austrasian campaign in 588 ended with a severe Frankish defeat, and Emperor Maurice, who had sent 50,000 *solidi* to the Franks for support against the Lombards, recalled the money when the degree of Frankish military engagement was deemed insufficient (*Hist.*, VI, 42 and VIII, 18). In 590, Childebert II concluded a peace treaty with the Lombards, thus ending Byzantine hopes of moving the Lombards out of Italy with Frankish help (see also Arnold, Chapter 21, this volume). It also marked the end of eastern Rome's policy of sending huge sums of money west, a step to which the "pseudo-imperial" gold coinage minted in Provence may be connected (Uhalde 2001; Loseby 2016, p. 464; Fischer 2019). From then on, Frankish–Byzantine cooperation was directed against the Avars in the Balkans rather than the Lombards in Italy (Pohl 2002; see Hardt, Chapter 20, this volume).

A World Crisis, an "Eternal Peace," and Frankish Expansion Eastward (ca. 628–634)

The usurpation of Phocas in 602 and the final phase of the Merovingian *bella civilia* (civil wars) may lie behind the fact that our sources tell us hardly anything about Byzantine–Frankish relations in the period between 602 and ca. 628, when Byzantium also lost control of its Spanish territories in Southern Spain. We may suspect that the dynastic turnover of 613 contributed to this development, as the Austrasian branch exterminated in 613 had had the closest links to Byzantium. It may be significant that, following the Persian conquest of Jerusalem in 614, the Visigothic King Sisebut concluded a treaty with Emperor Heraclius and adopted Byzantine policies by compulsorily baptizing the Jews of the Iberian peninsula. As some of them took refuge in Gaul, King Chlothar II of Neustria, who became sole king in 613, does not seem to have adopted Heraclius's policy (Esders 2018b). Moreover, shortly after 615, the Frankish mints of Provence gave up minting coins with the image of Emperor Heraclius, replacing him with the bust and name of Chlothar II instead (Rigold 1954, pp. 102, 117, 119; James 1988, p. 119; Grierson and Blackburn 1990, pp. 111–119).

Although Chlothar II reigned until 629, it is only with the succession of his son, Dagobert I, as sole ruler over the whole kingdom that information on closer contact between Constantinople and Francia may be found. In the meantime, dramatic wars against Persia and the siege of Constantinople (626) distracted eastern Rome's attention from the West (Bowersock 2012), and they lost the Spanish provinces at this time. The Frankish chronicler Fredegar, writing around 660 (Collins 2007; Fischer 2014), reports how the Slavic group of the Wends separated from the Avars and settled under their Frankish leader Samo on Frankish territory in a treaty concluded with Dagobert (*Chron.* IV, 68; Curta 1997, pp. 148–163). According to the same source, the people of the Frankish kingdom next to the frontier with the Slavs and Avars encouraged Dagobert to campaign in their frontier zone to subdue them until the frontiers of the "public hand" (*manus publica*) came under Frankish rule (*Chron.* IV, 58; Fritze 1994, pp. 85–89; Esders 2009, pp. 299–308; see also Hardt, Chapter 20, this volume). This seems to be connected to the fact that Emperor Heraclius and King Dagobert concluded an eternal peace (*pax perpetua*) (*Chron.* IV, 65) around 629/630. This agreement coincided with a new settlement policy pursued by Heraclius, who installed some converted groups of Croats and Serbs in the western Balkans against the Avars (Konstantinos Porphyrogennetos, *De administrando imperio* 31; Lilie 1985; Thanner 1989; Budak 1993; Pohl 2002, pp. 261–268, 276–277; see, however, Borri 2011), and possibly also a failed attempt by Amandus of Maastricht to convert Slavs in the areas along the Danube (Esders 2016). Dagobert's adoption of Heraclius's religious policy of forcing the Jews to convert to Christianity (Fredegar, *Chron.* IV, 66) may also have been a result of the treaty of 629/630 and seems to echo papal policy of the time (Rouche 1977; Esders 2009, pp. 263–272, Esders 2018a). A disastrous Frankish defeat against the Wends caused Dagobert to launch a reorganization of the east Frankish frontier in 633/634 by creating a subkingdom of Austrasia ruled by his underage son Sigibert III, for which purpose the Ripuarian Law code was compiled.

THE IMPACT OF MONOTHELITISM AND OF THE LATERAN SYNOD OF 649 ON MEROVINGIAN GAUL

Monothelitism, a Christological dogma propagated by Emperor Heraclius from 638, marks another issue that exercised a profound impact on Franco-Byzantine relations. A passage in the *Life* of Bishop Eligius of Noyon mentions that "a wicked heresy which originated in eastern lands began to pullulate" in the early years of King Clovis II (*Vita Eligii* I.33; see Bayer 2007, pp. 485–486; Berschin 2010), apparently referring to monothelitism, while the following section (*Vita Eligii* I.34; Sarti 2019) reports on Pope Martin I, the Lateran Synod of 649, and imperial attempts to remove the pope from his see. The Lateran Synod brought about a remarkable shift in the definition and geographical setting of religious groups within the Roman Empire and beyond (Booth 2013). Theologians critical of monothelitism such as Maximus Confessor exerted a powerful influence over the debates held in 649, which ultimately led to the condemnation of both Heraclius's *Ekthesis* and Constans II's *Typos* (Brandes 1998, pp. 142–149; Winkelmann 2001, pp. 85–90, 125–131). While bishops from Italy and North Africa gathered around the papacy, whose primacy was acknowledged even by Chalcedonian bishops from Palestine, the synod sent shockwaves throughout the Mediterranean, with the papacy urging the western kingdoms of Visigothic Spain (García Moreno 2002, Esders 2019b) and Merovingian Gaul to adopt its position. The position of the Merovingian kingdoms toward monothelitism had to take into account theological as well as political factors, as the Lateran Synod of 649 was framed by two usurpations of the imperial title. First, Gregory, exarch of Carthage, propagated the anti-monothelite cause and revolted against Constans II from ca. 645 to 647, until he was beaten and killed by the Arabs near his residence at Sbeitla. Shortly after the Lateran Synod, Olympius, exarch of Ravenna, was dispatched to Rome in 649 or 650 to suppress the anti-monothelite opposition, but eventually changed sides and had himself proclaimed emperor. He died in Sicily in 651/652, allegedly fighting an Arab attack. This development eventually led to the collapse of anti-monothelite opposition in Rome, the arrest of Pope Martin I and Maximus Confessor, and the condemnation of both as traitors (Brandes 1998; Howard-Johnston 2010, pp. 157–162; Booth 2013, pp. 300–313).

When seen in the general context of these crucial theological and political developments in the later 640s, it is striking that the two Merovingian kingdoms apparently pursued different policies with regard to the Lateran Synod. Pope Martin asked the Austrasian king, Sigibert III, to convoke an Austrasian synod that would adapt the Lateran Council's decisions and condemn monothelitism. To achieve this, Martin forwarded the conciliar acts along with a letter to Amandus, bishop of Maastricht from 647 to 649. In this letter, he requested that Amandus encourage the Austrasian king to send a delegation of bishops to Rome who "may act as delegates of the apostolic see and transmit without fail the proceedings of our council together with these our synodical letters to our most clement prince," that is, Emperor Constans II (*Concilium Lateranense*, 422–424; transl. Price, p. 411; see Scheibelreiter 1992; Winkelmann 2001, p. 128; Wood 2007, pp. 239–240). Amandus, though not a bishop of a prominent see at that time, was nonetheless the appropriate person to address, as he had baptized Sigibert and thus had been the underage king's godfather (Mériaux 2019). That Amandus resigned his position as bishop of Maastricht shortly thereafter suggests that King Sigibert did not follow the papal suggestion to convoke an Austrasian synod. Principally, he rejected the pope's plan to drag him into his conflict with Constantinople.

Moreover, in a letter of ca. 650, Sigibert forbade the Aquitanian bishop Desiderius of Cahors from taking part in a synod announced by Archbishop Vulfoleodus of Bourges (Desiderius of Cahors, *Letters* II, 17; Esders 2019b). He resided in the Neustro-Burgundian territory subject to Sigibert's brother King Clovis II, while many of the suffragan bishops of the metropolitan see of Bourges, which comprised the former Roman province of *Aquitania prima*, had their dioceses in territories that belonged to the Aquitanian possessions of the Austrasian kingdom of Sigibert III. This was true not only for Cahors, where Desiderius was bishop, but also for the bishoprics of Toulouse, Rodez, and Albi, which belonged to Bourges in an ecclesiastical sense and to Austrasia in a political sense. In contrast, Clovis II, Sigibert's brother and ruler of the Neustro-Burgundian kingdom, reacted differently to Pope Martin's request. Very likely in 650, Clovis ordered the bishops under his rule to assemble at a synod at Chalon-sur-Saône in northern Burgundy. The bishops, who had assembled "in zeal for religion and for love of the orthodox faith," consequently confirmed the definition of faith given at the Council of Nicaea in 325. They also confirmed the Council of Chalcedon, held in 451 in its entirety, while revealingly omitting any reference to the fifth ecumenical council that had condemned the Three Chapters. Moreover, they excommunicated and deposed Archbishop Theodore of Arles "regarding indecent life as well as violation of canon law" (*Concilia Galliae*, 303, 308–310). While all archbishops from Clovis's kingdoms of Neustria and Burgundy were present at Chalon, no Aquitanian bishop subject to Sigibert's rule took part.

In 650, it was very difficult to practice loyalty to the king as there were two kings with different opinions and an archbishopric whose territory overlapped with both of their kingdoms. The reservation of the Austrasian court in accepting the Lateran synod does not appear to have been primarily theologically motivated, but rather emanated from political considerations around not risking a political break with Byzantium, with which in particular the Austrasian kingdom shared political interests relating to Avars, Slavs, and Lombards. That the issue of monothelitism had divided the episcopate and clergy of the Frankish kingdoms around 650, appears to be reflected in the condemnation to hell of Archbishop Vulfoleodus of Bourges for his being deceitful in the *Vision of Barontus* (*Visio Baronti* 17), written around 675 from an Austrasian standpoint (see Esders 2019b). By contrast, the *Chronicle of Fredegar*, whose author can be linked to the Columbanian network centered around the monastery of Luxeuil that also included Amandus (Fox 2014, pp. 118–132), adopted the position of the Lateran Synod by claiming that Emperor Heraclius pursued "the heresy of Eutyches, abandoned the Christian faith and married his sister's daughter," finally "finishing his days in agony, tormented with fever" (Fredegar, *Chronicon* IV, 65–66; transl. Wallace-Hadrill, p. 55 ; Esders 2009, pp. 201–202). However, Fredegar's detailed account of Constans II's fight against the Arabs, out of chronological order (*Chronicon* IV, 81; see Esders 2013, 2019c; Fischer 2014), is free from this Christological bias. It provides a remarkable snapshot taken in a period of deep uncertainty around 658, with an astonishing Frankish awareness of the Roman Empire's struggle to survive.

CONSTANS II'S SOJOURN IN ITALY (663–668) AND FRANKISH ACCEPTANCE OF THE SIXTH ECUMENICAL COUNCIL (680/681)

In 662, Emperor Constans II moved to Italy and eventually took up residence in Syracuse, possibly in reaction to the Arab incursions and to protect Sicily and North Africa, but not least to intervene in Lombard Italy, where the Arian king Grimoald's union of Lombard groups of northern and southern Italy posed an enormous challenge to Roman rule over Italy (Corsi 1983, pp. 79–105; Haldon 1997, pp. 59–60; Prigent 2010;

Esders 2013). Although, according to Paul the Deacon, Constans II's campaigns against the Lombards soon resulted in failure so great that hopes of reconquering Italy were dashed (*Hist. Langob.* V, 6–12), the imperial presence in Italy had a profound impact on power structures and policies beyond the Alps. A Frankish campaign launched from Provence into northern Italy to strengthen Grimoald's opponents may have followed a Byzantine–Frankish alliance (*Hist. Langob.* V, 1–5; Bognetti 1966, p. 337; Christou 1991, p. 209). Indeed, there may have been an alliance between Grimoald and his namesake, the Austrasian mayor of the palace since ca. 656, directed against the Agilolfings in Bavaria as a common enemy (Jarnut 1976, pp. 331–333). According to Paul the Deacon, this treaty caused King Grimoald's adversary Perctarit, who had taken refuge to Gaul in 662 with the help of Queen Dowager Balthild and her Neustrian mayor of the palace Ebroin, who managed to extend Neustrian rule over Burgundy (*Hist. Langob.* V, 2), to flee further north to Britain (*Hist. Langob.* V, 32). He may have hoped to forge an alliance between an Anglo-Saxon kingdom and a group of Lombards against King Grimoald. These alliances also had many repercussions in Gaul, from whence alliances extended beyond the Channel (Picard 1991; Wood 1994, pp. 176–179). The failure of the mayor Grimoald's coup d'état in 661 or 662 led to a rise in the power of Balthild and Ebroin of Neustria and Burgundy. In southern Gaul, this event can be related to a series of trials in which prominent officials and several bishops were accused of treason, deposed from their offices, and exiled, or even executed around 663 (*Vita S. Aunemundi* 2, AA SS 7. September, 744; *Vita Wilfridi* 4 and 6; *Passio Leudegarii* I, 2; Mordek 1991, p. 38; Ewig 1993, p. 80). It is against this background that we must see Bede's famous report of Theodore of Tarsus's detention by the Neustrian mayor Ebroin. Theodore, freshly appointed eighth archbishop of Canterbury, crossed Gaul in 668 with his companion Hadrian, formerly abbot of a monastery in Naples. Hadrian was detained by Ebroin on suspicion that the two intended to forge an alliance between the kings of Britain and the Roman emperor, who was then in Syracuse intriguing against Ebroin's kingdom (*Historia ecclesiastica gentis Anglorum* IV, 1; Ekonomou 2007, p. 163).

After the assassination of Constans II in Syracuse in 668 or 669, his successor, Constantine IV, was installed in Constantinople with papal support. After having fought against Arab raids (Kaplony 1996), he sought to suppress monothelitism and return to orthodoxy. According to the Byzantine historian Theophanes, upon learning of the emperor's plans, "the inhabitants of the West... namely the Chagan of the Avars as well as the kings, chieftains, and *castaldi* who lived beyond them, and the princes of the western nations, sent ambassadors and gifts to the emperor, requesting that peace and friendship should be confirmed with them. The emperor acceded to their demands and ratified an imperial peace with them also" (Theophanes, *Chronicle* AM 6169 (677/678) and AM 6171 (678/679), pp. 355–359; trans. Mango and Scott 1997, pp. 495–500; Esders 2019a). On the eve of the ecumenical council, relations between the Roman Empire and its western kingdoms were restored by imperial peace treaties, and Constantine concluded one with the Lombards, acknowledging their position in Italy in general terms for the first time (Pohl 2002, p. 278). Although the Franks are not mentioned explicitly, it seems clear that they must have been among the nations Theophanes mentioned.

In 679, Pope Agatho ordered provincial councils to be held at the Lateran. To this effect, they prepared a joint western statement and instructed the ecumenical council to be assembled at Constantinople the following year (Levison 1948), emphasizing that the western patriarchate was composed of the Lombards, Slavs, Franks, Gauls, Goths, and Britons, who were united with Rome in a deep "harmony of faith." They emphasized that the papacy strove with all its might "that the commonwealth of your Christian empire may be shown to be more sublime than all the nations" (*Concilium Universale Constaninopolitanum Tertium*, 134; trans. Percival 1955, pp. 352–353, slightly altered). In the list of subscriptions attached to the joint statement, some of the Italian bishops were from the Lombard kingdom and three were titled "legate to the synod for the provinces of Gaul" (*legatus per Galliarum provincias*), that is, Bishop Deodatus of Toul, Archbishop Felix of Arles, and Deacon Taurinus of Toulon (*Concilium Universale Constantinopolitanum Tertium*, 148–149, nos. 48, 51, and 54). While the latter two had apparently been sent to Rome by the Neustro-Burgundian mayor of the palace, Ebroin, Deodatus of Toul had come from the Austrasian court along with Bishop Wilfrid of York, who subscribed as the "legate to the synod for *Britannia*" (*Concilium Universale*; Wood 2013, pp. 208–220; Ó Carragáin and Thacker 2013, pp. 222–225). The subscriptions again document the split of the Merovingian episcopate of the kingdoms of Austrasia and Neustro-Burgundy. The Austrasian branch with Deodatus of Toul and his Anglo-Saxon associate Wilfrid of York also had Lombard connections to King Perctarit (Jarnut 1982, pp. 62–63; Christou 1991, pp. 221–225), who had allowed a provincial synod to take place in Milan in 679 or 680. In contrast, the episcopate of Neustro-Burgundy at this time appears to have been occupied with Ebroin's harsh treatment of bishops at the synod of Malay-sur-Roi in September 679 (Esders 2019a), as the otherwise unattested Felix of Arles and the deacon from Toulon do appear to have been somewhat spurious representatives at the Lateran Synod.

One may assume that in the years 679/680 the constellation of Mediterranean politics changed completely in both political and religious terms. For while Constantine IV promulgated the decrees of the council in all parts of the Roman Empire by imperial edict, it was by treaties as well as by papal intervention that the western rulers came to accept the council's decrees for their churches. This attests to some sort of "contractualization" in the process of implementing imperial religious policy, which, after lengthy negotiations, was also adopted for Spain following Visigothic acknowledgment of the ecumenical council's decisions in 684 (Vallejo Girvés 2012, pp. 420–427). The different paths followed by both Merovingian kingdoms in activating their networks may have come to an end through the murder of Ebroin in 680 or 681, which apparently happened with Pippinid support (Esders 2019a), and through the Battle of Tertry in 687.

Byzantine–Frankish Relations and Mediterranean Connectivity around 700

The outline given here has focused on the political and religious relations between Byzantium and the Merovingians as part of larger networks in the post-Roman West. It is notable that the "Pirennian" picture (Pirenne 1937), largely drawn from economic evidence of a rupture or decline in the seventh century (for the debate, see McCormick 2001; Wickham 2005; Effros 2017), appears questionable when Mediterranean connectivity around the large councils is taken into account. From the intense, Mediterranean-wide ecclesiastical and diplomatic interaction centered around these councils, a very different picture of Merovingian connectivity emerges. Ecclesiastical elites continued to see the Roman Empire as a reference system that determined their actions at least to some extent—that is, with regard to orthodoxy (Herrin 1992). Reports on pilgrimages like the one undertaken by Adamnan (Hoyland and Waidler 2012), transfers of relics (McCormick 2001, pp. 283–318), and Latin translations of widely circulating texts such as the apocalypse of Pseudo Methodius (written in Syriac around 670, attested in the West in Latin around 717) suggest that in the late Merovingian period contacts could also be intense at times (Wood 2019).

It seems that the rise of the Pippinid mayors of the palace did not mark a break in such wide-ranging political, religious, and economic connectivity, provided that a report that credits Pippin with having received embassies from "Greeks and Romans, Lombards, Huns (Avars), Slavs and Saracens" around 690 (*Annales Mettenses priores*, ad ann. 690), given by the Annals of Metz, can be trusted. Although this impression may have been an idealized back-projection of Carolingian "internationalism," given the Mediterranean connectedness that is so evident in the debates about the Quinisext Council (Trullanum) of 692 that spread from Constantinople as far as Visigothic Spain, there seems to be no reason to doubt that the Merovingian kingdoms were part of a connected Mediterranean world around 700.

Works Cited

Ancient Sources

Agathias. J. D. Frendo. (trans.). (1975). *Agathias, The Histories.* Corpus fontium historiae Byzantinae, Series Berolinensis 2a. Berlin: Walter de Gruyter.

Annales Mettenses priores. B. von Simson (ed.). (1905). MGH SRG in us. schol. 10. Hanover: Hahn.

Bede, *Historia ecclesiastica gentis Anglorum*. B. Colgrave and R. A. B. Mynors (eds. and trans.). (1969). *Ecclesiastical History of the English People*. Oxford: Oxford University Press.

Capitularia regum Francorum. A. Boretius (ed.). (1883). MGH LL, Sect. 2.1. Hanover: Hahn.

Codex Iustinianus. P. Krüger (ed.). (1915). *Codex Iustinianus*. Berlin: Weidmann.

Concilia Galliae A. 511–A. 695. C. de Clercq (ed.). (1963). Corpus Christianorum, Series Latina 148A. Turnhout: Brepols.

Concilium Lateranense a. 649 celebratum. R. Riedinger (ed.). (1984). Acta conciliorum oecumenicorum II, 1. Berlin: De Gruyter.

Concilium Universale Constantinopolitanum Tertium (680–681): Concilii actiones I–XVIII. R. Riedinger (ed.). (1992). Acta conciliorum oecumenicorum II, 2, 2. Berlin: De Gruyter.

Constantine Porphyrogennetos. G. Moravcsik (ed.). (1985). *Konstantinos Porphyrogennetos, De administrando imperio*. Corpus fontium historiae byzantinae 1. Washington, DC: Dumbarton Oaks Center for Byzantine Studies.

Desiderius of Cahors, *Letters*. W. Arndt (ed.). (1892). *Desiderii episcopi Cadurcensis epistolae*, in *Epistulae Merowingici et Karolini aevi (1)*. MGH Epp. 3 (pp. 191–214). Berlin: Weidmann.

Epistolae aevi merowingici collectae. W. Gundlach (ed.). (1892). *Epistolae Merowingici et Karolini aevi (I)*. MGH Epp. 3 (pp. 434–468). Berlin: Weidmann.

Epistolae Arelatenses. W. Gundlach (ed.). (1892). *Epistolae Arelatenses genuinae*, in *Epistolae Merowingici et Karolini aevi (I)*. MGH Epp. 3 (pp. 1–83). Berlin: Weidmann.

Epistolae Austrasiacae. W. Gundlach (ed.). (1892). In *Epistolae Merowingici et Karolini aevi (I)*. MGH Epp. 3 (pp. 110–153). Berlin: Weidmann.

Evagrius, *Ecclesiastical History*. M. Whitby (trans.). (2000). *The Ecclesiastical History of Evagrius Scholasticus*. Liverpool: Liverpool University Press.

Fredegar, *Chronicle*. J. M. Wallace-Hadrill (ed. and trans.). (1960). *The Fourth Book of the Chronicle of Fredegar with Its Continuations*. Oxford: Oxford University Press.

Gregory of Tours, *Histories*. B. Krusch and W. Levison (eds.). (1951). *Gregorii episcopi Turonensis libri historiarum X*. MGH SRM 1.1. Hanover: Hahn.

Grierson, P., and Blackburn, M. (1986). *Medieval European Coinage, with a Catalogue of the Coins in the Fitzwilliam Museum, Vol. I: The Early Middle Ages (5th–10th centuries)*. Cambridge: Cambridge University Press.

Justinian, *Novels*. R. Schoell and W. Kroll (eds.). (1895). *Iustiniani Novellae, Corpus iuris civilis* 3. Berlin: Weidmann.

Marcellinus Comes, *Chronicle*. B. Croke (ed.). (1995). *The Chronicle of Marcellinus*. Sydney: Australian Association for Byzantine Studies.

Mordek, H. (ed.) (1995). *Bibliotheca capitularium regum Francorum manuscripta. Überlieferung und Traditionszusammenhang der fränkischen Herrschererlasse*. Munich: Monumenta Germaniae Historica.

Passio of Leudegar of Autun. B. Krusch (ed.). (1910). *Passiones Leudegarii episcopi et martyris Augustodunensis I/II*, in *Passiones vitaeque sanctorum aevi Merovingici 3*, MGH SRM 5. (pp. 249–356). Hanover: Hahn.

Paul the Deacon, *Hist. Langob*. L. Bethmann and G. Waitz (eds.). (1878). *Paulus Diaconus, Historia Langobardorum*. MGH SRL 1. Hanover: Hahn.

Price, R. (trans.) (2009). *The Acts of the Council of Constantinople of 553*. 2 vols. Liverpool: Liverpool University Press.

Price, R. (trans.) (2014). *The Acts of the Lateran Synod of 649*, with annotations by P. Booth and C. Cubitt. Liverpool: Liverpool University Press.

Procopius, *Wars*. H. B. Dewing (ed. and trans.). (1914–1940). *Procopius of Caesarea, Buildings, History of the Wars, and Secret History*. 7 vols. Cambridge, MA: Harvard University Press.

Schwartz, E. (ed.). (1940). *Vigiliusbriefe*. Sitzungsberichte der Bayerischen Akademie der Wissenschaften, Philosoph.-hist. Abt., 2. Munich: C. H. Beck.

The Seven Ecumenical Councils of the Undivided Church. H. R. Percival (trans.). (1955). *Nicene and Post-Nicene Fathers II/14*, edited by P. Schaff and H. Wace. Grand Rapids, MI: Eerdmanns.

Theophanes, *Chronicle*. C. G. De Boor (ed.). (1883). *Theophanis Chronographia*, Vol. 1. Leipzig: B. G. Teubner.

Theophanes, *Chronicle*. C. Mango and R. Scott (trans.). (1997). *The Chronicle of Theophanes Confessor. Byzantine and Near Eastern History AD 284–813*. Oxford: Oxford University Press.

Visio Baronti monachi Longoretensis. W. Levison (ed.). (1910). *Passiones vitaeque sanctorum aevi Merovingici 3*, MGH SRM 5 (pp. 368–394). Hanover: Hahn.

Vita S. Aunemundi. (1760). *Acta Sanctorum*. Septembris vii, Antwerpen, pp. 694–696.

Vita Wilfridi. B. Colgrave (ed. and trans.). (1927). *The Life of Bishop Wilfrid by Eddius Stephanus*. Cambridge: Cambridge University Press.

Vitae Eligii Noviomagensis libri duo. B. Krusch (ed.). (1902). *Passiones vitaeque sanctorum aevi Merovingici 2*, MGH SRM 4 (pp. 663–741). Hanover: Hahn.

Modern Sources

Bachrach, B. S. (1994). *The Anatomy of a Little War. A Diplomatic and Military History of the Gundovald Affair (568–586)*. Boulder, CO: Westview Press.

Bayer, C. M. M. (2007). "Vita Eligii." In H. Beck, D. Geuenich, and H. Steuer (eds.), *Reallexikon der Germanischen Altertumskunde* (vol. 35, pp. 461–552). Berlin: De Gruyter.

Becher, M. (2011). *Chlodwig I. Der Aufstieg der Merowinger und das Ende der antiken Welt*. Munich: C. H. Beck.

Berschin, W. (2010). "Der heilige Goldschmied. Die Eligiusvita—ein merowingisches Original?" *Mitteilungen des Instituts für österreichische Geschichtsforschung* 118: 1–7.

Beisel, F. (1993). *Theudebertus magnus rex Francorum. Persönlichkeit und Zeit*. Idstein: Schulz-Kirchner Verlag.

Bognetti, G. P. (1966). *L'età longobarda*. Vol. 2. Milan: Giuffrè editore.

Booth, P. (2013). *Crisis of Empire. Doctrine and Dissent at the End of Late Antiquity*. Berkeley: University of California Press.

Borri, F. (2011). "White Croatia and the Arrival of the Croats: An Interpretation of Constantine Porphyrogenitus on the Oldest Dalmatian History." *Early Medieval Europe* 19: 204–231.

Bowersock, G. W. (2012). *Empires in Collision in Late Antiquity*. Waltham, MA: Brandeis University Press.

Brandes, W. (1998). "'Juristische' Krisenbewältigung im 7. Jahrhundert? Der Prozess gegen Papst Martin I. und Maximus Homologetes." In L. Burgmann (ed.), *Fontes Minores X* (pp. 141–212). FrankfurtamMain: Klostermann.

Brandes, W. (2009). "Thüringer/Thüringerinnen in byzantinischen Quellen." In H. Castritius, D. Geuenich, and M. Werner (eds.), *Die Frühzeit der Thüringer. Archäologie, Sprache, Geschichte* (pp. 291–327). Berlin: De Gruyter

Budak, N. (1993). "Frühes Christentum in Kroatien." In G. Hödl and J. Grabmayer (eds.), *Karantanien und der Alpen-Adria-Raum im Frühmittelalter* (pp. 223–234). Vienna: Böhlau.

Cameron, A. M. (1968). "Agathias on the Early Merovingians." *Annali della Scuola Normale Superiore di Pisa. Classe di Lettere e Filosofia* Ser. 2, vol. 37: 95–140.

Cameron, A. M. (1976). "The Early Religious Policies of Justin II." In D. Baker (ed.), *The Orthodox Churches and the West* (pp. 51–67). Oxford: Basil Blackwell.

Cameron, A. M. (1985). *Procopius and the Sixth Century*. Berkeley: University of California Press.

Ó Carragáin, E., and Thacker, A. (2013). "Wilfrid in Rome." In N. J. Higham (ed.), *Wilfrid of York. Abbot, Bishop, Saint* (pp. 212–230). Donington: Shaun Tyas.

Caspar, E. (1933). *Geschichte des Papsttums von den Anfängen bis zur Höhe der Weltherrschaft, 2: Das Papsttum unter byzantinischer Herrschaft*. Tübingen: J. C. B. Mohr.

Chazelle, C., and Cubitt, C. (eds.) (2007). *The Crisis of the Oikoumene. The Three Chapters Controversy and the Failed Quest for Unity in the Sixth-Century Mediterranean*. Turnhout: Brepols.

Christou, K. P. (1991). *Byzanz und die Langobarden. Von der Ansiedlung in Pannonien bis zur endgültigen Anerkennung (500–680)*. Athens: Historical Publications St. D. Basilopoulos.

Chrysos, E. K. (1992). "Byzantine Diplomacy, A.D. 300–800: Means and Ends." In J. Shephard and S. Franklin (eds.), *Byzantine Diplomacy* (pp. 25–39). Aldershot: Ashgate.

Claude, D. (1997). "Niedergang, Ende und Renaissance der Präfekturverwaltung im Westen des römischen Reiches (5.–8. Jh.)." *Zeitschrift der Savigny-Stiftung für Rechtsgeschichte, Germanistische Abteilung* 114: 352–379.

Collins, R. (1983). "Theodebert I., *Rex Magnus Francorum*." In P. Wormald, D. Bullough, and R. Collins (eds.), *Ideal and Reality in Frankish and Anglo-Saxon Society. Studies Presented to John Michael Wallace-Hadrill* (pp. 7–33). Oxford: Oxford University Press.

Collins, R. (2007). *Die Fredegar-Chroniken*, Hanover: Hahn.

Collins, R. (2016). "Gregory of Tours and Spain." In A. C. Murray (ed.), *A Companion to Gregory of Tours* (pp. 498–515). Leiden: Brill.

Corsi, P. (1983). *La spedizione italiana di Costante II*. Bologna: Patron.

Curta, F. (1997). "Slavs in Fredegar and Paul the Deacon: Medieval *gens* or 'Scourge of God'." *Early Medieval Europe* 6: 141–167.

Drauschke, J. (2011). "Diplomatie und Wahrnehmung im 6. und 7. Jahrhundert: Konstantinopel und die merowingischen Könige." In M. Altripp (ed.), *Byzanz in Europa. Europas östliches Erbe* (pp. 244–275). Turnhout: Brepols.

Dumézil, B. (2008). *La reine Brunehaut*. Paris: Fayard.

Effros, B. (2017). "The Enduring Attraction of the Pirenne Thesis." *Speculum* 92: 184–208.

Ekonomou, A. J. (2007). *Byzantine Rome and the Greek Popes. Eastern influences on Rome and the papacy from Gregory the Great to Zacharias, A.D. 590–752*. Lanham, MD: Lexington Books.

Esders, S. (1997). *Römische Rechtstradition und merowingisches Königtum. Zum Rechtscharakter politischer Herrschaft in Burgund im 6. und 7. Jahrhundert*. Göttingen: Vandenhoeck & Ruprecht.

Esders, S. (2009). "Herakleios, Dagobert und die 'beschnittenen Völker'. Die Umwälzungen des Mittelmeerraums im 7. Jahrhundert in der fränkischen Chronik des sog. Fredegar." In A. Goltz, H. Leppin, and H. Schlange-Schöningen (eds.), *Jenseits der Grenzen. Studien zur spätantiken und frühmittelalterlichen Geschichtsschreibung* (pp. 239–311). Berlin: De Gruyter.

Esders, S. (2013). "Konstans II. (641–668), die Sarazenen und die Reiche des Westens. Ein Versuch über politisch-militärische und ökonomisch-finanzielle Verflechtungen im Zeitalter eines mediterranen Weltkrieges." In J. Jarnut and J. Strothmann (eds.), *Die Merowingischen Monetarmünzen als Quelle zum Verständnis des 7. Jahrhunderts in Gallien* (pp. 189–241). Munich: Fink.

Esders, S. (2014). "'Avenger of All Perjury' in Constantinople, Ravenna and Metz. St Polyeuctus, Sigibert I and the Division of Charibert's Kingdom in 568." In A. Fischer and I. N. Wood (eds.), *Western Perspectives on the Mediterranean. Cultural Transfer in Late Antiquity and the Early Middle Ages (400–800)* (pp. 17–40). London: Bloomsbury.

Esders, S. (2016). "*Nationes quam plures conquiri.* Amandus of Maastricht, Compulsory Baptism and 'Christian Universal Mission' in 7th century Gaul." In J. Kreiner and H. Reimitz (eds.), *Motions of Late Antiquity: Essays on Religion, Politics, and Society in Honor of Peter Brown* (pp. 201–229). Turnhout: Brepols.

Esders, S. (2018a). "The Prophesied Rule of a 'Circumcised People'. A Travelling Tradition from the Seventh-Century Mediterranean." In Y. Hen, and T. F. X. Noble (eds.), *Barbarians and Jews. Jews and Judaism in the Early Medieval West* (pp. 119–154). Turnhout: Brepols

Esders, S. (2018b). "Kingdoms of the Empire, AD 608–616. Mediterrane Konnektivität, Synchronität und Kausalität als analytisches und darstellerisches Problem der Frühmittelalterforschung." In W. Pohl, M. Diesenberger, and B. Zeller (eds.), *Neue Wege der Frühmittelalterforschung. Bilanz und Perspektiven.* (pp. 93–135). Vienna: Verlag der Österreichischen Akademie der Wissenschaften.

Esders, S. (2019a). "'Great Security Prevailed in Both East and West': The Merovingian Kingdoms and the 6th Ecumenical Council (680/81)." In S. Esders, Y. Fox, Y. Hen, and L. Sarti (eds.), *East and West in the Early Middle Ages: The Merovingian Kingdoms in Mediterranean Perspective.* (pp. 247–264). Cambridge: Cambridge University Press.

Esders, S. (2019b). "King Chindasvinth, the 'Gothic Disease', and the Monothelite Crisis." *Millennium* 16: 175–212.

Esders, S. (2019c). "When Contemporary History is Caught Up by the Immediate Present: Fredegar's Proleptic Depiction of the Emperor Constans II." In S. Esders, Y. Hen, P. Lucas, T. Rotman (eds.), *The Merovingian Kingdoms and the Mediterranean World. Revisiting the Sources* (pp. 141–149). London: Bloomsbury.

Ewig, E. (1983). *Die Merowinger und das Imperium.* Opladen: Westdeutscher Verlag.

Ewig, E. (1993). "Die Klosterprivilegien des Metropoliten Emmo von Sens, das Reichskonzil von Mâlay-le-Roi (660) und der Sturz des Metropoliten Aunemund von Lyon (661/662)." In G. Jenal (ed.), *Herrschaft, Kirche, Kultur. Beiträge zur Geschichte des Mittelalters. Festschrift für Friedrich Prinz zu seinem 65. Geburtstag* (pp. 63–82). Stuttgart: Hiersemann.

Faussner, H. C. (1986). "Die staatsrechtliche Grundlage des Rex Francorum." *Zeitschrift der Savigny-Stiftung für Rechtsgeschichte, Germanistische Abteilung* 103: 42–103.

Feissel, D. (1993). "La réforme chronologique de 537 et son application dans l'épigraphie grecque: années de règne et dates consulaires de Justinien à Héraclius." *Ktema* 18: 171–188.

Fischer, A. (2014). "Rewriting History: Fredegar's Perspectives on the Mediterranean." In A. Fischer and I. N. Wood (eds.), *Western Perspectives on the Mediterranean. Cultural Transfer in Late Antiquity And The Early Middle Ages (400–800)* (pp. 55–76). London: Bloomsbury.

Fischer, A. (2019). "Money for Nothing? Franks, Byzantines and Lombards in the Sixth and Seventh Century." In S. Esders, Y. Fox, Y. Hen, and L. Sarti (eds.), *East and West in the Early Middle Ages. The Merovingian Kingdoms in a Mediterranean Perspective* (pp. 108–126). Cambridge: Cambridge University Press.

Fourlas, B. (2019). "Early Byzantine Church Silver Offered for the Eternal Rest of Framarich and Karilos—Evidence of 'The Army of Heroic Men' Raised by Tiberius II Constantine?" In S. Esders, Y. Fox, Y. Hen, and L. Sarti (eds.), *East and West in the Early Middle Ages. The Merovingian Kingdoms in a Mediterranean Perspective* (pp. 87–107). Cambridge: Cambridge University Press.

Fowden, G. (1993). *Empire to Commonwealth. Consequences of Monotheism in Late Antiquity.* Princeton, NJ: Princeton University Press.

Fox, Y. (2014). *Power and Religion in Merovingian Gaul. Columbanian Monasticism and the Frankish Elites.* Cambridge: Cambridge University Press.

Fritze, W. H. (1994). *Untersuchungen zur frühslawischen und frühfränkischen Geschichte bis ins 7. Jahrhundert.* FrankfurtamMain: Peter Lang.

García Moreno, L. A. (2002). "*Urbs cunctarum gentium victrix gothicis triumphis victa.* Roma y el Reino visigodo." In *Roma fra Oriente e Occidente* (pp. 239–322). Spoleto: Centro italiano di studi sull' alto medioevo.

Gillett, A. (2010). "Love and Grief in Post-Imperial Diplomacy: The Letters of Brunhild." In B. Sidwell and D. Dzino (eds.), *Power and Emotions in the Roman World and Late Antiquity* (pp. 127–165). Piscataway, NJ: Gorgias Press.

Goffart, W. (1957). "Byzantine Policy in the West under Tiberius II and Maurice: The Pretenders Hermenegild and Gundovald (579–585)." *Traditio* 13: 73–117.

Goffart, W. (2012). "The Frankish Pretender Gundovald: A Crisis of Merovingian Blood." *Francia* 39: 1–27.

Goubert, P. (1955). *Byzance avant l'Islam, II: Byzance et l'Occident sous les successeurs de Justinien, 1: Byzance et les Francs.* Paris: Picard.

Guillot, O. (1997). "Clovis 'Auguste,' vecteur des conceptions romano-chrétiennes." In M. Rouche (ed.), *Clovis, histoire et mémoire* (pp. 706–737). Paris: Presses de l'Université de Paris–Sorbonne.

Haldon, J. F. (1997). *Byzantium in the Seventh Century*: The Transformation of a Culture. Cambridge: Cambridge University Press.

Halfond, G. I. (2012). "Vouillé, Orléans (511), and the Origins of the Frankish Conciliar Tradition." In R. W. Mathisen (ed.), *The Battle of Vouillé, 507 CE: Where France Began* (pp. 151–166). Berlin: De Gruyter.

Hammer, C. I. (2008). *From ducatus to regnum. Ruling Bavaria under the Merovingians and Early Carolingians.* Turnhout: Brepols.

Handley, M. A. (2000). "Inscribing Time and Identity in the Kingdom of Burgundy." In G. Greatrex and S. Mitchell (eds.), *Ethnicity and Culture in Late Antiquity* (pp. 83–102). Cardiff: Classical Press of Wales.

Hartung, W. (1983). *Süddeutschland in der frühen Merowingerzeit: Studien zu Gesellschaft, Herrschaft, Stammesbildung bei Alamannen und Bajuwaren.* Wiesbaden: Franz Steiner.

Hauck, K. (1967). "Von einer spätantiken Randkultur zum karolingischen Europa." *Frühmittelalterliche Studien* 1: 3–93.

Heidrich, I. (1968). "Südgallische Inschriften des 5.–7. Jahrhunderts als historische Quellen." *Rheinische Vierteljahrsblätter* 32: 167–183.

Herrin, J. (1992). "Constantinople, Rome and the Franks in the Seventh and Eighth Centuries." In J. Shephard and S. Franklin (eds.), *Byzantine Diplomacy* (pp. 91–107). Aldershot: Ashgate.

Howard-Johnston, J. (2010). *Witnesses to a World Crisis. Historians and Histories of the Middle East in the Seventh Century.* Oxford: Oxford University Press.

Hoyland, R., and S. Waidler (2012). "Adomnán's 'De Locis Sanctis' and the Seventh-Century Near East." *English Historical Review* 129: 787–807.

James, E. (1988). *The Franks.* Oxford: Blackwell.

Jarnut, J. (1976). "Beiträge zu den fränkisch-bayerisch-langobardischen Beziehungen im 7. und 8. Jahrhundert (656–728)." *Zeitschrift für bayerische Landesgeschichte* 39: 331–352.

Jarnut, J. (1982). *Geschichte der Langobarden.* Stuttgart: Kohlhammer.

Jenks, M. (2000). "Romanitas and Christianitas in the Coinage of Theodebert I of Metz." *Zeitschrift für antikes Christentum* 4: 338–368.

Kaelble, M. (2009). "Ethnogenese und Herzogtum Thüringen im Frankenreich (6.–9. Jahrhundert)." In H. Castritius, D. Geuenich, and M. Werner (eds.), *Die Frühzeit der Thüringer. Archäologie, Sprache, Geschichte* (pp. 329–414). Berlin: De Gruyter.

Kaplony, A. (1996). *Konstantinopel und Damaskus. Gesandtschaften und Verträge zwischen Kaisern und Kalifen 639–750. Untersuchungen zum Gewohnheits-Völkerrecht und zur interkulturellen Diplomatie.* Berlin: Klaus Schwarz Verlag.

Langgärtner, G. (1964). *Die Gallienpolitik der Päpste im 5. und 6. Jahrhundert. Eine Studie über den apostolischen Vikariat von Arles.* Bonn: Hanstein.

Levison, W. (1948). "Die Akten der römischen Synode von 679." In W. Levison (ed.), *Aus rheinischer und fränkischer Frühzeit. Ausgewählte Aufsätze* (pp. 267–294). Düsseldorf: L. Schwann.

Lilie, R.-J. (1985). "Kaiser Herakleios und die Ansiedlung der Serben. Überlegungen zum Kapitel 32 des 'De administrando imperio'." *Südostforschungen* 44: 17–43.

Loseby, S. T. (2016). "Gregory of Tours, Italy, and Empire." In A. C. Murray (ed.), *A Companion to Gregory of Tours* (pp. 462–497). Leiden: Brill.

Mathisen, R. W. (2012). "Clovis, Anastasius, and Political Status in 508 C.E.: The Frankish Aftermath of the battle of Vouillé." In R. Mathisen and D. Shanzer (eds.), *The Battle of Vouillé, 507 CE. Where France Began* (pp. 79–110). Berlin: De Gruyter.

McCormick, M. (1989). "Clovis at Tours, Byzantine Public Ritual and the Origins of Medieval Ruler Symbolism." In E. K. Chrysos and A. Schwarcz (eds.), *Das Reich und die Barbaren* (pp. 155–180). Vienna: Verlag der Österreichischen Akademie der Wissenschaften.

McCormick, M. (2001). *Origins of the European Economy. Communications and Commerce, AD 300–900.* Cambridge: Cambridge University Press.

Mériaux, C. (2019). "A One-Way Ticket to Francia. Constantinople, Rome and Northern Gaul in the mid seventh century." In S. Esders, Y. Fox, Y. Hen, and L. Sarti (eds.), *East and West in the Early Middle Ages. The Merovingian Kingdoms in a Mediterranean Perspective* (pp. 138–148). Cambridge: Cambridge University Press.

Mordek, H. (1991). "Bischofsabsetzungen in spätmerowingischer Zeit. Justelliana, Bernensis und das Konzil von Mâlay (677)." In H. Mordek (ed.), *Papsttum, Kirche und Recht im Mittelalter. Festschrift für Horst Fuhrmann zum 65. Geburtstag* (pp. 31–53). Tübingen: Niemeyer.

Moreira, I. (1993). "'Provisatrix optima': St Radegund of Poitiers' Relic Petitions to the East." *Journal of Medieval History* 19: 285–305.

Obolensky, D. (1971). *The Byzantine Commonwealth: Eastern Europe, 500–1453.* London: Sphere Books.

Picard, J.-M. (1991). "Church and Politics in the Seventh Century: The Irish Exile of King Dagobert II." In J.-M. Picard (ed.), *Ireland and Northern France, AD 600–850* (pp. 27–52). Dublin: Four Courts Press.

Pirenne, H. (1937). *Mahomet et Charlemagne.* Brussels: Nouvelle Société d'éditions.

Pohl, W. (1997). (ed.), *Kingdoms of the Empire: The Integration of Barbarians in Late Antiquity.* Leiden: Brill.

Pohl, W. (2002). *Die Awaren. Ein Steppenvolk in Mitteleuropa 567–822 n. Chr.* 2nd ed. Munich: C. H. Beck.

Pohlsander, H. A. (2000), "A Call to Repentence. Bishop Nicetius of Trier to the Emperor Justinian." *Byzantion* 70: 457–473.

Prigent, V. (2010). "La Sicile de Constant II: l'apport des sources sigillographiques." In A. Nef and V. Prigent (eds.), *La Sicile de Byzance à Islam* (pp. 157–188). Paris: De Boccard.

Rigold, S. E. (1954). "An Imperial Coinage in Southern Gaul in the Sixth and Seventh Centuries?" *Numismatic Chronicle* 6. ser. 14: 93–133.

Rouche, M. (1977). "Les baptêmes forcés de Juifs en Gaule mérovingienne et dans l'Empire d'Orient." In V. Nikiprowetzky (ed.), *De l'antijudaisme antique à l'antisémitisme contemporain* (pp. 105–124). Lille: Presses Universitaires de Lille.

Sarti, L. (2019). "The Digression on Pope Martin I in the Life of Eligius of Noyon (1.33–34). A Testimony to Late Seventh-Century Knowledge Exchange between East and West?" In S. Esders, Y. Fox, Y. Hen, and L. Sarti (eds.), *East and West in the Early Middle Ages. The Merovingian Kingdoms in a Mediterranean Perspective* (pp. 149–164). Cambridge: Cambridge University Press.

Scheibelreiter, G. (1989). "*Vester est populus meus.* Byzantinische Reichsideologie und germanisches Selbstverständnis." In E. K. Chrysos and A. Schwarcz (eds.), *Das Reich und die Barbaren* (pp. 203–220). Vienna: Verlag der Österreichischen Akademie der Wissenschaften.

Scheibelreiter, G. (1992). "Griechisches—lateinisches—fränkisches Christentum. Der Brief Martins I. an den Bischof Amandus von Maastricht aus dem Jahre 649." *Mitteilungen des Instituts für Österreichische Geschichtsforschung* 100: 84–102.

Schieffer, R. (1991). "Der Papst als Patriarch von Rom." In M. Maccarrone (ed.), *Il primato del vescovo di Roma nel primo millennio* (pp. 433–451). Vatican City: Libreria Ed. Vaticana.

Schreiner, P. (1985). "Eine merowingische Gesandtschaft in Konstantinopel (590?)." *Frühmittelalterliche Studien* 19: 195–200.

Shanzer, D. (1998). "Dating the Baptism of Clovis: The Bishop of Vienne vs. the Bishop of Tours." *Early Medieval Europe* 7: 29–57.

Steinacher, R. (2010). "The Herules. Fragments of a History" In F. Curta (ed.), *Neglected Barbarians* (pp. 321–364). Turnhout: Brepols.

Stueber, T. (2019). "The Fifth Council of Orléans and the Reception of the 'Three Chapters Controversy' in Merovingian Gaul." In S. Esders, Y. Hen, P. Lucas, and T. Rotman (eds.), *The Merovingian Kingdoms and the Mediterranean World. Revisiting the Sources* (pp. 93–102). London: Bloomsbury.

Thanner, A. (1989). *Papst Honorius I. (625–638).* St. Ottilien: Eos-Verlag.

Thompson, E. A. (1980). "Procopius on Brittia and Brittannia." *Classical Quarterly* N.S. 30: 498–507.

Uhalde, K. (2001). "The Quasi-Imperial Coinage and Fiscal Administration of Merovingian Provence." In R. W. Mathisen and D. Shanzer (eds.), *Society and Culture in Late Antique Gaul. Revisiting the Sources* (pp. 134–165). Aldershot: Ashgate.

Vallejo Girvés, M. (2012). *Hispania y Bizancio. Una relación desconocida.* Madrid: Editorial Akal.

Wickham, C. (2005). *Framing the Early Middle Ages. Europe and the Mediterranean, 400–800.* Oxford: Oxford University Press.

Widdowson, M. (2008). "Gundovald, 'Ballomer' and the Politics of Identity." *Revue Belge de Philologie et d'histoire* 86: 607–622.

Winkelmann, F. (2001). *Der monenergetisch-monotheletische Streit.* FrankfurtamMain: Peter Lang.

Wood, I. N. (1983). *The Merovingians and the North Sea.* Alingsås: Viktoria bokförlag.

Wood, I. N. (1992). "Frankish Hegemony over England." In M. Carver (ed.), *The Age of Sutton Hoo: The Seventh Century in North-Western Europe* (pp. 235–241). Woodbridge: Boydell & Brewer.

Wood, I. N. (1994). *The Merovingian Kingdoms, 450–751*. London: Longman.

Wood, I. N. (2007). "The Franks and Papal Theology, 550-660." In C. Chazelle and C. Cubitt (eds.), *The Crisis of the Oikoumene: The Three Chapters Controversy and the Failed Quest for Unity in the Sixth-Century Mediterranean* (pp. 223–241). Turnhout: Brepols.

Wood, I. N. (2013). "The Continental Journeys of Wilfrid and Biscop." In N. J. Higham (ed.), *Wilfrid of York. Abbot, Bishop, Saint* (pp. 200–211). Donington: Shaun Tyas.

Wood, I. N. (2014a). "The Burgundians and Byzantium." In A. Fischer and I. N. Wood (eds.), *Western Perspectives on the Mediterranean: Cultural Transfer in Late Antiquity and the Early Middle Ages, 400–800 AD* (pp. 1–15). London: Bloomsbury.

Wood, I. N. (2014b). "The Political Structure of the Burgundian Kingdom." In M. Meier and S. Patzold (eds.), *Chlodwigs Welt: Organisation von Herrschaft um 500* (pp. 383–396). Stuttgart: Steiner.

Wood, I. N. (2019). "Contact with the Eastern Mediterranean in the Late Merovingian Period." In S. Esders, Y. Fox, Y. Hen, and L. Sarti (eds.), *East and West in the Early Middle Ages. The Merovingian Kingdoms in a Mediterranean Perspective* (pp. 281–296). Cambridge: Cambridge University Press.

Zuckerman, C. (1998). "Qui a rappelé en Gaule le Ballomer Gundovald?" *Francia* 25: 1–18.

CHAPTER 17

::::::::::::::::::::::::::::::::::::

THE MOVEMENT OF
PEOPLE AND THINGS
BETWEEN BRITAIN AND
FRANCE

In the Late- and Post-Roman Periods

::::::::::::::::::::::::::::::::::::

ROBIN FLEMING

OUR ideas about the history of the economic links between Anglo-Saxons and Franks in the fifth and early sixth centuries can be productively reframed in four ways. First, emphasizing the material evidence for these connections rather than textual descriptions of them is a useful exercise. Although the material evidence is scarce, it is more reliable and extensive than our textual witnesses, many of which were written by people, like Procopius, who knew little about Britain, or they were penned retrospectively, long after the events they purport to describe. Second, we need to reformulate the language we use when thinking about these connections, in particular, the terminology we employ when describing the people and things moving across the Channel during this period. "Franks," as we shall see, are almost impossible to identify in the archaeological record of the fifth century, and "Anglo-Saxon" is not a meaningful category in this early period. So, we need to rethink what the relationships were between people and things on both sides of the Channel without resorting to anachronistic notions of ethnicity. Third, it is important to consider networks of exchange not only between eastern Britain and the Continent during this period, but also between western Britain and the Continent because in the sixth century, Frankish material culture was found across Britain, not just in its eastern half. Fourth and finally, when thinking about the early medieval connections between what are now France and England, it is fruitful to extend our examination back into the fourth century. Without taking into account the links between Britain and northern Gaul before the Roman state's withdrawal from Britain in the first decade of the fifth century, it is impossible to evaluate the persistence, novelty, or scale of the connections we find in the early medieval period. We will start with the last reframing first, and then take the second and third reframings in turn, depending, for all three, on material evidence.

LATE-ROMAN POTS, COINS, AND PEOPLE

Northern Gaul and Britain were part of the same regional economy in the late-Roman period, and goods, taxes, people, and ideas were constantly on the move between the two. Ceramics produced in northern Gaul and in Britain, which archaeologists have recovered on both sides of the English Channel, help us piece together the ways the economies on either side of the Channel were connected. In the fourth century, Argonne ware, produced west of Verdun, was the dominant regional fine ware. It was widely distributed between the Rhone and the Loire, regularly encountered in towns and forts along the Rhine, and available in parts of Britain, especially around the Thames and Solent estuaries (Blaszkiewicz and Jigan 1991; Tyer 1996, p. 136). *Céramique à l'éponge*, another tableware, was produced in western Gaul. It was used not only between the Gironde and the Loire in the fourth century, but also in southern Britain, mostly along the Solent estuary, the Kentish coast, and the mouth of the Thames. There was also a minor distribution of this ware along the Avon estuary (Tyers 1996, pp. 144–145). German marbled wares, in the form of slipped-ware jugs and flagons, were produced in the Mosel region and distributed along the middle and lower Rhine from Mainz to Nijmegen. They were also found around London and at coastal and military sites in Kent (Bird and Williams 1983; Tyers 1996, pp. 150–151; Swift 2010, p. 245). Finally, there is Mayen ware, northern Gaul's most common late-Roman coarse ware. It was ubiquitous on sites across modern-day Belgium and eastern France, and it was used throughout the Rhineland. It was also available in Britain from the middle of the fourth century. Finds are concentrated in the southeast, with the lion's share recovered at the important administrative and military centers of Canterbury, Richborough, Colchester, and London (Tyers 1996, pp. 151–152), but it was also used on less grand civilian sites along the coasts of Essex, Suffolk, Norfolk, Kent, Sussex, and Hampshire. It came in a variety of forms, but the most common in Britain was a jar with a lid-seated rim, a type of pot that may have served as a shipping container and thus arrived in Britain as packaging (Fulford and Bird 1975, p. 179; Pollard 1988, p. 149; Blockley 1995, vol. 2, pp. 737–740; Bruet, Vilvorder, and Delage 2010, pp. 420–422).

Pottery produced in Britain in the late-Roman period is also found in Gaul. BB1, a coarse ware produced on a very large scale in and around Poole Harbor in Dorset is regularly encountered in Brittany and Normandy, especially at Boulogne, but it is not found east of the Seine (Tuffreau-Libre, Mossman-Bouquillon, and Symonds 1995; Allen and Fulford 1996, p. 267; Dhaeze and Seillier 2005, pp. 628–630). A little New Forest ware, produced in Hampshire, and Alice Holt ware, made in Hampshire and Surrey, have also been recovered in Normandy (Fulford 1987, p. 98). Finally, fine ware produced in

Oxfordshire is mostly found in Gaul east of the Seine, especially around Boulogne, but it occasionally turns up as far west as Brittany (Fulford 1977, p. 49; Martin and Dufournier 1983; Allen and Fulford 1996, p. 249).

The ceramic pots produced on one side of the Channel and then transported to the other were not exported on a massive scale, nor were they shipped in their own right: the overwhelming majority of pottery used in northern Gaul and Britain during this period was locally made (for ceramics in the south of Gaul, see Bonifay and Pieri, Chapter 37, this volume). The transhipped pottery, rather, seems to have moved as subsidiary cargo. The bulk of the freight on boats departing from Britain and carrying British-made pots would have been the grain, salt, hides, and wool which was collected annually by the late-Roman state as *annona*, or tax-in-kind, and which it used to pay and feed imperial administrators and the army (see Sarti, Chapter 12, this volume).[1] Some of these shipments may have also been the result of state purchases through the system of *coemptiones*, that is, the acquisition, at a set price, of goods vital to the state and its army. The large number of troops along the Rhine frontier in the fourth century and the bustling western imperial capital at Trier would have required huge amounts of food-stuffs and raw materials, some of which had been produced in lowland Britain.

Thus, we can posit that some of the Oxfordshire ware found in Boulogne traveled southward toward London from kilns in Oxfordshire by piggybacking on carts and riverboats that were transporting grain and hides collected from the rich agricultural heartland of Britain for the *annona* or purchased through *coemptiones*. BB1 may have moved along the south coast of Britain and on to Gaul, serving as containers for salt produced in Dorset destined for soldiers serving on the Rhine frontier or for administrators dining in Trier (Gerrard 2008, pp. 121–124). In short, by following Romano-British pots, we can see the goods collected by the Roman state moving down the Thames, the Severn, and along Britain's southern and southeastern coasts. Many of these pots then moved across the Channel in large shipments destined mostly for imperial use via Richborough to the port at Boulogne (Fulford 1987, p. 102; Millett 2007, pp. 142–146). From there, the shipments moved on to military storehouses in the Rhineland, to the western imperial capital at Trier, or to the towns in the interior of northern Gaul where there were *fabricae*, military outposts, and imperial administrators, all of which were supported by the *annona* (Tyers 1996, p. 136; Esmonde Cleary 2013, p. 320).

The pottery from Gaul that ended up in Britain, on the other hand, marked the return trip of boats back to Britain: they were perhaps filled with barrels of wine alongside more archaeologically visible goods, such as quern stones and glass bowls engraved with mythological, biblical, or hunting scenes, both produced in the same region as Mayen ware and both found in Britain (Price 1978, p. 75; Grünewald and Hartmann 2014, p. 47). Much of the pottery from Gaul, as we have seen, was concentrated along the Thames and Solent estuaries and the Kentish coast, marking a zone where state shipments would have been organized (Bird and Williams 1983; Redknap 1988, p. 9; Fulford 1987; Tyers 1996, pp. 150–151). Pottery from Gaul has also been found at sites that were likely centrally involved in the administration of the *annona*—places like *Cunetio* (Mildenhall) in Wiltshire and Richborough, in Kent (Fulford 1977, p. 42).

Coin finds from the first half of the fourth century also indicate that Britain, northern Gaul, and the Rhineland formed a single, integrated economic region that centered on the Channel. In the early fourth century, for example, when both London and Trier were producing coins, coins from both mints were distributed equally on either side of the Channel (Fulford 1977, pp. 65–70; Allen and Fulford 1996, p. 267). Very large numbers of silver *siliquae*, moreover, are found in Britain. The distribution of both single *siliqua* accidentally lost by their owners (more than 1,600 of which have been recovered and reported through the Portable Antiquities Scheme since 1997), and large numbers of *siliquae* hoards (which range in size from a couple of coins to over 14,000) (Guest 2015), are concentrated in the heart of Britain's rural bread-belt (Bland, Moorhead, and Walton 2013, p. 121; Reece 2013). These coins arrived in their greatest numbers between the reigns of Constantine II and Julian (316–363), but they continued to flow into Britain in large numbers after 363 until 402 (Bland and Loriot 2010, p. 19; Walton and Moorhead 2016). One explanation for the presence of these coins in lowland Britain is that they are a reflection of the relationship between the region's agricultural production and the late-Roman state, since these coins were the means by which the state paid for the bulk purchase of basic goods needed to make up for the shortfalls not covered by the *annona*. Cargo ships loaded at the mouth of the Thames were only a two-day sail away from the mouth of the Rhine,[2] and even shipping bulk goods from Britain to Trier would have been faster and cheaper than bringing them from many seemingly closer regions in Gaul.[3] Thus, the drivers of the large-scale exchange of goods and money across the Channel were what Chris Wickham has called "bulk product hegemonies" (2005, p. 718). Although some of these transported goods would have been purchased and sold in commercial transactions that had nothing to do with the state, much of it would have been collected, moved, and distributed on the orders of imperial officials.

The scale of exchange witnessed by the ceramics and coins was made possible by impressive amounts of infrastructure built along both coasts and found in towns and villas across the northwestern provinces. The area around Richborough, in Kent, for example, helps us see the kinds of investments made by the state in order to facilitate large-scale exchange. Richborough had been a crucial port from the very beginning of the Roman period. It had long served as a military port and supply base, and it was likely the most important point of entry for goods into Britain for most of the Roman period. There was a major road leading directly from Rome to Boulogne, and with a short voyage one reached Richborough, which marked the start of the road network in Britain. Nearby was the late-Roman industrial site at Ickham, where near industrial-scale metal-working and leather and textile manufacturing took place. A number of lead seals dated 317–363 have been recovered at both Ickham and Richborough. They were once attached to sacks or bales of goods, which had been packaged for the state (Hassall and Tomlin 1979, 350–353; Millett and Wilmott 2003, p. 186; Millett 2007, pp. 141–146, 182–163, 343). Also in the neighborhood were numerous villas with large, above-ground grain-storage facilities, where the agricultural bounty of the countryside could be stored before shipment. Some, like the recently excavated stone-built aisled barn at Hog Brook, Deerton Street, Faversham, Kent, were not only very large, but they were elaborately decorated display buildings (Wilkinson 2009). Many villas in the region also had large-scale milling, parching, malting, and brewing facilities, all of which point to significant levels of production, storage, and transportation, not only to feed the quarter of a million or so civilians living in Britain who were not directly involved in the growing of their own food, but also soldiers stationed there and along the Rhine frontier (van der Veen 1989, p. 315; van der Veen and O'Connor 1998). On the other side of the Channel, across northern Gaul and the Rhineland, were large numbers of state-built granaries, which date to the late-Roman period (Fulford 2007; Roymans and Derks 2011, p. 18). Major imperial and elite investments in infrastructure made the levels of exchange between Britain and northern Gaul and the Rhineland possible. These buildings attest to the wealth and importance of the trans-Channel economic zone, stretching from the mouth of the Rhine all the way to Brittany, and across the sea to southern and eastern Britain.

The late-Roman state moved people as well as goods from northern Gaul and the Rhine frontier to Britain and back. Like the distribution of continental pottery and coins in Britain, evidence for mobile individuals centers on Britain's large administrative towns and military complexes. One way to track the more cosmopolitan men living in late-Roman Britain is through the fancy metalwork dress fasteners they wore. In the late-Roman period, men closely associated with the state adopted a uniform style of dress. They wore crossbow brooches, fancy belt sets, and prick spurs, which helped mark them as men in imperial service, whether they were soldiers, civilian administrators, or members of local elites. This trio of objects in Britain is generally all that survives from this costume, but it would have also included long-sleeved tunics embellished with decorative vertical strips and patches, and short, military-style cloaks (Kelly 2004, p. 20). We have detailed knowledge of this dress and its wide adoption from visual representations, most of which were made outside Britain and northern Gaul. But it is clear that many men in the northwestern provinces adopted it because some of them were buried with belt sets and crossbow brooches (Janes 1996, pp. 130–131; Cool 2010, p. 7; Esmonde Cleary 2013, pp. 83–84).

Many of the crossbow brooches and belt sets recovered from Romano-British cemeteries were made in state factories and had been given out to military men and administrators as donatives on special occasions. Some were manufactured in Britain, but others were fashioned in state workshops along the Danube frontier. Their variety of origins argues that these objects and the people who wore them could be highly mobile (Swift 2000, pp. 49–50).

Recent isotopic studies have revealed that late-Roman cemeteries in Britain where crossbow brooches and/or belt sets have been recovered contained the skeletons of people who had spent their early childhoods outside Britain. Extramural cemeteries at Winchester, York, Dorchester, Gloucester, and Scorton, near Catterick, in North Yorkshire all include men with crossbow brooches and/or official belt sets. The oxygen and strontium isotopic ratios preserved in the tooth enamel of some of these men make it unlikely that they were born in Britain, and, given their burial costumes, it is not unreasonable to argue that they had arrived there either as servants of the state or as soldiers (Eckardt et al. 2009; Booth 2014; Eckardt, Müldner, and Speed 2015). These foreigners, however, came from a variety of regions from across the Roman world, so there was considerably diversity not only among Roman Britain's native-born population, but among its foreigners (Müldner et al. 2011; Eckardt et al. 2014). At the same time, isotopic studies suggest that some of the locally born dead were buried in ways that made them look as if they had come from other parts of the empire, and that some of the foreign-born were buried in accordance with more local funerary rights. All of this suggests that a number of people in Britain had wide experience within the empire, whether locally born or not (Eckardt 2010, p. 250).

Isotopic studies have also helped to identify a number of foreign women, some with exotic grave-goods, others without, in York's, London's, and Winchester's extramural cemeteries (Leach et al. 2010; Montgomery et al. 2010). In addition, fifth-century funerary inscriptions as far afield as southern Gaul and Pannonia commemorate dead women who had been born in Britain (Handley 2011, p. 64 and nos. 53, 443, and 456). At the same time, impressive numbers of late-Roman bracelets from Britain have been recovered from the graves of women buried on the Continent. Distribution of these bracelets is limited to cemeteries closely associated with towns or military sites (Swift 2010, pp. 247–249). Like the crossbow brooches and belt sets buried with men, these bracelets argue for the movement of people closely associated with the state—in this case, women, who were likely accompanying their male relatives or owners from Britain to new imperial postings (Swift 2010, p. 250). There are almost 100 graves at Krefeld-Gellep, a cemetery attached to a late-Roman fortification on the lower Rhine dated from the second half of the fourth century to the first decades of the fifth, which include these bracelets (Swift 2010, pp. 265, 276).[4] Moreover, a number of the bracelet-wearing women were wearing more than one type of Romano-British bracelet, suggesting that they had collected them over some years and that they probably arrived in Gaul wearing them (Swift 2010, p. 266). This practice suggests that the population at Krefeld-Gellep in the late-Roman period, like that of many forts or administrative towns in Britain, was cosmopolitan (Swift 2010, p. 268). In the same cemetery, a significant minority of contemporary men were buried with crossbow brooches and/or belt sets (Swift 2010, p. 270). Not all the women buried with Romano-British grave-goods were necessarily from the same home communities. At a cemetery at the late-Roman fort at Oudenburg, in Belgium, for example, the grave of one bracelet-wearing woman included a Much Hadham ware face-pot from Hertfordshire, and another a Dales ware pot from Yorkshire (Swift 2010, p. 273).[5] So, people associated with the running and perpetuation of the late-Roman state could be highly mobile, and many must have traveled, like the pots, the bangles, and the crossbow brooches, via the Rhineland, Boulogne, and Richborough into Britain and back.

In short, we have evidence in the late-Roman period for a highly organized political economy that both facilitated and depended on the large-scale exchange of low-value commodities, which bound lowland Britain, northern Gaul, and the Rhineland together (for later trade, see Tys, Chapter 34, and Theuws, Chapter 38, this volume). Indeed, Chris Wickham has argued that the fiscal movement of goods is the thing that glued late-Roman supraregional economies like this one together (2005, p. 717). These goods and the economic and political needs that moved them were bound together by the large-scale movement of currency and imperial personnel, and required considerable infrastructure.

POST-ROMAN POTS AND PEOPLE

Given the pervasive links between northern Gaul, the Rhineland, and Britain in the fourth century, it is reasonable to ask how these connections and the large-scale movement of commodities, people, and coins that stood behind them fared in the two centuries after the Roman state's withdrawal from Britain. From the mid-sixth century on, there is ample evidence for links of all kinds—diplomatic, familial, cultural, and commercial—between English communities and Frankish kings and traders, particularly in Kent. Did these relationships develop organically out of late-Roman connections? Or were they forged in the fifth century, after the Roman state's withdrawal from Britain? Or is it true, instead, that the connections that facilitated the exchange of goods, people, and coins in this later period were built from scratch in the sixth century and beyond?

These questions are easier to pose than to answer. Because modes of production for the most visible kinds of Roman material culture collapsed in Britain in the first couple of decades after 400, people in the immediate post-Roman period used considerably less and quite different types of pottery, dress fittings, and building materials than had their immediate predecessors (Cooper 1996; Esmonde Cleary 2012, pp. 13–14; Fleming 2012; Gerrard 2013, p. 80; Fitzpatrick-Matthews and Fleming, in press). Because this new-style material culture was developing at the same time that migrants from the Continent were beginning to settle in Britain, and because some of it is clearly related to that found on the far side of the Rhine, this evidence has been used, not to think about connections between Britain and Continent in the ways done by scholars studying the period before 400, but rather as a means of determining the origins, ethnicity, and number of migrants who were moving into Britain.

Before looking at this new material culture and determining what it tells us about cross-Channel exchange in the post-Roman period, it is important to underscore the evidence demonstrating that the late-Roman economy had ceased to function in Britain by ca. 425, and that the long-standing mechanisms allowing the large-scale movement of goods, people, and coins across the Channel were no longer in operation. For one thing, when the imperial government withdrew from Britain, it stopped supplying it with currency (Abdy and Williams, p. 80). As a result, only miniscule numbers of fifth-century coins reached Britain after 408: less than three dozen have been found, most of them pierced and worn as jewelry (Abdy and Williams 2006; Bland and Loriot 2010, pp. 177–178, 338; Walton and Moorhead 2016). Once the shipment of coins stopped, the large-scale movement of basic commodities and taxes between Britain and the Continent was no longer a possibility (see Strothmann, Chapter 35, this volume, on coinage within Gaul). The end of the imperial coin supply also meant that administrators and soldiers still in Britain ceased to be paid by the state and that officials fresh from postings elsewhere in the Empire would no longer be sent to Britain.[6] Moreover, in the generations on either side of 400, Britain's villa estates, towns, and infrastructure associated with large-scale cereal production and transportation—all of which were heavily implicated in systems of imperial taxation and the money economy—ceased to be viable as well, and none survived past around 425. In the same decades that Roman Britain's economy imploded, northern Gaul was experiencing its own severe economic crisis (van Ossel and Ouzalias 2001; Halsall 2007, 383–387; Esmonde Cleary 2013, p. 429). It is hardly surprising, then, given the cascade of economic dislocations, that exchange links between the two regions did not endure.

Because the mechanisms, institutions, and infrastructure standing behind Roman cross-Channel exchange collapsed, it has long been suggested that the Franks should be credited with whatever trade was taking place between Britain and northern Gaul in the post-Roman period. Scholars working mainly before 1990—including Vera Evison and Sonia Chadwick Hawkes, who spent their careers excavating, classifying, and periodizing migration-period material culture, particularly artifacts recovered from cemeteries in Kent—used finds dated to the fifth century to build a case for early, high-status Frankish settlement in Britain. Based on this evidence, they argued that some of the men in England buried with fancy belt sets and weapons during this period were Frankish warriors who had formerly fought in Roman armies. Some had come to Britain as "invaders" and "conquerors," and others were invited to settle in lowland Britain in "strategic" regions (Hawkes 1961; Evison 1965). Archaeological evidence was thus used to support Gildas's claim that barbarian *foederati* had been invited into Britain in the early post-Roman period (Gildas, cap. 23.5).

This early Frankish presence in England helped explain why, by the sixth century, southern England, in particular Kent, was awash with Frankish material culture. The archaeological record makes clear, for example, that by the early sixth century, high-status women in Kent were wearing a distinctive costume—a plain, tabby-weave linen dress split at the neck and worn with a short, tight-fitting jacket, an outfit that required four or more brooches, rather than the two or three normally worn by women in other parts of lowland Britain. As a result, their dress was closer to that of Frankish women than it was to costumes worn elsewhere in England (Bender Jørgensen 1991, pp. 14–15, 17; Owen-Crocker 2004, pp. 90–102; Walton Rogers 2007, pp. 190–193). During this same period, many men in Kent had access to Frankish ring-swords, spears, belt buckles, and wheel-thrown pottery (Evison 1979, pp. 21–22, 26; *Novum Inventorium Sepulchrale*).

Building on these ideas, other scholars argued that Merovingian kings came to wield hegemonic power in Kent, and in return, they gave the kingdom of Kent "favored nation status" and granted the Kentish king a monopoly over Frankish goods traded within England (Chadwick-Hawkes 1970; Wood 1983, pp. 16–17; Huggett 1988; Wood 1992; Behr 2000, pp. 46–47; Welch 2002, 2007, pp. 191–192). By the second half of the sixth century, Frankish metalwork, glass, and pottery were found across much of southern England thanks to these arrangements (Parker Pearson, van De Noort, and Woolf 1993, p. 312; Harrington and Welch 2014, pp. 174–210). Indeed, Jean Soulat has identified more than 800 "Merovingian" finds in England dated 450–650 (2010, p. 50). Sixth-century

"Anglo-Saxon" brooches and pottery recovered in cemeteries on the Frankish side of the Channel have, in turn, been used to argue that official enclaves of "Anglo-Saxon" traders were involved in moving goods from Francia into Kent via this monopoly (Welch 1991; Soulat 2009). So, a history of Frankish activity in fifth-century Britain combined with a narrative of official Frankish political influence in sixth-century Kent, explained both the development of early medieval kingship in England and the history of its material culture.

Although many archaeologists no longer hold that Frankish warriors were settled in Britain in the fifth century, this idea continues to have its supporters (Welch 1993, 2002, 2007, pp. 199–200; Soulat 2009, 2011; Harrington and Welch 2014, p. 180). Theories about the hegemonic powers of Merovingian kings over Kent also continue to haunt modern historical narratives of the period.[7] It is important, therefore, to think carefully about Britain's belt set and weapon burials—which sit at the heart of these theories—and to lay out an alternative interpretation of their meaning.

It is, of course, possible that some of the men in fifth-century Britain buried with belt sets and weapons were the descendants of families who had moved from the far side of the Rhine into Gaul and had fought in Rome's armies. Similar burials are also found in northern Gaul (Hills and Hurst 1989; Theuws 2009; Esmonde Cleary 2013, pp. 82–90). We now understand, however, that contemporaries encountering men dressed or buried in this way in Gaul would have viewed them as late-Roman provincials or as members of local elite families rather than as "Franks." Indeed, it is difficult to identify self-consciously "Frankish" burials in Gaul until the very end of the fifth century (Halsall 2000; Effros 2003; Böhme 2009; Theuws 2009). It is unlikely, therefore, that men buried in Britain with similar belt sets and weapons in the fifth century were signaling Frankish ethnicity. It is more likely that they were telegraphing the same message as were people in Gaul: they were presented as people who were part of a broader, late-Roman world.

Britain's belt set and weapon burials, like those of the so-called Gloucester Goth, the prone weapon burial discovered outside of Richborough's defenses, and the "warrior" burial discovered at Dykes Hill in 1874, are increasingly being thought about as late Roman rather than "barbarian" (Booth 2014, pp. 268–269). Analysis of a recently excavated second Dykes Hill burial suggests that this man, too, in spite of the fact that his elaborate belt set and axe were made on the Continent and that his oxygen isotope signature suggests he was born outside of Britain, should nonetheless be interpreted as a late-Roman official, rather than an invading barbarian warrior. Indeed, the fact that he was buried in a late-Roman, extramural cemetery places him firmly in a late-Roman milieu (Booth 2014). Although he may have lived as late as about 420, his dress, burial, and the location of his grave all argue that we should understand him as a late-Roman provincial rather than a conquering barbarian. Similarly, a careful reevaluation of the fifth-century "Anglo-Saxon" settlement of Mucking and its cemeteries also suggests that the burials found there with belt fittings might be better understood as evidence for the continuation of local late-Roman traditions than as a sign of the arrival of "Germanic" *foederati* (Lucy 2016).

Other evidence from the fifth century also shows that sporadic contact continued between elites in Britain and in Gaul, but that participants in these contacts from Gaul were members of Roman rather than Frankish communities. Bishops Germanus of Auxerre and Lupus of Troyes, for example, traveled from Gaul to Britain to deal with the threat of Pelagianism, suggesting that the jurisdiction of some churchmen in late-Roman Gaul continued to stretch across the Channel and into Britain (Petts 2014, p. 74). Similarly, a distinctive style of brooch and belt set, made in the Quoit Brooch style, were also being worn by and buried with high-status individuals on both sides of the Channel in the fifth century (Inker 2000). This, too, suggests episodic contact between Britain and Roman Gaul in the fifth century.

If we pay close attention to chronology, it is clear that almost all the Frankish and Frankish-style objects found in lowland Britain and the vast majority of the so-called Anglo-Saxon pots and brooches found on the other side of the Channel date to the sixth century and beyond. Additionally, very little of this material dates to the fifth century (Soulat 2009, pp. 133–136; Soulat, Bocquet-Liénard, and Hincker 2012; Harrington and Welch 2014, pp. 183–205). This argues for a genuine hiatus in the persistence of late-Roman networks across the channel, and the break suggests that the mechanisms standing behind the movement of goods in the sixth century had little to do with those operating in the fourth century. If early Frankish settlement and hegemony over Kent are now seen as unlikely, how can we explain the impressive amounts of Frankish material culture found in Britain by the sixth century?

Zones of interaction between Britain and the Continent were reoriented in important ways in the immediate post-Roman period. Contacts across the North Sea into coastal Germany and Scandinavia had been rare in Britain during the Roman period, but from the mid-fifth century on, there was an uptick in the movement of people, ideas, and things between eastern Britain and lands to the north and east of the Roman *limes* (Hines 2013; Morris 2015, pp. 424–427). Like the connections that were springing up to facilitate traffic across the Channel, these new networks developed over the course of the late fifth century, and by the early sixth century, an important new zone of exchange across the North Sea had been stitched together (Deckers and Tys 2012; Hines 2013; see also Tys, Chapter 34, this volume). During the same period, there is also evidence for strong links developing between the terp (or artificial mound) settlements of coastal Netherlands and eastern England, with some communities in both regions participating in similar burial customs and using similar pottery, brooches, and combs (Hamerow, Hollevoet, and Vince 1994; Knol 2009; Deckers and Tys 2012, pp. 117–123; Soulat, Bocquet-Liénard, Savary, and Hincker 2012). It seems, then, that coastal communities on both sides of the North Sea and the Channel—in a zone that stretched from southern Norway past the mouth of the Rhine and into coastal northern France and along the eastern coast of Britain—came, by the early sixth century, to have considerable contact and that the people living in this region were connected rather than divided by the sea.

Many of the communities participating in these sixth-century exchange networks found in coastal Kent, Flanders, and the Rhine delta were not particularly high status, but they nonetheless had access to what we think of as exotic and/or high-status material culture, much of it Frankish (Fleming 2009; Loveluck 2013, pp. 191–192). The Frankish goods being used, for example, as grave goods in Kent in the sixth century were not limited to the fanciest 1 percent of Kentish graves, or even to its most extravagant 20 percent, but are found, rather, in graves of quite middling people—perhaps the best-off 40 percent, if their graves are anything to go by (Richardson 2005, vol. 2, Tables 141–145 and pp. 242–248; Brookes 2007, pp. 138, 142). At the same time, there is evidence that many households in this coastal zone had boats (Fleming 2009, pp. 6–7; Deckers and Tys 2012). Thus, access to Frankish imports in Kent, far from being restricted by monopolistic trade controlled by Frankish and Kentish kings, was remarkably open. Kentish evidence makes it unlikely that one king, and one king alone, was doling out the cornucopia of Frankish goods found in large numbers of graves belonging to people of quite different social ranks, excavated from cemeteries across the length and breadth of eastern Kent. The trans-Channel activities of relatively large numbers of Kentish households, so it seems, brought sufficient wealth to an impressive numbers of them in the sixth century—to enable them to acquire Frankish swords and wine and to dress their women in Frankish finery. This scenario suggests that communities of at least part-time mariners, who depended, in part, on boats and exchange to make a living, were moving the kinds of goods local would-be elites used to proclaim their exalted status, in particular, Frankish wine, pottery, and metalwork. It also indicates that members of the households of traders and ship captains involved in the trade had access to these goods as well.

Among the people living in eastern Britain involved in trans-Channel and trans-North Sea trade may have been groups of circular migrators, that is, people whose families had migrated to England but who continued to journey between their families' old communities on the Continent, in places such as lower Normandy, Frisia, or southwest Norway and their new ones along the east coast of Britain. This was a well-known phenomenon among historically attested immigrant groups (Anthony 1997). People like these may have been central in early maritime exchanges, distributing goods to allies, cousins, social betters, and even "customers" on both sides of the sea and teaching others, by example, of the opportunities available to men willing to act as skippers and traders (Fleming 2009).

A quite different situation from the one just described was found in western Britain. There is evidence of interaction between eastern Mediterranean traders and British elites from the western part of Britain from around 475 to the middle of the sixth century. A package of highly standardized goods, made up mostly of ceramics (and their contents), but also including a little glass and a few other archaeologically visible high-value goods, was brought from the eastern Mediterranean into Britain, via the Atlantic seaways by Byzantine traders, who were likely trading their wares in exchange for tin (Campbell 2007, pp. 128–130). These wares, once they arrived in western Britain, were traded almost exclusively with the masters of a small number of exceptionally high-status sites (Campbell 2007, p. 132). The networks that stood behind this trade were not the same as the ones that had been in operation in the fourth century. The sites where eastern Mediterranean wares were being exchanged in this later period do not overlap with those operating in the fourth century. There is, moreover, about a half a century break between the time when Roman goods ceased coming into Britain from the Mediterranean in the early fifth century, and the resumption of trade between the two regions in the later fifth century (Campbell 2007, pp. 125–126). This new exchange network continued until ca. 550. This network, in turn, overlapped for a few decades with another new network, one that eventually came to replace it. This newer network was run by Franks, who were bringing shipments of archaeologically visible glass and a range of pottery vessels called E ware, which was probably produced in Poitou-Charentes (Campbell 2007, pp. 46–49). Some of this Frankish material has been recovered in coastal Wales and southwest Britain, but impressive amounts are also found in Ireland and western Scotland (Doyle 2014). The Frankish material in western Britain is not, however, found at the same sites as the ones with the earlier, eastern Mediterranean material. Judging from where this material has been recovered, it is likely that Frankish merchants, like their Byzantine predecessors, were trading with elites at major high-status centers, and these men, in turn, distributed Frankish exotica to their friends and allies through gift exchange (Campbell 2007, pp. 133–135). Like the evidence for resuming trade in eastern Britain, both the earlier Mediterranean trade and the later Frankish trade were the result of the development of new networks of exchange not in operation in the fourth century. And like those developing in eastern post-Roman Britain, neither was involved with the exchange of low-value bulk commodities. All of these things argue that late-Roman systems had ceased to operate, and the people and mechanisms behind trade in the fifth and especially sixth centuries were new.

The differences between the external exchange networks operating in eastern and western Britain during the fifth and sixth centuries are instructive. First, goods arriving in the west of Britain came from western France, and Franks dealt directly only with elites who controlled important sites. In the east of Britain, on the other hand, goods from the other side of the Channel (as well as the North Sea) were more widely distributed, and it seems that many more people on both sides of the sea—not all of them Franks and not all of them high status—were both involved in these exchanges and had greater access to continental goods. Proximity to the Continent and a tradition of relatively widespread access to boats doubtless made this more of a possibility in eastern Britain than in the west of Britain, where trade along the Atlantic seaways required greater resources and know-how.

A close examination of material evidence suggests that Roman networks of exchange, which bound Britain, northern Gaul, and the Rhineland into a single economic zone, collapsed in the early fifth century. The institutions, people, and commodities implicated in this trade, and the mechanisms and infrastructure that facilitated it, did not survive the withdrawal of the Roman state from Britain. In the second half of the fifth century, archaeological evidence suggests that new trans-sea networks of exchange were beginning to emerge, which stretched across the Channel and the North Sea and from western Francia to the Irish Sea. The people, places, and goods entangled in these early medieval networks were different from those of the Roman period, and the scale of exchange was much smaller. Franks came to be important players in both western

Britain and eastern lowland Britain, but their roles in the two zones were quite different. In the west, Franks dominated the Atlantic trade and limited their interactions to the most important local elites. In the east, however, although local elites avidly collected and displayed Frankish material culture, its trade and distribution were much broader, and many more people were involved in its exchange—local Kentish boat owners, Frisians, traders from southern Scandinavia, as well as Franks. All of these groups would be poised to expand their operations in the early seventh century, when England's earliest towns began to develop.

Notes

1. Several late fourth-century texts note that grain was being shipped to the Rhine frontier from Britain (Ammianus Marcellinus, xviii, 2, 3; Taylor 2002, p. 845).
2. Based on calculations of the least expensive transportation available during the summer months, using the Orbis Stanford Geospatial Network Model of the Roman World, search from *Londinium* to *Lugdunum Canefatium* (Scheidel and Meeks 2012).
3. The calculation, using Orbis, from London to Trier using the cheapest method in the summer months is 44 days (Scheidel and Meeks 2012). The same calculation from Lyon to Trier is 52.4 days. Scheidel notes that maritime transport made Britain, during the good sailing months, a place from which it was relatively easy to transport goods to other parts of the Empire (Scheidel 2014, p. 16).
4. The cemetery contains more than 4,000 graves, about 640 datable graves from the fourth century, 50 from the fifth century, and 600 from the sixth century (Bloemers and Thijssen 1990, p. 145).
5. This is the only Hadham ware vessel identified on the Continent (Brulet, Vilvorder, and Delage 2010, p. 266).
6. However, many troops had already been withdrawn from Britain on a number of occasions in the late-Roman period, most famously under Constantine III (Collins and Breeze 2014, pp. 65–66, 70).
7. For some examples and a critique, see Collins and McClure 2008 and Fleming 2009.

Works Cited

Ancient Sources

Ammianus Marcellinus. J. C. Rolfe and J. C. (eds.). (1935–1939). *Rerum gestarum libri qui supersunt*. Cambridge, MA: Harvard University Press.
Gildas. M. Winterbottom (ed. and trans.). (1978). *Gildas, The Ruin of Britain and Other Works*. Chichester: Phillimore.

Modern Sources

Abdy, R., and Williams, G. (2006). "A Catalogue of Hoards and Single Finds from the British Isles c. AD 410–675." In B. Cook and G. Williams (eds.), *Coinage and History in the North Sea World, c. AD 500–1250* (pp. 11–74). Leiden: Brill.

Allen, J. R. L. & Fulford, M. G. (1996). "The Distribution of South-East Dorset Black Burnished Category I Pottery in South-West Britain." *Britannia* 27: 223–281.

Anthony, D. W. (1997). "Prehistoric Migration as Social Process." In J. Chapman and H. Hamerow (eds.), *Migration and Invasion in Archaeological Explanation* (pp. 21–32). BAR, International Series 664. Oxford: BAR.

Behr, C. (2000). "The Origins of Kingship in Early Medieval Kent." *Early Medieval Europe* 9: 25–52.

Bender Jørgensen, L. (1991). "The Textile of the Saxons, Anglo-Saxons and Franks." *Studien zur Sachsenforschung* 7: 11–23.

Bird, J., and Williams, D. F. (1983). "German Marbled Flagons in Roman Britain." *Britannia* 14: 247–252.

Bland, R., and Loriot, X. (2010). *Roman and Early Byzantine Gold Coins Found in Britain and Ireland*. London: Royal Numismatic Society.

Bland, R., Moorhead, T. S. N., and Walton, P. J. (2013). "Finds of Late Roman Silver Coins from Britain: The Contribution of the Portable Antiquities Scheme." In F. Hunter and K. Painter (eds.), *Late Roman Silver: The Traprain Treasure in Context* (pp. 117–166). Edinburgh: Society of Antiquaries of Scotland.

Blaszkiewicz, P., and Jigan, C. (1991). "Le problème de la diffusion et de la datation de la céramique sigillée d'Argonne décorée à la molette des IVème–Vème siècles dans le nord-ouest de l'Empire." In L. Rivet (ed.), *Actes du Congrès de Cognac. 8–11 Mai 1991. Société Française d'étude de la Céramique Antique en Gaule* (pp. 385–415). Marseille: SFECAG.

Blockley, K. (1995). *Excavations in the Marlowe Car Park and Surrounding Areas*, 5 vols. Canterbury: Canterbury Archaeological Trust.

Bloemers, J. H. F., and Thijssen, J. R. A. M. (1990). "Facts and Reflections on the Continuity of Settlement at Nijmegen between AD 400 and 750." In J. C. Besteman, J. M. Bos, and H. A. Heidinga (eds.), *Medieval Archaeology in the Netherlands. Studies Presented to H. H. van Regteren Altena* (pp. 133–150). Maastricht: Van Gorcum.

Böhme, H. W. (1974). *Germanische Grabfunde des 4.–5. Jahrhunderts zwischen unterer Elbe und Loire. Studien zur Chronologie und Bevölkerungsstruktur*. Munich: Verlag C. H. Beck.

Böhme, H. W. (2009). "Migrants' Fortunes: The Integration of Germanic Peoples in Late Antique Gaul." In D. Quast (ed.), *Foreigners in Early Medieval Europe* (pp. 131–148). Mainz: Verlag des Römisch-Germanischen Zentralmuseums.

Booth, P. (2014). "A Late Roman Military Burial from the Dyke Hills, Dorchester on Thames, Oxfordshire." *Britannia* 45: 243–273.

Brookes, S. (2007). *Economics and Social Change in Anglo-Saxon Kent AD 400–900: Landscapes, Communities and Exchange*. BAR, British Series 431. Oxford: Archaeopress.

Brulet, R., Vilvorder, F., and Delage, R. (2010). *La céramique romaine en Gaule du Nord: dictionnaire des céramiques; la vaisselle à large diffusion*. Turnhout: Brepols.

Campbell, E. (2007). *Continental and Mediterranean Imports to Atlantic Britain and Ireland, AD 400–800*. York: Council of British Archaeology.

Chadwick-Hawkes, S. (1970). "Early Anglo-Saxon Kent." *Archaeological Journal* 126: 186–192.

Collins, R., and Breeze, D. (2014). "*Limitanei* and *comitatenses*: Military Failure at the End of Roman Britain?" In F. K. Haarer (ed.), *AD 410: The History and Archaeology of Late and Post-Roman Britain* (pp. 61–72). London: Society for the Promotion of Roman Studies.

Collins, R., and McClure, J. (2008). "Canterbury and Wearmouth-Jarrow: Three Viewpoints on Augustine's Mission." In S. Barton and P. Linehan (eds.), *Cross, Crescent, and Conversion: Studies on Medieval Spain and Christendom in Memory of Richard Fletcher* (pp. 17–42). Leiden: Brill.

Cool, H. E. M. (2010). "A Different Life." In R. Collins and L. Allason-Jones (eds.), *Finds from the Frontier* (pp. 1–9). York: Council of British Archaeology.

Cooper, N. J. (1996). "Searching for the Blank Generation: Consumer Choice in Roman and Post-Roman Britain." In J. Webster, and N. J. Cooper (eds.), *Roman Imperialism: Post-Colonial Perspectives* (pp. 85–98). Leicester: University of Leicester.

Deckers, P., and Tys, D. (2012). "Early Medieval Communities around the North Sea: A 'Maritime Cuture'?" In R. Annaert, K. De Groote, Y. Hollevoet, F. Theuws, and D. Tys (eds.), *The Very Beginning of Europe? Cultural and Social Dimensions of Early-Medieval Migration and Colonisation (5th–8th Century)* (pp. 81–88). Brussels: Flanders Heritage Agency.

Dhaeze, W., and Seillier, C. (2005). "La céramique de l'égout collecteur du camp de la Classis Britannica à Boulogne-sur-Mer (Pas-de-Calais)." *Actes du congrès de Blois, S.F.E.C.A.G.* 44: 609–638.

Doyle, I.W. (2014). "Early Medieval E Ware Pottery: An Unassuming But Enigmatic Kitchen Ware?" In B. Kelly, N. Roycroft, and M. Stanley (eds.), *Fragments of Lives Past: Archaeological Objects from Irish Road Schemes* (pp. 81–94). Dublin: National Roads Authority.

Eckardt, H. (2012). "Foreigners and Locals in *Calleva*." In M. Fulford (ed.), *Silchester and the Study of Romano-British Urbanism* (pp. 247–256). Portsmouth, RI: *Journal of Roman Archaeology* Supplementary Series.

Eckardt, H., Chenery, C., Booth, P., Müldner, G., Evans, J. A., and Lamb, A. (2009). "Oxygen and Strontium Isotope Evidence for Mobility in Roman Winchester." *Journal of Archaeological Science* 36: 2816–2825.

Eckardt, H., Müldner, G., and Lewis, M. (2014). "People on the Move in Roman Britain." *World Archaeology* 46: 534–550.

Eckardt, H., Müldner, G., and Speed, G. (2015). "The Late Roman Field Army in Northern Britain? Mobility, Material Culture and Multi-Isotope Analysis at Scorton (n. Yorks)." *Britannia* 46: 191–223.

Effros, B. (2003). *Merovingian Mortuary Archaeology and the Making of the Early Middle Ages*, Berkeley: University of California.

Esmonde Cleary, S. (2012). "The Ending(s) of Roman Britain." In D. A. Hinton, S. Crawford, and H. Hamerow, eds., *The Oxford Handbook of Anglo-Saxon Archaeology* (pp. 13–29). Oxford: Oxford University Press.

Esmonde Cleary, S. (2013). *The Roman West, AD 200–500: An Archaeological Study*. Cambridge: Cambridge University Press.

Evison, V. I. (1965). *The Fifth-Century Invasions South of the Thames*. London: Athlone Press.

Evison, V. I. (1979). *A Corpus of Wheel-Thrown Pottery in Anglo-Saxon Graves*. London: Royal Archaeological Institute.

Fitzpatrick-Matthews, K., and Fleming, R. (2016). "The Perils of Periodization: Roman Ceramics after 400 CE." *Fragments* 5: 1–33.

Fleming, R. (2009). "Elites, Boats and Foreigners: Rethinking the Rebirth of English Towns." *Città e campagna prima del mille, Atti delle Settimane di Studio* 56: 393–425.

Fleming, R. (2012). "Recycling in Britain after the Fall of Rome's Metal Economy." *Past and Present* 217: 3–45.

Fleming, R. (in press). *The Material Fall of Roman Britain*. Philadelphia: University of Pennsylvania Press.

Fulford, M. (1977). "Pottery and Britain's Foreign Trade in the Later Roman Period." In D. P. S. Peacock (ed.), *Pottery and Early Commerce: Characterization and Trade in Roman And Later Ceramics* (pp. 35–84). London: Academic Press.

Fulford, M. (1987). "La céramique et les échanges commerciaux sur la Manche à l'époque romaine." In *Les céramiques gallo-romaines et romano-britanniques dans le nord-ouest de l'Empire. Place de la Normandie entre le continent et les îles britanniques. Actualités des recherches céramiques en Gaule. Actes du congrès de Caen, 28–31 mai, 1987* (pp. 95–106). Marseille: Société Française d'Etude de la Céramique Antique en Gaule.

Fulford, M. (2007). "Coasting Britannia: Roman Trade and Traffic around the Shores of Britain." In C. Gosden, H. Hamerow, P. de Jersey, and G. Lock (eds.), *Communities and Connections: Essays in Honour of Barry Cunliffe* (pp. 54–74). Oxford: Oxford University Press.

Fulford, M., and Bird, J. (1975). "Imported Pottery from Germany in Late Roman Britain." *Britannia* 6: 171–181.

Gerrard, J. (2008). "Feeding the Army from Dorset: Pottery, Salt and the Roman State." In S. Stallibrass and R. Thomas (eds.), *Feeding the Roman Army: The Archaeology of Production and Supply in North West Europe* (pp. 116–127). Oxford: Oxbow Books.

Gerrard, J. (2013). *The Ruin of Roman Britain: An Archaeological Perspective*. Cambridge: Cambridge University Press.

Grünewald, M., and Hartmann, S. (2014). "Glass Workshops in Northern Gaul and the Rhineland in the First Millennium AD As Hints of a Changing Land Use—Including Some Results of the Chemical Analysis of Glass from Mayen." In D. Keller, J. Price, and C. Jackson (eds.), *Neighbours and Successors of Rome* (pp. 5–57). Oxford: Oxbow Books.

Guest, P. (2015). "The Burial, Loss, and Recovery of Roman Coin Hoards in Britain and Beyond: Past, Present, and Future." In J. Naylor and R. Bland (eds.), *Hoarding and the Deposition of Metalwork from the Bronze Age to the 20th Century: A British Perspective*. BAR, British Series 615 (pp. 101–116). Oxford: Archaeopress.

Halsall, G. (2000). "Archaeology and the Late Roman Frontier in Northern Gaul: The So-Called 'Föderatengräber' Reconsidered." In W. Pohl and H. Reimitz (eds.), *Grenze und Differenz im frühen Mittelalter* (pp. 167–180). Vienna: Österreichische Akademie der Wissenschaften.

Halsall, G. (2007). *Barbarian Migrations and the Roman West, 376–568*. Cambridge: Cambridge University Press.

Hamerow, H., Hollevoet, Y., and Vince, A. (1994). "Migration Period Settlements and 'Anglo-Saxon' Pottery from Flanders." *Medieval Archaeology* 38: 1–18.

Handley, M. (2011). *Dying on Foreign Shores: Travel and Mobility in the Late-Antique West*. Portsmouth, RI: Journal of Roman Archaeology.

Harrington, S., and Welch, M. (2014). *The Early Anglo-Saxon Kingdoms of Southern Britain AD 450–650*. Oxford: Oxbow Books.

Hassall, M. W. C., and Tomlin, R. S. O. (1979). "Roman Britain in 1978." *Britannia* 10: 339–356.

Hawkes, S. C. (1961). "Soldiers and Settlers in Britain, Fourth and Fifth Century." *Medieval Archaeology* 5: 2–70.

Hills, C. M., and Hurst, H. R. (1989). "A Goth at Gloucester." *Antiquaries Journal* 69: 154–158.

Hines, J. (2013). "The Origins of East Anglia in a North Sea Zone." In D. Bates and R. Liddiard (eds.), *East Anglia and Its North Sea World in the Middle Ages* (pp. 16–44). Woodbridge: Boydell Press.

Huggett, J. W. (1988). "Imported Grave Goods and the Early Anglo-Saxon Economy." *Medieval Archaeology* 32: 63–96.

Hunter, F., and Painter, K. (eds.). (2013). *Late Roman Silver: The Traprain Treasure in Context*. Edinburgh: Society of Antiquaries of Scotland.

Inker, P. (2000). "Technology as Active Material Culture: The Quoit-Brooch Style." *Medieval Archaeology* 44: 25–52.

Janes, D. (1996). "The Golden Clasp of the Late Roman State." *Early Medieval Europe* 5: 127–153.

Kelly, C. (2004). *Ruling the Later Roman Empire*. Cambridge, MA: Harvard University Press.

Knol, E. (2009). "Anglo-Saxon Migration Reflected in Cemeteries in the Northern Netherlands." In D. Quast (ed.), *Foreigners in Early Medieval Europe* (pp. 112–129). Mainz: Verlag des Römisch-Germanischen Zentralmuseums.

Leach, S., Eckardt, H., Chenery, C., Müldner, G., and Lewis, M. (2010). "A Lady of York: Migration, Ethnicity and Identity in Roman Britain." *Antiquity* 84: 131–145.

Loveluck, C. (2013). *Northwest Europe in the Early Middle Ages, c. AD 600–1150*. Cambridge: Cambridge University Press.

Loveluck, C., and Tys, D. (2006). "Coastal Societies, Exchange and Identity along the Channel and Southern North Sea Shores of Europe, AD 600–1000." *Journal of Maritime Archaeology* 1: 140–169.

Lucy, S. (2016). "Odd Goings-on at Mucking: Interpreting the Latest Romano-British Pottery Horizon." *Internet Archaeology* 41. Retrieved from http://dx.doi.org/10.11141/ia/41/6.

Martin, T., and Dufournier, D. (1983). "Recherches sur la diffusion de la 'Black burnished ware' sur le littoral bas-normand au IVe s. de notre ère." In *Actes du 105e Congrès des Sociétés Savantes* (pp. 65–83). Paris: CTHS

Millett, M. (2007). "Roman Kent." In J. H. Williams (ed.), *The Archaeology of Kent to AD 800* (pp. 135–186). Woodbridge: Boydell Press.

Millett, M., and Wilmott, T. (2003). "Rethinking Richborough." In P. Wilson (ed.), *The Archaeology of Roman Towns: Studies in Honour of John S. Wacher* (pp. 184–194). Oxford: Oxbow Books.

Montgomery, J., Evans, J., Chenery, C., Pashley, V., and Killgrove, K. (2010). "'Gleaming White and Deadly': Using Lead to Track Human Exposure and Geographic Origins in the Roman Period in Britain." In H. Eckardt (ed.), *Roman Diasporas: Archaeological Approaches to Mobility and Diversity in the Roman Empire* (pp. 199–226). Portsmouth, RI: Journal of Roman Archaeology.

Morris, F. M. (2015). "Cross-North Sea Contacts in the Roman Period." *Oxford Journal of Archaeology* 34: 415–438.

Müldner, G. H., Chenery, C., and Eckardt, H. (2011). "The 'Headless Romans': Multi-Isotope Investigations of an Unusual Burial Ground from Roman Britain." *Journal of Archaeological Science* 38: 280–290.

Novum Inventorium Sepulchrale. (2007). Kentish Anglo-Saxon Graves and Grave Goods in the Sonia Hawkes Archive, 1st Edition. Retrieved from http://inventorium.arch.ox.ac.uk.

Owen-Crocker, G. R. (2004). *Dress in Anglo-Saxon England*. 2nd ed. Woodbridge: Boydell Press.

Parker Pearson, M., van De Noort, R., and Woolf, A. (1993). "Three Men and a Boat: Sutton Hoo and the East Saxon Kingdom." *Anglo-Saxon England* 22: 27–50.

Petts, D. (2014). "Christianity and Cross-Channel Connectivity in Late and Sub-Roman Britain." In F. K. Haarer (ed.), *AD 410: The History and Archaeology of Late and Post-Roman Britain* (pp. 73–88). London: Society for the Promotion of Roman Studies.

Pollard, R. J. (1988). *The Roman Pottery of Kent*. Retrieved from http://www.kentarchaeology.org.uk/Research/Pub/RPofK/Contents.htm.

Price, J. (1978). "Trade in Glass." In J. du, P. Taylor and H. Cleere (eds.), *Roman Shipping and Trade: Britain and the Rhine Provinces* (pp. 70–78). London: Council of British Archaeology.

Redknap, M. (1988). "Medieval Pottery Production at Mayen: Recent Advances, Current Problems." In D. R. M. Gaimster, M. Redknap, and H.-H. Wegner (eds.), *Zur Keramik des Mittelalters und der beginnenden Neuzeit im Rheinland.* (pp. 3–37). BAR International Series 440. Oxford: Archeopress.

Reece, R. (2013). "Silver after 350 and the Lost Generation." In F. Hunter and K. Painter (eds.), *Late Roman Silver: The Traprain Treasure in Context* (pp. 167–174). Edinburgh: Society of Antiquaries of Scotland.

Richardson, A. (2005). *The Anglo-Saxon Cemeteries of Kent*, 2 vols. BAR, British Series 391. Oxford: Archaeopress.

Roymans, N., and Derks, T. (2011). "Studying Roman Villa Landscapes in the 21st Century. A Multi-Dimensional Approach." In N. Roymans and T. Derks (eds.), *Villa Landscapes in the Roman North: Economy, Culture and Lifestyle* (pp. 1–44). Amsterdam: Amsterdam Archaeological Studies.

Scheidel, W. (2014). "The Shape of the Roman World: Modelling Imperial Connectivity." *Journal of Roman Archaeology* 27: 7–32.

Scheidel, W., and Meeks, E. (2012). *Orbis: The Stanford Geospatial Network Model of the Roman World*. Retrieved from http://orbis.stanford.edu/#.

Soulat, J. (2009). *Le materiel archéologique de type Saxon et Anglo-Saxon en Gaule mérovingienne*. Saint-Germain-en-Laye: Association française d'Archéologie mérovingienne.

Soulat, J. (2010). "Des Mérovingiens en Angleterre." *Histoire et image médiévales*, 34: 49–55.

Soulat, J. (2011). "Between Frankish and Merovingian Influences in Early Anglo-Saxon Sussex (Fifth–Seventh Centuries)." In S. Brookes, S. Harrington, and A. Reynolds (eds.), *Studies in Early Anglo-Saxon Art and Archaeology: Papers in Honour of Martin G. Welch* (pp. 62–71). BAR, British Series, 527. Oxford: Archaeopress.

Soulat, J., Bocquet-Liénard, A., Savary, X., and Hincker, V. (2012). "Hand-Made Pottery Along the Channel Coast and Parallels with the Scheldt Valley." In R. Annaert, K. De Groote, Y. Hollevoet, F. Theuws, and D. Tys (eds.). *The Very Beginning of Europe? Cultural and Social Dimensions of Early-Medieval Migration and Colonisation (5th–8th Century)* (pp. 215–224). Brussels: Flanders Heritage Agency.

Swift, E. (2000). *The End of the Western Roman Empire: An Archaeological Investigation*. Stroud: Tempus Publishing.

Swift, E. (2010). "Identifying Migrant Communities: A Contextual Analysis of Grave Assemblages from Continental Late Roman Cemeteries." *Britannia* 41: 237–282.

Taylor, A. (2002). "Supplying the Frontier Zones: The Role of the East Anglian Fens." In P. Freeman, J. Bennet, Z. T. Fiema, and B. Hoffman (eds.), *Limes XVIII: Proceedings of the XVIIIth Congress of Roman Frontier Studies* (pp. 843–850). BAR International Series 1084, 2 vols. Oxford: Archaeopress.

Theuws, F. (2009). "Grave Goods, Ethnicity and the Rhetoric of Burial Rites in Late Antique Northern Gaul." In T. Derks and N. Roymans (eds.), *Ethnic Constructs in Antiquity: The Role of Power and Tradition* (pp. 293–319). Amsterdam: Amsterdam Archaeological Studies.

Tuffreau-Libre, M., Mossman-Bouquillon, A., and Symonds, R.P. (1995). "La céramique dit black-burnished dans le nord de la France." In L. Rivet (ed.), *Actes du Congrès de Rouen 25–28 Mai 1995: productions et importations dans le nord-ouest de la Gaule et relations avec la Bretagne romaine: actualité des recherches céramiques* (pp. 91–112). Marseille: Société française d'étude de la céramique antique en Gaule.

Tyers, P. (1996). *Roman Pottery in Britain.* London: B. T. Batsford.

van der Veen, M. (1989). "Charred Grain Assemblages from Roman-Period Corn Driers In Britain." *Archaeological Journal* 146: 302–319.

van der Veen, M., and O'Connor, T. (1998). "The Expansion of Agricultural Production in the Late Iron Age and the Roman Period." In J. Bayley (ed.), *Science in Archaeology: An Agenda for the Future* (pp. 127–44). London: Historic England.

van Ossel, P., and Ouzalias, P. (2001). "Rural Settlement Economy in Northern Gaul in the Late Empire: An Overview and Assessment." *Journal of Roman Archaeology,* 13: 133–166.

Walton, P. J. (2011). *Rethinking Romano-British Coins: An Applied Numismatic Analysis of the Roman Coin Data Recorded by the Portable Antiquities Scheme.* Unpublished Ph.D. dissertation, University College London.

Walton, P., and Moorhead, S. (2016). "Coinage and Collapse? The Contribution of Numismatic Data to Understanding the End of Roman Britain." *Internet Archaeology* 41. Retrieved from http://dx.doi.org/10.11141/ia.41.8.

Walton Rogers, P. (2007). *Cloth and Clothing in Early Anglo-Saxon England: AD 450–700.* York: Council for British Archaeology.

Welch, M. (1991). "Contacts across the Channel between the Fifth and the Seventh Centuries: A Review of the Archaeological Evidence." *Studien zur Sachsenforschung* 7: 261–269.

Welch, M. (1993). "The Archaeological Evidence for Federated Settlement in Britain in the Fifth Century." In F. Vallet and M. Kazanski (eds.), *L'armée romaine et les barbares du IIIᵉ au VIIᵉ siècle* (pp. 268–278). Paris: Association Française d'Archéologie Mérovingienne.

Welch, M. (2002). "Cross-Channel Contacts between Anglo-Saxon England and Merovingian Francia." In S. Lucy and A. Reynolds (eds.), *Burial in Early Medieval England and Wales* (pp. 122–131). Leeds: Society of Medieval Archaeology.

Welch, M. (2003). "Migrating hoards?" In M. Ecclestone (ed.), *The Land of the Dobunni. A Series of Papers Relating to the Transformation of the Pagan Pre-Roman Tribal Lands into Christian, Anglo-Saxon Gloucestershire and Somerset from the Symposia of 2001 and 2002* (pp. 65–67). Gloucester: Committee for Archaeology in Gloucestershire and Council of British Archaeology South West.

Welch, M. (2007). "Anglo-Saxon Kent." In J. H. Williams (ed.), *The Archaeology of Kent to AD 800* (pp. 187–248). Woodbridge: Boydell Press and Kent County Council.

Wickham, C. (2005). *Framing the Early Middle Ages: Europe and the Mediterranean, 400–800.* Oxford: Oxford University Press.

Wilkinson, P. (2009). *An Archaeological Investigation of the Roman Aisled Stone Building at Hog Brook, Deerton Street, Faversham, Kent 2004–5.* Unpublished report, Kent Archaeological Field School.

Wood, I. (1983). *The Merovingian North Sea.* Alingås: Viktoria Bokförlag.

Wood, I. (1992). "Frankish Hegemony in England." In M. Carver (ed.), *The Age of Sutton Hoo* (pp. 235–241). Woodbridge: Boydell Press.

CHAPTER 18

DE GENTE SCOTTORUM MONACHI

The Irish in Merovingian Settlement Strategy

JEAN-MICHEL PICARD

IRISH involvement in Merovingian politics started quite late, at the end of the sixth century. It was not an organized campaign but, rather, the result of encounters between individuals who found a common interest in joint ventures. However, it did not happen by chance, and it can be seen as a consequence of the expansion of Christianity in Ireland from the late fifth century, especially as a result of the success of monasticism there. Often described as a missionary movement by the historiography of the nineteenth and twentieth centuries, Irish involvement in the Merovingian kingdoms from the 590s had little to do with missionary zeal. We know now, mostly thanks to twenty-first-century archaeological work and better readings of the original medieval sources, that the territories in which they operated were not inhabited by pagans in need of conversion. Certainly, Merovingian patronage for Irish monastic foundations was not only motivated by piety but was also a major element in the settlement strategy of kings and magnates in newly acquired or difficult areas of their territories.

EARLY CONTACTS: THE IRISHMAN COLUMBANUS AND THE FRANKISH ELITES

The foundation of monasteries in the border area of the kingdoms of Burgundy and Austrasia in the early 590s by the Irishman Columbanus provides the first example of the process of cooperation between Merovingian kings and the Irish (see Jonas, *Vita Columbani* I, 6, 18–19, 24, 27–30; Wood 1994, pp. 181–202; O'Hara 2009, Fox 2014, pp. 21–31; see Diem, Chapter 15, this volume). Columbanus had left the monastery of

Bangor in Ulster shortly before 590 in order to found his own community, where he could practice the kind of asceticism developed by the early fathers of monasticism in the Egyptian desert and in Cappadocia. Far from being a wandering pilgrim, Columbanus seems to have carefully chosen his itinerary, targeting royal residences as places of destination. His excellent control of Latin, his knowledge of theology and mathematical sciences, and his superior eloquence allowed him to impress the kings and their advisors. Messengers must have been sent ahead of his arrival at court as, in all instances, the kings seem to have been aware of his reputation as a remarkable holy man. Columbanus's monastic foundations on the continent were all the result of an agreement between saint and king as part of a strategy that suited both parties. The first monastic foundation at Annegray, on the southwest edge of the Vosges Mountains, in 590 or 591, was in fact a royal foundation commissioned by King Guntram, king of Burgundy and saint (died 592). The forest of the Vosges was fiscal land, and Columbanus's settlement there could not have happened without the king's consent. The king of Burgundy kept a tight control on his forest, and, in his *Histories*, for the year 590, Gregory of Tours tells how King Guntram had his own chamberlain killed for having hunted in the Vosges without his permission. Our main source for Columbanus's career on the continent is the *Vita Columbani*, written in 640 by Jonas, monk of Bobbio, twenty-five years after the saint's death in 615. While an invaluable document for Columbanus's legacy and for the position and role of the communities he founded, it is not always reliable as to the events that took place during the saint's life. Intent on developing the theme of eremitism in the *Vita Columbani*, Jonas portrays Annegray—the first monastery founded by Columbanus in 591—as a deserted place set in a wilderness. As it was situated on one of the roads connecting Burgundy to the Moselle Valley and giving access to the capital cities of Metz and Trier, Annegray certainly was not a desert. Before Columbanus's arrival, the site already had a religious significance, first dedicated to Diana in the imperial and late Roman times, and then to St. Martin in the early medieval period. It is also situated along the line of several small forts whose function must have been the protection of the road connecting the border area east of the Moselle to the Luxeuil Valley.

The several episodes in the *Vita Columbani* (Jonas, *Vita Columbani* I, 6, 18, 24, 27, 30) relating the encounter of Columbanus with kings lead us to understand that the choice of the Annegray–Luxeuil area in 591 was strongly influenced by King Guntram or his heir to the throne Childebert II, that of Bregenz in 611 was influenced by King Theudebert, and that of Bobbio in 613 by Agilulf, king of the Lombards. In all three cases, the monastic foundations are situated in liminal areas, removed from the main royal residences, and where royal control needed strengthening (on royal courts, see Hen, Chapter 10, this volume). While Jonas, in the *Vita Columbani*, stresses the deserted nature of these places and the fact that the saint had the final choice for the location of his foundations, diplomatic sources and the evidence of recent archaeological work tell us a different story. Excavations carried out since 2005 (see Bully 2014) have revealed that Luxeuil was a substantial town in the late sixth century. It was a trading town situated at the crossroad of two main roads, one going from west to east and linking the cities of Langres and Basel and the other going from south to north and linking the capital cities of Châlons and Metz. The hot mineral waters of the Luxeuil baths kept attracting visitors. Small industries, especially pottery, were fully functioning. The population was large enough to support two Christian churches, one dedicated to St. Martin and the other to the Virgin Mary. The morality of the inhabitants or the religious zeal of the clergy may not have been perfect, as Jonas implies, but they were not pagans and did not need to be converted to Christianity. Columbanus's work in Burgundy was that of a reformer.

The Irish monastic model, as exemplified at Iona, Bangor, or Clonmacnoise, included a lay population within the community. In medieval Irish texts, the term *manach* (derived from Latin *monachus*) means not only "monk," but also "monastic tenant." The small community of holy men, devoted to prayer, to the study of sacred scripture, and to writing and ascetic practices, was supported by a larger population of laypeople, men and women, who were expected to adhere to the stricter way of life inspired by the monastic ideal. An important practice brought in by the Irish to the continent was that of regular private penance, as opposed to the ritual of public penance, which was a rare occasion in the life of a Christian in continental Europe (see Uhalde, Chapter 45, this volume). In an Irish context, people were expected to confess often, and specific penance was applied, depending on the nature of the sins committed. Constant reminding about self-control, respect of the others, duties to one's superiors and love of God contributed to peace and stability within the social group, and, apart from considerations about the salvation of their own souls, such an environment certainly appealed to the Merovingian rulers.

Columbanus was very successful in this enterprise (see Drews, Chapter 6, this volume). Like St. Patrick in Ireland, who in his *Confession* tells us how he recruited the sons and daughters of the Irish nobility to become the first monks and nuns of his new Christian communities (Patrick, *Confessio*, § 41), Columbanus also attracted the children of the aristocratic families in the kingdoms of Burgundy and Austrasia. According to Jonas, "people flocked from all directions seeking the remedy of penance," to such an extent that Columbanus had to build a third monastery in nearby Fontaine in order to cater for a community that had grown to several hundred monks in less than three years. Fontaine was situated in a wide valley along the River Roge and produced the grain needed for the three communities created by Columbanus. Like his model, Columba of Iona, Columbanus entrusted the running of each of his monasteries to a prior (*praepositus*), keeping for himself the overall guidance of all three as abbot. By creating a network of foundations similar to that of the Irish *paruchia*, Columban contributed to the reorganization of a territory, with specialization of the production in different areas, leading to circulation and exchange of goods and a functioning economy. The Irish settlement in the Luxeuil region was meant to be permanent. In fact, it lasted for twenty years until Columbanus lost the king's favor, another reminder that nothing could have been achieved without active royal support.

After the death of King Childebert II in 595, Burgundy was given to his young son Theuderic, who was still a minor and reigned under the guidance of his grandmother, Queen Brunhild. In spite of her later reputation as a Jezebel (Jonas, *Vita Columbani* I, 31;

Nelson 1978; see James, Chapter 11, this volume) Brunhild was in fact a generous patron of the church, and Theuderic used to visit Luxeuil regularly to seek the advice of the saint. The conflict between the royal family and Columbanus started in 608 when Theuderic, who had been living with several concubines, repudiated his wife and sent her back to her father in Spain. While perfectly legal under Frankish law, this behavior could not be condoned by a church leader trying to reform Christian society. Columbanus insisted that Theuderic should stop all adulterous relationships and refused to bless the children born out of legitimate wedlock. According to Jonas (*Vita Columbani* I, 18), Theuderic could have been persuaded to renounce his way of life and do penance, but Brunhild saw the saint's reproaches as interference in Merovingian affairs and a challenge to royal power. As a result, Columbanus was expelled from Luxeuil in 610. The monasteries he had founded were not dissolved and were allowed to continue functioning under the leadership of his continental disciples.

The subsequent events (Jonas, *Vita Columbani* I, 24, 27, 30) show that the enmity of the Burgundian court did not diminish Columbanus's appeal and that his skills as church leader were much in demand among Merovingian rulers. He first called at Rouen, the capital of Neustria in 610, where he was received with open arms by King Chlothar II, who made most generous offers in order to convince him to establish new foundations in his own kingdom (Jonas, *Vita Columbani* I, 24). Columbanus, aware of Neustria's weak position in the raging civil war between the three Merovingian kingdoms, refused on the grounds that his presence on Neustrian soil would make the conflict even worse. His next call was Metz, the capital of Austrasia, where he reluctantly accepted the offer of King Theudebert to settle at Bregenz on the eastern border of his kingdom, on new territories that had just come under Frankish control. We know from a letter he sent to his monks in 610 that Columbanus was not keen on missionary work among pagans (Columbanus, *Epistula* IV, 5). The settlement strategy envisaged by Theudebert was a failure. Instead of reaching agreement with them, Columbanus found himself in conflict with the local populations; Theudebert's weakened position in the civil war against his brother Theuderic meant that he could not get the military support he might have needed. When Theudebert finally lost the war at Tolbiac in May 612, Columbanus abandoned Bregenz and moved down south to seek the patronage of Agilulf, king of the Lombards (see Arnold, Chapter 21, this volume).

The Lombards had converted to Christianity in the mid-sixth century but were Arians. However, under the influence of his Bavarian queen, Theodolinda, Agilulf had recently converted to Catholicism, thus strengthening his position as king in Italy. At first, Columbanus's superior scholarship and eloquence was put to use in Milan to convince the Arians of their errors and help with the move toward Catholicism for the whole of the Lombard people. The foundation of Bobbio in 614 on a territory that was granted by Agilulf to Columbanus for building his own monastery fits in the strategy of Lombard expansion toward the Mediterranean Sea and Rome. Like Luxeuil, Bobbio was situated at the junction of several roads: one in the northwest to southeast direction, connecting Pavia, the capital of the Lombards, to central Italy and Rome, via Pontremoli; another road went from northeast to southwest, linking Piacenza to Genoa. From

Bobbio, one could also walk the fifty miles down to the Mediterranean Sea at Chiavari, crossing the Apennines at the Forcella Pass, or walk the thirty miles west to Tortona, leading to the important city of Asti. Excavations over the past ten years (Destefanis 2010, 2012; Conversi and Destefanis 2014) have revealed several Lombard settlements in the valleys connecting Bobbio to Piacenza and Pavia. These valleys had been cultivated since Neolithic times and had been assimilated to the Roman world since around 200 BCE. Long before Columbanus's arrival, the Trebbia Valley population was Christian and Bobbio already had a basilica dedicated to St. Peter. Columbanus died in 615, and the development of the new monastery was left to his successor, Attala, a Luxeuil monk, a native of Burgundy. The settlement strategy at Bobbio (see Zironi 2004, pp. 9–46) was quite similar to that at Luxeuil: a royal foundation, in a liminal territory, where foreign monks were put in charge of reorganizing a local population according to the stricter rules of the monastic ideal.

Coming from an Irish society where, in each of the hundred, and possibly more, small kingdoms, the king was at the head of a highly structured social hierarchy, Columbanus would have seen the king as his main counterpart. Irish abbots were used to dealing directly with kings, not only in religious matters, but also in terms of the organization of society. When early Irish law was written down in the seventh century, abbots and bishops were given equal status (and equal financial compensation) with the king of the túath. The túatha (lit. "people"), in spite of their small size, had all the attributes of kingdoms and their identity was based on the knowledge that each family in that population group ultimately descended from a common heroic ancestor. While the institution of kingship was guaranteed by law and customs, the practical position of a king in a given generation rested not only on his personal aura but also on the strength of his own family ties. In Francia, kingship operated on a much larger scale, and Merovingian kings had to negotiate with—and take the advice of—a complex network of powerful magnate families. During the long civil war between the descendants of Clovis (561–613), when the Frankish realm was frequently divided into two, three, or four kingdoms, the magnate families could decide to support one or the other of the kings, regardless of territorial divisions. One of these families, the Pippinids, eventually eliminated the Merovingian dynasty and ruled a unified Frankish kingdom as the new Carolingian dynasty (see Fouracre, Chapter 2, this volume).

The Irish quickly understood the workings of Frankish society and sought patronage not only from kings, but also from the powerful families of magnates. In between the foundation of Luxeuil and that of Bobbio, Columbanus had acquired the patronage of the Faronid family, whose land base was on the border of Austrasia and Neustria, along the Marne Valley. The *Life of Columbanus* relates, in between the visits to King Chlothar II of Neustria and King Theudebert III of Austrasia in 610–611, another visit of Columbanus to two powerful landowners in the region of Meaux, Audechar, and Chagneric, both of whom belonged to the Faronid extended family (Jonas, *Vita Columbani* I, 26). His visit must have left a strong impression on their children since, in the 630s, the three sons of Audechar (Ado, Rado, and Audoin) not only held important positions at the court of Dagobert I, king of the reunited Frankish kingdom, but also founded monasteries following the rule of St. Columbanus (see Fox 2014, pp. 70–81). Among the children of Chagneric, Chagnoald was a monk at Luxeuil before being appointed bishop of Laon, his brother Faro became bishop of Meaux and his sister, Fara, became abbess of Faremoutiers. All three supported the foundation and running of monasteries following the rule of Columbanus. The Faronids were part of a larger family network called the Agilolfings, who controlled territories not only in Austrasia, Neustria, and Burgundy, but also in Bavaria and northern Italy. In the seventh century, the dukes of Bavaria and several kings of the Lombards were Agilolfings. Queen Theodolinda of Lombardy belonged to the Agilolfing family of Bavaria, and it is likely that it was through the Faronid–Agilolfing network that Columbanus joined the court of Lombardy and was granted Bobbio.

Barely apparent in 615, when Columbanus died, the strategy of cooperation between monastic leaders and kings becomes obvious after 632 when the kingdoms of Austrasia, Neustria, Burgundy, and Aquitania were reunited under the single kingship of Dagobert I. In territories newly acquired by the king or located in border areas, we can observe a recurring pattern: rather than relying on the local aristocracy and the local clergy, the king supported the foundations of monastic settlements headed by abbots who were strangers to these areas and claimed to follow the model of Luxeuil or the rule of Columbanus. In newly conquered Aquitania, Dagobert and his treasurer, Eligius, founded the monastery of Solignac (near Limoges) in 632 (see *Eligii Charta cessionis Solemniacensis*). The first abbot was Remacle, a monk of Luxeuil, and the rule followed was that of Columbanus. The charter of foundation (signed among others, by Chagnoald, Audoin, and Rado, mentioned above) makes it clear that no bishop could claim authority over the monastery, whose abbot answered to nobody else but the king, the most glorious prince (*gloriosissimus princeps*). In addition, should the monks and their abbot relax the demanding rule of Columbanus in subsequent years, the abbot of Luxeuil would be put in charge of Solignac and take action (including punishment) in order to implement the reform. In Flanders, the Christian mission supported by Dagobert I was given to Amandus, a native of Aquitaine, who founded Elnone (later St-Amand) in 636. The financial investment was considerable since the royal donation for the abbey of St-Amand was estimated at 25,000 acres (see Platelle 1962, p. 38). In the lower Seine Valley, in the large wooded area belonging to the royal fisc, Dagobert's son, Clovis II, supported the foundation of Jumièges (654) by Philibert, another native of Aquitaine also influenced by Columbanian monasticism (*Vita Filiberti* I, 5–8; Picard 1995). Nearby, he gave the land of Fontenelle (founded in 648, now St-Wandrille) to Wandregisel, a native of Austrasia (*Vita Wandregiseli* c. 13–14). At the diocesan level, the Christian mission in the lower Seine Valley was managed by Audoin (mentioned above), who also was a stranger to the region. A powerful man at the court of Dagobert, with the high rank of *referendarium* (head of the royal chancery), Audoin remained an influential person both in ecclesiastical and political circles until his death in 684. His election as bishop of Rouen in 641 when he was still a layman lends support to the view that, from the 640s, the Neustrian kings and their mayors of the palace were trying to secure better control of their peripheral territories by placing their own agents on the ground rather than relying on local powers. This is not to say that the Christianization or re-Christianization of northern Gaul by the Frankish aristocracy was only a calculated political maneuver. In fact, there is plenty of evidence that the spiritual reform started by Columbanus at the beginning of the century had a lasting effect, especially in northern and eastern Francia (see O'Hara 2009).

Expansion of the Irish Presence in the Seventh Century

While Columbanus was a major influence in the spread of monasticism as a development strategy among the Frankish magnates, the work of his circle was not the only Irish involvement in the politics of the Merovingian kingdoms. For example, as bishop of Meaux, Faro (mentioned above) granted land at Breuil (now St-Fiacre) and Aubigny to the Irishmen Fiachra and Killian in the 640s (*Vita Faronis* c. 97–100). Both are known from Carolingian sources: the *Life of Saint Faro*, written between 868 and 872 by Hildegar, bishop of Meaux and the *Life of Killian of Aubigny*. However, these texts tell us little about these saints as historical figures. They are celebrated for their holiness and their asceticism. Their monastic settlements are described as small, and we can only assume that, while they were recruited by the Faronids to establish communities in the forest of Brie for Fiachra and in the upper Scarpe Valley for Killian, their influence remained limited in the seventh century. Nevertheless, continuity was ensured by the cult of the relics of these Irish saints, and Hildegar reports that the miracles wrought at the shrine of St. Fiachra drew pilgrims to the region of Meaux already in the ninth century (*Vita Faronis* c. 98).

Beside the monastic foundations sponsored by the Faronids in the Marne Valley (Jouarre, Rebais, and Faremoutiers), there were others supported by the royal family of Neustria and their mayors of the palace. Between 642 and 644, King Clovis II and his mayor, Erchinoald, granted land to the Irishman Fursey at Lagny-sur-Marne, on the site of a royal villa for the foundation of a monastery (*Vita Fursei* c. 9; *Virtutes Fursei* c. 10–14). Fursey (see Moreira, Chapter 42, this volume) had left the Irish monastery of Louth, where he was abbot, in the early 630s and had crossed the sea to England where he founded a first monastery at Cnobheresburg in East Anglia. Royal patronage was also sought for this monastery, which was endowed first by King Sigeberht and then by King Anna of the East Angles. Following a pattern not uncommon in Irish *paruchiae*, Fursey was succeeded in Cnobheresburg by a family member, his brother Foillán. This pattern was to be repeated in Francia. When Fursey died in January 649, Erchinoald brought his remains to his own estate at Péronne and established a monastery under the authority of Foillán (*Vita Fursei* c. 10; *Virtutes Fursei* c. 18–19; *Additamentum Nivialense*). In donating land and buildings to a new monastic community Erchinoald, like other Frankish aristocrats, certainly had religious motives, but he also had political reasons. Situated on the Somme, Péronne was removed from the center of Neustria (between the Oise, the Marne, and the upper Seine). In order to break the power of the local magnates, secular and ecclesiastical, Erchinoald needed the help of outsiders who were dependent on him. It is quite possible that the coming to France of Fursey and his brothers took place in the context of wider links between the Franks, the Anglo-Saxons, and the Irish. Erchinoald belonged to the powerful Mauronti family (Geary 1985; Le Jan 1995, p. 438). His brother Sigefrid was Count of Ponthieu, the territory in the lower Somme Valley across Kent on the other side of the Channel. Another brother was Adalbald, lord of Douai and patron of the monastery of Marchiennes founded by Amandus around 640. They had an alliance with the royal family of Kent through the marriage of their sister Emma to Eadwald, king of Kent. In this context, it is unlikely that the relationship between Fursey and Erchinoald was due to a chance encounter. In the 640s, the Mauronti were rivals of the Faronids and were certainly looking for the same type of personnel for reorganizing their rural territories.

The mission Erchinoald assigned to Foillán was not easy, as Péronne was not fully under his control. The text of the *Miracles of St Fursey* mentions a conflict between Erchinoald and Berchar, duke of Laon, over the relics of Fursey in 649 (*Virtutes Fursei* c. 18–19). Berchar controlled territories in the Somme Valley and in that instance he moved against Erchinoald with a large army, claiming that Péronne belonged to him by right (*iure*) since he had been duke (*dux*) in that territory before anyone else. In fact, none of the Irish establishments outside their own kingdoms in Ireland could have survived without the military backup of the warrior elite who supported them. When the Agilolfing duke of Bavaria was temporarily unable to control the territory around Bregenz, Columbanus had to abandon his monastery there and move down south toward Italy. In England, the attacks of Penda, king of Mercia, against the kingdom of East Anglia were probably the cause of Fursey's departure from Cnobheresburg. We do not know the reasons for Foillán's expulsion from Péronne, whether it was linked to the warring activities of Berchar or due to a disagreement between Foillán and Erchinoald. In any case, the Irish had to leave Péronne in 650/651 and found patronage further north in Austrasia with the Pippinids, who were the rivals of both the Faronids and the Mauronti, over whom they would eventually triumph as founders of the Carolingian dynasty. Before the arrival of Foillán and his monks, the Pippinids had already been engaged in establishing monastic settlements in Austrasia. After the death in 640 of Pippin I, mayor of Austrasia, his wife, Itta, another native of Aquitaine, had founded a monastery at Nivelles, headed by her daughter Gertrude (*Vita Geretrudis* c. 2–3). Foillán was given land by Grimoald, the son of Pippin I, to establish a monastic community at Fosses, some 25 miles southeast of Nivelles (*Additamentum Nivialense*). Irish monks also became part of the community at Nivelles and certainly were responsible for the introduction of the cults of St. Patrick and St. Brigit in that community. Details of the dealings between Fursey's brothers and the magnate families in Austrasia show how close the relationship was in political matters.

In the 650s, the Pippinids were the dominant group in Austrasia. They also had interests in Neustria and had formed an alliance with the powerful family of the

Widonids, originally based in the Trier region, but active in Burgundy, Neustria, and Aquitaine. In 656, after the death of Sigebert III, king of Austrasia, the Pippinids were confident enough in their own power to plan the removal of the legitimate heir to the throne, the young Dagobert II, born in 651, in order to replace him by Grimoald's own son, who had been adopted by Sigebert III before 650 under the Merovingian name of Childebert (see Picard 1991; Fouracre 2008)). The child Dagobert was tonsured and sent to a monastery in Ireland, while Childebert "the Adopted" reigned as king of Austrasia from 657 to 662. The final details of the successful coup were agreed to at a council meeting (*placitum*) held at Nivelles on January 16, 657, where Grimoald met Dido, bishop of Poitiers, member of the Widonid family. Our main source for this event is a short text known as the *Additamentum Nivialense de sancta Fuilano (The Nivelles Supplement on Saint Foillán)*, written soon after 657, which was added to the manuscripts of the *Life of Saint Gertrude*, written at Nivelles between 663 and 670. Contemporary or near-contemporary accounts are rare for the history of the seventh century, and the evidence offered by the Nivelles writer is precious. The text infers that Foillán had been part of the plot but was murdered two and a half months before. Very few Irish monks were killed in the seventh century, and one can only assume that the stakes were high enough for the enemies of the Pippinids to commission the killing of a holy man. It would appear that the kind of advice and counsel given by Foillán to Grimoald went beyond spiritual matters and was felt to be dangerous enough in some quarters, possibly among the Wulfoad-Gundoinids or the Mauronti, who both had the means to strike in that part of Austrasia.

THE FRANKS AND IRELAND: COMMERCIAL AND PERSONAL TIES

By the 640s, the Irish would have been aware of the potential dangers of settling in Francia. The Franks were known to them through commercial dealings and personal contacts. Trade between Ireland and Frankish Gaul was not extensive, but it was regular. Wine was the main import from Gaul, as it was in demand not only from Christian communities who needed it for the celebration of the Eucharist, but also from the Irish warrior elite for whom this luxury item played an important part in the manifestation of their generosity. The place of wine in early Irish society is well attested, both in narrative and in legal texts dating from the seventh and eighth centuries (see Picard 2004). Other items of Frankish origin found in excavations in Ireland include pottery, glass, weapons and a few coins (see O'Sullivan et al. 2014, pp. 255–269). The coins do not appear to have been used as currency but, rather, as tokens of friendship or memorabilia. The geographical origin of the objects found in Ireland point toward the estuary of the Loire River as the main area for trading exchanges between Ireland and the Merovingian kingdom. For example, the two Merovingian gold tremissis found in Ireland (Hall 1973/1974, p. 82) were minted in Beaufay and Le Mans, a region with direct waterway access to the Loire Valley (on Merovingian numismatics, see Strothmann, Chapter 35, this volume). Finds of E-ware pottery, produced in western France, are common in Ireland (Doyle 2014; see Fleming, Chapter 17, this volume). These include jars, with or without lids, beakers, pitchers, and bowls. The jars with lids may have been used as containers to import luxury or exotic foodstuffs coming from the Mediterranean area (see Bonifay and Pieri, Chapter 37, this volume), but the bulk of the pottery was imported as tableware, bringing a continental cachet, style, and prestige to their owners. Though attested on fifty-five different sites, these finds are concentrated in northeast Leinster and around Strangford Lough (O'Sullivan et al. 2014, pp. 256–260). This may only reflect the level of activity of archaeologists in the Eastern provinces rather than the true distribution pattern for the whole of Ireland, but, in any case, it confirms that both Columbanus in Co. Down and Fursey in Co. Louth left Ireland from regions that had direct commercial contacts with the Merovingian world. The letter Columbanus sent to his monks of Luxeuil in 610 and the *Life of Saint Philibert* (both mentioned above) confirm the existence of regular trade between Ireland and Nantes and also Noirmoutier in the seventh century. Situated strategically between Aquitaine and Brittany, the point of export for the nearby production of wine, wheat, salt, metalwork and pottery, the estuary of the Loire Valley was a region of rivalry and competition among Merovingian rulers who vied to control it. The Pippinids also were interested in that area, and the donation of Grimoald to the abbey of Stavelot-Malmedy includes the ports of Vetraria and Sellis as well as the revenue of tax levied on boats transporting goods on the Loire River (*Chartae Stabulenses*, no. 4, pp. 12–13). The involvement of Dido, bishop of Poitiers, in the abduction and exile of King Dagobert II would make better sense if the route chosen was that of the regular trade through the Loire estuary. Whether Dido accompanied the young Dagobert all the way to Ireland is not known.

In any case, other Frankish aristocrats are known to have stayed in Ireland, to have been involved in both church and lay politics, and to have been in a position to inform their Irish contacts about the current state of Frankish affairs. One of them was Agilbert, a member of the Faronid family, a close relation of Audechar (mentioned above), who spent several years in Leinster in the 640s, possibly studying at Rathmelsigi, a monastery renowned for the quality of its teaching and for attracting foreign students, mostly from Anglo-Saxon England (see Ó Cróinín 1984). His career as church leader started in the late 640s–early 650s as bishop of Wessex at Dorchester-on-Thames. In 664, he took part in the Synod of Whitby in that capacity and, like Wilfrid, defended the cause of the *Romani*, who advocated the practices and rituals of the Roman church, against the *Hibernenses*, who were partisans of the old customs and traditions practiced in the early church in Ireland and Britain. From the 630s and throughout the seventh century, the Irish church went through an active period of development and transformation. Accepting new ideas, new customs, and new scientific knowledge was a slow process and certainly not uniform across the whole of Ireland. Debate, opposition, and rivalry existed among the different Christian communities or networks of communities. Franks and Anglo-Saxons living in Ireland would have taken part in the controversies and sided with the *Romani* networks. Whitby saw the defeat of the *Hibernenses* in England but not the end of the relationship between the Anglo-Saxon clergy and the Irish who shared the same views on church organization and beliefs.

Another Frank known to have been in Ireland in the 630s was Madelgarius, a prominent member of an Austrasian family based in Hainault, with close links to the Merovingian courts of Chlothar II (613–629) and Dagobert I (629–639) (Moisl and Hamann 2002). He was married to Waldetrud, the niece of Gundoland and Landeric, majors of the Palace of Chlothar II. His presence in Ireland and his participation at the Battle of Mag Ráth in 637 are linked to Dagobert's involvement in the politics of the Anglo-Saxon royal families of Kent and Deira. Mag Ráth was probably one of the most important battles fought on Irish soil in the seventh century since it sealed the fate of the Irish in Scotland—from then they had to renounce their claims on their territories in Ireland—and confirmed the prominence of the Cenél Conaill, a branch of the Uí Néill, as the most serious contenders for the high kingship of Ireland for the rest of the seventh century, alternately with the Síl nÁedo Sláine, another branch of the Uí Néill. On the one hand, Mag Ráth was part of the series of battles in the deadly feud within the Uí Néill family which lasted for most of the first half of the seventh century. On the other hand, the involvement of Irish Cruithni, of the Cenél nGabráin from Scottish Dál Ríata, of British troops from Strathclyde, of Anglo-Saxon warriors in both camps, and a battalion of Frankish warriors indicates that what was at stake was not just the high kingship of Ireland and the control of Ulster, but also the balance of power in northern Britain in the vacuum left after the death of King Aethelfrith of Northumbria in 616.

In spite of the large coalition gathered under the leadership of Congal Cáech, king of Ulster (the list of his allies included Domnall Brecc, king of Dál Riata; the Uí Néill branches of Cenél nÉogain and Clann Cholmáin; Oswiu, aetheling of Bernicia, married to Fin, daughter of Colmán Rímid, king of Cenél nÉogain; Madelgar, envoy of King Dagobert I, who was a kinsman of Queen Æthelburg of Deira, a protector of her children and therefore with a strong interest in the royal succession in Northumbria), Domnall mac Áeda, king of the Cenél Conaill and high king of Ireland, won this battle, which lasted for several days. Fighting also took place at sea, with a naval battle between Cenél Conaill and Cenél nÉogain, which was fought off the Mull of Kintyre (*Annals of Ulster*, CE 637). In terms of numbers, Mag Ráth involved thousands of men (*Cath Maige Rath* 1842). We know from Fredegar's *Chronicle* that a retinue of 300 men for a Frankish warlord was considered small (Fredegar, *Chronicle* c. 24–25). Dagobert would not have sent Madelgarius across the Channel with less. Like the Battle of Degsastan fought in Britain in 603, which also involved multinational forces, the Battle of Mag Ráth supposed careful logistic planning with meetings between potential allies. On each side, churches provided support for their patrons, not only in terms of prayers, rituals, or relics—often brought to the battlefield—but in the active participation of ecclesiastics in embassies and negotiations.

In the seventh century, the Cenél Conaill were the patrons of the *paruchia* of Colum Cille, a large organization based in Iona, with monasteries in both Ireland and Scotland. In 637, the abbot of Iona was Ségéne mac Fiachnaí, from the Cenél Conaill family, leader of the Irish party in the Easter controversy (*Hibernenses*), and responsible for the establishment of Irish monasteries in Northumbria, at the request of King Oswald. On the opposite side, the family of Congal Cáech, the Dál nAraidi, sponsored a network of churches founded by St. Patrick, which eventually came under the leadership of Armagh, rivals of the *paruchia* of Colum Cille for the primacy over all the Irish churches and champions of the *Romani* side. The monastery of Louth, where Fursey and his brothers had settled, had been founded by a disciple of St Patrick and would have been associated with this network. The foundations of monasteries in England and northern France by Fursey and his brothers, Foillán and Ultán, in the 630s and 640s were not isolated undertakings but must be understood in the context of family alliances across kingdoms on both sides of the Channel and extending to the Irish world.

The murder of Foillán (see *Additamentum Nivialense*) highlights an important trait of the position of the Irish in Merovingian politics: by the mid-seventh century, the Irish were de facto in the position of clients or vassals of the powerful magnates who were patrons of their monasteries. In situations of conflict, their fate was linked to that of the party they belonged to. Apart from the murder of Foillán, which is a case of extreme reaction, we find other examples of Irish involvement during the violent conflicts that followed the death of Chlothar III, king of Neustria and Burgundy, in spring 673. The Neustrian magnates, led by Leudegar, bishop of Autun, and his brother Gaerinus, count of Paris (belonging to the Widonid family and nephews of Bishop Dido of Poitiers), revolted against the mayor of the palace, Ebroin, and, with the help of Wulfoald, major of the palace in Austrasia, successfully defeated Ebroin (*Passio Leudegarii* c. 5–6; *Liber Historiae Francorum* c. 45; Fredegar, *Chronicle*, c. 2). Ebroin was tonsured and sent to the monastery of Luxeuil, which had attracted the patronage of the Wulfoad-Gundoinids under the successors of Columbanus. The alliance between Leudegar and Wulfoald did not last long. Wulfoald, now mayor of the palace in Neustria as well as in Austrasia, was able to capture Leudegar and send him to Luxeuil by the end of 673. The rule of Wulfoald came to an end in autumn 675 when Childeric II, the Austrasian king he had installed on the throne of Neustria, was assassinated by a conspiracy of Neustrians warriors, probably organized by Ebroin from his prison in Luxeuil (*Liber Historiae Francorum* c. 45; Fredegar, *Chronicle* c. 2). Wulfoald's position in Neustria had become too dangerous, and he barely escaped with his life to Austrasia. After their release from Luxeuil, Ebroin and Leudegar, who had briefly reconciled against Wulfoald, resumed their feud with renewed energy and violence. In 675, the Neustrian magnates led by Gaerinus and Leudegar reinstated King Theuderic III on the throne and appointed as mayor of the palace one of their relatives, Leudesius, son of Erchinoald, the patron of Fursey, and founder of Péronne.

The events of the following year show not only the complexity of family loyalties and feuds in Merovingian politics, but also the role played by Irish ecclesiastics in the strategy of Frankish magnates. After the death of Childeric II, the Austrasians needed a king, and someone, either among the Pippinids or among the Wulfoald-Gundoinids, remembered the existence of King Sigebert's son, Dagobert, who was exiled in Ireland twenty years previously. The successful return of Dagobert II from Ireland took place between April and June 676 and could not have happened without Irish involvement (see Picard 1991). During the spree of arrests and killings ordered by Ebroin in the following months, leading to the horrific deaths of Leudegar and Gaerinus in August 676, Ultán, who had succeeded his brother, Foillán, as abbot of Fosses and Péronne, was asked by Ebroin to detain in the monastery of Péronne Amatus, bishop of Sion in Switzerland, accused of plotting against the king and his mayor of the palace. Like Luxeuil, Péronne was not just a monastery and a center of spiritual activity and learning, but also a stronghold, a center of power, where men could be detained when political imperatives required it.

THE WIDER NETWORK: BRETONS AND ANGLO-SAXONS

Given their role in the settlement strategy and in the political affairs of the Merovingian elite, it is interesting to note that the Irish refused assimilation and did not try to blend with the societies in which they lived. While cooperating with the Frankish elite, they kept their own identity and were perceived by others as being Irish. In 604, in a letter to the pope, Columbanus was able to claim his identity, saying that, in Luxeuil "we are in our homeland since we do not use any Gaulish rule, but living in the desert, we follow the rules of our ancestors" (Columbanus, *Epistulae*, III, 2). In 805, when the *Annals of Metz* were written, Péronne was still known as *Perrona Scottorum* (Péronne of the Irish) (*Annales Mettenses*, p. 12). In continental annals, charters, and hagiographical texts, Irish ecclesiastics are always identified as *Scoti*. Their role was not static and one can observe a progression throughout the seventh century. Originally, the cooperation between the Frankish elite and Irish monks was about land settlement. On the one hand, Irish religious leaders requested lands where they could build the ideal communities envisaged by the founders of the monastic movement of sixth-century Ireland. On the other hand, the Frankish magnates saw the practical aspect of Irish monasticism. A social organization based on obedience, strict self-control, manual work, regular control through confession, and respect of a hierarchy was perfectly suited for the kind of territorial control needed by expanding family groups whose wealth depended on the successful management of large territories. Furthermore, lacking family connections in the territories allocated to them, the Irish were more likely to remain faithful to the lords who had provided lands and protection. This does not mean the spiritual aspect was not an important motive for the foundation of these monasteries. Frankish leaders were concerned with the salvation of their souls and especially with their future in the afterlife. These leaders highly respected the Irish clerics not only for their knowledge, but also for their ascetic way of life, which clearly marked them as holy men. As the relationship developed, the cooperation expanded into other areas of social and political life. Under the Carolingians, Irish clerics were used as political advisors, propagandists, and, most of all, teachers, implementing Charlemagne's new education policy. Their role in settlement strategy in newly conquered or liminal territories continued, as the appointment of Fergal as abbot of St. Peter at Salzburg in 747 shows.

The historiography of the nineteenth and early twentieth centuries has presented the Irish as an exception in the Merovingian world. While remarkable, their contribution was not unique. A similar pattern of settlement and cooperation with Frankish rulers can be observed with the Britons (on England, see Fleming, Chapter 17, this volume). As we have seen with the foundation of Jumièges and Fontenelle (St-Wandrille), the Merovingians were interested in securing the important trade access that was the Seine estuary (the same can be said of the Loire and the Somme). The foundation of Pentale (now St-Samson-de-la-Roque) in the 540s by Samson, former abbot of Llanilltud in Wales and renowned for his strict brand of ascetic monasticism, was a joint operation by Samson and King Childebert I, who granted lands in the lower Seine Valley at the meeting of the rivers Risle and Seine (*Vita Samsonis* I, 53). Samson was included in the king's ecclesiastical circle, and his name is found among the signatories of the Synod of Paris (561–562) convened by King Childebert I (*Concilia aevi Merovingici*, p. 146; Pontal 1986, pp. 122–126).

Forty years later, when Columbanus reached Annegray at the foot of the Vosges Mountains, Breton communities were already installed in the area. During his first winter in the Vosges in 591, as food supplies went low and famine threatened, Columbanus's community was saved from starvation by the Breton abbot Carantoc, who sent a cartful of food to his Irish neighbors (Jonas, *Vita Columbani* I, 7). Following in the footsteps of the Britons and the Irish, Anglo-Saxon ecclesiastics were also recruited in the later seventh century to fulfill similar functions. In 676, when Dagobert II was brought back from Ireland, the person in charge of the operation was no longer a Frankish magnate, but Wilfrid, bishop of York. From the mid-seventh century, the Pippinids had wished to extend their influence into Frisia. Inspired by the Irish experience, Wilfrid had wanted to live a life of exile on the continent (*Vita Wilfridi* c. 2–4). As a young man he had spent three years in Lyon around 655 and had good contacts in the Frankish church. In spite of (and perhaps because of) his close relationship with bishop Agilbert of Paris, who was a Faronid, Neustria was forbidden territory for him on account of Ebroin's enmity toward him. When Wilfrid successfully established Christian communities in Frisia under the protection of King Aldgisl, Ebroin went as far as offering a large sum of gold to Aldgisl for killing Wilfrid (*Vita Wilfridi* c. 26–27). In the 690s, with the help of the Pippinids, then the new overlords of Frisia, the work of Wilfrid was continued by other Anglo-Saxon monks, Swithbert and Willibrord, who had both studied in Ireland at the monastery of Rathmelsigi. Swithbert established communities among the Bructeri in the Ruhr region but had to leave that area due to increasing attacks from the Saxons (Bede, *Historia Ecclesiastica* V, 9). He finally founded a monastery on an island on the Rhine (now Kaiserswerth), which was granted to him by Plectrude, wife of Pippin II.

As for Willibrord (see Wood 1994, pp. 317–321), his mission in Frisia was a success, and he is still remembered as the apostle of the Frisians. Like Columbanus and Wilfrid before him, he sought the support of Rome and was granted the archbishopric of Utrecht, where he built a cathedral and founded a monastery. However, his most famous monastic foundation, Echternach, was another Pippinid undertaking. The initial grant of the monastery lands in 698 was given by Irmina, abbess of Oeren and mother of Plectrude, and the lavish construction of the church in 700 was financed by Pippin II (*Monumenta Epternacensia*, pp. 50–55). Monasteries could not have survived in Frisia without the military backup of the Pippinids. Thus, when Pippin II died in 714, the Frisians, under the leadership of King Radbod, took control of the territories conquered by the Franks and destroyed churches and monasteries. Willibrord had to flee the country and was able to come back only after Radbod died in 719, under the military protection of Charles Martel, son of Pippin II and grandfather of Charlemagne.

The contribution of the Irish to the creation of a monastic landscape in Merovingian Gaul cannot be separated from that of the Britons and the Anglo-Saxons. Contacts between the various people of the British Isles were close and their networks were interwoven. In spite of their differences and sometimes bitter opposition (as in the case of the Easter controversy), they were perceived by the Franks as coming from the same world—to such an extent that, in the Carolingian era, the term *Scotus* could be applied indifferently to people coming from Ireland, Brittany, Wales, or England. For instance, according to the *Life of Alcuin*, written around 825, when the Anglo-Saxon Alcuin was dying in Tours in 805–806, he was visited by Aigulf, another Anglo-Saxon. This visit drew the following comment from the monks of Tours: "This Briton or Irish (*Britto uel Scoto*) has come to visit that other Briton, who is lying down inside" (*Vita Alcuini* c. 18).

By then, the Franks were no longer dealing with isolated individuals like Columbanus, Fursey, Fiachra, or Killian, but with hundreds of insular clerics working in scriptoria, in schools, or more generally in the administration of the Carolingian court. Territorial expansion toward the East had also changed the nature of new monastic foundations. The aim of the rulers' strategy was no longer the reorganization of rural or urban population in regions that had known Romanization and early Christianity. The Saxons and the Slavs were pagans, and the Carolingians had to devise the kind of strong-armed missionary strategy that would remain that of imperial powers until modern times.

WORKS CITED

Ancient Sources

Additamentum Nivialense de Foillano. B. Krusch (ed.). (1902). MGH SRM 4 (pp. 449–451). Hanover: Hahn Verlag.

Additamentum Nivialense de Foillano. P. Fouracre and R. A. Gerberding (trans.). (1996). *Late Merovingian France. Story and Hagiography 640–720* (pp. 327–329). Manchester: Manchester University Press.

Annales Mettenses. B. von Simson (ed.). (1905). MGH SRG 10. Hanover: Hahn Verlag.

Annales Mettenses. P. Fouracre and R. A. Gerberding (trans.). (1996). *Late Merovingian France. Story and Hagiography 640–720* (pp. 330–370). Manchester: Manchester University Press.

Annals of Ulster. S. Mac Airt and G. Mac Niocaill (ed. and trans.). (1983). *The Annals of Ulster, to AD 1131*. Dublin: Dublin Institute for Advanced Studies.

Bede, *Historia ecclesiastica gentis Anglorum*. B. Colgrave and R. A. B. Mynors (ed. and trans.). (1981). *Bede's Ecclesiastical History of the English People*. Oxford: Clarendon Press.

Cath Maige Rath. J. O'Donovan (ed. and trans.). (1842). *The Banquet of Dun na n-Gedh and the Battle of Magh Rath* (pp. 90–320). Dublin: Irish Archaeological Society.

Chartae Stabulenses. J. Halkin and C. G. Roland (eds.). (1909). *Recueil des Chartes de l'Abbaye de Stavelot-Malmedy*. Vol. I. Brussels: Kiessling.

Columbanus, *Letters*. G. S. M. Walker (ed.). (1970). *Epistulae* (pp. 2–59). *Sancti Columbani Opera*. Dublin: Dublin Institute for Advanced Studies.

Concilia aevi Merovingici. F. Maassen (ed.) (1893). *MGH, LL* 3.1. Hanover: Hahn Verlag.

Eligii Charta cessionis Solemniacensis. B. Krusch (ed.). (1902). MGH SRM 4 (pp. 743–749). Hanover: Hahn Verlag.

Fredegar. J. M. Wallace-Hadrill (ed. and trans.). (1960). *The Fourth Book of the Chronicle of Fredegar with Its Continuations*. London: Nelson.

Gregory of Tours, *Historiarum libri decem*. B. Krusch and W. Levison (eds.). (1885). MGH SRM 1.1. Hanover: Hahn Verlag.

Gregory of Tours, *Historiarum libri decem*. L. Thorpe (trans.). (1974). *Gregory of Tours: The History of the Franks*. London: Penguin Classics.

Jonas of Bobbio, *Vita Columbani*. B. Krusch (ed.). (1905). *Ionae vitae sanctorum Columbani, Vedastis, Iohannis*. MGH SRG, 37. Hanover: Hahn Verlag.

Jonas of Bobbio, *Vita Columbani*. A. O'Hara and I. Wood, I (trans.). (2017). *Jonas of Bobbio. Life of Columbanus, Life of John of Réomé, and Life of Vedast* (pp. 85–239). Liverpool: Liverpool University Press.

Liber Historiae Francorum. B. Krusch (ed.). (1888). MGH SRM, 2 (pp. 215–328). Hanover: Hahn Verlag.

Liber Historiae Francorum. B. S. Bacharach (trans.). (1973). *Liber Historiae Francorum*. Lawrence: Coronado Press.

Monumenta Epternacensia. L. Weiland (ed.). (1874). MGH SS 23 (pp. 11–72). Hanover: Hahn Verlag.

Passio Leudegarii. B. Krusch (ed.). (1910). MGH SRM 5 (pp. 282–322). Hanover: Hahn Verlag.

Patrick, *Confessio*. L. Bieler (ed.). (1993). *Libri Epistolarum Sancti Patricii Episcopi*. Dublin: Royal Irish Academy.

Patrick, *Confessio*. P. McCarthy (trans.). (2011). *My Name Is Patrick*. Dublin: Royal Irish Academy.

Virtutes Fursei abbatis Latiniacensis. B. Krusch (ed.). (1902). MGH SRM 4 (pp. 440–449). Hanover: Hahn Verlag.

Vita Alcuini. W. Arndt (ed.). (1902). MGH, SS 15/1 (pp. 182–197). Hanover: Hahn Verlag.

Vita Audoini episcopi Rotomagensis. W. Levison (ed.). (1910). MGH SRM 5 (pp. 553–567). Hanover: Hahn Verlag.

Vita Audoini episcopi Rotomagensis. P. Fouracre and R. A. Gerberding (trans.). (1996). *Late Merovingian France. Story and Hagiography 640–720* (pp. 133–165). Manchester: Manchester University Press.

Vita Eligii episcopi Noviomagensis. B. Krusch (ed.). (1902). MGH SRM 4 (pp. 663–742). Hanover: Hahn Verlag.

Vita Eligii episcopi Noviomagensis. J. A. McNamara (trans.). (2001). "Dado of Rouen, Life of St. Eligius of Noyon." In T. Head (ed.). *Medieval Hagiography: An Anthology* (pp. 137–168). New York: Routledge.

Vita Faronis. B. Krusch (ed.). (1910). MGH SRM 5 (pp. 184–203). Hanover: Hahn Verlag.

Vita Filiberti. B. Krusch (ed.). (1910). MGH SRM 5 (pp. 568–606). Hanover: Hahn Verlag.

Vita Fursei. B. Krusch (ed.). (1902). MGH SRM 4 (pp. 434–440). Hanover: Hahn Verlag.

Vita Fursei. O. Rackham (trans.). (2007). *Transitus Beati Fursei: A Translation of an 8th Century Manuscript Life of St Fursey.* Norwich: Fursey Pilgrims.

Vita Geretrudis. B. Krusch (ed.). (1888). MGH SRM 2 (pp. 453–464). Hanover: Hahn Verlag.

Vita Geretrudis: P. Fouracre and R. A. Gerberding (trans.). (1996). *Late Merovingian France. Story and Hagiography 640–720* (pp. 319–326). Manchester: Manchester University Press.

Vita Killiani Albiniacensis: A. Poncelet (ed.). (1901). "Vita S. Killiani confessoris Albiniacensis." *Analecta Bollandiana* 20: 432–444.

Vita Leodegarii: B. Krusch (ed.). (1910). MGH SRM 5 (pp. 282–322). Hanover: Hahn Verlag.

Vita Samsonis. P. Flobert (ed.) (1997). *La Vie ancienne de saint Samson de Dol.* Paris: Éditions du CNRS.

Vita Wandregiseli. B. Krusch (ed.) (1910). MGH SRM 5 (pp. 13–24). Hanover: Hahn Verlag.

Vita Wilfridi. B. Colgrave (ed. and trans.). (1927). *The Life of Bishop Wilfrid. by Eddius Stephanus.* Cambridge: Cambridge University Press.

Modern Sources

Bully, S. (2014). "Les origines du monastère de Luxeuil (Haute-Saône) d'après les récentes recherches archéologiques." In M. Gaillard (ed.), *L'empreinte chrétienne en Gaule du IVe au IXe siècle* (pp. 311–355). Turnhout: Brepols.

Conversi, R., & Destefanis E. (2014). "Bobbio e il territorio piacentino tra VI e VII secolo: questioni aperte e nuove riflessioni alla luce dei dati archeologici." *Archeologia Medievale* 41: 289–312.

Destefanis, E. (2010)."Il comprensorio della Val Tidone tra antichitàe medioevo: strutture insediative, economia, organizzazione religiosa." In A. Scala (ed.), *Appunti di toponomastica piacentina. Bacino del Tidone e aree limitrofe* (pp. 31–60). Piacenza: Edizioni Riviste Tipografia Legatoria Commerciale.

Destefanis, E. (2012). "Bobbio come monastero 'di valle' nell'Appennino nord-occidentale (VII–XII secolo)." In L. Pani Ermini (ed.), *Le valli dei monaci: atti del convegno internazionale di studio: Roma, Subiaco, 17–19 maggio 2010* (pp. 703–732). Spoleto: Centro italiano di studi sull'Alto Medioevo.

Doyle, I. W. (2014). "Early Medieval E Ware Pottery: An Unassuming but Enigmatic Kitchen Ware?" In B. Kelly, N. Roycroft, and M. Stanley (eds.), *Fragments of Lives Past: Archaeological Objects from Irish Road Schemes* (pp. 81–93). Dublin: National Roads Authority.

Fouracre, P. (2008). "Forgetting and Remembering Dagobert II: The English Connection." In P. Fouracre and D. Ganz (eds.), *Frankland: The Franks and the World of the Early Middle Ages: Essays in Honour of Dame Jinty Nelson* (pp. 70–89). Manchester: Manchester University Press.

Fox, Y. (2014). *Power and Religion in Merovingian Gaul. Columbanian Monasticism and the Frankish Elites.* Cambridge: Cambridge University Press.

Geary, P. (1985). *Aristocracy in Provence. The Rhône Basin at the Dawn of the Carolingian Age.* Stuttgart: Anton Hiersemann.

Hall, R. (1973/1974). "A Check List of Viking-Age Coin Finds from Ireland." *Ulster Journal of Archaeology* 36/37: 71–86.

Le Jan, R. (1995). *Famille et pouvoir dans le monde franc (VIIᵉ-Xᵉ siècle). Essai d' anthropologie sociale*. Paris: Publications de la Sorbonne.

Moisl, H., and Hamann, S. (2002). "A Frankish Aristocrat at the Battle of Mag Ráth." In M. Richter and J.-M. Picard (eds.), *Ogma. Essays in Celtic Studies in Honour of Próinséas Ní Chatháin* (pp. 36–47). Dublin: Four Courts Press.

Nelson, J. (1978). "Queens as Jezebels: The Careers of Brunhild and Balthild in Merovingian History." In D. Baker (ed.), *Medieval Women* (pp. 31–77). Oxford: Blackwell.

Ó Cróinín, D. (1984). "Rath Melsigi, Willibrord, and the Earliest Echternach manuscripts." *Peritia* 3: 17–42.

O'Hara, A. (2009). "The *Vita Columbani* in Merovingian Gaul." *Early Medieval Europe* 17/2: 126–153.

O'Sullivan, A., McCormick, F., Kerr, T., and Harney, L. (2014). *Early Medieval Ireland, AD 400–1100: The Evidence from Archaeological Excavations*. Dublin: Royal Irish Academy.

Picard, J.-M. (1991). "Church and Politics in the Seventh Century: The Irish Exile of King Dagobert II." In J.-M. Picard (ed.), *Ireland and Northern France 600–850* (pp. 65–90). Dublin: Four Courts Press.

Picard, J.-M. (1995). "Aquitaine et Irlande dans le Haut Moyen Age." In J.-M. Picard (ed.), *Aquitaine and Ireland in the Middle Ages* (pp. 17–30). Dublin: Four Courts Press.

Picard, J.-M. (2004). "*Et in Hibernia*: Le vin dans l'Irlande du haut Moyen Age." In A. Tenaguillo y Cortázar (eds.), *Le vin dans ses oeuvres* (pp. 205–218). Bordeaux: CEPDIVIN.

Platelle, H. (1962). *Le temporel de l'abbaye de Saint-Amand, des origines à 1340*. Paris: Librairie d'Argences.

Pontal, O. (1986). *Die Synoden im Merowingerreich*. Paderborn: Schöningh.

Wood, I. (1994). *The Merovingian Kingdoms, 450–751*. London: Longman.

Zironi, A. (2004). *Il monastero longobardo di Bobbio: crocevia di codici, uomini, culture*. Spoleto: Fondazione centro italiano di studi sull'alto medioevo.

CHAPTER 19

"ALORS COMMENÇA LA FRANCE"

Merovingian Expansion South of the Loire, 495–510

RALPH W. MATHISEN

THE end of the fifth century and the beginning of the sixth was a crucial period for Gaul as the Franks contended for supremacy with the Visigoths of Toulouse. In the 470s, it had looked as if the Goths, under King Euric (466–484), would reign supreme.[1] In 475, the feeble Emperor Julius Nepos (474–475) ceded the Auvergne to Euric in exchange for a reduction of Visigothic pressure on Provence (Mathisen 1979, pp. 268–271). Subsequently, according to the historian Jordanes, after the exile of Nepos and the forced retirement of the usurper Romulus in 476, "Euric, king of the Visigoths, recognizing the feebleness of the Roman empire, delivered Arles and Marseille to his own authority."[2] By this time, of course, there was no authority left that could resist the Visigothic advance. The capture of the remaining cities of Provence was accomplished not, it seems, by force, but by simple occupation. The Visigothic realm now extended beyond the Rhône River in the east, to the Mediterranean Sea in the south, and to Loire in the north. The Goths also defeated the Bretons of Armorica in about 468 but failed to occupy the territory.[3] Otherwise, Euric's ambitions knew no bounds. In 473, Euric sent his Roman general Vincentius "like a Master of Soldiers" along with the Counts Alla and Sindilla to invade Italy.[4] The invasion failed, however, and Vincentius was killed. Then, in 484, Euric planned to invade Italy again, but he died before the plan could be put into effect (on Italy, see Arnold, Chapter 21, this volume).

Meanwhile, in 481/482, the ambitious Frank Clovis succeeded his father Childeric as ruler of one of several Frankish groups and began to forge a united Frankish kingdom (James 1988a, pp. 79–91; Wood 1994, pp. 41–49). After his victory over the Gallo-Roman Syagrius in 486, even the Visigoths, under Euric's son Alaric II (e.g., Vallet 1995, p. 37), were menaced by the expanding Frankish kingdom. The defeated Syagrius had taken refuge with Alaric, and Clovis threatened to attack if Alaric refused to turn him over (e.g., James 1988b, pp. 9–12; MacGeorge 2002, pp. 111–136). Alaric, demonstrating what Gregory of Tours called "customary Gothic cowardice," complied.[5] Gregory's view largely has become that of modern historiography: that Alaric was an ineffectual weakling (on Gregory, see Reimitz, Chapter 22, this volume). Herwig Wolfram, for example, notes a widespread belief that Euric's "incompetent successor Alaric gambled away the kingdom" (Wolfram 1988, p. 243). As the following discussion will show, however, a close analysis of the evidence suggests otherwise: that Alaric in fact was an effective ruler who did the best he could with what he had (as suggested in Mathisen 1997b, 1999, 2001, 2008, 2012a, 2012b; Mathisen and Sivan 1999). But Clovis and the Franks simply turned out to be much more of a threat to Visigothic rule than anyone would have expected.

THE CAMPAIGN OF 495/496

Clovis's threat of 486 soon became a reality. The latter half of the 490s saw a series of poorly known Frankish attacks upon Aquitania (Hodgkin 1888, vol. 3, p. 392 n. 1; Bachrach 1970; Wolfram 1988, p. 191; James 1988a, p. 86). A continuation of the chronicle of Prosper of Aquitaine notes under the year 496, "Alaric, in the twelfth year of his reign, captured Saintes."[6] Such a statement, of course, presupposes that someone, presumably the Franks (Wolfram 1988, p. 191; James 1988a, p. 86), already had captured Saintes at some earlier time. It may be, moreover, that Frankish ability to conduct such campaigns resulted from Visigothic commitments elsewhere, and, in particular, from increasing Visigothic interest in consolidating their holdings in Spain. The so-called Chronicle of Saragossa (actually a compilation of marginal addenda), for example, tells of significant Visigothic involvements in Spain. In 494, there was a Visigothic invasion of Spain; and, in 496, "Burdelenus assumed a tyranny in Spain."[7] However, presumably distracted in 496 by the Frankish attack on Saintes, the Visigoths could not respond to this revolt until 497: "The Goths seize territory in Spain and Burdelenus is betrayed by his support-ers, taken to Toulouse, placed within a bronze bull, and incinerated in a fire."[8]

The Visigothic ability to retake Saintes in 496 might have improved when Clovis was forced to confront the Alamanni in the same year. The subsequent battle was so hard fought that Clovis, on the point of defeat, later was said to have promised to become a Christian if the Franks emerged victorious.[9] And win they did. Subsequently, on Christmas Day, probably in 496 or 497, Clovis's baptism as a Nicene Christian was car-ried out, stage-managed to have the greatest positive effect on the Nicene Gallo-Roman population.[10] Gallo-Roman bishops not even living in the Frankish kingdom, such as Avitus of Vienne, were notified of the celebration.[11] Given that the Visigoths were Homoian Christians (not "Arians," as they usually are called in both ancient and mod-ern works), it generally has been assumed that Clovis's baptism as a Nicene helped to gain the favor of Romans in the Visigothic kingdom, despite the fact that the Homoian Creed of Rimini, issued in 359, had been legitimated by the Roman government in 386.[12]

Two events related to Clovis's southward expansion that seem to have occurred before his baptism now can be given a suggested context. For one thing, Gregory reports that "at the time of King Clovis" the Franks besieged Nantes, at the mouth of the Loire, for sixty days or more. They eventually were put to flight by an apparition of St. Similinus; the Frankish commander Chilo was so overwhelmed that he converted to Christianity.[13] If the campaign had occurred after Clovis's baptism, one would suppose that Clovis's generals certainly would already have been Christian as well. So it may be that the siege of Nantes occurred at the time of the campaign against Saintes, ca. 495–496.[14]

A curiously comparable tale is found in a letter dated around the 560s written by Nicetius, bishop of Trier, to Chlodeswintha, queen of the Lombards. Nicetius claimed that at some time prior to his victory over the Burgundians in 500, Clovis, after hearing of miracles done at the tomb of Martin, "humbly fell at the doorstep of the lord Martin and promised to be baptized without delay."[15] If one credits this report, its omission from the extant works of Gregory of Tours, who usually missed no opportunity to glorify Tours and St. Martin, certainly stands in need of some explanation. Now, such a visit necessarily must have occurred before Clovis's baptism, and therefore, either before, or at least not long after, his victory over the Alamanni. Prior to 507, Tours supposedly was in Visigothic territory, albeit in a very exposed position, on the border between the two kingdoms. So what was Clovis doing there not only before 507, but also before his baptism in 496/497? One possibility is that Clovis actually captured the city, perhaps during the Saintes campaign; after all, there was only one major stop, Poitiers, on the road from Tours to Saintes.[16]

As for Gregory's omission of Clovis's promise, it is clear that if such a promise was made, it was not kept. For Gregory himself reported Clovis's dramatic Alamannic promise, which clearly had captured the public imagination. And given that Clovis was in fact baptized at Reims to boot, from Gregory's point of view, an ostentatious, yet unfulfilled, promise at Tours without any concrete benefit to Tours would have reflected scant credit upon St. Martin. Yet, one wonders if Gregory's tale about Chilo, who actually did convert after witnessing a miracle in the neighborhood of Tours, reflects an echo of the story about Clovis being impressed by the miracles of St. Martin at Tours. If so, there might be some basis of truth to Nicetius's report that Clovis suggested that he might be baptized while he was at Tours.

However that may be, it would appear that Clovis's Aquitanian offensive of 495/496 ended in dismal failure. After some initial successes, including the capture of Tours, Saintes, and presumably Poitiers as well, the campaign had stalled. The siege of Nantes failed, the Visigoths recalled their forces from Spain, and Clovis himself was distracted by the Alamanni. Saintes, and presumably Tours and any other Frankish acquisitions, were retaken by the Goths. So for Clovis, perhaps the only concrete result of this campaign may have resulted from his promise at Tours (and perhaps elsewhere), which could have been intended as a play upon the sympathies, and prejudices, of the Nicene Gallo-Roman population of the Visigothic kingdom. If so, it may have had its desired effect.

One Gaul who was much affected by these developments was Volusianus, bishop of Tours. Perhaps just prior to the Frankish campaigns of ca. 495/496, Volusianus wrote to

Ruricius, bishop of Limoges c. 485–507, that he was "stupefied by fear of the enemies,"[17] an apparent reference to the Franks. Subsequently, Volusianus was not trusted by the Visigoths: "Having been considered suspect by the Goths because he wished to subject himself to the rule of the Franks and having been condemned to exile in the city of Toulouse, he died there."[18] Now, the anxiety Volusianus expressed to Ruricius does not suggest a person actively colluding with the enemy he purported to fear. So, perhaps Volusianus's "collusion" was more circumstantial in nature: Volusianus not only owned *praedia* (estates) deep in Frankish territory at Baiocasses (Bayeux), but all of his suffragan sees also were located north of the Loire.[19] So he, or any bishop of Tours, of necessity would have had to maintain at least a working relation with the Franks. And, if the Franks ever did hold the city in the course of their campaigns, Volusianus would have been all the more suspect. Given that he died around 496,[20] he may have been exiled after the Visigothic recapture of Saintes and, in this interpretation, Tours as well.

THE CAMPAIGN OF 498

During the next two years, Clovis seems to have concentrated on consolidating his position within his own kingdom, but by 498 he again was ready to try his luck toward the south. His strategic position may have been strengthened by an alliance, perhaps facilitated by his baptism, with the Christian "Arborychi" (Armoricans?) living in Lugdunensis III, modern Brittany, northwest of Tours (Procop. *Bell.* 1.12.13; Bachrach 1970). This alliance would have given him access to the Visigothic kingdom south of the Loire. Moreover, in the passages dedicated to the year 498, the aforementioned continuator of Prosper states, "In the fourteenth year of Alaric the Franks captured Bordeaux and transferred it from the authority of the Goths into their own possession, having taken captive the Gothic Duke Suatrius."[21]

There is no indication as to how long the Franks occupied cities such as Saintes or Bordeaux. Being so far from the Frankish kingdom, they could not have hoped to have held them for long. Saintes seems to have been recaptured quickly, and the same may have been the case with Bordeaux. Moreover, it also is unclear whether the seizures of Saintes and Bordeaux resulted from large-scale attacks by land that somehow escaped notice in the other sources or from surprise seaborne raids.[22] Other evidence attests that the coastal areas near Saintes and Bordeaux, at least, were vulnerable to attack from the sea at this time. For example, the *vita* (*Life*) of Bishop Vivianus of Saintes speaks of a raid on Saintes, apparently in the 460s: "In fact, it happened at a certain time that a multitude of barbarian Saxon enemies, accompanied by many ships, threatened the place that is called Marciacus[23] through their love of depredation."[24] This attack was beaten off. Sidonius Apollinaris, in a letter to the Roman aristocrat Namatius, the admiral of the Visigothic king Euric, spoke of coastal raids by the Saxons ca. 470, "In the midst of your duties you wandered the shores of the Ocean in opposition to the curved raiding ships of the Saxons, of whom however many oars you see, you think that you see the same number of arch-pirates."[25] (see also Fleming, Chapter 17, this volume). There is no reason to think that the Franks could not have conducted similar raids.[26]

DIPLOMATIC ENGAGEMENTS, 500–502

Ill will between the Visigoths and Franks continued. Shortly after the raid of 498, in the midst of a Burgundian civil war in 500, the Burgundian king Gundobad (ca. 473–516) recaptured Vienne from his brother Godegesil (ca. 473–500) and sent his Frankish captives "in exile to king Alaric at Toulouse."[27] After Gundobad's ultimate victory, the attendance of the bishop of Avignon at the Visigothic Council of Agde in 506 suggests that the Visigoths even gained control over Avignon for their troubles.

The strengthening of the Visigothic position might have given Alaric a bargaining chip he could use to reach a settlement with Clovis. Just after 500, Alaric and Clovis met at Ambiacum (modern Amboise) in the middle of the Loire River and restored direct diplomatic relations (Mathisen and Sivan 1999, pp. 56–57; Becher 2011, p. 215). Gregory of Tours reports:

> Alaric, king of the Goths, when he saw king Clovis unrelentingly defeating various nations, sent ambassadors to him, saying, "If my brother wishes, he might decide that, with God's blessing, we should meet." Clovis did not reject this suggestion and came to him. And meeting on an island of the Loire, which was next to the village of Amboise in the territory of Tours, they ate and drank together, and having promised friendship to each other, they departed in peace.[28]

Alaric's reference to Clovis's victories would have been especially appropriate, not to mention ironic, if Clovis's own victory over the Burgundians earlier in 500, on the side of Godegisel, were meant. As for any settlement that was reached, Gregory portrays the two as bosom banquet buddies. Alaric presumably returned his Frankish "guests" and was probably happy to be rid of them. Clovis would have returned any Visigothic territory he held, but it seems doubtful that by this time there was any. Indeed, it might seem that, if anything, Alaric was left with the upper hand. He had been able to counteract any previous Frankish offensives, and it had been he who had summoned Clovis to the conference, not the other way around.

THE PRELUDE TO WAR, 505–507

The status quo seems to have been maintained between the two kingdoms until about 505, when the situation for the Visigoths worsened. For one thing, Alaric's erstwhile friend Gundobad seems to have turned against him, and the Burgundians besieged

Arles; the bishop, Caesarius, was exiled to Bordeaux after being accused of plotting to betray the city (*Vita Caesarii* 1.21 in Morin 1942). At the same time, the Goths faced continuing problems in Spain.[29] As for Clovis, ca. 505, he undertook another campaign against the Alamanni, in which the Alamanni were totally defeated; Theoderic, the Ostrogothic king of Italy, settled their remnants in Raetia and ordered Clovis to let them be.[30] These developments left Clovis free to renew his attacks on the Visigoths.

Faced with this northern threat, Alaric attempted to fortify his Gallo-Roman support. In the year 506, he permitted the issuance of a civil law code based on existing Roman statutes. Gallic jurists published the *Breviarium Alarici* (Breviary of Alaric), or *Lex Romana Visigothorum* (Roman Law of the Visigoths), which enjoys the distinction of being the main transmitter of the *Codex Theodosianus* (Theodosian Code), originally issued by the eastern emperor Theodosius II (402–450) in 437 (Lambertini 1990). The Breviary was intended to supplant the Theodosian Code in the minds and lives of the Romans of Aquitania. It was distributed by two Gallo-Romans, the *vir spectabilis* (respectable gentleman) Count Timotheus and the *vir spectabilis* Anianus. Its prologue proclaimed that it had been issued "So that all the obscurity of Roman laws and ancient jurisprudence, led into the light of a better intelligence with the assistance of bishops and the nobility, might be made clear and so that nothing might remain in doubt," and it asserted that "the assent of the venerable bishops and chosen provincials has strengthened" it.[31]

The work is a typical product of Roman provincial jurisprudence. It complemented, but did not replace, the *Codex Euricianus* (Code of Euric), by giving the Visigothic *imprimatur* to a large amount of existing Roman legislation. In doing so, it reinforced the notion that the Visigothic kings were the direct successors of the Roman emperors. But this is not to say that the *Breviarium* merely copied the Theodosian Code. Far from it. For one thing, some Roman legislation, such as that on *hospitium* (the quartering of soldiers), *agri deserti* (land forfeited to the government because its taxes had not been paid), and heretics, was omitted (on the military, see Sarti, Chapter 12, this volume). Other laws were revised. The Breviary repeated the Roman prohibition in the 370s of intermarriage between Romans and barbarians, but substituted the words *Romani* and *barbari* for *provinciales* (provincials) and *gentiles* (barbarians in Roman military service), a curious instance of the Visigoths self-identifying as barbarians.[32]

The *Breviarium* also included extensive legal commentaries (*interpretationes*) on the Theodosian constitutions. Although it generally has been assumed that Alaric's Gallo-Roman legal advisors completed the task of assembling and issuing the code within just a few months, it is possible that the work might have been going on for a very long time in private Gallic legal circles (Matthews 2002). If so, the Gauls cagily used Alaric's dire straits to their own advantage in securing his approval for work that already was largely complete.

The Nicene bishops of Aquitania, meanwhile, were allowed to congregate not far from Narbonne in the small coastal town of Agde, the first Aquitanian council since the arrival of the Goths, indeed, the first since the late fourth century (on Gallic councils, see Halfond, Chapter 13, this volume). The council was overseen by Caesarius of Arles, who had been allowed to return from exile in Bordeaux. The prologue to the council begins:

"When in the name of the Lord, with the permission of Our Lord the Most Glorious, Magnificent and Pious King [Alaric] the blessed synod had gathered, and there with our knees bent to the ground we prayed for his kingdom and for his long life, so that the Lord might expand the realm of him who had permitted to us the opportunity to meet."[33] This apparently servile wording demonstrates the extent to which the Visigothic king proposed to control the ecclesiastical life of the kingdom.

The council's forty-eight canons demonstrate that the Aquitanian bishops had a lot of catching up to do. The bishops' primary concern was for regulating ecclesiastical life of both clergy and laity. One canon repeated the aforementioned restriction on mixed marriages found in the *Breviary*: "It is not proper to mix marriages with any heretics, and to give them sons or daughters, but [it is proper] to accept them, if they promise that they are going to become Catholic Christians."[34] The "heretics" in question presumably would have been Homoian Visigoths (on heretics, see Drews, Chapter 6, this volume). It is unclear, moreover, whether the initiative to prevent marriages between Romans and Visigoths came from Romans or Visigoths. The final canon, meanwhile, decreed hopefully, "It is fitting that a synod be summoned each year, according to the dictates of the fathers."[35]

The formal Visigothic role in conducting church councils was attested at the Council of Agde not only in the prologue and penultimate canon, but also in its Canon 35, where a *praeceptio regia* (royal command) became a valid excuse for absenting oneself from a church council.[36] One is not sure, however, how to interpret this clause. Does it refer to bishops who were in exile, as perhaps the case with Verus of Tours,[37] to bishops away on royal business, or simply to bishops who were able to cadge an excused absence from the king? Furthermore, the council convened not in the province of Arles but in the same province as the Visigothic capital of Toulouse. There even was in attendance "Petrus episcopus de Palatio" ("Bishop Peter, from the palace") (*CCSL* 148.213). If the word *palatium* refers to the royal court, and it is difficult to envision what else it could mean, one might wonder whether Petrus was a Nicene or a Homoian.[38] Visigothic oversight of church councils also is seen in plans for the subsequent council, to be held at Toulouse in 507, which was to be organized by a certain Eudomius, apparently a Gallo-Roman *consiliaris* (counselor) of Alaric.[39]

At some unspecified time, Alaric also intervened in a case involving the church of Narbonne. Between 508 and 511, the Ostrogothic king Theoderic, who now controlled the city, addressed the *dux* Ibba,

> Why indeed do we debate past issues, when there is nothing we need to correct? And therefore we, who do not desire to be involved in illicit presumptions in the administration of the church, command you by present authority, according to the ruling of Alaric of excellent memory, that, with a view toward fairness, you see to it that the possessions of the church of Narbonne, which are held occupied by certain invaders, are restored.[40]

So, at some point Alaric had issued a ruling apparently in support of the Nicene ecclesiastical establishment at Narbonne.[41] On balance, therefore, it would seem that, except in cases involving state security, Alaric's relations with the Gallo-Roman church were harmonious.[42] One therefore, perhaps, should speak of a continuation, rather than the inception, of a policy of conciliation in 506.

Meanwhile, Clovis's plans to attack Alaric continued apace. Gregory of Tours notes that he declared, "I take it very ill that these Arians should hold so large a part of Gaul. Let us go and overcome them with God's help, and bring their land under our rule."[43] Several reports suggest that, despite Alaric's conciliatory efforts, Clovis was making inroads into the loyalty of Alaric's Roman subjects, perhaps as a result of his adoption of Nicene Christianity, for Gregory of Tours wrote, "At that time, many Gauls wished with the greatest desire to have the Franks as masters."[44] At Tours, for example, Volusianus's successor, Verus (ca. 497–507), had suffered the same fate as his predecessor: "And he, because of his enthusiasm for the same cause, was considered suspect by the Goths, and having been carried off into exile, he died."[45] Just what had made Verus's loyalty suspect is unclear. One wonders whether his failure to attend the Council of Agde indicates that he was in exile already, or whether it might have influenced the decision to exile him: if the bishop of Tours had proven unreliable once, he was not to be trusted again.

It also was just before 507, it seems, that Quintianus, bishop of Rodez, already exiled from Africa, was faced with both civic dissension and accusations of treachery: "After a quarrel had arisen between the citizens and the bishop, a suspicion came to the Goths who then were stationed in the aforementioned city that the bishop wished to subject himself to the rule of the Franks, and having considered the matter, they decided to run him through with a sword."[46] Quintianus, having been apprised of this plot, took refuge at Clermont. There is, however, at least one problem with this account: Clermont, too, was in the Visigothic kingdom, and even closer to the Franks. So this story may be more representative of the general anxiety that prevailed in the Visigothic kingdom just before Clovis's invasion than of any actual dealings Quintianus had with the Franks: for any of Quintianus's parishioners who were looking to cause trouble for the embattled bishop, a false accusation of treachery could have been just the thing.

At the same time, moreover, the ambitious Ostrogothic king Theoderic was casting his diplomatic net as widely as possible by using marriage alliances. He himself married Audofled (*PLRE II*, 185), a sister of Clovis; his sister, Amalafrida (*PLRE II*, 63), was married to the Vandal king Thrasamund; one daughter, Ostrogotho Areagni (*PLRE II*, 138–139), married the Burgundian prince, later king, Sigismund; another daughter, Theodegotha (*PLRE II*, 1068), married Alaric II; and his niece, Amalaberga (*PLRE II*, 549–550), married Hermanfridus, king of the Thuringians. In early 507, Theoderic undertook to expand his influence into Gaul by posing as a peacemaker in individual letters to Clovis, Alaric, and Gundobad, and a joint letter to the kings of the Heruls, Warni, and Thuringians.[47] To Alaric, for example, Theoderic suggested, "Because the hearts of your ferocious peoples are made soft by long peace, beware suddenly sending into danger those whom it is known do not have sufficient experience in such portentous times."[48] Theoderic advised prudence: "Therefore, restrain yourself until I can send my ambassadors to the king of the Franks, so that the judgment of your friends may dissolve your quarrel."[49]

It was Clovis, however, whom Theoderic blamed for aggression against the Goths. He urged the Germanic kings to send ambassadors advising Clovis "either to restrain himself, in consideration of equity, from an attack on the Visigoths and to abide by the laws of nations, or he himself, who believed that the opinion of such great men should be disregarded, would suffer an attack by all them."[50] In a letter to Clovis himself, Theoderic threatened retaliation if he did not yield to arbitration, saying, "Throw down your sword.... He who believes that these warnings should be condemned will suffer us and our friends as enemies."[51]

THE BATTLE OF VOUILLÉ, 507 CE

Clovis was in no mood to subordinate himself to Theoderic (Mathisen 2012c). In the spring of 507, Clovis undertook his threatened invasion of the Visigothic kingdom.[52] The two armies met at Vouillé, just outside of Poitiers. One result of Alaric's policy of conciliation was the participation of Gallo-Romans on his side. These included a large contingent from Clermont, led by Apollinaris, the Count of Clermont and the son of Sidonius, and the leading figure of the Arvernian aristocracy (Greg. Tur. *Hist.* 2.37). And another tradition tells of an Avitus from Périgueux, who engaged in military service at this time "so that he could fight against the hostile army of the Franks."[53]

All for nought. The end result was the destruction of the Visigothic army and the death of Alaric. The *Gallic Chronicle of 511* reports: "Alaric, king of the Goths, was killed by the Franks. Toulouse was burned by the Franks and Burgundians, and Barcelona was captured by Gundobad, king of the Burgundians."[54] According to the Chronicle of Saragossa, "At this time a battle between the Goths and Franks was fought at Vouillé. King Alaric was killed in the clash by the Franks and the kingdom of Toulouse was destroyed."[55] Isidore of Seville, moreover, writing in the mid-seventh century, summarized the reign of Alaric II and its aftermath:

> Alaric...was reigning at Toulouse. After spending his youth in leisure and good times, he was finally incited by the Franks....Clovis, king of the Franks, desired to rule Gaul and declared war against him, having gained the assistance of the Burgundians. And he killed Alaric who was overcome near Poitiers after the Gothic army had been put to flight...and after his death the kingdom of Toulouse was destroyed and occupied by the Franks. Furthermore, when Theoderic, the king of Italy, learned of the death of his son-in-law, he immediately set out from Italy and defeated the Franks, and restored part of the kingdom, which had been occupied by the forces of the enemy, to the rule of the Goths.[56]

The blame for the end of the Visigothic kingdom of Toulouse was placed squarely at the feet of Alaric. After his death, the kingdom was dismembered by the Franks and the Ostrogoths.

FIGURE 19.1. Plaque erected at the site of Vouillé. (Photo by Ralph Mathisen)

After Vouillé, Clovis's son Theuderic advanced from Poitiers to occupy Albi, Rodez, and Clermont. Clovis left Poitiers, wintered in Bordeaux, and then, in 508, went to Toulouse and Angoulême before he returned to Tours. During the next year, Clovis occupied much of the rest of the kingdom of Toulouse. All that remained to the Visigoths in Gaul was Septimania, a coastal strip focused on Narbonne. The kingdom of the Visigoths now became the kingdom of Toledo and was firmly entrenched in the Iberian peninsula.

The Gothic kingdom of Toulouse thus came to an end after a brief eighty-seven-year existence, and the history of post-Roman Gaul was to be written not by the Visigoths but by the Franks. The Battle of Vouillé became memorialized in French history as one of the primary moments in the creation of the French nation, and it even has been commemorated by changing the name of Vouillé to "Vouillé-la-Bataille," where a plaque today states, "Alors commença la France" ("Then France began") (Fig. 19.1).

Notes

1. For Euric's preeminent status, see in particular Sid. Apoll., *Epist.* 4, 22 and 8.3; also, for example, Stroheker 1937; Thompson 1963; Sivan 1989; Mathisen and Sivan 1999.
2. Jord., *Get.* 244: "Euricus rex Visigothorum Romani regni vacillationem cernens Arelatum et Massiliam propriae subdidit dicioni."
3. Jord., *Get.* 237–238, dating the event to the reign of Anthemius (468–471) and connecting it with Riothamus; see Greg. Tur., *Hist.* 2.18 for the location.

4. *Chron. gall. 511* no. 653: "Vincentius uero ab Eorico rege quasi magister militum missus ab Alla et Sindila comitibus Italia occiditur."

5. Greg. Tur., *Hist.* 2.27: "Chlodovechus vero ad Alarico mittit, ut eum redderet, alioquin noveret, sibi bellum ob eius retentionem inferred. at ille metuens,...ut Gothorum pavere mos est, vinctum legatis tradidit"; cf. Fredegar, *Chron.* 3.15; *Liber historiarum Francorum* 9. Wolfram (1988, p.191), suggests that Syagrius might not have been handed over immediately. For Visigothic fears of the Franks after ca. 493, see Procop., *Bell. goth.* 1.12.21.

6. *Auct. prosp. haun.*, s.a. 496: "Alaricus anno XII regni sui Santones obtinuit."

7. *Chronicon Caesaraugustanum*, s.a. 496: "Burdunelus in Hispania tyrranidem assumit."

8. *Chronicon Caesaraugustanum*, s.a. 496: "Gotthi intra Hispanias sedes acceperunt et Burdunelus a suis traditus et Tolosam directus in tauro aeneo impositus igne crematus est" (ibid.).

9. Greg. Tur., *Hist.* 2.30: "Iesu Christi...tuae opis gloriam devotus efflagito, ut, si mihi victuriam super hos hostes indulseris...credam tibi et in nomine tuo baptizer...te nunc invoco, tibi credere desidero, tantum ut eruar ab adversariis meis."

10. Greg. Tur., *Hist.* 2.31, at Reims. See Spencer 1994 for refutations of attempts to date the baptism to after 500 AD; see also Rouche 1997; for a strong argument for a date of 507/511, see Shanzer 1998. As a result of his baptism, Clovis may have lost a good part of his Frankish support, so his desire to come to an agreement with the Visigoths could have been based in part on his realization that this was likely to happen.

11. Avit., *Epist.* 46. Krusch and Levison 1951, p. 76 n. 3, suggest that Avitus was actually invited to take part.

12. *C. Th.* 16.1.4 (386): "Damus copiam colligendi his, qui secundum ea sentiunt, quae temporibus divae memoriae Constanti...Ariminensi concilio...decreta sunt"; see Mathisen 2009a, also Weedman 2007.

13. Greg. Tur., *Glor. mart.* 60. Chilo is omitted in *PLRE II*.

14. It may be at this time that Ruricius of Limoges wrote (*Epist.* 2.8) to Bishop Aeonius of Arles (c. 490–502) on behalf of the priest Possessor, whose brother had been taken captive "ab hostibus" in the area of Angers, situated on the Loire between Tours and Nantes.

15. *Epist. aust.* 8: "Humilis ad domni Martini limina cecidit et baptizare se sine mora promisit, qui baptizatus quanta in heritocos Alaricum vel Gundobadum reghum fecerit."

16. Pietri 1983, p. 133, suggests that the Franks held the city during 494–496; note also James 1988a, p. 86.

17. Ruric., *Epist.* 2.65: "Nam quod scribis te metu hostium hebetem factum."

18. Greg. Tur., *Hist.* 10.31: "Suspectus habitus a Gothis, quod se Francorum ditionibus subdere vellet, apud urbem Tholosam exilio condempnatus, in eo obiit"; cf. 2.26. Elsewhere (*Hist.* 2.29), Gregory claims that Volusianus was exiled to Spain.

19. Volusianus is painted in rather stronger terms by Sidonius (*Epist.* 7.16), who requested his aid in controlling the fractious monks of the monastery of Abraham in the Auvergne. *Praedia*: Sid. Apoll., *Epist.* 4.18.2.

20. According to Gregory (*Hist.* 2.26, 10.31); see Duchesne [1907–1915] 2.305, Volusianus (*PLRE II*, 1183) was bishop for seven years and his successor Verus for eleven. Given that Verus sent his deacon Leo to represent him at the Council of Agde in 506 (*CCSL* 148.219), and that his successor Licinius was in office by 507 (Greg. Tur., *Hist.* 2.29), Verus's death must have been in late 506 or early 507. This would put his tenure at about 496–507 and Volusianus's around 489–496. Gregory's statement elswhere (*Hist.* 2.43) that Clovis died in the eleventh year of Licinius, must be mistaken, unless, perhaps,

Licinius had begun serving as bishop of Tours while Verus was still living in exile. On the bishops of Tours, see Mathisen (1984).

21. *Auct. prosp. haun.*, s.a. 498: "Ann. XIIII Alarici Franci Burdigalam obtinuerunt et a potestate Gothorum in possessionem sui redegerunt capto Suatrio Gothorum duce."

22. Ruricius's eighty-three letters, for example, give no indication of hostilities save for the reference to Volusianus noted above.

23. Perhaps Marsas in the département of Geronde, not far from Bordeaux.

24. *Vita Viviani* 7: "Accidit etiam quodam tempore, ut multitudo hostium Saxonum barbarorum cum plurimis navibus ad locum qui dicitur Marciacus amore depraedationis incumberet."

25. Sid. Apoll., *Epist.* 8.6: "Inter officia...litoribus Oceani curvis inerrare contra Saxonum pandos myoparones, quorum quot remiges videris, totidem te cernere putes archipiratas."

26. As Bachrach 1970, p. 26, who also suggests that the chronicler may have mistaken Saxon raiders for Franks.

27. Greg. Tur., *Hist.* 2.33: "Tolosae in exilium ad Alaricum regem"; for the date, see Marius episcopus Aventicensis, *Chronica*, s.a. 500.

28. Greg. Tur., *Hist.* 2.35: "Igitur Alaricus rex Gothorum, cum videret Chlodovechum regem gentes assidue debellare, legatos ad eum diriget, dicens, 'Si frater meus velit, insederat animo, ut nos Deo propitio pariter viderimus.' Quod Chlodovechus non respuens, ad eum venit. Coniunctique in insula Ligeris, quae erat iuxta vicum Ambaciensem territorium urbis Turonicae, simul locuti, comedentes pariter ac bibentes, promissa sibi amicitia, pacifeci discesserunt." This incident conventionally is dated to 502 AD, as by Wolfram 1988, p. 192; Gregory merely places the meeting between Gundobad's victory in 500 and Clovis's invasion of Aquitania in 507.

29. "*Chronicon Caesaraugustanum*," s.a. 506: "Dertosa a Gotthis ingressa est. Petrus tyrannus interfectus est et caput eius Casaraugustam deportatum est."

30. Cass., *Var.* 2.41; Hodgkin (1888, 3.390–391); Barnish (1992, pp.38–44); and *PLRE II*, 233–234.

31. "Ut omnis legum Romanarum et antiqui iuris obscuritas adhibitis sacerdotibus ac nobilibus viris in lucem intellegentiae melioris *deducta* resplendeat et nihil habeatur ambiguum...venerabilium episcoporum vel electorum provincialium nostrorum roboravit adsensus" (Mommsen, Meyer, and Krueger, 1905, 1.xxxiii–xxxv).

32. *C Th* 3.14.1; this clearly Roman alteration may have escaped the notice of the *Breviarium*'s Visigothic sponsors. Barbarian peoples generally avoided referring to themselves as "barbarians" at the same time that they referred to other barbarian peoples as "barbarians." See Mathisen 2009b.

33. "Cum in nomine domini ex permissu domini nostri gloriosissimi magnificentissimi piissimique regis...sancta synodus convenisset, ibique flexis in terram genibus, pro regno eius, pro longaevitate...deprecaremur, ut qui nobis congregationis permiserat potestatem, regnum eius dominus...extenderet." See CCSL 148.192.

34. "Quoniam non oportet cum omnibus hereticis miscere connubia, et vel filios vel filias dare, sed potius accipere, si tamen se profitentur christianos futuros esse catholicos." CCSL 148.228. See Mathisen 2008.

35. "Synodum etiam secundum constituta patrum annis singulis placuit congregari": CCSL 148.212.

36. Such a clause also would have excused bishops who were in exile; see Hefele and Leclercq 1907, p. 977, who see this as the only explanation.

37. If this were the case, even the exiled Verus was permitted to send his deacon to represent him.

38. Cf. the *Edictum Chlotharii II* (614 CE), "de palatio," "de palatio nostro" (*CCSL* 148A.283–284). Hefele-Leclercq 1907, p. 977, and Morin 1942, vol. 2, p. 54 n. 15, suppose that Petrus served as bishop of Roman Nicenes at the Visigothic court, although such a bishop-without-portfolio is otherwise unattested in the Nicene church, and one wonders why these Romans could not have attended the local Nicene church. Petrus may have been a Homoian bishop who trailed along with the Visigothic court: see Mathisen 1997a.

39. Krusch, MGH AA 8.lxv, assumes that Eudomius was a bishop, but not only did no Eudomius attend the Council of Agde, but this Eudomius presumably is to be identified with the *vir magnificus* Eudomius, clearly a secular noble, with whom Ruricius of Limoges corresponded (*Epist.* 2.39).

40. Cass., *Var.* 4.17.2: "Cur enim priora quassemus, ubi nihil est quod corrigere debeamus? Atque ideo praesenti tibi auctoritate praecipimus ut possessiones Narbonensis ecclesiae, secundum praecelsae recordationis Alarici praecepta, <quae> a quibuslibet pervasoribus occupata teneantur, aequitatis facias contemplatione restitui, qui versari nolumus in ecclesiae dispendio praesumptiones illicitas." It is unclear whether this controversy was related to Gregory of Tours's complaint that Alaric lowered the roof of the cathedral of Narbonne because it obstructed his view (*Gloria martyrum* 91).

41. Visigothic involvement in the church of Narbonne began as early as 462, when the prince Fridericus complained to Hilarus of Rome about the ordination of Hermes as bishop; see Hilarus, *Epist*, "Miramur fraternitatem."

42. For a different spin on these events, see Rouche 1979, pp. 43–50.

43. Greg. Tur., *Hist.* 2.37; Nicene Christians incorrectly and insultingly referred to the Homoian Visigoths as "Arians."

44. Greg. Tur., *Hist.* 2.35: "Multi iam tunc ex Galliis habere Francos dominos summo desiderio cupiebant."

45. Greg. Tur., *Hist.* 10.31: "Et ipse pro memoratae causae zelo suspectus habitus a Gothis in exilio deductus vitam finivit."

46. Greg. Tur., *Hist.* 2.36: "Orto inter cives et episcopum scandalo, Gothos qui tunc in antedicta urbe morabantur suspicio attigit, quod se vellet episcopus Francorum ditionibus subdere, consilioque accepto, cogitaverunt eum perfodere gladio"; also Greg. Tur. *Vit. pat.* 4.1.

47. Cass., *Var.* 3.1–4; see Arnold in this volume; also Saitta (1988) and Shanzer (1996–1997).

48. Cass., *Var.* 3.1.1: "Quia populorum ferocium corda longa pace mollescunt, cavete subito in aleam mittere quos constat tantis temporibus exercitia non habere."

49. Cass., *Var.* 3.1.3: "Quapropter sustinete, donec ad Francorum regem legatos nostros dirigere debeamus, ut litem vestram amicorum debeant amputare iudicia."

50. Cass., *Var.* 1.3.2: "Ut aut se de Wisigotharum conflictu considerata aequitate suspendat et leges gentium quaerat aut omnium patiatur incursum, qui tantorum arbitrium iudicat esse temnendum."

51. Cass., *Var.* 3.4.3–4: "Abicite ferrum...ille nos et amicos nostros patietur adversos qui talia monita...crediderit esse temnenda."

52. One of Clovis's soldiers stole hay from a poor man of Tours, which would not have been a serious problem in the summer or fall, and Clovis could not cross the Vienne because it was swollen by heavy rains (Greg. Tur. *Hist.* 2.37).

53. *Vita s. Aviti eremitae* 1: "Ut contra hostilem Francorum aciem pugnaturus."

54. *Chron. gall. 511* s.a. 507: "Occisus Alaricus rex Gothorum a Francis. Tolosa a Francis et Burgundionibus incensa et Barcinona a Gundefade rege Burgundionum capta."

55. *Chronicon Caesaraugustanum* s.a. 507: "His diebus pugna Gotthorum et Francorum Voglada facta. Alaricus rex in proelio a Francis interfectus est: regnum Tolosanum destructum est."

56. Isid. Hisp., *Hist. goth.* 36: "Alaricus…apud Tolosensem regnans, qui cum a pueritia vitam in otio et convivio peregissit, tandem provocatus a Francis in regione Pictavensis urbis proelio inito extinguitur eoque interfecto regnum Tolosanum occupantibus Francis destruitur…" [version 1]. adversus quem Fluduicus Francorum princeps Galliae regnum affectans Burgundionibus sibi auxiliantibus, bellum movit fusisque Gothorum copiis ipsum postremum regem apud Pictavis superatum interfecit. Theudericus autem Italiae rex dum interitum generi comperisset, confestim ab Italia proficiscitur, Francos proterit, partem regni, quam manus hostium occupaverat, recepit Gothorumque iuri restituit" [version 2].

Works Cited

Ancient Sources

Auct. prosp. Haun. T. Mommsen (ed.). (1892). *Auctarium Prosperi Hauniensis.* MGH: AA 9 (pp. 309–337). Berlin: Weidmann.

Avit., *Epist.* R. Peiper (ed.). (1883). *Alcimi Ecdicii Aviti Viennensis episcopi. Opera quae supersunt.* MGH: AA 6.2. Berlin: Weidmann.

Barnish, S. J. B. (trans.). (1992). *The Variae of Magnus Aurelius Cassiodorus Senator.* Liverpool: Liverpool University Press.

Cass., *Var.* A. Fridh (ed.). (1973). *Magni Aurelii Cassiodori Variarum libri XII.* CCSL 46. Turnholt: Brepols.

CCSL 148. C. Munier (ed.). (1963). *Concilia Galliae: A.314–A.506.* CCSL 148. Turnhout: Brepols.

Chron. gall. anno 511. T. Mommsen (ed.). (1892). MGH: AA 9 (pp. 647–666). Berlin: Weidemann.

"*Chronicon Caesaraugustanum*" (a collection of marginalia). T. Mommsen (ed.). (1894). MGH: AA 11 (pp. 221–222). Berlin: Weidmann.

C. Th. T. Mommsen, P. M. Meyer, and P. Krüger (eds.). (1905). *Theodosiani libri XVI cum constitutionibus Sirmondianis et leges novellae ad Theodosianum pertinentes,* 2 vols. Berlin: Weidmann.

Epistulae austrasicae. W. Gundlach (ed.). (1892). MGH: Epistulae 3 (pp. 110–153). Berlin: Weidmann.

Fredegar, *Chron.* B. Krusch (ed.). (1888). Fredegarius Scholasticus, *Chronicarum libri IV.* MGH: SRM 2 (pp. 1–193). Hanover: Hahn.

Greg. Tur., *GM.* B. Krusch (ed.). (1885). *Liber in gloria martyrum.* MGH: SRM 1.2 (pp. 211–294). Berlin: Weidmann.

Greg. Tur., *Hist.* B. Krusch and W. Levison (eds.). (1951). *Historiae.* MGH SRM 1.1. Hanover: Hahn.

Greg. Tur., *Vitae Patrum.* B. Krusch and W. Levison (eds.). (1885). *Liber vitae patrum opere Georgi Florenti Gregori Toronici.* In *Gregorii Turonensis Opera. Miracula et opera omnia.* MGH SRM 1.2 (pp. 661–744). Hanover: Hahn.

Hilarus. *Epist.* W. Gundlach (ed.). (1892). "Miramur fraternitatem." MGH: Epistulae 3 (pp. 22–23). Berlin: Weidmann.

Isid. Hisp., *Hist. Goth.* T. Mommsen (ed.). (1894). *Isidori Iunioris episcopi Hispalensis historia Gothorum.* MGH: AA 11 (pp. 391–388). Berlin: Weidmann.

Jord., *Get.* T. Mommsen (ed.). (1882). *De origine actibusque Getarum.* MGH: AA 5.1. Berlin: Weidmann.

Jord., *Get.* C. C. Mierow (trans.). (1915). *Jordanes, The Origin and Deeds of the Goths.* Princeton, NJ: Princeton University Press.

Liber historiarum Francorum. (1888). B. Krusch (ed.). MGH: SRM 2 (pp. 215–269). Hanover: Hahn.

Marius episcopus Aventicensis, *Chronica.* T. Mommsen (ed.). (1894). MGH: AA 11 (pp. 225–239). Berlin: Weidmann.

PLRE II. J. R. Martindale (ed.). (1980). *The Prosopography of the Later Roman Empire. Volume II. A.D. 395–527.* Cambridge: University of Cambridge Press.

Procop., *Bell. goth.* H. B. Dewing (ed.). (1919). *Procopius, Gothic War. History of the Wars* 3. The Loeb Classical Library 107. Cambridge, MA: William Heinemann.

Ruric., *Ep.* B. Krusch (ed.). (1887). *Ruricii epistulae.* MGH: AA 8 (pp. 299–350). Berlin: Weidmann.

Ruric., *Ep.* R. Mathisen (trans.). (1999). *Ruricius of Limoges and Friends: A Collection of Letters from Visigothic Aquitania.* Liverpool: Liverpool University Press.

Sid. Apoll., *Epistulae.* C. Leutjohann (ed.). (1887). *Gai Sollii Apollinaris Sidonii epistulae et carmina,* MGH: AA 8. Berlin: Weidmann.

Vita s. Aviti eremitae in Sarlatensi Petrocoriensis. (1863). *Acta Sanctorum quotquot toto orbe coluntur.* June IV (pp. 291–294). Paris: Carnandet.

Vita Caesarii. G. Morin (ed.). (1942). *Sancti Caesarii Episcopi Arelatensis opera omnia.* Maredsous: Sanctum Benedictinum.

Vita Viviani. B. Krusch (ed.). (1896). *Vita s. Viviani episcopi Santonensis.* MGH: SRM 3 (pp. 92–100). Hanover: Hahn.

Modern Sources

Bachrach, B. S. (1970). "Procopius and Chronology of Clovis' Reign." *Viator* 1: 21–31.

Becher, M. (2011). *Chlodwig I. Der Aufstieg der Merowinger und das Ende der antiken Welt.* Munich: Beck.

Duchesne, L. (1907–1915). *Fastes épiscopaux de l'ancienne Gaule,* 2nd ed. 3 vols. Paris: Fontemoing.

Hodgkin, T. (1888). *Italy and Her Invaders.* Oxford: Clarendon Press.

James, E. (1988a). *The Franks.* London: Paragon.

James, E. (1988b). "Childéric, Syagrius et la disparition du royaume de Soissons." *Revue archéologique de Picardie* 3–4, 9–12.

Lambertini, L. (1990). *La codificazione di Alarico II.* Turin: Giappichelli.

Mathisen, R. (1979). *Ecclesiastical Factionalism and Religious Controversy in Fifth-Century Gaul.* Washington, DC: Catholic University Press.

Mathisen, R. (1984). "The Family of Georgius Florentius Gregorius and the Bishops of Tours." *Medievalia and Humanistica* 12: 83–95.

Mathisen, R. (1997a). "Barbarian Bishops and the Churches 'in barbaricis gentibus' during Late Antiquity." *Speculum* 72: 664–697.

Mathisen, R. (1997b). "The 'Second Council of Arles' and the Spirit of Compilation and Codification in Late Roman Gaul." *Journal of Early Christian Studies* 5: 511–554.

Mathisen, R. (2001). "The Letters of Ruricius of Limoges and the Passage from Roman to Frankish Gaul." In R. Mathisen and D. Shanzer (eds.), *Society and Culture in Late Antique Gaul. Revisiting the Sources* (pp. 101–115). Aldershot: Ashgate.

Mathisen, R. (2008) "D'Aire-sur-l'Adour à Agde: Les relations entre la loi séculaire et la loi canonique au fin du royaume de Toulouse." In M. Rouche and B. Dumézil (eds.), *Le Bréviare d'Alaric. Aux origines du Code civil* (pp. 41–52). Paris: PUPS.

Mathisen, R. (2009a). "Ricimer's Church in Rome: How an Arian Barbarian Prospered in a Nicene World." In N. Lenski and A. Cain (eds.), *The Power of Religion in Late Antiquity* (pp. 307–326). Aldershot: Ashgate.

Mathisen, R. (2009b). "*Provinciales, Gentiles,* and Marriages between Romans and Barbarians in the Late Roman Empire." *Journal of Roman Studies* 99: 140–155.

Mathisen, R. (2012a) "The First Franco-Visigothic War and the Prelude to the Battle of Vouillé." In R. Mathisen and D. Shanzer (eds.), *The Battle of Vouillé, 507 CE: Where France Began* (pp. 3–10). Berlin: Walter de Gruyter.

Mathisen, R. (2012b) "Vouillé, Voulon, and the Location of the *Campus Vogladensis.*" In R. Mathisen and D. Shanzer (eds.), *The Battle of Vouillé, 507 CE: Where France Began* (pp. 43–62). Berlin: Walter de Gruyter.

Mathisen, R. (2012c). "Clovis, Anastasius, and Political Status in 508 C.E." In R. Mathisen and D. Shanzer (eds.), *The Battle of Vouillé, 507 CE: Where France Began* (pp. 79–110). Berlin: Walter de Gruyter.

Mathisen, R., and Sivan, H. (1999). "Forging a New Identity: The Kingdom of Toulouse and the Frontiers of Visigothic Aquitania." In A. Ferreiro (ed.), *The Visigoths. Studies in Culture and Society* (pp. 1–62). Leiden: Brill.

MacGeorge, P. (2002). *Late Roman Warlords.* New York: Oxford University Press.

Matthews, J. (2002). "Interpreting the *Interpretationes* of the *Breviarium.*" In R. Mathisen (ed.), *Law, Society, and Authority in Late Antiquity* (pp. 11–32). Oxford: Oxford University Press.

Pietri, L. (1983). *La Ville de Tours de IVe au VIe siècle.* Rome: Ecole Français de Rome.

Rouche, M. (1979). *L'Aquitaine des Wisigoths aux Arabes, 418–781: Naissance d'une région.* Paris: Éditions de l'École des hautes études en sciences.

Rouche, M. (ed.). (1997). *Clovis, histoire et mémoire,* vol. 1: *Le baptême de Clovis, l'événement;* vol. 2: *Le baptême de Clovis, son écho à travers l'histoire.* Paris: PUPS.

Saitta, B. (1988). "Teoderico di fronte a Franchi e Visigoti (a proposito della battaglia di Vouillé)." In *Cultura e società nell'Italia medievale. Studi per Paolo Brezzi,* 2 vols., 748–753. Rome: Istituto storico italiano per il Medio Evo.

Shanzer, D. (1996–1997). "Two Clocks and a Wedding: Theodoric's Diplomatic Relations with the Burgundians." *Romanobarbarica* 14: 225–258.

Shanzer, D. (1998). "Dating the Baptism of Clovis: The Bishop of Vienne vs. the Bishop of Tours." *Early Medieval Europe* 7: 29–57.

Sivan, H. (1989). "Sidonius Apollinaris, Theodoric II, and Gothic-Roman Politics from Avitus to Anthemius." *Hermes* 117: 85–94.

Spencer, M. (1994). "Dating the Baptism of Clovis." *Early Medieval Europe* 3: 97–116.

Stroheker, K. F. (1937). *Eurich, König der Westgoten.* Stuttgart: Kohlhammer.

Thompson, E. A. (1963). "The Visigoths from Fritigern to Euric." *Historia* 12: 105–126.

Vallet, F. (1995). *De Clovis à Dagobert. Les mérovingiens.* Paris: Gallimard.

von Hefele, K. J., and Leclercq, H. (1907). *Histoire des conciles d'après les documents originaux.* 2.1. Paris: Letouzy.

Weedman, M. (2007). "Hilary and the Homoiousians: Using New Categories to Map the Trinitarian Controversy." *Church History* 76: 491–510.

Wolfram, H. (1988). *History of the Goths,* trans. T. J. Dunlap. Berkeley: University of California Press.

Wood, I. N. (1994). *The Merovingian Kingdoms 450–751.* London: Routledge.

CHAPTER 20

THE MEROVINGIANS, THE AVARS, AND THE SLAVS

MATTHIAS HARDT

THE FRANKS EAST OF THE RHINE AND NORTH OF THE DANUBE

BETWEEN the sixth and early eighth century, the Merovingians were involved with the peoples and rulers who resided east of the Rhine and north of the Danube.[1] Some of the regions beyond these rivers had been part of the Roman Empire only briefly and others not at all. Politically, economically, and culturally, they were structured in a completely different manner than the Gallic and Germanic provinces that formed the basis of the Merovingian kingdom in the fifth and sixth centuries. Beyond the former imperial frontiers, there was no Roman infrastructure on which "barbarian" rule could build. Instead, those relationships that had initially emerged through peaceful and military contact with the Roman Empire in the first few centuries of the common era continued to develop.

While there is no room here to describe this process in detail, the Thuringian kingdom emerged from the constellation of peoples that archaeologists call the "Hassleben-Leuna group" after the two most important cemeteries in central Germany. Archaeologists have noted that the population of the late third and fourth centuries favored rich burials for high-status individuals, including lavish jewelry and imported silver and bronze table- and drinking wares that originated in the Roman Empire. After the end of Attila's empire in 454, which had also included Thuringians, the Thuringian kingdom became the dominant power beyond the former Roman frontier of the provinces of Germania, Raetia, and Noricum. Its kings were probably based in the mountain basins around Weimar and Erfurt, north of the Thuringian forest, whence they ruled in varying intensity over an area that stretched from the lower Rhine to the middle course of the Danube, and from the middle Elbe to the middle Main. They were dynastically related to the early Merovingians (such as Childeric I), and to inhabitants of the Ostrogothic kingdom of Theoderic the Great (Castritius, Geuenich, and Werner 2009). The open landscapes between the Elbe and Weichsel were only thinly settled after many Goths, Vandals, and Burgundians migrated into the Roman Empire. Scholars today debate whether the subsequent emergence of the Slavic world in this area was the consequence of immigration from the northeastern Carpathians and the area along the middle and lower Danube, or whether it resulted from the assimilation of the local groups to Sklaviniai communities, which were originally settled in the area by the Byzantine imperial administration. There is also extensive discussion as to what role the Avars played in this process (Fritze 1979; Herrmann 1985, pp. 21–32; Brather 2001, pp. 51–62; Curta 2001; Kobyliński 2005, pp. 525–540; Pohl 2008, pp. 27–31).

After the Thuringian kingdom was broken up in 531 by the Franks and the Thuringian king Herminafrid was murdered in Zülpich on the lower Rhine in 534 (Kälble 2009, pp. 345–346; see also James, Chapter 11, this volume), King Theudebert I wrote a letter to Emperor Justinian I ca. 545 (Kaiser and Scholz 2012, no. 17, p. 124) in which he explained that he ruled from the Danube and the borders of Pannonia to the ocean. North of the Thuringians and their provinces, the Frankish king mentioned Swabians (Norsavi), Saxons, and Jutes (Eucii) (Schlesinger 1975, pp. 14–15; Ewig 1983, pp. 19–20; Kälble 2009, pp. 340–341, 348–349). However, the Franks struggled to assert and maintain their claim of having subdued the groups mentioned in the letter. The *gentes ultra Renum* (peoples east of the Rhine) were sometimes called upon as military allies in intra-Merovingian conflicts, as was done by Kings Sigebert I and Theudebert II and Queen Brunhild, but they otherwise proved to be rather unreliable members of the Frankish kingdom (Schlesinger 1975, pp. 25–26; 1985, p. 336; Kälble 2009, pp. 350–351).

THE MEROVINGIANS AND THE EMERGENCE OF THE BAVARIANS

After Theudebert wrote this letter to Justinian I, the Bavarians emerged at the southeastern extremity of the Frankish kingdom (Fehr and Heitmeier 2012). Their consolidation can be directly connected to the Merovingians' need to secure and stabilize their southeastern frontiers against the Avars, Slavs, and Lombards (Hardt 2003; Wolfram 1987, pp. 83–106). Formerly, Theodoric the Great's Ostrogothic kingdom was often seen as the driving force behind this ethnogenesis on former Roman soil (Kahl 1989, pp. 164, 217, 223; Wolfram 1995a, p. 64; Wolfram 1995b, p. 22), despite the fact that the Ostrogoths had already ceded their rule over the northern Alpine territories to the Frankish kings in 537 (Schneider 1987, pp. 27–28; see Arnold, Chapter 21, this volume). As early as 540, Frankish bishops ordained priests in Aguntum, Virunum, and Teurnia, thereby demonstrating the presence of the Frankish kingdom in the eastern Alps (Berg 1989, pp. 65–66, 82–84; Hardt 2003, p. 438). It was probably King Theudebert I who brought the regions between the Danube and the Alps under Frankish rule and who was behind a Swabian-Alamannic campaign against the Veneto (Jarnut 1986, pp. 47–49; Kahl 1989, pp. 176–177).

Thus, it must also have been the Merovingians who established a duchy in order to organize the territories newly acquired from the Ostrogoths (Jarnut 1986, pp. 49–53). With the Agilolfings, they installed a family capable of influencing the northeastern Alpine foothills according to the wishes of the Franks. Initially, the Agilolfings had their core territory in the southwestern Visigothic periphery and later in the Austrasian-Burgundian part of the Frankish kingdom (Werner 1965, pp. 106–115; Jarnut 1986, pp. 12–14, 28–40, 57–68). Jörg Jarnut has convincingly argued that the Frankish King Theudebald, who himself had a Roman mother, deliberately chose Garibald, a member of the noble Agilolfing family that had broad connections to the Visigoths, Swabians, Franks, Burgundians, and Romans, to help oversee the integration of the newly emergent *gens* in Raetia (Jarnut 1986, p. 56).

The appointment of a *dux* (duke) by the Frankish king was what led to the creation of an institution actively concerned with the organization of the various non-Roman and Roman (on Romanness, see Pohl 2014) groups and federations living in the former province of Raetia (Jarnut 1986, p. 47). Near the former centers of Augsburg and Regensburg, drawing on Regensburg's military significance (Rettner 2002), the groups living around the former legionary fortress—called Baiuvarii, or men from the land of Baiahaim—were bound to play a crucial and, eventually, through ethnogenesis, a decisive role (Reindel 1981, pp. 471–473).

Irrespective of whether the name "Baiuvarii" referred to a tribal core originating from Bohemia or another area northeast of the Danube called Baia (Hardt 2015), the ethnogenesis of the Bavarians took place in the territory they later settled. Thus, the Agilolfingian *duces*, who were soon to gain an almost king-like position (Wolfram 1967, pp. 161–184), must have had a decisive influence on the crystallization of Bavarian identity and ethnic self-awareness. As soon as they were first mentioned in the written sources, the Bavarians formed a frontier society in the Frankish kingdom, set against another newly arrived player, the Avars, who came to dominate the situation in the southeast over the coming centuries.

MEROVINGIAN KINGS AND AVAR KHAGANS

Before settling in the area along the middle Danube and Tisza rivers in 568, the Avars first appeared at the eastern borders of the Frankish kingdom in 562. Allegedly, they were on their way to Gaul (Gregory of Tours, *Libri historiarum decem* IV, 23, pp. 155–156); Paul the Deacon later reported that they arrived at the Elbe *in Thuringia* (Paulus Diaconus, *Historia Langobardorum* II, 10, p. 79; Ewig 1983, pp. 26–27; Fritze 1979, pp. 524–525; Kälble 2009, pp. 342, 349–350; on Avar warfare, Curta 2015, pp. 70–75, 88). Most likely, after the looting of the Antian kingdom northeast of the Carpathians, they had traveled westward along the northern edge of the mountain range, crossing what at that time was the very thinly settled region of Silesia (Kobyliński 2005, p. 531). They may have been acting on Byzantine orders, with the aim of opening a second front toward the Franks, who at that time were fighting against Narses in northern Italy (Fritze 1979, pp. 527–528; Pohl 1988, pp. 45–46; Fritze 1994, p. 21). On that occasion, Sigebert I was victorious, but—most likely at the initiative of the leader of the Avars, the khagan (Pohl 1988, pp. 175–178)—entered into an *amicitia* (friendship) with the Avars (Gregory of Tours, *Libri historiarum decem* IV, 23, p. 155; Fritze 1979, pp. 528–529). A few years later, in 566, the Avars returned after Emperor Justin II terminated the agreement that was valid until that point (Fritze 1979, pp. 529–531). This time, as Gregory of Tours mentions, they were well versed in magical practices and used fantastic enchantments to curtail the Franks' resistance (on magic, see Klingshirn, Chapter 41, this volume). As a consequence, Sigebert was vanquished and was taken prisoner. Only by employing the *ars donandi* (Hannig 1986) was he able to convince Khagan Baian to enter a *foedus* (treaty) with him and withdraw Baian's army within three days once it had received sufficient supplies (Gregory of Tours, *Libri historiarum decem* IV, 29, pp. 161–162; Menander Protector fragment 23, pp. 141–142; Fritze 1979, pp. 525–526, 531–532). Perhaps it was the khagan's aspiration to defeat all neighboring groups and his goal to counteract the defeat of 562 that made him lead a campaign into the far-off border areas of Thuringia (Wolfram 1987, p. 347; Pohl 1988, p. 47). The former scholarly contention that Sigebert I had to relinquish the territories east of the Saale River as a result of his treaty with Baian, who in turn ordered Slavs to settle there instead of the emigrated Germanic groups, is not supported in the written sources (Fritze 1979, p. 532).

Owing to the demise of the Thuringian kingdom, the Lombards had gained in strength first north and then also south of the Danube. After they left Pannonia and following the settlement of the Avars in the Danube-Tisza area in 568, Sigebert I negotiated a peace with Byzantium. In practical terms, it can only be read as an alliance against the Lombards and Avars (Gregory of Tours, *Libri historiarum decem* IV, 40, p. 172; Fritze 1979, p. 533).

BAVARIANS, SLAVS, AND AVARS

The changes in political and tribal structure in the middle Danube area, caused by the emigration of the Lombards and the arrival of the Avars, were accompanied by the first appearance of Slavic groups at the eastern borders of the Frankish kingdom in the last decades of the sixth century. Slavic presence is documented archaeologically by cremation burials found at Groß-Prüfening, west of Regensburg (Eichinger and Losert 2004; Losert 2011). It is possible that the Slavs were in the employ of the Bavarian dukes. From the time of Tassilo I, this duchy had increasingly gained in importance and was established in opposition to the Slavs in the east Alpine area of what had been central

Noricum along the Drava and as a bulwark against the Avars just beyond them (Störmer 1977, pp. 2–4; Fritze 1979, pp. 518, 536–539; Kahl 1989, pp. 194–200; Wolfram 1995b, pp. 39–46). The sole real Bavarian victory was recorded in 592 and was swiftly followed by a defeat in 595; it was only around 610, as late as the reign of Garibald II, that a defeat at Aguntum was followed by another victory (Wolfram 1985, pp. 126–128; 1995a, pp. 78–79). Nevertheless, the Agilofingian fight against their eastern neighbors provided an early opportunity for the consolidation of their position. Having defeated the Bavarians in 595, the Avars rode again to Thuringia against the Franks the following year (Fritze 1979, pp. 538–541). As was the case in the earlier conflicts, after their victory against a Frankish army, they retreated after receiving tribute from Queen Brunhild (Paulus Diaconus, *Historia Langobardorum* IV, 11, p. 120; Ewig 1983, pp. 48–49; Fritze 1979, pp. 540–541).

DAGOBERT I AND SAMO

A connection between the rise of the Avars and the expansion of the Slavs as the Merovingians' eastern neighbors is particularly evident in the seventh century. In the year 630, Frankish historians recorded confrontations between King Dagobert I and the Slavs living in the eastern border areas of the Frankish kingdom (Fredegar IV, 48, pp. 144–145; Hardt 2002a, 2002b; Fritze 1994, pp. 73–108; Curta 1997). According to the chronicle of the writer referred to as Fredegar, Dagobert I planned to "subjugate the Avars and Slavs and the other people up to the borders of the Byzantian Empire" (Fredegar IV, 58, p. 150). As early as the fortieth year of the rule of the Frankish king Chlothar II (around 623/624), the same chronicle reported that a Frank named Samo from the *pagus Senonago* (today understood as Soignies in the Hennegau or as the area around Sens, but see Schütz 1992, pp. 46–49), together with some other like-minded traders, journeyed to a Slavic group, which was referred to as the Winedi (Wends) by their Germanic-speaking neighbors. They had just launched an uprising against their oppressive subjection to the Avars. The Slavs were likely forced to provide the Avars with winter quarters. Fredegar described the relationship between the two groups as characterized by the Avars' military exploitation of Slavic warriors and use of sexual violence against Slavic women. His text might preserve elements of an earlier Slavic narrative, some parts of which are also present in the Primary Chronicle of Nestor, composed in the early twelfth century in Old Russian (Curta 1997, pp. 148–151).

According to Fredegar's account, Samo took part in the rebellion, which was mostly carried out by the sons born of the rapes endured by the Slavic women. He proved himself in battle and was therefore made king by the Slavs. With Samo as leader, they achieved many victories against the Avars (Fredegar IV, 48, pp. 144–145; on the written sources, see Curta 1997; Collins 2007, pp. 50–51). As a ruler, Samo also was able to stave off claims that the Slavs owed *servicium* (service) to the Frankish king Dagobert I.

Instead, Samo ensured that *amicicia* (friendship) was maintained (Fredegar IV, 68, pp. 154–155; Ewig 1983, pp. 51–52). After a quarrel over Frankish traders who had been robbed and murdered in Samo's kingdom, Dagobert I marched Austrasians, Alamanni, and allied Lombards against Samo's Slavs. While the Merovingian king's "barbarian" supporters remained successful, the Austrasians themselves were defeated at the Wogastisburg fortress (*ad castro Wogastisburc*) (Fredegar IV, 68, p. 155; Schlesinger 1975, p. 39; Brachmann 1990, pp. 17–33; Kälble 2009, p. 352). From this point forward, Slavs plundered in Thuringia and other peripheral regions of the eastern Frankish kingdom. Samo's reputation rose to such a degree that even *dux* Dervan of the Slavic Sorbs, who had already (*iam olim*) been affiliated with the Frankish kingdom, joined Samo (Fredegar IV, 68, p. 155; Brachmann 1990, pp. 17–19; Eggers 2001). Irrespective of whether "Samo" was the name of the successful leader of the Slavs or whether this term refers solely to the title of an autocratic ruler (for: Kunstmann 1979, 1980; Pohl 1988, pp. 256–259; against: Schütz 1992, pp. 54–55), and whether Samo traded in weapons and slaves (Verlinden 1933) or only in the semiprecious stone almandine, in the course of this war he became the victorious leader of Slavs at the periphery of the Avar khaganate. There, he continued to rule successfully for thirty-five years and—according to Fredegar—sired twenty-two sons and fifteen daughters with twelve women *ex genere Winodorum* (of Slavic origin) (Fredegar IV, 48, p. 145).

The heated scholarly debates surrounding these narratives in the chronicle of the writer known as Fredegar are ongoing (Curta 1997, pp. 143–148, 163–167) and the question of the location of the Wogastisburg fortress can similarly not yet be answered. Although nowadays the center of Samo's kingdom is thought to have been in close proximity to the Avar core territories and hence in the southeast of Austria or Hungary, it cannot be denied that the Frankish army suffered its defeat at the eastern edge of the Austrasian part of its kingdom. This conflict therefore probably occurred not in the Bavarian-Carantanian southeast but somewhere in Main-Franconia (Brachmann 1990, pp. 18–19, 26–27). Despite these reflections, the sometimes inventive hypotheses (Losert 1993, pp. 254–257; Sage 1996, p. 225; Schmale and Störmer 1997, p. 82) identifying Wogastisburg (Brachmann 1990, pp. 19–20) with the sites of Burk near Forchheim (Jakob 1987, pp. 191–197; Brachmann 1990, p. 20; Sage 1996, pp. 199, 210, 225, 242) or the Burgberg of Bamberg (Brachmann 1990, p. 28; Sage 1996, pp. 195–199, 204–207), both on the left bank of the Regnitz and with other places in Upper Franconia (Brachmann 1990, p. 20, 27–28; Schütz 1992, pp. 56–59; Losert 1993, p. 256; Sage 1996, p. 242), remain speculative and have not been proven. Yet, these propositions are based on the interpretation of sources that, for this time, are at least as informative as the report regarding Samo's victory at Wogastisburg in the so-called Chronicle of Fredegar (Fredegar IV, 68, p. 155), which need not necessarily be accepted as a report based on hard historical facts (Curta 1997, pp. 143–148, 163–167). Specifically, these sources comprise the interpretation of the region's place names, which, however, do not furnish definitive evidence for an identification of Wogastisburg. Archaeological data at least show the early use of Bamberg's Burgberg by Slavic groups (Sage 1990, p. 46; Sage 1996, p. 204; Sage 2007, p. 51). Yet, currently, neither the early Slavic settlement structures uncovered to date in Upper Franconia nor the earliest Slavic strata of the region's place names can be identified securely, let alone dated precisely (Eichler 1985, pp. 292–293).

Fredegar's account of Samo problematizes both Avar-Slav and Frankish-Slav relations. It makes clear that the military expansion of the Avar khaganate was closely related to the diffusion of the Slavs, who served as warriors in this series of conflicts (Fritze 1994, pp. 19–22). When referring to the Slavs ruled by the Avars, Fredegar used the Germanic legal term *befulci*, or "wards," possibly hinting at a kind of dependency— perhaps contractually regulated or sealed by an oath—of the Slavs upon the Avars (Schütz 1991, 1992, pp. 51–53). Potentially, the Slavic language was the means of communication, the "lingua franca" among the many groups ruled by the Avar khagan, and perhaps it is this function that led to its rapid and considerable expansion after the sixth century (Pritsak 1983). Theophylact Simocatta recorded a claim made by some Slavic prisoners of the Byzantine emperor Mauricius that the influence of the Avar khagan reached as far as "the Slavs at the end of the western ocean" and that the khagan had tried to convince this group, hitherto interpreted as being the Baltic Slavs (Herrmann 1972; Kobyliński 2005, pp. 531–532), to support his military campaigns against Byzantium (Theophylact Simocatta, *Historiae* VI, 2, para. 10–16, pp. 223–224). Although this passage has since been interpreted as an invention of the Byzantine historiographer himself (Wołoszyn 2014), the area influenced by the Avars did reach as far as the eastern frontier of the Frankish kingdom, as shown by the military displays of 562, 566, and 595 in eastern Thuringia. Yet it is not explicitly mentioned whether in the first half of the seventh century this area was already settled by those Sorbs who, according to Fredegar, *ex genere Sclavinorum erant et ad regnum Francorum iam olem aspecserant* (were of Slavic origin and belonged to the Frankish realm for a long time; Fritze 1979, pp. 541–545; Eggers 2001, pp. 70–71). At this time, they may have been elsewhere on the eastern border of the Frankish kingdom, only later reaching the areas between the Elbe and Saale, where their presence is not attested in the reworked version of the Royal Frankish Annals until the year 782.[2]

RADULF AND THE SLAVIC FRONTIER

Undoubtedly, however, the Slavs, even if not necessarily the Sorbs, plundered the borders of Thuringia, and it was against them that Dagobert I planned a military campaign, set to begin in Mainz in 632. Apparently, this campaign was never realized. Nonetheless, Saxons in the area between Unstrut and Saale were freed from the obligation of paying a tribute of 500 cows that had been levied since the reign of Chlothar I. Instead, they were given the task of defending the frontier (Fredegar IV, 74, p. 158). Yet, as early as 633, Slavs again invaded Thuringia, allegedly on the order of Samo. The situation was only diffused once Austrasia obtained its own subordinate king in the person of Dagobert I's son Sigebert III, who resided at Metz and was supported by Bishop Kunibert of Cologne and the *dux* Adalgisel (Fredegar IV, 75, pp. 158–159; Kälble 2009, pp. 352–353).

Equally successful was Radulf, who was appointed a *dux* by Dagobert (Butzen 1987, pp. 142–145). He was the son of a certain Chamar and had several confrontations with a Slavic army (*exercitus Winedorum*), which he succeeded in driving off. As a result, he soon refused the fealty of Adalgisel and, after Dagobert I's death, rebelled against Sigebert III (Fredegar IV, 77, p. 159). In 641, the Austrasians organized a campaign against him. Yet, this operation failed because Radulf sought refuge in a "wooden castle" (*castrum lignis monitum*), which overlooked the Unstrut River in northern Thuringia and because the leaders of the Austrasian army, Adalgisel and Grimoald, disagreed with one another. After a heavy defeat, which cost—among others—the lives of Bobo, the *dux* of Auvergne, Aenovales, the *comes* of Saintois, and the *domesticus* Fredulf, it was only through negotiation that the Frankish army was able to secure safe passage back to the Rhine. Radulf now considered himself the *rex in Toringia* but recognized the overlordship of the Franks. He established an *amicitia* with his Slavic neighbors (Fredegar IV, 87, pp. 164–165; Lindner 1969, pp. 57–58; Schlesinger 1985, pp. 336–337; Butzen 1987, p. 151; Kälble 2009, pp. 353–355). It is possible that the duchy of the Heden family in Main-Franconia was established at the same time as that in Thuringia, also with the objective of securing the borders against Slavic groups. The duchy did not go back to Radulf but at most to *dux* Chrodobert, who led the Alamannic army against Samo in 631. However, information regarding the early years of the Main-Franconian duchy is very thin on the ground (Lindner 1969, pp. 55–74; but see Butzen 1987, pp. 148–160; Kälble 2009, pp. 356–358). Similarly, the timing of the incursion of the Main-Franconian Hedens into Thuringia is as difficult to pinpoint as its end, which could be related to Charles Martel asserting himself as mayor of the palace in 718/719 (Kälble 2009, pp. 360–361). The organization of the frontier, against, among others, the Slavs, was probably a crucial factor in the enduring self-definition and self-confidence of the Thuringians within the Merovingian kingdom (Kälble 2009, p. 370). According to Willibald's *Vita Bonifatii*, the eastern border of Thuringia ran only a little east of Erfurt (*Vitae Sancti Bonifatii* c. 8, p. 44); at the time of Charlemagne, the Saale was seen as the boundary to the Slavic Sorbs.[3] When Karlmann and Pippin the Younger, the mayors of the palace, fought the Saxons in 748, they were also supported by a *rex* or *reges Winidorum* (Fredegar Cont. 31, p. 181; Schlesinger 1985, pp. 343–344).

THE BAVARIANS AND THE MURDER OF THE BULGARIANS

The uprising of the Slavs in which Samo was involved was part of a larger array of internal upheavals in the Avar khaganate after the failed siege of Constantinople in 626. Another group involved in these conflicts was the Bulgarians, who—according to Fredegar— sought to gain dominance within the khaganate but were defeated. As a consequence, 9,000 Bulgarians are alleged to have been driven out of Pannonia and subsequently turned to Dagobert I for help. The king of the Franks is said to have ordered the Bavarians to provide shelter for the refugees over the winter. After the Bulgarians were distributed among individual households, Dagobert I consulted with the Franks and then ordered the Bavarians to kill the Bulgarians, including their wives and children, on an agreed-upon night. This order to murder the refugees was apparently carried out by the Bavarians; only a certain Alzeco with 700 men, women, and children found refuge in a *marca Vinedorum* (in the lands of the Slavs) and later lived for many years with Walluch, the *dux Winedorum* (Fredegar IV, 72, p. 157; Wolfram 1987, p. 341; Kahl 1989, pp. 187–188, 202). Between 656 and 671, the Bulgarians moved on to join the Lombards and were mostly settled in Benevento (Paulus Diaconus, *Historia Langobardorum* V, 29, p. 154; Wolfram 1987, pp. 341–342).

BAVARIANS AND CARANTANIANS: THE WENDISH MARCHES

Walluch, the ruler of the Wends, was most likely a leader of the Carantanians, who were probably initially followers of Samo. After Samo's death, Walluch managed to retain his independence in the face of both the Avars and his Bavarian and Lombard neighbors (Wolfram 1987, p. 341; Kahl 2002, pp. 140–141). The name of this *gens*, which may also have included groups of Croatians and Dulebes, as well as Romans (Wolfram 1987, pp. 342–343), is derived from the Karnburg fortress in the Zollfeld area, below the Ulrichsberg (Wolfram 1987, p. 342). Paul the Deacon reported that the son of the Friulian duke Lupus fled there after his father's death in 665 (Paulus Diaconus, *Historia Langobardorum* V, 22, p. 152; Wolfram 1987, p. 342). Around 740, the Carantanian ruler Boruth had come into a relationship of subservience to the Bavarians after the two groups had together repelled Avar attacks (Störmer 1977, p. 3; Wolfram 1985, p. 137; 1987, pp. 342–343, 349). As early as 743, Carantanian warriors are reported to have marched against the Franks in the army of the Bavarian Duke Odilo (Störmer 1977, p. 3; Wolfram 1985, p. 137; 1987, pp. 342–343, 349).

The jurisdiction of Salzburg over Carantania probably dates to the time of these upheavals, from which the Frankish mayor of the palace (and later king) Pippin the Younger eventually emerged victorious. In his political strategies against the Lombards, Pippin attempted to gain influence in the northeastern foreland of the Italian Lombard kingdom. After the successful campaign of the Bavarian duke Odilo against the Avars and Carantanians, he entrusted the recently established (739) bishopric to the care of Cacatius (*Gorazd*) and Cheitmar (*Hotimir*), the son and nephew of the Carantanian leader Boruth, whom the latter had been obliged to send as hostages to the monastery of (Herren-)Chiemsee (*Conversio* c. 4, p. 104; Wolfram 1981, pp. 145–146; Dopsch 2000, p. 667). After the death of Boruth around 750 and his short-term successor Gorazd, probably in 752, Cheitmar was returned to the Carantanians. It is perhaps already at this point that he was established as their ruler (Štih 2008, p. 37; Štih 2010, pp. 278–292; Wolfram 2012, pp. 119–120) in a ceremony using the so-called Prince's Stone, the base of an Ionian column placed in the ground upside-down (*Conversio* ca. 4, p. 104; Dopsch 1995, pp. 111–113; Fräss-Ehrfeld 1997, p. 6; Kahl 2002, pp. 143–146; Wolfram 2012, pp. 122–124). The Christian Cheitmar had to defend his regime against pagan uprisings in 763 and 765; after his death in 769, there was further unrest. Renewed victory over the Carantanians in 772 thus became an opportunity for Tassilo III to establish—in the person of Waltunc—a Carantanian leader well disposed toward the Bavarians (Prinz 1966, p. 19; 1977, pp. 30–32; Wolfram 1968, p. 165; 1995a, p. 89).

BAVARIANS, AVARS, AND THE FIRST ATTEMPTS AT CHRISTIANIZATION

In 595, the Avars assisted their former Slavic enemies and brought about a Bavarian defeat; after this defeat, for about a century there are no more indications of military conflicts with the Avars on the eastern border of the Frankish kingdom. Only at the end of the seventh or in the early eighth century can one reconstruct an Avar attack on Lorch on the Enns River. This information is contained in the *vita* of St. Emmeram, who is said to have been prevented from undertaking missionary work among the Avars by an upheaval at the mouth of the Enns during the rule of Duke Theodo (680–717/718) (Arbeo von Freising, *Vita Haimchramni* 5, p. 33–34; Wolfram 1975, p. 57; 1987, p. 121; Kahl 1989, p. 201). Between the rivers Traun and Enns, and further to the east up to the Vienna Woods, lay a thinly populated frontier zone that formed a natural separation between the Bavarians and the areas ruled by the Avars (Kahl 1989, pp. 204–210). The Aquitanian Amandus, coming from the lands along the Meuse, had already attempted to do missionary works among the Slavs in this area during the reign of Samo but had been unsuccessful (Wolfram 1987, p. 118; Curta 1997, pp. 153–154). About ten years later, St. Rupert traveled as far as the Enns in search of an area to proselytize but then settled in Salzburg (Wolfram 1975, pp. 57–58; 1981, pp. 127–128; 1987, p. 121; Dopsch 2000, p. 662), whence he founded the Maximilianszelle in Pongau-Bischofshofen in 711/712. It experienced its first Slavic attack in 720/730 (Dopsch 2000, pp. 663–664).

BONIFACE AND THE BISHOPRICS OF REGENSBURG, ERFURT, AND WÜRZBURG

The mayor of the palace, Charles Martel, also stabilized the eastern periphery of the Frankish kingdom by enlarging its ecclesiastical organization. To this end, he and his administration also supported the Anglo-Saxon missionaries Willibrord, Pirmin, and

Winfrid-Boniface. Equipped with an order by Pope Gregory II and a letter of protection from Charles Martel, Boniface first worked in Hesse and Thuringia between 721 and 735. In 732, Pope Gregory III made him an archbishop with responsibilities for converting the region, and in 737, Boniface became the papal legate for Germania. In this function, he first visited the Bavarians, where in 739, and with the help of Duke Odilo (Jarnut 1977, pp. 278–281; Wolfram 1995a, p. 84), he provided the existing Christian congregations in the Agilolfing duchy (Couser 2010) with a Roman-influenced constitution (Semmler 1998, pp. 14–15). Boniface established bishoprics (Reindel 1964, pp. 307–309; Kaiser 1990, pp. 60–62; Wolfram 1995a, pp. 110–111) at Regensburg, Freising, Passau, and Salzburg, but without making Regensburg an archbishopric and without being able immediately to delimit these dioceses in a linear fashion (Schmidinger 1985, pp. 93–95; Störmer 1990, pp. 126–127). In the late Merovingian period, Salzburg, which had finally become a metropolis in 798, led the mission to the Carantanian Slavs (*Conversio Bagoariorum*); in the Carolingian period, Regensburg was set to become the base for an early mission in Bohemia.

Two years after the implementation of the bishopric plan in Bavaria, Boniface initiated the foundation of bishoprics in Main-Franconian Würzburg, on the Hessian Büraburg near Fritzlar (Hardt 2018, pp. 646–649), and in Thuringian Erfurt. His objective was to organize a Christian presence which was much less well established than in Bavaria (Hardt 2005, pp. 13–15). Finally, in 741/742, Boniface wrote to the new pope Zachary II in Rome that at "a place called Erphesfurt and which has long been a fortress of heathens and country dwellers," (*in loco, qui dicitur Erphesfurt, qui fuit iam olim urbs paganorum rusticorum*), he had established one of the three bishoprics serving the German peoples (*Die Briefe des heiligen Bonifatius und Lullus,* no. 50, p. 81; Gockel 1995, p. 82; Heinemeyer 1995, pp. 45–51). In contrast to the description of the other two episcopal sees, the Anglo-Saxon missionary expended particular effort in describing the locations at which the future bishop of Erfurt was to care for the spiritual well-being of his parishioners.

This bishopric was established in a proto-urban settlement at the intersection of the Gera River and a road leading from the Rhineland via Hesse and Thuringia into the Slavic territories. A further north–south path linking the Thuringian valleys to the areas around Würzburg and Bamberg on the Main via the Oberhof pass also joined the river at this point. The fortress (*urbs*) mentioned by Boniface was probably located on the Petersberg, northwest of the later town.

Thus, Boniface chose as the seat of the future bishop a *locus iam olim urbs paganorum et rusticorum Erphesfurt*. In other words, it was an interregionally frequented central place in an exposed position in the center of the country, located along busy long-distance routes and equipped with a royal fortress. Despite such promising conditions, the bishopric of Erfurt had no real future. Boniface was also frustrated by the resistance of the Frankish episcopate to his attempts to provide an appropriate see for his archbishopric in Cologne and had to settle for Mainz. As a result, in his lifetime, he abolished the bishoprics of Erfurt and Büraburg for the benefit of the metropolitan diocese, a questionable course of action from the point of view of church law. Erfurt, now the see of an archdeacon, remained closely tied to Mainz without being able to take up its appropriate role as a bishopric. Boniface's biographer Willibald defended the missionary's course of action with the argument that he "had reserved for himself the churches in the boundary area between the Franks and the Saxons and Slavs and there, until the glorious day of his death, ceaselessly showed these peoples the narrow path to the kingdom of heaven" (Fritze 1954; Schlesinger 1985, p. 348).

The true significance of the settlement Erfurt for the relationship of the Merovingian kingdom with the Slavs and Avars is shown by the hagiographic report describing the events that led to the foundation, on March 12, 744, of the abbey in Fulda (Hardt 2018, pp. 649–654) in which Boniface was buried after his martyrdom in Frisian Dokkum in 754. According to his *vita*, around 740, the Benedictine abbot Sturm, while looking for a suitable place to build the abbey along the banks of the eponymous river in what is now eastern Hesse, met a group of Slavs accompanied by a "translator" (Eigil of Fulda, *Vita Sturmi* c. 7, p. 139; Hardt 2018). They were traveling westward along the road leading from east central Europe via Erfurt to the middle Rhine area and further to Verdun, a town that had grown rich through the slave trade (Hardt 2005, pp. 31–33; Hardt 2008, 2013, 2014). With the active participation of the Frankish toll stations, the Slavic principalities on the eastern edge of the Merovingian kingdom supplied slaves to the Emirate of Cordoba—via Erfurt and Mainz—and to the growing city of Venice via Regensburg. Most certainly, Boniface's attempts to establish the ecclesiastical organization of the eastern borders of the Merovingian Frankish kingdom were also aimed at the control and regulation of such economic interactions with Avars and Slavs.

Notes

1. This chapter is dedicated to Jörg Jarnut in honor of his seventy-fifth birthday.
2. "Sorabi Sclavi, qui campos inter Albim et Salam interiacentes incolunt" (*Annales regni Francorum et Annales qui dicuntur Einhardi* ad a. 782, p. 61).
3. "Salam fluvium, qui Thuringos et Sorabos dividit" (Einhard, *Vita Karoli Magni* c. 15, p. 18).

Works Cited

Ancient Sources

Annales regni Francorum et Annales qui dicuntur Einhardi. F. Kurze (ed.). (1950 [1895]). MGH SRG 6. Hanover: Hahn.

Arbeo von Freising, *Vitae sanctorum Haimhramni et Corbiniani*. B. Krusch (ed.). (1920). MGH SRG 13 (pp. 1–99). Hanover: Hahn.

Die Briefe des heiligen Bonifatius und Lullus. M. Tangl (ed.). (1916). MGH Epistolae selectae 1. Berlin: Weidmann.

Die Conversio Bagoariorum et Carantanorum und der Brief des Erzbischofs Theotmar von Salzburg. F. Lošek (ed.). (1997). MGH Studien und Texte 15. Hanover: Hahn.

Conversio Bagoariorum et Carantanorum. H. Wolfram (ed.). (2012). *Conversio Bagoariorum et Carantanorum. Das Weißbuch der Salzburger Kirche über die erfolgreiche Mission in Karantanien und Pannonien.* 2nd ed. Ljubljana/Laibach: Slovenska Akad. Znanosti in Umetnosti & Zveza Zgodovinskih Društev Slovenije.

Eigil of Fulda, *Die Vita Sturmi.* P. Engelbert (ed.). (1968). Veröffentlichungen der Historischen Kommission für Hessen und Waldeck 29. Marburg: Elwert.

Einhard, *Vita Karoli Magni.* G. Waitz (ed.). (1965 [1911]). MGH SRG 25. Hanover: Hahn.

Fredegar, *Chronicarum quae dicuntur Fredegarii scholastici libri IV cum continuationibus.* B. Krusch (ed.). (1984[1888]). MGH SRM 2 (pp. 1–193). Hanover: Hahn.

Gregory of Tours, *Decem libri historiarum.* B. Krusch and W. Levison (eds.). (1951). MGH: SRM 1.1. Hanover: Hahn.

Kaiser, R., and Scholz, S. (2012). *Quellen zur Geschichte der Franken und der Merowinger: vom 3. Jahrhundert bis 750.* Stuttgart: Kohlhammer.

Menander Protector, *Fragmenta.* E. Doblhofer (ed. and trans.). (1955). *Byzantinische Diplomaten und östliche Barbaren. Aus den Excerpta de legationibus des Konstantinos Porphyrogennetos ausgewählte Abschnitte des Priskos und Menander Protektor übersetzt.* Byzantinische Geschichtsschreiber 4. Graz: Styria.

Paulus Diaconus, *Historia Langobardorum.* L. Bethmann and G. Waitz (eds.). (1964[1878]). MGH: Scriptores rerum Langobardicarum (pp. 12–187). Hanover: Hahn.

Theophylactus Simocatta, *Historiae.* C. De Boor and P. Wirth (eds.). (1972). Bibliotheca Scriptorum Graecorum et Romanorum Teubneriana. Stuttgart: Teubner.

Vitae Sancti Bonifatii archiepiscopi Moguntini. W. Levison (ed.). (1905). MGH SRG 57. Hanover: Hahn.

Modern Sources

Berg, H. (1989). "Bischöfe und Bischofssitze im Ostalpen- und Donauraum vom 4. bis zum 8. Jahrhundert." In H. Wolfram and A. Schwarcz (eds.), *Die Bayern und ihre Nachbarn, Teil 1. Berichte des Symposions der Kommission für Frühmittelalterforschung 25–28. Oktober 1982, Stift Zwettl, Niederösterreich* (pp. 61–108). Österreichische Akademie der Wissenschaften, philosophisch-historische Klasse, Denkschriften 179. Veröffentlichungen der Kommission für Frühmittelalterforschung 8. Vienna: Verlag der Österreichischen Akademie der Wissenschaften.

Brachmann, H. (1990). "Als aber die Austrasier das Castrum Wogastisburc belagerten . . . (Fredegar IV, 68)." In E. Eichler (ed.), *Onomastica Slavogermanica XIX* (pp. 17–33). Abhandlungen der Sächsischen Akademie der Wissenschaften 73, 2. Berlin: Akademie-Verlag.

Brather, S. (2001). *Archäologie der westlichen Slawen: Siedlung, Wirtschaft und Gesellschaft im früh- und hochmittelalterlichen Ostmitteleuropa.* Ergänzungsbände zum Reallexikon der Germanischen Altertumskunde 30. Berlin: Walter de Gruyter.

Butzen, R. (1987). *Die Merowinger östlich des mittleren Rheins: Studien zur militärischen, politischen, rechtlichen, religiösen, kirchlichen, kulturellen Erfassung durch Königtum und Adel im 6. und 7. Jahrhundert.* Mainfränkische Studien 38. Würzburg: Freunde Mainfränkischer Kunst und Geschichte.

Castritius, H., Werner, M., and Geuenich, D. (eds.). (2009). *Die Frühzeit der Thüringer. Archäologie, Sprache, Geschichte.* Ergänzungsbände zum Reallexikon der Germanischen Altertumskunde 63. Berlin: Walter de Gruyter.

Collins, R. (2007). *Die Fredegar-Chroniken.* MGH: Studien und Texte 44. Hanover: Hahn.

Couser, J. (2010). "Inventing Paganism in Eighth-Century Bavaria." *Early Medieval Europe* 18: 26–42.

Curta, F. (1997). "Slavs in Fredegar and Paul the Deacon: Medieval Gens or 'Scourge of God'?" *Early Medieval Europe* 6: 141–167.

Curta, F. (2001). *The Making of the Slavs: History and Archaeology of the Lower Danube Region c. 500–700*. Cambridge Studies in Medieval Life and Thought, 4th Series. Cambridge: Cambridge University Press.

Curta, F. (2015). "Avar Blitzkrieg, Slavic and Bulgar Raiders, and Roman Special Ops: Mobile Warriors in the 6th-Century Balkans." In I. Zimonyi and O. Karatay (eds.), *Eurasia in the Middle Ages: Studies in Honour of Peter B. Golden* (pp. 69–89). Wiesbaden: Harrassowitz.

Dopsch, H. (1995) "*. . . in sedem Karinthani ducatus inthronizavi . . .*: Zum ältesten gesicherten Nachweis der Herzogseinsetzung in Kärnten." In L. Kolmer and P. Segl (eds.), *Regensburg, Bayern und Europa. Festschrift für Kurt Reindel zum 70. Geburtstag* (pp. 103–136). Regensburg: Universitäts-Verlag.

Dopsch, H. (2000). "Salzburg als Missions- und Kirchenzentrum." In R. Bratož (ed.), *Slowenien und die Nachbarländer zwischen Antike und karolingischer Epoche. Anfänge der slowenischen Ethnogenese 2* (pp. 659–692). Situla 39. Ljubljana: Narodni Muzej Slovenije.

Eggers, M. (2001). "Samo—Der erste König der Slawen." *Bohemia* 42: 62–83.

Eichinger, E., and Losert, H. (2004). "Ein merowingerzeitliches Brandgräberfeld östlich-donauländischer Prägung bei Großprüfening." *Das archäologische Jahr in Bayern*: 98–101.

Eichler, E. (1985[1962]). "Zur Etymologie und Struktur der slawischen Orts- und Flussnamen in Nordostbayern." *Wissenschaftliche Zeitschrift der Karl-Marx-Universität Leipzig, Gesellschafts- und sprachwissenschaftliche Reihe* 11, 365–395. [Reprinted in E. Eichler (ed.), *Beiträge zur deutsch-slawischen Namenforschung (1955–1981)* (pp. 269–99). Leipzig: Zentralantiquariat der Deutschen Demokratischen Republik.]

Ewig, E. (1983). *Die Merowinger und das Imperium*. Rheinisch-Westfälische Akademie der Wissenschaften: Geisteswissenschaften, Vorträge G 261. Opladen: Westdeutscher Verlag.

Fehr, H., and Heitmeier, I. (eds.). (2012). *Die Anfänge Bayerns: Von Raetien und Noricum zur frühmittelalterlichen Baiovaria*. Bayerische Landesgeschichte und europäische Regionalgeschichte 1. St. Ottilien: EOS-Verlag.

Fräss-Ehrfeld, C. (1997). "Fürstenstein—Symbol der Kärntner Geschichte." In A. Huber (ed.), *Der Kärntner Fürstenstein im europäischen Vergleich. Tagungsbericht Symposium Gmünd 20. bis 22. September 1996* (pp. 1–13). Seeboden: Stadtgemeinde Gmünd.

Fritze, W. H. (1954). "Bonifatius und die Einbeziehung von Hessen und Thüringen in die Mainzer Diözese: Bemerkungen zu einer unerklärten Stelle in Willibalds Bonifatius-Vita." *Hessisches Jahrbuch für Landesgeschichte* 4: 37–63.

Fritze, W. H. (1979). "Zur Bedeutung der Awaren für die slawische Ausdehnungsbewegung im frühen Mittelalter." *Zeitschrift für Ostforschung* 28: 498–545.

Fritze, W. H. (1994). *Untersuchungen zur frühslawischen und frühfränkischen Geschichte bis ins 7. Jahrhundert*. Europäische Hochschulschriften Reihe 3, Geschichte und ihre Hilfswissenschaften 581. Frankfurt-am-Main: Peter Lang.

Gockel, M. (1995). "Erfurts zentralörtliche Funktionen im frühen und hohen Mittelalter." In U. Weiß (ed.), *Erfurt in Geschichte und Gegenwart* (pp. 81–94). Schriften des Vereins für die Geschichte und Altertumskunde von Erfurt 2. Weimar: Böhlau.

Hannig, J. (1986). "Ars donandi. Zur Ökonomie des Schenkens im früheren Mittelalter." *Geschichte in Wissenschaft und Unterricht* 37: 149–163. Reprinted in R. van Dülmen (ed.) (1988). *Armut, Liebe, Ehre. Studien zur historischen Kulturforschung* 1 (pp. 11–37). Frankfurt-am-Main: Fischer-Taschenbuch-Verl.

Hardt, M. (2002a). "Aspekte der Herrschaftsbildung bei den frühen Slawen." In W. Pohl and M. Diesenberger (eds.), *Integration und Herrschaft. Ethnische Identitäten und soziale Organisation im Frühmittelalter* (pp. 249–255). Österreichische Akademie der Wissenschaften, philosophisch-historische Klasse, Denkschriften 301. Forschungen zur Geschichte des Mittelalters 3. Vienna: Verlag der Österreichischen Akademie der Wissenschaften.

Hardt, M. (2002b). "Slawisch-germanische Beziehungen an der mittleren Donau in der Merowingerzeit nach schriftlichen Quellen." In J. Tejral (ed.), *Probleme der frühen Merowingerzeit im Mitteldonauraum* (pp. 129–135). Spisy archeologického ústavu AV CR Brno 19. Brno: Archäologisches Institut.

Hardt, M. (2003). "The Bavarians." In H.-W. Goetz, J. Jarnut, W. Pohl, and S. Kaschke (eds.), *Regna et Gentes. The Relationship between Late Antique and Early Medieval Peoples and Kingdoms in the Transformation of the Roman World* (pp. 429–461). Transformation of the Roman World 13. Leiden: Brill.

Hardt, M. (2005). "Erfurt im Frühmittelalter: Überlegungen zu Topographie, Handel und Verkehr eines karolingerzeitlichen Zentrums anlässlich der 1200sten Wiederkehr seiner Erwähnung im Diedenhofer Kapitular Karls des Großen im Jahr 805." *Mitteilungen des Vereins für Geschichte und Altertumskunde von Erfurt* 66, Neue Folge 13: 9–39.

Hardt, M. (2008). "Fernhandel und Subsistenzwirtschaft: Überlegungen zur Wirtschaftsgeschichte der frühen Westslawen." In U. Ludwig and T. Schilp (eds.), *Nomen et Fraternitas. Festschrift für Dieter Geuenich zum 65. Geburtstag* (pp. 741–763). Ergänzungsbände zum Reallexikon der Germanischen Altertumskunde 62. Berlin: Walter de Gruyter.

Hardt, M. (2013). "Slavs, Medieval Migration." In *The Encyclopedia of Global Human Migration*. Oxford: Blackwell Publishing Ltd. (DOI: 10.1002/9781444351071.wbeghm492).

Hardt, M. (2014). "Slawen." In M. Borgolte (ed.), *Migrationen im Mittelalter. Ein Handbuch* (pp. 171–180). Berlin: Akademie-Verlag.

Hardt, M. (2015). "Boier und Baiern?" In M. Karwowski, V. Salač, and S. Sievers (eds.), *Boier zwischen Realität und Fiktion. Akten des internationalen Kolloquiums in Český Krumlov vom 14.-16. 11. 2013* (pp. 385–390). Kolloquien zur Vor- und Frühgeschichte 21. Bonn: Habelt.

Hardt, M. (2018). "Hessen im frühen Mittelalter." In H. W. Böhme and C. Dobiat (eds.), *Handbuch der hessischen Geschichte*. Vol. 5: *Grundlagen und Anfänge hessischer Geschichte bis 900* (pp. 635–713). Veröffentlichungen der Historischen Kommission für Hessen 63. Handbuch der hessischen Geschichte 5. Marburg: Historische Kommission für Hessen.

Heinemeyer, K. (1995). "Erfurt im frühen Mittelalter." In U. Weiß (ed.), *Erfurt in Geschichte und Gegenwart* (pp. 45–66). Schriften des Vereins für die Geschichte und Altertumskunde von Erfurt 2. Weimar: Böhlau.

Herrmann, J. (1972). "Byzanz und die 'Slawen am äußersten Ende des westlichen Ozeans'." *Klio* 54: 309–319.

Herrmann, J. (ed.). (1985). *Die Slawen in Deutschland: Geschichte und Kultur der slawischen Stämme westlich von Oder und Neiße vom 6. bis 12. Jahrhundert. Ein Handbuch.* Veröffentlichungen des Zentralinstituts für Alte Geschichte und Archäologie der Akademie der Wissenschaften der DDR 14. Berlin: Akademie-Verl.

Jakob, H. (1987). "Der Name Vogast und Wogastisburc." *Jahrbuch für fränkische Landesforschung* 47: 191–197.

Jarnut, J. (1977). "Studien über Herzog Odilo (736–748)." *Mitteilungen des Instituts für Österreichische Geschichtsforschung* 85: 273–284.

Jarnut, J. (1986). *Agilolfingerstudien: Untersuchungen zur Geschichte einer adligen Familie im 6. und 7. Jahrhundert.* Monographien zur Geschichte des Mittelalters 32. Stuttgart: Hiersemann.

Kälble, M. (2009). "Ethnogenese und Herzogtum Thüringen im Frankenreich (6.–9. Jahrhundert)." In H. Castritius, M. Werner, and D. Geuenich (eds.), *Die Frühzeit der Thüringer. Archäologie, Sprache, Geschichte* (pp. 329–413). Ergänzungsbände zum Reallexikon der Germanischen Altertumskunde 63. Berlin: Walter de Gruyter.

Kahl, H.-D. (1989). "Die Baiern und ihre Nachbarn bis zum Tode des Herzogs Theodo (717/18)." In H. Wolfram and A. Schwarcz (eds.), *Die Bayern und ihre Nachbarn 1. Berichte des Symposions der Kommission für Frühmittelalterforschung 25–28. Oktober 1982, Stift Zwettl, Niederösterreich* (pp. 159–225). Österreichische Akademie der Wissenschaften, philosophisch-historische Klasse, Denkschriften 179. Veröffentlichungen der Kommission für Frühmittelalterforschung 8. Vienna: Verlag der Österreichischen Akademie der Wissenschaften.

Kahl, H.-D. (2002). *Der Staat der Karantanen: Fakten, Thesen und Fragen zu einer frühen slawischen Machtbildung im Ostalpenraum (7.–9. Jh.). Slovenija in sosednje dežele med antiko in karolinško dobo. Začetki slovenske etnogeneze—Slowenien und die Nachbarländer zwischen Antike und karolingischer Epoche. Anfänge der slowenischen Ethnogenese; Supplementum.* Ljubljana: Narodni Muzej Slovenije.

Kaiser, R. (1990). "Bistumsgründung und Kirchenorganisation im 8. Jahrhundert." In H. Dickerhof, E. Reiter, and S. Weinfurter (eds.), *Der heilige Willibald—Klosterbischof oder Bistumsgründer* (pp. 29–67). Eichstätter Studien, Neue Folge 30. Regensburg: Pustet.

Kobylinski, Z. (2005). "The Slavs." In P. Fouracre (ed.), *The New Cambridge Medieval History* 1 *c. 500–700* (pp. 524–546). Cambridge: Cambridge University Press.

Kunstmann, H. (1979). "Was besagt der Name Samo, und wo liegt Wogastisburg." *Die Welt der Slaven* 24, Neue Folge 3: 1–21.

Kunstmann, H. (1980). "Samo, Dervanus und der Slovenenfürst Wallucus." *Die Welt der Slaven* 25, Neue Folge 4: 171–177.

Lindner, K. (1969). *Untersuchungen zur Frühgeschichte des Bistums Würzburg und des Würzburger Raumes.* Veröffentlichungen des Max-Planck-Instituts für Geschichte 35. Göttingen: Vandenhoeck & Ruprecht.

Losert, H. (1993). "Die slawische Besiedlung Nordostbayerns aus archäologischer Sicht." In K. Schmotz (ed.), *Vorträge des 11. Niederbayerischen Archäologentages* (pp. 207–270). Buch am Erlbach: Leidorf.

Losert, H. (2011). "Das Brandgräberfeld von Regensburg-Großprüfening und die frühen Slawen in Pannonien—in Gedenken an Marek Dulinicz, Warschau († 2010)." In O. Heinrich-Tamáska (ed.), *Keszthely-Fenékpuszta im Kontext spätantiker Kontinuitätsforschung zwischen Noricum und Moesia* (pp. 475–489). Castellum Pannonicum Pelsonense 2. Budapest: Verlag Marie Leidorf.

Pohl, W. (1988). *Die Awaren: Ein Steppenvolk in Mitteleuropa 567–822 n. Chr.* Munich: Beck.

Pohl, W. (2008). *Die ethnische Wende des Frühmittelalters und ihre Auswirkungen auf Ostmitteleuropa.* Oskar-Halecki-Vorlesung 2006: Jahresvorlesung des GWZO. Leipzig: Leipziger Universitäts-Verlag.

Pohl, W. (2014). "Romanness: A Multiple Identity and Its Changes." *Early Medieval Europe* 22(4): 406–418.

Prinz, F. (1966). "Zur Herrschaftsstruktur Bayerns und Alemanniens im 8. Jahrhundert." *Blätter für deutsche Landesgeschichte* 102: 11–27.

Prinz, F. (1977). "Nochmals zur 'Zweiteilung des Herzogtums der Agilolfinger." *Blätter für deutsche Landesgeschichte* 113: 19–32.

Pritsak, O. (1983). "The Slavs and the Avars." In *Gli Slavi occidentali e meridionali nell' alto medioevo* 1 (pp. 353–435). Settimane di studio del centro italiano di studi sull' alto medioevo 30. Spoleto: Presso la Sede del Centro.

Reindel, K. (1964). "Die Bistumsorganisation im Alpen-Donau-Raum in der Spätantike und im Frühmittelalter." *Mitteilungen des Instituts für Österreichische Geschichtsforschung* 72: 277–310.

Reindel, K (1981). "Die Bajuwaren: Quellen, Hypothesen, Tatsachen." *Deutsches Archiv für Erforschung des Mittelalters* 37: 451–473.

Rettner, A. (2002). "Von Regensburg nach Augsburg und zurück—Zur Frage des Herrschaftsmittelpunkts im frühmittelalterlichen Bayern." In G. Helmig, B. Scholkmann, and M. Untermann (eds.), *Centre—Region—Periphery. Medieval Europe Basel 2002,* 1: *Keynote-Lectures to the Conference Sections 1–2. 3rd International Conference of Medieval and later Archaeology* (pp. 538–545). Hertingen: Folio-Verlag.

Sage, W. (1990). "Zur Bedeutung des Bamberger Domberges für die Geschichte des Obermaingebietes." In E. Eichler (ed.), *Onomastica Slavogermanica* 19. *Hans Walther zum 70. Geburtstag* (pp. 39–50). Abhandlungen der Sächsischen Akademie der Wissenschaften, Philologisch-Historische Klasse 73, 2. Berlin: Akademie-Verlag.

Sage, W. (1996). "Frühgeschichte und Frühmittelalter." In W. Sage (ed.), *Oberfranken in vor- und frühgeschichtlicher Zeit* (pp. 161–180). Bayreuth: Bayerische Verlags-Anstalt.

Sage, W. (2007). "Dom und Domberg zu Bamberg." In L. Göller (ed.), *1000 Jahre Bistum Bamberg 1007–2007. Unterm Sternenmantel* (pp. 51–55). Petersberg: Imhof.

Schlesinger, W. (1975). "Zur politischen Geschichte der fränkischen Ostbewegung vor Karl dem Großen." In W. Schlesinger (ed.), *Althessen im Frankenreich,* pp. 9–61. Nationes 2. Sigmaringen: Thorbecke.

Schlesinger, W. (1985). "Das Frühmittelalter." In H. Patze and W. Schlesinger (eds.), *Geschichte Thüringens* 1 (pp. 317–380). Grundlagen und frühes Mittelalter Mitteldeutsche Forschungen 48/1. Cologne: Böhlau.

Schmale, F.-J., and Störmer, W. (1997). "Die politische Entwicklung bis zur Eingliederung ins Merowingische Frankenreich." In A. Kraus (ed.), *Handbuch der Bayerischen Geschichte* 3/1. *Geschichte Frankens bis zum Ausgang des 18. Jahrhunderts* (pp. 70–88). Munich: Beck.

Schmidinger, H. (1985). "Das Papsttum und die bayerische Kirche—Bonifatius als Gegenspieler Virgils." In H. Dopsch and R. Juffinger (eds.), *Virgil von Salzburg. Missionar und Gelehrter* (pp. 92–101). Salzburg: Amt d. Salzburger Landesregierung, Kulturabt.

Schneider, R. (1987). "Fränkische Alpenpolitik." In H. Beumann and W. Schröder (eds.), *Die transalpinen Verbindungen der Bayern, Alemannen und Franken bis zum 10. Jahrhundert* (pp. 23–49). Nationes 6. Sigmaringen: Thorbecke.

Schütz, J. (1991). "Zwei germanische Rechtstermini des 7. Jahrhunderts. Fredegari: befulci—Edictus Rothari: fulcfree." In R. Ibler, H. Kneip, and K. Trost (eds.), *Festschrift für Erwin Wedel. Typoskript-Edition Hieronymus* (pp. 409–414). Slavische Sprachen und Literaturen 20. Munich: Hieronymus.

Schütz, J. (1992). "Fredegar: Über Wenden und Slawen—Chronicon lib. IV cap. 48 et 68." *Jahrbuch für fränkische Landesforschung* 52: 45–59.

Semmler, J. (1998). "Bonifatius, die Karolinger und 'die Franken'." In D. R. Bauer, R. Hiestand, B. Kasten, and S. Lorenz (eds.), *Mönchtum—Kirche—Herrschaft 750–1000* (pp. 3–49). Sigmaringen: Thorbecke.

Štih, P. (2008). "Von der Urgeschichte bis zum Ende des Mittelalters." In P. Štih, V. Simoniti, and P. Vodopivec (eds.), *Slowenische Geschichte. Gesellschaft—Politik—Kultur* (pp. 14–118).

Veröffentlichungen der Historischen Landeskommission für die Steiermark 40. Zbirka Zgodovinskega Časopisa 34. Graz: Leykam.

Štih, P. (2010). "Die Kärntner Herzogseinsetzung zwischen Geschichte und Vorstellungen: Probleme ihrer Überlieferung, Entwicklung und ihres Verlaufs sowie der Rezeption bei den Slowenen." In S. Nikolay (ed.), *Der Kärntner Fürstenstein im Bild. Darstellungen eines europäischen Rechtsdenkmals* (pp. 26–299). Ljubljana/Laibach: Hermagoras Verlag.

Störmer, W. (1977). "Die Agilolfinger im politischen Kräftefeld vom 6. bis zum 8. Jahrhundert." In Oberösterreichisches Landesmuseum (ed.), *Baiernzeit in Oberösterreich. Das Land zwischen Inn und Enns vom Ausgang der Antike bis zum Ende des 8. Jahrhunderts. Ausstellung des Oberösterreichischen Landesmuseums im Schlossmuseum zu Linz anlässlich der 1200jährigen Wiederkehr der Gründung des Stiftes Kremsmünster durch Herzog Tassilo III* (pp. 1–12). Kataloge des Oberösterreichischen Landesmuseums 96. Linz: Oberösterreichisches Landesmuseum.

Störmer, W. (1990). "Die bayerische Herzogskirche." In H. Dickerhof, E. Reiter, and S. Weinfurter (eds.), *Der heilige Willibald—Klosterbischof oder Bistumsgründer* (pp. 115–142). Eichstätter Studien, Neue Folge 30. Regensburg: Pustet.

Verlinden, C. (1933). "Problèmes d' histoire économique franque. 1. Le Franc Samo." *Revue belge de philologie et d' histoire* 12: 1090–1095.

Werner, K. F. (1965). "Bedeutende Adelsfamilien im Reich Karls des Großen." In H. Beumann (ed.), *Karl der Große. Lebenswerk und Nachleben 1. Persönlichkeit und Geschichte* (pp. 83–142). Düsseldorf: Schwann.

Wolfram, H. (1967). *Intitulatio I.: Lateinische Königs- und Fürstentitel bis zum Ende des 8. Jahrhunderts.* Graz: Böhlau.

Wolfram, H. (1968). "Das Fürstentum Tassilos III., Herzogs der Bayern." *Mitteilungen der Gesellschaft für Salzburger Landeskunde* 108: 157–179.

Wolfram, H. (1975). "Grenze und Mission. Salzburg, vom heiligen Rupert zum heiligen Virgil." *Mitteilungen der Gesellschaft für Salzburger Landeskunde* 115: 51–79.

Wolfram, H. (1981). "Die Zeit der Agilulfinger—Rupert und Virgil." In H. Dopsch (ed.), *Geschichte Salzburgs. Stadt und Land* 1 (pp. 121–156). Vorgeschichte—Altertum—Mittelalter, 1. Teil. Salzburg: Pustet.

Wolfram, H. (1985). "Ethnogenesen im frühmittelalterlichen Donau- und Ostalpenraum (6. bis 10. Jahrhundert)." In H. Beumann and W. Schröder (ed.), *Frühmittelalterliche Ethnogenese im Alpenraum* (pp. 97–151). Nationes 5. Sigmaringen: Thorbecke.

Wolfram, H. (1987). *Die Geburt Mitteleuropas. Geschichte Österreichs vor seiner Entstehung 378–907.* Vienna: Kremayr & Scheriau Siedler.

Wolfram, H. (1995a). "Grenzen und Räume. Geschichte Österreichs vor seiner Entstehung." Österreichische Geschichte 378–907. Vienna: Ueberreuter.

Wolfram, H. (1995b). "Salzburg, Bayern, Österreich: Die Conversio Bagoariorum et Carantanorum und die Quellen ihrer Zeit." *Mitteilungen des Instituts für Österreichische Geschichtsforschung,* Ergänzungsband 31. Vienna: Böhlau & Oldenbourg.

Wołoszyn, M. (2014). *Theophylaktos Simokates und die Slawen am Ende des westlichen Ozeans—die erste Erwähnung der Ostseeslawen?* Krakow: Instytut Archeologii i Etnologii Polskiej Akademii Nauk.

CHAPTER 21

THE MEROVINGIANS AND ITALY

Ostrogoths and Early Lombards

JONATHAN J. ARNOLD

THIS chapter provides an overview of Merovingian relations with the Ostrogoths and Lombards from the late fifth to the early seventh century. Although the Ostrogothic and Lombard kingdoms are synonymous with Italy, the boundaries of their respective realms fluctuated greatly during this era, often as a consequence of their interactions with the Franks. Nor did these interactions and the changes they engendered occur in a vacuum, as they were part of a larger geopolitical milieu that included many other "barbarian" peoples and especially the Byzantine Empire. This chapter thus focuses on acts of diplomacy, alliance, and war between the Franks, Ostrogoths, and Lombards, but not in isolation from broader contemporary developments, and how these shaped the medieval future of Italy and Gaul. At times these peoples were friends; other times they were locked in epic struggles, often in collusion with their barbarian or Byzantine neighbors. In short, Merovingian relations with the barbarian kingdoms of Italy during this period began and ended diplomatically, with marriage alliances and peace; however, for much of the sixth century, the Franks, Ostrogoths, and Lombards were fierce rivals and only occasional allies, who frequently proved themselves unreliable and untrustworthy to their supposed "friends."

AMALS AND MEROVINGIANS

Ostrogothic relations with the Merovingians properly begin with the arrival of the Amal king Theoderic the Great and his polyethnic army in Italy in 489. These "Ostrogoths" had been sent by the Byzantine emperor Zeno to depose the current ruler of Italy, Odovacer, who himself had deposed the last western emperor in 476. Of earlier interactions there is precious little information, as the late fifth century is a shadowy period for Italy and Gaul. The sixth-century historian Jordanes relates that Theoderic's father and uncles, in the employ of the Huns, had fought at the famous Battle of the Catalaunian Plains (451) against certain Roman, Visigothic, and Frankish forces, which may have included Clovis's relatives (*Getica* 191; 199). Bishop Gregory of Tours, likewise, recounts that Childeric had once cooperated with Odovacer in two campaigns, one against Angers (although this Audovacer may be some other individual) and another against the Alamanni, who were then threatening Italy (*Histories* 2.18–19). Nonetheless, when exactly these events occurred and how they colored Clovis's own relations with Italy at the time of Theoderic's invasion cannot be determined. What can be said is that Clovis, unlike the other "barbarian" rulers in Gaul, did not involve himself in Theoderic's struggle for Italy but seems to have kept his distance (see Hen, Chapter 10, this volume).

The capitulation of Ravenna and the subsequent murder of Odovacer in 493 left Theoderic master of Italy. Whatever Zeno's plans had been, Theoderic assumed direct control of a state whose Roman inhabitants had perpetuated many aspects of late imperial governance and who continued to view Italy as the western Roman Empire. Despite some initial difficulties, in 497 Theoderic's position as the independent ruler of this "Italian Empire," as it was sometimes called, was formally recognized by Zeno's successor, Anastasius, who even restored to Italy the insignia of the western emperors. Whether Theoderic employed these markers/trappings of imperial authority is moot. Far more important are the implications for the identity of the Ostrogothic state and how this informed Theoderic's international relations, not least with the Franks. A patrician and former consul who had received numerous honors in Constantinople, Theoderic could justly present himself and indeed be accepted in Italy (and beyond) as the Roman ruler of the West and the heir of its emperors, a *princeps Romanus* as he himself and others put it (Arnold 2014).

Thus, as the ruler of a Roman rather than necessarily Ostrogothic Italy, Theoderic attempted to secure his frontiers and ensure peace by establishing close ties with the "barbarians" of the West. Marriage alliances were a ready solution and by this time in keeping with late imperial practices (Demandt 1989; Herrin 2013, pp. 304–307). The exact chronology of the earliest of these alliances is not fully known, but they occurred in the years immediately following Theoderic's conquest of Italy (ca. 493–500) and later allowed him to invoke kinship (*affinitas*) as a rationale against bloodshed. A number of sources refer to these marriages (e.g., *Anonymus Valesianus* 63; Jord., *Get.* 295–299; Procopius, *Wars* 5.12.21–23; Gregory, *Hist.* 3.4, 3.29). Peace was established with the Burgundian king Gundobad, for instance, when his son, Sigismund, married Theoderic's daughter, Ostrogotho Ariagne. Another daughter, Theodegotha, was married to the Visigothic king Alaric II, whose support had proven crucial during the contest for Italy. Meanwhile, Theoderic himself took Clovis's sister, Audofled, as his wife, an act that united Merovingian and Amal lines and doubtless speaks to Clovis's growing power. Indeed, by the late fifth century Clovis had ceased to be a minor player in Gaul and had established an important union of his own by marrying Gundobad's niece, Chlothild. Finally, rounding out these initial alliances was the marriage of Theoderic's sister, Amalafrida, to the Vandal king Thrasamund (Wolfram 1988, pp. 308–313; Moorhead 1992, pp. 51–53; on elite women, see James, Chapter 11, this volume).

Beyond such alliances, diplomacy was another technique that Theoderic used regularly, although the evidence is not complete. In the late 490s, the ruler of Italy complained about the gifts he needed to give incessantly to foreign envoys for the sake of peace (Ennodius, *Vita Epiphanii* 188). Decades later, one rather active Italian diplomat recorded twenty-five missions on his epitaph, some of which, no doubt, were directed to the Merovingian court (Gillett 2003, pp. 290–319). A handful of these missions are revealed in the official correspondence collected in the *Variae* of Cassiodorus, a leading statesman of the Ostrogothic regime. In 506, for instance, Theoderic sent Clovis a citharist at the Frankish king's earnest request (*Variae* 2.40–41). These and other gifts, such as a set of clocks sent to Burgundy around the same time, were professed markers of friendship and goodwill. As Theoderic confided to the Italo-Roman aristocrat Boethius, who helped procure these items, "charming delights frequently produce what weapons fail to accomplish" (*Var.* 1.45). But the words that accompanied these gifts also demonstrate that they were a form of dominance and allowed Theoderic to stake important claims to Romanness. Clovis's citharist, for example, was intended to imitate Orpheus and "to tame the savage hearts of the barbarians" (*Var.* 2.40). Gundobad's clocks, likewise, were designed to help the "beastly" Burgundians "put down their barbarous ways" (*Var.* 1.46). Indeed, despite marriage alliances, talk of kinship, and gift-giving, all the rulers of Gaul, even Theoderic's Visigothic cousins, were still described as the traditional nemeses of Rome, as uncouth and potentially dangerous barbarians (Arnold 2012, pp. 120–121; Arnold 2014, pp. 251–253). Beyond the Alps, beyond Italy's new frontier, there remained "fierce and very savage peoples," according to Theoderic; "barbarians whose oaths could not be trusted" (*Var.* 2.52, 7.4).

The arrival of a new Orpheus at Clovis's court was in fact well timed, for the Frankish king had just crushed the Alamanni in a major battle, killing their king and sending refugees fleeing into Ostrogothic territory. Along with the requested citharist, therefore, Theoderic sent his brother-in-law an appropriate congratulations for his victory, but also a plea to restrain himself and to be moderate in his conquests by not pursuing the remnants of the Alamanni into his own lands. "Those who appear to have taken refuge in the defense of your kin deserve to escape by the right of friendship" (*Var.* 2.41). The request appears to have been honored by Clovis, as Theoderic soon settled these Alamanni within the frontiers of Rhaetia and Noricum, rendering them, according to one Italian panegyrist, "guardians of the Latin Empire," perhaps with an eye to further Frankish expansion (Ennodius, *Panegyricus* 72). Indeed, by 506 it was becoming increasingly clear in Italy that tensions in Gaul were mounting. Civil wars had already occurred in Burgundy and led to the death of a Burgundian king, in part with Clovis's assistance. Clovis himself had continued to expand, consolidating his position as the sole king of the Franks. Finally, Clovis and Alaric II, once on friendly terms, had become estranged and even began to prepare for war. Although Gregory of Tours describes the impending campaign as a Catholic crusade against the Arian Visigoths (*Hist.* 2.37), Theoderic's letters imply that the dispute was a trivial matter of words and blind resentment, and that both parties had been incited to violence by some unnamed and delighted onlooker, likely the Byzantine emperor Anastasius, who now feared Theoderic's growing power (*Var.* 3.1 and 3.4; Meier 2009, pp. 229–230; Arnold 2014, pp. 265–266). That Gundobad may have been behind the intrigue is also quite possible, given his role in the war that followed and his family's professed allegiance to Constantinople (Avitus of Vienne, *Epistulae* 93–94; on Byzantine relations, see Esders, Chapter 16, this volume).

Regardless, Theoderic strove to use Roman reason and diplomacy to prevent war in Gaul, sending a number of embassies that pushed for arbitration and made frequent references to the marital ties that bound all parties involved. Clovis, specifically, was reminded of "the sacred laws of kinship" and admonished to put down his sword and to terminate existing quarrels "through the mediation of friends" (*Var.* 3.4). Alaric, on the other hand, was asked to consider the horrors of war and told to restrain himself. "Wait until we send envoys to the king of the Franks," he pleaded, "for we wish nothing [so terrible] to arise between men joined to us by affinity" (*Var.* 3.1). Theoderic nevertheless realized that his words might fall on deaf ears. In the same letter to Clovis, he claimed that he found it unlikely that his brother-in-law would scorn his advice, threatening that doing so would render the Ostrogoths and their allies Clovis's adversaries. This threat became a promise in the missive directed to Alaric, to whom Theoderic avowed, "He who strives to be your opponent will rightly find me as his adversary." Nor was Theoderic bluffing when he threatened Clovis with the enmity of his allies. Letters were also dispatched to the Franks' eastern neighbors, to the kings of the Warni, Heruli, and Thuringians (*Var.* 3.3), the latter of whose king, Herminifrid, had recently married Theoderic's niece Amalaberga, becoming the newest member of his system of marriage alliances (*Var.* 4.1; *Anon. Vales.* 70). These peoples, too, were asked to send missions to the Frankish court. Yet the letters addressed to them contain some of the harshest criticism of the Merovingian king and were presumably written in the aftermath of Theoderic's earlier, failed embassies. Indeed, according to these letters, Clovis was an "arrogant man" planning an "abominable war." It was imperative for the Frankish king to yield before justice or "suffer the attack of all those whose arbitration he believed worthy of scorn." "Let me say what I feel plainly," Theoderic continued, "he who is willing to act unlawfully is disposed to weaken the kingdoms of us all…if [Clovis] should prevail against so great a kingdom, he will doubtless dare to attack you too" (*Var.* 3.3). It was an ominous prediction, as later events would demonstrate.

Theoderic, therefore, strove for peace but also planned for war. Despite such planning, it seems that the Frankish invasion of Aquitaine and the defeat and death of Alaric II at Vouillé in 507 caught the Ostrogothic king by surprise (see Mathisen, Chapter 19, this volume). Worse still, Clovis's collusion not only with the Byzantine emperor Anastasius but also with the Burgundian king Gundobad suddenly revealed itself, also taking Theoderic by surprise. In the northwest, Burgundians raided the province of Liguria. Meanwhile, in the southeast, a Byzantine fleet devastated the coast of Apulia in a "daring act of piracy" that allowed "Romans to seize a dishonorable victory from other Romans" (Marcellinus, *Chronicon* 508; Schwarcz 1993, pp. 788–790; Arnold 2014, pp. 268–269). Only in the summer of 508 was Italy secure enough for Theoderic to react to the situation in Gaul, mustering his forces and then deploying them across the Alps in an attempt to halt the advancing Franks and Burgundians. The battles that followed in Provence, Septimania, Aquitaine, and Spain over the next three years are conveniently absent from the triumphalistic and pro-Frankish narrative of Gregory of Tours; so too is the participation of Clovis's Burgundian allies (Ewig 1976, p. 124; Delaplace 2000, pp. 78–79; Loseby 2016, pp. 478–479; see also Reimitz, Chapter 22, this volume).[1] Yet the campaign witnessed major Gothic victories over the Franks, Burgundians, and eventually even the Visigoths, most notably at Arles, Carcassonne, and Barcelona, all with serious repercussions for the immediate future of Gaul and Spain (Schwarcz 1993, pp. 791–794; Delaplace 2000, pp. 83–87; Arnold 2014, pp. 270–272). Theoderic, according to Jordanes, won "a great victory over the Franks in Gaul" (*Get.* 302); according to Cassiodorus, "he had defeated the Franks and acquired Gaul for his empire" (*Chronica* 508).

ROMAN GAUL

That Clovis returned to Paris, received an honorary consulship from the Byzantine emperor, donned imperial attire, and was hailed as consul and Augustus is well known from the pages of Gregory of Tours (*Hist.* 2.38). Yet, back in Italy, Ostrogothic victories against the Franks and others in Gaul also served to legitimize Theoderic as the true heir of the Roman emperors (Arnold 2014, pp. 272–274; Arnold 2016, pp. 86–87). In a now fragmentary panegyric, Cassiodorus declared to the Senate that Theoderic had "bridled with his *imperium* the proud barbarians" and made Gaul Roman again (*Orationum Reliquiae*, p. 466). Another senator went further, hailing Theoderic as "always Augustus" and granting him a long list of imperial titles, including "propagator of the Roman name" and "conqueror of the barbarians" (*Inscriptiones Latinae Selectae* 827). Theoderic, too, celebrated his triumphs in Gaul, likely minting around this time a commemorative triple solidus that bore his portrait in an overtly Roman way, with traditional victory iconography and the inscriptions "most invincible *princeps*" and "conqueror of the barbarians" (Arnold 2013). He likewise encouraged his Gallic provincials, now "restored to their ancient liberty," to "cast off barbarism" and wrap themselves "in the morals of the toga" (*Var.* 3.17). Finally, Theoderic even invited Anastasius, the emperor who had conspired with and then honored Clovis, to share in his Gallic exploits, announcing his elevation of a Gallo-Roman named Felix to the consulship of 511. "What could be thought more desirable," the emperor was asked, "than that Rome is restoring her nurslings to her bosom?" (*Var.* 2.1; Arnold 2014, pp. 290–294).

Meanwhile, it seems that relations between the Ostrogoths and all parties in Gaul, including the Franks, normalized to some extent in the wake of Felix's consulship. The sources are admittedly weak, but Gothic-Roman rule appears to have become entrenched in the region during this period (for what follows, see Delaplace 2005, pp. 46–50; Arnold 2014, pp. 278–289; Arnold 2016, 87–91). The frontier in Burgundy, already fixed along the Durance River, was maintained; funds were sent to Arles to rebuild the city's battle-tested walls; soldiers were stationed in important cities, like Arles and Marseille; and occasionally fresh recruits were even deployed for Gaul's continued protection, including federate Gepids from Pannonia sometime in the mid-520s. The Ostrogothic government also took action to ensure that this war-torn region would recover, and aspects of Italy's imperial administration were put in place, including the appointment and arrival of the praetorian prefect Liberius. To the west of the Rhône and in Spain, Theoderic assumed the role of king of the Visigoths, nominally as his grandson Amalaric's guardian, but perhaps with every intention of making the unification of both Gothic kingdoms permanent. At the same time, Ostrogothic soldiers and officials were placed in key cities, like Narbonne and Barcelona, and seem to have mingled with the remnants of the Visigothic army and its nobility (Procop., *Wars* 5.12.43–49). As late as the mid-520s, Theoderic still maintained that these Goths had been sent to the region "to fight for the sake of liberty" (*Var.* 5.39). Perhaps more importantly, his Gothic soldiers continued to engage in occasional skirmishes and "fierce struggles" with the Franks, in the process reclaiming some of Aquitaine, notably the cities of Rodez and Albi (Jord, *Get.* 296; Gregory, *Hist.* 3.21; Ewig 1976, pp. 123–128).

Still, and despite the minor conflicts of this period, Franks and Goths briefly found a common enemy in the Burgundian kingdom of Sigismund. Although Gregory of Tours is, once more, a poor source for these events and does not mention the Goths (*Hist.* 3.5–6; Wood 1994, pp. 52–53), Cassiodorus and Procopius provide evidence for a joint Frankish-Ostrogothic campaign, usually dated to 523 and following Sigismund's murder of his son, Sigiric, who was Theoderic's grandson and a potential successor. Both sources indicate that the Franks did all the fighting but that the Ostrogothic regime reaped the rewards. On the one hand, Procopius suggests that Theoderic intentionally delayed deploying his army but still acquired part of Gaul per an earlier arrangement with the Franks (*Wars* 5.12.24–32). Cassiodorus, on the other hand, claims that the Ostrogothic general Tuluin protected Gaul while the Franks and Burgundians were engaged in disputes and thus, without fatigue or peril, "acquired a province for the Roman Republic" (*Var.* 8.10). Other sources make it clear that these newly acquired lands pushed the Ostrogothic frontier in Provence north to the Isère (Moorhead 1992, pp. 213–216; Delaplace 2003, pp. 483–484).

As Jordanes recounts, "The Goths never yielded to the Franks while Theoderic lived" (*Get.* 296), an assertion that is difficult to deny. Yet, the death of Theoderic in 526 witnessed the Merovingians' renewed aggression in the region, which tested notions of Ostrogothic and Roman supremacy. Even before Theoderic's death, the Franks remained a concern. In Ravenna, there was fear that Theoderic's chief representative in Spain was planning a revolt and that the Franks might exploit the situation (Procop., *Wars* 5.12.50–54). Neither came to fruition; however, Theoderic's concerns do make clear the vulnerability of Ostrogothic possessions west of the Rhône and along the Frankish frontier, a problem that was solved when Theoderic died and Amalaric succeeded as the independent ruler of the Visigoths. The Visigothic kingdom thus went its own way, but its loss may have actually benefited the Ostrogothic state, which fell to Theoderic's other grandson Athalaric, a ten-year-old boy whose mother, Amalasuintha, served as regent and had

Merovingian blood in her veins. Although their ceded territory soon became a major target for Frankish expansion, Gothic losses were now at the expense of the Visigoths and posed an indirect rather than direct threat to the Ostrogothic regime. Indeed, with their Gallic prefecture now restricted to Provence, the Ostrogoths had a much smaller and arguably more manageable border to defend, a border that, into the 530s, was not shared with the Franks (Arnold 2016, p. 92). Nonetheless, the regency of Amalasuintha was vulnerable, both at home and abroad, and the Franks appear to have taken full advantage.

As Procopius relates, there was no one to oppose the Franks after Theoderic died (*Wars* 5.13.1). Worse still, according to Jordanes, "The Franks held [Athalaric] in contempt, having no confidence in the rule of a child and planning for war" (*Get.* 305). But whether the armies of Chlothar, Childebert, or Theuderic ever set their sights on Ostrogothic possessions during this period is less certain. Clearly, the Ostrogoths' neighbors were the main objects of their aggression. While this may have raised alarms in Ravenna, there is little evidence to suggest that Amalasuintha attempted, like her father, to intercede on her allies' behalf. In fact, Jordanes indicates that the Ostrogothic regime looked to its own interests, claiming that Athalaric restored to the Franks, at their insistence, certain long-held lands in Gaul that Theoderic had conquered, an act that allowed the young king to possess his remaining Gallic lands in peace (*Get.* 305; *Romana* 367). The account is contradicted by other sources and is thus confused, but it may refer to Frankish conquests in formerly Ostrogothic but by then Visigothic Aquitaine and Septimania, which met with no Ostrogothic reprisals. Gregory of Tours (*Hist.* 3.23) even relates that Theuderic's son, Theudebert, may have briefly occupied Ostrogothic Arles during these campaigns, probably in 531/532,[2] although the silence of the more reliable and contemporary *Life of Caesarius of Arles* renders this doubtful. The final conquest of long-allied Thuringia in ca. 531/534 also met with no Ostrogothic response, sending the Thuringian queen, Theoderic's niece Amalaberga, fleeing to Italy and, more alarmingly, removing an important buffer to the north of the Alps, which had blocked Frankish access to Italy (Wood 1998, pp. 235–236).

More disturbing, and eventually worthy of intervention, were the Merovingians' repeated attempts in the late 520s and early 530s to conquer Burgundy, a kingdom that shared a very long and historically dangerous frontier with Italy and Provence. Fear of a Frankish Burgundy made strange bedfellows. As already seen, Theoderic had once joined Clovis's sons in their war against the Burgundian king Sigismund. Amalasuintha, however, now allied with Sigismund's successor, Godomar, and even came to his assistance in the face of a Frankish invasion, probably in 532/533. The details are somewhat difficult to reconstruct, but a short panegyric delivered before the Roman senate in 533 provides the main evidence (Cass., *Var.* 11.1.12–13; Favinet-Ranson 1998, pp. 289–291). In it, Cassiodorus praised the "vast expedition" of the Goths, which supposedly so terrified the arrogant and heretofore victorious Franks that they declined to join battle. It also celebrated the bloodless death of Amalasuintha's kinsman, Theuderic I, who had "prided himself for a long time in his mighty name" (an allusion to Theoderic the Great) but had been "overcome by his feebleness more than fighting." Turning next to Godomar,

Cassiodorus made clear the connection between Amalasuintha's triumph and her current relations with Burgundy. Now devoted and obedient, Godomar was said to have "handed himself over completely" to the mistress of Italy, perhaps a reference to some form of client or tributary status. In exchange, he received "what he had lost in battle... his own possessions," either lands that had been liberated from the Franks or, as many have suggested, the territory north of the Durance that Theoderic had annexed a decade earlier (Wolfram 1988, p. 335; Klingshirn 1994, pp. 245–246; Favinet-Ranson 1998, p. 290). Whatever the case, Cassiodorus was confident that the restoration of these lands, along with Godomar's allegiance, would create "a safer [Burgundian] kingdom." The events were even hailed in Italy with the same imperial and Roman language utilized decades earlier in celebration of Theoderic's Gallic victories, although such optimism soon proved to be misplaced. In 533, Amalasuintha could be described as "blessed," since she had "either defeated the enemies of the Republic or joined them to her *imperium* through her voluntary munificence." But in 534 the situation was markedly different; the Franks had invaded Burgundy yet again, and they were now led by Childebert, Chlothar, and Theuderic's successor, Theudebert. This time, Ostrogothic support was nowhere to be found, Godomar was slain, and his kingdom was partitioned among its Merovingian conquerors. The Burgundian buffer once separating the Ostrogoths from the Franks suddenly disappeared.

Amalasuintha was thus able to count, if only for a moment, a major victory over the Franks that might have made her father proud. Although the Franks still succeeded in expanding their realm at the expense of her allies and came to share a lengthy border with the Ostrogothic kingdom, Italy and Provence nonetheless remained untouched during her regency. Her death, or better murder, in 535 at the instigation of her cousin and royal consort, Theodahad, would serve as the principal justification for the Byzantine invasion of Italy and the lengthy Gothic War that followed, events that quickly altered Frankish relations with the Ostrogoths, the Empire, and Italy itself. But at the time of Belisarius's landing in Sicily, according to Procopius, the Goths were still successfully defending Gaul against their ancient Frankish enemies and holding their own, just as they had always done (*Wars* 5.13.15–19).

THE GOTHIC WAR

Gregory of Tours reports that Amalasuintha's Merovingian cousins felt the need to avenge her "shameful death" and thus extorted 50,000 pieces of gold from Theodahad by threatening to kill him and seize his kingdom (*Hist.* 3.31). However, the bishop's story cannot be verified, and his representation of Ostrogothic and Italian history should be used with caution (Loseby 2016, p. 477). Nevertheless, the origin of Gregory's tale may have something to do with the account of Procopius, who relates that Theodahad did enter into negotiations with Childebert, Chlothar, and Theudebert in 536, but for a military alliance against the Byzantines, who had taken Sicily and appeared poised to take

Dalmatia. Threatened by these developments, Theodahad offered to cede all remaining Ostrogothic possessions in Gaul in addition to 20 *centenaria*, that is, 2,000 Roman pounds of gold (*Wars* 5.13.14). Yet, unbeknownst to Theodahad, these Merovingian kings had already eagerly promised to fight as the allies of Emperor Justinian, who purchased Frankish assistance with a gift of money (*Wars* 5.5.8–10). Meanwhile, nothing came of Theodahad's proposal, as the Ostrogothic army revolted and elected Witigis as its king. Theodahad was promptly executed, while the Franks made good on their alliance with Justinian, engaging the Goths in Provence (*Wars* 5.11.17) and apparently sending Burgundians, Alamanni, and Suevi, all subject peoples, to raid Liguria, Aemilia, and Venetia in 536 (Cass., *Var.* 12.7; 12.28; *Epistolae Austrasicae* 19, with Ewig 1983, p. 19). Their audacity and "barbaric savagery," according to Cassiodorus, offered Witigis fresh triumphs, allowing "the fame of the present empire to suddenly beam forth as if the rising sun" (*Var.* 12.28).

Such words are consistent with the Roman and imperial ideologies of prior Ostrogothic regimes, yet they also provide the final evidence for a specifically Ostrogothic perspective on the Franks and events unfolding in Italy. After 536, the Goths and their Roman partisans are silent, and one must rely on Byzantine and Frankish sources instead. Chief among these is the account of Procopius, who relates that, despite Witigis's early victories, the dangers of fighting a war along multiple fronts were not lost on the Gothic king. After much deliberation, he decided to make peace with the Franks and to seek their military assistance by offering the same terms as Theodahad (*Wars* 5.11.17–18; 5.13.17–26). As a further incentive, Witigis also offered to give up his hegemony over the Alamanni in Rhaetia and Noricum, effectively abandoning these provinces to Frankish rule (Agathias, *Histories* 1.6). Chlothar, Childebert, and Theudebert gladly accepted these terms and agreed to become "especially friendly to the Goths." However, because of their current alliance with the emperor, they promised to support the Goths in secret, namely, by deploying more subject nations to Italy rather than actual Frankish troops (*Wars* 5.13.27–29).

By early 537, therefore, Ostrogothic rule had ended both in Provence and in Italy's Alpine provinces, the former divided among all the Merovingian kings, the latter coming under the rule of Theudebert alone. Theudebert, however, would be the only Merovingian king to involve himself directly in the Gothic War, in part because his Austrasian kingdom shared the largest frontier with Italy, and in part, as will be seen, because of his own ambitions. The sources are somewhat laconic but make clear that in 537/538 he dispatched an army of some 10,000 Burgundians to Liguria, which, he claimed, were acting of their own volition. While Witigis remained in Ravenna, these forces joined with a portion of the Gothic army and attempted to vindicate the region from the Byzantines (*Wars* 6.12.38–40, 6.21.13). In 538/539, they took Milan by storm, supposedly demolishing the city and committing a number of atrocities against its inhabitants. All males, according to Procopius, were killed, while the women were enslaved and given to the Burgundians as payment (*Wars* 6.21.39). Even senators and priests who sought sanctuary in churches, according to another source, were not spared (Marius of Avenches, *Chronica* 538).

Nothing further is heard of these Burgundians, who likely returned home with their spoils. Yet the outrages committed at Milan may have struck a nerve in Ravenna, as

Witigis began searching for alternative allies in the winter of 538/539, fearing the trustworthiness of the Merovingians, who were still technically Justinian's allies. Hoping that the Franks might be convinced to remain neutral, he appealed first to the Lombard king Waccho but was turned down because the Lombards were already friends and allies of the emperor (*Wars* 6.22.10–12); they were also friends of Theudebert, who had been betrothed to Waccho's daughter, Wisigard, and probably married her around this time (Gregory, *Hist.* 3.27; Löhlein 1932, p. 29). Witigis next appealed to the Persians, who were sympathetic and whose preparations for war against Justinian so alarmed the emperor that he hastened to make peace with the Ostrogoths (*Wars* 6.22.15–22).

Still, Witigis's hope for Frankish neutrality was ill placed. In the spring of 539, Theudebert himself crossed into Liguria with a large army. Although he secretly intended to conquer much of Italy for himself, the local Goths believed that the Franks had finally come to assist them and offered no resistance. Nonetheless, Theudebert revealed his true intentions at Pavia, crossing the Po and then slaughtering the city's population. Procopius's accusation that the Franks sacrificed Gothic women and children according to pagan rites is probably fanciful, but it does echo the anti-Frankish propaganda of the Theoderican era (*Wars* 6.25.1–10; James 1988, p. 97; Rohr 2001, pp. 26–27). Theudebert then continued south into Aemilia, encountering and defeating both an Ostrogothic and a Byzantine army; the former fled to Ravenna, and the latter to Tuscany (*Wars* 6.25.11–16). Plundering followed, including the subjugation and ransacking of Genoa; however, by the end of the summer, Theudebert's army was suffering from starvation and disease, leading the Frankish king to come to terms with Belisarius (*Wars* 6.25.17–24; Marcell., *Chron. addit.* 539.4). No mention is made of conditions; nor does one hear of similar agreements with the Ostrogoths. What is clear, at least, is that Theudebert returned to Gaul with most of his army, leaving behind an occupational force led by the dukes Butilinus, Mumolenus, and Amingus (Jonas, *Life of John of Réomé* 15; Paul the Deacon, *History of the Lombards* 2.2; cf. Jord., *Rom.* 375; Gregory, *Hist.* 3.32). These and possibly other officials continued to exact tribute from portions of Liguria and possibly the Cottian Alps (Löhlein 1932, p. 35), rendering Theudebert an Italian monarch in his own right. Although Frankish envoys arrived in Ravenna early the next year, offering to renew their alliance and to share the rule of Italy with the Goths, Witigis was not convinced. In fact, he and the Gothic nobility determined that the Franks were completely untrustworthy and opted to make peace with the Byzantines instead (*Wars* 6.28.7–23). By May of the same year, the gates of Ravenna were opened to Belisarius and the first phase of the Gothic War had concluded.

FRANKISH ITALY

Theudebert, meanwhile, celebrated his Italian victories in an overtly Roman and imperial way, much as Theoderic the Great had done following his Gallic campaign roughly three decades earlier. Indeed, this "great king," as he was later remembered (Gregory, *Hist.* 3.25; Marius, *Chron.* 548), went further, minting a variety of high-quality gold coins throughout the 540s that bore his name and likeness, accompanied by traditional symbols of victory and a number of Roman imperial legends, including "conqueror of the barbarians," "victory of the Augusti," and "peace and liberty" (Prou 1892, pp. 9–16; Collins 1983, pp. 28–30). These were not commemorative pieces like Theoderic's triple solidus, but actual currency that blatantly infringed upon the Byzantine emperor's prerogatives and thus speak to Theudebert's imperial pretensions (*Wars* 7.33.5–6). Nor were such pretensions lost on the emperor in Constantinople, whose own frontiers now appeared threatened by Frankish, and specifically Theudebert's, imperialism (Agath., *Hist.* 1.4; *Epist. Aust.* 20; see also Esders, Chapter 16, this volume). In fact, it may have been with an eye to checking further Frankish expansion in the Balkans that Justinian turned to the Lombards, heretofore friendly to the Franks, and invited them to settle in Pannonia Savia and eastern Noricum (*Wars* 7.33.7–9; Ewig 1983, p. 21; Christou 1991, pp. 76–86). The act, which occurred late in Theudebert's reign, may have upset Franco-Lombard relations to some extent, sowing the seeds for a Frankish duchy in Bavaria (Hammer 2011, pp. 228–231) and leading to an "unhappy" marriage between Theudebert's son, Theudebald, and the Lombard princess, Wuldetrada (Gregory, *Hist.* 4.9; Paul, *Hist. Lomb.* 1.21).

Nevertheless, the narrative sources leave much to be desired with respect to Frankish operations in the Alps and Italy during the 540s and how these colored Merovingian relations with the Ostrogoths. What is clear is that Theudebert's dukes consolidated and then expanded their positions, especially in the wake of the revolts that began in neighboring Transpadane cities and reignited the Gothic War. Initially abortive, these revolts soon led to the rise of the Gothic king Totila (r. 541–552), whose campaigns against the Byzantines proved extremely effective and resulted in the Goths' virtual reconquest of Italy. The details are again shadowy, but Theudebert benefited from the situation and even cooperated with Totila at times, even if he supposedly mocked the Gothic king and denied him the Merovingian bride he requested (*Wars* 7.37.1–2). Indeed, by the time of Theudebert's death in 547/548, Procopius relates that the Franks had gained control over not only portions of Liguria and the Cottian Alps, but also, and with Totila's consent, the largest part of Venetia, leaving only a few forts to the Goths and certain coastal towns to the Byzantines (*Wars* 8.24.6–10). The Franks thus increased their Italian holdings, while Totila acquired their assistance and a valuable Frankish buffer that might block the Byzantine land route to Italy. Moreover, the Franks proved trustworthy and reliable allies for once, as Justinian's attempts to win over Theudebert's successor, Theudebald, came to nothing. Instead, the young Merovingian continued to hinder the Byzantine war effort (Marius, *Chron.* 548.1; *Wars* 8.24.11–30), and in 552, the Frankish buffer in Venetia served its purpose, barring General Narses from entering Italy on the pretense that his massive army included a number of Lombards within its ranks. By 552, it seems, the Lombards had become the Franks' "bitterest enemies," while the Ostrogoths were considered their good friends (*Wars* 8.26.12–19; Agath., *Hist.*1.5.3).

Despite this obstacle, Narses and his army proceeded along the Byzantine-held coast, eventually encountering and defeating the Goths at the decisive Battle of Taginae in July of 552. Totila lost his life, while the remnants of the Gothic army withdrew to Pavia and rallied behind Teias, who was proclaimed king. Teias quickly sought to renew his predecessor's Frankish alliance, sending envoys to Gaul with a large sum of money. Although the Franks in Venetia assisted the Goths at this time, preventing the Byzantines from taking Verona, Teias's envoys to the court of Theudebald were unsuccessful and received no Frankish assistance (*Wars* 8.33.5–7; 8.34.17–18). Late that year, the Gothic army engaged Narses in yet another decisive contest at Mons Lactarius and was annihilated. Teias, too, lost his life, while many Goths were forced to come to terms with Narses, returning to their homes and agreeing to become subjects of the emperor (Schmidt 1943, pp. 3–6; Wolfram 1988, pp. 359–361).

Ostrogothic kingship thus ended in Italy; yet the Franks retained their north Italian enclave, and pockets of Gothic resistance persisted throughout the peninsula. Soon, the Goths residing north of the Po sought another Frankish alliance, offering Theudebald money and warning that, with the Gothic race exterminated, the Franks might be next (Agath., *Hist.* 1.5.1). Although the Merovingian king rejected the offer, two members of his court accepted it. These were the brothers Butilinus and Leutharis, who were dukes of the Alamanni, a people once subject to the Ostrogoths. As seen above, Butilinus was a veteran of Theudebert's Italian campaign of 539 and may have been residing in Italy or perhaps Rhaetia or Noricum at the time (Löhlein 1932, p. 47). In 553, the two dukes led a very large army comprised of Franks and Alamanni and were quite successful against the Byzantines, reaching as far as the strait of Messina (Agath. *Hist.* 2.1; cf. Gregory, *Hist.* 3.32). Many Goths opened their gates to them, while the Transpadane Goths even considered making Butilinus their king (Agath., *Hist.* 1.15.6; 2.2). An Ostrogothic Italy ruled by an Alamannic king was not to be, however. In 554, Leutharis and his army headed for home, intending to send Butilinus reinforcements; they arrived safely in Frankish Venetia but were then decimated by an outbreak of plague. Meanwhile, Butilinus and his army encountered Narses near Capua. The Franks and Alamanni were routed and slaughtered, and Butilinus himself was killed.

What hope there was for an Ostrogothic Italy probably died with Butilinus, yet joint Franco-Gothic resistance to Narses continued. The sources are, again, fragmentary, but it is clear that Chlothar, who succeeded to Theudebald's kingdom in 555, remained concerned with the situation in Italy, even if he was distracted by affairs closer to home. Indeed, Narses pressed his advantage after the defeat of Butilinus and invaded northern Italy the following year. Although Chlothar's Franks held their own, the "army of the Republic" eventually defeated them and "occupied the part of Italy that King Theudebert had acquired," meaning the Cottian Alps and Liguria (Marius, *Chron.* 556.4). In Venetia, meanwhile, Franks and Goths continued to oppose the Byzantines, agreeing to a ceasefire by 560. Probably within this context Chlothar, sole king of the Franks since 558, sought to strengthen ties with the neighboring Lombards, who were still Byzantine allies. He thus offered his daughter, Chlodoswintha, to the Lombard king Alboin and married Theudebald's widow, the Lombard princess Wuldetrada, to the Frankish duke of Bavaria, Garibald (Gregory, *Hist.* 4.3; 4.9; Löhlein 1932, p. 49; Ewig 1983, pp. 24–25). However, Chlothar's death in 561 led to a series of conflicts among his successors and coincided with renewed hostilities in northern Italy. The latter were led by the Gothic count Widin and supported by the Frankish duke of Venetia, Amingus, another veteran of Theudebert's invasion. Despite some success, their forces were eventually crushed and Amingus was killed (Menander Protector, *Fragmenta* 3; Paul, *Hist. Lomb.* 2.2). By 562/563, Verona and Brescia, the centers of Gothic resistance, had surrendered and, with this, both an Ostrogothic and a Frankish Italy ceased to exist (Malalas, *Chronicle* 18.140; Agnellus, *Book of the Pontiffs of Ravenna* 90; Löhlein 1932, pp. 49–51; Schmidt 1943, p. 7).

Merovingians and Lombards

Italian unity under Byzantine rule was nonetheless short-lived and faced a number of obstacles, including financial and physical exhaustion, plague, and the continued threat of the Franks. Although Sigibert, who succeeded to the Austrasian kingdom, may have supported an uprising of the Heruli near the Brenner pass in 565/566 (Löhlein 1932, pp. 51–52), the Franks remained preoccupied with domestic concerns, not least a series of civil wars and two invasions by the Avars (on which see Hardt, Chapter 20, this volume). Still, the arrival of the Lombards in Italy in 568/569 may represent a concerted effort by the Byzantine government to defend the war-torn north against a potential Frankish (or other barbarian) invasion using trusted allies and veterans of the Gothic War. That Venetia offered little resistance to their approach may even suggest that the Byzantines had intended to settle the Lombards in this province, only recently wrested from the Franks (Christie 1991; Christou 1991, pp. 108–114). Alternatively, the Lombard king Alboin realized how vulnerable Italy was at this time and simply took advantage of the situation.

Whatever the case, the Lombards were joined by Saxons and other peoples, rendering their army just as polyethnic as Theoderic's. Turning on their former allies, they entered Italy and conquered much of Venetia and Liguria over the next three years. Raiding parties were also sent into central and southern Italy, while as early as 569 certain dukes began crossing the Alps and plundering the kingdom of Burgundy, then ruled by Sigibert's brother and rival Guntram. The reasons for these Gallic expeditions are uncertain, as is the current status of Franco-Lombard relations. Alboin's Merovingian wife had recently died, but his alliance with the Austrasian kingdom may have persisted and led Sigibert to incite Lombard forces against his brother (Christie 1995, pp. 80–81). Regardless, Lombard and Saxon assaults on Burgundy and Provence became a regular phenomenon for the next five years, during which time Alboin and his successor Clef (r. 572–574) were busy consolidating control over much of Italy. These Gallic campaigns met with mixed results, however. The "strong army" dispatched in 569 perished miserably, and its survivors were sold into slavery (Paul, *Hist. Lomb.* 3.1–2; Marius, *Chron.* 569). In contrast, the army sent in 570 returned to Italy with "incalculable spoils," having defeated and killed the Frankish patrician Amatus and made "so great a slaughter of the Burgundians that the number of slain men could not be calculated" (Paul, *Hist. Lomb.* 3.3). Frankish victories followed under the capable generalship of Amatus's successor,

Eunius Mummolus, who defeated multiple incursions by the Lombards and Saxons, the latter of which were eventually resettled in Sigibert's Austrasian kingdom (Gregory, *Hist.* 4.42; Fredegar, *Chronicle* 3.68; Paul, *Hist. Lomb.* 3.4–6). A final Lombard invasion occurred in 574, following the death of King Clef and the beginning of a ten-year inter-regnum in Italy. This campaign was led by the dukes Zaban, Amo, Rodan, Taloard, and Nuccio, who split their forces and plundered the regions around Arles, Grenoble, Valence, and Saint-Maurice. Taloard and Nuccio were defeated and killed by the Frankish dukes Wiolic and Theudefred. Near Embrun, likewise, Mummolus annihilated the joint forces of Rodan and Zaban, pursuing them across the Alps and causing Amo to retreat (Gregory, *Hist.* 4.44; Marius, *Chron.* 574; Fred., *Chron.* 3.68; Paul, *Hist. Lomb.* 3.8). The chief Lombard dukes in Italy then sued Guntram for peace in 575, ceding the regions around Aosta and Susa, offering to pay an annual tribute of 12,000 solidi and agreeing to some form of alliance (Fred., *Chron.* 3.68; 4.45; Löhlein 1932, pp. 55–60; Christie 1995, pp. 81–82).

Guntram remained on friendly terms with the Lombards for the rest of his reign (d. 592), despite repeated attempts by his fellow Merovingians and the Byzantines to convince him to alter his policies. The Byzantine strategies included appeals from the papacy and even a Constantinopolitan-backed coup in 584/585 known as the Gundovald affair, which aimed to replace Guntram with a more sympathetic king (Goffart 1957; Ewig 1983, pp. 29–36). Meanwhile, though failing to dislodge the Lombards on their own, the Byzantines had better luck with the Austrasian court and individual Lombard dukes, which they plied with subsidies (Menander, *frag.* 22 and 24). Sigibert had already established peace with the emperor in 571/572, and his pro-Byzantine policies continued during the minor rule of his son, Childebert II, who was proclaimed king in 575. Indeed, Austrasian intervention against the Lombards began as early as 575/576, when the Frankish duke Chramnichis invaded Italy and took the fortress of Nano near Trent, likely in support of the Byzantine general Baduarius. Both, however, were defeated, and in the aftermath the Lombard duke of Trent, Euin, not only consolidated his control over the region but also established a marriage alliance with Garibald of Bavaria, an important event with long-term repercussions (Paul, *Hist. Lomb.* 3.9–10; Löhlein 1932, pp. 62–64; Christie 1995, p. 86; Hammer 2011, pp. 231f.).

In the short term, however, the alliance may have helped to secure a temporary peace between the Austrasian court and the Lombards, against whom no action was taken for the rest of the decade. Still, the Byzantines continued to lobby for Frankish intervention in Italy, agreeing to subsidize an Austrasian mission in 581 that proved abortive (*Epist. Aust.* 48; Goffart 1957, pp. 77–80; Ewig 1983, p. 28 n. 111). A few years later, the emperor Mauricius complained that Childebert had received 50,000 solidi to "drive the Lombards out of Italy" and had not fulfilled his promises (Gregory, *Hist.* 6.42). However, only in 584 did Childebert, or more likely his generals, lead a large army of Franks into Italy. The account of Gregory of Tours, which was later sanitized by Paul the Deacon, relates that the Lombards submitted to Childebert's authority immediately, giving him gifts and promising to become his faithful subjects (cf. *Hist.* 6.42 and Paul, *Hist. Lomb.* 3.17; also Fred., *Chron.* 3.92; John of Biclarum, *Chronicle* 584.4). Such an outcome failed to please the emperor, who demanded his solidi back to no avail, but it soon convinced the independent Lombard dukes to elect Clef's son, Authari, as their king. Although Fredegar suggests that they did so with the expressed permission of the Franks (*Chron.* 4.45), Childebert was pressured to undertake a new mission to Italy the following year, as the Byzantines had stumbled upon the young king's sister and nephew in Spain and were, in effect, holding them hostage (Goffart 1957, pp. 107–116; Ewig 1983, pp. 37–46). In 585, therefore, an army of Franks and Alamanni invaded Italy but accomplished nothing (Gregory, *Hist.* 8.18; Paul, *Hist. Lomb.* 3.22).

In the meantime, Authari continued to expand against the Byzantines and, much like Theoderic and Totila before him, sought a Merovingian bride as a means of establishing peace between both peoples. Childebert even promised the Lombard king his sister, Chlodosinda, but then, in 587, betrothed her to the Visigothic king Reccared instead (Gregory, *Hist.* 9.25; Paul, *Hist. Lomb.* 3.28). Adding further insult to injury, Childebert caved to imperial pressure the same year, sending another army to Italy that met with some success (John, *Chron.* 587.3). He even attempted to win his uncle, Guntram, to the cause, claiming that he intended to reconquer the lands of his father, presumably in Lombard-held Venetia (Gregory, *Hist.* 9.20). At any rate, Guntram declined to participate, while the Austrasian troops sent across the Alps in 588 were cut to pieces by the Lombards. "So great was the slaughter of the Frankish army there," Gregory recorded, "that nothing like it could be remembered" (*Hist.* 9.25; cf. Paul, *Hist. Lomb.* 3.29). The following year, Authari sought a new marriage alliance with Garibald of Bavaria, who may have been aiming at establishing an independent duchy or even kingdom with Lombard support (Hammer 2011, pp. 231–233). Whatever the case, Childebert's forces subsequently invaded Bavaria and deposed Garibald, whose daughter, Theudelinda, managed to escape to Verona; there she married Authari in 589, proving herself a very influential queen for the next three decades (Paul, *Hist. Lomb.* 3.30; Balzaretti 1999). That same year, war was averted with Childebert through Lombard envoys, who promised the king tribute and military aid (Gregory, *Hist.* 9.29).

Nevertheless, in 590 Childebert and his Franks made one final attempt to dislodge the Lombards from Italy, this time in support of a major campaign led by the Byzantine exarch, Romanus. While Romanus's efforts were remarkably successful, capturing cities and fomenting Lombard revolts, Childebert's dukes showed themselves to be disappointingly unreliable (Christou 1991, pp. 144–145; Christie 1995, pp. 87–89). The forces of Audovald and some seven dukes attacked the region around Milan. At the same time, another thirteen dukes led by Cedinus entered the duchy of Trent, captured a number of forts, and penetrated as far as Verona. By the late summer, however, these Frankish forces were suffering from disease and starvation (on military provisioning, see Sarti, Chapter 12, this volume). "Wandering all over Italy for three months," they failed to make additional headway against the Lombards, who simply "barricaded themselves in very secure places" (Gregory, *Hist.* 10.3; cf. Paul, *Hist. Lomb.* 3.31). Although Romanus later complained that he had intended to join forces with the Franks, march on Pavia, and then capture the Lombard capital and king, his allies upset these plans. Some had already departed for Gaul; the rest remained with Cedinus, who, despite Romanus's instructions, negotiated a separate ten-month truce with Authari, exacted oaths of allegiance, and then returned home (*Epist. Aust.* 40).

Following this campaign, relations between the Franks and Lombards normalized considerably, setting the tone for the rest of this century and much of the next. Authari sent envoys to Guntram and Childebert in the fall of 590, seeking peace and concord, promising to be "true and obedient," and agreeing to continue paying an annual tribute (Gregory, *Hist.* 10.3; Paul, *Hist. Lomb.* 3.34). However, the Lombard king died in the midst of these negotiations, and a series of embassies followed on behalf of his successor, Agilulf (r. 590–616), the last of which was led by Duke Euin of Trent and established what proved to be an enduring peace (Gregory, *Hist.* 10.3; Paul, *Hist. Lomb.* 3.35–4.1). Indeed, despite the vicissitudes of contemporary Merovingian politics, Agilulf maintained good relations with the Franks for the entirety of his reign, agreeing to multiple treaties of "perpetual peace," securing a Merovingian bride for his son and successor, Adaloald, and eventually negotiating for the termination of the Lombards' annual tribute (Paul, *Hist. Lomb.* 4.13, 4.30, 4.40; Fred., *Chron.* 4.45). Frankish friendship and neutrality aided Agilulf considerably during this period, allowing him to consolidate and then expand his kingdom at the expense of the Byzantines. In 605 the emperor Phocas agreed to a truce. In 610, Lombard envoys secured a peace in Constantinople that would last for more than thirty years (Ewig 1983, pp. 59–61; Christou 1991, pp. 146–159; Christie 1995, pp. 89–91). Gone from Italy were the Ostrogoths; gone were the Franks, who would not mount another successful invasion of the peninsula until the Carolingian era. Truly, the Lombards had arrived.

Notes

1. I would like to express my gratitude to Simon Loseby for providing me with a copy of his essay in advance of its publication.
2. This style of dating will be used whenever an exact year cannot be determined but likely falls within the range provided. Thus, in this instance, the event probably happened in 531, 532, or even both.

Works Cited

Ancient Sources

Agathias, *Histories*. J. D. Frendo (trans.). (1975). *Agathias, The Histories*. Berlin: Walter de Gruyter.
Agnellus, *Book of the Pontiffs of Ravenna*: D. M. Deliyannis (ed.). (2006). *Agnelli Ravennatis Liber Pontificalis Ecclesiae Ravennatis*. CCCM 199. Turnhout: Brepols.
Anonymus Valesianus. J. Moreau (ed.). (1968). *Excerpta Valesiana*. Leipzig: B. G. Teubner.
Avitus of Vienne, *Epistulae*. R. Peiper (ed.). (1883). *Alcimi Ecdicii Aviti Viennensis episcopi Opera quae supersunt*. MGH AA 6.2. Berlin: Weidmann.
Cassiodorus, *Chronica*. T. Mommsen (ed.). (1894). *Cassiodori Senatoris chronica ad a. DXIX*. MGH AA 11. (pp. 109–161). Berlin: Weidmann.
Cassiodorus, *Orationum Reliquiae*. L. Traube (ed.). (1894). *Cassiodori orationum reliquiae*. MGH AA 12. (pp. 457–484). Berlin: Weidmann.
Cassiodorus, *Variae*. T. Mommsen (ed.). (1894). *Cassiodori Senatoris Variae*. MGH AA 12. Berlin: Weidmann.

Ennodius, *Vita Epiphanii*. F. Vogel. (ed.). (1885). *Magni Felicis Ennodii Opera*. MGH AA 7 (pp. 84–109). Berlin: Weidmann.

Ennodius, *Panegyricus*. C. Rohr (ed. and trans.). (1995). *Der Theoderich-Panegyricus des Ennodius*. MGH: Studien und Texte 12. Hanover: Hahn.

Epistolae Austrasicae. W. Gundlach (ed.). (1892). MGH Epist. 3 (pp. 110–153). Berlin: Weidmann.

Fredegar, *Chronicle*. B. Krusch (ed.). (1888). *Chronicarum quae dicuntur Fredegarii Scholastici libri IV. Cum Continuationibus*. MGH SRM 2 (pp. 1–194). Hanover: Hahn.

Gregory of Tours, *Histories*. B. Krusch and W. Levison (eds.). (1951). *Gregorii episcopi Turonensis libri historiarum X*. MGH SRM 1.1. Hanover: Hahn.

Inscriptiones Latinae Selectae. H. Dessau (ed.). (1974). *Inscriptiones Latinae Selectae*. 3 vols. Berlin: Weidmann.

John of Biclarum, *Chronicle*. T. Mommsen (ed.). (1894). *Iohannis abbatis Biclarensis chronica a. DLXVII-DXC*. MGH AA 11. (pp. 207–220). Berlin: Weidmann.

Jonas, *Life of John of Réomé*. B. Krusch (ed.).(1896). *Vita Iohannis abbatis Reomaensis auctore Iona*. MGH SRM 3 (pp. 502–517). Hanover: Hahn.

Jordanes, *Getica*. T. Mommsen (ed.). (1882). *De origine actibusque Getarum*. MGH AA 5.1 (pp. 53–138). Berlin: Weidmann.

Jordanes, *Romana*. T. Mommsen (ed.). (1882). *De summa temporum vel origine actibusque gentis romanorum*. MGH AA 5.1 (pp. 1–52). Berlin: Weidmann.

Life of Caesarius of Arles. B. Krusch (ed.). (1896). *Vitae Caesarii episcopi Arelatensis libri duo auctoribus Cypriano, Firmino, Viventio episcopis, Messiano presbytero, Stephano diacono*. MGH SRM 3 (pp. 433–501). Hanover, Hahn.

Malalas, *Chronicle*. E. Jeffreys, M. Jeffreys, and R. Scott (trans.). (1986). *The Chronicle of John Malalas*. Melbourne: Australian Association for Byzantine Studies.

Marcellinus, *Chronicon*. T. Mommsen (ed.). (1894). *Marcellini v. c. comitis chronicon ad a. DXVIII continuatum ad a. DXXXIV. Additamentum ad a. DXLVIII*. MGH AA 11. (pp. 37–108). Berlin: Weidmann.

Marius of Avenches, *Chronica*. T. Mommsen (ed.). (1894). *Marii episcopi Aventicensis chronica a. CCCCLV–DLXXXI*. MGH AA 11. (pp. 225–239). Berlin: Weidmann.

Menander, *Fragmenta*. R. C. Blockley (ed. and trans.). (1985). *The History of Menander the Guardsman: Introductory Essay, Text, Translation, and Historiographical Notes*. Liverpool: Francis Cairns.

Paul the Deacon, *History of the Lombards*. L. Bethmann and G. Waitz (eds.). (1878). *Pauli historia Langobardorum*. MGH SRL 1. Hanover: Hahn.

Procopius, *Wars*. H. B. Dewing (trans.). (1914–1928). *Procopius*. 5 vols. Cambridge, MA: Harvard University Press.

Modern Sources

Arnold, J. J. (2012). "The Battle of Vouillé and the Restoration of the Roman Empire." In R. W. Mathisen and D. Shanzer (eds.), *The Battle of Vouillé, 507 CE: Where France Began* (pp. 111–136). Berlin: Walter de Gruyter.

Arnold, J. J. (2013). "Theoderic's Invincible Mustache." *Journal of Late Antiquity* 6(1): 152–183.

Arnold, J. J. (2014). *Theoderic and the Roman Imperial Restoration*. New York: Cambridge University Press.

Arnold, J. J. (2016). "Ostrogothic Provinces: Administration and Ideology." In J. J. Arnold, M. S. Bjornlie, and K. Sessa (eds.), *A Companion to Ostrogothic Italy* (pp. 73–97). Leiden: Brill.

Balzaretti, R. (1999). "Theodelinda, 'Most Glorious Queen': Gender and Power in Lombard Italy." *The Medieval Journal* 2(2): 183–207.

Christie, N. (1991). "Invasion or Invitation? The Longobard occupation of northern Italy, A.D. 568–569." *Romanobarbarica* 11: 79–108.

Christie, N. (1995). *The Lombards: The Ancient Longobards.* Oxford: Blackwell.

Christou, K. P. (1991). *Byzanz und die Langobarden: von der Ansiedlung in Pannonien bis zur endgültigen Anerkennung (500–680).* Athens: S. D. Basilopoulos.

Collins, R. (1983). "Theodobert I, 'Rex Magnus Francorum.'" In P. Wormald (ed.), *Ideal and Reality in Frankish and Anglo-Saxon Society: Studies Presented to J. M. Wallace-Hadrill* (pp. 7–33). Oxford: Blackwell.

Delaplace, C. (2000). "La 'Guerre de Provence' (507–511), un épisode oublié de la domination ostrogothique en Occident." In *Romanité et cité chrétienne: Permanences et mutations intégration et exclusion du Ier au VIe siècle: Mélanges en l'honneur d'Yvette Duval* (pp. 77–89). Paris: De Boccard, 2000.

Delaplace, C. (2003). "La Provence sous la domination ostrogothique (508–536)." *Annales du Midi* 115(244): 479–499.

Delaplace, C. (2005). "La Provence dans la géostratégie des royaumes wisigoth et ostrogoth (418–536): une occupation décisive pour la Gaule du Sud à l'époque mérovingienne." In X. Delestre, P. Périn, and M. Kazanski (eds.), *La Méditerranée et le monde mérovingien: témoins archéologiques* (pp. 45–51). Aix-en-Provence: Association Provence Archéologie.

Demandt, A. (1989). "The Osmosis of the Late Roman and Germanic Aristocracies." In E. K. Chrysos and A. Schwarcz (eds.), *Das Reich und die Barbaren* (pp. 75–86). Vienna: Böhlau.

Ewig, E. (1976). "Die fränkischen Teilungen und Teilreiche (511–613)." In H. Atsma (ed.), *Spätantikes und fränkisches Gallien: Gesammelte Schriften (1952–1973)* 1 (pp. 114–171). Munich: Artemis.

Ewig, E. (1983). *Die Merowinger und das Imperium.* Opladen: Westdeutscher Verlag.

Favinet-Ranson, V. (1998). "Portrait d'une régente. Un panégyrique d'Amalasonthe (Cassiodorus, *Variae* 11,1)." *Cassiodorus* 4, 267–308.

Gillett, A. (2003). *Envoys and Political Communication in the Late Antique West, 411–533.* Cambridge: Cambridge University Press.

Goffart, W. (1957). "Byzantine Policy in the West under Tiberius II and Maurice: The Pretenders Hermenegild and Gundovald (579–585)." *Traditio* 13: 73–118.

Hammer, C. I. (2011). "Early Merovingian Bavaria: A Late Antique Italian Perspective." *Journal of Late Antiquity* 4(2): 217–244.

Herrin, J. (2013). *Unrivalled Influence: Women and Empire in Byzantium.* Princeton, NJ: Princeton University Press.

James, E. (1988). *The Franks.* Oxford: Blackwell.

Klingshirn, W. E. (1994). *Caesarius of Arles: The Making of a Christian Community in Late Antique Gaul.* Cambridge: Cambridge University Press.

Löhlein, G. (1932). *Die Alpen- und Italienpolitik der Merowinger im VI. Jahrhundert.* Erlangen: Palm & Enke.

Loseby, S. T. (2016). "Gregory of Tours, Italy, and the Empire." In A. C. Murray (ed.), *A Companion to Gregory of Tours* (pp. 462–497). Leiden: Brill.

Meier, M. (2009). *Anastasios I: Die Entstehung des Byzantinischen Reiches.* Stuttgart: Klett-Cotta.

Moorhead, J. (1992). *Theoderic in Italy.* Oxford: Clarendon Press.

Prou, M. (1892). *Les monnaies mérovingiennes.* Paris: C. Rollin & Feuardent.

Rohr, C. (2001). "Ennodio Panegirista di Teoderico e il conflitto fra Ostrogoti e Franchi." In F. Gasti (ed.), *Atti della prima Giornata Ennodiana: Pavia, 29–30 marzo 2000* (pp. 21–29). Pisa: Edizioni ETS.

Schmidt, L. (1943). "Die letzten Ostgoten." *Abhandlungen der Preußischen Akademie der Wissenschaften, Philosophisch-historische Klasse* 10: 1–15.

Schwarcz, A. (1993). "Die *Restitutio Galliarum* des Theoderich." In *Teoderico il Grande e i Goti d'Italia: atti del XIII Congresso internazionale di studi sull'Alto Medioevo, Milano 2–6 novembre 1992* (pp. 787–798). Spoleto: Centro italiano di studi sull'alto Medioevo.

Wolfram, H. (1988). *History of the Goths,* trans. T. J. Dunlap. Berkeley: University of California Press.

Wood, I. (1994). *The Merovingian Kingdoms, 450–751.* London: Longman.

Wood, I. (1998). "The Frontiers of Western Europe: Developments East of the Rhine in the Sixth Century." In R. Hodges and W. Bowden (eds.), *The Sixth Century: Production, Distribution and Demand* (pp. 231–253). Leiden: Brill.

PART V

MEROVINGIAN WRITTEN CULTURE

CHAPTER 22

THE HISTORY OF HISTORIOGRAPHY IN THE MEROVINGIAN PERIOD

HELMUT REIMITZ

THE historiography of the Merovingian period can hardly be described as "Merovingian."[1] None of the historical texts written between the end of the fifth and the middle of the eighth century presents its history from the perspective of Merovingian rulers or their families. The *Chronicle* of Marius of Avenches continues the Christian world chronicle, written first in Greek by Eusebius and later translated into Latin and expanded by Jerome (Favrod 1991). Although Marius wrote at the end of the sixth century (about three generations after the establishment of Merovingian rule over most of Gaul), he employed a historiographical model that grounded his chronicle firmly in the past of the Christian Roman Empire. Marius probably died in 594, the same year as another historian of the Merovingian period, Gregory of Tours. Instead of extending the Eusebius/Jerome chronicle, Gregory wrote his *Ten Books of Histories* (*Decem libri historiarum*: *DLH*) building on the model of Eusebius's *Church History* (Krusch and Levison 1951). However, Gregory did not continue Eusebius's text or Rufinus's late fourth-century Latin translation and addition. Rather, he articulated a distinctive post-Roman and postimperial perspective focusing on the long past of Christian Gaul as the foundation of a new, authentically Christian society in a post-Roman kingdom.

In the seventh and eighth centuries, history became more Frankish but not more Merovingian. Roughly two generations after Marius and Gregory, an anonymous compiler followed Marius by building on the model of the Christian world chronicle (Krusch 1888a; Wallace-Hadrill 1960). Unlike Marius, however, this compilation (which received its name—the *Chronicle of Fredegar*—only in the early modern period) did not just continue the Eusebius/Jerome chronicle. The older chronicle was thoroughly revised and reworked to provide the seventh-century Frankish kingdom and its elites with a more substantial role in the history of the world. But the chronicle does not present us with a narrative from a royal or Merovingian perspective. Rather, it represents the expectations, hopes, and fears of Burgundian and Austrasian elites during a time when the centers of gravity in the Merovingian kingdoms were shifting westward to the regions along the Seine and Oise away from Austrasia and Burgundy.

It was in the region around Paris where the last history of the Merovingian period was written. In the fourth year of King Theuderic IV's rule (726/727), another anonymous author wrote the *Book on the History of the Franks* (*Liber historiae Francorum*; Krusch 1888c). He (or she) was, in the words of Richard Gerberding, a "staunch Merovingian legitimist" (Gerberding 1987, p. 146). This may be true, but the narrative focuses on the changing balance of power between kings and elites and between the different political networks in the Merovingian kingdoms, rather than on the kings themselves. The emphasis lies not on the deeds of the Merovingian kings but on the cooperation of the elites (and in particular the elites in the western parts of the kingdom) with their kings as the key to political success and social stability for the Frankish kingdom.

The Merovingian histories have long been regarded as truly "dark" products of a "dark" age. Written or transmitted in a Latin that has been regarded far below the ideal of a "classical" Latin, they were seen as products of authors of limited skill, and as evidence for the general decline of Latin culture after the fall of the western Roman Empire (Wood 2016). The authors themselves seem to have confirmed such judgments. Gregory of Tours, for instance, started his general preface to all the *Ten Books* with an apology. With the decline of the *studium litterarum*, no "grammarian skilled in the art of dialectic" could be found who was able to depict the events of Gregory's turbulent and confused times. Thus, Gregory undertook the task, even though he admitted that he was only able to do so "in rather simple speech" (*in incultu effatu*). In doing so, he was also encouraged by members of his own community who, to Gregory's great surprise, said that only few would "understand the learned words of the rhetorician but many the simple speech of the common people" (*Philosphantem rhetorem intellegunt pauci, loquentem rusticum multi*) (*DLH*, preface; Krusch and Levison 1951, p. 1).

In the last few decades, however, research on early medieval historiography has assessed such generalizations more critically. As such, historians have developed much more complex and productive approaches. They have done so by taking the literary strategies of the extant texts and the achievements of their authors far more seriously (on Gregory, see Goffart 2005, originally published 1988; Wood 1994b, 1994c; Heinzelmann 2001, [1994]; Brown 2002; see the bibliography in Murray 2016a). As for the passage from Gregory's preface, Walter Berschin has suggested that Gregory did not just employ the widely used and expected topos of modesty at the beginning of his *Ten Books*. He also constructed the sentence *philosphantem rhetorem intellegunt pauci, loquentem rusticum multi* as a consciously rhetorical clause (1986, pp. 298–299). As Berschin remarked, the clause might not have been one Cicero would have preferred (1986, p. 299), but it nevertheless presented Gregory to other educated contemporaries as a well-versed grammarian and rhetorician.

The paradox that Gregory built into his general preface was, however, not just a literary play to convince and excite insiders. It responded to the challenge that post-Roman authors faced in reconciling Roman history and culture with post-Roman political social and religious realities. At the time of Gregory of Tours, "Gaul had still a recognizable Roman face" (Brown 2008, pp. 3, 7). Gregory and most of his contemporaries were well aware that they operated within Roman structures and traditions. But they also recognized that they were living in a distinctly post-Roman world. Whoever wished to use what remained of Roman cultural, social, and political resources understood that such frameworks needed to be handled in new and creative ways.

THE HISTORIOGRAPHICAL LEGACY OF THE ROMAN WORLD

The need to reconfigure the remaining resources of the Roman world was particularly obvious for the writing of history in the post-Roman West. The Merovingian world inherited a rich and varied historiographical legacy from the Roman world (for recent overviews, see Inglebert 2001 [part 2], 2014; Ghosh 2016). As different as these histories were, many situated the history of the world within an imperial framework, defining the place of individuals and communities in a larger social whole through their distinctly Roman relationships (Potter 2011; O'Gorman 2011, with further references). The historiographical projects embarked upon by Christian historians of the fourth century were no exception in this regard (see Whitby 2011). As Arnaldo Momigliano observed long ago, the typically Christian genre of church history was strongly shaped by the context of its origins, when the church and the Christian people had emerged victorious in the Roman Empire under Constantine (Momigliano 1992; Kelly 2010; Maier 2010).

The same was true for Eusebius's other highly influential historiographical project: the Christian world chronicle. Building on the work of Julius Africanus, Eusebius constructed a historiographical structure, which made the fulfillment of God's plan visible through a synoptic presentation of biblical history and the history of other kingdoms and empires. (McKitterick 2006; Grafton and Williams 2008, pp. 133–177; Burgess and Kulikowski 2013, pp. 119–131). The history of the world was organized into different columns called *fila* or *tramites regnorum* sketched out over a double page. Each file presented the succession of prophets, kings, or rulers of different peoples, beginning with the biblical peoples but then juxtaposing them with series of the rulers of other peoples, such as columns of the Athenians, the Argives, the Latins, and the Macedonians. Over the course of history, however, one column after the other either terminated or was absorbed into the Roman world, and the history eventually collapsed into one single column of a Christian Roman world.

As Eusebius was the first to deploy this structure, historians have often considered him to be the progenitor of a long tradition of Christian world chronicles or Christian universal chronicles (see, for instance, Krüger 1985, but cf. now the comprehensive survey of Inglebert 2014). Such a classification, however, ignores the apologetic background of their composition. Eusebius did not write only to organize time. The conception of the Christian world chronicle was also closely linked to arguments of Christian authors about the Antiquity of the Christian tradition, which they presented as being older than Greco-Roman culture. The universal interest of these chronicles was thus primarily apologetic. In so doing, they built on a long tradition of chronography (Nuffelen 2010; Kulikowski and Burgess 2013, pp. 110–126; Inglebert 2014, pp. 250–260, 357–366). These apologetic and polemical aspects of the genre still played an important role for Jerome's late fourth-century Latin translation and continuation of Eusebius's chronicle, which achieved greater success in the Latin West than Eusebius's original had in the Eastern Greek speaking parts of the Empire (McKitterick 2006; Kulikowski and Burgess 2013, pp. 125–131; Wood 2015; McMahon 2019). Eusebius and his successors did not merely shape history; they also gave it a direction. In so doing, they provided later generations of historians with a historiographical structure they could continue even beyond the end of the western Roman Empire. A number of extensions of Jerome's chronicle from the fifth- and sixth-century West survive today. However, the authors of these later histories continued the world chronicle, with a much narrower focus on events and signs of the regions and places they lived in (Kulikowski and Burgess 2013, pp. 129–133, 184–187). Although the horizons of their chronicles shrank, their efforts to link themselves to larger historical debates about Christianity and empire show that the large majority of Christians still lived "in a world where grandiose imperial structures seemed the norm" (Brown 2008, p. 6).

Marius of Avenches was one such historian. He wrote his chronicle during the last decades of the sixth century in southern Gaul. In addition to continuing the chronicle of Jerome, Marius used existing continuations, such as the one by Prosper of Aquitaine, for the years before he began his own addition with the year 455.[2] Marius's "chain of chronicles," however, was the last continuation of Jerome's chronicle that has come down to us from post-Roman Gaul, and it does not seem to have been widely read, since only one manuscript copied in the later Carolingian period survives (Favrod 1991, pp. 49–52; Wood 2010). We still have manuscripts of Jerome's chronicle from the Merovingian period. None of them, however, transmits the text with a continuation (Helm 1956, pp. x–xi, xiii). These manuscripts show that scribes and scholars of the Merovingian period were still interested in the narrative offered by the chronicle of Jerome. Yet, its continued application to the present state of Merovingian Gaul came to be less and less attractive. What we observe is a growing understanding that it was necessary to write distinct histories for a distinct time—a time that was not "Roman time." No other source better illustrates this phenomenon than the first comprehensive post-Roman history written in Gaul: Gregory of Tours's *Ten Books of Histories*.

THE FIRST POST-ROMAN HISTORY: GREGORY OF TOURS AND HIS *DECEM LIBRI HISTORIARUM*

Gregory of Tours[3] and Marius were roughly contemporaries. Gregory also knew Jerome's chronicle well and used it frequently in his first book (Krusch and Levison 1951, pp. xix–xx) and even referred to Jerome as his source at the beginning of the second

(*DLH* II, preface; Krusch and Levison 1951, p. 36). Unlike Jerome, Gregory did not compile a comprehensive account of Roman history (Mitchell 2002): Gregory's featured list of Roman emperors was extremely selective. In many places, his adapted dating system highlighted his alternative historical focus. Gregory did not enumerate the succession of emperors since Caesar and Augustus, instead counting the succession of persecutors of the church: Trajan, for example, was the third since Nero to order the persecution of Christians (*DLH* I, 27; Krusch and Levison 1951, p. 21). After Trajan, only Gallienus, Diocletian, and Constantine were mentioned as rulers of the *imperium Romanum*. The history of Roman rule and rulers appeared only as a pale background to the history of Christian saints, martyrs, and bishops.

Gregory emphasized historical continuities not with Rome but rather with the long past of Christian Gaul (Brown 2002). In doing so, Gregory oriented himself toward the model of ecclesiastical historiography as it had been developed by Eusebius (Halsall 2007; Reimitz 2015, pp. 44–50). Like Eusebius of Caesarea, who had claimed for himself the honor of having invented ecclesiastical history (Schwartz and Mommsen 1999, pp. 6–8), Gregory structured his narrative in ten books. Gregory likely knew Eusebius's history through one of the Latin translations and continuations that had been in circulation since the beginning of the fifth century (Heinzelmann 2003). Despite Eusebius's influence, Gregory had no intention of building on the Eusebian model of ecclesiastical history, which tied the history of the church so closely to that of the Roman Empire (Momigliano 1992). The focus on providence and fulfillment of Christianity in Gregory's historiographical project was the same as that of Eusebius, but the distinct social and political horizons of his post-Roman kingdom required a completely novel historical narrative, from beginning to end.

After starting his *Histories* with Adam and Eve and a brief sketch of biblical and classical history, Gregory quickly shifted focus onto the Christianization of Gaul and ended the first book with the life and death of St. Martin, his eminent predecessor as bishop of Tours (on the plan and structure of the *Histories*, see Heinzelmann 2001, pp. 94–152). The second book recounted the beginning of the political reorganization of Gaul with the death of the first Christian Merovingian ruler, Clovis, at its end (511). Books three and four continued the history into Gregory's own times. The remaining six books dealt with the 570s to the 590s, which roughly coincided with the time of Gregory's episcopate in Tours (573–594). In this part of the *Histories*, Gregory appeared as bishop of Tours and an acting and speaking character in his own text. In this double role as actor and author, Gregory used his *Histories* to explore the possibilities and limits of the unfolding of a truly Christian society after the end of the Roman Empire and before the crystallization of a new order (Heinzelmann 2001; Brown 2002, 2013, pp. 154–159; Reimitz 2016a; Rousseau 2016, but see also the comments of Brown 2015, pp. 155–157).

To be sure, Gregory was well aware that, in writing this new history, he, like Eusebius before him, needed to deal with the duality of the church as a divine institution and its less ethereal relationships with other social and political institutions (cf. Heinzelmann 2001, with Momigliano 1992). At the beginning of his second book, Gregory described his work as a history reporting the deeds of the saints and the slaughters of the peoples *mixteconfusequae* "in a messy and confused order" (*DLH* II, preface; Krusch and

Levison 1951, p. 36, transl. Thorpe 1974, p. 103). According to Gregory, this was just what history was if one wanted to follow the models of the venerable and ancient account from the biblical books (*DLH* II, preface; Krusch and Levison 1951, p. 36). For Gregory, Christianity's topsy turvy history within the Roman Empire was another episode in its long history, and this "imperial" episode was much less important than many might have thought (Brown 2013, pp. 154–159).

The emancipation from the boundaries set by the historical genre and the Roman Empire in which they had been defined was crucial for Gregory's historiographical project. It enabled Gregory to develop a vision of Christianity in which the relations of the divine church with worldly social and political institutions needed to be imagined in ways very different from how they had been organized in the Roman past.

Imagined Communities and Public Relations: The Audience and Reception of the Histories

The writing of the *Histories* was a lifelong project for Gregory. He seems to have worked on them for decades and regularly revised earlier parts (for an overview of the different positions regarding the process of composition, see: Murray 2016b). Like his other works, Gregory might have worked with variable intensity, taken long breaks, and even changed his plans while working on them (Shaw 2016). Because Gregory worked and reworked older parts of his *Histories* until the end of his life, the historical narrative itself does not appear to have come to a well-defined and planned conclusion. The last chapter of the *Histories* relates events of the year 591 (Heinzelmann 2001, pp. 84–87). However, from the final capstone that he prepared as a sort of epilogue, we know that Gregory did not finish his work until 594. It consisted primarily of a catalog of the bishops of Tours that summed up their achievements and legacies and counted the years of their episcopate. Arriving at his own *gesta*, he recounted the churches he built, rebuilt, and consecrated, as well as the works he had written. Before Gregory ended this epilogue with his own final date, he dramatically appealed to his successors as bishops of Tours to keep his literary legacy just as he had left it:

> I conjure you by the coming of our Lord Jesus Christ and by Judgment Day feared by all sinners, that you never permit these books to be destroyed or rewritten—by selecting them only in part or by omitting sections—otherwise you will be left in confusion by the Last Judgment and be condemned with the Devil. Rather, keep them in your possession, intact and unchanged, just as I have left them.
> (*DLH* X, 31; Krusch and Levison 1951, p. 535)

The dramatic appeal at the end of his *Histories* suggests that Gregory imagined a rather narrow audience for this work: his successors as bishop of Tours. But it is also possible to conclude from his appeal to his successors that Gregory might have anticipated a wider distribution and hoped that his successors at Tours were the most trustworthy in keeping his literary legacy intact and unchanged.

Gregory's concerns that his work might be manipulated after his death were quite justified and had been articulated by many other late-antique historians, not least Eusebius and Rufinus (Heinzelmann 2003; Mülke 2008). Gregory himself had rewritten Jerome's chronicle by "selecting passages in part and omitting sections" (see the introduction in *DLH*; Krusch and Levison 1951, pp. xix–xx). We could thus see Gregory's exhortation at the end of his *Histories* as evidence of his expectation of their wider distribution and reproduction beyond the episcopal archives of Tours.

The wider public sphere, which Gregory could imagine as an audience of his *Histories*, is well attested in the stories he recounted in his ten books. Those stories provide us with ample evidence for literary exchange and public communication in the Merovingian world through sermons and public speeches, legal negotiations in court, councils, letter exchanges, and more formal messages to kings, officials, and nobles (for a comprehensive survey that builds heavily on Gregory's *Histories*, see Riché 1995, especially pp. 220–290, see also Wood 1990, 2016; Dumézil 2007, 2016; Gioanni 2009; Diefenbach and Müller 2013; Mathisen 2013; Williard 2014; see also Gillett, Chapter 25; Halfond, Chapter 13; Hen, Chapter 10; Kreiner, Chapter 24; and Rio, Chapter 23, this volume).

A letter from Felix of Nantes, for instance, in which the bishop accused Gregory's brother, Peter, of having killed the appointed bishop of Langres in order to become bishop himself, triggered an elaborate defense mechanism from Gregory (*DLH* V, 5; Krusch and Levison 1951, pp. 200–203). Felix had sent the letter to Gregory directly (as Gregory mentioned). But it also seems that Gregory assumed that the message had been spread more widely and he needed to respond to it. Gregory mentioned that he also sent a letter to Felix. In the *Histories*, the letter exchange created the image of a public dispute, which Gregory also used to mock the bishop of Nantes:

> Oh, had you only become bishop of Marseille! Instead of bringing your cargos of oil and other wares, its ships could have carried only papyrus, which would have provided more opportunities for your pen to write libels against good people. As it is, only the lack of papyrus cuts short your evil verbosity.
>
> (*DLH* V, 5; Krusch and Levison, p. 200)

Gregory appears to have liked this joke so much that he presented it as a word-for-word quotation from the letter. It seems unlikely that he would have waited until the final publication of his *Histories* to present it to people who may have found it funnier than Felix did. We may assume that Gregory's joke was distributed among a wider audience than just Felix. His target audience was most likely members of his own network whom Gregory expected to have received the letters sent out by Felix with the denunciation of his brother. The story of Gregory's literary feud with Felix may thus also help us speculate about the arenas of communication in his world. It was a world of stories, both pious and impious. And it was a world whose structures of communication and literary exchange were still defined by Roman traditions of creating and maintaining social ties through literary networks (Wood 1990, 2018; Mathisen 1999; Gioanni 2001; Dumézil 2007; Müller 2013; Williard 2014; Mratschek 2016; for the seventh century, see also Shanzer 2010; Hen 2012; Mathisen 2013).

One of the co-opted members of the Merovingian elite who was in close contact with both Gregory and Felix was Venantius Fortunatus, whose poetry is our best evidence of the importance of literary exchange to social positioning in the later sixth century (George 1992; Roberts 2009; Ehlen 2011). Soon after his move from Italy to Gaul, Venantius achieved a permanent place in the Merovingian upper class, ending his life as bishop of Poitiers. Members of Gregory's family and network were among Venantius's very first supporters, and Gregory remained his patron until the end of his life (Roberts 2016). But in the decade after Venantius's arrival in Gaul, he was on good terms with Felix too. In his poems, Venantius praised Felix's unmatched guardianship of *romanitas*, and he mentioned having received a number of letters from the bishop of Nantes (George 1992, pp. 114–123; Roberts 2009, pp. 139–164; Roberts 2016, pp. 37–47). It may well have been that the poet received letters from both bishops, each one with a different version of the story about Peter.

Above all, however, the exchange of letters and other literary works between Venantius and Gregory of Tours is documented in the poet's writing. The exchange between the two friends continued throughout Gregory's life. In one poem, Venantius thanked Gregory for a book with sacred songs that Gregory had written. He also praised Gregory the pastor for sharing them not only with him but with his flock (Venantius, *Carm.*, V, 8b, Leo 1881, p. 119). Gregory was likely thinking of his friendship with Venantius when, in his appeal to his successors to keep his work complete and intact, he gave permission for it to be rewritten in verse (*DHL* X, 31; Krusch and Levison 1951, p. 536).

Unfortunately, we do not have the letters and poems that Gregory wrote, and it is impossible to reconstruct the social network of his literary friendship any more precisely. Presumably, strong overlaps with the network appeared in Venantius's poetry. Dedicatees of Venantius's poems are also favorably portrayed in Gregory's *Histories* (Reimitz 2015, pp. 92–93). Of course, this is not to suggest that the social network that Venantius built up overlapped entirely with Gregory's. Nevertheless, their close connections offer an idea of the literary and social networks in which Gregory imagined the circulation and distribution of his *Histories*.

Gregory, however, did not see the reception of the *Histories* as limited by the boundaries of a specific in-group. Like Gregory, many members of his familial and social network were deeply involved in the political and social fabric of the kingdom. The communicative frameworks this network created and re-created provided Gregory with ample opportunity to imagine them as channels for further distribution in the "meshwork of culture and structure" of a heterogeneous and highly stratified society (Preiser-Kapeller 2012, p. 2).

The wider the imagined audience of the *Histories* became, the more uncertain became the question of how and by whom copies were reproduced. The more important issue was that members of Gregory's familial and spiritual network kept his works "intact and complete just as he had left them" (*DLH* X, 31; Krusch and Levison 1951, p. 536). After all,

Gregory had provided members of his family with a venerable and prestigious history in the long narrative of Christian Gaul (Wood 2002). The same was true for his successors at the episcopate of Tours whom Gregory probably expected to come from his family as well. As Gregory mentioned in the *Histories*, with the exception of five bishops, all of his predecessors in the see of Tours had been members of his family (*DLH* V, 49; Krusch and Levison 1951, p. 262).

Whether or not Gregory's successors as bishops of Tours adhered to the appeal at the end of his *Histories* to keep his work "intact and complete just as he had left them," his predictions regarding the dissemination of his works were quite accurate. The unusually high number of extant Merovingian manuscripts makes clear that the *Histories* were widely copied soon after Gregory's death. The manuscript record also shows that the text circulated exactly as Gregory had feared they would: Merovingian and Carolingian historians and copyists compiled different versions, omitting not only chapters but even entire books (Bourgain and Heinzelmann 1997; Bourgain 2016; Reimitz 2016b). Within a generation after the end of the *Histories*, Merovingian compilers produced a six-book version in which they omitted the last four books. In the first six books, too, a series of chapters were left out. This six-book version became quite popular in the Merovingian period (Reimitz 2015, pp. 133–140). This was not the only rewriting of Gregory's *Histories*. Another Carolingian version began to circulate early in the ninth century. Although it included material from all ten books, it still omitted many chapters and divided the text into nine books adding as a tenth book, the "Fourth Book of the Chronicle of Fredegar," including its continuations up to the death of Charles Martel (Reimitz 2016b, pp. 540–563).

Although Merovingian and Carolingian transmission of Gregory's *Histories* clearly shows that subsequent historians and compilers distributed his historiographical vision far from how he "had left it," Gregory does seem to have succeeded in preserving an authoritative version. Most of the heavily edited manuscripts of his text have survived, with traces proving that the complete version of Gregory was available to copyists and readers of these rearranged *Histories*. In some instances, the complete text was used to check, or sometimes even to complement, the versions made by compilers who had "selected some parts and omitted others" (Krusch 1932, pp. 722–723; Bourgain and Heinzelmann 1997, pp. 274–275; Heinzelmann 2001; Hilchenbach 2009, pp. 41–50, 79).

THE RECONFIGURATION AND CONTINUATION OF THE ROMAN PAST IN THE SEVENTH CENTURY: *THE CHRONICLE OF FREDEGAR*

The popularity of Gregory's *Histories*, however, did not mean that the writing and rewriting of chronicles came to an end in the Merovingian kingdoms. As briefly mentioned, some of the oldest extant manuscripts of the Eusebius/Jerome chronicle date from the Merovingian period, when they were copied without any continuation by later chroniclers. Merovingian historians, however, also continued their own version of the Eusebius/Jerome chronicle, adopting its model but also adapting it to the circumstances of their post-Roman world. The oldest extant redaction of such a world chronicle was compiled in the eastern parts of the Merovingian kingdoms around 660 (Wood 1994c; Collins 2007; Fischer 2014).[4] The *Chronicle of Fredegar* received its "author" only in the early modern period, and we do not know the identity of the seventh-century historian who wrote it. In any case, the chronicle was clearly produced under very different conditions from those of Gregory and the Merovingian compilers of his *Histories* (cf. Reimitz 2015, pp. 190–199). Horizons and perspectives of the chronicle's narrative indicate that the oldest extant redaction originated in a milieu with strong connections to the members of the Pippinid family and networks (Wood 1994c; for the historical context, see Scholz 2015, pp. 225–229, 237–260; Wood 1994a, pp. 221–238). It was a place in which Gregory's *Histories* were read too. The compilers used the Merovingian six-book version for their narrative of the events until the death of Chilperic in 584 (Reimitz 2015, pp. 172–174). Nevertheless, they presented their version of the *Histories* in a different historiographical structure, embedding it in a chain of chronicles (Wood 2010).

This chain of chronicles starts with a version of the *Liber generationis* of Hippolytus of Rome to which are added a chronological computation running from Adam to the Frankish king Sigibert II (d. 613), Isidore of Seville's account on the creation of the world, a list of patriarchs, kings, and emperors to the Byzantine emperor Heraclius (d. 641), and followed by a rewriting of the chronicle of Jerome with its continuation by Hydatius (Burgess 1993; Wieser 2019). Unlike Hydatius, however, the Fredegar compilers not only continued the Jerome chronicle as a means of connecting their history to a Christian and Roman past, but they also fundamentally reworked the texts of their predecessors. There are a number of interpolations in the excerpts from Jerome and Hydatius, and the chroniclers also added a number of interesting chapters to the end of their version of Hydatius's chronicle. The compilers then included their own version of Gregory of Tours, calling it a book of excerpts from the chronicle of Gregory, the bishop of Tours (*liber, quod est scarpsum de cronica Gregorii episcopi Toronaci*) at the beginning of the next book (Krusch 1888a, p. 89).

After the death of Chilperic in 584 (where the six-book version of Gregory's *Histories*, which the compilers of the chronicle used, ended), the compilers of the chronicle provided their own account of the events up to the early 640s. In this part of the chronicle, labeled by its modern editor, Bruno Krusch, as the "Fourth Book," a series of remarks show that it was still worked on after 642 (Kusternig 1982, p. 10). The compilers clearly intended to continue their chain of chronicles into their own time, which probably coincided with the regency of Balthild, the wife of Clovis II, who reigned for her minor sons after the death of her husband in 658 or 659 (Wood 1994c).

The fact that the chronicle has come down to us in incomplete form, coupled with its "Merovingian" style and language, has led scholars to neglect its compilers' generic choices and literary strategies (but see Fischer 2014 and forthcoming; Reimitz 2015, Chapter 7; Wood 2015). With the choice of the *Liber generationis* at the beginning of the chain of chronicles, the chronicler made it clear that this history should be connected to the tradition of the Latin Christian world chronicle and Christian chronography. The alterations to the individual texts that were chosen, however, clearly show that this was a history for a post-Roman time too. Stories about the Franks' mythological origins going all the way back to the heroes of Troy most clearly illustrate this historiographical tactic (Ewig 1998; Coumert 2007, pp. 295–324; Reimitz 2015, pp. 166–174; see Coumert, Chapter 5, this volume). Unlike the compilers of other chains of chronicles, such as Marius of Avenches, however, the Fredegar compilers also fundamentally reworked most of the treatises included in their work. Additional information and a number of stories are interpolated into the excerpts from Jerome, Hydatius, and Gregory of Tours through which the chronicle integrated Roman and Frankish myth and history (see Reimitz 2015, pp. 199–212).

Yet, the chronicle did not just augment the prestige of Frankish history and identity. Its compilers also developed a new view of the world for a post-Roman period. They fundamentally reorganized their optical arrangement to provide a narrative in which stories about the Franks became part of a multifaceted vision of a world divided among different peoples. In the extant manuscripts of the Chronicle of Eusebius and Jerome, the visual arrangement of the text structured history as a history of kingdoms, empires and peoples (see above, p. 465). In Jerome's text, the different columns dedicated to different *regna* and peoples eventually ran together into a single column, that of the Romans, which continued the narrative until the Christianization of the Roman Empire. The compilers of the Chronicle of Fredegar did not want to depict such a process. Jerome's text in the Chronicle does not appear as a synoptic presentation of the columns of peoples and their realms. Rather, from the very beginning it was organized as a linear text. In such a presentation, every story about a community or a people could be considered as a discrete history or "file" and was presented as part of the history of the world just like the peoples, kingdoms, and empires that had been assigned a column in the chronicle of Eusebius/Jerome (Reimitz 2015, pp. 222–231, with illustrations). The compilers thereby organized world history as a series of peoples and kingdoms which Roman imperial history never absorbed. Instead, the Frankish kingdoms became part of a world that had always been divided among peoples. A new social and political ordering of the world had replaced the old order that the Roman Empire had represented. In altering the historical imagination of the social world , the chronicle provided its readers not only with its own interpretation of the Roman past. It also had an eye on the Roman Empire of the present—the Byzantine Empire—whose social and moral decline and religious and political failures were carefully registered (e.g., Fredegar, *Chronicae* IV, 66; Krusch 1888a, pp. 153–154; see Esders, Chapter 16, this volume). Byzantium was not a world they failed to understand: They may have understood it all too well, through the eyes of disgruntled, disillusioned Byzantines (Esders 2009, 2014; Fischer forthcoming).

The chronicle's broad Mediterranean horizons were also connected to more local social and political networks in the Merovingian kingdoms. As Ian Wood has convincingly argued, the oldest extant redaction was most likely produced in the context of the Pippinid network after the failed attempt to create familial bonds between the Pippinids and the Merovingian kings, the so-called Grimoald coup (Wood 1994c; for the Grimoald coup, see Becher 1994; Wood 1994c; Offergeld 2001, pp. 253–257; Hamann 2003). The text's critical portrayal of the Merovingians, the stress on the importance of the Frankish elites in the history of the kingdom and the positive representation of members of the Pippinid network, such as Pippin I, Arnulf of Metz, Kunibert of Cologne, and Pippin's son Grimoald, fit well within this context.

While traces of the Austrasian-Pippinid network are at work in the rewriting of Gregory's *Histories* and the independent continuation of the narrative up to the 640s, earlier layers shine through as well. A number of passages focus on the long past of the Burgundian regions and the important role performed by elites in the Burgundian parts of the Merovingian kingdom (e.g., Fredegar, *Chronicae* II, 46; Krusch 1888a, p. 68). These traces help us to understand the extant redaction of the chronicle as an effort to appropriate an older historical view and integrate the Pippinid network into it (Reimitz 2015, pp. 195–197).

One of the commonalities present in the chronicle was a shared Frankish past reaching back to the heroes of Troy. In more recent times, their Frankish descendants were represented as the essential element for the kingdom's stability and well-being. This conception of Frankish identity was not a regional one. It was defined by the willingness of members of the elite to take on responsibility for the balance between different political and social groups and different kings in an ethnically heterogeneous world. It was their care for the greater good of the entire kingdom that distinguished these self-styled Franks. Yet, in the chronicle, nearly all of the "Frankish" elites who took on the responsibility came from the Burgundian and Austrasian regions of the Merovingian kingdom (Reimitz 2015, pp. 176–190).

The importance of this common past for the elites in the Austrasian and Burgundian parts of the kingdom might well have been another reason for the generic choice of the historians who worked on the *Chronicle of Fredegar*. After the establishment and promotion of new political, social, and religious centers in northwestern Gaul in the wake of Chlothar II's ascension, many of these elites must have been concerned about the preservation of their prominent roles that had been established in the former Burgundian-Austrasian kingdom under Sigibert I and Brunhild and their descendants. The broad horizons of a chronicle with its imperial past and its actualization in a post-Roman "Mediterranean perspective" (Fischer 2014) might also have represented the political expertise and experience of this distinctive governing class of the powerful Austrasian-Burgundian kingdom during the decades before and after 600. They had acted as ambassadors and military leaders for missions across the whole Mediterranean, and they had successfully governed the ethnically and socially diverse territories of the Merovingian kingdoms.

The manuscript transmission of the *Chronicle of Fredegar* may also remind us that the process of its compilation did not end with the composition of its oldest extant redaction around 660. In fact, the extant manuscripts document the work on the *Chronicle* as a continuing project. There is one Merovingian exemplar of the chronicle written in the first decades of the eighth century, but not one later medieval copy of this Merovingian exemplar has come down to us. Other manuscripts that are extant from the Carolingian period onward transmit various versions of the chronicle. In nearly every manuscript, the chain of chronicles has come down to us in different arrangements, with further additions but also omissions of passages and texts (Reimitz 2015, pp. 236–239; for more comprehensive descriptions of the manuscripts, see Collins 2007).

The most spectacular rearrangement, produced after 751, also hints at the circulation and dissemination of the text in the Merovingian period. Further preservation and editing of the text most likely took place at the cultural and religious centers of the Pippinid network. About a hundred years after the compilation of the oldest extant redaction of the chronicle, the Carolingian descendants of the Pippinid family rearranged the "chain of chronicles" and continued it into their own time. They hoped that their rearrangement and continuation of the chronicle would help to legitimate the usurpation of the Frankish throne by members of the Carolingian family around the middle of the eighth century. (Collins 2007, pp. 3–7, 82–95; Reimitz 2015, pp. 295–334). By editing the *Chronicle of Fredegar*, Carolingian compilers could build on the work of their Merovingian predecessors, who had not only portrayed the Carolingians' Pippinid and Arnulfing ancestors in a highly favorable light, but also critically questioned the Merovingian monopoly on royal power.

However, in the second half of the eighth century, Carolingian historians and students had more choices to make beyond the ever-growing body of historiographical visions inspired by the work of Gregory of Tours and the Fredegar chroniclers. When the last editor and continuator of the Carolingian reworking of the Merovingian Fredegar-chronicle ended his narrative with his account of the year 768, an additional and particularly powerful conception of Frankish identity and history was already circulating widely in the post-Merovingian world: the *Liber historiae Francorum (Book on the History of the Franks)*, which was written (and already rewritten) during the last decades of the Merovingian period.

A PROVIDENTIAL PAST: BIBLICAL AND FRANKISH HISTORY IN THE LAST DECADES OF THE MEROVINGIAN PERIOD

The author of this *Liber historiae Francorum* (*LHF*) finished his text in 726/727, the fourth year of the penultimate Merovingian king, Theuderic IV (d. 737).[5] The political constellation and power balance had changed fundamentally in the Merovingian kingdoms since the compilation of the oldest redaction of the *Chronicle of Fredegar* in the 660s. The descendants of Pippin I and Arnulf of Metz had established themselves as the most powerful family in the Merovingian world, ruling with, and increasingly on behalf of, the Merovingian kings (Wood 1994a, pp. 270–287; Fouracre 2000; Fischer 2012). The anonymous author of the *LHF* was probably a monk or a nun in Soissons (probably at

Saint Medard or the convent of Notre Dame, see Gerberding 1987, pp. 146–172; Nelson 1990, pp. 194–195; Hartmann 2004) and responded to the changes in the topography of power in the Merovingian kingdoms from a distinctly western Frankish perspective. In the *LHF*, the "real" Franks were identified as the elites of the northwestern regions of the kingdom, around Paris and along the Seine and Oise. The importance of members of this elite for the political stability and success of the Frankish kingdom was emphasized repeatedly in the text (see Reimitz 2015, pp. 248–252; with further references).

The author of the *LHF* was not the first one to do so. We find this trend in hagiographical works such as the *Life of Balthild* and the *Life of Audoin*, which were written decades earlier (Ewig 1976, p. 153). The emphasis on the western regions should be understood as a response to the rise of the Pippinid family under Pippin II (d. 714), whose political networks and power bases were primarily in the eastern parts of the Merovingian kingdom. By the time the author of the *LHF* finished his text in 726/727, Pippin's son, Charles Martel, who had succeeded his father as mayor of the palace, had established himself as the *de facto* ruler of the whole kingdom. When Theuderic IV died in 737, the Carolingian mayor continued to govern the kingdom without a Merovingian king until his death in 741. In 743, his sons, Pippin and Carloman, reestablished a Merovingian king but deposed and replaced him soon after the middle of the century (see Fouracre, Chapter 2, this volume, with further literature). That was something the author of the *LHF* could not know when he ended his history about twenty-five years before the deposition of the last Merovingian king. The last chapters of the *LHF* documented the political consolidation of the kingdom under Charles Martel and the successful cooperation of the mayor with the king in Paris and western Frankish elites (see Gerberding 1987, pp. 169–172).

The history presented by the *LHF* begins Frankish history in a way similar to the *Chronicle of Fredegar*, focusing on the Franks' Trojan origins. However, it developed a very different Frankish history from these prestigious origins. Unlike the *Chronicle of Fredegar*, the author of the *LHF* presented an uninterrupted line of kings ruling over the Franks from the destruction of Troy up to the author's own lifetime, also including an early king, Faramundus (Pharamond), who did not appear in the chronicle (*LHF* c. 4; Krusch 1888c, p. 244). The author of the *LHF* also gave a very different account of the conquest of Gaul, strongly emphasizing the establishment of Frankish rule in the northwestern parts of Gaul. Whereas in the *Chronicle of Fredegar*, the Franks arrived at the regions along the Rhine and expanded their rule from these regions westwards, the *LHF* carefully orchestrated the crossing of the Rhine as an important event in Frankish history comparable to the crossing of the Jordan by the people of Israel (*LHF* c. 5; Krusch 1888c, pp. 245–246). The conquest of the regions along the Seine and Oise, which became the heartlands of the future Frankish kingdom, was also embellished with biblical motifs and allusions (Dörler 2013; Reimitz 2015, pp. 258–263).

The obvious differences in the Trojan myth have often been regarded as an indication that the author of the *LHF* was not familiar with the *Chronicle of Fredegar* (Gerberding 1987, p. 17; Anton 2003, p. 192). Yet, there are some conspicuous commonalities indicating that historians have underestimated the historiographical horizons of the *LHF*'s author (Coumert 2007, pp. 330–332; Reimitz 2015, pp. 251–258). As more recent studies on Merovingian culture and particularly late Merovingian culture have made clear, however, there is enough extant evidence from Merovingian scriptoria and cultural centers, particularly in the first decades of the eighth century, to show that the *LHF* came from a vibrant cultural world of well-informed and connected historiographical activity (see, for instance,Hen 1995; Ganz 2010; Kreiner 2014, pp. 125–155; Wood, 2018; Ganz 2019).

The author of the *LHF* was well aware of alternative historical perspectives, as is clear in the rewriting of Gregory's *Histories*. Like the compilers of the Fredegar chronicle, the author of the *Liber* was working with the abridged Merovingian version of Gregory, which started in the *Liber* soon after its account of the Franks' Trojan origins. As with the *Chronicle of Fredegar*, the clash with Gregory's legacy emerged not only in the form of a contradictory argument but also through a comprehensive rewriting of his *Histories*. However, the author of the *LHF* also offered a more explicit statement on competing views on Frankish history in her or his account of the life and death of Clovis II (d. 657). In the *LHF*, Clovis was presented in quite an unfavorable light. He was a fornicator and defiler of women, and he was bloated by gluttony and drunkenness. For the author of the *LHF*, this was reason enough to exclude any account of the king's death from the historical record. S/he knew that there were many more stories about the king, many of which were positive. Yet, as the different *scriptores* had left quite contradictory and incoherent reports, s/he decided to disregard them altogether (*LHF*, c. 44; Krusch 1888c, p. 316). However, the author of the LHF was not necessarily referring to other histories. For example, different portrayals of Clovis have come down to us mainly in hagiographical texts, above all in the life of Clovis's wife Balthild (written soon after her death in 680; see Gerberding and Fouracre 1996, p. 225). The passage clearly demonstrates that the author of the *LHF* regarded his historical work as part of a wider debate about the Frankish past.

For her or his intervention into these debates, the author of the *LHF* chose a form of historical writing that was strongly inspired by the narrative of the most important *historia* of the Christian world: the biblical history of the chosen people (van Uytfanghe 1987; O'Loughlin 2013; Wood 2014; Buc 1994; Hen 1998; Heydemann 2013, and still de Lubac 1959–1964). To be sure, this history had already played an important role in Gregory's *Histories* and the *Chronicle of Fredegar*. Both texts, albeit in very different ways, begin with a sketch of Old Testament history. Gregory developed important typologies in his first book that he returned to later in his narrative (Heinzelmann 2001, pp. 139–145). As we have seen, the compiler of the *Chronicle of Fredegar* did not just juxtapose biblical history with other histories available in the Eusebius/Jerome chronicle, but also started the chain of chronicles with extensive lists of biblical prophets, kings, and peoples alongside nonbiblical kings and emperors. With their historical-exegetical beginnings, these two works articulated very different imaginings of the social world. Gregory's *Histories* presented biblical history as a prefiguration of a Christian world that was organized along the distinctions between Christianity and paganism, orthodoxy and heresy. The synchronization of biblical with other histories provided the Fredegar-chronicler with the historical foundations needed to illustrate a world divided among peoples. The author of the *LHF* took a different approach to biblical *historia*: he rewrote it as a history of the Franks. In employing biblical motifs, style, and narrative patterns, this history presented the Franks as the new chosen people. This history mirrored the biblical chosen people as a history full of failures, errors, and efforts to find the right paths to attain God's support once more (Reimitz 2015, pp. 258–259, 275–276).

The author of the *LHF* was not alone in experimenting with the integration of biblical *historia* and the writing of the history of post-Roman societies. About 500 miles northwest of the monastery in Soissons, in which the author of the *Liber historiae Francorum* finished her or his text in 726/727, one of the foremost scholars of the early medieval Latin West, the venerable Bede was working on the *Ecclesiastical History of the English People*. Bede, who finished his history in 731, also exploited analogies between the kingdom of Israel and his own times to provide a shared past for the Saxons in Britain (McClure 1983; Goffart 2005; DeGregorio 2011; Thacker 2011; Brown 2013, pp. xl, 9, 349–354; Wood 2014, Wood forthcoming). To be sure, the two histories were very different historiographical projects and responded to quite different social, religious, and political challenges. Nevertheless, there are also striking parallels. Like Bede, the author of the *Liber historiae Francorum* added elements from epic traditions to their merging of biblical and ethnic history. In doing so, the author of the *LHF*—like the authors of Fredegar's chronicle—made a distinct generic choice linking the history of the Franks to a biblical and providential vision of history. (For the appeal to Old Testament models in late-antique historiography, see Brown 2013, pp. 9, 278–279). This choice not only presented the heroes of Frankish history as "avatars of a militant Israel" (Brown 2013, p. 279), but also helped mark the difference of this specific historical vision from those of earlier historians of the Merovingian world.

Conclusion

In a recent article, Ian Wood suggested that historians understand Merovingian culture not in terms of the decline or dissolution of the cultural landscape of the Roman classical world but, above all, in terms of the transformation and reorganization of knowledge. (Wood 2016). This is indeed well documented in the writing and rewriting of history by Merovingian authors. The investigation of these texts demonstrates that the transformation of historical knowledge and culture demanded a higher degree of sophistication, expertise, and originality than modern scholars have been willing to allow for the authors of Merovingian histories for a long time. Not only do the extant historical works from the Merovingian period testify to the historical sophistication and education of their authors. They also show that their authors were well aware of a variety of histories, historical interpretations, models, and genres.

In this light, it might be helpful to look to newer approaches to genre theory in order to better understand the specific genre choices of Merovingian historians. To be sure, modern scholars have more often than not used genre to emphasize the discontinuities between early medieval historians with the models of classical or late classical history.

Such an interpretation was based on rigid formal approaches to linguistic standards as well as the use of genre in defining texts as members or outliers of these generic categories defined by classical or imagined classical standards. More recent approaches to genre theory, however, have suggested more productive ways of looking at genre as historically fluid systems defined by communicative acts based on "pre-constituted horizon of expectations…to orient readers' [public's] understanding and to enable a qualifying reception" (Jauss 1999; Torgersen 2016, pp. 72–74). They suggest how to study generic choices as a "particular way texts and audiences worked with and upon each other to create and modify patterns of reading" (Torgesen 2016, p. 74).

As we have seen, Merovingian historians clearly understood that their works would have to stand up to historical scrutiny as one historical interpretation among many. At the time when the *LHF* was written, one of the most influential sources of competition was still the historical vision created by Gregory of Tours. This is most obvious in the efforts the author of the *LHF* made to rewrite Gregory's *Histories*. In doing so, s/he was just as selective as the author of the *Chronicle of Fredegar* more than three generations before, and also supplemented the new version with additional stories and perspectives. In their awareness of alternative versions and interpretations of history, we might understand the work of these historians better if we take their generic choices more seriously than we have usually done. They all worked with the preconception of a genre to define the subject of their historical inquiry, while attempting to transform the expectations and patterns of reading and writing history in a post-Roman world. We might speculate that the generic choice of the Christian world chronicle by the Fredegar chronicler was the most suitable form for meeting the expectations held by social and political elites in the former Austro-Burgundian kingdom. With the two most prominent genres of Christian history already taken by Gregory and the *Chronicle*, the author of the *LHF* decided to employ the model of biblical history.

Understanding the choice of genre of the different historians as part of their literary and historiographical strategies might also help us to understand why the histories of the Merovingian period were so different. There is also, however, a more political side to the explanation of how these authors found the literary and historical room for maneuver—*Spielräume*—to present history so differently. It brings us back to the observation with which I started this chapter, namely, that Merovingian history can hardly be labeled "Merovingian." As different as these histories were, they shared one commonality. All three Merovingian historians positioned themselves as talking to, not from, the centers of royal power. One hardly gets the impression that their authors were writing in reaction to, or in agreement or disagreement with, an established royal or central narrative of Merovingian-Frankish history (see Coumert, Chapter 5, this volume). Such a narrative does not even seem to have existed by the 720s.

A dominant historical narrative was absent as much for historiographical as for historical reasons. As I have argued elsewhere at greater length, the available *Spielräume* of Merovingian historians were directly or indirectly related to the strategies with which the Merovingian kings established themselves as rulers over most of the former Gallic provinces of the former Roman Empire from the beginning of the sixth century onward

(Reimitz 2015, pp. 98–112). In their efforts to stabilize their rule over a highly heterogeneous kingdom, they established themselves equidistant from the different groups and groupings of the emerging Merovingian world. They were interested neither in imposing a historical master narrative of their own to legitimate their rule, nor in supporting stronger historical profiles of any other social or political group in their kingdom. This situation created ample room for Gregory of Tours to maneuver. He ultimately integrated all these different groups and communities—real or imagined—into his Christian vision of community for the Merovingian kingdom. And with the impressive success of his *Histories*, he passed to later generations his vision as well as the *Spielräume* he had used to create this vision.

In short, the legacy of Gregory's *Histories* provided a rich and capacious resource to find a place in the history of Gaul. The text's manuscript tradition demonstrates how the seventh and eighth centuries preserved the interpretative space that Gregory had exploited and reinforced. This maneuverability was also used *against* Gregory's historical vision, which further expanded the horizons of the possible and multiplied opportunities for their appropriation. In spite of, or perhaps precisely because of, the conflicts in the second half of the seventh and early eighth centuries, the Merovingian kings remained in their equidistant position from different attempts at appropriation. Through their positioning, the Merovingian kings guaranteed a balance of power that would otherwise have been difficult to imagine. Even in the late seventh century, their monopoly of rule relied on a positioning of kingship that granted elites equal access to the royal court. As the Pippinid/Carolingian mayors of the palace increasingly monopolized access to the throne, the rules for the writing of history began to change. It is striking that with the rise of the Carolingians, we observe the emergence of a more centralized production of historical texts. For the first time in the history of post-Roman Gaul, only the kings and their historians offered suggestions for a shared past and a common future. But this is a different history–the history of a truly Carolingian historiography.

Notes

1. I should like to thank Peter Brown, Jamie Kreiner, Walter Pohl, and Ian Wood for many conversations and comments on earlier drafts; Ryan Low helped to improve the English of this work at a very early stage (when it was much longer and much more difficult to read and comprehend), and last but not least I am greatly indebted to Bonnie Effros and Isabel Moreira for their infectious enthusiasm, and their kind help, care, and patience as editors of this volume.

2. The extant manuscript, however, transmits Marius's part as a continuation of the Gallic chronicle of 452 and has only the entries of Prosper for 453 to 455. See Favrod 1991, p. 51; Wood 2010, pp. 68–69.

3. The most important edition is still Krusch and Levison 1951; for other editions and translations before 1984, see Repertorium 1964–2007, vol. 5, pp. 233–237; in the course of the 1980s, Gregory of Tours became an "academic industry" (Wood 2002, p. 29). Many of the studies on Gregory's *Decem libri historiarum* played an important role in the development of new approaches to early medieval historians and historiography: Goffart 2005 (orig.

publ. 1988); Heinzelmann 2001 (orig. published 1994), English transl. 2001; Wood 1994b; Breukelaar 1994; see the contributions in Murray 2016a; but see also the contributions in Mitchell and Wood 2002; and Gauthier and Galinie 1997; for an excellent overview of research on Gregory before the year 2000; see also Patzold 2000.

4. The most comprehensive modern edition is still Krusch 1888a; for other editions and translations before 1974, see Repertorium 1964–2007, vol. 4, pp. 555–556. Cf. also the update at http://www.geschichtsquellen.de/repOpus_02325.html (2017-03-06), under Pseudo-Fredegarius, scholasticus, *Chronicon*; for translations and introductions after 1974: see Devillers and Meyers 2001 (French); Kusterning 1982 (German), for more recent discussions, see also Wood 1994c; Collins 2007; Fischer 2014; and Reimitz 2015, pp. 166–239.

5. The relevant edition is still Krusch 1888c; for other editions and translations before 1997, see Repertorium 1964–2007, vol. 7, pp. 266–267; cf. the update at http://www.geschichtsquellen.de/repOpus_03269.html (2017-03-06) under *Liber historiae Francorum*; see also the recent French translation and introduction in Lebecq 2015; cf. also Gerberding 1987; Wood 1995; Dörler 2013, Reimitz 2015, pp. 240–281.

Works Cited

Ancient Sources

Eusebius of Caesarea, *Historia Ecclesiastica*. E. Schwartz and T. Mommsen (eds.). (1999). *Eusebius Werke* 2.1: Die Kirchengeschichte, Die griechischen christlichen Schriftsteller der ersten Jahrhunderte 6.1, 2nd ed. by F. Winkelmann. Berlin: Akademie-Verlag.

Fredegar, *Chronicle*. B. Krusch (ed.). (1888a). *Chronicarum quae dicunt Fredegarii Scholastici libri IV cum Continuationibus*. MGH SRM, 2 (pp. 1–167). Hanover: Hahn.

Fredegar, *Continuations*. B. Krusch (ed.). (1888b). *Chronicarum quae dicunt Fredegarii Scholastici libri IV cum Continuationibus*. MGH SRM 2 (pp. 168–193). Hanover: Hahn.

Fredegar, *Chronicle*. J. M. Wallace-Hadrill (ed. and trans.). (1960). *The Fourth Book of the Chronicle of Fredegar with Its Continuations*. London: Nelson.

Fredegar, *Chronicle*. O. Devillers and J. Meyers (eds. and trans.) (2001). *Fredegaire. Chronique des temps Mérovingiens. Livre IV et continuations*. Turnhout: Brepols.

Gerberding, R., and Fouracre, P. (trans.). (1996). *Late Merovingian France: History and Hagiography, 640–720*. Manchester, NY: Manchester University Press.

Gregory of Tours, *Histories* (DHL). B. Krusch, W. Levison, and W. Holtzmann (eds.). (1951). *Decem libri historiarum*. MGH SRM 1.1. Hanover: Hahn.

Gregory of Tours, Histories. L. Thorpe (trans.). (1974). *The History of the Franks*, London: Penguin.

Hydatius, Chronicle. R. W. Burgess (trans.). (1993). *The Chronicle of Hydatius and the Consularia Constantinopolitana*. Oxford: Clarendon.

Liber historiae Francorum. B. Krusch (ed.). (1888c). MGH SRM 2 (pp. 215–328). Hanover: Hahn.

Liber historiae Francorum. S. Lebecq (trans.). (2015). *La Geste des rois des Francs: Liber historiae Francorum*. Classiques de l'histoire de moyen âge 54. Paris: Les belles lettres.

Marius of Avrenches, *Chronicle*. J. Favrod (ed. and trans.). (1991). *La Chronique de Marius d'Avenches (455–581). Texte, traduction et commentaire*. Lausanne: Section d'histoire, Faculté des lettres, Université de Lausanne.

Ruricius of Limoges, *Letters*. Mathisen, R. (trans.). (1999). *Ruricius of Limoges and Friends. A Collection of Letters from Visigothic Aquitania*. Liverpool: Liverpool University Press.

Venantius Fortunatus, *Carmina*: F. Leo (ed.). (1881). MGH AA 4, 1. Berlin: Weidmann.

Modern Sources

Anton, H.-H. (2003). "Origo gentis. Die Franken." In *Reallexikon der Germanischen Altertumskunde*, 2nd ed., vol. 22. Berlin: Walter de Gruyter.

Becher, M. (1994). "Der sogenannte Staatsstreich Grimoalds. Versuch einer Neubewertung." In J. Jarnut, U. Nonn, and M. Richter (eds.), *Karl Martell in seiner Zeit* (pp. 119–147). Beihefte der Francia 37. Sigmaringen: Thorbecke.

Berschin, W. (1986). *Biographie und Epochenstil im lateinischen Mittelalter*, 1: *Von der Passio Perpetuae zu den Dialogi Gregors des Großen*. Stuttgart: Anton Hiersemann.

Bourgain, P. (2016). "The Works of Gregory of Tours: Manuscripts, Language, and Style." In A. C. Murray (ed.), *A Companion to Gregory of Tours*, pp. 141–188. Leiden: Brill.

Bourgain, P., and Heinzelmann, M. (1997). "L'oeuvre de Grégoire de Tours: la diffusion des manuscrits." In N. Gauthier and H. Galinie (eds.), *Grégoire de Tours et l'espace Gaulois* (pp. 273–317). Supplément à la Revue archéologique du Centre de la France 13.1. Tours: Féderation pour l'édition de la Revue archéologique du Centre.

Breukelaar, A. (1994). *Historiography and Episcopal Authority in Sixth-Century Gaul: The Histories of Gregory of Tours Interpreted in Their Historical Context*. Göttingen: Vandenhoeck & Ruprecht.

Brown, P. (2002). "Gregory of Tours: Introduction." In K. Mitchell and I. N. Wood (eds.), *The World of Gregory of Tours* (pp. 1–27). Boston: Brill.

Brown, P. (2008). "Christendom c. 600." In T. F. X. Noble and J. Smith (eds.), *Cambridge History of Christianity* (pp. 1–18). Cambridge: Cambridge University Press.

Brown, P. (2012). *Through the Eye of a Needle: Wealth, the Fall of Rome, and the Making of Christianity in the West, 350–550 AD*. Princeton, NJ: Princeton University Press.

Brown, P. (2013). *The Rise of Western Christendom. Triumph and Diversity, 200–1000*, 3rd anniversary edition. London: Wiley-Blackwell.

Brown, P. (2015). *The Ransom of the Soul: Afterlife and Wealth in Early Western Christianity*. Cambridge, MA: Harvard University Press.

Buc, P. (1994). *L'ambiguïté du livre: Prince, pouvoir, et peuple dans les commentaires de la Bible au moyen âge*, Collection théologie historique 95. Paris: Editions Beauchesne.

Burgess, R. W., and M. Kulikowsi. (2013). *Mosaics of Time. The Latin Chronicle Traditions from the First Century BC to the Sixth Century AD*, 1: *Historical Introduction to the Chronicle Genre from Its Origins to the High Middle Ages*. Turnhout: Brepols.

Collins, R. (2007). *Die Fredegar-Chroniken*. MGH Studien und Texte. Hanover: Hahn.

Coumert, M. (2007). *Origines des peuples. Les récits d'origine des peuples dans le Haut Moyen Âge occidental (550–850)*. Collection des études augustiniennes. Série moyen âge et temps modernes 42. Paris: Institut d'études augustiniennes.

DeGregorio, S. (2011). "Bede and the Old Testament." In S. DeGregorio (ed.), *The Cambridge Companion to Bede* (pp. 127–141). Cambridge: Cambridge University Press.

De Lubac, H. (1959–1964). *Exégèse medieval. Les quatre sens de l'écriture*. 2 vols. Paris: Aubier.

Devillers, O., and Meyers, J. (2001). *Frédégaire. Chronique des temps Mérovingiens. Livre IV et continuations*. Turnhout: Brepols.

Diefenbach, S., and Müller, G. (2013). *Gallien in Spätantike und frühem Mittelalter. Kulturgeschichte einer Region*. Berlin: Walter de Gruyter.

Dörler, P. (2013). "The *Liber Historiae Francorum*—A Model for a New Frankish Self-Confidence." *Networks and Neighbours* 1: 23–43.

Dumézil, B. (2007). "Gogo et ses amis: écriture, échanges et ambitions dans un réseau aristocratique de la fin du Ve siècle." *Revue historique* 643: 553–593.

Dumézil, B. (2016). "Les vrais-faux messages diplomatiques mérovingiens." In B. Dumézil and L. Viessière (eds.), *Épistolaire politique* 2 (pp. 19–47). Paris: Presses de l'Université Paris Sorbonne.

Ehlen, O. (2011). *Venantius-Interpretationen. Rhetorische und generische Transgressionen beim neuen Orpheus*. Stuttgart: Franz Steiner.

Esders, S. (2009). "Herakleios, Dagobert und die 'beschnittenen Völker'. Die Umwälzungen des Mittelmeerraums im 7. Jahrhundert in der fränkischen Chronik des sog. Fredegar." In A. Goltz, H. Leppin, and H. Schlange-Schöningen (eds.), *Jenseits der Grenzen. Studien zur spätantiken und frühmittelalterlichen Geschichtsschreibung* (pp. 239–311). Millennium Studien 25. Berlin: Walter de Gruyter.

Esders, S. (2014). "'Avenger of All Perjury' in Constantinople, Ravenna, and Merovingian Metz. St Polyeuctus, Sigibert I, and the Division of Charibert's Kingdom in 568." In A. Fischer and I. N. Wood (eds.), *Western Perspectives on the Mediterranean. Cultural Transfer in Late Antiquity and the Early Middle Ages, 400–800 AD* (pp. 23–76). London: Bloomsbury.

Ewig, E. (1976). "Die fränkischen Teilungen und Teilreiche (511–613)." In E. Ewig (ed.), *Spätantikes und Fränkisches Gallien* 1 (pp. 114–171). Beihefte der Francia, 3.1. Munich: Jan Thorbecke.

Ewig, E (1998). "Trojamythos und fränkische Frühgeschichte." In D. Geuenich (ed.), *Die Franken und die Alemannen bis zur "Schlacht von Zülpich" (496/497)* (pp. 1–30). Reallexikon der Germanischen Altertumskunde, suppl. vol. 19. Berlin: Walter de Gruyter.

Feldherr, A., and Hardy, G. (eds.). (2011). *The Oxford History of Historical Writing*. 1: *Beginnings to AD 600*. Oxford: Oxford University Press.

Fischer, A. (2012). *Karl Martell. Der Beginn karolingischer Herrschaft*. Stuttgart: Kohlhammer.

Fischer, A. (2014). "Rewriting History: Fredegar's Perspective on the Mediterranean." In A. Fischer and I. N. Wood (eds.), *Western Perspectives on the Mediterranean. Cultural Transfer in Late Antiquity and the Early Middle Ages, 400–800 AD* (pp. 55–76). London: Bloomsbury.

Fischer, A. (forthcoming). *Die Fredegar-Chronik. Komposition und Kontextualisierung*.

Fouracre, P. (2000). *The Age of Charles Martel*. London: Routledge.

Ganz, D. (2010). "Fragmentierung von patristischen Texten im früheren Mittelalter." In C. Gastgeber, C. Glassner, K. Holzner-Tobisch, and R. Spreitzer (eds.), *Fragmente: Der Umgang mit lückenhafter Quellenüberlieferung in der Mittelalterforschung* (pp. 151–159). Vienna: Verlag der Österreichischen Akademie der Wissenschaften.

Ganz, D. (2018). "In the Circle of the Bishops of Bourges." In S. Esders and Y. Hen (eds.), *East and West in the Early Middle Ages: The Merovingian Kingdoms in Mediterranean Perspective* (pp. 265–280). Cambridge: Cambridge University Press.

Gauthier, N., and Galinie, H. (1997). *Grégoire de Tours et l'espace Gaulois*, Supplément à la Revue archéologique du Centre de la France 13.1. Tours: Féderation pour l'édition de la Revue archéologique du Centre.

George, J. W. (1992). *Venantius Fortunatus. A Latin Poet in Merovingian Gaul*. Oxford: Oxford University Press.

Gerberding, R. (1987). *Rise of the Carolingians and the Liber Historiae Francorum*. Oxford: Oxford University Press.

Gerberding, R., and Fouracre, P. (1996). *Late Merovingian France: History and Hagiography, 640–720*. Manchester, NY: Manchester University Press.

Ghosh, S. (2016). *Writing the Barbarian Past. Studies in Early Medieval Historical Narrative*. Leiden: Brill.

Gioanni, S. (2001). "Fonctions culturelles, sociales et politiques de l'amicitia épistolaire dans la correspondance d'Ennode de Pavie." *Lalies* 21: 165–181.

Gioanni, S. (2009). "La langue du pourpre et la rhétorique administrative dans les royaumes ostrogothique, burgunde et franc." In F. Bougard, R. Le Jan, and R. McKitterick (eds.), *La culture de haut moyen âge: une question des élites* (pp. 13–38). Turnhout: Brepols.

Goffart, W. (2005). *Narrators of Barbarian History (AD 550–800). Jordanes, Gregory of Tours, Bede and Paul the Deacon*. 2nd ed. Notre Dame, IN: University of Notre Dame Press (first edition: Princeton, NJ: Princeton University Press, 1988).

Grafton, A., and Williams, M. (2008). *Christianity and the Transformation of the Book. Origen, Eusebius, and the Library of Caesarea*. Cambridge, MA: Harvard University Press.

Halsall, G. (2007). "The Preface to Book V of Gregory of Tours' *Histories*. Its Form, Context and Significance." *English Historical Review* 122: 297–317.

Hamann, S. (2003). "Zur Chronologie des Staatsstreichs Grimoalds." *Deutsches Archiv für die Erforschung des Mittelalters* 59: 49–96.

Hartmann, M. (2004). "Die Darstellung der Frauen im *Liber Historiae Francorum* und die Verfasserfrage." *Concilium Medii Aevi* 7: 209–237.

Heinzelmann, M. (2001). *Gregory of Tours. History and Society in the Sixth Century*. Cambridge: Cambridge University Press.

Heinzelmann, M. (2003). "La réécriture hagiographique dans l'œuvre de Grégoire de Tours." In M. Heinzelmann and M. Goullet (eds.), *La réécriture hagiographique dans l' occident médiéval: transformations formelles et idéologiques* (pp. 15–70). Beihefte der Francia 58. Sigmaringen: Thorbecke.

Helm, R. (1956). *Die Chronik des Hieronymus, Eusebius Werk*, 7: Die griechischen christlichen Schriftsteller der ersten Jahrhunderte 47. Berlin: Akademie-Verlag.

Hen, Y. (1995). *Culture and Religion in Merovingian Gaul, AD 481–751*. Leiden: Brill.

Hen, Y. (1998). "The Uses of the Bible and the Perception of Kingship in Early Medieval Gaul." *Early Medieval Europe* 7(3): 277–289.

Hen, Y. (2012). "Changing Places. Chrodobert, Bobo and the Wife of Grimoald." *Revue Belge de Philologie et d'Histoire* 89: 225–244.

Heydemann, G. (2013). "Biblical Israel and the Christian Gentes. Social Metaphors and Concepts of Community in Cassiodorus' *Expositio psalmorum*." In G. Heydemann and W. Pohl (eds.), *Strategies of Identification. Early Medieval Perspectives* (pp. 101–144). Cultural Encounters in Late Antiquity and the Middle Ages 13. Turnhout: Brepols.

Hilchenbach, K. (2009). *Das vierte Buch der Historien von Gregor von Tours. Edition mit sprachwissenschaftlich-textkritischem und historischem Kommentar*. 2 vols. Frankfurt: Peter Lang.

Inglebert, H. (2001). *Interpretatio Christiana: Les mutations des savoirs, cosmographie, géographie, ethnographie, histoire, dans la antiquité chrétienne*. Paris: Institut d'études Augustiniennes.

Inglebert, H. (2014). *Le monde, l'histoire. Essai sur les histoires universelles*. Paris: Presses Universitaires de France.

Jauss, H. R. (1999). "Theory of Genres and Medieval Literature." In H. R. Jauss (ed.), *Towards an Aesthetics of Reception* (pp. 76–109). Minneapolis: University of Minnesota Press.

Kelly, C. "The Shape of the Past. Eusebius of Caesarea and Old Testament History." In C. Kelly, R. Flower, and M. Stuart (eds.), *Unclassical Traditions. Alternatives to the Classical Past in Late Antiquity*, vol. I (pp. 13–27). Cambridge: Cambridge University Press.

Kreiner, J. (2014). *The Social Life of Hagiography in the Merovingian Kingdom*. Cambridge: Cambridge University Press.

Krüger, K.-H. (1985). *Die Universalchroniken*. Typologie des sources du moyen âge occidental 16. Turnhout: Brepols.

Krusch, B. (1932). "Die handschriftlichen Grundlagen der *Historia Francorum* Gregors von Tours." *Historische Vierteljahrschrift* 27: 673–723.

Kusternig A, (1982). *Die vier Bücher der Chroniken des sogenannten Fredegar, Ausgewählte Quellen zur Geschichte des 7. und 8. Jahrhunderts*, ed. H. Haupt (pp. 3–271). Freiherr vom Stein Gedächtnisausgabe 4a. Darmstadt: Wissenschaftliche Buchgemeinschaft.

Maier, H. O. (2010). "Dominion from Sea to Sea. Eusebius of Caesarea, Constantine the Great and the Exegesis of Empire." In M. Vessey, S. Betcher, R. A. Daum, and H. O. Meier (eds.), *The Calling of Nations. Exegesis, Ethnography and Empire in Biblical-Historical Present* (pp. 149–175). Toronto: Toronto University Press.

Mathisen, R. (2013). "Desiderius of Cahors. Last of the Romans." In R. Mathisen and S. Diefenbach (eds.), *Gallien in Spätantike und Frühmittelalter. Kulturgeschichte einer Region* (pp. 455–470). Berlin: Walter de Gruyter.

McClure, J. (1983). "Bede's Old Testament Kings." In P. Wormald (ed.), *Ideal and Reality in Frankish and Anglo-Saxon Society. Studies Presented to J. M. Wallace-Hadrill* (pp. 162–175). Oxford: Oxford University Press.

McKitterick, R. (2006). *Perceptions of the Past in the Early Middle Ages*. Notre Dame, IN: University of Notre Dame Press.

McMahon, M. (2019). "Polemics in Translation. Jerome's Fashioning of History in the Chronicle." In W. Pohl and V. Wieser (eds.), *Historiography of Identity 1: Ancient and Christian Models* (pp. 219–246). Turnhout: Brepols.

Mitchell, K. (2002). "Marking the Bounds. The Distant Past in Gregory's History." In K. Mitchell and I. N. Wood (eds.), *The World of Gregory of Tours* (pp. 295–306). Cultures, Beliefs and Traditions 8. Leiden: Brill.

Momigliano, A. (1992). "The Origins of Ecclesiastical Historiography." In A. Momigliano (ed.), *The Classical Foundations of Modern Historiography* (pp. 132–156). Sather Classical Lectures 54. Berkeley: University of California Press.

Mratschek, S. (2016). "The Letter Collection of Sidonius Apollinaris." In C. Sogno, B. K. Sorin, and E. Watts (eds.), *Late Antique Letter Collections. A Critical Introduction and Reference Guide* (pp. 309–336). Berkeley: University of California Press.

Muelke, M. (2008). *Der Autor und sein Text. Die Verfälschung des Originals im Urteil antiker Autoren*. Untersuchungen zur antiken Literatur und Geschichte 93. Berlin: Walter de Gruyter.

Müller, G. M. (2013). "Freundschaften wider den Verfall. Gemeinschaftsbildung und kulturelle Selbstverortung." In G. M. Müller and S. Diefenbach (eds.), *Gallien in Spätantike und Frühmittelalter. Kulturgeschichte einer Region* (pp. 421–454). Berlin: Walter de Gruyter.

Murray, A. C. (2006). *Gregory of Tours, The Merovingians*. Peterborough, Ontario: Broadview Press.

Murray, A. C. (ed.). (2016a). *A Companion to Gregory of Tours*. Leiden: Brill.

Murray, A. C. (2016b). "The Composition of the Histories of Gregory or Tours and Its Bearing on the Political Narrative." In A. C. Murray (ed.), *A Companion to Gregory of Tours* (pp. 63–101). Leiden: Brill.

Nelson, J. (1990). "Gender and Genre in Women Historians of the Early Middle Ages." In J. P. Genet (ed.), *L'historiographie médiévale en Europe* (pp. 143–163). Paris: Éditions du CNRS. (Repr. in J. Nelson (1996). *The Frankish World* (pp. 183–198). London: Routledge.

Offergeld, T. (2001). *Reges pueri. Das Königtum Minderjähriger im frühen Mittelalter*. 2 vols. MGH 50. Hanover: Hahn.

O'Gorman, E. C. (2011). "Imperial History and Biography at Rome." In A. Feldherr and G. Hardy (eds.), *The Oxford History of Historical Writing* (pp. 291–315). Oxford: Oxford University Press.

O'Loughlin, T. (2013). *Early Medieval Exegesis in the Latin West*. Aldershot: Routledge.

Patzold, S. (2000.) "Appendix." In R. Buchner (ed.), *Gregor von Tours: Zehn Bücher Geschichten* 2 (pp. 477–491). Ausgewählte Quellen zur deutschen Geschichte des Mittelalters, 2–3. 8th ed. Darmstadt: Wissenschaftliche Buchgemeinschaft.

Potter, D. (2011). "The Greek Historians of Imperial Rome." In A. Feldherr and G. Hardy (eds.), *The Oxford History of Historical Writing. Beginnings to AD 600* (pp. 316–344). Oxford: Oxford University Press.

Preiser-Kapeller, J. (2012). "Luhmann in Byzantium. A Systems Theory Approach for Historical Network Analysis." Working paper for the International Conference "The Connected Past: People, Networks and Complexity in Archaeology and History," Southampton, April 24–25, 2012. (http://oeaw.academia.edu/JohannesPreiserKapeller/Papers)

Reimitz, H. (2015). *History, Frankish Identity and the Framing of Western Ethnicity, 550–850*. Cambridge: Cambridge University Press.

Reimitz, H. (2016a). "After Rome, before Francia: Religion, Ethnicity, and Identity Politics in Gregory of Tours' *Ten Books of Histories*." In K. Cooper and K. Leyser (eds.), *Making Early Medieval Societies* (pp. 58–78). Cambridge: Cambridge University Press.

Reimitz, H. (2016b). "The Early Medieval Histories of Gregory of Tours' *Historiae*." In A. C. Murray (ed.), *A Companion to Gregory of Tours* (pp. 519–566). Leiden: Brill.

Repertorium. (1964–2007). *Repertorium fontium historiae medii aevi (primum ab Augusto Potthast digestum, nunc cura colegii historicorum e pluribus nationibus emendatum et auctum*. 11 vols. Rome: Instituto storico italiano per il medio evo. For updates on the page of the Repertorium "Deutsche Geschichtsquellen des Mittelalters," see: http://www.geschichtsquellen.de/index.html.

Riché, P. (1995). *Education et culture dans l'Occident barbare: VIe–VIIIe siècle*. 4th ed. Paris: Seuil.

Roberts, M. (2009). *The Humblest Sparrow. The Poetry of Venantius Fortunatus*. Ann Arbor: University of Michigan Press.

Roberts, M. (2016). "Venantius Fortunatus and Gregory of Tours: Patronage and Poetry." In A. C. Murray (ed.), *A Companion to Gregory of Tours* (pp. 35–61). Leiden: Brill.

Rousseau, P. (2016). "Gregory's Kings, The Theatre of the Modern and the Endurance of Romanitas." In J. Kreiner and H. Reimitz (eds.), *Motions of Late Antiquity. Essays on Religion, Politics and Identity in Honour of Peter Brown* (pp. 209–230). Turnhout: Brepols.

Scholz, S. (2015). *Die Merowinger*. Stuttgart: W. Kohlhammer.

Shanzer, D. (2010). "The Tale of Frodebert's Tail." In E. Dickey and A. Chahoud (eds.), *Colloquial and Literary Latin* (pp. 377–405). Cambridge: Cambridge University Press.

Shaw, R. (2016). "Chronology, Composition and Authorial Conception in Gregory of Tours' Miracula." In A. C. Murray (ed.), *A Companion to Gregory of Tours* (pp. 102–140). Leiden: Brill.

Thacker, A. (2011). "Bede and History." In S. DeGregorio (ed.), *The Cambridge Companion to Bede* (pp. 170–189). Cambridge: Cambridge University Press.

Torgerson, J. (2016). "Could Isidore's Chronicle Have Delighted Cicero?" *Medieval Worlds* 3: 65–82.

van Nuffelen, P. (2010). "Theology versus Genre? The Universalism of Christian Historiography in Late Antiquity." In P. Liddel and A. Fear (eds.), *Historiae mundi. Studies in Universal Historiography* (pp. 148–161). London: Bristol Classical Press.

van Uytfanghe, M. (1987). *Stylisation biblique et condition humaine dans l'hagiographie mérovingienne (600–750).* Brussels: AWLSK.

Whitby, M. (2011). "Imperial Christian Historiography." In A. Feldherr and G. Hardy (eds.), *The Oxford History of Historical Writing* (pp. 346–369). Oxford: Oxford University Press.

Wieser, V. (2019). "The Chronicle of Hydatius: A Historical Guidebook to the Last Days of the Western Roman Empire." In M. Gabriele and J. Palmer, *Apocalypse and Reform from Late Antiquity to the Middle Ages* (pp. 247–98). Turnhout: Brepols.

Williard, H. (2014). "Letter-Writing and Literary Culture in Merovingian Gaul." *European Review of History: Revue européenne d'histoire* 21(5): 691–710.

Wood, I. N. (1990). "Administration, Law and Culture in Merovingian Gaul." In R. McKitterick (ed.), *The Uses of Literacy in Early Medieval Europe* (pp. 63–81). Cambridge: Cambridge University Press.

Wood, I. N. (1994a). *The Merovingian Kingdoms 450–751.* London: Routledge.

Wood, I. N. (1994b). *Gregory of Tours.* Bangor: Headstart History.

Wood, I. N. (1994c). "Fredegar's Fables." In A. Scharer and G. Scheibelreiter (eds.), *Historiographie im frühen Mittelalter* (pp. 359–366). Veröffentlichungen des Instituts für Österreichische Geschichtsforschung 32. Vienna: Böhlau.

Wood, I. N. (1995). "Defining the Franks. Frankish Origins in Early Medieval Historiography." In S. Forde, L. Johnson, and A. V. Murray (eds.), *Concepts of National Identity in the Middle Ages* (pp. 47–57), Leeds Texts and Monographs, New Series 14. Leeds: University of Leeds School of English.

Wood, I. N. (2002). "The Individuality of Gregory of Tours." In I. N. Wood and K. Mitchell (eds.), *The World of Gregory of Tours* (pp. 29–46). Leiden, Cologne: Brill.

Wood, I. N. (2010). "The 'Chain of Chronicles' in London BL 16974." In R. Corradini and M. Diesenberger (eds.), *Zwischen Niederschrift und Wiederschrift. Historiographie und Hagiographie im Spannungsfeld von Edition und Kompendienüberlieferung* (pp. 68–78). Forschungen zur Geschichte des Mittelalters 15. Vienna: Verlag der Österreichischen Akademie der Wissenschaften.

Wood, I. N. (2014). "Who Are the Philistines." In C. Gantner, R. McKitterick, and S. Meeder (eds.), *The Resources of the Past in Early Medieval Europe.* Cambridge: Cambridge University Press.

Wood, I. N. (2015). "Universal Chronicles in the Early Medieval West." *Medieval Worlds* 1: 47–60.

Wood, I. N. (2016). "The Problem of Merovingian Culture." In S. Dusil, G. Schwedler, and R. Schwitter (eds.), *Exzerpieren—Kompilieren—Tradieren. Transformationen des Wissens zwischen Spätantike und Frühmittelalter* (pp. 199–222) Millennium Studien 64. Berlin: DeGruyter.

Wood, I. N. (2018). "Why Collect Letters?" In G. Müller (ed.), *Zwischen Alltagskommunikation und Literarischer Identitätsbildung. Kulturgeschichtliche Aspekte lateinischer Epistolographie in der Spätantike* (pp. 45–62). Stuttgart: Steiner-Verlag.

Wood, I. N. (forthcoming), "Bede's *Historia Ecclesiastica* and Anglian Northumbria." In G. Heydemann and H. Reimitz, *Historiographies of Identity 2: Post-Roman Multiplicity and New Political Identities*. Leiden: Brill.

CHAPTER 23

....

MEROVINGIAN LEGAL
CULTURES

....

ALICE RIO

HISTORIANS have used law and the exercise of justice as an important index of change in the transition from the late Roman Empire to the Merovingian kingdoms. In crude terms, the basic opposition between the two goes something like this: although it never *forced* anyone to use Roman law for private matters, the Roman Empire did have state officials placed in charge of courts; professional jurists and lawyers, trained in schools, providing expert advice on procedure to both litigants and officials; highly intrusive and coercive modes of proof and fact-finding, including the use of torture, and an apparatus of state-enforced punishment; and, perhaps most fundamentally, a distinction in principle between what was law and what was not law.[1] In Merovingian Francia, by contrast, one finds no known professional lawyer; venues for making legal decisions that coexisted more than they coordinated with each other; an emphasis on self-help; reliance on local consensus to determine the outcome of cases, with modes of proof that were often designed less to find out the facts of a case than to evaluate how much local support was available to the various parties; and acknowledgment of a wide variety of different sources of authority alongside written law. Naturally, self-help and local consensus all mattered under the Roman empire too; but that layer of Roman legal practice that had been structured by professional expertise as well as by state action becomes, by the early Middle Ages, practically impossible to find. Historiographical characterizations of this change were long dominated by a series of oppositions: Roman versus Germanic; literacy versus orality; rationality versus irrationality; technical knowledge versus folk tradition; coercion versus consensus; hierarchy versus community.

The decreasing emphasis on professionalism and technicality was mischaracterized by early French historians, such as Ferdinand Lot, as reflecting a lack of concern with law (Guillot 1995, pp. 653–654). This, however, cannot be correct, since legal matter of one kind or another makes up a very substantial proportion of the written evidence for this period, surviving in a variety of genres: law codes; private documents; records of judgments heard before the king (*notitiae* or royal *placita*); model documents in notaries' handbooks (*formulae*); and narrative treatments about particularly striking or lurid cases, as well as law-related miracle stories. All this suggests that people in Merovingian Francia in fact felt a pervasive concern with the legal realm, read broadly. Part of what lends a legal character to so much of our source material is that it is so hard to see the edges of the category of the "legal" during this period: there were all kinds of ways in which the behavior of individuals, including violent behavior, could be retrospectively read as a legitimate legal action or claim when constructing the narrative of a case. As we shall see, this is in itself a key aspect of this period: because legal behavior was neither specialized nor technical, it could be used to justify a wide spectrum of social action.

Legal Traditions, Roman and Frankish: The *Pactus Legis Salicae*

The notion of a clash between Roman and Germanic legal cultures—or rather, between Roman "law" and Germanic "custom"—was long identified as a major motor for change. Where nineteenth-century French historians, guided by surviving narrative sources, had often found chaos and anomia, German historians of the same era saw a world filled with law and with conflicting legal traditions (Brunner 1906). In their view, the earliest known version of Salic Law, the *Pactus Legis Salicae*, probably issued late in the reign of Clovis in the first decade of the sixth century, was a repository for the long-standing, ancestral customs of the Franks as a people (*Volksrecht*, or "people's law").[2] The idea, however, that Salic Law was distilling some kind of immemorial Frankish essence has become untenable. A key problem, highlighted by Patrick Wormald in the 1970s, lies in the haphazard character of the process of compilation. For him, the law codes of the northern European successor states assembled fragments of royal legislation alongside earlier materials to form a heterogeneous mixture of "custom, policy and judgment" (Wormald 1977, p. 115). He contrasted this with law codes from southern Europe, where he saw more continuous engagement with written legislation in practice. Wormald argued that northern European law codes were allowed to be such a mixed bag because they were essential neither to the practical business of lawmaking (for which the only thing that really mattered was the king's verbal command) nor of dispute settlement (since surviving examples of dispute settlement so rarely seem to contain any explicit reference to written law). Giving law a written form was more an ideologically driven afterthought, designed to project royal authority over Roman subjects, to borrow an important symbol of kingship from both Roman and biblical traditions, as well as, in some cases, to shore up dynastic legitimacy.[3] For Wormald, the operative distinction was therefore that between literacy and orality: the written word inherently represented a Roman and clerical perspective, and so necessarily constituted a distorting prism for all that was Frankish or lay.

These problems have only become further exacerbated. Wormald's argument had still left some room for the identification of a distinctively Frankish identity at work in Salic Law, even if he thought the written text was likely to misrepresent it. What was "Frankish," however, became an ever more elusive thing as ethnicity during this period became recognized as more fluid and situational than a simple choice between two rigid, homogeneous, and fully constituted cultural traditions would suggest. The notion of any clear opposition between "Roman" and "barbarian" in law increasingly came under fire during the 1980s (Wood 1986, p. 21; Amory 1993; Collins 1998; see Coumert, Chapter 5, this volume). If anything, ethnic distinctions in written law, such as those made between Franks and Romans as either victims or perpetrators in Salic Law, are now seen as contributing to the engineering of ethnic identity rather than merely reflecting it: a way of inventing tradition, and of turning into "Franks" people who may have been just as different from each other as they were from the Gallo-Roman elite—following the needs of the identity politics of the moment rather than any longstanding custom (see Reimitz, Chapter 22, this volume).

Salic Law has also come to be seen as ever less Frankish, more royal, and more late antique. The large extent to which later Merovingian royal capitularies were influenced by late Roman imperial legislation has been rightly stressed (Esders 1997), but arguments for Roman imperial influence have not been confined to them. A debate has lately been revived over the earliest known sixty-five-title version of Salic Law, which some historians think was made up of much earlier regulations intended to set rules for Frankish troops back when they still formed part of the Roman army (for this debate, see Poly 1993; Renard 2009; Ubl 2009, 2014; on the army, see Sarti, Chapter 12, this volume). Many other historians, while still subscribing to the traditional dating of the text to the reign of Clovis, had made arguments tending in a similar direction, and suggested a late Roman context as the background for at least some of the provisions included in the *Pactus*. This was done during the 1980s and 1990s in particular, when claims for a "long" Late Antiquity reached their highwater mark, and when the most severe level of doubt was cast over the extent of structural change brought about by the fall of Rome. Much of the material contained in the barbarian law codes that had up to then been regarded as entirely new and non-Roman was linked back to something known as "Roman vulgar law" (originally coined by Levy 1951; see Liebs 2008). This term refers to provincial legal practice under the late empire, which was argued to have been very different from the Roman law of the jurists and law books and was proposed as the true source for some of the practices subsequently recorded in the barbarian law codes (and so traditionally identified as barbarian rather than Roman). Since it remained essentially undocumented in surviving sources, however, Roman vulgar law functioned as something of a black box, from which arguments for continuity could always be generated (Wormald 1977, p. 112).

This tendency to Romanize the content of the barbarian law codes extended to those aspects that had up to then been seen as most iconically Germanic: for instance, the ordeal, which required accused persons to clear themselves by holding a heated iron or by retrieving an object from a boiling cauldron (innocence or guilt being assessed based on the healing of the wound); or oath-helping, in which the accused had to gather a set number of people to swear to his innocence with him (Wood 1986, pp. 17, 19). Some historians even read feuding and private vengeance through a Roman lens (Halsall 1999, pp. 17–18). (More on all of these later.) This approach offered a way of challenging the notion of the inherent superiority of Roman law, by crediting Roman provincial practice with those elements in the barbarian law codes that had been highlighted by previous generations of historians as the most glaringly irrational (Caenegem 1990). Vulgar law, then, was a way for historians to bridge Roman and Germanic cultures, which were coming to be seen as less and less different from each other (Wood 1986, pp. 20–22; Geary 1988; Collins 1998).

Even now that Roman vulgar law has lost some of its appeal as an argument (Ubl 2014, pp. 434–439), however, legal practice in Merovingian Gaul continues to be read largely in terms of an offshoot of late Roman legal culture, more than in the light of any distinctive Germanic contribution. This may be because this Germanic influence is so unknowable, and also because law codes themselves have so much fallen from grace as a source for actual legal practice—again following Wormald's argument that they were not referred to in the course of actual disputes.[4] In particular, the emphasis on continuity from the legal world of late Roman Gaul to that of the Merovingians grew as stronger claims were made, from the perspective of practice rather than prescription, for documentary sophistication, the use of writing, and literate skills (Classen 1977; Ganz 1983; Wood 1990).

Documentary Culture: The World of the Formularies

One notary's handbook, or "formulary," collected in Angers during the Merovingian period preserves a document in which a man declared a break-in at his home, as a result of which, along with some valuables, he lost "documents of sale, loan securities, transfers of property, donations, marriage gifts, dispute settlements, gifts, contracts, exchanges, agreements, deeds of security, annulments, judgments and records of judgment, contracts of obligation, and many others, too many to list one by one" (*Formulae Andecavenses* no. 32; for a full translation, see Rio 2008, pp. 74–75). Lists of this kind, just like lists of goods and appurtenances included in land transfers, attempted to cover every eventuality rather than offering an itemized description of what was really there. This one has nonetheless impressed modern historians, not only because it suggests a single layman might keep a wide range of different documents inside his home, but also because it implies that keeping such documents was essential to the effective holding of property, since the owner took such pains to have them replaced.

All this seems to imply a highly literate, indeed, bureaucratic system. Several more formulas from the Merovingian period deal with exactly the same problem of lost documents as a result of burglary or arson, or, in a touching example from Tours, when a couple decided to bury their documents in a safe place, only to find them later destroyed by rot (Lauranson-Rosaz and Jeannin 2001; Brown 2002). One of them, from Clermont, gives a doubly strong impression of the importance of the documentary process in that the claimants who lost their documents were apparently asking for them to be replaced through the city's *gesta municipalia* (*Formulae Arvernenses* no. 1; Wood 1986, pp. 12–13). The *gesta* were the municipal archives that under the Roman empire had housed registers of landed property, both as a reference for the settlement of disputes and as a source of information for tax assessment. Several other references to the *gesta* are found scattered in other formularies, as well as in the odd surviving testament (Brown 2012; Barbier 2014). The keenness of document holders to get their documents replaced; the variety and volume of documents they were expected to have in their possession; the reference to functioning public archives; even the very existence of formularies themselves, which contain models for the sale of a single field or urban plot, suggesting a routine use of documents even where only small items of property changed hands— all this suggests a society at ease with documents and resorting to them as a matter of course. If this picture is to be believed, the very unimpressive rate of survival of actual private legal documents from the Merovingian period (twenty-seven all told surviving as originals, fourteen of which preserved through the archive of the monastery of St. Gall: *Chartae Latinae Antiquiores* nos. 40–44, 50, 54, 101, 103, 159–162, 171, 185*, 564, 569*, 571, 580, 582, 592*, 594, 596, 635, 656, 659*, 670–671) would then represent a truly gigantic rate of loss.[5]

There is no doubting, of course, that the scale of loss from the early Middle Ages in general was such that surviving documentation can only ever represent the tip of an iceberg; the question is how big this one was. There can be no definitive answer to this question. Ian Wood once suggested that so few dispute documents survive from southern Gaul, in comparison with those from the north, because the *gesta* continued to function so well there and so prevented most disputes from reaching the courts. The smooth running of the literate system would then have been the very thing making it harder for us to detect. (This, however, would imply that the Merovingians had managed to get the *gesta* to work more effectively than they ever had under the Roman Empire itself, which would be surprising.) At the same time, Wood also noted that there is no evidence that anyone anywhere in fact ever won a case by having a claim checked out against information contained in the *gesta*, leading him to suggest the alternative possibility that entering documents into the *gesta* might by then have been "a formality with no real function" (Wood 1986, p. 14). Another way of interpreting these documents may be to think of the *gesta* neither as a coherent and fully functioning archiving system nor as a meaningless relic, but as a way of lending a particular kind of archaizing ritual formality to the action one wished to take, as well as to the document written up to record it (Rio 2009, pp. 177–182; Brown 2012). Whatever the public forum before which the transaction took place (a local assembly, for instance, or a comital court), it became translated in the document as a full-blown late-antique scene, for which a whole urban context, complete with long-defunct official positions, was conjured up that almost certainly found no correspondence in reality and did not always remain internally consistent (Brown 2012, pp. 355–357).

To read this kind of mention as evidence of continuity would, therefore, be stretching the concept past the breaking point. In the absence of state structures in a position to take responsibility for the recognition, processing, or enforcement of legal claims, written documents actually presented a fairly tenuous kind of guarantee for the future. As we shall see, there are some signs that people availed themselves of it above all when they had few alternative ways of asserting their wishes. Reference to the *gesta* represented an appeal to tradition and formality; what it did not do was achieve any sort of guarantee that the document would be heeded in the future. Perhaps the insistence on tradition and formality was intended as a way of trying to make up through solemnity what the action lacked in bureaucratic solidity. The continual use of Roman legal instruments, then, should not necessarily be counted as evidence for continuity: however identical the textual scripts used, they were being put to a fundamentally different use.

One way of making any document potentially irrelevant, for instance, was through an accusation of forgery, which required resorting to more flexible sources of memory, such as living witnesses or an assessment of whether what was written down corresponded to the current local understanding of the situation. One couple, whose testament was later turned into a formula, took care to say that erasures or scrapings on the parchment of their document should not be cited as evidence of tampering—a symptom of anxiety which suggests, perhaps paradoxically, that the more sophisticated an understanding of written instruments laypeople had, the more vulnerable documents were to being invalidated through claims of forgery (*Formulae Marculfi* II, 17). This couple was seeking to exclude certain people from their inheritance and were clearly expecting particularly intense opposition; they were trying to leave as few excuses as possible for their testament to be ignored or invalidated. Noncontentious cases may well have been much less often committed to writing, at least between laypeople. It is therefore important to avoid extrapolating from instances that seem to indicate a systematically literate and bureaucratic system: the fact that some formulas survive for recording the sale of a single field should not be taken to imply that it was ever the norm to use writing in such cases.

It may well be, then, that written documents were resorted to particularly when the actions they recorded were not supported, or not wholly supported, by commonly accepted norms, or when they amounted to doing something unusual. That is, writing may have been especially useful for recording actions that needed extra help to gain social or legal validity. This could explain why we find so many unorthodox cases in formularies (our main surviving source of information for transactions involving laypeople). For instance, it was no doubt precisely because he was explicitly flouting both written law and custom that one father had a document made leaving his daughter an equal share of her inheritance with her brothers, referring to the discrimination against women in inheritance matters in Salic Law as an "impious custom" (*Formulae Marculfi* II, 12; *Pactus Legis Salicae* 59, 6). He clearly hoped that the expression of his will in a written document would be sufficient to turn his wish into reality, though that point would presumably have largely depended on who the daughter could find to litigate by her side if her brothers decided to dispute the document.

This does not mean, of course, that formularies *only* contain strange or unrepresentative cases: the very fact that they were collected into handbooks suggests that they were thought likely to be needed again. But sorting out what was normal from what was not is one of the most difficult aspects of dealing with these texts. Although they had a genuine normative value, they were not documents of jurisprudence: they did not tell users *what* to do, but how to express correctly whatever it was that they wanted to do. If anything, it is likely that the more controversial the transaction that was being undertaken, the more irreproachably traditional and conservative the written form adopted had to be. What the people whose business left a trace in formularies were doing in their documents was not necessarily demonstrating their adherence to any particular existing legal norms, but instead using a legal form in order to tap into a legitimizing cultural discourse. People used legal documents and legal language because this offered them a way of signifying and claiming their right to do whatever it was they were doing. The father in the formula mentioned above did not bother to claim that his action was compatible with written law. Instead, he claimed validity for his chosen course of action by framing it in a correct legal form, and adopting a distinctive and formal legal register.

This could explain the keen interest in formal correctness in the production of documents represented by the spread of formularies themselves. Their textual transmission suggests a distinctive pattern of diffusion, of repeated and constant cross-fertilization and borrowing. The impression is of a widely diffused pool of available models that scribes shared with one another and that each individual scribe could then draw on to compose the collection that would best serve his own needs and those of his patrons or institution. This has two main implications: first, it suggests an enthusiastic quest for documentary norms in general; and second, it suggests, at the same time, that it did not really matter *where* these norms were obtained, as long as they were recognizably "proper" and respectable models. A single formulary could use some very old or very recent documents as examples, as well as some documents gathered from completely different geographical regions. The key point here is that this dissemination of norms seems to have been driven entirely by demand from end users (the scribes and their clients) rather than by any sort of imposition from above (Rio 2009, pp. 187–197).

This kind of nonbinding, deeply customizable legal norm was precious not because it referred to any well-defined or even generally accepted body of law or custom, but because it represented a way of translating one's social action into legal terms, thus claiming greater validity for it. Having a written document made did not tie down the scope of "legal" action to any particular rules; it simply allowed users to express what they were doing as something that involved legitimate, recognizable rights—no matter how creative they were being in the process. This, rather than any automatic value as evidence or bureaucratic need, was the added legitimacy that documents lent to their users' actions. In this context, legal language and practices did not correspond to a coercive system but to an exploitable resource.

The sheer breadth and variety of different available cultural models (Roman, Frankish, Christian, court- or community-centred) through which people could choose to express and frame their actions in legal terms made this resource an exceptionally rich and flexible one. The fact that there was no single authority capable of (nor, so far as one can tell, interested in) enforcing any set of rules that could be said to represent how things should be done left a great deal open to persuasion, rhetorical flourishes, and local power plays.

MODES OF PROOF: RITUAL CONSENTS

Although the later Merovingian royal *placita* do seem to place special emphasis on written documents, this should not necessarily be taken as a sign that royal courts were by then taking a different approach to modes of proof from either earlier royal courts or local ones. Many different legal *fora* were available to disputants in the early Middle Ages: royal tribunals, bishops' courts, abbots' courts, counts' courts, or local assemblies presided over by local "good men" (*boni homines*) or *rachymburgii*. None of these different venues seems to have particularly privileged one mode of proof over another—including ecclesiastical courts, which one would assume would have been the most deeply committed to writing. The formulary of Marculf, most likely compiled in the late seventh century, shows very similar ways of reaching legal judgments at the royal court to those in other formularies with a more local scope.

Nor does the use of written documents in later royal *placita* mean that there was a chronological development tending toward the growing importance of written instruments. If Childebert III, in a *placitum* from 697, ruled against Drogo, the son of the powerful mayor of the palace, in a dispute with an abbot, on the basis that Drogo had no way of proving his reconstruction of events through written documents, this should not be taken as a sign, as Olivier Guillot read it, that Childebert III was a "precursor of Charlemagne" and of Carolingian justice in privileging "rational proofs" and legal inquest over the oath-helping favored by his predecessors (Guillot 1995, pp. 726–731). Rather, it simply means that the king could use this argument opportunistically in order to turn the tables on Drogo and find against him. Drogo had argued his case forcefully before being undone by this bombshell, so he at least did not foresee that not having any documents to prove his side of the story would mean he would automatically lose the case. The fact that the judgment is attributed to an assembly of "leading men" who are described in the document as responsible for the judgment, leaving the king himself ostensibly out of it, suggests that the king needed substantial backup from the rest of the assembly in order to make this judgment stick. The use of written documents in dispute settlements did not obviate or replace the need for overwhelming consensus among those present: rather, accepting them as final proof was dependent on having managed to create such a consensus in the first place.

Even where, as in Childebert III's judgment against Drogo, a legal decision seems to have been based on a technical question (did Drogo have a document, or did he not?), these were not *legal* technicalities as we would understand them. They amounted more to ritual technicalities: that is, tools that either accuser or accused could use to establish a representation of their case which their audience could accept. The difference between the two is that legal rules are in principle stable, knowable in advance, and highly predictable; whereas ritual rules correspond more to a palette, which skilled practitioners needed to combine and deploy effectively in order to project the particular representation of themselves and their actions they wanted their audience to accept. The distinction is one of emphasis, rather than being cut-and-dried: I do not mean to say, of course, that where there is a set of technical legal knowledge there is not also plenty of courtroom ritual, as indeed can be seen today – rather, that in the Merovingian period the content of the legal rules invoked was as moveable a piece as any other aspect of this ritual. In this case, skill involved not a demonstration of knowledge of and adherence to a stable procedure, but the ability to adapt one's performance to particular circumstances, while still making it look like the most natural and traditional way of going about things (a key function of ritual).

In this sense, the process required to decide on the use of *any* proof demanded the establishment of a degree of common ground between the opposed parties. Nonparticipation was the sanction for failure to agree on a script and a clear sign of ritual dissent. Although Salic Law included punitive provisions for what should happen when one of the parties failed to turn up (*Pactus Legis Salicae* 56), formularies give no indication that such defaults automatically led to the loss of a case. In the Angers formulary, failing to appear to take an oath is treated in a virtually identical way to refusing to accept an oath once it had been sworn (compare *Formulae Andecavenses* nos. 12–15 with no. 16).

All forms of proof could also become fatally invalidated if a failure of ritual occurred, or was made to occur, later down the line. Oath-swearing with oath-helpers is the way of settling disputes most commonly found in notarial formularies and offers good examples of this. In principle, since the oath was typically sworn on relics, or at the very least in a religious building, it could be considered a variety of ordeal—the idea being that saints, unless in a particularly forgiving mood, could take violent exception to a false oath being sworn in their bodily presence. At the same time, stipulations made by courts show that further conditions still needed to be fulfilled in order for the oath to gain validity before its audience. Limits were sometimes placed on defendants' freedom in choosing oath-helpers: in one formula from Marculf setting out the conditions for an oath to be taken before the royal tribunal, the defendant had to select three of his six oath-helpers from a predetermined list of five names, the other three being left to his discretion (*Formulae Marculfi* I, 38). In other cases, oath-swearers had to be selected from among neighbors knowledgeable about the case. All these precautions must have been intended to ensure that the oath would be accepted. When it was not, the outcome could be disastrous, as in one case in Gregory of Tours's *Histories* in which an oath regarding a woman's adultery was rejected by her husband's family, resulting in a bloodbath inside the church (Gregory of Tours, *Libri historiarum decem* V, 32).

Since successful completion of the oath meant defeat for the other party, significant pressure would have needed to be brought upon the latter by the audience to accept it: in order to do its job, oath-swearing needed to mobilize, as well as to reflect, public opinion. Establishing a convincing narrative might require both accuser and defendant to act in apparently self-defeating ways by volunteering more or less stringent conditions for fulfillment of the oath. Skilled practitioners, if they felt things might not go their way, could find it worthwhile losing by setting a very low benchmark, if that meant delegitimizing their opponents' successful oath. Gregory of Tours did this himself when a man named Pelagius, whom Gregory describes as a habitual false oath-swearer, stole some sea urchins from him, which he had been intending to have for his dinner, and then demanded to clear himself by oath, bringing oath-helpers along. He apparently was able to mobilize a good deal of local support, so Gregory let him off the hook but undercut him ritually by accepting his oath alone, without oath-helpers. This action left Gregory sure to lose the argument, but at the same time resulted in something of a stalemate, by robbing his opponent of the full public vindication oath-helpers would have afforded him (Gregory of Tours, *Libri historiarum decem* VIII, 40).

Oath-helping is generally a mode of proof associated with community enforcement and establishment of consensus: it left room for public opinion to be brought to bear on the outcome. Both it and the ordeal have been placed in fundamental opposition with supposedly more state-driven, top-down forms of proof, such as written or oral testimony, including the use of torture.[6] One-to-one correspondence between modes of proof and sociological models, however, can only be established at the cost of a large degree of schematization. Ordeals, for instance, offer ambiguous evidence, judging from the divergent views expressed in the 1970s and 1980s. Peter Brown, for example, saw ordeals as "open-ended as a Rorschach test," their outcomes as determined by community consensus, and their disappearance as a mode of proof as signaling a "shift from consensus to authority." In contrast, Robert Bartlett saw them as dependent on the interpretation of authority figures, and typically imposed from above on low-status people (Brown 1975, pp. 139, 143; Bartlett 1986, pp. 36–37). Evidently, ordeals were capable of fulfilling the needs of both communities and authorities, rather than any one intrinsic social function.

The same kind of ambiguity also applies to torture, which has been seen as replacing oath-helping and the ordeal, developing hand in hand with the growth of the state. It does appear to have fulfilled largely the same function—that is, reaching a definite resolution when full proof was lacking, especially, at least at first, in the case of low-status defendants (Peters 1996, pp. 41–43; Bartlett 1986, pp. 136–143). Either way, torture has been associated more with the power of the state insofar as its main aim is associated with fact finding, however imperfect an instrument we now know it to be for this purpose, rather than opinion polling, which seems more the point in the case of oath-helping (and in some cases ordeals). It has been seen as a routine and important part of the judicial process in the late Roman Empire and from the twelfth century onward, but its importance has been played down for the early Middle Ages.[7]

Torture, however, abounds in Merovingian sources. In Salic Law, for instance, it was mandated in cases of serious accusations against slaves, who could not clear themselves in other ways. As the property of their master, community support was not a relevant consideration in their case, which automatically changed the rules of the game (*Pactus Legis Salicae* 40, 4). It is also pervasive in Gregory of Tours's *Histories* in which it is often performed for its own sake, as a punishment, and also very often as a way of extracting a confession, above all in cases of political accusations directly impinging on the safety of the king or his family (Gregory of Tours, *Libri historiarum decem* V, 39, 49; VI, 35, VII, 32, VIII, 11, 31, 41, and 44; IX, 3, 9, 38; X, 18–19, 21, 25). Torture, oath-helping and ordeal could evidently all coexist within the same legal ecosystem; the difference between them lay not in differences in social structures but in the level of commitment shown by the authorities involved in obtaining one particular outcome to the proceedings. Torture was simply used whenever kings did not want to leave things to chance or did not want to leave an opportunity for defendants to demonstrate that they had public support. When kings or state officials *really* wanted to impose a particular narrative, they certainly had the scope to do so, but this never amounted to a systematic effort. While torture and oath-helping clearly corresponded to completely different strategies, neither of them represents the true face of Merovingian justice more than the other.

Legal Practices and Sociological Models

Modes of proof were not the only instance in which legal practices coexisted despite being normally categorized by historians as belonging in radically different sociological contexts and therefore as being in principle mutually exclusive. The debate on feud and feuding offers perhaps the clearest example. Feuding (a highly structured process, counting in its own right as a type of legal behavior) was once thought to be a powerful organizing force for the whole of Frankish society. It is now disputed whether it even existed at all. The different positions in the debate partly rest on different definitions of what feuding is (compare Wallace-Hadrill 1958–1959, p. 122, and Halsall 1999, p. 9, each taking his own definition to be noncontroversial). There has been much debate over whether specific examples from narrative sources do or do not count as feud. The story of Sichar and Chramnesind told by Gregory of Tours has been a more or less constant reference point (Gregory of Tours, *Libri historiarum decem* VII, 47 and IX, 19). A complicated series of events involving revenge killings, arson, and theft of property were settled with great difficulty and flared up again a few years down the line. It was once taken as an exemplary feud (Monod 1886; Wallace-Hadrill 1958–1959, pp. 139–142), only to be reevaluated by several historians since the late 1980s as not really a feud at all (Sawyer 1987, pp. 29–31; Halsall 1998, p. 24; Depreux 2006).

Guy Halsall, who, in a classic article, mounted the most spirited attack against the applicability of the concept of feuding to early medieval societies, accepted the existence of customary vengeance, but not of feud. Halsall made a distinction between "tactical violence," aimed at ending a dispute once and for all, and "strategic violence," which only perpetuates the dispute, as in "true" feuding societies. Early medieval Europe, he argued, was not a true feuding society because most of the disputes in surviving sources tend to end either with the first vengeance killing or through compensation, as opposed to sparking a self-perpetuating cycle of violence (Halsall 1999, p. 15). In practice, however, Halsall's distinction between behavior he calls "tactical" and behavior he calls "strategic" may reflect only varying degrees of success on the part of the actors (as well as different ways of framing their actions in sources), rather than fundamentally different kinds of intention. In practice, the argument depends on how many moves might be necessary in order for retaliatory violence to merit being qualified as feud. The fact that one often finds relatively few moves in such sequences in early medieval source material could just as well be taken to confirm Michael Wallace-Hadrill's earlier view that the impact of feuding culture during the early Middle Ages was felt above all as a rarely actualized threat, with every possible pressure being brought to bear in order to avoid it or bring it to an end (Wallace-Hadrill 1958–1959).

Belief or disbelief in the feud has ultimately been dependent on historians' wider views about the nature of the Merovingian state and society. Feuding is often associated (particularly in older anthropological literature) with small-state or stateless societies, as well as with societies with extended family groupings (e.g., Campbell 1964, pp. 185–202). Neither of these views is now accepted as an accurate representation of Merovingian society, and arguments to this effect have often gone hand in hand with arguments against the existence of feuding. Peter Sawyer thus argued that, since extended kin was not very important in the early Middle Ages (Murray 1983), feuding could not have been very important either (Sawyer 1987). Similarly, Halsall's own arguments against the existence of feuding were rooted in the idea that the Merovingian state was not as powerless as was often assumed (Halsall 1999, p. 8).

The sense that feuding did not have a place in a Merovingian context thus depends on the premise that there has to be an exact one-to-one correspondence between legal practices and sociological profiles. But trying to characterize Merovingian society as a whole as being either a "feuding society" or not may be too blunt an approach. Rather, feud was a cultural reference point that individuals could choose to make use of or not. It was one available model of behavior among many others, and a way of ensuring legal legibility for one's actions.[8] In many cases, it appears essentially as a narrative device that people (whether at the time or retrospectively) could invoke to legitimize their chosen course of action.

Long-dormant feuds could sometimes be cited to justify actions taken for unrelated reasons. One famous example of this is Clothild's revenge: the widowed queen Clothild, immediately after her stepson had made an advantageous marriage into the Burgundian royal family, suddenly remembered a decades-old blood debt and urged her own sons to wage war against them (White 1996). The fact that the language of feud was here and elsewhere used as a transparent excuse does not invalidate the concept, nor does it mean that these episodes have nothing to do with feuding (Halsall 1998, p. 20). If anything, they demonstrate its relevance as a cultural construct, since even these far-fetched justifications only make sense in a context in which feud was both commonly understood and taken seriously as a cultural reference point, and in which it was at the same time also an instrument that people could use opportunistically to defend their actions. The fact that this story involves the Frankish royal family does not necessarily mean the same sort of opportunism was not also at work further down the social spectrum. The logic of feud did not determine people's actions with grim inevitability; rather, it allowed them to construct a narrative where acts of aggression could be read as legitimate. All the different episodes that historians have struggled to characterize as either "feud" or "not feud" offer ambiguous evidence because in all of them it was not feuding culture that was in the driver's seat. The individuals who invoked it were, and they were putting together a different itinerary each time, depending on what they were trying to do.

Sometimes, the narrative could be much more fragile, and the explanation of events in terms of feuding might be rejected by its intended audience. This is where we are more likely to find royal officials being led to intervene. One example in Gregory of Tours's *Life of the Fathers* shows a count imprisoning someone who had taken vengeance for the death of his brother without waiting for a judgment to approve this action (Gregory of Tours, *Liber vitae patrum* VIII.7). Halsall takes this story as evidence that retaliatory violence was not a sign of the weakness of the state (and therefore not really feud) because royal officials had the final say on whether or not it was legitimate: we would then be dealing with crime and punishment, the definition of which was ultimately controlled by the state, rather than private feuding—no more a "self-help mechanism . . . than telephoning the police today" (Halsall 1999, p. 20). The involvement of royal officials, however, does not necessarily mean that the process was controlled by the state: the state might try to establish ground rules, but that does not mean it got to choose the game. One could read this episode less as proof of the intrinsic power of the state and more as evidence of the failure to impose a feud narrative in this particular case. Gregory builds this failure into the framing of his story by describing the victim as an unnamed member of an enraged mob, killed during a riot. The killing is therefore presented as the result of generic public disorder, and not as the sort of killing that would legitimize the deployment of high-status vengeance in response. The practical distinction between the two could have been very tenuous without undermining the difference in symbolic terms. Clearly, not everyone could successfully stake their claim to a feuding register. A feuding narrative, then, had to be sold to its audience. The fact that actors were not being driven by feud as the one dominant cultural schema in their society, but instead were tendentiously deploying it as one possibility among many to lend legitimacy to their current or past actions, accounts for the often imperfect fit between the gold-standard, "classic" feuding reference point treated in poetry or (later) in Icelandic sagas (Miller 1990) and the cases we find described in Merovingian narrative sources.

The exercise may have been most difficult to navigate for very young elite males because they were not yet as well defined socially and because the narratives constructed about them at this point in their lives were likely to have important consequences for them in the long run. They may, therefore, have had to present themselves as especially hard-line in their pursuit of vengeance. For instance, it may seem puzzling that Chramnesind, having accepted compensation from Sichar for the killing of his father, uncle, and brother should have apparently become great friends with him; for Sawyer, this counts against the notion that this had really been a feud (Sawyer 1987, p. 31). But Chramnesind had probably made himself very vulnerable by agreeing to end the violence. Admitting that he still bore a grudge against Sichar without doing anything about it would have compounded this, leading to great pressure all round, for both public appearance and private self-image, to turn the friendship promised during the settlement into reality. Chramnesind's attempt ultimately failed, however, when Sichar mocked him for having accepted compensation rather than continuing the conflict. Chramnesind therefore had to kill Sichar, but this action was not in tension with his earlier friendship with him. Both had been motivated by the same sense of vulnerability and the constant need to frame and reframe his actions in an acceptable way. For other, less vulnerable people, both vengeance and compensation may simply have been available, nonbinding options, coexisting with many other ways of obtaining satisfaction—including deciding to acknowledge the right of state officials to intervene.

CONCLUSION

Different sources (or indeed different episodes in Gregory of Tours's *Histories*) seem to give us profoundly contradictory impressions about the nature of Merovingian legal processes, state, and society—on such fundamental matters as whether feud existed, whether legal documents mattered, and whether peacekeeping was chiefly community-driven or state-driven. This means that we should probably stop looking for one dominant legal *system*, which can only be done at the cost of dismissing much contradictory evidence. Instead, there was a multitude of different legal reference points, of which contemporaries could under certain circumstances avail themselves in order to justify their intended or past course of action. All these forms of legal solution were options open to those who were in a position to take advantage of them, rather than forming part of a more coherent or totalizing whole: they were above all scripts, combinations of symbols fine-tuned for the purposes of that one dispute or decision. This means that it is fundamentally very difficult to generalize from individual examples, and above all, that legal processes are best understood when decoupled from fixed sociological models. The fact that written documents were key to settling one dispute does not mean that they could necessarily be successfully deployed in other, different disputes; the fact that some "feud-like" conflicts were resolved by or before royal officials does not mean that royal officials could successfully intervene in all such conflicts.

That so many arguments in disputes seem to involve aspects of procedure (Fouracre 1986, p. 34) should not suggest that there was ever one conventional way of resolving them which might be discoverable by modern historians. Rather, it means that deciding on what the procedure should be, or which ritual and cultural script ought to be followed, was a key preliminary requirement of settling any dispute. Legal practices during this period should be understood less as manifestations of an overarching legal system and more as a series of ritual choices pieced together by participants to suit the needs of one particular event.

How much ritual choice one had available, how much scope to dictate the script or to refuse to participate, naturally depended largely on existing levels of agency and social status, since it required getting a substantial proportion of other participants to follow suit. In the case of poorer or marginal people, this scope was obviously very slight, as in the case of a poor man's daughter summarily enslaved for theft at her trial, immortalized in a poem by Venantius Fortunatus (*Carmina* V, 14).

This consideration has an impact on how to read evidence on the reach of the state during this period. Depending on how much power different types of participants had to manipulate these choices for their own ends, and on whether they were accuser or accused, *some* people might have the experience of living under a small state, while others might, at least sometimes, have the experience of living under a highly interventionist one. Provided one had the resources to make the claim stick, one could choose to behave *as if* there was a strong, Roman Empire-style state, or *as if* written instruments offered unquestionable authority. The Merovingian kingdoms were, in essence, small states with the memory of a big one. This expanded their range of available, justifiable forms of state action, but also meant that they could not deny alternatives.

Given the disappearance of most of the Roman state's infrastructure, it is remarkable that, throughout this period, so many of its legal concepts should have remained an enduringly attractive way of thinking about the world. Clearly, useful things could still be done within this tradition, in areas as diverse as the use of writing, or in the borrowing of its language of property to define authority over objects and people.[9] However, while much of what constituted the domain of the legal in the Merovingian kingdoms was derived from Roman antecedents, it is important not to mistake such borrowings for evidence of straightforward continuity. By this point, law was less a function of government than a form of cultural capital, manipulated and lent meaning by its end users.

In all societies, including our own, legal processes always require the building of a plausible, legible story, as well as audience management. What was perhaps special about Merovingian Francia, along with other post-Roman kingdoms, was that the range of equally acceptable different cultural frameworks one could use to piece that story together was so large. This was a period with an unusually wide variety of different ways to frame and explain one's social action in legal terms, none of which necessarily invalidated the others. This is why surviving sources present us with such apparently conflicting evidence. The conflict disappears, however, when one stops looking for a spirit of system behind each individual example. Law in the Merovingian period did not restrict or narrow people's choices; instead, it *expanded* their scope for legitimate social action, by offering them different possible approaches and solutions—all of which could nevertheless count as equally "legal" in character.

Notes

1. This is, naturally, an oversimplification. Roman provincial legal practice is currently a vibrant field of study: see especially Humfress 2013; Czajkowski and Eckhardt 2018.
2. As opposed to royal law (*Königsrecht*), for which historians looked more to lists of decisions known as capitularies. The dividing line, however, is fairly vague for the Merovingian period. The earliest known text of the *Pactus* in sixty-five titles is generally regarded as constituting the original core of the law code; the text after the sixty-fifth title consists wholly of capitularies (of these, titles 66 to 78 are anonymous, and these are followed by others issued by later Merovingian kings, of which the most important are the Edict of Chilperic and the *Pactus pro tenore pacis* of Childebert and Chlothar). Even within the "core" sixty-five titles, however, Beyerle identified a strand of more substantive legislation, which he distinguished from more "customary" material, such as compensation values (Beyerle 1924, pp. 220–225).
3. For a similar point made in the same year, see also Nehlsen 1977.
4. Although Wormald himself left more room than most historians of his generation for a Germanic identity underlying law codes. See Wormald 2003.
5. Shoichi Sato has made the comparison with Heian Japan, a demonstrably highly literate society from which hardly any documents survive (Sato 2000, pp. 160–161).
6. On the fallacy of the opposition between community and state enforcement in the early Middle Ages in general, see Taylor 2014.
7. For an argument that torture may have played more of a role in practice than the texts of early medieval documents suggest, at least in the Carolingian period, see Geary 2008, which also places ordeal and torture more in continuity than in opposition with each other.
8. On the idea of legibility, see especially Scott 1998.
9. For the example of the varied practical uses for the language and legal category of Roman slavery in the early Middle Ages, see Rio 2017.

Works Cited

Ancient Sources

Chartae Latinae Antiquiores. A. Bruckner and R. Marichal (eds.). (1954–). Dietikon/Zurich: Urs-Graf Verlag.

Formulae Andecavenses, Formulae Arvernenses and *Formulae Marculfi*. K. Zeumer (ed.). (1886). *Formulae Merowingici et Karolini Aevi*. MGH Leges 5. Hanover: Hahn.

Gregory of Tours, *Liber vitae patrum*. B. Krusch (ed.). (1969). MGH SRM 1.2 (pp. 661–743). Hanover: Hahn.

Gregory of Tours, *Libri historiarum decem*. B. Krusch and W. Levison (eds.). (1951). MGH SRM 1.1. Hanover: Hahn.

Pactus Legis Salicae. K. A. Eckhardt (ed.). (1962). MGH Leges nationum Germanicarum 4.1. Hanover: Hahn.

Venantius Fortunatus, *Carmina*. F. Leo (ed.). (1881). MGH AA 4.1. Berlin: Weidmann.

Modern Sources

Amory, P. (1993). "The Meaning and Purpose of Ethnic Terminology in the Burgundian Laws." *Early Medieval Europe* 2: 1–28.

Barbier, J. (2014). *Archives oubliées du haut Moyen Âge. Les gesta municipalia en Gaule franque (VIᵉ–IXᵉ siècle)*. Paris: Honoré Champion.

Bartlett, R. (1986). *Trial by Fire and Water: The Medieval Judicial Ordeal*. Oxford: Clarendon.

Beyerle, F. (1924). "Über Normtypen und Erweiterungen der Lex Salica." *Zeitschrift der Savigny-Stiftung für Rechtsgeschichte, Germanistische Abteilung* 44: 216–261.

Brown, P. (1975). "Society and the Supernatural: A Medieval Change." *Daedalus* 104: 133–151.

Brown, W. C. (2002). "When Documents Are Destroyed or Lost: Lay People and Archives in the Early Middle Ages." *Early Medieval Europe* 11: 337–366.

Brown, W. C. (2012). "On the *gesta municipalia* and the Public Validation of Documents in Frankish Europe." *Speculum* 87: 345–375.

Brunner, H. (1906). *Deutsche Rechtsgeschichte*. 2nd ed. Leipzig: Duncker & Humblot.

Caenegem, R. C. van (1990). "Reflexions on Rational and Irrational Modes of Proof in Medieval Europe." *Tijdschrift voor Rechtsgeschiedenis* 58: 263–279.

Campbell, J. K. (1964). *Honour, Family and Patronage: A Study of Institutions and Moral Values in a Greek Mountain Community*. Oxford: Clarendon.

Classen, P. (1977). "Fortleben und Wandel spätrömischen Urkundenwesens im frühen Mittelalter." In P. Classen (ed.), *Recht und Schrift im Mittelalter*, Vorträge und Forschungen 23 (pp. 13–54). Sigmaringen: Jan Thorbecke.

Collins, R. (1998). "Law and Ethnic Identity in the Western Kingdoms in the Fifth and Sixth Centuries." In A. P. Smyth (ed.), *Medieval Europeans* (pp. 1–23). New York: Palgrave.

Czajkowski, K., and Eckhardt, B. (2018). "Law, Status and Agency in the Roman Provinces." *Past and Present* 241: 3–31.

Depreux, P. (2006). "Une faide exemplaire? A propos des aventures de Sichaire: vengeance et pacification aux temps mérovingiens." In D. Barthélemy, F. Bougard, and R. Le Jan (eds.), *La vengeance, 400–1200* (pp. 65–85). Rome: Ecole française de Rome.

Esders, S. (1997). *Römische Rechtstradition und merowingisches Königtum: zum Rechtscharakter politischer Herrschaft in Burgund im 6. und 7. Jahrhundert*. Göttingen: Vandenhoeck & Ruprecht.

Fouracre, P. (1986). "'*Placita*' and the Settlement of Disputes in later Merovingian Francia." In W. Davies and P. Fouracre (eds.), *The Settlement of Disputes in Early Medieval Europe* (pp. 23–43). Cambridge: Cambridge University Press.

Ganz, D. (1983). "Bureaucratic Shorthand and Merovingian Learning." In P. Wormald with D. Bullough and R. Collins (eds.), *Ideal and Reality in Frankish and Anglo-Saxon Society: Studies Presented to J. M. Wallace-Hadrill* (pp. 58–75). Oxford: Basil Blackwell.

Geary, P. J. (1988). *Before France and Germany: The Creation and Transformation of the Merovingian World*. Oxford: Oxford University Press.

Geary, P. J. (2008). "Judicial Violence and Torture in the Carolingian Empire." In R. M. Karras, J. Kaye, and E. A. Matter (eds.), *Law and the Illicit in Medieval Europe* (pp. 79–88). Philadelphia: University of Pennsylvania Press.

Guillot, O. (1995). "La justice dans le royaume franc à l'époque mérovingienne." In *La giustizia nell'Alto Medioevo (secoli V–VIII)*, vol. 2 (pp. 653–731). Spoleto: Centro italiano di studi sull'alto medioevo.

Halsall, G. (1998). "Violence and Society in the Early Medieval West: An Introductory Survey." In G. Halsall (ed.), *Violence and Society in the Early Medieval West* (pp. 1–45). Woodbridge: Boydell and Brewer.

Halsall, G. (1999). "Reflections on Early Medieval Violence: The Example of the 'Blood Feud.'" *Memoria y Civilización* 2: 7–29.

Humfress, C. (2013). "Thinking Through Legal Pluralism: "Forum shopping" in the Later Roman Empire". In J. Duindam, J. D. Harries, C. Humfress and H. Nimrod (eds.), *Law and Empire: Ideas, Practices, Actors* (pp. 225–250). Leiden and Boston: Brill.

Lauranson-Rosaz, C., and Jeannin, A. (2001). "La résolution des litiges en justice durant le haut Moyen-Âge: l'exemple de l'*apennis* à travers les formules, notamment celles d'Auvergne et d'Angers." In *Le règlement des conflits au Moyen-Âge, XXXIe Congrès de la SHMES (Angers, juin 2000)* (pp. 21–33). Paris: Sorbonne.

Levy, E. (1951). *West Roman Vulgar Law: The Law of Property*. Philadelphia: American Philosophical Society.

Liebs, D. (2008). "Roman Vulgar Law in Late Antiquity." In B. Sirks (ed.), *Aspects of Law in Late Antiquity* (pp. 35–53). Oxford: All Souls College.

Miller, W. I. (1990). *Bloodtaking and Peacemaking: Feud, Law, and Society in Saga Iceland*. Chicago: University of Chicago Press.

Monod, G. (1886). "Les aventures de Sichaire." *Revue historique* 31: 259–290.

Murray, A. C. *(1983). Germanic Kinship Structure: Studies in Law and Society in Antiquity and the Early Middle Ages*. Turnhout: Brepols.

Nehlsen, H. (1977). "Zur Aktualität und Effektivität germanischer Rechtsaufzeichnungen." In P. Classen (ed.), *Recht und Schrift im Mittelalter* (pp. 449–502). Vorträge und Forschungen 23. Sigmaringen: Jan Thorbecke.

Peters, E. (1996). *Torture*. Expanded edition. Philadelphia: University of Pennsylvania Press.

Poly, J.-P. (1993). "La corde au cou: les Francs, la France et la loi salique." In H. Bresc (ed.), *Genèse de l'État moderne en Méditerranée: approches historique et anthropologique des pratiques et des représentations* (pp. 287–320). Rome: Ecole française de Rome.

Renard, E. (2009). "Le *Pactus Legis Salicae*, règlement militaire romain ou code de lois compilé sous Clovis?" *Bibliothèque de l'École des chartes* 167: 321–352.

Rio, A. (trans.). (2008). *Two Merovingian Legal Handbooks: The Formularies of Angers and Marculf*. Liverpool: Liverpool University Press.

Rio, A. (2009). *Legal Practice and the Written Word in the Early Middle Ages: Frankish Formulae, 500–1000*. Cambridge: Cambridge University Press.

Rio, A. (2017). *Slavery after Rome, 500–1100*. Oxford: Oxford University Press.

Sato, S. (2000). "The Merovingian Accounting Documents of Tours: Form and Function." *Early Medieval Europe* 9: 143–161.

Sawyer, P. H. (1987). "The Bloodfeud in Fact and Fiction." In K. Hastrup and P. M. Sørensen (eds.), *Tradition og Historieskrivning, Acta Jutlandica* 63 (pp. 27–38). Aarhus: Aarhus Universitetsforlag.

Scott, J. C. (1998). *Seeing Like a State: How Certain Schemes to Improve the Human Condition Have Failed*. New Haven, CT: Yale University Press.

Taylor, A. (2014). "*Lex scripta* and the Problem of Enforcement: Anglo-Saxon, Welsh and Scottish Law Compared." In J. Scheele and F. Pirie (eds.), *Legalism: Justice and Community* (pp. 47–75). Oxford: Oxford University Press.

Ubl, K. (2009). "L'origine contestée de la loi salique: une mise au point." *Revue de l'IFHA* 1: 208–234.

Ubl, K. (2014). "Im Bann der Traditionen. Zur Charakteristik der *Lex Salica*." In M. Meier and S. Patzold (eds.), *Chlodwigs Welt: Organisation von Herrschaft um 500* (pp. 423–445). Stuttgart: Franz Steiner.

Ubl, K. (2017). *Sinnstiftungen eines Rechtsbuchs: Die* Lex Salica *im Frankenreich*. Ostfildern: Jan Thorbecke.

Wallace-Hadrill, J. M. (1958–1959). "The Blood-Feud of the Franks." *Bulletin of the John Rylands Library, Manchester* 41: 459–487. Reprinted in J. M. Wallace-Hadrill. (1962). *The Long-Haired Kings and Other Studies in Frankish History* (pp. 121–147). London: Methuen.

White, S. D. (1996). "Clotild's Revenge: Politics, Kinship, and Ideology in the Merovingian Blood Feud." In S. K. Cohn Jr. and S. A. Epstein (eds.), *Portraits of Medieval and Renaissance Living: Essays in Memory of David Herlihy* (pp. 107–130). Ann Arbor: University of Michigan Press.

Wood, I. N. (1986). "Disputes in Late Fifth- and Sixth-Century Gaul." In W. Davies and P. Fouracre (eds.), *The Settlement of Disputes in Early Medieval Europe* (pp. 7–22). Cambridge: Cambridge University Press.

Wood, I. N. (1990). "Administration, Law and Culture in Merovingian Gaul." In R. McKitterick (ed.), *The Uses of Literacy in Early Mediaeval Europe* (pp. 63–81). Cambridge: Cambridge University Press.

Wormald, P. (1977). "*Lex scripta* and *verbum regis*: Legislation and Germanic Kingship from Euric to Cnut." In P. H. Sawyer and I. N. Wood (eds.), *Early Medieval Kingship* (pp. 105–138). Leeds: University of Leeds.

Wormald, P. (2003). "The *leges barbarorum*: Law and Ethnicity in the post-Roman West." In H.-W. Goetz, J. Jarnut, and W. Pohl (eds.), *Regna and Gentes: The Relationship between Late Antique and Early Medieval Peoples and Kingdoms in the Transformation of the Roman World* (pp. 21–53). Leiden: Brill.

CHAPTER 24

MEROVINGIAN HAGIOGRAPHY

JAMIE KREINER

GAUL was a noisy place in the Merovingian period. Would this volume exist if the kingdom had been quieter? The work of history writing, lawmaking, correspondence, liturgical celebration, monastic planning, and funerary commemoration, as other chapters in this collection make clear, reverberated through more parchment and papyrus and stone than survives from any other postimperial society of the West, although the eastern Mediterranean presents stiffer competition (Wickham 2005, pp. 41–42).

Hagiography was part of that noisy scene, and the genre attracted a significant amount of ambitious talent. By Martin Heinzelmann's calculations, 509 men and women who lived in Merovingian Gaul are celebrated in hagiographical texts, which is 43 percent of all the saints from Gaul and France who were commemorated in hagiography between the dawn of Christianity and the year 1500 (Heinzelmann 2010, pp. 27–31). The caveat is that many of these texts about Merovingian subjects may not have been Merovingian compositions: it was common practice for medieval hagiographers to write or rewrite texts about persons who had died long ago. But that also means that texts set in Antiquity and Late Antiquity—either in Gaul itself or as far afield as the deserts of Egypt—could plausibly be Merovingian manufactures (for a Carolingian parallel, see Diem and Müller 2010).

Although identifying the origins of many premodern hagiographical texts is still a work in progress (Goullet 2010, 2014), the hagiography that historians *have* been able to date securely to the Merovingian period still amounts to a great hoard. Gregory of Tours alone wrote six collections of miracle stories and saints' lives and translated a seventh: in the standard published edition, that material runs to 400 pages (Krusch 1969; Kitchen 2016). Martin Heinzelmann names almost seventy texts besides Gregory's that were definitely composed in Gaul before the seventh century (Heinzelmann 2010). By Marc van Uytfanghe's somewhat conservative count, twenty-one hagiographical texts were definitely written between 600 and 750, and an additional twenty-four texts could have either been written during that century and a half or in the Carolingian period—although several in this second category have since been confirmed as Merovingian as well (van Uytfanghe 2000; cf. Heinzelmann 2010, pp. 49–55, 66–82). These figures exclude texts that we know to have existed at one point but that no longer survive. The number would probably double if we included sermons, liturgies, and histories that resemble hagiography but are not strictly part of the genre. But no matter how we measure it, hagiography was a major part of Merovingian media culture.

Like the other forms of evidence that survive from the kingdom, hagiographical sources are not serene monuments to a crystalline social order. They are witnesses to energetic discussions that the inhabitants of Gaul were having about what exactly their "social order" should be. And like other written sources, hagiography was an active witness, not a passive one. The texts themselves participated in Gaul's debates about what was important, how the world should be seen and explained, and how different parts of Merovingian society should operate on the basis of those priorities. This chapter is about some of the advantages and disadvantages that this form of communication offered the women and men who used it.[1]

The Concept of the Saint

Hagiography is the work of writing about holy figures or saints. It is similar to biography, but unlike a biography, a hagiographical text narrates a story to demonstrate that the actions of its protagonist embody God's expectations for humanity. God himself usually endorses this course of action as the story unfolds, in the form of miracles or other kinds of special messages, such as visions or dreams (Moreira 2000, pp. 173–197; de Nie 2011; Keskiaho 2015, pp. 24–75). Hagiographers, and the early medieval scribes who copied their work, used different names for individual texts: a single work might be called a *vita* (life), *gesta* (deeds), *passio* (suffering), *acta* (acts, actions), or *historia* (story, history). No matter how these doings were labeled, the important thing was that, when the hagiographer related them, they would transparently show an underlying structure of some rational, ethical system that was consonant with divine understanding.

The difficulty was that ethical systems were not fixed or frozen. Even if God and his Word were changeless, the world was not. Because human and nonhuman environments were always shifting—because they were historical—determining what proper respect for God actually looked like in practice necessarily involved constant reinterpretation. As a result, every piece of hagiography involved a double argument: first, that a particular person ought to be praised for her or his accomplishments, and second and more fundamentally, that these accomplishments represented a legitimate ethics in the first place.

Each argument was necessarily calibrated to the other. Not only did the argument about an individual's reputation depend on developing a convincing tableau of the priorities and practices that Merovingian society ought to endorse. But also, in reverse, a text's social vision was constrained by the historical status and memory of its protagonist.

Celebrating the humility of an elite person, for example, and celebrating the humility of someone with only modest resources, produced entirely different effects. The first gesture was more impressive; the second risked undermining the reputation of someone whose status was already mediocre (Diefenbach 2013). Yet, as socially heterogeneous as the kingdom was—including the clergy themselves, as Steffen Patzold in particular has demonstrated—hagiographers chose overwhelmingly to write about men and women who were involved in the highest circles of Merovingian government (Fouracre 1990, pp. 29–37; Fouracre and Gerberding 1996; Patzold 2010; Walter and Patzold 2014; Patzold 2014). They did this partly because they were interested in redefining elite political culture and partly because it was much more difficult to make a successful social argument on the basis of undistinguished persons (Helvétius 2012; Kreiner 2014a, 2018). From this perspective, hagiography is autobiographical as well as biographical: it reflects the world of its author as much as, and often more so than, the world of its ostensible subject (Berschin 2014).

Sometimes these arguments are hard to see. Because we are so far removed from Merovingian culture, today the assertions that hagiographers made can seem like statements that anyone in Gaul would have endorsed rather than as new ways of interpreting the world. For example, a text called *The Life of Sadalberga*, which was written around 680, superficially seems to be an uncontroversial account of how the daughter of the duke of Alsace developed close friendships with two abbots of Luxeuil, married twice, had children, and eventually became the first abbess of a monastery that she founded in the city of Laon.[2] It seems (again, superficially) that Sadalberga's hagiographer praises the abbess for exhibiting character traits that any Christian in Gaul at the time would have automatically commended—such as generosity, humility, and dedication to prayer—and that the main "point" of the text was to suggest that Sadalberga should be recognized as a saint for so clearly conforming to that template (on gender and women, see Halsall, Chapter 8, and James, Chapter 11, this volume).

Such an interpretation presents us with two major problems. The first is that even seemingly stable "Christian traits" can ebb and flow: some Christians or Christian cultures may emphasize certain ideals over others or may introduce new ones or downplay what seems less relevant in a particular moment. Christians in Sasanian Persia studied their religion as a source of heroism and nobility; Christian reformers in Europe in the twelfth century emphasized the importance of poverty; and humanists working in fifteenth-century Italy included learnedness among Christian virtues worth praising (Constable 1996; Frazier 2005; Walker 2006; Payne 2015). Yet, to point out regional and chronological differences such as these is still to overgeneralize. Even within a single community, there were disagreements about what ideals mattered most. In Gaul, for example, the bishop and royal advisor Arnulf of Metz got into a terrible fight with King Dagobert about whether withdrawing from the court and becoming a monk was an appropriate move for a Christian of his stature (*Life of Arnulf*, p. 349; Kreiner 2014a, pp. 68–69).

The second problem is that any given ideal has an infinite number of possible applications. Peter Brown's work on wealth in the late Roman Empire and early medieval Europe has demonstrated that even when Christians agreed that generosity was crucial for the health of their communities and for their souls, it was not at all clear what "being generous" required, or what it should accomplish: who should give what to whom, and how much, and why? The answers to these questions varied enormously (Brown 2002, 2012, 2015). What that meant in Sadalberga's case was that praise for her humility, for instance, represented one among many possible interpretations of what humility should look like in practice. According to her hagiographer, it meant forsaking the distinctions of elite status and wealth for life in a monastery. It meant doing chores like cooking, instead of having others cook for her (*Life of Sadalberga*, pp. 63–64). But other Christians in Gaul thought of humility differently. For the abbot Romanus (or his hagiographer), it meant not wanting to stand physically above other monks, even when handling the Eucharist (*Life of the Jura Fathers*, p. 135). For the abbot and former courtier Wandregisel (or his hagiographer), it meant being willing to get his clothes dirty in front of other courtiers while he helped a random stranger dislodge his cart from the mud (*Life of Wandregisel*, p. 16).

Because it was possible to interpret "Christian values" in different ways, hagiographers worked to convince readers that their particular interpretations were legitimate ones. Sadalberga's hagiographer compared the abbess's choices to the departures of better known saints whom respected authors had already celebrated: Sadalberga was simply imitating (so her hagiographer suggested) what Jerome had praised in Paula and Melania, what Eusebius had said about Helena, and even what Abraham himself had done in the Bible (*Life of Sadalberga*, pp. 57, 64). The hagiographer also argued that Sadalberga's humility was a form of lawfulness: she was obeying her monastery's customary rules (or *Rule*), which included a system of chore rotation that the *Life* describes in unusual detail (pp. 61–63; on Rules, see Diem, Chapter 15, this volume). It is not the only time that this text adopts legal arguments. It also explains that Sadalberga only married a second time because the king commanded it—and that Dagobert was a ruler to be trusted (p. 55). It stresses that Sadalberga's monastery had properly documented its land transactions in order to discredit a claim that the abbess's brother had made to some of its land (p. 66). And it names an eyewitness to confirm one of Sadalberga's most bizarre miracles: the monk Landefrid, we are told, had heard the abbess scold him for stealing lettuce from the nuns' garden, despite the fact that Sadalberga was a half mile away and had only mouthed the words (pp. 62–63).

The hagiographer deployed these forms of defense because, although the *Life of Sadalberga* seems straightforward to us, it makes several larger-scale claims that would have surprised and sometimes unsettled other subjects, including other Christians, in the Merovingian kingdom. Sometimes those claims were highly localized. The *Life of Sadalberga* may have attempted, for example, to recover the reputation of Sadalberga's family following one of the most tumultuous decades in Merovingian politics, the 670s, when elites' alliances had fractured to the point of destabilizing the regular operation of royal law and administration (Wood 1994, pp. 221–238; Gaillard 2011; Fox 2014, pp. 145–146). But hagiography's vision often ranged further afield, and this one is no exception. At a time when the kingdom was debating what proper expenditure should look like, and what the criteria were for participation in royal politics, the *Life of Sadalberga* suggested that elite families should reconsider their commitments to their bloodlines, their family fortunes, and their connections to the court. It was possible, this hagiographer suggested, to generate profit, political capital, and even a long-term legacy by financing monastic institutions (Kreiner 2014a, 189–229). Likewise, the same narrative treated monasticism as basically coterminous with the institutions that had been founded or inspired by St. Columbanus, particularly those institutions that followed the model of Luxeuil. Because there were other monastic cultures in Gaul, and even other forms of "Columbanian" monasticism, this selective identification was another form of argument (Wood 1998; Diem 2005, forthcoming; Fox 2014, pp. 141–145). The text also stressed that the days before death were the best time to help the soul toward salvation, as a way of regaining control of a life that had inevitably been difficult to control—even though not everyone in the kingdom agreed that one's deathbed was the place to do this (Kreiner 2014b, pp. 121–122).

The Life of Sadalberga was therefore not merely a set of suggestions for how to be an elite woman or nun. The text offered a calculated vision of the Merovingian kingdom. It focused on particular frames of action, not only to highlight different policies that a person might hold but also, more fundamentally, to establish what kinds of situations were most worthy of scrutiny, what kinds of choices and behaviors were consequential and significant, and what kinds of goals were most worthy of attention in the first place. Marie-Céline Isaïa has characterized the difference this way: hagiography is not just a model for individuals to follow. It is also a normative discourse that attempts to change the measures by which an entire community or society sees and evaluates itself (Isaïa 2014).

The categorical concept of saintliness had become such an important vehicle for social argument in part because saints lived conspicuous lives of their own, outside of hagiography's pages. Many Christians in Gaul enfolded saints into their minds and movements, in ways that hagiographers sometimes tried to encourage or modify and in other cases merely took for granted (Van Dam 1993; Beaujard 2000). Some dedicated special altars or whole shrines and churches to the saints (Thacker and Sharpe 2002; Mériaux 2006). Some gave gifts of precious objects, money, or even property to the sanctuaries that housed them (Fouracre 1995; Magnani 2009). Some entered their names into martyrologies, calendars that commemorated saints' death dates (Lifshitz 2006). Some celebrated special masses or cycles of prayers for them (de Gaiffier 1954; Hen 1995, pp. 82–120; Rose 2005, 2009). Some buried their family members as close as possible to their tombs (Raynaud 2006). There were even numerous uses for pieces of saints' bodies or for items they had touched. Some Christians wore special pendants that contained such relics for personal protection, others swore oaths over them, others carried them in circuits around their cities, and yet others carefully labeled their relics with small strips of parchment, or preserved the labels that came tagged to the ones they had imported from more exotic locations (Fichtenau 1952; Boesch Gajano 1999; McCormick 2001, pp. 283–318; Esders 2014).

These cults were a culture, a way of developing new perspectives through received materials and meanings. There was no process resembling canonization in this period, no bureaucratic or centralized procedure that was needed to authorize holiness.

A saint was simply a person who received any of these forms of attention. But there was rarely a complete consensus about who deserved the distinction, so that as a result, not only did different saints and cults have different social statuses—meaning that some were more popular than others, or better connected, or more controversial (de Jong, Theuws, and van Rhijn 2001). More fundamentally, Christians rationalized their commitments to the saints in highly variable ways (Smith 1990; Boesch Gajano 1999; Sarris, Dal Santo, and Booth 2011; Bartlett 2013). To take three contrasting examples from Gaul: (1) visitors to the priest Eptadius (according to a *Life* that was probably written in the later sixth century) received a range of different things from him—good judgment, alms, royal assistance, sermons, pardons, redemption of captives, and healing miracles. (2) Eutropius of Orange, as Verus of Orange described him in the late fifth or early sixth century, was expected to intercede for his city by praying to God on their behalf, even once he was dead. And (3) according to the seventh-century hagiographer of Segolena of Troclar, God's main reason for making the saints famous was to encourage humans to obey his laws (*Life of Eptadius*; Verus of Orange, *Life of Eutropius*, pp. 53, 64; *Life of Segolena*, p. 631).

Not only was Gaul home to very different ideas about why and how saints should be venerated—and why a person might even deserve recognition as a saint in the first place. The disagreements ran even deeper. Not everyone in the kingdom believed in saints or in miracles. Some hagiographers told stories about persons who had doubted the powers of a saint in order to prove them wrong. Others believed in both saints and miracles, but they were unconvinced that dead persons, saintly or otherwise, were capable of doing anything for anybody. Even hagiographers hesitated. In the seventh century especially, they were more likely to focus on what their protagonists had accomplished when they were alive. In the process, the rate of miraculous activity at saints' tombs dropped— or at least, reports about such things did (Heinzelmann 1981; van Uytfanghe 2000; Kreiner 2014a, pp. 103–104).

It was a time for taking skeptical positions seriously: Italian, Byzantine, and East Syrian Christians were challenging the whole supposition of postmortem miracles on the grounds that they were completely illogical, unscientific even (Dal Santo 2012). Their arguments against saints' powers after death—and others' arguments *for* those powers— ran close to the contours of the debate in Gaul. So this contention between different Christian perspectives was, on a different scale, a sign of common ground in the early Middle Ages: the wider Mediterranean world was still linked by conversations such as this one (see Esders et al. 2019).

OLD AND NEW

Despite these ongoing ontological liabilities, many writers continued to be attracted to the discourse of sanctity. One important reason was that hagiography was an old, established form of evaluation. It was not that hagiographers stuck to the genre out of habit.

Rather, to a culture that was familiar with the genre's basic operations—with its logical and narratological structures—hagiography offered an efficient shorthand for communicating complex propositions. Anne-Marie Helvétius has shown, for example, that monastic writers in the eighth and ninth centuries found the idea of martyrdom to be a rich semantic field for interpreting the lives and deaths of many different kinds of people. To call someone a martyr made it possible to validate the work of political elites, missionary monks, and reformers (Helvétius 2014). Long before any of those hagiographers were born, Caesarius of Arles had reimagined asceticism as the modern form of martyrdom for his sixth-century congregation (Blennemann 2014)—for even in his day, martyrdom was a very old thing. When Caesarius stood in front of his congregation at Arles, Gaul had been reading and writing stories about martyrs for more than 300 years (Heinzelmann 2010, pp. 36–49).

As Gordon Blennemann has pointed out in his analysis of Caesarius's sermons, Merovingian writers such as the bishop of Arles were fully aware that each act of identifying a martyr—of interpreting someone as a martyr—revised the definition of "martyr," rather than merely reactivating it. But paradoxically, the constant work of comparing the present to the past simultaneously minimized and exaggerated the distance between them (Blennemann 2014). As a result, Merovingian listeners, readers, and writers developed a kind of split attitude toward martyrdom. They loved the ancient martyrs with few reservations and assessed modern applications of martyrdom cautiously and critically.

In the imperial period, the concept of martyrdom had been a subversive invention. It transformed the humiliation of criminal execution into a moral triumph by subordinating the Roman legal system to an understanding of justice based on divine law (Buc 1997; Liebs 2002). Early martyr stories focus tightly on explaining that subversion and demonstrating its legitimacy. This is the logic that structures the influential *Martyrdom of Polycarp*, written between 161 and 168. It is styled as a letter from the church of Smyrna addressed "to all the communities of the holy Church everywhere" (p. 7), and it presents Polycarp as a mirror image of Jesus, whose death enfolded in a hauntingly familiar narrative (Zwierlein 2014, vol. 2, pp. 102–106). The comparison to Christ was supposed to underline the idea that Polycarp, though executed by the Roman state, was oriented to an ethical system that superseded Roman law—but the letter also advances this claim in other ways. It reminds readers repeatedly that Polycarp was an old man, eighty-six years old in fact: how could he possibly be a threat to the Empire? It inverts the process of judgment and identifies the prosecutors as the truly "lawless" men (p. 11), and it depicts the crowd in the center of the stadium in a state of "unrestrained rage" (p. 9) who seem all the more irrational against Polycarp's calm self-composure. The text also argues that Polycarp's sentence to be burned alive was nothing compared to the endless fire that awaited the damned. Polytheists were obviously one target of these arguments, but they were not the only ones. Christians themselves were not in agreement about the legitimacy of martyrdom: well into Late Antiquity, they debated the ethics of complying (or not) with their rulers and with accepting death voluntarily (Boyarin 1999; Luijendijk 2008; Shaw 2011; Gemeinhardt 2014).

If the author of the *Martyrdom of Polycarp* had time-traveled to Merovingian Gaul, he would not have had to do so much explaining. Early medieval readers only needed the faintest of cues to know that they were dealing with a martyrdom: the idea was already familiar. Nor did they need to be persuaded that the deaths of Christians prosecuted by the Roman state had been victories for the "victims" rather than failures. And precisely because martyrdom was, by this period, so self-evident and so uncontroversial an interpretation of the imperial past, writers played with perspective in ways that their ancient models could not. When early medieval hagiographers wrote or rewrote the passions of ancient martyrs, they accentuated the difference between Christian and non-Christian characters, partly by pantomiming polytheist beliefs, but even more so by emphasizing how alien Christians would have seemed to polytheists at the time. In the seventh-century *Martyrdom of Priscus and His Companions*, an imperial official is baffled that Christians would worship "some crucified guy" (*nescio quis crucifixus*). The judge in *The Suffering of Afra* brashly and erroneously assumes that the Christian god categorically excluded prostitutes from redemption. The *Suffering of Juliana*, preserved in an early Carolingian legendary but almost certainly read and rewritten in the Merovingian period, pits its heroine against a prefect who is captivated by her beauty and does not want her to die. But Juliana mocks him for being afraid of a mere mortal, "shit-eating" emperor. In the same manuscript, *The Suffering of Babylas* relishes another prosecutor's confusion about why three little boys kept calling Bishop Babylas "father": surely Babylas must have had sex with their mother! (*Martyrdom of Priscus*, p. 366; *Suffering of Afra*, pp. 138–139; *Suffering of Juliana*, p. 659; Bottiglieri 2014, 641–656; *Suffering of Babylas*, pp. 568–569, 571).

The earliest hagiographers had developed martyrdom as an effort to reevaluate and accommodate Christians within the Empire without violating their legal responsibilities to God. As the *Martyrdom of Polycarp* pointed out, the only precondition for Christians to respect and uphold the imperial order was that "it does us no harm" (*Martyrdom of Polycarp*, p. 381). But Merovingian writers and their audiences seemed to relish thinking about what made Christianity historically distinctive. They felt no obligation to make either the imperial or Christian perspectives seem even remotely legible to each other. Hagiographers did this not only out of an interest in defining the special features of Christian identity of their own times by imagining what would have been strangest to societies in the past. They also recognized that hagiography's relationship to Christian audiences had changed. They anticipated and resisted complacency in a culture that would have known martyr stories as a genre—as a narrative framework of familiar characters, scenes, conflicts, and motifs—rather than as a radical politics. They were making these ancient confrontations seem weird and magnificent again.

Their technicolor visions of the past enlivened the concept of martyrdom, but they also made it harder to make sense of the present. Ancient saints in early medieval narratives behaved boldly and even incautiously. Their enemies gave only the flimsiest of excuses for pursuing them. Their tortures were exotic and nearly unending. And the martyrs endured all of it while bantering wittily with their tormentors and performing spectacular miracles. These were daunting precedents that made the work of contemporary hagiography difficult (Blennemann and Herbers 2014a, pp. 12–13; Kreiner 2014b, pp. 128–130). How could a writer represent a recent murder victim with the same panache and certainty without sacrificing the narrative's credibility?

According to the brilliant author of *The Suffering of Leudegar*, it was impossible. Leudegar was a bishop of Autun and an advisor to the Merovingian king Childeric II. Eventually, he was murdered in the late 670s by a faction of elites who were competing for influence at the court; his *Suffering* was composed about a decade later. But Leudegar's life did not unfold as smoothly as its models. Neither did his *Life*: his hagiographer had a lot of persuading to do, and that required confronting the past rather than erasing it (Fouracre 1990, pp. 9–11). The hagiographer carefully rationalized Leudegar's actions at court and in his home city, and simultaneously he had to make the case that his opponents had acted unethically. He also had to accommodate the fact that the "climax" of these conflicts seemed to be continually deferred: several times when it seemed that Leudegar was about to die, his antagonists changed their minds and let him go.

Leudegar's hagiographer was candid about these unexpected plot twists: "God did his servant the honor of this grace, that whenever he was handed over as an exile to be harmed, everyone extended him their respect and support instead" (*Suffering of Leudegar*, p. 315). But his remark was not merely an attempt to explain the surprises that Leudegar confronted. It also acknowledged the dilemma of having to narrate them, of having to package a messy and unresolved situation within a genre whose models were often considerably less complicated (Kreiner 2014b, pp. 128–133).

Most hagiographers working in Gaul reflected in some way on the challenges of their art form. Their most pervasive concern was that it was impossible to narrate a life in its full fleshiness. Writing was inescapably selective. Hagiographers had to be satisfied with saying a little about a lot. It seemed to them that they could never really capture the boundless good that their subjects had been capable of doing. *Quid plura?*—What else should I say?—was a common refrain. Honoratus of Marseille compared it to crafting a crown: one couldn't include every available gem! (*Life of Hilary of Arles*, pp. 81–82). So when hagiographers protested in their prefaces that they were unworthy to the task of writing, they probably meant it, at least a little bit. Not only did their subjects seem larger than life; writing could make anything seem smaller.

But hagiographers also saw the advantages of narrative economy. They were wary of boring their audiences. They also knew that a handful of well-edited episodes could be a rhetorically powerful form of representation: this genre was structurally designed to suggest that the biographical stood for the social and that the episodic had consequences for the eternal. And so rather than be deterred by the impossibility of being thorough, or by the profiles of saints that prior hagiographers had so expertly crafted, writer after writer took up the challenge of new narration.

PERSUASION AND PLEASURE

One of the joys and challenges of the work these writers left us is that, although it buzzed with erudition and political energy, it does not look the way we expect arguments to look. Merovingian hagiographers mastered the art of packaging complex conversations into seemingly simple stories. Take this scene from *The Suffering of Leudegar*, which stages a confrontation between Leudegar and Childeric II:

> Later, when [the king] was really shamefully drunk from wine, when others were fasting in anticipation of the holy liturgy, he entered the church. He made a racket, calling out for Leudegar by name, as if to put him to flight, while at the same time he terrified those who tried to intervene by threatening to strike them with his sword. He kept shouting out for him, and when he figured out that he was in the baptistery, he went in there, too, but at the brightness of so much light and at the scent of the baptismal oil, both of which were used for baptismal blessings there, he fell silent. And when [Leudegar] answered his cries—"I'm right here!"—[the king] didn't recognize him, and he moved on.   (p. 292)

The language here is vivid and brisk. The syntax is straightforward and the narrator is nearly invisible, seeming to surface only in words such as "shamefully" and "holy." For the most part, the scene seems to unfold by itself.

Most Merovingian hagiography moves this way, and in its stripped-down style, the actions and details themselves stand as arguments. It is significant not only that Childeric is drunk in a place where he should not be drunk and armed where he should not be armed; it also matters that he is committing these transgressions on Easter. In the Merovingian calendar, Easter was a time for Christians to mirror Jesus' sacrifice by acting selflessly for the benefit of other people. And yet here is the king, doing exactly the opposite of what the holiday required. Others are fasting; he is being self-indulgent. Worse, this indulgence makes him incautiously violent and unreceptive to guidance from his own advisor: his disregard for various legal customs as well as his disregard for liturgical and ethical propriety threatened the security of his own subjects. The hagiographer encoded these specific criticisms within the scene to suggest that Childeric had failed to fulfill his royal responsibilities, while by contrast Leudegar remained an exemplary public servant. And also, as part of the necessary double motion of hagiographical argument, he used the scene to reaffirm the particular set of principles that informed this judgment in the first place (Kreiner 2011).

This aesthetic was a deliberate rhetorical choice. It was informed by contemporary cognitive theory and by philosophies of action and responsibility. Many intellectuals in Gaul were thinking deeply about how memory, habit, and culture affected the choices that people made (Kreiner 2014a, pp. 88–139; 2014b). The hagiographers themselves figured that a memorable story—and the ideas that were laced through it—had the potential to transform its readers by "simmering" in their minds as long as they remembered it (*Life of Wandregisel*, p. 13). According to Sadalberga's hagiographer, a mind (*animus*) naturally tended to become complacent or "lukewarm" (*tepescere*) when times were good (*Life of Sadalberga*, p. 53). Literature was a kind of alternate source of energy that worked against that tendency. Through the simmering that a story generated, a reader would become increasingly persuaded that a narrative's sense of cause and effect—like, for example, the link that *The Suffering of Leudegar* made between selfishness and social endangerment—was real and consequential.

To enhance this persuasive process, the hagiographers designed their texts using mnemonic strategies that medieval and even modern memory specialists would recognize. They created scenic spaces (a church, a baptistery) within their stories with just enough detail to be visible but not so much that the vistas were crowded. They highlighted a few objects and gestures (a sword, staggering, making a racket) as a kind of significant shorthand that made the meaningful actions of their characters easier to visualize and recall (Martínez Pizarro 1989). They evoked sounds, tastes, smells, and tactile "imagery" (direct speech, yelling, silence, brightness, scented oil), which enriched these memories through different forms of sensory impression. Most importantly, they scaled down their complex views of politics into single biographical frames: in this cognitive economy, the singular stood for the whole (Kreiner 2014a, pp. 92–104, 140–142).

Besides being memorable, these scenes were also supposed to be pleasurable. As Mary Carruthers has demonstrated, there was a close connection in medieval rhetoric between aesthetics and persuasion. A work that was enjoyable or fascinating could draw a person in. It could make a reader (or listener, or viewer) more interested, curious, and appreciative (Carruthers 2013, pp. 45–79). Merovingian audiences would have agreed. Narratives were a vital form of communication whose form mattered as much as their function. The political "consultants" of the kingdom spoke to each other through stories or *fabulae*, recounting and reinterpreting literary or historical set pieces to offer informed judgments and advice. Those stories were also expected to be entertaining: an ideal advisor was *iocundus in fabulis*—a *delightful* storyteller. Not every story struck the perfect balance. Critics of storytelling suggested that *fabulae* consisted of nothing more than myths and gossip, and they suggested replacing them with more edifying instruction. But although one might disagree with the proportion of fun to functionality, or with the message that a story communicated, nobody suggested getting rid of interesting stories altogether (Kreiner 2014a, pp. 104–125; Reimitz 2015, pp. 199–212; Wood 2015).

We cannot know for sure that audiences enjoyed the hagiography they heard and read, but we *can* be sure that hagiographers were preoccupied with the question of what made a narrative pleasurable: they did not want to lose any minds to boredom. So the stories that they chose to tell, and the many stories that they chose not to tell, at least represent their best guesses about what other members of the Merovingian kingdom might appreciate. Several scenes, for example, doubled as both arguments and comedies. Jonas of Bobbio tells a cartoonishly goofy story about a monk named Fraimer who cut his thumb off with a plow. The story ends with a miraculous reattachment, but only after several gags and comically protracted delays (*Life of Columbanus*, pp. 234–235). Gregory of Tours complained that a royal treasurer illegally confiscated some sheep that were owned by the church of St. Julian. "What, does Julian eat sheep?" the official cackled to the shepherds. But Gregory has the last laugh: one day this treasurer had a bad fall in front of Julian's tomb, and when his servants eventually discovered him lying there they said, "Why have you been down on the ground all this time? You don't usually take so long to pray" (*Suffering and Miracles of Julian*, p. 121–122). *The Life of Arnulf* preferred slapstick: when courtiers insinuated that Arnulf was having sex with both the king and queen, God punished them by setting their pajamas on fire. They shot out of bed and started screaming for water, but even water couldn't extinguish the flames, so they rushed outside and hurled themselves into a pigpen, and they shrieked and rolled around in the dung while their genitals roasted to a crisp (p. 437).

Not all Merovingian jokes will be obviously identifiable as jokes to us now. The standards for delightful storytelling change. But the pleasures we do recognize were not just accidents or detours in a literature that focused primarily on religion and government and finance, as if jokes or even narratives more generally were a sugar coating that masked the moral medicine inside. Instead, the scenic vision of Merovingian hagiography *was* its ethics. Each episode was part of the social silhouette that the saints were said to outshine, part of the way that arguments were made, and part of the insurance that a story—and the frames of action and perception that it prized—would be remembered and retold.

ALTERNATE REALITIES: A BRIEF CASE AND CONCLUSION

One basic conclusion to draw from all of this is that, although hagiography was a traditional genre, it was not exactly conservative either. Every new act of identifying a saint altered the sense of what "sanctity" and social ethics were. It is worth stressing that this dynamic concept of culture is not exclusively poststructural or postmodern.[3] The hagiographical process was manifestly dialectical and discursive to Merovingian writers themselves. They responded to the world they inhabited, while recognizing that the categories by which they evaluated it (not only saintliness itself but also concepts such as humility, responsibility, bravery, or profit) could be redefined or even replaced with different forms of evaluation entirely. That is precisely what made these texts so argumentative and so stylistically savvy: hagiographers were aware of the alternatives.

This final section focuses on a single text to better demonstrate that limber, looping process. The text is called *The Interpolated Life of Germanus of Auxerre*. Its hagiographer, like most Merovingian hagiographers, is anonymous to us today, and at some point in the seventh century, she or he decided to revise and expand a text that had originally been written around 475, Constantius's *Life of Germanus of Auxerre* (Egmond 2006, 107–124). Despite its title, the *Interpolated Life* is no hack job. The "interpolations" consist of excerpts from other hagiographical texts that featured cameo appearances by Germanus, which the compiler carefully combined and supplied with a few extra comments in order to produce an entirely new work. One of the hagiographer's main objectives in "updating" Germanus's dossier was apparently to challenge the work of Gregory of Tours—which means we are dealing with a work with a fine-grained sense of difference, responding to an author who was himself dedicated to redefining a kingdom's sense of itself against other alternate realities.

Helmut Reimitz has shown how influential Gregory was for many generations of historians who succeeded him (Reimitz 2015). The *Interpolated Life* shows that hagiographers could be equally careful readers of Gregory, even when they disagreed with him as much as the historians did. The text's most visible riposte to the bishop of Tours was to rewrite an episode from his *Suffering and Miracles of Julian*. In Gregory's version, the citizens of Brioude ask Germanus to help them figure out the feast date of the village's homegrown saint. The *Interpolated Life* tells it differently: Germanus is the one to initiate the investigation, his announcement of his findings is far more imperious, and the bishop of Auxerre forces the inhabitants of Brioude to admit that their own searches had come up short. The result of these modifications is to suggest that the cult of Julian—one of the brightest stars in Gregory's spiritual constellation—was entirely dependent on the initiative and talent of an outsider (Gregory, *Suffering and Miracles of Julian*, p. 126; *Interpolated Life*, p. 215; Reimitz 2016, p. 537).

The *Interpolated Life* addresses Gregory more substantially in a section excerpted not from Gregory's own work but from a text called *The Revelation of Corcodemus and Conversion of Mamertinus*, which was probably written during the episcopacy of Gregory's contemporary, Aunarius of Auxerre (van Egmond 2006, pp. 97–107; *Interpolated Life*, pp. 206–211). The *Revelation* follows the path of a pagan named Mamertinus to Auxerre: he had been told by a cleric that he could cure his partial blindness and arthritis by seeking out Germanus in person. Mamertinus does not quite make it to the city before a storm hits, and he spends the night in a cemetery just south of the city. He falls asleep in a mausoleum, lying on top of a sarcophagus. In the middle of the night, being startled awake by a voice calling the deacon by name—"Saint Corcodemus! Saint Corcodemus! Deacon of Christ!"—he learns that this tomb belongs to the deacon.

Mamertinus eavesdrops on the long exchange that follows and in the process learns that this voice belongs to a subdeacon named Florentius. The subdeacon relays a message that Bishop Peregrinus is celebrating the night office and mass and wants Corcodemus and his subdeacons to be there. Corcodemus will not leave because he is watching over Mamertinus for the night. Peregrinus (via Florentius) insists. Corcodemus finally agrees to go, and one of his subdeacons takes Mamertinus along with them. At the church, Mamertinus is so curious about all the (dead) people assembled there that he cannot resist asking Corcodemus who they are. The deacon is happy to oblige: "The one standing in the middle is holy Peregrinus. He was a bishop and martyr, and Pope Sixtus sent him and me from Rome [to Gaul]. The two on the right are Amator and Bishop Marcellianus. On the left are saints Elladius and Valerian, who each succeeded Peregrinus as bishop in turn" (p. 207).

This series of personable introductions to the ancient personnel of the church of Auxerre is a subtle response to Gregory of Tours. It reconfigures the apostolic foundations of Gaul that Gregory had laid out in the very first book of his *Histories*.[4] Gregory had said that around the time that Pope Sixtus was martyred, seven men were ordained as bishops and sent to Gaul to preach. These seven men became the bishops of Tours, Arles, Narbonne, Toulouse, Paris, Clermont, and Limoges. The *Revelation of Corcodemus* brings this count of bishops to eight by inserting Peregrinus into that time and missionary project. So through Peregrinus, Auxerre becomes part of the early apostolic landscape, even though Gregory had not charted it that way.

Here too the hagiographer's style assists with the narrative's meaning: the saints Mamertinus sees are both ghostly and ordinary before him. He finds the whole ensemble surreal, and yet their chitchat is almost comically routine. The combination was surely meant to be memorable. Amator, for example, suggests that they all perform mass a little faster so that Peregrinus can get back home on time—because in the "real world" of Auxerre, Peregrinus was buried in a different place than that of the city's other early bishops (Atsma 1983, pp. 21–22; Picard et al. 1992, pp. 60–61). As the saints talk, work, and move through real landscapes, their strange charm fosters familiarity with Auxerre and the saintly genealogy that Gregory of Tours had "overlooked."

The text challenges another argument within Gregory's work, too. It claims that Mamertinus's experience entitled him to become an apostolic messenger because, although Mamertinus was not perfect, he had received visions from God. As a result, by rediscovering Corcodemus's tomb, he brought the deacon the recognition he deserved. In that regard, the hagiographer insists, he was no different than the apostles we meet in Acts: Mamertinus was functionally equivalent to Paul or to Barnabas (*Interpolated Life*, p. 206). Such a view countered a set of clues that Gregory had dropped across his writings, hinting that Gregory himself came from the most distinguished apostolic lineage in all of Gaul. Stringing those clues together reveals that Gregory's grandmother, Leocadia, was related to the very first martyr from the city of Lyon, a man named Vettius Epagatus. Vettius was martyred alongside his bishop, Irenaeus of Lyon, and Irenaeus had been sent to the city by none other than Polycarp of Smyrna. Polycarp in turn had been tutored by John—the apostle and evangelist! (Wood 2002; Reimitz 2015, pp. 45–46; Gregory of Tours, *Histories*, pp. 20–22; Gregory, *Life of the Fathers*, p. 230; Gregory, *Suffering and Miracles of Julian*, p. 124; Gregory, *Glory of the Martyrs*, pp. 71–72).

It is a meandering but unambiguous path: Gregory carried the blood that had been spilled alongside the students of St. John himself.[5] Other members of his family had emphasized that lineage in other ways. Gregory's brother Peter, and their great-grandfather Gregory of Langres, were buried in a mausoleum dedicated to John (Heinzelmann 2001, pp. 17–19). And Gregory of Langres might have been the author of a hagiographical cycle that followed John's apostolic trajectory through Polycarp, Irenaeus, and the disciples of Irenaeus, some of whom ended up in Dijon, which is where Gregory of Langres lived most of the time. Whoever the author of that cycle was, he or she envisioned a region that was stamped with apostolic footprints (van der Straeten 1961; Wood 2014, pp. 259–260).

Auxerre and its intellectuals were not trying to denigrate Gregory and his patrons. The city of Auxerre had churches dedicated to both Martin and Julian, and a synod that took place in the city makes clear that Martin's cult was very popular there by the late sixth century (Atsma 1983, pp. 24–29; Picard et al. 1992, pp. 61–62, 64–65; *Concilia Galliae*, p. 265). The presiding bishop of that synod, Aunarius of Auxerre, was also a dedicated fan of Martin, and Aunarius had worked with Gregory personally (Atsma 1983, pp. 73–77). The *Interpolated Life* was also obviously indebted to Gregory's research methods and his ideas: like Gregory's work, it was the product of comprehensive source collection and careful editing, and its effort to set Auxerre in a saintly genealogy and topography owes a great deal to Gregory's vision of Gaul.

But all those debts were precisely why Gregory's legacy was also something to challenge through the discourse of sanctity. The *Interpolated Life* and Auxerre were trying to establish new sources of authority, which first required putting the city on a map that Gregory had already made. More importantly, Auxerre challenged Gregory's ideas about leadership and influence. The bishops and abbots of Auxerre did not enjoy the same sources of prestige as Gregory's family did. They did not descend from senatorial families. Martyrs' blood had been shed on the city's behalf, but not as much of it as elsewhere, and the martyrs who *had* died there did not have networks that stretched back to the eastern Mediterranean, let alone to St. John. But the *Interpolated Life* suggested that these forms of endorsement did not matter as much as Gregory had said they did. What Auxerre's heroes represented instead was *effective* pastoral power. In order to be a good Christian leader, one needed only to be receptive to the subtle messages that God sent, and to persuade and enable others to participate in the same divine communication.

Mamertinus was a case in point. This pagan who stumbled onto Corcodemus's tomb ended up becoming an abbot of the most prestigious monastery in the diocese (*Interpolated Life*, p. 210; Atsma 1983, pp. 30–40; Picard et al. 1992, p. 57). And it was through Mamertinus that the author of the *Revelation of Corcodemus*, or possibly the compiler of the *Interpolated Life*, redefined what counted as apostolic. God, the hagiographer argued, had illuminated the whole world through Mamertinus—a pagan, a sinner! God "unlocked the tongues of both good and bad people alike to teach of his work" (p. 206). What mattered most was not Mamertinus's credentials but the fact that he had recognized and drawn attention to a moment and a place where the divine and earthly world had come together. The hagiographer called this moment, this night in the cemetery of Monte-Artre, a *spirituale negotium*, a spiritual exchange or transaction (p. 206). This give-and-take between heavenly and earthly systems mattered more than the identity of the messengers who advertised it. So this was a text that emphasized the *use* of power as a retroactive legitimation of that power. Such an argument may have appealed to other centers in Gaul at the time because political conditions were changing, all the more so after Gregory died in 594. The center of gravity was shifting northward, to Paris, especially after Clothar II took control of the entire kingdom in 613. On top of that, new social networks were forming around the new royal courts, and elite status was becoming more variegated than before (Wood 1994, pp. 140–272; Rosenwein 1999, pp. 57–96; Bougard et al. 2011; Loseby 2013; Reimitz 2015, pp. 159–239; Kreiner 2018). It may be that Auxerre's deemphasis of exclusive historical pedigrees was made with this political reshuffling in mind.

Despite all these differences, the *Interpolated Life* upheld Gregory's conviction that ecclesiastical leadership was a collaborative and beneficial force in the kingdom. Gregory's framework for seeing Gaul as a landscape of apostles and martyrs was his contribution to an ongoing conversation about leadership—about what justified leadership and what responsibilities it entailed (Kreiner 2014a, pp. 140–88; Reimitz 2015, pp. 25–97). Also, like Gregory's work—and like most hagiography after Gregory—the ethics of the *Interpolated Life* was eschatologically inflected (Heinzelmann 2001, pp. 153–172; Brown 2013, pp. 154–165; Kreiner 2014b; Reimitz 2015, pp. 65–69), meaning that hagiographical texts offered not only an improvement on society but also an incentive to change: God would reward the souls of the ones who heeded their particular recommendations. Even so, the hagiographers were all too aware that ethical reorientation was never instantaneous. It was a cultural process, even for the saints themselves. As the compiler of the *Interpolated Life* noted, in what were probably his or her own words (p. 217; van Egmond 2006, pp. 117–119), even Germanus himself benefited from other saints' encouragement and assurances that the heavenly Jerusalem really was a place that existed and that it was not so far away.

NOTES

1. Merovingian hagiography is a deep field of research. The best English-language introduction is Fouracre and Gerberding 1996; in French, one should also consult Heinzelmann 2010. Hagiography in English translation includes O'Hara and Wood 2017; de Nie 2015; Fouracre and Gerberding 1996; James 1991; van Dam 2004a, 2004b; Vivian et al. 1999; McNamara 2000; McNamara and Halborg 1992 (although not all texts in this collection are of Merovingian composition). Philippart and Goullet 1994–2014 is an essential resource for region-specific overviews of medieval hagiographical traditions, but the chapter on early medieval Gaul remains to be published. For a foothold in recent research, start with Goullet 2005; Renard et al. 2005; van Egmond 2006; Goullet et al. 2010; Bozóky 2012; Blennemann and Herbers 2014b; Isaïa and Granier 2014; and Kreiner 2014a.
2. My citations of Merovingian texts refer to the Latin editions, and the translations are mine. See n. 1 for Merovingian hagiography in English translation.
3. Many theorists whose work seem most "modern" to us were in fact informed by medieval philosophies of identity and culture: see, for example, Holsinger 2005; Cole 2014.
4. Van Egmond (2006, pp. 97–102) says the text could not have been written after 592 or 593, based on this text's agreement with an early draft of the Martyrology of Jerome on the feast date for Peregrinus. But the author's evident familiarity with Gregory's *Histories* suggests that the *Revelatio* postdated Gregory's work, which he completed in 594, or its author was familiar with an earlier draft of Gregory's text, or, as a third possible option, the compiler of the *Interpolated Life* rewrote this scene in response to Gregory's *Histories*.
5. In order to make this claim, Gregory has to modify his sources: according to Rufinus's Latin version of Eusebius's *Ecclesiastical History*, Vettius Epagatus was killed before Irenaeus even came to Lyon, and the *Historia ecclesiastica* does not say that Irenaeus was martyred at all. But Eusebius/Rufinus do say that Irenaeus was a student of Polycarp, and they and their sources repeatedly stress that Polycarp was educated by the apostle and evangelist John, the very man "who used to lay upon the breast of the Lord." Gregory conflates the two biographical trajectories in order to root his family in that genealogy. See Rufinus, *Historia ecclesiastica*, sections 3.23, 3.21, 3.36, 3.39, 4.14–15, and 5.1–5.

Works Cited

Ancient Sources

Concilia Galliae. C. De Clercq (ed.). (1963). *Concilia Galliae a. 511-a. 695*, vol. 2. Corpus Christianorum series Latina 148A. Turnhout: Brepols.

de Nie, G. (trans.). (2015). *Gregory of Tours: Lives and Miracles*. Dumbarton Oaks Medieval Library 39. Cambridge, MA: Harvard University Press.

Fouracre, P., and Gerberding, R. A. (1996). *Late Merovingian France: History and Hagiography, 640–720*. Manchester: Manchester University Press.

Gregory of Tours, *Glory of the Martyrs* [*Liber in gloria martyrum*]. B. Krusch (ed.). (1969). *Gregorii episcopi Turonensis miracula et opera minora* (pp. 34–111). MGH SRM 1.2, 2nd ed. Hanover: Hahn.

Gregory of Tours, *Histories* [*Libri historiarum X*]. B. Krusch and W. Levison (eds.). (1951). *Gregorii episcopi Turonensis Libri historiarum X*. MGH SRM 1.1, 2nd ed. Hanover: Hahn.

Gregory of Tours, *The Life of the Fathers* [*Liber vitae patrum*]. B. Krusch (ed.). (1969). *Gregorii episcopi Turonensis miracula et opera minora* (pp. 211–294). MGH SRM 1.2. 2nd ed. Hanover: Hahn.

Gregory of Tours, *The Suffering and Miracles of Julian* [*Liber de passione et virtutibus Iuliani martyris*]. B. Krusch. (1969). *Gregorii episcopi Turonensis miracula et opera minora* (pp. 112–134). MGH SRM 1.2. 2nd ed. Hanover: Hahn.

Honoratus of Marseille, *The Life of Hilary, Bishop of Arles* [*Vita Hilarii Arelatensis*]. S. Cavallin (ed.). (1952). *Vitae sanctorum Honorati et Hilarii, episcoporum Arelatensium*. Lund: Gleerup.

The Interpolated Life of Germanus of Auxerre [*Vita Germani interpolata*]. *Acta Sanctorum* (1731). July VII (pp. 201–221). Antwerp: Société des Bollandistes.

James, E. (trans.). (1991). *Gregory of Tours: Life of the Fathers*. 2nd ed. Liverpool: Liverpool University Press.

Jonas of Bobbio, *The Life of the Abbot Columbanus and His Disciples* [*Vitae Columbani abbatis discipulorumque eius libri II*]. B. Krusch (ed.). (1905). *Ionae Vitae sanctorum Columbani, Vedastis, Iohannis*. MGH SRG 37. Hanover, Leipzig: Hahn.

Krusch, B. (ed.). (1969). *Gregorii episcopi Turonensis miracula et opera minora*. MGH SRM 1.2. 2nd ed. Hanover: Hahn.

The Life of Arnulf [*Vita Arnulfi*]. B. Krusch (ed.). (1888). *Fredegarii et aliorum Chronica, Vitae sanctorum*. MGH SRM 2 (pp. 427–446). Hanover: Hahn.

The Life of Eptadius [*Vita Eptadii presbyteri Cervidunesis*]. B. Krusch (ed.). (1896). *Passiones vitaeque sanctorum aevi Merovingici et antiquiorum aliquot*. MGH SRM 3 (pp. 184–194). Hanover: Hahn.

The Life of Sadalberga [*Vita Sadalbergae abbatissae Laudunensis*]. B. Krusch and W. Levison (eds.). (1910). *Passiones vitaeque sanctorum aevi Merovingici (III)*. MGH SRM 5 (pp. 40–66). Hanover: Hahn.

The Life of Segolena [*Vita Segolenae*]. J. Mabillon (ed.). (1727). *Acta Sanctorum*, July V (pp. 630–637). Antwerp: Sociètè des Bollandistes.

The Life of the Jura Fathers [*Vita patrum Iurensium Romani, Lupicini, Eugendi*]. B. Krusch (ed.). (1896). *Passiones vitaeque sanctorum aevi Merovingici et antiquiorum aliquot*. MGH SRM 3 (pp. 125–166). Hanover: Hahn.

The Life of Wandregisel [*Vita Wandregiseli abbatis Fontanellensis*]. B. Krusch and W. Levison (eds.). (1910). *Passiones vitaeque sanctorum aevi Merovingici (III)*. MGH SRM 5 (pp. 1–24). Hanover: Hahn.

The Martyrdom of Polycarp [*Martyrium Polycarpi*]. O. Zwierlein (ed.) and Kölligan, D. (trans.), (2014). In *Editiones criticae* (pp. 6–44). Vol. 1 of *Die Urfassungen der Martyria Polycarpi et Pionii und das Corpus Polycarpianum*. Berlin: Walter de Gruyter.

The Martyrdom of Priscus and His Companions [*Martyrium Prisci et sociorum*]. *Acta sanctorum*. (1688). May VI (pp. 365–367). Antwerp: Société des Bollandistes.

McNamara, J. A. (trans.). (2000). "Dado of Rouen, Life of St. Eligius of Noyon." In T. Head (ed.), *Medieval Hagiography: An Anthology* (pp. 137–167). New York: Routledge.

McNamara, J. A., & Halborg, J. E. (trans.). (1992). *Sainted Women of the Dark Ages*. Durham, NC: Duke University Press.

O'Hara, A., and Wood, I. (trans.). (2017). *Jonas of Bobbio: Life of Columbanus, Life of John of Réomé, and Life of Vedast*. Liverpool: Liverpool University Press.

Rufinus. *Historia ecclesiastica*. E. Schwartz, T. Mommsen, and F. Winkelmann (eds.). (1999). *Eusebius Werke*. 2nd ed. Vol. 2, *Die Kirchengeschichte*. Berlin: Akademie.

The Suffering of Afra [*Passio Afrae*]. M. Goullet (ed.). (2011). "Conversion et passion d'Afra d'Augsbourg: Réouverture du dossier et édition synoptique des versions longue et brève." *Revue bénédictine* 121: 94–146.

The Suffering of Babylas [*Passio Babylae*]. M. Goullet (ed.). (2014). In M. Goullet and S. Isetta, *Le Légendier de Turin: Ms. D.V.3 de la Bibliothèque Nationale Universitaire* (pp. 559–572). Florence: SISMEL/Edizioni del Galluzzo.

The Suffering of Juliana [*Passio Iulianae*]. C. Bottiglieri (ed.).(2014). In M. Goullet and S. Isetta, *Le Légendier de Turin: Ms. D.V.3 de la Bibliothèque Nationale Universitaire* (pp. 657–669). Florence: SISMEL/Edizioni del Galluzzo.

The Suffering of Leudegar [*Passio Leudegarii episcopi et martyris Augustodunensis*]. B. Krusch and W. Levison (eds.). (1910). *Passiones vitaeque sanctorum aevi Merovingici (III)*, MGH SRM 5 (pp. 249–322). Hanover, Leipzig: Hahn.

Van Dam, R. (trans.). (2004a). *Gregory of Tours: Glory of the Confessors*. Reprint ed. Liverpool: Liverpool University Press.

Van Dam, R (trans.). (2004b). *Gregory of Tours: Glory of the Martyrs*. Reprinted with corrections. Liverpool: Liverpool University Press.

Verus of Orange, *The Life of Eutropius* [*Vita Eutropii*]. M. P. Varin (ed.). (1849). "Vie de saint Eutrope, évêque de l'Orange." *Bulletin du Comité Historique des Monuments Écrits de l'Histoire de France, Histoire-Sciences-Lettres* 1: 51–64.

Vivian, T., K. Vivian, and J. B. Russell (trans.). (1999). *The Life of the Jura Fathers*. Kalamazoo, MI: Cistercian Publications.

Modern Sources

Atsma, H. (1983). "Klöster und Mönchtum im Bistum Auxerre bis zum ende des 6. Jahrhunderts." *Francia* 11: 1–96.

Bartlett, R. (2013). *Why Can the Dead Do Such Great Things? Saints and Worshippers from the Martyrs to the Reformation*. Princeton, NJ: Princeton University Press.

Beaujard, B. (2000). *Le culte des saints en Gaule. Les premiers temps: D'Hilaire de Poitiers à la fin du VIᵉ siècle*. Paris: Cerf.

Berschin, W. (2014). "Biographie et autobiographie au Moyen Âge." In D. Barthélemy and R. Grosse (eds.), *Moines et démons: Autobiographie et individualité au Moyen Âge (VIIᵉ–XIIIᵉ siècle)* (pp. 5–11). Geneva: Librairie Droz.

Blennemann, G. (2014). "Martyre et prédication: Adaptations d'un modèle hagiographique dans les sermons de Césaire d'Arles." In M.-C. Isaïa and T. Granier (eds.), *Normes et hagiographies dans l'Occident (V⁴-XVI⁴ siècle): Actes du colloque international de Lyon 4–6 octobre 2010* (pp. 253–273). Turnhout: Brepols.

Blennemann, G., and Herbers, K. (2014a). "Das Martyrium als Denkfigur: Brüche und Entwicklungslinien in christlicher Perspektive." In G. Blennemann and K. Herbers (Eds.), *Vom Blutzeugen zum Glaubenszeugen? Formen und Vorstellungen des christlichen Martyriums* (pp. 7–20). Stuttgart: Steiner.

Blennemann, G., and Herbers, K. (eds.). (2014b). *Vom Blutzeugen zum Glaubenszeugen? Formen und Vorstellungen des christlichen Martyriums.* Stuttgart: Steiner.

Boesch Gajano, S. (1999). "Reliques et pouvoirs." In E. Bozóky and A.-M. Helvétius (eds.), *Les reliques: Objets, cultes, symboles* (pp. 255–269). Turnhout: Brepols.

Bottiglieri, C. (2014). "Passio Iulianae." In M. Goullet and S. Isetta, *Le Légendier de Turin: Ms. D.V.3 de la Bibliothèque Nationale Universitaire* (pp. 641–669). Florence: SISMEL/Edizioni del Galluzzo.

Bougard, F., Goetz, H.-W., and Le Jan, R. (eds.) (2011). *Théorie et pratiques des élites au haut Moyen Âge: Conception, perception et réalisation sociale.* Turnhout: Brepols.

Boyarin, D. (1999). *Dying for God: Martyrdom and the Making of Christianity and Judaism.* Stanford, CA: Stanford University Press.

Bozóky, E. (Ed.). (2012). *Hagiographie, idéologie et politique au Moyen Âge en Occident: Actes du colloque international du Centre d'Études supérieures de Civilisation médiévale de Poitiers, 11–14 septembre 2008.* Turnhout: Brepols.

Brown, P. (2002). *Poverty and Leadership in the Later Roman Empire.* Hanover, NH: Brandeis University Press/Historical Society of Israel.

Brown, P. (2012). *Through the Eye of a Needle: Wealth, the Fall of Rome, and the Making of Christianity in the West, 350–550 AD.* Princeton, NJ: Princeton University Press.

Brown, P. (2013). *The Rise of Western Christendom: Triumph and Diversity, A.D. 200–1000,* tenth anniversary rev. ed. Malden, MA: Wiley-Blackwell.

Brown, P. (2015). *The Ransom of the Soul: Afterlife and Wealth in Early Western Christianity.* Cambridge, MA: Harvard University Press.

Buc, P. (1997). "Martyre et ritualité dans l'Antiquité tardive: Horizons de l'écriture médiévale des rituels." *Annales: Histoire, Sciences sociales* 48: 63–92.

Carruthers, M. (2013). *The Experience of Beauty in the Middle Ages.* Oxford: Oxford University Press.

Cole, A. (2014). *The Birth of Theory.* Chicago: University of Chicago Press.

Constable, G. (1996). *The Reformation of the Twelfth Century.* New York: Cambridge University Press.

Dal Santo, M. (2012). *Debating the Saints' Cult in the Age of Gregory the Great.* Cambridge: Cambridge University Press.

de Nie, G. (2011). *Poetics of Wonder: Testimonies of the New Christian Miracles in the Late Antique Latin World.* Turnhout: Brepols.

Diefenbach, S. (2013). "'Bischofsherrschaft'": Zur Transformation der politischen Kultur im spätantiken und frühmittelalterlichen Gallien." In S. Diefenbach and G. M. Müller (eds.), *Gallien in Spätantike und Frühmittelalter: Kulturgeschichte einer Region* (pp. 91–149). Berlin: Walter de Gruyter.

Diem, A. (2005). *Das monastische Experiment: Die Rolle der Keuschheit bei der Entstehung des Klosterwesens.* Münster: LIT.

Diem, A. (forthcoming). "Disputing Columbanus' Heritage: The *Regula cuiusdam patris.*"

Diem, A., and Müller, H. (2010). "Vita, regula, sermo: Eine unbekannte lateinische Vita Pacomii als Lehrtext für ungebildete Mönche und als Traktat über das Sprechen (mit einer Edition der Vita Pacomii im Anhang)." In R. Corradini, M. Diesenberger, and M. Niederkorn-Bruck (eds.), *Zwischen Niederschrift und Wiederschrift: Frühmittelalterliche Hagiographie und Historiographie im Spannungsfeld von Kompendienüberlieferung und Editionstechnik* (pp. 223–272). Vienna: Österreichische Akademie der Wissenschaften.

Esders, S. (2014). "'Avenger of All Perjury' in Constantinople, Ravenna and Metz: Saint Polyeuctus, Sigibert I, and the Dvision of Charibert's Kingdom in 568." In A. Fischer and I. Wood (eds.), *Western Perspectives on the Mediterranean: Cultural Transfer in Late Antiquity and the Early Middle Ages, 400–800 AD* (pp. 17–54). London: Bloomsbury.

Esders, S., Hen, Y., Sarti, L., and Fox, Y. (eds.). (2019). *East and West in the Early Middle Ages: The Merovingian Kingdoms in Mediterranean Perspective.* Cambridge: Cambridge University Press.

Fichtenau, H. (1952). "Zum Reliquienwesen im früheren Mittlelalter. " *Mitteilungen des Instituts für Österreichische Geschichtsforschung* 60: 60–89.

Fouracre, P. (1990). "Merovingian History and Merovingian Hagiography." *Past and Present* 127: 3–38.

Fouracre, P. (1995). "Eternal Light and Earthly Needs: Practical Aspects of the Development of Frankish Immunities." In P. Fouracre and W. Davies (eds.), *Property and Power in the Early Middle Ages* (pp. 53–81). Cambridge: Cambridge University Press.

Fox, Y. (2014). *Power and Religion in Merovingian Gaul: Columbanian Monasticism and the Frankish Elites.* Cambridge: Cambridge University Press.

Frazier, A. K. (2005). *Possible Lives: Authors and Saints in Renaissance Italy.* New York: Columbia University Press.

Gaiffier, B. de. (1954). "La lecture des actes des martyrs dans la prière liturgique en Occident: À propos du passionnaire hispanique." *Analecta Bollandiana* 72: 134–166.

Gaillard, M. (2011). "Les *Vitae* des saintes Salaberge et Anstrude de Laon, deux sources exceptionelles pour l'étude de la construction hagiographique et du context sociopolitique." *Revue du nord* 93: 655–669.

Gemeinhardt, P. (2014). "*Non poena sed causa facit martyrem*: Blut- und Lebenszeugnis in der Alten Kirche: Sache, Kontext und Rezeption." In G. Blennemann and K. Herbers (eds.), *Vom Blutzeugen zum Glaubenszeugen? Formen und Vorstellungen des christlichen Martyriums* (pp. 23–39). Stuttgart: Steiner.

Goullet, M. (2005). *Écriture et réécriture hagiographiques: Essai sur les réécritures de Vies des saints dan l'Occident latin médiéval (VIIIᵉ-XIIIᵉ s.).* Turnhout: Brepols.

Goullet, M. (2010). "Introduction. " In M. Goullet, M. Heinzelmann, and C. Veyrard-Cosme (eds.), *L'hagiographie mérovingienne à travers ses réécritures* (pp. 11–25). Paris: Thorbecke.

Goullet, M. (2014). "Langue des textes ou langue des copistes?" In M. Goullet and S. Isetta, *Le Légendier de Turin: Ms. D.V.3 de la Bibliothèque Nationale Universitaire* (pp. 165–194). Florence: SISMEL/Edizioni del Galluzzo.

Goullet, M., Heinzelmann, M., and Veyrard-Cosme, C. (eds.). (2010). *L'hagiographie mérovingienne à travers ses réécritures.* Paris: Thorbecke.

Heinzelmann, M. (1981). "Une source de base de la littérature hagiographique latine: Le receuil de miracles." In E. Patlagean and P. Riché (eds.), *Hagiographie, culture et sociétés, IVᵉ-XIIᵉ siècles* (pp. 235–259). Paris: Études Augustiniennes.

Heinzelmann, M. (2001). *Gregory of Tours: History and Society in the Sixth Century*, trans. C. Carroll. Cambridge: Cambridge University Press. Originally published (1994) as *Gregor von Tours (538–594): "Zehn Bücher Geschichte," Historiographie und Gesellschaftskonzept im 6. Jahrhundert*. Darmstadt: Wissenschaftliche Buchgesellschaft.

Heinzelmann, M. (2010). "L'hagiographie mérovingienne: Panorama des documents potentiels." In M. Goullet, M. Heinzelmann, and C. Veyrard-Cosme (eds.), *L'hagiographie mérovingienne à travers ses réécritures* (pp. 27–82). Paris: Thorbecke.

Helvétius, A.-M. (2012). "Hagiographie et formation politique des aristocrats dans le monde franc (VII\u1d49–VIII\u1d49 siècles)." In E. Bozóky (ed.), *Hagiographie, idéologie et politique au Moyen Âge en Occident: Actes du colloque international du Centre d'Études supérieures de Civilisation médiévale de Poitiers, 11–14 septembre 2008* (pp. 59–80). Turnhout: Brepols.

Helvétius, A.-M. (2014). "L'idée du martyre dans l'hagiographie monastique franque (VIII\u1d49–IX\u1d49 siècles)." In G. Blennemann and K. Herbers (eds.), *Vom Blutzeugen zum Glaubenszeugen? Formen und Vorstellungen des christlichen Martyriums* (pp. 83–99). Stuttgart: Steiner.

Hen, Y. (1995). *Culture and Religion in Merovingian Gaul, A.D. 481–751*. Leiden: Brill.

Holsinger, B. (2005). *The Premodern Condition: Medievalism and the Making of Theory*. Chicago: University of Chicago Press.

Isaïa, M.-C. (2014). "L'hagiographie, source de normes médiévales: Pistes de recherche." In M.-C. Isaïa amd T. Granier (eds.), *Normes et hagiographies dans l'Occident (V\u1d49–XVI\u1d49 siècle): Actes du colloque international de Lyon 4–6 octobre 2010* (pp. 17–42). Turnhout: Brepols.

Isaïa, M.-C., and Granier, T. (eds.). (2014). *Normes et hagiographies dans l'Occident (V\u1d49–XVI\u1d49 siècle): Actes du colloque international de Lyon 4–6 octobre 2010*. Turnhout: Brepols.

Jong, M. de, Theuws, F., and van Rhijn, C. (eds.). (2001). *Topographies of Power in the Early Middle Ages*. Leiden: Brill.

Keskiaho, J. (2015). *Dreams and Visions in the Early Middle Ages: The Reception and Use of Patristic Ideas, 400–900*. Cambridge: Cambridge University Press.

Kitchen, J. (2016). "Gregory of Tours, Hagiography, and the Cult of the Saints in the Sixth Century." In A. Murray (ed.), *A Companion to Gregory of Tours* (pp. 374–426). Leiden: Brill.

Kreiner, J. (2011). "About the Bishop: The Episcopal Entourage and the Economy of Government in Post-Roman Gaul." *Speculum* 86: 321–360.

Kreiner, J. (2014a). *The Social Life of Hagiography in the Merovingian Kingdom*. Cambridge: Cambridge University Press.

Kreiner, J. (2014b). "Autopsies and Philosophies of a Merovingian Life: Death, Responsibility, Salvation." *Journal of Early Christian Studies* 22(1): 113–152.

Kreiner, J. (2018). "Romanness in Merovingian Hagiography: A Case Study in Class and Political Culture." In W. Pohl et al. (eds.), *Transformations of Romanness: Early Medieval Regions and Identities*. Millennium-Studien 71. Berlin: Walter de Gruyter.

Liebs, D. (2002). "Umwidmung: Nutzung der Justiz zur Werbung für die Sache ihrer Opfer in den Märtyrerprozessen der frühen Christen." In W. Ameling (ed.), *Märtyrer und Märtyrerakten* (pp. 19–46). Stuttgart: Franz Steiner.

Lifshitz, F. (2006). *The Name of the Saint: The Martyrology of Jerome and Access to the Sacred in Francia, 627–827*. Notre Dame, IN: University of Notre Dame Press.

Loseby, S. (2013). "Lost Cities: The End of the *Civitas*-System in Frankish Gaul." In S. Diefenbach and G. M. Müller (eds.), *Gallien in Spätantike und Frühmittelalter: Kulturgeschichte einer Region* (pp. 223–252). Berlin: Walter de Gruyter.

Luijendijk, A. (2008). "Papyri from the Great Persecution: Roman and Christian Perspectives." *Journal of Early Christian Studies* 16(3): 341–369.

Magnani, E. (2009). "Almsgiving, *donatio pro anima* and Eucharistic Offering in the Early Middle Ages of Western Europe (4th-9th Century)." In M. Frenkel and Y. Lev (eds.), *Charity and Giving in Monotheistic Religions* (pp. 111–121). Berlin: Walter de Gruyter.

Martínez Pizarro, J. (1989). *A Rhetoric of the Scene: Dramatic Narrative in the Early Middle Ages*. Toronto: University of Toronto Press.

McCormick, M. (2001). *Origins of the European Economy: Communications and Commerce, A.D. 300-900*. Cambridge: Cambridge University Press.

Mériaux, C. (2006) *Gallia irradiata: Saints et sanctuaires dans la nord de la Gaule du haut Moyen Âge*. Stuttgart: Steiner.

Moreira, I. (2000). *Dreams, Visions, and Spiritual Authority in Merovingian Gaul*. Ithaca, NY: Cornell University Press.

Patzold, S. (2010). "Zur Sozialstruktur des Episkopats und zur Ausbildung bischöflicher Herrschaft in Gallien zwischen Spätantike und Frühmittelalter." In M. Becher and S. Dick (eds.), *Völker, Reiche und Namen im frühen Mittelalter* (pp. 121–140). Munich: Fink.

Patzold, S. (2014). "Bischöfer, soziale Herkunft und die Organisation lokaler Herrschaft um 500." In M. Meier and S. Patzold (eds.), *Chlodwigs Welt: Organisation von Herrschaft um 500* (pp. 523–543). Stuttgart: Franz Steiner.

Payne, R. (2015). *A State of Mixture: Christians, Zoroastrians, and Iranian Political Culture in Late Antiquity*. Berkeley: University of California Press.

Philippart, G., & Goullet, M. (eds.). (1994–2014). *Hagiographies: Histoire internationale de la littérature hagiographique latine et vernaculaire en Occident des origines à 1550*. 6 vols. Turnhout: Brepols.

Picard, J.-C. et al. (eds.) (1992). *Province ecclésiastique de Sens (Lugunensis Senonia)*. Vol. 8 in N. Gauthier and J.-C. Picard (eds.), *Topographie chrétienne des cités de la Gaule des origins au milieu du VIIIᵉ siècle*. Paris: de Boccard.

Raynaud, C. (2006). "Le monde des morts." In M. Heijmans and J. Guyon (eds.), *Antiquité tardive, haut Moyen Âge et premiers temps chrétiens en Gaule méridionale. Première partie: réseau des cites, monde urbain et monde des morts. Gallia* 63: 137–156.

Reimitz, H. (2015). *History, Frankish Identity and the Framing of Western Ethnicity, 550-850*. Cambridge: Cambridge University Press.

Reimitz, H (2016). "The Early Medieval Editions of Gregory of Tours' *Histories*." In A. Murray (ed.), *A Companion to Gregory of Tours* (pp. 519–565). Leiden: Brill.

Renard, E., et al. (eds.). (2005). "*Scribere sanctorum gesta*": *Recueil d'études d'hagiographie médiévale offert à Guy Philippart*. Turnhout: Brepols.

Rose, E. (2005). *Missale Gothicum*. Corpus Christianorum series Latina 159D. Turnhout: Brepols.

Rose, E. (2009). *Ritual Memory: The Apocryphal Acts and Liturgical Commemoration in the Early Medieval West, c. 500-1215*. Leiden: Brill.

Rosenwein, B. (1999). *Negotiating Space: Power, Restraint, and Privileges of Immunity in Early Medieval Europe*. Ithaca, NY: Cornell University Press.

Sarris, P., Dal Santo, M., and Booth, P. (2011). *An Age of Saints? Power, Conflict and Dissent in Early Medieval Christianity*. Leiden: Brill.

Shaw, B. (2011). *Sacred Violence: African Christians and Sectarian Hatred in the Age of Augustine*. Cambridge: Cambridge University Press.

Smith, J. M. H. (1990). "Oral and Written: Saints, Miracles, and Relics in Brittany, c. 850–1250." *Speculum* 65: 309–343.

Straeten, J. van der. (1961). "Les actes des martyrs d'Aurélien en Bourgogne." *Analecta Bollandiana* 79: 115–144.

Thacker, A., and Sharpe, R. (eds.). (2002). *Local Saints and Local Churches in the Early Medieval West*. Oxford: Oxford University Press.

Van Dam, R. (1993). *Saints and Their Miracles in Late Antique Gaul*. Princeton, NJ: Princeton University Press.

van Egmond, W. S. (2006). *Conversing with the Saints: Communication in Pre-Carolingian Hagiography from Auxerre*. Turnhout: Brepols.

van Uytfanghe, M. (2000). "Pertinence et statut du miracle dans l'hagiographie mérovingienne (600–750)." In D. Aigle (ed.), *Miracle et karāma* (pp. 67–144). Bibliothèque de l'École des Hautes Études Sciences Religieuses 109. Turnhout: Brepols.

Walker, J. T. (2006). *The Legend of Mar Qardagh: Narrative and Christian Heroism in Late Antique Iraq*. Berkeley: University of California Press.

Walter, C., and Patzold, S. (2014). "Der Episkopat im Frankenreich der Merowingerzeit: eine sich durch Verwandtschaft reproduzierende Elite?" In S. Patzold and K. Ubl (eds.), *Verwandtschaft, Name und soziale Ordnung* (pp. 109–139). Berlin: Walter de Gruyter.

Wickham, C. (2005). *Framing the Early Middle Ages: Europe and the Mediterranean, 400–800*. Oxford: Oxford University Press.

Wood, I. (1994). *The Merovingian Kingdoms, 450–751*. London: Longman.

Wood, I. (1998). "Jonas, the Merovingians, and Pope Honorius: *Diplomata* and the *Vita Columbani*." In A. C. Murray (ed.), *After Rome's Fall: Narrators and Sources of Early Medieval History. Essays Presented to Walter Goffart* (pp. 99–120). Toronto: University of Toronto Press.

Wood, I. (2002). "The Individuality of Gregory of Tours." In K. Mitchell and I. Wood (eds.), *The World of Gregory of Tours* (pp. 29–46). Leiden: Brill.

Wood, I. (2014). "The Cult of Saints in the South-East of Gaul in the Fifth and Sixth Centuries." In M. Gaillard (ed.), *L'empreinte chrétienne en Gaule du IVe au IXe siècle* (pp. 257–269). Turnhout: Brepols.

Wood, I. (2015). "*Iocundus in fabulis*: The Value of Friendly Advice." In L. Jégou et al. (eds.), *Splendor Reginae: Passions, genre et famille. Mélanges en l'honneur de Régine Le Jan* (pp. 329–340). Turnhout: Brepols.

Zwierlein, O. (2014). *Die Urfassungen der Martyria Polycarpi et Pionii und das Corpus Polycarpianum*. 2 vols. Berlin: Walter de Gruyter.

CHAPTER 25

....

LETTERS AND COMMUNICATION NETWORKS IN MEROVINGIAN GAUL

....

ANDREW GILLETT

LETTERS are a familiar source material for the study of Merovingian Gaul, as for other periods of Late Antiquity and the Middle Ages, and some letters and letter collections are particularly well known. Nonetheless, as a source of evidence for the period, letters may not yet have been put to best use. Letters are regularly employed as evidence for specific historical situations—such as Radegund's relations with the Gallic episcopacy and the eastern imperial court, or Boniface's correspondence with the papacy—or are subjected to classicist, literary-critical analysis of authorial style and intent. The frame of reference for interpretation and historiographic use of letters is thus often circumscribed by narrative situations or literary evaluation. Of course, letters can and should be used, in conjunction with other evidence types, to examine particular historical events or persons. But letters inherently suggest a wider frame of reference than other available historical materials. Just as a page on a contemporary social media site not only describes one individual and their contacts, but also indicates the existence of a medium to support a sprawling network of purposeful and constructed interconnections, so, too, letters from Merovingian Gaul are a synecdoche for practices and infrastructure that linked elites and others within and outside Gaul in multiple ways. Letters do not constitute events themselves, like the publication of laws and the issue of charters do, nor are they records of events, like the minutes of church council discussions and decisions (*acta*) are: by its nature, the event to which an epistolary text alludes—a communicative transaction—is conceived but not executed at the time the letter is composed. The later preservation of the text need not indicate whether the contact even occurred, except in the very rare instances when we can know that our extant text is descended from an original document accepted into the hands of the recipient (saints' *vitae* offer a few examples, notably, *The Life of Amandus*, book 2, chapter 2; or *The Life of Desiderius of Cahors*, chapters 9–11). Letters instead are signs of processes, the by-products of the conduct of relations between parties and of facilities to support such conduct. Letters are epiphenomena to social and political networks.

The use of letters can be reframed beyond historical reconstruction and literary-critical analysis to serve as indicators of wider social frameworks: the enabling communicative networks that helped government, church, and aristocracies to function in the Merovingian period, as they had in the late Roman period. Such a shift reflects a trend over the last two decades to approach textual and material evidence less from a hermeneutic approach than from one of a functional analysis (cf. Mostert 1999, 2012). One pertinent example of such attention is the increasing understanding of the operations of the late Roman state as a vast system of governmental communication among many levels of government, and between them and a wide range of social strata (Matthews 2000; Millar 2006).

Discussions of early medieval letters often entail an unexpressed and unexamined assumption that communications tended to occur sporadically and generally only in the instances attested by specific extant texts—the supposition, for example, that Frankish royal courts were in contact with the eastern empire and the bishops of Rome largely only on the isolated occasions recorded by narrative histories and surviving letters. But absence of evidence is not evidence of absence. The relatively high number of surviving epistolary texts from Gaul between the late-fifth and eighth centuries suggests, prima facie, a period characterized by lively networks and what is now termed connectivity, an image rather at odds with dour traditional depictions of the Merovingian period, and early medieval western Europe in general, as one of increasing fragmentation and isolation. Such an interpretation, of course, requires due reserve. The extant evidence provides nothing like the data needed to measure the quantities, frequency, or range of letter exchange through different areas and times of early medieval Gaul. Moreover, the existence of evidence of communicative networks for certain regions cannot be extrapolated homogeneously for the whole period. All the same, some evidence does suggest a regular hum of communication, of unexceptional exchanges that constituted the largely obscured backdrop of texts that do survive. Extant letters marking certain standard events—such as announcements and acknowledgments of episcopal and royal accessions—may indicate not episodic and exceptional contacts, but rather examples of the normal observation of such courtesies, a level of regular exchange and communication that was pervasive and conventional.

Over 500 individual letters sent within, to, or from Gaul between the late-fifth and mid-eighth centuries are preserved, in addition to a large number of references to the use of letters in historical and hagiographic narrative sources (see the Checklists below; for an earlier survey of the evidence: Leclercq 1929, col. 2856–2857, 2874–2876; cf. Wood 1990; Hen 1995, pp. 38–39). This is a substantial corpus of material for study. Its use, however, is subject to several major caveats and distinctions, regarding the nature of preservation and the functions of preserved texts. The following discussion offers a profile of the materials available for the study of letters themselves as documents and of communicative practices. It starts, however, with a silhouette of the materials that are not available and a consideration of why this matters.

What is Missing

For all premodern studies, awareness of lost materials is a constant, unwelcome incubus. But in the case of letters, for the whole Roman and postimperial world, letters belong to a particular category of loss. "Ancient letters" brings to mind the major literary collections, headed by Cicero's *Letters to Friends* (*Ad familiares*) and Pliny's ten, self-edited *Books of letters* (*Epistolarum libri*). These literary letters and their later imitators, however, represent only the most extreme apex of ancient letters at their most *précieux*, and are far from representative of actual epistolary communications. The difference between such published, edited collections and the great mass of ancient personal and business letters is not unlike the distinction between published books of letters of politicians and celebrities and the bulk of regular correspondence today: an extreme minority of documents, selected because of the exceptional position of their author, and serving something of the same encomiastic purpose (Gibson 2012). Some idea of both the qualitative and quantitative differences between the materials we have for Merovingian Gaul and the materials that once existed is gained by comparison not with the republican and early imperial Roman past, but with Egypt in the Ptolemaic, Roman, Coptic/Byzantine, and early Islamic periods. Late-antique Egypt and Merovingian Gaul are comparable regions because of their high levels of economic activity, of which literary production was a consequence (Wickham 2005). Very large amounts of original documents on papyrus and other materials, written predominantly in Greek, Latin, or Coptic but also in Syriac, Armenian, and, from the seventh century, Middle Persian and Arabic, are extant from Egypt, so much so that only a proportion has been edited. Indeed, more documents are regularly uncovered in situ by fieldwork, a situation barely imaginable to an early western European medievalist. Late Antiquity is well represented, though the overall number of extant documents tapers off after the fourth century. Of those materials, letters form only one part, fewer in number than private and governmental business documents but nonetheless a substantial corpus. Total numbers, estimated at about 1,000 thirty years ago, are now more than double that (Parsons 1980, p. 3; Palme 2011, pp. 361–363). There were of course significant differences between Gaul and Egypt in Late Antiquity: the former was postimperial, and the latter firmly part of the eastern Roman Empire until its annexation by first the Iranian and then the Islamic empires. For Gaul, there is only minimal evidence of multilingualism and multiliteracy, while for Egypt, there are abundant indications. But both also shared comparable economic and social structures that determined cultural practices: large agricultural estates generating active economies supporting elites and their cultural activities, and a socially dominant church in which extensive monastic institutions developed alongside ecclesiastic structures. Late-antique Egypt gives some idea of what Merovingian Gaul might have looked like if climatic conditions in Gaul did not prevent the preservation of papyrus.

Several striking features of Roman-Byzantine letters in Greek and Coptic throw the nature of Merovingian evidence into relief. First, the sheer quantity of extant texts, which in turn is a fraction of the imaginable scale of either lost or as-yet undiscovered materials, preclude any scholar from presuming to be familiar with all available Egyptian materials. A complex, international cooperation is required to enable scholars to be aware of both existing collections of documents and new finds (*Trismegistos*: http://www.trismegistos.org). By contrast, the single MGH *Epistolae Merowingici et Karolini aevi* volume of 1892, edited mainly by Wilhelm Gundlach, while not containing every Merovingian-era epistolary text, does include all letter collections transmitted in manuscript form. Second, Egyptian papyri texts in general were produced on behalf of a wide social range of users, from aristocrats to very humble small landowners, the latter a class invisible in Merovingian-era letters and barely discernible in other texts of the period. This wider social range also brings into view a broader field of quotidian activities, and creates a far less elite-centered picture of late-antique Egypt than is the case with contemporary late Roman and Merovingian Gaul. One consequence is that the authority that dominates documents from the late Roman period is the taxation collection system, not the church (Bagnall 1993, 2011). Third, there is a near-complete disjuncture between extant Egyptian papyri documents and texts preserved in manuscript. No original papyri versions survive of texts written by the great ecclesiastical or monastic figures of the Egyptian church, such as Athanasius, bishop of Alexandria, or Shenoute, abbot of the White Monastery. By contrast, none of the eighty-odd original letters contained in the archive of Pisenthios, the seventh-century bishop of Koptos, have been transmitted in the Coptic manuscript tradition. This disjuncture is particularly acute for letters: not only are no texts preserved in both papyri original and manuscript copy, but papyri letters and letters transmitted in manuscript collections are fundamentally different in purpose, topic, style, and length. The high literary style and theological concerns that characterize manuscript texts, though not totally absent from original papyrus materials, are not dominant features of them (Choat, 2013a, b). If all Egyptian papyrus documents from Late Antiquity (or earlier) had been destroyed, their scale and nature could not be deduced from the existing corpus of Egyptian texts in Greek and Coptic preserved in the manuscript tradition. Texts transmitted in the manuscript tradition and texts preserved in original individual papyri or papyrological archives would give very different pictures of late-antique Egypt if both were not available. For Coptic-language texts especially, the almost exclusively ecclesiastical nature of manuscript literary texts produces a world of bishops and abbots which, with some tweaks in genre, looks very much like Merovingian Gaul. Scholars in late-antique Egypt are gifted with the opportunity to work with both documentary and manuscript materials. This opportunity brings with it the salutary necessity to address disciplinary assumptions that arise from the nature of the materials themselves (Bagnall 1995, pp. 90–108). Early medievalists, lacking documentary materials apart from the few dozen papyrus and parchment Merovingian charters, need to make that much greater an imaginative effort to contextualize manuscript materials and to resist internalizing their conventions as normative. Fourth, though some groups of surviving papyri documents do concern single individuals, because they were preserved as one person's archive of personal and business transactions, most do not, and the factors of preservation are not "authorial" in the way that most manuscript-transmitted documents, particularly sole-authored manuscript letter collections, are. From a modern perspective, one consequence is that it is sometimes the case, where a cluster of texts survives, that the nature of the evidence itself foregrounds networks in which multiple individuals participated, rather than the corpus of a single author (Ruffini 2008).

In short, the near-contemporary Egyptian material enables us to imagine a Merovingian world for which there was a quantum scale of evidence for epistolary communications, a society in which the practice of communication across distance was not restricted to elites, conventions of letter writing existed other than the highly literary and predominantly ecclesiastical practices of our extant texts, and evidence for multiple participants in social networks was available. This is in contrast to an older scholarly image of late-antique Gaul as a world of sporadic, exceptional contacts, often occasioned by crises, restricted to royal, aristocratic, and ecclesiastical elites who possessed the financial and cultural resources to participate in communications, and who, as egregious figures whose writings were worthy of preservation, dominate our visions of the period.

WHAT IS EXTANT: TRANSMISSION AND FORM

The evidence we do have for letters and, through them, of communicative networks in Merovingian Gaul, all comes from the manuscript tradition in three main forms: manuscript copies of letters, either as letter collections or, more rarely, as individual texts; letters embedded verbatim (apparently) in other texts; and narrative texts that refer to the use of letters. For manuscript transmission of letters, either as collections, sole documents, or embedded texts, it is obvious but essential to stress that the fact of selection at the time of the original copying of the document, and subsequent decisions to re-copy it, fundamentally shaped both the purpose and format of the text as an artifact, and therefore its use as a source (Rio 2008, pp. 8–17). A manuscript copy does not present the same text as an original document, even if the editor or copyist has not interfered with the original wording.

At the most basic level, manuscript copies do not look like ancient letters. The texts we see in manuscripts and editions frequently omit both verbal and metatextual data: the address written on the outside of a folded sheet of papyrus, and the seal to fasten it; the eschatocol formula with date and place of dispatch; and the personal signature (*subscriptio*) conventionally included at the end of a letter, written in the sender's autograph handwriting, as distinct from the hand of the scribe who prepared the text. (Some manuscript texts exclude *subscriptiones* altogether, while others incorporate them visually into the text of the letter. Most papal letters in *The Letters of Arles*, *The Letters of Boniface and Lull*, and the separately transmitted texts in *Collected Letters of the Merovingian Era* feature both dating formulae and *subscriptiones*, even when other texts in the same collections do not. A small number of texts specifically note that the *subscriptio* is "in the author's own hand" [*manu propria*], for example, *The Letters of Desiderius of Cahors* Book 1, Chapter 2; *The Life of Desiderius of Cahors*, Chapter 10: Herchenefreda, mother of Bishop Desiderius; perhaps *Epistolae Austrasicae*, no. 42.5: the emperor Maurice.) The excision of the main text of a letter, to be presented economically on the expensive page of a parchment codex, preserves only part of the information of the original textual document (Gillett 2012a, pp. 833–835).

Even then, the text of the letter itself indicates only a residue of the original act of communication for which it had been prepared and for which it was often only a secondary element, serving to authenticate more important oral and semiotic components—"live" elements. All letters were prepared for delivery by a person, whether a simple carrier (*portitor*) to hand over the object or an envoy (*legatus*) who would deliver a substantial oral message and perhaps also read out the actual letter and conduct subsequent discussions with the recipient. Notwithstanding the technology of written documentation, communication in the ancient and medieval worlds remained a fundamentally person-to-person action between sender, bearer, and recipient; the bearer, literally a medium, often disappears from our view, but it is essential to imaginatively re-create this role to understand how contact happened (Gillett 2003; Allen 2013). Elite letters of friendship (*amicitia*) were also often accompanied by gifts ranging from the extravagant to the homely (Williams 2014). Any oral message of course conveyed information outside the texts we have preserved, but so too did semiotic, contextual messages: the social status of the letter bearer, his bearing and performance (gesture, emphasis), and the nature of any gift. So a letter reveals only part of the information of an act of communication, and a manuscript copy of a text in turn conveys only part of the information of the original document.

Beyond those factors lie the standard textual considerations of editorial intervention in the preservation of letters, especially in the assemblage of a letter collection: whether the original editor and subsequent users and copyists manipulated the texts they had in producing their own versions. Letter collections (*libri epistolarum*), as a category of evidence, while obviously vital in preserving at least partial evidence of original documents and the contacts that generated them, must be regarded as related to but separate from actual epistolary documents. The relationship between *libri epistolarum* and actual letters is at least as distant and complex as that between charters and cartularies, the former an original document, the latter a copy preserved for recordkeeping in manuscript form and liable to intentional emendation or accidental miscopying.

One final but fundamental issue concerns the distinction of letters (*epistolae*) from other types of texts, in particular legal documents. A letter of greeting from one aristocrat to another is a simple enough example of a letter, understood as a specific communication from one person to another. But other document types are sometimes called *epistola*. Wills (*testamenta*) are sometimes labeled *epistola* in the copies we have, and we also have witnesses in their signature lists, an expression of their function as a communication from the testator to the party charged with carrying out the provisions of the document. A range of other legal documents often present the form of letters: an address to a recipient, sometimes a formal introduction, and the use of the second person throughout. Some royal dispute-settlement documents (*placita*) and the majority of the documents included in the *Formulary* of Marculf are composed in this way, cast as communications of specific times between specific correspondents. These legal instruments will not be discussed here (except, in the Checklist of Narrative References, to note Gregory of Tours's references to the issue of *placita* as letters).

LIBRI EPISTOLARUM: SINGLE AUTHORS

The bulk of extant Merovingian-era letters are preserved in the format of *libri epistolarum*, continuing the Roman and Hellenistic practices of collecting, editing, and issuing a selection of letters for circulation. The fourth and fifth centuries of the Roman Empire saw the period of peak preservation, and perhaps production, of letter collections (this should not be conflated with actual use of letters: the production and preservation of *libri epistolarum* seems to have been a late Roman elite "habit," accentuated by the medieval selection of texts for preservation, but this "epistolary-collection habit" must be understood as a separate phenomenon from quotidian use of channels of communication). Although late-antique letter collections display distinct generic features, there were no defined subcategories of *libri epistolarum*; different works varied in their contents and purpose. Here, for convenience, a simple distinction will be drawn between single-author collections of letters, literary in nature (sometimes including a limited number of letters received by the central author, and other literary works by him), and multiauthor collections, generally comprising "official" correspondence gathered for reuse as sources of authority. Single-author collections of letters by senior aristocrats and bishops had become a major literary activity, represented in Gaul by the letters included in the works of Ausonius and the nine books of letters of Sidonius, modeled on Pliny's letter-collection. Such collections served as monuments of their authors' literary skills and careers, and as models for imitation. When edited for circulation by the author, books of letters also served as extensions of the same patterns of *amicitia*, whether secular or ecclesiastic, for which many of the letters were originally composed. The circulation of *libri* of letters, often issued seriatim, was itself a means of engaging with patrons and peers (marked by the "dedicatory letter" with which some edited collections were prefaced; cf. Pliny, *Letters* I 1 and Sidonius Apollinaris, *Letters* I 1). Other sole-author collections were collected and circulated as an act of familial or ecclesiastic piety after the author's death. The preservation of letters in the form of manuscript letter collections, therefore, is not a matter of chance; multiple factors were involved in promoting the memory of the author. The high survival of collections of letters by bishops may be in part a result of selective medieval transmission, but it is also a sign of the growing development of episcopal networks across the Mediterranean in the post-Constantinian period, and the use of letter collections as a source of theological and disciplinary authority.

Although there are no sole-author letter collections extant from the early decades of the Merovingian kingdom, two collections from southern Gaul in the transitional period from late-Roman to postimperial rule (under the Visigothic, Burgundian, Ostrogothic, and then Frankish regimes) attest to *amicitia* and episcopal networks adjacent to early Merovingian Gaul. These are the large collection of letters of Bishop Avitus of Vienne (MGH AA 6.2) and the smaller collection of Bishop Ruricius of Limoges, a younger contemporary and distant relative of Sidonius Apollinaris (MGH AA 8, pp. 299–350; Mathisen 1999; Shanzer and Wood 2002). Both collections have survived through precarious transmission. While sole-author collections by their nature valorize one figure and obscure the networks in which they participated, the collections of Avitus and Ruricius include a small number of received letters, which somewhat expand our view of their social context. Moreover, there is further temporal, geographical, and social overlap between Avitus's and Ruricius's collections and the body of correspondence to and from Bishop Caesarius of Arles (which is preserved in a number of sources; Klingshirn 1994a; 1994b) and the letters to Gallic correspondents in the archival letter collection of Ennodius of Pavia, which allows partial reconstruction of the social networks that formed the context for these collections (Mathisen 1981, 2003).

Gregory of Tours, who cites the published letter collections of Sidonius Apollinaris and Avitus of Vienne, also attests the circulation of the otherwise lost books of letters of his contemporary bishop Ferreolus of Uzès in the late sixth century, written "in the style of Sidonius" (*quasi Sidonium secutus*; Greg. Tur., *Hist.*, II 24, 25, 34, VI 7; *PCBE*, 4:1, p. 764). It is striking that Gregory's careful enumeration of his own writings does not include a collection of letters. Gregory also omits mention of books of letters that circulated in his time and that he knew very well, as he was both the addressee of many of the letters and the dedicatee of several of the collected *libri*: the works of his client, the Italian poet Venantius Fortunatus (MGH AA 4.1-2). Along with works of encomia and hagiography, Fortunatus's eleven *libri* of literary works include five prose letters and more than sixty letters in verse (in addition to some fifty poems in epistolary form addressed to Radegund and Agnes of the monastery of Sainte-Croix in Poitiers, though it is uncertain whether these served as actual letters; see Roberts 2009, pp. 244–319). Fortunatus's letters are unusual, though not unique, not only for being in verse but also for being products of a nonecclesiastic. Most or all the verse letters were written before he became bishop of Poitiers at a date after 591. Moreover, about a third of his verse letters are written to secular figures (with another third to his patron, Gregory of Tours). Again, a slightly wider view of the late-sixth century aristocratic network within which Fortunatus operated can be achieved by complementing his letters with the much smaller clutch of letters of aristocratic *amicitia* from one of Fortunatus's correspondents, the senior Austrasian official Gogo, preserved in the collection *Epistolae Austrasicae* (*Ep. Austr.* 13, 16, 22, cf. 48; Dumézil 2007, 2009; Williard 2014).

On a different scale, the smaller collection of Columbanus, written from both Luxeuil and Italy in the first decades of the seventh century, also contains both prose and verse letters, arranged separately in that order (MGH *Ep.* 3, pp. 154–190). The slim collection of two *libri* of letters of Bishop Desiderius of Cahors, from the 630s to 650s, preserved by a single manuscript, again presents a strict, though different, binary arrangement: one *liber* of fifteen letters sent by Desiderius (including letters to kings Dagobert I and Sigibert III), and a second *liber* of twenty-one letters received by the bishop (five correspondents are common to both books). Presumably, this arrangement reflects an original archival system for file copies and received documents (MGH *Ep.* 3, pp. 191–214). Desiderius's *libri* are therefore one instance where a network of correspondents can be glimpsed, albeit on a very limited scale and still centered on a single individual. Strikingly, the late eighth-century *Vita* of Desiderius includes three letters he received from his mother, Herchenefreda, as examples of her frequent correspondence (*crebae … epistolae*) with him, although none of Herchenefreda's letters are included in the *libri epistolarum* (MGH SRM 4, pp. 569–570). These rare texts by a woman, addressed to her son, precede by a century the *Liber manualis*, Dhuoda's handbook of advice to William. Two of Herchenefreda's letters are hortatory, while one is deeply personal, grieving the loss of her other sons.

Finally, the lengthy collection of one hundred and fifty letters often referred to as the letters of bishops Boniface and Lull of Mainz in fact does not closely resemble even the varied conventions of sole-authored letter collections (MGH *Ep.* 3, pp. 215–433). Less than half (seventy) of the letters are from or to either Boniface or Lull; there are almost as many letters sent to Boniface as sent by him (thirty-seven to thirty-three) and over twice as many letters received by Lull as sent by him (twenty-four to eleven); and the collection includes letters by some eighteen authors altogether, from Britain and Italy as well as Gaul, including three popes, two Arnulfing mayors of the palace, and several abbots, abbesses, and bishops. Most but not all these documents directly concern the bishops of Mainz. As a group, popes Gregory II, Gregory III, Zacharias, and Stephen III are the largest presence in the collection after Boniface and Lull, sending or receiving some thirty-three letters, either as correspondences with the bishops of Mainz or as confirmations of their position. The letter collection, which also includes a number of nonepistolary documents and some anonymous texts, is an institutional collection of the bishopric of Mainz, naturally foregrounding its first two bishops.

LIBRI EPISTOLARUM: MULTIPLE AUTHORS

Multiauthored collections are a different and important form of text. Most extant multiauthored collections represent sources of authority. From at least the fifth century, both the unofficial gathering of papal letters as collections of *decreta*, and the private and later official editing of imperial laws (*constitutiones*), which were originally epistolary in form and function, as sources of law, represent the reuse of letters as sources of authority (Matthews 2000; Jasper 2001; Millar 2006; Gillett 2012a). Examples of letter collections as sources of authority from postimperial Gaul all consist of letters from the bishops of

Rome: a number of manuscript collections of fifth- to early sixth-century papal letters concerning the status of the bishopric of Arles, collectively known as the *Epistolae Arelatenses* in the modern edition (MGH *Ep.* 3, pp. 1–83); the papal letters establishing the archbishoprics of Boniface and Lull and the foundation of the monastery of Fulda in the collection discussed earlier; and the ninety-nine letters of popes to Carolingian major domos and kings in the *Codex Carolinus*, gathered at the order of Charlemagne (MGH *Ep.* 3, pp. 469–657). (The preface to the *Codex Carolinus* states that both letters from popes and from the east Roman Empire [*de imperio*] were collected, but no imperial letters are extant; it is possible that a discrete subsection of the collection was lost at an early date.) Papal-Gallic correspondences are of course the cornerstones of modern histories of the period: for example, the letters of Gregory I to Frankish rulers concerning ecclesiastical discipline and the Augustinian mission to Britain, and especially the Carolingian orientation toward the Roman papacy. But it comes as something of a surprise to the reader of Gregory of Tours to discover that at least one of the sons of Clovis, Childebert I (r. 511–558), known primarily for his fratricidal conflicts and other military adventures, corresponded regularly with popes Vigilius and Pelagius I concerning the bishopric of Arles, possibly continuing connections with Rome begun by Clovis (*Ep. Arel.* 48–49, 51–52, 54, cf. 40–41, 43–45; *Ep. Aevi Merow. Coll.* 5 in MGH *Ep.* 3, p. 444; for Clovis: *Book of the Pontiffs* 54). Vigilius was so confident of Childebert's good will that, as an unwilling guest of Emperor Justinian I in Constantinople, he wrote to Bishop Aurelianus of Arles asking him, inter alia, to petition Childebert to write in turn to the Gothic king Totila, who had recently occupied the city of Rome, requesting that Totila, as an Arian, refrain from involving himself in the already tortuous politics of the Three Chapters controversy (*Ep. Arel.* 45 = *Acta* of the Second Council of Constantinople, 553, Session VII 10.5, Price 2009, p. 95).

A different, and quite unusual, multiauthored letter collection is the small book of forty-eight letters from the late-fifth to late-sixth centuries, named the *Epistolae Austrasicae* by its MGH editor Wilhelm Gundlach, who considered that all letters in the collection had been sent to or from correspondents in Austrasia (MGH *Ep.* 3, pp. 110–153; the most recent editor of the collection prefers the title *Liber epistolarum*, which appears in a later hand on the front folio of the sole manuscript: Malaspina 2001, p. 5). The collection's two modern editors proposed that a lost original, assembled in or soon after the date of the latest documents at the end of the sixth century, lay behind the unique ninth-century manuscript. A recent study, however, has proposed a Carolingian date for the act of editing, which, if correct, would make the sole manuscript the actual original collection (Barrett and Woudhuysen 2016; cf. Gillett 2019). The collection includes letters by multiple senders and recipients, including fourteen Gallic bishops, two bishops in the eastern empire and one in Milan, an abbot, four Frankish kings, one Frankish queen and one Frankish-Lombard queen, a Frankish-Gothic prince, six senior Gallic court officials or aristocrats, two eastern emperors, two empresses, an exarch in Italy, four senior palatine officials at Constantinople, two imperial eastern nobles in Sicily, one Lombard duke, and a papal representative in Constantinople (*apocrisiarius*). This is an astonishingly broad range of members of various elites across the Mediterranean within such a short compass. Several preexisting sets of letters, drawn from either existing letter collections or archival file copies, seem to have been used, although the letters are not always clustered by either author or recipient. The collection is divided into two equal but distinct halves: twenty-four letters from a variety of bishops, aristocrats, and kings, followed by a second group of twenty-four letters between the courts of Childebert II, the emperor Maurice, and his exarch in Italy (Goubert, 1956, pp. 95–202). It is the only collection of Merovingian-era letters that is provided with a table of contents, and the letters appear to be arranged in broadly chronological order (all but one lack dating formulae), starting with Bishop Remigius of Reims's two letters to Clovis and ending with a series of letters from Childebert II, a time span very similar to the postbiblical narrative of Gregory of Tours's *Histories* (part of one of Remigius's letters appears also in Greg. Tur., *Hist.* II 31). No other letter collection of the period shares all these indications of editorial care and purpose.

The form of each Merovingian letter collection is to an extent *sui generis*; there is no indication that any standard form was considered normative. The functions of the collections must be regarded as equally diverse. Analyses of the texts and deployment of their evidence must proceed from a combination of the broad background of Roman-era single- and multiauthor letter collections and interpretation of the unique characteristics of the form of each collection. Several collections exist in single manuscripts (*Epistolae Austrasicae*, the letters of Bishop Desiderius, the *Codex Carolini*). While, of course, that is not unusual for any pre-Carolingian text, in some cases unique survival may indicate that the collections were never intended for circulation as part of *amicitia* networks or for dissemination of authoritative works, but were produced as reference resources for individuals or institutions.

Libri Epistolarum from Outside Gaul

Two further collections, both from Italy, warrant mention for their evidence of communicative actions and practices outside Gaul. Cassiodorus's *Variae* of the late fifth-early sixth century famously includes two letters to Clovis, both in the context of the complex diplomacy of the Gothic king of Italy, Theoderic (Cass., *Variae*, II 41 with 40, III 4 with 1–3). From a Gallic perspective, the letters indicate the wider Mediterranean framework within which the new Merovingian dynasty operated from its first generation. From the late sixth century, the *Registrum epistolarum* of Pope Gregory I is particularly important as evidence of long-distance patterns and practices of contact. Gregory writes to the court of Austrasia-Burgundia (in the person of the dowager queen, Brunhild, her son, Childebert II, and her infant grandsons kings, Theuderic and Theudebert), and to the court of Neustria (under the child king Lothar II), as well as to a significant number of Gallic bishops, abbots, abbesses, and senior officials. His knowledge of current and changing ecclesiastic personnel indicates a flow of information being received from Gaul, not all of which will have been through the papal *rector* of lands in Gaul

(Markus, 1997, pp. 168–187). The far-flung communicative network evidenced in Gregory's *Registrum* overlaps with the letters between the Austrasian royal court and the emperor and exarch included in the *Epistolae Austrasicae*, and Gregory's letters provide context for the directions and modes of communication employed by Childebert (Gillett 2012b). (Like Gregory's *Registrum*, too, the Austrasian court's knowledge of current palatine personnel in Constantinople indicates a regular receipt of information beyond what is visible in Gregory of Tours's *Histories*, which are sometimes wrongly taken as including a full outline of contacts between Austrasia and Constantinople). Though not a complete copy of his archive, Gregory's *Registrum* provides a fuller picture of a pope's relations with the church and government of Gaul than the more selective range of texts preserved in that region. In addition to mapping Gregory's relations with the potentates of Gaul, the *Registrum* also sometimes incidentally reveals the vertiginous depth of our lack of knowledge of the range of contacts across the Mediterranean in the late sixth century. Replying in 597 to a letter from Queen Brunhild, requesting that Bishop Syagrius of Autun be granted the pallium, Gregory states that he agrees to the request, against his better judgment, because the emperor Maurice had told Gregory's *apocrisiarius*, the papal representative in Constantinople, to advise the pope that the emperor supported Brunhild's wish (Greg. I, *Regist.* VIII 4). This is unique evidence that the court of Austrasia used its relations with Constantinople to leverage its relationship with the bishop of Rome. (Gregory likewise uniquely attests that treaties made a generation earlier between Justinian I and Gothic kings in Spain were documented in dual copies as treaties [*pacta*], to be preserved by both parties in their archives [*cartofilacium*]; Greg. I, *Regist.* IX 229.)

INDIVIDUAL LETTERS

Outside the specific collections of *libri epistolarum*, a number of copies of original letters are preserved, either as single letters included with other documents in manuscripts or embedded in other forms of text. Nineteen individual letters, preserved singly or in pairs in diverse manuscripts, were gathered by Gundlach under the title *Epistolae aevo Merowingici collectae* ("Collected Letters of the Merovingian Era") in his MGH *Epistolae* volume; seven of the letters are from popes (MGH *Ep.* 3, pp. 434–468).

A number of historical and hagiographic sources incorporate apparently full texts of letters as part of their narrative. Gregory of Tours includes three letters concerning the revolt of the nuns of Poitiers in 590, including Radegund's letter of foundation (Greg. Tur., *Hist.* IX 39, 41, 42; Cherewatuk 1993; Jeffrey 2002). The *Vita* of bishop Desiderius of Cahors, as mentioned earlier, includes three letters his mother, Herchenefreda, wrote to him, as well as two letters of Dagobert supporting Desiderius's episcopal elevation (MGH SRM 4, pp. 569–573). A third text type that sometimes includes copies of letters is the church council *acta*: letters associated with a council are sometimes incorporated into the *acta* as part of the documentation of the council (Halfond, 2009; see Halfond,

Chapter 13, this volume). The nature of the association varies. Some letters were documents preceding the council (i.e., letters of invitation from the host bishop to bishops to attend the council). Others were produced or received there (e.g., synodical letters to the king under whose authority the bishops assembled, and communiqués of council decisions to nonattendant bishops and their replies) or were issued subsequently and attached to the *acta* (e.g., papal confirmation of *acta*) (see 'Checklist of Extant Letters, Late Fifth to Mid-Eighth Centuries').

Narrative Accounts of Letter Exchange

Both single-author *libri epistolarum* and individually preserved texts inevitably focus attention on the authors and the particular situations that generated the documents. Even the multiauthor collections represent a series of specific situations rather than preserve records of ongoing exchanges. There are, for example, no equivalents from Merovingian Gaul of even the two-way exchange between Ausonius and Paulinus of Nola concerning Paulinus's adoption of the religious life, and there are few examples of repeated communication between the same correspondents, let alone records of exchanges among multiple correspondents that would outline the operation of communications among bishops within a province or throughout a clique of nobles. Moreover, the bulk of the mostly ecclesiastical and royal correspondence is formal, literary, and driven by specific issues—directly equivalent to the Greek and Coptic epistolary material preserved in manuscript from Egypt and distinct from more quotidian, often formulaic, and sometimes iterative documents preserved in original papyri. Even where, as mentioned earlier, some overlap exists for early and late sixth-century social networks and for late sixth-century ecclesiastical and political networks, the extant collections preserve only a small selection out of a much larger cross-work of communications. But such parallels do at least indicate the situation of specific documents and issues in broader, if largely lost, contexts.

A different perspective is given by casual references to the dispatch and reception of letters in narrative sources, particularly by Gregory of Tours's *Histories*. In the early Books of the *Histories*, Gregory uses circulated letter collections as sources of information and as part of his praise of past bishops (Greg. Tur., *Hist.* II 24, 25, 31, 34). He also includes two anecdotes of letters being used in secret or fraudulently, in the sorts of wily tales that appealed to him (Greg. Tur., *Hist.* III 23, IV 44). From Book Five onward—the period covered by Gregory's own episcopate—Gregory's narrative regularly mentions the sending of letters as part of the conduct of public and ecclesiastical affairs (he also continues to note the circulation of literary collection of letters, and deceptions using false messages: Greg. Tur., *Hist.* VI 7; VII 34, X 31.5, cf. *Glory of the Martyrs* 46). These practices are for the most part unobtrusive in his narrative; neither the detailed index of Krusch and Levison's MGH edition nor Margerete Weidemann's analytical handbook to Gregory's work provides full references for the terms *epistolae* and *litterae* in Gregory's text, noting only royal *placita* and the several letters that Gregory reproduces in full (MGH SRM 1.1, pp. 599, 612; Weidemann, 1982, I, pp. 6–8). Like most ancient authors, Gregory uses a variety of terms to refer to documents dispatched with messengers, both prosaic (letters, writings, pages; *litterae, epistolae, scripta, pagina*) and functional (orders, submissions; *praeceptum, suggestio*; *Hist.* III, 34, VI 32, VII 31, IX 40, 42). Mention of letters and of messages in general should be understood as very selective: Gregory's references to letters are mostly minor, neutral details, or occasionally elements in wry episodes of chicanery (very occasionally, Gregory casts letters in a spiritual context: *Hist.*, V 14; *Lives of the Fathers* VIII 9). Gregory has no interest in detailing the functional processes of either government, church, or society, but nevertheless includes a considerable number of incidental details that demonstrate the ubiquity of casual use of letter exchange to support government and church functions and the organization of the aristocracy, and something of the infrastructure supporting these contacts.

Gregory describes kings who regularly issue letters of instruction to their senior military and civilian officials, the *comites* and *duces* (including battlefield instructions; *Hist.* III 23, IX 9, X 5), and also, regularly, to bishops (e.g., *Hist.* VI 32, VIII 2, IX 33). (Senior royal officials also issue letters of authority in their own name: *Hist.* IX 19). Kings issue authenticating *epistolae cum auctoritate* to whole regions, either to proclaim their authority after one of the not-infrequent redistributions of royal authority over the multiple Merovingian kingdoms, to announce the new appointment of *duces* and *comites*, or to institute other policies (*Hist.* V 44, IX 30; *Lives of the Fathers* XVII 3). What we do not see in these accounts is how these letters of command to whole regions were intended to be disseminated: whether by public posting, as late Roman imperial edicts were, or by delivery to *comites*, bishops, or other *seniores* representing cities; or even by public reading. The recipient is unspecified, and therefore the process of public dissemination remains unclear. Another form of correspondence issued to more than one individual is shown by royal letters, not to individual bishops but to bishops throughout whole regions or kingdoms (*Hist.* VI 36, X 19 twice). The relatively short time frame attested for dispatch and reply in these episodes indicates the use of multiple messengers to deliver the instructions simultaneously, a conventional system for prompt communication with the episcopate at a group level. Moreover, kings communicate with each other, not only to negotiate the major dramatic political issues of succession, alliance, and division of authority, but also to coordinate relations with outside powers and policies in regard to the church (e.g., *Hist.* VIII 13). External to Gaul, kings communicate with popes and with the eastern imperial court (*Hist.* V 20), illustrated by letters in the collections discussed earlier—though none of the letters or embassies described by Gregory can be identified with any of the extant letters, including Childebert II's embassies to the emperor Maurice and the same king's letters to the emperor in the *Epistolae Austrasicae*.

Bishops, who are addressed *en bloc* by kings, likewise regularly communicate among themselves, both as groups and as individuals. Gregory mentions church councils preparing documents to be sent to absent bishops, a situation illustrated also by the synodical letters preserved with conciliar *acta* (*Hist.* V 49). But he also refers to bishops preparing joint letters when they are not together in council and to individual bishops, and other senior church figures, writing to a range of their peers for advice (*Hist.* VIII 31, IX 20, 41, 42). These scenarios indicate the ability of bishops to communicate among themselves at a distance while in their own sees, with sufficient ease and regularity as to be able to develop common policies both on regular matters and issues of crisis, such as the Poitiers nunnery revolt (*Hist.* VI 15, 32, VIII 31, IX 39). Bishops wrote to each other individually. In one bitter exchange, Gregory scored a point by commenting on the frequency of his interlocutor's messages (*Hist.* V 5). We also see Gregory himself writing to kings and queens on a range of issues (*Hist.* VI 10; 32). Besides the episcopacy, the other group depicted by Gregory as acting in concert to produce letters to present a single interest is the loosely defined nobility of Austrasia (*maiores* and *seniores*) (*Hist.*, VI 24, VII 36, IX 40).

A significant number of anecdotes in Gregory's narrative concern anxieties about communications, a concern that modern governments share. Secret communications among the kingdom's elite are a recurring issue (*Hist.* VI 22, 24, VII 30, 36, VIII 2, IX 28, X 19), even when kings themselves make use of secret letters (*occultae litterae*) to conduct business (*Hist.*, III 23, IX 9). The difficulty of establishing the genuineness of letters also recurs. In several sly stories, Gregory uses the ambiguity of letters' claim to represent individuals to display the guile or shrewdness of his protagonists; the balance of verisimilitude and storytelling in these particular episodes may be debateable (*Hist.* IV 44, VII 34). Elsewhere, however, Gregory treats his reader to forensic accounts of court trials in which examiners test whether letters are genuine or forged (*Hist.*, VI 22, 24, X 19). These anxieties, as much as Gregory's neutral mentioning of other letter exchanges, indicate the ready existence of the free movement of messengers throughout the landscape.

The trial scenes mentioned earlier give some description of the mechanics of the preparation of letters: the role of chancellery officials in providing authenticating signatures; the use of trained scribes; and the maintenance of archival copies in shorthand of sent letters and preservation of received letters (*Hist.* X 19). Gregory gives some glimpse of the resources available to the kings: an unspecified form of transport referred to with the term for official public transportation under the Roman Empire (*evectio publica*) (*Hist.*, IX 9), the speed expected of royal messages and replies to them (*Hist.* IX 30, X 5). But one would wish to know much more about the resources that supported this speed and the systems that facilitated multidirectional communications such as those between kings and multiple bishops or among bishops throughout a province.

Gregory's frequent, yet very incomplete, references to the use of letters in his own times create a picture that suggests not only that letter usage was common among the sixth-century Gallic elite, but more specifically that communication networks were essential infrastructure. They facilitated the operation of the royal government, the functioning of the episcopacy, and very likely the affairs of the secular aristocracy as well.

LEARNING COMMUNICATION

The ability to produce written texts and supply representatives able to accompany them successfully was a significant need for royal and ecclesiastical courts and aristocratic houses. Saints' *Lives* regularly refer to the training in literacy received by young members of the nobility and church (Heinzelmann 1990; see also Kreiner, Chapter 24, this volume). Some detail of more specific interest in learning how to use the potential of letter exchange and spoken representation is given by the *Formulary* of Marculf and the *Epistolae Austrasicae*. Marculf's *Formulary*, which was intended as a form of training manual (Marculf, *Praef.*; Rio 2009, pp. 20–26; see also Rio, Chapter 23, this volume), includes a large number of legal documents composed in an epistolary format (i.e., an address from sender to recipient or recipients, use of the second person), though they are not letters in the modern sense. It also includes a number of model letters of types familiar from letter collections: royal diplomatic letters, seasonal greetings between bishops and royalty, and letters of recommendation addressed to bishops, abbots, and aristocrats. These models (a small portion of the total formulary) indicate the role of letter writing in scribal training, not only for composition but perhaps also for outlining the occasions for which letters performed standard functions.

A second, less obvious text that may have served as a model for composition of both standard types of letters and the wider potential of epistolary communication, is the *Epistolae Austrasicae*. Though carefully assembled, the intended function of this collection is not clear; its broadly chronological arrangement from Clovis to Childebert II may indicate a historical interest. But in its striking variety, it may also represent a set of models of diverse letter types. The collection includes letters for a variety of epistolary situations: ecclesiastical and aristocratic *amicitia*, acknowledgments of royal accessions, letters of ecclesiastical discipline to multiple recipients, and letters of spiritual consolation for bereavement (*consolatio*). It also displays letters of different style, from the relatively simplistic Latin of Bishop Nicetius of Trier to the excessively florid language of the letters of Childebert II and Brunhild. It also includes examples of particular techniques, including *prosopopoeia*—the rhetorical device or writing in the character of another person, employed by courtiers who drafted letters in the name of monarchs (Gillett 2010). Beyond individual documents, however, the collection also appears to reveal an interest in the function of a large-scale embassy as a whole. Two sets of letters of Childebert II and Brunhild to the emperor Maurice and several members of his court—one set of fifteen letters and one of five—present highly repetitive content (*Ep. Austr.* 25–39, 43–46). It seems likely that the letters have been preserved not for their redundant content but for their "metadata" that is, as an example of how an embassy could engage figures close to the emperor as local advocates to support the aims of the Frankish rulers, a technique used also by the papacy (Gillett 2012b).

It is not new to note that the Merovingian state and church were in many respects a bureaucratic world in which documents were valorized and produced extensively

(Classen 1977; Ganz and Goffart 1990; Wood 1990; Murray 2005; Hen 2007; Brown et al. 2013; Barrett and Woudhuysen 2016). Among the other forms of written documentation that supported Merovingian society—such as charters, laws, and poetry—epistolary contact should also be considered as infrastructure for the functioning of government, church, and aristocracy. Every church council and every political negotiation was the product of extensive and sophisticated communications. The factors of preservation and loss of documents conceal from us how widespread and at what levels of society the regular use of letters was, and how the nature of the surviving evidence in manuscript collections causes a misleading focus on individual authors and situations rather than the regularity of the communicative practices that they demonstrate. But narrative accounts in the historical and hagiographic texts allow that activity to be recovered to an extent. The letters we have are valuable texts in themselves, but they are also pointers to an interconnected series of social and political networks that enabled the complex functioning of Merovingian society.

A Checklist of Extant Letters, Late Fifth to Mid-Eighth Century

Following is a list of letters sent within, to, or from Merovingian Gaul, preserved fully or in part in the manuscript tradition. It is intentionally inclusive; for example, it counts all the letters in the collections of Columbanus and of Boniface and Lull, including those written in Italy in the former and in Britain in the latter. It does not, however, include pre-Merovingian era documents preserved in early medieval Gaul, or some document types that are sometimes referred to as *epistolae* but did not actually have an epistolary function—for example, wills (*testamenta*). Epistolary documents in Marculf's *Formulary* are noted but not included in the following count. For an earlier survey of texts, see Leclercq 1929, col. 2856–2857, 2874–2882.

The total number of letters included here is 563.

Letter Collections from Merovingian Gaul

Venantius Fortunatus, MGH AA 4.1–2 (5 prose letters plus 65 verse letters; Roberts 2009, p. 245)

Columbanus, MGH *Ep.* 3 (7 letters, excluding 4 poems)

Desiderius of Cahors, MGH *Ep.* 3 (36 letters)

Boniface and Lull, MGH *Ep.* 3 (150 letters)

Epistolae Arelatenses, MGH *Ep.* 3 (56 letters)

Epistolae Austrasicae, MGH *Ep.* 3 (48 letters)

Codex Carolinus, MGH *Ep.* 3 (99 papal letters)

Individually Transmitted Letters

Epistolae aevi Merowingici collectae, MGH *Ep.* 3 (19 letters)

Letters in Merovingian Church Councils,
Sources Chrétiennes 353, 354 (8 letters)

Conc. Orléans 511: synodical letter to Clovis

Conc. Épaone 517: Bishop Avitus's letter of invitation, and Bishop Viventiolus of Lyon to the bishops of the council

Conc. Carpentras 527: synodical letter to Bishop Agricius of Antibes

Conc. Orange 529: Pope Boniface II to Bishop Caesarius of Clermont confirming the council's *acta*

Conc. Clermont 535: synodical letter to Theudebert I (requesting protection of bishops' private lands in the event of partitions of the kingdom)

Conc. Tours 567: cf. a separately transmitted letter of Bishop Euphrasius of Tours and his suffragans to their *plebs*

Conc. Chalon 647/653: synodical letter to Bishop Theudorius of Arles

Letter Collections from Italy

Cassiodorus, *Variae*, MGH AA 12
  Variae, II 41, III 4 (2 letters)

Gregory I, *Registrum epistolarum*, CSEL 140, 140a
  (65 letters; cf. Markus, 1997, p. 209)
  I 45, III 33, V 31, 58–60, VI 5–6, 50–60, VII 12, 21, 33, VIII 4, IX 158, 209, 212–227, XI 9–10, 34, 38, 40–51, 56, XIII 5–7, 9–11, XIV 12
  (Cf. Gregory's letters to the mission of Augustine to Britain, sent via Gaul: XI 35, 36, 37, 39, possibly Bede, *HE* I 27 = MGH 2, *Ep.* XI 56a)

Letters Embedded in Other Texts

Gregory of Tours, *Histories*, MGH SRM 1.2, IX 39, 41, 42 (3 letters)

Vita Desiderii Cadurcae, 9–14, MGH SRM 4, pp. 569–573: Herchenefreda, Dagobert (5 letters)

Vita Eligii Noviomagensis II, MGH SRM 4, pp. 741: dedicatory letters (2 letters)

Vita Amandi II auctore Milone, 2, MGH SRM 5, pp. 452–456: Pope Martin I to Amandus = *Acts of the Lateran Synod, 649*: Martin I, *Encyclical Letter* 2 (1 letter)

Acts of the Second Council of Constantinople, 553, Session VII 10.5: Vigilius to Aurelianus of Arles = *Epistolae Arelatenses*, 45

Formulae

Formulary of Marculf, MGH Leges 5

Model letters
  Royal diplomatic letters: I 9–10
  Seasonal greetings between bishops and royalty: II 42–45
  Letters of recommendation: II 46–47, 49–51

A CHECKLIST OF NARRATIVE REFERENCES TO LETTER EXCHANGES, LATE FIFTH TO MID-EIGHTH CENTURY

This list only includes narrative scenes with specific references to letters; many other scenes that mention oral messages will, of course, have assumed the presence of authenticating letters.

References to Letters by Gregory of Tours

Histories, MGH SRM 1.1
  Terms used: *litterae, epistolae, scripta, praeceptum, suggestio, pagina*
  Full texts of letters: IX 39, 41, 42
  Citations of letters: II 3, 31
  Citations of letter collections: II 24, 25, 34, VI 7, X 31.3
  Narrative descriptions: Royalty:
    Correspondence between royalty: III 23, VIII 13, IX 9
    Royal commands: III 23, VI 32 *bis*, IX 9, 30, 33, X 5
    Royal proclamations: V 44, VI 36
    Royal commands to bishops: X 19
    Imperial letters to kings: II 38
    Correspondence with pope: V 20
  Narrative descriptions: Officials:
    Officials' letters: IX 19
  Narrative descriptions: Bishops:
    Synodical letters: V 49, IX 20, 39, 41
    Bishop to synod: IX 41, 42
    Bishops' letters: individual: V 5
    Bishop to multiple bishops: VIII 31
    Bishop to royal: VI 10, VI 32, VIII 2

Bishop's letter of recommendation: VI 15, 32
Narrative descriptions: Nobles:
    Nobles' joint letter: VI 24, VII 36
    Nobles to king: IX 40
Narrative descriptions: Other:
    Letter to saint: V 14
Fraud letters: IV 44, VII 34
Secret letters: III 23, VI 22, VII 30, IX 9, IX 28
Letters used as evidence in trials: VI 22, 24, X 19
Evidence for production and dispatch of letters: X 19

Miraculae, MGH SRM 1.1
    Citation of letter: *In glor. martyr.* 46
    Royal proclamation: *Vita patrum*, XVII 3
    Letter as relic: *Vita patrum*, VIII 9

References to Letters in Saints' *Vitae*

The following represents a survey only of scenes involving letters, referred to as *epistolae* or, less often, *litterae*. Some of the texts were of course produced or reworked in the Carolingian period. The scenes include regular letter exchanges, royal commands, and use of letters as relics, but the scenes exclude *testamenta*.

MGH SRM 2:
    Vita Arnulfi, 16
    Vita Balthildis, 9
    Baudonivia, *Vita Radegundis*, II 7, 10, 16
MGH SRM 3:
    Vita Iohannis abbatis Reomanensis, 10
    Vita Caesarii ep. Arelatensis, I 3, II 47
    Vita Gaugerici ep. Camaracensis, 7
    Vita patrum Iurensium Romani, Lupicini, Eugendi, 10, 12
    Vita Eptadii presbyteri Cervidunensis, 12, 18
    Vita Eparchii conf., 13
MGH SRM 4:
    Ionas, *Vita Columbani abbat.*, 19, 30
    Vita Amati abbat. Habendensis, 12
    Vitae Galli conf.:
        Vita Galli vetustissima, 1, 3
        Wettinus, *Vita Galli conf.*, 15, 20, 21, 24, 26, 28
        Walafrid Strabo, *Vita Galli conf.* I 3, 15, 19, 20, 21, 24, 26, 28, II 10

Vita Austrigisili ep. Biturigi, 5, 11
Audoin (Dado) of Rouen, *Vita Eligii Noviomagensis*, I 33, II 21
Vita Desiderii Cadurcae, 8–15 (including the full texts listed above), 19
MGH SRM 5:
  Vita Amandi ep. Triecti, I 13, II 1–2
  Vita Lantberti abbat. Fontanellensis et ep. Lugdunensis, 3, 4
  Ursinus, *Vita Leudegarii ep. Augustodunensis*, II 24
  Passio Praeiecti ep. Et Martyris Arverni, 13
MGH SRM 6:
  Nicolaus, *Vita Landibert ep. Traiectensis*, Prologus (p. 408)
  Vita Aldegundis abbatiss. Malbodiensis, 17
  Vita Odiliae abbatiss. Hohenburgensis, 7
  Arbeo, *Vita Corbiniani ep. Baiuvariorum*, 38; *Vita Corbiniani retracta B*, 7 (p. 605), 30
  Vita Boniti ep. Arverni, 17
  Stephanus, *Vita Wilifridi ep. Eboracensis*, 27, 29, 43, 58
MGH SRM 7:
  Venantius Fortunatus, *Vita Germani ep. Parisiaci*, 57
  Vita Rigoberti ep. Remensis, 14

Other Narrative References to Letter Exchanges

Fredegar, *Chronica*, MGH SRM 2, IV 89 (letters to nobles)
Procopius, *History of the Wars*, V 5.8–10 (Justinian to Frankish kings)
Acts of the Second Council of Constantinople, 553, Session VII 10.5: Vigilius to Aurelianus
  of Arles = *Epistolae Arelatenses*, 45 (request to ask Childebert to write to Totila)
Acts of the Lateran Synod, 649: Martin I, *Encyclical Letter* 2 to Amandus of Maastricht
  (Martin writes to Sigisbert III, cf. *Vita Eligii*, 33)

WORKS CITED

Ancient Sources

Avitus of Vienne. R. Peiper (ed.). (1883). *Alcimi Ecdicii Aviti Viennensis episcopi opera quae supersunt*. MGH AA 6.2. Berlin: Weidmann.

Boniface and Lull. W. Gundlach (ed). (1892). *Bonifatii et Lulli epistolae*. MGH Epistolae 3 (pp. 215–433). Berlin: Weidmann.

Caesarius of Arles. G. Morin (ed.) (1937–1942). *Caesarii episcopi Arelatensis opera omnia*. 2 vols. CCSL 103, 104. Turnhout: Brepols.

Cassiodorus. A. Fridh (ed.). (1894). *Variarum libri XII*. CCSL 96. Turnhout: Brepols.

Codex Carolinus. Gundlach, W. (ed.). (1892). MGH Epistolae 3 (pp. 469–657). Berlin: Weidmann.

Columbanus, *Epistolae*. W. Gundlach (ed.). (1892). MGH Epistolae 3 (pp. 154–190). Berlin: Weidmann.

Davis, R. (trans.) (1989). *The Book of the Pontiffs*. Liverpool: Liverpool University Press.

de Clercq, C. (ed.) (1963). *Concilia Galliae: A.511–A.695*. CCSL 148A. Turnhout: Brepols.

Desiderius of Cahors. W. Gundlach (ed.). (1892). *Desiderii episcopi Cadurcensis-epistolae*. MGH Epistolae 3 (pp. 191–214). Berlin: Weidmann.

Dewing, H. (trans.) (1914–1940). *Procopius: Wars*. Cambridge, MA: Harvard University Press.

Duchesne, L. (ed.). (1886–1892). *Le Liber pontificalis*. Paris: Thorin.

Fredegar, *Chronica*. B. Krusch (ed.). (1888). MGH SRM 2 (pp. 1–194). Hanover: Hahn.

Gregory I, *Reg*. D. Norberg (ed) (1982). *Registrum epistolarum*. CCSL 140, 140a. Turnhout: Brepols.

Gregory of Tours, *GM*. B. Krusch (ed.). (1885). *Liber in gloria martyrum*. MGH SRM 2 (pp. 34–111). Hanover: Hahn.

Gregory of Tours, *Hist*. B. Krusch and W. Levison (eds.). (1937–1951). *Decem Libri Historiarum*. MGH SRM 1.1. Hanover: Hahn.

Gregory of Tours, *LVP*. B. Krusch (ed.). (1885). *Liber vitae patrum*. MGH SRM 2 (pp. 211–294). Hanover: Hahn.

Gundlach, W. (1892). *Epistolae aevi Merowingici collectae*. MGH Epistolae 3 (pp. 434–468). Berlin: Weidmann.

Gundlach, W. (1892). *Epistolae Arelatensis*. MGH Epistolae 3 (pp. 1–83). Berlin: Weidmann.

Gundlach, W. (1892). *Epistolae Austrasicae*. MGH Epistolae 3 (pp. 110–153). Berlin: Weidmann.

Klingshirn, W. (trans.). (1994b). *Caesarius of Arles: Life, Testament, Letters*. Liverpool: Liverpool University Press.

Krusch, B. (ed.). (1902). *Vita Desiderii Cadurcae*. MGH SRM 4 (pp. 547–602). Hanover: Hahn.

Krusch, B., and Levison, W. (eds.). (1887–1920). *Passiones vitaeque sanctorum aevi Merovingici*. MGH SRM 2–7. Hanover: Hahn.

Marculf, *Formulae Merowingici et Carolini aevi*. K. Zeumer (ed.). (1886). MGH Legum 5. (pp. 32–112). Hanover: Hahn.

Mathisen, R. (trans.). (1999). *Ruricius of Limoges and Friends: A Collection of Letters from Visigothic Gaul*. Liverpool: Liverpool University Press.

Milo, *Vita Amandi II*. B. Krusch (ed.). (1910). MGH SRM 5 (pp. 450–483). Hanover: Hahn.

Price, R. (trans.). (2009). *The Acts of the Council of Constantinople of 553, with Related Texts on the Three Chapters Controversy*. Liverpool: Liverpool University Press.

Price, R., Booth, P., and Cubitt, C. (trans.). (2014). *The Acts of the Lateran Synod of 649*. Liverpool: Liverpool University Press.

Procopius. G. Wirth (ed) (1962–1964). *Opera omnia*. Leipzig: Teubner.

Rio, A. (trans.) (2008). *The Formularies of Angers and Marculf: Two Merovingian Legal Handbooks*. Liverpool: Liverpool University Press.

Ruricius of Limoges, *Epistulae*. B. Krusch (ed.). (1887). MGH AA 8 (pp. 299–350). Berlin: Weidmann.

Shanzer, D., and Wood, I. (trans.). (2002). *Avitus of Vienne: Letters and Selected Prose*. Liverpool: Liverpool University Press.

Venantius Fortunatus. F. Leo and B. Krusch (eds.). (1881–1885). *Opera*. MGH AA 4.1–2. Berlin: Weidmann.

Modern Sources

Allen, P. (2013). "Prolegomena to a Study of the Letter-Bearer in Christian Antiquity." *Studia Patristica* 62: 481–490.

Bagnall, R. (1993). *Egypt in Late Antiquity*. Princeton, NJ: Princeton University Press.

Bagnall, R. (1995). *Reading Papyri, Writing Ancient History*. London: Routledge.

Bagnall, R. (2011). *Everyday Writing in the Graeco-Roman East*. Berkeley: University of California Press.

Barrett, G., and Woudhuysen, G. (2016). "Assembling the Austrasian Letters at Trier and Lorsch." *Early Medieval Europe* 24(1): 3–57.

Brown, W., Costambeys. M., Innes, M., and Kosto, A. (eds.) (2013). *Documentary Culture and the Laity in the Early Middle Ages*. Cambridge: Cambridge University Press.

Cherewatuk, K. (1993). "Radegund and Epistolary Tradition." In K. Cherewatuk and U. Wiethaus (eds.), *Dear Sister: Medieval Women and the Epistolary Genre* (pp. 20–45). Philadelphia: University of Pennsylvania Press.

Choat, M. (2013a). "The Epistolary Culture of Monasticism between Literature and Papyri." *Cistercian Studies Quarterly* 48: 227–237.

Choat, M. (2013b). "Monastic Letter Collections in Late Antique Egypt: Structure, Purpose, and Transmission." In S. Torallas Tovar and J. Pedro Monferrer-Sala (eds.), *Cultures in Contact: Transfer of Knowledge in the Mediterranean Context* (pp. 73–90). Cordoba: Oriens Academic.

Classen, P. (1977). *Kaiserrekript und Königsurkunde*. Thessaloniki: Byzantion.

Dumézil, B. (2007). "Gogo et ses amis: écriture, échanges et ambitions dans un réseau aristocratique de la fin du VIe siècle." *Revue historique* 309(3): 553–593.

Dumézil, B. (2009). "Le Patrice Dynamius et son réseau: culture aristocratique et transformation des pouvoirs autor de Lérins dans la seconde moitié du VIe siècle." In Y. Codou and M. Lauwers (eds.), *Lérins, une île sainte de l'Antiquité au Moyen Age* (pp. 167–194). Turnhout: Brepols.

Ganz, D., and Goffart, W. (1990). "Charters Earlier than 800 from French Collections." *Speculum* 65: 906–932.

Gaudemet, J., and Basdevant, B. (eds.) (1989). *Les canons des conciles Mérovingiens [VIe–VIIe siècles]*, 2 vols., SC 353–354. Paris: Les éditions du Cerf.

Gibson, R. (2012). "On the Nature of Ancient Letter Collections." *Journal of Roman Studies* 102: 56–78.

Gillett, A. (2003). *Envoys and Political Communication in the Late Antique West, 411–533*. Cambridge: Cambridge University Press.

Gillett, A. (2010). "Love and Grief in Post-Imperial Diplomacy: The Letters of Brunhild." In B. Sidwell and D. Dzino (eds.), *Power and Emotions in the Roman World and Late Antiquity*. Piscataway NJ: Gorgias Press.

Gillett, A. (2012a). "Communication in Late Antiquity: Use and Reuse." In S. Johnson (ed.), *Oxford Handbook of Late Antiquity* (pp. 815–846). Oxford: Oxford University Press.

Gillett, A. (2012b). "Advise the Emperor Beneficially: Lateral Communication in Diplomatic Embassies between the Post-Imperial West and Byzantium." In A. Becker and N. Drocourt (eds.), *Ambassadeurs et ambassades au coeur des relations diplomatiques: Rome, Occident Médiéval, Byzance (VIIIe s. avant J.-C.– XIIe s. après J.-C.)* (pp. 257–285). Metz: Centre de recherché universitaire Lorrain d'histoire.

Gillett, A. (2019). "Telling Off Justinian: Theodebert I, the *Epistolae Austrasicae*, and Communication Strategies in Sixth-Century Merovingian-Byzantine Relations." *Early Medieval Europe* 27: 161–194.

Goubert, P. (1956). *Byzance avant l'Islam*, vol. 2.1: *Byzance et les Francs*. Paris: A. et J. Picard.

Halfond, G. (2009). *The Archaeology of Frankish Church Councils, AD 511–768*. Leiden: Brill.

Heinzelmann, M. (1990). "*Studia sanctorum*. Education, milieu d'instruction et valeurs éducatives dans l'hagiographie en Gaule jusqu'à la fin de l'époque mérovingienne." In M. Sot (ed.),

Haut moyen-âge: Culture, education et société: Etudes offertes à P. Riché (pp. 105–138). Nanterre: Editions Publidix.

Hen, Y. (1995). *Culture and Religion in Merovingian Gaul, AD 481–751.* Leiden: Brill.

Hen, Y. (2007). *Roman Barbarians: The Royal Court and Culture in the Early Medieval West.* Houndmills: Palgrave.

Jasper, D. (2001). "The Beginning of the Decretal Tradition." In D. Jasper and H. Fuhrmann (eds.), *Papal Letters in the Early Middle Ages* (pp. 3–133). Washington, DC: Catholic University of America.

Jeffrey, J. (2002). "Radegund and the Letter of Foundation." In L. Churchill et al. (eds.), *Women Writing Latin, 2: Medieval Women Writing Latin* (pp. 11–23). New York: Routledge.

Klingshirn, W. (1994a). *Caesarius of Arles: The Making of a Christian Community in Late Antique Gaul.* Cambridge: Cambridge University Press.

Leclercq, H. (1929). "Lettres Chrétiennes." In F. Cabrol and H. Leclercq (eds.), *Dictionnaire d'archéologie chrétienne et de liturgie* (col. 2683–2885). Paris: Librairie Letouzey et Ané.

Malaspina, E. (2001). *Il* Liber epistolarum *della cancelleria austrasica (sec. V–VI).* Rome: Herder.

Markus, R. (1997). *Gregory the Great and His World.* Cambridge: Cambridge University Press.

Mathisen, R. (1981). "Epistolography, Literary Circles, and Family Ties in Late Roman Gaul." *Transactions of the American Philological Society* 111: 95–109.

Mathisen, R. (trans.). (1999). *Ruricius of Limoges and Friends: A Collection of Letters from Visigothic Gaul.* Liverpool: Liverpool University Press.

Mathisen, R. (2003). *People, Personal Expression, and Social Relations in Late Antiquity.* Ann Arbor: University of Michigan Press.

Matthews, J. (2000). *Laying Down the Law.* New Haven, CT: Yale University Press.

Millar, Fergus. (2006). *A Greek Roman Empire: Power and Belief under Theodosius II, 408–450.* Berkeley: University of California Press.

Mostert, M. (ed.). (1999). *New Approaches to Medieval Communication.* Turnhout: Brepols.

Mostert, M. (2012). *A Bibliography of Works on Medieval Communication.* Turnhout: Brepols.

Murray, A. (2005). "The New MGH Edition of the Charters of the Merovingian Kings." *Journal of Medieval Latin* 15: 246–278.

Palme, B. (2011). "The Range of Documentary Texts: Types and Categories." In R. Bagnall (ed.), *The Oxford Handbook of Papyrology* (pp. 358–394). Oxford: Oxford University Press.

Parsons, P. (1980). "Background: The Papyrus Letter." *Acta colloquii didactici classici octavi (Didactica Classica Gandensia)* 20: 3–18.

Rio, A. (2009). *Legal Practice and the Written Word in the Early Middle Ages: Frankish Formulae, c. 500–1000.* Cambridge: Cambridge University Press.

Roberts, M. (2009). *The Humblest Sparrow: The Poetry of Venantius Fortunatus.* Ann Arbor: University of Michigan Press.

Ruffini, G. (2008). *Social Networks in Byzantine Egypt.* Cambridge: Cambridge University Press.

Weidemann, M. (1982). *Kulturgeschichte der Merowingerzeit nach den Werken Gregors von Tours.* 2 vols. Mainz: Römisch-Germanisches Zentralmuseum.

Wickham, C. (2005). *Framing the Early Middle Ages: Europe and the Mediterranean, 400–800.* Oxford: Oxford University Press.

Williams, J. (2014). "Letter Writing, Materiality, and Gifts in Late Antiquity: Some Perspectives on Material Culture." *Journal of Late Antiquity* 7(2): 350–358.

Williard, H. (2014). "Letter-Writing and Literary Culture in Merovingian Gaul." *European Review of History: Revue européenne d'histoire* 21: 691–710.

Wood, I. N. (1990). "Administration, Law and Culture in Merovingian Gaul." In R. McKitterick (ed.), *The Uses of Literacy in Early Mediaeval Europe* (pp. 63–81). Cambridge: Cambridge University Press.

Wood, I. N. (1993). "Letters and Letter Collections from Antiquity to the Middle Ages: The Prose Works of Avitus of Vienne." In M. A. Meyer (ed.), *The Culture of Christendom: Essays in Medieval History in Commemoration of Denis T. Bethell* (pp. 29–43). London: Bloomsbury Academic.

CHAPTER 26

MEROVINGIAN EPIGRAPHY, FRANKISH EPIGRAPHY, AND THE EPIGRAPHY OF THE MEROVINGIAN WORLD

MARK A. HANDLEY

THE task of briefly summarizing the inscriptions from the Merovingian world is a difficult one. By definition every individual inscription is unique, while the evidence stretches across all of Gaul and over the entirety of the period from the end of Roman control over northern Gaul, through the rise of Clovis to the end of Merovingian rule. In an attempt to encapsulate key aspects of this evidence, I begin with the microcosm of the epigraphy of the Merovingian family itself, before broadening slightly to the epigraphy of the Franks where my focus is on the commemoration of non-Merovingian royals, those inscriptions that refer expressly to Franks, and finally the inscriptions alleged to have been written in "Frankish." I then broaden the perspective to provide a survey of the evidence from the entirety of the Merovingian world.

MEROVINGIAN EPIGRAPHY

The Merovingians were the single most commemorated dynasty of their time. There are no royal Vandal epitaphs; the two royal epitaphs from Visigothic Spain are so scurrilous as to make it certain they were not ever raised (Eugenius of Toledo, *Carm.* 25–26). The Suevic kings recorded on inscriptions are found in dating clauses (Ferreiro 1997; Nuñez 1979, no. 15). Two Burgundian kings (Hanhavaldus in late fourth-century Trier, and Gundobad in late fifth-century Geneva) are recorded as actors in inscriptions

(*ILCV*, nos. 44–45), but there is no epitaph for either of them, although there is an epitaph for the Burgundian queen Caratene (*ICG*, no. 31; Kampers 2000). Early Berber (Desanges 1996), British (e.g. Nash-Williams 1950, no. 33, p. 176), Gepid (Cetinkaya 2009), and Anglo-Saxon (Sharpe 2005) royalty were commemorated with epitaphs, but no more than one per dynasty. There are no epitaphs for an Ostrogothic royal, but there are a few for Lombard kings (Everett 2001; Rubeis 2000). By contrast, there are nine known epitaphs of members of the Merovingian family and at least one other epitaph for a non-Merovingian royal Frank.

Three of the Merovingian epitaphs were composed by Venantius Fortunatus, and another three by an anonymous tombstone poet who was familiar with at least some of Fortunatus's epitaphs and was working at much the same time. Each composed a trip-tych consisting of epitaphs for a queen and two young princes. The epitaphs composed by the anonymous court poet are no longer extant. They survive as part of a collection of epitaphs contained in a ninth-century manuscript (BN Lat. No. 2832), which most likely included an earlier collection put together in Burgundy in the late sixth century (Handley 2000).[1] The epitaphs were composed for King Guntram's queen Austrechild (d. 580, *ICG*, no. 218[2]), and her two sons, Chlodomer and Chlothar (d. 576, *ICG*, nos. 219–220). Edmond Le Blant's nineteenth-century edition placed the epitaphs at Orléans, but he admits that his only reason for doing so was that Orléans was Guntram's chief residence (*ICG*, pp. 315–316). The Burgundian focus of the manuscript collection of epi-taphs (including as it does the epitaphs of four bishops of Vienne and another epitaph of the woman Silvia, which was then found in Vienne in 1860 [*RICG XV*, no. 101]), might suggest an original location closer to Lyon or Vienne, but it is not impossible that the compiler traveled further afield for these royal epitaphs than for the others. The already-mentioned epitaph of Queen Caratene survives via the same Burgundian collection.

Austrechild is otherwise known only through Gregory of Tours's *Ten Books of History*, and the chronicle of Marius of Avenches. She was Guntram's second wife (*DLH* IV.25), and the former servant of one of Guntram's courtiers (*DLH* V.20). She survived the young sons she had with Guntram (Marius, *Chronicle*, s.a. 576), the two commemorated via the same poet, and would have remained a pale shadow of a character if not for her actions on her deathbed. To encourage additional wailing and lament at the time of her own death, and in frustration at their failed attempts to save her, she ordered that the doctors who had treated her should be killed at the moment of her death. Gregory likens her sinful actions to Herod (*DLH* V.25) but confirms that King Guntram carried out this wish. Marius gives the names of the two doctors as Donatus and Nicolaus (Marius, *Chronicle*, s.a. 580).

Gregory's portrait of Austrechild is naturally untempered by reference to her epitaph. Modern scholarship has unnecessarily followed suit (e.g., Dailey 2015, pp. 92–93, 99; Martmann 2009, p. 74). The opportunity to compare and contrast Gregory's evidence with other contemporaneous evidence on the same subject has been universally missed. Austrechild's epitaph (presumably commissioned by King Guntram) does not liken her to Herod, does not see her as sinful, and does not give any space to her feelings about health care professionals. Instead, she is praised in glowing terms as the "mother of kings, a surpassing royal wife, the light of her homeland, the world, and the court" *regum genetrix et regia coniux/praecellens lumen patriae lux orbis et aulae*. Her charity is praised in general, if unstinting, terms: "she sent her wealth to heaven in advance of herself and resolved to transfer her earthly kingdom."

Austrechild's epitaph can be usefully compared not just with Gregory's account, but with the epitaph composed by Fortunatus for the contemporaneous Queen Theudechild (*Carm.* IV.25). She was the granddaughter of Clovis and brother of Theudebert (*PLRE III, s.n.* Theudechildis and Wareman, 1986), and is portrayed as generous and charitable, secretly providing largesse to the poor, the widowed, orphaned, and exiled. We are told that her "brother, father, husband, grandfather and forebears" were of a royal line and that she was the builder of churches (*templorum domini cultrix*). Theudechild's church building activity is confirmed by an extant inscription from Sens: *Hunc regina locum monachis construxit ab imo Theuchildis* (*ICG*, no. 216). This same inscription records Theudechild as being buried at Sens: "her body is buried in this tomb." This may mean that we need to see Fortunatus's epitaph for Theudechild as being raised in Sens, or being a composition in the literary form of an epitaph but perhaps, in this instance, without any intent to have the words carved.

The two other royal epitaphs composed by Fortunatus were for the princes Chlodobert (d. 580, *Carm.* IX.4), and Dagobert (d. 580, *Carm.* IX.5), the sons of Chilperic I. The second is an acrostic poem in that the first letter of each line spells out a word, in this instance the prince's name *Dagobercthus*. Although not all acrostic poems were necessarily carved, the use of this device combined with the text being in the form of an epitaph suggests that Dagobert's poetic epitaph was designed to be placed on a monument. There are enough other instances of poetic inscriptions known primarily through manuscript transmission but where fragments or parts of the text have now been discovered[3] that we can have some confidence in this conclusion.

The last three Merovingian epitaphs all come from Saint-Germain-des-Prés in Paris. Two of the epitaphs, the first of which was found in 1643, were last seen in the seventeenth century. Regarding the first, two sarcophagi were discovered near the door to the cloister in the north of the church. One of these carried the inscription: *Tempore nullo volo hinc tolantur ossa Hilperici/precor ego Ilpericus non auferantur hinc ossa mea* (Montfaucon 1729, p. 175; Périn 1996, p. 34). "I wish that Chilperic's bones will never be removed from here. I, Chilperic, pray that my bones will not be removed from here." This has been identified as Chilperic I, who is known from Gregory to have been buried at Saint-Germain in 584 (*DLH*, VI.46). The early modern account of the inscription contains an image of its text (Fig. 26.1). It is impossible to know how accurate this representation is. Nonetheless, the ligatures, superscript contraction marks, superscript letters, lozenge-shaped Os, and Z-shaped Ss can all be paralleled from the other inscriptions of the sixth and seventh centuries. Therefore, some care may have been taken to render the inscription as accurately as possible.

The second Merovingian epitaph from Saint-Germain-des-Prés was found in March 1656, but the account of the discovery dates from 1724. A number of sarcophagi were found, one of which had a lid with an inscription placed above the head—CHILDR REX

.TEMPRE NZLoVo HINCToLIANT RoSSAHILPERIE

PEREGoILPERIES No AFERANVR HINOSSAMEA

FIGURE 26.1.   Epitaph of Chilperic I, after Montfaucon, 1729, p. 175.

with a contraction mark over the L and D—*Child(e)r(icus) rex* (Bouillart 1724, p. 253; Montfaucon 1729, p. 175; Périn 1996, p. 34; James 1992, pp. 250–251). Since Childeric I had died before the foundation of Saint-Germain-des-Prés (*PLRE II*, s.n. Childericus 1), this epitaph is likely to have been the epitaph of Childeric II murdered in 675 (Wallace-Hadrill 1960, p. 81). The inscription and sarcophagus were lost before they were even first reported. No image has come down to us.

The third and last Paris epitaph was uncovered in an archaeological dig carried out between 1970 and 1974 in the chapel of St. Symphorian at Saint-Germain-des-Prés (Fleury 1981; Dérens 1973). During the excavations, a sarcophagus was found in the northeastern angle of the chapel, built into the structure and seemingly in its original location. The sides of the sarcophagus were decorated with tight patterns of geometric striations, as was the lid. The lid of the sarcophagus was broken in three pieces. One of those was carved with the outline of a cross and carried the inscription GILDEBTUS/ REX FR. This should be expanded to read *Gildeb(er)tus rex Fr(ancorum)*. Because Fleury published it in *Cahiers de la Rotonde*, the low-circulation in-house journal of the Commission du Vieux Paris, the inscription has been almost entirely overlooked since it was found.

No less a figure than Jean Mallon published the *editio princeps* of this last inscription, dating the script to between the sixth and eighth centuries (Mallon 1981). He was troubled by the initial G-, suggestive of aspiration of the sound, but declared that a reading of CH- or H, was "perfectly impossible, the G is certain." He took comfort from the appearance of the name "Gildobertus" in a seventh-century document from Tours (Gasnault 1975, p. 69). The spelling of Austrechild's name as Austregild in her epitaph, in Marius of Avenches, and in a significant number of the manuscripts of Gregory of Tours, adds further weight to the view that the surprising G should not be allowed to interfere with the weight of archaeological and palaeographical evidence that suggests this is most likely the epitaph of Childebert I (d. 558),[4] the king responsible for the foundation of Saint-Germain-des-Prés and who had originally dedicated the church to the cult of Saint Vincent of Saragossa (*DLH* IV.20). In light of this identification, this inscription is the earliest original text referring to a Merovingian king as *Rex Francorum*— "king of the Franks."[5]

Eight of the nine epitaphs for Merovingian royal figures date from the last half of the sixth century, with one outlier a century later. There appears to have been a moment when it was almost standard for recently deceased members of the family to receive an epitaph. This moment cannot be attributed to the influence of Venantius Fortunatus, as it had started before him.

In addition to the epitaphs, members of the Merovingian family are known to have had inscribed signet rings (e.g., Childeric I, Aregund, and Balthild; see Effros 2003, pp. 29–32; Earenfight 2013, pp. 62–63). Merovingian royalty are also epigraphically recorded as patrons of ecclesiastical establishments. The inscription from Sens recording the patronage of Theudechild has already been mentioned (*ICG*, no. 216), but other instances are known from Courbehaye (between Orléans and Chartres)—*Clotarius rex istam dotavit ecclesiam* (Ollagnier and Joly 1994, p. 172)[6]—and from Le Ham in Normandy (*ICG*, no. 91).

FRANKISH EPIGRAPHY: NON-MEROVINGIAN ROYALS

Before and during the reign of Clovis, there were a number of different Frankish kingdoms (see Fouracre, Chapter 2, and Hen, Chapter 10, this volume). The Merovingian kingdom was but one of these kingdoms; the others included the kingdom of King Ragnachar centered at Cambrai and that of King Sigibert at Cologne. Count Arbogast in Trier, despite his name, perhaps underplayed any Frankish element to his rule. The teleology of the Merovingian rise is as good a reason as any to remind ourselves of the originally fractured nature of postimperial power, especially in northern Gaul and especially among the Franks.

Into this fractured political landscape must be inserted Queen Ragnehild (Schwinden 1991, no. 2). She was commemorated via a now-lost epitaph at Karden on the Moselle, approximately two-thirds of the way between Trier and the Rhine. She was recorded as being twenty years and six months at her death, and she was commemorated by an unnamed *vir*—more than likely her husband. The epitaph reads:

> *Conditum hic / tumulom requi / esc[i]nt membra / riginae / Ragnehildi fi / mini qui vixit in se / colum annus XX viginti et mensis / VI sex oviit in pace / ipsas kal(endas) enni / as et vir ipsius fi / mini titolum / posuit [...] in pa / ce.*

> (In this tomb lie the bones of the wife Queen Ragnehild, who lived in the world twenty years and six months. She died in peace in the Kalends of June and her husband set...this stone in peace.)

The quality of the Latin would perhaps have been more recognizable to the graffiti scratchers of Pompeii than to Cicero. It is what classicists like to call "vulgar" Latin: the masculine *qui* instead of the feminine *quae*; *ovitt* for *obiit*; *fimini* for *feminae*; *ennias* for *iunias*; *titolum* for *titulum* and so on. Leaving these attempts to reflect the spoken language to one side, albeit accepting that divergence from the strictures of classical Latin grammar and orthography can make interpretation more difficult, we must find room for Queen Ragnehild in the political landscape of the fifth- or very early sixth-century Moselle-Rheinland.

No such queen is known from the Merovingian family, although the names of some Merovingian queens (such as Clovis's first wife) are unknown to us (see James, Chapter 11, this volume). As a matter of probability, a twenty-year-old woman is unlikely to have forged her own kingdom. We should see her as either the wife or the daughter of an established king. That the king is unnamed should perhaps not trouble us: Guntram was not named in Austrechild's epitaph, nor were the family members of Queen Theudechild named in hers.

It is tempting to link Ragnehild in some way to the already-mentioned Ragnachar of Cambrai, who was himself a relative of Clovis. Ragnachar had two brothers, Rignomer and Riccha; this suggests a family habit of names beginning with Rig- or Rag-. Ragnachar and his family had a fairly broad field of activity, with Ragnachar joining Clovis in the attack on Syagrius, and the brother Rignomer being killed at Le Mans (*PLRE II*, s.n. Ragnachar, Richarius, Rignomeris). Nonetheless, the 330 kilometers from Cambrai to Karden poses a significant challenge to any such connection, and we would be unwise to posit a kingdom for Ragnachar that stretched anywhere close to this distance. It is possible that Ragnehild was a relative who survived the deaths of the rest of her family at Clovis's hands and was in semi-exile at Karden. However, it is just as likely that she had no connection at all to that family and was attached to a quite different kingdom: a kingdom that is not attested by Gregory and thus is otherwise unknown to us.

Considerable doubt, however, must be attached to the epitaphs of two further "royals" from late-antique Gaul. In the twelfth century, Emperor Henry VI ordered the expansion of the city walls of Cologne. The building work cut through a late Roman cemetery. Many hundreds of graves and inscriptions were found. At the time, this was interpreted as physical proof for the truth of the preexisting cult of Ursula and the 11,000 virgins of Cologne, and the area became known as the *ager Ursulanus*. As a result, a number of works record the inscriptions found (Schmitz 2008, 2015; Montgomery 2010, pp. 9–23; Militzer 2016). For our purposes the most relevant is the *Liber Revelationem* of Elisabeth of Schönau from the mid-twelfth century. In this work, Abbot Gerlach of Deutz tasks Elisabeth with discovering the link between a series of epitaphs and Ursula. One of the epitaphs was that of the virgin Verena. Elisabeth was able to enter into a series of visions in which she spoke with Verena and Verena was able to provide details and context of the people recorded on the inscriptions, and how they fit into the narrative of Ursula's martyrdom. Included were the likes of Pope Cyriacus, said to be the nineteenth pope. Elisabeth is surprised by this information, as having checked the lists of popes she could find no Cyriacus. Verena has the answer. Cyriacus was systematically stricken from the historical record by the Roman curia as punishment for abandoning his office and joining with Ursula on her voyage from Rome to Cologne.

Another epitaph was that of Aetherius. The text of his epitaph is recorded as reading: *Aetherius qui vixit annos viginti quinque fideles in pace recessit* ([Here lies] the faithful Aetherius who lived twenty-five years [and] departed in peace)—a perfectly plausible late-antique epitaph. Elisabeth goes on to say that below this—and carved in *capitalibus literis* (capital letters)—was the word *rex* (king), which is then described in terms suggesting that this word may have been a monogram. Near the epitaph of King Aetherius was found an epitaph reading only *Demetria regina* (Queen Demeteria) (*ICG*, no. 352; Clark 2000, pp. 219–220). Under Verena's tutelage, Elisabeth comes to know that Aetherius was the betrothed of Ursula and Demetria was his mother. Another epitaph, reading *Florentina puella*, is revealed as being the epitaph of Aetherius's sister.

In the late nineteenth century, Edmond Le Blant considered the inscriptions to be genuine. Certainly, if these inscriptions were genuine, they would have to be explained through the short-lived existence of an Aegidius/Syagrius style postimperial Roman kingdom in the northern Rhineland. This would be a kingdom otherwise unknown from the sources, but it is safe to say that our knowledge of events in fifth-century Cologne is not sufficient to exclude this possibility. We certainly know that by the end of the fifth century there was a kingdom centered on Cologne, as Gregory of Tours records the kings Sigibert the Lame and his son Chloderic as based in Cologne (*DLH* II.37 and II.40). Although Sigibert may not have been descended from Aetherius, it may be that we would have to see Sigibert's kingdom as descended from that of Aetherius.

Although there probably was some sort of secular power figure in Cologne, we should discount the possibility that this was Aetherius. While a significant number of late-antique and early medieval epitaphs were found as a result of Cologne's twelfth-century wall building, there is no more reason to make Aetherius a fifth-century king in Cologne than there is to squeeze a new pope Cyriacus into the list of popes.

Inscriptions of Franks

Two individuals expressly identified as "Franks" are known from inscriptions (on Franks, see Coumert, Chapter 5, this volume). Both are recorded in fourth-century inscriptions, and in neither instance is the name of the Frank recorded. In an entirely apt contradiction, one fought against the Romans and the other fought for the Romans.

The first instance is the unnamed killer of Viatorinus *protector* (Schmitz 1995, no. 12). The epitaph of Viatorinus from Cologne records that he was killed by a Frank in *barbaricum* near Divitia—*occisus in barbarico iuxta Divitia a Franco*. "Divitia" was the name of the fort on the barbarian side of the Rhine built to defend the bridge across the river. Presumably, Viatorinus had been on some sort of patrol outside the walls of Divitia and had met his fate at the hands of the unnamed Frank.

The other Frank is recorded from near Budapest (Aquincum) on the Danube. His epitaph is justly famous: *Francus ego cives Romanus miles in armis/egregia virtute tuli bello mea dextera sem[p]er* (I am a Frankish citizen, a Roman soldier under arms/with outstanding valor I have always gone into battle, my weapon in my hand) (*CIL III*, no. 3576; trans. in James 2009, p. 168). Although it is possible that Francus was the man's name, most observers see the man as an unnamed Frank who died while serving in the Roman army. Whether we identify him as a Frank who was a Roman citizen and soldier or as a Frankish citizen who was a soldier is a question without an answer. Certainly, a variety of non-Roman groups adopted the language of citizenship in this period, so a Frankish citizen cannot be ruled out. Although straying slightly outside of the Franks, we can note the female *civis Alamanna* (Alemannic citizen) commemorated at Florence in 423 (*CIL XI*, no. 1731), as another example of the use of civic terminology.

Mention can also be made of the mysterious *Brandobrici*, an otherwise unknown group recorded on an epitaph from Luzinay in Burgundy from the year 527 (*RICG XV*, no. 270): *sub (h)unc conss(ulem) Brandobrici redimtionem a D(o)<m>(i)<n>o Gudomare rege acceperunt*—"during this consulship the Brandrobrici accepted their redemption from the Lord King Godomar." We would dearly love to know more about the episode and about this group.

INSCRIPTIONS IN "FRANKISH"

The Frisians had runes; the Alemanns had runes; the Continental Saxons had runes, as did the insular Anglo-Saxons (on the Anglo-Saxons, see Fleming, Chapter 17, this volume). The north and east of the Merovingian world had no shortage of peoples who had adopted the runic script. With the exception of Anglo-Saxon England, however, the study of these runic inscriptions is largely excluded from the mainstream of analysis.

It is difficult to know what would be more surprising—the idea that the Franks would not have used runes when they were used by so many neighboring peoples or that the Franks did use runes, but this fact is so little known. Although one could get to the end of many books about the Franks without ever reading about Frankish runic inscriptions, there is in fact a growing corpus of inscriptions, some of which were found over a century ago, with other finds much more recent (see Looijenga 2003; Fischer 2005).

In runological terms, there is no difference between the runic inscriptions found to the east of the Rhine and those to the west. Focusing just on those found west of the Rhine—those most clearly to be identified as Frankish—examples include the silver bow fibula found in 1872/1873 in a woman's grave within the row cemetery at Freilaubersheim (Rheinland-Pfalz) (Fig. 26.2). The runes read: "boso:wraetruna/Þkda[.]ïna: golida"— *Boso wrote (the) runes, DaÞina greeted you* (Looijenga 2003, pp. 241–242). In Charnay (Saône-et-Loire) in France, another silver bow fibula was found in 1830. It reads: "fuÞarkgwhnijïpzstb[...] :uÞfnÞai:id dan:liano/iïa, *fuÞark*"—*May Liano get to know Idda* (Looijenga 2003, pp. 235–236). At Arlon in Belgium, a silver bulla was found in 1936 as an artifact within a row grave cemetery. The inscription is damaged but reads: "godun[...]o[...]e[...]s rasuwa[m]ud wo[.]gt," suggestive of Rosamund making the runes and/or bulla for Goda (Looijenga 2003, pp. 227–228).

New runes continue to be found. For example, in 1990 a disc brooch was found in a sixth-century woman's grave at Chéhéry (Ardenne). Remarkably, this brooch has a bilingual inscription. It reads in Latin *Deo s(anct)o de(dicatus) e(st)*, and then **ditan** in runes, which may be a woman's name (Looijenga 2003, p. 264). In 2008, a new runic inscription on a sword pommel was found in grave 11 at Saint-Dizier reading **alu**

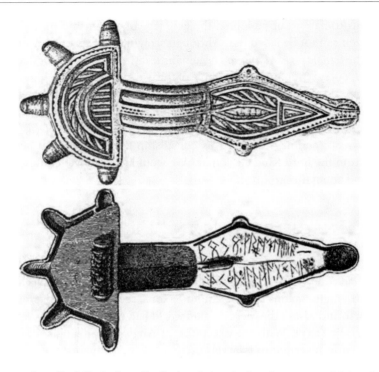

FIGURE 26.2. Inscribed fibula from Freilaubersheim. (© Landesmuseum Mainz. Reproduced with permission)

(Fischer, Croix, and Soulat 2008). More recently still in 2011, a silver spoon containing runes was found within a lavishly furnished grave at Ichtratzheim. This is another bilingual item. In addition to a small cross, the spoon is inscribed *Matteus* and then in runic **lapela**—*spoon*, and **abuda** a sequence of uncertain meaning (Fischer et al. 2014).

No doubt further finds will continue. The importance of this corpus cannot be underestimated. A person who wants to argue that the Franks were merely an evolved form of the late Roman army, born of the frontier but still essentially Roman, has to be able to explain the use of a Germanic language and the runic script by the Franks.

SCHOLARSHIP ON THE EPIGRAPHY OF THE MEROVINGIAN WORLD

There are approximately 3,500 extant or recorded Christian inscriptions from Gaul in the period from roughly 300 to 750 CE.[7] Although there are some in Greek (Decourt 2004; Siede and Schwinden 2012), and even fewer raised by Jews (Noy 1993, nos. 189–192; see Fig. 26.3), complete with Hebrew *shalom* and a menorah (on Jews, see

FIGURE 26.3. Jewish building inscription from Auch (Noy 1993, no. 189). © Musée d'archéologie nationale, Saint-Germain-en-Laye. Reproduced with permission.

Drews, Chapter 6, this volume), the vast majority are in Latin and are Christian in content and/or context. The runic inscriptions are not in stone.

The publication of these inscriptions is devastatingly fragmented.[8] The great nineteenth-century volumes of Edmond Le Blant (*ICG* and *NR*) and Otto Hirschfeld (*CIL* vols. 12 and 13), while utterly indispensable, have long since passed their sell by date. For France, three volumes of the "nouveau Le Blant"—*Receuil des inscriptions chrétiennes de la Gaule antérieures de la renaissance carolingienne*—covering the period to 750 CE have appeared since 1975, the most recent in 1997. Unlike the original Le Blant, this series does not include inscribed portable objects—*instrumentum domesticum*. The published volumes to date cover the late Roman provinces of Belgica Prima (*RICG I*), northern Viennensis (*RICG XV*), and Aquitania Prima (*RICG VIII*). Two further volumes, one by Marc Heijmans combining southern Viennensis, Narbonensis Prima, and Alpes Maritimae, and the other by Morgane Uberti for Aquitania Secunda and Novempopulana should appear soon (for now see Treffort and Uberti 2010; Heijman 2015). The timetable for the remaining volumes is even more uncertain.

The unpublished (but online) dissertation of Paul Reynolds from 2000 provides an edition and English translation of the inscriptions then known from the provinces of Lugdunensis Prima, Viennensis, Narbonensis Prima, and Alpes Maritimae (Reynolds 2000). In addition, the series *Corpus des inscriptions de la France médiévale* with its twenty-six volumes to date includes inscriptions dating from the mid-eighth century but not before. New volumes in this series appear on a regular basis. The Swiss inscriptions were fully published (subject to new finds and the very occasional omission) in five volumes of *Corpus Inscriptionum Medii Aevi Helvetiae* between 1977 and 1997 (*CIMAH I-V*), and Stéphanie Lambot compiled an edition of the early medieval inscriptions of Belgium in her doctoral dissertation, to be published at a future date (Lambot 2007). Finally, regional corpora exist, such as Walter Boppert's edition for the Middle Rhine (Boppert 1971) or the publication of the corpus from Brittany under a team led by Wendy Davies (Davies et al. 2000). There are also modern editions devoted to specific towns such as Maastricht, Andernach, and Cologne (Boppert 1986, 1988; Schmitz 1995).

In terms of keeping up with finds of inscriptions published across innumerable local journals, scholars can benefit from the work of the team at *L'Année épigraphique*. This journal seeks to publish in summary form all the new finds, or significant reinterpretations, for any given year. It is usually published several years after the year the respective volume is covering—for instance, the volume for 2013 was announced as published in September 2016. No disrespect is intended to the editors to note that their emphasis is on the Roman period rather than the early Middle Ages. Nonetheless, it remains an invaluable resource for the Merovingian period. As a measure of this, for the years 2000–2007, *L'Année épigraphique* published forty-eight inscriptions from late-antique and early medieval Gaul.

Of the stone inscriptions, the vast majority are epitaphs. There are also many hundreds of graffiti (discussed below); a fair number of building inscriptions recording acts of patronage; and then much smaller numbers of other kinds of inscriptions such as the two epitaphs from Briord in Burgundy that doubled as records of manumissions. They record in one instance the name of the slave Arenberga freed *pro redemtionem animae suae* (for the redemption of her soul) and in the other instance, the names of six slaves freed by Manneleubus (*RICG XV*, nos. 258 and 261). There is one inscribed relic list (also discussed later in this chapter).

Before discussing the evidence for secular and ecclesiastical life that comes from the inscriptions, a brief word needs to be said about their manufacture. In this context, perhaps the most important inscription in Gaul is that shown in Fig. 26.4 (*NR*, no. 170). Although it is an incomplete inscription from Arles from the late fifth or early to mid-sixth century, its importance derives from its incompleteness. Substantial portions of the inscription were never carved. What is apparent is that the name—*Leonidius*—was carved, but otherwise no personal details were offered. The formulaic words are

FIGURE 26.4. Epitaph of Leonidius © CNRS Centre Camille Jullian, Aix-en-Provence. Reproduced with permission.

there—*qui vixit annus pl(us) m(inus)*, "who lived more or less…years"—but there is a blank space where the age should be. Similarly, we see the phrase *obit sub die*, "He died on the day…," which would normally be followed by a date, and then after a wholly blank line we see *indictione*, which would normally be followed by the year of the indiction, a fifteen-year cycle originally tied to taxation.

This inscription clearly shows that the stone was largely prepared ahead of time with the formulaic words before the grieving customer even walked into the workshop to provide the personal details of the loved one. Therefore, here we see the process of preparing an inscription, at least in the large urban centers where we can and should envisage dedicated epigraphic workshops. It is in this light that scholars need to be careful tying formulaic expressions to the specific commemorands (i.e., those doing the commemorating). The commemorands may have been only supplying purely factual information such as the name, age, and date of death. There was always, of course, scope for individuality; one could pay more and get a personalized text. In some ways such texts become all the more significant precisely because they represent a conscious decision to divert from the norm.

The epitaphs themselves survive in a wide variety of forms. Most have little or nothing known about their archaeological context, giving us relatively limited understanding of their physical placement and their precise nature as monuments. Brittany is perhaps the region where we have the best information because the majority of inscriptions there were either placed onto standing stones or were found scratched onto sheets of slate and placed above the body and then buried within a grave (see Davies et al. 2000).

THE DEMOGRAPHICS OF EARLY MEDIEVAL EPIGRAPHY

Textually, the majority of early medieval epitaphs carry one of the archetypal Christian funerary formulae—*hic requiescit, hic iacet, hic quiescit*—often then followed by *in pace* and then the person's name. The image conveyed is expressly that of the Christian dead in repose awaiting the resurrection. In many cases, the epitaph is then accompanied by an age at death and/or a date that may be described as the day of death or the day of burial. The occupation or rank of the person may also be recorded, as may other incidental details.

The ages recorded on epitaphs make clear that, outside Trier, children were rarely commemorated. The preponderance of ages ending in 0 or 5 is evidence both for widespread age rounding and age ignorance. Combining analysis of the age and gender of the commemorands reveals a pattern across Gaul of women tending to be commemorated when they were of childbearing age. By comparison, male commemoration was proportionately less common in the teens and twenties but then peaked and stayed at higher levels for longer into the seventies and eighties.[9]

FIGURE 26.5. Inscribed sarcophagus Sigofrido from Luxeuil. (© Sébastian Bully. Reproduced with permission)

Whereas some epitaphs consist of just a name (see, e.g., Fig. 26.5), others again are lengthy poetic compositions. This last category is largely reserved for figures otherwise known to us through other sources—bishops and royal persons (see Heinzelmann 1976 for the episcopal epitaphs). Over ten years ago, I listed 152 examples of secular status recorded on the inscriptions from Gaul between 300 and 750, ranging from kings to senators, officeholders, and slaves, and 312 examples of ecclesiastics ranging from bishops, through the myriad ranks of the church down to catechumens and pilgrims (Handley 2003, p. 40). Specific female examples include the seventh-century Bertichildis *filia inl(ustris)* from Bingen on the Rhine (Boppert, 1971, s.n. Bertichildis) or the 45-year-old Cheldofrida *dom(i)na* commemorated at Inden-Pier (Kreis Düren) west of Cologne (Engemann and Rüger 1991, no. 42). In Trier, we find the likes of the *vicarius* Hlodericus from the early eighth-century (*RICG I*, no. 135), Flavius Gerontius the *trebunus* from the sixth or seventh century (*RICG I*, no. 107), and Ursacius the *cursor dominicus* (the lord's, i.e., king's, messenger) from the sixth century (*RICG I*, no. 138).

This is not the place to list new examples found since then but merely to reiterate the point that those raising inscriptions in the Merovingian world saw no bar to proclaiming status on a publicly inscribed text. Indeed, the fact that the epitaphs (other than the few found *within* a grave) are *public* texts should reinforce this point. The mere engagement in public monumental display should go some way toward confirming the conclusion that the commemorands were participating in acts of competitive display through which raising a textual monument was a marker of status. The one known price of an epitaph from seventh-century Lyon (11 *solidi*) supports this conclusion and ties in with other known prices from Spain, Rome, and Salona (Handley 2003, pp. 38–39).

We should then envisage the epigraphic population as largely excluding the poor. Although a significant minority expressly recorded their status, for the majority of the others we should posit them as either largely made up of the non-noble free, with some significant or disposable wealth, or as those aspiring to such a position, and using the raising of monument as a step in that process.

DISTRIBUTION: NORTH AND SOUTH, URBAN AND RURAL

Unusually for any of the genres of written evidence that survive from this period, the inscriptions survive in roughly equal numbers from north and south of the Loire. The reason for this can be summed up in one word: Trier. This one northern town has over 1,300 published inscriptions,[10] including 300 recently published inscriptions found in excavations in the town's northern cemetery of St. Maximinus (Merten 2018). Not only does this one town dominate the distribution in the north, it dominates the surviving evidence from the entirety of Gaul. Its corpus is approximately 6½ times larger than the next biggest civic corpus from Vienne. No town in Spain has half as many inscriptions. In the entirety of the late-antique and early medieval West, only Carthage and Rome have more inscriptions.

The other northern locations with sizeable concentrations are Cologne, Mainz, Andernach, Tours, Paris, Metz, and Amiens. Between them, these towns have approximately 250 inscriptions. By contrast, many other notable towns across the north places, such as Auxerre, Orléans, Nantes, Reims, and Soissons, have corpora numbering five or less.

In the south, the Rhône Valley runs through the core territories of epigraphic use. Vienne, Lyon, and Arles between them have approximately 500 inscriptions, with Vienne having over 200 of those. As with the north, however, we then drop to a series of towns with much smaller numbers: Marseille and Narbonne each have fifty to sixty inscriptions, and then Clermont, Vaison, and Bordeaux each have between twenty and thirty, and Autun, Grenoble, Geneva, Orange, Alba, Viviers, Toulouse, and Poitiers have between ten and twenty.

As the above figures suggest, approximately 70 percent of the inscriptions that survive from late-antique and early medieval Gaul survive from urban contexts. This figure is based on using towns with bishoprics as the definition of "urban." This does not mean that 30 percent come from genuinely rural contexts. The only sizable collection from a rural cemetery is that from Neuvicq-Montguyon (Charente-Maritime) in the southwest of Gaul, where the inscriptions are on sarcophagi and are brief in the extreme, often consisting of just a name (Maurin 1971). These have been published before, but we await their re-publication as part of Morgane Uberti's *RICG* edition.

CHRISTIANITY AND CHURCH BUILDING

Inscriptions also record church building activity. From west to east, these could range from the church of St. Martin raised by an uncertainly named abbot in late seventh-century Liguge—*N(…) abba edificavi basilica s(an)c(t)i Martini* (Coquet 1954), to another church of St. Martin built at Windisch in modern Switzerland in the sixth or seventh century. It was sponsored by Ursinos the bishop and at least one other named benefactor—*In onore s(an)c(ti) Martini e(pis)c(o)p(i). Ursinos ebescubus [...] Detibaldus + Linculfus ficit* (*CIMAH* III, no. 6).

These inscriptions are a continuation of a tradition of recording church building through inscriptions. Earlier examples include Bishop Rusticus of Narbonne in the 440s recording in stone the long list of donors (including other churchmen, government officials, and laymen), to his episcopal building efforts (*ICG*, no. 617; Marrou 1970). Another example from 455 is the priest Othia who built a basilica in honor of the holy martyrs Vincent, Agnes, and Eulalia in completion of a vow—*sui baselicam ex voto suo in hon(ore) s(ancto)r(u)m mart(yrum) Vincenti, Agnetis et Eulalia* (Chalon 2010).

MONKS, NUNS, AND MONASTERIES

The commemoration of individual monks and nuns across wide areas of Merovingian Gaul provides invaluable evidence for the spread of monasticism outside those regions of the Rhône Valley, Clermont, and Tours in which our written sources congregate in the fifth and sixth centuries (see Diem, Chapter 15, this volume). Later in the seventh and eighth centuries, when our written evidence changes and more charters begin to appear, and where Columbanian monasteries shine brightest in the textual evidence, the commemoration of individual monks and nuns again provides granular reminders that monasticism was everywhere. The epigraphic evidence for monasticism in northern Gaul before 600 was largely published by Hartmut Atsma (1976), but additional finds since then have further filled out the picture with significant additional evidence from Metz, Cologne, and Remagen. At Trier, there is an epitaph of one Gerola *presbiter atque monachus* (priest and monk), and there is another reference to *turba fratrum* (multitude of brethren). In addition, there is the already-mentioned inscription raised by Theudechild at Sens recording the foundation of a monastery in the early sixth century (Handley 2003, pp. 48–49).

The inscriptions, however, provide evidence not just of monks and monasteries, but evidence from within monasteries. Only a few years ago it would have been entirely sensible to draw strong contrasts in the monastic displays of monumental epigraphy in the early medieval West. The contrast would have been between the significant epigraphy from monasteries in Britain and Ireland such as Clonmacnoise, Iona, and Whitby, and the almost complete lack of similar collections from the great continental monasteries, including those from Francia. This seeming contrast first started to crack with excavations at San Vincenzo al Volturno in Italy (Mitchell 1990). The publication of significant collections from monasteries such as Bobbio (Destefanis 2004), Reichenau (Geuenich, Neumüllers-Klauser, and Schmid 1983), and Saint Maurice d'Agaune (*CIMAH* I, nos. 3–21), as well as new finds from Luxeuil (for one of which, see Fig. 26.5) identified by Sébastian Bully (Bully, Bully, and Čaušević-Bully 2014), and the old, but almost entirely unpublished finds from Monte Cassino (Pantoni 1958), have made any such apparent contrast disappear.

It is not just monumental inscriptions that are being published from Merovingian monasteries. Over the last ten years, excavations by Etienne Louis at the nunnery of Hamage (Nord); have produced a collection of hundreds of inscribed goblets. These are yet to be fully published, but those that have appeared in print show a variety of texts, including personal names such as *Aughilde* or invocations such as *Amen*, and other texts perhaps unexpected in an ascetic environment such as *Mitte plino* +: "fill me up" (Fig. 26.6A and 26.6B).

Absent this last example, it might have been possible to interpret the goblets as practice writing pieces with students reusing shards of broken goblets before being let loose on parchment. Instead, despite many of the texts being very short and fragmentary with only a few letters surviving, we need to associate at least some of the texts with use of the goblets as drinking vessels. That the lettering is scratched into the colored wash makes clear that the letters were added after firing and not before. What is more, although the challenge of scratching onto a curved surface should not be underestimated, the lettering is often accomplished and includes some decorative letter forms such as a lozenge-shaped O, as well as a mixture of capitals and minuscule forms such as the e at the end of *mitte*, as well as half-uncial letters A, M, and E seen in *Amen* (Fig. 26.6A).

(A)

(B)

FIGURES 26.6A AND 26.6B Inscribed goblets from Hamage. (© CAD-Arkeos. Reproduced with permission of Étienne Louis)

THE CULT OF SAINTS

The path to the study of the cult of saints in the Merovingian world laid by the volumi-nous quantity of Merovingian hagiography is well trod (see Kreiner, Chapter 24, this volume). Inscriptions have rarely contributed to these studies. Admittedly, there is no large corpus of inscribed relic lists and liturgical calendars such as we have from Visigothic Spain. What there is, however, is a corpus of little-studied inscriptions that shines light on different aspects of the cult of saints. The large, diverse body of religious graffiti speaks to the popular take-up of certain cults in a way that hagiographical texts rarely can. The building inscriptions like those discussed above recording dedications to certain cults show localized promotion and adoption of certain cults by local clerics—whether bishops or priests. Epitaphs with occasional textual references to a saint show the tangible impact of such promotion: the surviving family seeking a particular saint's intercession for their loved one. An example is the collection of inscriptions from seventh-century Lyon referencing St. Laurence (e.g., *ILTG*, nos. 297, 298).

There is also one inscribed relic list that survives from Merovingian Gaul. It is from Céleyran in *Narbonensis Prima*. It records the deposition of relics of the holy martyrs *s(an)c(to)r(um) mar(tyrum) riliqiae*. The saints listed are Cassianus, Marcellus, and Martinus. The priest Hilarius dedicated these relics, and the inscription then goes on to record the giving of the basilica of Sts. Saturninus and Marcellus, and the giving of a house *ad cap(u)<d> pontis* for the lighting of the saints (*NR*, no. 445). The identity of these saints has been the subject of some debate. Saturninus, Martinus, and Cassianus are names all known from the North African *Acts of the Abitinian Martyrs* (Tilley 1996). While possible, at least as likely an identification for these saints (and one that explains the inclusion of Marcellus) is as follows: Saturninus of Toulouse, Martin of Tours, John Cassian, and Marcellus of Chalon-sur-Saône.

Moving to the less formal inscriptions, a total of approximately 450 graffiti survive from Christian Gaul in the period up to, and including, the eighth century (Treffort 2004; Handley 2017). The four most significant sites are Trier (131—in Binsfeld, 2006), Bielle (Pyrénées-Atlantiques) (127—in Leclercq 1925), Minerve (Hérault) (95—in *ICG*, no. 610), and Vouneuil-sous-Biard (Vienne) (36—in Treffort 2009). The many hundreds of painted and scratched graffiti on the altar slab at Reichenau may start just a little too late to be Merovingian (Geuenich et al. 1983).

At Trier, the graffiti come from the walls of the Liebfrauenkirche within the walls of the city and are dated to the fourth and fifth centuries. The cult that attracted these graf-fiti is unknown. At Minerve, the graffiti were scratched onto an altar slab associated with the cult of Rusticus of Narbonne. Another little-known cult was the subject of the graffiti at Bielle which were scratched onto the columns of the church. There the cult is of Vivianus of Saintes. A different type of find spot is evidenced by the site of Vouneuil-sous-Biard where the graffiti were carved into stucco paintings. The cult associated with this last site is unknown. The surviving graffiti require further study and, in some cases, proper publication. As a means of reaching beyond the canonical texts of *Monumenta*

Germaniae Historica and inching closer to properly popular devotion, however, their testimony is invaluable.

CONCLUSION

The epigraphy of the Merovingian world is in flux. New finds continue at a challenging pace. No other area in Merovingian studies requires the assimilation of wholly new written evidence at a similar rate. New editions and regional studies are needed to allow scholars to keep abreast of these developments. The lack of up-to-date editions and commentaries only exacerbates the entry-level challenges that face those who would like to understand this evidence, but who are immediately faced with the daunting task of just trying to access and collect it.

These challenges apply to the monumental inscriptions, but as part of this work, special attention needs to be given to inscriptions on portable objects—the likes of the metalwork inscribed with runes and Latin inscriptions, and the goblets from Hamage. Inscriptions such as these, as well as the hundreds of graffiti, show literacy being used in different and informal ways. They show lay literacy in action outside legal transactions and the recording of deaths. The insights to be gleaned from the inscriptions are not, however, limited to new insights into the pretensions of the "great and good." As this contribution has sought to show, the inscriptions, once collected and published and made available, help to broaden and deepen our understanding of any number of issues, ranging from the popular uptake of certain cults and the recording of otherwise unknown senior officeholders to the commemoration of the Merovingian dynasty itself.

NOTES

1. The manuscript is now available online in high-quality photos. For the folio containing the epitaph of Austrechild, see http://gallica.bnf.fr/ark:/12148/btv1b85722439/f243.image.
2. "Austregilde" is the spelling in the manuscript. Austrechild is most often used in modern studies, although *PLRE* III uses Austregildis. Marius of Avenches also uses Austregildis; see Marius in MGH AA, *Chronica Minores*, p. 239. The spellings in the manuscripts for Gregory vary between Austerghilde, Austrigildis, Austregild, and Austrigild; see MGH SRM I, pp. 156, 215, 241.
3. Taking just examples from Gaul: for a carved fragment of the *Martinellus*, see Pietri 1974; for the epitaph of Sidonius Apollinaris recorded in a tenth- or eleventh-century manuscript but rediscovered in 1991, see Prévot 1993; for the epitaph of Abbot Hymnemodus of Agaune, known from the *Vita abbatum Acaunensium absque epitaphiis*, and partially rediscovered in 1896, see *CIMAH I*, p. 41; and for the already-discussed epitaph of Silvia in Vienne, see *RICG XV*, no. 101.
4. In any event, we should be slow to impose upon the inscriptions the strictures of a modern view as to correct spelling, and slow also to extract linguistic significance from variations in orthography. An example of a *laissez-faire* attitude to spelling comes from the name

Daniel spelled *Dagnihild* (*CIMAH II*, no. 15). The inscription's mention of *duo leones* makes it clear that Daniel was the intended name. Handley (2003, p. 168) listed seventy-six variant spellings of *vixit* that survive from the inscriptions.

5. Goetz (2003, pp. 323–324), relying on the charter evidence, can find no examples of a Merovingian being described as "King of the Franks" from before 596. Reimitz (2015, p. 98) gives the earliest example of this terminology as the Edict of Guntram from 585. Reimitz does this despite acknowledging the existence of the Saint-Germain-des-Prés inscription. Neither Goetz nor Reimitz mentions the *Vita Sanctae Genovefae*, c. 26 and its reference to *Childericus Rex Francorum*; see MGH SRM 3, p. 226.

6. The inscription is no longer extant but was recorded in the nineteenth century. The identification of the king as Chlothar III should be considered uncertain.

7. In 2003, I concluded that there were 2,941 inscriptions in late antique and early medieval Gaul. Since then, the numbers have continued to increase. Taking just the most obvious examples: over a hundred new graffiti from Trier were published in Binsfeld (2006); thirty-two new inscriptions from Marseille were published in Decourt, Gascou, and Guyon (2005), and see Merten (2018) for 300 newly published inscriptions from Trier.

8. For a general introduction to Latin inscriptions, see Cooley 2012. For a general introduction to Christian epigraphy, see Carletti 2008. Both are excellent, and both emphasize the evidence from Italy.

9. See the different discussions of age and gender in Handley 2003, pp. 65–109, Halsall 2003; Schmitz 2003; Perez, Chapter 9, this volume).

10. It has been a source of much confusion that *RICG I* published only 246 inscriptions from Trier. In addition to that volume, we must also consult (1) Gose 1958, which published 538 inscriptions later not included in *RICG I*; (2) Merten 1990, which added 103 inscriptions; and (3) Binsfeld 2006, which took the number of known Christian graffiti from the town from 28 to 131, and Merten 2018.

Works Cited

Ancient Sources

Acts of the Abitinian Martyrs. M. Tilley (trans.). (1996). *Donatist Martyr Stories: The Church in Conflict in Roman North Africa* (pp. 25–50). Liverpool: Liverpool University Press.

CIFM. R. Favreau et al. (ed.). (1975–). *Corpus des inscriptions de la France médiévale*. 26 volumes to date. Paris: CNRS Editions.

CIL III. T. Mommsen and O. Hirschfeld (eds.). (1873–1902). *Inscriptiones Asiae, provinciarum Europae Graecarum, Illyrici Latinae*. Corpus Inscriptionum Latinarum 3. Berlin: Berlin-Brandenburg Academy of Sciences and Humanities.

CIL XI. E. Bormann (ed.). (1888–1926). *Inscriptiones Aemiliae, Etruriae, Umbriae Latinae*. Corpus Inscriptionum Latinarum 11. Berlin: Berlin-Brandenburg Academy of Sciences and Humanities.

CIL XII. O. Hirschfeld (ed.). (1888). *Inscriptiones Galliae Narbonensis Latinae*. Corpus Inscriptionum Latinarum 12. Berlin: Berlin-Brandenburg Academy of Sciences and Humanities.

CIL XIII. O. Hirschfeld and C. Zangmeister (eds.). (1899–1916). *Inscriptiones trium Galliarum et Germaniarum Latinae*. Corpus Inscriptionum Latinarum 13. Berlin: Berlin-Brandenburg Academy of Sciences and Humanities.

CIMAH I. C. Jörg (ed.). (1977). *Die Inschriften des Kantons Wallis bis 1300. Corpus Inscriptionum Medii Aevi Helvetiae. Die Frühchristlichen und mittelalterlichen Inschriften der Schweiz 1.* Freiburg: Universitätsverlag Freiburg.

CIMAH II. C. Jörg (ed.). (1984). *Die Inschriften der Kantone Freiburg, Genf, Jura, Neuenberg und Waadt. Corpus Inscriptionum Medii Aevi Helvetiae. Die Frühchristlichen und mittelalterlichen Inschriften der Schweiz 2.* Freiburg: Universitätsverlag Freiburg.

CIMAH III. W. Kettler (ed.). (1992). *Die Inschriften der Kantone Aargau, Basel-Stadt, Basel-Land, Bern und Solothurn bis 1300. Corpus Inscriptionum Medii Aevi Helvetiae. Die Frühchristlichen und mittelalterlichen Inschriften der Schweiz 3.* Freiburg: Universitätsverlag Freiburg.

CIMAH IV. W. Kettler and P. Kalbermatter (eds.). (1992). *Die Inschriften der Kantone Luzern, Unterwalden, Uri, Schwyz, Zug, Zürich, Schaffhausen, Thurgau, St. Gallen und des Fürstentums Liechtensteins bis 1300. Corpus Inscriptionum Medii Aevi Helvetiae. Die Frühchristlichen und mittelalterlichen Inschriften der Schweiz 4.* Freiburg: Universitätsverlag Freiburg.

CIMAH V. M. Bernasconi Reusser (ed.). (1997). *Le iscrizioni dei cantoni Ticino e Grigioni fino al 1300. Corpus Inscriptionum Medii Aevi Helvetiae. Die Frühchristlichen und mittelalterlichen Inschriften der Schweiz 5.* Freiburg: Universitätsverlag Freiburg.

Clark, A. L. (trans.). (2000). *Elisabeth of Schönau: The Complete Works.* New York: Paulist Press.

Eugenii Toletani Episcopi Carminae. F. Vollmer (ed.). (1915). MGH AA 14. Berlin: Weidmann.

Favrod, J. (ed. and trans.). (1991). *La Chronique de Marius d'Avenches (455–581). Texte, traduction et commentaire.* Lausanne: Section d'histoire de la Faculté des lettres.

Gasnault, P. (ed.). (1975). *Documents comptables de Saint-Martin de Tours à l'époque mérovingienne.* Paris: Bibliothèque nationale.

ICERV. J. Vives (ed.). (1969). *Inscripciones Cristianas de la España Romana y Visigoda.* 2nd ed. Madrid: J. M. Viader.

ICG. E. Le Blant (ed.). (1856–1865). *Inscriptions chrétiennes de la Gaule antérieures au VIIIe siècle.* 2 vols. Paris: Imprimerie Impériale.

ILCV. E. Diehl (ed.). (1927–1931). *Inscriptiones Latinae Christianae Veteres.* Berlin: Weidmann.

ILTG. P. Wuilleumier (ed.). (1984). *Inscriptions latines des Trois Gaules.* Paris: CNRS Editions.

NR. E. Le Blant (ed.). (1892). *Nouveau Recueil des inscriptions chrétiennes de la Gaule antérieures au VIIIe siècle.* Paris: Imprimerie Nationale.

PLRE II. J. R. Martindale (ed.). (1980). *Prosopography of the Later Roman Empire, A.D. 395–527.* Cambridge: Cambridge University Press.

PLRE III. J. R. Martindale (ed.). (1992). *Prosopography of the Later Roman Empire, A.D. 527–641.* Cambridge: Cambridge University Press.

RICG I. N. Gauthier (ed.). (1975). *Recueil des inscriptions chrétiennes de la Gaule antérieures à la Renaissance carolingienne 1: Belgica Prima.* Paris: CNRS Editions.

RICG VIII. F. Prévot (ed.). (1997). *Recueil des inscriptions chrétiennes de la Gaule antérieures à la Renaissance carolingienne 8: Aquitania Prima.* Paris: CNRS Editions.

RICG XV. F. Descombes (ed.). (1985). *Recueil des inscriptions chrétiennes de la Gaule antérieures à la Renaissance carolingienne 15: Viennensis du Nord.* Paris: CNRS Editions.

Vita abbatum Acaunensium absque epitaphiis. B. Krusch (ed.). (1920). MGH SRM 7 (pp. 329–36). Hanover: Hahn.

Vita Sanctae Genovefae. B. Krusch (ed.). (1986). MGH SRM 3 (pp. 204–238). Hanover: Hahn.

Wallace-Hadrill, J. M. (trans.). (1960). *The Fourth Book of the Chronicle of Fredegar with Its Continuations.* London: Thomas Nelson.

Modern Sources

Atsma, H. (1976). "Die Christlichen Inschriften Galliens als Quelle für Klöster und Klosterbewohner bis zum Ende des 6. Jahrhunderts." *Francia* 4: 1–57.

Binsfeld, A. (2006). *Vivas in Deo. Die Graffiti der frühchristlichen Kirchenanlage in Trier*. Trier: Bischöfliches Dom- und Diözesanmuseum Trier.

Boppert, W. (1971). *Die frühchristlichen Inschriften des Mittelrheingebietes*. Mainz am Rhein: Philipp von Zabern.

Boppert, W. (1986). "Die frühchristlichen Grabinschriften aus der Servatiuskirche in Maastricht." In *Sint-Servatius Bisschop van Tongeren-Maastricht. Het vroegste Christendom in het Maasland* (pp. 65–96). Limburg: Borgloon-Rijkel.

Boppert, W. (1988). "Die frühchristliche Grabinschriften von Andernach." *Andernacher Beiträge* 3: 121–144.

Bouillart, J. (1724). *Histoire de l'abbaye royale de Saint-Germain des Prez*. Paris: Gregoire Dupuis.

Bully, S., Bully, A., and Čaušević-Bully, M. (2014). "Les origins du monastère de Luxeuil (Haute-Saône) d'après les récentes recherches archéologiques." In M. Gaillard (ed.), *L'empreinte chrétienne en Gaule du IVe au début du IXe siècle* (pp. 311–355). Turnhout: Brepols.

Carletti, C. (2008). *Epigrafia dei cristiani in Occidente dal III al VII secolo*. Bari: Edipuglia.

Çetinkaya, H. (2009). "An Epitaph of a Gepid king at Vefa kilise camii in Istanbul." *Revue des Études Byzantines* 67(1): 225–229.

Chalon, M. (2010). "L'inscription d'une église rurale du territoire narbonnais au ve siècle." *Pallas* 84: 145–175.

Cooley, A. (2012). *The Cambridge Manual of Latin Epigraphy*. Cambridge: Cambridge University Press.

Coquet, J. (1954). "L'inscription tumulaire de Ligugé (fin du VIIe siècle)." *Revue Mabillon* 44: 97–104.

Dailey, E.T. (2015). *Queens, Consorts, Concubines: Gregory of Tours and Women of the Merovingian Elite*. Leiden: Brill.

Davies, W., et al. (2000). *The Inscriptions of Early Medieval Brittany. Les inscriptions de la Bretagne du haut Moyen Age*. Aberystwyth and Oakville: Celtic Studies Publications.

Decourt, J. C. (2004). *Inscriptions grecque de la Gaule*. Lyon: Maison de l'Orient et de la Méditerranée.

Decourt, J. C., Gascou, J., and Guyon, J. (2005). "L'épigraphie." In M.-P. Rothé and H. Tréziny (eds.), *Carte Archéologique de la Gaule*, Vol. 13.3: *Marseilles et ses alentours* (pp. 160–216). Paris: Académie des Inscriptions et Belles-Lettres.

Dérens, J. (1973). "A propos des fouilles de la chapelle Saint-Symphorien de Saint-Germain des Prés: la basilique de Saint-Vincent puis Saint Germain des origines au XIe siècle." *Document-Archéologique* 3: 11–27.

De Rubeis, F. (2000). "Le iscrizioni dei re Longobardi." In F. Stella (ed.), *Poesia dell'Alto Medioevo Europeo: manoscritti, lingua e musica dei ritmi Latini* (pp. 223–237). Florence: SISMEL.

Desanges, J. (1996). "A propos de Masties imperator berbère et chrétien." *Ktema* 21: 183–188.

Destefanis, E. (2004). *Materiali lapidei e fittili di età altomedievale da Bobbio*. Piacenza: Tip le.co.

Earenfight, T. (2013). *Queenship in Medieval Europe*. London: Palgrave.

Effros, B. (2003). *Merovingian Mortuary Archaeology and the Making of the Early Middle Ages*. Berkeley: University of California Press.

Engemann, J., and Rüger, C. B. (eds.). (1991). *Spätantike und frühes Mittelalter. Ausgewählte Denkmäler im Rheinischen Landesmuseum Bonn*. Cologne: Rheinland Verlag.

Everett, N. (2001). "Liutprandic letters amongst the Lombards." In J. Higgitt, K. Forsyth, and D. Parsons (eds.), *Roman, Runes and Ogham. Medieval Inscriptions in the Insular World and on the Continent* (pp. 175–189). Donington: Shaun Dyas.

Ferreiro, A. (1997). "Veremundo R(eg)e: Revisiting an Inscription from San Salvador de Vairão (Portugal)." *Zeitschrift für Papyrologie und Epigraphik* 116: 263–272.

Fischer, S. (2005). *Roman Imperialism and Runic Literacy—the Westernization of Northern Europe (150–800)*. Uppsala: Department of Archaeology and Ancient History.

Fischer, S., Croix, S., and Soulat, J. (2008). "Les pommeaux avec inscriptions runiques à l'époque mérovingienne." In C. Vareon (ed.), *Nos ancêtres les Barbares, voyage autour de trois tombes de chefs francs* (pp. 70–83). Saint-Dizier: Somogy éditions d'art.

Fischer, S., Graf, M. H., Fossurier, C., Châtelet, M., and Soulat, J. (2014). "An Inscribed Silver Spoon from Ichtratzheim (Bas-Rhin)." *Journal of Archaeology and Ancient History* 11: 1–25.

Fleury, M. (1981). "Les fouilles récentes de la chapelle Saint-Symphorien (ou des Catéchismes) de l'église Saint-Germain-des-Prés." *Cahiers de la Rotonde* 4: 17–32.

Geuenich, D., Neumüllers-Klauser, R., and Schmid, K. (1983). *Die Altarplatte von Reichenau-Niederzell*. Hanover: Monumenta Germaniae Historica.

Goetz, H.-W. (2003). "Gens, Kings and Kingdoms: the Franks." In H.-W. Goetz, J. Jarnut, and W. Pohl (eds.). *Regna and Gentes: The Relationship between Late Antique and Early Medieval Peoples and Kingdoms in the Transformation of the Roman World* (pp. 307–344). Leiden: Brill.

Gose, E. (1958). *Katalog der frühchristlichen Inschriften in Trier*. Berlin: Verlag Gebr. Mann.

Halsall, G. (2003). "Burial Writes: Graves, 'Texts' and Time in Early Merovingian Northern Gaul." In J. Jarnut and M. Wemhoff (eds.), *Erinnerungskultur im Bestattungsritual. Archäologisch-Historisches Forum* (pp. 61–74). Munich: Wilhelm Fink Verlag.

Handley, M. A. (2000). "Epitaphs, Models and Texts: A Carolingian Collection of Late Antique Inscriptions from Burgundy." In A. Cooley (ed.), *The Afterlife of Inscriptions* (pp. 47–56). London: Institute of Classical Studies.

Handley, M. A. (2003). *Death, Society and Culture. Inscriptions and Epitaphs in Gaul and Spain, AD 300–750*. Oxford: British Archaeological Reports.

Handley, M. A. (2017). "Scratching at Devotion: Graffiti, Pilgrimage And Liturgy in the Late Antique and Early Medieval West." In K. Bolle, C. Machado, and C. Witschel (eds.), *The Epigraphic Cultures of Late Antiquity* (pp. 555–594). Stuttgart: Franz Steiner Verlag.

Heijman, M. (2015). "Les inscriptions paléochrétiennes d'Arles." In L. Clemens, H. Merten, and C. Schäfer (eds.), *Frühchristliche Grabinschriften im Westen des Römischen Reiches* (pp. 151–160). Trier: Kliomedia.

Heinzelmann, M. (1976). *Bischoffsherrschaft in Gallien. Zur Kontinuität römischer Führungsgeschichten von 4. bis zum 7. Jahrhundert: soziale, prosopographische und bildungsge-schichtliche Aspekte*. Munich: Artemis Verlag.

James, E. (1992). "Royal Burials among the Franks." In M. Carver (ed.), *The Age of Sutton Hoo. The Seventh Century in North-Western Europe* (pp. 243–254). Woodbridge: Boydell and Brewer.

James, E. (2009). *Europe's Barbarians AD 200–600*. London: Routledge.

Kampers, G. (2000). "Caretena—Königin und Asketin. Mosaiksteine zum Bild einer burgundischen Herrscherin." *Francia* 27(1): 1–32.

Lambot, S. (2007). *Les inscriptions latines en Belgique: de l'époque mérovingienne jusqu'à 1100. État de la recherche, établissement d'un corpus, évolution, analyse et perspectives pour l'avenir.* 4 vols. Unpublished doctoral thesis, Université libre de Bruxelles.

Leclercq, H. (1925). "Graffites." In H. Leclercq (ed.), *Dictionnaire d'Archéologie Chrétienne et de Liturgie* 6.2 (cols. 1453–1542). Paris: Librairie Letouzey et Ané.

Looijenga, T. (2003). *Texts and Contexts of the Oldest Runic Inscriptions.* Leiden: Brill.

Louis, E. (2014). "Une église monastique du haut Moyen Âge dans le nord de la France: le case de Hamage." In M. Gaillard (ed.), *L'empreinte chrétienne en Gaule du IVᵉ au début du IXᵉ siècle* (pp. 357–385). Turnhout: Brepols.

Mallon, J. (1981). "Le graffite Gildebertus rex francorum découvert à Saint-Germain-des-Prés." *Cahiers de la Rotonde* 4: 33–35.

Marrou, H.I. (1970). "Le dossier épigraphique de l'évêque Rusticus de Narbonne." *Rivista di archeologia Cristiana* 46(3–4): 331–349.

Martmann, M. (2009). *Die Königin im frühen Mittelalter.* Stuttgart: Kohlhammer.

Maurin, L. (1971). "Le cimetière mérovingien de Neuvicq-Montguyon (Charente-Maritime)." *Gallia* 29(1): 151–189.

Merten, H. (1990). *Katalog der frühchristlichen Inschriften des Bischöflichen Dom- und Diözesanmuseums Trier.* Trier: Bischöfliches Dom- und Diözesanmuseum Trier.

Merten, H. (2015). "Frühchristliche Grabinschriften in Trier. Stand der Bearbeitung." In L. Clemens, H. Merten, and C. Schäfer (eds.), *Frühchristliche Grabinschriften im Westen des Römischen Reiches* (pp. 29–36). Trier: Kliomedia.

Merten, H. (2018). *Die frühchristlichen Inschriften aus St. Maximin bei Trier.* Trier: Selbstverlag des Museums am Dom Trier.

Militzer, K. (2016). "The Church of St Ursula in Cologne: Inscriptions and Excavations." In J. Cartwright (ed.). *The Cult of St Ursula and the 11,000 Virgins* (pp. 29–40). Cardiff: University of Wales Press.

Mitchell, J. (1990). "Literacy Displayed: The Use of Inscriptions at the Monastery of San Vincenzo Al Volturno in the Early Ninth Century." In R. McKitterick (ed.), *The Uses of Literacy in Early Medieval Europe* (pp. 186–225). Cambridge: Cambridge University Press.

Montfaucon, B. de. (1729). *Les Monuments de la monarchie Françoise.* Vol. 1. Paris: Gandouin et Giffart.

Montgomery, S. B. (2010). *St. Ursula and the Eleven Thousand Virgins of Cologne. Relics, Reliquaries and the Visual Culture of Group Sanctity in Late Medieval Europe.* Bern: Verlag Peter Lang.

Nash-Williams, V. (1950). *The Early Christian Monuments of Wales.* Cardiff. University of Wales Press.

Noy, D. (1993). *Jewish Inscriptions of Western Europe. 1. Italy (Excluding the City of Rome), Spain and Gaul.* Cambridge: Cambridge University Press.

Nuñez, M. (1979). "Inscripciones de la Galicia altomedieval." *Revista de Guimarães* 89: 293–320.

Ollagnier, A., and Joly, D. (eds.). (1994). *Carte archéologique de la Gaule 28: L'Eure-et-Loire.* Paris: Fondation Maison des Sciences de l'Homme.

Pantoni, A. (1958). "Documenti epigrafici sulla presenza di settentrionali a Montecassino nell'alto medioevo." *Benedictina* 12: 205–238.

Périn, P. (1996). "Saint-Germain des-Prés: première nécropole des rois de France." *Médiévales* 31: 29–36.

Pietri, L. (1974). "Les tituli de la Basilique Saint-Martin édifiée à Tours par l'évêque Perpetuus (3ᵉ quart du Vᵉ siècle)." In *Mélanges d'histoire ancienne offerts à William Seston* (pp. 419–431). Paris: de Boccard.

Prévot, F. (1993). "Deux fragments de l'épitaphe de Sidoine Apollinaire." *L'Antiquité tardive* 1: 223–229.

Reimitz, H. (2015). *History, Frankish Identity and the Framing of Western Ethnicity, 550 to 850.* Cambridge: Cambridge University Press.

Reynolds, P. (2000). *A Comparative and Statistical Survey of the Late Antique and Early Medieval Inscriptions of South-Eastern Gaul (c. 300–750 AD).* Unpublished PhD, Leicester. Available online at https://lra.le.ac.uk/handle/2381/30792.

Schmitz, W. (1995). "Die spätantiken und frühmittelalterlichen Grabinschriften in Köln (4.–7. Jahrhundert n. Chr.)." *Kölner Jahrbuch* 28: 643–776.

Schmitz, W. (2003). "Requiescit in pace. Die Abkehr des Toten von der Welt der Lebenden. Epigraphische Zeugnisse der Spätantike als Quellen der historischen Familienforschung." In T. Grünewald and S. Seibel (eds.), *Kontinuität und Diskontinuität. Germania inferior am Beginn und am Ende der römischen Herrschaft* (pp. 374–413). Berlin: Walter de Gruyter.

Schmitz, W. (2008). "Mittelalterliche Ausgrabungen auf dem ager Ursulanus in Köln. Antike Inschriften im Licht mittelalterlicher Märtyrerverehrung." In D. Boschung and S. Wittekind (eds.), *Persistenz und Rezeption. Weiterverwendung, Wiederverwendung und Neuinterpretation antiker Werke im Mittelalter* (pp. 217–236). Wiesbaden: Dr Ludwig Reichert Verlag.

Schmitz, W. (2015). "Spätantik-frühmittelalterliche Grabinschriften vom ,ager Ursulanus' in Köln." *Rheinische Vierteljahrsblätter* 79: 20–31.

Schwinden, L. (1991). "Zu den frühchristlichen Inschriften von Karden an der Mosel." *Trierer Zeitschrift* 54: 249–275.

Sharpe, R. (2005). "King Caedwalla's Roman Epitaph." In K. O'Brien O'Keefe and A. Orchard (eds.), *Latin Learning and English Lore: Studies in Anglo-Saxon Literature for Michael Lapidge*, Vol. 1 (pp. 171–193). Toronto: University of Toronto Press.

Siede, M., and Schwinden, L. (2012). *Inscriptiones Graecae Treverenses. Edition der spätantiken und frühchristlichen griechischen Inschriften in Trier mit Übersetzung und Kommentar.* Trier: Wissenschaftlicher Verlag Trier.

Treffort, C. (2004). "Les 'graffitis' sur tables d'autel aux époques pré-romane et romane. Notes à propos des inscriptions de l'autel de Gellone." In X. Barral y Altet and C. Laurason-Rosaz (eds.), *Saint-Guilhem-le-Désert. La fondation de l'abbaye de Gellone. L'autel medieval* (pp. 137–146). Montpellier: Amis de Saint-Guilhem-le-Désert.

Treffort, C. (2009). "La table d'autel à graffiti découverte à Vouneuil-sous-Biard." In C. Sapin (ed.), *Les stucs de l'antiquité tardive de Vouneuil-sous-Biard (Vienne)* (pp. 24–28). Paris: CNRS Editions.

Treffort, C., and Uberti, M. (2010). "Identité des défunts et statut du groupe dans les inscriptions funéraires des anciens dioceses de Poitiers, Saintes et Angoulême entre le IVᵉ et la Xᵉ siècle." In L. Bourgeois (ed.), *Wisigoths et francs autour de la bataille de Vouillé, 507. Actes des XXVIIIe Journées internationals d'archéologie mérovingienne* (pp. 193–214). Saint-Germain-en-Laye: Association française d'archéologie mérovingienne.

Wareman, P. (1986). "Theudechildis Regina." *Classica et Medievalia* 37: 199–201.

PART VI

MEROVINGIAN LANDSCAPES

CHAPTER 27

....

THE ROLE OF THE CITY IN MEROVINGIAN FRANCIA

....

S. T. LOSEBY

IN the 530s, the final subjugation of the Burgundian kingdom and the Ostrogothic concession of Provence left the Merovingians with undisputed mastery over the whole of Roman Gaul and Germany but for Visigothic Septimania and the Breton peninsula. Across much of their dominions, they inherited a network of cities and dependent territories (known as *civitates*) that had emerged substantially unscathed from the political upheavals of the breakdown of the western empire. Whereas the more extensive units of imperial administrative organization in Gaul, the dioceses and provinces, were respected neither during the piecemeal expansions of the "treaty-breaking peoples" in the course of the fifth century (Sidonius, *Ep.* 6.6) nor by the ensuing divisions of the Merovingian polity, the vast majority of existing cities retained both their territorial integrity and their significance as centers of social organization, as embodied in the sphere of ecclesiastical administration by their bishops (see Halfond, Chapter 13, this volume). In some regions, the *civitas* system had required some reconstitution in the aftermath of disruption to the established pattern during the disintegration of Roman authority, as was probably the case along the Channel coast or in the vicinity of the Rhine frontier, where no fifth-century bishops are attested from either of the two provinces of Germania.[1] But the urban network inherited by the Merovingians would prove unsustainable only on the fringes of their power, up in the Alpine valleys, among the small fortress cities of Roman Novempopulana in the foothills of the Pyrenees, or in the wild Breton west, where, in revealing contrast to most of Francia, the ancient framework of cities and their dependent territories came, in obscure circumstances, to be completely superseded (Pietri 1987).

Despite changes such as these, all but 5 of the 113 *civitates* originally included in the *Notitia Galliarum*—a list of Gallic cities by province initially compiled in a secular administrative context around 400—became the seats of bishops during the

Merovingian era.[2] Within this fundamentally stable framework, local economic circumstances, perceived pastoral needs, or specific political circumstances dictated the relocation of a handful of *civitas* capitals within enduring city territories, and the creation of a few additional sees through the subdivision of existing cities (Kaiser 1990). Even so, modifications of this nature had been taking place since the inception of the urban network in the aftermath of the Roman conquests. Their overall effect was far from radical; all but one of the *civitates* among which the heartlands of Gaul had been distributed at the time when the *Notitia* was drawn up were still in existence in the late sixth century. While we can assume that many features of the world of Gregory of Tours would have alarmed a late fourth-century Gallic aristocrat such as Ausonius, its armature of *civitates* would have seemed reassuringly familiar, even if the cities themselves no longer lived up to the (already idealized) depictions of them in the latter's *Order of Famous Cities*.

This widespread pattern of continuity is significant, but one might reasonably wonder how far it is indicative of the conservatism of ecclesiastical organization, as enshrined in a rubric added to the *Notitia Galliarum* that set out its ongoing value as a point of reference in disputes over metropolitan authority (Harries 1978, pp. 29–30), rather than of any contemporary features that distinguished these cities as a category of settlement beyond their possession of a bishop. The prominence of such bishops in Merovingian sources, and our comforting capacity to track their urban locations—and occasional gallivanting—through, in particular, the witness lists of church councils, might similarly be thought to delude us into privileging the former Roman cities over other long-established or newly emerging categories of settlement, whether *vici* ("small towns"), *castra* ("fortresses"), trade hubs, monasteries, or rural royal and aristocratic residences, that may have been coming to serve as equally significant foci of territorial organization, social power, or economic activity (see Bourgeois, Chapter 28, this volume). But in order both to appreciate and to qualify the extent to which cities remained distinct in function or appearance from other categories of settlement, and how their roles and built environments evolved over the Merovingian era, we had best begin with a brief sketch of the Roman legacy on which their inherited preeminence had been based.

THE LATE ROMAN URBAN LEGACY

By the time the Merovingians assumed control of most of Gaul, the heyday of the vast majority of its cities lay in the distant past. Most of them had peaked in the second century, as the efforts of several generations of local elites to buy into the imperial value system and cement their local standing by supporting the development of ordered urban landscapes and equipping them with the array of public buildings and amenities characteristic of Roman civilization, not to mention lavish townhouses for themselves, reached their monumental apogee. The archaeological evidence now provides ample indication that the upkeep of these extensive and expensive built environments began to prove

unsustainable for a mixture of economic and cultural reasons even before the accelerated changes of the third century encouraged a significant shift in the balance of social
power from devolved civic institutions toward an expanded imperial bureaucracy
(Esmonde Cleary 2013, Chapter 3). The majority of Gallic cities therefore went into Late
Antiquity on a long-term trajectory of material decline, whether in terms of their extent,
the steady regression of which is in some measure quantifiable, or, more subjectively, in
the coherence and sophistication of their layouts, as the political culture that had generated their development and guaranteed their maintenance was progressively eroded.
This drift toward more utilitarian expressions of urbanism was gradual and uneven, and
by no means peculiar to Gaul. It had reached a critical stage by the fifth century, when it
was exacerbated (though not instigated) by the gathering political and military crisis of
the western empire. Its various archaeological markers, such as the contraction or fragmentation of built-up areas, the dereliction, spoliation, or colonization of public buildings and spaces, and the progressive deterioration of urban infrastructure, now began to
proliferate (Loseby 2006, with Brogiolo 2011, Chapter 2, for the west in general). Just as a
handful of key imperial political or military centers, notably Trier and Arles, had to
some extent been insulated from these trends by higher levels of investment deriving
from their privileged roles within the imperial system, so it can be hypothesized that the
seats of the rulers of the emerging successor states, most plausibly Visigothic Toulouse,
but probably also Burgundian Lyon and Geneva and Clovis's Paris, benefitted similarly
from royal patronage in the decades around 500. Even so, these various symptoms of
decay came to accumulate, sooner or later, in every late-antique Gallic city.[3] The structured layouts and monumental schemas characteristic of classical Roman urbanism had
thus been widely and substantially degraded long before the Merovingian kingdoms
became established.

   This long-term involution in the built environments of Gallic cities was nevertheless
mitigated, and the form that it took substantially shaped, by the restructuring of late-
antique urban landscapes around city walls and churches that took place in response to
the new and pressing social priorities of security in this world and salvation in the next.
Around a sixth of Gallic cities had already acquired a wall circuit during the early imperial period, usually as a monumental assertion of their legal status as colonies, but most
were only equipped with defenses at some point between the later third and fifth centuries, in a period when the more utilitarian conception of urbanism was already taking
hold. These new ramparts were usually designed to incorporate only part—sometimes
the merest fraction—of the expansive urban landscapes of earlier centuries (Loseby
2006, pp. 75–83). The city walls of Tours, for example, completed around the mid-fourth
century, enclosed some 9 hectares of a settlement which at its peak had extended over
more than eight times that area (Galinié 2007, pp. 355–361), while at Clermont, now
thought to have sprawled across as much as 150 hectares at its later second-century
apogee, the early fifth-century defenses encompassed fewer than 3 hectares.[4] Here the
circuit was centered on the old forum complex, situated atop the *Clarus mons* which
would subsequently lend its name to the city. Elsewhere, however, defensive considerations cut right through the spatial logic of existing layouts, as the architects of similar

fortifications excluded established monumental centers and unceremoniously exploited redundant public buildings and funerary monuments as a convenient source of construction materials. These new city walls, punctuated by monumental gates and numerous towers, with patterns picked out in decorative brickwork, were certainly designed to impress as well as deter (Garmy and Maurin 1996; Guilleux 2000). But their immediate purpose in a context of mounting internal and external insecurity was evidently to protect urban populations (and stockpiled resources) against potential threats, particularly in the increasingly militarized environment of northern Gaul. These precautions were amply justified in the fifth century, when many of these circuits, including the exiguous walls of Clermont, were put repeatedly to the test. Through the Merovingian period too, these defenses not only made cities into strongholds, but loomed over their inhabitants as the dominant secular monumental legacy of the Roman era, both materially and conceptually.

The fortification of each city was the product of a specific historical context (all too often imperfectly known), but one that carried long-lasting topographical consequences. Once established, a wall circuit became a defining, but often dormant feature of the urban landscape: costly to maintain and difficult to defend effectively, but imprudent or infeasible to demolish in light of its potential utility and formidable scale. By contrast, the Christianization of urban power and space was an incremental and polyfocal process that would continue throughout the Merovingian period and beyond. But again the parameters within which it played out on the ground were determined in the fourth and fifth centuries, as the organization of the church was mapped onto the urban framework of the empire. Sooner or later, almost every Gallic city acquired a resident potentate in the person of its bishop, whose pastoral oversight lent a significant new dimension to the concept of the city-territory. In the cities themselves, meanwhile, the bishops began to preside over a fresh wave of Christian building patronage that gradually revolutionized the spatial logic of existing urban landscapes.

This regeneration began slowly, but over the fifth century it gathered momentum as the cult of the saints acquired an increasing grip on the collective spiritual imagination and became the new focus for the munificence of Gallo-Roman elites (Beaujard 2000, Chapter 2; more generally, Brown 1981; on religious architecture, see Chevalier, Chapter 30, this volume). Even as political crisis was reaching its climax in Gaul in the years around 470, this heady combination of piety and patronage inspired a wave of expansive urban building projects. Bishops such as Perpetuus of Tours or Patiens of Lyon embarked on monumental upgrades of the humble shrines of their respective late fourth-century predecessors, Martin and Justus, to render them worthier of the holy power that they were perceived to contain (Sidonius, *Ep.* 2.10; Gregory, *Hist.* 2.14). By around 500, most Gallic cities had not only developed an episcopal complex at their cores, typically consisting of one or more churches, a baptistery, a bishop's residence, and sundry annexes (all located within the walls, where they existed; e.g., Bonnet 2012), but were also coming to be encircled by an array of churches springing up in the sanctified suburban cemeteries around their fringes. These basilicas were built to enshrine the tombs of local martyrs and confessors, some of them long remembered by their communities, while others were more or less serendipitously "invented" to match, particularly as the sixth century progressed (Gauthier 2014, pp. 377–381). It was this relatively new and radical reconceptualization of urban space around the interplay of extramural saintly shrine and intramural episcopal complex that Clovis would exploit on his triumphant progress from St. Martin's church to Tours cathedral after his victory at Vouillé. Indeed, he soon made his own contribution to it by sponsoring the building of the church of the Holy Apostles in Paris for his own burial (Gregory, *Hist.* 2.38, 2.43).

Over the centuries immediately prior to their takeover by the Franks, the cities of Gaul had therefore undergone a threefold transformation that did much to frame Merovingian urbanism. On the one hand, the monumental cityscapes and sophisticated infrastructures of earlier periods were already in an advancing state of deterioration, variously neglected, despoiled, or repurposed, while the regulated layouts formerly characteristic of classical urbanism were slowly falling apart. On the other hand, the recent fortification of most cities, and the progressive Christianization of almost all of them, reflected an adaptation of urban culture and landscapes to contemporary social priorities that would equip most of these centers to retain their significance through the Merovingian period. Finally, although the scanty evidence makes it difficult to assess the formal operation of civic administration in late-antique Gaul, some influential members of the Gallic elite were being driven by the breakdown of the western empire to take a renewed interest in sources of social status and legitimation available at the level of the city, particularly, though not exclusively, within the context of the church (Jussen 2001; Müller 2003). As we shall see, this narrowing of their horizons did not encourage a full-scale resurgence of civic government along earlier imperial lines, since the old city councils were becoming obsolete even in what was left of the empire (Liebeschuetz 2001, Chapters 3–4; Laniado 2002). However, it did ensure that aristocratic competition for power did not simply revolve around the emerging courts of barbarian rulers, but was given renewed impetus at the level of the humble *civitas*.

Urban Powers, Functions, and Landscapes

Any exploration of the changing roles and social dynamics of Gallic cities in the period during and immediately after the breakdown of the western empire is hampered primarily by the deficiencies of the available sources, and further complicated by the fragmentation of power between the multiple Roman and barbarian "successor states" that initially developed out of regional military command structures. While striving in broad terms to exercise their authority through the existing machinery of local government, these nascent kingdoms took different approaches to its maintenance. The Merovingian absorption of the Roman urban legacy was therefore mediated through an intervening phase of diverse political experiences and regional administrative solutions, onto which no uniform system of rule was ever reimposed; Provence, for example, retained the office of patrician, a hangover from Ostrogothic rule, through to the eighth century (Buchner 1933, pp. 86–104). But by the time Gregory of Tours leads us out of this evidential quagmire into a world of fully fledged Frankish rule, it is the *civitates* that emerge as the basic framework through which Merovingian power was projected across Gaul. The perils of taking Gregory's portrayal of Gallic society at face value are as familiar as they are difficult to circumvent, given the absence of other textual evidence of comparable volume or detail. Even so, there is every reason to think that the framing of his representation of Gaul around its cities, while no doubt accentuated by his predominantly urban and episcopal perspective, reflects their paramount administrative and conceptual position within contemporary society.

In part, this predominance had been achieved by default. It derived originally from the virtual disappearance of the upper tiers of Roman territorial organization from the secular sphere along with the empire, and latterly from the sluggishness with which similarly extensive and stable political entities were reconstituted under the Merovingians after they had eliminated rival Gallic regimes.[5] Historians are often tempted to project the *tria regna* of Austrasia, Burgundy, and Neustria back into their accounts of later sixth-century Francia, if only to serve as heuristic labels for contending kingdoms, but the teleology that this implicitly imposes is thoroughly misleading. It lends Gregory's world a political order that it did not as yet possess and, even in the late sixth century, was still by no means guaranteed to eventuate. Admittedly, the fourfold division of the kingdom between Chlothar I's sons in 561 had, in broad terms, aggregated clusters of *civitates* into continuous political territories with the significant exception of the division of Sigibert's share between the Rhineland, the Auvergne, and Provence, which arguably triggered as much internecine conflict as Chilperic's aggrandizement. But, even so, Gregory still conceived the sons and grandsons of Clovis as ruling from their respective urban seats—Paris, Soissons, Orléans, and Reims (*Hist.* 4.22)—over dominions that were accumulations of individual cities. Although the last two of these kingdoms do correspond in embryo to seventh-century Burgundy and Austrasia, Gregory hardly ever resorted to such terminology in describing them, and he would have needed one of his visions to foresee the impending emergence of the Neustrian kingdom.[6] In truth, the sixth-century divisions of Frankish rule between anything from one to four Merovingians were as yet too provisional to be firmly or meaningfully defined in terms of fixed territories. Instead, as the incoherence of the redistribution of Charibert's share of the kingdom between his three surviving brothers on a city-by-city basis in 567 vividly demonstrates, royal authority was conceived and determined at the level of the *civitates*, which, like pieces of Merovingian Lego, could readily be assembled into larger territorial entities, but might just as easily be pulled apart and put back together in different and haphazard ways.[7]

The negotiation of royal power at the level of the individual *civitas* is thus a leitmotif of the contemporary books of Gregory's narrative. It is audible, for example, in the oaths of loyalty sworn, with varying degrees of enthusiasm, by citizens to kings, in the reading of the Treaty of Andelot with its detailed allocations of control over specific cities, and at its most inescapable in the city-by-city clangor of civil war. The determination of allegiance on the basis of individual *civitates* made for political instability precisely because it was so mutable and open to challenge. This was particularly evident at critical moments when cities changed hands, as, for example, on the death of a ruler such as Charibert, or the arrival of an aspiring Merovingian such as Gundovald, or along the faultlines between conflicting kingdoms, one of which was straddled, to Gregory's discomfort and despair, by the *civitas* of Tours. The concomitant advantages of this fissile system of rule lay in the administrative convenience for rulers of using cities and their dependent territories, as under the empire, as mechanisms through which resources could be extracted. But the novelty was that the *civitates* were now employed as flexible units of account not only in allocating such resources—supposedly equally—among themselves, but in allocating them in endowment to their wives and children.[8] For the first century of Frankish rule at least, the Merovingian kingdoms were made of their cities.

In ruling through the cities, the Merovingians arrived at a hybrid arrangement that retained, in simplified form, the ranks, offices, and associated machinery of late Roman provincial military administration but, in the absence of functioning provinces, brought them to bear at the level of the *civitates*. While the kings continued to extract taxes and services through the cities, the allocation and delivery of these obligations accordingly passed from the competence of civic administrations into the hands of centrally appointed officials and their underlings. In Gregory's day, the most significant of these burdens was still the land tax (Kaiser 1979; Goffart 1982). His strident hostility to such impositions makes it difficult to gain a sense of their continuing frequency or scale, but it is revealing that some of his fellow bishops remained more concerned to mitigate the impact of such charges than to denounce them outright. In 589, for example, Maroveus of Poitiers successfully petitioned Childebert II to update the tax registers in order to redistribute the burden more equitably among his community. However, when the royal officials who had carried out the reassessment moved on, perhaps heartened by their efforts, to Tours, Gregory dismissed their books as obsolete and treated them to a lengthy but selective history of his city's tax exemption, originally granted by Chlothar I out of respect for St. Martin; he promptly had his resistance vindicated, first by divine judgment and then by royal confirmation.[9] Anecdotes such as these confirm that a bureaucratic, document-based framework for the collection of taxes did continue to exist in the late sixth century. But they also illustrate how it was inequitably and unevenly applied, both within and between *civitates*, whether because the necessary information about landholding was becoming increasingly outdated, because powerful interest groups—notably Franks and clerics—were looking to avoid liability, or because more substantive attempts to overhaul the existing tax regime were prone to generate fierce opposition, such as the riot of the people of Limoges against the imposition of Chilperic's *discriptiones novas* in 579 (*Hist.* 5.28). These were all problems that were only going to increase with time. Even so, although the tax system was creaking under the strains of becoming too outdated to work and too contentious to repair, it continued in the late sixth century to be administered through the *civitates*.

The labor services that kings extracted through cities were in all probability grounded similarly in late Roman precedents, though the few surviving references to the continuing imposition of *publicae actiones* are more concerned to grumble generically about such burdens than to specify their content (e.g., Conc. Orléans 541, c.13; *Vita Balthildis* 6). They included a duty to participate in local peacekeeping duties (Murray 1988), but also a more novel obligation to perform military service. The precise origin of the latter development is again lost in the evidential void that separates the professional armies, imperial or federate, of the late empire from the city-based levies that routinely make up a significant component of the Frankish military in Gregory's narrative, which attests to such musters from a swathe of nineteen *civitates* (or fractions thereof) extending across Gaul from Bayeux to Toulouse.[10] The militarization of Gallic society over the intervening period provides one necessary (if perhaps not altogether sufficient) explanation of this shift (Esders 2014), which was presumably achieved through the extrapolation of existing peacekeeping or defensive duties to incorporate periods of active service (see Sarti, Chapter 12, this volume). No normative sources exist to explain the precise nature, application, or duration of the new obligation, but the anecdotal evidence suggests that it initially applied to the free population at large. In principle, it fell alike upon local Gallo-Roman grandees, such as the *magni viri* of the Auvergne who were swept away in the waters of the Rhône when sent against Arles by Sigibert in 568 (*Hist.* 4.30), and upon the poor and those in the service of the church, whom the kings sought to sanction for their failures to comply (e.g., *Hist.* 5.26, 6.12, 7.42; cf. more widely *Lex Ribuaria* 65, 1–2). It is probably significant that although no *civitas*-based musters are mentioned prior to the above humiliation of the magnates of Clermont, Gregory takes their existence entirely for granted. In conjunction with the absence of evidence for the existence of similar levies either from cities in the former Burgundian and Ostrogothic kingdoms or from the core Frankish territories in the northeast of the kingdom, this may suggest that they came into being earlier in the sixth century, as Merovingian power expanded southwestwards into regions with few resident Franks, but functioning fiscal machinery. But whatever its origin, the grafting of this military obligation onto existing frameworks for demanding services through the cities seems clear.

The responsibility for seeing that these royal demands for taxes and services from the populations of the *civitates* were met no longer fell upon the city councils of the imperial era, but upon a single, centrally appointed official, the count of the city (*comes civitatis*), and his subordinate staff. The initial development of this office is again obscure, but it seems to have originated in a late imperial innovation that, in a context of political emergency, dispensed with the conventional late-antique separation of civil and military powers to establish a designated official with executive authority in key centers such as Marseille, and perhaps Trier (Claude 1964, pp. 4–11; Müller 2003, pp. 67–80).[11] This creation of a direct chain of command between ruler and city, shortcircuiting intervening layers of bureaucracy and moribund or malfunctioning local administrations, caught the *Zeitgeist*, and it was apparently embraced by several of the successor states. It can be difficult at first, however, to distinguish city-based counts from other holders of the generic title of *comes*, who can rarely be tied to individual cities.[12] Nevertheless, we can tell from Gregory's incidental references that Autun had its own count by the late fifth century, Clermont in the 520s and Tours by the 550s, and in total he mentions such offi- cials from twenty-three different *civitates* scattered through every part of Frankish Gaul except for Provence (Weidemann 1982, vol. 1, pp. 63–80). It therefore seems reasonable to infer that over the course of the sixth century the *comes civitatis* (or, in the northeast, his vernacular equivalent, the *grafio*: Murray 1986) had become the lynchpin for the mediation of royal authority through the cities. It fell to these counts and their ill- attested subordinates to administer justice and maintain local order on the king's behalf, and to supervise the rendering of revenues and services from city-territories to the crown (see the summary in Murray 2016, pp. 221–223). We catch glimpses of Count Macco of Poitiers, for example, striving to suppress Waddo's outlaw sons, making his annual trip to court to pay the sums due to the fisc, and summarily putting down the revolt in the Sainte-Croix nunnery once he had covered his back by securing Childebert's written authority to do so. In microcosm, Macco was thereby exhibiting the faithfulness and diligence that a surviving royal formula of appointment expected of such officials (*Hist.* 10.21, 10.15; Marculf 1.8).

In fulfilling such tasks, the dutiful count was obliged to work alongside the local bishop, who was based alongside him in the city (where, like boxers, they seem often to have resided in opposite corners of the wall circuit: Brühl 1975). Their territorial sphere was coterminous, and their responsibilities routinely and variously over- lapped, whether formally, as in the judicial sphere, or informally, through their mutual obligation to work for the good of their communities. Although canonically his elec- tion was arrived at through local consensus, the bishop, like the count, was effectively a royal official in that his appointment was subject to the king's approval, bestowed in exchange for gifts and services past or promised. This process came increasingly to favor candidates drawn from leading local families or parachuted in from careers in royal service, who often came from the same gene pool as the counts. But while in practice bishops were similarly political figures, in principle they answered to a higher lord. In working for the well-being of their flocks in this world and their salvation in the next, they could draw locally, alongside their judicial powers, upon their control of liturgical observances, spiritual sanctions, and the steadily increasing material resources of their churches. They could also rely collectively on a corporate identity expressed through the canons of church councils in which they repeatedly reiterated their concerns for the weaker members of society and the rights of the church, some- times, as at Mâcon in 585 or Paris in 614, in direct counterpoint to royal edicts (Heinzelmann 1988; Gauthier 2000; Halfond 2010). Whereas counts could be hired and fired by kings at will, bishops were appointed for life, barring their conviction by their peers of a serious offense, or else their murder, which could prove somewhat easier to arrange (Fouracre 2003). In the words that Gregory puts into his mouth to damn him, Chilperic, after denouncing the foibles of individual bishops and lament- ing the rise of church wealth at the expense of the fisc, supposedly asserted that "no one at all rules except the bishops; our honor perishes and has passed to the bishops of the cities" (*Hist.* 6.46).

Whether or not Chilperic really made this protestation, the supremacy of Gallic bishops over their cities has been widely emphasized, not only by our sources, often hagiographic in nature and generally far more sympathetic than the king (see Kreiner, Chapter 24, this volume), but also in the strand of modern scholarship that has sought to reify their powers into a particular system of civic lordship known as *Bischofsherrschaft* or *bischöflichen Stadtherrschaft*. This is generally assumed to have originated in the peculiarly Gallic phenomenon of the fifth-century colonization of the episcopate by scions of late Roman senatorial families. Whether they usurped (Prinz 1974), were delegated (Heinzelmann 1976, 1988; Durliat 1996), or shaped to their own ideals and advantage (Jussen 1995, 2001) the considerable rights and responsibilities originally vested in the role by the Roman state, their takeover of episcopal office would then have bequeathed to their Merovingian successors a combination of institutionally grounded and socially constructed powers that equipped them to lord it over their communities to an extent unparalleled in other western successor states.

This paradigm is variously problematic, not least in this assumption of a precocious aristocratic monopolization of episcopal office that endowed it with ready-made social and cultural capital. At least a third of the bishops of the Merovingian era are sadly nonentities, at least to us, in that the memorials that they left in their own cities, to borrow Gregory's touching phrase (*Hist.* 8.39), have not survived. Perhaps as many as another third live on only through the bare record of their names in conciliar subscriptions and episcopal lists. Finally, among the remaining bishops of whom we have some substantive knowledge, only a very small (and by the nature of the sources probably overrepresented) proportion are demonstrably of noble, let alone senatorial origin (Patzold 2010, 2014). In short, the Gallic episcopate, like that of Africa or Italy (Eck 1983; Gasparri 2008), is likely, at least at first, to have been composed of a mixed bag of grandees, courtiers, worthy citizens, career clerics, and holy men. Many of these appointees, unlike Ruricius of Limoges, could not have claimed to be lending prestige to their cities by taking office, but were acquiring it from their newfound dignity (Ruricius, *Ep.* 2.33, snubbing Caesarius of Arles; cf. Fortunatus, *Carm.* 3.23).

Most Gallic bishops, therefore, were probably not as predestined to urban supremacy by their elite backgrounds as the historiography has tended to assume. Even so, the powers into which they came upon entering office were considerable, and royal oversight of their elections came over time to benefit rich and well-connected candidates. In bringing their authority to bear upon their communities, however, bishops still faced the problem of their lack of coercive power, which, when not miraculously supplied by God and his saints, was presumably provided by the counts. Such routine cooperation rarely proves newsworthy, though one vivid, if extreme exception is provided by Macco's decisive intervention in putting down the Sainte-Croix nunnery revolt in Poitiers after the failed attempts of the local bishop to mobilize the community and of his episcopal peers to mediate (*Hist.* 10.15; see James, Chapter 11, this volume). More frequently, however, our sources depict bishops and counts in structural and stereotyped opposition, particularly when showing how episcopal obligations to the unfortunate could oblige them to obstruct the mundane efforts of secular officials to do their duty, for example by resuscitating a criminal sentenced to hang by a count "more cruel than any beast" (*Vita Amandi* 14), or by employing the explosive charge of episcopal *virtus* to release captives by blowing the doors off prisons ("with a great bang": *Vita Eligii* 2.15; in general, see Wiesheu 2001). We might assume, nevertheless, that their mutual obligations to rulers and complementary moral and coercive powers over their communities would generally have fostered a less dramatic working relationship between the two officials, particularly in the judicial sphere, where the temporary resolution of the dispute between Sichar and Chramnesind shows how pragmatic collaboration could supervene over normative procedures.[13]

When the relationship between bishop and count did irretrievably break down, it was usually because its latent potential for conflict was compounded by personal antipathies. This is visible, for example, in Gregory's vituperative denunciation of the upstart Leudast (*Hist.* 5.48–49), the family rivalries that lurked behind generations of jockeying for comital and episcopal power in Clermont (Wood 1983), or the vengeance wrought from beyond the grave by Bishop Heraclius upon Count Nantinus of Angoulême, burnt black on his deathbed (*Hist.* 5.36). Most revealing of all, perhaps, are the similar tensions that frequently arose in the late sixth century when a city changed hands and its new ruler inherited a bishop whose political allegiances lay elsewhere, as epitomized by the trials and tribulations of Bishop Theodore in the divided city of Marseille, where he was repeatedly harassed by the local secular authorities and arraigned by Guntram over his dubious loyalties, but never convicted or deposed (*Hist.* 6.11, 6.24, 8.12, 8.20). Such episodes illustrate, paradoxically, both the potential predicament and the relative security of a bishop's position within his city. In Gregory's mind, there could be only one winner, at least ultimately, in this type of intraurban power struggle, and he took pains to emphasize Theodore's virtue and explicitly to remind his audience of the respect for bishops that the grisly fate of Nantinus should inspire in them. But he knew from bitter experience that the "pastoral power" held by bishops over their communities was always open to challenge (P. Brown 2012, Chapters 28–29).

The oversight of urban communities by two pivotal figures, both of whom were in effect appointed by the crown, illustrates the ongoing significance of cities within the Merovingian polity even as it marks a radical departure from the civic institutions and magistracies to which much local authority had routinely been devolved under the empire. Persons of superior standing do nevertheless remain visible on urban stages in the assorted guises of *maiores, seniores, priores, honorati, magnifici*, and sometimes mere *cives*. Such individuals seem, moreover, to play an influential role within their communities, often collectively and in conjunction with the bishop, at moments of ceremonial consensus or political crisis.[14] The qualifications for inclusion in this urban leadership group are never transparent, but this sporadic prominence of its members is wholly consistent with developments in other western successor states. In the eastern empire, too, a similar shift in civic government during the later fifth and sixth centuries from formally constituted city councils to informal coteries of notables, essentially leading local landowners operating under episcopal oversight, had come steadily to be enshrined in law (Laniado 2014). Even so, in Francia the collections of formulae of the sixth to early ninth century that survive from various cities meanwhile continued to include provisions for registering documents in municipal archives (*gesta municipalia*) that called for the participation of old-style city councils and an associated cast of late Roman municipal officials in an elaborate formal procedure. The application of these templates in actual transactions is confirmed, moreover, by surviving documents that adhere broadly to these norms, such as a donation by the bishop of Poitiers to Philibert's new monastery at Noirmouter in the late 670s, witnessed by seven individuals who style themselves as *curiales*.[15] Unless we posit the existence of two discrete categories of city-based notables, it seems reasonable to infer that the *maiores* (and their ilk) of the narrative sources and the *curiales* of the formulae and charters were essentially the same people. To explain why similar municipal officials and institutions scarcely feature in the narrative sources, or for that matter elsewhere in the formulae, one might then suppose that for the specific purposes of registering or witnessing documents this small elite group within the *civitas* community assumed a set of personal and corporate identities particular to that discourse, which in other spheres of their activity had been superseded.[16]

The privileged civic actors denoted by this confusing superfluity of terms lack any clearly defined roles other than the socially significant task of document registration. Like their eastern counterparts, they need not have been permanent urban residents, but probably maintained townhouses for use during the major religious festivals which they and the clergy were notionally expected to keep with the bishop in the city, or the saintly feast days with which kings tended to synchronize their arrivals in cities and merchants their markets.[17] Their influence meant, nonetheless, that the exercise of episcopal authority over them could be more a matter of continuous negotiation than a guaranteed right. In looking to live up to his billing as the "hope of the flock," "father of the people," and "lover of the city," the practiced epithets with which Fortunatus introduced the new shepherd of Tours to his flock in 573 (*Carm.* 5.3, with Roberts 2009, pp. 106–122, and more widely, Coates 2000), a bishop such as Gregory could exploit his family and high-level political connections, orchestrate saints' cults, build new churches, and restore old ones. However, he had to be constantly mindful of internal opposition in doing so (Van Dam 1993, Chapter 2).

One of Gregory's first acts in Tours was to establish an oratory in the bishop's house to associate his family's saints with St. Martin. Its dedication was attended by a large group of white-robed clerics and deacons, the illustrious order of *cives honorati*, and lots of lesser folk, to whom Gregory explicated a frightening flash of saintly power (*GC* 20). But some of the very citizens and clergy who participated in this ritualized celebration of urban consensus under episcopal authority, reported by Gregory in uncharacteristically formal terms, were presumably among those who over the next twenty years sought to undermine his position by supporting the villainous official Pelagius, handing over tax books to Childebert's collectors, and, more perilously, exploiting the wider political situation to conspire with Count Leudast to seek their bishop's deposition (*Hist.* 8.40, 9.30, 5.48–49). In acting as "defender of the people," to appropriate another of Fortunatus's stock of episcopal epithets (*Carm.* 3.5), the prudent bishop also had to be ready to defend himself against rival sources of urban power by whatever means was most appropriate to his background and personality. By his own account, at least, Gregory relied primarily on saintly vindication. His contemporary Badegisel of Le Mans, an ex-mayor of the palace fast-tracked into the episcopate, perhaps played to his strengths in focusing instead on aggressive land management, battering his citizens in court, and performing enigmatic *militias saeculares*. Such "savage" behavior earned him Gregory's contempt, and apparently cost him his place in the later *Acts of the Bishops of Le Mans*. It nevertheless serves to confirm how episcopal primacy over urban communities was something that had to be fought for, and could be pursued through a variety of strategies (*Hist.* 6.9, 8.39; Weidemann 2002, vol. 1, pp. 62–63).

This uneasy primacy of bishop over leading citizens, however it was achieved, made for a very different species of civic politics from that of earlier centuries. Even so, as has been persuasively argued in regard to the contemporary cities of the eastern empire, it was not necessarily a weaker one (Whittow 1990), albeit for somewhat different reasons. In Merovingian Gaul, as we have seen, the simplification of the political structure had devolved more power down to the level of the cities than before. Personal identification with one's *civitas* community was also regularly and variously reinforced, regardless of the character of municipal administration, by shared experience and collective action. The inhabitants of each *civitas* were encouraged to come into town for major religious occasions, but also prayed and processed together according to the rhythms of their city's particular festal calendar, which regularly incorporated commemorations of the local "special patrons" buried in the city's suburban cemeteries, as well as supplementary rituals of communal expiation in times of crisis (Hen 1995, pp. 82–120). Leading citizens and clerics sat in court together (*Hist.* 5.48), and it was their voices that spoke loudest in episcopal elections, even if a hard-won civic consensus could still be summarily trumped by royal intervention. The people of Tours, Limoges, or Poitiers had long paid their taxes together, or sought to avoid doing so, and now they were required to fight alongside each other too, often against the inhabitants of neighboring *civitates* in rival kingdoms. During vacuums in royal power, they even took up arms to that end without waiting to be asked (*Hist.* 7.2). In confirmation of its allegiance, moreover, each *civitas* was bound to a particular king by an oath, extracted by the count from all inhabitants regardless of their ethnicity (Marculf 1.40; Esders 2005, 2016, pp. 458–460; see Rio, Chapter 23, this volume). The surviving formula for its administration envisages the holding of assemblies in cities, villages, and fortresses (*civitates, vici et castra*), but in our narrative sources it is generally the cities that feature as the decisive settings for the formal determination of local loyalties. These situations offer perhaps the clearest signs of the *civitates* functioning as political communities, but also the strict limits on their capacity for self-determination.

Such episodes tend to be described in detail only on the contentious occasions when existing or aspirant rulers demanded an oath of allegiance from *civitates* with established loyalties to other kings. This was particularly the case in the aftermath of Chilperic's death, when Gundovald laid claim to various southwestern *civitates*, and Guntram looked to assert his authority over cities that had been held, rightfully or not, by his late brother. In general, the inhabitants of these various cities, headed by the bishop and unspecified citizens, were disinclined to change their sworn allegiances and strove with varying resolution to resist. But what they lacked was the military means to put their wishes into effect. The citizens of Toulouse made ready to oppose Gundovald, rallied by Bishop Magnulf, but backed down upon sight of his army. Since Magnulf persisted in his insubordination, he was beaten up and exiled (*Hist.* 7.27). When Guntram sent in his counts to take the oath from Tours and Poitiers, both cities wanted to renew their former ties to Childebert II, but the king deployed the *civitas* levy from Bourges, whose plundering soon led Tours to capitulate and to advise the "bishop and citizens" of Poitiers to do the same, at least for now. The Poitevins were eventually coerced, in the absence of military support, into swearing an oath to Guntram, but soon broke it again, only for repeated ravagings to compel their reluctant submission; Bishop Maroveus was held responsible for their infidelity and had to ransom himself and his people (*Hist.* 7.12–13; 7.24). The citizens of Angers, loyal to Chilperic's infant son Chlothar, successfully drove out Guntram's nominee as count, only for him to come back with a duke (and presumably an army) to reassert his authority, even though regional resistance to Guntram's nominees continued (*Hist.* 8.18; 8.42). In these and similar cases, we see the familiar direct relationship between rulers and cities, occasionally brokered by individual magnates, but not by any intervening political structures. In short, it is clear that the *civitas* community remained a highly significant element in the late sixth-century *Spielräume*, the fields of action and perception within which identity was negotiated through social practice, and represented by the likes of Gregory and Fortunatus.[18] But while a city's leaders might hope to choose their political destiny, they lacked any effective means of resistance to royal power, and they were thinking strictly within the confines of Merovingian rule, not aspiring to go it alone.

In the later Merovingian period, this civic *Spielraum* gradually diminished in importance.[19] The secular significance of the cities had derived, as we have seen, from the transplantation of late-Roman provincial military administration to the *civitas* level, where it had formally superseded local curial government, but not the informal operation of the cities as political communities. This hybrid arrangement was a viable solution to the problem of exploiting the Roman legacy in the absence of an imperial superstructure, but by the seventh century it was coming to outlive its usefulness, and thereby its grounding in the cities. One clear symptom of its degradation was the managed decay of the land tax, which was logistically difficult to administer, politically impossible to reform, and no longer required to fund a professional army or salaried bureaucracy (Wickham 2005, pp. 110–115). Franks and clerics, for their different reasons, resisted liability, while the kings themselves hollowed the system out through grants of immunities to individuals, churches, and communities. Chlothar II effectively formalized existing trends by ruling out fiscal innovations, thereby ending any prospect of substantive reform, and by edging closer to conceding blanket exemptions from public dues to all the lands of favored individuals and institutions (Goffart 1982, pp. 17–19). Although taxation would linger on piecemeal to the end of the Merovingian period, it lost its systemic character. As such exactions came increasingly to be collected by lay and clerical landowners from their own estates, they became divorced from the city-based framework through which they had been imposed. When royal grants of immunity begin to survive from the mid-seventh century onward, it is telling that they concentrate not on rewarding the past and prospective services of their recipients with superfluous exemptions from fixed taxation, but on the granting of judicial privileges. In particular, these featured the exclusion of the count and his staff from the extraction of services, the exercise of jurisdiction, and the maintenance of order on the lands of the beneficiaries (Murray 2010).

The proliferation of such concessions redistributed public authority without necessarily weakening it, but it did much to dissolve the judicial and territorial competence of the count. That office, as we have seen, had effectively been invented to broker the relationship between rulers and cities, but it was now becoming superseded by a system of social organization structured around lay and ecclesiastical landholding. Meanwhile, in some cities at least, the count was subordinated to the authority of the bishop. Although counts are still visible in later seventh- and eighth-century sources, it becomes more difficult to tie them to specific cities, and especially to imagine that they were still managing a system of royal administration integrated through the *civitates* (Claude 1964, pp. 25–32). When the Carolingians sought to reinvigorate such a system, they kept the office of count and invested it with similar responsibilities. Even so, they radically revised their expectations of its holders and anchored it not in the *civitates* but in their constituent *pagi*, the subsidiary units of territorial organization that were already becoming increasingly prominent in later Merovingian sources.[20]

It is no coincidence that the gradual erosion of the administrative significance of the *civitates* at the local level occurred alongside the belated consolidation of the shape-shifting sixth-century kingdoms into more stable political entities. This development was enduringly (if somewhat fortuitously) cemented during the pivotal reign of Chlothar II, and was given scope to mature through the ensuing half-century or so of relative internal stability. In marked contrast to Gregory of Tours, later Merovingian narrative sources routinely think in terms of the larger territorial frameworks of the *tria regna*, Austrasia, Burgundy, and Neustria. These entities often managed with only one king, but continued to form three distinct kingdoms and magnate communities, as highlighted, for example, at the accession of Childeric II in 675 (*Vita Balthildis* 5, *Passio Leudegarii I* 7). One illustration of the new dominance of these conceptions is that the military levies of individual *civitates*, so prominent in Gregory's accounts of internecine Frankish warfare, all but vanish from our sources, replaced by the less ambiguous struggles of Austrasians versus Neustrians.[21] Whether their disappearance should be ascribed to changes in Merovingian military organization (see Sarti, Chapter 12, this volume), and therefore regarded as a further indication of a decline in the extraction of obligations through the framework of the *civitates*, or whether it is symptomatic of a wider cultural shift in the assumptions of our sources and their audiences about the appropriate frameworks in which to represent such warfare, the implications are not dissimilar. The *civitas* was now being definitively superseded as the dominant context for the exercise or representation of collective identity by the centralization of political practice around the royal courts. In exchange for magnate engagement, kings now often delegated their local rights directly to lay or ecclesiastical landowners, the wealthier of whom frequently held estates across numerous city-territories (Fouracre 1998). The bonds between central and local authorities were no longer forged through the cities and the rusting fiscal infrastructure inherited from the empire, but through the office- and landholding of the aristocrats themselves.

The magnetic pull of the royal courts did not, however, lead to the emergence of a firmly-established Frankish capital, as it would in Visigothic Spain or Lombard Italy, or even to the lasting dominance of particular centers within the *tria regna*. Instead, the Merovingians seem increasingly to have given up on cities as privileged settings for representation of their power. The sixth-century kings can generally be seen, with some variations of emphasis (Loseby 1998, pp. 262–263), to gravitate between their appointed *sedes* (or a favored alternative) and a couple of estates in its immediate vicinity. While they often transacted the business of their kingdoms from the nearby estates, they still assigned a certain symbolic value to cities for public appearances and ritual occasions, and sponsored the building of churches in their suburbs. Chilperic in particular, with his persistent designs on Paris, and his provision of circuses both there and at Soissons (*Hist.* 5.17), exhibits some interest in urban ideologies of rule, perhaps inspired as much by the contemporary efforts of Leuvigild in Spain as by past or present imperial models. But if Chilperic ever dreamed of creating a Frankish equivalent of Toledo, or even founding his own Chilpopolis, his son Chlothar II, whose sole rule was inaugurated by the holding of magnate assemblies in Paris, soon shifted the focus of his regime to the various royal villas round about. His eventual preference for Clichy and the nearby shrine of St-Denis was consolidated under Dagobert I, and although this did not last, the disassociation of Merovingian rule from cities endured. Royal power continued thereafter to be exercised from a shifting array of rural palaces, and courts hardly ever assembled in urban settings (Barbier 1990; see Hen, Chapter 10, this volume). The ideological significance of cities in Merovingian rule had never been pronounced, but it disappeared during much the same period as the role of the *civitates* within secular administration fell into decline. In this case, moreover, the contrast with the consolidation of royal urban centers in other western successor states is strikingly direct.

These various developments still left cities with their bishops, whose standing within society was hardly diminished by a consolidation of political culture around office- and landholding. By the seventh century, the Frankish church had accumulated control over vast estates (Wood 2013). Meanwhile, its leaders enjoyed privileged status as partners of the crown in leading their wandering flocks toward the sheepfold of the lord (Marculf 1.5), in many cases after honing their talents and building lifelong connections at the royal courts. The epitome of such prelates is Desiderius of Cahors, whose correspondence and later *Life* reveal him in such formidable command of all aspects of the spiritual and practical management of his see, from votive crowns to wooden waterpipes, that we can easily forget how he only assumed office after his brother and predecessor Rusticus, a career cleric, was murdered by members of his own community (*Vita Desiderii* 8, 11; Durliat 1979). The death of Rusticus is left unexplained, but the similar fates suffered by several later seventh-century bishops were often the result of a toxic combination of court politics and internal *civitas* rivalries that in the *Lives* of Leudegar of Autun or

Praiectus of Clermont seems remarkably little altered, unless in its deadly consequences, from the problems that Gregory or Theodore had faced in their cities a century earlier (*Passio Leudegarii I, Passio Praiecti*). But if the power of the bishops and the political risks attached to its exercise were now arguably greater than ever, the integrity of episcopal authority over their city-territories was meanwhile being weakened.

Bishops had long faced difficulties in exercising spiritual and managerial prerogatives over the churches of their dioceses in the face of lay proprietary interests (Pietri 2005). These problems were greatly accentuated by the seventh-century monastic boom, especially in northern Francia (Atsma 1976), which saw favored communities, urban and rural, obtain royal privileges that restricted episcopal control over them or removed it altogether (Ewig 1979a). This "deterritorialization" of episcopal authority (Lauwers and Ripart 2007) would prove neither as extensive nor as irreversible as the breaking of the bonds between count and *civitas*, but it may have contributed to an erosion of the distinction between the "pastoral power" of the bishops and the authority wielded by other leading landowners and officeholders. In the early eighth century, this blurring of boundaries culminated in some bishops behaving much like secular magnates in those areas where central authority was temporarily weak: bearing arms, leading military expeditions, leaving their spiritual responsibilities to others, and even holding sees in plurality, which would have been inconceivable a century earlier (Ewig 1979b; Kaiser 1981). The so-called episcopal republics that fleetingly emerged, though superficially based on the *civitates*, were really products of this secularized and suprapastoral conception of the bishop's lordship. Although they proved short-lived, when the Carolingians strove to reassert episcopal authority within their dioceses, they would do so primarily by rebuilding personal ties between the bishops and their clergy rather than by reasserting fundamental principles of territorial administration over fragmented lordships.

Finally, although extensive discussion of the built environments of Merovingian cities lies beyond the scope of this chapter, it is worth emphasizing how little either the projection of royal power through the *civitates* or the eventual rise of the politics of land altered the trajectories of a generalized decay in urban landscapes and their restructuring around walls and churches which, as we saw, were already well under way before Clovis rode triumphantly into Tours. Specifically, the ongoing performance of the secular administrative functions of cities now required little more than a "palace" for the count, storage facilities for goods or documents, and probably the upkeep of a public space for assemblies and markets. More generally, the archaeological evidence shows how urban environments continued to become progressively more discontinuous and polycentric, as clusters of settlement, generally more basic in form and conception than the urban housing of earlier periods, were interspersed with areas given over to cultivation or left derelict, as in cities throughout the post-Roman west (e.g., Galinié 1997; more generally Brogiolo 2011, pp. 131–146). The structures of earlier periods remained an inescapable feature of these landscapes, but while some were passively left to the ravages of time, others were vigorously robbed of their materials or adapted to new uses: amphitheaters and theaters transformed into fortresses or filled up with housing, basilicas, baths, and temples converted into churches, warehouses turned into monasteries, public spaces or private houses occupied by craftsmen or cluttered with refuse, and street frontages preserved for centuries as estate boundaries. The new form of urbanism had limited use for the values of the old, but took every advantage of the solidity of its buildings and the utility of their materials.

Despite their omnipresence, our written sources show scant regard for these relics of the Roman past unless they happened to provide a context for a demonstration of holy power or the construction of saintly memory (Effros 2001). Moreover, the extent to which the Merovingians sought, as the Ostrogoths had done, to control the transformation of the classical monumental legacy is almost entirely hypothetical. Although episcopal care for urban communities could extend to flood defense, water-supply, or house-building projects (e.g., Fortunatus, *Carm.* 3.10, 9.9; Gregory, *Hist.* 5.45; Desiderius, *Ep.* 1.14), we lack any direct confirmation that they or other public authorities, such as the counts or notional municipal administrations, were assigned regular responsibility for building regulation or infrastructural maintenance, or that their rulers took any interest in such matters. The notable exceptions were the city walls, the one element of the late Roman secular monumental legacy routinely acknowledged by our sources, which retained an abiding, if intermittent, relevance. But even their upkeep, probably another of the labor services that could be demanded of the local population, has largely to be inferred from the frequency of siege warfare. One might assume that such circuits usually existed in a state of benign neglect, hastily redressed in times of danger, as implied by an instruction from Chilperic to his dukes and counts to withdraw to their cities and repair their defenses in anticipation of attack (*Hist.* 6.41). Similarly, the wall-building projects undertaken by two seventh-century bishops, Desiderius of Cahors and Leudegar of Autun, probably did not entail extensive new building, but rather the restoration of existing circuits or even the provision within cities of small defended enclosures, a precursor of later developments. The potential gulf between the vaunting tone of hagiographical descriptions of episcopal building activity and its material reality would be emphasized if the ditch and bank recently excavated around the cathedral complex at Autun is, as seems plausible, identifiable with the defenses built by Leudegar (*Vita Desiderii*, 16–17; *Passio Leudegarii I*, 2; Balcon-Berry and Berry 2014, pp. 196–198).

Meanwhile, both inside and outside the notional perimeter of the walls, churches continued to proliferate. In contrast to the paucity of our information about other types of building, the textual and (to a lesser extent) archaeological evidence attests to the likely existence of over 800 urban and suburban religious establishments by the end of the Merovingian period, now systematically catalogued in the invaluable *Topographie chrétienne* series (Gauthier et al. 1986–2014). These numbers do not seem all that impressive at first glance when distributed between well over 100 centers, but they must significantly underrepresent the sum total of Christian urban building activity. Those cities about which we happen to be better informed (sometimes through a sequence of incidental references, but more often thanks to the survival of a single revealing source) had typically accumulated a dozen or more churches and monasteries by the middle of the eighth century, and, in the case of Metz, as many as forty-four.[22] These foundations varied immensely in their scale and sophistication, and some of them proved ephemeral.

Even so, they cumulatively demonstrate the enduring attraction of the cities as focal points of monumental patronage, often provided and orchestrated by bishops, but also forthcoming from members of their clergy, from kings in their favored centers, or from pious lay donors such as Duke Launebod and his wife Beretrude in Toulouse (Fortunatus, *Carm.* 2.8), or the wealthy widow Eustadiola, who established a monastery and three churches in Bourges in the mid-seventh century (*Vita Eustadiolae* 3, 8).

The spatial distribution of these foundations in and around each city was the product of sundry local variables. In broad terms, nevertheless, it perpetuated and consolidated the distinction that had emerged in the fifth century between an intramural episcopal complex and extramural saintly shrines, though later in the Merovingian period this came to be complicated by the proliferation of monasteries, with their sometimes substantial enclosures, both inside and outside the city walls (Gaillard and Sapin 2012). Any centripetal effects of such defenses on the experience or conception of urban space were therefore broken down by the ongoing pull of churches which were often located at some remove from the ramparts and in some cases would eventually generate discrete settlement nuclei. The outcomes were loose and fragmented urban landscapes that had lost the inherent coherence of their Roman predecessors. They could nevertheless be rationalized into a whole that was at once conceptually symbolic and topographically realistic by invoking the triple ring of protection afforded urban communities by intramural bishop, city walls, and suburban churches (e.g., Gregory, *VP* 4.2, 17.4), or momentarily knitted together on feast days by liturgical processions between central and peripheral shrines. But while these were undoubtedly impressive and important occasions in the life of each *civitas* community, their splendor is likely to have derived more from the associated ephemera of bells and banners, or the dress and demeanor of the participants, than from the crumbling and discontinuous landscapes through which they moved, which are assigned remarkably little value by our sources. The gleaming roofs or perpetual illumination of the churches that shone out at either end of these routes should not blind us to the grimy and disheveled realities of Merovingian urbanism, as revealed by the archaeological evidence from cities such as Tours.[23] Instead, it was probably the very brightness of the contrast that made cult sites seem like anticipations of the heavenly glory to come.

Even so, notwithstanding their material simplification, most Merovingian cities remained distinct from other central places—monastic powerhouses of prayer, specialist production centers, royal palaces and aristocratic estate centers, and the dynamic but unstable emporia—because of their greater concentration of functions and their continuous and multivalent associations with power.[24] Their enviable locations on road and, especially, riverine axes of communication left them well placed to act as exchange hubs and market centers for surplus production, particularly once rural economies began to revive, and to provide the range of specialist services to their hinterlands that distinguishes them archaeologically from other categories of settlement (Claude 1985; Henning 2007; for minting, see also Strothmann, Chapter 35, this volume; for rural communities, see Peytremann, Chapter 31; and Theuws, Chapter 38, this volume). With the emergence of charter evidence at the very end of the Merovingian period, moreover, we find increasing confirmation that rurally based magnates and institutions maintained significant urban holdings, and came into cities to play out the politics of land. The boom in rural church foundations in the seventh century had not precluded the ongoing endowment of new or existing urban churches and monasteries. In a world where holy sites had become vital to the power of elites, the cities still presented an abundance of investment opportunities and continued to function as theaters for aristocratic munificence and competition for local power. Even if the Frankish kingdoms had eventually ceased to be integrated though the *civitates*, and any Merovingian conception of urbanism was reduced to its essentials of walls and churches, the cities still remained privileged settings for public action and display.

NOTES

1. The absence of recorded bishops does not necessarily equate with abandonment of settlement, however, as the archaeology of fifth- and early sixth-century Cologne now amply demonstrates (Eck 2007).

2. Harries 1978 remains the best summary of the shifting purpose and complex history of this text, updated long into the Middle Ages. The sum total of the numbers of cities given in the provincial headers yields 113 *civitates*, though this does not correspond to the actual number listed (alongside *castra* and one *portus*) in any of its extant versions, which is generally slightly higher. Those without Merovingian-era bishops are Jublains, Boulogne, *Boatium*, *Rigomagensium*, and Castellane. For these and other cities that lost their status, see Loseby 2000 and Beaujard and Prévot 2004 for overviews, Ferdière (ed.) 2004 for case studies, and Bourgeois, Chapter 28, this volume, for recent updates.

3. Trier: Witschel 2004/2005; Arles: Loseby 1996; Heijmans 2004; Toulouse: Guyon 2000; Geneva and Lyon: Bonnet and Reynaud 2000; Paris: Dierkens and Périn 2000, pp. 271–277.

4. At Clermont, the recent reexamination of a section of the late-antique circuit in the rue Boirot showed that it was erected over the demolition layer of a late fourth-century building, supporting its earlier attribution to the early fifth century on typological grounds (Maurin 1992). Its walls were supposedly in a dilapidated state by the early 470s (Sidonius, *Ep.* 7.7–8). A sense of their extent can be obtained from a visit to the Saxon Shore fort at Pevensey, which encloses a nearly identical area.

5. For a comprehensive demolition of one of the supposed indicators of post-Roman provincial continuity, Clovis's takeover of Belgica Secunda, see now Barrett and Woudhuysen 2016.

6. For these references, see Loseby 2013, p. 236 n. 65.

7. Ewig 1976 remains the classic overview of the various partitions. The incoherence of the 567 division by comparison with that of 561 is highlighted by the maps in James 1988, pp. 171–172.

8. Chilperic gave Galswinth five cities on their marriage, for example, for the inheritance of which specific provision was made in the Treaty of Andelot (*Hist.* 9.20).

9. Gregory, *Hist.* 9.30, which pretends Tours had never slipped from Childebert's control. For the original concession, cf. *Hist.* 4.2.

10. For a list and discussion of these references, see Bachrach 1972, pp. 65–72, and Weidemann 1982, vol. 2, pp. 238–241.

11. The only explicit reference to an imperial *comes civitatis* comes from Marseille around 470: Sidonius, *Ep.* 7.2. The precise status of the *comes* Arbogast in Trier is less certain.

12. For example, in Visigothic Gaul: Euric, *Code* 322, Dumézil 2008; Burgundian Gaul: Heftner 2002, Gregory, *VP* 7.1; Ostrogothic Gaul: Cassiodorus, *Var.* 3.34.

13. Gregory, *Hist.* 7.47, with James 1983, who emphasizes that Gregory offers only one example of explicit jurisdictional conflict between bishops and counts, which is left unresolved (*VP* 8.3). Such cooperation is also envisaged, for example, in *Formulae Andecavenses* 32.

14. Durliat 1997; Weidemann 1982, vol. 2, pp. 307–319, who categorizes these individuals more rigidly than Gregory's flexible terminology allows.

15. The fullest assemblage and analysis of this material are now provided by Barbier 2014; for alternative perspectives, see also Rio 2009, especially pp. 177–182, W. C. Brown 2012.

16. Merovingian narrative sources contain no explicit references to city councils, *curiales*, or municipal officials such as the *curator*, and only four to *defensores*, which are put in the context of a wider sixth-century decline in the significance of that office by Schmidt-Hofner 2014.

17. For elite residences in cities, see Claude 1997, pp. 331–333; charters and wills confirm that magnates generally owned townhouses alongside their rural holdings (e.g., Bertram, *Testamentum* 24–25, 30, 36, 71).

18. For available *Spielräume*, see Reimitz 2015, especially chapter 9, an analysis that concentrates more on the emergence of Frankish identity than the disappearance of the potential alternatives.

19. For a fuller version of some of the following arguments, see Loseby 2013.

20. Davis 2015, especially pp. 95–99. The problem of the survival or emergence of the *pagus* lies beyond the scope of this chapter, but see Esders 2012.

21. *Civitas* levies appear just twice in Fredegar (4.73, 4.87), for example, alongside dozens of references to armies described in terms of larger territorial entities.

22. For lists by city, see Gauthier et al. 1986–2014, vol. 16.2; for example, Arles (15 religious establishments), Autun (13), Auxerre (29), Bordeaux (11), Bourges (15), Cahors (14), Clermont (25), Geneva (12), Le Mans (20), Lyon (21), Marseille (15), Paris (29), Reims (22), Tours (15), and Vienne (15); the numbers here refer to securely attested cases only. Meanwhile, around one-fifth of the centers discussed have no reported churches at all. For the erratic and highly skewed distribution of the data, see Gauthier 2014, pp. 363–364.

23. For a far more optimistic reading, see Dey 2015, pp. 160–174. On Tours, see: Galinié 2007.

24. For multivalency, see Theuws 2001 in reference to the emerging urban center of Maastricht, though the idea applies equally well to long-established cities.

WORKS CITED

Ancient Sources

Ausonius, *Opera*. R. P. H. Green (ed.). (1999). *Ausonius, Opera*. Oxford: Clarendon.

Bertram of Le Mans, *Testamentum*. M. Weidemann (ed.). (1986). *Das Testament des Bischofs Berthramn von Le Mans vom 27. März 616. Untersuchungen zu Besitz und Geschichte einer fränkischen Familie im 6. und 7. Jahrhundert*. Mainz: Verlag des Römisch-Germanischen Zentralmuseums.

Cassiodorus, *Variae*. T. Mommsen (ed.). (1894). MGH: AA 12. Berlin: Weidmann.

Codex Euricianus. A. D'Ors. (1960). *El Código de Eurico*. Madrid: Consejo Superior de Investigaciones Científicas.

Concilia Galliae A.511 – A.695. C. de Clercq (ed.). (1963). CCSL: 148A. Turnhout: Brepols.

Desiderius of Cahors, *Epistulae (Ep.)*. D. Norberg (ed.). (1961). *Epistulae sancti Desiderii Cadurcensis*: Acta Universitatis Stockholmiensia 6. Stockholm, Göteborg, Uppsala: Almquist and Wiksell.

Formulae Andecavenses. K. Zeumer (ed.). (1886). *Formulae Merowingici et Karolini Aevi*. MGH LL 5 (pp. 1–25). Hanover: Hahn.

Fredegar. B. Krusch (ed.). (1888). *Chronicarum quae dicuntur Fredegarii Scholastici Libri IV cum continuationibus*. MGH: SRM 2 (pp. 1–193). Hanover: Hahn.

Gregory of Tours, *Gloria confessorum (GC)*. B. Krusch (ed.). (1885). MGH SRM 1.2 (pp. 294–370). Hanover: Hahn.

Gregory of Tours, *Vitae patrum (VP)*. B. Krusch (ed.). (1885). MGH: SRM 1.2 (pp. 211–294). Hanover: Hahn.

Gregory of Tours, *Historiae (Hist.)*. B. Krusch and W. Levison (eds.). (1937[1951]). MGH: SRM 1.1. Hanover: Hahn.

Lex Ribuaria. F. Beyerle and R. Buchner (eds.). (1954). MGH LL 3.2. Hanover: Hahn.

Marculf, *Formularum libri duo*. K. Zeumer (ed.). (1886). *Formulae Merowingici et Karolini Aevi*. MGH LL 5 (pp. 32–112). Hanover: Hahn.

Passio Leudegarii I. B. Krusch (ed.). (1910). *Passio Leudegarii episcopi et martyris Augustodunensis I*. MGH SRM 5 (pp. 282–322). Hanover: Hahn.

Passio Praeiecti. B. Krusch (ed.). (1910). *Passio Praeiecti episcopi et martyris Arverni*. MGH SRM 5 (pp. 212–248). Hanover: Hahn.

Ruricius of Limoges, *Epistulae (Ep.)*. B. Krusch (ed.). (1887). MGH: AA 8 (pp. 299–350). Berlin: Weidmann.

Sidonius Apollinaris, *Epistulae (Ep.)*. A. Loyen (ed. and trans.). (1960[2008]). *Sidoine Apollinaire, Oeuvres, t. 2–3: Lettres*. Paris: Les Belles Lettres.

Venantius Fortunatus, *Carmina*. M. Reydellet (ed. and trans.). (1994–2004). *Venance Fortunat, Poèmes*. 3 vols. Paris: Les Belles Lettres.

Vita Amandi, B. Krusch (ed.). (1910). *Vita Amandi episcopi I*. MGH SRM 5 (pp. 395–449). Hanover: Hahn.

Vita Balthildis. B. Krusch (ed.). (1888). *Vita sanctae Balthildis*. MGH SRM 2 (pp. 475–508). Hanover: Hahn.

Vita Desiderii. B. Krusch (ed.). (1902). *Vita Desiderii Cadurcae urbis episcopi*. MGH SRM 4 (pp. 547–602). Hanover: Hahn.

Vita Eligii. B. Krusch (ed.). (1902). *Vita Eligii episcopi Noviomagensis*. MGH SRM 4 (pp. 663–742). Hanover: Hahn.

Vita Eustadiolae. (1742) [1867]). AASS Iun. 2 (pp. 131–133). Paris: Victor Palme.

Modern Sources

Atsma, H. (1976). "Les monastères urbains du nord de la Gaule." *Revue d'histoire de l'Eglise de France* 62: 163–187.

Bachrach, B. S. (1972). *Merovingian Military Organisation 481-751*. Minneapolis: University of Minnesota Press.

Balcon-Berry, S., and Berry, W. (2014). "Le groupe épiscopal d'Autun au haut moyen âge." In M. Gaillard (ed.), *L'empreinte chrétienne en Gaule du IVᵉ au IXᵉ siècle* (pp. 173–200). Turnhout: Brepols.

Barbier, J. (1990). "Le système palatial franc: genèse et fonctionnement dans le nord-ouest du regnum," *Bibliothèque de l'École des chartes* 148: 245–299.

Barbier, J. (2014). *Archives oubliées du haut Moyen Âge. Les* gesta municipalia *en Gaule franque (VIᵉ-IXᵉ siècle)*. Paris: Honoré Champion Éditeur.

Barrett, G., and Woudhuysen, G. (2016). "Remigius and the 'Important News' of Clovis Rewritten," *Antiquité tardive* 24: 471–500.

Beaujard, B. (2000). *Le culte des saints en Gaule. Les premiers temps. D'Hilaire de Poitiers à la fin du VIᵉ siècle*. Paris: Éditions du Cerf.

Beaujard, B., and Prévot, F. (2004). "Introduction à l'étude des capitales 'éphémères' de la Gaule (Iᵉʳ s.—début VIIᵉ s.)." In A. Ferdière (ed.), *Capitales éphémères. Des capitales de cités perdent leur statut dans l'antiquité tardive* (pp. 17–37). Revue Archéologique du Centre de la France, supp. 25. Tours: FÉRACF.

Bonnet, C., with Peillex, A. (2012). *Les fouilles de la cathédrale Saint-Pierre de Genève. Les édifices chrétiens et le groupe épiscopal*. Geneva: Librarie Droz.

Bonnet, C., and Reynaud, J.-F. (2000). "Genève et Lyon, capitales burgondes." In G. Ripoll and J. M. Gurt (eds.), *Sedes regiae (ann. 400–800)* (pp. 241–266). Barcelona: Reial Acadèmia de Bones Lletres.

Brogiolo, G. P. (2011), *Le origini della città medievale*. Mantua: SAP Società Archeologica.

Brown, P. (1981). *The Cult of the Saints: Its Rise and Function in Latin Christianity*. Chicago: University of Chicago Press.

Brown, P. (2012). *Through the Eye of a Needle. Wealth, the Fall of Rome, and the Making of Christianity in the West, 350–550 AD*. Princeton, NJ: Princeton University Press.

Brown, W. C. (2012). "The *gesta municipalia* and the Public Validation of Documents in Frankish Europe." In W. C. Brown et al. (eds.), *Documentary Culture and the Laity in the Early Middle Ages* (pp. 95–124). Cambridge: Cambridge University Press.

Brühl, C. (1975). *Palatium und Civitas. Studien zur Profantopographie spätantiker Civitates vom 3. bis zum 13. Jahrhundert. Band I: Gallien*. Cologne: Böhlau Verlag.

Buchner, R. (1933). *Die Provence in merowingischer Zeit: Verfassung—Wirtschaft—Kultur*. Stuttgart: Kohlhammer.

Claude, D. (1964). "Untersuchungen zum frühfränkischen Comitat." *Zeitschrift der Savigny-Stiftung für Rechtsgeschichte, Germanistische Abteilung* 81: 1–79.

Claude, D. (1985). "Aspekte des Binnenhandels im Merowingerreich auf Grund der Schriftquellen." In K. Düwel et al. (eds.), *Untersuchungen zu Handel und Verkehr der vor- und frühgeschichtlichen Zeit in Mittel- und Nordeuropa, Vol. 3, Der Handel des frühen Mittelalters* (pp. 9–97). Göttingen: Vandenhoeck and Ruprecht.

Claude, D. (1997). "Haus und Hof im Merowingerreich nach den erzählenden und urkundlichen Quellen." In H. Beck and H. Steuer (eds.), *Haus und Hof in ur- und frühgeschichtlicher Zeit* (pp. 321–334). Göttingen: Vandenhoeck and Ruprecht.

Coates, S. (2000). "Venantius Fortunatus and the image of episcopal authority in late antique and early Merovingian Gaul." *English Historical Review* 115: 1109–1137.

Davis, J. R. (2015). *Charlemagne's Practice of Empire*. Cambridge: Cambridge University Press.

Dey, H. W. (2015). *The Afterlife of the Roman City. Architecture and Ceremony in Late Antiquity and the Early Middle Ages*. Cambridge: Cambridge University Press.

Dierkens, A., and Périn, P. (2000). "Les *sedes regiae* mérovingiennes entre Seine et Rhin." In G. Ripoll and J. M. Gurt (eds.), *Sedes regiae (ann. 400–800)* (pp. 267–304). Barcelona: Reial Acadèmia de Bones Lletres.

Dumézil, B. (2008). "Le comte et l'administration de la cité dans le Bréviare d'Alaric." In M. Rouche and B. Dumézil (eds.), *Le Bréviare d'Alaric. Aux origines du Code civil* (pp. 73–90). Cultures et civilisations médiévales, 44. Paris: Presses de l'Université Paris-Sorbonne.

Durliat, J. (1979). "Les attributions civiles des évêques mérovingiens: l'exemple de Didier, évêque de Cahors (630–655)." *Annales du Midi* 91: 237–254.

Durliat, J. (1996). "Évêque et administration municipale au VIIᵉ siècle." In C. Lepelley (ed.), *La fin de la cité antique et le début de la cité médiévale de la fin du IIIe siècle à l'avènement de Charlemagne* (pp. 273–286). Bari: Edipuglia.

Durliat, J. (1997). "*Episcopus, civis* et *populus* dans les *Historiarum Libri* de Grégoire." In N. Gauthier and H. Galinié (eds.), *Grégoire de Tours et l'espace gaulois* (pp. 185–193). Revue Archéologique du Centre de la France, suppl. 13. Tours: FÉRACF.

Eck, W. (1983). "Der Episkopat im spätantiken Africa: organisatorische Entwicklung, soziale Herkunft und öffentliche Funktionen." *Historische Zeitschrift* 236: 265–295.

Eck, W. (2007). "Köln im Übergang von der Antike zum Mittelalter." *Geschichte in Köln* 54: 7–26.

Effros, B. (2001). "Monuments and Memory: Repossessing Ancient Remains in Early Medieval Gaul." In M. de Jong and F. Theuws (eds.), *Topographies of Power in the Early Middle Ages* (pp. 93–118). Transformation of the Roman World 6. Leiden: Brill.

Esders, S. (2005). "Treueidleistung und Rechtsveränderung im frühen Mittelater." In S. Esders and C. Reinle (eds.), *Rechtsveränderung im politischen und sozialen Kontext mittelalterliche Rechtsvielhaft* (pp. 25–62). Münster: LIT Verlag.

Esders, S. (2012). "Zur Entwicklung der politischen Raumgliederung im Übergang von der Antike zum Mittelalter—Das Beispeil des *pagus*." In O. Dally et al. (ed.), *Politische Raüme in vormodernen Gesellschaften. Gestaltung—Wahrnehmung—Funktion* (pp. 195–211). Rahden: Verlag Marie Leidorf.

Esders, S. (2014). "Nordwestgallien um 500. Von den militarisierten spätrömischen Provinzgesellschaft zur erweiteren Militäradministration des merovingischen Königtums." In M. Meier and S. Patzold (eds.), *Chlodwigs Welt. Organisation von Herrschaft um 500* (pp. 339–361). Stuttgart: Franz Steiner Verlag.

Esders, S. (2016). "Gallic Politics in the Sixth Century." In A. C. Murray (ed.), *A Companion to Gregory of Tours* (pp. 429–461). Leiden: Brill.

Esmonde Cleary, S. (2013). *The Roman West, AD 200–500: An Archaeological Study*. Cambridge: Cambridge University Press.

Ewig, E. (1976). "Die fränkischen Teilungen und Teilreiche (511–613)." In E. Ewig, *Spätantikes und fränkisches Gallien. Gesammelte Schriften (1952–1973)*, Vol. 1 (pp. 114–171). (Beihefte der Francia 3/1). Munich: Artemis Verlag.

Ewig, E. (1979a). "Beobachtungen zu den Klosterprivilegien des 7. und frühen 8. Jahrhunderts." In E. Ewig, *Spätantikes und fränkisches Gallien. Gesammelte Schriften (1952–1973)*, Vol. 2 (pp. 411–426). Beihefte der Francia 3/2. Munich: Artemis Verlag.

Ewig, E. (1979b). "Milo *et eiusmodi similes*." In E. Ewig, *Spätantikes und fränkisches Gallien. Gesammelte Schriften (1952–1973)*, Vol. 2 (pp. 189–219). Beihefte der Francia 3/2. Munich: Artemis Verlag.

Ferdière, A. (ed.) (2004). *Capitales éphémères. Des capitales de cités perdent leur statut dans l'antiquité tardive*. Revue Archéologique du Centre de la France, suppl. 25. Tours: FÉRACF.

Fouracre, P. (1998). "The Nature of Frankish Political Institutions in the Seventh Century." In I. Wood (ed.), *Franks and Alamanni in the Merovingian Period: An Ethnographic Perspective* (pp. 285–301). Woodbridge: Boydell Press.

Fouracre, P. (2003). "Why Were So Many Bishops Killed in Merovingian Francia?" In N. Fryde and D. Reitz (eds.), *Bischofsmord im Mittelalter* (pp. 13–35). Veröffentlichungen des Max-Planck-Instituts für Geschichte 191. Göttingen: Vandenhoeck and Ruprecht.

Gaillard, M., and Sapin, C. (2012). "Monastères et espace urbain au haut Moyen Âge." *Mélanges de l'Ecole française de Rome: Moyen Âge* 124: 27–37.

Galinié, H. (1997). "Tours de Grégoire, Tours des archives du sol." In N. Gauthier and H. Galinié (eds.), *Grégoire de Tours et l'espace gaulois* (pp. 65–80). Revue Archéologique du Centre de la France, suppl. 13. Tours: FÉRACF.

Galinié, H. (ed.). (2007). *Tours antique et médiéval, lieux de vie, temps de la ville, 40 ans d'archéologie urbaine.* Revue Archéologique du Centre de la France, suppl. 30. Tours: FÉRACF.

Garmy, P., and Maurin, L. (eds.). (1996). *Enceintes romaines d'Aquitaine. Bordeaux, Dax, Périgueux, Bazas.* Documents d'archéologie française 53. Paris: Éditions de la Maison de Sciences de l'Homme.

Gasparri, S. (2008). "Recrutement social et rôle politique des évêques en Italie du VIe au VIIIe siècle." In F. Bougard, D. Iogna-Prat, and R. Le Jan (eds.), *Hiérarchie et stratification sociale dans l'occident médiéval (400–1100)* (pp. 137–160). Collection Haut Moyen Âge 6. Turnhout: Brepols.

Gauthier, N. (2000). "Le réseau de pouvoirs de l'évêque dans la Gaule du haut Moyen-Âge." In G. P. Brogiolo, N. Gauthier, and N. Christie (eds.), *Towns and their territories between late Antiquity and the early Middle Ages* (pp. 173–208). Transformation of the Roman World 9. Leiden: Brill.

Gauthier, N. (2014). "Christianisation et espace urbain." In F. Prévot, M. Gaillard, and N. Gauthier (eds.), *Topographie chrétienne des cités de la Gaule des origines au milieu du VIIIe siècle, vol. 16.2: Christianisation et espace urbain: atlas, tableaux, index* (pp. 359–399). Paris: Éditions de Boccard.

Gauthier, N., et al. (1986–2014). *Topographie chrétienne des cités de la Gaule des origines au milieu du VIIIe siècle* (16 vols.). Paris: Éditions de Boccard.

Goffart, W. (1982). "Old and New in Merovingian Taxation." *Past and Present* 96: 3–21.

Guilleux, J. (2000). *L'enceinte romaine du Mans.* Saint-Jean-d'Angély: J.-M. Bordessoules.

Guyon, J. (2000). "Toulouse, la première capitale du royaume wisigoth." In G. Ripoll and J. M. Gurt (eds.), *Sedes regiae (ann. 400–800)* (pp. 219–240). Barcelona: Reial Acadèmia de Bones Lletres.

Halfond, G. I. (2010). *The Archaeology of Frankish Church Councils, AD 511–768.* (Medieval Law and Its Practice 6). Leiden: Brill.

Harries, J. (1978). "Church and State in the *Notitia Galliarum.*" *Journal of Roman Studies* 68: 26–43.

Heftner, H. (2002). "*Comites, iudices, iudices deputati.* Untersuchungen zum Gerichtswesen im südgallischen Burgunderreich (443–534)." *Concilium medii aevi* 5: 119–141.

Heijmans, M. (2004). *Arles durant l'Antiquité tardive. De la Duplex Arelas à l'Urbs Genesii.* Collection de l'Ecole française de Rome 324. Rome: École Française de Rome.

Heinzelmann, M. (1976). *Bischofsherrschaft in Gallien.* Beihefte der Francia 5. Munich: Artemis Verlag.

Heinzelmann, M. (1988). "Bischof und Herrschaft vom spätantiken Gallien bis zu den karolingischen Hausmeiern. Die institutionellen Grundlagen." In F. Prinz (ed.), *Herrschaft und Kirche: Beiträge zur Entstehung und Wirkungsweise episkopaler und monasticscher Organizationsformen* (pp. 23–82). Monographien zur Geschichte des Mittelalters 33. Stuttgart: Anton Hiersemann Verlag.

Hen, Y. (1995). *Culture and Religion in Merovingian Gaul, AD 481–751*. Leiden: Brill.

Henning, J. (2007). "Early European Towns: The Development of the Economy in the Frankish Realm between Dynamism and Deceleration, AD 500–1100." In J. Henning (ed.), *Post-Roman Towns, Trade and Settlement in Europe and Byzantium, Vol. 1: The Heirs of the Roman West* (pp. 3–40). Millennium Studien 5/1. Berlin: Walter de Gruyter.

James, E. (1983). "*Beati pacifici*: Bishops and the Law in Sixth-Century Gaul." In J. Bossy (ed.), *Disputes and Settlements. Law and Human Relations in the West* (pp. 25–46). Cambridge: Cambridge University Press.

James, E. (1988). *The Franks*. Oxford: Blackwell.

Jussen, B. (1995). "Über *Bischofsherrschaften* und die Prozeduren politisch-sozialer Umordnung in Gallien zwischen Antike und Mittelater." *Historische Zeitschrift* 260: 673–718.

Jussen, B. (2001). "Liturgy and Legitimation, or How the Gallo-Romans Ended the Roman Empire." In B. Jussen (ed.), *Ordering Medieval Society. Perspectives on Intellectual and Practical Modes of Shaping Social Relations* (trans. P. Selwyn) (pp. 147–199). Philadelphia: University of Pennsylvania Press.

Kaiser, R. (1979). "Steuer und Zoll in der Merowingerzeit," *Francia* 7: 1–18.

Kaiser, R. (1981). *Bischofsherrschaft zwischen Königtum und Fürstenmacht. Studien zur bischöflichen Stadtherrschaft im westfränkisch-französischen Reich im frühen und hohen Mittelalter.* Pariser Historische Studien 17. Bonn: Ludwig Röhrscheid Verlag.

Kaiser, R. (1990). "Bistumsgründungen im Merowingerreich im 6. Jahrhundert." In R. Schieffer (ed.), *Beiträge zur Geschichte des Regnum Francorum*. Beihefte der Francia 22. Sigmaringen: Jan Thorbecke Verlag.

Laniado, A. (2002). *Recherches sur les notables municipaux dans l'empire protobyzantin*. Paris: Association des Amis du Centre d'Histoire et Civilisation de Byzance.

Laniado, A. (2014). "From Municipal Councillors to 'Municipal Landowners'. Some Remarks on the Evolution of Provincial Elites in Early Byzantium." In M. Meier and S. Patzold (eds.), *Chlodwigs Welt. Organisation von Herrschaft um 500* (pp. 545–565). Stuttgart: Franz Steiner Verlag.

Lauwers, M., and Ripart, L. (2007). "Représentation et gestion de l'espace dans l'occident médiéval (V^e–XIIIe siècle)." In J.-P. Genet (ed.), *Rome et l'état moderne européen: une comparaison typologique* (pp. 115–171). Collection de l'École Française de Rome 377. Rome: École Française de Rome.

Liebeschuetz, J. H. W. G. (2001). *The Decline and Fall of the Roman City*. Oxford: Oxford University Press.

Loseby, S. T. (1996). "Arles in Late Antiquity: *Gallula Roma Arelas* and *urbs Genesii*." In N. Christie and S. T. Loseby (eds.), *Towns in Transition: Urban Evolution in Late Antiquity and the Early Middle Ages* (pp. 45–70). Aldershot: Ashgate.

Loseby, S. T. (1998). "Gregory's Cities: Urban Functions in Sixth-Century Gaul." In I. Wood (ed.), *Franks and Alamanni in the Merovingian Period. An Ethnographic Perspective* (pp. 239–270). Woodbridge: Boydell Press.

Loseby, S. T. (2000). "Urban Failures in Late Antique Gaul." In T. R. Slater (ed.), *Towns in decline, AD 100–1600* (pp. 72–95). Aldershot: Ashgate.

Loseby, S. T. (2006). "Decline and Change in the Cities of Late Antique Gaul." In J.-U. Krause and C. Witschel (eds.), *Die Stadt in der Spätantike—Niedergang oder Wandel?* (pp. 67–104). Historia Einzelschriften 190. Stuttgart: Franz Steiner Verlag.

Loseby, S. T. (2013). "Lost Cities. The End of the *Civitas*-System in Frankish Gaul." In S. Diefenbach and G. M. Müller (eds.), *Gallien in Spätantike und Frühmittelalter. Kulturgeschichte einer Region* (pp. 223–252). Millennium-Studien 43. Berlin: Walter de Gruyter.

Mathisen, R. W. (1993). *Roman Aristocrats in Barbarian Gaul. Strategies for Survival in an Age of Transition*. Austin: University of Texas Press.

Maurin, L. (1992). "Remparts et cités dans les trois provinces du Sud-Ouest de la Gaule au Bas-Empire (dernier quart du IIIe siècle-début du Ve siècle." In *Villes et agglomérations urbaines antiques du sud-ouest de la Gaule: histoire et archéologie* (pp. 365–389). Aquitania, suppl. 6. Bordeaux: Fédération Aquitania.

Müller, C. (2003) "Kurialen und Bischof, Bürger und Gemeinde—Untersuchungen zur Kontinuität von Ämtern, Funktionen und Formen der 'Kommunikation' in der gallischen Stadt des 4.–6. Jahrhunderts." Dissertation, University of Freiburg.

Murray, A. C. (1986). "The Position of the *grafio* in the Constitutional History of Merovingian Gaul." *Speculum* 64: 787–805.

Murray, A. C. (1988). "From Roman to Frankish Gaul: *centenarii* and *centenae* in the Administration of the Merovingian Kingdom." *Traditio* 44: 59–100.

Murray, A. C. (2010). 'Merovingian Immunity Revisited." *History Compass* 8: 913–928.

Murray, A. C. (2016). "The Merovingian State and Administration in the Times of Gregory of Tours." In A. C. Murray (ed.), *A Companion to Gregory of Tours* (pp. 191–231). Leiden: Brill.

Patzold, S. (2010). "Zur Sozialstruktur des Episkopats und zur Ausbildung bischöflicher Herrschaft in Gallien zwischen Spätantike und Frühmittelater." In M. Becher and S. Dick (eds.), *Völker, Reiche und Namen im frühen Mittelalter* (pp. 121–140). Mittelalter Studien 22. Munich: Wilhelm Fink.

Patzold, S. (2014). "Bischöfe, soziale Herkunft und die Organisation lokaler Herrschaft um 500." In M. Meier and S. Patzold (eds.), *Chlodwigs Welt. Organisation von Herrschaft um 500* (pp. 523–543). Stuttgart: Franz Steiner Verlag.

Pietri, L. (1987). "L'organisation de la province." In L. Pietri and J. Biarne, *Topographie chrétienne des cités de la Gaule, vol. 5: Province ecclésiastique de Tours* (pp. 11–17). Paris: Éditions de Boccard.

Pietri, L. (2005). "Les *oratoria in agro proprio* dans la Gaule de l'Antiquité tardive: un aspect des rapports entre *potentes* et évêques." In C. Delaplace (ed.), *Aux origines de la paroisse rurale en Gaule* (pp. 235–242). Paris: Éditions Errance.

Prinz, F. (1974). "Die bischöfliche Stadtherrschaft im Frankenreich von 5 bis 7 Jahrhundert." *Historische Zeitschrift* 217: 1–35.

Reimitz, H. (2015). *History, Frankish Identity and the Framing of Western Ethnicity, 550–850.* Cambridge: Cambridge University Press.

Rio, A. (2009). *Legal Practice and the Written Word in the Early Middle Ages. Frankish formulae, c. 500–1000.* Cambridge: Cambridge University Press.

Roberts, M. (2009). *The Humblest Sparrow. The Poetry of Venantius Fortunatus.* Ann Arbor: University of Michigan Press.

Schmidt-Hofner, S. (2014). "Der *defensor civitatis* und die Entstehung des Notabelnregiments in den spätrömischen Städte." In M. Meier and S. Patzold (eds.), *Chlodwigs Welt. Organisation von Herrschaft um 500* (pp. 487–522). Stuttgart: Franz Steiner Verlag.

Theuws, F. (2001). "Maastricht as a centre of power in the early middle ages." In M. de Jong and F. Theuws (eds.), *Topographies of Power in the Early Middle Ages* (pp. 155–216). Transformation of the Roman World 6. Leiden: Brill.

Van Dam, R. (1993). *Saints and Their Miracles in Late Antique Gaul*. Princeton, NJ: Princeton University Press.

Weidemann, M. (1982). *Kulturgeschichte der Merowingerzeit nach den Werken Gregors von Tours*. 2 vols. Mainz: Verlag des Römisch-Germanischen Zentralmuseums.

Weidemann, M. (2002). *Geschichte des Bistums Le Mans von der Spätantike bis zur Karolingerzeit: Actus pontificum Cenomannis in urbe degentium und Gesta Aldrici*, 3 vols. Mainz: Verlag des Römisch-Germanischen Zentralmuseums.

Whittow, M. (1990). "Ruling the Late Roman and Early Byzantine City: A Continuous History." *Past and Present* 129: 3–29.

Wickham, C. (2005). *Framing the Early Middle Ages. Europe and the Mediterranean, 400–800*. Oxford: Oxford University Press.

Wiesheu, A. (2001). "Bischof und Gefängnis: zur Interpretation der Kerkerbefreiungswunder in der merowingischen Hagiographie." *Historisches Jahrbuch* 121: 1–23.

Witschel, C. (2004/5). "Trier und das spätantike Städtewesen im Westen des römischen Reiches." *Trierer Zeitschrift* 67–68: 223–272.

Wood, I. (1983). "The Ecclesiastical Politics of Merovingian Clermont." In P. Wormald, D. Bullough, and R. Collins (eds.), *Ideal and Reality in Frankish and Anglo-Saxon Society: Studies Presented to J. M. Wallace-Hadrill* (pp. 34–55). Oxford: Basil Blackwell.

Wood, I. (2013). "Entrusting Western Europe to the Church, 400–750." *Transactions of the Royal Historical Society* 23: 37–73.

CHAPTER 28

THE FATE OF SMALL TOWNS, HILLTOP SETTLEMENTS, AND ELITE RESIDENCES IN MEROVINGIAN-PERIOD GAUL

LUC BOURGEOIS

THE history of places of power in the Merovingian realm has long been focused on three types of site: cities, monasteries, and royal palaces.[1] Whereas urban archaeology has made it increasingly possible to move beyond the exclusive study of Christian topography and consider more widely the transition from the ancient city to the medieval town, it has made hardly any progress in other areas, such as identifying the features of urban settlement or changes in the wall circuits constructed at the end of antiquity (on cities, see Loseby, chapter 27, this volume). At the same time, our knowledge of the material forms of royal residences from the fifth to the eighth century remains almost nonexistent. With the exception of the very classicizing palace of Toulouse, identified as a fifth-century residence of the Visigothic kings, only fragments of the Merovingian palaces of Vitry-en-Artois (Pas-de-Calais), Malay-le-Grand (Yonne), and Marlenheim (Bas-Rhin) have been revealed by archaeological excavations in the course of the last thirty years (Bourgeois 2006).

In contrast, in the last fifteen years, there have been marked advances in the categorization of more modest places of power. Four of them will be the subject of this discussion: ancient administrative centers that were downgraded before the sixth century; Gallo-Roman small towns that evolved in the course of the fifth to eighth centuries; the large variety of hilltop settlements that were either reoccupied or created *ex nihilo*; and nonfortified residences of the rural elites. Despite their apparent diversity, these four types of modest centers of power reveal numerous similarities to one another. There is no shortage of examples of slippage between these categories, and architectural references to Antiquity are common at the majority of these sites. Indeed, field research has largely discredited nineteenth-century paradigms of historical research that created these categories, and which sometimes remain deeply engrained even today.

Because it hardly makes sense to present an analysis that matches settlements—often occupied over long periods of time—with different phases of Frankish conquest, it seems a better option to introduce a broader perspective to the discussion. Constrained by the varying pace of research in different regions, I will concentrate here on some of the best documented cases (Fig. 28.1), which are scattered across the western parts of the Merovingian kingdoms and pertain to the period extending from the fifth to the mid-eighth century.

FIGURE 28.1. Location of the sites mentioned in this chapter.

DOWNGRADED CAPITALS, UPGRADED SMALL TOWNS, AND ISOLATED CATHEDRALS

Although the network of capital cities inherited from the early Roman Empire furnished most of the episcopal seats attested in the Merovingian period, the church generally adopted a pragmatic approach. The church avoided placing bishops in settlements that were less active due to depopulation, poor connections to the communication network, or their location on threatened frontiers (on bishops, see Halfond, chapter 13, this volume). Across the entire expanse of ancient *Gallia transalpina*, close to forty administrative centers (roughly half of those that existed originally) based in ancient cities either lost their political status in late antiquity or could not house or maintain an episcopal seat during the following centuries. If the streamlining of the administrative map in the second century caused the downgrading of some smaller cities in the region of Narbonne, this reorganizing activity accelerated in the late third and early fourth centuries during the Tetrarchy (293–306) and continued until the sixth century.

In the early 2000s, a conference on the topic of demoted cities provided the broad brushstrokes of the state of our knowledge of most of these sites (Ferdière 2004), but without according sufficient attention to the fate of these settlements over the course of the early Middle Ages. In Gaul the downgraded capitals of the third to sixth centuries were concentrated north of the line separating Brittany and the Netherlands and south of the line linking the Basque country with Alsace. Thus, it was specifically the regions characterized by cities of average size (in the north) or of small size (in the south) that saw the most downgrades. By contrast, in central France, which was filled with large *civitates* (cities with their appertaining territories), some small Roman towns were actually promoted to the status of episcopal centers. However, this reorganization did not result in the disappearance of the original episcopal administrative centers, which generally lost only part of their territories in the process. In the ecclesiastical province of Sens, for example, Orléans, a *vicus* (secondary town) that benefited from its location on the Loire, was put on a par with the older city of Chartres some time before 346. Moreover, in a second example, two secondary settlements were upgraded to cities at the expense (but not the eclipse) of Autun: Auxerre (before 346) and then Nevers (probably by the Burgundian king Gundobad after 486, when Clovis took control of the region of Auxerre [Picard et al. 1992, pp. 52, 145]). Unlike some other cities, Autun survived as an ecclesiastical and administrative center. Other attempts to create administrative centers, however, proved unsustainable. In 511, Adventinus, the bishop of Chartres, appears to have resided in the *castrum* (fortification) of Châteaudun. This was the administrative center of the *pagus* (district) that Sigibert I, who did not control Chartres, temporarily detached from the rest of the diocese between 567 and 575, and that still had a count around 585 (Picard et al. 1992, pp. 43–45). Although Châteaudun survived, it never evolved into a major administrative center.

Elsewhere, some administrative centers in downgraded cities were not equipped with defenses and never became episcopal sees. Five cases of episcopal transfer are explored here. In each case, the relative isolation of these demoted centers has allowed archaeologists the exceptional ability to conduct excavations and uncover evidence of their earlier prominence and subsequent demise. The first example is the ancient capital of Jublains (*Noviodunum*, Mayenne), which possessed a regular layout (covering about 25 hectares), though its construction appears not to have been fully completed, and it was partially deserted before the end of the second century. At the start of the third century, however, the southwestern fringes of the city saw the construction of an immense hall, which has been interpreted as a public granary. In the late third century, this building was protected with fortifications. In the fourth century, the development of cemeteries in the heart of the urban center and the growing scarcity of imported products are indicators of the progressive decline of the trade and communications network that had once supplied the city. However, a church dedicated to Sts. Gervasius and Protasius (the same as the nearby cathedral of Le Mans) was installed at the heart of the ancient Roman baths and would later form the heart of the medieval town (Bocquet and Naveau, in Ferdière 2004, pp. 173–182) (Fig. 28.2A).

Although Jublains appears to have remained the head of a city-territory at the end of the fourth or the beginning of the fifth century, by the time it was mentioned in the will of Bertram of Le Mans (616) (Weidemann 1986), the settlement was no more than a *vicus* (secondary town) or *oppidum* (fortified settlement). The former city was probably absorbed into the diocese of Le Mans before 453, and it is doubtful that it was at any point the residence of a bishop. Yet, there are four indicators of its past importance: Bishop Bertram of Le Mans distinguished the church of Jublains by the title *sancta ecclesia* (bishop's church—using *ecclesia* rather than usual *basilica*), which no doubt signaled its local religious importance. Moreover, until the sixth or seventh century, the site remained a *vicus* and then the center of a small Carolingian civil district (*condita*), and coins were issued in its name in the second half of the seventh and the first half of the eighth centuries (on numismatics, see Strothmann, chapter 35, this volume). Although the physical appearance of Jublains is now modest, a variety of traces of its earlier status thus remain. Finally, when the counts of Maine erected their new castle in Mayenne around 900, they reused Roman stones taken from Jublains, an operation that contributed symbolically to the legitimization of the new center of power (Early 2001, pp. 283–284).

Other small towns were protected by fortifications and received an episcopal see but apparently did not manage to maintain their ecclesiastical prerogatives. Such was the case with our second example of a demoted city: Augst (*Augusta Raurica*) in Switzerland (Schwartz in Ferdière 2004, pp. 103–126) (Fig. 28.2B). Between 240 and 270, an earthquake and then military troubles brought about the decline of this city. Around 276, the civil and military population took refuge in a reduced walled area beside the ancient *forum* before occupying the bank of the Rhine and the new *castrum Rauracense*, at the site of modern Kaiseraugst, around 290–300. Excavations undertaken at Kaiseraugst have revealed continuous occupation of the site throughout the early Middle Ages.

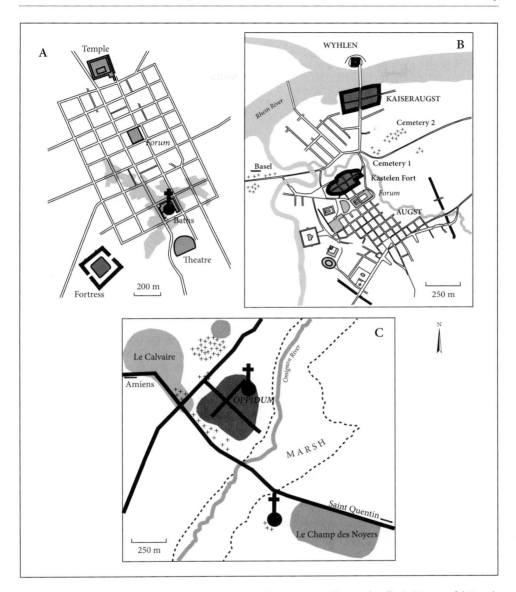

FIGURE 28.2. A: Jublains (Mayenne); B: Augst and Kaiseraugst (Switzerland); C: Vermand (Aisne).

The two rich cemeteries that bordered the walled settlement, and the funerary structures associated with them, marked the importance of this site until the 720s. These
cemeteries were then abandoned in favor of a burial site in the vicinity of a large church,
which had been built within the settlement walls at the beginning of the fourth century
and which was then extended with a baptistery and various rooms that probably constituted the bishop's residence. Although an *episcopus* (bishop) *Rauracorum* participated
in a synod in 346, it is impossible to determine if the bishopric was at this date located at

the *castrum* of Kaiseraugst, or whether this name referred to the entire territory of the city. While later sources are rare, two documents of the ninth century invoke a temporary transfer of the episcopal see into eastern Frankish hands and some resulting vacancies in the see of Kaiseraugst at the end of the fifth and then during the sixth century. At the beginning of the seventh century, Bishop Ragnachar was again based in the *castrum*, but he nonetheless held the double title of bishop of Augst and Basel. The transfer of the episcopal see to Basel was attested in a tangible manner during the years 805–823, when Bishop Haito built (or rebuilt) a cathedral there. This third site was not a new foundation. From the end of the fourth century, the *castrum* of Basel (*Basilea*), 10 kilometers to the east of Kaiseraugst, was protected by a rampart enclosing 6 hectares, and it was designated a city in the *Notitia Galliarum*. Around 540–600, the cemetery of Basel-Bernerring (Martin 1976) included the burials of many members of the Frankish nobility. As a consequence of this transfer, *Augusta*—as it was known in the eighth century—was still described as a *civitas* in 825 but was no more than a *villa* by 891–894.

In still other cases, some hesitation could occur before a newly established political capital and episcopal center was definitively fixed in a particular location. In our third example, dated between the third and sixth centuries, the localization of the centers of power in Vermandois (Aisne and Oise) fluctuated between the communities of Vermand and Saint-Quentin (Collard and Gaillard in Ferdière 2004, pp. 83–102). Vermand (Fig. 28.2C), a vast Gaulish *oppidum* and the original administrative center following the Roman conquest, was rapidly relieved of its status by the new central place of Saint-Quentin (*Augusta Viromanduorum*), about 10 kilometers to the east. However, Saint-Quentin itself experienced a major decline after 250, whereas renewed activity was recorded in the fourth and fifth centuries at the *oppidum* of Vermand and in the unfortified neighborhoods that surrounded it. In this case, the old Gaulish site again became the administrative center of the city, and it was probably there that the first bishops, documented from 511, were located (Duchesne 1915, pp. 99–102). Although referred to as a *civitas* in the first version of the *Inventio prior* of Saint-Quentin (late seventh to early eighth century), Vermand was, however, no longer described as more than a *castrum* in the Carolingian recensions of this text. According to this legendary account, the pious woman who rediscovered the holy man Quentin's remains in the Somme River wanted to bring them back to Vermand. However, the body of the saint became so heavy when they arrived at Saint-Quentin that it was necessary to bury him at this location (Collart and Gaillard in Ferdière 2004, p. 88). The cult at Saint-Quentin, attested from the sixth century, was reinforced after the translation of the relics into the abbey church conducted by St. Eligius around 650 (Audoin, *Vita Eligii*, II, 6), which led to the rapid expansion of the monastery and its associated settlement. In the ninth century, Saint-Quentin was the residence of the local lay authority, the count of Vermandois. But an earlier decision determined the decline of Vermand: during the rule of Bishop Medard (died c. 560), the episcopal see was transferred to Noyon, in the south of the diocese, and Vermand was henceforth no longer either the political or religious capital of the territory that carried its name.

Some kinds of decline also resulted from competition between neighboring episcopal sees. In our fourth example, Cimiez (Alpes-Maritimes) was the administrative center of a Roman city-territory, whereas Nice, located just 2 kilometers further south, was a mere *portus* (port) attached administratively to Marseille. However, a bishop is attested at Nice in 381, whereas there is no known bishop at Cimiez before 439. This anomaly relates to the fact that the two settlements belonged to two different ecclesiastical provinces: the first, that of the bishop of Embrun, who was then trying to create an ecclesiastical province, and the second, that of Aix in Narbonensis Secunda. The interventions of the papacy from 462 helped resolve this conflict over status. The bishop, henceforth the only one, was still called the *episcopus ecclesiae Cemelensis* in 554, but we know that he resided in Nice in 585. Finally, in 614, the prelate signed as being *ex civitate Nicia*, and the episcopal complex installed in the midst of the ancient baths of Cimiez had thus lost its privileges (Ardisson in Ferdière 2004, pp. 247–254).

In contrast to all of the preceding examples, which saw a bishop installed in the most dynamic or best defended settlement, the fifth and final case, the cathedral complex of Maguelone (Hérault), is today located on an isolated islet jutting out of a saltwater lake on the coast of Languedoc. Some recent excavations have revealed the existence of a vast funerary basilica linked to a cemetery of the sixth and early seventh centuries to the east of the cathedral of Saint Peter and Paul. The existence of a harbor settlement that reached its greatest extent in the fifth century explains the creation of this episcopal see, detached from the bishopric of Nîmes between 506 and 589, probably at the instigation of the Visigothic regime. The abandonment of the associated settlement appears almost complete after Charles Martel's conquest of the site in 737, but it did not involve the transfer of the cathedral structures, which remained isolated on their islet until 1536 (Barruol, Raynaud, and Garnotel 2004; Raynaud 2004).

The decline of some ancient *civitates* and the early transfer of some episcopal sees thus brought the multiplication of "ghost cities," whose fate during the Merovingian period and beyond appears to have been relatively varied. In some cases, simple villages often made use of numerous sanctuaries or an important church (Jublains). In others, they shifted from the focal point of the settlement to a hilltop fortification, which proved fatal to the ancient settlement at the base of the valley, as occurred at Augst. By contrast, some episcopal centers moved downhill toward a more practical and active site (as was the case at Nice). In other examples, like Vermand, political or economic competition made the choice logical to locate an episcopal center further away. Only in rare cases like Maguelone was a cathedral maintained in a deurbanized location.

The Fate of Small Towns of Roman Origin and New Places of Power in the Region of Poitou

If the fate of the administrative centers of ancient city-territories has attracted keen interest, the same cannot be said for settlements of secondary rank. Small towns have long been studied within the framework of chronological periods and traditional disciplines: archaeologists of Antiquity have thus been more inclined to work with Gallo-Roman settlements, whereas medieval towns have long been a research field reserved for medieval historians and art historians. This divided approach (Bur 1993) has led to the idea of the end of a "first urban network," namely, that most ancient small towns disappeared between the third and fifth centuries. This process of deurbanization was followed by the birth, between the tenth and the twelfth centuries, of a "second urban network," centered around castles and monasteries. Between these two high points, the early Middle Ages has long been considered a period with a relative absence of urban phenomena outside of the administrative centers of cities. However, the constant expansion of archaeological evidence, recent interest in the transition between Antiquity and the Middle Ages, and a growing practice of conducting research over the *longue durée,* have opened up new perspectives on the fate of small settlements in the Merovingian period. Even so, the practical organization of these settlements after the fourth century remains poorly understood. But by assessing all types of available information on civil, religious, and economic power exercised in these sites or their vicinity at the start of the Middle Ages, their importance among the "central places" of this period may be evaluated more accurately.

This type of analysis is still little developed in France, with the exception of the pioneering work undertaken by Gabriel Fournier on the Auvergne (Fournier 1962, pp. 127–200). We will concentrate here on a similar regional survey carried out since then in the region of Poitou (Bourgeois 2005). The results of this investigation appear to be generally applicable to most other regions in Gaul for which we currently possess only limited studies.

The *Civitas Pictonum* constituted the largest city-territory in ancient Gaul: it extended over about 250 kilometers from west to east, from the Atlantic to the first foothills of the Massif Central (Fig. 28.3). Its eastern part, present Haut-Poitou, benefited from a relatively dense network of small towns, which were strung out along large roads and navigable waterways. Lower Poitou was marked by lower levels of urban density, but for a long time it was not the subject of archaeological research. The best studied sites are of very variable scale: they range from settlements with regular urban layouts covering more than 100 hectares and possessing vast complexes of public buildings (temples, theaters, baths) to modest posting stations located along the roads.

While some settlements in this territory seem to have been completely or partially abandoned before the end of the second century, it is above all at the end of the third and during the course of the fourth centuries that signs of decay accelerated. The privatization of oversize public buildings and then their progressive dismantling constituted the first signs of such decline, even if sometimes it was experienced in stages (e.g., the transition from organized worship to individual devotion in one of the temples at Antigny (Vienne) (Bourgeois 2000a, pp. 87–90). This development was accompanied by the abandonment of most artisanal quarters on the periphery. However, these trends were not universal. At the beginning of the fifth century, for instance, the ceramic workshops of Civaux (Vienne) exported their wares as far as insular Britain, and metallurgical activities continued in Rom (Deux-Sèvres), probably in the context of a new road station of the *cursus publicus* (state-run transportation system along Roman routes). Similarly, since urban settlements

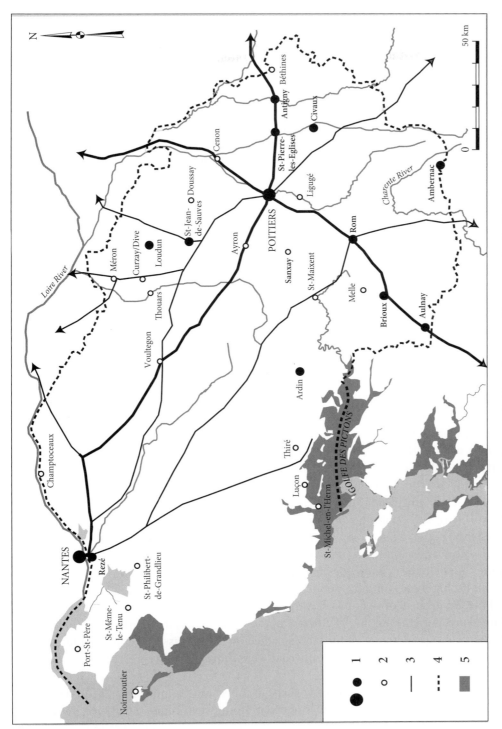

FIGURE 28.3. The diocese of Poitiers in the Merovingian period. (1): settlements of Roman origin cited in the text; (2): other Merovingian "central places"; (3): principal Roman roads; (4): frontiers of the territory; (5): land overtaken by the sea since Antiquity.

could have taken more elusive forms, including structures made of wood that leave few traces, we do not always know the extent of their decline.

Even if this cursory overview offers some chronological nuances, its broader outline matches the traditional image of a progressive disappearance of the "first urban network" at the end of Antiquity. To go beyond that, we need to nuance our investigation of these sites and give closer attention to evidence that is both rare and heterogeneous in order to push the analysis a little further.

The study of place names displayed on the gold triens (pl. trientes; more often called tremisses) coinage minted between 560 and 675 provides an additional means of documenting the centers of Poitevin power in the Merovingian period. The reverse of these coins is struck with the name of the moneyer, whose standing continues to be debated. These individuals were responsible for issuing coins on behalf of the fisc (the royal lands), a city, a *vicus*, or a church. They have been variously considered to have been functionaries working in the name of the fisc, goldsmiths, controllers of public money, or private individuals (see also Strothmann, Chapter 35, this volume). In the neighboring city of Limoges, the future St. Eligius and his father fulfilled the first two of these functions (Audoin, *Vita Eligii*, I, 3). The diversity of settlements identified on the face of the coins, the low volume of coin issues, and the fact that certain moneyers worked at more than one location or used the same dies for stamping coins, suggests that either their workshops were itinerant or centralized workshops stamped the gold stock furnished by the localities from which the coins were issued.[2]

The forty-five locations from which gold coins were issued in Poitou were of very diverse standing (Bourgeois 2005, pp. 558–562). Of course, the network of ancient Gallo-Roman towns is represented by Poitiers, but many secondary settlements also issued coins. Some appear to have been isolated in the countryside (as at Ambernac); others were described in Merovingian written sources as administrative centers of *pagi* (Brioux-sur-Boutonne, Thiré), were *vici* (Ardin), or were located at traditional river ports (Rezé, Bessac-Niort). Other ports attested from the Merovingian period should also be added to this list (Saint-Même-le-Tenu, Cenon). The list of known mint sites also includes early fortifications (Thouars), abbeys (e.g., Ligugé or Saint-Philibert-de-Grand-Lieu), and estates belonging to the royal fisc (Méron), which were often conceded to bishops (Ardin) or to large monasteries (Curçay-sur-Dive). Finally, some of the other place names found on coins from Poitou correspond to local centers established by the church in the countryside (among others, Béthines and Voultegon).

This list highlights both the political and economic influence of small Roman towns, and the importance of river ports. Although the volume of gold coin issues cannot be defined precisely, the number of different moneyers issuing coinage in the same location suggests a rough hierarchy of the places named on the tremisses. It appears, therefore, that centers like Thiré, Rezé, and Ambernac were almost as well represented by moneyers as the city of Poitiers.

The situation changed around 675, when silver became the monetary standard in the Merovingian kingdoms. The number of places from which coins were issued was then significantly reduced. From that time on, Poitiers took the top rank in minting deniers and obols (half-deniers) in the name of the city or its churches (the cathedral, Saint-Hilaire, or Sainte-Croix). The powerful rural monasteries of Saint-Maixent and Ligugé likewise continued to issue coins, as did the port of Rezé, the administrative center of the *pagus* of Brioux and the large estate (*curtis*) that Saint-Martin of Tours possessed at Doussay. But it is Melle that took on particular importance: its silver and lead mines rapidly became the most important of the Frankish world. The *vicus* that developed here around the church of Saint-Pierre was established on the leftover waste from processing ore (Téreygeol 2010). This site shows no evidence of such minting activity before the sixth to seventh century, and so it is probably necessary to see it as a Merovingian foundation. The emergence of new "central places" was equally marked around another strategic region for the Merovingian economy (Bourgeois 2005, pp. 562–563): the saltworks established here on either side of the mouth of the Loire and, further south, in the "gulf of Pictons". In 652–653, the abbey of Stavelot-Malmédy, patronized by the Pippinid Grimoald, received some rights over the *portus Vetraria* (Port-Saint-Père), a move that represented the first intervention in this region by an ancestor of the Carolingian dynasty. Nearby, the river port of Saint-Même-le-Tenu was a place from which gold coins were issued in the years 585–675 and, before 821, some warehouses there were given to the abbey of Micy by Louis the Pious. Likewise, it was on the Atlantic coast that Ansoald, the bishop of Poitiers, presided over the foundation between 677 and 682 of three new monasteries linked to ports: Noirmoutier, Saint-Michel-en-l'Herm, and Luçon.

Outside these zones, in which the control of strategic products led to the development of new establishments, the traditional network of settlements inherited from Antiquity continued to play an important role. However, it is not generally within the borders of Gallo-Roman small towns that one can find evidence of continuity but on their immediate fringes. For example, the area of the ancient Roman settlement of Vieux-Poitiers ("Old-Poitiers") at Naintré has revealed no traces of Merovingian activity. A few hundred meters further east, however, on the banks of the Vienne River, the port and *vicus* of Cenon are cited by multiple sources of the seventh to eighth century. The presence of two early churches and a vast cemetery here demonstrates the displacement of the settlement to the point at which the main road from Poitiers to Tours crossed the river (Bourgeois 2000b, pp. 178–181). In quite a few cases, a village that exercised specific functions in the course of the Middle Ages arose on the edge of an abandoned ancient city (Rom, Sanxay, Vendeuvre-du-Poitou, etc.). This shift could have resulted from the development of a new settlement around an ancient suburban cemetery and any religious buildings located there. At Aulnay, for example, the church of Saint-Pierre was established over the tombs of soldiers from the ancient Roman military camp, on the edge of the Roman settlement, and alongside the old road from Poitiers to Bordeaux. The associated settlement shifted in the tenth century toward the nearby hill, near a viscount's castle, and the church was left isolated.

The churches and cemeteries associated with such sites often reveal specific characteristics. In the neighboring Touraine region, the list of the oldest episcopal foundations transmitted by Gregory of Tours illustrates the foundation by bishops of religious complexes in the countryside dependent upon the cathedral and the frequent choice of small towns of Gallo-Roman origin for these implantations (Zadora-Rio 2008, pp. 21–25, 77–78). There is no such documentation for Poitou, but a number of indicators suggest that the situation was quite similar. The site of Civaux furnishes a good archaeological illustration of this phenomenon. In this Roman settlement, which already housed a Christian community at the beginning of the fifth century, a Gallo-Roman temple was reused in the Merovingian period to establish a church dedicated to Sts. Gervasius and Protasius and associated with a small baptistery (Boissavit-Camus and Bourgeois 2005, pp. 159–161).

In the diocese of Poitiers, fifteen other sites preserve traces of clusters of church buildings established in imitation of cathedral complexes and including: a principal building (most frequently dedicated to St. Peter, patron of the cathedral of Poitiers, or else to foreign saints who had an early cult in Gaul); a nearby structure, probably for the purpose of baptism and always dedicated to John the Baptist; and sometimes a third church established nearby and associated with the relics of a local confessor saint. To give but one example, the village of Saint-Jean-de-Sauves, located next to a Gallo-Roman settlement, formerly included two churches dedicated to St. John the Baptist and Pope Clement I (Boissavit-Camus and Bourgeois 2005, p. 164). In Merovingian sources, such centers were often identified as *vici* and were served by archpriests, as in the case of the Poitevan *vicus* of Bessay, where Gregory of Tours mentioned one such archpriest in an anecdote in his *Glory of the Martyrs*, (Godding 2001, pp. 215–247).

Sometimes much later, such a complex was described as the *ecclesia matrix* (mother church) of the neighboring district. At Saint-Pierre-les-Églises (Chauvigny), the parish church, which at one time was associated with two other sanctuaries, remained isolated in the midst of the ruins of the former Roman town. The parish church nonetheless preserved some prerogatives over nearby parishes. We should note also that a not insubstantial portion of this network continued to form part of the patrimony of the bishops of Poitiers until the eighteenth century (Boissavit-Camus and Bourgeois 2005, p.164).

If the majority of cemeteries associated with Merovingian settlements in Poitou were modest in size (less than 250 graves), some very large cemeteries also have been identified in this region. All appear to have been linked to small Roman towns. The example of Civaux, with its thousands of sarcophagi, is famous, but this phenomenon may be found elsewhere, as, for example, at Cenon, Saint-Pierre-les-Églises, Brioux-sur-Boutonne, or Aulnay (Bourgeois 2005, p. 548). The list of regional cemeteries that have produced epitaphs and decorated sarcophagi includes Poitiers and some large monasteries, but this list again privileges the larger settlements that had their roots in Antiquity. The cemetery of Antigny, which took over from the Roman settlement of Gué de Sciaux, has, for example, yielded a remarkable collection of decorated sarcophagi and names of the dead. The quantity and quality of the tombs demonstrate that such sites still possessed a power of attraction that exceeded their local framework and that they remained privileged foci for the elites. Finally, the Roman tradition of the suburban cemetery continued in some former Roman towns, as at the foot of the *castrum* of Loudun, where the suburb of Martray (*martyretum*), with its two churches, constituted a veritable neighborhood of the dead from Late Antiquity to the eighteenth century (Bourgeois 2000a, p. 44).

Lay centers of power are more difficult to discern for the Merovingian period. The public character of some large fortified sites is evident, as at Champtoceaux, residence of Duke Austrapius in the 560s, and then of Pippin III during the conquest of Aquitaine (Gregory of Tours, *Historiae* IV, 18; Fred. *Cont.* IV, 51). Similarly, when Childeric II allocated the revenues of the domain of Ardin to the church of Le Mans in 669 (Weidemann 2002, Nr. 7), he showed the relationship between this former ancient settlement and the lands of the fisc, an association that can be confirmed for several Carolingian examples in Poitou. By contrast, the administrative consistency of the *pagi minores*, territorial entities of a lower rank than a city, remains more difficult to determine. The increase in the number of sources in the Carolingian epoch illustrates more clearly the predilection of public power for the centers that had deep roots in the past, where viscounts or *vicarii* (magistrates) were installed. Even some sites that had been deserted since the end of Antiquity appear to have conserved a symbolic place in political memory: thus, it was in the ruins of Vieux-Poitiers that the sons of Charles Martel met in 742 (Fred. *Cont.* IV, 25). Even if the network of "central places" was partially renewed during the Merovingian period, without a doubt at least some major sites inherited from Antiquity, the material appearance of which could be modest, conserved their *aura* as public places. Their antiquity helped legitimize the actions of successive local powers who acted from them.

Instead, the actual rupture with the past only occurred in the tenth to eleventh century: new urban centers attracted authorities, just as they did communication routes. Even if certain castral or monastic towns succeeded earlier settlements, many other traditional places of power lost their last public prerogatives in these later centuries. Only the episcopate made conservative choices in fixing the numerous seats of archdeacons and deacons in villages that were heirs to small Roman towns, like Brioux-sur-Boutonne, Sanxay, and Rom (Bourgeois 2005, pp. 549–550). These "living fossils" were maintained until the time of the French Revolution.

FORTIFIED SETTLEMENTS, HILLTOP SETTLEMENTS

References to fortified sites other than *civitas* capitals are relatively numerous in the written sources of the fifth to eighth century. Most appear in contemporary narratives as strongholds to conquer (which proves their strategic interest), or as refuges for the population. These references have given birth to the concept of the walled refuge, which has long dominated French historiography. As recently as 2000, André Debord described such sites, often inherited from the Iron Age, as having a function that was "inadvertently residential", and denied them any importance as political, administrative, and economic centers (Debord 2000, pp. 27–31). This kind of interpretation arises from a variety of causes, including: an absence of extensive excavations (or excavations that focus only on the earlier phases from these sites); a very pessimistic reading of early medieval developments; and confidence that fortifications akin to the medieval castle could not have existed before around 1000. Nevertheless, the sources of the fifth and sixth centuries describe both fortified palaces and the foundation of walled settlements furnished with a wall. Without material proof, however, such evidence has been regarded as the product of nostalgic yearnings for Antiquity.

Once again, the pioneering work of Gabriel Fournier on the Auvergne outlined very early the complexity of these hilltop sites and their importance in the control of territories (Fournier 1962, pp. 401–409). But it was only with the project organized by Laurent Schneider on hilltop settlements in the Mediterranean regions of France that the great diversity of this kind of site became apparent (e.g., Schneider 2004). Since then, although research has extended to the east and center of France, the coast of the Channel, the North Sea, and the Atlantic remain to be studied. The size of such hilltop installations appears to have been extremely variable: spanning from a few hundred square meters to more than 100 hectares. Their density in the regions that have been best studied appears relatively high: for example, more than a hundred sites of this period have been identified along the Mediterranean coast between Marseille and Spain, twenty in the Auvergne, and fifty in Franche-Comté. In the regions that remain to be studied, one should mention, among others, the banks of the Loire, where a series of large fortifications of the fifth to sixth century dot the landscape between Champtoceaux and Blois. Similar indications exist for Normandy and Burgundy. With the multiplication of excavations, always limited and conducted on challenging terrain, it is now possible to outline a typology that reveals the variety of forms and functions of hilltop sites and to catch a glimpse of the rhythms of their creation and abandonment.

It makes sense to accept the existence of a certain number of foundations among the hilltop sites that were purely military in their conception. But in Gaul the fortifications that simply sheltered a garrison defending frontiers or communication routes appear to have been both few in number and early in date. Several small hilltop sites in northern Gaul established between the last third of the third century and the beginning of the fifth century housed a military contingent or auxiliaries of Germanic origin, including Franks. They have never been the subject of exhaustive excavations, and they remain documented above all by their cemeteries. All of them were occupied for only a relatively brief period (Brulet 2008). We can likewise note the two fortresses of Cluses (Pyrénées-Atlantiques), which flanked a pass controlling the route of the *Via Domitia* through the Pyrenees. They probably marked the frontier with the Iberian peninsula from the 350s and clearly constituted sites with a military purpose. But occupation at these sites too does not seem to have extended beyond the fifth century (Castellvi 1995).

By contrast, the dozens of hilltop settlements occupied from the mid-fifth century that have been partially excavated in France practically never reveal evidence of weaponry. To be sure, the installation of people in these hilltop sites that were difficult to access, and the resources expended on the construction of their walls, testify to defensive concerns, but these fortifications could equally have symbolized the status of these settlements and a desire for display by the powers that were established there. More than the exterior appearance of these sites, it is their interior organization that reveals their true nature: elite residences that controlled the neighboring territory, peasant settlements, harvest storage sites, artisanal and religious centers, and even veritable urban creations.

In effect, the will to found true fortified towns *ex nihilo* remained significant in Mediterranean Gaul during the fifth and sixth centuries. At the beginning of this period, this desire was evoked by a famous inscription in the name of the former praetorian prefect of the Gauls, a man named Dardanus. When this powerful person founded his *Theopolis* in the mountains above Sisteron (Alpes de Haute-Provence), his first concern was to protect it with "walls and gates" (*CIL* XII, 1524). Although this "City of God" has not been found, this type of settlement is now exemplified by sites like the Roc de Pampelune (Argelliers, Hérault) (Schneider 2008, pp. 40–46) (Fig. 28.4A). Established to the north of Montpellier on a large outcrop with a surface area of 2 hectares, it was founded between the late fifth century and 540, its dynamism thereafter weakening until the site's definitive abandonment in the seventh century. Just as other hilltop settlements, it was organized over two terraces. The upper terrace was occupied by a church that was

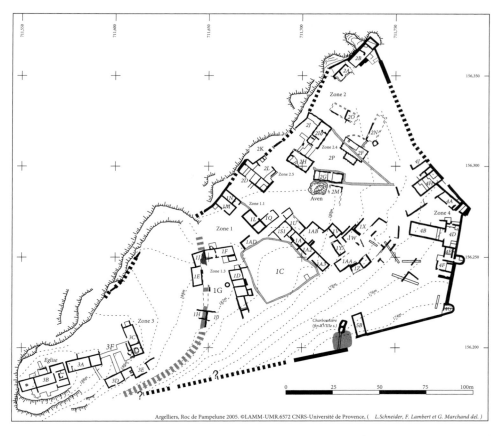

FIGURE 28.4. A: Le Roc de Pampelune (Argelliers, Hérault) (L. Schneider, F. Lambert, and G. Marchand).

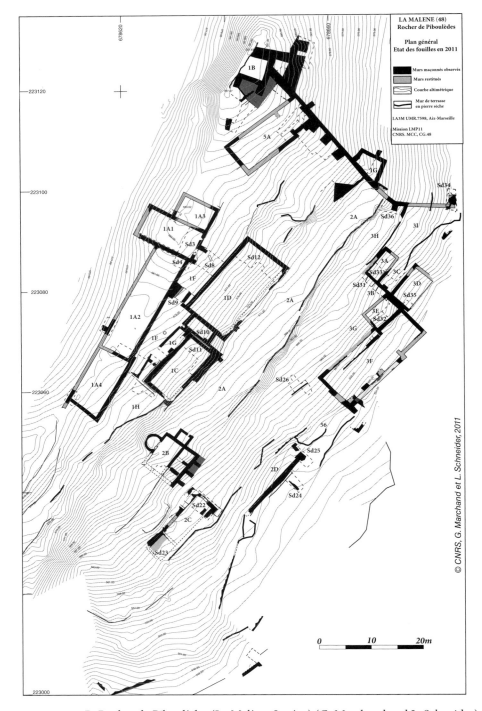

FIGURE 28.4. B: Rocher de Piboulèdes (La Malène, Lozère) (G. Marchand and L. Schneider).

the last building on the site to be abandoned. Extended by a baptistery, it contained a rich marble sarcophagus. The baptismal complex is associated with a series of buildings interpreted by the excavator as the residence of a group of priests who served the sanctuary. Below it, the principal terrace was organized in a way that bears no relationship to the regular layout of the classical city: it consisted of the juxtaposition of courtyards bordered by stone buildings with tile roofs. Each of these units included a vast principal house with an upper story, and housing units of one or two rooms of standardized dimensions. The stone rampart, which was fairly thin, was punctuated by some small towers. The principal activity of the inhabitants was artisanal and was linked to metalworking: both ferrous and nonferrous metals (copper alloys and perhaps gold) were subjected to different processes in the course of their transformation, revealing a high level of technical competence. Glass was also transformed on this site and surrounding ones, its manufacture no doubt exploiting forests that today are long gone. The settlement was integrated fully into the Mediterranean exchange network, as is shown by, among other things, the diversity of late amphorae found at the site (on Mediterranean trade, see Bonifay and Pieri, chapter 37, this volume).

During Late Antiquity and the early centuries of the Middle Ages, many hilltop sites with Iron Age fortifications were also reoccupied. In these cases, the walls and the earlier urban layouts often determined to a great extent the nature of the later oRampartion. This is the case at the well known site of Saint-Blaise (Saint-Mitre-les-Remparts, Bouches-du-Rhône) established between two saltwater marshes on the coast of Languedoc (Fig. 28.5A). The early medieval occupation was not on virgin terrain because an important protohistoric settlement had previously existed here over two terraces that formed a plateau of 5.5 hectares, protected by a powerful rampart closing off access to the outcrop. But this first settlement was almost fully abandoned at the end of the second century BCE, and it was not until the mid-fifth century CE that it was progressively reoccupied. The first three quarters of the sixth century saw the reconstruction of a wall punctuated by towers of diverse forms and bordered by a church (church A); the development of the occupied areas partially respected the layout of the Hellenistic streets and the appearance of a vast extramural cemetery. This renaissance was contemporary with the Frankish conquest of Provence with the support of the Byzantine Empire (536–537), and the structure of the new enclosure wall was consistent with a Byzantine style. The first phase of post-Roman occupation, which privileged the "lower quarter" of the site, was partially given up at the end of the sixth century, when Church A was abandoned and the orientation of the layout of certain quarters was changed. This reorganized layout included a large house equipped with an absidial reception room, and church B was linked to a baptistery. From the seventh century, however, the settlement shrank progressively toward a "high quarter" at the summit of the plateau. Over the course of the following centuries, only a small settlement called the *castellum vetus* (old fortification) survived on the outcrop, clustered around the churches that succeeded sanctuary B. Below Sainte-Blaise, the port of Fos-sur-Mer was able to maintain close ties with the *oppidum*, which was particularly important for the salt trade (Valenciano 2015).

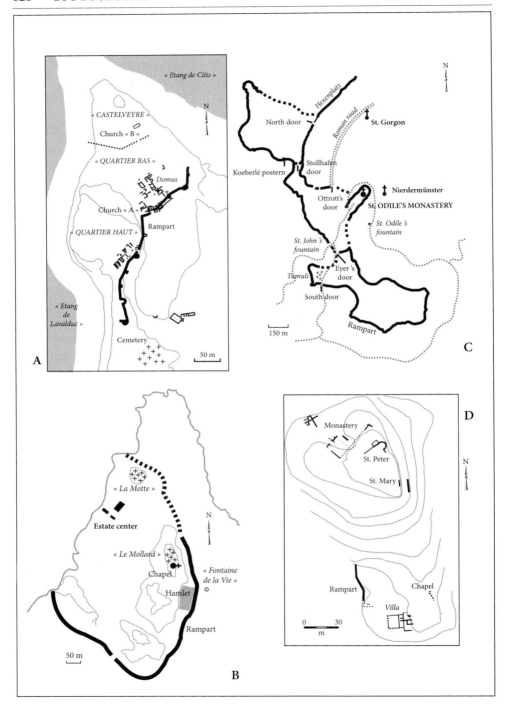

FIGURE 28.5. A: Saint-Blaise (Saint-Mitre-les-Remparts, Bouches-du-Rhône)(after Valenciano);
B: Larina, general map (Hières-sur-Amby, Isère)(after Porte); C: Le Mont-Sainte-Odile (Ottrott,
Bas-Rhin)(after Steuer); D: Le Saint-Mont (Saint-Amé Vosges)(after Kraemer).

Other hilltop settlements, which have revealed structures far more modest than those of Roc de Pampelune, appear equally to have been dedicated principally or even exclusively to metallurgical activities. Nicolas Clément has recently renewed the study of elevated settlements controlling access between the Rhône Valley and the Ardèche by the Eyrole and Baravon passes that fall into this category (Clément 2011, III-2, pp. 62–74; 111–119). At Chastelas de Baravon (Gras, Ardèche), these structures occupy an area of 2 hectares, but there is no sign of any wall around them. This site has revealed small individual residences, constructed in dry stone covered with perishable materials and flanked by paths. The earliest finds associated with these sites go back to the mid-fifth century, but their occupation appears to have been particularly dense in the sixth century, just before their subsequent decline. However, this site has produced neither traces of high-quality architecture nor Mediterranean imports. Baravon appears to have been superseded in the course of the seventh century by the hilltop settlement near the Ferme de Retz (Lagorce, Ardèche). This settlement presents the same characteristics as its predecessor. Enclosed by a simple clay-bonded wall, it was occupied for several generations by metalworkers who were involved in all of the stages of producing iron from imported refined materials.

Other fortified sites could serve as public or private storage places. A passage from Cassiodorus's *Variae* III, 41, relates how, before 526, Theodoric sent stocks of Italian wheat destined for the troops of the Visigothic-Ostrogothic kingdom. They were stored in Marseille before being distributed among the *castella* (forts). While such "citadel-storage places" similar to those of North Africa or Muslim Spain have not been identified clearly in Gaul, sites like Lombren (Vénéjan, Gard) and Clapas-Castel (La Canourgue, Lozère) could have sheltered peasant communities of the late fifth and sixth centuries (Soutou 1964; Charmasson 1970). They had drystone ramparts sheltering simple buildings of one or two rooms, some of which may have constituted storage spaces, enclosures for animals, or gardens (on rural settlements, see Peytremann, chapter 31, this volume).

Alongside these sites with modest structures and finds, contemporary texts, like archaeology, demonstrate that elites of the fifth to eighth century often inhabited collective fortified settlements, where they benefited fairly late from long-distance Mediterranean trade. The vast settlement of Sant-Peyre (Bouquet, Gard), for example, represents a residence in the Roman tradition occupied at the end of the seventh century or the beginning of the eighth by a magnate who posssesed large amphorae from the Byzantine region and an Umayyad seal (Pellecuer and Pène 2002). But throughout the period considered here, some aristocratic residences occupied the entirety of fortified spaces. The famous description by Sidonius Apollinaris of the *burgus* (fortress) of Pontius Leontius (Bourg, Gironde) provides some details of the features of this luxury senatorial residence of the mid-fifth century (*Carm.* XXII, ed. Loyen, I, pp. 132–143). A century later, Venantius Fortunatus offered a description of the fortified palace of Nicetius, bishop of Trier (526–566/569) on the banks of the Moselle, which echoed Sidonius's account. Founded on a rocky outcrop, this palace was surrounded by a wall, and its gate was defended by a tower equipped with artillery (*gemino ballista*). The principal residence, which was comparable to a *castellum*, included a marble colonnade and extended over three or four levels. An aqueduct supplied the site with water and also turned the wheel of a mill (Venantius Fortunatus, *Carmina* III, 12).

These descriptions of fifth- and sixth-century poets might seem like literary evocations strongly colored by the mores of classical culture. However, the hilltop palace of La Malène (Lozère) allows us to concretize the existence of such sites (Fig. 28.4B). Dominating the gorges of the Ardèche, this narrow spur (0.5 hectare) was separated from a neighboring plateau by a wall and a buttressed tower. A large hall decorated with paintings was discovered under this tower. In the middle of the site, the residential building, more than 40 meters long, was composed of an immense cellar with an arcaded upper story above. A cistern for supplying water to baths and a mausoleum or church occupied the lower part of the site. The finds associated with La Malène show that its inhabitants continued to follow a Roman way of life at this late date. It seems to have been the *castrum Melena* in which Bishop Hilary of Gévaudan took refuge ca. 530. Founded at the end of the fifth century or at the beginning of the sixth, from 507, this site was effectively on the frontier between the Franks and the Visigoths, and its key role may have been to control the production of the mint of Banassac, one of the most active in the Merovingian realm. The occupation of the hilltop spur continued until the mid-seventh century, or possibly even a little later (Schneider and Clément 2012).

Other archaeological undertakings have revealed less prestigious residences, which nevertheless still attest to elite occupation of fortified settlements. The very classical structure discovered on the upper terrace of the *oppidum* of Notre-Dame de la Consolation at Jouques (Bouches-du-Rhône) (Fig. 28.6A) could thus signal the privatization of a collectively occupied fortification. The lower part of this plateau of roughly 30 hectares dominating the valley of the Durance was fortified from the Iron Age and reoccupied during the fifth and sixth centuries, specifically by a church. The upper terrace has revealed a residential complex comprising a main building oriented east–west, completed later by a new wing perpendicular to it. The presence of decorated capitals, stucco, and cement floors compensated for the modest quality of its masonry. Evolving over the course of the seventh and eighth centuries, this ensemble survived until the start of the ninth century (Michel d'Annoville 2005).

The large rocky outcrop of Larina (Hières-sur-Amby, Isère) remains one of the most fully excavated hilltop settlements known to date (Porte 2011). Established on a limestone spur overlooking the Rhône River, a rampart close to a kilometer long defended almost 21 hectares (Fig. 28.5B). Probably built in the Iron Age, it was restored during the Merovingian epoch. The topography of the site, which was very irregular, included many hills and a cultivatable depression. Some dry stone huts, dispersed or in groups, may represent a complementary early medieval settlement, while the successive stages of the principal residence occupied a small plateau of 4 hectares to the northwest of the site (Fig. 28.6E). A first stage (end of the fourth to early fifth century) comprised dispersed wooden huts, associated with a *fanum* (pagan sanctuary) and quarries. They were replaced in the second quarter of the fifth century by a new group of habitations and farming annexes with wooden elevations on a pebble foundation. These buildings, which were the object of numerous transformations, have been interpreted by the

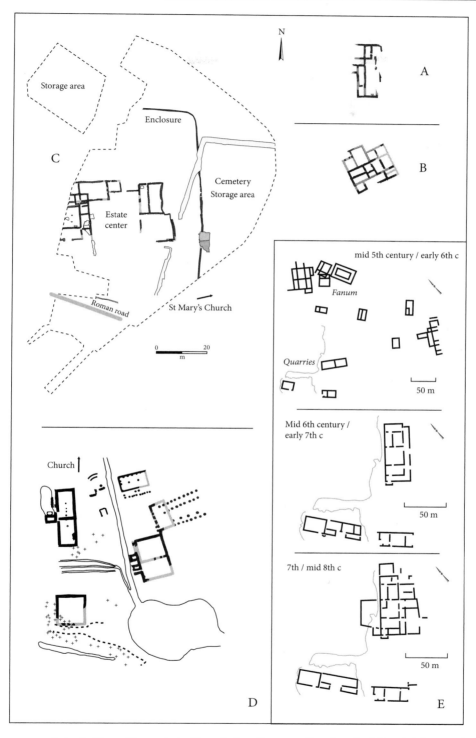

FIGURE 28.6. A: Notre-Dame de la Consolation (Jouques, Bouches-du-Rhône) (after Michel d'Anoville); B: Saint-Romain-de-Jalionas (Isère) (after Porte); C: Pouthumé (Châtellerault, Vienne) (after Cornec); D: Serris (Seine-et-Marne) (after Gentili); E: Larina, estate (Hières-sur-Amby, Isère) (after Porte).

excavator as the satellites of a *villa* established on the plain. Close to the settlement, a cemetery of 123 graves (at a site called la Motte) was used during the years 440–550.

The first half of the sixth century, which corresponded to the arrival of the Merovingians in the region, was marked by an important rupture. A new architectural program at Larina was at that time put steadily into action. It consisted of a large residence associated with two agricultural buildings. The residential complex consisted of a rectangular structure originally composed of four rooms, but which was gradually enlarged until it attained a surface area of 1,200 square meters. Built on a stone foundation, it perhaps also had an upper floor. Stock-rearing, however, seems to have been the main activity on the site, and one sees the appearance of finds of northern origin. At the same time, the cemetery of La Motte was abandoned for a new cemetery, located on the highest hill of the site. The principal funerary space, which was first established around a mausoleum at the summit, was relocated in a second phase around a chapel that housed high-status tombs.

The excavator Patrick Porte has observed that, at the beginning of the seventh century at the earliest, an evolution took place in the residential building, which seems to have been divided among three groups of inhabitants and was used for different functions. The exterior gallery was thus destroyed to create rooms linked to agricultural production. The funerary chapel, reconstructed after a fire, was progressively augmented with many annex rooms, and a funerary enclosure in dry stone (a structure lacking mortar) appeared in the cemetery. Several dominant groups also seem to have coexisted here. The complex was willingly abandoned during the course of the eighth century, and the openings of the principal building were walled in.

The site of Larina testifies to a contrasting evolution. It seems to have represented the annex of a residence in the valley below until the emergence of the vast residential and funerary complex in the course of the sixth century shows the site's autonomy. Even if one of the stages of the residential building included an exterior gallery reminiscent of ancient architectural tradition, the Roman way of life quickly disappeared.

We have already noted the frequency of religious structures, and, in particular, baptismal and funerary churches, present in the midst of large hilltop settlements occupied from the fifth century. Moreover, these were often the only buildings that survived the desertion of these sites. For example, in the Auvergnat *castrum* of La Couronne (Molles, Allier), a building established on a terrace bordering the enclosure was significantly enlarged in the years 425–430, just before its transformation into a church (Martinez et al. 2018). The site reached its apogee in the sixth and at the beginning of the seventh centuries, when the building was completed by a series of annexes, including a possible baptistery, before being burned down. The church was, however, reconstructed around the year 1000 on a site that appears to have been abandoned in the interim.

The power of the church is equally apparent at certain sites in the form of monasteries (on monasticism, see also Diem, Chapter 15, this volume). Above all, they sheltered communities of women: this logic of protecting nuns merges with the observations of Hartmut Atsma (1976, p. 184) on the cities in northern Gaul, where female monastic communities were for the most part established within city walls.

In the eastern part of modern France, two famous sites illustrate well this reuse of hilltop fortifications for the establishment of a monastery. The first is Le Saint-Mont (Saint-Amé, Vosges), where earlier excavations have recently been subject to new interpretations (Kraemer 2008) (Fig. 28.5D). The site was established on the southern edge of the Vosges Mountains, at an intersection of land and river routes. Tied to a woodland (*saltus*) that was probably part of the Merovingian fisc, the *castrum Habendum*, also known as the *Vosagi castrum*, was controlled at the start of the seventh century by the ancestors of Romaric, the former duke of Austrasia. With Amé, a monk of Luxeuil, Romaric founded a female monastery ca. 620, which was rapidly moved to the interior of the *castrum*. The least steep access to the site was blocked by a 400-meter-long rampart of dry stone. This first barrier, which protected a surface a little larger than 4 hectares, was reinforced by an internal earthen rampart that was clad with granite, which followed the terrain of the upper part of the mountain. The interior of this second enclosure was divided into three terraces. The lower part revealed traces of a residence traditionally identified as the residence of Romaric and linked to Merovingian finds. In a second phase, this sector sheltered numerous graves and was still used for burial as late as the eleventh century. A funerary basilica, which was likely constructed in the seventh century and surrounded by numerous tombs, occupied the middle terrace. The monastic complex was constructed in the upper part of the enclosure. It consisted of the abbey church of Saint-Pierre and the funerary church of Sainte-Marie. A cemetery focused around a mausoleum that contained a decorated Merovingian sarcophagus was established between the two sanctuaries. Other chapels (Saint-Michel, Saint-Sépulcre, Sainte-Croix) are attested later in the cartulary of St-Mont (Bridot 1997). The ensemble was deserted ca.820 for Remiremont in the nearby valley, but that abbey refounded a priory at St-Mont in the twelfth century.

One hundred kilometers to the northeast, the "pagan wall" that surrounded the mountainous outcrop of Mont-Sainte-Odile (Ottrott, Bas-Rhin), with its perimeter of 10.5 kilometers, is suggestive more of a desire for ostentation than a need for defense (Fig. 28.5C). Its construction, moreover, harked back clearly to the monumental architecture of antiquity; it made use of large ashlars assembled with the assistance of wooden clamps. The monumentality of this site is likewise underlined by the gate towers with a vaulted passage surmounted by an upper storey. The dating of a sample of wood from the site indicates that the building was constructed ca. 670, a date compatible with the finds from within the site. The 120 hectares enclosed by the wall were organized into three neighboring spaces. The southern area has revealed rich burials under a mound dated to the end of the Merovingian period. The middle terrace, which reutilized a Neolithic-period fortification, contained a monastery and the only cultivable land on the plateau. The masters of this site were the dukes of Alsace, who probably made it the seat of their power. The function of this fortified complex evolved with the foundation of the female monastery of Hohenburg, of which Odile, the daughter of Duke Eticho, became the first abbess at the turn of the seventh and eighth centuries (Steuer 2012).

These two examples illustrate the functional evolution of certain large fortified sites in which a monastic complex might replace a lay complex and perpetuate the power of its owners in a different form. Such abbeys could equally be established beneath a *castrum*, as was the case at Loches (Indre-et-Loire), where Gregory of Tours indicates that the *castrum* was built in his time above a monastery founded by St. Ursus and the neighboring *vicus* (Gregory of Tours, *Historiae* X, 31 and *VP* XVIII, 1–3). The frequency of this complementarity between a hilltop settlement and a residence at the base of a valley needs more systematic study. It could involve the pairing *castrum/vicus*, as at Château-Thierry (Aisne), a link between *castrum* and *portus* (Champtoceaux, Maine-et-Loire), or the control of main roads, small towns of Roman origin, and saltmines, as in the Jura (Billouin and Gandel 2013). It would also be of interest to understand more about the coupling of rural *castra* and *curtes* (centers of large estates)—which are better attested in the Carolingian period—and the relationship between *castra* and the lands of the fisc.

Sometimes, neighboring fortifications also seem to have been the products of a combined program, as attested by three sites near the Donzère Gorge (Drôme and Ardèche). From the end of the fifth century, this area of the Rhône Valley saw the development of the vast *oppidum* of Saint-Saturnin, the probable fortified aristocratic residence of Château-Porcher, and on the opposite bank of the river, the walled town of Viviers, which became the location of the episcopal group, transferred from the former city of Alba (Clément 2011, t. III-2, pp. 44–54, 179–206). It is nonetheless necessary to admit that such policies of fortification remained in part in the hands of Roman authorities until ca. 475–477, even in territories occupied by the Burgundians, Visigoths, and the Franks. The movement to create hilltop sites in the Auvergne, which began at the turn of the fourth to fifth century, or the initial emergence of fortifications in the French Jura in the second quarter of the fifth century, should be understood from this perspective. By contrast, the vast program initiated ca. 500 in the city of Nîmes occurred after the Visigoths were no longer under imperial authority. This allowed them to establish a new network of fortified cities in the mountainous regions that were not urbanized in Antiquity or in which few *villae* survived from the Gallo-Roman period. The second phase of the creation of the sites in the Jura (late fifth to early eighth century) likewise reveals a political strategy specific to the barbarian kingdoms regarding fortification. Whatever their chronology, such investment of resources raises questions about both the new geography of places of power and the reorganization of the territory of Roman cities (Schneider 2008).

Over the course of their territorial expansion, the Franks took over and completed these networks of fortifications. However, the fate of these hilltop sites varied by region. The wave of abandonments of hilltop sites that marked the seventh century requires, for example, a nuanced reading: the fact that archaeological excavations are only concerned with deserted sites has led scholars to overestimate the failures, and it is under modern settlements (like Anduze, Gard), that one should look for the more lasting foundations. Moreover, after the sixth century, these installations are less monumental and yield finds that are more difficult to date. But some fortifications long remained in use, like the important site of Pont-de-Roide (Doubs), which moved to the base of a neighboring valley around the year 1000, or the *castra* on the banks of the Loire River, still urbanized today. Others received a masonry enclosure in the seventh century (Camp du Château at

Salins-les-Bains, Jura: Gandel 2014) or contained a new form of occupation at the turn of the seventh and eighth century (the *oppidum* of Sainte-Candie in Roquebrune-sur-Argens, Var). Finally, in the Carolingian epoch, some *castra* that appear to have been deserted or very disorganized gave their name to administrative districts, without revealing whether they still constituted centers of power or if they merely marked, among learned elites, the memory of formerly important sites (Schneider 2008).

OPEN ELITE RESIDENCES: FROM RESIDENCES IN THE ANCIENT STYLE TO THE "VILLAGE MANOR"

Elite residences observed in fortified sites now have some parallels among open settlements. The rare examples excavated make it possible to sketch out three main architectural types. In southern Gaul, we have already covered the late survival of architectural principles dating from Antiquity, such as the tendency to incorporate symmetry in designs, external galleries, or apsidal rooms. Such classical referents are not at all surprising in regions in which aristocratic *villae* survived until the sixth century, or even a little later (see Chavarría Arnau, Chapter 29, this volume). These references are, for example, still very apparent in the seventh century in the Merovingian residence of Saint-Romain-de-Jalionas (Isère). This building was established in a vast Gallo-Roman *villa*, which had been luxuriously redesigned in the fourth and fifth centuries. After a hiatus of a century, a new construction of close to 400 m² replaced the main building of the ancient *villa* (Fig. 28.6B). Built in reused stones and tiles, it had a symmetrical layout, with axial reception rooms and a gallery with corner pavilions to the exterior. The ensemble perhaps included an upper story. Nearby, a funerary chapel containing high-status tombs was established in a late-antique structure (Porte 2011, I, pp. 367–368, 403).

A second model of elite residence developed further to the north, as is attested by the site of Pouthumé (Châtellerault, Vienne) in the seventh to eighth century. The main focus here was a courtyard surrounded by buildings that opened to the south, occupying in total a surface area of about 1,500 square meters (Fig. 28.6C). A rectangular residential building with an estimated length of 18 meters closed its western side. It included an enormous central hall (about 65 square meters), surrounded by smaller rooms probably with an upper floor above. The entry points, by foot from the courtyard and by cart from the south, were neatly separated. The hypothesis of a comfortable dwelling place in the north and probable service rooms in the south is equally reinforced by the differences in the quality of the foundations of the masonry walls. This plan, consisting of a large central structure (perhaps an *aula* or hall?) surrounded by two levels of small rooms, has parallels in the Carolingian epoch such as in Thier d'Olne (Engis, Belgium). At Pouthumé, the eastern wing was a vast building with two naves. It contained a grain dryer, linked to an enclosure, and the courtyard was closed to the north by a ruined structure. Just on the edge of the ditched enclosure that marked the edges of this settlement, there was a small, semi-buried wooden structure, perhaps a funerary building, which has been dated to the years 663–795. It was surrounded by a cemetery and storage silos. At the time of its abandonment, the residence was briefly replaced by a single rectangular building. Beside it, funerary activity grew and continued until the tenth to the eleventh century. East of the cemetery, texts then attest to the existence of a church dedicated to the Virgin. The discovery of an epitaph of a kinsman of the dukes of Aquitaine from the beginning of the tenth century shows that this site continued to house members of the elite (Cornec and Farago-Szekeres 2010).

In a third model, now well attested in northern France, the buildings were arranged in a looser manner around one or two courtyards (see Peytremann, Chapter 31, this volume). The dwelling of Ruelles at Serris (Seine-et-Marne), part of a village founded at the start of the seventh century, corresponds to this type of layout. From the origin of this site, an enclosure established in its southwest part contained a "manor" (Fig. 28.6D). It was organized around a courtyard, closed on the west side by a residential building more than 30 meters long, perhaps with an upper story. Some of the buildings in this residence were the only structures of the settlement with a stone foundation. Two of them were associated with groups of graves characterized by a high percentage of women and quality dress accessories. The presence of window glass and a Byzantine scale weight, the importance of pork (whereas beef was predominant in the rest of the village), the consumption of peacocks, white bread, and sturgeon, among other things, strongly distinguished the inhabitants of this part of the site (on animals and diet, see Yvinec and Barme, Chapter 33, this volume). This ensemble was deserted at the end of the eighth century or at the start of the ninth for another elite settlement, constructed on wooden posts and established just to the south of the preceding habitation (Gentili and Valais 2007). The frequent association of such estate centers with villages and places of worship that survive today demonstrates the durable imprint of these estate centers on the organization of the countryside.

RUPTURES, CONTINUITIES, MEMORY

The four categories of site covered in these pages allow us to reflect variously on the hierarchy of "central places" during the Merovingian period, from cities to an administrative center or a large estate. Nevertheless, this archaeological rereading, initiated in the early 2000s, remains very patchy and it will be necessary to expand the inventories and excavations to discern all of the diversity of these settlements and the historical context of their establishment.

It is now clear that the concept of "fortified refuge" and the hypothesis of a multiplication of hilltop sites in response to the menace of invasions have lost virtually all of their value for the early centuries of the Middle Ages. Whatever the area of the sites under study, each new excavation reveals lasting settlements whose forms and functions are extremely varied. They reconnected with the geographical rationale that had prevailed in the pre-Roman period and marked a rupture with the infrastructures of power that had prevailed in Antiquity. Besides geopolitical choices, the change from intensive agriculture to more varied production could also help to explain the investment in hilltops for metalworking and glassworking or the extension of stock-rearing.

The cities and secondary settlements inherited from Antiquity often remained points of anchorage of lay and ecclesiastical power, no doubt because they enjoyed the legitimacy of traditional "public places." But this legitimacy was displayed above all in new forms, by the foundation of baptismal and monastic churches, by the burial of the dead at such sites, and by the geography of relics. The long-term survival of these settlements was more certain when they were inserted in new configurations of political space and networks of exchange. In other cases, this survival was more symbolic than real. Finally, the first excavations of the rural residences of Merovingian elites furnish some "missing links" between the model of the Gallo-Roman villa and the demesne centers of the medieval period.

Romanitas clearly remained an architectural reference point for the elites who decided on the creation or maintenance of most of these sites. But these references to the past appear more and more superficial as one moves later in time and toward the north. For example, the centers of power that replaced the older small towns were located on the fringes of their original areas, adopted previously unused forms, and exercised new functions: arguments for topographical and functional continuity thus must be nuanced. At the same time, external galleries, symmetrical layouts, and apsidal rooms remained quite late as features in elite residences, but these architectural formulas lost a large part of their functional significance with the disappearance of *otium* (leisure time). Moreover, the construction techniques employed increasingly limited the luxurious character of such dwellings. *A contrario*, the analysis of fortifications of the fifth to eighth century reveals borrowings from the classical architectural vocabulary for the defense of cities that were more symbolic than pragmatic. This dialectic between the renewal of forms and functions, and the prestige of earlier models reflected and accompanied the reciprocal acculturation of elites of Gallo-Roman and Germanic origin.

NOTES

1. This chapter has been translated from French by Bonnie Effros, Isabel Moreira, and Simon Loseby.
2. For a review of different hypotheses regarding the status of Merovingian-era moneyers, see Boyer 2018, pp. 148–177.

WORKS CITED

Ancient Sources

Audoin, *Vita Eligii Noviomagensis*. B. Krusch (ed.). (1902). MGH: SRM 4 (pp. 663–742). Hanover: Hahn.

Bridot, J. (ed.). (1997). *Chartes de l'abbaye de Remiremont, des origines à 1231*. ARTEM 2. 2nd ed. Turnhout: Brepols.

Cassiodorus, *Variae*. T. Mommsen (ed.). (1894). *Variae: Cassiodori senatoris chronica*. MGH: AA 12 (pp. 1–385). Berlin: Weidmann.

CIL XII. O. Hirschfeld (ed.). (1888). *Inscriptiones Galliae Narbonensis latinae. Corpus inscriptionum latinarum*, 12. Berlin: Reimer.

Fredegar, *Chronicon*. J. M. Wallace-Hadrill (ed. and trans.). (1960). *The Fourth Book of the Chronicle of Fredegar with Its Continuations*. London: Nelson.

Gregory of Tours, *Liber vitae patrum (VP)*. B. Krusch (ed.). (1885). *Liber vitae patrum*. MGH: SRM 1.2 (pp. 211–294). Hanover: Hahn.

Gregory of Tours, *Historiarum libri decem (Historiae)*. B. Krusch and W. Levison (eds.). (1937[1951]). MGH: SRM 1.1. Hanover: Hahn.

Sidonius Apollinaris, *Carmina*. A. Loyen (ed. and trans.). (1960[2008]). *Poèmes* 1. Paris: Les Belles Lettres.

Venantius Fortunatus, *Carmina*. M. Reydellet (ed. and trans.). (1994). *Carmina* 1. Paris: Les Belles Lettres.

Weidemann, M. (1986). *Das Testament des Bischofs Berthramm von Le Mans vom 27. März 616. Untersuchungen zur Besitz und Geschichte einer fränkischen Familie im 6. und 7. Jahrhundert*. Mainz: RGZM; Bonn: Habelt.

Weidemann, M. (2002). *Geschichte des Bistums Le Mans von der Spätantike bis zur Karolingerzeit*. Actum pontificum Cenommanis in urbe degentium *und* Gesta Aldrici, 3 vols. Mainz: RGZM; Bonn: Habelt.

Modern Sources

Atsma, H. (1976). "Les monastères urbains du nord de la Gaule." *Revue d'histoire de l'Église de France* 62: 163–187.

Barruol, G., Raynaud, C., and Garnotel, A. (2004). "Villeneuve-les-Maguelone: la basilique funéraire de Maguelone." In *ADLFI, Archéologie de la France-Informations*, Retrieved from http://adlfi.revues.org/12053 [accessed April 25, 2016].

Billouin, D., and Gandel, P. (2013). "Les sites de hauteur de l'Antiquité tardive et du haut Moyen Âge en Franche-Comté." *Archéologie médiévale* 43: 284.

Blary, F. (2013). *Origines et développements d'une cité médiévale: Château-Thierry*. Amiens: Revue archéologique de Picardie.

Boissavit-Camus, B., and Bourgeois, L. (2005). "Les premières paroisses du Centre-Ouest de la France : études de cas et thèmes de recherche." In C. Delaplace (ed.), *Aux origines de la paroisse rurale en Gaule méridionale (IVᵉ–IXᵉ siècles)* (pp. 159–172). Paris: Errance.

Bourgeois, L. (2000a). *Les petites villes du Haut-Poitou de l'Antiquité au Moyen Âge: formes et monuments*, vol. 1. Chauvigny: APC.

Bourgeois, L. (2000b). "De Vieux-Poitiers à Châtellerault: le confluent de la Vienne et du Clain de l'Antiquité au Moyen Âge. " *Bulletin de la société des antiquaires de l'Ouest*, 5th ser., IV, 163–194.

Bourgeois, L. (2005). "Le poids du passé: les pôles de pouvoir traditionnels dans le Poitou des VIᵉ-XIᵉ siècles." In C. Arrignon et al. (eds.), *Cinquante ans d'études médiévales: à la confluence de nos disciplines* (pp. 537–572). Turnhout: Brepols.

Bourgeois, L. (2006). "Les résidences des élites et les fortifications du haut Moyen Âge en France et en Belgique dans leur cadre européen: aperçu historiographique (1995–2005)." *Cahiers de civilisation médiévale* 49: 113–142.

Boyer, J.-F. (2018). *Pouvoirs et territoires en Aquitaine du VIIe au Xe siècle : enquête sur l'administration locale.* Stuttgart: Steiner.

Brulet, R. (2008). "Fortifications de hauteur et habitat perché de l'Antiquité tardive et du début du haut Moyen Âge, entre Fagne et Eifel." In H. Steuer, V. Bierbauer, and M. Hoefer (eds.), *Höhensiedlungen zwischen Antike und Mittelalter von den Ardennen bis zur Adria* (pp. 13–70). Berlin: Walter de Gruyter.

Bur, M. (ed.). (1993). *Aux Origines du second réseau urbain: les peuplements castraux dans les pays de l'Entre-Deux.* Nancy: Presses universitaires.

Castellvi, G. (1995). "*Clausurae* (Les Cluses, P.-O.): forteresses de frontière du Bas Empire romain." In A. Rousselle (ed.), *Frontières terrestres, frontières célestes dans l'Antiquité* (pp. 81–104). Perpignan: Presses universitaires de Perpignan.

Charmasson, J. (1970). "Un *oppidum* du Bas Empire: Lombren à Vénéjan (Gard)." *Archéologia* 36: 54–61.

Clément, N. (2011). *L'occupation du sol dans le* pagus *d'Alba-Viviers (Ardèche) entre le Ve et le Xe siècle,* 5 vol. (Doctoral dissertation). Lyon: Université Lyon II.

Cornec, T., and Farago-Szekeres, B. (2010). "L'habitat et les cimetières du haut Moyen Âge de Pouthumé (Châtellerault, Vienne)." In L. Bourgeois (ed.), *Wisigoths et Francs autour de la bataille de Vouillé (507). Recherches récentes sur le haut Moyen Âge dans le Centre-Ouest de la France* (pp. 97–111). Saint-Germain-en-Laye: Association française d'archéologie mérovingienne.

Debord, A. (2000). *Aristocratie et pouvoir. Le rôle du château dans la France médiévale.* Paris: Picard.

Duchesne, L. (1915). *Fastes épiscopaux de l'ancienne Gaule, III: les provinces du Nord et de l'Est.* Paris: Fontemoing.

Early, R. (2001). "Les origines du château de Mayenne: apports archéologiques." In A. Renoux (ed.), *"Aux marches du palais". Qu'est-ce qu'un palais médiéval?* (pp. 273–287). Le Mans: Publications du LHAM.

Ferdière, A. (ed.). (2004). *Capitales éphémères: des capitales de cités perdent leur statut dans l'Antiquité tardive, actes du colloque de Tours, 6–8 mars 2003.* Tours: FERACF.

Fournier, G. (1962). *Le peuplement rural en Basse Auvergne durant le haut Moyen Âge.* Paris: Presses universitaires de France.

Gandel, P. (2014). "Salins-les-Bains (Jura), Camp du Château." *Archéologie médiévale* 44, 283–284.

Gentili, F., & Valais, A. (2007). "Composantes aristocratiques et organisation de l'espace au seun de grands habitats ruraux du haut Moyen Âge." In P. Depreux (ed.), *Les élites et leurs espaces. Mobilité, rayonnement, domination (du VIe au IXe siècle)* (pp. 99–134). Turnhout: Brepols.

Gooding, R. (2001). *Prêtres en Gaule mérovingienne.* Subsidia hagiographica, 82. Brussels: Societé des Bollandistes.

Kraemer, C. (2008). "Du *Castrum Habendum* au *Monasterium Habendum*: le Saint-Mont et ses relations avec le peuplement de la Moselotte et de la haute vallée de la Moselle." In J. Guillaume and E. Peytremann (eds.), *L'Austrasie: sociétés, économies, territoires, christian-isation, Actes des XXVIe Journées internationales d'archéologie mérovingienne, Nancy, 22–25 septembre 2005* (pp. 205–219). Nancy: Presses Universitaires de Nancy.

Martin, M. (1976), *Das fränkische Gräberfeld von Basel-Bernerring.* Basel: Archäologischer Verlag and Mainz: von Zabern.

Martinez, D. et al. (2018). "L'église paléochrétienne de l'établissement fortifié de hauteur de La Couronne à Molles (Allier, Auvergne)." *Archéologie médiévale* 48: 1–36.

Michel d'Anoville, C. (2005). "L'occupation de l'*oppidum* de Notre-Dame de la Consolation à Jouques (Bouches-du-Rhône) durant l'Antiquité tardive et le haut Moyen Âge." In X. Delestre et al. (eds.), *La Méditerranée et le monde mérovingien: témoins archéologiques, actes des XXIIIe Journées internationales d'archéologie mérovingienne, Arles 11–13 octobre 2002* (pp. 129–133). Aix-en-Provence: Provence Archéologie.

Pellecuer, C., and Pène, J.-M. (2002). "Bouquet, Saint-Peyre (Gard)." In J.-L. Fiches (ed.), *Les agglomérations gallo-romaines en Languedoc-Roussillon* (pp. 889–902). Lattes: Lattara.

Picard, J.-C., et al. (ed.). (1992). *Topographie chrétienne des cités de la Gaule, VIII: Province ecclésiastique de Sens* (Lugdunensis Senonia). Paris: De Boccard.

Porte, P. (2011). *Larina de l'Antiquité à l'époque mérovingienne*, 2 vols. Biarritz: Atlantica-Séguier.

Raynaud, C. (2004). "Territoires du sud du Montpelliérais." In *ADLFI, Archéologie de la France-Informations*. Retrieved from http://adlfi.revues.org/12098 [accessed April 25, 2016].

Schneider, L. (2004). "Entre Antiquité et haut Moyen Âge: traditions et renouveau de l'habitat de hauteur dans la Gaule du Sud-Est." In M. Fixot (ed.), *Paul-Albert Février de l'Antiquité au Moyen Âge, actes du colloque de Fréjus, 7–8 avril 2001* (pp. 173–200). Aix-en-Provence: Publications de l'Université de Provence.

Schneider, L. (2008). "Cité, *castrum* et 'pays': espace et territoires en Gaule méditerranéenne durant le haut Moyen Âge. L'exemple de la cité de Nîmes et du *pagus* de Maguelone." In P. Cressier (ed.), *Le château et la ville, espaces et réseaux, actes du colloque Castrum 8, Baeza, 2002* (pp. 29–69). Madrid: Casa de Velásquez.

Schneider, L., and Clément, N. (2012). "Le *castellum* de La Malène en Gévaudan. Un 'rocher monument' du premier Moyen Âge (VIe–VIIe s.)." In A. Trintignac (ed.), *Carte archéologique de la Gaule: la Lozère (48)* (pp. 317–328). Paris: Académie des Inscriptions et Belles-Lettres.

Soutou, A. (1964). "L'éperon barré de Clapas-Castel à La Capelle (Lozère)." *Gallia* 22(1): 189–208.

Steuer, H. (2012). "Studien zum Odilenberg im Elsass." *Zeitschrift für Archäologie des Mittelalters* 40: 27–69.

Téreygeol, F. (2010). "Y-a-t-il un lien entre la mise en exploitation des mines d'argent de Melle (Deux-Sèvres) et le passage au monométallisme argent vers 675?" In L. Bourgeois (ed.), *Wisigoths et Francs autour de la bataille de Vouillé (507). Recherches récentes sur le haut Moyen Âge dans le Centre-Ouest de la France* (pp. 251–261). Saint-Germain-en-Laye: Association française d'archéologie mérovingienne.

Valenciano, M. (2015). *Saint-Blaise/*Ugium: de l'agglomération tardo-antique au castrum médiéval. Relectures et regard nouveau*, 2 vols. (Doctoral dissertation). Aix-en-Provence: Aix-Marseille Université.

Zadora-Rio, E. (ed.). (2008). *Des paroisses de Touraine aux communes d'Indre-et-Loire: la formation des territoires*. Tours: FERACF.

CHAPTER 29

THE FATE OF LATE-ROMAN VILLAS IN SOUTHERN GAUL BETWEEN THE SIXTH AND SEVENTH CENTURIES

ALEXANDRA CHAVARRÍA ARNAU

THE transformation and end of late-Roman villas have been the subject of extensive scholarly discussion, and most of the archaeological features of this process have been exhaustively researched in most of the regions once incorporated into the Roman Empire (e.g., Lewit 1992/2004; Van Ossel 1992; Brogiolo and Chavarría Arnau 2005; Chavarría Arnau 2007; Castrorao Barba 2014; for a general synthesis, see Chavarría Arnau and Lewit 2004). All the same, there is still disagreement over the interpretation of these developments.

Scholars recognize that the transformation of villas in the late-Roman and post-Roman periods and their eventual abandonment in the early medieval period was chronologically and geographically diverse. Generalizing about the fate of villas, which resulted from complex processes, is highly problematic due to the difficulty of obtaining reliable occupation sequences, especially when a variety of patterns of villa evolution has been discerned in different regions. In general terms, however, it seems that changes in the use of villas in northern Gaul began from the third century on, especially in areas close to the Roman frontiers. This development was followed in the fourth century by the abandonment of Roman villas in Britain (Van Ossel and Ouzoulias 2000). In contrast to the picture in the north, however, the majority of villas in the Mediterranean basin did not undergo radical transformation before the fifth century. Only in exceptional cases did villas continue to be occupied, with high standards of decoration and commodities, during the sixth century. Most examples of continued occupation in the sixth century come from three regions: the area around Ravenna (the former capital of the western Roman Empire), southern Italy (recent data in Pensabene and Sfameni 2014), and southwestern Gaul (Balmelle 2001, pp. 71–75). By the end of the sixth century, villas and the aristocratic late-Roman lifestyle that they supported had vanished from the rural landscape, never to appear again.

To understand what happened to villas, it is necessary to broaden our perspective. Rather than focusing exclusively on villas, we must seek a more comprehensive assessment of how late-Roman rural territories and properties were organized and how different kinds of settlements, and the cities to which they were connected, evolved during the period under consideration (Brogiolo and Chavarría Arnau 2020). Another possible avenue of research is to examine the broad variety of cemeteries in a specific territory and collect more systematic data to determine whether there were changes in population distribution patterns that may have had an impact on the occupation and abandonment of villas (for example, Chavarría Arnau 2019).

Two general features can be identified in southern Gaul during the Merovingian period. First, extensive archaeological research shows that smaller dispersed settlements such as farms and nucleated forms of settlement (*vici*), continued to function more or less as they had during Roman times (Parodi, Raynaud, and Roger 1987; Favory et al. 1994; Archeomedes 1998; see Peytremann, Chapter 31, this volume). Second, a new kind of fortified settlement emerged in this period. The development of hilltop settlements (*castella* and *castra* in contemporary written sources) during the fifth century in southeast Gaul has been widely studied by Laurent Schneider (2004, 2005), and elsewhere in Gaul by Luc Bourgeois (see Chapter 28, this volume). The phenomenon has parallels in Alpine areas (northern Italy and Slovenia; see Brogiolo 2014) and probably also in Spain, although in this region the archaeological evidence is still fragmentary (Vigil Escalera 2015). The correlation between the reduction in the number of aristocratic monumental villas and the contemporary growth of fortified settlements has led scholars to propose a substitution of one type of settlement with the other. Scholars have also claimed that some villas were fortified, or that some references to *castra* or *castella* in contemporary texts may signal the existence of fortified villas or villages (Ripoll and Arce 2000). The *burgus* of Pontius Leontius, described by his friend Sidonius (Carmina 22) at Bourg, near Bordeaux, has often been translated as "fortified villa" (e.g., Percival 1992, p. 158; Wickham 2005, p. 171; Robert 2011). However, in this case, Sidonius's use of the term should be translated more accurately as hilltop or tower due to his emphasis on its fortifications and their elevated character.

However, the vocabulary employed to refer to Roman settlements seems to have not only evolved over time, but it also varied according to the author in question. It is thus necessary to consider what kind of text is under analysis, such as whether it is legal or literary, and be very cautious of the context and circumstances in which it was written. This need for caution applies not only to the term *castellum* (which has been interpreted in different circumstances as villa, village, or hilltop settlement), but also to the meaning of the word *villa* itself, which some scholars propose evolved during the early Middle

Ages to signify a "village" (Francovich and Hodges 2003). Vocabulary is thus a significant challenge because changes in the usage of these words have been used as a basis for interpreting the transformation of rural property during this period (Carrié 2012–2013). In reality, as we will see, although some words were multivalent, and thus had a variety of meanings depending on the context in which they were used, it is difficult to deny that in legal sources the terms *civitas, villa, vicus,* and *castellum* continued to represent different realities and functions.

One of the key questions we must ask in analyzing the end of Roman villas relates to the properties on which these habitations were constructed and, in particular, to the real meaning of the end of villas in terms of the agricultural territory they exploited. Did the end of these residential buildings signal the abandonment of the properties in which they were located? Did this end indicate changes in the way these properties were managed? A second significant and much debated question relates to how what contemporary sources refer to as barbarian populations and their settlement affected the late-antique system of rural exploitation. The objectives of this chapter are thus two-fold: first, to discuss the varying potential of the written and archaeological sources for a reconstruction of the structure of properties and rural settlements and buildings (for northern Gaul, see Peytremann, Chapter 31, this volume); and second, to assess in what ways the evolution of villas was related to the properties within which they were constructed and whether the new owners of these properties, whether ecclesiastics, monks, or barbarians, had any impact on these developments.

WRITTEN SOURCES AND PROPERTY STRUCTURES

Contemporary scholarship has developed sophisticated tools for the analysis of written sources. Above all, we must recognize their subjectivity and treat them with caution, calling into question modern interpretations that can be even more unreliable than the sources themselves. Let us consider two examples in which scholarly interpretations of written sources have differed significantly. The first concerns an inscription of the early fifth century that has been interpreted as evidence for fortified villas. The second relates to a corpus of seventh-century writings that provides insight into the ecclesiastical residences and the survival strategies employed by some aristocratic families.

THE CASE OF VILLAS AND FORTIFICATIONS

An inscription dated to 409 (*CIL* XII, 1524), written on a stone near Sisteron (Alpes-de-Haute-Provence), refers to the ex-praetorian prefect of Gaul: *vir inlustris Claudius*

Postumus Dardanus, whom Jerome described as "the most noble of the Christians, among the nobles the most Christian" (Hunt 1992: 272–273). Generally, this stone has been viewed as attesting to a shift from residential villas to fortified properties (Chatilllon 1943; Marrou 1954; Matthews 1975, pp. 322–324; Whittaker 1993, p. 292). The text of the inscription states:

> Claudius Postumus Dardanus, illustrious man and invested with the dignity of patrician, former consul of the province of Vienne, former master of the office of appeals, former quaestor, former praetorian prefect of the Gauls, and Nevia Galla, most noble and illustrious woman, the family matriarch, in a place known as Theopolis, have furnished a viable road by cutting away on both sides the flanks of the mountain and having procured walls and gates; having accomplished this work on their own land, they wanted to make it accessible for the security of all, with the help of Claudius Lepidus, brother and companion of the above named man, former consul of (the province of) Germania prima, and former master (of the office) of the archives, former count of private affairs. So that their zeal with regard to the well being of all and as a witness of the public recognition may be demonstrated.[1]

The inscription's passage about walls and gates has been interpreted as proof of the fortification of private properties like Theopolis by members of the Gallo-Roman aristocracy during this period (Matthews 1975, pp. 322–324; Whittaker 1993, p. 292, among others). In reality, the inscription says something very different: Claudius Postumus Darnanus (Martindale 1980, pp. 346–347) and his mother Nevia Galla, with the help of his brother, the *vir inlustris* Claudius Lepidus, fortified a road (VIARUM VSVM PRAESTITERVNT), not a villa or a property. That is, the inscription's reference to cutting both sides of hills (CAESIS VTRIMQVE MONTIVM LATERIBVS), and giving it gates and walls (MURUS ET PORTAS DEDERUNT) refers to a road, which was important and in public use, and which was fortified with an enclosure (*clausura*). A similar example has been documented on the other side of the Pyrenees near the site of Saint Julia de Ramis, close to the city of Girona (Burch et al. 2006). The inscription is thus important because it demonstrates the involvement of two senior officials of the empire circa 400 in issues related to transportation and communication as the Roman state was in the process of developing a defense system (for more on inscriptions, see Handley, Chapter 26, this volume). Hence, it appears to have nothing to do with the structure of agricultural property and the private fortifications of villas.

Another interpretative approach places villas in competition with the *castella* as an alternative location of aristocratic residences. As Laurent Schneider (2004) has observed, *castella* could have different characteristics in terms of location, size, presence of fortifications, and number and types of buildings. They also had different functions and chronologies, with some *castra* developing in the same place as earlier settlements (as at Bouquet/San Peyre in the department of Gard), whereas others were founded by the late fifth century or the beginning of the sixth century, thus coinciding with the extension of Ostrogothic rule to Provence, with examples at Lombren (Gard),

Saint Blaise (Bouches-du-Rhône), and Roc de Pampleune (Hérault). One of the most important roles of *castra* seems to have been that of a small central place that administered a territory and perhaps also coordinated its defence. They were probably the residences of the military elites, Roman and barbarian alike, from the fifth century onward. However, a problem that remains unresolved is how to understand their relationship to the luxury villas of the previous century or the senatorial class that had inhabited them (on the military, see Sarti, Chapter 12, this volume). The inscription of Theopolis suggests that at least some members of the Gallo-Roman aristocracy, perhaps because of their role in the power hierarchy, were directly involved in the construction of fortifications.

However, this passage does not suggest that the aristocracy had moved to the countryside. Archaeological evidence and written sources for regions like southern Gaul, Italy, and Spain reveal that besides *castra* and *villae*, elites probably continued to occupy permanent residences in the cities because urban centers continued to be the focus of political power and influence (see Wickham 2005, p. 691, for a review of the evidence, and Guyon 2013 for this specific territory). The presence or absence of proprietors in the countryside, as revealed by the architecture of villas and their decoration, was connected to a certain lifestyle focused on *otium* (leisure) and was not necessarily linked to the management of properties. The latter could be accomplished by dependent workers known as *actores*. We must therefore emphasize that to understand what happened in the late Roman countryside in southern Gaul and elsewhere in the Mediterranean basin, our attention must shift from villas to properties. In southern Gaul, there are some important documents that offer interesting insights into these estates.

Aristocratic Properties during the Seventh Century

A series of written documents dated between the years 600 and 680, relating to the territory north of Toulouse (Haute-Garonne), describes how the countryside looked 200 years after the end of most of the villas and offers some hints as to what had happened to late-Roman properties. The documents in question are the will of Desiderius of Auxerre (Sot 2002, pp. 84–110), the *Vita* of Desiderius of Cahors (Arndt 1957), forty-two letters relating to Desiderius of Cahors, seventeen of which he wrote (Desiderii episcopi Cadurciensis, *Epistulae*), and the will of Nicezius and his wife, Irmintrudis, and their bequest to the abbey of Moisac dated to 680 (Boyer 1962; Boudartchouk 2007). These sources contain 178 references to rural properties. And on 135 occasions, properties are described by the word *villa*, which does not seem to refer to a particular building but more generally to a rural property containing different buildings. Moreover, *praedium* (landed property with buildings) is mentioned eleven times; *ager/arum* (field) two times; and *hospiciolum*, meaning "small house," five times. We find the words *curtis indomnicata*, with the meaning of a central place on a property, two times. Finally, there are three references to a *castrum*, an *oppidum*, and a *fiscum* (see the analysis of place names and properties in Hautefeille 2006 and—specifically for the will—Ravier 1999 and Chambon 2001).

What, then, do these documents say about rural properties and the fate of late Roman villas? First, it is important to emphasize that during the seventh century, the word *villa* was used indiscrimatly to refer to a property or to buildings, a polysemy that had already begun in the first century with Pliny the Elder (Carrié 2012). The problems raised by the word *villa*, the evolution of its meaning, and the words used from Late Antiquity to refer to buildings with residential areas in rural contexts is extremely complicated. Already by the fourth century, in his agricultural treatise, the Roman agronomist Palladius did not use the word *villa* to refer to the residential building of the property, but instead substituted the word *praetorium* (*Opus Agriculturae* I, 8). The same term was used later by other authors like Cassiodorus (*Variae* VII, 5, 4; XI, 14, 3; XII, 22) and Sidonius Apollinaris (*Carmina* I, 18, 7). In the sixth and seventh centuries, the word used in Visigothic sources to refer to rural residences seems to be *uillula*, a word that already had appeared in the *Vita* of Melania the Younger in the fourth century. Throughout the whole period, legal texts and councils continued to refer to *villa*, as well as *vicus* and *castellum* and, at the top of what generally seem to have been hierarchies of settlements, *civitas*.

A second point to be noted is that many properties were composed of scattered parcels of land (as they had been in ancient Rome and Late Antiquity), and sometimes depended on a central place, which in these late seventh-century documents were called *curtis indomnicata*. It is also important to emphasize that in contemporary evidence of seventh-century agrarian organization, there is no trace of militarization. Only one castle appears in the will of Desiderius of Auxerre, the *Vita* of Desiderius of Cahors, and the will of Nicezius and Irmentrudis. Furthermore, there is no clear trace of the nucleation of the rural population into villages, which apparently occurred only later, at least in this region. As Jean-Michel Carrié has demonstrated recently in an extensive and well-documented analysis of the meaning and evolution of the term *villa* in late-antique and early medieval sources, the term cannot be translated as "village," which has often been accepted as an equivalent by scholars studying other early medieval texts (2012, 2013). As late as the ninth century, the texts clearly referred to private properties in the hands of a single *possessor,* rather than to a system dominated by some kind of cooperative peasant economy or village communities. If any nucleated sites existed, they must have corresponded to groups of families working the lands of more powerful *possessores* (to whom texts likely referred to as *mancipia*).

In conclusion, at least for the region north of Toulouse, seventh-century texts reveal that the rural landscape and its organization are not likely to have changed greatly after the end of the Roman Empire. This continuity is attested by the survival of the word *villa*, which defined the agrarian structure. What did change, however, was the identity of the proprietors, through a series of progressive transformations that the written sources clearly describe.

ECCLESIASTICAL LANDOWNERS

The main difference that may be observed between the late-Roman system of landhold-ing and that visible in the Merovingian countryside relates to the replacement of much of the late Roman aristocracy with the church hierarchy, at least in part. However, as Ralph Mathisen has argued in a seminal book (1993), in southern Gaul these elites came from similar backgrounds.

The documents that testify most clearly to this transition and the passage of property from secular to ecclesiastical hands include the seventh-century sources described above. To them we may add the will of Bertrand, bishop of Le Mans, dated March 27, 616 (Weidemann 1986; Linger 1995). The text of his testament refers to seventy-four *villae*, thirteen *colonicae* (farmhouses), twelve *loca* (places), five *reicolae* (property), seven *pos-sessiones*, and one *castro*, revealing a structure very similar to the information conveyed in the documents discussed earlier. The will sometimes mentions the buildings located on the property (*domibus*), but they seem to be related to the farmers (*mancipia, manci-piis*) and not the owner of the property, who clearly resided in the city.

In the introduction to the will, the bishop specifies how these properties came into his possession: inheritance, donation (by kings or private persons), purchase, and exchange. The main beneficiaries of the will were the churches of Sts. Peter and Paul that he built and the cathedral of St. Mary, with some minor bequests to his nephews and other churches. The will also reveals the complex processes of gifts and usurpations that took place during this period, and how kings employed land to punish or gratify the nobility and churches of the time, the transfer of land being an extraordinary tool for those in power (a subject discussed in Linger 1995).

Overall, these texts show that many seventh-century properties had fallen into the hands of bishops as well as, probably, other members of the church (on bishops, see Halfond, Chapter 13, this volume). These bishops generally belonged to the old Roman senatorial aristocracy of Gaul which, as Sidonius Apollinarus already noted in 470 in a letter sent to his friend Ecdicius, was the only way that aristocrats could survive the cur-rent political landscape: aristocrats could escape to safer territories or enter the church. The best option of all was to become a bishop.[2] Omatius, the brother of Constantius (Martindale 1980, p. 321), became the bishop of Tours; following a military career, Leontius, linked to the family of Emperor Avitus and Sidonius Apollinaris, became the bishop of Bordeaux by 549 (Fortunatus, *Carmina* 1, 15, 9–10); Felix, bishop of Nantes (549-55), stemmed originally from an important senatorial family of Aquitania (PLRE IIIA, sv Felix 5, 481–482); or Chronopius, bishop of Périgueux (503–533) (PLRE IIIA, sv Cronopius, p. 363). All of these examples confirm that Sidonius's advice was followed by many nobles of the fifth and sixth centuries as a "strategy of survival," as Ralph Mathisen (1993) has expressed it. In the following century, the situation does not seem to have changed: the bishop of Auxerre, Desiderius (618), was described as a *vir nobilissimus*, and we know that the bishop of Cahors (590–655), was the son of Salvius from Albi and

Haerchemfreda (described as *honestissima*), and the brother of Syagrius, who was count of Albi in 618. Desiderius and his two elder brothers spent their youth in the royal court in the company of many aristocrats forging ties that would last for the rest of their lives (for Desiderius of Cahors and his circle, see Mathisen 2013).

This evidence reveals that important aristocratic local families continued with their way of life, properties, and probably villas at least until the middle of the sixth century and sometimes even longer. However, it seems that, at least in some cases, there was a tendency to exchange civil life for ecclesiastical responsibilities. Sometimes the choice involved a more ascetic way of life (Balmelle 2001, pp. 46–47). Another strategy, not mentioned by Sidonius, was to enter the barbarian hierarchy and become part of a new, militarized elite. Finally, we must not forget that some civil aristocrats also existed (such as Nicezius and his wife, Irmintrudis), but they are hard to find because of the bias of the written sources toward a particularly "ecclesiastical" picture of society. Archaeology and material culture can thus offer a broader picture and provide a critical perspective for understanding the conditions that contributed to the end of villas in Merovingian Gaul.

ARCHAEOLOGICAL EVIDENCE: VILLAS, MONASTERIES, AND THE LOCATION OF ÉLITE RESIDENCES

It is striking to consider that, whereas villas dominated in the western empire in 300, they had almost disappeared by 500. If we explore what happened in northern Gaul, Britain, or some areas of Spain, where most villas were abandoned by the end of the fourth century or the first decades of the fifth, we can see that in southern Gaul, the end of the villas was a slightly later process. Despite their heavily rhetorical nature, the writings of Sidonius Apollinaris (mainly 460–470), allow us to think that in southeastern Gaul, aristocratic *otium* based on the villa and its associated way of life continued throughout the fifth century. Belief in this continuity is also supported by archaeological evidence, which has revealed a good number of villas with baths, colonnades, mosaics, and other forms of monumental display. All of these attest to the likely veracity of Sidonius's descriptions (Balmelle 2001). It is important, however, to emphasize that these villas are not in any way evidence for any massive flight from urban contexts to rural properties, as we may see from the evidence in some passages of Sidonius that criticized villa owners who abandoned their political responsibilities in the cities (*Epistulae* I, 6 and VIII, 8). On the contrary, alternating between town and country was a typical trait of the period, as already described by Ausonius in the fourth century: "I move from house to house, so enjoying both the countryside and the city."[3] Throughout the fifth century in southern Gaul, "villas exported an urban lifestyle into the countryside as long as such a style continued to exist in the cities" (Wickham 2005, p. 468). Similarly, more fragmented evidence of these kinds of residences have been documented archaeologically (Heijmans 2006). From the beginning of the sixth century, however, evidence of significant invest-ments in these residences (generally identified with mosaics) becomes rare, as noted by Catherine Balmelle (2001), who refers to a number of villas with significant fifth- and sixth-century occupation like Sorde-l'Abbaye (Landes), Plassac (Gironde), Saint-Laurent-des-Combes (Gironde), Saint-Sever (Landes), and Saint-Jean at Bonnieux (Vaucluse).

The main problem for archaeologists is to clarify where people such as Nicezius and his wife, Irmintrudis, as well as other aristocrats whose residences are sometimes men-tioned by sources, lived. A shift toward wooden structures can be envisaged in some cases, but the architecture of churches and some scattered references in the written sources reveal that stone was still widely used for elite buildings during the early Middle Ages (Wickham 2005, p. 506). We can assume that bishops lived in distinctive residences like the one built by Desiderius when he arrived in Cahors (by 630), constructed with large square stones (*quadris lapidibus*), narrow windows (*fenestras obliquas*), porticoes, and stairs (Ray 1953).

Other quality buildings have been unearthed at some fifth- and sixth-century hilltop sites such as Larina (Isère) (Porte 2001), Chateau Porcher (Rhône-Alps), and Bouquet/San Peyre (Gard). The last-named was dated to the end of the seventh or the beginning of the eighth century (Pellecuer and Pène 2002; see also Bourgeois, Chapter 28, this volume). The importance of this last site is demonstrated not only by the construction technique of the building using squared stones but also by the imported ceramics from the eastern Mediterranean (for more on ceramics, see Bonifay and Pieri, Chapter 37, this volume). These included cylindrical amphorae of type Keay LXIA, VIIIA, and a seal with a kufic inscription from Umayyad times, for example, revealing aristocratic demand for luxury products coming from the East. The presence of imported products from the Mediterranean in the main buildings points to the survival of elites living in hilltop settlements during this period (Bourgeois 2006) rather than in villas. By contrast, although villas were, in many cases, still inhabited, this was probably not by high-status owners. Evidence of post-holes, hearths, and other signs of "para-sitic" occupation suggests that these individuals occupied these villas in only a partial fashion. In many cases, however, villa occupation could reflect the presence of slaves (*mancipia*) of the landholders mentioned in the texts.

Many early medieval churches and monasteries in southern Gaul seem to have been built in the same locations that large villas had previously occupied (for information on Merovingian church architecture, see Chevalier, Chapter 30, this volume). The chal-lenge in general is to understand the relationship between the residential and religious building, that is, whether the church was built while the villa was still in use, or when the villa had been abandoned and was a ruin. In the former case, we can assume that the church was built by the lay inhabitants of the residence, while in the latter case we can-not be sure whether the owner of the property was from the laity or the clergy.[4] John Percival has linked the existence of churches in villas with the presence of ascetic communities at those sites, but on the basis of current evidence, the likelihood of this connection is still difficult to assess (Percival 1997; on monasteries, see Diem, Chapter 15, this volume).

One of the few cases in which a church seems to have been built in a still functioning villa (late fifth or early sixth century) has been documented in the baths of the magnificent villa of Séviac (Montréal du Gers) (Balmelle 2001, pp. 386–390). Catherine Balmelle refers to the discovery of interesting material remains in the villa such as LR4 amphorae and quality glass dishes. Since their chronology is very broad (fifth to sixth century), however, it is not possible to specify whether they pertained to the phase in which the villa was being monumentalized (mid-fifth century) or to the later period when the church was built. At a later phase (seventh century), a second church was built close to the preceding one, with a cemetery developing nearby. Probably associated with this later period are post-holes, hearths, and other elements in the rooms of the former villa, revealing some kind of low-status settlement.

Conclusion

The texts we have examined here provide new perspectives on our understanding of the early medieval countryside and on future directions for research. Those we have analyzed show some developments in southern Gaul that shared features with the general evolution of the landscape in other regions, but also some peculiarities that are the product of a substantial corpus of written sources relating to a small area of Gaul. These texts reveal how ecclesiastical properties were organized during the seventh century, and they give important insight into the frequent association of villa and church. The written sources that we have mentioned suggest that churches were not necessarily linked to the late Roman villa owners, as has been a common interpretation, but mainly occurred on ecclesiastical properties. If wills and donations such as those that we have examined were a general phenomenon, it seems apparent that ecclesiastical properties were composed of extremely fragmented and scattered properties.

Archaeological evidence also reveals that ecclesiastical authorities did not occupy the residences, as they were generally abandoned or, sometimes, reoccupied by people of lower status—probably the rural population that depended on the owners. Villas therefore disappeared because their owners could not maintain or were not interested in (depending on the case) the kind of life that was represented by the villa. However the abandonment of the villas did not imply the end of private aristocratic landholdings, which survived at least during the next two centuries. By contrast, our texts rarely refer to villages, a lacuna that could be due to the type of documents we are dealing with. Neither do they describe a militarized countryside, probably because the territory in question was not in a frontier zone.

This reconstruction of the final decades of the late Roman villa has so far made little reference to the arrival of barbarian populations in southern Gaul from the fifth century on (on this issue, see Coumert, Chapter 5, and Fouracre, Chapter 2, this volume). The debate on how barbarian settlement—and particularly for our case, Visigoths and Franks—was carried on in the different provinces is still lively (mainly between Walter Goffart and his supporters defending the distribution of taxes from fiscal properties and those who argue against it and defend the idea of a distribution of land leading to sustained settlement: see Goffart 1980, 2006, 2013, on the one hand, and Barnish 1986, Sivan 1987, Liebeschuetz 1997, and Porena 2012, on the other, all of them with further bibliography). The archaeological evidence showing the presence of nonlocal individuals occupying parts of former villas (with settlements or cemeteries, or probably both) makes clear that, at least in some cases, new occupants settled on these properties (e.g., see Raynaud 2015).[5] Nonetheless, discussion still continues on the identification of "barbarian" material in the south of Gaul (see Kazanski and Périn 2010; for the counterargument, see Patrello, Chapter 39, this volume). We must probably envisage different kinds of occupation depending on the chronology, the owner of lands in question (whether public or private), and so on, a situation that might change over time. New research is needed to solve a historical problem that archaeologists cannot ignore, perhaps by use of biological sciences such as ancient DNA and isotopic studies that may shed light on migration (see Czermak, Chapter 7, this volume).

Notes

1. "Claudius Postumus Dardanus, vir inlustris et patriciae dignitatis, ex consulari provinciae Viennensis ex magistro scrinii libellorum, ex questore, ex praefecto pretorio (sic) Galliarum, et Nevia Galla, clarissima et inlustris femina, mater familias eius, loco cui nomen Theopoli est viarum usum, caesis utriumque montium lateribus, praestiterunt, muros et portas dederunt, quod in agro proprio constitutum tuetioni omnium voluerunt esse commune, adnitente etian (sic) viro inlustri comite ac fratre memorati viri Claudio Lepido, ex consulari Germaniae Primae, ex magistro memoriae, ex comite rerum privatarum, ut erga omnium salutem eorum studium et devotionis publicae titulus posset ostendi" (CIL, XII, 1524).
2. "Si nullae a republica vires, nulla praesidia si nullae, quantum rumor est, Anthemii principis opes, statuit te auctore nobilitas seu patriam dimittere seu capillos." (Sidonius Apollinaris, Epistulae 2, 1., 4).
3. "Transeo et alternis rure uel urbe fruor." (Ausonius, De Herediolo, III, 31–32).
4. This problem has led to extensive discussion by scholars in Italy and Spain. The divergence of views centers on whether private owners rather than bishops led the process of Christianization of the late-antique countryside (with different positions represented by A. Chavarría Arnau 2007 and Cantino Wataghin 2013).
5. For example, in Gelleneuve (Mouchan-de-Gers), a fourth-century villa was reused for the site of a Merovingian cemetery with approximately eighty graves, many of which included grave-goods; at Pompogne (Lot-et-Garonne, Aquitania seconda), a late-antique villa was used for a Merovingian cemetery after its abandonment in the sixth century; at Pastissé at Preignan (Gers-Novempopulane), a late-antique villa was replaced by Merovingian graves dating to the sixth and seventh centuries; at Sainte Colombe Le Bourg (Gironde, Aquitaine Seconde), a late-antique villa was reused for a Merovingian cemetery in the sixth and

seventh centuries; La Turraque (Beaucaire-sur-Baise, Gers) was the creation of a large cemetery with sarcophagi and earth graves associated with wood structures, possibly indicating the presence of a settlement inside a former villa. For all of these, see the catalogue published by Balmelle 2001. Some cemeteries have also been documented in relation to other kinds of structures (*mansiones*), as was the case at Monferrand (Auche) or Isle-Jourdan (Boudartchouk and Bach 1996; Boudartchouk 1998; Mérel-Brandeburg 2005).

WORKS CITED

Ancient Sources

Ausonius, *Works*. H. G. Evelyn-White. (trans.). (1919). *Ausonius, Works*. Cambridge, MA: Harvard University Press.

CIL XI. O. Hirschfeld (ed.). (1962[1888]). *Inscriptiones Galliae Narbonensis Latinae*. Berlin: Walter de Gruyter.

Desiderii episcopi Cadurciensis, *Epistulae*. W. Arndt (ed.). (1957). CCSL 117 (pp. 309–342). Turnhout: Brepols.

PLRE IIIA. J. R. Martindale (1992). *The Prosopography of the Later Roman Empire*. 3: A.D. 527–641. Cambridge: Cambridge University Press.

Sidonius Apollinaris, *Epistulae et Carmina*. C. Luetjohann (ed.). (1961[1887]). MGH AA 8 (pp. 1–264). Berlin: Weidmann.

Venantius Fortunatus, *Carmina*. M. Reydellet (ed.). (1994). *Venance Fortunat, Poèmes, tome I (livres I–IV)*. Paris: Les Belles Lettres.

Vita Desiderii Cadurciensis. W. Arndt (ed.). (1957). CCSL 117 (pp. 343–401). Turnhout: Brepols.

Modern Sources

Arce, J. (1997). "*Otium et negotium:* The Great Estates, 4th to 7th Centuries." In L. Webster and M. Brown (eds.), *The Transformation of the Roman World, AD 400–900* (pp. 19–32). London: British Museum Press.

Archeomedes. (1998). *Des oppida aux métropoles, archéologues et géographes en vallée du Rhone*. Paris: Anthropos.

Balmelle, C. (2001). *Les demeures aristocratiques d'Aquitaine. Société et culture de l'Antiquité tardive dans le Sud-Ouest de la Gaule*. Aquitania, Suppl. 10. Bordeaux: Ausonius.

Barnish, S. J. B. (1986). "Taxation, Land and Barbarian Settlement." *Papers of the British School at Rome* 54, 170–195.

Boudartchouk, J.-L. (1998). "L'habitat rural et le souterrain médiéval de "Pech de Bonal" (Fontanes, Lot)." *Archéologie du Midi médiéval* 15/16: 67–105.

Boudartchouk, J.-L. (2007). "La 'charte de Nizezius': encore un faux de l'abbaye clunisienne de Moissac?" *Annales du Midi* 119: 269–308.

Boudartchouk , J.-L., and Bach, S. (1996). "La nécropole franque du site de la Gravette, l'Isle Jourdain (Gers)." *Aquitania* 14: 153–156.

Bourgeois, L. (2006). "Les résidences des élites et les fortifications du haut Moyen Âge en France et en Belgique dans leur cadre européen: aperçu historiographique (1955–2005)." *Cahiers de civilisation médiévale* 49: 113–141.

Boyer G. (1962). "Remarques sur la charte de Nicezius." In G. Boyer (ed.), *Mélanges d'Histoire du droit Occidental* (pp. 236–246). Paris: Sirey.

Brogiolo G. P. (2014). "Costruire castelli nell'arco alpino tra Ve VI secolo." In S. Gelichi (ed.), *Quarant'anni di Archeologia medievale in Italia. La rivista, i temi, la teoria, i metodi* (pp. 143–156). Florence: All'Insegna del Giglio.

Brogiolo, G. P., and Chavarría Arnau, A. (2005). *Aristocrazie e campagne da Costantino a Carlomagno*. Florence: All'Insegna del Giglio.

Brogiolo, G. P., and Chavarría Arnau, A. (2020). *Archeologia Postclassica. Temi, strumenti, prospettive*. Rome: Carocci.

Buffat, L. (2005). "De la villa antique à la villa médiévale. L'évolution des centres domaniaux dans l'ancienne cité de Nîmes aux premiers siècles du Moyen Âge." In X. Delestre, P. Périn, and M. Kazanski (eds.), *La Méditerranée et le monde mérovingien: témoins archéologiques. Actes des XXIIIᵉ Journées internationales d'archéologie mérovingienne, Arles, 11–13 octobre 2002* (pp. 161–176). Bulletin Archéologique de Provence, Suppl. 3. Aix-en-Provence: Association Provence Archéologie.

Burch, J., et al. (2006). *Excavacions arqueològiques a la muntanya de Sant Julià de Ramis 2*. Sant Julia de Ramis: Ajuntament de Sant Julia de Ramis.

Cantino Wataghin, G. (2013). "Vescovi e territorio: l'Occidente tra IV e VI secolo." In *Acta XV Congressus internationalis archaeologiae christianae* (pp. 431–462). Vatican City: PIAC.

Carrié, J.-M. (2012). "Nommer les structures rurales entre la fin de l'antiquité et le haut Moyen Âge: le repertoire lexical gréco-latin et ses avatars modernes (1ᵉʳ partie)." *Antiquité tardive*, 20: 25–46.

Carrié, J.-M. (2013). "Nommer les structures rurales entre la fin de l'antiquité et le haut Moyen Âge: le repertoire lexical gréco-latin et ses avatars modernes (2ᵉᵐᵉ partie)." *Antiquité tardive* 21: 13–21.

Castrorao Barba, A. (2014). "Continuità topografica in discontinuità funzionale: trasformazioni e riusi delle ville Romane in Italia tra III e VIII secolo." *European Journal of Post-Classical Archaeologies* 4: 259–296.

Chambon, I. P. (2001). "Observations et hypothèses sur la charte de Nizezius (Moissac a. 680): contributions à la protohistoire du gallo-romain et à la connaissance de la période mérovingienne dans la région toulousaine." *Revue des Langues Romanes* 105: 539–605.

Chatilllon, F. (1943). "*Locus Cui Nomen Theopoli Est*." *Essai Sur Dardanus, préfet du prétoire des Gaules au vᵉ siècle*. Gap: Imprimerie Ribaud Frères.

Chavarría Arnau, A. (2007). *El final de las villae en Hispania (siglos IV–VII)*. Bibliothèque de l'Antiquité Tardive 7. Brepols: Turnhout.

Chavarría Arnau, A. (2019). "The Topography of Early Medieval Burials: Some Reflections on the Archaeological Evidence from Northern Italy (Fifth-Eighth Centuries)." In J. Escalona, O. Vésteisson, and S. Brookes (eds.), *Polity and Neighbourhood in Early Medieval Europe* (pp. 83–120). Turnhout: Brepols.

Chavarría Arnau, A., and Lewit, T. (2004). "Recent Research on Late Antique Countryside: A Bibliographical Essay." In W. Bowden and L. Lavan (eds.), *Recent Research on Late Antique Countryside* (pp. 3–51). Late Antique Archaeology 2. Leiden: Brill.

Favory, F., et al. (1994). *Les campagnes de la Gaule Méditerranéenne dans l'Antiquité et le haut Moyen Âge. Etudes microregionales*. Documents d'archeologie française 42. Paris: Éd. de la Maison des sciences de l'homme.

Francovich, R., and Hodges, R. (2003). *Villa to Village. The Transformation of the Roman Countryside in Italy, c. 400–1000*. London, Duckworth.

Goffart, W. (1980). *Barbarians and Romans, 419–584: The Techniques of Accommodation*. Princeton, NJ: Princeton University Press.

Goffart, W. (2006). *Barbarian Tides: The Migration Age and the Later Roman Empire.* Philadelphia: University of Pennsylvania Press.

Goffart, W. (2013). "Administrative Methods of Barbarian Settlement in the Fifth Century: The Definitive Account." In S. Dieffenbach and G. M. Müller (eds.), *Gallien im Spätantike und Frühmittelalter. Kulturgeschichte einer region* (pp. 46–56). Berlin: Walter de Gruyter.

Hautefeille, L. (2006). "La *villa* et les autres structures de peuplement dans les pays de Moyenne Garonne au VIIe s." In *Nouveaux regards sur les villae d'Aquitaine: bâtiments de vie et d'exploitation, domaines et postérités médiévales, Actes de la table ronde de Pau, 24 et 25 novembre 2000* (pp. 351–362). Hors série n° 2 d'Archéologie des Pyrénées Occidentales et des Landes. Pau: Université de Pau.

Heijmans, M. (2006). "Les habitations urbaines en Gaule méridionale durant l'Antiquité tardive." *Gallia* 63: 47–57.

Hunt, E. D. (1992). "Gaul and the Holy Land in the Early Fifth Century." In J. Drinkwater and H. Elton (eds.), *Fifth-Century Gaul: A Crisis of Identity?* (pp. 264–274). Cambridge: Cambridge University Press.

Kazanski, M., and Périn, P. (2010). "Archéologie des Wisigoths en Gaule." In *El tiempo de los "bárbaros." Pervivencia y transformación en Galia e Hispania (ss V–VI d.C.)* (pp. 123–133). Zona Arqueoloógica n. 11. Alcalá de Henares: Museo Arqueológico Regional.

Lewit, T. (2004/1992). *Villas, Farms and the Late Roman Rural Economy (Third to Fifth Centuries AD).* BAR International Series 568. Oxford: BAR.

Lewit, T. (2003). "'Vanishing Villas': What Happened to Elite Rural Habitation in the West in the 5th and 6th Centuries A.D.?" *Journal of Roman Archaeology* 16: 260–275.

Lewit, T. (2005). "Bones in the Bathhouse: Re-evaluating the Notion of 'Squatter Occupation' in 5th-7th Century Villas." In G. P. Brogiolo, A. Chavarría Arnau, and M. Valenti (eds.), *Dopo la fine delle ville: evoluzione nelle campagne tra VI e IX secolo* (pp. 251–262). Documenti di Archeologia 39. Mantua: Società Archeologica Padana.

Liebeschuetz, J. H. G. W. (1997). "Cities, Taxes and the Accommodation of the Barbarians: The Theories of Durliat and Goffart." In W. Pohl (ed.), *Kingdoms of the Empire: The Integration of Barbarians in Late Antiquity*, pp. 135–151, Leiden: Brill.

Linger, S. (1995). "Acquisition et transmission de propriétés d'après le testament de Bertrand du Mans (27 mars 616)." In E. Magnou-Nortier (ed.), *Aux sources de la gestion publique*, 2: "L'invasio" des "villae" ou la "villa" comme enjeu de pouvoir (pp. 171–194). Lille: Presses universitaires de Lille.

Marrou, H.-I. (1954). "Un lieu-dit *Cité de Dieu*." In *Augustinus Magister* 1 (pp. 101–110). Paris: Bibliothèque Augustinienne.

Martindale, J. R. (1980). *The Prosopography of the Later Roman Empire (PLRE)* 2. Cambridge: Cambridge University Press.

Mathisen, R. W. (1993). *Roman Aristocrats in Barbarian Gaul: Strategies for Survival in an Age of Transition.* Austin: University of Texas Press.

Mathisen, R. W. (2013). "Desiderius of Cahors: Last of the Romans." In S. Dieffenbach and G. M. Müller (eds.), *Gallien im Spätantike und Frühmittelalter. Kulturgeschichte einer Region* (pp. 455–469). Berlin: Walter de Gruyter.

Matthews, J. (1975). *Western Aristocracies and the Imperial Court.* Oxford: Clarendon Press.

Mérel Brandenbourg, A.-B. (2005). "A propos du mobilier metallique découvert à Peyre Clouque, Montferrand (Aude)." In X. Delestre, P. Périn, and M. Kazanski (eds.), *La Méditerranée et le monde mérovingien: témoins archéologiques. Actes des XXIIIe Journées internationales d'archéologie mérovingienne, Arles, 11–13 octobre 2002* (pp. 193–205).

Bulletin Archéologique de Provence, Suppl. 3. Aix-en-Provence: Association Provence Archéologie.

Parodi, A., Raynaud, C., and Roger, J.-M. (1987). "La Vaunage du IIIe siècle au milieu du XIIe siècle. Habitat et occupation des sols." *Archéologie du Midi médiéval* 5: 3–59.

Pellecuer, C., and Pène, J.-M. (eds.) (2002). *Carte Archéologique de la Gaule: Gard* 30/2. Paris: Académie des Inscriptions et Belles-Lettres.

Pensabene, P., and Sfameni, C. (2014). *La villa restaurata e i nuovi studi sull'edilizia residenziale tardoantica, Atti del convegno internazionale del Centro Interuniversitario di Studi sull'edilizia abitativa tardoantica nel Mediterraneo* (CISEM) (Piazza Armerina 7–10 November 7–10, 2012). Bari: Edipuglia.

Percival, J. (1992). "The Fifth-Century Villa: New Life or Death Postponed?" In J. Drinkwater and H. Elton (eds.), *Fifth-Century Gaul: A Crisis of Identity?* (pp. 156–164). Cambridge: Cambridge University Press.

Percival, J. (1997). "Villas and Monasteries in Late Roman Gaul." *Journal of Ecclesiastical History* 48(1): 1–21.

Porena, P. (2012). *L'insediamento degli ostrogoti in Italia*. Roma: L'Erma di Bretschneider.

Porte, P. (2001). "Le domaine rural de Larina de l'Antiquité au Moyen Âge (Hières-sur-Amby, Isère)." In X. Delestre, P. Périn, and M. Kazanski (eds.), *La Méditerranée et le monde mérovingien: témoins archeologiques. Actes des XXIIIe Journées internationales d'archéologie mérovingienne, Arles, 11–13 octobre 2002* (pp. 219–224). Bulletin Archéologique de Provence, Suppl. 3. Aix-en-Provence: Association Provence Archéologie.

Ravier, X. (1999). "Remarques sur la charte de Nizezius." *Nouvelle Revue d'Onomastique* 33–34: 111–142.

Ray, R. (1953). "Un grand bâtisseur au temps du roi Dagobert: S. Didier, évêque de Cahors." *Annales du Midi* 65(23): 287–294.

Raynaud, C. (2015). "Gallo-romains, wisigoths, septimaniens? Les nécropoles en Septimanie du Ve au VIIIe siècle et le paradigme ethniciste." In J. A. Quiros Castillo and S. Castellanos (eds.), *Identidad y etnicidad en Hispania. Propuestas teóricas y cultura material en los siglos V-VIII* (pp. 313–332). Bilbao: Universidad del Pais Vasco.

Ripoll, G., and Arce, J. (2000). "The Transformation and End of Roman Villae in the West (Fourth-Seventh Centuries). Problems and Perspectives." In G. P. Brogiolo, N. Gauthier, and N. Christie (eds.), *Towns and Their Territories between Late Antiquity and the Early Middle Ages* (p. 63–114). Transformation of the Roman World 9. Leiden: Brill.

Robert, R. (2011). "La description du Burgus de Pontius Leontius: entre realité et objet de mémoire littéraire (Sidoine Apollinaire, Carm., 22)." In C. Balmelle, H. Eristov, and F. Monier (eds.), *Décor et architecture en Gaule entre l'Antiquité et le haut Moyen Âge, Actes du colloque international (Université de Toulouse II-Le Mirail 9–12 octobre 2008)* (pp. 377–390). Aquitania, Suppl. 20. Bordeaux: Fédération Aquitania.

Schneider, L. (2004). "Entre Antiquité et haut Moyen Âge: tradition et renouveau de l'habitat du hauteur dans la Gaule du sud-est." In M. Fixot and P.-A. Février (eds.), *De l'Antiquité au Moyen Âge, Actes du colloque de Fréjus, 7 et 8 avril 2001* (pp. 173–200). Aix-en-Provence: Université de Provence.

Schneider, L. (2005). "Dynamiques spatiales et transformations de l'habitat en Languedoc méditerranéeen durant le haut Moyen Âge (VIe–IXe s.)." In G. P. Brogiolo, A. Chavarría Arnau, and M. Valenti (eds.), *Dopo la fine delle ville: Le campagne tra VI e IX secolo, 10 Seminario sul tardo antico e l'alto medioevo (Gavi 8–10 maggio 2004)* (pp. 287–312). Documenti di Archeologia, 40. Mantua: Società Archeologica Padana.

Sivan, H. (1987). "On *Foederati, Hospitalitas* and the Settlement of the Visigoths in AD 418." *American Journal of Philology* 108: 759–772.

Sot, M. (ed.). (2002). *Les gestes des évêques d'Auxerre* 1. Paris: Belles Lettres.

van Ossel, P. (1992). *Établissements ruraux de l'Antiquité tardive dans le nord de la Gaule*. 51eme Suppl. à Gallia. Paris: Editions du Centre National de la Recherche Scientifique.

van Ossel, P., and Ouzoulias, P. (2000). "Rural Settlement Economy in Northern Gaul in the Late Empire: An Overview and Assessment." *Journal of Roman Archaeology* 13: 133–160.

Vigil Escalera, A. (2015). *Los primeros paisajes altomedievales en el interior de Hispania: registros campesinos del siglo V d.C.* Bilbao: Universidad del País Vasco, Servicio Editorial.

Weidemann, M. (1986). *Das Testament des Bischofs Berthramm von Le Mans vom 27. März 616: Untersuchungen zu Besitz und Geschichte einer Fränkischen Familie im 6. 7. Jahrhundert*. Monographien 9. Mainz: R. Habelt.

Whittaker, Dick. (1993). "Landlords and Warlords in the Later Roman Empire." In J. Rich and G. Shipley (eds.), *War and Society in the Roman World* (pp. 277–302). London: Routledge.

Wickham, Chris. (2005). *Framing the Early Middle Ages: Europe and the Mediterranean, 400–800*. Oxford: Oxford University Press.

CHAPTER 30

···

MEROVINGIAN
RELIGIOUS
ARCHITECTURE
Some New Reflections

···

PASCALE CHEVALIER

ANYONE launching a simple search by typing the words "Merovingian architecture" into an electronic browser is likely to be very disappointed. The longest account in English, in six lines, is to be found in the sixth edition of the *Columbia Encyclopedia*. It observes coldly: "Little remains of the architecture of the Merovingian period, although contemporary sources, such as the writings of Gregory of Tours, indicate that building activity was substantial."[1] This page offers a list of four sites where constructions were found (Auxerre, Jouarre, Lyon, and Poitiers), whereas other websites add St. Peter's in Vienne. That is not many for a large territory that included, as early as the 530s, not only the territory of modern France but also the borderlands of Switzerland, Belgium, the Netherlands, and Luxemburg, in addition to the Rhine and Meuse valleys. Fortunately for the reader, archaeology makes it possible to correct this quite despairing first impression. In this chapter, I present a few thoughts on the architecture of the Merovingian era that includes, in fact, hundreds of extant representative examples (Fig. 30.1).

It would be unwise in this short contribution to review all the sites and studies of Merovingian churches in an effort to survey the entire vision of a form of religious architecture that was expressed in quite simple but majestic masses and forms. Gregory of Tours recorded somewhat enigmatic descriptions of these churches (Vieillard-Troïekouroff 1976; Guyon 1997; Duval 2002),[2] as did Venantius Fortunatus in his *Opera poetica* (Leo 1881) and writers of chronicles like Fredegar (Krusch 1888). Hagiographical works are also important sources for this inquiry (Gauthier and Picard 1972–2012; Prévot 2003), despite the fact that their objective was not to inform the twenty-first-century reader about the basilicas that formed the background of their stories or poems.

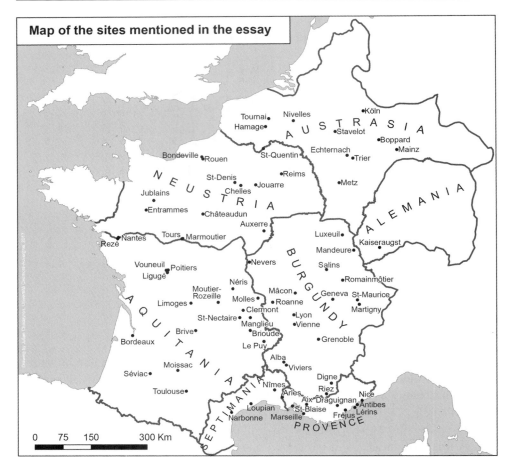

FIGURE 30.1. Map of the sites mentioned in the chapter. (Drawing by Julien Chadeyron, Université Clermont Auvergne).

The material remains of churches that have been excavated reveal central plans (which are rare) or, more commonly, timber-roofed basilicas that are single-naved or that boast three aisles separated by elegant colonnades (Duval 1991), depending on the classical or early Christian tradition from which they drew. At the east end, they usually have a single semicircular protruding apse with a vaulted half-dome (or occasionally a rectangular one). Some display a transept or, in the "Tau" plan, two eastern annex rooms that evoke one. At the west end, one finds an entrance hall, sometimes an *atrium*, funerary side porticoes or galleries, and various other annexes including baptisteries, of which the most famous have a central plan (octagonal, with the exception of Poitiers, Fig. 30.2, at Aix, Fréjus, Marseille, and Riez). Underground crypts are still rather unusual (Sapin 2014; on the Hypogée des Dunes, see Coon, Chapter 46, this volume). All of this architecture is constructed of small stones and/or brick masonry, coated with mortar, without decoration on the exterior (again aside from the Poitiers baptistery, Fig. 30.3),

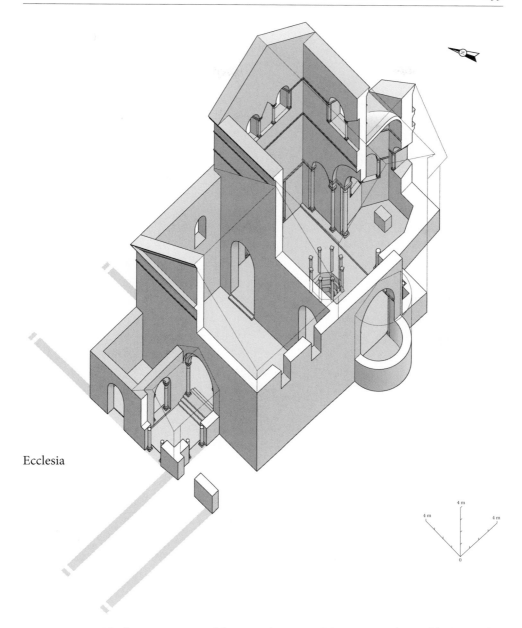

Ecclesia

FIGURE 30.2. Ideal reconstruction of the seventh-century Merovingian phase of the Baptistère Saint-Jean in Poitiers. (Drawing by Xavier d'Aire, from Boissavit-Camus 2014, p. 225, fig. 258)

but the interiors are often articulated with arches and niches, sometimes in superimposed rows. In what follows, I give attention to a few of the main categories of churches and offer a selection of important buildings, some partially known, others recently discovered, that illustrate, each in its own way, a facet of early medieval or so-called Merovingian architecture.

FIGURE 30.3. North façade of the eastern *aula* of the Baptistère Saint-Jean in Poitiers. (Photo by Jean-François Amelot, from Boissavit-Camus 2014, p. 193, fig. 203)

STEADY ADVANCES IN RESEARCH
IN THE PAST HALF-CENTURY

On the eve of World War II, the seminal work of the French scholar Jean Hubert (1938, 1952) defined the architectural expression of the early medieval period as *préroman* or "pre-Romanesque." In essence, he defined it as a function of what it was yet to be. We find this same meaning in the German word *Vorromanik* and of course in the title of the famous *Vorromanische Kirchenbauten*, the first large published corpus devoted to churches in Germany prior to the Ottonians, which covered the Germanic areas under Merovingian rule (Oswald, Schaefer, and Sennhauser 1966–1971). Between the 1950s and 1980s, archaeologists and historians of art and architecture attempted to define the contours, timing, and formal vocabulary of this religious architecture. The beginning and the end of this period were symbolically demarcated in France by the fifth International Congress of Christian Archaeology (CIAC in French) held at Aix-en-Provence in 1954 and the eleventh CIAC (Lyon, Vienne, Grenoble, Geneva, Aosta) in 1986 (on the history of Merovingian archaeology in France, see Effros, Chapter 4, this volume). French historiography on the subject is marked by the contributions of scholars such as Émile Mâle (1950), Aliette de Maillé (1971), May Vieillard-Troïekouroff (1976), Paul-Albert Février (1981), Christian Sapin (1986), Carol Heitz (1987), Jean-François Reynaud (1998), Gabrielle Démians d'Archambault (2001), and so on. In addition to the German authors of the huge *Vorromanische Kirchenbauten*, we should also cite Joseph Mertens in Belgium (1979), and Hans-Rudolf Sennhauser (2012a, 2012b) and Charles Bonnet (1977, 2006) in Switzerland, whose expert advice helped many better understand the geographical territory considered in this chapter.

More recently, the development of rescue excavations, alongside more traditional planned excavations, has correlated with a resurgence of scientific interest in Christian archaeological heritage. This research has resulted in the publication, initiated by Noël Duval, of the collective and multidisciplinary book *Naissance des arts chrétiens* (Duval 1991), which introduced the *Les premiers monuments chrétiens de la France* (Duval 1995, 1996, 1998). Organized by region and by site, as in the *Vorromanische Kirchenbauten*, the three volumes of Duval's coordination of a "national" corpus offer a snapshot of what was known about early Christian monuments dated between the fourth and the eighth centuries from both older excavations and newer French research of the 1990s. The *Vorromanische Kirchenbauten* volumes were completed in the same years (Jacobsen, Schaefer, and Sennhauser 1991), shortly before the great exhibition *Die Franken, Wegbereiter Europas* (1996). With respect to urbanism, the forty years of investigation that have resulted in sixteen volumes of the *Topographie chrétienne des cités de la Gaule* have shed light on the materiality of urban monuments, which have also benefited from historical and epigraphic research (Gauthier and Picard 1972–2012; Prévot, Gaillard, & Gauthier 2014; on cities, see Loseby, Chapter 27, this volume; on epigraphy, see Handley, chapter 26, this volume). These corpuses remain essential references and work instruments for the French, Belgian, Dutch, Luxemburg, German, and Swiss territories included in the early medieval kingdoms of Neustria, Austrasia, and Burgundy. They also contributed to the successful completion of the *Corpus architecturae religiosae europeae (IV–X saec.)* (Chevalier et al. 2012; Chantinne and Mignot 2012; Faccani and Ristow 2012).[3]

There are also some catalogs that address religious architecture within a more limited geographical scope: for Austrasia (Päffgen and Ristow 1996), Switzerland (Bujard, Jäggi, and Meier 2005), southwestern Gaul (Colin 2008), northern Gaul (Mériaux 2006), Brittany (Guigon 1997–1998), the Rhineland (Ristow 2007), and general books and articles on given regions such as Provence (Guyon and Heijmans 2001, 2013) and the Auvergne (Martinez and Morel 2012), or on thematic questions like the origins of the rural parish in southern Gaul (Delaplace 2005), and the Merovingian royal foundations in Paris and Saint-Denis (Kluge-Pinsker 1996). Of note are also the published contributions of two symposia reporting on the latest archaeological discoveries (Paris-Poulain, Istria, and Nardi-Combescure 2009; Gaillard 2014). At the very time when the Musée national du Moyen Âge in Paris (the Musée Cluny) successfully presented in Paris a beautiful exhibition, *Les Temps mérovingiens,* on the Merovingian arts (Bardiès-Ponti, Denoël, and Villela-Petit 2016; in particular, Bully 2016), the monuments of the southern regions of Gaul remain the most, and best, studied because of the good state of their conservation, regional density, and the tradition of research stimulated by Paul-Albert Février. The most recent studies include synthetic overviews of early Christian communities in the south of Gaul (*Gallia* 63, 2006; *Gallia* 64, 2007, and in particular, Guyon and Heijmans 2001, 2013; Beaujard et al. 2007). More generally, research conducted during the last two decades has benefited from the development of stratigraphic and structural archaeological methods (Boissavit-Camus et al. 2003) as well as from archaeometric analyses. Without dismissing existing work on typological classification and formal analysis, but rather by contextualizing those data by reference to historical and artistic data, this new reading of the archaeological evidence provides a clarification of relative chronologies and documentation of construction methods, which in some cases has led to more accurate absolute chronologies.

THE ANTIQUE AND EARLY CHRISTIAN ROOTS OF MEROVINGIAN ARCHITECTURE

Given that the second word in the title of this chapter is "religious," I wish to say a few words about Christianization prior to the Merovingian period and the preexisting structures that form the substrate of and lay the patterns for Merovingian architecture. The view of Christianization has changed significantly in the last twenty years; recent excavations and research are leading to ever more convincing ways to consider the conversion process and the buildings that accompanied it. These trends are best seen over the very long term, thus overcoming the tendency to see the Merovingian period in isolation rather than as being intimately connected both to what came before and what followed it. We now understand better the emergence in Gaul of a landscape actually converted to Christianity, thanks to the investigations undertaken in the *Topographie chrétienne des cités de la Gaule* (*TCCG*) (Gauthier and Picard 1972–2012; Prévot, Gaillard, and Gauthier 2014) and recent syntheses on rural parishes (Delaplace 2005, 2015).

The first monumental signs of the new faith are quite late, even in those areas of southern Gaul (*Gallia* 63, 2006, p. 64, 2007) and the Rhône Valley which were reached early by the Christian missions. Those that can be dated with certainty before 400 CE are extremely rare. As in other areas of the Roman Empire, it took time for the faithful and their pastors to have the desire, financial means, and political weight to express their religiosity in public ways. Until the 390s, Christianity was still competing with the official imperial religion. The process of spatial conquest by the new faith, which can be measured through the growing presence of Christian structures for worship, never stopped, but it advanced very gradually in the countryside as in the towns, in successive waves that lasted beyond the chronological period under study here.

In the late-antique urban world of the 350s to 450s, buildings related to the freshly triumphant faith contributed pragmatically to the monumental adornment of the capital cities of the *civitates*. Subsequently, both there and in the countryside, the growth of a network of Christian structures played a part in the new sociocultural paradigm and therefore appears to have been a distinctive feature of the period. In terms of Christian topography, the fifth century marked a turning point, when the practices of antique patronage underwent a true conversion—in every sense of the word (Anton 1996; Lepelley 1997; Duval and Pietri 1997). Although inscriptions displaying church dedications by a bishop are rarely preserved as they are for Rusticus of Narbonne (Mérel-Brandenburg 1999, p. 45; Prévot 2003), we can see how highly ranked Gallo-Roman clergymen and notables gave new meaning to their generosity. After Clovis's baptism, Frankish elites mimicked Gallo-Roman bishops by favoring pious foundations at the expense of the maintenance, renovation, and construction of other public buildings in their cities. This emphasis promoted the appropriation and reuse of older structures and monuments. Their spoliation worked particularly to the benefit of churches. As early as the first half of the fifth century, for instance, the *vita* of St. Hilarius records a cleric named Cyrillus dismantling Arles's theater for its marble elements to build a Christian basilica at the express order of Bishop Hilary of Poitiers: "... *qui basilicis praepositus construendis, dum marmorum crustas et theatri proscenia celsa deponeret,...*" (*Vita Hilarii* 20, Honoratus of Marseille 1995, pp. 134–137).

The phenomenon also existed in rural areas, with *villae* reused for their building materials as well as for their land base (see Chavarría Arnau, Chapter 29, this volume). Early monasteries were important recipients of such properties (see Diem, Chapter 15, this volume). The so-called presbyterial or baptismal complexes—the ancestors of parish churches (Delaplace, 2005)—which often reproduced the *mater ecclesiae* and its surroundings on a reduced scale (Codou et al. 2007, 61–66), provided the local faithful with a possible element of identification with, and belonging to, a community. Within the rural world, the erection of "parish," funerary, votive, monastic, and other kinds of churches laid out a new geography that would develop further during the Middle Ages. The progressive acquisition of territorial control by Merovingian kings typically occurred in lands already richly endowed with religious architecture that took a variety of forms and fulfilled multiple functions.

Some Good News About Cathedrals and Monasteries

We may now turn to the Merovingian monuments themselves. In the section that follows, we will measure the progress that has been made in our understanding of cathedral complexes on the one hand, and monasteries on the other, by the growing number of publications devoted to them in recent years.

Cathedrals were the first churches to be built (*ecclesia mater, senior, prima, major*). Most of them were already standing at the beginning of the Merovingian period, during which time they evolved, as is evidenced by written sources, epigraphy, and, in a score of emblematic cases, in archaeology. In addition to short accounts in the *TCCG*, an essay by Françoise Prévot (2003), and a synthetic paper by Brigitte Boissavit-Camus and Christian Sapin (2013), a number of monographs and shorter texts have appeared recently that synthesize the evidence published in the past few years. They relate to the cathedrals and complexes of Arles (Heijmans 2006, 2014), Bordeaux (Migeon 2006), Clermont (Chevalier 2014b; Chevalier and Fray 2014), Digne (Démians d'Archambault 2001), Fréjus (Fixot 2012), Geneva (Bonnet 2006, 2012), Cologne (Ristow 2002), Lyons (Reynaud and Richard, 2011), Martigny (Faccani 2010), Nantes (Monteil 2013), Nice (Bouiron, Guilloteau, and Mercurin 2012), Poitiers (Boissavit-Camus 2014, Fig. 30.4), Reims (Berry 2010), Rouen (Le Maho 1994, 2013), Tournai (Brulet 2012), as well as to the current excavations in the Mainz Alterdom (Untermann 2014). In addition, significant progress is being made in our understanding of the contexts of cathedrals, as evidenced by the proceedings of a symposium on bishops' palaces (Balcon-Berry et al. 2012), about which we knew so little just a few years ago.

Cathedrals frequently consisted of two parallel churches (Alba, Bordeaux, Lyons, Rouen, Tours, Trier, and Viviers) or even three (Geneva). They invariably included a baptistery as well as the bishop's *domus ecclesiae*, access spaces (entrance hall, *atrium*, porticoes), economic and domestic areas, and offices. The cathedral complex formed a distinct urban district, as large as 1.6 hectares in Trier or one-eighth of the *intra-muros* city in Geneva (Prévot 2003). Among the extant components visible today, baptisteries have drawn particular attention, especially in southeastern Gaul. New examples have been added to the list of baptisteries that have been identified, which remain few in number compared, for example, to early medieval Italy. The baptisteries of Geneva (Bonnet 2012), Nevers (Bonnet et al. 1995), Poitiers (Boissavit-Camus 2014) and that of Clovis's baptism in Reims (Berry 1996, 2010) have been carefully (re)considered. In addition, a new baptistery has been identified in Grenoble (Baucheron, Gabayet, and de Montjoye 1998), which is tetrafoil in plan, recalling the baptistery at Venasque. And the baptistery in Le Puy has been re-dated to the Merovingian era (Chevalier 2014a).

Four other baptisteries not associated with cathedrals have also been found during rescue excavations: the first, in Brioude (Gauthier 2004), is an important pilgrimage site (following the model of St. Peter's in Rome, St. Martin's in Tours, and Saint-Maurice's in

FIGURE 30.4. The eastern apse of the Baptistère Saint-Jean in Poitiers, general vue. (Photo by Jean-François Amelot, from Boissavit-Camus 2014, p. 219, fig. 252)

Agaune). The second is located in a small town, Roanne (Loire), with two successive constructions of *piscinae* (baptismal pools; Le Nezet-Celestin 2009). In a third example, the *castrum* of Mandeure (Doubs), the *piscina* was abandoned in the Merovingian phase (Cramatte, Glaus, and Mamin 2012, pp. 10–15; on fortified sites, see Bourgeois, Chapter 28, this volume). Finally, the fourth baptistery is thought to have been constructed in Molles-La Couronne (Allier), a fortified hill site; the pool would have had a wooden internal casing (Martinez and Morel 2012). Laid down in simple rectangular annexes, all the newly discovered *piscinae* were either octagonal or circular. Brigitte Boissavit-Camus's study (2008) of the hydraulic infrastructure used in baptismal constructions has enhanced our understanding of these sites.

In recent years, another type of architectural complex dated to the Merovingian period—the monastery—has emerged in excavations of material remains but unevenly and only partially. Nonetheless, several current research programs offer the promise of further discoveries (Bully 2009), particularly concerning the conditions of the installation, topography, and organization of early monastic sites. In 2004, Christian Sapin (2008b) proposed a state of the art research project entitled "L'archéologie des premiers monastères en France (V[e]-déb. XIe s.)." One may perceive the progress achieved in just ten years, for example, at the *4e Journées d'Etudes monastiques* organized in Baume-les-Messieurs in 2014, which was devoted to the origin of monastic sites on the basis of written sources and archaeological data (Bully and Sapin 2016), or at the international symposium *Colomban et son influence. Moines et monastères du haut Moyen Âge en Europe*, held in Luxeuil-les-Bains in 2015 (Bully, Dubreucq & Bully 2018).

Following the model of study employed at St. Germain in Auxerre (Sapin 2000), it has taken years to investigate centuries-old complexes like Agaune (Antonini 2015), Chelles, and Saint-Denis, the last-named of which had no less than three churches aligned to the north of the pilgrimage and royal burial basilica (Wyss 1996; Périn and Wyss 2015). It has also taken time to reevaluate earlier excavations conducted at Nivelles thanks to urban public works (Mertens 1979; van Hove et al. 2012; Chantinne and Mignot, 2014) and to explore in greater depth the foundations of Saint Martin in Ligugé (Boissavit-Camus 2010) and Marmoutier (Lorans 2012). Recently, scholars have also dared to discuss the crypt of Jouarre more critically, which from the nineteenth century was an iconic, almost untouchable cultural monument (de Maillé, 1971; de Mecquenem, 2007). Work has also begun on the excavation of large monastic sites such as Echternach (Krier 1996), Luxeuil (Bully et al. 2014), Lérins (Codou 2014), and Stavelot Abbey (Lambotte and Neuray 2009; Neuray 2013). Merovingian architectural remains have also been found unexpectedly, such as at the small nunnery in Hamage (Nord), which is now thought to have had an early medieval phase (Louis 2014).

URBAN AND RURAL CHRISTIAN TOPOGRAPHY: MANY CHURCHES FOR MANY FUNCTIONS

Other phenomena have recently attracted the attention of scholars, such as the insertion of churches in preexisting urban centers or in the *suburbia* of towns where the necropolises were located. These observations have resulted in large studies dedicated to the Christian topography of early medieval cities (Gauthier and Picard, 1972–2012; Prévot 2003; *Gallia* 63, 2006; Prévot, Gaillard, and Gauthier 2014, especially Guyon 2006; Bonnet 2006 on

Geneva; Reynaud 1998 on Lyon; Guyon 2000 on Marseille; Borgard and Michel d'Annoville 2013 on Riez).

Today, funerary churches are better understood than they were in the past (Gauthier and Picard 1972–2012; Mérel-Brandenburg 2005; Moliner 2006; *Gallia* 63, 2006; Colardelle 2008; Ristow 2009; Prévot, Gaillard, and Gauthier 2014…), as are the deceased they housed in large numbers. Scholars today are employing new methods of funerary archaeology to investigate cemeteries (see Effros, Chapter 4, this volume), and containers such as sarcophagi in which the dead were laid to rest (Cartron, Henrion, and Scullier 2015). The famous Hypogée des Dunes of Mellebaudis in Poitiers (see Coon, Chapter 46, this volume) is the subject of an important archaeological study coordinated by Bénédicte Palazzo-Bertholon and Cécile Treffort (2010). A little-known mausoleum in Saint-Romain en Gal at the gates of the city of Vienne (Isère) is also the subject of a recent study (Prisset 2015). The most recent discovery made before this chapter was written is that of a burial church in Nîmes.[4] The archaeology of settlement structures and landscapes (see Peytremann, Chapter 31; Bourgeois, Chapter 28, this volume), along with rescue archaeology, have made it possible to reevaluate the status of rural churches and the new structures by which the landscape was occupied (for southern Gaul, see *Gallia* 64, 2007, in particular Codou et al. 2007; on the area of Geneva, see Terrier 2002; Terrier, Odenhardt-Donvez, and Fauduet 2007; on the Neuchâtel area, see Bujard 2013).

The reuse and adaptation of ancient structures for Christian worship, whether they were well preserved or more or less ruined, have caused much ink to flow. Sites adapted to Christian use included public or private baths as found in Cimiez and Entrammes (Naveau 1993), Jublains, Néris-les-Bains, Moissac, and Poitiers (Boissavit-Camus 2014), Riez and Reims; townhouses as in Trier or Geneva; *villae rusticae* as in Loupian or Séviac; a portion of the forum as in Aix and Clermont, or civic basilicas as in Saint-Pierre-aux-Nonnains in Metz (Heber-Suffrin 1995); buildings inside a fortification as in Kaiseraugst (Faccani 2012; see Bourgeois, Chapter 28, this volume), Molles-La Couronne (Martinez and Morel, 2012); and abandoned temples. Furthermore, the *memoriae* (shrines) of recognized saints were often transformed into churches—as at St. Seurin in Bordeaux (Cartron et al. 2009), St. Julian in Brioude (Chevalier 2008), St. Martial in Limoges (Lhermite 2012), and Saint-Quentin (Gaillard et al. 2011). In other instances, the mausolea of probable familial origin, like those of Agaune (Antonini 2015), Moutier-Rozeille (Roger 2016), Brive-la-Gaillarde (Cantié, Lhermite, and Proust 2007), Grenoble (Colardelle 2008), and Limoges (Lhermite et al. 2015) likewise became churches. These sites have attracted significant interest and recently led to an international symposium (Sapin and Chevalier 2012). Much has been done on the developments around saints' tombs since Werner Jacobsen's article in *Speculum* (1997). There has been an important survey of fifth- and sixth-century sanctuaries published by Christian Sapin (2008a). And an exceptional double grave has been found in the burial basilica in Marseille located on the rue Maraval. It was fenced off by a screen, with an oil circulation system that allowed oil to be poured into the grave of two saints whose names are currently unknown; the oil was collected at the bottom, perhaps to allow the faithful to fill eulogia bottles with holy oil as in the Middle East (Moliner 2006).

Learning About an Old Friend: The Baptistery in Poitiers

New archaeological research on some iconic Merovingian monuments has warranted the large-scale revision of earlier ideas. Such is the case of the famous baptistery of Saint-Jean in Poitiers, an epistemological milestone for early medieval Western architecture, which was assessed by a multidisciplinary team between 1995 and 2002 (Boissavit-Camus 2014). The extant building is the result of a long diachronic sequence (ten periods, fourteen phases), that began with an antique structure and ended with its restoration to the form thought to have been that of its Romanesque iteration by the Commission des Monuments Historiques in the nineteenth and twentieth centuries. At the beginning of the fifth century, a preexisting room was adapted for baptism, and was then shaped by successive additions until it gained a cruciform plan (Figs. 30.2 and 30.5). Playing with ancient aesthetic canons, the monumental outside decor of the seventh century employed an ornamental polychrome repertoire combining limestone and terracotta, late-antique marble *spolia* (reused from earlier structures), and Merovingian limestone sculpture (Fig. 30.3). The pilasters and slabs, with carved roses and crosses (Fig. 30.6A,B),

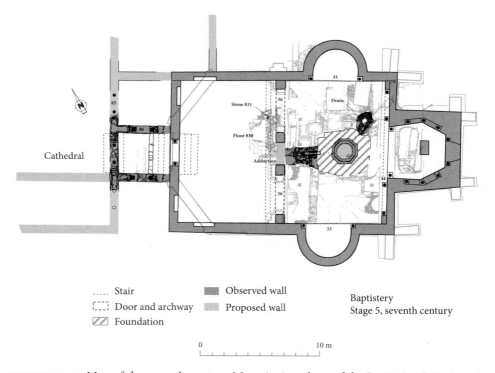

FIGURE 30.5. Map of the seventh-century Merovingian phase of the Baptistère Saint-Jean in Poitiers. (Drawing by Serge Dalle, after Brigitte Boissavit-Camus and Jean-François Raynaud, from Boissavit-Camus 2014, p. 203, fig. 216)

(A)

(b)

FIGURE 30.6. A. Carved stone slab and pediment and B. Smaller stone and terracotta pediment on the north façade of the Baptistère Saint-Jean in Poitiers. (Photo by Jean-François Amelot, from Boissavit-Camus 2014, p. 365, fig. 423–424)

evoked "Visigothic" sculpture from Spain and suggested that Poitiers was an important artistic center in the seventh century.

The remains of an outer triangular pediment carried by a series of brackets on the eastern end of St. Sebastian's Church in Manglieu (Puy-de-Dôme) reveal some similarity with the baptistery of Saint-Jean in Poitiers (Martinez and Morel 2012). The architectural decoration inspired by classical and early Christian trFoundations suggests the possible Merovingian dating of the eastern part of the building, where researchers had already noted a triumphal arch supported by two antique column shafts carrying one reused late-antique and one Merovingian capital.

Antique *spolia* are so common in Merovingian architecture that they contribute to its overall definition, even if there are exceptions to this practice. The reuse and recycling of materials can be explained by both the need to economize the construction process and the desire to affirm a link with antiquity, even in buildings that are of a somewhat earlier date, as in the case of Poitiers (Boissavit-Camus 2014). There are various sorts of *spolia*, including sculpted capitals (Fig. 30.7), large stone blocks, and *tegulae* (tiles). As for the last, recent attention to roofing issues allows us to reconstruct several religious and prestigious secular buildings with timber roofs that must have been covered with Merovingian

FIGURE 30.7. Marble capital, reused in the seventh-century eastern apse of the Baptistère Saint-Jean in Poitiers. (Photo by Jean-François Amelot, from Boissavit-Camus 2014, p. 514, pl. 42A)

tegulae or, more rarely, lead tiles, as in the cathedral of Rouen (Le Maho 1994). This strongly contradicts older stereotypes of Merovingian roofs being made of only stone slabs or perishable materials, although two of the poems of Venantius Fortunatus evoke resplendent *stagnea tecta* (tin roofs) (Venantius Fortunatus. *Opera poetica*, Carmen I.8 and III.7).

Meeting New Friends
in Le Puy and Luxeuil

In addition to the baptistery of Poitiers and well-known examples in Provence, archaeologists have uncovered several early medieval baptisteries in recent years, including Grenoble, Le Puy, Roanne, Brioude, Mandeure, Molles-La Couronne, and perhaps Strasbourg. At Le Puy-en-Velay, a multidisciplinary team undertook an excavation connected with a comprehensive analysis of the walls and adornment of the baptistery of Saint-Jean (Chevalier 2014a). Formerly "well dated" to the tenth century, the initial phase of construction has proved to be much earlier and dates from the very end of the fifth or sixth century, thanks to the analysis of its architecture and decoration combined with ^{14}C dating and archaeometric examination of the mortars used in its walls. In this phase (Fig. 30.8), the building had a large, single timber-roofed nave, whose walls were punctuated by large columns supporting high arches with internal twin blind arches. The apse had four lobed niches and a rectangular eastern one, and it displayed two superimposed arcades; it had a huge central window and a half-dome vault with a flat ending on the eastern side (Fig. 30.9). It exhibited distinctive basilical architecture, giving a strong emphasis on the inner walls animated with blind arcades, with one level of wall arches in the nave and two levels in the apse. This decor may be compared to that of La Daurade in Toulouse, Saint-Laurent in Grenoble (Colardelle 2008) (Fig. 30.14), Saint-Pierre in Vienne, or the eastern apses of the Poitiers (Boissavit-Camus 2014) and Venasque baptisteries.

Similar decor has been discovered during excavations in the outer crypt added to the east of the cemetery church in Luxeuil abbey (Bully et al. 2014) (Fig. 30.10). This small quadrangular room, which is nonhypogeal and very likely vaulted, was built around 600 as an *augmentum* (added room) of Saint-Martin's early Christian basilica. It was intended to accommodate a major grave (maybe that of the founder, St. Colombanus, who died in Bobbio). It gave rise to a necropolis of sarcophagi located *ad sanctos* where monks were buried in the seventh century. Its architecture and decor referred to Roman and late-antique models of mausoleums, including the famous Hypogée des Dunes (Poitiers). This latter small building of the seventh century was subterranean, vaulted, and decorated with paintings and shallowly carved relief sculpture. It hosted the sarcophagi of men whose memory was honored with epitaphs and an altar (Palazzo-Bertholon and Treffort 2010; on Merovingian epigraphy, see Handley, Chapter 26, this volume).

FIGURE 30.8. The Baptistère St. Jean in Le Puy-en-Velay during the excavations supervised in 2010 by Sophie Liegard. (Photo by Bernard Galland)

Saint-Martin in the abbey of Luxeuil (Bully et al. 2014) was a three-aisled basilica whose nave opened on a narrow square apse flanked by slightly protruding annex rooms (Fig. 30.11). A similar partition of the space was found in the so-called Tau plan of single or three-aisled churches, such as the fifth-century example in Mandeure (Cramatte, Glaus, and Mamin 2012), the sixth-century (cathedral?) basilica of Champs Saint-Martin in Rezé (Pirault 2009) and the seventh-century church of Château-sur-Salins (Billoin and Gandel 2014), in Notre-Dame-de-Bondeville (Langlois 2001), to mention

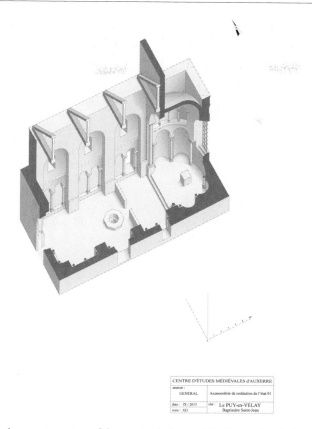

CENTRE D'ÉTUDES MÉDIÉVALES d'AUXERRE

secteur :	
GENERAL	Axonométrie de restitution de l'état 01
date : IX / 2013	site : Le PUY-en-VELAY
nom : XD	Baptistère Saint-Jean

FIGURE 30.9. Ideal reconstruction of the original phase of the Baptistère St. Jean in Le Puy-en-Velay, end of the fifth to sixth century. (Reconstruction by Xavier d'Aire-CEM Auxerre)

only four of the most recent discoveries. The fifth-century church in Molles-La Couronne (Martinez and Morel 2012) was distinctive because of its semicircular apse opening on a single nave appropriated from a late-antique building (Fig. 30.12A–B); two side-annex rooms were added in the seventh century to form a layout that recalls the church of Romainmôtier in Switzerland.

SOPHISTICATION VERSUS SIMPLICITY: THE CONTRAST BETWEEN STONE AND WOODEN CONSTRUCTION

But far more elaborate architectural formulas also existed. In Grenoble, the completion of a long and thorough archaeological investigation (Colardelle 2008) has clarified the complicated evolution of the church of Saint-Laurent, which was rebuilt on a cruciform plan

FIGURE 30.10. Excavation of St. Martin's church in the abbey of Luxeuil: the so-called crypt of Saint Valbert, built around 600. (Photo by Sébastien Bully)

in the sixth century; the quadrangular arms of the cross opened onto a central square space while eleven small semicircular apses punctuated the lower part of their walls. In the seventh century (Fig. 30.13), the new vaulting decorated with stucco was supported by a set of twenty columns with beautiful Corinthian capitals and carved abacus blocks (Saint-Oyand's crypt; Fig. 30.14). By contrast, the inner articulation and the original architectural plan are much less evident in the famous iconic monument of Merovingian architecture: the hall-crypt of Saint-Paul in Jouarre Abbey (de Maillé 1971). Recent

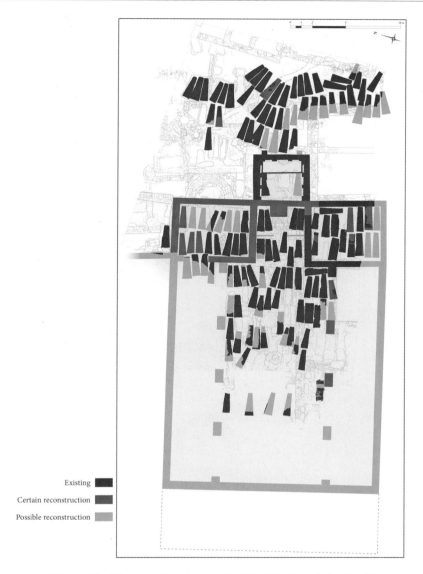

FIGURE 30.11. Map of the Merovingian phase of St. Martin's Church in the abbey of Luxeuil. (Drawing by Laurent Fiocchi, from Bully et al. 2014, p. 327, fig. 8d)

studies (de Mecquenem 2007) have questioned its homogeneity and Merovingian dating, and hypothesized that it was a Romanesque reconstruction that included Roman and Carolingian structures. According to this interpretation, the sarcophagi, the columns, and their heterogeneous fifth- or sixth-century marble capitals must have been displayed there in a new setting that makes it difficult to imagine the original one.

In the small nunnery site of Hamage (Nord) (Louis 2014), important excavations have brought to light the remains of two phases of construction from the eighth century in

(A)

(B)

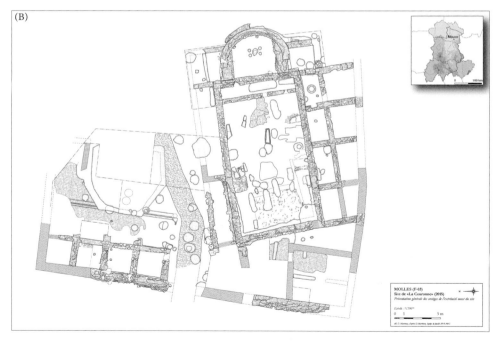

FIGURE 30.12A-B. Aerial view and map of the church at the fortified site of Molles-La Couronne. (Photo and drawing by Damien Martinez)

FIGURE 30.13. Ideal reconstruction of the seventh-century Merovingian phase of Saint Lawrence in Grenoble: the crypt has been vaulted. (Drawing by Martin Keller, from Colardelle 2008, p. 193)

FIGURE 30.14. The crypt of St. Oyand beneath St. Lawrence in Grenoble: walls date from the sixth century, and columns and vaults were added in the seventh century. (Photo by Frédérick Pattou)

the one-aisled church of Sainte-Marie. More than that, Hamage reminds us that religious buildings in stone masonry coexisted with timber-framed, one- or three-aisled buildings with a rectangular apse. They were especially widespread in the eastern and northern Merovingian territories (apart from Fehring 1967; Bonnet 1997; and the *Vorromanische Kirchenbauten*; for the north of France, see Cattedu et al. 2009; for the Geneva region, see Terrier 2002; and recently near Tours, see Ben Kaddour 2015). Surprisingly, this vernacular mode of construction did not necessarily lack refinement: the apse window of the church of Hamage had a colorful stained glass in lead frames.

SOME NEW CLUES ABOUT CHURCH ADORNMENT

A better understanding of the decor of Merovingian buildings is one of the main contributions of research in the last several decades. Despite the survival of a few well-preserved examples (such as at Grenoble and Poitiers), mural painting in this period remains poorly understood. But the existence of so-called mosaic stained-glass windows has been proved in the Merovingian phases of many churches and baptisteries: Brioude, Château-sur-Salins (Billoin and Gandel 2014); Hamage, Limoges, Luxeuil-les-Bains (Bully et al. 2014); Notre-Dame de Bondevillle (Langlois 2001); Rezé (Pirault 2009); Mandeure (Cramatte, Glaus, and Mamin 2012); Stavelot (Lambotte and Neuray 2008, 2009); and others. The identification of these colorful settings accelerated after a symposium held in 2006 (Balcon-Berry, Perrot, and Sapin 2009; Balcon-Berry Velde 2016).

At the same time, stucco decorations—another art form that depends on the legacy of classical traditions (Balmelle, Eristoff, and Montel 2011)—appear in a new light, thanks to an exhibition (Sapin 2004) and another conference. Among the different locations in which these have been discovered (including Bordeaux, Caudebec, Grenoble, Luxeuil, Marseille, Nantes, Poitiers, Saint-Denis, Toulouse, and Tours), the exceptional decor of the church of Vouneuil-sous-Biard stands out (Sapin, Treffort, and Palazzo-Bertholon 2009). An assessment based on architectural style and ^{14}C analyses gave it a precise date in the late fifth or beginning of the sixth century; the technical use of lime stucco rather than plaster stucco and the pattern choices was still very Roman. The decorative repertoire displayed a molded blind arcade housing standing figures (saints, apostles, prophets?), meeting the aesthetic canons of early Christian art (Fig. 30.15).

The traditions of Roman antiquity (Balmelle, Eristoff, and Montel 2011) are still strongly expressed in Merovingian architectural sculpture, mosaic floors (Arles, Digne, and others) and parietal mosaics. During the sixth century, the large diffusion of scattered glass *tesserae* (mosaic tiles), sometimes gilded, as in Nevers, Mâcon, Tours, Poitiers, and Bordeaux, shows that, as is the case for stucco, Merovingian wall mosaics should be compared to contemporary masterpieces in Rome and Ravenna (Italy) or Poreč (Croatia), something that is confirmed by written sources. What is new and original is

FIGURE 30.15. Reconstruction of the stucco decoration in the apse of the church in Vouneuil-sous-Biard. (Drawing by Gilles Fèvre, CEM-Auxerre)

the interaction of architectural glass, mosaics, and stained glass windows, which contributed to the luminosity of the interior church space. And again, archaeology can sometimes clarify the dating of formerly known decors as for the mosaic pavement of Saint-Quentin (Fig. 30.16), which has now been attributed to the seventh or early eighth century (Gaillard et al. 2011).

In the reconstructed luxurious decoration of church interiors, one should not forget more ephemeral or temporary elements such as woven and embroidered textiles (tablecloths, curtains, wall hangings, clerical vestments, and so on). There were also liturgical vessels, thuribles (censers), crosses, and votive crowns in metalwork. Last, but not least, were the incensing and lighting, made possible by myriad oil lamps made of glass and metal, which lit the night offices and the great feasts (see, e.g., Beghelli and Pinar Gil 2013).

Liturgical Appropriation
of Church Interiors

Before concluding, I would like to draw attention to items associated with the liturgical function of Merovingian churches (see Bailey, Chapter 44; Rose, Chapter 43, this volume). The liturgy found material expression in the furniture that organized the space used within the church for worship, furniture that the literary, hagiographic, and canonical texts sometimes evoked. Once again, churches in the Merovingian regions are found to

FIGURE 30.16. The Merovingian mosaic floor in Saint-Quentin. (Photo by Fabrice Henrion, CEM-Auxerre)

be relatively poor in liturgical features compared to churches in the Mediterranean and Balkan regions.[5] Furthermore, French scholars have long been quite cautious in their discussion of liturgy compared to German scholarship, for example. Even in this regard, however, French scholars are now making significant progress in assessing liturgical features such as the altar, the only piece of furniture that is indispensable to these celebrations.

In more than twenty churches in modern France, one can now reconstruct the place of the masonry or carved altar base in the chancel, in the apse, or in the choir (just thirteen were known to Thomas Creissen in 2009). It should be noted that two *loculi* (niches) for relics were discovered in Saint-Nectaire (Chevalier 2009) and Molles-La Couronne (Martinez and Morel 2012) (Fig. 30.17). Despite the lack of a true corpus of sculptures like the Spoleto series for Italy and despite the dispersion of existing elements, our knowledge of the appearance of the altar has now benefited from the publication of Yumi Narazawa's PhD (2015) for southern Gaul, in addition to the reflections of Anne-Bénédicte Mérel-Brandenburg (2005) and Thomas Creissen (2009), among others. Dozens of altars can now be virtually reconstructed even if their traces have disappeared in situ: they appear as rectangular tables on four or more columns and as tables on a carved foot or on a pedestal of solid masonry, with or without a *loculus* for relics. A *ciborium* (canopy over the altar) is known, for example, in Tournai (Belgium) and Draguignan (Var), but there is a lack of tangible and well-dated evidence everywhere else.

Remains of the seats used by the clergy in the church are even more discrete. Thomas Creissen (2009) counted only five stone-built collective benches, and wooden *synthrona*

FIGURE 30.17. Apse of the church in Molles-La Couronne, with traces of the four table feet and the *loculus* for the altar relics. (Photo by Damien Martinez)

(bench-like amphitheater-style seating), with or without *cathedra* (a bishop's chair),[6] are most likely the explanation. The *presbyterium*,[7] where the celebrants stood and sat, was always separated by a screen from the space allotted to the laity. Known as the *cancellum*, this screen (about a meter high) fenced off an enclosure reserved for the clergy alone. Accessible from the front side, it spanned the width of the nave when the church was one-aisled or took the shape of a rectangular low platform protruding westward in a three-aisled church. Whereas many scattered fragments prove their existence, the remains of the anchor of "classical" altar screens made of pillars and stone or marble slabs are extremely rare. More common are thin walls (there are fifteen examples in Gaul), whose masonry was coated with lime mortar or stucco and embossed, as in the eastern church of the cathedral complex in Geneva (Bonnet 2012). It is assumed that the altar screen was made of wood, at least in the case of Saint-Lubin in Châteaudun (Eure-et-Loir).

Generally called a *solea* (see endnote 7), an elevated axial walkway promoting the dramaturgical nature of the processions, sometimes extended into the nave (Antibes, Digne, Rezé, Entrammes, Jublains, Saint-Blaise, Viviers, and the north church of the cathedral in Geneva). This walkway should not be confused with other narrower walkways, which are also fenced off with parapets, leading to an *ambo* (lectionary) (Ristow 2006). This circular, oval, or polygonal platform, used for the liturgy of the word, has been found in Boppard, Cologne, and Trier in Germany, Tournai in Belgium (Brulet 2012), Arles (Heijmans 2006, 2014) with huge dimensions, perhaps at Vienne in France, and in the north church of Geneva cathedral in Switzerland (Bonnet 2012).

Crypts, like the one at the Clos de la Lombarde in Narbonne, sometimes also had an altar and a *loculus* for relics In the same way, some baptisteries displayed complete liturgical furnishings: altar, *presbyterium* fenced by a screen, *ambo*, and a *ciborium* above the *piscina*; the four elements are present in the sixth-century phase of the Geneva cathedral (Bonnet 2012).

CONCLUSION

For nearly 270 years, between the end of the Roman Empire and the advent of the Carolingian dynasty, the Merovingian territories experienced an intense flowering of religious construction, which recent archaeology can finally document in an improved form. Witnesses constructed of stone (or wood) reveal a society progressively Christianized under the leadership of bishops, clerics, and monks, as well as by the Merovingian sovereigns. A new monumental landscape reshaped both cities and the countryside. Without any break with classical antiquity, the Merovingian centuries fit into a continuous legacy. The various forms of Christian monuments of the fifth to eighth century illustrate this heritage, sometimes through an extreme simplification of antique patterns, and the significant development of aesthetic tastes now enriched by the arrival of immigrant populations. Within a slowly mutating world, religious buildings appear as a catalyst for cultural exchanges, as places of visibility and gathering, as well as true "témoins de la véritable fièvre bâtisseuse qui avait saisi l'ensemble du *regnum Francorum*" (witnesses of the true building fever that seized all of the kingdom of the Franks) (Guyon 1997, p. 199). Our picture of religious architecture in Merovingian Gaul is gradually becoming more accurate. We now know much more about the establishment, planning, forms and sizes, construction techniques, ornamentation, and liturgical and functional content of all these structures, which were so varied in size and use, and which reveal extensive artistic plurality.

NOTES

1. www.learn.columbia.edu/ma/htm/cl/ma_cl_gloss_merov.htm.
2. These are found in Gregory of Tours's *Historiarum libri decem*; *Liber in gloria confessorum*; *Liber in gloria martyrum*; and *Liber vitae patrum* with such regularity that it is impossible to list them all here.
3. This European project, launched in Zagreb in 2002, has brought together dozens of researchers from ten countries, including archaeologists, historians, and art historians (about sixty of whom are in France). This new corpus covers a longer period than that considered here, in order to explain the complexity of the evolution of these church sites from the late fourth century to the first decades of the eleventh century. One may find the CARE-France project online database at the following address: http://care.huma-num.fr/care.
4. Reported online June 23, 2016: www.inrap.fr/decouverte-de-l-eglise-la-plus-ancienne-de-nimes-11341.

5. This part of the chapter expands on some material comparisons discussed in the CROMART program of Zagreb University.

6. The *synthronon* is a collective semicircular benched seating, attached to the base of the apse, which sometimes incorporated a central throne (*cathedra*), meant for the bishop or the main attending priest.

7. To visualize a *presbyterium*, one can use, as has Sible de Blaauw (de Blaauw 2012), the ecclesial features of San Clemente (sixth century) in Rome, which epitomizes almost ideally the words used in the *ordines romani* and is valid for the rest of the West. The *presbyterium* includes the apse (with its *synthronon*) and the platform of the higher choir, the altar area a few steps below, after other steps the lower choir slightly raised above the nave, and to the front of the lower choir "the so-called *solea* [although the word never occurs in Western written sources]."

WORKS CITED

Ancient Sources

Fredegar. B. Krusch (ed.). (1888). *Chronicarum quae dicuntur Fredegarii Scholastici libri IV. cum Continuationibus.* MGH SRM 2. Hanover: Hahn.

Fredegar. J. M. Wallace-Hadrill (ed. and trans.). (1960). *The Fourth Book of the Chronicle of Fredegar: With Its Continuations.* London: Nelson.

Gregory of Tours, *Historiarum libri decem.* B. Krusch and W. Levison (eds.). (1951). MGH SRM 1.1. Hanover: Hahn.

Gregory of Tours, *Liber in gloria confessorum.* B. Krusch (ed.). (1969). MGH SRM 1.2 (pp. 284–370). Repr. ed. Hanover: Hahn.

Gregory of Tours, *Liber in gloria martyrum.* B. Krusch (ed.). (1969). MGH SRM 1.2 (pp. 34–111). Repr. ed. Hanover: Hahn.

Gregory of Tours. *Liber vitae patrum.* B. Krusch (ed.). (1969). MGH: SRM 1.2 (pp. 211–294). Repr. ed. Hanover: Hahn.

Honoratus of Marseille. *La vie d'Hilaire d'Arles.* S. Cavallin and P.A. Jacob (ed. and trans.). (1995). Sources Chrétiennes 404. Paris: Editions du Cerf.

Venantius Fortunatus. *Opera poetica.* F. Leo (ed.). (1881). MGH AA 4.1. Berlin: Weidmann.

Modern Sources

Anton, H. H. (1996). "Bischof und *civitas*—Kirchliche Grundlagen und politische Dimensionen bischöflicher Amtsführung im Frankenreich." In *Die Franken, Wegbereiter Europas. Vor 1500 Jahren: König Chlodwig und seine Erben [Katalog der Ausstellung]* (pp. 373–380). Mainz: Reiss-Museum Mannheim.

Antonini, A. (2015). "Archéologie du site abbatial (des origines au Xᵉ siècle)." In B. Andenmatten and L. Ripart (eds.). *L'abbaye de Saint-Maurice d'Agaune 515–2015*, Vol. 1: *Histoire et archéologie* (pp. 59–109). Gollion: Infolio.

Balcon-Berry, S., Baratte, F., Caillet, J.-P., and Sandron, D. (eds.). (2012). *Des "Domus ecclesiae" aux palais épiscopaux. Actes du colloque international—Autun 2008.* Bibliothèque de l'Antiquité Tardive 23. Turnhout: Brepols.

Balcon-Berry, S., Perrot, F., and Sapin, C. (eds.). (2009). *Vitrail, verre et archéologie entre le Vᵉ et le XIIᵉ siècle. Actes de la table ronde au Centre d'études médiévales d'Auxerre – 15–16 juin 2006.* Paris: CTHS.

Balcon-Berry, S., and Velde, B. (2016). "Evolution et caractères techniques et esthétiques du verre plat et du vitrail de l'Antiquité tardive à l'époque carolingienne." In S. Balcon, B. Boissavit-Camus, and P. Chevalier (eds.), *La mémoire des pierres, Mélanges d'archéologie, d'art et d'histoire en l'honneur de Christian Sapin* (pp. 141–153). Bibliothèque de l'Antiquité Tardive 29. Turnhout: Brepols.

Balmelle, C., Eristoff, H., and Montel, F. (eds.). (2011). *Décor et architecture en Gaule entre l'Antiquité et le haut Moyen Âge: mosaïque, peinture, stuc. Actes du colloque international de Toulouse—octobre 2008. Aquitania*, Suppl. 20. Bordeaux: Ausonius.

Bardiès-Ponti, I., Denoël, C., and Villela-Petit, I. (eds.). (2016). *Les temps mérovingiens. Trois siècles d'art et de culture (451–751). Catalogue d'exposition. Musée de Cluny—Musée national du Moyen Âge, 27 octobre 2016–13 février 2017.* Paris: Éditions de la RMN.

Baucheron, F., Gabayet, F., and de Montjoye, A. (1998). *Autour du groupe épiscopal de Grenoble: deux millénaires d'histoire.* Documents d'Archéologie en Rhône-Alpes, 16. Lyon: Alpara.

Beaujard, B., Bonifay, M., Codou, Y., Colin, M.-G., Guyon, J., Heijmans, M., Raynaud, C., and Schneider, L. (2007). "En guise de conclusion." *Gallia* 64: 57–83.

Beghelli, M., and Pinar Gil, L. (2013). "Corredo e arredo liturgico nelle chiese tra VIII e IX secolo. Suppellettili antiche e moderne, locali e importate tra archeologia, fonti scritti e fonti iconografiche." *Jahrbuch des Römisch-Germanischen Zentralmuseums Mainz* 60: 697–762.

Ben Kaddour, C. (2015), "Un édifice religieux sur poteaux plantés du haut Moyen Âge à Sainte-Catherine-de-Fierbois (Indre-et-Loire)." *Bulletin du centre d'études médiévales d'Auxerre|BUCEMA* [En ligne], 19.1. http://cem.revues.org/13966.

Berry, W. (1996). "Das Baptisterium der Kathedrale von Reims." In *Die Franken, Wegbereiter Europas. Vor 1500 Jahren: König Chlodwig und seine Erben [Katalog der Ausstellung]* (pp. 200–205). Mainz: Reiss-Museum Mannheim.

Berry, W. (2010). "Le groupe cathédral primitif. VIᵉ–XIIᵉ s." In T. Jordan (ed.), *Reims* (pp. 37–41). Collection La grâce d'une cathédrale. Strasbourg: La Nuée bleue.

Billoin, D., and Gandel, P. (eds.). (2014). *Château-sur Salins et Prétin: sept millénaires d'occupation.* Collection Archéologie dans le Jura. Ornans: Communauté de communes du Pays de Salins & Association Fortis.

Boissavit-Camus, B. (2008). "L'eau dans les baptistères paléochrétiens de la Gaule: problèmes archéologiques et perspectives d'études." In A.-M. Guimier-Sorbets (ed.), *L'eau. Enjeux, usages et représentations* (pp. 251–260). Colloques de la Maison de l'archéologie & ethnologie René-Ginouvès 4. Paris: Les éditions de la Maison Archéologie & Ethnologie, René-Ginouvès.

Boissavit-Camus, B. (2010). "Les édifices cultuels de Ligugé (Vienne)." In L. Bourgeois (ed.). *Wisigoths et Francs, autour de la bataille de Vouillé (507): recherches récentes sur le haut Moyen Âge dans le Centre-Ouest de la France. XXVIIIᵉ Journées d'archéologie mérovingienne—Vouillé-Poitiers 2007* (pp. 215–235). Saint-Germain-en-Laye: Association française d'archéologie mérovingienne.

Boissavit-Camus, B. (ed.). (2014). *Le baptistère Saint-Jean de Poitiers. De l'édifice à l'histoire urbaine.* Bibliothèque de l'Antiquité Tardive 26. Turnhout: Brepols.

Boissavit-Camus, B., Barraud, D., Bonnet, C., Fabioux, M., Guyon, J., Heber-Suffrin, F., Prigent, D., Pulga, S., Reynaud, J.-F., Sapin, C., and Vergain, P. (2003). "Archéologie et restauration, instaurer de véritables études archéologiques préalables." *Bulletin monumental* 161–163: 195–222.

Boissavit-Camus, B., and Sapin, C. (2013). "De la cathédrale paléochrétienne à la cathédrale romane." *Les Cahiers de Saint-Michel de Cuxa* 44: 19–38.

Bonnet, C. (1977). *Les premiers édifices chrétiens de la Madeleine à Genève*. Geneva: Société d'histoire de d'archéologie.

Bonnet, C. (1997). "Les églises en bois du haut Moyen Âge d'après les recherches archéologiques." In N. Gauthier and H. Galinié (eds.), *Grégoire de Tours et l'espace gaulois, Actes du congrès international Tours, 3–5 novembre 1994* (pp. 217–236). Revue archéologique du centre de la France, Suppl. 13, 1997. Tours: FERACF.

Bonnet, C. (2006). "Éléments de topographie chrétienne à Genève (Suisse)." *Gallia* 63: 111–115.

Bonnet, C., in collaboration with A. Peillex, G. Faccani, I. Plan, M. Berti, and M. Campagnolo. (2012). *Les fouilles de la cathédrale Saint-Pierre de Genève. Les édifices chrétiens et le groupe épiscopal*. Geneva: Société d'histoire et d'archéologie.

Bonnet, C., Oudet, B., Picard, J.-C., Reynaud, J.-F., and Sapin, C. (1995). *La cathédrale de Nevers: du baptistère paléochrétien au chevet roman (VI*e*–XI*e* siècles)*. Paris: Société française d'archéologie.

Borgard, P., and Michel d'Annoville, C. (2013). "Le groupe épiscopal de Riez : insertion et évolution des bâtiments au sein de la ville à la fin de l'Antiquité et au Moyen Âge." In S. Guizani (ed.). *Urbanisme et architecture en Méditerranée antique, Actes du colloque international de Tunis (24–26 novembre 2011)* (pp. 293–305). Tunis: Institut supérieur des sciences humaines.

Bouiron, M., Guilloteau, E., and Mercurin, R. (2012). "Nice, la colline du château. L'ancienne cathédrale et les fortifications de la ville médiévale et moderne." In *Congrès archéologique de France. 168*e* session. Nice et Alpes-Maritimes* (pp. 155–163). Paris: Société française d'archéologie.

Brulet, R. (ed.). (2012). *La cathédrale Notre-Dame de Tournai. L'archéologie du site et des monuments anciens*. 3 vols. Etudes et documents. Archéologie 27–29. Namur: Service public de Wallonie-UCL.

Bujard, J. (2013). "Lieux de culte et peuplement neuchâtelois (VI*e*–XVIII*e* siècle)." In A. Richard, F. Schifferdeckers, J.-P. Mazimann, and C. Belet-Gonds (eds.), *Le peuplement de l'Arc jurassien de la Préhistoire au Moyen Âge. Deuxièmes Journées archéologiques Frontalières de l'Arc Jurassien* (pp. 485–501). Besançon-Porrentruy: Presses universitaires de Franche-Comté/Office de la Culture/Société jurassienne d'émulation.

Bujard, J., Jäggi, C., & Meier, H.-R. (2005). "Les églises." In R. Windler, R. Marti, U. Niffeler, and L. Steiner (eds.), *La Suisse du Paléolithique à l'aube du Moyen Age*, vol. 6: *Haut Moyen-Âge* (pp. 119–144). Basel: Société suisse de préhistoire et d'archéologie.

Bully, S. (2009). "Archéologie des monastères du premier millénaire dans le Centre-Est de la France. Conditions d'implantation et de diffusion, topographie historique et organisation." *Bulletin du centre d'études médiévales d'Auxerre* 13: 257–290.

Bully, S. (2016). "L'architecture religieuse." In I. Bardiès-Ponti, C. Denoël, and I. Villela-Petit (eds.), *Les temps mérovingiens. Trois siècles d'art et de culture (451–751)* (pp. 24–27). Paris: Éditions de la RMN.

Bully, S., Bully, A., Čaušević-Bully, M., and Fiocchi, L. (2014). "Les origines du monastère de Luxeuil (Haute-Saône) d'après les récentes recherches archéologiques." In M. Gaillard (ed.), *L'empreinte chrétienne en Gaule (de la fin du IV*e* au début du VIII*e* siècle)* (pp. 311–355). Turnhout: Brepols.

Bully, S., and Sapin, C. (eds.). (2016). *L'origine des sites monastiques : confrontation entre la terminologie des sources textuelles et les données archéologiques. Actes des 4*e* journées d'études monastiques, Baume-les-Messieurs, 4–5 septembre 2014. Bulletin du centre d'études médiévales d'Auxerre|BUCEMA* [En ligne], Hors-série no. 10. https://cem.revues.org/14463.

Cantié, G., Lhermite, X., and Proust, E. (2007). "Brive-la-Gaillarde, église Saint-Martin: de la *memoria* mérovingienne à la collégiale." In *Congrès archéologiques de France: 163ᵉ session, Corrèze, 2005* (pp. 105–123). Paris: Société française d'archéologie.

Cartron, I., Barraud, D., Henriet, P. and Michel, A. (eds.). (2009). *Autour de Saint-Seurin : lieu, mémoire, pouvoir des premiers temps chrétiens à la fin du Moyen Âge. Actes du colloque de Bordeaux – 12–14 octobre 2006.* Bordeaux: Ausonius.

Cartron, I., Henrion, F., and Scuillier, C. (eds.) (2015). *Les sarcophages de l'Antiquité tardive et du haut Moyen Âge: fabrication, utilisation, diffusion. Actes des XXXᵉ Journées internationales d'archéologie mérovingienne—Bordeaux 2009.* Aquitania, Suppl. 34. Bordeaux: Ausonius.

Cattedu, I., Carré, F., Gentili, F., Delahaye, F., Langlois, J.-Y., and Couanon, P. (2009). "Fouilles d'églises rurales du haut Moyen Âge dans le Nord de la France. Des questions récurrentes." In D. Paris-Poulain, D. Istria, and S. Nardi Combescure (eds.), *Les premiers chrétiens dans le territoire de la France actuelle. Hagiographie, épigraphie et archéologie : nouvelles approches et perspectives de recherche. Actes du colloque international d'Amiens – 18–20 janvier 2007* (pp. 205–233). Rennes: PUR (Collection Archéologie et Culture).

Chantinne, F., and Mignot, P. (2012). "Prémices du projet CARE en Belgique." *Hortus Artium Medievalium* 18(1): 183–187.

Chantinne, F., and Mignot, P. (2014). "La collégiale Saint-Gertrude de Nivelles. Réexamen du dossier archéologique." *Hortus Artium Medievalium* 20: 513–519.

Chevalier, P. (2008). "La crypte de Saint-Julien de Brioude, 'memoria' de la première basilique?" In A. Dubreucq, C. Lauranson-Rosaz, and B. Sanial (eds.), *Saint-Julien et les origines de Brioude, Actes du Colloque international—Brioude (22–25 Septembre 2004)* (pp. 280–287). Brioude–Saint-Etienne: Almanach de Brioude-CERCOR.

Chevalier, P. (2009). "De la fosse d'autel à l'armoire aux reliques: réalités archéologiques des dépôts de reliques dans l'Antiquité tardive et au Moyen Âge." In S. Bonnardin, X. Hamon, M. Lauwers, and B. Quilliec (eds.). *Du matériel au spirituel. Réalités archéologiques et historiques des "dépôts" de la Préhistoire à nos jours. Actes des XXIXᵉ Rencontres internationales d'archéologie et d'histoire d'Antibes—2008* (pp. 421–434). Antibes: CEPAM.

Chevalier, P. (2014a). "Au cœur du groupe épiscopal du Puy, le baptistère Saint-Jean." In M. Gaillard (ed.). *L'empreinte chrétienne en Gaule (de la fin du IVᵉ au début du VIIIᵉ siècle)* (pp. 201–214). Turnhout: Brepols.

Chevalier, P. (2014b). "Le long temps des archéologues." In H. Simon (ed.), *Clermont, l'âme de l'Auvergne* (pp. 26–38). Collection La grâce d'une cathédrale. Strasbourg: La Nuée bleue.

Chevalier, P., and Fray, J.-L. (2014). "La première cathédrale et l'évangélisation des Arvernes." In H. Simon (ed.), *Clermont, l'âme de l'Auvergne* (pp. 309–311). Strasbourg: La Nuée bleue (Collection La grâce d'une cathédrale).

Chevalier, P., and Sapin, C., in collaboration with L. Granjon, E. Leclercq, A. Millereux, and M. Savonnet (2012). "Les avancées du corpus CARE en France (2008–2011)." *Hortus Artium Medievalium* 18(1): 85–96.

Codou, Y. (2014). "Aux origines du monachisme: le dossier de Saint-Honorat de Lérins." In M. Gaillard (ed.). *L'empreinte chrétienne en Gaule (de la fin du IVᵉ au début du VIIIᵉ siècle)* (pp. 291–310). Turnhout: Brepols.

Codou, Y., Colin, M.-G., Le Nézet-Célestin, M., Fauduet, I., and Odenhardt-Donvez, I. (2007). "La christianisation des campagnes (IVᵉ–VIIIᵉ s.)." *Gallia* 64, 57–83.

Colardelle, R. (2008). *La ville et la mort. Saint-Laurent de Grenoble, 2000 ans de tradition funéraire.* Bibliothèque de l'Antiquité Tardive 11. Turnhout: Brepols.

Colin, M.-G. (2008). *Christianisation et peuplement des campagnes entre Garonne et Pyrénées, IVᵉ–Xᵉ siècles*. Archéologie du Midi Médiéval, Suppl. 5. Toulouse: CAML.

Cramatte, C, Glaus, M., and Mamin, Y. (2012). "Une église du 5ᵉ siècle dans le *castrum* de Mandeure." *Archäologie Schweiz/Archéologie suisse/Archeologia Svizzera* 35: 4–15.

Creissen, T. (2009). "L'aménagement du sanctuaire dans les églises de France avant l'an Mil." *Hortus Artium Medievalium* 15(1): 87–103.

De Blaauw, S. (2012). "Origins and Early Developments of the Choir." In S. Frommel and L. Lecomte (eds.), *La place du chœur: architecture et liturgie du Moyen Âge aux temps modernes. Actes du colloque de l'EPHE-INHA* (pp. 25–32). Paris: Picard.

Delaplace, C. (ed.). (2005). *Aux origines de la paroisse rurale en Gaule méridionale (IVᵉ–IXᵉ siècles). Actes du Congrès international de Toulouse – 21–23 mars 2003*. Paris: Errance.

Delaplace, C. (2015). "Local Churches, Settlement, and Social Power in Late Antique and Early Medieval Gaul: New Avenues in the Light of Recent Archaeological Research in South-East France." In J. Sanchez-Pardo and M. Shapland (eds.), *Churches and Social Power in Early Medieval Europe. Integrating Archaeological and Historical Approches* (pp. 419–450). Turnhout: Brepols.

de Maillé, A. (1971). *Les cryptes de Jouarre*. Paris: Picard.

de Mecquenem, C. (2007). "Les cryptes de Jouarre: un bilan archéologique provisoire (1840–20)." In *Medieval Europe Paris – 2007*. Paris: Université Paris I. http://www.medieval-europe-paris-2007.univ-paris1.fr/C.Demecquenem.pdf.

Demians d'Archambault, G. (2001). "Les fouilles de l'ancienne cathédrale de Digne: état des questions." *Comptes rendus des séances de l'Académie des Inscriptions et Belles Lettres* 145(1): 409–439.

Denis, J. (2006). "Le baptistère de Limoges (Haute-Vienne)." *Gallia* 63: 125–129.

Duval, N. (ed.). (1991). *Naissance des arts chrétiens. Atlas des monuments paléochrétiens de la France*. Paris: Imprimerie Nationale.

Duval, N. (1995). *Les premiers monuments chrétiens de la France*. Vol. 1: *Sud-Est et Corse*. Atlas archéologiques de la France. Paris: Picard.

Duval, N. (1996). *Les premiers monuments chrétiens de la France*. Vol. 2: *Sud-Ouest et Centre*. Atlas archéologiques de la France. Paris: Picard.

Duval, N. (1998). *Les premiers monuments chrétiens de la France*. Vol. 3: *Ouest, Nord et Est*. Atlas archéologiques de la France. Paris: Picard.

Duval, N. (2002). "Les descriptions d'architecture et de décor chez Grégoire de Tours et les auteurs gaulois : le cas de Saint-Martin de Tours." In B. Beaujard (ed.), *La naissance de la ville chrétienne. Mélanges en hommage à Nancy Gauthier* (pp. 21–58). Tours: Publications de la MSH « Villes et territoires ».

Duval, Y., and Pietri, L. (1997). "Evergétisme et épigraphie dans l'Occident chrétien (IVᵉ–VIᵉ s.)." In C. Christol and O. Masson (eds.), *Actes du Xᵉ Congrès International d'épigraphie grecque et latine* (pp. 371–396). Paris: Publications de la Sorbonne.

Faccani, G. (2010). *Martigny (VS), Pfarrkirche Notre-Dame. Römischer Gebäudekomplex, spätantike Bischofskirche, mittelalterliche Pfarrkirche*. Studien zu Spätantike und Frühmittelalter 2. Hamburg: Verlag Dr. Kovac.

Faccani, G. (2012). *Die Kastellkirche von Kaiseraugst*. Forschungen in Augst 42. Basel: Museum Augusta Raurica.

Faccani, G., and Ristow, S. (2012). "Vorromanische Kirchenbauten online—ein internationales Projekt." *Hortus Artium Medievalium* 18(1): 179–182.

Fehring, G. P. (1967). "Die Stellung des frühmittelalterlichen Holzkirchenbaus in der Architekturgeschichte." *Jahrbuch RGZM* 14: 179–197.

Février, P.-A. (1981). *Le Groupe épiscopal de Fréjus.* Collection Petites notes sur les grands édifices. Paris: Caisse nationale des monuments historiques et des sites.

Fixot, M. (ed.) (2012). *Le groupe épiscopal de Fréjus.* Bibliothèque de l'Antiquité Tardive 25. Turnhout: Brepols.

Fizellier-Sauget, B. (ed.). (1999). *L'Auvergne de Sidoine Apollinaire à Grégoire de Tours: histoire et archéologie. Actes des XIIIᵉ Journées internationales d'archéologie mérovingienne— Clermont-Ferrand 1991.* Clermont-Ferrand: Institut d'études du Massif central.

Die Franken, Wegbereiter Europas (1996). *Vor 1500 Jahren: König Chlodwig und seine Erben [Katalog der Ausstellung im Reiss-Museum Mannheim 8. September 1996 bis 6. Januar 1997].* 2 vols. Mainz: Reiss-Museum Mannheim.

Gaillard, M. (ed.). (2014). *L'empreinte chrétienne en Gaule (de la fin du IVᵉ au début du VIIIᵉ siècle).* Turnhout: Brepols.

Gaillard, M., Rabel, C., Sapin, C., Vallet, F., and Villette, J.-L. (2011). *Aux origines de Saint-Quentin : de la tradition littéraire à la réalité archéologique. Catalogue d'exposition.* Saint-Quentin: Musée Antoine Lécuyer.

Gallia 63. (2006). *Antiquité tardive, haut Moyen Âge et premiers temps chrétiens en Gaule méridionale. Première partie: réseau des cités, monde urbain et monde des morts.* http://www.persee.fr/issue/galia_0016-4119_2006_num_63_1.

Gallia 64. (2007). *Antiquité tardive, haut Moyen Âge et premiers temps chrétiens en Gaule méridionale. Seconde partie: monde rural, échanges et consommation.* http://www.persee.fr/issue/galia_0016-4119_2007_num_64_1.

Gauthier, F. (2004). "Inscriptions paléochrétiennes découvertes dans le baptistère de Saint-Julien de Brioude." *Hortus Artium Medievalium* 10: 211–215.

Gauthier, N., and Galinié, H. (eds.) (1997). *Grégoire de Tours et l'espace gaulois, Actes du congrès international Tours, 3–5 novembre 1994.* Revue archéologique du centre de la France, Suppl. 13. Tours: FERACF.

Gauthier, N., and Picard, J.-C. (eds.). (1972–2012). *Topographie chrétienne des cités de la Gaule des origines au milieu du VIIIᵉ siècle* 15 vols. Paris: De Boccard.

Guigon, P. (1997–1998). *Les églises du haut Moyen Âge en Bretagne.* 2 vols. Saint-Malo: Centre régional d'archéologie d'Alet.

Guyon, J. (1997). "L'architecture religieuse chez Grégoire de Tours." In N. Gauthier and H. Galinié (eds.), *Grégoire de Tours et l'espace gaulois, Actes du congrès international Tours, 3–5 novembre 1994* (pp. 197–207). Revue archéologique du centre de la France, Suppl. 13. Tours: FERACF.

Guyon, J. (2000). "La topographie chrétienne de Marseille pendant l'Antiquité tardive et le haut Moyen Âge." In F. Prévot (ed.), *Romanité et cité chrétienne : permanence et mutations, intégration et exclusion du Iᵉʳ au VIᵉ siècle, Mélange en l'honneur d'Y. Duval* (pp. 391–407). Paris: De Boccard.

Guyon, J. (2006). "Émergence et affirmation d'une topographie chrétienne dans les villes de la Gaule méridionale." *Gallia* 63: 85–110.

Guyon, J., and Heijmans, M. (eds.). (2001). *D'un monde à l'autre. Naissance d'une chrétienté en Provence IVᵉ–VIᵉ siècle. catalogue d'exposition.* Arles: Musée de l'Arles Antique.

Guyon, J., and Heijmans, M. (eds.). (2013). *L'Antiquité tardive en Provence (IVᵉ–VIᵉ siècle). Naissance d'une chrétienté.* Arles: Actes Sud.

Heber-Suffrin, F. (1995). "Saint-Pierre-Aux-Nonnains." In *Congrès archéologique de France. 149ᵉ session. Les Trois-Évêchés et l'ancien duché de Bar* (pp. 495–515). Paris: Société française d'archéologie.

Heijmans, M. (2006). "L'église paléochrétienne de l'enclos Saint-Césaire à Arles (Bouches-du-Rhône)." *Gallia* 63: 121–124.

Heijmans, M. (2014). "A propos de la mise à jour de la *Topographie chrétienne des Cités de la Gaule*: réflexions sur le cas d'Arles." In M. Gaillard (ed.), *L'empreinte chrétienne en Gaule (de la fin du IVᵉ au début du VIIIᵉ siècle)* (pp. 151–171). Turnhout: Brepols.

Heitz, C. (1987). *La France pré-romane. Archéologie et architecture religieuse du haut Moyen Âge du IVᵉ siècle à l'an Mille.* Paris: Errance.

Hubert, J. (1938). *L'art préroman.* Collection Les monuments datés de la France. Paris: Éditions d'art et d'histoire.

Hubert, J. (1952). *L'architecture religieuse du haut Moyen Âge en France.* Paris: Imprimerie nationale.

Jacobsen, W. (1997). "Saints' Tombs in Frankish Church Architecture." *Speculum* 72(4): 1107–1143.

Jacobsen, W., Schaefer, L., and Sennhauser, H. R. (1991). *Vorromanische Kirchenbauten. Katalog der Denkmäler bis zum Ausgang der Ottonen. Nachtragsband.* Veröffentlichungen des Zentralinstituts für Kunstgeschichte in München 3.2. München: Prestel.

Kluge-Pinsker, A. (1996). "Königliche Kirchen der Merowinger in Paris und Saint-Denis." In *Die Franken, Wegbereiter Europas. Vor 1500 Jahren: König Chlodwig und seine Erben [Katalog der Ausstellung]* (pp. 423–434). Mainz: Reiss-Museum Mannheim.

Krier, J. (1996). "Echternach und das Kloster das hl. Willibrord." In *Die Franken, Wegbereiter Europas. Vor 1500 Jahren: König Chlodwig und seine Erben [Katalog der Ausstellung]* (pp. 466–478). Mainz: Reiss-Museum Mannheim.

Lambotte, B., and Neuray, B. (2008). "Stavelot/Stavelot: ancienne abbatiale, état d'avancement des fouilles dans le secteur occidental des nefs et de l'avant-corps ottoniens." *Chronique de l'archéologie wallonne* 15: 153–155.

Lambotte, B., and Neuray, B. (2009). "Stavelot/Stavelot : ancienne abbatiale, vestiges du milieu du VIIᵉ siècle jusqu'à 881." *Chronique de l'archéologie wallonne* 16: 121–125.

Langlois, J.-Y. (2001). "Seine-Maritime. Une église du VIIᵉ siècle à Notre-Dame de Bondeville." *Bulletin Monumental* 159(2): 173–175.

Le Maho, J. (1994). "Les fouilles de la cathédrale de Rouen de 1985 à 1993. Esquisse d'un premier bilan." *Archéologie Médiévale* 24: 1–49.

Le Maho, J. (2013). "La cathédrale des origines." In J.-C. Descubes (ed.), *Rouen, primatiale de Normandie* (pp. 13–25). Collection La grâce d'une cathédrale. Strasbourg: La Nuée bleue.

Le Nezet-Célestin, M. (2009). "Le baptistère de Roanne, place Maréchal de-Lattre-de-Tassigny (Loire)." In D. Paris-Poulain, D. Istria, and S. Nardi Combescure (eds.), *Les premiers chrétiens dans le territoire de la France actuelle. Hagiographie, épigraphie et archéologie: nouvelles approches et perspectives de recherche. Actes du colloque international d'Amiens – 18–20 janvier 2007* (pp. 195–202). Collection Archéologie et Culture. Rennes: PUR.

Lepelley, C. (1997). "Evergétisme et épigraphie dans l'Antiquité tardive : les provinces de langue latine." In M. Christol and O. Masson (eds.), *Actes du Xᵉ Congrès International d'épigraphie grecque et latine* (pp. 335–352). Paris: Publications de la Sorbonne.

Lhermite, X. (2012). "Abbaye Saint-Martial de Limoges recherches en cours sur l'église Saint-Pierre du Sépulcre." *Bulletin de la Société archéologique et historique du Limousin* 140: 1–19.

Lhermite, X., Marty, A., Misme, A.-C., Poulain, P. and Verliac, G.-A. (2015). "1 rue de la Courtine (Limoges): du mausolée antique à l'église Sainte-Marie de la Courtine." *Archéologie en Limousin* 1: 1–16.

Lorans, É. (2012). "Aux origines du monastère de Marmoutier: le témoignage de l'archéologie." *Annales de Bretagne et des Pays de l'Ouest* 119(3): 178–203.

Louis, É. (2014). "Une église monastique du haut Moyen Âge dans le nord de la France: le cas d'Hamage." In M. Gaillard (ed.), *L'empreinte chrétienne en Gaule (de la fin du IVᵉ au début du VIIIᵉ siècle)* (pp. 357–385). Turnhout: Brepols.

Mâle, É. (1950). *La fin du paganisme en Gaule et les plus anciennes basiliques chrétiennes*. Paris: Flammarion.

Martinez, D., and Morel, D. (2012). "L'architecture religieuse de l'Auvergne entre Antiquité tardive et haut Moyen Âge." *Hortus Artium Medievalium* 18(1): 97–121.

Mérel-Brandenburg, A.-B. (1999). "Installations et mobilier liturgique en Septimanie. Antiquité tardive—Haut Moyen Âge (IVᵉ–VIIᵉ s.)." *Hortus Artium Medievalium* 9: 45–56.

Mérel-Brandenburg, A.-B. (2005). "Le complexe architectural et funéraire de Peyre Clouque à Montferrand (Aude) (IVᵉ–VIIᵉ s.)." *Hortus Artium Medievalium* 9: 143–154.

Mériaux C. (2006). *Gallia irradiata. Saints et sanctuaires dans le nord de la Gaule du haut Moyen Âge*. Stuttgart: Steiner Verlag (Beiträge zur Hagiographie, 4).

Mertens, J. (1979). *Le sous-sol archéologique de la collégiale de Nivelles*. Nivelles: Musées communaux.

Migeon, W. (2006). "Le groupe épiscopal de Bordeaux (Gironde)." *Gallia* 63: 117–119.

Moliner, M. (2006). "La basilique funéraire de la rue Malaval à Marseille (Bouches-du-Rhône)." *Gallia* 63: 131–136.

Monteil, M. (2013). "La cathédrale des origines." In J.-P. James (ed.), *Nantes* (pp. 15–27). Collection La grâce d'une cathédrale. Strasbourg: La Nuée bleue.

Narazawa, Y. (2015). *Les autels chrétiens du Sud de la Gaule (Vᵉ–XIIᵉ siècles)*. Bibliothèque de l'Antiquité tardive 27. Turnhout: Brepols.

Naveau, J. (1993). "Les thermes et l'église paléochrétienne d'Entrammes. Données nouvelles sur le plan et les élévations." *Société d'histoire de la Mayenne* 16: 15–54.

Neuray, B. (2013). " L'abbaye de Stavelot." In O. Vrielynck (ed.), *L'archéologie en Wallonie. L'époque mérovingienne* (pp. 42–43). Carnets du Patrimoine 114. Namur : Institut du Patrimoine wallon.

Oswald, F., Schaefer, L., and Sennhauser, H. R. (1966–1971). *Vorromanische Kirchenbauten. Katalog der Denkmäler bis zum Ausgang der Ottonen*. 3 vols. Veröffentlichungen des Zentralinstituts für Kunstgeschichte in München 3/1. Munich: Prestel.

Päffgen, B., and Ristow, S. (1996). "Christentum, Kirchenbau und Sakralkunst im östlichen Frankenreich (Austrasien)." In *Die Franken, Wegbereiter Europas. Vor 1500 Jahren: König Chlodwig und seine Erben [Katalog der Ausstellung]* (pp. 407–415). Mainz: Reiss-Museum Mannheim.

Palazzo-Bertholon, B., and Treffort, C. (2010). "Pour une relecture de l'hypogée des Dunes à Poitiers: approche méthodologique et interdisciplinaire." In L. Bourgeois (ed.), *Wisigoths et Francs, autour de la bataille de Vouillé (507): recherches récentes sur le haut Moyen Âge dans le Centre-Ouest de la France. XXVIIIᵉ Journées d'archéologie mérovingienne—Vouillé-Poitiers 2007* (pp. 151–169). Saint-Germain-en-Laye: Association française d'archéologie mérovingienne.

Paris-Poulain, D., Istria, D., and Nardi Combescure, S. (eds.). (2009). *Les premiers chrétiens dans le territoire de la France actuelle. Hagiographie, épigraphie et archéologie : nouvelles approches et perspectives de recherche. Actes du colloque international d'Amiens – 18–20 janvier 2007*. Rennes: PUR (Collection Archéologie et Culture).

Périn, P., and Wyss, M. (2015). "La basilique mérovingienne. VIᵉ–VIIᵉ s." In P. Delannoy (ed.), *Saint-Denis, dans l'éternité des rois et des reines de France* (pp. 34–47). Collection La grâce d'une cathédrale. Strasbourg: La Nuée bleue.

Pirault, L. (2009). "La basilique des Champs-Saint-Martin à Rezé (Loire-Atlantique." In D. Paris-Poulain, D. Istria, and S. Nardi Combescure (eds.), *Les premiers chrétiens dans le territoire de la France actuelle. Hagiographie, épigraphie et archéologie : nouvelles approches et perspectives de recherche. Actes du colloque international d'Amiens – 18–20 janvier 2007* (pp. 181–194). Rennes: PUR (Collection Archéologie et Culture).

Prévot, F. (2003). "La cathédrale et la ville en Gaule dans l'Antiquité Tardive et le Haut Moyen Âge." *Histoire urbaine* 7(1): 17–36.

Prévot, F., Gaillard, M., and Gauthier, N. (eds.). (2014). *Topographie chrétienne des cités de la Gaule des origines au milieu du VIIIᵉ siècle*. Vol. 16. *Quarante ans d'enquête (1972–2012)*. 2 vols. Paris: De Boccard.

Prisset, J.-L. (2015). *Saint-Romain-en-Gal aux temps de Ferréol, Mamert et Adon. L'aire funéraire des thermes des Lutteurs (IVᵉ–Xᵉ siècles)*. Bibliothèque de l'Antiquité Tardive 28. Turnhout: Brepols.

Reynaud, J.-F. (1998). "*Lugdunum Christianum.*" *Lyon du IVᵉ au VIIᵉ s: topographie, nécropoles et édifices religieux*. DAF 69. Paris: Maison des Sciences de l'Homme.

Reynaud, J.-F., & Richard, F. (2011). "Le groupe épiscopal de Lyon, IVᵉ–XVᵉ s." In P. Barbarin (ed.), *Clermont, l'âme de l'Auvergne* (pp. 15–38). Collection La grâce d'une cathédrale. Strasbourg: La Nuée bleue.

Ristow, S. (2002). *Die frühen Kirchen unter dem Kölner Dom. Befunde und Funde vom 4. Jahrhundert bis zur Bauzeit des Alten Domes*. Studien zum Kölner Dom 9. Cologne: Verlag Kölner Dom.

Ristow, S. (2006). "Zur Gestaltung des Ambo in Gallien, Germanien, Raetien und Norikum im Frühmittelalter." In M. Altripp and C. Nauerth (eds.), *Architektur und Liturgie. Akten des Kolloquiums vom 25. Bis 27. Juli 2003 im Greifswald (Spätantike—Frühes Christentum—Byzanz)* (pp. 223–232). Wiesbaden: Reichert Verlag.

Ristow, S. (2007). *Frühes Christentum im Rheinland. Die Zeugnisse der archäologischen und historischen Quellen an Rhein, Maas und Mosel*. Cologne: Rheinischer Verein für Denkmalpflege und Landschaftsschutz. Münster: Aschendorff für Denkmalpflege und Landschaftsschutz.

Ristow, S. (2009). *Die Ausgrabungen von St. Pantaleon in Köln. Archäologie und Geschichte von römischer bis karolingisch-ottonischer Zeit*. Zeitschrift für Archäologie des Mittelalters, Beiheft 21. Bonn: Habelt.

Roger, J. (2016). "Moutier-Rozeille." *ADLFI. Archéologie de la France—Informations [en ligne], Limousin*. http://adlfi.revues.org/16116.

Sapin, C. (1986). *La Bourgogne préromane. Construction, décor et fonction des édifices religieux*. Paris: Picard.

Sapin, C. (ed.). (2000). *Archéologie et architecture d'un site monastique, 10 ans de recherche à l'abbaye Saint-Germain d'Auxerre*. Auxerre: CEM and Paris: CTHS.

Sapin, C. (ed.) (2004). *Le stuc. Visage oublié de l'art médiéval. Catalogue d'exposition*. Poitiers: Musée Sainte-Croix.

Sapin, C. (2008a). "Archéologie des tombeaux des grands sanctuaires de Gaule aux Vᵉ–VIᵉ siècles: état des recherches et réflexions." In A. Dubreucq, C. Lauranson-Rosaz, and B. Sanial (eds.), *Saint-Julien et les origines de Brioude, Actes du Colloque international—Brioude (22–25 sept. 2004)* (pp. 1–30). Brioude–Saint-Étienne: Almanach de Brioude-CERCOR.

Sapin, C. (2008b). "L'archéologie des premiers monastères en France (V^e-déb. XIe s.), un état des recherches." In F. De Rubeis and F. Marazzi (eds.), *Monasteri in Europa occidentale (secoli VIII–XI): topografia e strutture. Atti del Convegno Internazionale, Castel San Vincenzo, 27–29 settembre 2004* (pp. 83–348). Roma: Viella.

Sapin, C. (2014). *Les cryptes en France: pour une approche archéologique.* Paris: Picard.

Sapin, C., and Chevalier, P. (eds.). (2012). *Mausolées & églises IVe-VIIIe siècles. Actes du colloque international de Clermont-Ferrand—3–5 novembre 2011. Hortus Artium Medievalium* 18(2): 239–385.

Sapin, C., Treffort C., and Palazzo-Bertholon, B. (2009). *Les stucs de l'Antiquité tardive de Vouneuil-sous-Biard (Vienne).* Supplément à Gallia. Paris: CNRS éditions.

Sennhauser, H. R. (2012a). "Zur Geschichte der Christlichen Archäologie in der Schweiz (1. Folge), Schweizer Altertumsforscher und Christliche Archäologie." *Römische Quartalschrift für Christliche Altertumskunde und Kirchengeschichte* 107(1–2): 21–48.

Sennhauser, H. R. (2012b). "Zur Geschichte der Christlichen Archäologie in der Schweiz (2. Folge), Denkmäler des frühen Christentums in der Schweiz: Zum Stand der Forschung." *Römische Quartalschrift für Christliche Altertumskunde und Kirchengeschichte* 107(3–4): 163–201.

Terrier J. (2002). "Les églises dans la campagne genevoise." *Zeitschrift für Archäologie und Kunstgeschichte* 59: 195–206.

Terrier J., Odenhardt-Donvez, I., and Fauduet, I. (2007). "Une archéologie pour aborder la christianisation de l'espace rural: l'exemple de la campagne genevoise." *Gallia* 64: 85–91.

Untermann, M. (2014). "Einzigartiger Kirchenbau aus dem 7. Jahrhundert in Mainz Nachgewesen." *Archäologie online.* http://www.archaeologie-online.de/magazin/einzigartiger-kirchenbau-aus-dem7-jahrhundert-in-mainz-nachgewiesen_32519.

Van Hove, M.-L., Chantinne, F., Willems, D., Colette, O., Dietrich, A., Godefroid, A., and Yernaux, G. (2012). "Dans la clôture d'une grande abbaye : premiers résultats des recherches archéologiques menées sur la place de Nivelles (2009–2011)." *Medieval and Modern Matters* 3: 165–209.

Verslype, L. (ed.). (2007). *Villes et campagnes en Neustrie. Sociétés—Économies—Territoires—Christianisation. XXVe Journées d'archéologie mérovingienne—Tournai 2004.* Montagnac: Éditions Mergoil.

Vieillard-Troïekouroff, M. (1976). *Les monuments religieux de la Gaule d'après les œuvres de Grégoire de Tours.* Paris: Librairie Honoré Champion.

Wyss, M. (ed.) (1996). *Atlas historique de Saint-Denis, des origines au XVIIIe siècle.* DAF 59. Paris : Éditions de la Maison des sciences de l'homme.

CHAPTER 31

RURAL LIFE AND WORK IN NORTHERN GAUL DURING THE EARLY MIDDLE AGES

EDITH PEYTREMANN

How did people live and work in northern Gaul during the Merovingian period, an epoch of significant change?[1] The end of the Roman Empire and its political-economic system brought substantial changes to the political and economic life of northern Gaul (Fig. 31.1). The emergence of the Frankish kingdoms, with new actors and different rulers, added to and transformed the previously existing economic infrastructure. These transformations directly affected rural society, which was organized in different ways and regained some importance to the detriment of urban society. The countryside began to be exploited and used differently than had previously been the case.

These changes were progressive, but from the archaeological data, we can distinguish just two main phases of transformation in the countryside of northern Gaul during the early Middle Ages (Peytremann 2003). The first began around the end of the fifth century and was complete by about the middle of the seventh century. The second started in the mid-seventh century and finished around the end of the eighth century. Within each of these phases, several points will be highlighted in an effort to understand the modifications that affected the rural world. This chapter begins by addressing the modalities of rural settlement and the different forms of occupation that existed in each phase, before it turns to an examination of how lands were exploited and raw materials transformed.

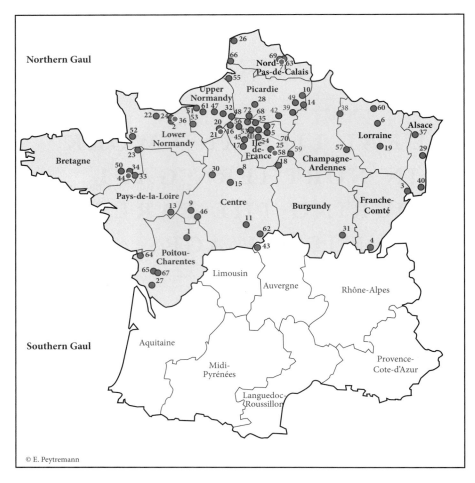

FIGURE 31.1. Location of sites mentioned in the chapter over the background of the French administrative regions:

1: Pouthumé (Vienne), 2: Biéville-Beuville (Calvados), 3: Delle (Territoire-de-Belfort), 4: Pratz (Jura), 5: Serris (Seine-et-Marne), 6: Prény (Meurthe-et-Moselle), 7: Chessy (Seine-et-Marne), 8: Ingré (Loiret), 9: Truyes (Indre-et-Loire), 10: Goudelancourt-Lès-Pierrepont (Aisne), 11: Saint-Florent-sur-Cher (Cher), 12: Genlis (Côte-d'Or),13: Distré (Maine-et-Loire), 14 Juvincourt-et-Damary (Aisne), 15: Saran (Loiret), 16: Herblay (Val-d'Oise), 17: Saint-Maurice-Montcouronne (Essonne), 18: Villeroy (Yonne), 19: Messein (Meurthe-et-Moselle), 20: Guichainville (Eure), 21: Marcilly (Eure), 22: Mondeville (Calvados), 23: Montours (Ille-et-Vilaine), 24: Giberville (Calvados), 25: Saint-Germain-Laxis (Seine-et-Marne), 26: Hames-Boucres (Pas-de-Calais), 27: Saint-Georges-des-Coteaux (Charente-Maritime), 28: Saleux (Somme), 29: Sermersheim (Bas-Rhin), 30: Fréteval (Loir-et-Cher), 31: Sevrey (Saône-et-Loire), 32: Tournedos-sur-Seine (Eure), 33: Gennes-sur-Seiche (Ille-et-Vilaine), 34: Châteaugiron (Ille-et-Vilaine), 35: Louvres (Val-d'Oise), 36: Cormelles-le-Royal (Calvados), 37: Marlenheim (Bas-Rhin), 39: Condé-sur-Aisne, 40: Riediesheim (Haut-Rhin), 41: Paris, 42: Chelles (Oise), 43: Saint-Victor (Allier), 44: Châteaugiron, 45: Villiers-le-Bâcle (Essonne), 46: Sainte-Catherine-de-Fierbois (Indre-et-Loire), 47: Val-de-Reuil (Eure), 48: Guerny (Eure), 49: Athies-sur-Laon (Aisne), 50: Chantepie (Ille-et-Vilaine), 51: Saint-Vigor-d'Ymonville (Seine-Maritime), 52: Courbépine (Eure), 53: La Courneuve (Seine-Saint-Denis), 54: Servon (Seine-et-Marne), 55: Le Translay (Somme), 56: Avernes (Val-d'Oise), 57: Saint-Dizier (Haute-Marne), 58: Vert-Saint-Denis (Seine-et-Marne), 59: La Saulsotte (Aube), 60: Vitry-sur-Orne (Moselle), 61: La Londe (Seine-Maritime), 62: Farges-Allichamps (Cher), 63: Wandignies-Hamage (Nord), 64: Houmeau (Charente-Maritime), 65: Port-Berteau (Charente-Maritime), 66: Quentovic (Pas-de-Calais), 67: Taillebourg (Charente-Maritime), 68: Villiers-le-Sec (Val-d'Oise), 69: Guesnain (Nord), 70: Tremblay-en-France (Seine-Saint-Denis), 71: Dechy (Nord), 72: Villiers-sous-Saint-Leu (Oise)

Land Use and Rural Settlement Forms from the Late Fifth to the Mid-Seventh Century

The Merovingian countryside was the product of the human shaping of the landscape from as early as the Neolithic period. Forests, fields, and waterways had undergone numerous transformations: deforestation, a return to heaths, the creation of hedges to demarcate land and byways for movement, and the channeling of rivers, among other processes. These features form an open landscape, a term that archaeologists employ to describe regions that were deforested and heavily affected by human intervention in the form of cultivated lands, the existence of built structures, and so on. This picture contrasts markedly with the impression of a densely forested wilderness created by contemporary hagiographical texts like the sixth-century *Life of the Jura Fathers* (Martine 2004). Early medieval historians have long depended on this work, whose accuracy they have overemphasized in portraying this period.

Archaeological sites dated to the early Merovingian period allow us to distinguish three main types of rural settlement in northern Gaul. The first, to adopt the terminology employed by geographers, corresponds to what we might describe as a dispersed habitat. This form of settlement was characterized by a sparse network of isolated farms (or units of agricultural exploitation). Among these dispersed habitations, we may distinguish those that were the legacy of earlier occupation from those that were created during the sixth and the first half of the seventh century. In effect, a significant proportion of known habitation sites were established on territory formerly occupied by Roman farmsteads. These new settlement sites might be established in the residential quarters of these sites (*pars urbana*), the working buildings (*pars rustica*), or simply in a field adjacent to the old Roman structures. However, continuity of occupation at such sites from one form of use to the other is difficult to demonstrate except in some regions of France such as Poitou-Charente. There, sites inhabited from the early Roman Empire through to the Carolingian period are more common, such as L'Houmeau near La Rochelle.[2] In most instances, however, as, for example, in the valley of Tautecourt in Lorraine (Frauciel 2013), the Roman establishments in northern Gaul were abandoned at the end of the third century and rarely show evidence of late-antique activity. For this reason, some of these sites have sometimes been described as opportunistic or temporary (Carpentier and Hincker 2013).

The second form of rural occupation during the early Merovingian period corresponds to loosely grouped settlements (Peytremann 2003). In this case, farms formed a denser network than in the examples of dispersed settlements, and the distance between them varied from 10 to 100 meters. This form of rural settlement generally included two to five farms. In rare cases, this type of rural settlement displayed the same characteristics as those of the first form in that it was established in a landscape that had previously been developed or built upon, or, even more rarely, upon virgin territory. Often connected to road system, such hamlets might be open or, alternatively, delineated by a ditch.

The last type of rural occupation described here takes the form of a nucleated settlement in which farms stood adjacent to one another and could number ten or more. Seldom documented archaeologically, the nucleated settlements of this period were often installed in a developed landscape. They present all of the characteristics of a village, with neighboring farms, enclosures, ditches, and byways. The sites of Prény (Lorraine) (Frauciel 2013) and Genlis (Bourgogne) (Catteddu 1992) correspond to this form of rural occupation.

Among the dispersed habitations (the first type), whether they were the heirs to a Roman site or newly established, appear some that exhibit elite characteristics. However, archaeological examples of such sites from the early Merovingian period are quite rare, and only four have been identified in northern France (Peytremann 2013a). These four elite residences—Biéville-Beuville in Normandy (Hincker 2007), Pouthumé in Poitou-Charente (Cornec and Farago-Szekeres 2010), Delle and Pratz in Franche-Comté (Billoin 2003, 2010)—have in common the fact that they were equipped with an exceptional structure with a surface area greater or equal to 100 square meters, generally constructed on stone sills or built entirely of stone. At least three of these sites also contained rich finds, notably in the form of metal tools and glassware. The residences of Pouthumé[3] and of Biéville-Beuville, situated in valleys, were enclosed and organized around a courtyard of approximately 400 square meters. They possessed facilities rarely found on farms of this period, such as a meat-drying shed and a smokehouse. The residences of Delle and Pratz, by contrast, were located on hilltop sites and occupied strategic positions (see Bourgeois, Chapter 28, this volume). Unfortunately, the limited number and quality of information from such sites do not allow us to understand their place in the network of contemporary settlements, and in particular whether they played a "centralizing" role, at least for the storage and distribution of agricultural production.

These three different forms of occupation were not exclusive, and more than one type was often present in the same area. Some archaeologists have described this mix of different modes of settlement as "polynuclear occupation." This is, for example, the phenomenon that one observes in the region of Goudelancourt-Lès-Pierrepont (Picardy) where the polynuclear habitat consisted of at least one agricultural unit located at the site called "Les Fontaines" together with the loosely grouped habitat "Le Fossé Saint-Martin" located roughly 500 meters from the farm (Peytremann 2003). Subject to variations between regions and landscapes, these different types of human settlement formed hierarchical networks that probably had economic as well as other links. Political and religious connections can also be envisaged among the settlement sites in a given region.

If continuity in building use is rarely certain, the continued functioning of the layout of the landscape is more frequently attested. Parcels of land were frequently maintained, as were some property boundaries such as ditches at Chessy in the region of Paris (Bonin 2000). Similarly, road networks changed little over time.

When excavations allow us to understand the topographical organization of these remains, it appears that units of agricultural exploitation (farms) were generally of modest size, rarely exceeding 1.5 hectares. Sometimes, it is possible from extant remains to recognize the bipartite organization of a single farm such as Grandes Maisons in Truyes (Centre) or Goudelancourt-Lès-Pierrepont (Picardie). At the latter, one finds a concentration of sunken huts and ditches at the northern end of the site, while to the south, beyond a ditch, were located surface constructions, including a dwelling equipped with a chimney, and a well. These farms could be open or included within an enclosure, sometimes as part of a system of landed plots (examples of which may be found in Normandy, Brittany, Pays-de-La-Loire, and, less frequently, Picardy) (Carpentier and Hincker 2013). In cases of enclosed habitations, which were generally associated with other enclosures devoid of structures, it is easier to understand the nature of agricultural exploitation in its totality: the dwelling, the agricultural outbuildings, animal breeding spaces, and lands under cultivation. By contrast, interpreting the structures established amidst Roman ruins is a more complex task. Often, only the sunken features (sunken huts, ovens, ditches, and so on) are preserved. The difficulty of understanding such sites is partially attributable to the absence of a sense of the organization of their buildings.

Farmsteads included at least one surface construction, usually built on posts, but sometimes on stone basements and more rarely on sill beams located under walls. Such main structures were supplemented by multiple outbuildings of varied architectural types: semi-sunken huts serving a variety of purposes, small constructions raised on posts for storage (granaries, haylofts, etc.), other postbuilt structures (barns, stables, etc.), pits (silos, quarries, dumps, etc.), ovens for domestic usage, and sometimes wells for water. During this period, sunken huts were present in abundance in some regions (Lorraine, Alsace, Île-de-France, Normandy, and Picardy), but rare in others (Brittany, Pays-de-la-Loire, and the western part of the Centre region). Sometimes sunken huts are the only buildings revealed in excavation of rural sites (Carpentier and Hincker 2013).

At the start of the Merovingian period in the sixth century around 25 percent of agricultural settlement sites were created *ex nihilo* in an area that was not built on during Antiquity (Peytremann 2003). Whereas some of these settlements were occupied for an average of two centuries, it is important to note that many were abandoned at some period or other. Archaeological investigations conducted in the context of modern villages are insufficiently numerous at present to weigh this evidence, but they offer a new perspective on a Merovingian rural settlement pattern long characterized as ephemeral (Mahé-Hourlier and Poignant 2013). The early results of this new approach to research tend to show, as Patrick Périn (1992) had anticipated, that a number of modern French villages have been occupied continuously from at least the Merovingian period.

Since the late 1980s in France, historians and archaeologists have conducted a fairly lively debate on the topic of Merovingian-era villages. Some scholars, like Robert Fossier (1982), cannot conceive of the idea of villages in the Merovingian period. In his opinion, the rural settlements that then existed lacked certain emblematic structures such as castles and churches and more "permanent" construction materials than earth and wood. Others, such as Périn (2004), relied on discoveries from the first rescue excavations and the distribution of Merovingian-period cemeteries to suggest not only that villages existed in the Merovingian period but also that a good number of these lie at the origin of modern villages today. More recent work (Peytremann 2003) has demonstrated that the tenets of Fossier's research are obsolete because his argument did not sufficiently take into account the chronology of existing archaeological sites.

SURFACE AND SUNKEN STRUCTURES FROM THE LATE FIFTH TO THE MID-SEVENTH CENTURY

Archaeologists typically distinguish constructions established at ground level from those that involved the digging of some form of foundation of varied depth. With respect to surface constructions, several building techniques have been documented in the northern half of Gaul in this period. The three principal ones correspond to buildings constructed on posts, stone basements, and sill beams. A fourth technique of surface construction, which might be termed mixed, utilized both stone basements and posts (as seen notably at the sites of Louvres in the Île-de-France and at Saint-Florent-sur-Cher in the Centre region, now known as the Centre-Val de Loire). In the great majority of cases, the elevations of these structures were fabricated in wattle-and-daub, or more rarely from adobe, wooden planks, or stone. A type of postbuilt construction was characteristic of the sixth and seventh centuries, and is found over much of the northern half of France (Alsace, Burgundy, Brittany, Franche-Comté, Normandy, Lorraine), southwestern Germany, and Switzerland (Peytremann 2013b, p. 302). It consisted of structures with load-bearing walls characterized by a significant number of posts positioned close together (Fig. 31.2). The layout of the buildings, which were rectangular, usually with a single nave, could include several rooms or a lateral gallery, as at the sites of Prény (Lorraine) and Genlis (Bourgogne). Double-nave plansf are also attested archaeologically, as again at Genlis and also Chessy (Île-de-France). Traditionally, the central row of post-holes has been interpreted as support for the ridge beam of the frame. In recent work drawing on experimental archaeology and ethnography (Epeaud and Gentili 2009), protohistorical and medieval archaeologists have shown that erecting such structures was a complex and costly undertaking. The roofs of these buildings were made from perishable materials, mostly thatch, but also, depending on local resources, rushes and wooden tiles. The doors of some of these buildings were equipped with latches as attested, for example, by the discovery of a key at the site of Herblay (Île-de-France) (Valais and Laforest 2009).

Among the excavated structures found at Merovingian sites of the late fifth and early seventh centuries are the buildings of modest size (less than 14 square meters) that are known as sunken-feature buildings (SFBs) that are considered typical of the early medieval period; there are also some larger structures. Depending on the region in which they are found and the state of their preservation, these structures can vary in depth

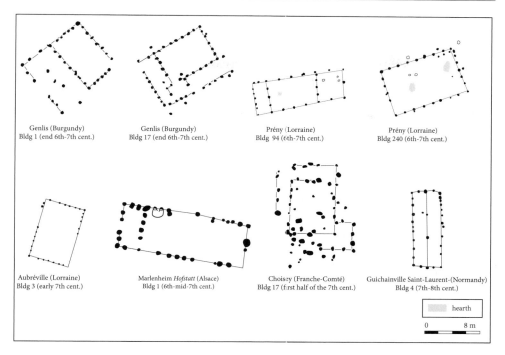

Genlis (Burgundy)
Bldg 1 (end 6th-7th cent.)

Genlis (Burgundy)
Bldg 17 (end 6th-7th cent.)

Prény (Lorraine)
Bldg 94 (6th-7th cent.)

Prény (Lorraine)
Bldg 240 (6th-7th cent.)

Aubréville (Lorraine)
Bldg 3 (early 7th cent.)

Marlenheim *Hofstatt* (Alsace)
Bldg 1 (6th-mid-7th cent.)

Choisey (Franche-Comté)
Bldg 17 (first half of the 7th cent.)

Guichainville Saint-Laurent-(Normandy)
Bldg 4 (7th-8th cent.)

hearth

0   8 m

FIGURE 31.2. Load-bearing walls of Merovingian buildings.

from a dozen to several dozen centimeters. The huts consisted of a varied number of posts, often between two and six, which helped to bear the frame and the building of walls that were mostly made from wattle-and-daub. The use of stone basements and sill plates is sometimes also in evidence. The appearance of these small structures was extremely variable depending on whether they had flooring over a crawl space (as was generally the case in the shallower structures), or whether the level of occupation was at the bottom of the sunken feature. In the first case, it is possible to envisage the structure serving the function of storage or habitation, whereas in the second case, the hypothesis of small workshops, notably for weaving, or, alternatively, storage places, is possible. As far as the larger sunken buildings are concerned, their function was identical to that of the surface constructions, whether for use as dwellings or as agricultural or artisanal outbuildings.

The numerous pits with assorted layouts discovered at settlement sites served a variety of functions that are not always easily identified. These might have included silos for grain stocks, storage, clay extraction, garbage dumps, latrines, and ditches related to artisanal or agricultural activities. This is notably the case for small rectangular ditches equipped with four post-holes interpreted as the base for a wine press, as at Saint-Germain-Lès-Corbeil (Île-de-France) (Peytremann 2003) and at Château-Gonthier (Pays-de-la-Loire) (Valais et al. 2009). Farmsteads were often equipped with a well or ovens for culinary, or more rarely, artisanal usage. Culinary ovens were frequently dug underground from the facings of a ditch or built at surface level in stone or cob (a building material made of a mixture of subsoil and other natural elements). Some sites were also equipped with grain- or meat-dryers.

FARMING AND ARTISANAL ACTIVITIES IN THE EARLY MEROVINGIAN PERIOD

The principal activities of early medieval rural populations were agricultural. The recent increase in the number of archeozoological and botanical publications, linked to the rise of preventive archaeology in France, has been the source of more precise information about Merovingian agriculture. A separate study of livestock and diet is contained in this volume (see Yvinec and Barme, Chapter 33) and so will not be addressed here. Meanwhile, arable farming was practiced in line with the care that individual crops required, either in fields or, for more demanding plants, in gardens situated closer to habitation sites. Thus, these sites were more easily enriched with manure. Wheat (*Tricitum sp.*), barley (*Hordeum vulgare* ssp. *vulgare*), rye (*Secale cereale*), and oats (*Avena sp.*) were the grains most frequently cultivated in northern Gaul, with wheat clearly dominant among them. Einkorn, an older form of wheat (*Tricitum monococcum.*), spelt (*Tricitum spelta*), and millet (*Panicum Miliaceum*) are also attested but in smaller quantities. The majority of sites display a polyculture of grains, alternating between winter grains, including wheat, rye, and einkorn, and summer grains, including six-row barley and oats (see Squatriti, Chapter 32, this volume). Leguminous crops such as peas (*Pisum sativum*), lentils (*Lens culinaris*), fava beans (*Vicia faba* var. *minor*), or vetch, a cover crop (*Vici sativa*), could be cultivated either in fields or in gardens. Several oleaginous plants were cultivated, including hemp and flax, from which textile fibers were extracted. The principal fruits cultivated in early medieval Gaul were plums, apples, pears, and Morello cherries. Many sites also reveal the cultivation of plants that served as condiments and/or for medicinal purposes like coriander (*Coriandrum sativum*), dill (*Anethum graveolens*), and celery (*Apium graveolens*).

These different crops required a significant male workforce to work the land, sow, and harvest and a female workforce (Kuchenbuch 1991) for cultivating gardens, weeding, and harvesting. Agricultural tools for this period remain poorly understood but a priori did not differ from those in use since Antiquity. Nevertheless, we can note the presence of an ard share (light plow) at the site of Herblay *Gaillon le Bas* (Île-de-France) and a pick-axe and billhook (a tool with a sickle-shaped blade for pruning) at Prény *Tautecourt* (Frauciel 2011). Following recent work on metal finds (Guillemot 2011, 2012; Raffin 2014, 2015) found in the context of rural occupation sites, it appears that agricultural equipment was generally rare at the start of the Merovingian period.

A variety of artisanal activities have been identified not only in the midst of farms, hamlets, and villages but also away from built environments. One of the recurrent activities practiced in a rural milieu, albeit not exclusively so, was metallurgy. Some recent publications allow us to understand the general outline of its organization (Cabboï et al. 2007). Many changes, starting in the course of Late Antiquity, characterize Merovingian iron working. For example, the structure of shallow furnaces was modified during the course of the third century to give way to the type (known as *Bellaire*) (Cabboï et al. 2007), which is typical of the Merovingian period and allowed a higher yield of iron. Moreover, the large-scale sites of earlier production gave way to smaller entities, which specialized in just one or two stages of the chain of production. The reduction of ore was carried out in workshops that were often located at some distance from occupation sites like those of Frouard in Lorraine or Saint-Maurice-Moncouronne in the Île-de-France, whereas the forging of iron was done within settlements, as was the case at the sites of Villeroy *La Plaine d'Herbier* (Burgundy), Villiers-sous-Saint-Leu (Picardy), and Vitry-sur-Orne (Lorraine). However, some semi-grouped settlement sites (farms or hamlets) do show that reduction and postreduction processes could occur close to settlements, like those of Guichainville *Saint-Laurent* (Normandy) and Meissein (Lorraine).

The metallurgy of copper alloys is more rarely observed among archaeological remains. However, such activities have been identified at the sites of Marcilly-la-Campagne, Giberville (Normandy), and Saint-Germain-Laxis (Île-de-France), for example, thanks to the presence of a few crucibles or a furnace, as at Vieux in Normandy. The site of Hames-Boucres in the Pas-de-Calais (François, Meurisse-Fort, and Saussus 2012) differs from the preceding examples in the sense that no vestiges of habitation were found in association with a pit that contained numerous fragments of bivalve ceramic molds for the production of different objects and more than sixty crucibles, showing the existence of a workshop that produced jewelry on request. The discovery of cut red glass suggests that other artisans must also have been associated with manufacture of this jewelry.

Archaeological evidence for ceramic production at the beginning of the Merovingian period reveals a diversity of organizational forms (Thuillier and Louis 2015). Small workshops, generally equipped with one or two kilns, whether associated with habitation or set apart from it (Fréteval and Ingré in the Centre region, Gennes-sur-Seiche in Brittany, Trémentine *La Frétellière* in Pays-de-la-Loire), coexisted with larger production centers like those of Saran *La Médicinerie* or Sevrey in Burgundy (Thuillier and Louis 2015). In addition, ceramic production sites were installed in urban centers, as shown by the discovery of workshops in Merovingian cities on the Meuse like Huy and Maastricht (Plumier and Regnard 2005). Some changes in ceramic production from the ancient period are discernible, notably in the locations from which clay was procured but also in the number of active workshops, which were *a priori* less numerous than they had been in the early imperial period in any given territory.

Another characteristic activity, many aspects of which are, however, still poorly understood, is weaving. Textile production is usually assumed from the presence of some sunken-feature buildings, interpreted as workshops, of tools such as punches fabricated from bone, and of stone or ceramic weights that served as ballast for weft threads of vertical looms. This activity has been documented both in farmsteads like

Cormelles-le-Royal (Normandy) (Carpentier 2003) and in semi-grouped settlements like that of Guichainville *Le Long Buisson* (Carré et al. 2011).

By contrast, bone working, notably of deer antlers, is up to now little attested in archaeological excavations for this period. The known examples tend to demonstrate that, as in the case of weaving, such activity was carried out by small workshops that *a priori* were installed in sunken-feature buildings (Prény in Lorraine, Marlenheim in Alsace, and Condé-sur-Aisne in Picardy) (Peytremann 2003; Châtelet 2009; Frauciel 2011).

Archaeology leaves little evidence of other artisanal activities. Some crafts like leather working leave few traces, and the tools associated with it have still not been identified. Such activity is, however, supposed at the site of Prény because of the discovery of a shoemaker's knife and the scoring tool of a saddler. Occasionally, the discovery of tools or structures such as lime kilns testify to activities that are often difficult to identify. Thus, the discovery of a matrix, scale, and a half-finished object suggests goldsmithing activity at the sites of Giberville *La Delle-sur-le-Marais* in Normandy and Riediesheim in Alsace. For the early Merovingian period, however, no traces of glass production have yet been found in northern Gaul in archaeological excavations, despite the significant number of glass vessels that have been uncovered in graves of the same era (but see Pion et al., Chapter 36, this volume).

Recent excavations have allowed us to refine our knowledge of artisanal activities in rural contexts. It is still difficult to understand all the features of this kind of production, but it nonetheless appears that a significant proportion of metal and ceramic production occurred in small workshops. Larger production centers were infrequent or located elsewhere, perhaps in urban centers, as can be envisaged for some activities that are absent from the countryside. Recent excavations into the dark earth (Galinié 2004) found in urban contexts have revealed the presence of pollutants like lead, which confirm substantial artisanal activity in urban contexts (Borderie 2011). Among the questions raised by these discoveries are whether production was continuous or seasonal and whether products were made on demand or in bulk.

A last category of activities, those linked to streams and rivers, have hitherto been poorly integrated into research on the rural world of early medieval Gaul but can now be addressed here. In the last thirty years, the development of subaquatic and wetland archaeology (Rieth and Serna 2010) has led to the discovery of infrastructures linked both to traffic (bridges, the development of riverbanks, shipwrecks, etc.) and to economic activities (fishing, milling, etc.). Systematic study and dendrochronological dating of wooden remains have made it possible to establish the chronology of such sites and to demonstrate the presence of riverine activities during the Merovingian period. Indeed, the exploitation of the resources of rivers is now better understood thanks to the discovery of the ballast of fishing nets and the remains of fisheries. Although finds of this nature are still rare, the examples of Paris, at Quai Branly on the Seine River, Chelles on the Marne River, and Saint-Victor on the Cher River, testify to a continuity of riverine activity from the late Roman Empire to the Merovingian period (Peytremann, 2016). This continuity with the Roman period thus calls into question the common assumption that it was monks who were chiefly responsible for the installation of riverine infrastructure.

Early medieval dug-out canoes and boats found over the last half century in rivers such as the Charente, Brivet (Pays-de-la-Loire), and the Saône (Burgundy) likewise allow us to better understand the transport by river that was frequently used. These vessels were also associated with coastal navigation, as is demonstrated by the river- and seagoing vessel of Port-Berteau (Charente) dated to 600 (Rieth, Carrière-Desbois, and Serna 2001). Chance finds of surviving implements also testify to river traffic as in the case of an iron boat hook discovered at the site of Herblay (Valais 1998) on the banks of the Seine. These important data reinforce the image of an open Merovingian rural world in which people and merchandise regularly circulated.

In summary then, up to the seventh century, archaeological excavation of domestic and artisanal sites has allowed us to sketch something of an outline of rural life at the beginning of the Merovingian period. The countryside offered an open landscape in which built and cultivated spaces, prairies, moors, and managed forests were juxtaposed. The Roman network of plots of land and communication routes was still in use and largely determined the organization of built spaces. People lived in structures built in large part from wood and earth. Stone, used widely in the Roman period, was now of secondary importance. Some artisanal activities, such as metalworking and ceramic production, underwent changes in their organization when compared with Antiquity, notably with the progressive disappearance of large centers of production or, in the case of ceramics, their diminution in favor of small workshops manufacturing specialized products destined for local consumers. By contrast, it is more difficult to get a precise idea of the functioning of farmsteads and to understand their relationship to one another at the local level. The discovery of elite settlement sites is also still too infrequent to determine their role in these networks. A military presence, as important as it was in this period (see Sarti, Chapter 12, this volume), is not documented in excavations of settlement sites on the plains. Essentially, it is found only in evidence from funerary sites and hilltop settlements.

Land Use and Rural Settlement from the Mid-Seventh to the Late Eighth Century

The second phase of Merovingian rural activity addressed here spans from the mid-seventh to the late eighth century in northern Gaul. Although the precise dating of this phase varies by region, this epoch was characterized by changes that tipped rural society toward that which was characteristic of the Carolingian Middle Ages. Nevertheless, this change occurred in the Merovingian era, a rural transition that has been interpreted as signaling the end of Antiquity. From the mid-seventh century onward, the countryside underwent new changes, most notably the creation of new plots of land. Some of these changes followed orientations identical to those of Antiquity, as at Mountours or at

Châteaugiron in Brittany (Catteddu 2001) and were defined differently by region, whether by hedges, ditches, or both. However, some of these plots disregarded the alignments established in Antiquity and ancient property boundaries that were no longer effective. Some new roads were added on to the existing road system, and new communication networks were created. Some types of land, like valley bottoms that had been little used hitherto, witnessed construction for the first time, as can be seen at the site of Distré in the Pays-de-la-Loire (Valais 2012), in Seine-Saint-Denis in the Île-de-France (Gonçalves-Buissart, Lafarge, and Le Forestier 2012), and in the region of Nord-Pas-de-Calais.

Although the three main types of rural settlement we have outlined remained identical in this second phase, their proportions changed in relation to each other. The number of dispersed habitats (isolated farms, etc.) tended to decline in favor of semi-grouped habitats (hamlets) and grouped habitats (villages), which were often organized in a linear pattern along either side of a road but could also take a more nuclear form. These changes indicate an increase in the built-up area and/or the density of constructions within settlements. Some modifications are also perceptible in the composition of settlements. Alongside the juxtaposed farms, marked off by hedges, ditches, or grassy embankments, were added plots of land exclusively dedicated to storage (silos and barns), to cooking (ovens and sometimes wells), and to sunken-feature buildings possibly for artisanal purposes, thus forming specialized quarters in the midst of the hamlets or villages. This concentration of similar activities within a specific area of a settlement has frequently been interpreted as evidence of a collective or even communal life. However, it could just as easily reflect the infrastructures belonging to a rich landowner, which were grouped together for ease of use and management, as is thought to have been the case for the site of Sermersheim in Alsace (Peytremann, 2018).

Settlement sites having an elite component or corresponding to an elite residence are also attested for the end of the Merovingian period. The number of such sites does not, however, greatly increase from the earlier Merovingian period; six sites have been identified to date, all of which were enclosed and included at least one notable building. In the case of Serris in Île-de-France (Gentili and Valais, 2007), for instance, an elite farm was located in the midst of a semi-grouped settlement. The buildings constructed on stone flashings were organized, as before, around a courtyard, the dimensions of which exceeded 800 square meters. It is more difficult to understand the topographical layout of the farm at Prény, which is thought to have been an elite settlement, due to the limited excavation of the site. There, too, the farm was organized around a courtyard of around 700 square meters and possessed a remarkable building combining elevation on stone flashings and wooden posts. Among the changes that had occurred since the previous period, it should be noted that the size of the courtyard had been enlarged and some of the infrastructure such as the drying sheds had disappeared.

It was also from the mid-seventh century to the end of the eighth century that Christian religious or funerary structures appear within settlements, testifying to the slow but steady spread of Christianity in Gaul. At first, these buildings were located on the edges of agglomerations as at Saleux, Sainte-Catherine-de-Fierbois (Centre) (Ben Kaddour 2015), (Fig. 31.3) or Tournedos-sur-Seine (Normandy) (Catteddu et al. 2009).

FIGURE 31.3. Layout of a religious building of the seventh to ninth century at Sainte-Catherine-de-Fierbois (Indre-et-Loire). DAO: C. Ben Kaddour & N. Tourancheau (Ben Kaddour 2015).

These religious edifices were postbuilt and had an identical layout: rectangular, with a square chancel to the east. Churches could sometimes be built on stone flashings, as at Mondeville (Normandy), where the building had an offset chancel, or at Villiers-le-Bâcle in Île-de-France (Peytremann 2003). Some examples of stone buildings are known, however, including the church of Saint-Genest in Villemomble (Île-de-France) (Gonçalves-Buissart et al. 2012), which was probably dependent on a settlement, the remains of which are hidden under the current village. In the case of Pouthumé (Poitou-Charentes) (Cornec and Farago-Szekeres 2010), a sunken postbuilt structure is associated with sarcophagus burials and is located on the periphery of an elite farm. At some sites, the introduction of a religious building at a site was accompanied by that of a small farm intended to supply the religious structure, like those thought to have existed at the sites of Mondeville, Tournedos-sur-Seine, and Sissones in Picardy (Peytremann 2003). Besides the main building, such units were characterized by the presence of structures for grain storage and were generally located in close proximity to religious buildings and cemeteries.

Changing mentalities regarding perceptions of the dead resulted in a modification of the locations in which they were buried. From the mid-seventh century, two phenomena occurred contemporaneously to one another. The first was the appearance of cemeteries in the midst of settlements such as the one at Mondeville, Val-de-Reuil, *Le Chemin aux Errants* in Normandy, and Serris (Lorren 1981; Adrian et al. 2014). In the last-named case, some privileged tombs were located close to a chapel. The second phenomenon involved the appearance of isolated graves, dispersed or in larger groups, that were often placed along the edges of plots of land or communication routes, or even near disused buildings on the margins of the contemporary built environment.

Within the farms themselves, some changes are also perceptible. They mainly relate to the organization of on-site structures, which tended to be more coherent and were frequently laid out around a courtyard, as at Guerny Guichainville *Saint-Laurent* in Normandy, Athies in Picardy (Harnay 2015), and Chantepie in Brittany (Béthus 2011), or along main roadways, as, for example, at Vitry-sur-Orne, *Vallange* (Lorraine) (Gérard 2012). The buildings and facilities found in farms are more diversified than those in the earlier Merovingian period.

Renovated Structures, from the Mid-Seventh to Late Eighth Century

Between the mid-seventh and late eighth centuries, changes are also visible in building types, especially with regard to surface-level constructions. In Lower Normandy during this period, the earlier sunken huts disappeared in favor of larger buildings, which were generally built on stone flashings. This type of construction tended to become widespread in the north of Gaul. Postbuilt structures were also more numerous, often with two naves and of a larger size. Internal partitions were likewise more common, and structures combining the functions of dwelling and stable, or stable and storage, or dwelling and storage, are attesued, for example, at Fleury and at Saint-Vigor-d'Ymonville (Normandy) (Peytremann 2003; Carré et al. 2011), and at Juvincourt-et-Damary (Picardy) (Harnay 2015). (Fig. 31.4). The plan of these buildings was more varied than earlier in the Merovingian period, and layouts with one or two apsidal ends can be seen in Normandy at the sites of Courbépine, Fleury, and Saint-Georges-des-Coteaux in Poitou-Charente. In some regions, new materials such as plaster were used as coverings (La Courneuve in Île-de-France). Tile was once again employed for the roofing of some structures as at Saran.[4] Although no technological or morphological changes are attested in domestic ovens, it does however appear, at least in the Île-de-France region (Bruley-Chabot 2003), that they were a lot less common within farming units. Instead, they were grouped together in the midst of a single plot. Overall, buildings were of a better quality.

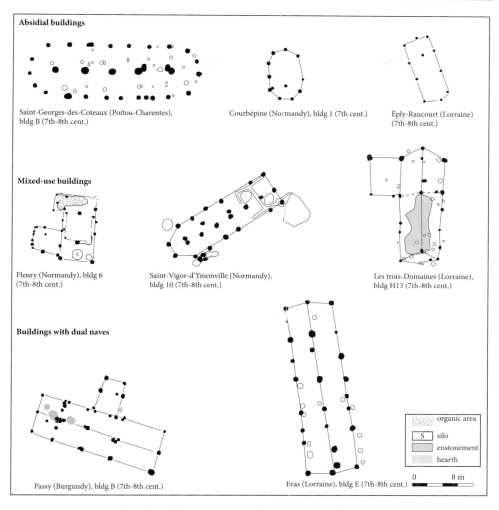

Absidial buildings

Saint-Georges-des-Coteaux (Poitou-Charentes), bldg B (7th-8th cent.)

Courbépine (Normandy), bldg 1 (7th cent.)

Éply-Raucourt (Lorraine) (7th-8th cent.)

Mixed-use buildings

Fleury (Normandy), bldg 6 (7th-8th cent.)

Saint-Vigor-d'Ymonville (Normandy), bldg 10 (7th-8th cent.)

Les trois-Domaines (Lorraine), bldg H13 (7th-8th cent.)

Buildings with dual naves

Passy (Burgundy), bldg B (7th-8th cent.)

Bras (Lorraine), bldg E (7th-8th cent.)

organic area
S | silo
enstonement
hearth

0   8 m

FIGURE 31.4. Seventh-and eighth-century buildings constructed on posts.

FARMING AND ARTISANAL CRAFTS IN THE LATE MEROVINGIAN PERIOD

In broad terms, farming practices did not change significantly between the beginning and the end of the Merovingian period. The available data, however, do allow us to identify regional variations such as the importance of oat and barley cultivation in the west of France, in contrast to the east, where these crops were of only secondary importance. In the Île-de-France, wheat and rye dominated cultivation. The cultivation of "naked" grains increased to the detriment of those that were hulled or "dressed" (see Squatriti, Chapter 32, this volume). Millet continued to be cultivated in Franche-Comté and in the Touraine, whereas it tended to disappear in other regions. It is highly likely, moreover, that fields were maintained through crop rotation. Some settlements indicate specialization in cereal production (Chantepie in Brittany) or in the preparation of carcasses for export.

North of the Loire, the extension of viticulture can probably be associated with the spread of Christianity and the development of religious establishments in the country-side. The introduction of a new type of fruit tree is perhaps linked to this development. The recent discovery at Sermersheim in Alsace of the pit of a peach in a late-seventh or eighth-century context from an artisanal site associated with a religious establishment points in this direction. Plants for making textiles, like linen and hemp, are more abundantly represented. Discoveries of iron tools confirm the development of grain cultivation: an ard share and sickle at Chantepie, sickles at Ensisheim in Alsace, at Serris, Villiers-le-Sec, and Servon in the Île-de-France, and at Tournedos-sur-Seine, a scythe and an ard share found in association with two sickles. The scale of remains linked to milling, whether hand-powered (Chantepie) or hydraulic (Saleux), also suggests extensive grain cultivation. These discoveries also tend to reveal a slightly larger and more diversified range of metal tools, including a billhook at Serris, a tool to remove thistles at Avernes in the Île-de-France, a pitchfork in Translay in Picardy, and so on.

Even if the metallurgical infrastructure did not undergo any particular modifications in the period under review, some changes were perceptible in the ways in which production was organized. From the eighth century centers of large-scale production first appear, such as the production site of Ludres in Lorraine (Cabboï et al. 2007). However, the available archaeological data do not show whether such production sites were integrated into settlements. Furthermore, metalworking activity within settlements became more common than in the earlier Merovingian period. Sites now exhibited several phases in the manufacturing process as at Guichainville *Le Long Buisson* in Normandy, and Saint-Dizier *Le Seugnon, Toupot,* and *Millot* in Champagne where extraction, reduction, and postreduction activities have been attested. At Vert-Saint-Denis, *Les Fourneaux*, in the Île-de-France, the scale of iron ore extraction and the preparation and reduction of ore suggests that this village was above all dedicated to metallurgical production (Peytremann 2003; Cabboï et al. 2007; Carré et al. 2011;). The presence of these large centers, however, did not rule out the existence of smaller and more specialized workshops, principally in relation to forging, as at Prény, where the manufacture of belt buckles has been suggested (Frauciel 2013). This coexistence of different types of manufacture shows that the several levels of production probably responded to various authorities. By contrast, metalworking in copper alloys remained just as rare as in the early Merovingian period. Perhaps it was a more urban craft or took place in centers of a specific type such as abbeys (cf. *infra*).

Ceramic manufacture reverted to larger centers of production in some places. This centralization occurred slowly, however, and at different times in different regions. The centers of Saran and Sevrey (Thuillier and Louis 2015), which had existed since the beginning of the Merovingian period, continued and increased their production. The same growth has been documented at the workshops of Trémentine *La Frétellière*, even if they cannot be considered a priori as a center of mass ceramic production.

Other centers emerged such as Saulsotte in Champagne and La Londe in Normandy. Small workshops with a single kiln and production to meet local demand nonetheless continued to flourish like those of Farges-Allichamps in the Centre region, Dechy in Nord-Pas-de-Calais, and Saint-Maurice-Montcouronne in Île-de-France.

Occasionally, other craft industries or artisanal structures have been identified in later Merovingian settlements, such as a lime kiln found in Pays-de-la-Loire. Although not many have yet been fully excavated, some villages, little documented archaeologically, can be identified as having an economic structure that focused mainly on manufacturing. The most characteristic example is the village of Wandignies (Nord) situated near the female monastery of Hamage (Louis 2015). Apart from the craft production (weaving, bone working, metalworking in copper alloys, and glass making) known from within the monastic enclosure itself, ceramic and metallurgical production (reduction and postreduction) and bone working (including the manufacture of ice skates) are attested within the lay settlement.

Developments on rivers, mainly fisheries and mills, were also more numerous from the mid-seventh century and can in this case be linked to the development of monastic and lay estates. The mill of Saleux (Catteddu 1997) was constructed around the end of the seventh century. Harbor infrastructure on rivers was developed at sites such as Quentovic, Taillebourg, and elsewhere, sometimes in connection with abbeys, as has been observed in Normandy. A river dock of the first half of the eighth century has, for example, been discovered at the site of Guerny in Normandy (Carré et al. 2011).

These finds and features allow us to continue the tale of rural life into the second part of the Merovingian period. The countryside experienced a period of growth that is apparent both in the organization of the landscape with the creation of defined plots of land, an expansion of communication networks, and riverine developments, and in economic activities, whether they were agricultural or artisanal. This growth is equally perceptible within settlements, the built-up areas of which expanded. The number of isolated farms dropped, probably in favor of semi-grouped hamlets. Wood remained the most common building material, but stone was increasingly present, notably in the foundations of buildings. The appearance of structures with mixed functions suggests that there was a concentration of activities in such locations. New elements find room within villages or hamlets, whether specialized zones, cemeteries, and/or religious buildings. Although elite residences are well attested, they remain too few in number for us to fully understand their contribution to rural organization.

RESULTS AND FUTURE PROSPECTS FOR RESEARCH

Following this examination of rural archaeological data from northern Gaul during the Merovingian period, it is possible to make some important observations. From a historiographical perspective, excavations since the 1990s have significantly augmented the small number of Merovingian sites in the northern half of France identified by Claude Lorren and Patrick Périn (1995). These new data give us a more precise understanding of rural occupation in the late Roman Empire and at the beginning of the Merovingian period. The traditional hypothesis of a break in rural settlement occupation between Late Antiquity and the beginning of the Merovingian period is being abandoned in favor of a more nuanced view. Some settlements clearly show continuous occupation from the first to the tenth century, without a break in occupation per se but rather in the mode of occupation. This is now well documented by a transition from stone to wood for building around the fourth century and by a transition from dispersed to semi-grouped habitats. The site of Val-de-Reuil (Normandy) (Adrian et al. 2014), excavated in 2012 over 8 hectares, offers a good example of continuity. The site of Mondeville in Normandy,[5] can therefore no longer be seen as exceptional but must instead be understood within the possible framework of continuity of occupation.

The increase in the number of excavations of occupied sites in northern Gaul dating from the Merovingian era also allows us to refine our knowledge of the rural economy, especially for the early part of this period. In fact, artisanal activities appear more extensive than had previously been thought, and it is now possible to form some idea of the organization of production, particularly of metalwork and ceramics. Overall, the new data confirm that the second half of the seventh and eighth centuries mark the break. The new examples of cemeteries established within settlements, and the construction of new religious structures, all date to this pivotal period.

From a methodological perspective, the much greater accessibility of data derived from rescue excavations, thanks to online repositories of excavation reports and the publication of overviews for Normandy and Picardy (Carré et al. 2011; Carpentier and Hincker 2013; Harnay 2015), and of research projects in Pays-de-la-Loire, Île-de-France, Picardy, and the Centre region (Gentili, Lefèvre, and Mahé 2009; Valais 2012), provide valuable tools for those working on the Merovingian countryside. The various studies associated with archaeological investigations, particularly those related to the life sciences and earth sciences and initiated about twenty years ago, have begun to bear fruit. They provide new data, especially on the organization of the landscape, agricultural practices, or climate. Coupled with archaeological observations, these studies offer new perspectives on the socioeconomic organization of the Merovingian countryside. The complementary nature of the observations carried out on large to very large excavation sites like Villiers-le-Sec, Châteaugiron, Saran, and Serris, and on smaller areas of modern villages like Tremblay-en-France in the Île-de-France, Guesnain in the Nord, Marlenheim in Alsace, and other locations, also contribute to a better understanding of the formation and chronological development of villages (Mahé-Hourlier and Poignant 2013). These excavations refine and/or contradict existing models, whether regarding the transformation of late-antique villas into early medieval villages, or the formation of villages in the year 1000. On the other hand, the compartmentalization of research into fields such as riverine archaeology, or metallurgical and ceramic studies is regrettable in the sense that these divisions impede more global studies of the economy of the Merovingian countryside.

From our current understanding, it appears that life in Merovingian rural contexts was dynamic, a view that is completely at odds with the traditional description of an abandoned countryside that was having difficulty recovering from the end of the empire and the settlement of "barbarians." From the outset, the results from cemetery excavations contradicted this vision by providing evidence of certain artifacts (glass, weapons, and so on) that must have been manufactured in relatively large quantities, and provide evidence of social stratification. The data derived from excavations of domestic contexts now also attest to a continuity of economic life in the countryside but one that was different from the one that existed at the end of Antiquity. In the present state of research, it appears that artisanal productions from the late fifth to the mid-seventh century were made in small workshops. Their production was largely to meet local demand and made to order. Some more important centers, notably those for ceramic production, distributed their wares on a wider scale (see Tys, Chapter 34, this volume). The remnants and the small scale of the workshops concerned are often suggestive of seasonal activity. The idea that has sometimes been advanced of peasants engaged in artisanal activity is, by contrast, increasingly rejected by archaeologists, based on the technical skills that these crafts required, both with respect to crafts that required heat (metalworking, ceramic and glass production) and those that involved working in products derived from animals (bone and leather) or wood.

Questions remain, however. The available data do not, for example, settle either way the regularly advanced hypothesis of the existence of itinerant artisans, and still less the question of their social status (but see Theuws, Chapter 38, this volume). The absence of a major center for the production of weapons or glass in northern Gaul remains problematic, given the funerary deposits contained in early medieval graves. The discovery of boats confirms—if it was necessary to do so—that riverine exchange continued, but it is not possible to evaluate its importance, particularly in relation to the Roman period. Similarly, the framework of agricultural production at the beginning of the Merovingian period remains poorly defined by the archaeological data. Finally, the presence of elite residences suggests that the use of estates, probably derived from ancient villas (see Chavarría Arnau, Chapter 29, this volume), endured, though probably in reduced numbers. However, it is not possible to tell how these lands were cultivated or by whom. The creation of substantial numbers of dispersed farms probably indicates the presence of small, independent landowners.

The overall analysis of recent data has confirmed that there was a period of change , as previously identified, dating from the mid-seventh to the late eighth century. The changes documented in settlements and in the countryside in which they were installed testify to the establishment of new frameworks, in some cases already long identified from the written sources (Iogna-Prat and Zadora-Rio 2005; Devroey 2006). The implementation of a parish network and the development of large lay and ecclesiastical estates are linked to the appearance of religious structures within settlements and to the development of cereal and vine cultivation, an infrastructure of mills and ports, and larger artisanal production centers. It is worth questioning the significance of marked regional differences, as identified in this chapter. Might the presence of semi-grouped or dispersed habitations, often associated with enclosures, in western France, where sunken-feature buildings are less frequent, reflect the survival of small, independent landowners focused on agricultural production, while the development of grouped settlements, including zones devoted to specialized activities, point to the development of great estates and indirect exploitation? Although this latter hypothesis may be drawn too strongly here, it would nevertheless merit closer examination, based in particular on the topographical, constituent, and economic differences between excavated settlements. This hypothesis does not imply the disappearance of the small, independent landowner, who can also be found in semi-grouped or grouped habitats. For example, the modest consumption of wild game at the sites of Saleux (Picardy) and Villiers-le-Sec (Île-de-France) has been interpreted as a possible indication of the presence of free men (Loveluck 2013).

The next steps for research on the rural world are multidirectional. Some studies attest to a continuation of existing research, whereas others are more innovative in that they are the product of new methodological developments and the collection of new data. Studies dealing with the transitional period between the end of the late empire and the start of the Merovingian period are very important to our understanding of the changes that affected the rural world. Too long shackled by historical dating frameworks and by divisions between research specialties, projects undertaken jointly by Roman archaeologists and those working on the Merovingian period are currently expanding—notably those concerned with the ceramic material that will improve our ability to date sites and understand levels of production and exchange. Having a relatively large body of data, we can now analyze settlement sites and their development more closely, so as to be able, as a first step, to distinguish them from one another. An examination of this corpus indicates, in effect, that the convenient label of "rural settlement" conceals a range of sites with dwellings, agricultural and artisanal structures, and organizational and topographical forms, that are themselves greatly varied.

This first step is decisive in enabling us to refine the definition of the frameworks of agricultural and artisanal production, be they social, political, or religious. While research on "elites" has in recent years been the focus of much scholarship, it appears that the archaeological data must be reconsidered in order to identify and define a social hierarchy more equivalent to the complexity of Merovingian society suggested by study of the written sources (Loveluck 2013). The elements considered as markers of the elite are, as described above, still insufficient in number to construct a social model based solely on their presence or absence. This problem is similar to that presented by the evidence attesting to the establishment of parish networks. This evidence remains limited, and its archaeological interpretation must be treated with caution: do the ecclesiastical units identified at Mondeville, Tournedos, and Sissonne attest to a parish church to which was attached a priest residing nearby on his small farm? What elements allow archaeologists to distinguish private religious foundations from parish churches, and how can we recognize the transition from one such status to the other?

This analytical overview, and its definition of the frameworks of rural organization, has covered important issues such as the scale of observation of archaeological sites, and the proliferation of multidisciplinary approaches, in particular the growth of studies carried out in conjunction with historians. The debate addresses the reality of the perception of archaeological remains and more specifically critiques our habit of interpreting them through the models of social evolution described here. Research in progress, some of which addresses a wider time frame, is being undertaken on the initiative of Belgian and British historians, and demonstrates the benefits of such approaches. Having long sought to identify Merovingian rural settlements principally on the basis of their features (houses, outbuildings, paths, and so on), researchers are extending their attention to the wider context of sites and must now try not only to understand the organization of the countryside and its evolution, but also to identify the principal actors and their roles within it.

Notes

1. This chapter has been translated from French by Bonnie Effros, Isabel Moreira, and Simon Loseby.
2. The sites mentioned in this chapter are displayed in the map in Figure 31.1.
3. The date of the creation of the elite farm of Pouthumé is likely in the mid-seventh century. However, its characteristics are closer to those observed at the beginning of the Merovingian period than those commonly attributed to the late Merovingian period.
4. Information offered by S. Jesset during a seminar, "La place de l'artisanat en milieu villageois (VIe–XIe s.)" organized by E. Peytremann at the University of Paris, January 27, 2011.
5. The site of Mondeville in Normandy, excavated by Claude Lorren in the early 1980s, has long remained the only known example of a settlement occupied from the Iron Age to the twelfth century.

Works Cited

Ancient Source

Martine, F. (ed. and trans.). (2004). *La vie des Pères du Jura*. Paris: Du Cerf.

Modern Sources

Adrian, Y.-M., Lukas, T., Roudié, N., and Thomann, A. (2014). "Val-de-Reuil Le Chemin des Errants—Zone C." *Bilan scientifique de la région Haute-Normandie*, 2012: 49–52.

Béthus, T. (2011). *Chantepie, Ille-et-Vilaine, Les rives du Blosne. Un habitat enclos du haut Moyen Âge (VIe–IXe siècle)*. Cesson-Sévigné: Inrap Grand Ouest.

Ben Kaddour, C. (2015). "Un édifice religieux sur poteaux plantés du haut Moyen Âge à Sainte-Catherine-de-Fièrebois (Indre-et-Loire)." *Bulletin du Centre d'Études Médiévales d'Auxerre* 19.1, doi:10.4000/cem.13966

Billoin, D. (2003). "Un atelier métallurgique du haut Moyen Âge à Pratz (Jura) 'Le Curtillet' (VIIe siècle)." In F. Passard, S. Gizard, J.-P. Urlacher, and A. Richard (eds.), *Burgondes, Alamans, Francs et Romains dans l'Est de la France, le Sud-Ouest de l'Allemagne et la Suisse, Ve–VIIe siècle après J.-C.: actes des XXIèmes Journées internationales d'Archéologie mérovingienne, Besançon, 20–22 octobre 2000* (pp. 255–265). Besançon: PUFC.

Billoin, D. (2010). "Un établissement rural mérovingien à Delle 'La Queue au loup' (Territoire de Belfort)." *Revue Archéologique de l'Est de la France* 59: 603–634.

Bonin, T. (2000). "Le site de Chessy et l'occupation du sol en Île-de-France (VIᵉ–Xᵉ siècles)." *Archéologie Médiévale* 29: 1–68.

Borderie, Q. (2011). *L'espace urbain entre Antiquité et Moyen Age: analyse géoarchéologique des terres noires: études de cas.* Thèse de doctorat de l'Université de Paris 1, sous la direction de J. Burnouf. Paris I, Panthéon-Sorbonne, Paris.

Bruley-Chabot, G. (2003). "Les fours culinaires en Île-de-France." In *L'habitat rural du haut Moyen Âge en Île-de-France. Programme collectif de recherche—Bilan 2002-2003.* (pp. 25–31). Guiry-en-Vexin: Centre de recherches archéologiques du Vexin français.

Cabboï, S., Dunikowski, C., Leroy, M., and Merluzzo, P. (2007). "Réflexions sur les formes d'organisation du travail du fer dans le nord de la France au Haut Moyen Âge, l'apport des découvertes archéologiques récentes." In *Medieval Europe, Paris, 2007 (4ᵉ Congrès International d'Archéologie Médiévale et Moderne)* (pp. 1–18). Université de Paris I. http://medieval-europe-paris-2007.univ-paris1.fr/S.%20Cabboi%20et%20al.pdf. [Consulted 14.05.2014].

Carpentier, V. (2003). "Cormelles-le-Royal (Calvados), Le chemin de Grentheville." *Archéologie Médiévale* 33: 207.

Carpentier, V., and Hincker, V. (2013). "L'habitat rural du haut Moyen Âge en Basse-Normandie. Arrêt sur vingt années de recherches archéologiques." In C. Lorren (ed.), *La Gaule, le monde insulaire du nord au haut Moyen Âge. Actualité de l'archéologie en Normandie (Vᵉ–Xᵉ s.). Actes des XXVIIᵉ Journées internationales d'archéologie mérovingiennes* (pp. 183–210). Saint-Germain-en-Laye: Association française d'archéologie mérovingienne.

Carré, F., Adrian, Y.-M., Zaour, N., Moesgaard, J. C., and Devillers, S. (2011). *L'archéologie en Haute-Normandie: bilan des connaissances. (Haute-Normandie. Service régional de l'archéologie).* Mont-Saint-Aignan: Publications des universités de Rouen et du Havre.

Catteddu, I. (1992). "L'habitat rural mérovingien de Genlis (Côte-d'Or)." *Revue archéologique de l'Est et du Centre-Est* 43(161): 39–98.

Catteddu, I. (1997). "Le site médiéval de Saleux 'Les Coutures': habitat, nécropole et églises du haut Moyen Âge. In G. De Boe and F. Verhaeghe (eds.), *Rural Settlements in Medieval Europe, Papers of the Medieval Europe Brugge 1997 Conference* (pp. 143–148). AAP rapporter, Vol. 6. Zellik: Insituut voor het Archaeologisch Patrimonius.

Catteddu, I. (2001). *Les habitats carolingiens de Montours et la Chapelle-Saint-Aubert (Ille-et-Vilaine).* Paris: MSH.

Catteddu, I., Carré, F., Gentili, F., Delahaye, F., Langlois, J.-Y., and Couanon, P. (2009). "Fouilles d'églises rurales dans le nord de la France. Questions récurrentes." In D. Paris Poulain, D. Istria, and S. Nardi Combescure (eds.), *Les premiers temps chrétiens dans le territoire de la France actuelle. Hagiographie, épigraphie et archéologie. Actes du colloque international d'Amiens. Université de Picardie Jules Verne, Faculté des Arts, 18–20 janvier 2007.* Rennes: PUR.

Châtelet, M. (2009). *Marlenheim «Hofstatt»(Bas-Rhin). Des inhumations en silo néolithiques au quartier artisanal carolingien, Rapport final d'opération* (vol. 3). Dijon, Sélestat: Inrap, PAIR.

Cornec, T., and Farago-Szekeres, B. (2010). "L'habitat et les cimetières du haut Moyen Âge de Pouthumé (Châtellerault, Vienne)." In L. Bourgeois (ed.), *Wisigoths et Francs autour de la bataille de Vouillé (507), Actes des XXVIIIᵉ Journées internationales d'Archéologie mérovingienne, Vouillé et Poitiers (Vienne, France)—28–30 septembre 2007* (pp. 97–111). Saint-Germain-en-Laye: AFAM.

Devroey, J.-P. (2006). *Puissants et misérables: système social et monde paysan dans l'Europe des Francs, VIe-IXe siècles.* Brussels: Académie royale de Belgique, Classe des lettres.

Epeaud, F., and Gentili, F. (2009). "L'apport de l'expérimentation archéologique pour la compréhension de l'architecture carolingienne à poteau planté: les exemples du chantier d'Orville (Val-d'Oise)." In *Actes des XXIXe Journées internationales d'Archéologie mérovingienne, Marle (Aisne) 26–28 septembre 2008. Revue Archéologique de Picardie* 1/2: 129–144.

Fossier, R. (1982). *Enfance de l'Europe. Aspects économiques et sociaux. 1/L'homme et son espace.* Paris: PUF.

François, S., Meurisse-Fort, M., and Saussus, L. (2012). "Hames-Boucres, 'Fonds d'Hames', 2010. Fouille, atelier de bronzier mérovingien". http://archeologie.pasdecalais.fr/ Archeologue/Notices-scientifiques/Hames-Boucres-Fond-d-Hames-2010-Fouille-atelier-de-bronzier-merovingien. [Consulted 11.03.2016]

Frauciel, M. (ed.). (2011). *Prény (Meurthe-et-Moselle) "Tautecourt," "Frichamp," "Bois Lasseau" : TVG EST Lot 33 : Fouilles TGV Est n°83 et 88, évaluations n°219 et 221* (Vol. 1). Metz: INRAP Grand-Est Nord.

Frauciel, M. (2013). "Le vallon de Prény 'Tautecourt' (Meurthe-et-Moselle), de l'habitat mérovingien à la grange monastique médiévale." In N. Mahé-Hourlier and S. Poignant (eds.), *Archéologie du village, archéologie dans le village dans le nord de la France (V^e–XIIIe siècles). Actes de la table ronde, 22–24 novembre 2007, M.A.N.* (pp. 55–65). Saint-Germain-en-Laye, Associaton française d'archéologie mérovingienne.

Galinié, H. (2004). "L'expression 'terres noires' un concept d'attente. In L. Verslype and R. Brulet (eds.), *Terres noires, Dark earth. Actes de la table ronde internationale, Louvain-la-Neuve, 9–10 nov. 2001* (pp. 1–11). Louvain-la-Neuve: UCL.

Gentili, F., Lefèvre, A., and Mahé, N. (2009). *L'habitat rural du haut Moyen Âge en Île-de-France. 2e supplément au Bulletin archéologique du Vexin français et du Val-d'Oise.* Guiry-en-Vexin (Val-d'Oise): Centre de recherches archéologiques du Vexin français et le Collectif d'archéologie rurale du haut Moyen Âge.

Gentili, F., and Valais, A. (2007). "Composantes aristocratiques et organisation de l'espace au sein de grands habitats ruraux du haut Moyen Âge." In P. Depreux, F. Bougard, and R. Le Jan (eds.), *Les élites et leurs espaces. Mobilité, rayonnement, domination (du VIIe au XIe siècle). Actes de la rencontre de Göttingen des 3, 4 et 5 mars 2005* (pp. 99–134). Turnhout: Brepols.

Gérard, F. (2012). "La structuration du village pour une économie agraire planifiée à la fin du IXe siècle en Lorraine. Les sites de Vitry-sur-Orne et de Demange-aux-Eaux." *Archéopages* 34: 38–47.

Gonçalves-Buissart, C., Lafarge, I., and Le Forestier, C. (2012). "Les habitats ruraux du haut Moyen Âge en Seine-Saint-Denis. Etats des Lieux." *Archéopages* 34: 48–57.

Guillemot, A. (2011). *Le mobilier métallique en contexte d'habitat rural du premier Moyen Âge, (V^e–XIIe siècle), en Île-de-France.* Mémoire de master 1 de l'Université de Paris I sous la direction de E. Peytremann et J. Burnouf. Paris I, Panthéon-Sorbonne.

Guillemot, A. (2012). *Le mobilier métallique en contexte d'habitat rural du premier Moyen Âge, (V^e–XIIe siècle), en Seine-et-Marne et dans le Val-d'Oise.* Mémoire de master 1 de l'Université de Paris I sous la direction de E. Peytremann et J. Burnouf (2 vols.). Paris I, Panthéon-Sorbonne.

Harnay, V. (2015). "Le haut Moyen Âge." In D. Bayard, N. Buchez, and P. Depaepe (eds.), *Quinze ans d'archéologie préventive sur les grands tracés linéaires en Picardie, part 2. Revue archéologique de Picardie,* no. 3/4: 233–308.

Hincker, V. (2007). "Un habitat aristocratique en Neustrie. Le site du château à Biéville-Beuville (Calvados, Normandie, France)." In L. Verslype (ed.), *Villes et campagnes en Neustrie.*

Sociétés—Économies—Territoire—Christianisation. Actes des XXVᵉ Journées internationales d'Archéologie mérovingiennes de l'AFAM. (pp. 175–189). Montagnac: Monique Mergoil.

Iogna-Prat, D., and Zadora-Rio, É. (2005). "Formation et transformations des territoires paroissiaux." *Médiévales. Langues, Textes, Histoire* 49: 5–10. doi:10.4000/medievales.1200 [Consulted 11.03.2016]

Kuchenbuch, L. (1991). "Opus feminile." In H.-W. Goetz (ed.), *Weibliche Lebensgestaltung im frühen Mittelalter* (pp. 140–175). Cologne: Böhlau.

Lorren, C. (1981). "Le village de Saint Martin de Mondeville (Calvados). Premiers résultats des fouilles (1978–1980)." In A. van Doorselaer (ed.), *De Merovingische beschaving in de Sheldevallei. Actes du colloque international de Courtrai, 28–30 octobre 1980* (pp. 169–198). Courtrai: Vereniging voor oudheidkundig bodemonderzoek in West-Vlaanderen.

Lorren, C., and Périn, P. (eds.). (1995). *L'habitat rural du haut Moyen Âge: (France, Pays-Bas, Danemark et Grande-Bretagne).* Rouen: Association française d'Archéologie mérovingienne.

Louis, E. (2015). "Les indices d'artisanat dans et autour du monastère de Hamage (Nord)." In S. Bully and C. Sapin, *Au seuil du cloître: la présence des laïcs (hôtelleries, bâtiments d'accueil, activités artisanales et de services) entre le Vᵉ et le XIIᵉ siècle. Actes des 3èmes journées d'études monastiques, Vézelay, 27–28 juin 2013.* Bulletin du centre d'études médiévales d'Auxerre, Hors-série n. 8, doi:10.4000/cem.13684. [Consulted 10.09.2015]

Loveluck, C. (2013). *Northwest Europe in the Early Middle Ages, c. AD 600–1150: A Comparative Archaeology.* Cambridge: Cambridge University Press.

Mahé-Hourlier, N., and Poignant, S. (eds.) (2013). *Archéologie du village, archéologie dans le village dans le nord de la France (Vᵉ–XIIIᵉ siècles): actes de la table ronde des 22–24 novembre 2007, M.A.N.* Saint-Germain-en-Laye: Association française d'Archéologie mérovingienne.

Périn, P. (1992). "La part du haut Moyen Âge dans la genèse des terroirs de la France médiévale." In M. Parisse and X. Barral I Altet (eds.), *Le roi de France et son royaume autour de l'an mil, actes du colloque Hugues Capet 987–1987. La France de l'an mil, Paris-Senlis, 22–25 juin 1987* (pp. 225–234). Paris: Picard.

Périn, P. (2004). "The Origin of the Village in Early Medieval Gaul." In N. Christie, ed., *Landscapes of Change. Rural Evolutions in Late Antiquity and the Early Middle Ages* (pp. 255–278). Burlington: Ashgate.

Peytremann, E. (2003). *Archéologie de l'habitat rural dans le nord de la France du IVᵉ au XIIᵉ siècle* (2 vols.). Saint-Germain-en-Laye: Association française d'archéologie mérovingienne.

Peytremann, E. (2013a). "Identifier les résidences des élites au sein des habitats ruraux du VIᵉ au XIᵉ s." In J. Klápště (ed.), *Hierarchies in Rural Settlements* (pp. 183–197). Turnhout: Brepols.

Peytremann, E. (2013b). "Le bâti dans les campagnes françaises du VIᵉ au XIᵉ siècle." In L. Lakovleva, O. Korvin-Piotrovskiy, and F. Djindjian (eds.), *L'archéologie du bâti en Europe* (pp. 298–12). Kiev: Presses de l'académie des sciences d'Ukraine.

Peytremann, E. (ed.). (2016). *Des fleuves et des hommes à l'époque mérovingienne. Territoire fluviale et société au premier Moyen Âge (Vᵉ–XIIᵉ siècle).* Saint-Germain-en-Laye: Association française d'archéologie mérovingienne-Revue Archéologique de l'Est.

Peytremann, E. (2018). *En marge du village: la zone d'activités spécifiques et les groupes funéraires de Sermersheim (Bas-Rhin) du VIᵉ au XIIᵉ siècle.* Dijon: Revue Archéologique de l'Est.

Plumier, J., and Regnard, M. (eds.). (2005). *Colloque Commerce et économie le long des voies d'eau à l'époque mérovingienne de Verdun à Maastricht.* Namur, Belgique: Ministère de la Région wallone, Direction générale de l'aménagement du territoire, du logement et du patrimoine, Division du patrimoine.

Raffin, A. (2014). *Le petit mobilier métallique médiéval en contexte d'habitat rural dans les Pays de la Loire (V^e–XVIes.).* Mémoire de master 1 de l'Université de Nantes sous la direction d'Y. Henigfeld et V. Legros (2 vols.). Université de Nantes, Nantes.

Raffin, A. (2015). *Le mobilier métallique médiéval en contexte d'habitat rural dans les Pays de la Loire (V^e–XVIes).* Mémoire de master 2 de l'Université de Nantes sous la direction d'Y. Henigfeld et V. Legros (2 vols.). Université de Nantes, Nantes.

Rieth, E., Carrière-Desbois, C., and Serna, V. (2001). *L'épave de Port Berteau II (Charente-Maritime), un caboteur fluvio-maritime du haut Moyen Âge et son contexte nautique.* Paris: Édition de la Maison des Sciences de l'Homme.

Rieth, E., & Serna, V. (2010). "Archéologie de la batellerie et des territoires fluviaux au Moyen Âge." In J. Chapelot (ed.), *Trente ans d'archéologie médiévale en France. Un bilan pour un avenir* (pp. 291–304). Caen: Publications du Centre de recherches archéologiques et historiques anciennes et médiévales.

Thuillier, F., and Louis, É. (eds.). (2015). *Tourner autour du pot: Les ateliers de potiers médiévaux du Ve au XIIe siècle dans l'espace européen : actes du colloque international de Douai (5–8 octobre 2010).* Caen: Presses Universitaires de Caen.

Valais, A. (1998). "Herblay, site de Gaillon-le-Bas : un habitat du Bas-Empire et de l'époque mérovingienne en Vallée de Seine." In X. Delestre and P. Périn, (eds.), *La datation des structures et des objets du haut Moyen Âge : méthodes et résultats, Actes des XVe Journées internationales d'Archéologie mérovingienne, Rouen, Musée des Antiquités de la Seine-Maritime, 4–6 février 1994* (pp. 207–212). AFAM v. 7. Saint-Germain-en-Laye: AFAM.

Valais, A. (2012). *L'habitat rural au Moyen Âge dans le Nord-Ouest de la France: Deux-Sèvres, Ille-et Vilaine, Loire-Atlantique, Maine-et-Loire, Mayenne, Sarthe et Vendée,* Vol. 1. Rennes: Presses universitaires de Rennes.

Valais, A., Arthuis, R., Nauleau, J.-F., and Moréra-Vinçotte, I. (2009). "Les enclos du haut Moyen Âge de Vauvert à Château-Gontier (Mayenne)." *Revue Archéologique de l'Ouest* 26: 205–227.

Valais, A., and Laforest, P. (2009). "Herblay (Val-d'Oise) 'Gaillon-le-Bas.'" In F. Gentili and A. Lefèvre (eds.), *L'habitat rural du haut Moyen Âge en Île-de-France. Programme collectif de recherche—Bilan 2004–2006.* (pp. 199–208). Guiry-en-Vexin: Centre de recherches archéologiques du Vexin français.

CHAPTER 32

··

GOOD AND BAD PLANTS IN MEROVINGIAN FRANCIA

··

PAOLO SQUATRITI

AVITUS, the bishop of Vienne, was delighted and relieved when, some time before 507, he discovered a partial copy of his book *The Deeds of Spiritual History* at the house of a friend. It was a stroke of luck because Avitus had lost his own manuscript some years earlier in the violence caused by rival Burgundian kings' struggle to control his city. Moreover, he was lucky because this biblical epic, strong evidence that he knew Genesis and classical literary norms, was later much admired and secured the bishop's medieval reputation (Avitus of Vienne, *Historia Spiritualis*, pp. 24–31).

It was also a lucky find because *The Deeds* afford a glimpse into the botanical imaginary of early Francia. In its third section, Avitus relates that God issued his sentence on Adam, along with his successors, for the Edenic transgression. A crestfallen first man learned that he would no longer bask in the environmental perfection of paradise. From now on, the soil, previously lush with beautiful vegetation, would be uncooperative, and "pure seed" was a thing of the past. Instead, thorns and thistles would sprout, and, even when human cultivation appeared to return a semblance of order to the landscape, it would be an illusion. For where wheat was sown, the weeds darnel and wild oats would grow, and Adam, like his progeny, would only with the gravest difficulty manage to gather grain and make bread. God thus lowered humans to the status of ruminants: they would have to feed on herbs and grasses, and they would suffer from the same bloated bellies as bovines (Avitus of Vienne, *Historia Spiritualis* c. 155, pp. 278–280).

Avitus's careful attention in *The Deeds* to the botanical dimensions of humanity's banishment from Eden was not new. It derived from a long, Christian exegetical tradition (Bouteneff 2008). Thus, to the extent that it was Christian, Dark Age Francia was predisposed to appreciate Avitus's refined awareness of plants, their varieties, origins, hierarchies, and meanings. This chapter explores Merovingian plant lore as it can be divined in written texts; it also probes the history of some plants as revealed by archaeology.

While a comparison of such disparate evidence brings out many incongruities, it also demonstrates that human–plant interactions between 500 and 750 in the Frankish area were at least as dynamic as these relationships had been in earlier epochs in the same regions. Merovingian botanical history, the changes and continuities in crop regimes and weed populations, as well as people's evaluation of the goodness or badness of plants, both reflected and drove changes in rural settlement, production, and culture.

Good and Bad Plants

Like beauty, weeds are very much in the eye of the beholder. One person's pest is another person's food, ornament, fodder, building material, or fuel. A decade and a half before he died, the preeminent Latin theologian of the first millennium, Augustine of Hippo (d. 430), acutely identified the central ambiguity in plants, and the difficulty of making hard and fast distinctions between the good ones and the bad ones. In one of his commentaries on Genesis, he pointed out that people's economic activities alone, and no particular botanical characteristic, elevated some plants to the status of useful crop and lowered others into bleak weediness. To Augustine, all plants had equal ecological utility, supporting their ecosystems in ways *Homo oeconomicus* often could not appreciate (*De Genesi ad litteram* 3.18.27–28). It would have made perfect sense to Augustine, then, that medical texts in the early Middle Ages took an opposing view of notorious weeds from that of cultivators. While stinging nettles "are known to everyone," only pharmacologists considered them valuable, a cure for jaundice and colic, and able to ease deep coughs in the lungs (Everett 2012, p. 368). Blind to this medical silver lining, farmers and horticulturalists simply eradicated the plant wherever it arose, as Walafrid Strabo advocated in his poem *Hortulus* of ca. 830 (Walafrid Strabo, *Liber de Cultura Hortorum*).

This underlying uncertainty about the status of plants left etymological traces. Latin lacked a term for weeds, as indeed do the Romance languages that derive from Latin (André 1950, p. 160). Latin's "bad herbs" or "noxious herbs" were still just herbs. Such plants might easily slip over the border into more neutral semantic territory. Virgil had used the Latin *herba* without qualifiers to mean weed (*Georgics* 1.69), which further confused things. As Virgil was a supreme linguistic authority, the *Georgics* were much consulted throughout the first millennium. They influenced many, including Walafrid when he composed *Hortulus* (Gaulin, 1990, pp. 110–116, 128–129).

Consequently, Merovingian authors were unsure how to classify their plants. Some seemed indisputably good. The leaves that pious people were accustomed to sprinkle on the ground around holy places, including inside churches, were beneficent and laudable. They perfumed the air, adding an olfactory dimension to the experience of holiness and perhaps re-created paradise's verdure. Those who spread these "herbs" won prizes from holy patrons, and those who sucked their juices obtained lifelong health benefits (Gregory of Tours, *Libri Historiarum X*, pp. 239, 305, 333; *Liber Vitae Patrum*, pp. 686, 696; *Liber in Gloriae Confessorum*, p. 806). But the same plants could become very bad indeed. For instance, "herbs" were downright lethal to the starving (Gregory of Tours, *Libri Historiarum X*, p. 365). When bishops begged their audiences to end their superstitious practices, the proscribed activities included "incantations over herbs and dragging sheep through hollow trees" (*Vita Eligii*, p. 706). Indeed, to the seventh-century chronicler Fredegar, it was perfectly reasonable to divorce a woman accused of being an herb dealer (*herbariam*), as well as a prostitute (Fredegar, *Chronica*, p. 108). It seems that weeds, witchcraft, and wantonness went hand in hand.

As to the more respectable plants that sustained civilization, the Council of Frankfurt (794) assigned the lowest value to oats, then barley, then rye, with wheat, presumably *Triticum aestivum*,[1] highest in a hierarchical arrangement matching that of Diocletian's Price Edict of 301 (Comet 1979, p. 141). Over the course of the eighth century, the Frankish elite evaluation of the worth of grains seems to have changed little. An accounting document drawn up around 700 for the clergy of the church of Saint Martin in Tours lists landholdings in Anjou, Poitou, and the environs of Tours itself, although most of the toponyms it uses are unidentifiable. It registers rents in kind that scores of tenants owed the church and does so in a rigid order that appears to reflect the relative status for the redactors of each kind of grain rather than their relative quantities in the rents. Here, too, wheat (*triticum*) always opens the listings, rye follows, then barley, and finally oats. Spelt, a hulled wheat (or "dressed," having adherent husks on its kernels), receives six mentions and seems irrelevant in the pecking order (Gasnault 1975, pp. 12–19; Devroey 1990, pp. 234–236). In central Francia, by contrast, Merovingians preferred "naked" wheat (whose kernels easily separate from the husks—see Peytremann, Chapter 31, this volume). Indeed, not long after the compilation of Tours's account book, wheat's unrivaled prestige led to it being pronounced alone suitable for making the liturgical host (Devroey 2003, p. 102). But rye had made inroads and came before oats and barley in the consideration of the literate.

Merovingian hagiographers sustained a similar sense of cultivated plants' worth. In the upside-down world of Christian asceticism, wheat was a controlled substance: sixth- and seventh-century holy people avoided it to prove their humility and their ability to endure hardship. Thus, to eat "barley bread" or even "barley bread with ashes mixed in" was most meritorious to saintly Merovingians, though they had to do this modestly, without letting anyone know of their wheat-avoidance (e.g., Gregory, *Liber Vitae Patrum*, p. 687; Constantius, *Vita Germani*, p. 252; *Vita Bavonis*, p. 542). A version of the *Vita* of Amandus, bishop of Maastricht (d. ca. 675), written in the 800s, extols the holiness of "eating barley bread, the fodder of peasants' animals, mixed with ashes" (Milo, *Vita Amandi*, p. 464). In a single instance, the ascetic queen Radegund was said to have consumed rye bread instead of barley, but always hiding her frugality under a condiment (*Vita Sanctae Radegundis*, p. 371). In other words, Merovingian ascetical practice was grounded in a vegetarian gastronomic imaginary ruled by wheat and, in consequence, by white bread: abstention from wheat was wondrous.

Despite the claims of Merovingian writers, the social stigma of dark bread and the high status of wheat are not confirmed by archaeological finds. Seventh-century dwellings at Serris-les-Ruelles east of Paris, are so unlike each other that they suggest residents of different status lived in them, yet the inhabitants drew on granaries containing similar supplies (see Peytremann, Chapter 31, this volume). In fact, the silo in one of the more lavish residences contained the most rye. People presumably munched on dark bread, no matter what the conventions of hagiographers or the preferences of St. Martin's clergy. There were evidently other ways to display social superiority (de Hingh and Bakels 1996; Ferdière et al. 2006, p. 178).

Overall, Merovingian texts seldom presented plants as absolutely, irrevocably bad or good. Even wheat, a plant that enjoyed exceptional status, bore the whiff of pride, as the ascetics who studiously avoided it demonstrate. Other plants (or herbs) drifted from approbation to hostility, depending on circumstances. Only "zizania," branded devilish by the Gospel (see the final section in this chapter), was always bad and dragged in its wake "lolium," presumably the *Lolium temulentum* called darnel in English. Otherwise Augustine seems to have been right: it was people's variable activities, not any inherent qualities of plants, that rendered some vegetation noxious and some desirable.

Ordinary people in Francia's fields seem to have had fewer doubts about which plants were good, and which needed to be eliminated. Although studies of the topic are rare, on balance it seems that Merovingian rule coincided with a decline of unwanted plants in agricultural areas. If comparison of the grain stores in rural settlements from different periods is a reliable guide, Roman fields in Gaul had been rather weedy, while early medieval ones tended to be much cleaner. For example, wild oats (*Avena fatua*) and corncockle (*Agrostemma githago*) abounded in granaries at Bibracte (in Roman Burgundy), while Roman rule in the Aisne Valley coincided with a peak in weed variety and dissemination (Wlethold 1996; Bakels 1999). On the other hand, the contents of late-antique, Frankish-era granaries in modern-day Belgium were quite pure, containing almost only crop seeds. Similarly, samples of the contents of silos from Merovingian-period sites in the Swiss Jura, despite considerable variation in local agrarian strategies, consistently deliver low percentages of arable field weeds, which is surprising as growing cereals ("naked" and hulled wheats, rye, oats) was one foundation of all villagers' livelihood (Vermeulen 2001, p. 64; Brombacher and Hecker 2015).

A synthetic study of Roman- and Merovingian-era grain stores in Rhineland Germany proposes that the Roman custom of eliminating weed seeds by sorting and winnowing *after* storage, just prior to consumption, lost favor in late antique times (Rösch 1998). Thus, Dark Age grain stores were cleaner because more intensive weeding reduced unwanted "bad" plants in the field: what entered the granary was virtually ready to eat. The apparent switch from more careful winnowing and sieving to more careful weeding is difficult to assess in terms of efficiency but was definitely not neutral. Modern agronomical statistics show 10 to 35 percent crop losses from weeds and justify the development and deployment of increasingly complex and expensive weed control (Ziska and Dukes 2011, p. 16).

It is true that infesting plants mattered less in preindustrial agriculture, which was always less uniform than modern agribusiness and thus less susceptible to weeds. It is also possible that Rhenish farmers in the Roman era were indifferent to the bad plants in their fields because once crops had a big enough head start, they did not suffer much from volunteers' competition for light or water. Most weeds, in any case, affect soil quality little. Thus, harvest sizes were not visibly changed by weeds that germinated after crops, and cultivators for whom quantities harvested (rather than quality) were the main preoccupation might forego weeding. Following this logic, we might postulate that when bulk production, for commercial purposes, was the primary goal, farmers dealt with weeds differently than when they aimed at household subsistence. A further reason for Roman-era farmers to leave weeds alone may have been that they felt confident they could cull weed seeds from their distinctive grains before consumption. When hulled grains like spelt, whose large seeds are easy to distinguish from those of most common field weeds, lost favor in later Roman times, greater fastidiousness in the fields could develop (Rösch 1998, p. 119).

Yet it seems clear that the conditions of production in late-Roman and Merovingian countrysides also contributed to reduced weed populations: smaller farms, more diversified cultivation, and less monocropping limited opportunities for unwanted plants to grow (Rösch 1992, p. 209; 1998). Hence, postclassical crops reached granaries with fewer intruders mixed in, not just because Merovingian farmers grew grains that were hard to tell apart from the seeds of common weeds, or because they did not sell their harvests, but also because subsistence farmers' more biodiverse agriculture prevented specialized infesting plants from building up their presence, as they tend to do where the same crops are sown year after year in the same fields. While the result seems to have been that weeds in Merovingian territories flourished less than before (at least in northern and eastern Francia), inevitably some species of weed, notably corn marigold and stinking chamomile, found postclassical conditions most agreeable and blossomed more than ever. For weeds are opportunistic, and even when some species struggle in a particular set of circumstances, others fill the vacancy. The Genesis writer knew that no agroecosystem can entirely free itself of them.

But hope springs eternal, and Gregory of Tours tells an admonitory tale in his *Life of St. Martin* about "a certain woman, having taken her weeding hoe," who went to clear her crop field of darnel on the feast of St. John the Baptist, in late June (*De Virtutibus Beati Martini*, p. 628). Gregory's story confirms that removing bad plants was a low-status occupation, assigned to Merovingian children and women, as it remains in many rural societies. Despite her excellent intentions and technique (using a hoe, rather than plucking by hand, aids soil aeration and moisture retention), this woman was painfully incapacitated for violating the feast day. She obtained release only after months of prayer at St. Martin's tomb. Gregory's story reveals the tensions between agricultural operations a farmer might deem urgent and the rigidities of the Christian calendar. In Mediterranean conditions, weeding by hoe had to await April, by which time winter-sown crops had strong enough roots to withstand the treatment. In northern fields, the weeding season began later, about the middle of June (Comet 1992, pp. 167–170). Throughout Francia, however, in broadcast-sown fields lacking tidy rows (all fields before early modern times), such hoeing was very slow work. To Gregory's hoe-wielding woman, this investment of time was worthwhile, presumably because her crops' undesirable competitors had not yet gone to seed, at which point their potential as "green manure" or fodder ended and they might have to be uprooted and burned. In this sense, the timely attack on bad plants was a way of saving labor in a weed-conscious agroecosystem. To sixth-century cultivators, weeding at the proper time was therefore worth the risk of divine displeasure, and to Gregory it was fitting that divine chastisement took the form of enforced time off from work.

The timing of weed removal had another dimension, related to the spread of new methods of cultivation during the Merovingian period. Devroey (2006) and other scholars have discovered, in northern Francia around the middle of the first millennium, the first experiments in three-field rotation, though for most Merovingian farmers, two-field rotations remained the norm. Both systems for exploiting the soil sustainably had repercussions for good and bad plants and how they intermingled (see Jones et al. 2010, pp. 70–72). For if any rotation had the potential to create conditions amenable to certain "obligate" weeds (that do well only in agriculture), three-field rotations in particular were good for the bad plants. By multiplying types of conditions, three-field rotations facilitated the diversification and local dissemination of weeds, even if weed population size was restricted and opportunities for long- and medium-distance travel were few (Bakels 1999, p. 76).

Three-field rotation was an "intensification" that called for more labor, including more weeding, partly because it made bad plants out of good ones. On the fallow field, or on the field being cultivated with a spring-sown crop, plants that germinated from escaped seeds of last year's crop were a natural outcome; but to the farmer, they were weeds and maybe also confirmed what Genesis said about the unexpected germination of plants different from what one sowed (Pradat 2001, p. 157; Peytremann 2003, p. 338; Ruas 2007, pp. 159–160). In this case, only the passage of time and human classifications transformed a good plant into an undesired one: botanically, nothing had changed. Perhaps plants' basic ambiguity, adumbrated by Augustine and recognized by early medieval plant taxonomists, like the author of the *Alphabet of Galen*, derived from such situations (Everett 2012). For in that Latin compilation of Hellenistic plant lore, whose earliest manuscript dates from the 600s, hyssop was both a wild *and* a cultivated plant. It depended on how one looked at it, or, to be more exact, when.

Among the conditions of production that shifted after 400 and changed people's perspectives was demand. With Roman authority evaporating throughout the western provinces of the empire, the circulation of goods slowed, including that of bulk commodities like agricultural products (Zug Tucci 1990, pp. 868–869). Although archaeologists now discern numerous traces of a lively, interconnected commercial world along the coasts of the North Sea from the sixth century on (Loveluck 2013; Zech-Matterne et al. 2014, pp. 37–41), the gradual end to Roman state exactions, and the gradual contraction of urban demand, had consequences for all plants, good and bad. A cascade of effects on plant communities, and how people understood them, derived from Merovingian farms' increasing self-sufficiency.

For instance, one can plausibly correlate the demise of wheat as the premier crop in Gallo-Roman fields to the fact that wheat was the preferred form of tax payment near Roman army bases (Lewit 2009; Esmonde Cleary 2013, pp. 266–267; Zech-Matterne et al. 2014). Until the 400s, wheat had enjoyed continuous centuries of increasing significance in Gaul, a success driven by some of this grass's ecological characteristics. For wheat gave good yields even in dry climate conditions; in addition, its seeds had a sweeter taste and more gluten than other grains, all of which were positive attributes for bread makers and eaters. Above all, wheat seeds were tenuously attached to their glumes, so they were less bulky and lighter than other grain seeds after minimal processing. Thus, the fashion for eating bread and the trend toward transporting grain far from places of production conspired to elevate "naked" wheat above other grains in Roman Gaul. Wheat's "naked" kernels convinced many growers to abandon grains that were less demanding on the soil than wheat and more resistant to pests, many of which were "dressed." But if these grains required more labor to be separated from their ears and husks, and weighed 30 percent more than "naked" grains before their husks were removed, they still had some advantages (Jasny 1944; Ruas 2007, p. 150; Zech-Matterne et al. 2014, p. 29). Indeed, when commercial networks withered, wheat went into a partial eclipse, especially in many northern fields. In autarchic conditions, other grains flourished.

These shifts also redesigned the possibilities of "obligate" weeds, namely, the ones that do well only in agricultural contexts. Judging from pollen deposits (e.g., Barbier et al. 2002), the contraction of arable agriculture in the fourth and fifth centuries greatly reduced the populations of plants dependent on farmers' "disturbances." The Roman transfer of grains from region to region, and mostly toward the areas where soldiers were stationed, had also allowed numerous weed seeds to migrate into new areas. For example, the persistent presence in northern Gaul of *Myagrum perfoliatum*, a southern weed unsuited to local soil and climate, implies repeated reintroductions, piggybacking on more formal grain exchanges (Zech-Matterne et al. 2014, p. 39). From Late Antiquity, however, unsupported by the Roman state's extractions and redistributions, the dissemination of weeds became harder, and *Myagrum* disappeared from the north.

Fortunately for the bad plants, there remained several means of conveyance. Human mobility during the Germanic migrations is an obvious instance. Still, the flows of weeds did not follow the directions taken by barbarians, and there was no botanical stampede from north to south or east to west, as one might expect. In southern Germany, for instance, between the fifth and seventh centuries, the successful biological invaders ("adventive" weeds) were crafty plants from the Mediterranean area, especially members of the Caucalidion group (Rösch 1998), a sign that postclassical botanical flows did not always align with political and demographic ones.

Preindustrial farmers, moreover, worried about the viability of their seed grain. Many thought that after a few years (in early modern Languedoc, four), seeds selected from one's own crop were too "accustomed" to one's soil, which lowered their suitability. In order to improve their crops' reliability, as opposed to yields (an important distinction as explained in Kingsbury 2009, pp. 40–43), farmers traded with not-too-proximate neighbors, sometimes by visiting designated sites such as markets and fairs. For weed dissemination, such exchanges of seed lacked the massive efficiency of the grain movements organized by the Roman state but still gave weed seeds useful rides (Le Roy Ladurie 1966, pp. 54–56; Comet 1992, pp. 144–146).

In the biography of the holy Merovingian king Dagobert (d. 679), the peasants near Reims compelled their ruler, who happened to be traversing their territory, to sow their wheat "with his own hand." The episode ended with the predictable bumper crop that ripened earlier than usual, proving Dagobert's sanctity. Still, the passage also reveals a rural world where good kings were competent sowers, a difficult art, and carrying seed across fields made a difference (*Vita Dagoberti*, p. 515; Comet 1992, pp. 151–154). Thus, the *Vita* of Dagobert provides a glimpse of one way for weeds to move among fields, mingling with the good plants people preferred.

Among weeds' allies were domestic animals. The well-attested development of free-range animal husbandry in Merovingian times (see Yvenic and Barme, Chapter 33, this volume; Loveluck 2013, p. 69) could accelerate the diffusion of bad plants. Cattle, goats, and sheep carried weed seeds on their fur, in their hooves and intestines, and from the fallow land they grazed onto cultivated fields after harvest. Spread on agricultural fields by farmers, their manure was another disseminating agent. This continuous transfer blurred botanical distinctions between grassland vegetation and crop weed, or between cultivated and uncultivated land (Karg 1995).

In sum, in the early Frankish centuries, the fortunes of both good and bad plants fluctuated. Both kinds of plant adapted to and exploited human activities. Roman Gaul had hardly been a monocropped factory farm, but Merovingian agriculture tended toward more regional variety and the integration of more kinds of grains and other crops (legumes) in the same territories (Rösch 2008; Catteddu 2009). Southern Francia's agrarian systems, and therefore also its weed associations, displayed greater resilience than those of the northern territories. South of the Loire, wheat and barley remained predominant crops well into the eighth century (Ruas 1998, 2005). In the north, settlement change, reorganization of the rural economy, and a redesigned rural landscape fit together (Nissen Jaubert 2012, p. 301). In the transition from Roman to Merovingian landscapes, open pasture was increasingly mixed in among cereal fields, woods, and marshes; archaeologists have uncovered examples of such landscapes along the Selle River, in the Scarpe Valley, in what is today northern Belgium, and at the Rhine delta (Noël 1990, pp. 81–85; Barbier et al. 2002, pp. 149–151; Louis 2004; Loveluck 2013, pp. 57, 67). Greater biodiversity in these regions included new types of grain, like rye and oats, and of course new weed associations. While Gaul's economy grew more regionalized from the fifth century, one outcome found everywhere was more farms geared to producing subsistence for their farmers. For these agricultural producers, diversification was in fact a risk-controlling strategy in increasingly autarchic circumstances of production (Devroey 2003, pp. 34, 49; Peytremann 2003; Ferdière et al. 2006, pp. 134–139; Cattedu 2009;). It was also a new opportunity for some bad plants.

THE REVOLUTIONS OF RYE

The literary sources are silent on the subject, but both pollen records and finds in granaries indicate that rye increasingly asserted itself across Europe beginning in the fourth century. This quiet revolution was accompanied by some other grains' equally swift advances and retreats (some of which were evoked in the preceding section), redefining what was in people's fields and on their tables. The causes and effects of rye's surprising rise in the context of late-antique Gaul's cereal transition are worth pondering. How did a plant that was appallingly bad to Roman experts like Pliny the Elder (whose *Natural History* 18.40 called rye *deterrimum*, or "very awful") become good, at least to its cultivators?

Before attempting to answer that question, we must address some regional inconsistencies. For the cereal history of southern Frankish territories was more static than that of the northern heartlands. The reasons why farmers' evaluation of good crops and bad crops south of the Loire was more stable seem not to have been environmental. For in the Mediterranean regions of early modern France, rye *did* make inroads. Moreover, ninth-century monastic records from Brescia suggest that a process similar to what happened north of the Loire swept the early medieval Lombard plain: rye became a significant presence in northern Italy, at southern French latitudes (Comet 2004, pp. 49–51). Meanwhile, parallel cereal transformations ("dressed" grains replaced by rye) took place in late-antique Scandinavia (Grabowski 2011), central Europe (Dreselrova and Koçar 2013), and the Balkans (Henning 1987, pp. 99–101). Viewed synoptically, these changes in postclassical cereal culture look like an acceleration in the surge of "naked" grains across western Eurasia. Southern Francia's limited enthusiasm for rye and faithful adherence to barley (and wheat) thus are exceptions in this Dark Ages picture.

Rapid shifts in crop regimes like the one that swept across late-antique northern Francia are rare in agrarian societies but not unknown. In early modern Languedoc, apparently because of the demographic collapse resulting from epidemics after 1347, barley almost vanished from the fields and barley bread from peasant tables. In a mere three generations, between 1397 and 1480, what Le Roy Ladurie called "the revolution of wheat" swept away the ancient regime of cereals, then millennia old. But later, during the 1500s, a dual alimentary system emerged, and increasingly impoverished Languedoc peasants began to eat rye bread, leaving wheat to the privileged (1966, pp. 179–184). This development represented the beginning of a generalized "de-cerealization" of Mediterranean agriculture, a three-century phase when Mediterranean lowlands virtually stopped growing grain (an activity outsourced northwards, especially to the Baltic regions), and when other cultivations like vineyards, orchards, and pasture prevailed, usually on hillsides. This conspicuous change in the cereal regime of vast portions of the Mediterranean, including France, was related to the Little Ice Age that left lowlands hydrologically vulnerable and to Amsterdam's ascendancy in the Atlantic age, but more particularly to population decline (Tabak 2008, pp. 117–128). There are some obvious parallels between these early modern developments and the Merovingian ones: a greater diversity of agricultural production, a higher profile for smallholders, and a demographic trough, all seem related to the rise of rye in the middle of the first millennium.

Scholarly consensus holds that the replacement of barley and wheats with rye and oats did not radically redesign Frankish productive systems. However, these changes did enable the cultivation of previously "marginal" soils and facilitate three-field rotations (oats are spring sown and so compatible with winter-sown wheat and rye) that were integral to the medieval "agricultural revolution." Rye demanded less of the soil than "naked" wheat did (indeed, it could be sown on the same ground several years running), abbreviated the agricultural season somewhat by maturing earlier than wheat, and thereby reduced farmers' exposure to crop loss (Körber-Grohne 1987, p. 42). Thus, the late-antique success of rye expanded production possibilities and reduced risk without radically shaking up the agrarian order (Devroey 2006, p. 363).

Though part of a longer trend whereby Europeans came to prefer "naked" over "dressed" grain, rye's replacement of barley and the wheats emmer, einkorn, and spelt (all of which are "dressed") was also a godsend to field laborers, to those responsible for grain processing and storage, and to cooks. The shift freed Dark Age cultivators from at least one tiresome postharvest operation, an advantage conspicuous enough, perhaps, to motivate them to alter their growing strategies. For, severed from their stalks and brought in from the fields, most grains had to be dried. This was because grain was gathered slightly unripe, so that it would not break off the stalk during harvesting, and therefore was moist and vulnerable to fungi (van Ossel 1992, pp. 135–145). In northern Francia's conditions, therefore, it was usual to spread freshly harvested grains to dry in a sheltered space, hoping to prevent the formation of molds during storage: the *Vita Dalmati* (p. 549) records how anxious peasants felt about damp crops entering granaries. In fact, the Salic Law mentions two kinds of drying facility: the *spicaria* for grain on the ear and the *machola*, where whole sheaves could be stacked. Only after this preliminary drying did threshing, winnowing, and storage in (often underground) granaries occur (Sigaut 1981; Zug Tucci 1990, pp. 878–892).

Once dry, light threshing made rye kernels fall clean from the ear. They differed in this regard from "dressed" grains that called for a second procedure to separate the nutritious seed from its protective glumes. Archaeologists tend to think the many small, seemingly inefficient ovens near Merovingian houses were for toasting "dressed" grains, making it easier to remove their husks (van Ossel 1992, pp. 143–145; Hanusse et al. 2014, pp. 18–19). The procedure so altered the grain that it could no longer germinate or be used to make leavened bread (Moritz 1955; Devroey 2003, pp. 102–104). All grains had to be winnowed, but rye, unlike "dressed" grains, permitted people to skip a step that was risky because, performed outdoors and dependent on weather, it was laborious, and called for artificial heat that added a cost in fuel.

Dried, threshed, and winnowed rye was ready to eat, but was also lighter and less voluminous than "dressed" grains. Though "naked" grains were more liable to pests than grains tightly ensconced in tough husks, on Francia's scaled-back farms, rye also had the potential to elude that drawback. Merovingian grain stores were modest, smaller than the thirty quintals beyond which spoilage rates become problematic. Rye quite suited people with limited storage, who might have to move grains around and hence preferred lighter "naked" kernels but did not aim at growing big marketable surpluses (Zech-Matterne et al. 2014, p. 29).

Once in the kitchen, rye could be prepared in several ways, but it was sufficiently glutinous to make bread (Sigaut 1981). Rye thus suited communities of bread eaters worried about sparing labor. As bread became the uncontested "staff of life," reinforced in its preeminence by Christian culture, that was a big asset (Comet 2004). Rye matched wheat in ease of processing and in the storage space it occupied, but it also offered some high-quality side-products, such as the long supple stalks people wove into many useful implements.

In other words, rye combined several advantages in a sustainable package. In a rural landscape of dispersed settlement and small-scale production, growing numbers of northern Merovingian farmers appreciated the combination enough to adopt the new crop. Pliny's "worst" grain became good because it brought numerous advantages in cultivation, storage, and consumption to an agrarian economy of small farms and limited exchanges.

Of course, Merovingian agriculturalists also had to assess some drawbacks in rye before taking the plunge and adopting it. While ancient agronomists like Pliny thought rye yields extraordinary, wheat generally yields more per seed and requires no more soil preparation. When rye ripens, harvesters have to stoop low to cut the stems close to the roots in such a way that stalk and ear remain intact, as the stalks are prized for thatching. Thus, harvesting rye could be more exhausting than harvesting grains like wheat, whose culm is hollow and whose stems can be left in the field. Another consequence of the desire to use the stalks was that, after harvest and before threshing, rye required more space than wheat to dry (Guadagnin 1988, pp. 162–163; Comet 1992; Ferdière et al. 2006, pp. 92–93).

Rye's most notorious liability was its susceptibility to the fungus *Claviceps purpurea*, or ergot. An infected crop of rye would spread ergotism to anyone who ate the alkaloids contained in the parasitical fungus. Although other grains also host ergot, the human sickness associated with the fungus (ergotism) is especially linked to rye consumption, notably in cool and damp years. Several samples of rye from the Merovingian excavated site of Develier in the Swiss Jura had *Claviceps purpurea* on them, some of the oldest witnesses to the presence of the fungus in Switzerland (Brombacher, Hecker 2015, p. 338). Yet there are no known references in Merovingian texts to outbreaks that might be identified as ergotism, and though such palaeodiagnosis is arduous, scholars assign to the *Annales Xantenses'* entry for 857 the first European appearance of this painful disease of the intestinal tract and, in some cases, of the circulatory system. Thus, if rye brought toxic fungi into Merovingian food, no one was aware of the fact or acknowledged it. Rye remained a good plant despite its disadvantages.

As emphasized earlier, changes in agricultural regime entailed changes in weed communities. By becoming a good plant that people wanted to sow in their fields, rye created new conditions for field weeds. Unlike oats, the other grain to make large inroads in early medieval Europe, rye was sown before winter set in, so rye fields offered an ample window of opportunity for weed colonization before harvest (Comet 1992, p. 230; Comet 2004, pp. 162–165). Therefore, in northern conditions, rye fields were weedier than oat, or other spring-sown grain fields (Ziska and Dukes 2011, p. 16).

The bad plants best adapted to the northwestern European rhythms of rye production were corncockle (*Agrostemma githago*) and cornflower (*Centaurea cyanus*) (Ferdière et al. 2006, p. 185; Ruas 2007, p. 163, and 1998, p. 197; Grabowski 2011, pp. 482–483). Cornflower managed to increase its north European presence at the same time and in the same regions as rye, immune to the slowing of commerce that earlier supported this weed's dissemination (Körber-Grohne 1987, p. 45). Corncockle, meanwhile, learned to mimic rye so well that its seeds ended up in several Merovingian granaries, and presumably also in many loaves of bread. Since corncockle is toxic and causes considerable misery, and exceptionally even death, in humans who ingest its saponins, the triumph of this bad plant in fields sown with rye was far from inconsequential, even if not recorded (Mabey 2012, p. 72).

Late-antique cultivators sought antidotes to the weediness of rye fields. One traditional method of weed control was to sow rye so densely that it outcompeted weeds. Carbonized remains of crops suggest that in southern Denmark around the year 400, the spontaneous flora in adjacent cultivated fields could be quite different, presumably because the crop seed sown there had different provenances. Regardless, these rye fields were "very clean" (10–20 weeds/m²) because densely sown (Steen-Henriksen 2003). But this approach was not suitable everywhere, and wise cultivators carefully gauged their sowing. In Mediterranean conditions, for instance, sparse sowing recommended itself, as each plant sought scarce moisture. The ensuing competition could stunt development and reduce yields, particularly in fields where the farmer sowed several grains, an ancient method whereby Mediterranean farmers attenuated the risk of total crop loss in the event of a blight (Sallares 1991, pp. 305, 377–387).

Overall, the salient feature of rye's history in the Merovingian period was the mounting popularity of this grain (less in southern Francia, admittedly), no matter how weedy the rye fields or how infested with ergot. This success has naturally intrigued historians. In the past, the tendency to ethnicize food systems led scholars to link the dissemination of rye with Germanic or Slavic migrants, despite the fact that the northwestern European rise of this grain began before there were likely many barbarian settlers in the Roman Empire (Jasny 1944; Behre 1992, p. 150). As the ethnic hypothesis has fallen out of favor, climate determinism has come to the fore. Rye's hardiness, its dependence on a hard frost for germination, its ability to endure cold and wet conditions, and its long roots that give it resistance to spring and summer drought have seemed relevant to scholars convinced of a late-Roman "downturn" in European climate (Ruas 2005, p. 407; McCormick 2013, pp. 83–86; Henning 2014, pp. 335–336).

Rather than any particular (and so far unfathomed) late-antique climate regime giving rye an advantage over more delicate grains, we might postulate on the basis of the present discussion that this cereal's sheer versatility gave it a competitive edge over barley and wheat and convinced Merovingian farmers who could to sow it more often. (Behre 1992, p. 149). Whatever conditions climate "worsening" might have brought, colder and wetter weather did not alone drive early medieval peasant strategies. For the diffusion of sorghum in Italy coincided with that of rye in the peninsula, as well as in Francia: yet sorghum originated in Africa and needs hot, humid conditions to grow well (Castiglioni and Rottoli 2010). The biggest changes in cereal regimes began before there is evidence of climatic "degradation" in the western provinces where rye took off. They accelerated in the sixth to seventh century in what appear to have been quite dissimilar climate conditions. Since rye enjoyed a second expansion from the tenth century, when the European climate is thought to have warmed up, climate cannot have been the sole, or main, determinant of whether people planted it (Ferdière et al. 2006, pp. 134–136).

In a properly multicausal reconstruction of the rye revolution, peasant agency, increasingly rehabilitated in Dark Age archaeology (Loveluck 2013), should be taken into account. For Merovingian peasants used their experience to make choices and could have chosen to grow more barley, a grain that also endures cold and dry conditions well, matures early, and has culms that make fine fodder (Amouretti 1979, p. 59; Plotnicov 1999); and though barley tends to make better beer than bread, people could make do (Sallares 1991, pp. 367–368). In southern Francia, that was evidently the choice the majority made. Yet in the period between the fourth and eighth centuries, in several parts of the Merovingian sphere, it made sense for people and rye to accommodate one another because rye demanded a labor regime that was sustainable (no doubt also for climatic reasons) and rewarded its patrons with an array of products they were culturally and socially predisposed to appreciate.

DAMNABLE DARNEL

Merovingian writers showed more acute concern for some bad plants than others. Prickly and thorny weeds, a major worry of late ancient Bible readers impressed by the "thorns and thistles" (Genesis 3.18) that were agricultural man's lot, were a leitmotif in Merovingian literature. Since thistles and nettles are visibly different from grains, their absence from the archaeological record, made mostly of grain deposits, is natural. The interest of Merovingian authors, attuned to observe around themselves plants made significant by their readings, derived from literary more than agricultural contexts. Perhaps in consequence, Merovingian Francia's hagiography did not associate the thorny bad plants with agricultural spaces: in fact, prickly plants tended to appear in wild places (e.g., *Vita Bertuini*, p. 181; Gregory, *Liber in Gloriae Confessorum*, p. 799). Thereby these redoubts of asceticism could call to mind the thorny crown of Jesus (see *Vita Walfridi*, p. 199), though burgeoning thorn bushes might also signal the lack of human care for buildings (e.g., Gregory, *Libri Historiarum X*, pp. 70–71; *Vita Carileffi*, p. 390). Instead, for a sickle-wielding harvester, bent low to cut a sheath of grain, such plants represented a major nuisance: unlike other weeds, which had a few redeeming qualities, prickly plants made poor fodder and poor thatching material.[2]

The bad plant that most interested Merovingian literati was not thorny at all. Because Jesus, in one of his rare directly recorded interventions (Matthew 13.24–30), had told of a good farmer whose wheat field became infested with a weed maliciously sown there by an enemy, Christian readers, including Merovingian ones, paid close attention to this weed and its ways. But exactly what weed Jesus had in mind is unknown, and his spokesman Matthew, in attempting to render it into Greek, was stumped. Therefore, he introduced a new word into Greek lexica, *zizanion*, to convey Jesus' botanical meaning.

Scholars have, inevitably, lavished considerable attention on determining what species of noxious plant the word signified in first-century, eastern Mediterranean circles, but with inconclusive results (see Zohary 1982). Similar perplexity no doubt pervaded early Christian groups who read the Gospel parable. Jerome sagely left *zizania* in the Vulgate without attempting to render it into Latin. Yet at around the time Jerome published his translation of the Bible, uncertainty attenuated, and the identity of the bad plant, the weed chosen by demonic forces to ravage the fields of upstanding cultivators, was finally revealed. From the later fourth century, commentators rendered *zizania* as *aira* for those who read Greek and *lolium* for Latin readers. Thus, in his *Two Books of Instruction*, a compendium of difficult and obscure terms Latinists should know, Bishop Eucherius of Lyon (d. 449) listed the mysterious Gospel weed unambiguously as *lolium* (Eucherius of Lyon 1894, pp. 146–148).

The fourth-century interpretive lurch toward *lolium* authorizes the identification of the worst of weeds with darnel (*Lolium temulentum*), and although modern and ancient botany do not always align, in this case it seems that late Roman *lolium* and Linnaeus's *Lolium* were the same plant: the drawing of *aira* in the "Vienna Dioskurides," one of late antiquity's most famous manuscripts, confirms it (Cod. Vindobonensis med. Gr. 1, f. 71r).

What made *Lolium temulentum* stand out and may have encouraged the identification is its toxicity. Both chemicals in the weed itself and those in a parasite it is liable to host can poison hapless darnel eaters. To become lethal, the doses ingested have to be high, yet the nausea, headaches, weakness, vomiting, and intense gastric distress suffered by people who eat darnel seeds are surely sufficient to justify the suspicion surrounding this weed in many agrarian societies (Saharan nomads instead consider it a delicacy for guests: Comet 1992, pp. 290–291). That darnel is such an excellent imitator of wheat, barley, and rye seeds, and therefore could strike its victim unawares, no doubt contributed to its reputation. Duplicitous as well as poisonous, darnel was the quintessential "bad herb."

Indeed, darnel demonstrated imitative ingenuity over the long duration. It responded to human cropping strategies, and it mutated in order to survive alterations in taste and fashions in cultivation such as those that characterized the postclassical period. Early on, when emmer (*Triticum dicoccum*) was a preferred grain of farmers in Gaul, *lolium* developed bigger seeds. As "naked" grains displaced hulled ones like emmer, *lolium* again changed, for if its seeds were to pass through threshing, winnowing, and seed selection, to be resown with next year's crop, it had to mimic a new paragon. Human choices and techniques thus selected traits in darnel, and the species adapted, as it had done before in ancient Greece (Sallares 1991, p. 339).

Darnel was a plant equipped to do well in preindustrial fields. It was tough and able to cope with the quite different environments of continental and Mediterranean Europe. In addition, its botanical characteristics included considerable genetic variation among individuals, high numbers of offspring, and short generation time, so it could evolve as quickly as humans altered the odds of survival through their agrarian ways (see Russell 2011, p. 40). Agronomical research in Ethiopia, where *Lolium temulentum* is a significant nuisance, shows that different strains of the weed prevail (hulled or "naked") according to whether or not it grows among "naked" grains. Unintentionally, Ethiopian farmers increase the diversity of darnel's genes and thus its ability to adapt to different conditions. Their farming methods, especially their simultaneous cultivation of different landraces of crops, exchange of crop seeds, and hand weeding, contribute to this end (Senda and Tominaga 2004).

In spite of its admirable flexibility, in the end, darnel's most effective weapon in negotiations with people was the usual one of agricultural weeds: mimicry. The bad plant darnel resembled the plants people deemed good and grew (like rye or wheat) enough that its seeds regularly got mixed up with those farmers sowed as crops. Even darnel's growth cycle came to resemble that of edible grains: leaf shape and seed appearance were similar, and darnel became indehiscent, meaning that the seeds stayed on the ear at harvest.

Perhaps this astonishing malleability is what lay behind the belief of Merovingian writers that *lolium* and other weeds were not distinct species of plant but, rather, perversions of rye or wheat. This idea was old, first advanced by the protobotanist Theophrastus, a student of Aristotle. But it did make sense of observed phenomena: one sowed grain but reaped darnel, pretty much realizing the dire warning in Genesis 3. The late seventh-century author of the *Vita* of abbess Sadalberga (d. 665) told of the spiritual weeding carried out by a holy man in the valley of the Doubs River, "lest the crop of the Lord . . . might grow into wild oats and darnel" (*Vita Sadalbergae*, p. 54). In other contexts, Avitus of Vienne ascribed to windborne seeds the sprouting of spiritual darnel (*Operae* 1883, p. 57). But a preoccupation with the shape-shifting of apparently good plants that grew into bad ones undergirded Avitus's discussion of the pure seed of Eden and its corruption in postlapsarian conditions, so that what one planted was not what grew, a mysterious subterranean transformation having changed the nature of the seeds.

Jesus' fearsome weed *zizania* reverberated through the literature of late-antique Gaul. Hilary of Poitiers, Prosper of Aquitaine, Arnobius Junior, Vincent of Lérins, John Cassian, and, of course, Avitus of Vienne, all cited the weed in different contexts. Gregory of Tours referred to it too, usually as a metaphor for doctrinal impurity: the wheat field was the orthodox church, and the darnel was pullulating dissent, illicitly intermingling itself. Gregory's use of *zizania* as both a symbol and a real plant depended on some familiarity with rustic ways, as well as on knowledge of Matthew's Gospel and late-antique exegesis. By weaving the three together, Gregory established what a bad plant was: a plant that God had singled out for human edification but one whose presence in Frankish fields confirmed everything one had read about it (Gregory, *Libri Historiarum X*, p. 376, 379; *Liber de Miraculis Andrea Apostoli*, p. 838; *De Virtutibus Beati Martini*, p. 628).

Yet a plant with such a redoubtable literary reputation as an infesting weed left scant vestiges in the archaeobotanical record. Tiny seeds are always hard to uncover, but

Lolium temulentum appears more seldom in published reports of botanical finds from Merovingian Francia than other field weeds, like corncockle (*Agrostemma githago*), endowed with similarly sized seeds. In seventh-century contexts at Villiers-le-Sec in the vicinity of Paris, it is unclear if the darnel came from arable or other zones (Guilbert 1988, p. 197), while at nearby sites it was absent (Ruas 1988).

Here the well-known wall that separated early medieval theoretical botany from agricultural practice emerges clearly. Merovingian writers had to present plants plausibly but did so according to fixed canons, responding to a literary tradition. The points of contact between a text about crops, fields, weeds, or vegetation and the actual plants that grew in Francia were few (Gaulin 1990; Devroey 1990, pp. 224–225). Thus, it was principally the scriptural reputation of *lolium*, which writers thought to be the plant Jesus had mentioned as an insidious infestation of grainfields, that raised its profile. Beyond the halls of Frankish scriptoria, this most nefarious and capable bad plant barely survived in obscurity.

Conclusion

Contemporary debates about which plants are autochthonous, deserving conservation efforts, and which are exotic, invasive, and should be eradicated, reveal Western people's anxieties about the most pressing issues of the times, like permeable national borders and flows across them. Yet, historians have yet to include plants in their narratives about the past. Thus, neither textually nor archaeologically informed Merovingianists see history being made when they observe the ineluctable regularities in the life cycles of annual plants. Even trees, whose longer lives make them seem permanent, and which therefore attract disproportionate attention, matter only when people cut them down (deforestation) or fail to (afforestation). Apparently immutable, plants appear passive. At most, they reflect human social and economic change. Instead, this chapter has proposed that plants' characteristics, aptitudes, and adaptability outfitted them to participate in historical processes in Merovingian Francia, for example, by making specific styles of cultivation possible. Plants, too, effected the economic, social, and cultural transformations of Roman Gaul, both by growing as they did in real Frankish fields and by flourishing so luxuriantly in Merovingian imaginations.

Notes

1. "Wheat" encompasses two genera and some 600 species of grasses, so is really an ethnobotanical construct (Head et al. 2012). My discussion assumes that the "wheat" in Merovingian sources was usually the "naked" *T. aestivum* species that predominates in the coeval archaeological record, but the Latin texts are ambiguous.
2. In backwoods Mexican corn fields, thistles are considered a problem only for harvesters: Vieyra-Odilon and Vibrans 2001, p. 431.

Works Cited

Ancient Sources

Avitus of Vienne, *Historia Spiritualis*. N. Hecquet-Noti (ed.). (2001). *Avit de Vienne, Histoire Spirituelle*, 1. Paris: Les Éditions du Cerf.

Avitus of Vienne, *Operae quae supersunt*. R. Peiper (ed.). (1883). MGH: AA 6.2. Berlin: Weidmann.

Constantius, *Vita Germani Episcopi Autissiodorensis*. W. Levison (ed.). (1920). MGH: SRM 7 (pp. 225–283). Hanover: Hahn.

De Vita Sanctae Radegundis Libri Duo. B. Krusch (ed.). (1988). MGH: SRM 2 (pp. 364–395). Hanover: Hahn.

Eucherius of Lyon, *Instructionum Libri Duo*. C. Wotke (ed.). (1894). *S. Eucherii Lugdunensis Opera Omnia* 1 (pp. 65–161). Vienna: F. Tempsky.

Fredegar, *Chronica*. B. Krusch (ed.). (1888). MGH: SRM 2 (pp. 18–168). Hanover: Hahn.

Gregory of Tours, *De Virtutibus Beati Martini Episcopi*. B. Krusch (ed.). (1885). MGH: SRM 1.2 (pp. 585–561). Hanover: Hahn.

Gregory of Tours, *Liber de Miraculis Beati Andreae Apostoli*. B. Krusch (ed.). (1885). MGH: SRM 1.2 (pp. 821–46). Hanover: Hahn.

Gregory of Tours, *Liber in Gloriae Confessorum*. B. Krusch (ed.). (1885). MGH: SRM 1.2 (pp. 744–720). Hanover: Hahn.

Gregory of Tours, *Liber Vitae Patrum*. B. Krusch (ed.). (1885). MGH: SRM 1.2 (pp. 661–644). Hanover: Hahn.

Gregory of Tours, *Libri Historiarum X*. B. Krusch, and W. Levison (eds.). (1951). MGH: SRM 1.1. Hanover: Hahn.

Milo, *Vita Amandi Episcopi II*. B. Krusch (ed.). (1910). MGH SRM 5 (pp. 449–485). Hanover: Hahn.

Pliny the Elder, *Naturalis Historia*. L. Jan (ed.). (1878). *Naturalis Historia Libri XXXVII*. Leipzig: Teubner.

Vita Bavonis Confessoris Gandavensis. B. Krusch (ed.). (1878). MGH: SRM 4 (pp. 534–545). Hanover: Hahn.

Vita Bertuini Episcopi Maloniensi. B. Krusch and W. Levison (eds.). (1920). MGH: SRM 7 (pp. 177–182). Hanover: Hahn.

Vita Carileffi abbatis Anisolensis. B. Krusch (ed.). (1896). MGH: SRM 3 (pp. 389–394). Hanover: Hahn.

Vita Dagoberti III Regis Francorum. B. Krusch (ed.). (1888). MGH: SRM 2 (pp. 511–524). Hanover: Hahn.

Vita Dalmati Episcopi Ruteni. B. Krusch (ed.). (1896). MGH: SRM 3 (pp. 543–549). Hanover: Hahn.

Vita Eligii Episcopi Noviomagensis. B. Krusch (ed.). (1902). MGH: SRM 4 (pp. 663–741). Hanover: Hahn.

Vita Sadalbergae Abbatissae Laudunensis. B. Krusch and W. Levison (eds.). (1910). MGH: SRM 5 (pp. 40–66). Hanover: Hahn.

Vita Walfridi I, Episcopi Eboracensis. B. Krusch, and W. Levison (eds.). (1913). MGH: SRM 6 (pp.193–163). Hanover: Hahn.

Walafrid Strabo, *Liber de Cultura Hortorum*. E. Dümmler (ed.). (1884). MGH: Poetae Latini Aevi Carolini 2 (pp. 335–350). Berlin: Weidmann.

Modern Sources

Amouretti, M. (1979). "Les céréales dans l'antiquité." In M. Gast and F. Sigaut (eds.), *Les techniques de conservation* 1 (pp. 57–69). Paris: Editions MSH.

André, J. (1950). *Lexique des termes de botanique en Latin*. Paris: Klincksieck.

Bakels, C. (2005). "Crops Produced in the Southern Netherlands and Northern France during the Early Medieval Period." *Vegetation History and Archaeobotany* 14: 394–399.

Bakels, C. (1999). "Archaeobotanical Investigations in the Aisne Valley, Northern France, from the Neolithic up to the Early Middle Ages." *Vegetation History and Archaeobotany* 8: 71–77.

Barbier, D., et al. (2002). "Une source pollinique et son exploitation." *Histoire et sociétés rurales* 18: 137–158.

Behre, K. (1992). "The History of Rye Cultivation in Europe." *Vegetation History and Archaeobotany* 1: 141–156.

Bouteneff, P. (2008). *Beginnings. Ancient Christian Readings of the Biblical Creation Narrative.* Grand Rapids, MI: Baker.

Brombacher, C., and Hecker, D. (2015). "Agriculture, Food, and Environment During Merovingian Times." *Vegetation History and Archaeobotany* 24: 331–342.

Castiglioni, E., and Rottoli, M. (2010). "Il sorgo (*Sorghum bicolor*) nel medioevo in Italia settentrionale." *Archeologia medievale* 27: 485–495.

Catteddu, I. (2009). *Archéologie médiévale en France.* Paris: La Découverte.

Comet, G. (2004). "Les céréales du bas empire au moyen âge." In M. Barceló (ed.), *The Making of Feudal Agricultures?* (pp. 120–176). Leiden: Brill.

Comet, G. (1992). *Le paysan et son outil.* Rome: EFR.

Comet, G. (1979). "À propos de diverses céréales au moyen âge." In M. Gast and F. Sigaut (eds.), *Les techniques de conservation* 1 (pp. 39–43). Paris: Editions MSH.

de Hingh, A., and Bakels, C. (1996). "Palaeobotanical Evidence for Social Difference?" *Vegetation History and Archaeobotany* 5: 117–120.

Devroey, J. (1990). "La céréaliculture dans le monde franc." *Settimane di studio del Centro italiano di studi sull'alto medioevo* 37: 221–253.

Devroey, J. (2003). *Économie rurale et société dans l'Europe franque (VIe–IXe siècles).* Paris: Belin.

Devroey, J. (2006). *Puissants et misérables.* Louvain-la Neuve: Academie Royale de Belgique.

Dreslerova, D., and Koçár, P. (2013). "Trends in Cereal Cultivation in the Czech Republic from the Neolithic to the Migration Period (5500 BC–AD 580)." *Vegetation History and Archaeobotany* 22: 257–268.

Esmonde-Cleary, S. (2013). *The Roman West, AD 200–500.* Cambridge: Cambridge University Press.

Everett, N. (2012). *The Alphabet of Galen.* Toronto: University of Toronto Press.

Ferdière, A., et al. (2006). *Histoire de l'agriculture en Gaule, 500 av. J.-C.–1000 apr. J.-C.* Paris: Editions Errance.

Gasnault, P. (1975). *Documents comptables de Saint-Martin de Tours à l'époque mérovingienne.* Paris: Bibliothèque nationale.

Gaulin, J. (1990). "Traditions et pratiques de la literature agronomique pendant le haut moyen âge." *Settimane di studio del Centro italiano di studi sull'alto medioevo* 37: 103–135.

Grabaowski, R. (2011). "Changes in Cereal Cultivation During the Iron Age in Southern Sweden." *Vegetation History and Archaeobotany* 20: 479–494.

Guadagnin, R. (1988). "Matériaux et technqiues de construction." In *Un village au temps de Charlemagne* (pp. 153–166). Paris: Reunion des Musées Nationaux.

Guilbert, P. (1988). "Étude des pollens prélevés dans les couches archéologiques de Villiers-le-Sec." In *Un village au temps de Charlemagne* (pp. 196–198). Paris: Reunion des Musées Nationaux.

Haas, J. (2006). *Die Umweltkrise der 3. Jahrhundert n. Chr. im Nordwesten des Imperium Romanum*. Stuttgart: Franz Steiner Verlag.

Hanusse, C., et al. (2014). "L'habitat de la Sente à Grentheville (Calvados), VIᵉ-Xᵉ siècles." *Archéologie médiévale* 44: 1–49.

Head, L., et al. (2012). *Ingrained. A Human Bio-geography of Wheat*. Farnham: Ashgate.

Henning, J. (2014). "Did the 'Agricultural Revolution' Go East with the Carolingian Conquest?" In J. Fries-Knoblach, H. Steuer, and J. Hines (eds.), *The Baiuvari and Thuringi* (pp. 331–359). Woodbridge: Boydell and Brewer.

Henning, J. (1987). *Südosteuropa zwischen Antike und Mittelalter*. Berlin: Akademie Verlag.

Jasny, N. (1944). *The Wheats of Classical Antiquity*. Baltimore: Johns Hopkins University Press.

Jones, G., et al. (2010). "Crops and Weeds." *Journal of Agricultural Science* 37: 70–77.

Karg, S. (1995). "Plant Diversity in the Late Medieval Cornfields of Northern Switzerland." *Vegetation History and Archaeobotany* 4: 41–50.

Kingsbury, N. (2009). *Hybrid*. Chicago: University of Chicago Press.

Körber-Grohne, U. (1987). *Nutzpflanzen in Deutschland*. Stuttgart: Theiss Verlag.

LeRoy Ladurie, E. (1966). *Les paysans de Languedoc*. Paris: SEVPEN.

Lewit, T. (2009). "Pigs, Presses, and Pastoralism." *Early Medieval Europe* 17: 77–91.

Louis, E. (2004). "A De-Romanized Landscape in Northern Gaul." In W. Bowen et al. (eds.), *Recent Research on the Late Antique Countryside* (pp. 479–504). Leiden: Brill.

Loveluck, C. (2013). *Northwest Europe in the Early Middle Ages, AD 600–1150*. Cambridge: Cambridge University Press.

Mabey, R. (2012). *Weeds, the Story of Outlaw Plants*. London: Profile Books.

McCormick, M. (2013). "What Climate Science, Ausonius, Nile Floods, Rye, and Thatch Tell Us about the Environmental History of the Roman Empire." In W. Harris (ed.), *The Ancient Mediterranean Environment Between Science and History* (pp. 61–88). Leiden: Brill.

Moritz, L. (1955). "Husked and 'Naked' Grain." *The Classical Quarterly* 5: 129–134.

Nissen Jaubert, A. (2012). "Ruptures et continuités dans l'habitat rural en pays de la Loire." In A. Valois (ed.), *L'habitat rural au moyen âge dans le nord-ouest de la France* 1 (pp. 295–314). Rennes: PUR.

Noël, R. (1990). "Pour une archéologie de la nature dans le nord de la 'Francia.'" *Settimane di studio del Centro italiano di studi sull'alto medioevo* 37: 763–820. Spoleto: CISAM.

Peytremann, E. (2003). *Archéologie de l'habitat rurale dans le nord de la France du IVᵉ au XIIᵉ siècle*. Saint-Germain-en-Laye: AFAM.

Plotnicov, L. (1999). "Introduction." In L. Plotnicov and R. Scaglion (ed.), *Consequences of Cultivar Diffusion* (pp. ix–xx). Pittsburgh: University of Pittsburgh.

Pradat, B. (2001). "Les écofaits: céréales et adventices." In *L'occupation de l'âge du fer dans la vallée de l'Auron à Bourges* (pp. 150–163). Bourges: FERACF.

Rösch, M. (1992). "The History of Cereals in the Region of the Former Duchy of Swabia (Herzogtum Schwaben) from the Roman to the Post-Medieval Period." *Vegetation History and Archaeobotany* 1: 193–231.

Rösch, M. (1998). "The History of Crops and Crop Weeds in Southwestern Germany from the Neolithic Period to Modern Times." *Vegetation History and Archaeobotany* 7: 109–125.

Rösch, M. (2008). "New Aspects of Agriculture and Diet of the Early Medieval Period in Central Europe." *Vegetation History and Archaeobotany* 17: 225–238.

Ruas M. (1988). "Alimentation végétale, pratiques agricoles et environment du VIIᵉ au Xᵉ siècle." In *Un village au temps de Charlemagne* (pp. 203–211). Paris: Reunion des Musées Nationaux.

Ruas, M. (1998). "Les plantes consommées au moyen âge en France méridionale d'après les semences archéologiques." *Archéologie du Midi médiévale* 15–16: 179–204.

Ruas, M. (2005). "Aspects of Early Medieval Farming from Sites in Mediterranean France." *Vegetation History and Archaeobotany* 14: 400–415.

Ruas, M. (2007). "La parole des grains." In A. Durand (ed.), *Plantes exploitées, plantes cultivées* (pp. 149–170). Aix en Provence: Presses de l'Université de Provence.

Russell, E. (2011). *Evolutionary History*. Cambridge: Cambridge University Press.

Sallares, R. (1991). *The Ecology of the Ancient Greek World*. London: Duckworth.

Senda, T., and T. Tominaga (2004). "Genetic Diversity of Darnel (*Lolium temulentum* L.) in Malo, Ethiopia." *Economic Botany* 58: 568–577.

Sigaut, F. (1981). "Identification des techniques de conservation et de stockage des grains." In M. Gast et al. (eds.), *Les techniques de conservation des grains à long terme* 2 (pp. 156–180). Paris: CNRS.

Steen-Henriksen, P. (2003). "Rye Cultivation in the Danish Iron Age." *Vegetation History and Archaeobotany* 12: 177–185.

Tabak, F. (2008). *The Waning of the Mediterranean, 1550–1870*. Baltimore: Johns Hopkins University Press.

Van Ossel, P. (1992). *Etablissements ruraux de l'Antiquité tardive dans le nord de la Gaule*. Paris: CNRS.

Vermeulen, F. (2001). "Les campagnes de la Belgique septentrionale et des Pay-Bas méridionales au IVᵉ et Vᵉ siècles." In P. Ouzoulias et al. (ed.), *Les campagnes de la Gaule à la fin de l'antiquité* (pp. 45–68). Antibes: APDCA.

Vieyra-Odilon, L., and H. Vibrans (2001). "Weeds as Crops." *Economic Botany* 55: 426–443.

Wlethold, J. (1996). "Late Celtic and Early Roman Plant Remains from the Oppidum of Bibracte, Mont Beuvray (Burgundy, France)." *Vegetation History and Archaeobotany* 5: 105–116.

Zech-Matterne, V., et al. (2014). "L'essor des blés nus en France septentrionale. In X. Deru, R. González Villaesclusa (ed.), *Consommer dans les campagnes de la Gaule romaine* (pp. 23–49). Lille: Revue du Nord.

Ziska, L., and Dukes, J. (2011). *Weed Biology and Climate Change*. Ames: Wiley/Blackwell.

Zohary, M. (1982). *Plants of the Bible*. Cambridge: Cambridge University Press.

Zug Tucci, H. (1990). "Le derrate agricole." *Settimane di studio del Centro italiano di studi sull'alto medioevo* 37: 865–902.

....

CHAPTER 33

LIVESTOCK AND THE EARLY MEDIEVAL DIET IN NORTHERN GAUL

....

JEAN-HERVÉ YVINEC AND MAUDE BARME

DURING the transition between Late Antiquity and the early Middle Ages, namely, during the Merovingian period, a number of important economic and social transformations took place in northern Gaul that included the relationship of humans with animals.[1] It is vital to approach choices relating to animal production and consumption within the context of two factors that likely influenced the social and economic conditions that framed this relationship: climate and plague.

First, it is important to note that climatic changes in the mid-sixth century were linked to a series of volcanic eruptions. The consequent cooling, a development known as the Late Antique Little Ice Age, lasted from about 536 to about 600 (Büntgen et al. 2016) and may have caused food shortages, even famines. Second, the climatic changes at the start of the early Middle Ages may have been a significant factor in triggering the outbreak of plague, which recent genetic analyses have identified as *yersinia pestis*, in western Europe, including Germania (Harbeck et al. 2013). Although current research does not allow us to estimate the extent of the epidemic, the plague is thought to have had a considerable sociodemographic impact on the populations of Gaul.

Beyond the possible influence of the plague, the climate crisis probably affected modes of production and agro-systems, which likely necessitated adaptation (Nissen Jaubert 2006). Bio-archaeological research, to which archaeozoology belongs, contributes precisely to the identification and understanding of transformative processes linked to cultural, economic, and environmental evolution. Thus, the archaeozoological data produced in the last thirty years have begun to fill out our knowledge of animal husbandry in the Merovingian period, and, in some cases, offer historians and archaeologists an opportunity to reorient modern perspectives formed on the basis of written and art historical sources (Alexandre-Bidon and Manne 1988; Dierkens 2008a; Dierkens, Le Bec, and Périn 2008).

The current overview, dedicated to the relations that existed between humans and animals, concerns the northern third of what is now France, a territory where the hold of Germanic culture was strongest. This analysis addresses the same geographic area as Edith Peytremann's chapter (Chapter 31 of this volume); it likewise remains limited to the available sources. However, whereas the dynamism of French conservation archaeology (*archéologie préventive*) in the last three decades has dramatically expanded the amount and type of research possible on this period, the unsystematic publication of these studies remains a challenge. Many surveys can only be undertaken by consulting unpublished excavation reports whose data, in many cases, must remain confidential. Moreover, only the literature produced by Inrap (Institut National de Recherches Archéologiques Préventives) has been made steadily available in digital form (Base Dolia), meaning that some data remain inaccessible.[2] These conditions have not facilitated the advance of synthetic archaeozoological studies addressing vast geographical zones, including those on the Merovingian period; significant obstacles of this nature explain why such surveys do not currently exist (on the structural challenges of French archaeology, see Effros, Chapter 4, this volume). However, recent surveys have been conducted on a *regional* scale, such as those undertaken in the region of Douai (Yvinec 1996), the Île-de-France (Frère and Yvinec 2008), and Normandy (Lepetz and Yvinec 2002), and in a diachronic appraisal of northern France during Late Antiquity (Jouanin and Yvinec 2019) and from the medieval period through the beginning of the modern era (Clavel and Yvinec 2010). Finally, one must cite the "thematic incursions," often within a more ambitious spatial-temporal framework, that seek to develop an understanding of a single or specific aspect of existing interactions between humans and animals, such as the social and economic implications of the introduction of donkeys to the north of Gaul in the seventh or eighth century, or the maintenance of the stature of horses in the early Middle Ages discussed later in this chapter. In the analysis undertaken here, the data have been supplied by the authors and their affiliated colleagues at the Centre de Recherche Archéologique de la Vallée de l'Oise and at Inrap.

At first sight, examination of the dataset reveals a striking disparity among the bone assemblages found at rural sites, which constitute the large majority of locations under study, and those yielded by urban and privileged sites, which are significantly rarer. This disproportionate representation of rural sites is the first difficulty encountered in creating a synthetic discourse. It may also reflect the significant ruralization of society as an initial outcome of the early Middle Ages.

From a chronological perspective, in the period of transition between the end of Antiquity and the start of the early Middle Ages, there were not a significant number of contemporary settlements. Moreover, they generally do not yield much beyond small bone samples. However, thanks to conservation archaeology, this so-called period of "transition" has become increasingly well documented. In just the northern third of France, thirty-five sites have been catalogued recently informing us about the period between the late fourth and the early sixth century.[3] At the heart of this corpus of data, the Île-de-France distinguishes itself as the best documented sector of this geographic region. Over the period studied in this chapter, one sees a drastic reduction in the number of sites. The transition between the fourth and fifth centuries, then the fifth century, and finally the transition between the fifth and sixth centuries, are illustrated, respectively, by twenty, three, and two archaeological sites each. These figures reflect both the methodological challenge of dating and singling out transitional archaeological sites, and an archaeological reality corresponding to less dense territorial occupation during these transitions.

Over the course of the sixth century, the corpus of sites studied is thus markedly reduced. This lacuna testifies to the increased continuity of human settlement in this region that has effectively erased or made inaccessible evidence from this period. Moreover, although the techniques for dating archaeological sites are regularly improving in accuracy, the date ranges obtained for certain bone samples remain imprecise. At present, we cannot date specific sites more precisely than within a century. This deficiency has impeded our ability to synthesize the data summarily attributed to the Merovingian and Carolingian periods.

We must be aware, therefore, that the bones gathered offer only a general reflection of a past reality: like any source, they necessarily involve limits, insufficiencies, and so on. In fact, taphonomic factors (features of an archaeological site associated with natural processes of decay) and human agents can interfere with or destroy the samples that survive, thus distorting the image or images obtained (see Yvinec 1997, especially the methodological section). For example, in a rural environment, the widespread practice of spreading waste as a fertilizer causes the relative poverty of animal bone assemblages. This phenomenon, combined with the destructive action of dogs in such contexts, makes it necessary to analyze what are often assemblages of a restricted size. This makes their interpretation all the more delicate.

Moreover, the results of this analysis must be put into perspective in a systematic way, notably through comparisons among sites. Synthetic analytical information emerges best by juxtaposing sites and, most importantly by asking how the respective proportions of animal species changed across sites and over time. At the same time, the ratio of species distribution among bone remains does not testify directly to which animals were being raised on site. It is necessary to contextualize the data by considering animal size together with other variables, above all the factors of human dietary choice that operated in different milieux (among producers and consumers, in rural and urban settings, and so on).

THE EVOLUTION OF LIVESTOCK HUSBANDRY

Merovingian domestic livestock was similar to that in present-day northern France, apart from a few notable differences. With respect to livestock, one can observe the presence of beef cattle, pigs, and domestic ovicaprids (sheep and goats) during the Merovingian period.

As for equines, the horse was already durably implanted in the territory at the start of the early Middle Ages, but this was not true of the donkey. The donkey, which was well known to the Romans, was totally absent from the north of France until the Merovingian period. Donkeys were not truly integrated with northern equine livestock until later in this period, during the course of the seventh and eighth centuries, at which point they appear on about 12 percent of surveyed sites. The frequency in the appearance of donkey osteological remains then grew exponentially, appearing on sites 75 percent of the time by the end of the Carolingian period. However, the evidence of donkeys remains weak in comparison to that of horses, with the proportion of donkey bones oscillating between 5 and 15 percent of assemblages found from members of the horse family (*equidae*). The introduction of the donkey in northern Gaul in the Merovingian period, coupled with the rapid embrace of this species, merits attention because it is emblematic of the capacity of contemporaries for evolution and adaptation.

Even if the details of the factors that contributed to this success remain difficult to determine, we can point to the many inherent advantages of this species: the donkey is a rustic animal whose care is not an intensive obligation. Not only can the donkey carry a packsaddle but it is endowed with remarkable endurance and is capable of bearing heavy loads relative to its size. Best adapted to the transportation of small quantities of merchandise, at least over short and middle distances, the donkey can meet emerging needs on an individual level, or those of small communities. Thus, the new favor that the donkey enjoyed ultimately translated to agricultural exploitation on a modest scale, or at least the necessity of greater modularity in the circulation of commodities (i.e., more circulation hubs). In this sense, these previously unacknowledged factors could prove influential in explaining supervening modifications in the socio-economic organization and/or modes of exploiting the land in the late Merovingian and Carolingian periods.

De facto, the adaptation of the donkey also makes it possible to envisage the existence of hybrids, among which the mule prominently figures. However, identifying the evidence of the presence of mules often comes up against the limits of the criteria of anatomical distinction: osteometrically speaking, it is very difficult to distinguish mules from donkeys. The tests that have been conducted only allow us to think that hybrids were, at best, very little represented.

The farmyard consisted, in an almost systematic fashion, of hens and geese. One may add the peacock, whose presence was exceptional. This latter species must have fulfilled an ornamental and symbolic function, although it is also possible that it was consumed (Dutton 2004, pp. 43–68). To give an example, the peacock is well attested at one elite Merovingian residence, the demesne farm of Serris-Les-Ruelles, in the Île-de-France (Gentili and Mahé 1999). It is also found later in Compiègne, in the palace complex, amidst the leftovers from feasting (Yvinec 1997). The status of the mallard duck remains less easy to determine since osteological criteria do not allow us to make a distinction between wild and domestic forms. Alexandra Liarsou has recently proposed the possibility of the domestication of this taxon before the early Middle Ages (Liarsou 2013). In support of this hypothesis, Liarsou makes use of textual sources and emphasizes the fact that there is no evidence of a change in the size of the animal, even if this must have accompanied the process of domestication. She notes, among other sources, the

Capitulare de Villis (794) (Magnou-Nortier 1998, art. 40), which included ducks among ornamental birds like the peacock. If the duck was thus regularly maintained in captivity for diverse purposes, proof of its domestication continues to be difficult to attest. Perhaps it is necessary to admit, as Liarsou suggests, that contemporaries preferred to preserve the duck's wild attributes and thus its status as game. An analogous choice of animals being maintained for symbolic reasons are deer (*cervids*) (Vigne 1993). Finally, the bones of rock pigeons only seem to appear in isolated cases, but it is not possible to determine if they had been domesticated.

THE SIZE AND ROBUSTICITY OF ANIMALS

Animal bones, whatever the context of their discovery, inform us about the height of the withers and the robusticity of livestock. Indeed, the dimensions of the bones, measured across all of the sites studied, make a description of farm animals possible. At the start of the Middle Ages, animal bones were characterized by modest size and relative gracility, although regional differences and local specificities are discernable.

A comparison of the evolution of the size of domestic mammals between the Gallo-Roman period and the modern period, which is helpful to this discussion, was undertaken by means of an index or average (with a base of 100 at the end of the Gallic period, retained for all species studied). It emerges from this comparison that Roman influence brought an important augmentation in the height of domestic species. This has classically been interpreted as the product of three factors: the intensification of exchange, the circulation of animals over long distances, and the renewal of zootechnical knowledge. Starting with the Merovingian period, this tendency reversed itself: one may observe an abrupt reduction in the height of the withers of the animals studied, excepting horses. The evolution of the index reveals that the trend toward a reduction in the size of the animal was accentuated during the Carolingian period: the height of the withers reached its lowest value, which continued until the fifteenth, or even the seventeenth century, depending on the species under consideration. Only an augmentation of the size of hens was recorded earlier, in the twelfth to thirteenth century.

Many hypotheses have been proposed to explain the causes of this regression in the size of the principal domestic taxa. Certain authors attribute this phenomenon to a loss in received zootechnical knowledge that occurred at the end of the Roman period. Others evoke the possibility that in this period there was a wish to privilege the smaller species, rendering it easier to master the quantities of fresh meat destined for immediate consumption. Thus, there was no need for conservation procedures (drying, salting, and so on). This last interpretation is not entirely convincing since poultry is implicated in this phenomenon of decreased size in the same way as cattle. It therefore suggests, at least in this case, that an intentional zootechnical approach aimed at the better mastery of quantities of meat can be excluded. Finally, the interesting proposition of J.-P. Devroey

(2003) associates this trend with a change in modes of production, which became more family-based, coupled with a modification in social demand.

These factors probably played a role but they leave one question unresolved. The marked decrease in the size of farm animals, which started in the Merovingian period and finished in the Carolingian period, continued for many centuries. For this reason, it is necessary to question the causes of the continuity and longevity of this phenomenon into the Middle Ages: why did demographic and economic growth, and then the rapid expansion of cities and the demand that it entailed, not positively influence the size of livestock during the course of the central Middle Ages? Perhaps, this stagnation owed its relative permanence to significantly impoverished genetic diversity. The weakening of the routes of long-distance exchange during the early Middle Ages led to a reduction and regionalization of commercial activity; it provoked, locally but concomitantly, a consequent reduction in the genetic admixture necessary for maintenance of the size of animals. Later, the progressive reestablishment of the movement of livestock, which was especially favored by the growth of fairs in the course of the early Middle Ages, failed to hold back the stagnation of the size of the livestock. In any event, the increase in the size of livestock, which has been identified as occurring around the sixteenth century, seems to have resulted from a concerted and reasoned initiative aimed at renewing agropastoral techniques in this region through the contribution of "new blood" to local livestock.

As for the horse, it has already been mentioned that it escaped the global movement toward decreased size of livestock in the early Middle Ages. The attention given to maintaining the stature of these animals was related perhaps to the consideration that it received in elite spheres: the horse's symbolic value was coupled with its growing martial prestige. More generally, the quality of these privileged auxiliaries of human activities, which were destined for riding or for the work of pulling, were largely conditioned by their size (Baillif-Ducros and Yvinec 2015).

Thus, it is possible that in order to ensure the continued existence of the Roman equestrian heritage, early medieval horse breeders developed new zootechnical strategies, those in which cross-breeding depended on long-distance exchanges and the practice of diplomatic gifts, or perhaps a mixture of these two practices. From this point of view, the evolution of the size of horses during the early Middle Ages allows us to posit the capacity of contemporaries to preserve the size of one species for the few who wished for it. In this respect, the ascendance of economic and/or social demand appears to have been a determining factor once again. Because the horses were destined for the circulation of people and merchandise, they had greater opportunities to spread over a larger territory than cattle on the hoof. In this sense, the utility of the animals tended to favor the circulation of genes and thereby the preservation of their size.

We should remark, moreover, that rare evidence proves that there were deliberate efforts to import certain prestige animals, despite the fact that this enterprise was without a doubt not the practice of the majority of animal breeders. Thus, the few cases of polycerate or many-horned sheep (*ovis polyceratus*) identified in the catchment basin of the Seine River (Putelat 2005) testify to an attempt to introduce these remarkable animals into the territory, apparently via the establishment of commercial exchanges across the Channel and the North Sea.

Along the same lines, the discovery of a sternal cleft (*thoracique bifide*), belonging to a representative of the genus *Bos* (domestic and wild cattle), deserves some attention. In this case, skeletal remains with this congenital malformation to the rib cage were identified among samples collected in the port zone of Quentovic, which, moreover, also yielded a case of polyceracy—in other words, livestock with more than two horns (Oueslati 2012). This osteological particularity, described as classical with respect to humped cattle (*zebu*), may be observed on shorthorn cows (Grigson 1984, 1996), probably the result of hybrids in the range of the humped cattle. However, this morphological category is equally found among the representatives of the subspecies *Bos taurus* (domestic cow) in the continental European domain: in this instance, the scholarly literature reports a sternal cleft in the skeletal remains of the Swiss Simmental breed (Duerst 1931, cited by Epstein 1955). The factors that could shape the expression of this osteological particularity remain partially unknown. This anatomical variation may have been the result of a cross-breeding between *Bos taurus* and *Bos taurus indicus*, which long antedates modern examples of such cross-breeding. Although the data require prudence and the significance of the appearance of this osteological characteristic among the Merovingian cattle of Quentovic remains subject to caution, this bone fragment should nevertheless arouse curiosity. The phenomenon could possibly indicate a genetic admixture of two animals that were closely related. This outcome would imply that the most southern and eastern varieties were carriers of a genetic patrimony inherited from the *Bos taurus indicus* (zebu). This hypothesis, the validity of which cannot be confirmed prior to release of the results of genetic analysis that are forthcoming, suggests that there was a manifest intention to reinvigorate livestock in these northern regions. There is evidence for this objective in the introduction of the many-horned sheep, as also seen in the case of the adoption of the donkey.

HUSBANDRY PRACTICES

The respective frequency of the principal domesticated mammals (cows, pigs, sheep, and goats) remains a privileged marker of agro-pastoral organization in a given territory. These animals remain closely connected with human activities: as draft animals, riding animals, and pack animals, and as sources of primary alimentary material (meat, milk, marrow, and so on) or other essential resources for ends that were not exclusively dietary (wool, bone, horns, hide, leather, body fat, and so on).

The strategies of producers who raised livestock are reflected in both the relative proportion of species (which are expressed in the number and mass of animal remains), and the selection of individual animals within a herd (evidenced by the marks of slaughter). This latter form of evidence permits us to understand the economic utility of the animals that were chosen for slaughter because the marks can distinguish animals that were immature, butchered, culled, and so on. Although such an analysis relies essentially on data from rural sites, in particular the data involving animals, consumer preferences would also have made a difference, through particular demands that breeders would have sought to supply. Ultimately, study of the bones of the principal domesticated species seeks, among other things, to identify the nature and goal of animal husbandry. In the end, it involves determining a schema of production, at least partially, and understanding the modifications that affected it.

DOMESTIC OVICAPRIDS

The principal and common characteristic of all the transitional sites studied remains the very small number of remains of domestic ovicaprids (sheep and goats). During this short period, consumption of sheep and goat meat declined drastically: our research in the northern third of Gaul shows a significant decrease in the number of domestic caprines over a wide geographical area, in both rural and urban areas.

During the Gallo-Roman period, the overall proportion of domestic ovicaprid remains, within the three principal subspecies (cows, pigs, and ovicaprids), reached about 20 percent on average. This number dropped to 13 percent during the phase corresponding to the fourth and fifth centuries, that is, the start of Late Antiquity. The decline was bolstered during the course of the fifth century in that the frequency of the remains of domestic ovicaprids was confined to 4.7 percent, a figure that is confirmed on settlement sites dated to the fifth and sixth centuries, with a value that did not exceed a threshold of 6.3 percent.

The distinction that existed between a rural milieu on the one hand, and an urban and privileged milieu on the other, does not invalidate this pattern of decline in the number of domestic ovicaprids found in bone assemblages. On the contrary, the causes of this phenomenon remain difficult to discern. Did it reflect a desirable adaptation to agropastoral patterns that are unknown to us? Or was the decline due to new economic imperatives, such as difficulty in selling sheep and goat products destined for southern, Romanized regions through weakened trade networks? Or, finally, was the decline in caprine numbers a response to uncontrolled constraints, whether epizootic (disease) or environmental, such as the decline of available pasture?

Whatever the cause, this situation did not extend beyond the Merovingian period. Rather, the present synthesis of data indicates a likely rapid renewal in interest in domestic ovicaprids in the Carolingian period because their number reached 22 percent, a figure roughly equivalent to their representation in the Gallo-Roman period. In the eighth century, certain settlements reveal a new increase in the frequency of sheep and goats, for example, in the bone assemblages gathered at Fontaine-Notre-Dame (Nord) (Marcy, forthcoming) dated between the seventh century and the end of the Carolingian period, in which the frequency of domestic ovicaprid remains grew from 20 to more than 40 percent.

In the northern third of Merovingian Gaul, the rise in the proportion of domestic caprines between the Merovingian and Carolingian period appears to be slightly less notable than at the settlement of Fontaine-Notre-Dame. In the latter case, the head-count grew from a third to perhaps half. On average, the number of domestic ovicaprids moved overall from 22 to 29 percent. This upsurge in the breeding of sheep and goats could have corresponded to an early boom in the production of wool. In fact, the increase in the number of remains of domestic ovicaprids was sometimes accompanied by a change in the management of the herds concerned, composed mostly of sheep. From the late eighth century, and particularly at Fontaine-Notre-Dame, an analysis of the age at which animals were butchered reveals that a growing number of individuals were slaughtered later (at six to ten years of age). However, this observation cannot be made uniformly in the territory studied. At other sites that are contemporary and geographically close, the production of milk and meat was more readily favored, as was the case at Bourlon (Pas-de-Calais) (Marcy 2013).

Pigs and Cattle

As for other domestic mammals, the preponderance of cattle in the course of the fourth century was followed by the relative importance of pigs during the fifth century, at a number of sites (Kreiner 2017). However, this preponderance of pigs did not last through the early Merovingian period except in a few habitats. Overall, a rapid change led once again to an increased representation of bovine cattle among the samples found in the settlements concerned.

Furthermore, this sequence of phenomena, that is to say, the rise in the remains of pigs to the detriment of cattle in the fifth century, and then the resurgent remains of cattle thereafter, occurred with some variability that seems to have reflected the geographical region in question. Undoubtedly, these fluctuations testify to regional heterogeneity in economic organization. Thus, in the Île-de-France, in the well-documented area of Serris-Les-Ruelles, only the older phases of the site of Jossigny, which was newly established in the sixth and seventh centuries, reveal the predominance of pigs in terms of the proportions of remains (Gentili and Sethian 2012). By contrast, at the end of the Merovingian period, the number of cattle grew again in significance, now accounting for close to two-thirds of the number of bone remains among the three principal domestic taxa, a frequency analogous to that which was observed at the site of Serris itself in the same period. A comparable situation may be observed in the department of Aisne in Picardy, at which there was a single settlement dated from the sixth century at the earliest, yielding samples in which pigs prevailed over the other domestic mammals. By contrast, Merovingian assemblages found at other sites in the same territory presented elevated numbers of cattle.

Likely linked to the ruralization of society from the beginning of the early Middle Ages, this episodic prevalence of the pig, circumscribed in time and/or place, suggests that there was a temporary decrease in agropastoral activities linked to fulfilling local needs in a "small-scale economy," or even an adaptation to an autarkic mode of functioning. However, in those settlements that reveal this brief primacy of pigs, the rapid return to preponderant numbers of cattle in rural milieux testifies to the vitality of Merovingian agropastoral dynamics.

Although the pattern described previously does not always apply, at certain sites the primacy of cattle among the samples can be consistently verified. Thus, at Saint-Pathus "les petits Ormes" (Seine-et-Marne), cattle dominated from the third to fourth century, from the fourth to fifth century, then from the fifth to sixth century (Hurard 2011). Likewise, at the Burgundian site of Malay-le-Grand "Paquis" (Yonne), the dominant proportion of cattle remained remarkably stable during three phases of successive occupation, namely, from the fifth to the early seventh century (Lamotte 2007).

These observed differences at the earliest Merovingian settlement sites remain obscure because until now the analysis has been made on a relatively limited corpus of data. The state of research does not permit sound testing of the potential correlations between the examples at rural sites and husbandry patterns—something that requires particular care in the formulation of proposed interpretations.

That the overriding percentage of cattle remains was unchanged, or was restored after a short period of dominance of hogs at numerous settlements that have provided assemblages, signals a rise in the involvement of bovine cattle after the sixth century. This phenomenon may reveal recognized needs in terms of the labor force and the need for other animal products. These imperatives varied in relation to the agropastoral models in use. For example, crop production, already largely practiced during Antiquity, generated a need to return to oxen for plowing.

This hypothesis seems to be confirmed by the analysis of data relative to the age of animals at slaughter. Although husbandry strategies remained largely focused on the production of meat from young and fattened animals (54 percent), they also reserved a good number of animals for the "major cull" of old age, putting them to death only after they were over nine years old (26 percent). The pattern of slaughter, based on 288 examples, reveals two age groups that are poorly represented among the breeding and dairy stock, namely those slaughtered at an "intermediate" adult age, and those between four and a half and nine years, respectively (Frère et Yvinec 2008). Thus, the range of regional slaughter achieved in the north of France presents a homogeneous practice, and thus the trustworthiness of the results appears to be sound.

Even if there was a dominant husbandry practice at work, there was also a certain amount of regional adaptation. In the bottom of the great alluvial valleys, like that of the Seine, with more sandy soils, it appears that there was a greater emphasis on ovicaprids (Yvinec 2003). The strongest presence of bovines occurred little by little in the maritime plain zones and to the east of the plain of the Rhine. At times, environmental changes also induced successive modifications of the pastorage choices as has been demonstrated in the work of Stéphane Frère and Benoît Clavel (Frère and Yvinec 2008; Clavel and Yvinec 2010). Thus, in the zone of the maritime plain, one notes the gradual draining of the area by humans, the establishment of saltmarsh sheep, and then the ultradomi-nance of cattle husbandry.

THE GROWING PRESENCE OF THE HORSE

As for the Gallo-Roman period, the frequency with which horse bones are discovered remains fairly low, even in rural milieux: this species does not represent more than about 3.5 percent of the identified remains (Lepetz 1996). The consumption of horse meat was interrupted during this period, or at least became more rare. With the majority of the discards studied coming from alimentary garbage dumps, however, the actual represen-tation of these animals in the midst of settlements is necessarily lowered.

However, during Roman Antiquity, the equidae (members of the horse family, which typically include horse, donkey, and mule) reentered the population's diet, particularly in the countryside (Dierkens 2008b). From this point in time, the practices of horse butchers allow a better understanding of the place horses occupied in Merovingian agrosystems. During the early Middle Ages, the presence of members of the horse fam-ily in the bone-remain samples varied and depended on the methods used to gather the bones, particularly in rural contexts. Overall, horse remains are not abundant: their rep-resentation is limited to, on average, 4 percent, even if the number tended to grow grad-ually over time. By contrast, when the Carolingian period began, a substantial rise in the number of horses may be observed. This global movement is, however, not exempt from profound disparities, principally linked to the contexts considered. This is suggestive of an unequal acceptance of the practice of horse butchery: the presence of horse meat in the meat-based diet appears most popular in modest rural contexts.

The individual animals that were consumed frequently appear to have been young. This finding suggests a parallel between the mode of managing equine cattle and bovine herds: a percentage of the horses were specifically reared for alimentary purposes. Together with a possible exploitation of the work potential of horses, this might explain the numbers obtained at the "peasant" settlements, which were clearly higher than those of other contexts.

Finally, some differences can be observed at the local level. Thus, in the north of Île-de-France (Frère and Yvinec 2008), the discovery of horse remains appears to be two times higher than the average. This phenomenon increased, moreover, during the Carolingian period. In the Île-de-France, the homogeneity of the samples at many occu-pation sites concentrated in a restricted space, furnishes strong evidence of breeding or a locally intensified exploitation of members of the horse family. For this reason, it is appropriate to ask about what influence the proximity of centers of elite rule, whether lay or ecclesiastical, exerted on the size of horse populations. The value of the ceremo-nial and military interest of the horse, cultivated with aristocratic mentalities, could have motivated the privileging of this animal on the demesnes revolving around places of power. Incidentally, the specific location of the Pays de France, a plain located in the

Île-de-France north of Paris, which is rich in heavy silt but also the seat of the great abbeys and the presence of elite laity, could have initiated the allocation of horses to the work of plowing. This may have been the case even if it is generally thought that optimization of harness equipment did not occur until later.

FARMYARD MANAGEMENT

Overall, chickens furnished at least 80 percent of the remains found of poultry that were consumed. The remaining 20 percent were geese. Individual animals of all ages were consumed, even if the adults remained by far the most prominent. As for the consumption of eggs, it is difficult to estimate this quantitatively, but it must have constituted a strong incentive for raising hens.

This mode of exploitation contrasts strongly with the raising of flocks of geese, which was designed essentially to produce adults. It is thus legitimate to ask if this species was not raised with a view to its multiple end products, privileging what the animal could produce while still living (eggs, feathers, down, and so on). However, the slaughter of those animals at an adult age may have been a response to an alimentary need. Force-feeding was not efficacious until the autumn, when the animals reached an adult age. A fattened goose was thus necessarily arriving at its maturity, and its meat was greatly prized because it could be easily preserved in the form of potted or salted goose.

DIETARY CHOICES

In some respects, archaeozoology offers an essentially qualitative approach. However, it does not allow for a discussion of the place of meat products in the diet, and it provides even less information about the daily portion of meat. Nonetheless, archaeozoology allows us to clarify some alimentary preferences during the Merovingian period.

The place accorded to each of the principal domestic species in the diet (cows, pigs, ovicaprids), most notably because they made up an essential part of the meat supply, was a major factor that distinguished the social classes. There was a divide between the milieux of consumers and those of producers. Consumers privileged the excellent meat-providing species, namely, pork and poultry, whereas producers oriented their consumption in response to the necessities of husbandry requirements of the agro-systems that were in place and thus they nourished themselves with, above all, beef.

The rare evidence that survives from Merovingian urban settlements suggests, however, the limits of this consumer/producer split, which was doubtless constrained by the economic imperatives at play. Thus, beef probably constituted the principal meat resource for the urban food supply, as is illustrated by the case of the site of Quentovic (Oueslati 2012). However, as we have seen, many urban sites, especially in the earliest phases, were distinguished by the frequency of pig husbandry. It remains possible that the consumption of pork in the cities around the fifth century was a repercussion of the favor which the breeding of pigs gained in certain parts of the countryside during the same period (Seigne et al. 2007). However, these contradictory signals still resist interpretation, since study of Merovingian urban centers needs to be enriched still further. This issue illustrates the limits of this archaeological exercise, which is dependent on the state of research and thus does not always permit us to determine definitively the status of occupants and the dynamics governing excavated settlements.

Let us add that, even in the midst of villages, differences in dietary behavior are sometimes perceptible. The site of Bussy-Saint-George (Seine-et-Marne) is particularly illuminating in this regard. During the Merovingian settlement of this village, beef dominated in all of the collections of bone remains found, with the exception of remains gathered from the only real rubbish dump identified. This rubbish dump, associated with metallurgical activity, was characterized by an abundance of pig remains, as well as the presence of poultry two times higher than that observed in other sectors. Some activities of particular sectors of the site, even in the midst of the same village, show underlying social differences that are very much detectable on the basis of diet (Yvinec 1993a). This approach to demarcating social sectors has also been applied recently at Villiers-le-Sec, with respect to the frequency of sumptuous artifacts, notably those of glass (Gentili 2010), or all kinds of elite consumption (Gentili and Valais 2007). Growth of the corpus of sites excavated presently permits the isolation of certain settlements in which dietary behavior contrasted, inexplicably at first sight, with that observed in the majority of other rural settlements. One could cite the examples of the Merovingian and Carolingian sites of Huppigny à Vitry-sur-Orne (Moselle), Grosbliederstroff "Gungling" (Moselle), and also the farm Sassinot at Roissy-en-Brie (Seine-et-Marne). All present similar features, that is to say, a moderate spectrum of faunal remains, and seem to have borrowed as much from a rural milieu as from a privileged context, including little recourse to meat of the horse family, a meat diet of good quality, and a diet that favored pork and poultry. All of the settlements turn out to have been associated with artisanal activities or at least forms of production other than those of the cultivation of cereals or cattle husbandry.

Finally, some regional particularities are starting to emerge. For example, the dynamism of cattle breeding in the plain of Caen appears so vivid that beef predominated as much on the tables of peasants as those of the lords, such as was the case at Giberville and Biéville-Beuville (Calvados) (Saint-Jores and Hincker 2001; Hincker 2007). By contrast, elites tended to choose the most tender meat, coming from veal (10 percent were animals less than two years old) and, above all, animals on the threshold of their mature weight (55 percent were between two and four years old). Thus, the selection of animals based on age, among those of the same species, was an indicator of prosperity as pertinent as that of the choice of the species consumed: the most privileged more willingly set their sights on quality meats coming from young animals, which they often consumed in the form of fresh meat. At Giberville, pork consumption followed the same logic, with juveniles offering relatively strong representation, at least for the period considered: piglets less than six months old and young pigs of between six months and one year of age represented, respectively, 17 percent and 30 percent of the effective totals. As for animals that had arrived at their mature weight, they were generally butchered at the start of winter and transformed into preserved meat (salted, smoked, or dried). They totaled 42 percent of the remains observed, whereas the contribution of culled adult animals was limited to 11 percent (Saint-Jores and Hincker 2001).

Even so, the Merovingian peasantry was not reduced to nourishing itself uniquely from culled beef: their ordinary diet included a significant proportion of meat. Moreover, the residents of rural habitations were distinguished by their consumption of horse meat, which was widespread and represented a significant resource of protein. The practice of butchering horses in the countryside is indicated by numerous surviving traces of butchery marks on bone remains. Indeed, in these contexts, the frequency of these markings on the bones of horses prove to be similar to that observed on the remains of other animals that were consumed. However, the technique implemented for butchering and processing horse carcasses differed: it was characterized by the almost exclusive use of a thin and light blade, the handling of which was, in fact, more inconspicuous. Finally, individual horses of a young age occupied a notable place among the butchery profiles in rural settlements where the de-fleshing of horses was practiced. This coincidence suggests that at such sites, horses located there were mostly consumed (Frère and Yvinec 2008).

Finally, the place occupied by poultry in the consumption of meat constituted a final marker of social difference. Supplementary meats from the farmyard were not abundant in modest rural contexts, whether calculated in number of bones or as a proportion of total mass of remains.

SUPPLEMENTARY MEATS: WILD ANIMALS AND HUNTING STRATEGIES

The stand-off between historical and archaeozoological sources relative to the wild animals of northern France (Duceppe-Lamarre et al. 2002) suffices to convince us of the necessity of increasing our collection of data to understand better the composition of past fauna. The comparison of the two views produces strongly contrasting visions of the evidence. Archaeozoological studies are tied intimately to the dietary and cultural customs of the inhabitants of the territories studied. As such, the ancient bones do not furnish an objective and exhaustive image of the fauna present in wild spaces. Rather, the bone assemblages resulted from a choice, from strategies of selecting specific samples. However, archaeological observations complement the textual documentation usefully, especially hagiographical sources (see Kreiner, Chapter 24, and Squatriti, Chapter 32, this volume). Textual sources have their own biases, for example, in more readily connecting wild animals with their symbolic meaning than documenting their actual abundance in the environment (Guizard-Duchamp 2004). Wild animals encountered in the texts are noticeably different from those found in the bone samples. Thus, the stag and the hare, frequently present at archaeological sites, are missing from the written sources. By contrast, bears, wolves, serpents, ravens, and falcons, largely cited in the lives of holy persons, are rarely found among osteological assemblages, with the notable exception of deer. This dissonance, unavoidable in the context of an effort to describe ancient wild fauna, illustrates the need to acknowledge the results of the many disciplines contributing to the reconstruction of the environment of past societies.

The profound social and cultural changes that marked the end of the western Roman Empire caused new dynamics among game animals. Furthermore, the probable human demographic decline in this period may have had an impact on the proliferation of wild populations that were already present, in addition to the return of certain large wild mammals at least to the relatively well-preserved cores, such as the Vosges or the remainder of the great northern forests. From an environmental point of view, the lightened human pressure on these territories and the climactic changes that occurred from the sixth to seventh century must have worked conjointly. However, these combined effects probably marked certain sectors more profoundly, as some recent studies conducted in Alsace and Lorraine have indicated (Rodet-Belarbi and Forest 2010; Putelat et al. 2016). At privileged sites, even elite sites, in Alsace and Lorraine, remains of bears, aurochs, as well as, at the site of Ostheim, bisons or moose (*Alces alces*) have been found (Putelat et al. 2016). Finally, it is no doubt significant to observe the substantial presence of the bear at the very beginning of the Merovingian period, in the Île de France, and at sites like Compans "Ouest du parc" (Seine-et-Marne), and in lower Normandy, at Giberville (Séguier, Cammas, and Van Ossel 1997; Saint-Jores and Hincker 2001). This situation does not seem to have continued during the rest of the early Middle Ages.

The study of bone remains suggests that many mammal species and wild birds were hunted and, generally, consumed. Only some species appear to have been truly excluded from the dietary regimen, such as, for example, the wolf. In fact, this species is virtually absent from the archaeozoological samples of the early Middle Ages. This deficiency is not uniquely ascribable to the difficulty in discriminating between the skeletal remains of wolves and those of dogs. The strong antagonism that pitted man against wolf led to the banishment of this species from human habitats, no doubt in consequence of symbolic ideas anchored in the popular imagination. These included the wolf's resistance to taming, its attraction to blood, and the cultural classification of animals that were linked to these qualities. Thus, the wolf is hardly present in the form of skins or trophies in the domestic sphere (Yvinec 2009). As for the animals that were a source of furs (foxes, members of the weasel family, and so on), their presence in bone assemblages does not correlate with their actual frequency in the ecosystems. Among them, the fox was always the most abundant, no doubt because of its ability to profit from opportunities offered by human habitation and the human need to limit the fox's incursions into domestic spaces.

Four species destined for consumption were systematically privileged among the game available: hare, stag, roe deer, and boar. During the early empire, the hare dominated all of the bone assemblages despite the progressive growth relative to the proportion of stag bones (Lepetz 1996). By contrast, in the late empire, the representation of hare and stag in the consumption of game was equivalent. The Merovingian period saw continuity in this evolving overall pattern, so that stags came to dominate in the archaeological samples, in all contexts, with the hare second.

The first synthesis of the archaeozoological data (Yvinec 1993b) has indicated that the hunt was practiced as much by the aristocracy as by the peasantry because this prerogative was partially linked to the ownership of land. The ecclesiastical milieu was without a doubt an exception in this regard: the small amount of game consumed on these lands most probably came in the form of gifts, fees, and so on. Those of modest means appear to have engaged in opportunistic hunting, as is suggested by the recurrent discoveries of immature magpies and ravens or other unearthed birds. However, the stag remained the most abundant species, following the hare and, on interesting occasions, boar (Lepetz 1996). This suggests that peasant hunting was not limited to simple captures made in the fields.

The hunt of certain forms of large game appears to have depended on aristocratic preference. As Patrice Méniel has proposed, in the Gallic period, certain kinds of hunts (for boar, bear, and wolf) were reserved for elites, being the only individuals who had the means to undertake such activities (2002, pp. 223–230). In this period, Germanic cultural influence and the necessity of proving one's value, as much in the hunt as in war, may have motivated the progressive appropriation (or at least reinforced control) of the great forest spaces that were from then on dedicated to the hunt of large game (on warriors, see Sarti, Chapter 12, this volume). Bears and aurochs thus became the preferred prey of the high aristocracy and they remained so until the end of the Carolingian period (Hennebicque 1980). A relic of a probable bear hunt was found on the site of Giberville, in lower Normandy, and is thus dated to the sixth to seventh century. It takes the form of a tibia fragment, which bears the marks caused by dogs' teeth: these marks allow us to suppose the presence of flesh on the bone when it was discarded. In the absence of bears and elk, elites favored a species that was very combative, the boar, which is attested in the numerically higher presence of this species in seigneurial milieux. This wild mammal is most prevalent in the bone samples of Giberville, departing from the rule in which the stag prevailed among all of the other game (Saint-Jores and Hincker 2001).

Among wild birds, the corvidae (crow family) stands out above all species in a peasant milieu. As to the mallard, it remained a choice form of game in all milieux combined. However, it remains a challenge to distinguish between wild and domestic animals—a topic that will be debated further as more research is dedicated to understanding the early medieval farmyard.

Lastly, it is important to count aquatic species among the wild fauna that were hunted: the coasts and the waterways furnished shellfish and fish. Among the products of fishing, sturgeon remained a marker of elite milieux, as is attested by its recurrent presence in the trash pits of seigneurial and ecclesiastical sites throughout the early Middle Ages. They are found notably in the Merovingian monastic context of Wandignies-Hamage (Nord). This large species was rare and therefore appears to have been monopolized by the powerful, who apparently acquired them via donations, fees, purchases, or preemptive rights. Today, the data published regarding the activity of fisheries practiced in northern France concern mainly early Merovingian settlements (fifth to sixth century) and sites relatively far from the coast. Thus, one may cite two rural establishments at Vignely (Seine-et-Marne) (Bertin et al. 2003) and Bresle (Oise) (Clavel 2013), as well as the urban sector of the site of the Metz amphitheater (Moselle) (Clavel and Lepetz 2014). This first corpus indicates that the attendant species consumed remained closely linked to those found in nearby waters: fishing was focused first on the freshwater fish and the migratory species available near the sites concerned. Furthermore, even though the fish's flesh was clearly being used as food, it appears to have been only a supplementary resource, at least in a rural context. In the urban area of Metz, recourse to aquatic resources appears to have been more intensive than at rural sites such as Vignely or Bresle. Finally, it is important to note that Metz benefited from a supply of saltwater fish, attested by some remains of mackerel, black sea bream, and brill (*Scophthalmus rhombus*). These species encouraged food conservation, which made it possible to transport these foodstuffs to the interior of territories, and they likely reached Metz in this form. During the early Middle Ages, the consumption of saltwater shellfish was exceptional, and when we find traces of such usages, it is considered an indicator of privileged social status.

To close this "bestiary" section dedicated to wild species, we should observe that exotic animals, attested only rarely during the Gallo-Roman period (Lepetz and Yvinec 2002), disappeared from bone assemblages during the Merovingian period. Among the animals whose introduction and maintenance depended on human agency, only the peacock can perhaps be cited, even when this bird was profoundly integrated into the domestic sphere. As for fallow deer, its isolated subsistence in the first part of the early Middle Ages remains uncertain: for now, the osteological evidence only firmly connects its presence with the Carolingian period.

GAME AND THE STATUS OF CONSUMERS OF GAME

All archaeozoologists who have explored this question (among others Yvinec 1993b; Borvon 2012; and Putelat et al. 2016) recognize the evident connection between the status of inhabitants and the quantity of game they consumed. This connection is also detectable from the beginning of the early Middle Ages. Access to varied and quality meat products was conspicuous consumption: it remained a sign of opulence during the Merovingian period, as it had been in other times. In fact, the proportion of game uncovered on seigneurial sites appears to have been five times more common than game found on more humble rural sites, the number varying between 3 and 10 percent of the remains found. The elites not only devoted themselves to the hunt of large game but also, probably, orchestrated its consumption, thus adapting these practices into attributes of localized power.

Among the large wild mammals, the lay aristocracy preferred to consume the boar, an animal apparently valorized in the hierarchy of game for the qualities that its pursuit required. However, if one reasons on the basis of the number or mass of remains collected, stag meat remained the most abundant foodstuff on Merovingian tables. Finally, the hare appears to have been the second best represented wild species, but only in terms of the number of remains rather than by mass (which would favor wild boar).

To the extent that current studies of sites permit us to judge, those connected with ecclesiastical milieux only consumed a small amount of game. Thus, during the early phases of the settlement of the female monastery of Wandignies-Hamage, the consumption of game included some wild birds, representing about 0.44 percent of the bird remains (Yvinec 1996). More generally, the early medieval ecclesiastical sphere preferred hare, probably because it had fewer symbolic connotations than the large mammals. Along the same lines, the level of representation of the stag, the second form of game known in these milieux, remained among the lowest of the different centers of consumption. Finally, the boar remained rare at ecclesiastical sites, almost absent in fact, no doubt because of its ferocity and its associations with the secular aristocratic pasttime of hunting.

As for the exceptional Merovingian sites with an urban character, the bone samples that derive from such locations do not provide more than very small proportions of game, somewhere between 0 and 1 percent of the remains found. The port of Quentovic, of which many quarters have recently been the object of excavation (Oueslati 2012), is emblematic in this sense. The provision of meat has proved to be very homogeneous in this area and does not include more than a very small proportion of wild fauna, between 0 and 0.3 percent of the remains. These numbers seem even smaller given the fact that Quentovic's location on an estuary and on the coast was favorable to hunting birds.

Except for some elite sites, the contribution of wild fauna to the meat diet of Merovingians remained negligible, if not nearly nonexistent. This reality is even more acutely evident, moreover, if one attempts to make an indirect estimate of the mass of meat on the basis of the weight of the bone samples that have been collected. From this perspective, there was no major rupture between Antiquity and the Merovingian period. Such a conclusion might also help relativize the hypothesis according to which human pressure on the environment is alleged to have occurred during the early Middle Ages. Nonetheless, sociocultural factors should not be neglected in this matter because they could have also contributed to considerably limiting recourse to meat components of the diet. Finally, as observed earlier in this chapter, let us recall that the presence of some species, including peacocks, sturgeon, bears, and aurochs, could signal a privileged settlement.

Unwanted Guests at the Table and Synanthropes

Among commensal species, the black rat (*Rattus rattus*) merits our attention given its eminent role in propagation of the plague (Audoin-Rouzeau 2003; McCormick 2003).

This pest brought diseases into the domestic sphere that could be transmitted from animals to humans (zoonoses)—diseases that were already present in the wild and that could then devolve into an epidemic. Present during the early and late Roman Empire, it appears that populations of rodents subsequently decreased, although this trend is difficult to confirm since the presence of black rats is difficult to detect, especially in rural contexts, in the absence of systematic fine-sieving on archaeological sites (Audoin-Rouzeau and Vigne 1997). This decrease mirrored the severe decline of cities, on the one hand, and, on the other hand, the abandonment, in a rural context, of stone construction associated with cellars and latrines, which were without a doubt more favorable to the propagation of rats. The pronounced ruralization of society could have contributed to the absence of epidemic outbreaks in the north of France, at least during the second part of the early Middle Ages (but see Biraben and Le Goff 1969). In a rural environment, the propagation of disease was more quickly checked, and still more so when the networks of exchange were little developed. Frédérique Audoin-Rouzeau (2003) has convincingly demonstrated the implication of growing numbers of sellers of cloth, hats, shoes, and rags for the rise of modern plague since these items provided prime vectors for the plague in that they transported the fleas of infected rats.

The cat, the natural predator of rats, owes probably part of its success as a species to its prey, which allowed it to expand rapidly across even the most remote countryside (Bobis 1990; Lepetz and Yvinec 2002). The rapid expansion of the cat population began in the course of the fourth and fifth centuries, the remains of cats being documented at one of every three sites studied. The expansion of this population thereafter continued throughout the early Middle Ages at varied rates. It was so large that, by the end of the Merovingian period, at least one in two rural sites excavated bears witness to the presence of cats. It was no different at any of the relatively large settlements.

The strong diffusion of cats must have limited the population of wild rodents, in general, and black rats, in particular, in the immediate environment of rural homes. In this sense, this animal ensured the existence of a sort of "sanitary barrier." However, the role of the cat in a period of outbreak is equally important since the cat was regularly in contact with wild rodents. Cats were potentially an agent of transmission between rats and their counterparts colonizing a particular habitat. In this sense, rats remained an important link in a complex chain of interactions, in the midst of which cats could intervene. Beyond feline implication in the transport of contaminated fleas, cats could equally contract the plague, including its pneumonic form. Thus, the animal was itself a vector of disease and was capable thereby of infecting humans (Nelson, Madon, and Tilzer 1986), notably by airborne transmission (Rust et al. 1971).

During the early Middle Ages, the dog remained a precious helper in multiple domains (hunting, pastoral activities, and so on). As to the practice of consuming dog meat, it was abandoned at the beginning of the Gallo-Roman period and was not reestablished in Merovingian custom. However, rare examples of consumption of dog meat can be identified. For example, the site of Bourlon produced an interesting witness to such practice: the femur of a large dog, dating from the eighth century, carries some fine traces of defleshing and disarticulation (Yvinec 2014). Certain cultural traits, reminiscent of pre-Roman heritage or more recent Germanic influences, could perhaps explain localized cases. Occasional examples of the consumption of dog flesh can be found as late as the twentieth century in France, Germany, and Switzerland. However, these practices perhaps responded more to necessity born of specific difficulties (e.g., food shortages, famines) rather than a deeply anchored dietary practice. As Victor Hugo wrote during the siege of Paris in 1870, dogs and cats were frequently on the menu during the food shortages that affected the city (Hugo 1953, p. 87; Taithe 1999, p. 8).

CONCLUSION

The place of animals was incomparably more important in the Merovingian period than in modern society. Animals had considerable economic importance, and human relations with animals were richer and more complex than in present times. On the economic scale, the dominance of bovines, among livestock, owed much to their multifunctional use. The multiple contributions that cows provided during their lifetimes were as important for rural society as the products that resulted after their death. Moreover, toward the end of the period and from the start of the Carolingian period, one notes the growing role of sheep. All of the developments observed here were almost synchronous in large geographical territories. From the beginning of the early Middle Ages, choices were established, or redeployed, regarding the management of cattle, and probably of agrosystems as well, that were applicable on a large territorial and chronological scale.

The disappearance of Gallo-Roman techniques of mass butchery and the break in the chain of the artisanal handling of beef with respect in central places of slaughter were caused by the ruralization of society. From the point of view of the movement of animals and their products over distances, the Merovingian period appears to have brought a halt to these practices with the decline of urban centers in the post-Roman period.

NOTES

1. This chapter has been translated from French by Bonnie Effros, Isabel Moreira, and Jamie Kreiner, to whom the authors give their sincere thanks.
2. Catalogue of the documentation and the digital library of Inrap may be found here: http://dolia.inrap.fr
3. This work was presented in the context of a "Workshop on Late Antiquity," organized by Fabienne Pigière (Pigière, Akeret, and Kühn 2019).

WORKS CITED

Ancient Sources

Magnou-Nortier, É. (1998). "Capitulaire *De Villis et curtis imperialibus* (vers 810–813): texte, traduction et commentaire." *Revue historique* 607 (July–September): 643–690.

Modern Sources

Alexandre-Bidon, D., and Manne, P. (1988). "La vie quotidienne à travers les enluminures carolingiennes, du VIIIe au Xe siècle." In R. Guadagnin (ed.), *Un village au temps de Charlemagne. Moines et paysans de l'abbaye de Saint-Denis du VIIe siècle à l'an Mil. [Catalogue d'exposition] Musée national des arts et traditions populaires, 29 novembre 1988–30 avril 1989* (pp. 340–353). Paris: Editions de la Réunion des Musées Nationaux.

Audoin-Rouzeau, F. (2003). *Les chemins de la peste: Le rat, la puce et l'homme.* Rennes: Presses universitaires de Rennes.

Audoin-Rouzeau, F., and Vigne, J.-D. (1997). "Le rat noir (*Rattus rattus*) en Europe antique et médiévale: les voies du commerce et l'expansion de la peste." *Anthropozoologica* 25/26: 399–404.

Baillif-Ducros, C., and Yvinec, J.-H. (2015). "Le cheval de monte aux VIe-VIIe siècles en Gaule du nord. Croisement des données archéologiques et ostéologiques." *Archéopages* 41: 14–19.

Rodet-Belarbi, I., and Forest, V. (2010). "Les chasses au Moyen Âge: quelques aspects illustrés par l'archéozoologie en France méridionale." *Archéopages: archéologie et société*: 52–59.

Bertin, P., Clavel, B., Dalnoki, O., Mahé, N., and Yvinec, J.-H. (2003). "Une occupation mérovingienne précoce au bord de la Marne. Le site de Vignely, la Noue Fenard (Seine-et-Marne)." In P. Ouzoulias and P. Van Ossel (eds.), *Dioecesis galliarum: document de travail* 6 (pp. 120–178). Paris: Diocesis Galliarum.

Biraben, J.-N., and Le Goff, J. (1969). *La peste dans le haut moyen âge.* Paris: A. Colin.

Bobis, L. (1990). *Contribution à l'histoire du chat dans l'occident médiéval: étude critique des sources.* Thesis. Paris: École nationale de Chartes.

Borvon, A. (2012). *Acquisition des ressources animales, alimentation carnée et distinction sociale en Anjou de la fin du Xe au début du XIIe siècle. Étude archéozoologique du site de Montsoreau (Maine-et-Loire).* Doctoral dissertation. Université Paris I Panthéon-Sorbonne.

Büntgen, U., Myglan, V. S., Ljungqvist, F. C., McCormick, M., Di Cosmo, N., Sigl, M., Jungclaus, J., Wagner, S., Krusic, P. J., Esper, J., Kaplan, J. O., de Vaan, M. A. C., Luterbacher, J., Wacker, L., Tegel, W., & Kirdyanov, A. V. (2016). "Cooling and societal change during the Late Antique Little Ice Age from 536 to around 660 AD." *Nature Geoscience* 9(3): 231–236.

Clavel, B. (2013). "Les restes archéo-ichtyologiques témoins de la dégradation du milieu dulçaquicole dans le nord de la France." In F. Guizard, J. Heude, and C. Beck (eds.), *Eaux de la vie: pour une histoire de la biodiversité des cours d'eau. 13e Rencontres internationales de Liessies. Revue du Nord*, (hors série n°19): 41–55.

Clavel, B., and Lepetz, S. (2014). "La consommation des poissons en France du nord à la période romaine. Marqueur socio-culturel et artefacts taphonomiques." In X. Deru and R. González Villaescusa (eds.), *Consommer dans les campagnes de la Gaule romaine. Actes du Xe congrès de l'Association AGER. Revue du Nord* (hors-série n°21): 93–108.

Clavel, B., and Yvinec, J.-H. (2010). "L'archéozoologie du Moyen Age au début de la période Moderne dans la moitié nord de la France." In J. Chapelot (ed.), *Trente ans d'archéologie médiévale en France. Un bilan pour un avenir. IXe Congrès international de la Société d'archéologie médiévale—Vincennes, 16–18 juin 2006* (pp. 71–87). Caen: Publications du CRAHM.

Devroey, J.-P. (2003). *Économie rurale et société dans l'Europe franque (VIe-IXe siècles). Tome 1: Fondements matériels, échanges et lien social.* Paris: Belin.

Dierkens, A. (2008a). "Grande cuisine romaine à la table des premiers rois mérovingiens: contexte historique et enjeux culturels." In A. Dierkens and L. Plouvier (eds.), *Festins mérovingiens. Mémoires de l'Association Française d'Archéologie Mérovingienne* 17 (pp. 9–21). Brussels: Le livre Timperman.

Dierkens, A. (2008b). "Réflexions sur l'hippophagie au Haut Moyen Âge." In A.-M. Brisebarre, A.-E. Delavigne, and B. Lizet (eds.), *Viandes et sociétés: les consommations ordinaires et extra-ordinaires. Journées scientifiques 27–28 novembre 2008* (p. 12). Paris: Muséum national d'Histoire naturelle.

Dierkens, A., Le Bec, C., and Périn, P. (2008). "Sacrifice animal et offrandes alimentaires en Gaule mérovingienne." In S. Lepetz and W. Van Andringa (eds.), *Archéologie du sacrifice animal en Gaule romaine. Rituels et pratiques alimentaires. Festins mérovingiens* (pp. 279–299). Montagnac: Mergoil.

Duceppe-Lamarre, F., Lepetz, S., and Yvinec, J.-H. (2002). "Caractériser la faune sauvage par l'apport conjoint des os et des textes (Nord de la Gaule, Antiquité et Haut Moyen Âge)." In A. Corvol (ed.), *Forêt et faune. Journée d'Etudes Environnement, Forêt et Société, XVIe–XXe siècle* (pp. 11–24). Cahiers d'Etudes 12. Paris: IHMC-CNRS.

Duerst, J. U. (1931). *Grundlagen der Rinderzucht.* Berlin: Julius Springer.

Dutton, P. (2004). *Charlemagne's Moustache and Other Cultural Clusters of a Dark Age.* New York: Palgrave Macmillan.

Epstein, H. (1955). "Phylogenetic Significance of *spina bifida* in Zebu Cattle." *Indian Journal of Veterinary Science and Animal Husbandry* 25: 313–316.

Frère, S., and Yvinec, J.-H. (2008). "Elevage et alimentation carnée en Île-de-France durant le haut Moyen Âge." In F. Gentili and A. Lefèvre (eds.), *L'habitat rural du haut Moyen Âge. Bilan 2004–2006 des travaux du PCR. Bulletin archéologique du Vexin français et du Val-d'Oise,* 2nd supplément: 11–20.

Gentili F. (2010). " L'organisation spatiale des habitats ruraux du haut Moyen Âge: l'apport des grandes fouilles préventives. Deux exemples franciliens: Serris « Les Ruelles » (Seine-et-Marne) et Villiers-le-Sec (Val-d'Oise)." In J. Chapelot (ed.), *Trente ans d'archéologie médiévale en France. Un bilan pour un avenir. IXe Congrès international de la Société d'archéologie médiévale—Vincennes, 16–18 juin 2006* (pp. 119–131). Caen: Publications du CRAHM.

Gentili, F., and Mahé, N. (1999). *Les Ruelles de Serris (Seine-et-Marne) (77.049.002AH), village du Haut Moyen Age: DFS de sauvetage urgent, du 01/08/97 au 31/10/97.* Paris: AFAN; Saint-Denis: SRAIF.

Gentili F., and Sethian, E. (2012). *L'habitat rural du haut Moyen Âge de Jossigny Pré Chêne (VIe-XIe s.).* Rapport final d'opération. Paris: Inrap/CIF.

Gentili F., and Valais, A. (2007). "Composantes aristocratiques et organisation de l'espace au sein de grands habitats ruraux du haut Moyen Âge." In P. Depreux, F. Bougard, and R. Le Jan (eds.), *Les élites et leurs espaces: mobilité, rayonnement, domination (VIe-XIe s.). Actes de la rencontre organisée par la Mission historique française en Allemagne—Göttingen (Allemagne), 3–5 mars 2005* (pp. 99–134). Turnhout: Brepols.

Grigson, C. (1984). "Bifid Dorsal Spines and Bos indicus? A reply to Stallibrass." *Journal of Archaeological Science* 11(2): 177.

Grigson, C. (1996). "Early Cattle around the Indian Ocean." In J. E. Reade (ed.), *The Indian Ocean in Antiquity* (pp. 41–74). London: Kegan Paul International, British Museum, Columbia University Press.

Guizard-Duchamp, F. (2004). *L'homme et les espaces du sauvage dans le monde franc (V^e-IXe siècles).* Thèse de doctorat d'histoire de l'Université de Lille III—Charles de Gaulle. Paris I: Panthéon-Sorbonne.

Harbeck, M., Seifert, L., Hänsch, S., Wagner, D. M., Birdsell, D., Parise, K. L., Wiechmann, I., Grupe, G., Thomas, A., Keim, P., Zöller, L., Bramanti, B., Riehm, J. M., and Scholz, H. C. (2013). "Yersinia pestis DNA from Skeletal Remains from the 6th Century AD Reveals

Insights into Justinianic Plague." *PLoS Pathogens* 9.5: e1003349. doi:10.1371/journal. ppat.1003349 [Consulted 04.06.2016]

Hennebicque, R. (1980). "Espaces sauvages et chasses royales dans le nord de la Francie, VIIe–IXe siècles." In *Le paysage rural: réalités et représentations. Actes des congrès de la Société des historiens médiévistes de l'enseignement supérieur public, 10e congrès—Lille (France), 1979. Revue du Nord* 62, n° spécial 244: 35–60.

Hincker, V. (2007). "Un habitat aristocratique en Neustrie. Le site du château à Biéville-Beuville (Calvados, Normandie, France)." In L. Verslype (ed.), *Villes et campagnes en Neustrie (IVe-Xe siècles). Sociétés—Économies—Territoire—Christianisation. Actes des XXVe Journées internationales de l'Association française d'Archéologie mérovingiennes (AFAM)—Tournai (Belgique): 17–19 juin 2004* (pp. 175–191). Europe médiévale 8. Montagnac: Monique Mergoil.

Hugo, V. (1953). *Carnets intimes, 1870-1871*, H. Guillemin (ed.). 7th ed. Paris: Gallimard.

Hurard, S. (2011). *Saint-Pathus (Seine-et-Marne) « Les Petits Ormes » (77). Longue durée d'occupation du Néolithique à l'époque moderne. Mutations d'un habitat rural du Bas-Empire à la fin du premier Moyen Age. Rapport final d'opération.* 4 vols. Inrap/CIF/SRA.

Jouanin, G., and Yvinec, J.-H. (2019). "Changes in faunal spectra in northern France during Late Antiquity." *Quaternary International* 499(A): 92–100.

Kreiner, J. (2017). "Pigs in the Flesh and Fisc: An Early Medieval Ecology." *Past and Present* 236: 3–42.

Lamotte, D. (2007). *Malay-le-Grand, Yonne, Rue des Écoles, Rapport de diagnostic.* Inrap GES, Dijon.

Lepetz, S. (1996). *L'animal dans la société gallo-romaine de la France du Nord.* Revue archéologique de Picardie 12. Amiens: Revue archéologique de Picardie.

Lepetz, S., and Yvinec, J.-H. (2002). "Présence d'espèces animales d'origine méditerranéennes en France du nord aux périodes romaine et médiévale: actions anthropiques et mouvements naturels." In A. Gardeisen (ed.), *Mouvements ou déplacements de populations animales en Méditerranée au cours de l'Holocène* (pp. 33–42). BAR, International Series 1017. Oxford: British Archaeological Reports.

Liarsou, A. (2013). "Le canard colvert (Anas platyrhynchos L.): une espèce domestique dont l'homme a souhaité conserver le caractère sauvage ?" Document de travail. En cours d'actualisation. https://hal.archives-ouvertes.fr/halshs-00801583/[Consulted 06.05.2016]

Marcy, T. (2013). *Canal Seine-Nord Europe, fouille 33–Nord-Pas-de-Calais, Pas-de-Calais, Bourlon. Une implantation rurale du haut Moyen-Age au lieu-dit « La Vallée de Marquion ».* Croix-Moligneaux: Rapport final d'opération, Inrap/Canal Seine-Nord Europe.

Marcy, T. (forthcoming). *Fontaine Notre-Dame « le petit Fontaine ».* Rapport final d'opération de fouille, Inrap, Service regional de l'archéologie du Nord—Pas-de-Calais, Lille.

McCormick, M. (2003). "Rats, Communications, and Plague: Towards an Ecological History." *Journal of Interdisciplinary History* 34(1): 1–25.

Méniel, P. (2002). "La chasse en Gaule, une activité aristocratique? L'aristocratie celte à la fin de l'Âge du Fer." Unpublished conference paper June 1999, Glux-en-Glenne, France. Collection Bribracte 5. https://halshs.archives-ouvertes.fr/halshs-00459279 [Consulted 01.17.2017].

Nelson, B. C., Madon, M. B., and Tilzer, A. (1986). "The Complexities at the Interface among Domestic/Wild Rodents, Fleas, Pets, and Man in Urban Plague Ecology in Los Angeles, County, California." In T. P. Salmon (ed.), *Proceedings of the Twelfth Vertebrate Pest Conference—San Diego (California): March 4-6 1986* (pp. 88–96). Davis: University of California.

Nissen Jaubert, A. (2006). "Le haut Moyen Age." In A. Ferdière, F. Malrain, V. Matterne, P. Méniel, A. Nissen Jaubert, and B. Pradat (eds.), *Histoire de l'Agriculture en Gaule: 500 av. J.-C.—1000 apr. J.-C.* (pp. 141–196). Paris: Éditions Errance.

Oueslati, T. (2012). "III.1.8. L'étude archéozoologique." In D. Cense-Bacquet (ed.), *La Calotterie (62), Chemin de Visemarais les "Prés à l'Eau" (AC 3P), "Le Visemarais est" (AC 40). Rapport final d'opération* (vol. 2, pp. 220–251). Lille: Archéopole/Service régional de l'archéologie du Nord-Pas-de-Calais.

Pigière, F., Akeret, O., and Kühn, M. (2019). "Editorial: Food production and land use at the transition from Antiquity to the Middle Ages in the Roman world." *Quaternary International* 499: 1–2.

Putelat, O. (2005). "Le bestiaire polycère." *Revue de Paléobiologie* 10: 293–301.

Putelat, O., Logel, T., Bocherens, H., Geigl, E.-M., De Lima Guimaraes, S., and Metz, B. (2016). "Une chasse aristocratique dans le Ried Centre-Alsace au premier Moyen Âge. L'apport de l'archéozoologie à la connaissance du site d'Ostheim 'Birgelsgaerten' (Haut-Rhin, France)." In E. Peytremann (ed.), *Des fleuves et des hommes à l'époque mérovingienne. Territoire fluviale et société au premier Moyen Âge (V^e-XIIe siècle). Actes des 33e Journées internationales d'Archéologie mérovingiennes—Strasbourg (Belgique): 28–30 septembre 2012* (pp. 255–270). Dijon: Revue Archéologique de l'Est.

Rust, J. H., Cavanaugh, D. C., O'Shita, R., and Marshall, J. D. (1971). "The Role of Domestic Animals in the Epidemiology of Plague. I. Experimental Infestion of Dogs and Cats." *Journal of Infectious Disease* 124(5): 522–526.

Saint-Jores (de), J.-X., and Hincker, V. (2001). "Les habitats mérovingiens et carolingiens de la Delle sur le Marais à Giberville (Calvados)." *Archéologie médiévale* 30–31: 1–38.

Séguier, J.-M., Cammas, C., and van Ossel, P. (1997). *Compans (Seine-et-Marne), l'Ouest du Parc (lots Spicers et Paneurolog), sauvetage urgent 1997*, Document Final de Synthèse, Saint-Denis, 1997.

Seigne, J., et al. (2007). "La fouille du site du 'Château', site 3." In H. Galinié (ed.), *Tours antique et médiéval: lieux de vie, temps de la ville. 40 ans d'archéologie urbaine* (p. 73). Tours: FERACF.

Taithe, B. (1999). *Defeated Flesh: Medicine, Welfare, and Warfare in the Making of Modern France*. Lanham: Rowman & Littlefield Publishers, Inc.

Vigne, J.-D. (1993). "Domestication ou appropriation pour la chasse: histoire d'un choix socio-culturel depuis le Néolithique. L'exemple des cerfs (Cervus)." In J. Desse, and F. Audoin-Rouzeau (eds.), *Exploitation des animaux sauvages à travers le temps*. Antibes: APDCA.

Yvinec, J.-H. (1993a). *Étude archéozoologique du site du Bussy-Saint-Georges "Les Dix-Huit Arpentes,"* Laboratoire d'archéozoologie de Compiègne, CRAVO-URA 1415.

Yvinec, J.-H. (1993b). "La part du gibier dans l'alimentation du haut Moyen Âge" In J. Desse and F. Audoin-Rouzeau (eds.), *Exploitation des animaux sauvages à travers le temps. Actes des XIIIe Rencontres internationales d'archéologie et d'histoire d'Antibes/IVe Colloque international de l'Homme et l'Animal—Antibes (France): 15–17 octobre 1992* (pp. 491–504). Juan-les-Pins: Éditions APDCA.

Yvinec, J.-H. (1996). "Eléments de synthèse sur l'alimentation carnée durant le haut Moyen Âge dans le Douaisis." In M. Colardelle (ed.), *L'homme et la nature au Moyen Âge. Actes du Ve Congrès International d'Archéologie Médiévale—Grenoble (France): 6–9 octobre 1993* (pp. 30–35). Paris: Éditions Errance.

Yvinec, J.-H. (1997). "Étude archéozoologique du site de la place des Hallettes à Compiègne (Oise) du haut Moyen Âge au XIIe s." In M. Petijean (ed.), *Fouilles de sauvetage sous la place du Marché à Compiègne (Oise), 1991/1993. L'évolution urbaine de l'aire palatiale du Haut*

Moyen Âge aux marchés médiéval et moderne. Revue archéologique de Picardie n° spécial 13: 171–210.

Yvinec, J.-H. (2003). "La faune." In F. David and A. Valais, "Un habitat occupé du VIIᵉ au XIIᵉ siècle: Les Cinq Chemins à Bauné (Maine-et-Loire)." *Archéologie médiévale* 33: 63–90.

Yvinec, J.-H. (2009). "Le loup, une espèce en ombre chinoise: point de vue archéozoologique." In F. Guizard-Duchamp (ed.), *Le loup en Europe du Moyen âge à nos jours. Actes du Colloque interdisciplinaire co-organisé par le Centre d'étude et de recherche en histoire culturelle (CERHIC-Reims) et le Centre de recherche Histoire, civilisations et cultures des pays du monde occidental (CRHICC-Valenciennes)—Reims (France): 9–10 novembre 2006* (pp. 109–118). Valenciennes: Calhiste/Presses universitaires de Valenciennes.

Yvinec, J.-H. (2014). "Étude archéozoologique." In T. Marcy (ed.), *Canal Seine-Nord Europe, fouille 33. Une implantation rurale du haut Moyen-Âge au lieu-dit "La Vallée de Marquion"* 2 (pp. 187–218). Croix-Moligneaux: Inrap.

PART VII

ECONOMIES, EXCHANGE, AND PRODUCTION

CHAPTER 34

MARITIME AND RIVER
TRADERS, LANDING
PLACES, AND EMPORIA
PORTS IN THE
MEROVINGIAN PERIOD
IN AND AROUND THE
LOW COUNTRIES

DRIES TYS

THROUGHOUT human history, communities inhabiting liminal coastal areas have been connected by the sea, which acted not so much as a barrier but rather as a facilitator of exchanges of all kinds (migrations, trade, and so on). Coastal regions and seascapes, therefore, act as arenas of contact, dialogue, and transition, as well as offering settings for conflict and the concentration of power. The North Sea coasts were connected in networks of trade and communication from at least the late Iron Age, if not earlier (Jöns et al. 2013). These coastal communities thus developed connections with one another, with some locations becoming ports and trade hubs by which goods and services were distributed throughout trading networks. Access to products and ideas from other regions gave these coastal societies their special character (Loveluck and Tys 2006; Jervis 2016; IJssenagger 2017). To understand the consequent rise, and dynamics of coastal trade and landing places between the sixth and eighth centuries, we must discuss how these free, coastal societies were involved in regional, interregional, or long-distance trade networks, as well as the political, social, and economic strategies of the people behind these networks (Hillerdal 2010; Loveluck 2013, pp. 9–14; Theuws and Bouwmeester 2013).

Interregional and long-distance trade in the North Sea area seems to have been continuous, but it apparently intensified from the late seventh century onward. The appearance of the sceatta, a late-seventh to mid-eighth-century silver penny that is found along the North Sea coasts of eastern England, Denmark, the Netherlands, and Belgium, shows that a shared silver currency was needed and that trade for profit had grown in importance. In the same period, more organized transshipment ports appeared in the coastal regions, namely, the so-called emporia (Fig. 34.1). We must use this term carefully since it was only found in two written sources, namely, the Venerable Bede's *Ecclesiastical History* in the early eighth century, which described Lundenwic as an emporium; and the *Annales Bertiniani* in the ninth century, in which only Quentovic and Dorestad are identified as emporia (Bede II.3; Nelson 1991; Lebecq 1992, p. 13).[1] This documentary lacuna does not preclude Lundenwic, Quentovic, and certainly Dorestad from being exceptional ports of trade. However, from a strict historical point of view, emporia are not a single category of site. Instead there was a wide range of larger or smaller ports

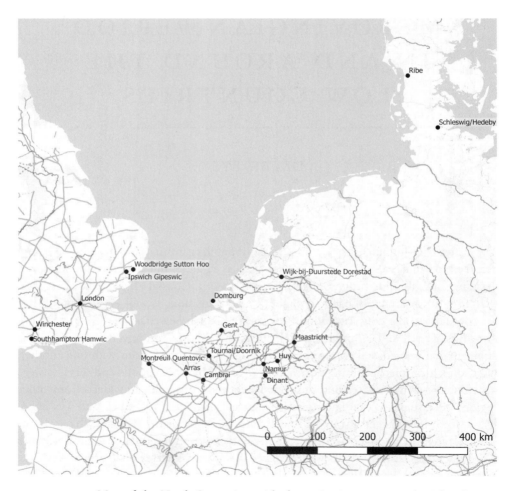

FIGURE 34.1. Map of the North Sea region with the main sites mentioned in the chapter, including the well-known ports of trade. In broader gray: the main Roman roads; in thinner and darker gray: the main rivers. Map produced by Dries Tys and Sarah Dalle.

of trade and trade-involved rural sites, each with its own contextual significance and development (Loveluck 2013; Deckers 2015; Costen and Costen 2016; Naylor 2016; Kalmring 2016). Since the 1990s, researchers have indeed become aware of a large number of landing places and exchange sites, including larger ports, which existed as a part of networks, each with its own physical features and position in the landscape (Theuws 2004, 2012; Loveluck and Tys 2006; Loveluck 2013). The early medieval coastal networks of exchange were much more complex and diverse than the simple emporium network model that was once advocated by connecting the major archaeological sites along the North Sea coast (Hodges 1982, 2012).[2]

In this chapter, I discuss the role of coastal and river societies in the early medieval economy and trade, and the character of the networks and exchanges in the centuries before the expansion of emporia in the second quarter of the eighth century. I also address the importance of bottom-up agency for the development of trade and exchange networks (see Theuws, Chapter 38, this volume), since coastal and riverine dwellers seem to have possessed some form of free status and large degrees of autonomy. This resulted from the specific environmental conditions of the landscapes in which they dwelled and the distance of those coastal areas from political centers. Nonetheless, this situation does not suggest that social stratification did not exist since some coastal dwellers had more wealth and social status than others.

The geographical focus of this chapter is the wide estuarine region of the Low Countries, between coastal Flanders in the south and Friesland in the north. This delta was, and still is, an intrinsic zone of exchange and communication. Its "hinterlands" are vast: reaching up to the Alps in the southeast and the region of Nancy and Mainz in the southwest, including areas where wine was produced, as well as timber, iron ore, ceramics, and many other commodities (see Verhulst 2002, p. 55). Via the Meuse and Moselle, connections could be made to the southern Frankish and Mediterranean exchange networks, while in the east the Danube connection was within reach (Kosian, Weerts, van Lanen, and Abrahamse 2013; Kosian, van Lanen, and Weerts 2016).[3] The delta lies opposite the coast of England, specifically the Thames estuary, which was not difficult to reach. With coastal navigation, Denmark and the rest of Scandinavia lay within reach of travelers and merchants.[4] The early medieval environment of the estuarine delta of the Low Countries was a moderately open landscape of tidal wetlands (close to the sea), peat bogs, and marsh and shrub wetlands behind the tidal areas and rivers (the Schelde, Maas, and Rhine being the most important).

According to the *Vita Eligii* in the mid-seventh to early eighth century, the delta was inhabited by "the Flemish" (or the inhabitants of the "watery lands," the saltmarshes in present coastal Belgium), the "Antwerpians" (or the inhabitants of lowlands on both sides of the River Schelde), the Frisians (probably a reapplied protohistoric name for the inhabitants of the wetlands in the north of the present Netherlands), the Suevi (or the "Sea-people" alongside the mouths of rivers in present Zeeland and Holland), and "other barbarians coming from the seacoast."[5] The identity of the early medieval population in the delta was clearly determined by the specific environment and topography of the area, and its location at the edge of the sea fostered connectivity with other coastal people alongside the North Sea rim. Missionaries had a hard time bringing these coastal dwellers closer to the Christian faith and, at a minimum, the actual conversion of the coastal areas lasted throughout the eighth century.

Historians and archaeologists have considered the dwellers from these coastal wetlands from Flanders to Friesland as wealthy "free peasant traders" or "marchands-paysans," rather than an aristocracy (Lebecq 1983, 1992; Schmid 1991; Heidinga 1997, pp. 31–32). This brings us to the topic of social property relations and trade.

The Bias of the Written Sources: Early Medieval Social Property Relations and Peasant Agency

The Merovingian period was for a long time dismissed as autarkic, in comparison with the apparently successful Roman villa-economy and the Carolingian manorial system (Pirenne 1923, 1925; see Effros 2017 on this debate). These views were a remarkable combination of nineteenth-century cultural historical reasoning on the one hand and liberal idealism on the other hand (Pirenne 1923). The legacy of this view has been hugely influential (Effros 2017). The rise of new landed aristocracies and more articulated social hierarchies related to the development of the manorial system were especially important in the development of a contextual framework to explain the rise and development of the larger ports of trade (formerly known as *emporia*), and were understood as a token of the success of the Carolingian renaissance (Hodges 1982, 2012, 2017; Halsall 1992, 2012; see also Loveluck 2013, p. 4). The social and political developments of the seventh and eighth centuries that led to new aristocracies, hierarchies, and governance were seen more specifically as the context for the development and control of long-distance trade for the purposes of acquiring luxury goods for gift exchange among new elites (Hodges 1982). The so-called emporia, as the most important ports of trade, were even seen as sites designed by royal architects for this elite-controlled long-distance trade (Hodges 2000; see Verhaeghe 2005, p. 270; Effros 2017, p. 197). The appearance of silver coinage (sceattas) in the same period was also used to explain these developments, since this process of monetization coincided with the payment in rents that were now due on several of the new larger landholdings from the end of the seventh century (Hodges 2017). The development of trade in the North Sea world was thus framed in a teleological discourse with Pirenne's model of the development of the liberal merchant towns of the later Middle Ages (Verhulst 1999; Wickham 2005, pp. 881–822).

However, we must be careful when discussing the importance of "elites" in the seventh and eighth centuries in western Europe. One of the biases is that there is a clear difference between what archaeologists and historians mean by elites. In archaeology, portable wealth and luxuries and the possession of a larger hall are often equated with the presence of elites, whereas in history, the aristocratization of society starts with the development of larger estates and properties leading to a manorial society. However, it is impossible to connect both concepts and prove that someone with portable wealth or a bead workshop on his or her farm is a larger landowner. Nor can the development of social differentiation from an archaeological point of view be connected to changing property relations or the fact that a peasant subsistence economy was evolving into a manorial economy. The visibility of manorial landowning in the documentary record is due to the emergence of ecclesiastical and government institutions that started to keep archival records to manage these landholdings, such as the *polypticha* (polyptychs). By comparison, the smaller estates and especially the holdings of free "peasant" landholders were always far less visible, since they only appeared in the documentary record when one of their holdings was donated to a monastery or similar institution.

The presence and impact of the early medieval allodial farmers only become fully visible via more complex reconstructions of property relations and detailed landscape analysis (Verhulst 1999; see also Bonassie 1991; Tys 2003, 2004; Wilkin 2010; Oosthuizen 2017). In coastal Flanders, a detailed retrogressive analysis of the landscape shows that the populations of these salt marshes, with terp-focused settlement hierarchies, were free proprietors probably from at least the seventh century onward (Tys 2003, pp. 266–273; Tys 2004). They may have owed some dues to regional lords, whether counts or kings, but with the exception of these obligations there is no evidence that they came under any other significant sociopolitical control. In the coastal areas of the Netherlands, including Friesland, personal freedom and free property rights (thus, technically speaking, of the "peasantry") dominated throughout the early Middle Ages. They were only threatened under the Carolingians, but without too much success (the problem of the so-called Koningsvrijen or "King's freemen") (Heidinga 1997, p. 23; Hoppenbrouwers 2001, pp. 42–43; Wickham 2005, p. 499). This observation does not contradict per se the presence of some social stratification, but allodial landholdings seem to have prevailed. Before the later Middle Ages, when farmers became tenants producing for larger landowners, there was no significant surplus extraction system or manorial development in Friesland or Holland, (Mostert 2009, p. 181). A similar situation may be recognized in northern Friesland, on the edge of northern Germany and southern Denmark, where people maintained their independence from landlords as allodial peasantry until the second half the sixteenth century (Meier 2013, p. 96). This was the case notwithstanding the fact that leading families with more wealth and status were present (Meier 2013). It is not surprising that the saltmarshes, peat bogs, and river wetlands of (early) medieval Friesland, Holland, Zeeland, and Flanders were most often used under common right (Tys 2003, p. 47; see Oosthuizen 2017 for the situation in the East-Anglian Fenlands).[6] This is of great importance for the social and economic strategies of free farming communities since commons provide negotiated opportunities for profitable economic activities such as sheep herding or reed production without the need to develop private properties (De Keyser and van Onacker 2016).

Allodial landownership in the Low Countries was much more frequent and widespread than what a literal reading of the contemporary texts would suggest (see Theuws, Chapter 38, this volume; Verhulst 2002; Loveluck 2013).[7] Alfons Dopsch had already argued that the archetypical large estates (*les grands domaines*) were not able to meet their own demands and that there was much more freedom of movement and room for surplus production, consumption, and exchange than in the manorial paradigm current in his time (1937, pp. 322–324, 329–334).[8] Historians such as Alexis Wilkin and Jean-Pierre Devroey see a plurality of "exploitation models" and social property relations in the early medieval southern North Sea region. All kinds of estates, free and unfree, were connected in different networks (Wilkin and Devroey 2012, pp. 255–260).

The longstanding presence of early medieval free landholdings related to the absence of surplus-extraction mechanisms and the presence of wealth and imports in the coastal areas tell us that we must be careful about generalizing the importance of manorial developments for the development of trade. Early medieval northwestern Europe was fragmented into a tapestry of territories, with microregional modes of production. Inside the borders of the former Roman Empire, economic and social agency could only be bottom-up and had to be negotiated (Wickham 2005, pp. 1–14; Devroey 2006; Banaji 2009; Effros 2017; see also Theuws, Chapter 38, and Fleming, Chapter 17, this volume).[9] No ruling class or "elite" had the means by which to impose unilateral decisions about production, consumption, distribution of wealth, ceremonies, or even religion for that matter, until at least the late eighth century, if not later (Innes 2005).

The free "peasantry" was, as suggested, not a homogeneous category: some had more or less land, or more or less wealth, and more or fewer slaves to help them with their landholdings and/or productive activities. It is important to understand that production for subsistence is not contradictory to strategies aimed at surplus production and sale and market integration; the distinction is that the profit motive was not the leading reproduction strategy (Brenner 2001; De Keyser and van Onacker 2016). For the early Middle Ages as well as afterward, it has become increasingly evident that free landholders were involved in interlocked regional and interregional exchange networks in which imports were exchanged for marketable commodities they produced themselves (Loveluck 2013; see Theuws, Chapter 38, this volume; De Keyser and van Onacker 2016). The archaeology of coastal settlements from Friesland to Flanders seems to confirm this.

The Bias of the Material Data: (In)Alienable Luxuries and Central Places

For some time, archaeology has confirmed the role of elites as the main promoters of social change, an idea that was promoted first by historians. They did so by relating luxury metalwork and imports to the presence of elites, even magnates.[10] The emporia were likewise interpreted initially as centers of elite gift exchange where aristocrats controlled the social and political distribution of prestigious items (see especially Hodges 1982, 2012; Hill 2001). These approaches fit very well in the processual paradigm of the 1970s and

1980s; they were heavily influenced by models borrowed from social anthropology on the importance of gift exchange for social reproduction (see Bazelmans 2003, 2009; Loveluck 2013). A recent example of this is Johan Nicolay's consideration of the access of Frisian terp dwellers to high-value materials, such as golden coins or tremisses, sceattas, and unique ornamented objects like the Wijnaldum Fibula. Nicolay interprets these as indicators of the development of horizontal networks between "leaders" and vertical networks between the leaders and their followers or clients (2017, p. 75). Nicolay and other authors have related high-status objects found in Friesland to the presence of political power from tribal (Iron Age) kings in Friesland, comparable to actors such as Redwald at Sutton Hoo and Scandinavian chiefs (not kings) (Nicolay 2003, 2014, 2017; Bazelmans 2003, 2009; Dijkstra and De Koning 2017). At Sutton Hoo, the king was buried with high-status objects relating to Scandinavia (weaponry), the Frankish world (Merovingian tremissi), as well as the eastern Mediterranean world (silver bowls), which testify to European maritime communications and connectivity.[11]

There are, however, some archaeological biases and interpretative problems with making a direct link between luxuries and power. The first problem is that many Frisian terp sites were excavated in the nineteenth century, when a large number of terp sites were leveled in a relatively careful way in search of rich organic deposits for use in improving the soil quality of Dutch arable fields (Nicolay 2003). In the process, a multitude of sixth- and (early) seventh-century artifacts from middens, production contexts, ritual contexts, and burial grounds were unearthed. However, most of the objects that were retrieved in the nineteenth and early twentieth centuries were chosen because of their attraction as luxury goods and pottery, whereas other items were ignored. This led to an overrepresentation of glass beads, gold, silver, and copper alloy artifacts, and a concurrent undercounting of bulk wares and commodities (on beads and garnets, see Pion et al., Chapter 36, this volume). Because of the rudimentary documentation and antiquarian approaches of those scholars, it is not possible to ascertain the actual activities, such as trade, craftsmanship, and ritual or ceremonial activities, of the Frisian terps. This skewing gives sites like Hogebeintum and Weinaldum the character of a (micro) regional central place (Nicolay 2003). (Fig. 34.2) The sixth- and seventh-century artifacts on more recently excavated terp sites indicate how strong links developed between the terp settlements of the coastal Netherlands and eastern England, with communities in both regions using similar pottery, brooches, and combs (Hamerow, Hollevoet, and Vince 1994; Deckers and Tys 2012, pp. 117–123; Soulat, Bocquet-Liénard, Savary, and Hincker 2012). By the early sixth century, the Frisian terp settlements were an integral part of the coastal communities on both sides of the North Sea and the Channel.

These observations lead us to the second issue, namely, that gift exchange of inalienable luxuries for social reproduction is not contradictory to short-term market transactions for profit by allodial landholders at ceremonial sites and gatherings (see Theuws 2004; Kalmring 2016; Theuws, Chapter 38, this volume,). The cultural biographies and trajectories of status-related luxuries are far more complex than suggested by the assumption that they were distributed in a top-down fashion. Research by Frans Theuws and his students has convincingly shown how artifacts could change from the sphere of long-term exchange to short-term exchange, and vice versa (Kars 2014;

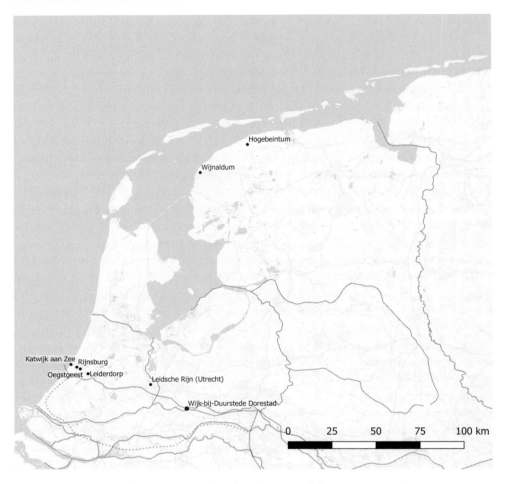

FIGURE 34.2. Map of the Netherlands with indication of the river sites and Frisian terp sites mentioned in the chapter. In broader gray: the main Roman roads; in thinner and darker gray: the main rivers. Map produced by Dries Tys and Sarah Dalle.

Tys 2018; see Theuws, Chapter 38, this volume). Exchange of both alienable and inalienable artifacts occurred in (cult-related) central places, such as the Scandinavian great hall complexes, along with ritual components, as at Lejre, Tissø, or Uppåkra (Vestergaard 1991; Jørgensen 2003, 2009).

The most important central places, where ceremonies, social reproduction, and trade were combined in the Low Countries' river delta, were the Merovingian religious centers on the Meuse River, such as the sixth- to eighth-century episcopal center at Maastricht, where no fewer than 12 *monetarii* (moneyers) produced golden tremissi between the sixth and late seventh century (Dijkman 1994; Theuws 2004) (Fig. 34.1). The archaeology of the site showed the presence of important organic deposits and "dark earth," which can probably be related to artisanal production of beads, combs, and pottery, and regional and interregional trade in the sixth and seventh centuries (Dijkman and Ervynck 1998).[12] Similar sites include Huy and Namur south of Maastricht. In Huy, a sixth- and seventh-century central place with twelve *monetarii*, trade and craft work-shops developed in relation to a very early church (*terminus ante quem* AD 634) (Péters and Fontaine-Hodiamont 2005). In Namur, archaeologists found a continuity of cult (Roman *fana*, followed by Merovingian burials and an early church) linked to artisanal production and trade throughout the fifth, sixth, and seventh centuries (Plumier et al. 2005). Both Adriaan Verhulst and Chris Loveluck have stressed the importance of the presence of free specialist craftsmen who sold alienable commodities at these central places for profit at a very early stage (Verhulst 2002, pp. 74–78; Loveluck 2013, pp. 18–19).[13] These early riverine central places were connected with hinterlands as well as other regions, via middlemen who traveled on the rivers and the North Sea in order to move these products through interlocked exchange networks. Other sites that could have acted as central places were the abbeys of Arras, Saint-Omer, and Ghent, and the episco-pal center Tournai, where dark earth and sceatta finds indicate the presence of early medieval crafts and trade around the basilica (Verhulst 1999; Brulet et al. 2004; Op den Velde and Metcalf 2014; Tys 2018) (Fig. 34.2).

Recent archaeological research has proved that Dorestad originated as a mainly secu-lar river-based central place in the time before the famous port and transshipment site (emporium) started to develop there. Not only does Dorestad appear to have been a center of some political significance before the port was developed, but so was a site called De Geer, northwest of the later port (Fig. 34.3). This site existed from at least the second half of the sixth century to the second half the eighth century, although there are also indications of a late-Roman military presence in addition to fifth-century artifacts such as glassware from the German Rhineland (van Doesburg 2010, p. 55; Jansma and van Lanen 2016). The site contained some striking luxuries from the sixth and seventh centuries, such as golden and silver pendants and brooches and an early sixth-century gold hoard, including coins of Justinian and the hacked pieces of a gold bar. Although Jan van Doesburg suggests that these might have come from the graves of an elite center or *curtis* (court), it is remarkable that this assemblage resembles the material culture from the Frisian terp settlements (2010, pp. 54–55). Another important element is the pres-ence of two moneyers of gold tremissi in Dorestad in the seventh century, well before the development of the famous port. The coins associated with Madelinus (630s–640s), coming from Maastricht, are especially well known and have been discovered in France and northwestern Europe (Pol 2010; Kosian, Weerts, van Lanen, and Abrahamse 2013; Kosian, van Lanen, and Weerts 2016). The significance of these tremissi is that, as in Maastricht, Namur, and Huy, these gold coins could have served equally as gifts for social reproduction, politically inspired payments, or larger mercantile transactions (Pol 2010). The dispersion of the Madelinus-associated coins in Gaul, northern Italy, and Catalonia indicates that the central place Dorestad was in a network with the south as much as with the northwest (Kosian et al. 2013; Kosian et al. 2016) (Fig. 34.3).

Dendrochronological research by Esther Jansma and her team reveals that between the second half of the sixth century and the end of the seventh century in Dorestad De

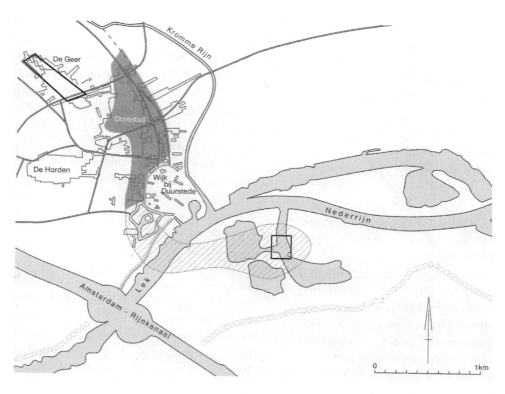

FIGURE 34.3. Expanse of the site Dorestad De Geer compared to the *emporium* or port of Dorestad. From: Van Doesburg 2010, p. 58, fig. 23.

Geer, both local (lower Rhine estuary) and German Rhineland oak timbers were used and traded (Jansma and van Lanen 2016; Jansma et al. 2017). This observation suggests that interregional trade circuits of commodities existed quite early and that these circuits were indeed interlinked with the circuit for the exchange of status-related objects, as argued by Verhulst and Loveluck (Verhulst 2002, pp. 74–78; Loveluck 2013, pp. 18–19). This, and the sites and data discussed earlier, raise the question of the significance of so-called luxuries such as beads or artifacts made of precious metals on sites that were clearly interlinked with trade circuits. Were these luxuries indeed testimonies of local elites? Or were they the result of trade for wealth, albeit in a context in which social negotiation and networking were of marked importance? The discovery of luxuries and imports in several river and coastal sites with a rural, nonelite character shows how dangerous it is to equate access to special artifacts automatically with elite formation. It also tells us that we have to be careful not to ignore the fact that wealth accumulation could be achieved by producing and exchanging bulk wares such as textile materials, raw iron and copper, food products, timbers, antlers, quern stones, or slaves, all of which left far fewer archaeological traces than the trade in luxuries (see Verhulst 2002; Loveluck and Tys 2006; Loveluck 2013).

PRODUCTIVE SITES, COMMODITIES, AND TRADE IN THE COASTAL LANDSCAPES OF THE DELTA REGION

Archaeological management, new academic projects, and a more positive attitude toward metal-detecting amateurs have nuanced our understanding of rural sites on the early medieval coastal plains of the Netherlands, Flanders, and northern France.[14] The relatively good soil conditions (clay, peat, and a high groundwater level) have enabled the survival of organic materials, which help us understand the economy of those sites. Recent archaeology confirms what Chris Loveluck and I wrote in 2006, namely, that the populations of low-lying coastal zones and river delta regions had remarkable access to an abundance of imported goods, so-called luxury items, and apparent material wealth. This was already the case from the sixth century onward (Loveluck and Tys 2006, p. 161).

In the river estuaries of Holland, large-scale excavations have brought to light remarkably wealthy rural sites alongside the branches of the Rhine (Fig. 34.2). The river site Leidsche Rijn (575–eighth century), downstream from Dorestad De Geer, for instance, was clearly a rural site focused on cattle for dairy production, manure, and arable farming. The site was also involved in crafts and trade (Nokkert et al. 2009; on animal husbandry in northern Gaul, see Yvinec and Barme, Chapter 33, this volume). One of the farms contained a workshop for antler working and comb production, as well as indications of amber and glass bead production (including the presence of Italian tesserae) and metal workshops (iron and bronze). On the side of "consumption," materials traded included goods such as saltwater fish, imported pottery, and jewelry (not related to burials) from the sixth and seventh centuries. Trade itself is also suggested by a gold tremissis from Chalon sur Saône and 27 sceattas (Porcupine and Wodan type) from the late seventh and early eighth centuries.[15] Although the sites' heydays were largely parallel to the start of the large port in Dorestad (late seventh century), it is clear that their involvement did not depend on the presence of the famous emporium and that they kept their typical peasant-mixed economies.

A site with a similar profile is Oegstgeest, which was a ripuarian site from the late sixth to the early eighth century, with a mixed economy focused on animal husbandry (and dairy farming), fisheries as well as crafts production (metalworking, comb production, amber processing, and leather shoe production) (De Bruijn 2018). Oegstgeest was clearly involved in the Rhenish as well as the North Sea trade network, with short-term exchange of commodities such as wood from southern Germany (again), with pigs on the import side and craft products, fish and dairy, meat, and leather on the export side (De Bruijn 2018). The dwellers obtained prestigious luxuries, either as an expression of the wealth they obtained or as objects with a long-term exchange value, such as the famous Oegstgeest bowl (first half of the seventh century), which had apparently an apotropaic function at the site (De Bruijn 2018).

Alongside the Oude Rijn estuary, we find several other "Merovingian" sites such as Rijnsburg, Katwijk, and the Merovingian phase of Leiderdorp with similar characteristics:

the mixed rural subsistence economy, the dominance of animal husbandry (cattle), the presence of crafts production (even a workshop of fake Madelinus coins in Katwijk and a bead workshop in Rijnsburg), and the presence of substantial quantities of imported commodities (in the case of Leiderdorp, grain and glass vessels) and sceattas indicating regional as well as intraregional trade (Dijkstra 2011; Theuws 2012; Verhoeven and Dijkstra 2017; Dijkstra and Verhoeven 2018). All of these sites originated in the late sixth or early seventh century, before Dorestad received its port infrastructure, and initially did not depend on the trade dynamics of the later emporium. These sites, as Menno Dijkstra and Arno Verhoeven rightly stress, were not trade settlements as such, although they were integrated in commodity trade and could have acted as microregional landing places (Verhoeven and Dijkstra 2017). They were peasant sites with a typical mixed and balanced farming economy, including the sale of commodities (craft products, fish, products related to cattle husbandry, and so on) to supplement their incomes. This income allowed them to import needed bulk wares such as grains or luxuries. This involvement in regional and interregional exchanges provided wealth and a material culture profile comparable to larger trading sites (Loveluck and Tys 2006; Dijkstra and Verhoeven 2018, pp. 729–730) (Fig. 34.4).

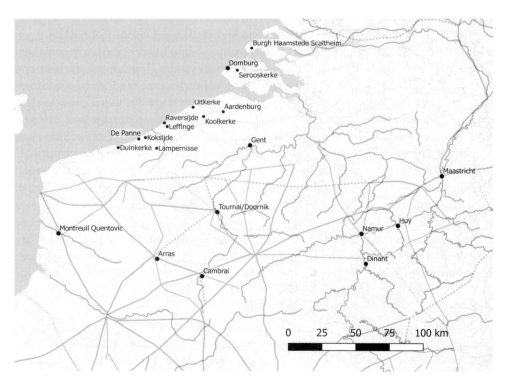

FIGURE 34.4. Map of the Belgian and French coastal plain of Flanders with the main sites mentioned in the chapter. In broader gray: the main Roman roads; in thinner and darker gray: the main rivers. Map produced by Dries Tys and Sarah Dalle.

These characteristics may also be recognized in sixth- to eighth-century sites in the saltmarshes of Zeeland and Flanders, and probably also Friesland (Loveluck and Tys 2006; Verhoeven and Dijkstra 2017) (Fig. 34.4). The saltmarshes of those regions became inhabitable from the fifth (Friesland) and second half of the sixth centuries (Flanders and Zeeland) onward, after a relatively short period of deterioration of environmental conditions in the late-Roman period (Baeteman 2013; Vos 2015). Geological and environmental data suggest that environmental conditions were calm in the tidal area, an observation that is not contradicted by archaeological findings (Tys 2013). The presence of early medieval terp settlements in Friesland is well known. Recent research has confirmed for Flanders and Zeeland the existence of a similar settlement hierarchy of farmsteads on the contemporary ground surfaces of silted-up tidal channel ridges, as well as on small dwelling mounds, such as the site Oude Werf. These consisted of nucleated settlements of multiple households located on communal terp mounds as at Leffinge and Bredene (Tys 2003, pp. 588–598, 2005; Loveluck and Tys 2006; Deckers 2014). The oldest (fifth- and early sixth-century) post-Roman settlements in the coastal wetlands of Flanders and Zeeland are found in the original dune belt and on the Pleistocene edge of the saltmarsh area (Deckers 2010; Dijkstra 2011; Hollevoet 2016).

There is evidence of specialist husbandry and commodity production, as well as cross-channel and coastal exchange from the sixth (Friesland) and seventh centuries (Flanders and Zeeland) onward (for more on animal husbandry in northern Gaul, see Yvinec and Barme, Chapter 33, this volume). The written sources suggest the importance of the production of wool and especially the so-called Frisian woolen coat or *pallia fresonica* (Lebecq 1983, pp. 382–383). This particular type of cloth was regarded as a high-quality product, valued for its warmth, its waterproof character, and especially its bright colors (Brandenburgh 2010). It was used for coats as well as for covers, and it was apparently produced in large quantities. However, its presence is difficult to read, if not absent, from an archaeological point of view, contrary to common brown or black woolen garments (Brandenburgh 2010). The general supposition is that it was produced mainly on Frisian terps, based on the presence of looms and other weaving instruments on these dwelling mounds, but there is no hard evidence for this theory.

The presence of sheep is also suggested by the attestations of *marisci* (sheep farm units) in eighth- and ninth-century written sources in Zeeland and Flanders (Verhulst 1959).[16] A specific donation of a *mariscus* in 794 states that it could feed 190 sheep in summer and 130 sheep in winter (Henderikx 1995, p. 77).[17] Wool and textile production was undoubtedly the main activity of these early medieval sheep farms, of which several hundred must have been scattered around in the large tidal landscape of Flanders and Zeeland. Beyond the exploitation of other tidal-borne resources and commodities like reeds, fowl, and (shell)fish, other activities at these sites likely involved the production of salt in at least some of the farms or centers. Evidence for salt production can be found in the contract for the transfer of seventeen *culinas ad sal faciendum* (saltpans) belonging to one farm in Zeeland to the abbey of Lorsch in 776 (Dekker 1971, p. 34).

Studies conducted on animal bone collections from terp settlements in present Friesland show, however, that the terp settlements in the saltmarshes were more involved in cattle breeding than in sheep herding. The statistics produced by most sites suggest around 60 to 70 percent cattle breeding versus about 30 percent sheep herding (Prummel 2001, 2006, 2008). Only at the site of Wijnaldum, which witnessed strong development after the second half of the seventh century, did sheep husbandry become more dominant (Prummel 2001). The early medieval sites in Zeeland and Flanders enjoyed a far greater share of sheep husbandry compared to the north. At the small dwelling mound of Oude Werf near the town of Ostend at which settlement started around 630 and continued to the eleventh century, the percentage of sheep bone was 74 percent versus 19 percent for cattle (Ervynck et al. 2012). At the site Uitkerke, Lissewegestraat, which may have started as early as the sixth century (on the basis of the presence of ceramics like biconic wares and Wölbwandtopfe from the Rhineland) and continued well into the ninth century, sheep bone represented 64 percent of the site assemblages versus 31 percent of cattle bone (van Remoorter 2016; Nijssen 2016). Material from the early to high medieval dwelling mound of Leffinge in Flanders, as well as the saltmarsh site Serooskerke in Zeeland, offered similar proportions (van Dijk et al. 2011; Pil 2016). Additional proof for the importance of sheep herding was found in the burial of sheep herding dogs in Oude Werf as well as Uitkerke-Lissewegestraat.

An important remark about the site Oude Werf is that nitrogen analysis of cattle bone proved that the cattle was raised and fed on grassland and not in the saltmarshes, contrary to the sheep from the dwelling mound (Ervynck et al. 2012, p. 157; Müldner et al. 2014). This could mean that meat from cattle was imported to saltmarsh sites from farms on the Pleistocene "mainland" and thus through commodity trade. Another remarkable result is that the kill-off pattern of sheep indicates a peak slaughter of younger animals, which would indicate the importance of the production of fleeces, while older animals were kept for wool production (Ervynck et al. 2012, pp. 157–160).[18] The sites Oude Werf and Uitkerke also possessed evidence for wool processing onsite (Deckers 2014; van Remoorter et al. 2016). Consideration of these data leads inevitably to the suggestion that the dwellers in the saltmarshes in the south of the estuary (Flanders and Zeeland) were much more systematically involved in sheepherding than those in the north (Friesland), where a more classical mixed-farming economy seems to have existed, at least before the eighth century. The data under discussion are still rather scarce, and we need more systematic analysis of animal bone from saltmarsh sites in north and south, but it is not impossible that the *pallia fresonica* were in fact produced in Flanders and Zeeland rather than in Friesland.[19] Another economic product that should not be forgotten in relation to wool production is the fabrication of precious ship sails (from the eighth century onward) (Kalmring 2010, pp. 371–373).[20]

The early medieval (sixth century and later) free farmers who lived in the unem-banked supra-tidal saltmarshes of Zeeland and Flanders, traded specialized products of sheep husbandry for other commodities such as wood, cereal, beef, and wine.[21] The subsistence strategy of the saltmarsh sheep farmers with their specialist products in the maritime regions was aimed at the demand of wool and fleeces in other regions, which involved them in exchange and the circulation of trade goods. The presence of significant quantities of imported pottery, such as black burnished wares from inland Belgium (seventh to eighth centuries) and Mayen from the Rhineland (sixth to eighth centuries), as well as imported copper alloy and even silver and golden luxury goods on several of these coastal sites show a similar trend toward the development of wealth (Fig. 34.5). We have noticed similar phenomena for the inhabitants of the terp sites in Friesland and the rural sites next to the Old Rhine in the Netherlands (Loveluck and Tys 2006; Tys 2010; Deckers 2010, 2014).

Several sites in the saltmarshes, as well as on the dune belt of coastal Flanders, also produced gold tremissi (the oldest found in Raversijde, dating from 527–565) and sceattas from the late seventh and eighth centuries (Deckers et al. 2017). In Koolkerke, at an unexcavated site close to a tidal channel near present-day Bruges, metal detecting brought to light a pseudo-Madelinus tremissis, a Series E sceatta, and large quantities of imported pottery (Deckers et al. 2017). They show the relationship between what happened in the seventh-century saltmarshes in Flanders and the Holland Rhine estuary we discussed earlier, which should not be surprising.

The majority of the sceattas in present-day coastal Flanders were discovered during early twentieth-century excavations in the dunes of De Panne (numbering twelve), in connection with some rare artifacts that were also encountered in Dorestad and Ribe in Denmark (Deckers 2010). It is not yet clear if these sceattas were deposited in a burial context, as was the case in a recently discovered burial ground in the dunes east of De Panne, dating from around 700, including a porcupine sceatta as grave gift (Dewilde et al. 2017). The De Panne site might have been a semi-ritual meeting place that succeeded an older Roman dune burial ground, although the material culture clearly pertains to wool processing (including wool shaving scissors and loomweights) and trade, with remarkable artifacts such as glass beads from between the mid-fifth to eighth century, an amber bead, and combs dated between the sixth and ninth centuries (Deckers 2010). The site is certainly reminiscent of the sites on the Old Rhine we discussed in the Netherlands. It is possible that De Panne was a landing place and beach site on the west bank of the estuary of the Yzer River connecting the productive sites in the saltmarshes with the North Sea coastal trade.

FIGURE 34.5. Sixth-century golden ring discovered in Vinkem at the edge of the coastal plain. From Deckers et al. 2017, p. 103, fig. 9.

The most remarkable beach site in the region is Domburg-Walicrum in the dunes of Walcheren in Zeeland, on the west bank of the original Schelde estuary, where no fewer than 866 sceattas from between 640 and 800 were discovered, in addition to 97 coins dated from between 500 and 670 and 69 Merovingian denarii dated from between 670 and 750 (Pol 1995; Deckers 2014; on numismatics, see Strothmann, Chapter 35. this volume). It is important to note that we are discussing a site that was almost entirely eroded during recent centuries, including a few burial grounds, which makes it difficult to compare (van Haperen 2013; Deckers 2014). However, just as in De Panne, we are dealing with a dune site with older Roman cult-related antecedents evolving into a large trade-related central place with a continuity of cult and assembly well into the seventh and eighth centuries. In the ninth century, the site was clearly related to royal power (and was given as a fief to Danish warlords), suggesting a royal villa or at least a high-status estate center in the dunes (Deckers 2014). The role of the site in the interregional and long-distance trade in the North Sea world is evident.[22] The great abundance of coins and remains of silver, copper alloy, and antler workshops allude to a Merovingian central place and possibly also to a landing place comparable to the De Geer site in Dorestad (Deckers 2014). The site clearly had a link to the saltmarsh dwellers, sheep husbandry sites in the saltmarshes, and trade in the Schelde estuary. It was also connected to the dune site on the east bank of the original Schelde mouth, the possible location of "Scaltheim" with material dating from the fifth to tenth century. This included no fewer than 97 sceattas (van der Valk and Beekman 2013).

The coastal areas spanning from Friesland, north of the estuary, to Flanders in the south comprised part of a vibrant rural economy based on peasant property relations. A few estates related to overlords must have been present as well (Deckers 2014; Hollevoet 2016). The coastal dwellers had a very specific production strategy aimed at specialized animal husbandry and market involvement. This can be seen in the archaeological signature of those coastal sites, including imports that refer to contact and trade especially (but not solely) with the Rhine and Meuse hinterlands and the other coastal regions of the southern North Sea area. None of these sites could have been regarded as ports of import trade, although it is certain that we need more information to understand the settlement hierarchy in these coastal regions. For instance, the communal dwelling mounds, such as Leffinge in coastal Flanders, possessed workshops and occupied a ritual and institutional role in their surroundings. They probably also had a role as a local market center (Tys 2004; Marchal et al. 2015).

THE DEVELOPMENT OF SPECIALIZED TRADE INFRASTRUCTURE AND COMMUNITIES

The overview of the sixth-, seventh-, and early eighth-century rural sites in the wetlands of the Low Countries testifies to the dynamic development of regional and interregional economic activity and trade. This seems comparable to John Naylor's analysis of eastern England (2016; see also Pestell and Ulmschneider 2003). In northwestern Europe, certain sites with favorable geographical locations and good communications evolved between the late seventh and early eighth centuries into permanent port and transshipment sites, commonly known as emporia (Naylor 2016; see also Loveluck 2013). Lundenwic was the hub of a trade or transshipment site on the Thames, Ipswich for East Anglia, while Hamwic related to a hinterland focused on Winchester and Wessex (Jervis 2016; on England, see Fleming, Chapter 17, this volume). On the continent, Quentovic formed a gateway to Picardy with important central places such as Arras and Cambrai but was equally related to the saltmarsh region between Saint-Omer and the coast of Calais and the east of coastal Flanders (Réveillion and Verslype 2010; Deckers 2016). In the Low Countries, a port of trade developed on a nodal point of the Rhine branches Kromme Rijn and Lek, namely, Dorestad, near to an older rural estate and a Roman fortress, with the huge tributary system of the Rhine as hinterland.

All these sites were initially quite small and rather unorganized, before their growth from the second quarter or middle of the eighth century onward (van Es and Verwers 2015, p. 358; Naylor 2016). Quentovic, which we did not discuss earlier and which is now the subject of new exploration under the direction of Laurent Verslype, was a trade settlement and minting place with a rather unorganized form of settlement before the end of the seventh century (Serna and Leroy 2016; Routier and Barbet 2016). In the seventh century, Ipswich had a surface area of only 6 hectares, whereas it extended 50 hectares in the eighth century. Lundenwic was not organized according to a gridlike pattern before 730. In Dorestad. only a small number of parcels of land and jetties developed on the riverbank near the older estate during the first quarter of the eighth century (van Es and Verwers 2015). (See Fig. 34.6.)

At the so-called northern emporium of Ribe, spatial organization evolved from being unorganized before 705, to achieving greater organization during the eighth century, to becoming a settlement with regular buildings from the late eighth century onward (Feveille 2012). We have to keep in mind, however, that even the organization of these sites was not spectacular. Richard Hodges sees a design by lords and architects in the layout of the emporia, such as the development of parcels alongside an axis (called "Hoogstraat" in Dorestad) parallel to the river (2000, 2017). This layout was, however, "basically very simple and easy to realize from a technical point of view," as Frans Verhaeghe stated (2005, p. 270). Moreover, developments alongside roads parallel to shores of rivers, or fjords for that matter, often occurred prior to the development of agglomerated developments, as is shown in the case of Hedeby and Ghent, for instance (Schultze 2005; Vermeiren et al. 2017).

As Frans Theuws wrote in 2004, the eighth-century expansion of the trade agglomerations in Dorestad, Lundenwic, and so on was exceptional. Eighth- and ninth-century Dorestad, of which no less than 80 percent has been excavated, had around 700 houses alongside 3 kilometers of river shore, including wells, jetties (for which 150,000 to 200,000 wooden piles were needed), workshops, and so on, leading to an estimate of approximately 10,000 inhabitants (van Es and Verwers 2015, p. 200; see also Willemsen

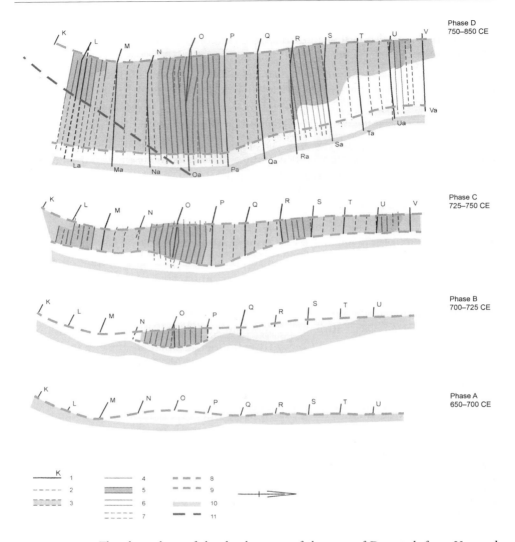

FIGURE 34.6. The chronology of the development of the port of Dorestad, from Van and Verwers 2015, p. 358, fig. VIII.

2009). Dorestad appears to have been foremost a port for trade and transshipment of bulk wares and crafted commodities rather than a center for luxury exchange. The main industries included:

1. Textile production (presence of circa 5,000 looms, or between 25 and 50 in use per year).
2. Trade and working of stone from the Rhineland and Meuse Valley (thousands of fragments of tephrite querns from the Eifel region as well as hundreds of fragments of limestone from the French Moselle Valley).

3. Iron working (related to iron ore production in the Veluwe east of Dorestad).
4. Wood working and trade (oak from Hessen and silver fir from the south of Germany).[23]
5. Trade and production of amber (5,000 or 18 kilograms of recovered material) (van Es and Verwers 2015, pp. 305–334).

Trade in tesserae, gold (ten touchstones recovered), and worked antler (combs), and, of course, later the production of Dorestad coins, were or became part of the economy but did not dominate its activities. The slave trade must have been present, although it cannot be recognized from an archaeological perspective.[24]

The economic turnover must have been of such importance that surplus extraction mechanisms were installed by the last quarter of the eighth century, which Frans Verhaeghe has described as "parasitic" (Verhaeghe 2005, p. 284; Kalmring 2016; Naylor 2016; Mallbosch 2017, pp. 215–218). It is important to understand that these tolls were not only new Carolingian creations, but were also levied on the circulation of merchandise and the sale of market goods, which means that they were only interesting to Carolingian lords because circulation and sale of goods flourished at these river sites earlier (Ganshof 1968, pp. 43–44). As Michael McCormick has expressed it, the *reges ex machina* explanation is no longer valid, and the interest and intervention of kings, offering guaranteed market peace and protection in return for custom duties, was the consequence rather than the cause for the growth of these ports of trade (2007, pp. 47, 61; see also Sindbaek 2007; Kalmring 2016).

Their location in specific environments, on nodal points in economic networks, or borderlands and meeting places of (regional) governance and sociopolitical entities caused certain sites to develop as more permanent fairs and meeting places, including the transshipment sites or emporia under discussion (McCormick 2007; Sindbaek 2007). Thus, their setting in a more complex landscape and settlement structure, where far more people were involved in commodity trade as well as luxuries exchange, shows how we have to consider the origin of these ports of trade as bottom-up and not top-down initiatives (Verhaeghe 2005; Sindbaek 2007; Hillerdal 2010; Croix 2015; Kalmring 2016). As Soren Sindbaek has observed, the motive for the crystallization of these hubs of trade with their workplaces and craft production was profit. Activity was undertaken foremost by farmers and traders, and not by elites who would have wanted to monopolize the dispersion of gift-exchange-related luxuries (2007; see also Naylor 2004, 2012; Henning 2007; Loveluck and Tys 2006; Loveluck 2012). The multitude of trade-related settlements, small marketplaces, river sites, and other small landing places throughout the eighth and ninth centuries shows how no emporium ever monopolized trade as such, and they were not the instruments of elite control (see also McCormick 2001, p. 420; Loveluck 2013, pp. 204–205; Costen and Costen 2016).

The actual construction and development of these ports can indeed not have been anything else but a bottom-up initiative, since there was almost no "state," nor was there a monopoly on "violence" by which to force economic agency on inhabitants (Innes 2005). Additionally, the whole period during which especially Dorestad started to develop was a period of warfare between "Frisians" and Carolingians followed by a disruption of the existing governance system. As Matthew Innes points out, only by the later eighth century did new governance mechanisms aimed at the integration of local elites become successful (2005, p. 75). Could it be, rather, that the absence of governance had a positive influence on the organization of free trade and the emancipation of merchants in so-called emporia or permanent fairs as Sven Kalmring (2016) calls them? In 1937, Alfons Dopsch had already remarked that early medieval craftsmen and merchants were, as far as he could see, mostly of free status. These merchants included groups such as the Frisian traders and the free manual workers who were recognized by Frisian law in the ninth century (Dopsch 1937, pp. 330, 334). Indeed, merchants were long considered lordless men, outside more traditional rural societies, where foreigners could be prosecuted and enslaved for being "strangers," unless they received some form of legal protection (Ganshof 1956; Kalmring 2016). Is it possible that the liminal position of the inhabitants of the wetlands of the Low Countries, with their allodial landholdings, produce from husbandry, maritime connections, and maybe also status as a fluid society, made them a world within worlds, as James Barrett describes them (2015)? Did these conditions provide the necessary social context for them to become free merchants?

CONCLUSION

In 2005, Frans Verhaeghe wrote that a better understanding of rural settlements was needed to establish a clearer picture of settlement hierarchies, communications and interactions, and the context for trade dynamics (p. 271). The overview presented here, with new knowledge and understanding of early medieval rural settlements in the Low Countries, proves him right. Ports of trade were embedded in the economic activities and networks of their respective hinterlands (see also Theuws 2004; Loveluck and Tys 2006; Loveluck 2013; Croix 2015). Here was a context of free coastal dwellers producing commodities in such quantities that they could sell them for profit in return for other commodities and objects for social reproduction. This occurred well before the eighth century, and these coastal dwellers did not end their way of life because of the arrival of the so-called emporia. New contributions by dendrochronologists, archaeozoologists, micromorphologists, and isotope specialists tell us about the environmental context of these rural sites as well as the significance of bulk trade goods or related data, such as wood, sheep bone, archaeozoological assemblages in general, and more. New research at the actual transshipment sites or emporia also provide additional data. The eighth-century emporia (alleged type B sites) were not places without a previous history, nor the result of direct intervention by central authorities, nor planned at the design tables of royal architects (Hodges 2000, 2017). On the contrary, they did not emerge in a vacuum. There was a network of rural producers and traders who were regionally connected (Theuws 2012). Consequently, we must avoid applying anachronistic, teleological schemes or models such as the development of urbanism to explain these developments (see also Henning 2007,

p. 6). No one in the Merovingian North Sea world had plans to regenerate towns after the crumbling of the Roman world. No one in the Merovingian North Sea world had conceived ideas about the development of commerce or markets for that purpose.

Production and exchange did exist for their own contextual reasons: the social reproduction of (free) landholders of an agrarian society, who had to negotiate affairs by gathering at assemblies where cult practices, governance, and fairs likewise occurred (Theuws 2004; Skré 2012; Kalmring 2016, pp. 15–16; Tys 2018). It certainly seems worthwhile to approach these agrarian societies and their dynamics from the perspective of the integration of governance and economy ("new institutional economics") in a regional setting, and to move beyond both archaeological and documentary biases. Research needs to proceed with an eye to contextual reproduction strategies. This approach will support a much more open and dynamic view of the early medieval economy, not only in the wetlands of Low Countries, but also elsewhere in the fascinating North Sea zone.

NOTES

1. The fourth northwestern landing place labeled as an emporium, albeit only at the end of the ninth century, was Dinant, a relatively important toll center and Carolingian mint in the Belgian Meuse valley (Verhulst 1999, p. 74).
2. It is worth noting that Richard Hodges is more careful in his argument in his 2012 book than he had been in 1982.
3. Under the reign of Charlemagne, the decision was made to create a channel called the "*Fossa Carolina*" between the river basin of the Rhine and that of the Donau in Bavaria near Eichstatt (Ettel 2007).
4. According to Adam of Bremen in the early eleventh century, merchant traffic between Denmark and the south systematically followed the coastal route via lower Saxony, the Netherlands, and Flanders before crossing to England from the Calais–Boulogne region, where the Channel is most narrow. The distance between Ribe and Flanders could be covered in two days when the winds were favorable (Lebecq 1983, pp. 196–197).
5. *Vita Eligii episcopi Noviomagensis*, p. 639. See Knol and IJssennagger 2017 on the complex history of the name "Frisians." The *Vita Eligii* referred to them as such in the middle of the seventh century but was rewritten in the early eighth century. However, this revision probably had no impact on the naming of the aforementioned group (Hen 1995, p. 196).
6. In Flanders, the later medieval landbooks regularly refer to a *hernesse* rent on wetlands under common landholding (both saltmarshes and river meadows). The word *hernesse* refers to flocks that were herded on the wetlands, while the actual rent, which belonged to the overlord (count or king), was symbolic rent for the use of these common haylands for herding. It is agreed that at least the common right structure goes back to the early Middle Ages, while the rent related to the so-called *wildernisregaal* or regalian right, on waste, unembanked lands. The place name *Lampernisse* in coastal Flanders, mentioned for the first time in 857, comes from the combination of *lamba* or lam and *hernesse*, the place where lambs were herded in the saltmarshes. Lampernisse was an allodial holding, until it was donated to the abbey of Saint-Bertin in St-Omer in 857. (On flocks in northern Gaul, see Yvinec and Barme, Chapter 33, this volume.)

7. We have to keep in mind that in the coastal regions of Flanders and Friesland, the free landholders kept their social and economic role until the later Middle Ages (de Langen 1992; Tys 2004).

8. Alfons Dopsch could in his time only refer to written documents when he deduced how indeed "finer as well as larger manufactured goods" were produced and exchanged in sixth-century (and later) central places such as Tours, and on annual markets, such as the seventh-century Saint-Denis market, where wine was brought from a great distance (1937, p. 322).

9. This far more complex development is described by Effros as "messy" (2017).

10. In historical usage, this term actually refers to an absolute top elite such as the most important royal advisors of the Carolingian emperors and kings in the ninth century, and not to local elites in the period before the ninth century (see, for instance, McKitterick 1983). This is yet another example of interdisciplinary terminological contamination between historians and archaeologists.

11. A site close to Sutton Hoo that testifies to these connections and is therefore interpreted as "royal" is Rendlesham (Scull, Minter, and Plouviez 2016).

12. On the discussion and interpretation of these dark earths, see Devos, Nicosia and Wouters 2019.

13. Henri Galinié defined similar sites such as Tours and the market area of Saint-Denis as nonurban towns (2000).

14. The urbanization of the area between Amsterdam and Rotterdam, also named Randstad, Holland, has caused a series of development projects, leading to a multitude of large-scale excavations. Similar active modernization of the landscape is not occurring in coastal Flanders, where urbanization in the coastal area remains limited and only the expansion of the port of Zeebrugge leads to large excavations. Expanding urbanization and industri-alization around Dunkirk has equally resulted in an increase of archaeological excavations on the northern French coastal plain (Lançon and Tys 2015; Desoutter, et al. 2016). In the Dutch provinces of Friesland and Groningen, on the one hand, and German Friesland, on the other, spatial pressure is minimal. In Flanders, additional academic research since 2006, as well as the introduction of a Flemish version of the Portable Antiquities Scheme, namely, www.vondsten.org, multiplied the number of sites of free landholders with luxuries and imports (Deckers 2014, 2015, 2016). These new initiatives have allowed a better assessment of the chronology of the coastal sites, as well as the economic and environmental study of these sites, such as the role of sheep husbandry (Ervynck et al. 2012; Müldner, et al. 2014).

15. It is suggested that the value of one cow was more or less 30 sceattas (Wynia 2010).

16. In 707, 12 *marisci* in the saltmarshes around Aardenburg were donated to the abbey of Saint Peter's near Ghent (Verhulst 1959; Henderikx 1995, p. 76).

17. The difference between the number of sheep in winter and summer is probably explained by seasonal slaughter for the winter and the breeding of lambs in the spring. However, the type of vegetation available, and its availability, might have been a factor in the winters before embankment. They may have just moved a proportion of the flock (a specific age group) to another feeding ground to overwinter. Nevertheless, seasonal slaughter was present in later periods, as testified by tithe specifications.

18. A remarkable rent from at least the eleventh century refers to this specific kill-off pattern; see Tys 2003, p. 494, and Archive Nationales de Paris, S5350: 16r°: "*Primo cest assavoir que la Maison de Sclipes a Rentes de Aigneaulx Mors par an selon que les vieux livres et registeres remonstrent a la somme de 80 lb 7 sol 10 den par, mais de ceste somme ylia en obscuer becop et demoura en obscuer jusques autant quil soit par acort messures les terres sus quoy la rente*

se doit estre assignes et souchy doit estre par le consent de Prinche Monseigneur le Conte de Flandres, Mon seigneur le Prevost de Saint Donas et de autres seigneurs a qui yl tient." The significance of the rent could be that fleeces obtained larger prices on the early markets compared to wool as such.

19. In this hypothesis, the reference to Frisia would thus have been to the coastal region of the entire Low Countries rather than to the present province.

20. Sails were so precious that they were in later times guarded under the roofs of churches (thanks to Sven Kalmring for the argument and information).

21. Other sites with a similar origin in the seventh and eighth centuries may, for instance, be found at Uitkerke-Groenwake and Lampernisse (Ervynck et al. 1999; Hermans 2009). In the French part of coastal Flanders, similar sites were excavated, ranging from the Merovingian period to the eleventh century (Lançon and Tys 2015).

22. Between the ninth and eleventh centuries, the activities of the site were transferred to the ringfort of Domburg, which was clearly integrated in a Scandinavian and possibly even Baltic trade network (Deckers 2014;Tys, Deckers, and Wouters 2016).

23. Not only was this wood produced locally but it was traded from the German hinterlands. This provides images of the Rhine that are comparable with Canadian or Scandinavian rivers. It also tells us that the construction of Dorestad did not necessarily go hand in hand with massive deforestation in the Dutch riverland itself (McCormick 2001, p. 653).

24. McCormick 2001, p. 654. The trade in slaves was certainly one of the most valuable and extensive sectors in early medieval trade, as Ganshof acknowledged in 1956.

Works Cited

Ancient Sources

The Annals of St-Bertin. J. L. Nelson (ed.). (1991). *The Annals of St-Bertin. Ninth-century histories, volume 1.* Manchester: Manchester University Press.

Bede, *Ecclesiastical History of the English People.* G. Hardin Brown and F. Biggs (eds.). (2017). *Bede. Part 1, Fascicles 1–4.* Amsterdam: Amsterdam University Press.

Vita Eligii Episcopi Noviomagensis. B. Krusch (ed.). (1902). *Passiones Vitaeque Sanctorum aevi Merovingici.* MGH SRM 4.2 (pp. 634–761). Hanover: Hahn.

Modern Sources

Baeteman, C. (2013). "History of Research and State of the Art of the Holocene Depositional History of the Belgian Coastal Plain." In E. Thoen, G. Borger, A. de Kraker, T. Soens, D. Tys, L. Vervaet, and H. Weerts (eds.), *Landscapes or Seascapes? The History of the Coastal Environment in the North Sea Area Considered* (pp. 11–29). Comparative Rural History of the North Sea Area 13. Turnhout: Brepols.

Banaji, J. (2009). "Aristocracies, Peasantries and the Framing of the Early Middle Ages." *Journal of Agrarian Change* 9(1): 59–91.

Bazelmans, J. (2003). "Beowulf: een man van aanzien." In E. Kramer, I. Stoumann, and A. Greg (eds.), *Koningen van de Noordzee* (pp. 33–40). Leeuwarden: Fries Museum.

Bazelmans, J. (2009). "The Early-Medieval Use of Ethnic Names from Classical Antiquity: The Case of the Frisians." In T. Derks and N. Roymans (eds.), *Ethnic Constructs in Antiquity. The Role of Power and Tradition* (pp. 321–338). Amsterdam: Amsterdam University Press.

Bonassie, P. (1991). "From One Servitude to Another: The Peasantry of the Frankish Kingdom at the Time of Hugh Capet and Robert the Pious (987–1031)." In P. Bonnassie (ed.), *From Slavery to Feudalism in South-Western Europe* (pp. 288–313). Cambridge: Cambridge University Press.

Brandenburgh, C. (2010). "Textile Production and Trade in Dorestad." In A. Willemsen and H. Kik (eds.), *Dorestad in an International Framework. New Research into Trade Centres in Carolingian* (pp. 83–88). Turnhout: Brepols.

Brenner, R. (2001). "The Low Countries in the Transition to Capitalism." In P. Hoopenbrowers and J. Luiten van Zanden (eds.), *Peasants into Farmers? The Transformation of Rural Economy and Society in the Low Countries (Middle Ages–19th Century in Light of the Brenner Debate* (pp. 275–338). Comparative Rural History of the North Sea Area 4. Turnhout: Brepols.

Brulet, R., Coquelet, C., Defgnée, A., Pigère, F. and Verslype, L. (2004). "Les sites à 'terres noires' à Tournai et le secteur des anciens cloîtres canoniaux. Etudes archéozoologique, palynologique et contextualisation." In *Terres noires. Dark Earth. Actes de la table-ronde international tenue à Louvain-la-Neuve, les 09 et 10 novembre 2001* (pp. 152–172). Louvain-la-Neuve: UCL.

Costen, M., and Costen, N. (2016). "Trade and Exchange in Anglo-Saxon Wessex, c AD 600–780." *Medieval Archaeology* 60(1): 1–26.

Croix, S. (2015). "Permanency in Early Medieval Emporia: Reassessing Ribe." *European Journal of Archaeology* 18(3): 497–523.

De Bruin, J. (2018). "Living in Oegstgeest 575–725 AD." In M. Kars, R. van Oosten, M. A. Roxburgh, and A. Verhoeven (eds.), *Rural Riches and Royal Rags? Studies on Medieval and Modern Archaeology, Presented to Frans Theuws* (pp. 20–25). Zwolle: SPA-uitgevers.

Deckers, P. (2010). "An Illusory Emporium? Small Trading Sites around the North Sea: De Panne as a Case Study." In A. Willemsen and H. Kik (eds.), *Dorestad in an International Framework. New Research into Trade Centres in Carolingian Times* (pp. 159–168). Turnhout: Brepols.

Deckers, P. (2014). *Between Land and Sea. Landscape, Power and Identity in the Coastal Plain of Flanders, Zeeland and Northern France in the Early Middle Ages (AD 500–1000).* Brussels: Vrije Universiteit Brussel.

Deckers, P. (2015). "The Maritime Cultural Landscape of Early Medieval Northumbria: Small Landing Places and the Emergence of Coastal Urbanism." In J. Barrett and S. J. Gibbon (eds.), *Maritime Societies of the Viking and Medieval World* (pp. 138–155). Society for Medieval Archaeology Monograph 37. Leeds: Maney.

Deckers, P. (2016). "Economy, Identity and Power. The Yser Estuary in the Early Middle Ages." In I. Leroy and L. Verslype (eds.), *Les cultures des littoraux au Haut Moyen Âge. Cadres et modes de vie dans l'espace maritime Manche-Mer du Nord du IIIe au Xe s* (pp. 77–88). Revue du Nord, Hors Série. Collection Art et Archeologie 24. Lille: Université de Lille.

Deckers, P., and Tys, D. (2012). "Early Medieval Communities around the North Sea: a 'Maritime Culture'?" In R. Annaert, K. De Groote, Y. Hollevoet, F. Theuws, D. Tys, and L. Verslype (eds.), *The Very Beginning of Europe? Cultural and Social Dimensions of Early-Medieval Migration and Colonisation* (pp. 81–88). Relicta Monografieën 7. Brussels: Flanders Heritage Agency.

Deckers, P., Fillet, R., van Ham-Meert, A., Makarona, C., Claeys, P., and K. Nys. (2017). *Een vergeten tijd gedetecteerd. Metaalvondsten uit de Vlaamse kuststreek, 600–1100 n.Chr.* West-Vlaamse Archaeologica 22. Roeselare: V.O.B.o.W.

De Keyser, M., and van Onacker, E. (2016). "Beyond the Flock. Sheep Farming, Wool Sales and Social Differentiation in a Sixteenth-Century Peasant Society: The Campine in the Low Countries." *Agricultural History Review* 64(2): 157–180.

De Langen, G. (1992). *Middeleeuws Friesland. De economische ontwikkeling van het gewest Oostergo in de Vroege en de Volle Middeleeuwen.* Groningen: Universiteit Groningen.

Dekker, C. (1971). *Zuid-Beveland, De historische geografie en de instellingen van een Zeeuws eiland in de Middeleeuwen.* Assen: Van Gorcum.

Desoutter, S., Elleboode, E., Lançon, M., and Routier, J.-C. (2016). "L'occupation carolingienne et post-carolingienne de la plaine maritime flamande française. Premier bilan." In I. Leroy and L. Verslype (eds.), *Les cultures des littoraux au haut Moyen Âge. Cadres et modes de vie dans l'espace maritime Manche-mer du Nord du IIIe au Xe s.* (pp. 127–165). Collection Art et archéologie 24. Villeneuve d'Ascq: Revue du Nord.

Devos, Y., Nicosia, C., and Wouters, B. (2020). "Urban Geoarchaeology in Belgium: Experiences and Innovations." *Geoarchaeology* 35: 27–41.

Devroey, J.-P. (2006). *Puissants et misérables. Système social et monde paysan dans l'Europe des Francs (VIe–IXe siècles).* Brussels: Académie royale.

Dewilde, M., Baetsen, S., and Wyffels, F. (2017). "Merovingisch grafveld en woonerf aan de Vlaamse kust. Een toevalsvondst in Koksijde." *Monumenten, Landschappen en Archeologie* 36(6): 39–47.

Dijkman, W. (1994). "Maas-Tricht, lieu de défense et centre réligieux." In P. Demolon, H. Galinié, and F. Verhaeghe (eds.), *Archéologie des villes dans le nord-ouest de l'Europe (VIIe-XIIIe s.). Actes du IVe Congrès International d'Archéologie Médiévale (Douai, 26, 27, 28 septembre 1991)* (pp. 35–39). Douai: Société archéologique de Douai.

Dijkman, W., and Ervynck, A. (1998). *Antler, Bone, Horn, Ivory and Teeth: The Use of Animals Skeletal Materials in Roman and Early Medieval Maastricht.* Maastricht: Gemeente Maastricht.

Dijkstra, M. (2011). *Rondom de mondingen van Rijn & Maas. Landschap en bewoning tussen de 3e en 9e eeuw in Zuid-Holland, in het bijzonder de Oude Rijnstreek.* Leiden: Universiteit Leiden.

Dijkstra, M., and de Koning, J. (2017). "'All Quiet on the Western Front?' The Western Netherlands and the 'North Sea Culture' in the Migration Period." In J. Hines and N. Ijssenagger (eds.), *Frisians and Their North Sea Neighbours. From the Fifth Century to the Viking Age* (pp. 53–74). Woodbridge: Boydell & Brewer.

Dijkstra, M., and Verhoeven, A. (2018). "Synthese. Vroegmiddeleeuws Leithon in een breder perspectief." In M. Dijkstra, A. Verhoeven, and K. van Straten (eds.), *Nieuw licht op Leithon. Archeologisch onderzoek naar de vroeg middeleeuwse bewoning in plangebied Leiderdorp-Plantage* (pp. 703–731). Amsterdam: University of Amsterdam Press.

Dopsch, A. (1937). *The Economic and Social Foundations of Europe.* London: Kegan Paul.

Effros, B. (2017). "The Enduring Attraction of the Pirenne Thesis." *Speculum* 92(1): 184–208.

Ervynck, A., Baeteman, C., Demiddele, H., Hollevoet, Y., Pieters, M., Schelvis, J., Tys, D., van Strydonck, M., and Verhaeghe, F. (1999). "Human Occupation Because of a Regression, or the Cause of a Transgression? A Critical View on the Interaction between Geological Events and Human Occupation History in the Belgian Coastal Plain during the First Millennium AD." *Probleme der Küstenforschung im südlichen Nordseegebiet* 26: 97–121.

Ervynck, A., Deckers, P., Lentacker, A., Tys, D., and van Neer, W. (2012). "Leffinge—Oude Werf: The First Archaeozoological Collection from a Terp Settlement in Coastal Flanders." In D. C. M. Raemaekers, E. Esser, R. C. G. M. Lauwerier, and J. T. Zeiler (eds.), *A Bouquet of Archaeozoological Studies. Essays in Honour of Wietske Prummel* (pp. 153–164). Groningen Archaeological Studies 21. Groningen: Barkhuis/Groningen University Library.

Ettel, P. (2007). "Fossa Carolina und Befestigungsanlagen am Main als Indikatoren der Integration der Frankenlande in das Frankenreich." In S. Freund, M. Hardt, and P. Weigel (eds.), *Flüse und Flusstäler als Wirtschafts- und Kommunikationswege* (pp. 121–151). Siedlungsforschung. Archäeologie-Geschichte-Geographie 25. Bonn: Siedlungsforschung.

Feveile, C. (2012). "Ribe: *Emporia* and Town in 8th–9th Century." In S. Gelichi and R. Hodges (eds.), *From One Sea to Another. Trading Places in the European and Mediterranean Early Middle Ages. Proceedings of the International Conference Comacchio 27th–29th March 2009* (pp. 111–122). Turnhout: Brepols.

Galinié, H. (2000). *Ville, espace urbain et archeologie*. Tours: Université de Tours.

Ganshof, F. L. (1956). *Het statuut van de vreemdeling in het Frankische Rijk*. Mededelingen van de Koninklijke Vlaamse Academie voor Wetenschappen, Letteren en Schone Kunsten van België. Klasse der Letteren, Jaargang XVIII, nr 3. Brussels: Koninklijke Vlaamse Academie voor Wetenschappen, Letteren en Schone Kunsten van België.

Ganshof, F. L. (1968). *Frankish Institutions under Charlemagne*. New York: Norton.

Halsall, G. (1992). "Social Change around A.D. 600: An Austrasian Perspective." In M. Carver (ed.), *The Age of Sutton Hoo. The Seventh Century in North-Western Europe* (pp. 265–278). Woodbridge: Boydell.

Halsall, G. (2012). "From Roman *fundus* to Early Medieval *grand domaine*. Crucial Ruptures between Antiquity and the Middle Ages." *Revue Belge de Philologie et d'Histoire* 90(2): 273–298.

Hamerow, H., Hollevoet, Y. and Vince, A. (1994). "Migration Period Settlements and 'Anglo-Saxon' Pottery from Flanders." *Medieval Archaeology* 38: 1–18.

Heidinga, A. (1997). *Frisia in the First Millenium—an Outline, Frisia Project*. Utrecht: Matrijs.

Hen, Y. (1995). *Culture and Religion in Merovingian Gaul, A.D. 471–751*. Leiden: Brill.

Henderikx, P. (1995). "De ringwalburgen in het mondingsgebied van de Schelde in historisch perspectief." In R. van Heeringen, P. Henderikx, and A. Mars (eds.), *Vroeg-Middeleeuwse ringwalburchten in Zeeland* (pp. 70–112). Amersfoort: Rijksdienst voor Oudheidkundig Bodemonderzoek.

Henning, J. (2007). "Early European Towns. The Development of the Economy in the Frankish Realm between Dynamism and Declaration AD 500–1100." In J. Henning (ed.), *Post-Roman Towns, Trade and Settlements in Europe and Byzantium. 1: The Heirs of the Roman West* (pp. 3–40). Berlin: Walter de Gruyter.

Hermans, M. (2009). *Analyse van het aardewerk uit de archeologische opgraving van de site Uitkerke Groenwake*. Brussels: VUB.

Hill, D. (2001). "150 years of the Study of *Wics*: 1841–1991." In D. Hill and R. Cowie (eds.), *Wics. The Early Mediaeval Trading Centres of Northern Europe* (pp. 3–6). Sheffield: Sheffield University Press.

Hillerdal, C. (2010). "Early Urbanism in Scandinavia." In P. J. J. Sinclair, G. Nordquist, F. Herschend, and C. Isendahl (eds.), *The Urban Mind. Cultural and Environmental Dynamics* (pp. 499–525). Uppsala: Uppsala University.

Hodges, R. (1982). *Dark Age Economics: The Origins of Towns and Trade, AD 600–1000*. London: Duckworth.

Hodges, R. (2000). *Towns in the Age of Charlemagne*. London: Duckworth.

Hodges, R. (2012). *Dark Age Economics. A New Audit*. London: Bloomsbury Academic.

Hodges, R. (2017). "Klavs Randsborg and the Ninth Century AD." *Acta Archaeologica*: 155–162.

Hollevoet, Y. (2016). "Entre Frisons, Francs et Anglo-Saxons: la Flandre maritime au haut Moyen Age." In I. Leroy and L. Verslype (eds.), *Les cultures des littoraux au haut Moyen Âge. Cadres et modes de vie dans l'espace maritime Manche-mer du Nord du IIIe au Xe s* (pp. 69–76). Revue Du Nord, Hors Série. Collection Art et Archeologie 24. Lille: Université de Lille.

Hoppenbrouwers, P. (2001). "Mapping an Unexplored Field. The Brenner Debate and the Case of Holland." In P. Hoppenbrouwers and J. Luiten van Zanden (eds.), *Peasants into Farmers? The Transformation of Rural Economy and Society in the Low Countries (Middle Ages–19th Century in Light of the Brenner Debate* (pp. 41–66). Comparative Rural History of the North Sea Area 4. Turnhout: Brepols.

IJssennagger, N. (2017). *Central Because Liminal. Frisia in a Viking Age North Sea World.* Groningen: Universiteit Groningen.

Innes, M. (2005). "Charlemagne's Government." In J. Story (ed.), *Charlemagne, Empire and Society* (pp. 71–89). Manchester: Manchester University Press.

Jansma, E., and van Lanen, R. (2016). "The Dendrochronology of Dorestad: Placing Early-Medieval Structural Timbers in a Wider Geographical Context." In A. Willemsen and H. Kik (eds.), *Golden Middle Ages in Europe—New Research into Early-Medieval Communities and Identities* (pp. 105–144). Turnhout: Brepols.

Jansma, E., van Lanen, R., and Pierik, H.J. (2017). "Travelling through a River Delta: A Landscape Archaeological Reconstruction of River Development and Long-Distance Connections in the Netherlands during the First Millennium AD." *Medieval Settlement Research* 32: 35–39.

Jervis, B. (2016). "Trade, Cultural Exchange and Coastal Identities in Early Anglo-Saxon Kent: A Ceramic Perspective." In A. Willemsen and H. Kik (eds.), *Golden Middle Ages in Europe—New Research into Early-Medieval Communities and Identities* (pp. 57–63). Turnhout: Brepols.

Jöns, H., Beuker, J. IJssennagger, N., and Kramer, E. (2013). "Das Besondere in der Fremde: Fernkontakte im Ems-Dollart-Raum." In J. F. Kegler (ed.), *Land der Entdeckungen: Die Archäologie des friesischen Küstenraums* (pp. 360–370). Aurich: Verlag Ostfriesische Landschaft.

Jorgensen, L. (2003). "Manor and Market at Lake Tisso in the Sixth to the Eleventh Centuries: The Danish 'Productive' Sites." In T. Pestell and K. Ulmschneider (eds.), *Markets in Early Medieval Europe, Trading and Productive Sites, 650–850* (pp. 175–207). Macclesfield: Windgather Press.

Jorgensen, L. (2009). "Pre-Christian Cult at Aristocratic Residences and Settlement Complexes in Southern Scandinavia in the 3rd–10th Centuries AD." In U. von Freeden, H. Friesinger, and E. Wamers (eds.), *Glaube, Kult und Herrschaft. Phänomene des Religiösen im 1. Jahrtausend n. Chr. in Mittel- und Nordeuropa. Akten des 59. Internationalen Sachsensymposions und der Grundprobleme der frühgeschichtlichen Entwicklung* (pp. 329–354). Frankfurt: Römisch-Germanische Kommission.

Kalmring, S. (2010). *Der Hafen von Haithabu.* Die Ausgrabungen in Haithabu 14. Neumünster: Wachholtz.

Kalmring, S. (2016). "Early Northern Towns as Special Economic Zones." In L. Homquist, S. Kalmring, and C. Hedenstierna-Jonsons (eds.), *New Aspects on Viking-age Urbanism c. AD 750–1100 AD. Proceedings of the International Symposium at the Swedish History Museum, April 17–20th 2013* (pp. 11–21). Stockholm: University of Stockholm.

Kars, M. (2014). "(Re)considering the Pre-Burial Life of Grave Goods: Towards a Renewed Debate on Early Medieval Burial Chronology on the Continent." *Medieval and Modern Matters. Archaeology and Material Culture in the Low Countries* 3: 107–134.

Knol, E., and N. IJssennagger. (2017). "Palaeogeography and People: Historical Frisians in an Archaeological Light." In J. Hines and N. IJssennagger (eds.), *Frisians and their North Sea*

Neighbours. From the Fifth Century to the Viking Age (pp. 5–24). Woodbridge: Boydell & Brewer.

Kosian, M., van Lanen, R., and Weerts, H. (2016). "Dorestad's Rise and Fall: How the Local Landscape Influenced the Growth, Prosperity and Disappearance of an Early Medieval Emporium: New Research into Early-Medieval Communities and Identities." In A. Willemsen and H. Kik (eds.), *Golden Middle Ages in Europe—New Research into Early-Medieval Communities and Identities* (pp. 99–104). Turnhout: Brepols.

Kosian, M., Weerts, H., van Lanen, R., and Abrahamse, J. E. (2013). "The City and the River. The Early Medieval Emporium (Trade Centre) of Dorestad; Integrating Physical Geography with Archaeological Data in Changing Environments." In W. Börner and S. Uhlirz (eds.) *Proceedings of the 17th International Conference on Cultural Heritage and New Technologies 2012*. CHNT 17. Vienna: Museum der Stadt Wien.

Lançon, M., and Tys, D. (2015). "L'occupation du littoral: un cas particulier." In P. Demolon (ed.), *Le haut Moyen Âge dans le nord de la France: Des Francs aux premiers comtes de Flandres, de la fin du IVᵉ au milieu du Xᵉ siècle* (pp. 87–91). Douai: Arkeos.

Lebecq, S. (1983). *Marchands et navigateurs frisons du haut Moyen Age.* 2 vols. Lille: Université de Lille.

Lebecq, S. (1992). "The Frisian Trade in the Dark Ages: A Frisian or a Frankish/Frisian Trade?" In A. Carmiggelt (ed.), *Rotterdam Papers VII* (pp. 7–15). Rotterdam: Bureau Oudheidkundig Onderzoek van Gemeentewerken Rotterdam.

Loveluck, C. (2012). "Central-Places, Exchange and Maritime-Oriented Identity around the North Sea and Western Baltic, AD 600–1100." In S. Gelichi and R. Hodges (eds.), *From One Sea to Another: Trading Places in the European and Mediterranean Early Middle Ages. Proceedings of the International Conference Comacchio 27th–29th March 2009)* (pp. 123–166). Turnhout: Brepols.

Loveluck, C. (2013). *Northwest Europe in the Early Middle Ages, c. AD 600–1150.* Cambridge: Cambridge University Press.

Loveluck, C., and Tys, D. (2006). "Coastal Societies, Exchange and Identity along the Channel and Southern North Sea Shores of Europe, AD 600–1000." *Journal for Maritime Archaeology* 1(2): 140–169.

Malbosch, L. (2017). *Les ports des mers nordiques à l'époque Viking (VIIᵉ-Xᵉ siècle).* Turnhout: Brepols.

Marchal, C., Deckers, P., Tys, D., and van Loock, S. (2015). "Archeologisch onderzoek van een middeleeuwse pastorie en de ontdekking van de vroeg- en volmiddeleeuwse terp in Leffinge. Een project in community archaeology." *Archaeologia Mediaevalis* 38: 152–154.

McCormick, M. (2001). *Origins of the European Economy. Communications and Commerce, AD 300–900.* Cambridge: Cambridge University Press.

McCormick, M. (2007). "Where Do Trading Towns Come from? Early Medieval Venice and the Northern *Emporia.*" In J. Henning (ed.), *Post-Roman Towns, Trade and Settlements in Europe and Byzantium. Volume 1: The Heirs of the Roman West* (pp. 41–68). Berlin: Walter de Gruyter.

McKitterick, R. (1983). *The Frankish Kingdoms under the Carolingians. 751–987.* Harlow: Pearson Education.

Meier, D. (2013). "From Nature to Culture: Landscape and Settlement History of the North-Sea Coast of Schleswig-Holstein, Germany." In E. Thoen, G. Borger, A. de Kraker, T. Soens, D. Tys, L. Vervaet, and H. Weerts (eds.), *Landscapes or Seascapes?: The History of the Coastal Environment in the North Sea Area Considered* (pp. 85–110). Comparative Rural History of the North Sea Area 13. Turnhout: Brepols.

Mostert, M. (2009). *In de marge van de beschaving. De geschiedenis van Nederland, o–1100*. Amsterdam: Bert Bakker.

Müldner, G., Britton, K., and Ervynck, A. (2014). "Inferring Animal Husbandry Strategies in Coastal Zones through Stable Isotope Analysis: New Evidence from the Flemish Coastal Plain (Belgium, 1st–15th century AD)." *Journal of Archaeological Science* 41: 322–332.

Naylor, J. (2004). *An Archaeology of Trade in Middle Saxon England*. British Archaeological Series 376. Oxford: BAR Publishing.

Naylor, J. (2012). "Coinage, Trade and the Origins of the English *Emporia*, ca. AD 650–750." In S. Gelichi and R. Hodges (eds.), *From One Sea to Another. Trading Places in the European and Mediterranean Early Middle Ages. Proceedings of the International Conference Comacchio 27th–29th March 2009* (pp. 237–266). Turnhout: Brepols.

Naylor, J. (2016). "Emporia and Their Hinterlands in the 7th to 9th Centuries AD: Some Comments and Observations from England." In I. Leroy and L. Verslype (eds.), *Les cultures des littoraux au haut Moyen Âge. Cadres et modes de vie dans l'espace maritime Manche-mer du Nord du IIIe au Xe s* (pp. 59–67). Revue Du Nord, Hors Série. Collection Art et Archeologie 24. Lille: Université de Lille.

Nicolay, J. (2003). "Een politiek machtscentrum in noordelijk Westergo. Goudvondsten uit het Fries-Groningse terpengebied." In E. Kramer, I. Stoumann, and A. Greg (eds.), *Koningen van de Noordzee* (pp. 55–74). Leeuwarden: Fries Museum.

Nicolay, J. (2014). *The Splendour of Power: Early Medieval Kingship and the Use of Gold and Silver in the Southern North Sea Area (5th to 7th Century AD)*. Groningen: University of Groningen.

Nicolay, J. (2017). "Power and Identity in the Southern North Sea Area: The Migration and Merovingian Periods." In J. Hines and N. Ijssennagger (eds.), *Frisians and Their North Sea Neighbours. From the Fifth Century to the Viking Age* (pp. 75–92). Woodbridge: Boydell & Brewer.

Nijssen, E. (2016). "Dierlijk botmateriaal." In O. Van Remoorter, S. Sadones, and R. Vanoverbeke (eds.), *Archeologische Opgraving Blankenberge, Lissewegestraat* (pp. 147–157). Ghent: Baac-Vlaanderen.

Nokkert, M., Aerts, A. and Wynia, H. (2009). *Vroegmiddeleeuwse bewoning langs de A2. Een nederzetting uit de zevende en achtste eeuw in Leidsche Rijn*. Basisrapportage Archeologie 26. Utrecht: Stadsontwikkeling gemeente Utrecht.

Oosthuizen, S. (2017). *The Anglo-Saxon Fenland*. Oxford: Oxbow.

Op den Velde, W., and Metcalf, M. (2014). "The Circulation of Sceattas in the Southern Low Countries." *Revue Belge de Numismatique et de Sigillographie/Belgisch Tijdschrift Voor Numismatiek En Zegelkunde* 160: 3–22.

Pestell, T., and Ulmschneider, K. (2003). "Introduction: Early Medieval Markets and 'Productive' Sites." In T. Pestell and K. Ulmschneider (eds.), *Markets in Early Medieval Europe. Trading and "Productive" Sites, 650–850* (pp. 1–10). Bollington: Windgather Press.

Péters, C., and Fontaine-Hodiamont, C. (2005). "Huy et le travail du verre à l'époque mérovingienne: étude préliminaire du matériel trouvé Rue Sous-le-Château et Place Saint-Séverin." In J. Plumier and M. Regnard (eds.), *Voies d'eau, commerce et artisanat en Gaule mérovingienne* (pp. 233–267). Études et Documents, Archéologie 10. Namur : Ministère de la Région walonne.

Pil, N. (2016). *Specialistisch rapport archeozoölogie: onderzoek van het vroeg middeleeuwse bot-materiaal van de site Leffinge*. Leiden: Universiteit Leiden.

Pirenne, H. (1923). "Un contrast économique: Mérovingiens et Carolingiens." *Revue belge de philologie et d'histoire* 2: 223–225.

Pirenne, H. (1925). *Medieval Cities: Their Origins and the Revival of Trade*, trans. F. D. Halsey. Princeton, NJ: Princeton University Press.

Plumier, J., Plumier-Torfs, A., Vanmechelen, R., Mees, N., and Robinet, C. (2005). "*Namuci fit. Namur du Ve au VIIe siècle.*" In J. Plumier and M. Regnard (eds.), *Voies d'eau, commerce et artisanat en Gaule mérovingienne* (pp. 219–231). Études et Documents, Archéologie 10. Namur : Ministère de la Région walonne.

Pol, A. (1995). "Middeleeuwse munten van het Domburgse strand." In R. van Heeringen, P. Henderikx, and A. Mars (eds.), *Vroeg-Middeleeuwse ringwalburchten in Zeeland* (pp. 44–49). Amersfoort: Rijksdienst voor Oudheidkundig Bodemonderzoek.

Pol, A. (2010). "Madelinus and the Disappearing of Gold." In A. Willemsen and H. Kik (eds.), *Dorestad in an International Framework. New Research into Trade Centres in Carolingian Times* (pp. 91–94). Turnhout: Brepols.

Prummel, W. (2001). "The Significance of Animals to the Early Medieval Frisians in the Northern Coastal Area of the Netherlands. Archaeozoological, Iconographic, Historical and Literary Evidence." *Environmental Archaeology* 6: 73–81.

Prummel, W. (2006). "Dierlijk bot." In A. Nieuwhof (ed.), *De wierde Wierum (provincie Groningen). Een archeologisch steilkantonderzoek* (pp. 31–45). Groningen: Groninger Instituut voor Archeologie.

Prummel, W. (2008). "Dieren op de wierde Englum." In A. Nieuwhof (ed.), *De Leege Wier van Englum. Archeologisch onderzoek in het Reitdiepgebied* (pp. 116–159). Groningen: Groninger Instituut voor Archeologie.

Réveillion, S., and Verslype, L. (2010). "Quentovic. Réalités et perspectives archéologiques." In S. Lebecq, B. Béthouart, and L. Verslype (eds.), *Quentovic. Environnement, archéologie, histoire. Actes du colloque international de Montreuil-sur-Mer, Etaples et Le Touquet et de la journée d'études de Lille sur les origines de Montreuil-sur-Mer (11–13 mai 2006 et 1er décembre 2006)* (pp. 510–521). Lille: Ceges.

Routier, J.-C., and Barbet, P. (with Foucray, B.). (2016). "Bilan des operations de l'Inrap à La Calotterie (2005–2007)." In I. Leroy and L. Verslype (eds.), *Les cultures des littoraux au haut Moyen Âge. Cadres et modes de vie dans l'espace maritime Manche-mer du Nord du IIIe au Xe s* (pp. 217–251). Revue Du Nord, Hors Série. Collection Art et Archeologie 24. Lille: Université de Lille.

Schmid, P. (1991). "Mittelalterliche Besiedlung, Deich- und Landesausbau im niedersächsichen Marschgebiet." In H. W. Böhme (ed.), *Siedlungen und Landesausbau zur Salierzeit I: in der Nördlichen Landschaften des Reiches* (pp. 9–36). Osnabrück: Kraemer & Hansen.

Schultze, J. (2005). "Zur Frage der Entwicklung des zentralen Siedlungskernes von Haithabu." In C. Dobiat (ed.), *Reliquiae Gentium. Festschrift für Wolfgang Horst Böhme zum 65. Geburtstag. Teil 1* (pp. 359–373). Rahden: Leidorf.

Scull, C., Minter, F., and Plouviez, J. (2016). "Social and Economic Complexity in Early Medieval England: A Central Place Complex of the East Anglian Kingdom at Rendlesham, Suffolk." *Antiquity* 90(354): 1594–1612.

Serna, V., and Leroy, I. (2016). "Interactions et occupations des milieux côtier et fluvial dans la longue durée: sources confluentes en Canche." In I. Leroy and L. Verslype (eds.), *Les cultures des littoraux au haut Moyen Âge. Cadres et modes de vie dans l'espace maritime Manche-mer du Nord du IIIe au Xe s.* (pp. 41–55). Revue Du Nord, Hors Série. Collection Art et Archeologie 24. Lille: Université de Lille.

Sindbaek, S. (2007). "Networks and Nodal Points. The Emergence of Towns in Early Viking Age Scandinavia." *Antiquity* 81: 119–132.

Skré, D. (2012). "Markets, Towns and Currencies in Scandinavia ca. 200–1000." In S. Gelichi and R. Hodges (eds.), *From One Sea to Another. Trading Places in the European and Mediterranean Early Middle Ages. Proceedings of the International Conference Comacchio 27th–29th March 2009* (pp. 47–64). Turnhout: Brepols.

Soulat, J., Bocquet-Liénard, A., Savary, X., and Hinckler, V. (2012). "Hand-Made Pottery along the Channel Coast and Parallels with the Scheldt Valley." In R. Annaert, K. De Groote, Y. Hooevoet, F. Theuws, D. Tys, and L. Verslype (eds.), *The Very Beginning of Europe? Cultural and Social Dimensions of Early-Medieval Migration and Colonisation* (pp. 215–224). Relicta Monografieën 7. Brussels: Flanders Heritage Agency.

Theuws, F. (2004). "Exchange, Religion, Identity and Central Places in the Early Middle Ages." *Archaeological Dialogues* 10(2): 121–138.

Theuws, F. (2012). "River-Based Trade Centres in Early Medieval Northwestern Europe. Some 'Reactionary' Thoughts". In S. Gelichi and R. Hodges (eds.), *From One Sea to Another. Trading Places in the European and Mediterranean Early Middle Ages. Proceedings of the International Conference Comacchio 27th–29th March 2009* (pp. 25–46). Turnhout: Brepols.

Theuws, F., and Bouwmeester, J. (2013). "Early Towns and Artisan Production in the Low Countries (500–1200). An Introduction to a Series of Workshop Papers." *Medieval and Modern Matters. Archaeology and Material Culture in the Low Countries* 4: 1–10.

Tys, D. (2003). "Landschap als materiële cultuur. De interactie tussen macht en ruimte in een kustgebied en de wording van een laatmiddeleeuws tot vroegmodern landschap. Kamerlings Ambacht, 500–1200/1600." Unpublished PhD thesis. Brussels: Vrije Universiteit Brussel.

Tys, D. (2004). "Domeinvorming in de 'wildernis' en de ontwikkeling van de vorstelijke macht—Het voorbeeld van het bezit van de graven van Vlaanderen in het IJzerestuarium tussen 900 en 1100." *Jaarboek voor Middeleeuwse Geschiedenis* 7: 31–83.

Tys, D. (2010). "The Scheldt Estuary as a Framework for Early Medieval Settlement Development." In A. Willemsen and H. Kik (eds.), *Dorestad in an International Framework: New Research on Centres of Trade and Coinage in Carolingian Times* (pp. 168–176), Turnhout: Brepols,

Tys, D. (2013). "The Medieval Embankment of Coastal Flanders in Context." In E. Thoen, G. Borger, A. de Krager, T. Soens, D. Tys, L. Vervaet, and H. Weerts (eds.), *Landscapes or Seascapes?: The History of the Coastal Environment in the North Sea Area Considered* (pp. 199–239). Comparative Rural History of the North Sea Area 13. Turnhout: Brepols.

Tys, D. (2018). "Cult, Assembly and Trade: The Dynamics of a 'Central Place' in Ghent in the County of Flanders, Including Its Social Reproduction and the Re-Organisation of Trade Between the 7th and 11th Centuries." In M. Kars, R. van Oosten, M. A. Roxburgh, and A. Verhoeven (eds.), *Rural Riches and Royal Rags? Studies on Medieval and Modern Archaeology, Presented to Frans Theuws* (pp. 171–178). Zwolle: Spa-uitgevers.

Tys, D., Deckers, P., and Wouters, B. (2016). "Circular, D-Shaped and Other Fortifications in 9th and 10th-Century Flanders and Zeeland as Markers of the Territorialisation of Power(s)." In N. Christie and H. Herold (eds.), *Fortified Settlements in Early Medieval Europe* (pp. 173–189). Oxford: Oxbow Books.

van der Valk, B., and Beekman, F. (2013). "Living in a Dynamic Landscape: The Dune Area on the Island of Schouwen, Province of Zeeland, during the Late Prehistory and Early Historical Period." In E. Thoen, G. Borger, A. de Kraker, T. Soens, D. Tys, L. Vervaet, and H. Weerts (eds.), *Landscapes or Seascapes?: The History of the Coastal Environment in the North Sea Area Considered* (pp. 127–144). Comparative Rural History of the North Sea Area 13. Turnhout: Brepols

van Dijk, J., Bouman, M., Moolhuizen, C., and Bos, J. (2011). "De voedseleconomie vanaf de Midden-IJzertijd tot en met de Late Middeleeuwen." In J. Dijkstra and F. Zuidhoff (eds.), *Kansen op de kwelder. Archeologisch onderzoek op Walcheren langs de N57* (pp. 109–130). Amersfoort: ADC ArcheoProjecten.

van Doesburg, J. (2010). "Villa Non Modica? Some Thoughts on the Interpretation of a Large Early Medieval Earthwork near Dorestad." In A. Willemsen and H. Kik (eds.), *Dorestad in an International Framework. New Research into Trade Centres in Carolingian Times* (pp. 51–58). Turnhout: Brepols.

van Es, W., and Verwers, W. (2015). *Excavations at Dorestad 4. The Settlement on the River Bank Area.* Nederlandse Oudheden 18. Amersfoort: Rijksdienst voor Cultureel Erfgoed.

van Haperen, A. (2013). "Natural and Anthropogenic Factors in the Origin and Evolution of the Dune Landscape on the Islands of the South-West Netherlands." In E. Thoen, G. Borger, A. de Kraker, T. Soens, D. Tys, L. Vervaet, and H. Weerts (eds.), *Landscapes or Seascapes?: The History of the Coastal Environment in the North Sea Area Considered* (pp. 111–126). Comparative Rural History of the North Sea Area 13. Turnhout: Brepols.

van Remoorter, O. (2016). "Aardewerk." In O. Van Remoorter, S. Sadones, and R. Vanoverbeke (eds.), *Archeologische Opgraving Blankenberge, Lissewegestraat* (pp. 111–143). Ghent: Baac-Vlaanderen.

van Remoorter, O., S. Sadones, and R. Vanoverbeke. (2016). *Archeologische Opgraving Blankenberge, Lissewegestraat.* Ghent: Baac-Vlaanderen.

Verhaeghe, F. (with C. Loveluck, and J. Story). (2005). "Urban Developments in the Age of Charlemagne." In J. Story (ed.), *Charlemagne, Empire and Society* (pp. 259–287). Manchester: Manchester University Press.

Verhoeven, A., and Dijkstra, M. (2017). "Leiderdorp, a Frisian settlement in the Shadow of Dorestad." In J. Moreland, J. Mitchell, and B. Leal (eds.), *Encounters, Excavations and Argosies. Essays for Richard Hodges* (pp. 329–340). Oxford: Archaeopress.

Verhulst A. (1959). "Historische geografie van de Vlaamse kustvlakte tot omstreeks 1200." *Bijdragen voor de Geschiedenis der Nederlanden* 14: 1–37.

Verhulst A. (1999). *The Rise of Cities in North-West Europe.* Cambridge: Cambridge University Press.

Verhulst A. (2002). *The Carolingian Economy.* Cambridge: Cambridge University Press.

Vermeiren, G., Bru, M.-A., and Steurbaut, P. (2017). "Langs Gentse wegen . . . Een kijk op de vroegstedelijke ontwikkeling." In K. De Groote and A. Ervynck (eds.), *Gentse geschiedenissen ofte nieuwe historiën uit de oudheid der stad en illustere plaatsen omtrent Gent* (pp. 7–22). Ghent: Stad Gent.

Vestergaard, E. (1991). "Gift-Giving, Hoarding and Outdoings." In R. Samson (ed.), *Social Approaches to Viking Studies* (pp. 97–104). Glasgow: Cruithne Press.

Vos, P. (2015). *Origin of the Dutch Coastal Landscape.* Groningen: Barkhuis.

Wickham, C. (2005). *Framing the Early Middle Ages. Europe and the Mediterranean 400–800.* Oxford: Oxford University Press.

Wilkin, A. (2010). "Le patrimoine foncier des élites dans la region de la Meuse moyenne, jusqu'au XIe siècle." In J.-P. Devroey, R. Le Jan, and L. Feller (eds.), *Les élites et la fortune au Haut Moyen Âge* (pp. 327–343). Turnhout: Brepols.

Wilkin A., and Devroey, J.-P. (2012). "Diversité des formes domaniales en Europe Occidentale." *Revue Belge de Philologie et d'Histoire* 90(2): 249–260.

Willemsen, A. (2009). *Dorestad, een wereldstad in de middeleeuwen.* Zutphen: Walburg Pers.

Wynia, H. (2010). *Dorp aan de rivier. Archeologisch onderzoek naar een nederzetting uit de tijd van Willibrord in Leidsche Rijn.* Utrecht: Gemeente Utrecht.

CHAPTER 35

THE EVIDENCE OF NUMISMATICS

"Merovingian" Coinage and the Place of Frankish Gaul and Its Cities in an "Invisible" Roman Empire

JÜRGEN STROTHMANN

MEROVINGIAN coinage minted ca. 585–670 offers some insight into the political system of Gaul in the seventh century.[1] It was not part of a fiscal system that depended on the Merovingian family itself or even on particular Merovingian kings. Rather, it was based on the political microcosms embodied by cities that had existed from the time of the Roman Empire. These elements of Roman civilization had a social, political, and economic impact and continued to function long after the official end of Roman rule in Gaul. It was especially those cities identified as *civitates*—that is, those recognized as the central places of political units with surrounding territories—that operated within such structures (for more on cities, see Loseby, Chapter 27, this volume). Although their function changed over the course of the long period spanning from the ancient to the early medieval period, their contributions to Gaul's political system continued well after the official end of the Roman Empire in the West. Churches, too, played an important role in sustaining the cultural and even political continuity of ancient civilization from Late Antiquity to early medieval Gaul by helping maintain systems like urban centers that had existed in the Roman period.

In this chapter, we will thus explore Merovingian coinage of ca. 585–670, which was minted with the names of a large number of political and even economic units. Among these toponyms were villages (mostly as main places of *pagi*—political units under the authority of *civitates*—or sometimes incorporated into the *civitates*), and nearly all of the central places of *civitates*, that is, all cities of the former late-Roman Gaul. Those who minted coins probably engraved so many place names on gold as a means of citing the entities that paid taxes. In other words, within Gaul's fiscal system, cities remained the main political units even through the Merovingian period (Strothmann 2008, p. 374). It is important to acknowledge this role of urban centers in the Merovingian world, which supplemented other facets of Roman tradition, culture, and even language that lived on in the post-Roman period. Indeed, the political culture of the Roman Empire did not cease at all: Antiquity did not end, and there was no "dawn" of the Middle Ages. Instead, the Merovingian period was a long era of transition.

THE SYSTEM OF MINTING

Although the writings of Gregory of Tours have shaped our understanding of the Merovingian period, it is important to recognize that the stories he composed could be misleading. He wrote the *Histories* from his own perspective, which may not have represented the many voices that must have existed in early medieval Gaul (see Reimitz, Chapter 22, this volume). His world was composed largely of the elites who were active in the Frankish realm (see Hen, Chapter 10, this volume). Gregory portrayed kings and their courts, as well as the bishops who figured as the main actors in the cities of Gaul (Loseby 1998, 2006, pp. 91ff.; Loseby 1998; on bishops, see Halfond, Chapter 13, this volume). The challenges historians face in understanding early medieval Gaul are thus not much different from those they face in studying the Roman Empire. Like Gregory, historians of the Roman world tended not to reveal much about the systems that upheld the Roman Empire but instead featured the actions of elites. Nonetheless, in the case of the Roman Empire, we have the benefit of a wealth of nonliterary sources coming from a greater proportion of the actors of the Roman world. In particular, inscriptions make us aware of the important role of cities and their political systems (see Handley, Chapter 26, this volume). Even in the case of the Roman Empire, however, we are misled if we think of it as an enormous Rome-centered hierarchical state of one or two monarchs, the senate, and the army (Eck 1999; Witschel 1999, p. 21; on the army, see Sarti, Chapter 12, this volume).

Is it possible to compare societies that have been seen traditionally as very different systems without taking an insider's view like that of Gregory? Some would deny that this approach is possible given the nature of our extant sources for Merovingian Gaul. Consequently, we must look for other kinds of relevant sources for post-Roman Gaul. In addition to turning to hagiographical sources, which are also an important resource for this epoch (see Kreiner, Chapter 24, this volume), we can look to the evidence of coinage. One may argue that numismatics speaks more independently than literary sources and does not narrate particular events or present an idealized picture of the period. Known in German as "Merowingische Monetarmünzen" (i.e., "Merovingian national coinage"), numismatic remains (coins) of this period represent a generally contemporary medium that was very close to the economic and political system. This evidence reveals significant information about the political and economic structures that existed in post-Roman Gaul.

(A)   (B)

FIGURE 35.1A AND 35.1B. Solidus, 4.39 g. The legend reads, A: D N ΛNΛSTΛS-IV-S PP ΛVG, and B: VICTORI-Λ ΛVGGGB//CONOB. Dahmen and Kluge 2017, No. 53. Münzkabinett der Staatlichen Museen zu Berlin, 18211576. Photography by Lübke and Wiedemann, Stuttgart.

To give a very general picture of what we now know about the minting of coins in the post-Roman West, it is clear that the post-Roman *regna* (kingdoms) initially began to mint copies of actual Roman coinage following eastern standards of weight and iconography. However, these coins often exhibited illegible copies of the inscriptions found on the earlier issues and thus were presumably without meaning for the use of the coins themselves (Hendy 1988; for Gaul, see Grierson 1986, Figs. 35.1A, 35.1B).

From the time of Constantine I, the Roman minting system had been based on the *solidus*, a pure gold coin weighing 4.55 grams (Abdy [2012] 2016, p. 591; Grierson 1986, p. 107). It was part of a financial system that mandated the payment of taxes in gold rather than via nonmonetary-exchanges. In many locations, once gold was collected as taxes, it was melted down to cast bullion and was transferred to mints, which in this period were very few in number. In the 460s, Emperor Valentinian thus decreed that taxes paid in gold had to be purified so that they could be melted down and minted as very fine *solidi* at about 99 percent purity (Moorhead [2012] 2016, p. 602). It is possible that the Merovingians continued this practice for nearly a century, albeit with more mints than before and at a lower level of purity. Moreover, we can assume that they copied eastern numismatic usages in accepting an imperial monopoly on the minting of gold. King Theudebert (533–547) was the first leader in the West to break this imperial privilege by putting his own name on golden coins, *solidi* and *tremisses* or *trientes*; a *tremissis* or *triens* had the value of a third of a *solidus* (Stahl [2012] 2016, pp. 645–650 and Kluge 2013, p. 88; Figs. 35.2A, 35.2B).

Around the year 585, however, and perhaps in some places a bit earlier, this so-called pseudo-imperial coinage disappeared. At this time, a new system of coinage was established. Although numismatic scholars speak of the emergence of a "national coinage" (especially Grierson 1986), the term *national* in this respect is very problematic because

(A) (B)

FIGURE 35.2A AND 35.2B. Solidus (Köln, 534–548), 4.39 g. The legend reads, A: D N THEOD-EBERTVS VI. B: VICTORI-A-A-VCCC I. Dahmen and Kluge 2017, No. 5. Münzkabinett der Staatlichen Museen zu Berlin, 18202270. Photography by Lübke and Wiedemann, Stuttgart.

there was no nationhood as we now know it but instead a kind of regnal coherence. We know next to nothing about the innovator or particular king who was responsible for this new minting system across Gaul. The most common coin was the *tremissis* or *triens*, which was a third of a *solidus* as before but weighed a little less than the earlier ones, regularly about 1.3 grams. In the years after 640, however, this gold coin systematically lost its purity, and at the end of its production it became pale in color because of its substantial silver content.[2] In about 670, the *tremissis* disappeared and gave way to *denarii*, silver coins that, after a short period of transition, lost all the typical markers of the so-called national coinage (Lafaurie 1969; Grierson 1986, pp. 138–154). The "Merovingian" system of coinage between 585 and 670 existed exclusively in the political space of Gaul, although the minting systems of Italy and Spain presumably followed similar principles (Hendy 1988, pp. 51–55). Although Merovingian coins of this era could not be found in the rest of the former empire, they played a central role in the trade between Gaul and England, as demonstrated by single finds, hoards, and the large ship burial of Sutton Hoo, the last of which contained thirty-seven Merovingian gold coins (Grierson 1986, pp. 124–125).

On the post-585 *tremissis*, in the middle of the front side, moneyers struck the image of the bust of a king or the emperor, turned to the right and wearing a diadem. In most cases, this portrait reveals no individual features. Around the bust, in a circle, there is typically an inscription bearing the name of a place, given in ablative; sometimes there are short sentences like "ALBENNO FIT" (Prou 1892, No. 1334) or "SIDVNIS CIVETATE FIT" (Dahmen and Kluge 2016, No. 326; see Figs. 35.3A, 35.3B), indicating a relationship between minting and a particular place. In many examples, we find more specific references to places like a *civitas* (a city in the Roman sense, a political unit with territory), *vicus* (village), *basilica* (church), *castrum* (fortification), or even *pons* (bridge) and

(A)   (B)

FIGURE 35.3A AND 35.3B. Triens, Sion, 1.22 g. The legend reads, A: GRΛTVS MVNITΛRIVS, and B: SIΔVNIS CIVETΛTE FIT. Dahmen and Kluge 2017, No. 326. Münzkabinett der Staatlichen Museen zu Berlin, 18207526. Photography by Lübke and Wiedemann, Stuttgart.

portus (harbor) (Berghaus 1985, pp. 197–200). All of these details show the character of these places within an economic system. These locations figured as juridical entities, that is, as active participants in the political system. Although some of these places may have merited low status in the Merovingian realm, there were a lot of them (see Bourgeois, Chapter 28, this volume). This usage suggests that the self-governed *civitates*, of which there were about 100 in Gaul, were the basis for the political order of Roman Gaul. This practice continued in the Frankish realm, as we can see in the division of the territory up to the Carolingian period. On some coins belonging to individual regions, we also find abbreviations, presumably standing for the actual mint itself—for example, CA for *Cabilonno* (Chalon-sur-Saône) or LEMO for *Lemovecas* (Limoges).

On the rear side of the *tremissis*, in its middle, we find a symbol, commonly a cross, and a circular inscription showing another name, this time standing for a person, sometimes with the term "MONETARIUS" or an abbreviation like "MONE" or "MON" (Figs. 35.4A, 35.4B). These persons were no doubt *monetarii*, or masters of the mint. What they actually did in practice is not entirely clear. What we do know, however, is that they were the officials who presided over the work of melting the gold, and perhaps they did this work themselves. Presumably, the cutting of dies belonged to the competence of another official, for we are aware of the die identities of different mints. Some issues bear the name of particular kings, whereas sometimes the name of the moneyer is included as well. We learn this in particular from the coins bearing the place names of Paris, Banassac, and Marseille (Grierson 1986, pp. 128–131).

In all, there are about 600 to 800 place names and about 1,200 different names of perhaps 2,000 people on these coins. Although this is not the place to deal with the questions raised by these personal names (Felder 2003, p. 22; Buchner et al. 2017; Strothmann 2017a), we are now certain that these names belonged to a group of officials, perhaps

(A)

(B)

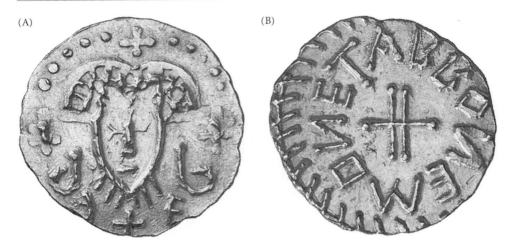

FIGURE 35.4A AND 35.4B. Triens, Limoges, 1.25 g. The legend reads, A: LE, and, clockwise from the top, B: ABBONE MONET. Dahmen and Kluge 2017, No. 271. Münzkabinett der Staatlichen Museen zu Berlin, 18206829. Photography by Lübke and Wiedemann, Stuttgart.

part-time moneyers, some of whom also worked as goldsmiths. One of them, Abbo of Limoges, was associated with the *moneta publica*, the public mint at Limoges. Another moneyer about whom we know something is Eligius, later bishop of Noyon, who was a kind of supermoneyer working at Marseille and Paris. Prior to his election and consecration as bishop of Noyon in 640/641, he was responsible for the issue of coins with royal names at these locations (see Lafaurie 1977). Eligius was Abbo's pupil and came from a Gallo-Roman family from the *civitas* of Limoges. He made his career after learning the craft of goldsmithing from Abbo at the royal court (Heinzelmann 2013, pp. 258–259). Unfortunately, regarding the other moneyers, we know little more than their names and the place names with which they were associated.

Of the places named on the coins, most are the central places of *civitates* (cities) and *pagi* (land districts), presumably representing their communities, and therefore a lot of them on the coins itself are qualified as *vici* (villages) and *civitates*, both of which are understood as political entities. The primary centers of *civitates* are known because there are literary references to their names (Strothmann 2017b). However, the *vici* often are not recorded in literary sources, so their identification and localization are based in most cases on numismatic knowledge of iconographic similarities and onomastic evidence that can tell us about the level of possibility that the name on a coin means a certain place we have in mind. A lot of work has been undertaken to compare the names on coins with modern place names and their onomastic history (Eufe 2013). However, it is important to recognize that most of the usual identifications of the current location of place names found on coins are based on weak evidence, even if most of them are probably localized correctly.

Some numismatists thought, and still think, of this system as revealing the absence of a formal system of minting coinage. They assume that a lot of "private" persons, like landlords, made their own coins, putting their names on their own issues (Grierson 1986;

Metcalf 2013; Carlà 2015, p. 154). This conclusion is based in part on the fact that roughly 75 percent of the moneyers' names are Germanic (Felder 2003, p. 26). In only a very few cases, however, do the moneyer's name and the place name show a possible connection, even though many places in Gaul established at this time had Germanic personal names and the suffix "-iacus" (Buchmüller-Pfaff 1999). By contrast, most place names on coins of this period were Roman in origin, based on Celtic and Latin linguistic usages, such as *Augustodunum* for Autun. So, on the basis of coin inscriptions, it cannot be assumed that moneyers worked for their own "private" interest.

Another assumption that seems problematic is that most of the place names on coins are thought to have been mint names. If this was an accurate assumption, there might have been as many as roughly 600 to 800 places in which coins were struck, and the process of minting must have been ephemeral rather than sustained at each location. Although there is no framework in place at present for establishing an absolute chronology of coinage, we can propose a relative chronology on the basis of numismatic iconography and the steadily decreasing weight and purity of the issues. By organizing the data in this fashion, we can see that some place names were not represented over the whole time span during which certain coins were minted. It appears that hundreds of mints were only used temporarily. Such a scenario therefore suggests that they were not the product of a "private" and regional money-making-system. Instead, the large number of place names should be seen as a product of a centralized political system across Gaul, but not with the main purpose of producing coins exclusively for regular exchange. In other words, the objective of the minting system was to coin money not for exchange but rather for fiscal purposes.

Merovingian Cities and Numismatic Evidence

For a better understanding of the role and composition of *civitates* in the seventh century, we must analyze the coinage itself, particularly the inscriptions found on them. On the coins, in most cases, the *civitates* are qualified as such. If this were only in reference to the place of the mint, it would seem that including the name of the *civitas* in the ablative form, as was customarily done for all place names, would not have been necessary. The term *civitas* in the written sources from the sixth to the early eighth century, especially in saints' lives, historical writing, and in charters, meant the political unit, but it also could be used as a synonym of *urbs* or *oppidum*, for larger and smaller cities, respectively. However, this usage seems to have been secondary. In the course of the eighth century, the term no longer meant the political unit, but primarily the city as a central place rather than as an *oppidum* (fortified place).

Extant early medieval coins provide us with very good evidence of the original form of a place name. In literary tradition, names often are spelled in the way that prevailed at the time of writing, whereas the place names themselves typically followed the evolution of language as manuscripts were copied and re-copied. By contrast, coins preserve the original spelling of a place name and its variants too. Thus, numismatic evidence provides a direct view of the state of a name in the period of our interest. However, not only the spelling of names was original in this way but sometimes even the actual name itself was original. Indeed, in some cases, names used for places might themselves change over time.

Surviving coin issues testify to several phases in the naming of cities, and it is evident that the different ways of referring to a *civitas* reveal a lot about the contemporary political situation and society (Strothmann 2013b, pp. 621–623). First, there are names of Celtic origin. However, when the *oppida* became Roman cities and received official names like Roman titles, they were often referred to by a title beginning with *colonia* or *municipium,* followed by the personal name, the *nomen gentile,* of the founder and the proper name of the city. In the West in the late third century, they mainly used the proper names of the cities, which often consisted of a Celtic–Latin hybrid name such as *Augustodunum* for Autun or *Caesarodunum* for Tours. These names were used until the end of the fourth century, as long as the system of gift-giving by the emperor and gratitude from the cities and their citizens continued to function. Typically, in the fifth century, a new name emerged, coming from the name of the people of the *civitas,* like the *Seduni,* the *Lemovecenses,* or the *Turonenses.* However, it seems that after giving the body politic of a *civitas* the name of its central location, the situation changed after the fifth century, and the close relationship between a central place and its territory became more relevant. Subsequently, in the seventh century, a lot of place names started to come from the peoples resident in that area, such as *Sedunum, Lemovecas,* and *Turonus.* These names referred to the *civitas* as a body politic in its territory. This qualification may be seen on the seventh-century coins like: "CIVITATE SIDVNIS" (Prou 1892, No. 1285), or "TVRONUS CIVI[TATE]" (Prou 1892, No. 310), which sometimes even operated without reference to the *civitas*: "LEMOVECAS" (Prou 1892, No. 1936).

To qualify as a body politic, the city required its own financial system. What was the state of civic finances? Did the cities themselves have income that they acquired by levying taxes on their own, or did they participate in public taxes? As Sebastian Schmidt-Hofner has shown for Late Antiquity through evidence recorded in the legal codes of the Codex Theodosianus and the Codex Iustinianus, cities had income for their own purposes in addition to the growing system of private charges such as repairing streets and bridges. Although two-thirds of their income went to the *sacrae largitiones* (the Roman office of public finance), the community was permitted to keep one-third for its own, as stated by Valentinian (Valentinian, CTh IV,13,7; see Schmidt-Hofner 2006, p. 221). This principle was cited again by Theodosius and Valentinian in 431 or 432 (Codex Iustinianus IV, 16, 13). In the case of church income, we know that this principle of dividing tax income into thirds survived into the early Middle Ages.

Although the constitutions of Valentinian and Theodosius, presumably did not affect regular taxes, we have to consider why the circulation of coins in the seventh century seems to correspond with this principle. Roughly one-third of single finds of coins stayed either in the places named on the coins or strayed less than 50 kilometers from the central point (Metcalf 2006, pp. 352–354). This portion of the extant coins could be understood as the funds necessary to repair the city's buildings, streets, and bridges. We have to be aware that the elites presumably refused to take on such heavy burdens on behalf of the urban community. Thus, we may infer that this income came from all the contributions the cities' inhabitants made to public offices as a whole. Indeed, taxes in the Merovingian period were not levied regularly to pay the military, but rather to fill the treasure of kings (see Hardt 2004). By contrast, cities had to defend themselves. Although there was no longer a great need to expend funds to maintain an army, significant amounts were needed for infrastructural repair which may have come from the cities' tax-collecting efforts of this nature.

Minting and State Finance

It is important to determine the main purpose of the production of coinage in the Merovingian period. Was it aimed at providing traders and consumers with money, thereby supporting the smooth operation of the economy? In the case of post-Roman Gaul, this reasoning seems unlikely. It is thus helpful at this point to turn to our main literary source describing the Merovingian minting system, the *Vita Eligii*, written at the end of the seventh century and authored by Eligius's friend, Bishop Audoin, also called Dado (Scheibelreiter 1989). Although older publications on Merovingian coinage dismissed this work as a later Carolingian fiction without reliable historical value, recent research suggests that the contents of the *vita* can be safely integrated into our understanding of this subject (on dating, see Bayer 2007; Heinzelmann 2013).

In a central passage of the *Vita Eligii*, Audoin related that the holy man Eligius went to the king and petitioned him for a place in which to erect a monastery for the spiritual welfare of both the king and his agent, Eligius. Consequently, he received the *villa Solemniacus* (Solignac) for this purpose (on villas, see Chavarría Arnau, Chapter 29, this volume). However, as he soon learned that the villa had recently been taxed, Eligius tried to get the tax-gold returned. At an unspecified location, the moneyer and possibly a second official (*domesticus simul ac monetarius*)—since in fact we do not know whether these were two separate officials or the same man (see Hendy 1988, p. 66; Strothmann 2017a)—had not been able to melt down the gold in time to hand it over to the king. As Audoin recounted in the *Vita Eligii*, the moneyer received a message that this gold was God's own and thus it was returned to Eligius (*Vita Eligii* I,15, pp. 680f.).

To clarify the details of this account, it is important to observe that the *villa Solemniacus* must have been granted to Eligius exempt from tax obligations; otherwise, Audoin would not have related this story. Moreover, if, after melting the gold, the *domesticus simul ac monetarius* struck coins rather than only making bullion, this account offers us a critical detail about the process of minting. The gold was transferred from the tax-paying villa to another place, where it was melted to be moved later to the king's possession. The numismatic evidence offers further elucidation of this account since there is an extant coin from Solignac (Felder 2003, p. 537 [No. 2014/1]; Boyer 2007, pp. 146, 150). The *Vita Eligii* thus suggests that this coin must have been struck before Eligius received tax-exempt status for the villa for religious purposes. If the place names on coins were mint names, the story told in the *Vita Eligii* would not have transpired in this manner. Instead, the place name on the coin appears to be the name of the place from which the gold came, as Alan Stahl (1982) already proposed. Melting the gold at a different place than its place of origin, as reported in the *Vita Eligii*, without minting it would not have allowed the name of the tax-paying location to be stamped on the coin. Moreover, even if bullion bearing the name of Solignac had been produced, it would not have been logical to melt it down another time for the purpose of minting coins with the name of Solignac. This logic suggests, then, that the place names on coins are to be identified with the sources of the tax-gold rather than with the places where they were minted. Therefore, gold from smaller places would have presumably been transported to a larger place, whereas the taxes from larger settlements like *civitates* did not need to be taken to another location to be melted down. This process offers an explanation for the grammalogues or symbols on some coins, like "CA" for Cabilonno (Chalon-sur-Saône), which remained for mint names (Strothmann 2012, p. 100).

From Late Antiquity, we know that nearly the same working process bound tax-collecting with minting. In the Roman Empire, taxes were drawn from juridical entities as a whole and from the time of Valentinian (ca. 368; Schmidt-Hofner 2008, pp. 191–195), they were melted down as bullion at nearby tax-collecting places, and thereafter, the bullion was transferred to the very rare mints. The story that the *Vita Eligii* tells us thus sounds very similar. Only one step in the working process was eliminated: the melting of gold for bullion as the form in which taxes were transported. An explanation for this variation is that an important difference between Roman and early medieval infrastructure was the steady loss of the centralized registration of property. We can see this in the increasing role of charters to replace municipal registration in the case of landed property (Wood 1994, p. 203; see also Classen 1955/1956). The coins presumably bear the only notice of the tax payment, and they included data about the group liable for tax payments and the quantity of taxes that were paid. This can be seen as a transitional period in minting that occurred between Late Antiquity and the early Middle Ages. If the minting system of Merovingian Gaul derived its main features from antiquity, not only in terms of its organization but also because it was a gold-based, monometallic system, we have to ask why. We will find the answer in the fact that at least some Roman successor states acted in a very similar political fashion to their predecessors.

In most societies, money is not made for the people and their wealth, but for the ruling elites and their needs. A person strikes coins because he or she needs something and aims to purchase it, whether it be a luxury item or the manpower of soldiers, as was the case in the Roman state. The state disbursed funds in this manner, and in the process of the purchase, the money involved reached people who provided the goods or services. The money then returned to the ruler when people paid tribute or taxes. The origin of tribute and taxes was nearly the same. Within the Roman Empire, the *civitates* paid taxes to counter military threats. This money thus supported the military system, which is not all that different from tribute received from the people of the provinces, like the cities of Greece before they became Roman in a legal sense, who paid the Roman state so as not to be ruled directly by the Roman emperors.

Therefore, in each case where a minting system operated, we have to ask what purpose minting served beyond its task of supplying people with coinage for trade. Without a doubt, the more sophisticated Roman state, and even the Merovingian kingdoms that succeeded it, needed money to participate in a financial system. However, in the course of fundamental political and economic change, we have to be aware of another potential answer to our question that relates to the transformation that occurred in the later Merovingian period in Gaul. That is, the shift of the monometallic monetary system from gold to silver in Gaul at the end of the seventh century reflected changes in the political system and the growing power of the mayors of the palace over the Merovingian kings in the Frankish realm following the Battle of Tertry (687). In the period in which silver coinage prevailed, the elites became more independent, and Gaul grew more politically fragmented than it had been before. We can surmise that the rulers of the land, rather than the kings, were minting new money, as may be seen in the coins of the patrician rulers (*patricii*) of Marseille like Nemfidius (Figs. 35.5A, 35.5B). Then, in what was another numismatic transition, no coins were minted that portrayed a king's face or name. What was the objective of the new ruling elites who opted to mint coins of their own and yet in a style breaking with earlier Roman tradition? In the new economy of *Grundherrschaft* (manorialism) (Wickham [2005] 2006), landowners needed money to buy goods and services, but the same money had to serve for the payment of rents from tenants in cases when these were not paid in kind.

If we look back to the period before Tertry, namely, the mid-seventh century, when gold coinage and the system of minting we have described finally prevailed, it is important to note that the inscriptions on the coinage bore no direct reference to the spatial order of the Frankish realm at all. As discussed earlier, no king had a monetary

(A)   (B)

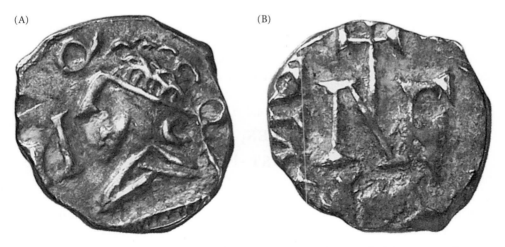

FIGURE 35.5A AND 35.5B. Denarius, 1.10 g. The legend reads, A: N–[M]FIDIVIS, and B: NE. Dahmen and Kluge 2017, No. 424. Münzkabinett der Staatlichen Museen zu Berlin, 18210744. Photography by Lübke and Wiedemann, Stuttgart.

system of his own, and the coins made no reference to Neustria, Austrasia, Burgundy, or Aquitaine as political units. Instead, we see the citation of cities of very high political importance like Chalon-sur-Saône and Paris with a large number of coins struck with their names (see the ranking presented by Kluge 2013, p. 66). Some cities occupied such a dominant position because of their economic importance. In the case of Chalon-sur-Saône, it was located on the main route from Marseille to the north and along the Saône River, which bound together the Rhône, Saar, Moselle, Rhine, and Seine rivers.

Looking more closely at the units named on coins, we see that some places were relevant only because of their economic status, whether as *pontes* (bridges) and *portus* (harbors), whereas other places had political standing, or, in the case of churches, they were juridically defined entities that were much the same as in Roman antiquity. If the *vici* on the coins, whether named as such or not, were the central places of *pagi*, which is true in many cases, then the majority of these coins bear the name of a political and juridical unit in Gaul beyond the *civitates*. However, the coins with the names of *civitates* make up almost the largest group among the coins with place names. It is possible that the coins that were struck, which bear the name of a *civitas*, were greater in number than all of the other coins struck in that time period (see the ranking of mints in Kluge 2013). In other words, the place names on coins are mostly those of political units that paid taxes in both Roman and Merovingian Gaul.

An additional source that reveals something about paying taxes in the late sixth century is Gregory of Tours's *Historiae* (IX, 30 and X, 7). He used these accounts about taxes primarily to complain about the urban populations of Gaul and to showcase the power of bishops, especially his own authority as the bishop of Tours. In one case, Gregory himself denied the obligation of the city of Tours to pay taxes to the king, noting that the will of St. Martin forbade that obligation. Consequently, the king transmitted the taxes to St. Martin. King Dagobert did this anew in the 630s (Garipzanov 2001, p. 99), a practice that presumably explains why we have coins from Tours bearing the name of Saint Martin and the word *racio*, presumably for "portion." The tax-gold went to the monastery of Saint Martin rather than not being paid at all, since after the sole exemption of the churches of Clermont-Ferrand (*Avernum*) described in another passage of the *Historiae* (X, 7) became a normal process in Frankish Gaul, charters show that the tribute of a whole city was conferred upon its churches and clerics (Kaiser 1979, p. 10).

Taxation, Cities, and Political Order in Post-Roman Gaul

Thus, it seems fairly clear that the practice of relying on cities and other political units to pay taxes was borrowed from the ancient Roman financial system. However, extracting taxes from these units was not easy for Merovingian political leaders. One reason for this difficulty was that each unit might go for a long time without paying, as much as ten years or more, and this caused inaccuracies. Whether this practice was regularly followed is not easy to confirm. However, it seems likely that this poorly defined state of affairs prompted Gregory of Tours's reaction to the attempt to levy taxes from Tours (*Historiae* IX, 30). More specifically, Gregory alleged that the former king had levied taxes and later abandoned that aim, and complained that King Childebert was now trying anew to get taxes from cities and especially from Tours and Poitiers. To do so, the agents of the king used earlier, now inaccurate, tax registers and, in the case of Poitiers, had updated them. Thus far, the exaction seems to have been regular. Yet, we do not know if this regularity was more than regional. Another reason for Gregory's reaction stemmed from the king's limited oversight of the cities. According to him, the cities were militarily on their own, taking responsibility for their own security, as was the case in their defense against Chuppa, a former agent of King Chilperic (*Historiae* X,5).

Thus, despite the fact that the Merovingian finance and minting systems were based on Roman precedents and political entities until the end of the seventh century (see Hardt 2013), the practical rule of the kings of this period was centralized and top-down in its administration. In Merovingian Gaul, the kings' courts were based at Soissons, Paris, or Chalon-sur-Saône, just as in the Roman Empire the administrative center was at first in Rome itself, then Trier and Milan in the West. The two systems required a lot of money to function, in terms of administering both the provinces and the military. In each case, the economic elites were subordinate to the political ones and were controlled by the political center. However, from the last third of the seventh century, and continuing into the Carolingian period, the economic elites no longer waited to be empowered with responsibilities or titles to act as political elites. Instead, they created their own spheres, a practice that resulted in the royal courts losing their role in integrating elites (Patzold 2013, p. 558). These developments affecting the political system were paralleled by the end of the practice of minting tax-gold from cities and the political takeover of the state by the land-based economic elites. The changes in monetary practice that occurred during the last third of the seventh century were thus far more radical than any financial developments that occurred between the late Roman period and the early decades of the Merovingian polities in Gaul.

When dealing with Merovingian Gaul, then, we have to be aware of the structural similarity between early medieval and Roman Gaul. Understanding the transition in the West from Roman Antiquity to the early medieval kingdoms requires a revised approach to the economic and political structures of both periods. When payments to hierarchical structures like the provincial administration and the military were cut, these disappeared almost immediately. By contrast, the underlying political entities, especially the cities, continued to function due to their character as social spaces and economic microsystems. Naturally, they changed in some respects, but for nearly 200 years, they continued to organize political space in an economic and political way. The bishops, who ruled a lot of these cities, as we know, were the only interfaces between civic society and the new Frankish elites who ruled with the kings. The churches offered some continuity, but more with respect to state-building rather than supporting the surviving infrastructure of the Roman Empire that the cities represented.

In order to understand changes in taxation and the role of coinage in the Merovingian period, we have to rethink the conception of rulership and gain a better understanding of whether authority came from the king or from urban- or land-based economic elites. To address this complex issue, we can look to surviving evidence from Merovingian urban centers. The Formularies of Angers, based partly on charters from roughly the end of the sixth century, show that the civic political organization and administration of the city of Angers, located directly north of the Loire, was already functioning despite the fact that the region was not as Roman-influenced as, for example, Aquitaine. Angers had a civic council and designated political leaders that represented the community, perhaps beyond the involvement of the bishop (*Formulae Andecavenses*; Bergmann 1981; see also Rio 2009, pp. 67–80).

Most sources for our knowledge of seventh-century Gaul reveal nothing about cities as essential political units. Interestingly, there are far fewer inscriptions in this period than in pre-Christian Roman Antiquity (see Handley, Chapter 26, this volume), and only a few charters from the sixth century survive, such as those that are preserved in the above-mentioned Formularies of Angers (see Rio, Chapter 23, this volume). Most current research largely links the decline of cities at the end of the sixth century with the decline of Roman culture more generally from the fifth century (Diefenbach 2013). Perhaps one reason for thinking this way relates to a change in the terminology associated with cities. In the central Middle Ages, after the resurrection of cities as political entities at the end of the eleventh century, an urban center was defined as a *comunis* and was given a proper name. In Antiquity, by contrast, a city's actions as a political body did not require that it adopt a special political name. The actors were the citizens, the *Andecaves*, *Turonenses*, *Mettenses*, and so on. Incorporating usages from ancient terminology allows us to see that when Gregory of Tours described such groups, he meant a body politic that coalesced around the actions of its inhabitants. It permits us to point to the greater continuity of functioning cities into the late sixth century.

Numismatic evidence begins to contribute to this discussion ca. 585, concurrent with the composition of the charters of Angers and Gregory of Tours's references to functioning cities. If we propose that the existing economic system viewed cities as political bodies of the Merovingian state and dealt with them in a political manner, including collecting taxes from them, a practice that ceased in the late seventh century, then we can see that the cities designated were legally defined political bodies. These cities continued to exist until the end of the Merovingian minting system and ceased only thereafter, or in some cases likely never ceased completely.

CITIES IN GAUL FROM ANTIQUITY TO THE SEVENTH CENTURY

Unfortunately, the development of the ancient constitutions of Roman cities, given by the emperors of the first and second century, is much less transparent in the sources than we would like, and very little is known about the functioning of Roman cities after the second century. However, we know that over time, from the foundation of Roman cities up to the end of the Roman West, emperors made a significant number of attempts to gain more direct control over cities in their realm. From the late second century, parts of city territories were cut off and made into political units of their own (Witschel 1999, p. 128), although we can assume that they had much less autonomy. In contrast, in Late Antiquity cities were bound more closely than before to the administration of the provinces. A main step in this direction across the empire occurred in the course of the third century with the installation of a *defensor civitatis*, whose responsibility was to take care of the Roman citizens against the actions of the elites (Jones, 1973, pp. 726–727; for the West, see Liebeschuetz [2001] 2007, pp. 126–127). However, this step also benefited the economic interests of a tax-spending emperor, who sought to increase his income by charging the elites and even the less wealthy inhabitants for infrastructural necessities like maintaining streets, water supply, and most civic buildings. As these changes occurred, the constitution of cities likewise evolved, with the elites under greater economic pressure, yet with greater power over the whole political system of the city, which was now controlled by the *defensor civitatis* and the increasingly hierarchical political order of the empire. With the end of the Roman state in the West, cities remained independent for some time before they fell under the control of the barbarian states. One can state that at the end of this process, cities were ruled by the economic elite itself. The leading actors of the urban centers were the magistrates, who may not have been elected by the *comitia* (assembly), and the *decuriones* (members of the city senate).

Evidence of the early medieval formularies, like those of Angers at the end of the sixth century and those of Marculf in the seventh century, shows the existence of constitutional rituals of enacting the formularies (on law, see Rio, Chapter 23, this volume). In the case of Angers, a kind of contract was negotiated between the king and his actors with the urban elites—in other words, between the ruler and the city. On the part of the king, the actor was called *vir magnificus illi prosecutor*, and on the side of the city, the actors were *vir laudabilis illi defensor, illi curator, illi magister militum vel reliqua[m] curia puplica, utique coticis puplici patere iobeatis* (Formulae Andecacenses Ia, p. 4). The highest authority in the city was now indeed the *defensor* (see Liebeschuetz [2001] 2007, p. 126). From Late Antiquity to the seventh century, the *defensor* moved from the provincial administration into the city itself, and a new magistrate was established in his place. Although the ancient institution of *duoviri* (a magistracy of two men) was lost in this process, the *decuriones* as civic council, acting at the forum (*curia puplica resedere in foro*), remained in place (*Formulares Andecavenses* Ia). There was thus a significant continuity between Angers's civic structure in the Roman Empire and in Late Antiquity. Even by this later period, moreover, cities were also tax-paying units overseen by the *decuriones*, with the level of taxes set by the administration of the empire.

In the late sixth century, Gregory of Tours likewise mentioned *descriptores* (*Historiae* IX, 30, "*discriptores*"), whose task was to establish the level of the city's tax assessment and obligations. The whole sum of the tax, which Gregory referred to as *census* as well as *tributa*, had to be paid, presumably by the civic institutions for the city as a whole.

Gregory's account was mostly intended to show that tax payments had been abandoned, since by this point in time they had apparently become very irregular and had to be repeatedly levied. Gregory nonetheless offered evidence of the levying of taxes in Tours as well as in Poitiers at the end of the sixth century (*Historiae* X, 30). In addition, we know from the *Vita Eligii* I,15) of regular tax payments made presumably by the whole *civitas* of Limoges before about 640.

Although the levying of taxes presumably became irregular after the end of the Roman provincial administration, the practice continued or was reenacted under the Merovingian kings. At first, they followed the manner in which the Roman administration undertook such activity, namely, by melting down tax-gold to bullion and then transporting it to the rare mints. If we integrate what Gregory of Tours had to say on this topic, we may see that a regular tax-levying system had been reinstated in at least some cities, like those of Poitiers and Tours, and presumably many others as well. This activity was undertaken at a very high level by officials, as Gregory recounted, such as the *maior domus* of the queen and the palace count of the king. Although Gregory was able to prevent the city of Tours from releasing its tax payments to the king while he was bishop (Gregory of Tours, *Historiae* X, 30), it is quite possible that this practice was invoked again after his death.

This passage in Gregory of Tours also suggests that we are witnessing the start of a new system of minting by moneyers, a system that, in the past, had been understood as the rise of a "national" coinage in the Frankish kingdoms. The cities formed the remaining constituents of an older, internal political order: they continued to be political bodies that could organize tax payments to central authorities. However, it must also be recognized that these political communities had already lost large parts of their original territories. This change is the reason that a lot of place names on coins are the names of *vici*, mostly the main places of *pagi*, which in earlier times were integrated parts of a *civitas*. Thus, the taxes levied from all tax-liable entities were not necessarily levied from cities but directly from all those entities that were under central control and could pay them. These entities also were political units, since we know that from Late Antiquity, *pagi* were political units such as the *civitates* with respect to their central administration and an inner political organization. But they were reduced in autonomy and territory starting from the second century, a process which had not ended by the seventh, as our coins show. The studies of Elisabeth Magnou-Nortier (1987; 1989, pp. 302f.) reveal that *pagi* could have an inner political organization and function as a body politic, even in the early medieval period.

In the first half of the seventh century, when Eligius learned his craft as a goldsmith, or perhaps somewhat later when Audoin composed the *Vita Eligii* at the end of the seventh century, there was a *publica fiscalis monetae officina* (*Vita Eligii* I, 3), a public fiscal office in Limoges. This small glimpse of one such arrangement suggests that, while cities had lost a large part of their territories, many nonetheless continued to serve as centers of administration for fiscal matters.

GAUL AS PART OF AN "INVISIBLE ROMAN EMPIRE"

The evolution of cities in the West from the first to the seventh century is largely a picture of increasingly reduced autonomy. Yet, although it is a story of change, it reveals more continuities than breaks. The cities of Merovingian Gaul were political bodies and played the same role for the state as they had during the Roman Empire. One may argue for the continuity of the basic structures of the Roman Empire even after the end of the provincial administration in the West. The main source of continuity with respect to politics came not from the churches but from the cities. As late as the seventh century, the activities surrounding the minting and levying of taxes in Merovingian Gaul were Roman in their origins. If we consider the Roman Empire to have been a political system consisting of a large number of political units, then we can state that this empire lived on in the Merovingian period as a kind of "invisible Roman Empire." Furthermore, churches took on a new role in the transition from Late Antiquity to the early Middle Ages. Presumably, they helped to support the communication between the basic political systems, the *civitates* and *pagi*, and the government of Gaul. As the role of the cities as political entities decreased following the last quarter of the seventh century, churches took the place of these entities, suggesting that their impact and political organization likewise owed much to the political culture of pre-Christian Roman Antiquity.

In future research, if we are to understand the role of the "invisible Roman Empire," we will need to expand our inquiry beyond Gaul to address all areas of the former Roman West. There are moments, which may be discerned even in the numismatic evidence, of a certain degree of overall regularity in the West. As mentioned earlier, the minting systems of the western *regna* followed similar principles. Adapting eastern Roman minting practices, the moneyers of the coinage of the *regna* followed the late-Roman gold standard. They had no significantly lower standard coinage in copper or silver. In Spain, for instance, the coinage of *trientes* was based on the *civitates*. And one source, *De fisco Barcinonense*, at the end of the sixth century, describes the close relationship between minting and the levying of taxes in Barcelona (Hendy 1988, p. 55). When Charlemagne went to Italy with the aim of governing the kingdom of the Lombards, he took over their minting system, which consisted of *trientes* graced with inscriptions telling of the political entities of northern Italy, presumably even revealing some level of state finances (Strothmann 2013c).

Interesting, too, is the frontier of the early medieval West, especially the Rhine. On the left bank of this river, no Merovingian minting took place; the tribute of the Saxons was not part of Gaul's finance system or its civilization. But even after the period of the so-called national coinage, the public minting activities of moneyers, the end of the entirely city-based political system, and the rising power of landlords as political actors did not bring about the end of the cultural space of the West, which continued to be based on Latin language and tradition. The Frankish realm was a political space in which the elites were part of the *regna* but not restricted by them. In the Merovingian period, the evidence of coinage allows us to see a state of Roman political culture in a long transformational process that led to the medieval state. Understanding this process, however, requires acknowledging that Roman political culture lived on as an "invisible Roman Empire" that shaped the early medieval West.

NOTES

1. The concept of an "invisible Roman Empire" is related to the research of "Nomen et Gens," a group of scholars investigating personal names from the fourth to the eighth century (see http://www.neg.uni-tuebingen.de/?q=de/ziele). This concept comes from research on Merovingian coinage and from our attempt to understand the particularities of the Merovingian minting system in the course of a large interdisciplinary project, consisting of numismatics, linguistics, and historical study, financed by Deutsche Forschungsgemeinschaft (DFG) during the years 2007–2009 (2015) in a project entitled "Die Merowingischen Monetarmünzen als interdisziplinär-mediaevistische Herausforderung." For more on this topic, see Jarnut and Strothmann 2013; especially Strothmann 2013a; Greule, Jarnut, Kluge and Selig 2017. On the concept of an "invisible Roman Empire," a colloquium on this topic was held at the University of Siegen in 2014, and a publication is currently in preparation.
2. For this minting system and its description, see: Grierson 1986 and Dahmen 2013. For catalogs see De Belfort 1892–1895 (generally); Prou 1892 (Bibliothèque Nationale, Paris); Depeyrot 1998 (generally); and Dahmen and Kluge 2017 (for Berlin).

WORKS CITED

Ancient Sources

Gregory of Tours, *Historiae*. B. Krusch and W. Levison (eds). (1951). *Gregory of Tours, Decem libri historiarum*. MGH SRM 1,1. Hanover: Hahn.

Vita Eligii Episcopi Noviomagensis. B. Krusch (ed.). (1902). *Passiones Vitaeque Sanctorum aevi Merovingici*. MGH SRM 4,2 (pp. 634–661). Hanover: Hahn.

Modern Sources

Abdy, R. (2016[2012]). "Tetrarchy and the house of Constantine." In William E. Metcalf (ed.), *The Oxford Handbook of Greek and Roman Coinage* (pp. 584–600). Oxford: Oxford University Press.

Bayer, C. M. (2007). "Vita Eligii." In *Reallexikon der germanischen Altertumskunde* 35 (pp. 461–424). Berlin: Walter de Gruyter.

Berghaus, P. (1985). "Wirtschaft, Handel und Verkehr der Merowingerzeit im Licht numismatischer Quellen." In K. Düwel, H. Jankuhn, H. Siems and D. Timpe (eds.), *Untersuchungen zu Handel und Verkehr der vor- und frühgeschichtlichen Zeit in Mittel- und Nordeuropa. Teil III: Der Handel des frühen Mittelalters* (pp. 193–213). Göttingen: Vandenhoeck and Ruprecht.

Bergmann, W. (1981). "Verlorene Urkunden des Merowingerreiches nach den Formulae Andecavenses. Katalog." *Francia* 9: 3–56.

Boyer, Jean François. (2007). "À propos des triens mérovingiens: Approche du système de collecte et de traitement de la recette fiscal en Limousin aux VIe-VIIe siècles." *Annales du Midi* 119: 141–157.

Buchmüller-Pfaff, M. (1999). *Siedlungsnamen zwischen Spätantike und frühem Mittelalter. Die-(i)acum-Namen der römischen Provinz Belgica Prima.* Berlin: Walter de Gruyter.

Buchner, S., Eller, N., Eufe, R., Greule, A., Hackl-Rößler, S., and Selig, M. (2017). "Die Legenden der merowingischen Münzen des Münzkabinetts Berlin aus sprachwissenschaftlicher Sicht." In A. Greule, J. Jarnut, B. Kluge, and M. Selig (eds.), *Die merowingischen Monetarmünzen als interdisziplinär-mediaevistische Herausforderung. Historische, numismatische und philologische Untersuchungen auf Grundlage des Bestandes im Münzkabinett der Staatlichen Museen zu Berlin* (pp. 125–154). Paderborn: Wilhelm Fink.

Carlà, F. (2015). "Wirtschaftliche Fragmentierung? Die spätantike Goldwährung und das Ende des römischen 'monetary system' (5.–7. Jh n. Chr.)." In D. Boschung, M. Danner, and C. Radtki (eds.), *Politische Fragmentierung und kulturelle Kohärenz in der Spätantike* (pp. 136–158). Paderborn: Wilhelm Fink.

Classen, P. (1955/1956). "Kaiserreskript und Königsurkunde. Diplomatische Studien zum römisch-germanischen Kontinuitätsproblem." *Archiv für Diplomatik* 1: 1–87; 2: 1–115.

Dahmen, K. (2013). "Die Merowingermünzen im Bestand des Berliner Münzkabinetts. Numismatische Grundlagen zur Monetarforschung." In J. Jarnut and J. Strothmann (eds.), *Die Merowingischen Monetarmünzen als Quelle zum Verständnis des 7. Jahrhunderts in Gallien* (pp. 155–168). MittelalterStudien 27. Paderborn: Wilhelm Fink.

Dahmen, K., and Kluge, B. (2017). "Bestandskatalog der merowingischen Münzen des Münzkabinetts der Staatlichen Museen zu Berlin." In A. Greule, J. Jarnut, B. Kluge, and M. Selig (eds.), *Die merowingischen Monetarmünzen als interdisziplinär-mediaevistische Herausforderung. Historische, numismatische und philologische Untersuchungen auf Grundlage des Bestandes im Münzkabinett der Staatlichen Museen zu Berlin* (pp. 155–292). Paderborn: Wilhelm Fink.

De Belfort, A. (1892–1895). *Description générale des monnaies mérovingiennes* (Vols. 1–5). Paris: Société française de numismatique.

Depeyrot, G. (1998). *Le Numéraire Mérovingien, l'Âge de l'Or.* Vols. 1–4. Wetteren: Collection Moneta.

Diefenbach, S. (2013). "Bischofsherrschaft. Zur Transformation der politischen Kultur im spätantiken und frühmittelalterlichen Gallien." In S. Diefenbach and G. M. Müller (eds.), *Gallien in Spätantike und Frühmittelalter. Kulturgeschichte einer Region* (pp. 91–149). Millennium-Studien 43. Berlin: Walter de Gruyter.

Eck, W. (1999). *Lokale Autonomie und römische Ordnungsmacht in den kaiserzeitlichen Provinzen vom 1. bis 3. Jahrhundert.* Munich: Oldenbourg.

Eufe, R. (2013). *Die Ortsnamen auf den merowingischen Monetarmünzen des Münzkabinetts des Bode-Museums Berlin.* Regensburg: University of Regensburg. [urn:nbn:de:bvb:355-epub-280698].

Felder, E. (2003). *Die Personennamen auf den merowingischen Münzen der Bibliothèque Nationale de France.* Bayerische Akademie der Wissenschaften, Philologisch-historische Klasse, Abhandlungen NF 122. Veröffentlichungen der Kommission für Namenforschung. Munich: Bayerische Akademie der Wissenschaften.

Garipzanov, I. H. (2001). "The Coinage of Tours in the Merovingian Period and the Pirenne Thesis." *Revue Belge de Numismatique* 147: 79–118.

Greule, A., Jarnut, J., Kluge, B., and Selig, M. (eds.). (2017). *Die merowingischen Monetarmünzen als interdisziplinär-mediaevistische Herausforderung. Historische, numismatische und philologische Untersuchungen auf Grundlage des Bestandes im Münzkabinett der Staatlichen Museen zu Berlin*. Paderborn: Wilhelm Fink.

Grierson, P. (1986). "The Franks and Frisians in the Merovingian Period." In M. Blackburn and P. Grierson (eds.), *Medieval European Coinage. With a Catalogue of the Coins in the Fitzwilliam Museum, Cambridge. I: The Early Middle Ages (5th–10th centuries)* (pp. 81–154; 460–507, plates). Cambridge: Cambridge University Press.

Hardt, M. (2004). *Gold und Herrschaft. Die Schätze europäischer Könige und Fürsten im ersten Jahrtausend*. Berlin: Akademie Verlag.

Hardt, M. (2013). "Was übernahmen die Merowinger von der spätantiken römisch-byzantinischen Finanzverwaltung?" In J. Jarnut and J. Strothmann (eds.), *Die Merowingischen Monetarmünzen als Quelle zum Verständnis des 7. Jahrhunderts in Gallien* (pp. 323–336). MittelalterStudien 27. Paderborn: Wilhelm Fink.

Heinzelmann, M. (2013). "Eligius monetarius: Norm oder Sonderfall?" In J. Jarnut and J. Strothmann (eds.), *Die Merowingischen Monetarmünzen als Quelle zum Verständnis des 7. Jahrhunderts in Gallien* (pp. 243–291). MittelalterStudien 27. Paderborn: Wilhelm Fink.

Hendy, M. F. (1988). "From Public to Private: The Western Barbarian Coinages as a Mirror of the Disintegration of Late Roman State Structures." *Viator* 19: 29–78.

Jarnut, J., and Strothmann, J. (eds.). (2013). *Die Merowingischen Monetarmünzen als Quelle zum Verständnis des 7. Jahrhunderts in Gallien*. MittelalterStudien 27. Paderborn: Wilhelm Fink.

Jones, A. H. M. (1973). *The Later Roman Empire 284–602. A Social, Economic and Administrative Survey*. Oxford: Basil Blackwell.

Kaiser, R. (1979). "Steuer und Zoll in der Merowingerzeit." *Francia* 7: 1–17.

Kluge, B. (2013). "Die merowingischen Monetarmünzen: Epochenwandel im Münzwesen—Münzwesen im Epochenwandel. Numismatische Handreichungen für Historiker." In J. Jarnut and J. Strothmann (eds.) *Die Merowingischen Monetarmünzen als Quelle zum Verständnis des 7. Jahrhunderts in Gallien* (pp. 33–92). MittelalterStudien 27. Paderborn: Wilhelm Fink.

Lafaurie, J. (1969). "Monnaies d'argent mérovingiennes des VIIᵉ et VIIIᵉ siècles: Les trésors de Saint-Pierre-les-Étieux (Cher), Plassac (Gironde) et Nohanent (Puy-de-Dôme)." *Revue Numismatique* 6(11): 98–219.

Lafaurie, J. (1977). "Eligius Monetarius." *Revue Numismatique* 6(19): 111–151.

Liebeschuetz, J. H. W. G. ([2001] 2007). *Decline and Fall of the Roman City*. Oxford: Oxford University Press.

Loseby, S. T. (1998). "Gregory's Cities: Urban Functions in Sixth-Century Gaul." In I. Wood (ed.), *Franks and Alemanni in the Merovingian period. An ethnographic perspective* (pp. 239–284). Woodbridge, NY: Boydell Press.

Loseby, S. T. (2006). "Decline and Change in the Cities of Late Antique Gaul." In J. U. Krause and C. Witschel (eds.), *Die Stadt in der Spätantike—Niedergang oder Wandel? Akten des internationalen Kolloquiums in München am 30. und 31. Mai 2003* (pp. 67–104). Stuttgart: Franz Steiner.

Magnou-Nortier, E. (1987). "Les pagenses, notables et fermiers du fisc durant le haut moyen âge." *Revue Belge de Philologie et d'Histoire* 65: 237–256.

Magnou-Nortier, E. (1989). "La gestion publique en Neustrie: les moyens et les hommes (VIIᵉ–IXᵉ siècles)." In H. Atsma (ed.), *La Neustrie. Les pays au Nord de la Loire de 650 à 850* (vol. 1, pp. 271–320). Sigmaringen: Thorbecke.

Metcalf, M. (2006). "Monetary Circulation in Merovingian Gaul, 561–674. A Propos Cahiers Ernest Babelon, 8." *Revue Numismatique* 6(162): 337–393.

Metcalf, M. (2013). "The Moneyers of Paris and Reims Compared. Strategies for Exploring the Work of Individual Moneyers." In J. Jarnut and J. Strothmann (eds.), *Die Merowingischen Monetarmünzen als Quelle zum Verständnis des 7. Jahrhunderts in Gallien* (pp. 455–465). MittelalterStudien 27. Paderborn: Wilhelm Fink.

Moorhead, S. (2016[2012]). "The Coinage of the Later Roman Empire, 364–498." In W. E. Metcalf (ed.), *The Oxford Handbook of Greek and Roman Coinage* (pp. 601–632). Oxford: Oxford University Press.

Patzold, S. (2013). "Eliten um 630 und um 700. Beobachtungen zur politischen Desintegration des Merowingerreichs im 7. Jahrhundert." In J. Jarnut and J. Strothmann (eds.), *Die Merowingischen Monetarmünzen als Quelle zum Verständnis des 7. Jahrhunderts in Gallien* (pp. 551–561). MittelalterStudien 27. Paderborn: Wilhelm Fink.

Prou, M. (1892). *Les monnaies mérovingiennes, Catalogue des monnaies françaises de la Bibliothèque Nationale.* Paris: C. Rollin & Feuardent.

Rio, A. (2009). *Legal Practice and the Written Word in the Early Middle Ages. Frankish Formulae, c. 500–1000.* Cambridge: Cambridge University Press.

Scheibelreiter, G. (1989). "Audoin von Rouen. Ein Versuch über den Charakter des 7. Jahrhunderts." In H. Atsma (ed.), *La Neustrie. Les pays au nord de la Loire de 650 à 850*, 2 vols. (vol. 1, pp. 195–216). Sigmaringen: Thorbecke.

Schmidt-Hofner, S. (2006). "Die städtische Finanzautonomie im spätrömischen Reich." In H.-U. Wiemer (ed.), *Staatlichkeit und politisches Handeln in der römischen Kaiserzeit* (pp. 209–248). Millennium-Studien 210. Berlin: Walter de Gruyter.

Schmidt-Hofner, S. (2008). *Reagieren und Gestalten. Der Regierungsstil des spätrömischen Kaisers am Beispiel der Gesetzgebung Valentinians I.* Munich: C. H. Beck.

Stahl, A. M. (1982). *The Merovingian Coinage of the Region of Metz.* Numismatica Lovaniensia 5. Louvain-la-Neuve: Institut Supérieur d'Archéologie et d'Histoire de l'Art. Seminaire de Numismatique.

Stahl, A. M. ([2012] 2016). "The Transformation of the West." In W. E. Metcalf. (ed.), *The Oxford Handbook of Greek and Roman Coinage* (pp. 633–654). Oxford: Oxford University Press.

Strothmann, J. (2008). "Königsherrschaft oder nachantike Staatlichkeit? Merowingische Monetarmünzen als Quelle für die politische Ordnung des Frankenreiches." *Millenium* 5: 353–381.

Strothmann, J. (2012). "Das 7. Jahrhundert in neuem Licht. Merowingische Monetarmünzen als Quelle für eine nachantike Gesellschaftsordnung Galliens." *Nouvelle revue d'onomastique* 54: 89–110.

Strothmann, J. (2013a). "Einleitung—Münzen, Epochenwandel und Interdisziplinarität." In J. Jarnut and J. Strothmann (eds.), *Die Merowingischen Monetarmünzen als Quelle zum Verständnis des 7. Jahrhunderts in Gallien* (pp. 13–20). MittelalterStudien 27. Paderborn: Wilhelm Fink.

Strothmann, J. (2013b). "*Civitas*-Hauptorte und ihre Benennungen als Quelle für den Wandel der politischen Struktur Galliens bis zum 8. Jahrhundert." In J. Jarnut and J. Strothmann (eds.), *Die Merowingischen Monetarmünzen als Quelle zum Verständnis des 7. Jahrhunderts in Gallien* (pp. 613–628). MittelalterStudien 27. Paderborn: Wilhelm Fink.

Strothmann, J. (2013c). "Susa und Aosta als merowingische Münzorte. Zu den Bedingungen der Kulturen im 'Alpenraum' in Antike und frühem Mittelalter." In M. G. Arcamone (ed.),

Lingua e Cultura nelle Alpi. Studi in onore di Johannes Kramer (pp. 693–713). Florence: Archivio per l'Alto Adige.

Strothmann, J. (2017a). "Merowingische Monetarmünzen und die Gallia im 7. Jahrhundert." In A. Greule, J. Jarnut, B. Kluge, and M. Selig (eds.), *Die merowingischen Monetarmünzen als interdisziplinär-mediaevistische Herausforderung. Historische, numismatische und philologische Untersuchungen auf Grundlage des Bestandes im Münzkabinett der Staatlichen Museen zu Berlin* (pp. 11–70). Paderborn: Wilhelm Fink.

Strothmann, J. (2017b). "Kommentare zu einigen Hauptorten Galliens." In A. Greule, J. Jarnut, B. Kluge, and M. Selig (eds.), *Die merowingischen Monetarmünzen als interdisziplinär-mediaevistische Herausforderung. Historische, numismatische und philologische Untersuchungen auf Grundlage des Bestandes im Münzkabinett der Staatlichen Museen zu Berlin* (pp. 403–446). Paderborn: Wilhelm Fink.

Wickham, C. ([2005] 2006). *Framing the Early Middle Ages. Europe and the Mediterranean, 400–800.* Oxford: Oxford University Press.

Witschel, C. (1999). *Krise—Rezession—Stagnation? Der Westen des römischen Reiches im 3. Jahrhundert n. Chr.* Frankfurt-am-Main: Marthe Clauss.

Wood, I. (1994). *The Merovingian Kingdoms, 460–751.* London: Longman.

CHAPTER 36

BEAD AND GARNET TRADE BETWEEN THE MEROVINGIAN, MEDITERRANEAN, AND INDIAN WORLDS

CONSTANTIN PION, BERNARD GRATUZE, PATRICK PÉRIN, AND THOMAS CALLIGARO

As a result of the availability of new scientific methods, the archaeological evidence for long-distance trade in the Merovingian period is now better verified than in the past. This new evidence points to a continuation of important trade connections between western Europe, India, and Southeast Asia, connections that were first established in the Greco-Roman period. Long-distance trade, principally maritime but also overland, between India and the Mediterranean in the Greco-Roman epoch is well attested both by texts and archaeological evidence, albeit more of the latter for India than for the West (Suresh 2004, 2007). There are few written sources that attest to the survival of such exchanges with the West in the early Middle Ages, but one notable exception is Cosmas Indicopleustes's *Christian Topography* (Wolska-Conus 1973), a sixth-century text by a Greek merchant who later became a monk. Indicopleustes, whose name literally means "traveler of the Indies," reported making a trip by sea to the southern coasts of India and testified to the precious textiles, spices, and gems that still reached the Mediterranean (Doehaerd 1971). Indian and Persian, and later Arabic documents also attest to this activity (Banaji 2012; Christides 2013). Until recently, the evidence was similarly limited for material remains. Beyond some textile remains preserved in the treasuries of churches or found in exceptional excavations like those of the Merovingian burials in the basilica of Saint-Denis near Paris, material evidence for these exchanges was rare.

This limited picture is no longer the case today thanks to recent excavations undertaken in western Europe and to pioneering laboratory work. It can now be confirmed that at the start of the Merovingian period, tiny glass "Indo-Pacific beads" and garnets from India and Sri Lanka were employed in large quantities in Gaul to produce decorative items. Both beads and garnets testify to the survival, at least until the end of the sixth century, of exchanges between the Indian subcontinent and the western Mediterranean world. This chapter focuses first on glass beads and then on garnets. It discusses the significance of recent advances in research that allows us to understand the sources of these materials, how far both kinds of artifacts traveled, and the purposes they served once they arrived in Merovingian territories.

Glass Beads: An Introduction

Glass beads are one of the most original and iconic artisanal productions of the Merovingian period. Despite their apparent profusion in early medieval graves, few production sites have been found up till now within Merovingian territories. This factor has led to lacunae in publications devoted to understanding the technology and mechanisms of the supply of this type of material. We are now closer to understanding some important aspects of these complex developments. Following a multidisciplinary study of glass beads (archaeological, archaeometric, and technological), several groups of beads have been shown to have distant origins, including Egypt and the Syro-Palestinian coast, the Middle East (probably Mesopotamia), and southern Asia (India and/or Sri Lanka).

The first half of this chapter offers an overview of current research carried out on pulled glass beads found in Merovingian contexts. More particularly, it focuses on one category of beads—miniature beads ($\varnothing \leq 2.5$ mm)—produced on the Indian subcontinent, which are found in quite large numbers in fifth- and sixth-century cemetery sites in Merovingian Gaul (Fig. 36.1). These tiny beads are commonly called Indo-Pacific beads in archaeological studies because of their wide distribution in the regions of the Indian Ocean and the Pacific.

The Technology of Drawn Glass Bead Manufacture

Unlike wound beads, which are fabricated by wrapping a mass (or "gather") of molten glass around a rotating metal rod (called a mandrel),[1] drawn or pulled beads are obtained by pulling a thin strand out of a gather of molten glass to create a glass tube. Their fabrication can be carried out in several ways that are difficult to identify from the finished object.[2] One method consists of gathering a mass of molten glass on the end of a

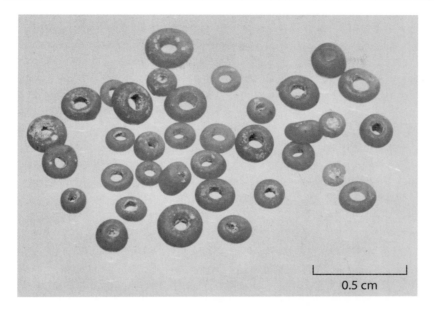

FIGURE 36.1. Green glass beads of Indo-Pacific type from India or Sri Lanka. Blanzac-Porcheresse "le Molle" (Charente), grave 931. Photo C. Pion © Hadès.

hollow metal rod (a pontil or blowpipe) and imprisoning an air bubble within it, either by blowing or by inserting a metal rod. Through use of a tool, the glass is drawn into a tube of the desired diameter and size (Fig. 36.2). The hole in the tubes is thus formed by drawing in the imprisoned air bubble rather than by perforating the glass. Subsequently, the glass tubes are cut up into beads.

The method by which the tube is sliced into beads varies. Judging from the shape of the edges of the beads found in Merovingian Gaul, two principal methods were employed: hot and cold cutting. Cold cutting is specific to beads of the "Indo-Pacific" type (Francis 2002, pp. 17–50): in this process, cold-drawn tubes are cut by a blade into small cylindrical segments. On the current Indian subcontinent, as in the village of Papanaidupet in southeastern India (Madras region),[3] the craftsman places a series of tubes (about a dozen) side by side on the cutting edge of a blade fixed on the ground and then cuts these tubes into smaller pieces by means of a second blade. This method enables a rapid and quasi-industrial production of beads with edges that display a more or less regular clean cut (Fig. 36.3A). These products can be used as is, but the majority of beads show a relatively pronounced degree of roundness as a result of subsequent treatment with heat (Fig. 36.3B).

Among Merovingian assemblages, beads fabricated by the second method of hot cutting are the most common. This approach consists of reheating a glass tube and segmenting it by squeezing it at regular intervals. This transformed tube is subsequently cut at the squeezed points to produce single or multiple segments. The edges of the beads present an umbilical shape, rarely rounded unless they have received cold finishing (polishing) or a heat treatment (re-firing). In practice, a fine metal rod is pushed into a

FIGURE 36.2. Drawing of a glass tube following the *lada* method (Gudo, Indonesia). Photo J. W. Lankton.

FIGURE 36.3. Drawn glass beads with edges cut when cold, including those in row A. with or in row B. without heat finishing. Photo C. Pion.

section of a tube to enable its manipulation and avoid the deformation or closing of the hole once softened.[4] The segmentation points can be made individually with a blunt instrument, such as a blade, or collectively by rolling the tube on a mold with a crenellated surface (Fig. 36.4).[5] The latter procedure is known to have begun in the Roman period and allows for the uniform segmentation of the glass tubes at regular intervals with a single action. This cutting technique likewise enables the large-scale production of beads with relatively standardized shapes: cylinders with rounded edges and "perfect" cylinders (perfectly straight edges) are among the most frequent in the Merovingian period; the tubular, fusiform (tapered), baluster (pillar), and ninepin shapes are much rarer (Fig. 36.5).

In the past few years, significant progress has been made in research on the origin of glass beads and the localization of their production areas, especially with regard to drawn glass technology (Gratuze and Pion 2019). The latter has required substantial technological skills and expertise. However, no trace of the fabrication or even the use of drawn tubes has been found in Merovingian Gaul, either in beadmaking or glassmaking workshops. Beads with edges indicating this segmentation technique and covered by silver or gold leaf are generally considered to be Levantine imports (Callmer 1977, p. 98; Greiff and Nallbani 2008, pp. 360–361; on golden beads: Spear 2001, p.133; Francis 2004, 508–509), as are probably most of the other beads with such edges. The latter were a key product of the Egyptian and Syro-Palestinian coasts, where they have been found in large quantities dating from the Hellenistic to the Islamic period (Francis 2002, p. 90; 2004, p. 508). All archaeologically known workshops using these techniques are located in the eastern regions of the Mediterranean basin (on ceramics from these regions, see Bonifay and Pieri, Chapter 37, this volume).[6]

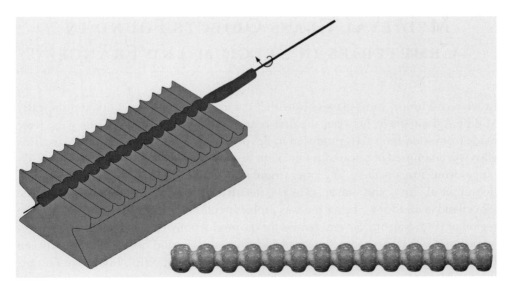

FIGURE 36.4. Proposed model of the segmentation of a glass tube at regular intervals by rolling it on a crenellated mold (photographic montage). Drawing after Spear 2001, 47, fig. 13.

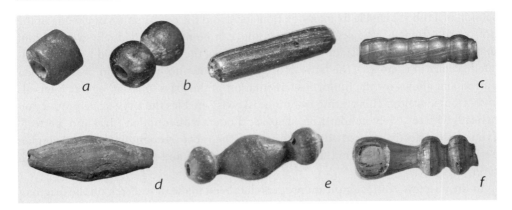

FIGURE 36.5. Principal shapes of drawn glass beads with umbilical shaped edges indicative of segmentation: A. Cylindrical "perfect," B. Cylindrical "rounded," C. Tubular undulating or not undulating, D. Fusiform, E. Baluster, F. Ninepin. Photo C. Pion.

With regard to beads of the Indo-Pacific type, the technique of their fabrication (cold-drawn tubes cut by a blade) and their morphology are identical to the beads produced on the Indian subcontinent during the same period. The hypothesis of their origin in South Asia has recently been confirmed by archaeometric analyses (see next section).

ARCHAEOMETRIC ANALYSES OF EARLY MEDIEVAL GLASS OBJECTS FOUND IN CEMETERIES IN BELGIUM AND FRANCE

In western Europe, most glass objects that circulated during Antiquity and the early Middle Ages, namely, between the first century BCE and the ninth century CE, were made from soda-lime glass produced in Egypt and on the Syro-Palestinian coast. This glass was composed of calcareous sand with very little alumina content (typically Al_2O_3 ranges from 2 to 3 percent, and rarely more than 4 percent) (Brill 1999; Schibille 2011; Rehren et al. 2015) and natron, which is relatively pure hydrated sodium carbonate (Shortland et al. 2006). The natron was probably collected in dry Egyptian lakes in the region of Wadi Natrum. Several centers for the production of raw glass (called "primary workshops") that probably functioned during this period were located between Lebanon and Egypt (Freestone et al. 2000, 2008; Rehren et al. 2010). In western Europe, the production centers of vessels and beads ("secondary workshops") worked from blocks of raw glass that came either from these primary workshops or from recycled glass (in the form of groisil, which is crushed common glass and/or tesserae, pieces of glass used predominantly in colored glass). The various archaeometric studies carried out on ancient and medieval glass objects have enabled the identification of several compositional subgroups (Freestone et al. 2000; Foy et al. 2003; Velde 2013; Velde and Motteau 2013; Rehren and Freestone 2015). These subgroups are probably related to the geographic origin of the primary workshops or particular combinations of elements. Overall, the material is nonetheless characterized by relative homogeneity in its composition (Picon and Vichy 2003; Foy et al. 2003; Foy and Picon 2005).

Regarding Antiquity and the early Middle Ages, a second type of soda-lime glass may be found occasionally. It was fabricated from a soda extracted from the ashes of halophytic plants (those that grow in saline conditions), such as *Salicornia sp.* or *Salsola sp.* This type of glass is distinguished from the preceding one by its higher content of potash (K_2O), magnesia (MgO) and phosphoric oxide (P_2O_5). Two families of plant ash soda glass have been identified. The first, found mainly in mosaic glass, is characterized by similar quantities of magnesia and potash.[7] It is frequently found among red and green glasses of classical Antiquity (Nenna and Gratuze 2009). The second type is characterized by magnesia levels that exceed those of potash. During Antiquity and the early Middle Ages, these types of glass were probably produced inland in Mesopotamia. The studies carried out on Sassanian soda-lime plant ash glass from Veh Ardasir (Iraq) provide evidence for the existence of subgroups distinguished by different magnesia/potash ratios (Mirti et al. 2009; Ganio et al. 2013). Starting in the ninth century, halophytic plant ash soda-lime glasses progressively replaced natron glass in the Mediterranean zone (Whitehouse 2002; Shortland et al. 2006; Phelps et al., forthcoming). During the same period, potash-lime glass made with the ash of forest plants appeared in western Europe (Wedepohl and Simon 2010; Velde 2013; Velde and Motteau 2013).

Most Merovingian glass objects were typically produced from different types of soda-lime natron glasses that originated from the Levantine and Egyptian coastal zones. However, late-antique and Merovingian glasses differ from those of the preceding periods in terms of their coloring and opacifying elements (those that make glass opaque). From the fourth and fifth centuries and spreading from the eastern toward the western Mediterranean, tin became increasingly important as the principal coloring and opacifying agent for yellow glass (with lead stannate, also referred to as lead tin yellow—$PbSnO_3$—replacing lead antimonate—$Pb_2Sb_2O_7$) and white glass (in which tin oxide replaced calcium antimonate $Ca_2Sb_2O_7$) (Tite et al. 2008). Although this development did not affect the color of white glass, the dominant yellow-orange in yellow glass changed to a lemon yellow hue. Whereas there seems to have been a technological innovation in relation to white glass, recent work by Marco Verità on the yellow tesserae of the Gorga collection (Italy) shows that opacification with tin yellow had been used since the second century CE (2013). Recent work carried out on the Merovingian necropoleis at Saint-Laurent-des-Hommes "Belou Nord" (Dordogne) (Poulain et al. 2013) and at Bossut-Gottechain (Belgium) (Mathis et al. forthcoming) also provides evidence for the appearance of new recipes for the production of black glass. This color appears to have been obtained by the addition of large quantities of iron and lead oxides (in variable proportions) to natron glass that probably had come from recycling.

The objects studied here include 576 glass beads from twenty-one necropoleis situated in Belgium and France (see Table 36.1). In addition to mosaic glass, four techniques of fabrication are represented within the sample studied: wound glass, drawn glass, folded glass, and perforated glass. They were analyzed by LA-ICP-MS (Laser Ablation Inductively Coupled Plasma Mass Spectrometry) at the Ernest-Babelon Center (IRAMAT, UMR 5060 CNRS/Université d'Orléans). Elements were quantified using a Thermo Fisher Scientific Element XR mass spectrometer associated with a Resonetics RESOlution M50e ablation device (ArF UV excimer laser, 193 nm). This method requires no preparation of the sample and is particularly well adapted both to composite objects and to very small objects like beads (Gratuze 2013). For this analysis, the beads were placed inside an ablation chamber. A microsample, invisible to the naked eye, was taken by a laser beam. The material sampled (a few micrograms) was carried to a plasma torch by a gaseous flow of argon and helium. The high temperature of the plasma (8000° C) dissociates and ionizes the material, whose different constituents are identified according to their mass. An electronic detector enables their quantification.

The results obtained enable the classification of the beads into four large groups (Table 36.2, Fig. 36.6) according to the principal constituents of the sand source (CaO, Al_2O_3) and the modifiers (MgO, K_2O, P_2O_5). Three of the groups (groups 1 to 3) are soda-lime glasses, elaborated either with natron or soda plant ashes commonly encountered in the Western world, as described earlier. Group 4 represents an unusual composition, characterized by the high content of alumina (Al_2O_3) and several (unusual) trace elements (Ti, Zr, U, Th, Ce, and Rare Earth Elements).

Group 1, the main group, consists of 356 beads made of soda glass of the natron type. They are characterized by low potash and magnesia content (< 1.5 percent), moderate alumina content (1.5 to 4 percent), and high lime content (4 to 12 percent). Most of the beads analyzed here correspond to this group, as do most glass objects produced during the Merovingian period. This means that they were probably fabricated using natron glass, possibly by reusing older objects. Different subgroups of beads may be distinguished by their composition. The main group is characterized by fairly homogeneous composition, although certain discrete variations can be observed that appear to be the result of recycling practices and the addition of glass of slightly different composition. Other variations may be related to particular coloring processes like the use of reducing agents or colorants of specific composition. For example, most amber-colored glass is differentiated from other natron glass by higher potassium, magnesium, and phosphorus content. These elements, usually associated with ash, were probably introduced into the glass by organic reducing agents. Some of the glass thus has a composition that is intermediate between the typical makeup of natron glass and that of soda plant ash glass. Similarly, the black glass is clearly distinct from the others. In fact, the coloring agents used for this hue, whether iron (Fe) and, in some cases, lead (Pb), have a strong impact on the elements usually brought by sands or modifiers (like alumina, potash, phosphorus oxide, etc.).

Group 2 consists of fifty-three red and green beads of the soda plant ash type, which are colored by copper. This glass is characterized by similar quantities of magnesia and

Table 36.1. Studied Sites and Corpus, with the Distribution of Beads among the Different Compositional Groups. This table does not reflect the real number of beads discovered on each site and their statistical distribution among groups, but only the number of objects selected for analysis. For some sites, only small Indo-Pacific beads were selected. However the absence of beads in Groups 3 and 4 mean that none of these types of beads have been visually identified among the glass objects discovered and studied on these sites

Site	Country	Total number of analyzed beads	Group 1	Group 2	Group 3	Group 4
Broechem (Anvers)	Belgium	49	29	16	4	
Baisy-Thy (Brabant wallon)	Belgium	25	7	18		
Bossut-Gottechain (Brabant wallon)	Belgium	41	25	2	8	6
Beerlegem (Flandre-Orientale)	Belgium	8	8			
Harmignies "Mont de Presles" (Hainaut)	Belgium	10	2			8
Pont-à-Celles-Viesville (Hainaut)	Belgium	32	22	3	7	
Verlaine "Oudoumont" (Liège)	Belgium	57	50	7		
Haillot "Matagne" (Namur).	Belgium	4	0		1	3
Arcy-Sainte-Restitue (Aisne)	France	34	27			7
Lucy-Ribemont (Aisne)	France	6	3			3
Pezens "Chapelle Sainte-Madeleine" (Aude)	France	27	6		3	18
Blanzac-Porcheresse "le Molle" (Charente)	France	45	29			16
Luxé "les Sablons" (Charente)	France	4				4
Saint-Laurent-des-Hommes "Belou Nord" (Dordogne)	France	143	124	6	2	11
La Mézière (Ille-et-Vilaine)	France	20	15			5
Vouciennes "le Maltrat" (Marne)	France	9				9
Quiéry-la-Motte "Le chemin de Beaumont" (Pas-de-Calais)	France	7				7
Estagel "las Tumbas" (Pyrénées-Orientales)	France	17	2	1		14
Saint-Denis "Basilique de Saint-Denis" (Seine-Saint-Denis).	France	25				25
Nîmes,"rue de Saint-Gilles" (Gard)	France	4				4
Harfleur, "Les Coteaux du Calvaire" (Seine-Maritime)	France	9	7			2

Table 36.2. Mean Chemical Compositions and Standard Deviation of Some Relevant Elements for the Different Groups of Glass Compared to Those of m-Na-Al 1 Glass Defined by Dussubieux (Dussubieux et al. 2010). Compositions expressed in weight percentage of oxides for major and minor elements and in ppm oxides for trace elements: 1 ppm = 0.0001%

%	Group 1	Group 2	Group 3	Group 4	m-Na-Al 1 glass
Na_2O	16.7±2.3	13.6±2.6	14.8±2.0	16.8±2.4	15.5±3.2
MgO	0.93±0.26	1.9±0.7	3.8±0.3	0.54±0.19	0.7±0.7
Al_2O_3	2.1±0.3	2.3±0.4	2.9±0.8	8.7±2.9	9.8±2.1
P_2O_5	0.16±0.16	0.71±0.38	0.23±0.07	0.09±0.09	
K_2O	0.63±0.18	1.7±0.7	2.2±0.5	1.4±0.5	2.3±0.9
CaO	7.7±1.1	8.3±1.2	7.0±0.6	2.3±1.0	3.0±1.3
MnO	0.96±0.74	0.45±0.33	0.08±0.07	0.06±0.02	0.10±0.10
TiO_2	0.14±0.05	0.16±0.03	0.14±0.04	0.61±0.18	0.60±0.28
ppm					
V_2O_5	45±19	45±12	30±4	149±35	203±84
Cr_2O_3	22±11	23±14	182±92	60±27	58±39
Rb_2O	8±2	10±3	15±4	35±9	63±27
SrO	721±185	791±159	472±53	370±156	415±161
ZrO_2	102±35	92±19	91±30	700±323	758±570
BaO	278±10	253±50	163±50	590±200	1040±480
La_2O_3	10±12	10±6	7±2	32±8	34±16
CeO_2	17±9	20±25	14±3	54±12	72±23
ThO_2	1.5±0.3	1.6±0.3	1.8±0.4	9.1±2.4	14±9
UO_2	1.3±0.2	1.1±0.2	0.7±0.1	7.6±2.6	12±11

potash, and presents characteristics close to those of soda plant ash glass identified among ancient mosaic glasses (Nenna and Gratuze 2009). Among the latter, red and green glass also dominates the glass beads made of soda plant ash glass. Thus, we can hypothesize that these objects, like those of the first group, come from the reutilization of ancient Roman glass (Verità et al. 2013). A continuous increase in the quantity of potash and magnesia is observed between the first group of natron glasses and Group 2, probably resulting from the recycling and mixture of different types of glass (Fig. 36.6).

Group 3 also consists of beads made of soda plant ash glass, but the twenty-five glass beads that compose this group are clearly distinguished from those of Group 2 by significantly higher concentrations of magnesia accompanied by a relatively low proportion of phosphorus. This type of glass is not often found among ancient Mediterranean productions and seems more closely related to the glass identified as being made in Mesopotamia (Mirti et al. 2009). It is unlikely that the beads of this type

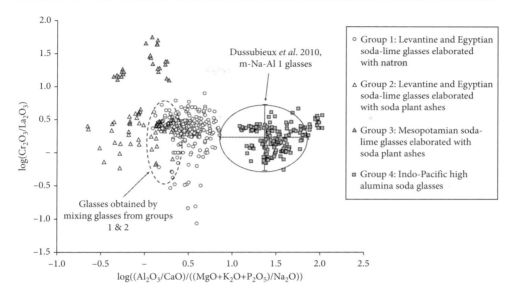

FIGURE 36.6. Distribution of the main chemical groups identified among the glass beads. Logarithm of the ratios between the main constituents of sands (Al_2O_3/CaO) and fluxes ($K_2O + MgO + P_2O_5/Na_2O$) versus the logarithm of the ratio between chromium and lanthanum oxides. Our groups are compared with the "m-Na-Al 1" Indo-Pacific glass group defined by L. Dussubieux (Dussubieux et al. 2010).

were produced by Merovingian craftsmen. Instead, they were almost certainly imported, probably from workshops located in Sassanian Mesopotamia. The lanthanum and chromium contents (Table 36.2, Fig. 36.6) which characterize Mesopotamian productions, distinguish this glass from other soda glass beads (Shortland et al. 2007).

The 142 glass beads from Group 4 appear to be very different from those of the three previous groups since they only include miniature Indo-Pacific beads ($\varnothing \leq 2.5$ mm). These beads are made from soda glass characterized by high alumina content (> 4 percent), low lime content (< 3 percent), and potash content higher than that of magnesia. The glass beads of this group are also characterized by levels of trace elements (cerium, thorium, uranium, and zirconium) that are clearly much higher than those in the other groups (Table 36.2). In comparison with glass coming from southern and southeastern Asia, it appears that this glass is in every respect similar to that of type "m-Na-Al 1" produced at the same time in southern Asia (Table 36.2, Fig. 36.6), particularly in southern India and Sri Lanka. Laure Dussubieux has identified this glass based on her analyses of beads and raw glass from sites dated between the fourth century BCE and the fifth century CE (Dussubieux et al. 2008, 2010). During this period, this type of glass did not circulate in the Mediterranean in the form of raw glass. With the exception of some Byzantine glass vessels (Schibille 2011; Rehren et al. 2015), which have been discovered mainly in Turkey, the only objects made with a luminous soda glass during the fifth and sixth centuries that have been found in the western Mediterranean world are the beads in question. Moreover, the fabrication technique of cold-cutting drawn tubes, the knowledge of which does not appear to have spread to the western Mediterranean, and the composition of the glass (high aluminous soda glass), indicate that these 142 beads did indeed come from the Indian subcontinent.

Several production sites are known for this period in southern and southeastern Asia, including Arikamedu, Karaikadu, and Manikollai (southeastern India), Anuradhapura, Giribawa, and Mantai (Sri Lanka), Khlong Thom, Khuan Lukpad, and Satingpra (Thailand), Kuala Selinsing (Malaysia), Muara Jambi (the Indonesian island of Sumatra), and Oc-èo (Vietnam) (Francis 2002, 2004; Bellina and Glover 2004; Dussubieux et al. 2008; Gratuze and Sarah 2012). However, due to the existence of many poorly dated sites in other coastal regions of India, it is possible that several production centers have not yet been identified (Bellina 2002). Given the current state of knowledge, it is not yet possible to attribute Merovingian finds to any specific archaeological site in southern India or Sri Lanka.

In all, Indo-Pacific beads have been found in forty-four Merovingian cemeteries, whose geographical distribution shows their wide diffusion (Fig. 36.7). Indeed, they are found throughout Merovingian Gaul and even beyond, in the current territories of the Netherlands, Germany, Switzerland, Spain and, although not indicated on the map, Serbia (the necropoleis of Viminacium and Singidunum III). These cemeteries contain a minimum of 114 graves that contain a total of 6,734 Indo-Pacific beads; no less than 3,037 of these beads were found at the French site of Saint-Laurent-des-Hommes "Belou Nord" (Dordogne). Thanks to exemplary collaborative work, it has been possible to conduct archaeometric analyses of 576 beads from twenty-one Merovingian sites (Table 36.1). Of these, 142 beads from sixteen sites reveal composition characteristic of Indo-Pacific glass.

From a morphological point of view, Indo-Pacific beads are the smallest of the Merovingian period, with a diameter of approximately 2 millimeters. The inventory of shapes (Fig. 36.8) is quite diverse, despite the fact that they are basically sections of tubes: namely, short cylinders with a degree of roundness that is more or less pronounced depending on the degree of re-firing. The chromatic spectrum is varied: green (6,291 examples), orange with a red core (233 examples), black (184 examples), yellow (18 examples), slightly translucent "milky" white (5 examples), and red (3 examples). The predominance of green (93 percent of the total studied here) may express a preference for this color. Furthermore, black, orange, red, yellow, and white beads are present only in the oldest graves dated to the *Proto-Mérovingien* or the *Mérovingien Ancien 1* (according to the standardized chronology for Merovingian-era grave-goods in northern Gaul) (Legoux et al. 2009), that is, between 440/450 and 520/530. The green beads show a longer duration of use. They derive mainly from contexts dated to the *Proto-Mérovingien* or the *Mérovingien Ancien 1* (forty-three graves), whereas they are less common in the *Mérovingien Ancien 1* or *Mérovingien Ancien 2* (twenty graves), between 470/480 and 560/570, and even rarer after the *Mérovingien Ancien 2* (three graves).

Therefore, Indo-Pacific beads were mainly traded between the mid-fifth and mid-sixth centuries in Europe, where they were mainly worn on necklaces or used to decorate the

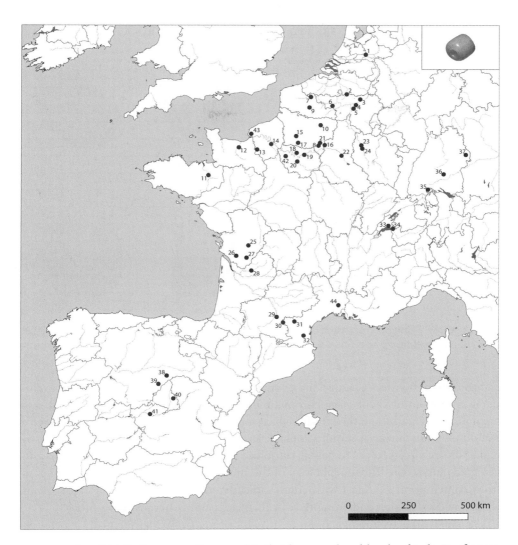

FIGURE 36.7. Distribution map of necropoleis that have produced beads of Indo-Pacific type from the Indian subcontinent. DAO C. Pion. 1. Rhenen "Donderberg" (NL) (?), 2. Bossut-Gottechain (BE), 3. Verlaine "Oudoumont" (BE), 4. Haillot "Matagne" (BE), 5. Spontin (BE), 6. Harmignies "Mont de Presles" (BE), 7. Marquette-lez-Lille "Haut-Touquet" (FR), 8. Armentières-sur-Ourcq (FR), 9. Quiéry-la-Motte "Le chemin de Beaumont" (FR), 10. Lucy-Ribemont (FR), 11. La Mézière (FR), 12. Saint-Martin-de-Fontenay (FR) (?), 13. Capelle-lès-Grands "Les Terres noires" (FR) (?), 14. Louviers "rue du Mûrier" (FR), 15. Bulles "Sainte-Fontaine" (FR), 16. Villers-Agron-Aiguisy (FR), 17. Montataire "La Coquetière" (FR), 18. Saint-Denis "Basilique de Saint-Denis" (FR), 19. Lagny-sur-Marne (FR), 20. Grigny (FR), 21. Arcy-Sainte-Restitue (FR), 22. Vouciennes "le Maltrat" (FR), 23. Verdun "Abbaye Saint-Vanne" (FR), 24. Dieue-sur-Meuse (FR), 25. Luxé "Sablons" (FR), 26. Chadenac "La Chapelle" (FR), 27. Blanzac-Porcheresse "le Molle" (FR), 28. Saint-Laurent-des-Hommes "Belou Nord" (FR), 29. Vernet "le Mouraut" (FR), 30. Molandier "Bénazet" (FR), 31. Pezens "Chapelle Sainte-Madeleine" (FR), 32. Estagel "las Tumbas" (FR), 33. Lausanne "Bel-Air" (CH) (?), 34. La Tour-de-Peilz "Clos d'Aubonne" (CH), 35. Schleitheim (CH), 36. Gammertingen (DE), 37. Lauchheim (DE), 38. Duratón (SP), 39. Espirdo-Veladiez (SP), 40. Alcalá de Henares (SP) (?), 41. El Carpio de Tajo (SP), 42. Vicq (FR), 43. Harfleur "rue de Saint-Gilles" (FR), 44. Nîmes "Les Coteaux du Calvaire" (FR). Although these beads are easily recognizable, their presence in five of the sites is probable but still needs to be confirmed by a visual examination of the material (cf. sites marked with a "?").

FIGURE 36.8. Principal shapes and colors of South Asian glass beads discovered in Merovingian Gaul. Photo C. Pion.

embroidery of textiles (Gratuze and Pion 2019). At this time, ornaments were exclusively composed of small monochromatic drawn beads with edges indicative of segmentation (sometimes in the hundreds) in small or very small formats. According to a well-known use during Antiquity, some glass colors imitated more precious and costly materials such as jet (black in color), turquoise (blue-green or green-blue in color), silver, gold, and so on. The morphology of the Indian beads was thus not very different from contemporary models with edges indicative of segmentation (Fig. 36.9). They were, however, smaller and presented a brilliant appearance because of re-firing.

Ultimately, the technological study of glass beads from Merovingian cemeteries, enriched by archaeometric analysis, leads to a better understanding of the mechanisms by which they were supplied. Moreover, the results provide insight into the great maritime and overland trade between the Indian, Mediterranean, and Merovingian worlds. During the second half of the fifth and the first third of the sixth centuries, bead craftwork appears to have been little developed in western Europe. The market was mainly supplied with products from the eastern Mediterranean, Egypt, and the Middle East, some of which were the Indo-Pacific models coming from the Indian subcontinent. These tiny beads, mainly green in color, perfectly matched the taste and usages of the time: principally, ornaments that were composed of miniature beads in monochromatic drawn glass. Their progressive rarity after 530 was probably related to a change of fashion in western Europe. The fashion of ornamentation with many small, monochrome beads, imitating more precious materials, progressively disappeared, as likely did the use of beads in embroidery. There was, however, considerable expansion in the local production of wound beads, which showed impressive diversity in shape as well as in color and decoration. The Merovingians thereafter developed an appreciation for

FIGURE 36.9. Morphological comparison of drawn glass beads with edges indicative of segmentation (A) and those of Indo-Pacific type (B). Photo C. Pion.

polychrome beads, and the contemporary craftsmen learned to exploit glass for its intrinsic ornamental qualities.

HISTORICAL AND ECONOMIC PERSPECTIVES ON GLASS BEADS

The presence of these glass beads in Merovingian Gaul provides evidence for trade between the Indian Ocean and the Merovingian world. Some ancient historians were familiar with the maritime and overland trade routes linking the Indian world and the Mediterranean world, and recorded their existence in textual sources such as the *Periplus of the Erythraean Sea*, a first-century CE maritime itinerary (Schoff 1912; Casson 1989; Boussac, Salles, and Yon 2012), and, as mentioned above, the sixth-century *Christian Topography* attributed to Cosmas Indicopleustes (Wolska-Conus [1968–1973] 2006). Among the Indian ports cited in the *Periplus* is that of Podoukê, identified as the site of Arikamedu (Mahadevan 1970). The site of Mantai, in northwestern Sri Lanka, has been identified with Modutti, cited in Ptolemy's second-century treatise *Geographia* (Berggren and Jones [2000] 2002; Francis 2004, p. 473). Beads were probably not objects of exclusive trade. Easy to transport in large quantities, they would have formed part of the cargos, included with spices, incense, textiles, precious and semiprecious stones, and so on, that came from the East and the Far East, brought through the Red Sea or the Arabo-Persian Gulf to the trading posts of the Syro-Lebanese coast. From there, they were traded to Europe alongside Levantine productions, including beads with metallic leaf and probably most of those having edges indicating segmentation.

As shown previously, however, a change of fashion in Merovingian Gaul perhaps explains why the Indian beads appear less frequently after 530, in contrast to garnets from the Indian subcontinent, which appear to have remained a desirable object of trade. By the end of the sixth century, however, Indian glass beads disappeared definitively from funerary contexts in Gaul. If the reasons for this interruption are still difficult to define, this break in supply coincides with that of the garnets, as will be demonstrated in the next section.[8]

The Origin of *Cloisonné* with Garnets

One of the most dramatic cultural manifestations of the period of the great migrations and the subsequent "barbarian kingdoms" was, without a doubt, the diffusion in the West of the so-called *polychrome* style (Périn 1993). This decorative art took two forms: the first, known as *cloisonné* style, corresponds to luxury objects covered by a mosaic of garnet inserted in a metallic setting, which developed in the fifth and sixth centuries. The second, a style featuring isolated gems and glass inlays on "mounted bezels" appeared in western Europe by the end of the sixth century. Art historians and archaeologists are still divided as to the origin and diffusion of these two styles, and the divergent theories can be supported by a comparative analysis of the stylistic and technical characteristics of the luxury objects, the dating of the materials from which these objects were made, and by the interpretation of their geographic distribution. By the 600s, as will be shown, Indian garnets ceased to be traded in the West, and garnets of local provenance were temporarily employed to produce the cloisonné style, without sustained success, possibly due to the lack of large and transparent garnets.

Cloisonné (from the French word *cloison meaning* partition wall) consists of a decor that is entirely or partially paved with thin platelets of red garnets finely cut and polished to match each cell, or very rarely with pieces of glass, especially red glass, which could only be procured with difficulty in Europe during the fifth and sixth centuries (Fig. 36.10). Garnet platelets were disposed in a geometric pattern, or sometimes featured zoomorphic shapes, formed by metal partition walls welded on their interior housing, which was likewise made of metal (gold, silver—often gilded, or copper alloys). The garnets and glass paste platelets typically were laid atop a thin metallic foil of gold or more frequently silver, sometimes gilded, which was generally embossed by stamping. This foil called *paillon* acted as a mirror reflecting the natural light.[9] In each case, the *cloisonné* decoration was determined by the shape of the supporting object (belt plates, brooches, decor on the sheaths of swords and scramasaxes, or liturgical objects in the Christian world) or the many independent motifs (animals, interlacings) that were purely geometrical or offered a figurative character (evoking the scales of fish or the feathers of birds, for instance).

FIGURE 36.10. Round brooches of Queen Aregund directly exposed to the extracted beam of the AGLAE accelerator for nondestructive analysis by the PIXE method of the garnets they contain. Photo T. Calligaro

Many scholarly publications, with sometimes diverging interpretations, have been dedicated to understanding the origin of the *cloisonné* style (Ambroz 1971; Zasetskaja 1982, 1999; Arrhenius 1985; Schukin and Bajan 1995; Kazanski and Périn 1996; Adams 2000, 2011). It is clear, however, that *cloisonné* appeared in the third and fourth centuries between Constantinople and Iran, and thus in the Near and Middle East. From there, it reached central and western Europe in steps, possibly conveyed by the Alano-Sarmatian vassals of the Sassanid Persians, as witnessed by a series of important discoveries: in Pietroassa and Simleul-Silvaniei (Romania) in the first third of the fifth century, followed by Apahida (Romania), Blucina (Moravia), and Bakodpuszta (Hungary) in the second half of the fifth century. Finds at Pouan (Aube) and Tournai (Belgium), as well as the tomb of Childeric I dated to the last third of the fifth century, provide the earliest evidence for the arrival of the cloisonné style in western Europe (Kazanski et al. 2000). Adapted by local artisans, this style, the most remarkable pieces of which may have been produced in centralized workshops in Byzantium or Ravenna, experienced a broad diffusion in the barbarian kingdoms of the West (Ostrogothic and Lombard Italy, Visigothic Spain, Merovingian Gaul, the Anglo-Saxon kingdoms, Germania, and Scandinavia and Vandal Africa). They included among them both objects of very high quality and less refined productions (on Merovingian examples, see: Vierck 1974, 1985; Fleury and France-Lanord 1998).

HISTORIOGRAPHICAL REMINDER OF THE GEOLOGICAL ORIGINS OF GARNETS USED BY EUROPEAN GOLDSMITHS

By the end of the nineteenth century, the red inlays of the *cloisonné* style were studied to determine their composition: glass, enamel, or stone (de Linas 1864) and their origin. Their resistance to being scratched by a steel blade revealed that they were almost always made of garnets, a red mineral, whereas the use of red glass paste was exceptional (Greiff and Banerjee 1994). The enormous quantity of garnets required to manufacture *cloisonné* items soon raised the question of their origin, a question left unanswered by the ancient texts, which were silent on this issue.

It is useful to summarize some important features of the garnets. They possess the requisite qualities to be classified as a precious stone: sufficient hardness to ensure durability (H = 7 equivalent to rock crystal); good transparency; a high refraction index (n = 1.75) giving a high gloss; and, above all, an attractive hue consisting of a palette of red shades ranging from pink to orange (Gilg et al. 2008). In contrast to most gems, however, the chemical composition of garnets is not constant. They form a mineral family of variable composition resulting from a mixture at the molecular level of mineralogical species called end members (e.g., pyrope $Mg_3Al_2(SiO_4)_3$, almandine $Fe_3Al_2(SiO_4)_3$ and spessartite $Mn_3Al_2(SiO_4)_3$). The archaeological garnets generally belong to the pyralspite group, which results from the mixing of pyrope, almandine, and spessartite end members (Deer et al. 1982; Kievlenko 2003; Frost et al. 2002; O'Donoghue 2006). The chemical composition of garnets depends on the nature of the host rock and the conditions of pressure and temperature during the metamorphic formation of the crystals. Their composition, which varies from one location to another, constitutes a potential fingerprint that can be exploited to determine its provenance.

Garnets are rarely mined from their host rock, which would be difficult but are rather gathered from secondary deposits called placers, which result from the natural weathering of the rocks. For instance, raw garnet crystals are commonly handpicked from alluvial deposits along the riverbanks or in gravel extracted from galleries dug in the sediments. While garnets are relatively common and their occurrences are widespread, deposits of gem quality (that is, stones that are large in size and transparent because they are free of inclusions and cracks) remain few.

Garnets adorning armament, jewelry, and clothing accessories from the early Middle Ages have been the subject of scientific investigations since the 1960s. The garnets studied were few in number and were investigated using different methods. All studies point out the presence of distinct garnet groups, sometimes bearing resemblance to garnets from India and Sri Lanka, but a general picture of the garnet supply could not be advanced. In the earliest study, O. Mellis considered garnets from early medieval artifacts excavated in Sweden (Mellis 1963). From the refraction index, the specific gravity, and the absorption spectrum, an approximate end-member percentage of each garnet could be assessed. The garnets were categorized into five groups on the ground of the almandine to pyrope ratios, but without a determination as to their geological provenance.

The disappointing outcomes of these first mineralogical studies led Helmut Roth, in a famous article (1980), to conclude that this geochemical approach was elusive and that a comprehensive archaeological approach supplemented with the study of written sources was to be preferred. Nevertheless, in 1982, Mavis Bimson, Susan La Niece, and Morven Leese analyzed 106 garnets mounted on luxury objects from the presumed royal tomb of the ship burial of Sutton Hoo (East Anglia, ca. 620/630) using X-ray fluorescence (Bimson, La Niece, and Leese 1982). The results were compared to those found for garnets from objects of the Merovingian period in Sweden, Germany, and Crimea. Despite the limitations of the analytical technique (magnesium could not be measured, hence the pyrope proportion), interesting results were obtained by comparing, with the help of statistical methods, garnets elsewhere on the same object as well as on other pieces. Most garnets from Sutton Hoo objects were found to be almandines of comparable composition to those of continental artifacts from the Merovingian period.

In 1985, Brigit Arrhenius dedicated one chapter of her monumental study of Merovingian *cloisonné* style to the characterization of garnets (1985). A set of sixty-five loose garnets were analyzed by X-ray diffraction and sorted into four groups according to slight differences in atomic distances. By comparing them with geological garnets from Bohemian deposits in the Czech Republic, Sri Lanka, and Austria, Arrhenius proposed that archaeological garnets of Group 1—almandines most often found on Merovingian objects—were coming from a deposit located in Zbyslav, Czech Republic. The garnets of Group 2, identified on objects found in Hungary, could have been exploited from deposits located in southwest Austria. By contrast, the garnets of Group 3 might come from deposits in Asia Minor, and those of Group 4 from deposits in Sri Lanka and India.

In 1997, Staf Van Roy and Lisa Vanhaeke published a gemological study of almandine garnets mounted on eight Merovingian objects from the Musées Royaux d'Art et d'Histoire, Brussels. Examining microscopic mineral inclusions trapped in the garnets, the authors distinguished two groups. Group 1 garnets had few inclusions (e.g., rutile needles, zircons), among which were notable microscopic dark crystals surrounded by a dark halo that were visually identified as uranium-rich inclusions. By contrast, the garnets of Group 2 contained many more inclusions, notably apatite, ilmenite, and zircon crystals. Drawing on the work of Eduard Josef Gübelin and John Koivula on inclusions in gems (Gübelin and Koivula 1986), they concluded that the studied almandines featured strong parallels to garnets from India and Sri Lanka, and so they dismissed the possibility, earlier proposed by Arrhenius, that these almandine garnets could originate from Austria.

In 1998, François Farges published the composition of 118 garnets on objects found in aristocratic tombs dating to the early Merovingian period excavated at Louvres-en-Parisis, France. The analytical method employed was PIXE (Particle Induced X-ray Emission)

(Dran, Calligaro, and Salomon 2000), implemented with the AGLAE particle accelerator of the Centre de Recherche et de Restauration at the Musées de France, as it is the case for our study (Pichon et al. 2015). Surprisingly, instead of almandine, which is commonly observed for these types of objects, pyraldine garnets were found. The study distinguished three types: Type I, which were pyraldine (40 percent pyrope and 60 percent almandine) possibly coming from Sri Lanka, Type II chromium-poor pyropes (60 percent pyrope and 30 percent almandine) of undetermined provenance, and Type III, chromium-rich pyrope (70 percent pyrope), considered to originate from Bohemia. While this work was the first to identify chromium-rich pyropes, especially on artifacts dated from an early period (end of the fifth century), the reanalysis of the same garnets showed that the composition of the other garnets was inaccurately determined (Calligaro 2008).

In 1998, Susanne Greiff published a study of 100 archaeological garnets mounted on objects from the collections of the Römisch-Germanisches Zentralmuseum in Mainz, Germany, supplemented by geological garnets from eighty-two deposits in Europe and Asia against which they could be compared. Two analytical techniques were employed: X-ray fluorescence and quantitative analysis by means of a scanning electronic microscope. Four groups of garnets named H, S1, S2, and S3, were distinguished according to their composition in iron, calcium, and manganese. These results were compared to the largest database of garnets available during this period. The garnets of Group H, the most numerous (58 percent), were almandines that showed great similarity with the geological garnets from India, and in particular, from Orissa and Madhya Pradesh. Group S1, composed of pyralspite garnets, could be paralleled with geological garnets from deposits in Tamil Nadu (India), Simplon (Switzerland), and Holt (Norway). Moreover, Group S2 could have come from Ratnapura (Sri Lanka) or from Tamil Nadu (India), whereas Group S3 did not correspond with any of the reference garnets considered. It should be noted that Greiff did not identify any pyrope in the archaeological garnets studied and so dismissed the possibility that they came from the vast majority of the deposits found in Scandinavia and central Europe.

Finally in 2000, Dieter Quast and Ulrich Schüssler studied 203 garnets from forty-eight Merovingian artifacts from the Württembergisches Landesmuseum collections in Stuttgart, Germany, using an electron microprobe (Quast and Schussler 2000). Garnets were sorted into two groups: Group 1 composed of the almandines and pyralspite showing great similarity with the reference garnets from India and Sri Lanka, without ruling out a possible Scandinavian or Alpine origin. Group 2 consisted of chromium-rich pyropes with close chemical composition to sixty-nine reference garnets from Třebenice, Měrunice, in Bohemia. The garnets of this group were of small size and were exclusively found on late objects after the second half of the seventh century. The authors interpreted these results as owing to a change in supply of the garnets during the course of the seventh century, when garnets conveyed to that point from Asia were replaced by Bohemian pyropes.

The synthesis of all the previous works is in fact complex. While all studies agree on the use of different types of garnets during the Merovingian period, it is difficult to compare the results obtained by different authors. Moreover, the methods used before 1999 did not provide accurate numbers, but often only points in composition plots. As Bimson later proposed (1985), it would have been useful to define a set of standard-reference garnets to standardize protocols and instruments employed to analyze these gems (Bimson et al. 1982).

THE RESULTS: EVIDENCE FOR SIX
GROUPS OF GARNETS

We report here the chemical composition of several thousand archaeological garnets from the Merovingian objects excavated. The results are compared first to data from the literature and second to measurements of reference geological garnets lent by geology and natural history museums, as well as samples gathered from placers in India and Sri Lanka and provided by the local geological surveys during four field missions (2011, 2012, 2013, 2017).

The PIXE method employed (particle-induced X-ray emission) makes it possible to measure a wide range of elements present in garnets, whose major constituents are Mg, Al, Si, Ca, Mn, Fe, and trace elements (less than 0.1 percent), such as Ti, Cr, Mn, Cu, Zn, Rb, Sr, Zr, and Y. The major constituents allow us to determine the proportions of end members (almandine, pyrope, spessartite, and grossular). The concentration in trace elements, notably titanium (Ti), chromium (Cr), and yttrium (Y), are particularly informative. Certain elements like zinc (Zn) or copper (Cu) were found at a concentration too low to be useful (on the order of a few parts per million or ppm). The composition of the major elements in a single garnet was generally found to be uniform. This was also the case for the trace elements, with the exception of yttrium, which can feature band-like variations.

The composition in Ca (in the form of lime oxide CaO) versus Mg (in the form of magnesia oxide MgO) is given in Figure 36.11. This diagram makes it possible to distinguish six groups of garnets, which is indeed remarkable, above all if one considers the extent of the geographical zone (most of Europe) and the range of the period covered (from the mid-fifth century to the early eighth century). The existence of these six groups is confirmed by the concentration of yttrium and chromium, chemical elements that are present in trace amounts, a fact not previously established. These groups resulted from the application of statistical methods of discriminant analysis and clustering (Baxter 2015) to the concentration values of the most significant elements with the help of the statistical processing software STATISTICA (Sá 2007).

The six groups identified include the following: two groups of almandines, labeled Type I and Type II, which were distinguished by similar content but distinct amounts of MgO and CaO; two groups of pyraldines called Type IIIa and Type IIIb; and two groups of pyropes, called Type IV and Type V. The diagram Y_2O_3 in relation to MgO (Fig. 36.12)

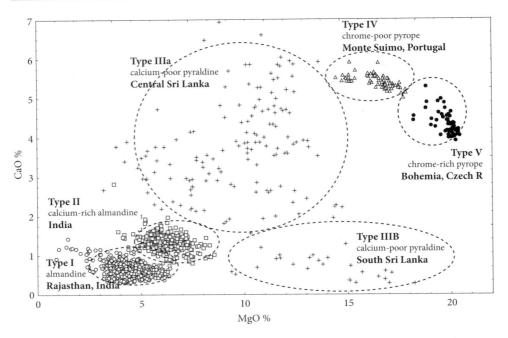

FIGURE 36.11. Diagram of CaO in terms of MgO providing evidence of the six types of garnets identified in Merovingian objects.

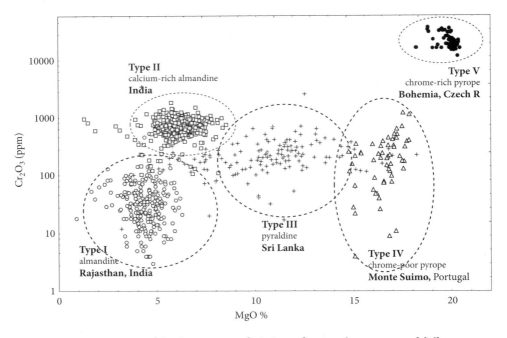

FIGURE 36.12. Diagram of Cr_2O_3 in terms of MgO confirming the presence of different types of garnets identified in Merovingian objects.

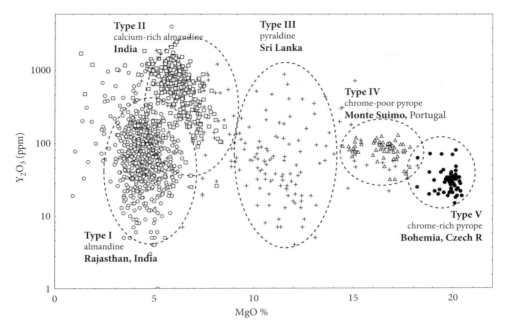

FIGURE 36.13. Diagram of Y_2O_3 in terms of MgO distinguishing in particular the Types I and II present in Merovingian objects.

allows us to distinguish clearly between almandines of Types I and II, whereas the diagram Cr_2O_3 versus MgO (Fig. 36.13) differentiates between two types of pyropes: Type V containing chromium (2 percent) and Type IV, which does not contain it. The table synthesizes the average compositions and the standard deviation of the six types, which are explained with reference to their contents, pure areas, as well as their frequency (Table 36.3).

Interesting correlations were observed between the six types of garnets within the objects. Types I and II are almost always associated in a single object; the same is true of Types IV and V. By contrast, the mixture of almandines (Types I and II) and pyropes (Types IV and V) is exceptional. The proportions between Type I and Type II, just as Types IV and V, are nonetheless variable from one object to the next. Types IIIa and IIIb are less common and are often found associated with almandines of Types I and II.

Where Merovingian Garnets Come From: Almandines of Type I and II

The majority of garnets found in Merovingian cloisonné are almandine of Types I and II. They are very common minerals, and their sources are numerous, notably Europe in the Alps, the Pyrenees, the Sierra Nevada, and the Bohemia Mountains (Gilg and

Table 36.3. Composition of Six Types of Archaeological Garnets

oxide percent	Type I 48% India Rajasthan		Type II 32% India ?		Type IIIa 6% central Sri Lanka		Type IIIb 2% south Sri Lanka		Type IV 5% Portugal Monte suímo		Type V 7% Czec rep. Bohemia	
Provenance	mean value	standard deviation	mean value	standard deviation	mean value	standard deviation	mean value	standard deviation	mean value	écart type	standard deviation	standard deviation
SiO_2	36.0	1.2	37.3	0.8	40.3	1.1	38.2	1.1	41.2	0.8	41.5	0.7
TiO_2	0.0	0.0	0.0	0.0	0.0	0.0	0.0	0.0	0.4	0.04	0.45	0.16
Al_2O_3	20.8	1.2	21.5	0.7	22.4	0.6	21.3	0.6	23.1	0.4	21.6	0.6
Cr_2O_3	0.0	0.0	0.06	0.04	0.0	0.0	0.0	0.0	0.0	0.0	2.2	0.7
FeO	37.5	2.2	32.1	1.5	19.7	2.6	25.7	2.6	12.7	1.6	8.9	0.5
MnO	0.4	0.5	1.2	0.9	0.3	0.4	0.5	0.4	0.4	0.03	0.3	0.03
MgO	4.4	0.7	6.2	0.9	12.7	2.3	12.3	2.3	16.3	0.9	19.8	0.5
CaO	0.7	0.3	1.4	0.6	3.0	1.5	1.3	1.5	5.4	0.2	4.3	0.28

Hyršl 2015). If one refers to Greiff's measurements of reference garnets (Greiff 1998), the almandine garnets of central Europe (the Alps, Bohemia) reveal a different composition from those Types I and II (with a composition less heavy in almandine and more elevated in grossular than for Types I and II). Greiff indicates some exceptions in Europe—for example, the deposit of Zirkenreuth in Bavaria in which the garnets are made of a larger proportion of almandine than those of Type I. The data on reference geological garnets published by Quast and Schüssler (2000), in particular in the form of a three-part diagram of almandine, pyrope, and andradite, show that Types I and II are similar to the garnets coming from India, one of which is localized in Rajasthan (Fig. 36.14). A more detailed study demonstrates that Type I corresponds to garnets from Rajmahal in the district of Tonk (Gilg et al. 2010, p. 99). By contrast, the garnets of Type II do not correspond to any of the analyzed reference geological garnets, but most of the time they are associated with archaeological objects with Type I garnets, which could suggest a neighboring geological origin. Moreover, one may observe that a few European garnet sources (Alméria in Spain, Mont-Blanc in the Alps, and so on) are similar to Type I.

These results confirm that the deposits in India constitute a plausible source of the almandines, but do not entirely rule out European deposits. More criteria are necessary to distinguish between stones originating in India and Europe. One important clue is the frequent presence of microscopic radioactive inclusions, which are uniquely observed in Type I garnets, identified as uraninite on the basis of μ-PIXE and μ-Raman analyses (Mazzoli et al. 2002). The uranium to lead ratio measured indicates that these garnets formed 1,500 Ma ago (the middle Proterozoic era). This information is crucial

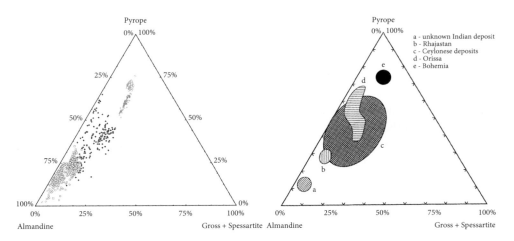

FIGURE 36.14. Comparison of ternary diagrams for the composition of garnets from Merovingian objects (left) and geological garnets from the literature (right). The axis represents the proportion of almandines, pyropes, spessartines, and grossular end members (Quast & Schüssler 2000). Note that Type V corresponds well to deposits in Bohemia, whereas Types I and II are similar to deposits in India. Types III (A and B combined) resemble deposits in Sri Lanka and Orissa.

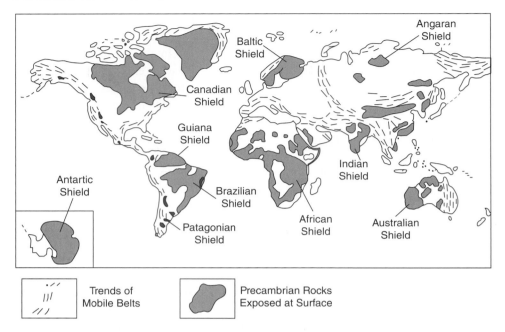

FIGURE 36.15. Distribution map of pre-Cambrian rocks exposed on the surface of the globe. Note that no Proterozoic rocks occur in western Europe. In northern Europe, the Baltic rocks are of suitable age, but garnets there have a different composition than the archaeological garnets. The only option left is the rocks in India.

because it makes it possible to reject their source as being from any of the geological formations in central and western Europe, which date from a later epoch.

Considering the distribution map of Proterozoic rocks exposed at the surface of the globe (Fig. 36.15) (Goodwin 2000) that have a similar geological age to Type I garnets (middle Proterozoic, noted as m-lPz on the map), one can identify two possible sources. First is the Baltic Shield, a large area of exposed igneous and metamorphic rocks, in the south of Norway, Sweden, and Finland dated to the middle and early Proterozoic. But our analyses and the data from the literature reveal that the reference garnets coming from this region have a chemical composition that is very different from that of the garnets of Type I (since their calcium and manganese content is markedly higher). This incompatibility was confirmed by a study of raw or partially cut archaeological garnets that were brought to light at sites in Norway, Sweden, and Denmark during the fourth through eighth centuries (Mannerstrand and Lundqvist 2003). Among the twenty-six archaeological garnets, only one belonged to Type I; the others were radically different, with, in particular, a systematic composition of CaO at the level of 4 percent, compared with less than 1 percent of Type I. This demonstrates that the garnets exploited in early medieval Scandinavia are clearly different from the garnets used in Merovingian objects. A Scandinavian origin of Type I almandines is consequently improbable.

The second possible source is the Indian subcontinent, where the very ancient Indian Shield presents two areas of comparable age to that of Type I garnets. The first is that of the mountain range of the Eastern Ghats, bordering the eastern side of India, extending from Orissa in the north, Andhra Pradesh in the southeast, to Tamil Nadu in the south (Naqvi and Rogers 1987). During the middle Proterozoic, this ancient formation underwent an intense metamorphism that could explain the presence of sillimanite needles present in Types I and II garnets. The Eastern Ghats contain deposits of garnets of gemmological quality as historically reported. The second area of interest in India is the Aravalli chain, a formation as ancient as the Eastern Ghats situated in the northeast of the country, historically famous for providing garnets of gem quality, notably in the region of Rajasthan.

Finally, one cannot completely eliminate the hypothesis that the garnets may have originated in Africa. In the epoch when the garnets of Types I and II were formed (1.5 Ga), the Indian and Ethiopian tectonic plates were still united. The Ethiopian plate consequently possesses a geological context similar to that of India, and one effectively finds outcrops of garnets in Kenya and Tanzania. This African route remains to be explored, particularly considering Pliny's notation that *carbunculi* or carbuncles—a term designating different red stones including garnets—were coming from Ethiopia, Carthage, and the Garamantes, and thus from Africa (Pliny the Elder, Book XXXVII, ch. 25).

Garnets of Type IIIa and IIIb, IV, and V

The garnets of intermediate composition between pyrope and almandines (known as pyraldines) form a cloud dispersed among many tighter groups of Types I and II on the one hand and Types IV and V on the other. Recent analyses have led us to distinguish Types IIIa and IIIb, which correspond to two distinct provenances on the basis of concentrations of calcium oxide (CaO) (Fig. 36.11). Type IIIa presents concentrations of CaO (4 percent) more elevated than Type IIIb (1.3 percent); it corresponds to outcrops of charnockite facies of Sri Lanka (Farges 1998), in particular to the shales of Trincomale in the northeast of the island. The composition of Sri Lanka's geological garnets published by Greiff (1998) and Schüssler et al. (2001) is in agreement with this hypothesis. Moreover, the measures that we have for the geological garnets collected from central Sri Lanka (Elahera area) confirm these results. With regard to the Type IIIb garnets, they could correspond with the garnets from southern Sri Lanka, as we have noted in analyzing the numerous geological garnets from this region (Ratnapura and Deniyaya areas). Moreover, garnet beads excavated in southern Sri Lanka (Ridiyagama archeological site, beginning of the 1st millennium CE) are of Type IIIa and IIIb (Calligaro 2011). Importantly, the pyraldine garnets of Type III have been identified among the objects dated to Antiquity, notably necklaces, pendants, and intaglios.

Type IV chromium-poor pyropes were never mentioned in earlier studies. The origin of these garnets, appearing in *cloisonné* at the end of the sixth century has been enigmatic for a long time. They occur, for instance, on objects from the late tombs of the basilica of Saint-Denis (Périn et al. 2005) and in the letters of the Visigothic crowns of Recceswinth (d. 642) (Calligaro et al. 2003). The fact that Type IV and Type V garnets are sometimes present in the same object (e.g., in the quatrefoil brooch from tomb 8 at Saint-Denis) suggests that they more likely originate from Europe than from India or Sri Lanka (Calligaro et al. 2007). H. Albert Gilg has proposed several non-Asiatic sources for these garnets of peculiar composition, notably Nigeria, Scotland (Elie Ness), and the more plausible source of Monte Suímo in Portugal (Gilg et al. 2010), which was exploited in the Roman period (Gilg and Hyršl 2015). The hypothesis of Asiatic origin cannot be definitively discarded because some of the reference garnets from Rajamundri, Andra Pradesh were also found to have a similar composition.

Type V, which consists of chromium-rich pyropes, clearly stands out from the preceding types. The most evident source of chromium-rich pyropes is in the central mountains of Bohemia, north of Prague, in the Czech Republic. The compositions we measured on reference pyropes from the alluvial outcrops in this region (Vestrev & Podsedice) closely agree with those published by Quast and Schüssler on pyropes of the same area (Třebenice and Měrunice) and strongly coincide with the archaeological garnets of Type V. There is thus little doubt that the garnets of Type V were coming from Bohemia. Note that while this famous deposit flourished during the nineteenth-century fashion fad for Bohemian jewelry, the presence of its garnets on Merovingian artifacts shows that it was exploited long before its first mention in sixteenth-century historical texts.

EVOLUTION OF GARNET SOURCES IN THE MEROVINGIAN PERIOD

The large number of garnets studied, together with the dating of the objects on which they occur (Legoux et al. 2009), has permitted study of the chronological evolution of the types of garnets goldsmiths used during the early Middle Ages. Like the diagram shown in Fig. 36.16, garnets of Types I, II, and III (the last of which are more rare) from Southeast Asia, form the large majority used until the late sixth century. From this period, these garnets gave way to European garnets of Type IV (likely from Portugal) and of Type V (from Bohemia). The latter two types are found on objects in tombs from the first third of the seventh century in the necropolis of Saint-Denis, France (the quatrefoil brooch from grave 8 and the belt from tomb 11). Type IV garnets are sometimes found exclusively, as is the case of the liturgical objects of the late sixth to early seventh centuries (the disc of Limons, near Puy-de-Dôme or the St. Eligius cross, conserved at the Bibliothèque Nationale de France).

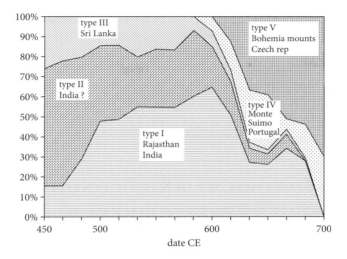

FIGURE 36.16. Evolution of garnet types employed during the Merovingian period (450–650). The almandine garnets from the Indian subcontinent disappeared circa 600 and were replaced by pyropes from Europe.

Table 36.4. Summary of Six Types of Garnets, Their Provenance, and the Period of Their Appearance

Type	Subtype	Country	Location	Confidence	Period	Remarks
I		India	Rajmahal, Tonk district	***	4th – 6th c. CE	
II		India	?	*	4th – 6th c. CE	
III	IIIa	Sri Lanka	Central	**	?th – 6th c. CE	Greco-Roman use
	IIIb	Sri lanka	Southern	**	? – 6th c. CE	
IV		Portugal	Monte Suimo	***	6th – 7th c. CE	Roman exploitation
V		Bohemia (Czech Republic)	Region of Vestrev	****	6th – 7th c. CE	

This scheme, based on six types of garnets and the chronology of their appearance, was found to be identical to the collections studied, spanning from France to Romania and from Germany to England. Table 36.4 summarizes the provenance and period of usage of the six types of garnets found on Merovingian objects, in addition to the degree of confidence with regard to their origin. However, this general scheme does not offer a strict guide to the distribution of garnets. For instance, Type I-II almandine garnets are occasionally found on late objects as well. This finding can be explained by the availability of Asian garnet stocks left over from earlier periods or by the recycling of garnets from older objects. While the Type V pyrope garnets appear extensively on late objects, they surprisingly also occur occasionally in early periods. For example, small cabochons of Type V garnets were found at Tournai (Belgium) on the sheaths of the sword and the scramasax of Childeric I (d. 481), and among loose garnets from the Gepid tombs of Apahida III in Romania (Bugoi et al. 2016). Despite these promising results, we must remain prudent in any analysis of new objects. Indeed, the extension of the program of study to Scandinavian countries and eastern Europe and to the period of Late Antiquity might call this scheme into question.

Historical and Economic Perspectives

There is only a little space remaining to outline how this approach to the origin of garnets used by European goldsmiths during the Merovingian period adds exciting and complex historical and economic perspectives. First of all, for the western and above all eastern written sources as well as for archaeological sources in India and, to a lesser extent, Sri Lanka, it is well established that commercial relations between the Indian subcontinent and the Mediterranean world go back to at least the second century BCE (Suresh 2004). From this period, Indo-Roman *emporia* are attested in India, such as at Pattanam on the southwest coast (Cherian et al. 2007, 2009), or at Arikamedu on its southeastern coast (Wheeler et al. 1946; Begley et al. 2004; Suresh 2007). Both of these sites have benefited from considerable excavation. As has been demonstrated, the Indian Ocean crossing, just as the Red Sea and its Egyptian *emporia* like Berenike, was preferred to the continental silk routes. Recent research indicates that the great Indian maritime trade was linked closely to the emergence of "kingdoms," or "states," in the south of India, which sustained this commerce and its shipping companies (Margabandhu 1965; Suresh 2004). Until the middle of the sixth century, as confirmed by the archaeological finds, these *emporia* still operated (Sidebotham 2011), but the situation deteriorated at the end of the sixth century with the Persian empire's control of the Red Sea.

The navigation of Indian commercial ships, and not of Mediterranean ones, as was long thought, did not hug the coast, notably along the Arabian peninsula, to avoid the threat of piracy. Instead the ships sailed further offshore and had armed men on board. They timed their passages to accommodate the monsoon season. Thus, it was in winter that they sailed up to the Red Sea, loaded with spices (pepper, cinnamon, nutmeg, cloves, cumin, galenga—from the ginger family, aloe, and so on), coconuts, perfume (incense, sandalwood), precious fabrics (Chinese silk), gems, and other luxury products and foodstuffs. Their return took place in the summer, their cargoes principally composed of amphorae of oil and wine, in addition to Greco-Roman luxury items, of which the archaeological remains are numerous throughout the Indian peninsula (Suresh 2004; Seland 2009). This maritime commerce seems to have started to decline in the

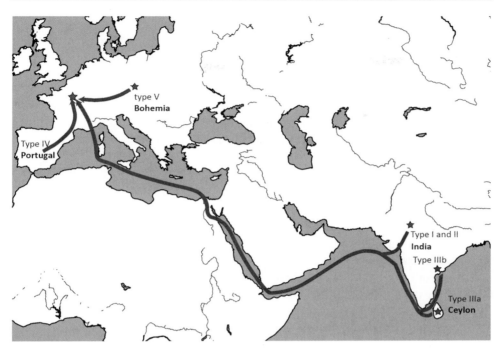

FIGURE 36.17. Map of the evolution of the supply of garnets over the course of the Merovingian period.

fourth century, no doubt as a consequence of the political troubles that affected the south of India, but, as Subra Suresh has proposed (2004), this trade must have continued until at least the proto-Byzantine period. We have been able to confirm this suggestion based on knowledge of the exportation of Indian garnets to Europe until the end of the sixth century. This economic factor was previously unknown to Indian researchers (Calligaro et al. 2002).

This rupture in the supply of eastern garnets to the West beginning in the late sixth century was first established by the pioneering work of Quast and Schüssler (2000) and Uta von Freeden (2000) (Fig. 36.17). They proposed that this rupture was the economic consequence of the Byzantines' loss of control of the Red Sea to the Sassanid Persians. In fact, it was in 570, during the reign of the Persian king Khusro I (531–579), that Yemen became a vassal state of the Sassanids, after the expulsion of the Ethiopians, who were the allies of Byzantium.

However, neither Western written sources nor Indian and Persian sources explicitly mention any interruption of maritime trade between the Indian Ocean, the Red Sea, and the Mediterranean from the late sixth century. Moreover, the archaeological evidence, just as the availability in the seventh century of amethysts from Sri Lanka for elite Merovingian jewelry, attests to the persistence of economic contact between India and the Mediterranean world after the loss of control of the Red Sea trade. It seems unlikely that Indian provisioning of the West via maritime trade in spices, perfumes, precious cloth, gems, and so on, ceased in the seventh century. The question remains: What is contained in Indian, Persian, and Arab written sources, which are richer in material than Western sources (Banaji 2012)?

The issue concerning the origin of garnets remains complex. According to our contacts in the Archaeological Survey in India and the National Museum of Archaeology in Delhi, garnets were undervalued and little used during the early centuries in India, and even then, uniquely as small-size beads and pendants. Garnet platelets, the kind used in *cloisonné*, were apparently unknown in India. In addition, the fifth and sixth centuries, when the highest number of Indian garnets appeared in Europe, correspond to a period during which they were practically absent from Indian archaeological discoveries.

While the Greco-Roman world did not express a particular taste for garnets apart from their use in prestige objects such as incised gems and medallions (Adams 2011), these gems, starting in the third- and fourth-century Sassanid world (notably via Alano-Sarmatian vassals) were diffused progressively through the cloisonné decoration of armament and jewelry. Moreover, these were found from across the Hunnic Empire to Gaul, where the tomb of Childeric is one of the oldest manifestations of the cloisonné style in the West, as is the contemporary tomb of Pouan (Aube) (Kazanski et al. 2000, pp. 166ff, 206ff). Beginning in the late sixth century and for a long time afterward, however, garnets became secondary gems (Fig. 36.18).

In bringing these remarks to a close, one cannot avoid asking about the market value of garnets that India exported to the Western world during at least two centuries. In fact, Indian garnets were the supply for both objects discovered in the tombs of elites and those coming from more modest inhumations in western Europe. These gems thus seem to have been broadly accessible, with only the nature of the objects on which they were found, notably in gold, differentiating the high-status from the more modest pieces. Nonetheless, there was thus sufficient economic interest in exporting garnets from Indian, where in this period they were used rarely, if at all, in local productions. If one extrapolates from contemporary examples, it is possible that these gems, esteemed in the West for two centuries, had a low cost of extraction and sufficient positive value to make them an object of complementary trade. But it is equally important to recognize that the location of garnet deposits, notably in Rajasthan, was remote. They were located opposite the maritime *emporia* of southern India in the Gulf of Bengal where the Greek merchant Cosmas Indicopleustes (Wolska-Conus 1973), indicated in the mid-sixth century that one could acquire these gems. Although their cost of extraction was apparently low, the long caravan route across the Indian subcontinent added supplementary costs in reaching ports for exportation to the West.

Finally it is necessary to ask, with regard to the internal transport of garnets across India, about the nature of the exported garnets. Were they exported raw or semi-worked? As we have observed in the case of Rajasthan, raw crystals of garnets are heavy and the waste after debitage (waste flakes) has a significant mass. Considering that India did not produce garnets in the form of platelets, one can propose that they only exported crystals suitable for *cloisonné*, which were selected beforehand and freed from their

FIGURE 36.18. Example of a *cloisonné* brooch worn empty, due to the lack of garnets. Hüfingen, Germany, circa 600. Photo P. Périn

useless gangue. It is unlikely that they were raw crystals, which were too heavy. However, this proposal remains hypothetical and has yet to be verified.

Conclusions

Many questions still merit deeper historical-economic examination. One of the principal issues is whether the rupture in the supply of garnets and pulled glass beads in western Europe reflected a much more general economic phenomenon than archaeological material viewed in isolation permits us to measure at this time. It would therefore be important to try to verify whether the other types of gems originating in Southeast Asia, like amethysts, continued to arrive in the West after the 600s. At the same time, one would like to know whether, when the great maritime commerce from the Red Sea did in fact decline, other routes, notably overland ones such as the well-known silk routes, were used instead.

NOTES

1. On the technique of wound glass, see the technological descriptions proposed in Spear 2001, pp. 45–51; Sode 2004, pp. 89–94; Siegmann 2006, pp. 928–932; Pion 2013; Pion 2014, pp. 53–72, which provide further bibliography. In addition, contemporary manuals intended for training in wound bead fabrication are particularly valuable for the technological study of archaeological material, particularly the richly illustrated Adams 2005.
2. Concerning the technique of drawn beads, we refer mainly to Francis 1990; Spear 2001, pp. 46–48; 130–135; Francis 2002, pp. 17–50; 90–92; Francis 2004, pp. 450–460; Siegmann 2006, pp. 932–937. More specifically on Merovingian beads, see: Pion 2014, pp. 36–52 and Gratuze and Pion 2019.
3. On Asian bead craft in the village of Papanaidupet, see mainly: Stern 1987; Francis Jr. 1990, pp. 10–13; Francis Jr. 2002, pp. 21–23; Francis Jr. 2004, pp. 452–453; Kanungo 2004.
4. An iron rod within a tube of drawn glass was discovered on the Egyptian site of Kôm el-Dikka (fifth to sixth centuries CE) at Alexandria (Arveiller-Dulong & Nenna 2011, p. 175).
5. The excavations of Kom el-Dikka at Alexandria, a site where the production of drawn beads is dated to between the end of the fifth and the sixth centuries, have uncovered a series of stone molds associated with drawn tubes of which some have not yet been "pinched" (Rodziewicz 1984, pp. 241–243, Fig. 265, pl. 72, n. 359–366).
6. Peter Francis Jr. (2002) counted three: at Rhodes (third to early second century BCE) and in Egypt, at the sites of Kôm el-Dikka (late fifth to sixth century CE) and Fustat (seventh to eleventh century CE). Beads were probably made on the island of Elephantine in the first century CE and possibly at Jerusalem, where the use of drawn tubes is reported (Arveiller-Dulong & Nenna 2011, p. 175).
7. When dealing with glass, the commonly accepted terminology is Na_2O for soda, K_2O for potash, Al_2O_3 for alumina, SiO_2 for silica, MgO for magnesia, and CaO for lime. Thus, we refer here to "natron soda-lime glass," "soda-lime natron glass," "halophytic plant ash soda-lime glass," "soda-lime plant ash glass," and "potash-lime glass" which are also referred to in the literature as "wood ash glass" or "forest plant ash glass."
8. The following sections have been translated from French by Bonnie Effros and Isabel Moreira.
9. The dissertation of Kathrin Vielitz (2003) regarding circular Merovingian cloisonné brooches dedicates important attention to the study of partitions, reflectors, and the technology of cloisonné. Regarding the metal used in the partitions, bronze was the most common in Mediterranean regions, in preference to iron, which nonetheless was characteristic of the Merovingian world proper. With respect to the motifs stamped on the reflectors, these appear to have varied by geographic zone: orthogonal grids were common in northern Gaul, rhomboid grids were above all to be found in the eastern part of the Merovingian kingdom, notably in southern Germany, and eye-shaped reflectors, which were very rare, were a possible evidence of a Mediterranean production.

WORKS CITED

Ancient Sources

Berggren, J. L. and A. Jones (eds. and trans.). ([2000] 2002). *Ptolemy's Geography: An Annotated Translation of the Theoretical Chapters*. Princeton: Princeton University Press.

Casson, L. (ed. and trans.). (1989). *The Periplus Maris Erythraei: Text with Introduction, Translation, and Commentary*. Princeton: Princeton University Press.

Wolska-Conus, W. (ed. and trans.). (1973). *Topographie chrétienne de Cosmas Indicopleustes*. Vols. 1 and 2. Paris: Editions du Cerf.

Pliny the Elder. (1972). E. de Saint-Denis (ed. and trans.). *Histoire Naturelle* de Pline l'Ancien. Paris: Les Belles Lettres.

Modern Sources

Adams, K. (2005). *The Complete Book of Glass Beadmaking*. New York: Lark Books.

Adams, N. (2000). "The Development of Early Garnet Inlaid Ornaments." In C. Balint (ed.), *Kontakte zwischen Iran, Byzanz und der Steppe im 6–7. Jahrhundert* (pp. 13–70). Budapest-Napoli-Roma: Varia Achaeologica Hungarica.

Adams, N. (2011). "The Garnet Millenium. The Role of Seal Stones in Garnet Studies." In C. Entwisle and N. Adams (eds.), *"Gems of Heaven." Recent Research on Engraved Gemstones in Late Antiquity, AD 200-600* (pp. 10–25). British Research Publication 179. London: British Museum Research Publication.

Ambroz, A. K. (1971.) "Problemy rannesrednevekovoj hronologii Vostocnoj Europy." *Sovetskaja Arheologija* 2: 96–123.

Arrhenius, B. (1985). *Merovingian Garnet Jewellery: Emergence and Social Implications*. Göteborg: Kungl. Vittershets Historie och Antikvitets Akademien.

Arveiller-Dulong, V., and Nenna, M.-D. (2011). *Les verres antiques du musée du Louvre*, Vol. 3: *Parures, instruments et éléments d'incrustation*. Paris: Somogy, Musée du Louvre Éditions.

Banaji, J. (2012). "Regions That Look Seawards: Changing Fortunes, Submerged Histories and the Slow Capitalism of the Sea." In *A Tale of Two Worlds: Comparative Perspectives on Indo-Mediterranean Trade* (pp. 1–17). Leiden: Brill.

Baxter, M. J. (2015). *Exploratory Multivariate Analysis in Archaeology*. Clinton Corners, NY: Eliot Werner Publications.

Begley, V., Francis, P., Jr., Karashima, N., Raman, K. V., Sidebotham, S. E., and Will, E. L. (eds.) (2004). *The Ancient Port of Arikamedu: New Excavations and Researches 1989–1992*. Paris: Centre d'histoire et d'archéologie, École française d'Extrême-Orient.

Bellina, B. (2002). "Peter Francis Jr.: Asia's Maritime Bead Trade—300 B.C. to the Present." *Bulletin de l'École française d'Extrême-Orient* 89: 380–385.

Bellina, B., and Glover, I. C. (2004) "The Archaeology of Early Contacts with India and the Mediterranean World from the Fourth Century BC to the Fourth Century AD." In I. C. Glover and P. Bellwood (eds.), *Southeast Asia: From Prehistory to History* (pp. 68–89). London: Routledge.

Bimson, M., La Niece, S., and Leese, M. (1982). "The Characterisation of Mounted Garnets." *Archaeometry* 24: 51–58.

Bimson, M. (1985). "Dark-Age Garnet Cutting." *Anglo-Saxon Studies in Archaeology and History* 4: 125–128.

Boussac, M.-F., Salles, J.-F., and Yon, J.-B. (eds.). (2012). *Autour de périple de la mer Erythrée*. In Topoi Supplement 11. Lyon: Maison de l'Orient et de la Méditerranée.

Brill, Robert H. (1999). *Chemical Analyses of Early Glasses* 2. Corning: Corning Museum of Glass.

Bugoi, R., Oanta-Marghitu, R., and Calligaro T. (2016). "IBA Investigations of Loose Garnets from Pietroasa, Apahida and Cluj-Someseni Treasures (5th Century AD)." *Nuclear Instruments and Methods in Physics Research B* 371: 401–406.

Calligaro, T. (2008). *Rapport d'étude*. Centre for Research and Restoration of the Museums of France (C2RMF) 16340.

Calligaro, T. (2011). *Rapport d'étude*. Centre for Research and Restoration of the Museums of France (C2RMF).

Calligaro, T., Colinart, S., Poirot, J.-P., and Sudres, C. (2002). "Combined External-Beam PIXE and μ-Raman Characterisation of Garnets Used in Merovingian Jewellery." *Nuclear Instruments and Methods in Physics Research B* 189: 320–327.

Calligaro, T., Dran, J.-C., and Poirot, J.-P. (2003). "Del estudio analytico de las gemas: Estudio por acelerador de las gemas del useo nacional de la Edad Media, Cluny." In A. Perea (ed.), *El tesoro visigodo de Guarrazar* (pp. 277–286). Madrid: CSIC Editions.

Calligaro, T., Périn, P., Vallet, F., and Poirot, J.-P. (2007). "Contribution à l'étude des grenats mérovingiens (Basilique de Saint-Denis et autres collections du Musée d'Archéologie nationale, diverses collections publiques et objets de fouilles récentes). Nouvelles analyses gemmologiques et géochimiques effectuées au Centre de Recherche et de Restauration des Musées de France." *Antiquités Nationales* 38: 111–144.

Callmer, J. (1977). *Trade Beads and Bead Trade in Scandinavia ca. 800–1000 A.D.* Acta Archaeologica Lundensia Series 4, no. 11. Bonn: Rudolf Habelt Verlag.

Cherian, P. J., Ravi Prasad, G. V., Dutta, K. I., Ray, D. K., Selvakumar, V., and Shajan, K. P. (2009). "Chronology of Pattanam: A Multi-Cultural Port Site on the Malabar Coast." *Current Science* 97(2): 236–240.

Cherian, P. J., Selvakumar, V., Shajan, K. P. (2007). "The Muziris Heritage Project Excavations at Pattanam." *Journal of Indian Ocean Archaeology* 4: 1–10.

Christidès, V. (2013). "Roman and Byzantine Naval Power in Decline in the Red Sea and the Indian Ocean." *Ekklesiastikos Pharos* 95(n.s. 24): 80–106.

de Linas, C. (1864). *Orfèvrerie Mérovingienne: les œuvres de Saint-Éloi et la verroterie cloisonnée*. Paris: Edition Didron.

Deer, W. A., Howie, R., and Zussman, J. (1982). "Rock-Forming Minerals." Vol. 1A: *Orthosilicates* (pp. 468–498). London: Longman.

Doehaerd, R. (1971). *Le haut Moyen Âge occidental. Economies et sociétés*. Paris: Presses Universitaires de France.

Dran, J.-C., Calligaro, T., and Salomon, J. (2000). "Particle Induced X-ray Emission." In E. Ciliberto and G. Spoto (eds.), *Modern Analytical Methods in Art and Archaeology, Chemical Analysis* 155 (pp. 135–166). New York: John Wiley.

Dussubieux, L., Gratuze, B., and Blet-Lemarquand, M. (2010). "Mineral Soda Alumina Glass: Occurrence and Meaning." *Journal of Archaeological Science* 37(7): 1646–1655.

Dussubieux, L., Kusimba, C. M., Gogte, V., Kusimba, S. B., Gratuze, B., and Oka, R. (2008). "The Trading of Ancient Glass Beads: New Analytical Data from South Asian and East African Soda-Alumina Glass Beads." *Archaeometry* 50(5): 797–821.

Farges, F. (1998). "Mineralogy of the Louvre's Merovingian Garnet Cloisonné Jewelry: Origins of the Gems of the First Kings of France." *American Mineralogist* 83: 323–330.

Fleury, M., and France-Lanord, A. (1998). *Les trésors mérovingiens de la basilique de Saint-Denis*. Woippy: Klopp Editions.

Foy, D., and Picon, M. (2005). "L'origine du verre en Méditerranée occidentale à la fin de l'Antiquité et dans le haut Moyen Âge." In X. Delestre, P. Périn, and M. Kazanski. (eds), *La Méditerranée et le monde mérovingien: témoins archéologiques, Actes des XXIIIᵉ Journées internationales d'archéologie mérovingienne, 11–13 octobre 2002, Arles* (pp. 99–110). *Bulletin archéologique de Provence*. Suppl. 30. Aix-en-Provence: Editions de l'Association Provence Archéologie.

Foy, D., Picon, M., Vichy, M., and Thirion-Merle, V. (2003). "Caractérisation des verres de la fin de l'Antiquité en Méditerranée occidentale: l'émergence de nouveaux courants commerciaux." In D. Foy and M.-D. Nenna (eds.), *Échanges et commerce du verre dans le monde antique, Actes du colloque de l'Association Française pour l'Archéologie du Verre, 7–9 juin 2001, Aix-en-Provence-Marseille* (pp. 41–86). Monographies Instrumentum 24. Montagnac: Éditions Monique Mergoil.

Francis, P., Jr. (1990). "Glass Beads in Asia, Part Two: Indo-Pacific beads." *Asian Perspectives* 29(1): 1–23.

Francis, P., Jr. (2002). *Asia's Maritime Bead Trade – 300 B.C. to the Present*. Honolulu: University of Hawai'i Press.

Francis, P., Jr. (2004). "Beads and Selected Small Finds from the 1989–92 Excavations." In V. Begley, P. Francis, Jr., N. Karashima, K.V. Raman, S. F. Sidebotham, and E. I. Will (eds.), *The Ancient Port of Arikamedu: New Excavations and Researches 1989–1992* (pp. 447–507). Mémoires archéologiques 22/2. Paris: École Française d'Extrême-Orient.

Freestone, I. C., Gorin-Rosen, Y., and Hughes, M. J. (2000). "Primary Glass from Israel and the Production of Glass in Late Antiquity and the Early Islamic Period." In M.-D. Nenna, (ed.), *La route du verre: ateliers primaires et secondaires de verriers du second millénaire av. J.-C. au Moyen-Age* (pp. 65–83). Travaux de la Maison de l'Orient Méditerranéen 33. Lyon: Maison de l'Orient Méditerranéen.

Freestone, I. C., Hughes, M. J., and Stapleton, C. (2008). "The Composition and Production of Anglo-Saxon Glass." In V. I. Evison. (ed.), *Catalogue of Anglo-Saxon Glass in the British Museum* (pp. 29–46). British Museum Research Publication 167. London: British Museum.

Frost, R. L., Cejka, J., Weier, M. L., and Martens, W. (2006). "Molecular Structure of the Uranyl Silicates—A Raman Spectroscopic Study." *Journal of Raman spectroscopy* 37: 538–551.

Ganio, M., Gulmini, M., Latruwe, K., Vanhaecke, F., and Degryse, P. (2013). "Sasanian Glass from Veh Ardašīr Investigated by Strontium and Neodymium Isotopic Analysis." *Journal of Archaeological Science* 40(12): 4264–4270.

Gilg, H. A., Gast, N., and Calligaro, T. (2010). "Vom Karfunkelstein." In L. Wamser (ed.), *Karfunkelstein und Seide: Neue Schätze aus Bayerns Frühzeit (Bayerische Geschichte)* (pp. 87–100). Regensburg: Pustet Verlag.

Gilg, H. A., and Hyršl, J. (2015). "Garnet Mines in Europe." In J. Toussaint (ed.), *Rouges & Noirs. Rubis, grenat, onyx, obsidienne et autres minéraux rouges & noirs dans l'art et l'archéologie* (pp. 145–173). Coll. Monographies du TreM.a, no. 67. Namur: Musée des Arts anciens du Namurois.

Gilg, H. A., Kile, D., Liebetrau, S., Modreski, P., Neumeier, G., and Staebler, G. (2008). *Garnet: Great Balls of Fire*. ExtraLapis No 11. Munster, IN: Lithographic Communications, LLC.

Goodwin, A. M. (2000). *Principles of Precambrian Geology*. London: Academic Press.

Gratuze, B. (2013). "Glass Characterisation Using Laser Ablation Inductively Coupled Plasma Mass Spectrometry Methods." In K. H. A. Janssens (ed.), *Modern Methods for Analysing Archaeological and Historical Glass* 1 (pp. 201–234). New Delhi, India: Wiley.

Gratuze, B., and Pion, Constantin (2019). "Des perles en verre provenant du sous-continent indien en Gaule mérovingienne." In E. Boube, A. Corrochano, and J. Hernandez (eds.), *Du Royaume Goth au Midi mérovingien, Actes des XXXIVᵉ Journées internationales d'archéologie mérovingienne, 6–8 novembre 2013* (pp. 449–472). Bordeaux: Ausonius.

Gratuze, B., and Sarah, G. (2012). "Analysis of Tamil Nadu Glass Beads: Application to the Study of Inland Glass Trade." In A. Murugaiyan (ed.), *New Dimensions in Tamil Epigraphy: Select Papers from the Symposia held at EPHE-SHP, Paris in 2005, 2006 and a Few Invited Papers*, Cre-A (pp. 129–143). Chennai: Cre-A Publishers.

Greiff, S. (1998). "Naturwissenschaftliche Untersuchungen zur Frage der Rohsteinquellen für frühmittelalterlichen Almandingranatschmuck rheinfränkischer Provenienz." *Jahrbuch des Römisch-Germanischen Zentralmuseums Mainz* 45(2): 599–645.

Greiff, S., and Banerjee, A. (1994). "Zerstörungsfreie Unterscheidung von Granat und Glas in Frühmittelalterlichen Granatfibeln. Eine Anwendung der Infrarot-Reflexionsspektroskopie." *Archäologisches Korrespondenzblatt* 24: 97–205.

Greiff, S., and Nallbani, E. (2008.) "When Metal Meets Beads. Technological Study of Early Medieval Metal Foil Beads from Albania." *Mélanges de l'École française de Rome. Moyen Âge* 120(2): 355–375.

Gübelin, E. J., and Koivula, J. I. (1986). *Photoatlas of Inclusions in Gemstones*. Zürich: ABC Edition.

Kanungo, A. (2004). *Glass Beads in Ancient India: An Ethnoarchaeological Approach*. British Archaeological Reports International, Series 1242. Oxford: BAR Publishing.

Kazanski, M., and Périn, P. (1996). "La tombe de Childéric et la question de l'origine des parures de style cloisonné." *Antiquités nationales* 28: 203–209.

Kazanski, M., Périn, P., and Vallet, F. (2000). *L'or des princes barbares. Du Caucase à la Gaule au Ve siècle après J.-C.*, catalogue de l'exposition du Musée des Antiquités nationales. Paris: Réunion des Musées nationaux.

Kievlenko E. Y. (2003). *Geology of Gems*, trans. A. Soregaroli. Littleton, CO: Ocean Pictures Ltd.

Legoux, R., Périn, P., and Vallet, F. (2009). *Chronologie normalisée du mobilier funéraire mérovingien entre Manche et Lorraine, Condé-sur-Noireau*. 3rd ed. (N° hors série du *Bulletin de l'Association française d'Archéologie mérovingienne*). Saint-Germain-en-Laye: Association française d'Archéologie mérovingienne.

Mahadevan, I. (1970). "The Ancient Name of Arikamedu." In N. Subramanian (ed.), *Parithimar Kalaijnan Nurrantu Vila Malar* (pp. 204–206). Madurai: V.S. Swaminathan.

Mannerstrand, M., and Lundqvist, L. (2003). "Garnet Chemistry from the Slöinge Excavation, Halland and Additional Swedish and Danish Excavations: Comparisons with Garnets Occurring in a Rock Context." *Journal of Archaeological Science* 30: 169–183.

Marganadhu, C. (1965). "Trade Contacts between Western India and the Greco-Roman World in the Early Centuries of the Christian Era." *Journal of the Economic and Social History of the Orient* 8(3): 316–322.

Mathis, F., Vrielynck, O., Leroy, A., Tregouet H., and Strivay, D. (forthcoming). "Les perles en verre de la nécropole de Bossut-Gottechain: recettes et fabrication." In *Archéométrie 2013. Actes du XIXe Colloque du Groupe des Méthodes Pluridisciplinaires Contribuant à l'Archéologie, Caen, 22–26 avril 2013*.

Mazzodi, C., Hanchar, J. M., Della Mea, G., Donovan, J. J., and Stern, R. A. (2002). "μ-PIXE Analysis of Monazite for Total U-Th-Pb Age Determination." *Nuclear Instruments and Methods in Physics Research B* 189: 394–399.

Mellis, O. (1963). "Mineralogische Untersuchungen an Granaten aus in Schweden gefundenen Schmuckgegenständen der Merowinger- und Karolingerzeit." *Arkiv för Mineralogi och Geologi* 3(15): 297–362.

Mirti, P., Pace, M., Malandrino, M., and Negro Ponzi, M. (2009). "Sasanian Glass from Veh Ardašīr: New Evidences by ICP-MS Analysis." *Journal of Archaeological Science* 36(4): 1061–1069.

Naqvi, A. M., and Rogers J. W. (1987). *Precambrian Geology of India*. Oxford Monographs on Geology and Geophysics 6. Oxford: Oxford University Press.

Nenna, M.-D., and Gratuze, B. (2009). "Étude diachronique de compositions de verres employés dans les vases mosaïqués antiques: résultats préliminaires." In K. H. A. Janssens, P. Degryse, P. Cosyns, J. Caen, and L. Van't dack (eds.), *Annales du 17ᵉ Congrès de l'Association Internationale pour l'Histoire du Verre, Anvers-2006* (pp. 199–205). Antwerp: Association internationale pour l'histoire du verre.

O'Donoghue, M. (2006). *Gems: Their Sources, Descriptions and Identification.* 7th ed. Amsterdam: Elsevier.

Périn, P. (1993). "L'Occident mérovingien: les styles colorés et les styles animaliers." In *Grand Atlas de l'Art Universalis* (pp. 236–239). Paris: Encyclopaedia *Universalis*.

Périn, P., Calligaro, T,. Buchet, L., Cassiman, J.-J., Darton, Y., Gallien, V., Poirot, J.-P., Rast-Eicher, A., Rucker, C., and Vallet, F. (2005). "La tombe d'Arégonde. Nouvelles analyses en laboratoire du mobilier métallique et des restes organiques de la défunte du sarcophage 49 de la basilique de Saint-Denis." *Antiquités nationales* 36: 181–206.

Phelps, M., Freestone, I. C., Gorin-Rosen, Y., and Gratuze, B. (forthcoming). "Plant Ash Glass in the Early Islamic Near East: Chronology, Characterisation and Origins of the Technology."

Pichon, L., Calligaro, T., Lemasson, Q., Moignard, B., and Pacheco, C. (2015). "Programs for Visualization, Handling and Quantification of PIXE Maps at the AGLAE Facility." *Nuclear Instruments and Methods in Physics Research* B 363: 48–54.

Picon, M., and Vichy, M. (2003). "D'Orient en Occident: l'origine du verre à l'époque romaine et durant le haut Moyen Âge." In D. Foy and M.-D. Nenna (eds.), *Échanges et commerce du verre dans le monde antique, Actes du colloque de l'Association Française pour l'Archéologie du Verre, 7–9 juin 2001, Aix-en-Provence-Marseille* (pp. 17–32). Monographies Instrumentum 24. Montagnac: Éditions Monique Mergoil.

Pion, C. (2013). "Les perles en verre en Gaule mérovingienne (vᵉ–viiiᵉ siècles). À la découverte d'un savoir-faire au service des dames." *Koregos, revue et encyclopédie multimédia des arts*, reporticle 5. http://www.koregos.org/.

Pion, C. (2014). *Les perles mérovingiennes: typo-chronologie, fabrication et fonctions.* 2 vols. Doctoral dissertation, Free University of Brussels.

Poulain, D., Scuiller, C., and Gratuze, B. (2013). "La parure en verre et en ambre de la nécropole mérovingienne de Saint-Laurent-des-Hommes (Dordogne)." *Bulletin de l'Association Française pour l'Archéologie du Verre*: 72–79.

Quast, D., and Schüssler, U. (2000). "Mineralogische Untersuchungen zur Herkunft der Granate merowingerzeitlicher Cloisonnéarbeiten." *Germania* 78(1): 75–96.

Rehren, T., Connolly, P., Schibille, N., and Schwarzer, H. (2015). "Changes and Consumption in Pergamon (Turkey) from Hellenistic to Late Byzantine and Islamic Times." *Journal of Archaeological Science* 55: 266–279.

Rehren, T., and Freestone, I. C. (2015). "Ancient glass: From Kaleidoscope to Crystal Ball." *Journal of Archaeological Science* 56: 233–241.

Rehren, T., Marii, F., Schibille, N., Swann, C., and Stanford, L. (2010). "Glass Supply and Circulation in Early Byzantine Southern Jordan." In J. Drauschke and D. Keller (eds.), *Glass in Byzantium—Production, Usage, Analyses* (pp. 65–81). RGZM-Tagungen 8. Mainz: RGZM.

Rodziewicz, M. (1984). *Alexandrie, 3: Les habitations romaines tardives d'Alexandrie à la lumière des fouilles polonaises à Kôm el-Dikka.* Warsaw: Editions scientifiques de Pologne.

Roth, H. (1980). "Almandinhandel und -verarbeitung im Bereich des Mittelmeeres." *Allgemeine und Vergleichende Archäologie-Beiträge* 2: 309–335.

Sá, J. (2007). *Applied Statistics Using Spss, STATISTICA, Matlab and R.* Berlin: Springer.

Schibille, N. (2011). "Late Byzantine Mineral Soda High Alumina Glasses from Asia Minor: A New Primary Glass Production Group." *PloS ONE* 6(4): e18970.

Schukin, M., and Bajan, I. (1995). "L'origine du style cloisonné de l'époque des Grandes Migrations." In F. Vallet and M. Kazanski (eds.) *La noblesse romaine et les chefs barbares (Actes du colloque international du Musée des Antiquités nationales, Saint-Germain-en-Laye, 1992), Condé-sur-Noireau* (pp. 63–75). Condé-sur-Noireau: Association française d'Archéologie mérovingienne et Musée des Antiquités nationales (Saint-Germain-en-Laye).

Schüssler, U., Rösch, C., and Hock R. (2001). "Beads from Ancient Sri Lanka. First Results of a Systematic Material Analysis." In *Ancient Ruhuna. Sri Lanka-German Archaeological Project in Southern Province* 1 (pp. 227–242). Mainz: Ph. von Zabern.

Schoff W. H. (1912). *The Periplus of the Erythrean Sea*. London: Longmans, Green.

Seland, E. H. (2009). "Shipwreck, Maroons and Monsters: The Hazards of Ancient Red Sea Navigation." In L. Blue, J. Cooper, R. Thomas, and J. Whitewright (eds.), *Connected Hinterlands* (pp. 179–185). *Proceedings of Red Sea Project IV (University of Southampton Sept. 2008)* Oxford : British Archaeological Reports.

Shortland, A., Rogers, N., and Eremin, K. (2007). "Trace Element Discriminants between Egyptian and Mesopotamian Late Bronze Age Glasses." *Journal of Archaeological Science* 34(5): 781–789.

Shortland, A. J., Schachner, L., Freestone, I., and Tite, M. (2006). "Natron as a Flux in the Early Vitreous Materials Industry: Sources, Beginnings and Reasons for Decline." *Journal of Archaeological Science* 33: 521–530.

Sidebotham, S. (2011). *Berenike and the Ancient Maritime Spice Route* (pp. 175–194).Oakland: University of California Press.

Siegmann, M. (2006). *Bunte Pracht. die Perlen der frühmittelalterlichen Gräberfelder von Liebenau, Kreis Nienburg/Weser, und Dörverden, Kreis Verden/Aller. Chronologie der Gräber, Entwicklung und Trageweise des Perlenschmucks. Technik der Perlen* 5. Beiträge zur Ur- und Frühgeschichte Mitteleuropas 28/5. Langenweissbach: Beier & Beran.

Sode, T. (2004). "Glass Bead Making Technology." In M. Bencard, A. K. Rasmussen, and H. B. Madsen (eds.), *Ribe Excavations 1970–76* 5 (pp. 83–102). Jutland Archaeological Society Publications 46. Esbjerg: Jutland Archaeological Society.

Spear, M. (2001). *Ancient Glass in the Israel Museum. Beads and Other Small Objects*. Jerusalem: The Israel Museum.

Stern, E. M. (1987). "Secret of Papanaidupet." *Glastechnische Berichte* 60(10): 346–351.

Suresh, S. (2004). *Symbols of Trade. Roman and Pseudo-Roman Objects Found in India*. New Delhi: Manohar Publishers.

Suresh, S. (2007). *Arikamedu: its Place in the Ancient Rome-India Contacts*. New Delhi: Embassy of Italy.

Tite, M., Pradell, T., and Shortland, A. (2008). "Discovery, Production and Use of Tin-Based Opacifiers in Glasses, Enamels and Glazes from the Late Iron Age Onwards: A Reassessment." *Archaeometry* 50(1): 67–84.

Van Roy, S., and Vanhaeke, L. (1997). "L'origine des grenats à l'époque mérovingienne." In *La vie archéologique* 48 (*Bulletin de la fédération des archéologues de Wallonie*) (pp. 124–137). Saint-Germain-en-Laye: Association française d'Archéologie mérovingienne.

Velde, B. (2013). "Glass Composition over Several Millennia in the Western World." In K. H. A. Janssens (ed.), *Modern Methods for Analysing Archaeological and Historical Glass* 1 (pp. 67–78). New Delhi: Wiley.

Velde, B., and Motteau, J. (2013). "Glass Compositions of the Merovingian Period in Western Europe." In K. H. A. Janssens (ed.), *Modern Methods for Analysing Archaeological and Historical Glass* 2 (pp. 387–398). New Delhi: Wiley.

Verità, M., Maggetti, M., Saguì, L., and Santopadre, P. (2013). "Colors of Roman Glass: An Investigation of the Yellow Sectilia in the Gorga Collection." *Journal of Glass Studies* 55: 21–34.

Vielitz, K. (2003). *Die Granatscheibenfibeln der Merowingerzeit*. Europe médiévale 3. Montagnac: Mergoil.

Vierck, H. (1974). "Werke der Eligius." In *Studien zur Vor- und Frühgeschichtlichen Archäologie* (*Festschrift für Joachim Werner zum 65. Geburtstag*) (pp. 309–380). Munich: C. H. Beck.

Vierck, H. (1985). "L'œuvre de saint Eloi, orfèvre, et son rayonnement." In P. Périn and L.-C. Feffer (eds.), *La Neustrie. Les pays au nord de la Loire de Dagobert à Charles le Chauve (VIIe-IXe siècle)* (pp. 403–409). Catalogue de l'exposition du musée des Antiquités de la Seine-Maritime. Rouen: Musée départementaux de la Seine Maritme.

Von Freeden, U. (2000). "Das Ende engzelligen Cloisonnés und die Eroberung Südarabiens durch die Sasaniden." *Germania* 78: 97–124.

Wedepohl, K. H., Simpon, K. (2010). "The Chemical Composition of Medieval Wood Ash Glass from Central Europe." *Chemie der Erde* 70: 89–97.

Wheeler, M., Ghosh, A., and Deva, K. (1946). "Arikamedu: an Indo-Roman Trading-Station on the East Coast of India." *Ancient India* 2: 17–124.

Whitehouse, D. (2002). "The Transition from Natron to Plant Ash in the Levant." *Journal of Glass Studies* 44: 193–196.

Zasetskaja, I. P. (1982). "Klassifikacija polihromnyh izdelij gunnskoj epohi po stilisticeskim dannym." In *Drevnosti epohi velikogo pererselenija narodov V-VIII vekov* (pp. 31–49). Moscow. [In German: "Klassifizierung polychromer Erzeugnisse der Hunnenzeit nach Stilmarken" (pp. 246–248).]

Zasetskaja, I. P. (1999). "Les steppes politiques à l'époque hunnique. Questions de chronologie." In J. Tejral, C. Pilet, and M. Kazanski (eds.), *L'Occident romain et l'Europe centrale au début de l'époque des Grandes Migrations* (pp. 341–356). Brno: Institut d'Archéologie de l'Académie des Sciences de la République tchèque.

CHAPTER 37

···

MEROVINGIAN GAUL AND THE MEDITERRANEAN

Ceramics and Trade

···

MICHEL BONIFAY AND DOMINIQUE PIERI

BORROWING the title of a recent book (Reynolds 2010), this chapter provides a short overview of trade relations between Merovingian Gaul and the Mediterranean. This survey is based on the ceramic evidence, without, however, forgetting links with contemporary texts and other categories of artifacts that convey additional information relative to trade such as coins and glass. In chronological terms, Merovingian Gaul is understood here to include the period from the beginning of the fifth century to the first half of the eighth century. This broad framework allows consideration of the present subject within the context of the lengthy transformation of the late-antique economy. Geographically, however, it is important to recognize that the state of the available evidence favors the southernmost parts of the territory progressively occupied by the Franks.

To address the question of whether it is legitimate to use pottery as a measure of the directions, nature, and intensity of trade in late antiquity, we rely on the response of Simon Loseby, who has noted that "the ubiquity and volume of the ceramic data, when combined with the possibility of assigning much of them an approximate provenance and date, opens up a host of comparative possibilities, whether diachronic or synchronic." He adds that "the *general* comparative potential of the ceramic data is greatly in excess of that afforded by the contemporary textual evidence," and he concludes that "it is reasonable to interpret the ceramic data as general indices of potential economic complexity" (Loseby 2007). Indeed, although the ceramic evidence does not obviate the importance of extant literary sources, it would be unwise to study the late-antique economy without taking into account the evidence for, and distribution of, amphorae and tableware, cooking ware, and lamps. Amphorae, in particular, were the primary containers for the transportation of liquid and semi-liquid foodstuffs across the Mediterranean, including oil, wine, and fish products. In addition, these observable

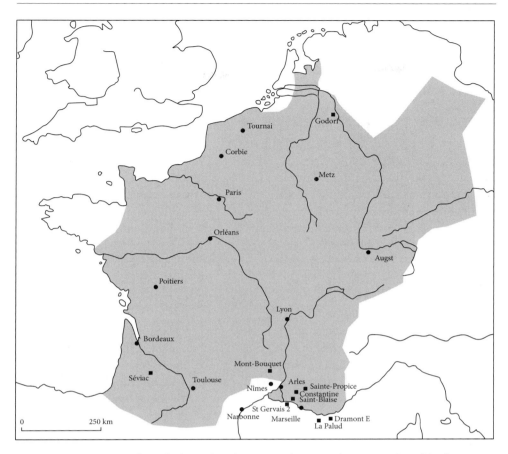

FIGURE 37.1. Map of Frankish Gaul in the 560s and principal sites mentioned in the text.

remains serve as proxies or indicators of trade in articles like grain and clothing that are largely invisible in the archaeological record (on trade of beads and garnets, see Pion et al., Chapter 36, this volume).

To achieve these objectives, this survey of the ceramic evidence is divided into three different periods: (1) the beginning of the fifth century until 536, when the Frankish kingdom obtained direct access to the Mediterranean Sea; (2) from 536 until the middle of the seventh century, the period when Merovingian Gaul was largely open to the Mediterranean world; and (3) from the late seventh century to the first half of the eighth century, a phase that reflected the gradual disappearance of Mediterranean imports from Frankish Gaul (Fig. 37.1). In order not to burden the text, we largely avoid giving specific bibliographic references to the artifacts attested to at different archaeological sites, but instead refer to more general essays on these topics that provide the relevant bibliography for anyone interested in engaging in further study of specific finds.

THE DOMINANCE OF AFRICAN IMPORTS
IN THE LATE FOURTH CENTURY

At the end of the fourth century, as was the case elsewhere in the western Mediterranean (Panella 1993), markets in southern Gaul were dominated by African imports of what was likely oil and *salsamenta* (salted fish) transported in medium-sized cylindrical amphorae of type Keay 25/Africana III (Bonifay and Raynaud 2007). In addition, local evidence reveals that a significant number of these amphorae also carried wine. By contrast, imports of Spanish amphorae were not rare in some cities like Arles and others mainly in the vicinity of Spain like Narbonne and Toulouse, which received Baetican oil (type Dressel 23), and fish sauces from Baetica (southern Iberia) and Lusitania (south-western Iberia) (types Almagro 50, 51a–b, 51c). Sicilian wine is also attested in late examples of MR1 amphorae, along with the first arrivals of Calabrian amphorae Keay 52. In addition, wine from the eastern Mediterranean is present in modest quantities, as was the case during the previous centuries, having been imported from Crete and Asia Minor in one-handled MR3 containers (Fig. 37.3).

By contrast, Mediterranean amphorae were far less abundant in more northern regions. However, their periodic discovery in these areas suggest that they traveled via two main trade routes. The first one was through the Rhône Valley, where a river port in Lyon dated to circa 400 contained about 30 percent African amphorae (Lemaître et al. 2011), including both Keay 25 and Keay 1B types with wine possibly from Algeria. The same kinds of amphorae are also found much further to the north, for instance, in Augst, Metz, and Tournai. The second trade route followed the terrestrial and fluvial route of the "Gallic isthmus," from Narbonne to Bordeaux, via Toulouse. Along this route, and particularly in Toulouse, the representation of African amphorae in urban contexts reaches 38 percent (Amiel and Berthault 1996).

This model of interpretation based on amphorae is nonetheless less than ideal if one seeks to gauge the amount of foodstuffs transported in perishable containers. It is important to remember that wine from Gaul and even from Italy might be imported in wooden barrels rather than ceramics. Moreover, one must recall that archaeology is generally unable to testify to the trade of grain, since it was transported in bags or even in bulk, first by boat and then, of course, by cart.

With respect to fine ceramics across southern Gaul, African Red Slip (ARS)[1] table-ware, which has long been highlighted in economic history (Fentress et al. 2004), dominates all the archaeological contexts dated to the fourth century (for more detail, see Bonifay and Raynaud 2007). This situation was well established as early as the mid-second century with inflows of ARS ware from the region of Carthage (the so-called category A), which was soon followed in the mid-third century by central Tunisian ARS ware (the so-called category C; for more details on this classification, see Bonifay 2004). From the mid-fourth century onward, however, the ceramic production from the lower Mejerda Valley (the area of El Mahrine, northern Tunisia) invaded the markets. This was true even in a city like Arles, which also saw the abundant arrival of tableware (*sigillée luisante*) from Gaul, mainly from the region of Savoy through the Rhône Valley (Bonifay and Raynaud 2007). In contrast, distribution patterns of ceramics are quite different in northern regions of Gaul, which continued to be supplied by a variety of regional productions deriving from the mid-Roman period such as Argonne ware (for more details on the classification, see Brulet, Vilvorder, and Delage 2010; see also Fleming, Chapter 17, this volume).

Nowadays, it is generally assumed that ARS ware did not normally travel from Africa along with amphora cargoes and that grain was the main product with which ARS traveled (Bonifay and Tchernia 2012). It is also thought that the seminal distribution of ARS ware throughout the Mediterranean did not move directly from Africa to the different provinces or towns but was largely dependent on the phenomenon of return cargoes from Rome. Indeed, the Eternal City was the general hub of most of the Mediterranean trade in the Roman period, through both the imperial supply system (*annona*) and private interprovincial trade. These observations support the current understanding that, by the start of the fifth century, the territories that progressively came under the control of the Frankish kings were still completely integrated in the Roman economic system.

PERIOD 1: FRANKISH EXPANSION IN A TIME OF ECONOMIC CHANGE (CIRCA 400–536)

We propose two distinct phases in the period between circa 400 and 536: one of upheaval during most of the fifth century, and a second of partial recovery at the beginning of the sixth century.

The Growing Popularity of Eastern Mediterranean Amphorae in the Fifth Century

As early as the beginning of the fifth century, the percentage of African amphorae clearly decreased. This drop reflected the increase of Spanish containers (Dressel 23, Almagro 51a-b) in the western part of Narbonensis, which came under Visigothic rule at this time, as was the case for most of the Iberian peninsula. However, this drop in the trade of African amphorae mainly mirrored the arrival of numerous and geographically diverse amphorae from the eastern Mediterranean. Throughout the fourth century, the commercial attractiveness of Constantinople had promoted the emergence of new productive regions, which were scarcely active until then but were thenceforth distinguished by their "export-oriented" production. These developments followed a proliferation of production centers in continental Greece, some of the Aegean islands (Samos, Chios,

Thasos), Crete, Cyprus, the western and southern edges of Asia Minor, the southern coastline of the Black Sea, the Levant, and Egypt (Pieri 2012). In southern Gaul, the arrival of impressive quantities of eastern Mediterranean ceramic is reflected in their very high percentages of ceramic finds during a large part of the fifth century: they represent up to an average of 30–45 percent of the amphorae recorded in the stratigraphies of Narbonne, Arles, and Marseille (Pieri 2005). Elsewhere in the western Mediterranean, including Rome, Tarragona, and Carthage, imports from the eastern Mediterranean seem to have followed the same trend in similar proportions (Reynolds 2010).

During the fifth century, the distribution of eastern Mediterranean amphorae in Gaul was irregular. They were very diversified in Narbonensis, with a multiplicity of types (including LRA 1A, 2A, 3, 4A, *bag-shaped* 1-2, Agora M273, Agora M334), while the morphological panorama was more limited in northern Gaul, with the nearly exclusive presence of type LRA 1 from Cilicia and LRA 4 from Gaza-Ashkelon (Le Bomin 2020). Eastern wine, which seems to have been the main foodstuff transported in these amphorae, was well known and celebrated by numerous fifth-century authors, including Sidonius Apollinaris (*Carmina*, 17.15) and Venantius Fortunatus (*De Vita S. Martini* 2). Such wine generally was of good quality and very expensive. Among the most appreciated vintages was Palestinian white wine produced in the Gaza region, which was reputed for its gustatory qualities as well as its medicinal properties and vaunted by the Greek physician Oribasius (*Collectionum Medicarum Reliquiae, libri IX–XVI*), the North African physician Cassius Felix (*De medicina* LXII), and the Byzantine physician Aetius of Amida (*Libri medicinales V–VIII*).

It is true that if we consider the differing capacities of amphorae, our calculations allow for a more balanced ratio of eastern Mediterranean and African products. Nevertheless, even if the quantity of foodstuffs transported by small eastern Mediterranean amphorae and gigantic African cylindrical containers was more or less the same in mid-fifth-century Marseille (Bonifay 2004), the nature of the African imports was probably more diversified: possibly fish sauces (type Keay 35B), possibly olive oil (type Keay 35A), and pickled olives (type Keay 25 and *spatheia*), as shown by the cargo of the fifth-century Dramont E shipwreck (Santamaria 1995). Finally, throughout the fifth century, Italian wine remained well attested, particularly in Marseille, with high percentages of Keay 52 amphorae from Calabria.

Declining Imports of African Red Slipware Tableware in the Fifth Century

Ceramic surveys have demonstrated generally that from the start of the fifth century, the distribution of ARS tableware, which reflected ongoing demand from the end of the first century CE due to its high quality, decreased everywhere in the Mediterranean (in the West: Fentress et al. 2004). This drop was particularly noticeable in Marseille in the middle and the second half of the fifth century. In addition, there was a change in the sources

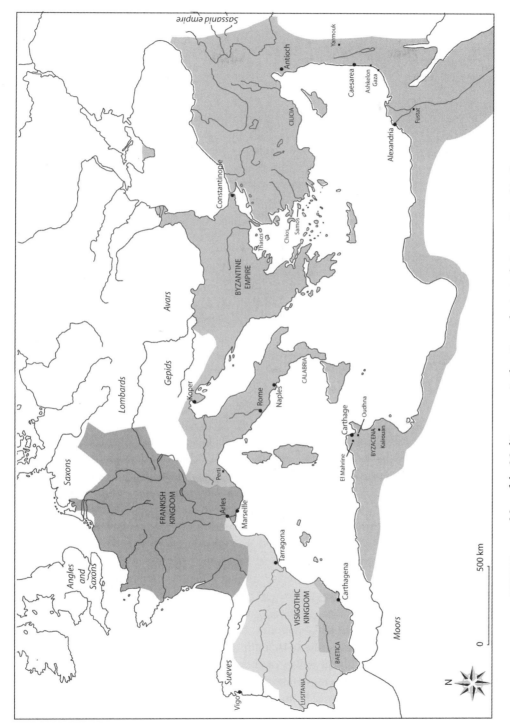

FIGURE 37.2. Map of the Mediterranean in the 560s and principal sites mentioned in the text.

for this supply, namely, the products from the region of Carthage (ARS ware D1 from the El Mahrine area) were progressively replaced on the markets in the south of Gaul by those of equivalent quality coming from central Byzacena (ARS ware C5) and the northern Hammamet gulf (Sidi Khalifa workshop) in eastern Tunisia. In addition, finds of these tableware imports were not regularly distributed over the territory. Well attested in major towns, in some large rural estates (La Gayolle and Eyguières, near Aix-en-Provence), and even in some hilltop settlements (Saint-Blaise, between Marseille and Arles, and Constantine, near Aix-en-Provence), they disappeared almost completely from certain regions, for instance, in eastern Languedoc (Bonifay and Raynaud 2007).

The declining evidence of ARS ware imports, which may be explained by a change in the general organization of trade in the western Mediterranean, was accompanied by a process of "import substitution" or "replacement," which found its most evident expression in the development of the local tableware known as *Dérivées-des-Sigillées Paléochrétiennes* (literally, early Christian derivatives of early Roman relief ceramics), first in Languedoc at the very end of the fourth century, and then in Marseille in the first half of the fifth century. Another more marginal phenomenon was the sudden appearance on the markets in the south of Gaul of tableware from the eastern Mediterranean, including most prominently "Late Roman C ware" from the region of Phocaea in western Anatolia, and "Late Roman D ware" from Cyprus or southern Anatolia.

Other Evidence of Mediterranean Trade in Gaul in the Fifth Century: Glass and Coins

As early as the second quarter of the fifth century, alongside a few imports of finished glass vessels from Egypt and Asia Minor, most of the glass commonly found in southern Gaul is characterized by its olive-green or yellow-brown coloration. These glass artifacts were produced from a new raw material coming into the region (the nature of the transport is completely unknown), which was shaped locally into previously existing forms like cut-rim goblets and cups. Chemical analyses of the glass suggest that ingots of this material were imported from Egypt and then manufactured in secondary workshops of southern, and in some cases, northern Gaul (for the importation of glass beads, see Pion et al., Chapter 36, this volume). In this period, there were no large distinctions between the glass of the southern and the northern regions of Gaul. This custom prevailed until the period between the 480s and 530s, when the production and distribution of glasses with opaque white trails prevailed in both regions (D. Foy in Bonifay and Raynaud 2007).

Along with the ceramic and glass evidence, the analysis of numismatics for the purpose of the history of trade continues to be a difficult issue (see Strothmann, Chapter 35, this volume), but a stratigraphical survey of about 100 coins found in the excavations of Marseille harbor shows that two monetary practices were common in this city, as well as in Africa, during the fifth century. First, old minted coins were systematically reused, provided that their size corresponded to that of contemporary coins. Second, a good portion of the coins used in the fifth century were molded on top of contemporary coins that had been struck, for example, under Valentinian III. They were then used in this fashion until the end of the century. The sustained use or reuse of older coins probably resulted from the increasing rarity of official mints (Brenot in Bonifay, Carre, and Rigoir 1998).

With respect to Mediterranean trade, extant texts are virtually silent in this period, with the exception of some of the letters of Sidonius Apollinaris. The Gallo-Roman aristocrat indicated in his correspondence that traders came to Marseille for business purposes and in order to make a profit (*Lib. VII, Epist. VII*), an observation that corroborates the ceramic evidence (see Drews, Chapter 6, this volume).

The Early Sixth-Century Revival of African Imports and the Diversification of Eastern Mediterranean Imports

Before either the Byzantine reconquest of Africa or the Frankish annexation of Provence, the import of ceramics from North Africa throughout southern Gaul recovered (Fig. 37.2). This revival may be seen in the arrival of new generations of amphorae (types Keay 55 and 62), whose percentages balance with imports from the eastern Mediterranean, roughly 30 percent for each at the start of the sixth century, whereas the remaining 40 percent are of Italian or unknown origin (Pieri 2005) (Fig. 37.3). These amphorae, well attested both in ports (Marseille and Toulon) and inland cities (Nîmes), are also present in finds at some rural sites (Eyguières and Camargue), and even in hilltop settlements (Saint-Blaise and Constantine) (Pieri 2005; Bonifay and Raynaud 2007). They are also noted in western Gaul, for example, in Bordeaux and in the *villa* of Séviac (Gers) (Amiel and Berthault 1996). The content of these amphorae is still debated, but they may have contained oil, fish sauces, or wine.

At the same sites, the proportion of ARS ware rose again in the sixth century. This tableware is particularly well attested in some hilltop settlements, which were then abandoned in the 530s. It made up, for example, more than half of the fine ware documented at Sainte-Propice, near Aix-en-Provence (Bonifay and Raynaud 2007). The origin of these imports shifted once again from central Byzacena and the northern Hammamet gulf to the Carthage region (Oudhna and "X" workshops). Similar products were not completely absent from northern contexts, as may be seen in the case of the Oudhna cup Hayes 97 of Godorf, south of Cologne (Hayes 1972, p. 150), which provides evidence of the revival of African imports.

As far as eastern Mediterranean amphorae are concerned, it seems that the sources of supply multiplied in the sixth century from what was observed previously: products from continental Greece (type LRA 2) and Syria-Palestine (*bag-shaped* 3 type from Caesarea and Jerusalem; for more details on the typology, see Pieri 2005) complemented the types already attested from Asia Minor and Gaza. The early sixth century was characterized by quite a large territorial distribution of these amphorae not only in

Mediterranean regions, but also in western Gaul, with examples in major cities (Toulouse, Bordeaux, and Poitiers), and to a lesser extent in small towns and rural areas of the same regions (Amiel and Berthault 1996; F. Berthault in Bonifay and Raynaud 2007). This period was also characterized by the heightened distribution of eastern Mediterranean tableware ("Late Roman C ware" from Phocaea) and cooking ware, including cooking pots and frying pans of Aegean origin, which testifies to the movement of substantial numbers of both goods and people.

Interpretations and Questions Regarding the Period Circa 400–536

Review of the ceramic documentation suggests that changes in Mediterranean trade did not follow but preceded the slow territorial dismantling of the Roman Empire over the course of the fifth century. Southern Gaul, even before being divided among the Visigoths, Ostrogoths, and Burgundians, did not escape this economic shakeup. How can we explain this modification in the quantity and origin of goods arriving in late Roman Gaul? One of the possible central causes was that Rome ceased to be the over-sized and dominant port of redistribution in the western Mediterranean. Indeed, there was likely a global drop in demand from inhabitants of the city, which may be explained by a progressive decline in population from the 410s, and then by collapse of the *annona* system circa 455. This change was probably also boosted by the new "liberal" economic policy of the eastern Roman Empire under the initiative of Theodosius, from the 390s onward. These important developments, and no doubt other complex microeconomic factors, may have caused a complete reorganization of Mediterranean trade networks. These changes had an impact on supply sources at the Mediterranean level, leading to a sudden upsurge in the number of eastern Mediterranean imports, the reorganization of production within Roman provinces (e.g., products from central Byzacena replacing those from Carthage), and the rise of a multitude of direct commercial shipping routes that replaced the complex network of the return cargoes from Rome.

Moreover, the penetration of Mediterranean imports into the markets of central and northern Gaul—as far as the ceramic evidence is concerned—appears to have been less frequent and more haphazard than in the past. It is plausible that insecurity affected inland roads, thus explaining these difficulties. For instance, the revival of the Atlantic shipping route may reflect the decision of traders to bypass possible obstacles blocking traditional terrestrial and fluvial routes in the second half of the fifth and the first third of the sixth centuries. This situation might explain the spectacular development of the port of Vigo in southwestern Galicia, a possible transshipment or intermediate port on the way to the British Isles and their tin and lead mines (Fernández 2014; on England, see Fleming, chapter 17, this volume).

Unfortunately, however, the present state of ceramic typologies makes it difficult to incorporate these observations into a precise chronological portrait. For instance, the

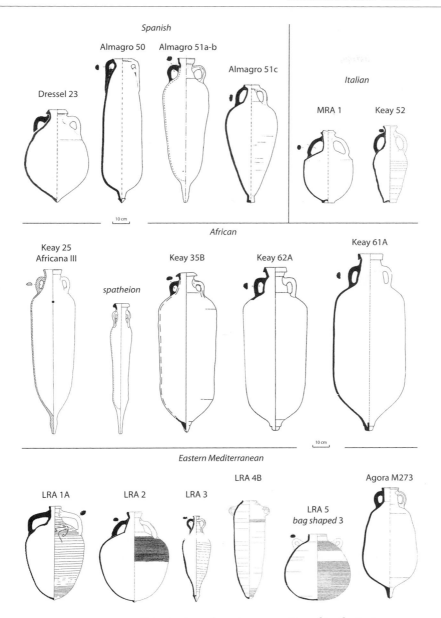

FIGURE 37.3. Principal amphora types mentioned in the text.

merchant ship that sank in the 430s at Cap du Dramont near Saint-Raphaël, in what is now the French Riviera (Santamaria 1995), held a cargo of ARS plates and at least six different amphora types. All of these originated from the Nabeul region in northeastern Tunisia and can be considered either "Late Roman" or "Vandal" depending on whether they date to before or after 439, a level of precision that is obviously impossible to reach through the ceramic evidence. Similarly, the ship that sank in the 530s in the bay of La Palud near the island of Port-Cros (one of the Hyères islands in the Var) (Long and Volpe 1998), while transporting a mixed cargo of African amphorae and eastern Mediterranean amphorae, may be interpreted as either "Late Vandal" or "Byzantine" depending on whether it sailed before or after 533. For the latter, if `the final destination of the shipment was Marseille, we do not know whether this city was still ruled by the Ostrogoths or whether it was already controlled by the Franks since it is unclear whether it sank before or after 536. In the same way, it is difficult to assign a series of prestigious large ARS plates Hayes 89B/90 found in Augst (pers. comm. S. Fünfschilling), Orléans (pers. comm. P. Dupont), and Ponthévrard (Barat, Séguier, and van Ossel 2011, Fig. 4.2-3) to either period 1 (fifth and early sixth centuries) or period 2 (mid-sixth to mid-seventh century).

PERIOD 2: THE FRANKISH KINGDOM AND THE MEDITERRANEAN, 536–CIRCA 650

With the annexation of Provence in 536, the Merovingian kingdom reached its maximum size and gained access to the Mediterranean Sea for the first time. Limited to a narrow corridor between Rhone and Alps, this coastal strip had its main harbor at Marseille, which, to all intents and purposes, became the kingdom's gateway to Mediterranean trade.

Marseille

Simon Loseby has described the city of Marseille as a late-antique success story (1992), a characterization that sums up the historical triumph of the city over its former rival Arles during the course of the fifth century. The latter was, from the end of the first century BCE, the main maritime and fluvial port of Roman Gaul. Marseille's wealth in the second half of the fifth century made possible the construction of a group of impressive episcopal buildings, including one of the largest baptisteries of the Roman world (larger than even that of Milan, an imperial capital). In the absence of the demographic and architectural contraction that affected so many other urban centers in Gaul in this period, Marseille also saw the erection of a new defensive wall that supplemented the older Hellenistic one, which was still standing at this time. Unlike Arles, moreover, Marseille did not suffer repeated sieges and became an urban refuge for a number of contemporary scholars such as Paulinus of Pella and Salvian, whose presence raised the intellectual standing of the city in the fifth century. A last, but certainly not least, important, difference with Arles may be found in the ceramic evidence. While contexts post-dating the mid-fifth century are rare in Arles, Marseille's archaeological record attests to massive arrivals of Mediterranean amphorae and table- and cooking wares throughout the fifth and early sixth centuries. At this date, Marseille was undoubtedly the main Mediterranean port of Gaul and remained so under Merovingian rule.

Although it is difficult or impossible to distinguish between the imports made before and after the Frankish annexation of Provence, the Merovingian kingdom's continued engagement in Mediterranean trade in the late sixth century and the first third of the seventh century is demonstrated by the large number of archaeological contexts with ceramics found in both Marseille and a few other regional semi-urban and rural areas (such as the hilltop agglomeration of Saint-Blaise). During this period, more substantial shipments of ARS wares arrived in Marseille than had been the case previously. These ceramics displayed a new panorama of forms (Hayes 91D, 105, 106, 107, 109A) and diversified origins, coming from the region of Carthage as well as Byzacena. The percentage of African amphorae (types Keay 62E, 61C, Bonifay 47, mainly from coastal Byzacena) equaled or even surpassed that of eastern Mediterranean containers (LRA 1B from Cyprus, LRA 2B from Argolid, LRA 4B from Gaza/Ashkelon, bag-shaped amphorae from Syria-Palestine, and LRA 7 from Egypt) (Fig. 37.3). African lamps and eastern Mediterranean cooking wares were also present, the latter even more numerous than in the past. The supply of Byzantine African, and eastern Mediterranean goods in Frankish southern Gaul during the years 575–625 was comparable to that found in contemporary Byzantine towns and strongholds in the western Mediterranean like Cartagena, Naples, Sant'Antonino di Perti, and Koper (Reynolds 2010) (Fig. 37.2).

When the Franks took possession of Marseille, they maintained the active minting of silver and copper coinage that the Ostrogoths had initiated at the beginning of the sixth century. This low-value coinage was probably necessitated by the growth of small-scale retail trade. Moreover, between circa 575 and 670, Marseille seems to have been one of the only cities in Merovingian Gaul to strike gold coins, first in the name of the eastern Roman emperor and subsequently in the name of the Frankish kings. These high-value coins were no doubt intended for major transactions (Loseby 1992).

Finally, the glass of the mid-sixth to mid-seventh century, probably blown in numerous regional workshops including Marseille, is characterized almost exclusively by a single form, the stemmed goblet (Isings 111; for more details on glass typology, see Foy in Bonifay and Raynaud 2007). In this case, even if the end products were locally manufactured, the raw material was still imported from Egypt or Syria-Palestine. Moreover, the morphology of these vessels was common to all of the Mediterranean regions (Foy in Bonifay and Raynaud 2007).

The archaeological evidence for this period corresponds with the textual data, which led Henri Pirenne to consider Marseille the Mediterranean gateway of Merovingian Gaul (Pirenne 1939). Gregory of Tours clearly shows the critical importance of this port for the Franks. The fratricidal struggles of succession that pitted the Merovingian princes against one another for possession of the valuable harbor demonstrate the jealousy with which they guarded this important trade hub that resisted the economic decline seen in Arles and elsewhere (Baratier 1969, pp. 87–99). Gregory's *Histories* also testify to imports that are invisible to archaeology, including spices, aromatics, skins and leather, papyrus, and slaves, for which Marseille was one of the principal markets (*Historiae* V, 5).

In some instances, however, the historical and archaeological sources contradict one another. According to Gregory, in 591, a ship arrived in Marseille from Spain with its usual cargo. Despite this important historical witness, Spanish imports to Marseille are not indicated by contemporary ceramic evidence. The same text (*Historiae* IX, 22) also tells us that at this time the plague was introduced into the city, while contemporary archaeological evidence suggests to the contrary that habitation and population experienced growth at roughly this same date (on the plague, see Horden, Chapter 14, this volume).

Mediterranean Goods in Northern Gaul

In northern Gaul, available archaeological data, mostly from cities and monasteries, provide a few examples of eastern Mediterranean amphorae in the sixth century (LRA 1 and LRA 4). The quantity of these goods is always very small in contrast to cities like Lyon and especially Bordeaux, where the supply was larger and more diversified. These finds include a couple of eastern amphora types (LRA 2 and bag-shaped), some African types (Keay 61), and an ARS assemblage dated to the late sixth century or early seventh century. This distribution is very similar to that found in Marseille.

It appears that the distribution of Mediterranean goods preferably followed the course of the rivers (including the northern Loire and Seine), given the fact that land routes were not always practical and could be taxed heavily. In the case of Bordeaux, we do not know exactly how Eastern and African goods reached the city (that is, whether by the Atlantic route or through the "Gallic isthmus"), but some differences with patterns seen in the Gallician port of Vigo could lead us to favor the second hypothesis.

The second half of the sixth century is the moment when early medieval texts mention Eastern wine most frequently. Authors like Corripus (*In Laudem Iustini Augusti minoris*, III, 87–89), Gregory of Tours (*De gloria confessorum*, LXIV, LXV), Venantius Fortunatus (*Vita Sancti Martini*, 2), and others make reference to its presence in Gaul. The use of this wine during the sixth century is attested as having been consumed by elites and was used in liturgical settings by high-ranking ecclesiastics. Thus, it seems that the same foodstuff was only the perquisite of elites in northern Gaul, while it was affordable for many more people in southern Gaul, in accordance with the customs inherited from the Roman past.

Sixth-century trade appears to have been largely in private hands. The involvement of the church was hardly noticeable in Gaul, despite the fact that bishops played an active role in the economic management of the territories and the strong likelihood that some portion of the imported Mediterranean foodstuffs were produced on ecclesiastical estates, whether in the eastern Mediterranean or in Africa. By contrast, the texts made numerous references to private traders, especially of eastern European origin, including Syrians and Jews, who were described as specialists in business (see Drews, Chapter 6, this volume). They appear to have lived sometimes in "colonies" installed inside major commercial cities, and they had their own communal activities (for more details, see Pieri 2005).

The Role of Regions of Production Between 536 and 650

The period 490–560 is considered the "golden age" of the proto-Byzantine economy (Pieri 2012). In the eastern Mediterranean, from the late fifth century, major economic reforms boosted trade and significantly increased the opulence of the empire. Anastasius introduced two fundamental reforms: the abolition of the *chrysargyron* (a tax impacting those who earned their incomes from sale and trade) and the introduction of a new copper coin, the *nummus*, which was favorable to trade (on cities, see Loseby, Chapter 27, this volume; on Merovingian coinage, see Strothmann, Chapter 35, this volume). Even after this, during the reign of Justinian, the economy was still in full expansion despite the fact that the empire had to face a series of challenges including earthquakes, plagues, and a war with Sassanid Persia. Some Eastern cities like Constantinople, Antioch, and Alexandria, the population of which reached or exceeded 300,000 inhabitants, supported expanded trade in luxury goods and facilitated the interregional and regional exchange of crucial foodstuffs (on the Byzantine Empire, see Esders, Chapter 16, this volume). Rural areas likewise experienced significant demographic increases, and in certain places free peasants succeeded in accumulating surpluses as a consequence of adapting their production to the demand of urban markets (see Theuws, Chapter 38, this volume).

By contrast, interpretations of the situation in Byzantine Africa is less clear. Some scholars have interpreted the period from 536 onward as a time of stagnation, or even of downturn, due in particular to the oppressive taxation of production (on this question, see Wickham 2005, p. 724). Nevertheless, the Arab conquerors, as recorded by the chroniclers, found an incredibly rich land endowed with prosperous olive groves and grain fields. In the course of their early raids in the 640s, they profited from their pillage of large quantities of foodstuffs and gold (Mrabet 1995).

Marseille, too, made important contributions to the Mediterranean economy, which was closely linked not just to trade but also to diplomatic and pilgrimage traffic, all of which were closely connected. For one, the Merovingian kings conducted foreign policy from this port, and it was the point of departure of most of their Mediterranean embassies. In addition, the harbor was the point of departure of numerous pilgrims, who made use of regular shipping routes. In turn, pilgrims played a significant role in the promotion of the Palestinian wines from the Holy Land (especially Gaza-Ashkelon) in Gaul. The archaeological evidence of pilgrimage is weak, but it can be perceived in glass medals and ceramic eulogy *ampullae* bearing the image of saints.

Yet, if access to the Mediterranean afforded by possession of the port of Marseille was such an advantage for the Merovingian kingdom(s), why do we not see more evidence of Mediterranean ceramic imports in northern Gaul? The fact that ARS tableware was not diffused north of Provence from the mid-sixth to the mid-seventh century was nothing new: the lack of distribution of Mediterranean goods in the north differed little from the situation during the Roman Empire. More significant, perhaps, was the low level of distribution of stemmed glass goblets in the north of Gaul. It perhaps signaled the existence of some cultural divisions between north and south, and simultaneously it confirmed the complete integration of the south in the Mediterranean world.

Many of the more profitable exchanges that transpired in early medieval Gaul, however, did not leave any archaeological traces. For instance, trade in luxury goods—such as spices—attested in the written record for northern Gaul and production places is hard to identify through material remains. Nevertheless, one may surmise that some portion of Mediterranean foodstuffs, when arriving in Marseille, could have been transferred into perishable containers such as barrels. Although barrels were more easily transportable on rivers and roads, they only exceptionally leave traces in the archaeological record. In this scenario, it is possible to imagine that only elites purchased Mediterranean products in their original containers.

Period 3: Did Mediterranean Trade in the Frankish Kingdom End between 650 and Circa 750?

The most dramatic improvements in our understanding of late-antique ceramics concern the late seventh century. Any hesitation that scholars once felt about dating western Mediterranean archaeological contexts containing ARS, African, and eastern Mediterranean amphorae to the very end of the seventh century disappeared with the discovery of the spectacular deposit at the Crypta Balbi in Rome, which the stratigraphy and coinage dated to the 690s (Saguì 1998). Some contexts in southern Gaul that have recently been surveyed have proved to be of similar composition. By contrast, Mediterranean ceramic evidence in northern Gaul during this period remains as invisible as ever.

In southern Gaul, four examples are offered here to highlight various facets of the late Merovingian economy. The first example comes from Marseille. Our knowledge of ceramic presence in Marseille has significantly increased as a consequence of the excavations conducted during the 1990s at the Place Jules-Verne, the Place Villeneuve-Bargemon, and the music hall Alcazar (Bien 2007). Dating a series of contexts at these three urban sites was made possible by assessment of the stratigraphy and coin finds (*follis* of Constantine IV): they pointed to the second half of the seventh century. The other chronological markers consist in the latest forms of the ARS tableware (Hayes 80B/99, 105B, 108, 109B), associated with the latest types of African amphorae (Keay 8A, 50, 61A), and some rarer Eastern late types (LRA 1C, 4C). Contacts with Egypt still are attested by the discovery of some bag-shaped amphorae from the Mariout area, while the link with Constantinople, not evidenced until now in the ceramic record, is made clear by a series of cooking wares of type Saraçhane 3. The latest assemblages, with similar imports (including some African and perhaps Italian globular amphorae), seem to be dated to the first third of the eighth century, according to the chronology of certain local potteries (Bien 2007).

The second example comes from Arles where excavations in the episcopal group of structures at Saint-Cesaire have recently revealed a context that appears very similar to the ones of Marseille, which are often seen as exceptional. Very late, and partially unclassified, ARS tableware is present (variants of Hayes 105), along with a large quantity of African amphorae (Keay 50, 61A, and 8A) and some unidentified containers. The chronology of this context can be pushed well into the first third of the eighth century, following ^{14}C (Carbon 14) analysis and their association with numerous local gray wares characteristic of the eighth-century regional patterns (Mukai et al., 2017).

Our third example is the shipwreck Saint-Gervais 2 at Fos-sur-Mer (Bouches-du-Rhône), which provided many artifacts, the majority of which were African in origin. These include the same African amphorae-type Keay 8A, a *spatheion* 3B, some sherds of ARS forms Hayes 108 and 109B, and an ARS lamp. However, the ship's main cargo was grain, as attested by the remains trapped in a gangue of pitch that spilled over when the vessel sank (Jézégou 1998). Besides the irony that this is almost the sole grain cargo that has been verified in the Mediterranean despite being of such a late date, in contrast to the historical evidence for robust trade in grain during the Roman period, the question must be raised as to the origin of the ship. Was it a coastal vessel supporting regional trade or an offshore vessel involved in a direct transaction between North Africa and Gaul? However, the most important question is not the origin of the ship, but the origin of the wheat. Even if the dominant hypothesis of "cabotage" (transport between two points by a ship of different origin) seems convincing, it is impossible to reject the hypothesis that this grain was imported from overseas, possibly Sicily or North Africa.

Finally, at Mont-Bouquet (Gard), in the eastern Languedoc scrubland, a burnt stronghold or house has been excavated, the cellar of which was found to hold a large number of amphorae. These included African amphorae of the same type as those found in Marseille, Arles, and Fos, globular amphorae of various origins, and a clay (possibly commercial?) seal with Arabic characters, the last named dated between 650 and 750 (Pellecuer and Pène 1996). Christophe Pellecuer has proposed that this possibly aristocratic house may have burned during the 730s, which brought conflict between Childebrand, Charles Martel's nephew, and the local aristocracies who were perhaps tempted to take the side of the Arabs against the burgeoning power of the Carolingians.

The ceramic evidence documented in recent research thus gives us a glimpse of the possible continuity of Mediterranean imports, even of basic foodstuffs like oil and grain, in southern Gaul as late as the end of the first third of the eighth century. However, it is impossible to gauge the real quantities of these arrivals, since our evidence is still relatively meager. Glass evidence, for instance, seems to back the idea that the level of imports was high. It appears that the practice of recycling broken glass became more frequent from the late seventh century onward, which may indicate a reduction in the import of raw material for glassmaking from overseas (Foy in Bonifay and Raynaud 2007).

Whereas discoveries of Mediterranean amphorae and tableware are rare in northern Gaul for the mid-sixth to the early seventh century, they are completely nonexistent, in current research, from the mid-seventh century onward for these regions. This observation is even more surprising given that, at the same time, the distribution of central Gallic "bistre" (yellowish-brown) coarse ware through the Rhône Valley to southern Gaul is well attested (Bonifay and Raynaud, 2007). In addition, the glass locally produced throughout Frankish Gaul once again became similar in color (blue) and morphology ("palm cups") (Foy in Bonifay and Raynaud 2007).

However, written texts from this period provide more relevant information. A series of surviving documents (see Loseby 2000) reveal that two northern monasteries, Saint-Denis and Corbie, were granted annual rents by the Merovingian kings. This income permitted them to purchase Mediterranean commodities useful to the monastic life, including oil for lighting purposes, papyrus, and different kinds of exotic herbs and fruits. Some scholars like Loseby have doubted that these goods were still easily available in the fiscal stockrooms (*cellaria fisci*) of Marseille or Fos at time that the privileges are supposed to have been written (716 in the case of Corbie). They thus suspect these Merovingian *tractoria* were in fact literary archaisms, or simple statements of intent, or even royal propaganda (Loseby 2000). However, recent discoveries in Marseille and Arles now make clear that these lists of goods may have been realistic for the early eighth century and could have been sourced from Marseille or Fos. However, it is worth bearing in mind that the quantities in question were not so enormous, considering that the 10,000 pounds of oil for Corbie represents the average volume of only forty African amphorae Keay 61 or 8A, if oil in fact was the real content of these amphorae. This figure represented just a tiny part of the normal load of a medium-sized late antique vessel.

INTERPRETATIONS AND QUESTIONS
REGARDING THE PERIOD 650–750

From the mid-seventh century onward, existing problems with dating artifacts from the Mediterranean are far from being resolved. Whereas dates for seventh century sites are more easily secured, it is often impossible to identify secure eighth century contexts. It is important to recognize that scholars do not unanimously accept the absolute chronology of ceramic evidence for the first third of the eighth century suggested for some contexts in the south of Gaul. The solution will probably come from advances in research on ceramic production areas since the question of the disappearance of Mediterranean imports in southern Gaul cannot be separated from the question of the collapse of the traditional production of amphorae and tableware in the main regions of production.

The ceramic evidence of the late seventh century and perhaps of the beginning of the eighth century in southern Gaul raises interesting issues about the effects of the Arab conquest on Mediterranean trade. The contexts of Marseille, Arles, and Mont-Bouquet show that Syro-Palestinian and Egyptian wine continued to arrive after the Battle of

Yarmouk (636) and the foundation of Fustat (Cairo, Egypt) in 641. Moreover, African oil, fish-sauces (the *liquamen* of the Corbie charter), possibly wine, and ARS tableware were still imported after the foundation of Kairouan (Tunisia) circa 670, and perhaps even after the fall of Carthage in 698/699. It is remarkable, in particular, that the latest African amphorae of type Keay 8A originate from regions like coastal Byzacena, which was conquered by the Arabs in the 670s. It is quite clear that this political change, similar to earlier ones like the Vandal conquest, hampered but did not break the continuity of trade, even if it is not yet understood how this trade, and the production of the goods entailed, were organized.

Extant charters of the late seventh century and the beginning of the eighth century show the sophisticated organization of taxes and custom-dues imposed by Merovingian authorities on the cargoes arriving in the Mediterranean ports and transiting through the Rhône corridor. One of the most interesting elements of this very lucrative activity for the Frankish kings was the *cellarium fisci*, understood as a warehouse in which the goods levied by agents of the king from the cargoes arriving from overseas were stored in Marseille and Fos. Probably this system already existed in an earlier period, but it is only described in detail, including its northerly manifestation, when it was close to its end.

Conclusion

Ceramic evidence, with the added witness of contemporary texts, confirms the continuity of trade between Merovingian Gaul and the Mediterranean until at least the first half of the eighth century. However, what was at stake on the eve of the "Dark Ages" is not the continuity of trade, but its *intensity* and *directions*, and also *when* or *if* it ended. In fact, reflecting on relations between Merovingian Gaul and the Mediterranean on the basis of the ceramic evidence means reconsidering once more the validity of historian Henri Pirenne's thesis (1939 [1937]), from an archaeological perspective. There has been much debate on this subject during these last decades. In particular, archaeologists Richard Hodges and David Whitehouse (1983), provided a new "current orthodoxy" (Loseby 1998: 204) by demonstrating that the end of the exchange-networks of antiquity were not due directly to the rapid and unexpected advance of the Arabs onto the southern shores of the Mediterranean. They argued that the latter only gave the "*coup de grâce*" to a system which was in progressive decline from the early fifth century.

In this debate, the case of mainly southern Merovingian Gaul suggests a scenario that is both compatible with and different from the latter hypothesis. On the one hand, it seems clear that great migrations, whether of the Franks, or the Arabs, were not directly responsible for breaking up the unity of the ancient world. On the other hand, the decline of the Roman economy was perhaps not as continuous as was once thought. At the root of this irreversible evolution was probably dysfunction within the imperial economic system by the early fifth century, well before the end of the Roman Empire itself. Perhaps this owed to the collapse of its main driver, demand, followed by a phase of stabilization on partially new footing at the beginning of the sixth century. This new organization of trade, characterized in southern Gaul by a change in the direction of flows of cargo and perhaps also growth of these exchanges, became increasingly rigid in the course of the first half of the sixth century. This inflexibility owed to the territorial reconfiguration of the western Mediterranean into three main blocks: the Byzantine empire in Italy, Africa, and southwestern Spain, the Visigothic kingdom in the remainder of Spain and Languedoc, and the Frankish kingdom(s) in the rest of Gaul. The situation changed again in the course of the first half of the seventh century, with the arrival of the Lombards in northern Italy, the loss of Byzantine territories in Italy and Spain, and general economic downturn in the eastern Mediterranean. From the mid-seventh century onward, ceramic evidence in southern Gaul showed a continuous retraction of imports until their assumed end in the 730s. Only at this moment does a true rupture seem to have occurred. However, the question remains as to whether this supposed collapse of trade between the Merovingian Gaul and the Mediterranean was "caused by a failure of production and distribution-networks in the Mediterranean [or] by a failure of demand on the Frankish market" (Loseby 2000, p. 191).

Mediterranean trade in this period likely did not offer the same quantity of production surpluses as in the past. The rarefaction of eastern amphorae in southern Gaul in the late seventh century can probably—at least in part—be related to a drop in wine production both in the regions that passed into Umayyad rule, and the regions that remained under Byzantine control. In Africa, we are ill informed about the first part of the Islamic period. However, the amphorae there, the production of which was almost industrial, and the large-scale manufacture of traditional foodstuffs like oil, *garum* (fish sauce), and wine that presumably accompanied it, probably ceased to be made during the first half of the eighth century. So, whereas in the earlier instance the failure of production seems to have preceded the rupture of trade, in the later instance in the first half of the eighth century, the failure of production and demand seem to have been contemporary to one another.

By contrast, if we consider that the fire of the house at Mont Bouquet was actually contemporaneous to the disorder that accompanied or preceded Childebrand's campaigns in the southern Rhône Valley, it is legitimate to ask whether the mayors of the palace deliberately sacrificed the openness of their kingdom to the Mediterranean for the sake of security against the Arab advance and political considerations like the struggle against the aristocracy of Provence. If they did so, it was perhaps because their nascent empire had already forged new exchange networks, more local and/or more northern ones, in which ancient roads no longer played a considerable role. In fact, within the framework of the Carolingian economy, the empire favored the riverine outlets of western and northern Gaul. There, new types of trading posts like Nantes, Rouen, Quentovic, and Dorestad were constructed mainly in contact with the British Isles and the Scandinavian and Slavic worlds (see Fleming, Chapter 17; Hardt, Chapter 20; and Tys, Chapter 34, this volume). Contact with the Mediterranean would then pass mainly through Russian rivers to the Baltic axis and Alpine passes (McCormick 2001).

When trying to explain the supposed end of Mediterranean trade in Merovingian Gaul, it is difficult to prioritize either the failure of the production of available goods or the drop in demand. We can only observe that the match between supply and demand, which boosted the tremendous development of "Roman" trade, even in its later phase at the start of the sixth century, no longer existed. Perhaps it was a sort of divorce by mutual consent.

Nevertheless, the idea of rupture is not unanimously accepted. Did long-distance exchange collapse in the 700s (Wickham 2005), or was a certain connectivity maintained (Horden and Purcell 2000)? This question leads to two others: Is ceramic evidence actually suited to making us aware of the realities of exchange networks in the "Dark Ages"? Or are ceramics only able to teach us which kinds of foodstuffs ceased to be imported (Eastern wine, African oil, and *garum*)? And, are they incapable, as for the previous periods, of offering evidence for a lot of other highly valuable goods such as those on the list of the Corbie charter, or the foodstuffs that were transported in perishable containers like wine in barrels? As a matter of fact, textual references to sea crossings starting from, or arriving to Marseille, were not rare during the second half of the eighth century and the main part of the ninth century (Ganshof 1938). For the time being, we have to wait for new archaeological approaches suited to checking these alternative thesis issues, as was the case in 1983, when Hodges and Whitehouse revisited Pirenne's thesis (on this question, see Effros 2017).

NOTE

1. African Red Slip Ware (ARS) is one of the most widely distributed forms of tableware throughout antiquity. It is found from Scotland in the north to Egypt in the south, and from Portugal in the west to Crimea in the east. Produced in the Roman provinces of Africa, mainly in the part of *Africa proconsularis* that today form part of Tunisia, ARS was made from the end of the first century CE to the end of the seventh century. This tableware is characterized by a smooth light red to orange slip and a very standardized panorama of forms (bowls, dishes, jugs, etc.), bearing various types of decoration: rouletted, molded, appliqué, stamped, and so on.

WORKS CITED

Ancient Sources

Aetius Amidenus, *Libri medicinales*. A. Olivieri (ed. and trans.). (1950). *Corpus Medicorum Graecorum* 8.2. Berlin: Akademie Verlag.

Cassius Felix, *De medicina*. A. Fraisse (ed. and trans.). (2002). *Cassius Felix, De la médecine*. Paris: Les Belles-Lettres.

Gregory of Tours, *Historiae*. R. Latouche (trans.). (1995). *Grégoire de Tours, Histoire des Francs*. 3rd ed. Paris: Les Belles-Lettres.

Gregory of Tours, *De gloria confessorum*. H. L. Bordier and N. Desgrugillers (ed. and trans.). (2003). *Grégoire de Tours, Vie des pères et des confesseurs*. Clermont-Ferrand: Paleo.

Oribasius, *Collectionum medicarum reliquiae*. H. Raeder (ed. and trans.). (1929). *Corpus Medicorum Graecorum* 6:1–2. Leipzig: A. M. Hakkert.

Sidonius Apollinaris, *Carmina*. A. Loyen (ed. and trans.). (1970). *Sidoine Apollinaire, Lettres*. Paris: Les Belles-Lettres.

Venantius Fortunatus, *De Vita S. Martini*. S. Quesnel (ed. and trans.). (1996). *Venance Fortunat, Œuvres*, vol. 4: *La vie de saint Martin*. Paris: Les Belles-Lettres.

Modern Sources

Amiel, C., and Berthault, F. (1996). "Les amphores du Bas-Empire et de l'Antiquité tardive dans le Sud-Ouest de la France. Apport à l'étude du commerce à grande distance pendant l'Antiquité." *Aquitania* 16: 255–263.

Barat, Y., Séguier, J.-M., and Van Ossel, P. (2011). "Les importations lointaines de céramiques au Bas-Empire en Île-de-France." In P. Van Ossel with P. Bertin and J.-M. Séguier (eds.), *Les céramiques de l'Antiquité tardive en Île-de-France et dans le bassin parisien. Volume II. Synthèses* (pp. 195–214). Diocesis Galliarum Document de travail n° 9. Nanterre: Librairie archéologique.

Baratier, E. (1969). *Histoire de la Provence*. Toulouse: Privat.

Bien, S. (2007). "La vaisselle et les amphores en usage à Marseille au VIIᵉ siècle et au début du VIIIᵉ siècle: première ébauche de typologie évolutive." In M. Bonifay and J.-C. Tréglia (eds.), *LRCW 2, Late Roman Coarse Wares, Cooking Wares and Amphorae in the Mediterranean. Archaeology and Archaeometry* (pp. 263–274). British Archaeological Reports Int. Ser. 1662. Oxford: Archaeopress.

Bonifay, M. (2004). *Études sur la céramique romaine tardive d'Afrique*. British Archaeological Reports International Series 1301. Oxford: Archaeopress.

Bonifay, M., and Raynaud, C. (2007). "Les échanges et la consommation." In M. Heijmans and J. Guyon (eds.), *Antiquité tardive, haut Moyen Âge et premiers temps chrétiens en Gaule méridionale* 2 (Vol. 64, pp. 93–161). Special issue of *Gallia*.

Bonifay, M. and Tchernia, A. (2012). "Les réseaux de la céramique africaine (Iᵉʳ–Vᵉ s.)." In S. J. Keay (ed.), *Rome, Portus and the Mediterranean* (pp. 315–336). Archaeological Monographs 21. London: British School at Rome.

Bonifay, M., Carre, M.-B., and Rigoir, Y. (1998). *Fouilles à Marseille. Les mobiliers (Iᵉʳ–VIIᵉ s.)*. Etudes Massaliètes 5. Paris: Errance.

Brenot, C. (1998). "Le monnayage." In M. Bonifay, M.-B. Carre, and Y. Rigoir (eds.), *Fouilles à Marseille. Les mobiliers (Iᵉʳ–VIIᵉ s.)* (pp. 358–360). Etudes Massaliètes 5. Paris: Errance.

Brulet, R., Vilvorder F., and Delage, R., with the collaboration of Laduron, D. (2010). *La céramique romaine en Gaule du Nord*. Turnhout: Brepols.

Effros, B. (2017). "The Enduring Attraction of the Pirenne Thesis." *Speculum* 92(1): 184–208.

Fentress, L., Fontana, S., Hitchner, B., and Perkins, P. (2004). "Accounting for ARS: Fineware and Sites in Sicily and Africa." In S. Alcock and J. Curry (eds.), *Side by Side Survey* (pp. 147–62). Oxford: Oxbow.

Fernández, A. (2014). *El commercio tardoantiguo (ss. IV–VII) en el Noroeste peninsular a través del registro cerámico de la ría de Vigo*. Roman and Late Antique Mediterranean Pottery 5. Oxford: Archaeopress.

Ganshof, F. (1938). "Notes sur les ports de Provence du VIIIᵉ au Xᵉ siècle." *Revue Historique* 183: 28–37.

Hayes, J. W. (1972). *Late Roman Pottery*. London: British School at Rome.

Hodges, R., and Whitehouse, D. (1983). *Mohammed, Charlemagne and the Origins of Europe*. London: Duckworth.

Horden, P., and Purcell, N. (2000). *The Corrupting Sea, A Study of Mediterranean History.* Oxford: Blackwell.

Jézégou, M.-P. (1998). "Le mobilier de l'épave Saint-Gervais 2 (VIIe siècle) à Fos-sur-Mer (Bouches-du-Rhône)." In M. Bonifay, M.-B. Carre, and Y. Rigoir (eds.), *Fouilles à Marseille. Les mobiliers (Ier–VIIes.)* (pp. 343–352). Etudes Massaliètes 5. Paris: Errance.

Le Bomin, J. (2020). "Mediterranean Pottery Imports in Western Gaul during Late Roman Period (Mid 3rd–Early 7th c. AD). State of Knowledge." In M. Duggan, M. Jackson, and S. Turner (eds.), *Ceramics and Atlantic Connections: Late Roman and Early Medieval Imported Pottery on the Atlantic Seabord. Proceedings of an International Symposium* at Newcastle University, March 2014). Roman and Late Antique Mediterranean Pottery 15. Oxford: Archaeopress.

Lemaître, S., Duperron, G., Silvino, T., Bonnet, C., Bonifay, M., and Capelli, C. (2011). "Les amphores africaines à Lyon entre le IIe et le Ve siècle: réflexions à propos de la circulation des marchandises sur l'axe rhodanien." In L. Rivet (ed.), *SFECAG, Actes du congrès d'Arles* (pp. 203–222). Marseille: SFECAG.

Long, L., and Volpe, G. (1998). "Le chargement de l'épave de la Palud (VIe s.) à Port-Cros (Var). Note préliminaire." In M. Bonifay, M.-B. Carre, and Y. Rigoir (eds.), *Fouilles à Marseille. Les mobiliers (Ier–VIIes.)* (pp. 317–342). Etudes Massaliètes 5. Paris: Errance.

Loseby, S. T. (1992). "Marseille: A Late Antique Success Story?" *Journal of Roman Studies* 82: 165–185.

Loseby, S. T. (1998). "Marseille and the Pirenne Thesis, I: Gregory of Tours, the Merovingian kings, and 'un grand port.'" In R. Hodges and W. Bowden (eds.), *The Sixth Century. Production, Distribution and Demand* (pp. 203–229). Leiden: Brill.

Loseby, S. T. (2000). "Marseille and the Pirenne Thesis, II: 'ville morte.'" In C. Wickham and I. L. Hansen (eds.), *The Long Eighth Century. Production, Distribution and Demand* (pp. 167–193). Leiden: Brill.

Loseby, S. T. (2007). 'The Ceramic Data and the Transformation of the Roman World." In M. Bonifay and J.-C. Tréglia (eds.), *LRCW 2, Late Roman Coarse Wares, Cooking Wares and Amphorae in the Mediterranean. Archaeology and Archaeometry* (pp. 1–14). British Archaeological Reports International Series 1662. Oxford: Archaeopress.

McCormick, M. (2001). *Origins of the European Economy, Communications and Commerce, AD 300–900.* Cambridge: Cambridge University Press.

Mrabet, A. (1995). "L'état économique de l'Afrique byzantine d'après les récits des chroniqueurs arabes." *Africa* 13: 123–133.

Mukai, T., Tréglia, J.-C., Heijmans, M., and Dantec, E. (2017). "Arles, enclos Saint-Césaire. La céramique d'un dépotoir urbain du Haut Moyen Âge: Milieu du VIIe-début du VIIIe siècle apr. J.-C. In D. Dixneuf (ed.), *LRCW 5, Late Roman Coarse Wares, Cooking Wares and Amphorae in the Mediterranean. Archaeology and Archaeometry* (pp. 171–200). Etudes alexandrines, 42–43. Alexandria: Centre d'Études Alexandrines.

Panella, C. (1993) "Merci e scambi nel Mediterraneo tardoantico." In *Storia di Roma, III, 2*, (pp. 613–697). Turin: Einaudi.

Pellecuer, C., and Pène, J.-M. (1996). "Les importations d'origine méditerranéenne en Languedoc aux VIIe et VIIIe s: l'exemple de San Peyre (Le Bouquet, Gard, France)." In G. P. Brogiolo (ed.), *Early Medieval Towns in the Western Mediterranean* (pp. 126–132). Documenti di Archeologia. Padua: SAP.

Pieri, D. (2005). *Le commerce du vin oriental à l'époque byzantine (V^e–VIIe siècles), Le témoignage des amphores en Gaule.* Bibliothèque archéologique et historique 174. Beirut: IFAPO.

Pieri, D. (2012). "Regional and Interregional Exchanges in the Eastern Mediterranean during the Early Byzantine Period. The Evidence of Amphorae." In C. Morrisson (ed.), *Trade and Markets in Byzantium* (pp. 27–49). Washington, DC: Dumbarton Oaks.

Pirenne, H. (1939 [1937]). *Mahomet et Charlemagne*, reprint 1992. Paris: PUF.

Reynolds, P. (2010). *Hispania and the Roman Mediterranean, AD 100–700. Ceramics and Trade.* London: Duckworth.

Saguì, L. (1998). "Il deposito della Crypta Balbi: una testimonianza imprevidibile sulla Roma del VII secolo?" In L. Saguì (ed.), *Ceramica in Italia: VI–VII secolo* (pp. 305–330). Florence: All'insegna del giglio.

Santamaria, C. (1995). *L'épave Dramont E à Saint Raphaël (Ve s. ap. J.-C.).* Archaeonautica 13. Paris: CNRS.

Wickham, C. (2005). *Framing the Early Middle Ages, Europe and the Mediterranean, 400–800.* Oxford: Oxford University Press.

CHAPTER 38

··

LONG-DISTANCE TRADE AND THE RURAL POPULATION OF NORTHERN GAUL

··

FRANS THEUWS

"GALLIA est omnis divisa in partes tres (...)." These famous opening words by Julius Caesar in his book on the Gallic Wars could have just as easily been written by an author about Merovingian Gaul 600 years later. Indeed, Merovingian Gaul was not a homogeneous entity. South of the Loire River, it was quite different from what was found to the north of the Seine River. Even northern Gaul was not a homogeneous whole (Fig. 38.1). Between the two rivers lay central Gaul, and a zone to the north of the Seine River formed a sort of transitional landscape between central and northern Gaul. Moreover, in each part of Gaul, different infrastructural, religious, sociopolitical, economic, and cultural structures were present, and alternative developments took place from the mid-fifth to the mid-eighth century in each of them. From an archaeologist's point of view, then, generalizations about Merovingian Gaul do not seem profitable. It is imperative to aim for higher chronological resolution in future research: Merovingian society of the sixth century was quite different from that of the first half of the eighth.[1]

Historians have emphatically stressed the uneven geographical, temporal, and social distribution of written sources in and on Merovingian Gaul (Wood 1994). Most texts refer to the southern and central parts of Gaul, and relatively few to the north; those documents that refer to the north are for the most part related to the activities of the Merovingian kings. Moreover, those persons who were in power and participated in a "culture savante" (Le Goff 1977) produced the majority of contemporary texts. Similarly, an uneven distribution characterizes the archaeological record. That of northern Gaul is dominated by evidence from cemeteries that are known by the thousands, many of which contained a multitude of graves with an innumerable number of skeletons and artifacts. However, when one proceeds southward from the Seine River

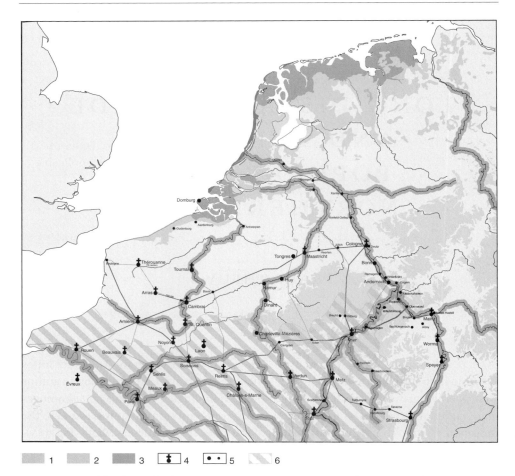

FIGURE 38.1. Northern Gaul in Merovingian times. Roman roads, rivers, and major centers. 1. land higher than 300 m (middle range mountains); 2. marshlands; 3. tidal flats; 4. bishops' seats; 5. *vici* and fortresses; 6. bishoprics with continuous bishops' lists. Along the rivers, a zone five kilometers wide is indicated.

in the direction of the Loire River and toward southern France, the number of cemeteries with an abundance of deposited objects gradually declines. Instead, cemeteries, including large ones, are found with numerous burials in sarcophagi almost devoid of grave-goods, although the rite of clothed burial was practiced in locations such as Marseille (Boyer et al. 1987; Young and Périn 1991; Halsall 1995a). In northern Gaul, not many rural places of religious significance have been excavated fully. By contrast, to the south, the urban fabric of the surviving Roman towns is better known than that in the north, where Merovingian urban archaeology has focused mainly on religious foundations (see the many contributions in Duval et al. 1991; *Die Franken* 1997, the volumes of *Topographie chrétienne des cités de la Gaule,* and the three volumes of *Les premiers monuments chrétiens de la France*). Because of this uneven distribution of sources, varying images emerge regarding the nature of society in distinct parts of Gaul. To what extent

these differences have been determined by the uneven distribution of sources is difficult to evaluate. If this uneven distribution could be shown to have been the result of
the degree to which these areas were excavated or suffered damage due to industrial
development or military campaigns that have transpired since then, one might propose
that the original situation once was more equal in all of Gaul (see Effros, Chapter 4, this
volume). Despite the relevance of such issues, the uneven distribution of the archaeological evidence is likely and largely the result of the unequal development of various
parts of Gaul in the late Roman and Merovingian periods. Because this chapter focuses
on the society in northern Gaul, the ideas presented here may not be applicable to
Gaul's central and southern regions.

NORTHERN GAUL: THE LAY OF THE LAND

The end of Roman rule changed the defense of the empire, and the disappearance of the
Roman army from the Rhine River had profound consequences for society in northern
Gaul. These changes must have leveled a great blow to the demand for goods generated
by the Roman state. The quantity of grain, leather, pottery, iron, and other goods that
had previously been produced for the state, must have declined enormously. So did the
villae (Roman estates) and centers responsible for producing these goods. The *villa*
landscape of northern Gaul had already suffered from decline in the decades around
200. Many *villae* were abandoned in the third century, and of those that survived, many
were lost at the beginning of the fifth century (Brulet 1990; van Ossel and Ouzoulias 2001;
Nieveler 2003, pp. 179–184; on villas in southern Gaul, see Chavarría Arnau, Chapter 29,
this volume). Some regions, like the area south and west of the lower Meuse River, were
almost completely abandoned. This area was repopulated from ca. 380/390 to ca. 450
and then nearly abandoned again (Theuws 2008a, 2008b; Heeren 2015). Other regions,
like Picardy, were studded with the ruins of *villae* (Agache and Bréart 1975).

What would Clovis have seen on his way to his baptism in Reims at the turn of the
fifth century? A lot of ruins, that is certain, and a lot of *agri deserti* (deserted fields).
Nonetheless, he still would have considered it a Roman landscape, even if one littered
with abandoned estates. He would also have seen that people lived among these ruins,
even if they did so under quite different conditions than in the second century (van
Ossel and Ouzoulias 2001). What this means is a matter of debate: were the lands of the
former *villae* still tilled? If they were tilled, was it under quite different conditions
regarding the social organization of production (see Peytremann, Chapter 31, this
volume)? Was it just the luxurious building of an absentee owner that had crumbled, or
did the estate as such not exist anymore? The type of ownership of these lands might
have changed drastically in many parts of late-Roman northern Gaul compared to the
villa system of previous centuries and what may still have been the case in southern Gaul
(Theuws 2009). Whatever the circumstances, northern Gaul must have looked quite
depopulated in the fifth century compared to the centuries before. However, as noted
earlier, in some areas, people were still present and trying to make a living.

In one way or another, a number of towns survived. It is evident that they had shrunk considerably in the fifth century. They must have suffered from a decline in demand, production, and thus the activities of investors in *villae* and town amenities. The survival of a town greatly depended on the presence of a bishop or the renewed presence of a bishop (see contributions in *Die Franken*, 1997, pp. 121–170; see also Bourgeois, Chapter 28, this volume). Although many towns must have had bishops at the end of the fourth century, in the north and along the Rhine, the reconstructed lists of bishops show discontinuities (Weidemann 1990) (Fig. 38.1). However, in the late fifth century or the first half of the sixth century, most sees in the region were reoccupied. The northernmost towns, including Forum Hadriani (near The Hague), Nijmegen, and Xanten, however, did not recover, and Tongres had to give way to Maastricht, where the bishop installed himself at an unknown date (Theuws 2001). However, this episcopal presence does not mean that northern Gaul was fully Christianized in the sixth century. In the countryside, there were few cultic places, and the creation of monasteries was a regular feature only from the mid-seventh century onward. Nonetheless, there are signs of rural Christianity if one interprets the production and distribution of glass and ceramic vessels from the Argonne and middle Meuse Valley near Namur, which were decorated with Christian symbols as a feature of a Christian substrate that is hardly visible in contemporary texts (Fig. 38.2). Yet, shortly after the turn of the sixth century, there was an end to the production of these objects, and one wonders whether this Christian substrate was a late-antique feature that gradually disappeared rather than representing an emerging Christian community. Thereafter, it seems that many bishops operated from an ivory tower in a land that showed hardly any signs of Christianity before the mid-seventh century. Moreover, one may suggest that they were more preoccupied with Merovingian politics than with local affairs (Wood 1994, pp. 71–87; see Halfond, Chapter 13, this volume).

In northern Gaul, a few towns profited from regular visits by the king. Some towns were qualified as *sedes regiae* (royal seats), including Paris, Soissons, Reims, and later Metz, a concept whose meaning is still debated (Dierkens and Périn 2000). Indeed, what royal presence meant in times of itinerant kingship is not entirely clear (see Hen, Chapter 10, this volume). Archaeology has not yet managed to demonstrate the presence of royal palaces in these towns, although they are mentioned in texts. Is this a sign that these structures were rather modest and that Merovingian kings did not invest in town palaces as their Mediterranean counterparts had?

In addition to towns, there were *vici* in the Merovingian period that may have had Roman antecedents but grew in importance in the sixth century. First were the *vici* along the Meuse River, including Charleville-Mézières, Dinant, Namur, Huy, and especially Maastricht (Plumier and Regnard 2005; Theuws 2007). A fortress characterized these sites in late-Roman times: in Maastricht, it protected a bridge; in other sites, fortresses often guarded important river crossings. Only exceptionally small fortresses survived the Roman period. These exceptions are mainly found along the major routes through northern Gaul (see Bourgeois, Chapter 28, this volume).

Roads connected all these sites in Roman times, and many of them must have remained in use in the Merovingian period. It has been suggested, for instance, that

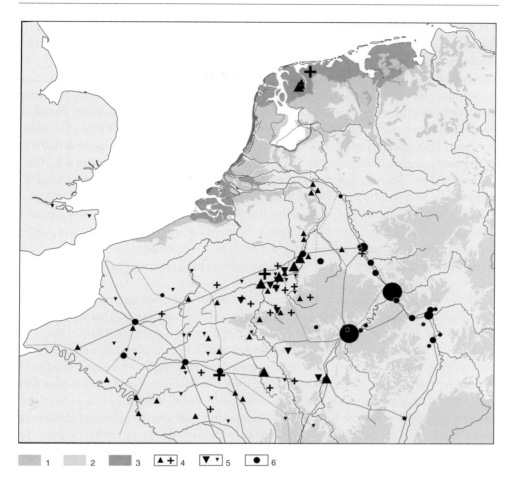

FIGURE 38.2. Northern Gaul. The distribution of red-slipped Argonne ware decorated with Christian symbols (after Dijkman 1992), Christian gravestones (after Boppert 1986), and glass bowls with Christian motifs (after van Wersch et al. 2010). 1. land higher than 300 meters (middle range mountains); 2. marshlands; 3. tidal flats; 4. Argonne ware with Christian symbols in settlements (triangles) and cemeteries (crosses); 5. glass bowls with Christian symbols; 6. Christian gravestones. The size of the symbols reflects the number of finds.

the name "Chaussée Brunehaut" for a stretch of Roman road indicated continued use of the road in the Merovingian period (Rouche 1985). It is unclear to what extent these roads were kept in order. Excavations in Maastricht have shown that the important road from Cologne in the direction of Tongres was kept up through the second, third, and probably fourth centuries, although there are no archaeological indications for the last date (Dijkstra and Flamman 2004, pp. 54–55; Theuws and Kars 2017). The road was not repaved until ca. 1300 (Dijkstra and Flamman 2004, p. 57). However, it must have been in use in the late-Roman and Merovingian period. It served a sixth- and seventh-century cemetery immediately to its south. Moreover, in 830, Einhard wrote that owing to his illness, it took him no less than ten days to get from Maastricht to Valenciennes, a distance of 170 kilometers (Dutton 1998, p. 149). He must have used old Roman roads that were still passable in the Carolingian period. The road from Cologne through Maastricht to Tongres can be followed to Cambrai, Amiens, and Rouen in an almost straight line, forming one of the main land arteries in northern Gaul. It is why minor fortified sites like Bavai and Jülich remained important. Another major land route must have led from Mainz to Trier and continued to Reims, Soissons, and Paris. This road is likely why the small fortresses of Arlon and Carignan remained so important. Another important east–west route was from Strasbourg to Metz, Verdun, Reims, Soissons, and Paris, with a number of smaller fortresses along it. Important north–south land routes were those from Cologne through Trier to Metz, Toul, and further south, the road along the Rhine River, and roads from Paris and Soissons to the south and north. Research in Maastricht (Vos 2004) and Cuijk (Goudswaard et al. 2001) shows that the bridges were repaired in the late Roman period. Many bridges associated with these routes must have still been in use in the Merovingian epoch.

While old Roman roads remained important, major rivers were the most important communication routes in northern Gaul (Guizard-Duchamp 2003). This was the case especially for the Rhine and Meuse rivers, as well as the Seine and Oise/Aisne. The Scheldt River seems not to have been as important as it became in later centuries.[2] The two towns along its upper reaches, Tournai and Cambrai, might rather have depended on land routes crossing rivers than the river routes themselves. The map in Figure 38.1 shows that almost all centers of importance were situated on the banks of a major river. Those towns, such as Tongres, Arras, and Thérouanne, that were not so situated, seem to have suffered as a result. They dwindled in favor of river-based centers like Maastricht (Guizard-Duchamp 2003, pp. 593–594). The move of the royal seat from Reims (a land-based town)[3] to Metz (a river-based town), might have been triggered not just by political factors but by its preferable position in the river-based Merovingian network system. In short, during the Merovingian period, communication seems to have changed from a road-based to a river-based system.[4]

This is not to say that all communications were by boat: roads along the rivers may have been just as important. While the rivers were central lines in corridors of communication, roads undeniably remained important. Where rivers mainly flowed from south to north (in the east), roads going east to west remained important. Similarly, where rivers flowed from east to west (in the west), north–south roads remained important. Places at the junctions of the main land routes and rivers became important centers: Cologne, Maastricht, Cambrai, Amiens, Paris, Verdun, Metz, Strasbourg, Trier, and Mainz. Strangely, no major center developed where the road from Trier to Reims crossed the Meuse River. Was this road in the end only of secondary importance? And is it possibly the case that one traveled from Trier first to Metz and then further west instead of taking the road through the uninhabited southern Ardennes? This is certainly a consideration. Finally, it is important to note that new centers rarely developed in coastal areas with the exception of Domburg and possibly Quentovic.

One issue that has not yet received sufficient attention in the study of northern Gaul is the region's relatively good infrastructure. The roads and rivers not only provided good transport options for royal, episcopal, and aristocratic trains, but the rural population also had good access to the traffic along these routes. If one maps zones of 50 kilometers on both sides of the major rivers like the Meuse, Rhine, Seine, Moselle, Somme, Aisne and Scheldt, which are zones in which the rural population could reach the river in one or two days, one can see that no one lived further than 50 kilometers from a major river (Fig. 38.3). This means that in northern Gaul, physically speaking, everyone had relatively easy access to regional, supraregional, and international traffic exchange along the area's major arteries. Moreover the places in which those areas overlap are interesting: the middle Dutch river area; the Middle Rhine, lower Moselle and lower Main area; the upper Moselle, upper Meuse and upper Aisne area; and the upper Somme, upper Scheldt and Aisne region. These infrastructural characteristics may have been an important prerequisite to the post-Roman economic development of northern Gaul.

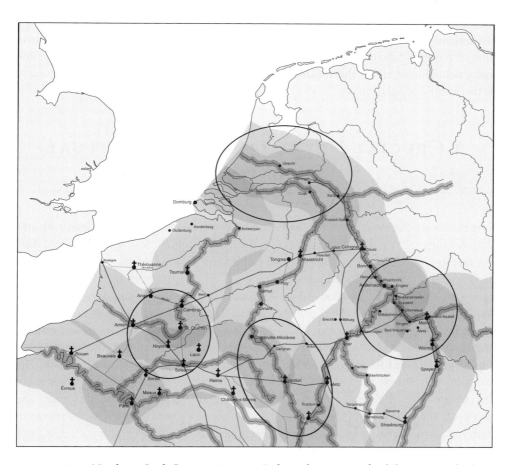

FIGURE 38.3. Northern Gaul. Communications. Indicated are zones of 50 kilometers wide along the major rivers, important Roman roads, and zones where one or two river zones overlap.

In this world of inherited Roman structures, the population began to grow in the second half of the fifth century, as revealed by cemetery evidence (see, for instance, Nieveler 2006). The first burials in many cemeteries date to the later fifth and early sixth centuries. However, not all regions in northern Gaul show this early development: in some regions, habitation only started in the second half of the sixth century. There is also a difference in the density of habitation. Usually, cemeteries in the French-speaking part of Belgium, for instance, are significantly larger (with hundreds of graves dating to the later fifth, sixth, and seventh centuries) than those in the southern Netherlands (usually less than 100 graves dating to the later sixth, seventh, and early eighth centuries). In Picardy, there are cases of cemeteries with more than 1,000 graves and at least five examples of cemeteries with more than 2,000 graves (*La Picardie*, 1986, p. 204). The number and size of cemeteries thus varied substantially from one region to another. Moreover, some regions were never colonized intensively like the middle-range mountains of the Ardennes, Eifel, and Westerwald. Others, in coastal peat areas, were not colonized at all. Habitation on the coast was limited to a ring of settlements directly on the coast and more intensively in the "terpen" (raised dwelling mounts) area in northern Netherlands and Germany (Nicolai 2014). An important element in the debate on post-Roman economic development in northern Gaul should be numbers: determining how many people lived in northern Gaul at various moments in time. The size of the early sixth-century population was modest in large parts of northern Gaul.[5]

A Crucial Development: New Ritual Repertoires

Cemeteries are the most important evidence for population growth in the later fifth and sixth centuries. From the nineteenth century on, many cemeteries were discovered during forestry and building activities and publicized because of the abundant goods deposited in the graves. Soon local museums started treasure hunting to fill their cabinets with the splendid objects from the graves (Effros 2012). This funerary wealth resulted from important ritual changes in the second half of the fifth century. The expanding population developed new repertoires of burial rites within one or two generations throughout northern Gaul and adjacent regions to the east. Center stage in this deposition rite was furnished burial (Young and Périn 1991; Halsall 1995a, 1995b; *Die Franken*, 1997; Effros 2002, 2003). The deceased were buried fully clothed. In graves of men and women, the metal fittings of belts are regularly found. In those of women, one also finds the remains of garments and, above all, fine jewelry. Likewise, in graves of both men and women, gender-neutral objects such as vessels of ceramic, glass, copper alloy, and wood were deposited. In the graves of many men, there were weapons, including swords, shields, lances, and seaxes. This burial rite was practiced by almost every family, even those in the smallest communities. The practice was widespread and contrasted with the far more austere burial style of the fifth century in northern Gaul. Why this lavish burial rite developed in this form is hotly debated. A whole series of interpretations have been advanced: some are less sophisticated, common-sense suggestions based on modern conceptions of death, dying, personhood, and property; others are directly related to interpretations of events and information found in written sources; and still others are ethnographically informed (Härke 2014). The intellectual history of northwestern Europe, from nationalism to postmodernism, has been visible in this debate (see Graceffa, Chapter 3, this volume). There is not yet a *communis opinio* as to why this ritual developed or the meaning behind its various facets.

An Immense Demand for Objects

Interpretation of the burial rite is important in understanding the nature of the early medieval economy and contribution of the world of ideas, norms, and values to it, to the point that it may be described as a "ritual economy" (Theuws 2004; McAnany and Wells 2008; Hodges 2012; Carver 2015). But it is the immense quantity of objects deposited in graves from the late fifth century onward that interests us here. What we now have in museum collections and archaeological depots is the tip of the iceberg. Many graves were reopened and objects taken out shortly after burial, and many cemeteries have not yet been discovered. Moreover, not all available material culture was deposited in graves. How did the rural population of northern Gaul obtain these objects? In what way was this new ritual demand satisfied? These questions touch on a central theme of historiography that has prevailed since the days of Henri Pirenne and Alfons Dopsch: the nature of the early medieval economy in (northwestern) Europe (McCormick 2001; Wickham 2005). Recent theories stress the role of elite demand in post-Roman economic development. Most outspoken on this subject is Chris Wickham's work, but he is certainly not alone in his opinion. Jean-Pierre Devroey (2006) has voiced the same opinion for a somewhat later period. He considers the needs of the "state" (to be interpreted as the court, the army, and the church) as offering important incentives for growth. Historians are in the good company of archaeologists like Heiko Steuer, whose model of early medieval exchange presents a top-down structured system of distribution controlled by the elite, in which the only trade is that in luxuries (1997, p. 392). At the bottom of his graphic representation of the model are free persons. By contrast, Steuer does not consider unfree individuals (who were likely tenants rather than slaves in the area to which the model relates), and probably assumes that the material needs of the unfree were satisfied through elite channels.

We can see, however, following Wickham, that legal status and economic agency need not be intimately connected (Wickham 2005, pp. 261–262). In these models, the rural population is not an important element of the economic development of northern Gaul. As an example, we can turn to one of Wickham's central observations: "elite consumption structured these large-scale systems.... Peasantries and the poor were not yet a sufficiently consistent, prosperous market for these economies of scale to exist just for them, particularly given the absence of sophisticated and responsive structures for the movement of goods" (Wickham 2005, pp. 706–707, 819; 2009, p. 222). However, both the immense number of objects in the graves of rural dwellers and the infrastructure of northern Gaul counter this argument. This model does not consider the men and women who deposited an enormous quantity of objects in the graves of their deceased relatives and friends to have been agents in the economy of Merovingian Gaul. Is this assumption justified? To answer this question, we can start with one certainty: the mass of the rural population was able to acquire large quantities of objects, of which only a (small?) part was deposited in graves. Again, how did they acquire them? There are two possible explanations (both of which are oversimplified, but will suffice here): either the economy developed top-down on the basis of elite demand and control of the production and distribution of products by the elite; or the economy developed bottom-up on the basis of a quantitatively large demand by the rural population that was able to acquire the objects needed in their rituals in a more or less open exchange system that triggered production. Of course, such an opposition will in the future have to be nuanced, but for the moment, it is interesting to analyze the second possibility, an alternative to currently prevalent models. Before we do so, however, it is useful to look more closely at the objects deposited in graves.

Types of Objects Deposited and Their Distribution Patterns

One only needs to browse the typochronological studies of material recovered to grasp the diversity of objects deposited in Merovingian-period graves (Siegmund 1998; Müssemeier et al. 2003; Legoux, Périn, and Vallet 2004). The main categories are metal belt and strap fittings that were at times exquisitely decorated; vessels (mainly tableware) of ceramic, glass, wood, and copper alloy; dress accessories like brooches, bracelets, beads, earrings, and finger rings; horse gear and spurs; weapons like swords, seaxes, axes, bow and arrows, lances, and shields; utensils like knives, shears, keys, spindle whorls, purses with contents, wooden boxes; many types of amulets like cowry shells and teeth of wild animals; and, finally, coins. Many dress accessories were made of gold, silver, or a copper alloy; belts and brooches were inlaid with precious stones and silver. And this list could be extended still further.

Research on individual types of objects and their distribution in northern Gaul and adjacent regions has shown that some of these objects originated from the same region in which the burials took place, but others came from regions hundreds of kilometers away or even from the Mediterranean and Near East (see Pion et al., Chapter 36, this volume). Jörg Drauschke (2011) studied the Mediterranean imports in southern Germany, but the distribution of many of the types of finds he studied likewise extended further north.[6] Impressive are the cowry shells deposited in graves of women in the sixth century which originated from the Red Sea and Indian Ocean. The distribution map shows that they were most likely brought to the north via the Alps rather than the Rhône corridor, which is often presented as the major north–south route in the Merovingian period (McCormick, 2001, p. 360). However, the distribution pattern depends to some extent on conservation conditions, which are poor in the sandy soils of the northwestern European plain. There might have been cowrie shells there as well, for they can be seen when conditions are favorable. One could argue that the number of cowry shells recovered up until now does not allow us to consider their regular flow northward. Yet, archaeology can state with certainty that their number will increase in the future, as will all categories of objects and types of graves.

Large numbers must also be involved in the flow of garnets into northern Gaul, either as an element of a finished object (brooches, for instance) or as raw materials. Scientific research has now demonstrated that these garnets originated from sources in India and Sri Lanka (Calligaro et al. 2006–2007; see Pion et al., Chapter 36, this volume). Hardly a cemetery dated to the sixth century exists in which no objects decorated with garnets are present. It was almost a common good available to inhabitants of even remote settlements. It is difficult to establish the precise social or juridical status of inhabitants of what were usually small local communities, or how diverse their social positions were. No detailed inventory of such material has been carried out in northern Gaul, as has been done by Drauschke (2011) in southern Germany, in which he demonstrates how much material from the Mediterranean was imported to this region. Finally, it is important to observe that not only finished objects but also raw materials came from the Mediterranean and Near East to satisfy the demand created by the new burial rites. The raw glass used to make bowls decorated with Christian motifs in the middle Meuse region came from the Near East (van Wersch, van Geesbergen, and Vrielynck 2010). The bowls themselves, however, must have been blown somewhere nearby, possibly in Namur.

Next to these exotic objects in graves were many finds made in the region of the cemetery or from less than a few hundred kilometers away. This phenomenon is implied by distribution maps of the types of objects found in graves, although many maps now need to be updated if they are to serve the purpose of an in-depth analysis of the circulation of objects. Some distribution patterns are determined by scholars' choices as to what criteria they use in defining artifactual types. An interesting example is the distribution pattern of a polyhedron type of earring (one among others) dating to the later seventh century (Fig. 38.4).[7] Most were of silver and could be made easily. They were mainly deposited in cemeteries in the Rhineland but occasionally also further west. One wonders what the western extension of the distribution pattern into the Netherlands and Belgium means. Did the women in whose graves the earrings were found originate in the Rhine Valley and migrate in fulfillment of marriage negotiations? Did the earrings travel to the West as commodities through trade, or did they arrive in the West as gifts in women's marriage networks? It is probable that all of these explanations are valid and that maybe more than one explanation may clarify the biography of an individual object. Discrete sets of earrings could have had unique and complicated biographies and changed from commodity to gifts and then back to commodities again (Kopytoff 1988).

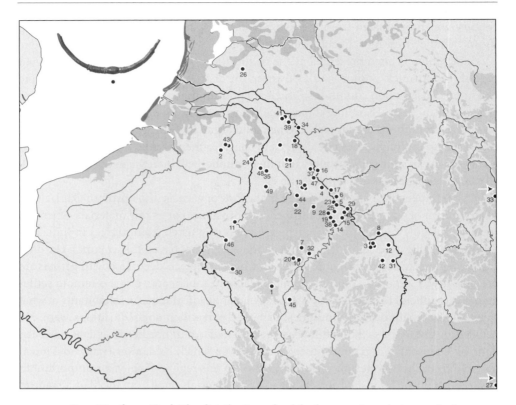

FIGURE 38.4. Northern Gaul. The distribution of polyhedron earrings dating to the later seventh century.

Another interesting problem is posed by the distribution pattern of a specific type of small ceramic bowl with a ribbed wall and foot in the seventh century. These vessels are found in the region of the middle Meuse Valley and the Moselle Valley, but not in the Rhine Valley (Fig. 38.5) (Theuws and van Haperen 2012). They are related to a similar type of beaker in northern France. However, archaeologists have traditionally understood pottery production in the Merovingian period to have been fairly regional. Of course, these beakers might have been produced in a single center and moved over considerable distances. Another possibility is that they were produced in several places, but that either their prototype, or the craftsmen-women who made them, traveled. Other types of objects that are almost identical, such as the silver inlaid iron belt fittings of the so-called Bülach type named after a cemetery in Switzerland (Werner 1953), are found all over northern Gaul and the regions to the east of it. It is difficult to believe that they were all made in one place. The alternative is that they were made in many places following a template that circulated. However, no single specimen is identical to another. Although a transfer of technical knowledge and information regarding how belt fittings should look must have circulated in Gaul early on, there was nonetheless an interplay of "norms" and "variability" that has hitherto been analyzed insufficiently. In fact, we are not well informed about the nature of nonagrarian production, its sociopolitical context, and the

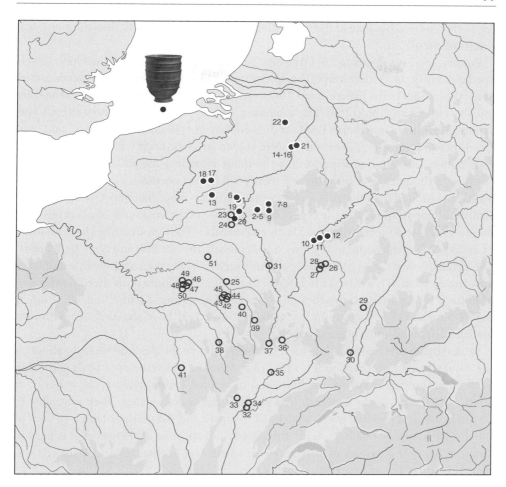

FIGURE 38.5. Northern Gaul. The distribution of ceramic beakers with ribbed walls and related beakers.

agents involved. These few examples show that there must have been complicated exchange systems in which objects, and knowledge of how to produce them, circulated. The same is true of beads that might have been important in cementing intergenerational (grandmother–mother–daughter) and lateral (sister–sister, friends) relations among women. Some easy-to-produce types are found all over northwestern Europe. The wide distribution of identical beads suggests that they were elements in the production of "encoded" material culture that enabled the communication and transmission of shared cultural concepts, as they are in recent societies studied by ethnographers.

Next to these fancy objects, the graves in cemeteries in northern Gaul contain enormous quantities of simple iron objects like knives, shears, pins, and keys, in addition to seaxes, lance heads, shield bosses and grips, axes, and arrows. In the seventh century, the majority of belt fittings were made of iron. Not only was the demand for iron large (see Peytremann for iron production in Chapter 31, this volume), but this demand was regularly renewed because of the deposition of objects in graves and thus their physical exit from circulation.[8]

Pottery, too, was deposited in large quantities: pottery production must have developed quickly in the sixth century. The production of wheel-thrown pottery never ceased in northern Gaul in the fifth century. The potters in the Argonne who started in the early fourth century still produced fine tableware in the early sixth century, which was exported all over northern Gaul and even beyond (Bakker, Dijkman, and van Ossel 1996). Thereafter, the products were copied in workshops with smaller regional distribution. The same observation may be made regarding the potters of Mayen near Koblenz, although the distribution of their products in northern Gaul seems to have been more limited than that of Argonne ware (Redknap 1999; Glauben, Grünewald, and Grunwald 2009). In view of the types of sites at which they are found, the continuity of these centers for potters testifies to a lasting demand for their products by all social strata of society. When the population grew considerably in the late fifth and early sixth centuries, production in the Argonne stopped. Although this may seem strange in a context of growing demand, it is a mistake to interpret a change from more centralized production of pottery to regionalized production as a sign of economic decline. Indeed, it might have been the other way around: regionalization could have signaled adaptation to increased demand and a bigger market.

In surveying this material, it is hard to underestimate the demand brought about by the rural population. Distribution maps of cemeterial and settlement finds show that local communities, even the smallest ones in remote places, had access one way or another to the networks in which this material culture circulated. They were able to obtain exotic and regional goods to deposit in graves and use on their tables. In view of the infrastructure of northern Gaul, this should not surprise us. However, it is hard to continue to see this density of distribution as an element of elite demand. Rather, it was demand created in large part by a growing rural population.

We now have to deal with the question posed above: how did the rural population of northern Gaul obtain these objects? One could instead, in line with current thinking, ask to what extent elites controlled the production and distribution of the goods circulating in rural communities. Although the absence of evidence need not be decisive, it is difficult to find the archaeological correlates of the elites who are supposed to have brought about or controlled the massive circulation of goods.

ELITE DEMAND AND CONTROL OF PRODUCTION AND CIRCULATION OF GOODS IN NORTHERN GAUL?

The majority of written sources from the Merovingian period deal with southern and central Gaul (Wood, 1994). Northern Gaul remains relatively invisible for a long time.

Our major informant for the sixth century, Gregory of Tours, mentions places in northern Gaul only sporadically in conjunction with his mention of "royal" towns (Wood 1994; Heinzelmann 1994; Gauthier and Galinié 1997). In the seventh century, historical sources shed some light on developments in the north when new elite groups struggled for power in Austrasia (Ewig 1980, pp. 18–29; Werner 1980, 1982; Wood 1994, p. 140; Fouracre 2005). There is no telling how old their power bases were, but they might have been fairly recent.

The name Austrasia developed only in the late sixth century and was used to designate the northeastern Merovingian kingdom (Ewig 1980, pp. 23–25; Cardot 1987, pp. 53–73, 181–188; Wood 1994, p. 145). This new designation was a sign that the elite of the region had become important in the politics of the kingdom only from that time onward. In the southern zone of northern Gaul where "towns" like Soissons, Reims, and Metz were located, the situation was somewhat different. Even there, however, we do not learn of powerful or large landowning, aristocratic groups with a continuous power base in the sixth century (Bergengruen 1958;[9] Weidemann 1993; LeJan 1995). The presence of "royal" seats need not be an indication of a stable aristocratic stratum in the zone with these towns. Kings were not permanently present, and it is a matter of debate whether more permanent royal services like chanceries and archives existed in those towns (see Rio, chapter 23, this volume). A recent reinterpretation of the origin of the *Epistolae Austrasicae*,[10] points to the presence of archives in Trier, but Trier was not a royal town, and the collected letters may have been dispersed over several religious institutions (Barret and Woudhuysen 2016). However, Trier seems to be an exceptional town in northern Gaul, and there must have been specific reasons why Metz was chosen above Trier. Perhaps, although Trier was a fine place with a noteworthy Roman past, its imperial past may have "prohibited" Frankish kings from choosing it as a residential site. Perhaps it was thought that a king who did so aspired to associated imperial prerogatives, something that had not yet been done. This interpretation suggests that Trier was possibly a no-go town for Frankish kings, and its splendid past contributed to its decline.

A longstanding and controversial debate has divided historians on the nature and even absence or presence of a Merovingian aristocracy in general, and more specifically in northern Gaul (see note 9). Wickham (2005, pp. 168–203) has addressed this debate: he has found it difficult to accept the near invisibility of an aristocracy in northern Gaul in the sixth century as a sign of its absence or relatively unimportant role. He countered with four arguments: (1) political logic: why would a new ruler destroy the contemporary aristocracy? (2) the instance of documentation for an aristocrat with landed property near Reims; (3) ceramic distribution patterns; and (4) a few instances of possible references to Frankish aristocrats and richly furnished graves. The first argument is a very general one and does not preclude the possibility that something of this nature happened. More importantly for our purposes, it starts from the premise that an important aristocracy was already present. Was it? And, if so, what indications do we have for their existence in northern Gaul? The second argument is based on a singular early will of a powerful bishop, Remigius of Reims, in one of the important towns in the southern zone of northern Gaul. His landed property was modest. Is this one example sufficient evidence to support an image of a landowning aristocracy that controlled the country-side in northern Gaul? Regarding the third argument, the relationship between central-ized pottery production and large-scale elite-controlled distribution networks rests on assumptions about the continuity of landowning elites that had maintained a taste for high-end goods. It is part of a set of larger and unfounded presuppositions that such production could not take place without elite control and/or elite demand (Wickham 2005, p. 797).[11] If this situation was the case, why did the production of Argonne ceramics stop when aristocratic power is thought to have become stronger?

If we turn in more detail to the fourth argument, Wickham refers both to richly fur-nished graves (see, however, below), and he mentions a few instances of Frankish aristo-crats like Guntram Boso named by Gregory of Tours. However, important men like Boso cannot easily be pinpointed to a specific region, nor do we know their regions of origin or the location of their power bases. Although we know that Guntram Boso was active in northern Gaul as well as Tours, and Gregory of Tours also mentions Boso's treasure (*Histories* X:11), we do not know where it was located and whether it was there all the time. In the end we have to conclude that there is, as there was before, little evi-dence in either written or archaeological sources for the presence of an omnipresent landowning aristocracy in northern Gaul in the sixth century.[12] Aristocratic control might have been somewhat stronger in the southernmost part of northern Gaul around towns like Paris, Soissons, Reims, and Trier. However, in the rest of northern Gaul, this control seems to have been largely absent. The decline of Cologne as a royal center and the rise of Reims and Metz suggest that the north was not as important as once thought in the power politics of the sixth-century Merovingian kingdom (Ewig 1980, p. 23).

Of course, there were bishops in northern Gaul, some of whom were recruited from local important families. Others, like Amandus, originated from Aquitaine, and thus from outside the region (Wood 1994, p. 78). Like important laymen, many bishops owed their position to the king (Wood 1994, pp. 71–87; see Halfond, Chapter 13, this volume). Bishops' seats were relatively few and far between in a large part of northern Gaul except in the transitional southern zone (Fig. 38.1). Their control of the world outside of urban settlements might have been relatively limited and quite different from the power base of bishops and their often small dioceses in southern and central Gaul typified by Bertramn of Le Mans (Weidemann 1986; Wood 1994, pp. 207–210), who has dominated our understanding of episcopal power in the sixth century.

We learn of important families in the Seine Valley and the north of Gaul in the sev-enth century (Bergengruen 1958; Le Jan 1995; Werner 1980, 1982). The Pippinids took several generations to create an uncontested power base, which was firmly secured only in the first half of the eighth century. In view of their originally limited power base, which centered on the middle Meuse Valley (Werner 1980, 1982; Dierkens 1985), it is surprising that they surfaced ultimately as the most powerful aristocratic group. They also relied on the power base and landed property of great women from other aristocratic groups like the family of Plectrude, Pippin II's first wife (Werner 1982; Wood 2004). Control of the rural population through development of more coherently organized properties seems to have occurred only in the later Merovingian and early Carolingian period (650 and 800, respectively). Landed estates, such as that of Adalgisl Grimo, a deacon of the church of Verdun, whose testament of 634 gives us the oldest glimpse of such a complex in the north of Gaul, appear to have been loosely organized (Levison 1948 [1932]; Werner 1980, pp. 31–59, with map on p. 34).

In the end, there is no denying the lack of significant textual evidence supporting the idea that a powerful landowning elite was present in northern Gaul in the early Merovingian period and that it closely controlled the majority of the rural population. This deficit precludes a model in which we can assume that the elite generally controlled both production and distribution (see Tys, Chapter 34, this volume). Nor was the Merovingian elite in northern Gaul so expansive that their demand quantitatively out-weighed that of the rural population. Thus, can we accept the premise that the aristoc-racy controlled to a significant degree the large-scale production of pottery, iron objects, glass vessels, and so on, and their distribution in even the smallest of settlements? Since the absence of textual evidence may not be decisive, given its limitations for this time period, we should turn to the archaeological correlates for the elite, including the oft-invoked subject of richly furnished graves.

One of the great enigmas of Merovingian archaeology in northern Gaul is the almost complete absence of elite residential sites in the archaeological record (Loveluck 2013, pp. 105–113). In those regions in which abundant settlement research has been carried out, all of the evidence relates to rural sites such as those in the Île-de-France (Peytremann 2003; Theuws 2008a). There are no Merovingian *villas* in the countryside as was the case in the Roman period. Is it possible that there was an elite stratum that did not show off with splendid residential sites? It is hard to believe. Did they all live among the Roman ruins in ancient towns or on hilltop settlements like Namur (see Bourgeois, Chapter 28, this volume)? Archaeology has yet to prove that this was the case. Moreover, although we know of the relationship between kings and towns, evidence that aristo-crats owned plots of land in towns is scarce (Bergengruen 1958, p. 65). Adalgisl Grimo had a house in Trier, but, in contrast to much of the other property he owned, it was not inherited. The archaeology of the living conditions in ancient Roman towns in the sixth and seventh centuries relates mainly to cult sites and cemeteries, not to residential quar-ters (Ristow 2007; Brulet 2015). Nor have we found remains of royal palaces.

What about the "rich" graves found in some of the cemeteries? First of all, there are just a modest number of these. This fact has not been accounted for sufficiently, although one could say that this modest number changes with each new discovery. This need not mean that new discoveries will prove that there were aristocracies because as these graves more common or less special, they also become less aristocratic. Burials at sites like Arlon in southern Belgium and Morken in the German Rhineland have long been used to support the idea of the presence of a Merovingian aristocracy (*Adel*) in northern Gaul (Böhner 1958; Roosens and Alenus-Lecerf 1963; Schlesinger and Werner 1973; Böhme 1993; Verslype 2010). Without question, these were above-average furnished graves and privileged graves. However, the traditional interpretation of these burials as the graves of aristocrats simply because they were well furnished with grave-goods has to be nuanced to a greater degree. There are multiple reasons why well-furnished graves were created (Theuws and Alkemade 1999; Theuws 2009, 2013). The argument that wealth in a grave reflected the wealth of the person buried, or that of his or her family, is too simple.

It has also been suggested that elite families separated themselves from the rest of the population by choosing exclusive burial grounds such as cult sites or separate burial grounds next to large cemeteries where the rest of the population was buried (Böhme 1993). However, the examples presented in such cases are a mixture of various types of burials with different histories and thus there are distinct reasons for their creation. The sixth-century group of well-furnished burials in places of worship like Saint-Denis, Cologne, and Maastricht consists almost entirely of women and children, a fact that was not considered by Horst-Wolfgang Böhme. This gender distinction is important to understand since it affected the meaning of these burials and their raison d'être. Such sites were first and foremost a means of creating relationships between families and the supernatural, rituals in which women, in view of their dominant presence in the graves, obviously played an important role.[13] Of course, some of these graves belonged to important high-ranking families, like those buried in Saint-Denis and Cologne. Yet, many other graves in places of worship may have belonged to families with only a local power base, such as the well-furnished graves found in Maastricht, Arlon, and Morken. Other well-furnished burials in ordinary cemeteries were often singular phenomena. In some cases, they were the founders' graves of the burial ground, and the wealth invested in their interments might have represented the effort of a larger constituency than that of a single leading family. Moreover, the interpretation of such graves as representing singular aristocratic persons is informed by modern conceptions of the relationship between power and wealth, and of individuality, which might not apply in the burial rites of northern Gaul in the Merovingian period (Theuws 2013).

In many cases, there is no continuous line of well-furnished burials through time that might be understood as an indication of the presence of a powerful family capable of an intergenerational transfer of power and wealth.[14] In exceptional cases where there are well-furnished burials in subsequent chronological periods, as in the sixth- to seventh-century cemetery of Krefeld-Gellep in the German Rhineland, there is no proof of a direct connection like a familial relationship between the man in the early well-furnished but rather inconspicuous grave in 1782, and the large chamber graves that were constructed in subsequent generations (Böhme 1993, pp. 424–426). Another example of a chronological series of graves starting in the late sixth century that is supposed to illustrate several generations of aristocrats are the chamber graves of the very small cemetery at Soest (Westphalia, Germany) (Peters 2011). There is a remarkable gender differential in this cemetery too: eight of ten chamber graves were those of women, a situation not unlike the places of worship mentioned earlier. The cemetery is exceptional in yet another respect: no fewer than thirteen horse burials were in the same area as the chamber graves of the women. Some of the horse graves were clearly related to the women's graves. Was this the burial ground of an aristocratic community with absentee men?[15] Or should we look differently on such a cemetery and consider it a kind of cultic burial place in which various local families buried a female member and horses in order to define their family's position in relation to one another and the supernatural? From this perspective, the burials found in Saint-Denis and Soest may not be so different. The grave-goods at both sites may not necessarily have been a representation of the status of the deceased as a single historical person (Kars 2012; Theuws 2013). Separation from other graves may have been desirable for other reasons.

The conceptual framework for interpreting rich graves has, up until now, been highly circumscribed and has ignored the fact that we are dealing with rites of passage in which the buried person was not necessarily a mirror image of the living person but a person with new, possibly ancestral, capacities.[16] The idea that the dead person represents a single historical person is vested in modern conceptions of personhood and individuality, if not our individualism (Fowler 2004; Theuws 2013). Early medieval conceptions of personhood might have been different (Bazelmans 1999). Lavish burials might have represented the totality of a society, group, or community; they may have been newly created ancestors who could protect (men with weapons in the grave) or guarantee fertility and continuity (women with lavish grave-goods).[17] Moreover, the interpretive framework has been haunted by modern conceptions of power and social status provided by texts. It is important to recall that the total set of well-furnished and privileged graves in northern Gaul is highly diversified and that the raison d'être of individual graves probably differed greatly. They cannot be considered en masse to support the idea of an omnipresent aristocracy separating itself from the rest of the population. Moreover, if one considers well-furnished graves as an indication of the presence of elite groups with a more than local/regional power base, an additional problem is created. Namely, if one maps well-furnished burials per generation or half century, one can easily see that few were contemporary. Significantly, the distribution of those groups was not very dense, although new discoveries might change this pattern. However, today, well-furnished graves are usually overidentified with aristocratic or elite status. The more well-furnished graves that come to light as new finds, the more we will understand that such graves were more common than we envisaged thirty years ago. Instead of seeing important aristocrats and royal dignitaries everywhere, we must take into consideration the internal diversity of local communities.

A final element we should consider in this context is the nature of the church's control of the rural population. Bishops could have controlled a part of the rural population, but as stated before, in northern Gaul their landed property does not seem to be as extensive as that of a bishop like Bertramn of Le Mans. Monastic control of rural communities cannot have been strong in northern Gaul in Merovingian times for the simple reason that there were hardly any monasteries in that region in the sixth century. In a number of towns, early clerical communities were associated with extramural *martyria* (shrines for martyrs).[18] Many rural monasteries were created from the mid-seventh century (see Diem, Chapter 15, this volume). They were concentrated in three regions: the Seine Valley, the Hainaut, and the Jura (Fig. 38.6). Outside these regions, there was not a dense distribution of monasteries, and they certainly did not have the vast landed property complexes of their Carolingian counterparts.[19] The landed property of Saint-Servatius,

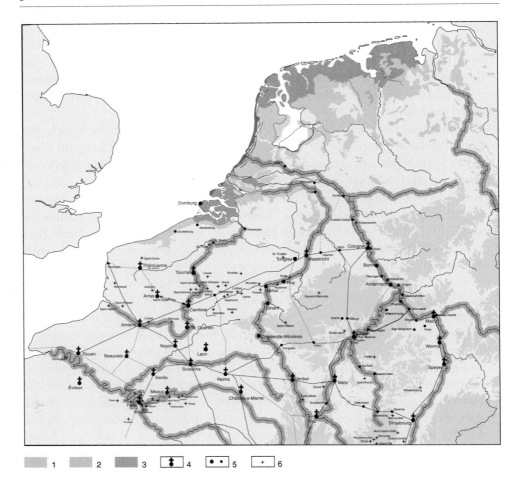

FIGURE 38.6. Northern Gaul. The distribution of Merovingian monasteries. Note the concentrations in the Seine/Marne Valley, the Jura, and Hainaut (provisional map).

in Maastricht, for instance, was relatively small (Hackeng 2006). Monastic control of the rural population in northern Gaul in Merovingian times must have been limited.

In concluding this section, I would like to suggest the following hypothesis: elite and ecclesiastical control of the rural population was relatively weak in northern Gaul in the sixth century and a large part of the seventh. Large complexes of landed property developed gradually in the seventh century, but their organization did not yet exercise the degree of control established by later Carolingian estates. An important feature of this hypothesis is that elite and ecclesiastical/monastic extraction of a surplus from the rural population was limited, too. When we add to this the fact that the Roman tax system probably ceased functioning in the north already in the fifth century (Wickham 2005, pp. 102–115), we can see that the skimming of the resources of the rural population in northern Gaul was limited. In other words, rural families might have been able to satisfy their ritual demands because there were not yet large funds of rent to be paid to the king, an aristocracy, or the church.

An Earlier Critique of the Top-Down Elite Economic Model

Christopher Loveluck and Dries Tys (2006) have critiqued the model of an elite-controlled early medieval economy. On the basis of the material culture recovered from settlement sites from the Merovingian and Carolingian periods, they have shown how rural communities in the coastal areas of the southern North Sea were embedded in international maritime exchange networks. The coastal areas, often considered as marginal, were, in their view, not that marginal, and they have hypothesized that the dwellers in those settlements obtained foreign goods independent of aristocrats, and thus showed a form of economic independence (see Tys, Chapter 34, this volume).[20] To indicate the international character of the find complexes on coastal settlement sites, they have coined the term "maritime material culture profile." However, whereas Loveluck and Tys have concluded that this level of exchange was a typical phenomenon for coastal communities, they have suggested that inland rural societies were much more exposed to aristocratic control than those on the coast. Thus, what might be called an "inland material culture profile," was likely less international and relatively poor in comparison to coastal communities.

Yet, like written sources, archaeological sources have their problems. The comparison between coastal and inland communities that Loveluck and Tys have made is between settlements in regions dominated by Holocene deposits (peat, clay) with settlement sites in regions with Pleistocene deposits (sand, among others things). Conservation conditions are quite different in both landscapes on the continent. Settlements in sandy regions in which the top layers of archaeological features contain most archaeological material have often been destroyed by agricultural activities in more recent times. Hence, settlements are relatively poor in find material, in terms of both metal finds and pottery. This situation at such inland settlement sites contrasts with nearby cemeteries, which often produce a lot of exquisite, nonlocal objects. Thus, if one makes a comparison between coastal and inland regions on the basis of cemetery finds, a completely different picture emerges: the coastal areas are very poor in grave-goods compared to the inland communities. Cemetery evidence thus shows that inland communities were not composed of relatively poor people with no access to foreign goods. The contrast Loveluck and Tys sketch on the basis of settlement evidence between "free" coastal communities with access to foreign goods independent of aristocratic control, and poorer inland communities depending on aristocracies, cannot be upheld.

A Hypothesis and its Implications

On the basis of what has been presented above, one may hypothesize that the absence of elite control of the economy is not likely to have been a characteristic specific to "free" coastal communities but was applicable more generally to communities in northern Gaul in the Merovingian period. Although elite control may have developed to some extent in the course of the seventh century, it is not likely that the rural population depended on the elite for the procurement of the goods they needed, not even of products that came from a distance. The sheer numbers of goods deposited in graves by the rural population indicates that they were able to obtain these items. This access must have been possible because of the presence of a relatively open exchange system that functioned on the basis of a well-developed communication infrastructure along rivers and ancient Roman roads.

The demand by the "mass" of the rural population was the first trigger for economic development in northwestern Europe. Indeed, it was not just ordinary demand based on the individual fulfillment of infinite needs in conditions of scarcity, but demand brought about by changing ritual repertoires with life-cycle rituals salient among them. Of these rituals, the conspicuous burial rite is most visible in archaeological terms. Defining gender positions was one of the central issues in the emerging burial rite, which suggests that this rite was intimately related to other life-cycle rites of women and men (on children, see Perez, Chapter 9, this volume). In the late fifth and sixth centuries, burial rites in which the deposition of clothing accessories, weapons, and vessels were prioritized became quite widespread in a relatively short period of time. Because of the deposition of these goods in burials, they did not continue to circulate and the demand for new products was renewed constantly. This pressure, in combination with a growing population, triggered increasing demand for raw materials to make such products, including iron, clay, wood, glass, and so on. This demand was satisfied by both local extraction and production, as well as by imports like garnets, raw glass, and cowry shells from, in some cases, areas well beyond the eastern Mediterranean.

This model of a bottom-up developing economy contrasts with the model suggesting that elite demand formed the most important incentive for economic development in post-Roman times. This idea actually follows from conceptions of a peasant economy or a peasant mode of production, in contrast to a feudal mode of production. The peasant mode of production model suggests that economic growth is not likely to occur in this mode because peasants are not supposed to increase production beyond their own needs or a certain level of production that is at the equilibrium between work and well-being (Wolf 1966; Devroey 2003). When there are no incentives from landlords who extract rents or a market system, production will not increase. This is a situation described by the concept of marginal utility defined by Chayanov (Devroey 2003, p. 150). In contrast, the extraction of rents in a feudal mode of production triggers an increase in production and thus economic growth.

There is a fundamental flaw in this thinking, which becomes clear when we look in greater detail at peasant household economics as explained by Eric Wolf (1966). A peasant household produces first its own caloric needs, then the caloric needs of the livestock, and finally a "replacement fund" that provides for nonagricultural activities, such as repairing the house and replacing a plow. On top of this production, peasants produce to meet social and religious obligations; they produce a "ceremonial fund," a concept that goes back to the early twentieth-century economist Thorstein Veblen (Wolf 1966, 7–9). Any peasant society produces in principle its necessary caloric needs, its "replacement fund," and its "ceremonial fund." In addition, peasants can produce "funds of rent" and a "surplus" to be sold. Eric Wolf defines peasants as rural cultivators who are encapsulated in the power of a dominant group of rulers (1966, pp. 3–4). When rural cultivators are not encapsulated in such power networks, as may have been the case with the majority of the Merovingian rural population in northern Gaul, it is better not to qualify them as peasants but simply as rural dwellers or rural cultivators. I prefer rural dwellers because they may have fulfilled a broader range of activities or separate "jobs" as farmers, craftsmen, and traders. To understand rural society in northern Gaul in post-Roman times, one must comprehend the nature of the "ceremonial fund." It is this "ceremonial fund" that increased considerably in the fifth and sixth centuries due to new ritual repertoires, which were probably related to life-cycle rituals. The rural dwellers' economy could thus grow considerably, independent of lords and markets. From our modern perspective, it might even take "irrational forms" such as burying riches in graves that normally would have to circulate in the constant renewal of relations (Platenkamp 2016). Growth caused by an increase in expenditure of the "ceremonial fund" means that the economy and rituals were closely related and that the value system was increasingly geared to the needs of those rituals. We might designate such an economy a "ritual economy" (McAnany and Wells 2008; Hodges 2012). As suggested, the rituals concerned would have mainly been life-cycle rituals. It is a matter of debate and future research by whom these life-cycle rituals were developed, how these were shared over large areas, and how a complex of encoded material culture became an important element in these rituals. An important development is the church's gradual control of those life-cycle rituals (Paxton 1990; Treffort 1996; Effros 2002), which led to a diversion of the invested "ceremonial fund" from the local community to the church. This diversion might not have at first had a coercive character but instead resulted from a changing ideology. The rural dwellers who became peasants might thus have "suffered" a double loss in the course of time: first, a transfer of part of the "ceremonial fund" to churches and clerics, and then, above that, the exaction of rents by both the church and the aristocracy. The close connection between rituals, values, and religion characterized the economy of early medieval northwestern Europe (Theuws 2004; Carver 2015; Theuws in press).

The next question to be asked is how the rural dwellers obtained the necessary goods. The above hypothesis suggests that the development of exchange in these goods, including trade, developed from the bottom up. A complicated exchange system with all kinds of actors, ranging from local, petty commodity producers to international traders from the eastern Mediterranean, developed in a way that might have been to a large extent outside elite control. However, in the Merovingian period, the elite may have started to extract a surplus from the streams of goods that developed in places like Fos and Marseille and much later in places like Quentovic and Dorestad.[21] Neither state nor royal control was necessary to create a complicated exchange system. The mass of objects found in cemeteries of even remote small communities argues against the idea of elite control of production and distribution. It seems unlikely that the elite could have controlled this steady stream of objects to any significant degree (see Tys, Chapter 34, this volume). Moreover, elite control of the rural population might not have been as strong in the north, as suggested by written sources that describe southern Gaul. Neither ecclesiastical nor monastic control of the rural population could have been strong because there were simply too few of these institutions.

This hypothesis of the nature of post-Roman economic development of northwestern Europe pushes us to reconsider economic models and the nature of exchange. It implies that rural communities had access to exchange networks that connected various parts of Europe and the Near East. The international component of exchange is as important as local and regional exchange, even if the volume of goods moving in regional exchange was larger than in local. Because demand was triggered by ritual needs, the population of northern Gaul may have perceived the exchange of foreign products to be as important as regional ones (McCormick 2001; Wickham 2005, p. 819). Objects that traveled great distances might have occupied a special place in the value system (Helms 1988). I suggested before that the early medieval economy, at least in northern Gaul, was dominated by an eclectic exchange system (Theuws 2012).[22] That is, the exchange system was not dominated by a particular type of exchange such as a market exchange, commodity exchange, or gift exchange. Rather, it was formed from a series of articulating forms of exchanges (Theuws 2012; see also Drauschke 2011). Moreover, in an eclectic economy, specific types of exchanges were not confined to specific agents. Almost all agents, from rural dwellers to kings, were involved in a variety of types of exchanges. Moreover, specific agents might not yet have had specific exclusive roles. Riverine dwellers might have acted at times as petty commodity producers selling some of their normal produce to those who passed by. Farmers might have acted as long-distance traders, or they could become warriors and travel large distances. Traders might turn into craftsmen, and so on. Moving forward, what we must study is to what extent commodity exchange existed, how commodities could become gifts (for instance, in women's networks, like the earrings described earlier), how they could become grave-goods (Kars 2013), and how the objects changed character in this process (Kopytoff 1988; Bloch and Parry 1989; Bazelmans 1999). What was the nature of mass-produced objects leaving workshops? Were they commodities? We also need to know how the exchange in raw materials took place, what their origins were, how production was technically organized, where it occurred, and how it was socially and cosmologically embedded. However, we also need to understand how the "normative solidarity" (Mann 1986, p. 45) that this system created also contributed to both a relatively coherent burial rite and an associated coherent encoded material culture in a large area such as northern Gaul and adjacent regions. At the same time, we need to assess why it could vary so much at the local level: what is the role of the agency of persons and local groups in relation to the structures of the various rituals, and was this agency the cause of so much variability? Finally, we also need in-depth research into the nature of rural communities. What was their size, how mobile were its members, and what opportunities were offered to rural dwellers in the absence of a dominant elite? What were the consequences for local social differentiation? How strong was local competition among rural dwellers in often very small communities, and was this competition reflected in the burial ritual? Does the evidence of cemeteries provide insight into this social differentiation, or do the rites, which might have addressed issues other than social organization and competition for power (*pace* Halsall 2010), mask the social structure of local communities? Much interesting research remains to be done.

FINAL REFLECTIONS ON NORTHERN GAUL

In his *Sources of Social Power*, Michael Mann (1986, pp. 15–16) coined the concept of interstitial emergence to refer to the emergence of social structures between the "pores" of the existing society. I would like to use this term in a very wide sense to indicate what happened in northern Gaul, where developments took place between the "pores" of Merovingian society at large dominated by power structures centered on the king. Models that depart from this power structure share what Mann has described as having a unitary view of society. It is time to abandon such models because the written sources dealing with society are produced by those in positions of power. Their texts are thus unlikely to reveal "interstitial emergence." We have to accept the existence of a variety of important social developments that are not documented in the written sources. Wickham (2005, p. 803) is correct in noting that northern Gaul reveals some surprising features such as the fact that its trade was second only to the intensity of exchange in the Nile Valley. Where our outlooks differ is in the nature and origins of the wealth in northern Gaul.

As I argued earlier in this chapter, it is not elite demand but the demand of the rural population that drove the economy. Rather than a top-down structured economy, the economy of northern Gaul in the Merovingian period was bottom-up. Characterized by a relatively open eclectic exchange system, it was supported by a good, functioning infrastructure and not a controlled exchange system based solely on gift exchange. The exchange system was bottom-up, created along arteries like the Rhine River that functioned long before the eighth century rather than becoming important only from that age onward (McCormick 2001). This type of economy is what makes northern Gaul special in the history of economic development in Europe. By contrast, Wickham's, Devroey's, and other scholars' models seems to have been valid for the second half of the eighth and ninth centuries. By that time, the aristocracy knew how to exploit the riches of the region: skimming off the wealth of the countryside by reorganizing landed property in bipartite estates and exacting rents; profiting from the wealth of trade by exacting tolls at places like emporia that had grown outside their control; and controlling coin production. In the long run, the economy of northern Gaul/Austrasia developed from an inclusive to an extractive economy (Acemoglu and Robinson 2013), creating immense differences in income made visible in both palaces and abbey churches. Like many other extractive economies, the Carolingian one failed too.

NOTES

1. Most of the ideas in this chapter were presented at a conference in Copenhagen in 2010. My paper has not yet been published, but Richard Hodges (2012) already discussed some of the ideas contained therein in his new edition of *Dark Age Economics* on the basis of the manuscript. Since then, I have presented the ideas in classes and conferences in Newcastle and Vienna (2014), and in my inaugural lecture at Leiden University (2014). The debates that followed these presentations have sharpened my views on this topic. The very fruitful debates on this subject in the Research Master Classes at Leiden University were/are a constant source of inspiration. The ideas presented led to an ERC Advanced Grant to carry out research on this topic. The project is titled 'Rural Riches'. https://www.merovingianarchaeology.org/blog/.

2. The sick Einhard intended to continue his voyage from Valenciennes to Gent by boat over the Scheldt River (Dutton 1998, pp. 149–151).

3. The winding La Vesle does not seem to have been a navigable river.

4. This is not to say that river transport had no share in the movement of goods in Roman times. Land routes, however, played a more dominant role.

5. In a planned project on the "Post-Roman Economic Development of Northwestern Europe," this will be one of the first research goals: to make an educated estimate of the size off the population over time.

6. Several types of objects were inventoried in the context of a research master class at Leiden University (Byzantine coins, amethyst beads, objects with garnets, and specific types of beads) by Mette Langbroek, Femke Lippok, Gwendolyn de Groote, Bas van de Weerd, and Dita Ausina. The research area was the Benelux, Nordrhein Westfalen, and the northern part of Rheinland Pfalz.

7. They are called "*Drahtohrringen mit aufgeschobenen Polyeder*" (see Theuws & van Haperen 2012, p. 75).

8. Objects might have remained in circulation in a mental sense; others were recovered from graves, but it is unlikely that they were reused in a practical sense due to corrosion (van Haperen 2017).

9. Alexander Bergengruen's work has received substantial criticism from both historians and archaeologists. Critique by historians addresses not only his central thesis that there was hardly an original, large Frankish landowning aristocracy in northern Gaul in the sixth century, but also questions the limited geographical scope of the sources and their editions in northern Gaul for his argument (Irsigler 1969, pp. 67–68). Walter Schlesinger and Joachim Werner (1973) used rich graves to counteract Bergengruen's thesis, which might not have been justified. Other historians like Franz Irsigler (1969) pointed to Gregory of Tours's terminology for leading persons to prove the existence of an ancient Frankish aristocracy by birth. Irsigler's book is full of presuppositions and is unconvincing. His interpretation of words and terms in Gregory of Tours's work seems to have been made with the preconceived conviction that there was an aristocracy by birth with bases of power independent of the king, whereas the majority of the elite in Gregory's work seems to have been related to the king. However, whereas Bergengruen dealt mainly with northern Gaul, others used material from southern regions and later periods in an encompassing model of the Frankish world that included northern Gaul. In this sense, perhaps Bergengruen, despite

the shortcomings of his work, was not that far wrong as far as northern Gaul was concerned. One of his central questions is still very up to date: considering the large number of newly created cemeteries, what was the role of a Frankish elite in the recolonization of northern Gaul in the late fifth and sixth centuries? We have no good answer (see also Goetz 1999, pp. 226–228). It might be negative: archaeologists can point to relatively few rich graves, and in most cemeteries there is nothing that might be considered "aristocratic" (*Adel* or even *Geburtsadel*, in German).

10. The *Epistolae Austrasicae* (a modern name) is a collection of letters, forty-eight in total, that mostly date to the sixth century (see Gillett, Chapter 25, this volume). It is a matter of debate when this collection was created. Some argue for a late sixth-century date, whereas Barret and Woudhuysen recently opted for an early ninth-century date (Barret & Woudhuysen 2016).

11. In the discussion on changes in pottery production, Wickham ignores the fact that most pottery produced in Mayen and the Argonne, and later fine tablewares, have been found in rural sites and cemeteries (2005, p. 797). Moreover, the poorly understood production of wheel-thrown cooking pots (*Wölbwandtöpfe*) must have been on a scale many times larger than that of fine tablewares. In Merovingian settlements, the number of cooking pot shards usually outweighs that of fine wares (sometimes by as much as 90 percent versus 10 percent). These pots were not produced on a mass scale to satisfy sophisticated tastes.

12. Wickham (2005, pp. 185–186) has nuanced his position to some extent by suggesting that seventh-century aristocrats did not control all regions and that there might have been microregions with "relatively independent peasantries."

13. Similar developments may be seen in England (Hamerow 2016). I thank Helena Hamerow for sending me what was at the time her unpublished manuscript.

14. This, as well as the gender bias, is often explained as a result of women staying at home. They died at the site of their residence whereas men were on the move to do their military residence whereas men were on the move to do their military service and political business and died elsewhere. However, in many cases, there is not a continuous line of well-furnished women's graves after the first generation of founders' graves and research on "elite" burials up till now has concentrated on men. A thorough analysis of women's graves in northern Gaul is overdue.

15. Peters (2011) avoids the term *aristocratic* and speaks of "elites." There is no doubt, however, that he means the highest ranking elites of the realm.

16. Halsall refutes this interpretation of ancestral capacities because it does not figure in the texts (Halsall 2010, pp. 245–246). It is worth asking whether this is a valid argument.

17. Guy Halsall observes that most lavish burials of women in the Metz region were those in the age category of twenty to forty (Halsall 1995b).

18. See the various contributions in the volumes of the series *Topographie chrétienne des cités de la Gaule des origines au milieu du VIIIe siècle.*

19. It is estimated that over the course of time, ecclesiastical institutions collected almost 40 percent of the cultural land in Gaul (Wood 2013).

20. In the words of Wickham, these might have been microregions that had "relatively independent peasantries" (2005, pp. 185–186).

21. It has been suggested that the late Merovingian and Carolingian "emporia" developed without royal control (among others, see McCormick 2007).

22. I borrowed this concept from ethnographic studies of peasants in the Amazon basin (for instance: Nugent 1993; Roopnaraine 2001).

WORKS CITED

Modern Sources

Acemoglu, D., and Robinson, J. A. (2013 [2012]). *Why Nations Fail: The Origins of Power, Prosperity, and Poverty.* London: Profile Books.

Agache, R., and Bréart, B. (1975). *Atlas d'archéologie aérienne de Picardie. La Somme Protohistorique et Romaine. Société des antiquaires de Picardie.* Amiens: Société des Antiquaires de Picardie.

Bakker, L., Dijkman, W., and van Ossel, P. (1996). "Corpus de la céramique sigillée d'Argonne de l'Antiquité Tardive." In *Société Française d'Etude de la Céramique Antique en Gaule, Actes du congrès de Dijon 1996* (pp. 423–426). Marseille: Société francaise d'Étude de la Céramique Antique en Gaule. (http://sfecag.free.fr[consulted February 5, 2016]).

Barret, G., and Woudhuysen, G. (2016). "Assembling the Austrasian Letters at Trier and Lorsch." *Early Medieval Europe* 24: 3–57.

Bazelmans, J. (1999). *By Weapons Made Worthy. Lords Retainers and Their Relationship in Beowulf.* Amsterdam: Amsterdam University Press.

Bergengruen, A. (1958). *Adel und Grundherrschaft im Merowingerreich. Siedlungs- und Standesgeschichtliche Studie zu den Anfängen des fränkischen Adels in Nordfrankreich und Belgien.* Vierteljahrsschrift für Sozial- und Wirtschaftsgeschichte Beihefte 41. Wiesbaden: Steiner Verlag.

Bloch, M., and Parry, J. (1989). "Introduction. Money and the Morality of Exchange." In J. Parry and M. Bloch (eds.), *Money and the Morality of Exchange* (pp. 1–32). Cambridge: Cambridge University Press.

Böhme, H. W. (1993). "Adelsgräber im Frankenreich. Archäologische Zeugnisse zur Herausbildung einer Herrenschicht unter den merowingischen Königen." *Jahrbuch des Römisch-Germanischen Zentralmuseums Mainz* 40: 397–434.

Böhner, K. (1958). "Das Grab eines fränkischen Herrn aus Morken im Rheinland." In W. Krämer (ed.), *Neue Ausgrabungen in Deutschland* (pp. 432–468). Berlin: Mann Verlag.

Boppert, W. (1986). "Die frühchristlichen Grabinschriften aus der Servatiuskirche in Maastricht." In C. G. de Dijn (ed.), *Sint-Servatius, bisschop van Tongeren-Maastricht. Het vroegste Christendom in het Maasland. Handelingen van het colloquium te Alden Biesen Bilzen, Tongeren en Maastricht 1984* (pp. 65–96). Borgloon-Rijkel: Provinciale Diensten voor het Kunstpatrimonium.

Boyer, R., et al. (1987). *Vie et mort à Marseille à la fin de l'Antiquité. Inhumations habillées des Ve et VIe siècles et sarcophage reliquaire trouveés à l'abbaye de Saint Victor.* Marseille: Atelier du Patrimoine.

Brulet, R. (1990). *La Gaule septentrionale au Bas-Empire. Occupation du sol et defense du territoire dans l'arrière-pays du Limes aux IVe et Ve siècles.* Trier: Rheinisches Landesmuseum.

Brulet, R. (2015). "Die Stadt Tournai in der Spätantike." In D. Quast (ed.), *Das Grab des fränkischen Königs Childerich in Tournai und die Anastasis Childerici von Jean-Jacques Chifflet aus dem Jahre 1655* (pp. 77–96). Mainz: Römisch-Germanischen Zentralmuseum.

Calligaro, T., Périn, P., Vallet, F., and Poiroit, J.-P. (2006–2007). "Contribution à l'étude des grenats mérovingiens (Basilique de Saint-Denis et autres collections du Musée d'Archéologie nationale, diverse collections publiques et objets de fouilles récentes)." *Antiquités Nationales* 38: 111–144.

Cardot, F. (1987). *L'espace et le pouvoir. Étude sur l'Austrasie Mérovingienne.* Paris: Sorbonne.

Carver, M. (2015). "Commerce and Cult: Confronted Ideologies in 6th–9th Century Europe." *Medieval Archaeology* 59: 1–23.

Devroey, J.-P. (2003). *Économie rurale et société dans l'Europe franque (VIe–IXe siècles). 1: Fondements matériels, échanges et lien social.* Paris: Éditions Belin.

Devroey, J.-P. (2006). *Puissants et misérables. Système social et monde paysan dans l'Europe des Francs (VIe–IXe siecles).* Brussels: Académie Royale de Belgique.

Die Franken, Wegbereiter Europas. König Chlodwich und seine Erben. (1996). Mainz: Zabern Verlag.

Dierkens, A. (1985). *Abbayes et Chapitres entre Sambre et Meuse (VIIe–XIe siècles). Contribution à l'histoire religieuse des campagnes du Haut Moyen Age.* Beihefte der Francia 14. Sigmaringen: Thorbecke Verlag.

Dierkens, A., and Périn, P. (2000). "Les *sedes regiae* mérovingiennes entre Seine et Rhin." In G. Ripoll and Gurt, J. M. (eds.), *Sedes regiae (ann. 400–800)* (pp. 267–304). Barcelona: Real Academia de Buenas Letras.

Dijkman, W. (1992). "La terre sigillée décorée à la molette à motifes chrétiens dans la stratigraphie maastrichtoise (Pays-Bas) et dans le nord-ouest de l'Europe." *Gallia* 49: 129–172.

Dijkstra, M., and Flamman, J. (2004). *Onderweg naar gisteren. Archeologisch onderzoek naar 2000 jaar wegopbouw langs de noordzijde van het Vrijthof te Maastricht.* Amsterdam: Diachron.

Drauschke, J. (2011). *Zwischen Handel und Geschenk. Studien zur Distribution von Objekten aus dem Orient, aus Byzanz und aus Mitteleuropa im östlichen Merowingerreich.* Rahden: Leidorf Verlag.

Dutton, P. E. (1998). *Charlemagne's Courtier. The Complete Einhard.* Peterborough: Broadview Press.

Duval, N., et al. (eds.). (1991). *Naissance des arts chrétiens. Atlas des monuments paléochretiens de la France.* Paris: Imprimerie Nationale Éditions.

Effros, B. (2002). *Caring for Body and Soul. Burial and the Afterlife in the Merovingian World.* University Park, PA: Penn State University Press.

Effros, B. (2003). *Merovingian Mortuary Archaeology and the Making of the Early Middle Ages.* Berkeley: University of California Press.

Effros, B. (2012). *Uncovering the Germanic Past: Merovingian Archaeology in France, 1830–1914.* Oxford: Oxford University Press.

Ewig, E. (1980). *Frühes Mittelalter.* Rheinische Geschichte in drei Bänden 1. Düsseldorf: Schwann Verlag.

Fouracre, P. (2005). "Francia in the Seventh Century." In P. Fouracre (ed.), *The New Cambridge Medieval History* 1 (pp. 371–396). Cambridge: Cambridge University Press.

Fowler, C. (2004). *The Archaeology of Personhood: An Anthropological Approach.* London: Routledge.

Gauthier, N., and Galinié, H. (eds.) (1997). *Grégoire de Tours et l'espace gaulois. Actes du congrès international Tours, 3–5 novembre 1994.* Tours: Fédération pour l'éditions de la Revue archéologique du Centre.

Glauben, A., Grünewald, M. B., and Grunwald, L. (2009). "Mayen am Übergang von Spätantike zu frühen Mittelalter." In O. Wagener (ed.), *Der umkämpfte Ort-Von der Antike zum Mittelalter* (pp. 135–156). Beihefte zur Medievistik 10. Frankfurt-am-Main: Peter Lang Verlag.

Goetz, H.-W. (1999). *Moderne Medievistik. Stand und Perspektiven der Mittelalterforschung.* Darmstadt: Wissenschaftliche Buchgesellschaft.

Goudswaard, B., Kroes, R. A. C., and van der Beek, H. S. M. (2001). "The Late Roman Bridge at Cuijk." *Berichten van de Rijksdienst voor het Oudheidkundig Bodemonderzoek* 44: 439–460.

Guizard-Duchamp, F. (2003). "Fleuves, forêts et territoire dans les sources narratives des VIe et VIIe siècles." *Revue du Nord* 82: 575–594.

Hackeng, R. A. W. J. (2006). *Het middeleeuwse grondbezit van het Sint-Servaaskapittel te Maastricht in de regio Maas-Rijn.* Maastricht: Regionaal Historisch Centrum Limburg.

Halsall, G. (1995a). *Early Medieval Cemeteries. An Introduction to Burial Archaeology in the Post-Roman West.* Glasgow: Cruithne Press.

Halsall, G. (1995b). *Settlement and Social Organisation: The Merovingian Region of Metz.* Cambridge: Cambridge University Press.

Halsall, G. (2010). *Cemeteries and Society in Merovingian Gaul. Selected Studies in History and Archaeology 1992–2009.* Leiden: Brill.

Hamerow, H. (2016). "Furnished Female Burial in Seventh-Century England. Gender and Sacral Authority in the Conversion Period." *Early Medieval Europe* 24(4): 423–447.

Härke, H. (2014). "Grave Goods in Early Medieval Burials. Messages and Meanings." *Mortality* 19: 41–60.

Heeren, S. (2015). "The Depopulation of the Lower Rhine Region in the 3rd Century. An archaeological perspective." In N. Roymans, T. Derks, and H. Hiddink (eds.), *The Roman Villa of Hoogeloon and the Archaeology of the Periphery* (pp. 271–294). Amsterdam: Amsterdam University Press.

Heinzelmann, M. (1994). *Gregor von Tours (538–594). Zehn Bücher Geschichte. Historiographie und Gesellschaftskonzept im 6. Jahrhundert.* Darmstadt: Wissenschaftliche Buchgesellschaft.

Helms, M. (1988). *Ulysses' Sail. An ethnographic odyssey of power, knowledge and geographical distance.* Princeton, NJ: Princeton University Press.

Hodges, R. (2012). *Dark Age Economics. A New Audit.* London: Bristol Classical Press.

Irsigler, F. (1969). *Untersuchungen zur Geschichte des frühfränkischen Adels.* Bonn: Rörscheid Verlag.

Kars, M. (2012). "(Re)considering the Pre-Burial Life of Grave Goods. Towards a Renewed Debate on Early Medieval Burial Chronology on the Continent." *Medieval and Modern Matters* 3: 107–134.

Kopytoff, I. (1988). "The Cultural Biography of Things. Commoditization as Process." In A. Appadurai (ed.), *The Social Life of Things. Commodities in a Cultural Perspective* (pp. 64–94). Cambridge: Cambridge University Press.

La Picardie, berceau de la France. Clovis et les derniers Romains. 1500ème anniversaire de la Bataille de Soissons 486–1986. (1986). Soissons: Société archéologique de Picardie.

Le Goff, J. (1977). *Pour un autre Moyen Âge. Temps, travail et culture en Occident: 18 essais.* Paris: Gallimard.

Le Jan, R. (1995). *Famille et pouvoir dans le monde franc VIIe–Xe siècle. Essai d'anthropologie sociale.* Paris: Sorbonne.

Legoux, R., Périn, P., and Vallet, F. (2004). *Chronologie normalisée du mobilier funéraire mérovingien entre Manche et Lorraine.* Paris: Association francaise d'Archéologie mérovingienne.

Levison, W. (1948 [1932]). "Das Testament des Diakons Adalgisel-Grimo vom Jahre 634." In *Aus rheinischer und fränkischer Frühzeit. Ausgewählte Aufsätze von Wilhelm Levison* (pp. 118–138). Düsseldorf: Schwann Verlag. (original publication *Trierer Zeitschrift* 7: 69–85).

Loveluck, C. (2013). *Northwest Europe in the Early Middle Ages, c. AD 600–1150. A Comparative Archaeology.* Cambridge: Cambridge University Press.

Loveluck, C., and Tys, D. (2006). "Coastal Societies, Exchange and Identity along the Channel and Southern North Sea Shores of Europe, AD 600–1000." *Journal of Maritime Archaeology* 1: 140–169.

Mann, M. (1986). *The Sources of Social Power. 1: A History of Power from the Beginning to A.D. 1760*. Cambridge: Cambridge University Press.

McAnany, P., and Wells, E. C. (2008). "Towards a Theory of Ritual Economy." In E. C. Wells and P. A. McAnany (eds.), *Dimensions of Ritual Economy* (pp. 1–16). Bingley: JAI Press.

McCormick, M. (2001). *Origins of the European Economy. Communications and Commerce, A.D. 300–900*. Cambridge: Cambridge University Press.

McCormick, M. (2007). "Where Do Trading Sites Come From? Early Medieval Venice and the Northern Emporia." In J. Henning (ed.), *Post-Roman Towns, Trade and Settlement in Europe and Byzantium, I, The Heirs of the Roman West* (pp. 41–68). Berlin: Walter de Gruyter.

Müssemeier, U., Nieveler, E., Plum, R., and Pöppelmann, H. (2003). *Chronologie der merowingerzeitlichen Grabfunde vom linken Niederrhein bis zur nördlichen Eifel*. Materialien zur Bodendenkmalpflege im Rheinland 15. Cologne: Rheinisches Amt für Bodendenkmalpflege.

Nicolai, J. (2014). *The Splendour of Power. Early Medieval Kingship and the Use of Gold and Silver in the Southern North Sea area*. Groningen: Barkhuis Publishing and the University of Groningen Library.

Nieveler, E. (2003). *Die merowingerzeitliche Besiedlung des Erftskreises und des Kreises Euskirchen*. Rheinische Ausgrabungen 48. Mainz: Verlag Phillip von Zabern.

Nieveler, E. (2006). *Geschichtlicher Atlas der Rheinlande. Beiheft IV/10. Merowingerzeitliche Besiedlung. Archäologische Befunde in den nördlichen Rheinlanden*. Bonn: Habelt Verlag.

Nugent, S. (1993). *Amazonian Caboclo Society. An Essay on Invisibility and Peasant Economy*, Providence, RI: Bloomsbury Academic.

Paxton, F. S. (1990) *Christianizing Death. The Creation of a Ritual Process in Early Medieval Europe*. Ithaca, NY: Cornell University Press.

Peters, D. (2011). *Das frühmittelalterliche Gräberfeld von Soest. Studien zur Gesellschaft in Grenzraum und Epochenumbruch*. Münster: Aschendorff.

Peytremann, E. (2003). *Archéologie de l'habitat rural dans le nord de la France du IVe au XIIe siècle*. 2 vols. Saint-Germain-en Laye: Association française d'archéologie mérovingienne.

Platenkamp, J. (2016) "Money Alive and Money Dead." In C. Haselgrove and S. Krmnicek (eds.). *The Archaeology of Money. Proceedings of the Workshop "Archaeology of Money," University of Tübingen, October 2013* (pp. 161–181). Leicester: Leicester Archaeological Monographs.

Plumier, J., and Regnard, M. (eds.). (2005). *Voies d'eau, commerce et artisanat en Gaule mérovingienne*. Namur: Ministère de la Région wallone.

Redknap, M. (1999). "Die römischen und mittelalterlichen Töpfereien in Mayen, Kreis Koblenz." *Berichte zur Archäologie an Mittelrhein und Mosel* 6: 11–401.

Ristow, S. (2007). *Frühes Christentum im Rheinland. Die Zeugnisse der archäologischen und historischen Quellen an Rhein, Maas und Mosel*. Münster: Aschendorf Verlag.

Roopnaraine, T. (2001). "Constrained Trade and Creative Exchange on the Barima River, Guyana." *Journal of the Royal Anthropological Institute* 7: 51–66.

Roosens, H., and Alenus-Lecerf, J. (1963). *Sépultures mérovingiennes au Vieux Cimetière d'Arlon*. Annales de l'Institut archéologique du Luxembourg Arlon 94. Arlon: Institut archéologique du Luxembourg.

Rouche, M. (1985). "Atlas historique." In P. Périn and L.-C. Feffer (eds.), *La Neustrie. Les pays au nord de la Loire de Dagobert à Charles le Chauve VIIe-IXe siècles* (pp. 431–454). Rouen: Musées departementaux de Seine-Maritime.

Schlesinger, W., and Werner, J. (1973). "Über den Adel im Frankenreich." In F. Petri (ed.), *Siedlung, Sprache und Bevölkerungsstruktur im Frankenreich* (pp. 544–550). Darmstadt: Wissenschaftliche Buchgesellschaft.

Siegmund, F. (1998). *Merowingerzeit am Niederrhein. Die frühmittelalterlichen Funde aus dem Regierungsbezirk Düsseldorf und dem Kreis Heinsberg.* Rheinische Ausgrabungen 34. Cologne: Rheinland Verlag.

Steuer, H. (1997). "Handel und Fernbeziehungen. Tausch, Raub und Geschenk." In *Die Alamannen* (pp. 389–402). Stuttgart: Theiss Verlag.

Theuws, F. (2001). "Maastricht as a Centre of Power in the Early Middle Ages." In M. de Jong and F. Theuws with C. van Rhijn (eds.), *Topographies of Power in the Early Middle Ages* (pp. 155–216). Leiden: Brill.

Theuws, F. (2004). "Exchange, Religion, Identity and Central Places in the Early Middle Ages." *Archaeological Dialogues* 10: 121–138, 149–159 (with comments by R. Hodges, 138–144 and J. Moreland, 144–149).

Theuws, F. (2007). "Where Is the Eighth Century in the Towns of the Meuse Valley?" In J. Henning (ed.), *Post-Roman Towns, Trade and Settlement in Europe and Byzantium, I, The Heirs of the Roman West* (pp. 153–164). Berlin: Walter de Gruyter.

Theuws, F. (2008a). "Settlement Research and the Process of Manorialization in Northern Austrasia." In S. Gasparri (ed.), *774 Ipotesi su una transizione. Atti del Seminario di Poggibonsi, 16–18 febbraio 2006* (pp. 199–220). Turnhout: Brepols.

Theuws, F. (2008b). "'Terra non est'. Zentralsiedlungen der Völkerwanderungszeit im Maas-Rhein-Gebiet." In H. Steuer and V. Bierbrauer (eds.), *Höhensiedlungen zwischen Antike und Mittelalter von den Ardennen bis zur Adria* (pp. 765–793). Berlin: Walter de Gruyter.

Theuws, F. (2009). "Grave Goods, Ethnicity, and the Rhetoric of Burial Rites in Late Antique Northern Gaul." In T. Derks and N. Roymans (eds.), *Ethnic Constructs in Antiquity. The Role of Power and Tradition* (pp. 283–319). Amsterdam: Amsterdam University Press.

Theuws, F. (2012). "River-Based Trade Centres in Early Medieval Northwestern Europe. Some 'Reactionary' Thoughts." In S. Gelichi and R. Hodges (eds.), *From one sea to another. Trading places in the European and Mediterranean Early Middle Ages. Proceedings of the International Conference Comacchio, 27th-29th March 2009* (pp. 25–45). Turnhout: Brepols Publishers.

Theuws, F. (2013). "Do All the Burials We Excavate Allow an Archaeology of Individuality and Individualism? An Introduction to the Sachsensymposion 2011." In B. Ludowici (ed.), *Individual and Individuality? Approaches towards an Archaeology of Personhood in the First Millenium AD* (pp. 9–15). Neue Studien zur Sachsenforschung 4. Hanover: Niedersächsischen Landesmuseum Hanover.

Theuws, F. (in press) "Peasant Agency, Long Distance Trade and the Early Medieval Economy." (Conference Proceedings Copenhagen 2010).

Theuws, F., and Alkemade, M. (1999). "A Kind of Mirror for Men. Sword Depositions in Late Antique Northern Gaul." In F. Theuws and J. Nelson (eds.), *Rituals of Power from Late Antiquity to the Early Middle Ages* (pp. 401–476). Leiden: Brill.

Theuws, F., and Kars, M. (eds.). (2017). *The Saint-Servatius Complex in Maastricht. The Vrijthof Excavations (1969–1970).* Merovingian Archaeology in the Low Countries 4. Bonn: Habelt Verlag.

Theuws, F., and van Haperen, M. (2012). *The Merovingian Cemetery of Bergeijk-Fazantlaan.* Bonn: Habelt Verlag.

Treffort, C. (1996) *L'église carolingienne et la mort. Christianisme, rites funéraires et pratiques commémoratives.* Lyon: Presses universitaires de Lyon.

van Haperen, M. (2017). "In Touch with the Dead: Early Medieval Grave Reopenings in the Low Countries." PhD Thesis, Leiden University.

van Ossel, P., and Ouzoulias, P. (2001). "La mutation des campagnes de la Gaule du nord entre le milieu du IIIe siècle et le milieu du Ve siècle. Où en est-on?" In M. Lodewijckx (ed.), *Belgian Archaeology in a European setting II* (pp. 231–245). Louvain: Leuven University Press.

van Wersch, L., van Geesbergen, D., and Vrielynck, O. (2010). "Les coupes en verre à décor chrétien découvertes en Belgique (fin V^e-début VIe siècle)." *Archéologie Médiévale* 49: 115–147.

Verslype, L. (2010). "La dotation funéraire des tombes dites de 'chefs' dans le nord-ouest de la Gaule du Ve au VIIe siècle." In K. de Groote, D. Tys, and M. Pieters (eds.), *Exchanging Medieval Material Culture. Studies on Archaeology and History Presented to Frans Verhaeghe* (pp. 303–315). Relicta monografieën 4. Brussels: Vlaams Instituut voor het Onroerend Goed.

Vos, A. D. (2004). *Resten van Romeinse bruggen in de Maas te Maastricht.* Rapportage Archeologische Monumentenzorg 100. Amersfoort: State Archaeological Service.

Weidemann, M. (1986). *Das Testament des Bischofs Bertramn von Le Mans vom 27. März 616. Untersuchungen zu Besitz und Geschichte einer fränkischen Familie im 6. und 7. Jahrhundert.* Römisch-Germanisches Zentralmuseum, Monographien 9. Mainz: Habelt Verlag.

Weidemann, M. (1990). "Die kirchliche Organisation der Provinzen Belgica und Germania vom 4. bis 7. Jahrhundert." In P. Bange and A. G. Weiler (eds.), *Willibrord, zijn wereld en zijn werk. Voordrachten gehouden tijdens het Willibrordcongres Nijmegen, 28–30 september 1989* (pp. 285–316). Nijmegen: Centrum voor Middeleeuwse Studies.

Weidemann, M. (1993). "Adel im Merowingerreich. Untersuchungen zu seiner Rechtsstellung." *Jahrbuch des Römisch-Germanischen Zentralmuseums Mainz* 40: 535–555.

Werner, J. (1953). *Das Alamannische Gräberfeld von Bülach.* Basel: Birkhäuser.

Werner, M. (1980). *Der Lütticher Raum in frühkarolingischer Zeit. Untersuchungen zur Geschichte einer karolingischer Stammlandschaft.* Göttingen: Birkhäuser.

Werner, M. (1982). *Adelsfamilien im Umkreis der frühen Karolinger. Die Verwantschaft Irminas von Oeren und Adelas von Pfalzel. Personengeschichtliche Untersuchungen zur frühmittelalterlichen Führungsschicht im Maas-Mosel-Gebiet.* Vorträge und Forschungen 28. Sigmaringen: Thorbecke.

Wickham, C. (2005). *Framing the Early Middle Ages. Europe and the Mediterranean 400–800.* Oxford: Oxford University Press.

Wickham, C. (2009). *The Inheritance of Rome: A History of Europe from 400–1000.* London: Allen Lane Publishers.

Wood, I. (1994). *The Merovingian Kingdoms 450–751.* London: Longman.

Wood, I. (2004). "Genealogy Defined by Women. The Case of the Pippinids." In L. Brubaker and J. M. H. Smith (eds.), *Gender in the Early Medieval World. East and West 300–900* (pp. 234–45). Cambridge: Cambridge University Press.

Wood, I. (2013). "Entrusting Western Europe to the Church." *Transactions of the Royal Historical Society* 23: 37–73.

Wolf, E. R. (1966). *Peasants.* Englewood Cliffs, NJ: Prentice Hall.

Young, B., and Périn, P. (1991). "Les nécropoles (IIIe–VIII^{e}siècle). Problèmes d'historiographie et de méthode." In N. Duval et al. (eds.), *Naissance des arts Chrétiens. Atlas des monuments paléochretiens de la France* (pp. 94–121). Paris: Imprimerie Nationale Éditions.

CHAPTER 39

BELT BUCKLES AND BURIALS IN SOUTHWESTERN GAUL

RALPH J. PATRELLO

AROUND 584 AD, Eberulf, a disgraced treasurer of the Merovingian kingdom of Neustria, sought refuge from his royal pursuers in the church of Tours.[1] The bishop, Gregory, recounted in his *Decem Libri Historiarum* that he admitted the official to sanctuary, albeit reluctantly considering Eberulf's habit of despoiling churches of their property. Indeed, Gregory spent a good portion of the chapter dedicated to Eberulf's sanctuary enumerating his crimes committed against the churches of Gaul, and specifically that of St. Martin. Gregory concluded this catalog of Eberulf's misdeeds with the tale of an instance in which the Merovingian official engaged the help of a local man to steal church lands. While his unnamed accomplice harassed the estate overseers, Eberulf seized the lands in question by producing counterfeit bills of sale. In closing, Gregory noted a peculiar exchange between the two men in which Eberulf presented his partner in crime with a "golden piece of his belt." On the surface, this appears to have been a straightforward exchange. The golden ornament would likely have had some value due to the material and would have been a wholly appropriate payment for playing a role in this Merovingian-era short con. Understood in the context of the sixth century, however, the exchange of a belt fragment implicated one of the ways in which people formalized bonds of allegiance, service, and status (Sarti 2013, pp. 222–232).

Notably, the anecdote Gregory offered about Eberulf is rare in contemporary sources. However, pieces of belt fittings, or incomplete belt sets, appear more frequently in archaeological contexts, specifically in graves. These items were broken apart and deposited in graves at a considerable rate. In the nineteen cemeteries surveyed here from southwestern Gaul,[2] nearly one in four graves containing plate buckles featured an incomplete set of fittings.

It is the contention of this chapter that incomplete sets uncovered during the excavation of cemeteries were often the result of intentional acts of fragmentation, in which plate buckles, elaborate, often large, bronze or iron belt fittings, were broken up, and one or several pieces were included in the burial assemblage [Fig. 39.1].[3] Rather than simply being included in the grave assemblage as "costume" and accoutrements, the items included in the grave were chosen for their significance to the memory of the deceased and the social strategies of those living who created the assemblage (Effros 2002, p. 19; Williams 2006, pp. 119–120; Halsall 2010, p. 175).

The meaning of this act, though only a hypothetical reconstruction, may have derived from the social role of the exchange of belts among the living. Contemporaries such as Gregory of Tours and Venantius Fortunatus described the central place buckle sets held in relationships of service and political dependence, circulating in relationships of allegiance and dependence among the social elite of the Merovingian kingdoms. Beyond simply representing such connections, something of the relationships and the power they conferred was contained in the buckle sets. Thus, while receiving a buckle from the king was ennobling, one could also be stripped of a belt set, thereby removing one's status.

The social significance of furnished burial in the confirmation (or indeed, establishment) of a family's status through memorialization of the deceased has long been recognized, and the fragmentation of belt sets may have served to reinforce this message in the burial rite. However, the treatment of objects prior to their deposition has not always

FIGURE 39.1. Plate buckle from Teilhet "Tabariane." Photo courtesy of The Walters Art Museum, Baltimore, Maryland.

featured in analyses of furnished burial, in part due to the difficulty in determining when alterations took place (Olivier 1999, pp. 125–126). The context of the grave can offer some clues: the placement of buckle fragments in the grave, often on or near areas of the body associated with belts, may have implied the existence of a complete set and may have drawn the viewers' attention to the missing pieces. While it is impossible to know where and with whom the rest of these partial sets resided, fragments emphasize the nature of grave-goods as links between the living, the dead, and the relationships that brought belt sets into being.

Plate buckles could be broken up with relative ease: they generally featured multiple articulated pieces including a plate, a buckle, and a tongue, connected by a metal pin (Lorren 2001, pp. 187–190). In addition, large rivets often adorned the plates. Some earlier forms also included back plates, small square or rectangular metal plates riveted to the plate buckle that sandwiched the belt leather as a means of attaching the buckle assembly. Later plate buckles featured perforated tabs, sewn or otherwise secured on the backside, attaching the buckle to the belt leather (Salin 1952, p. 315). Occasionally, counterplates rounded out the belt set. Finally, belt sets often included additional pieces such as ornaments, strap ends, and chatelaines, added to the belt leather by either rivets or perforated tabs.

Despite the many ways plate buckles could be disassembled, this phenomenon has received little attention in scholarship on the period.[4] In general, archaeologists prefer to work with whole objects, even though broken or incomplete items are frequently recovered though excavation (Chapman 2000a). This preference reveals itself through the ways archaeologists choose to represent the objects they recover. Line drawings, and later photography, both represent and distort artifacts to suit the researcher's purposes (Shanks 1997; Moser 2012, p. 303), and typically focus on whole objects. Although there is no a priori reason that past actors must have deposited belt buckles as complete sets, this is generally how archaeological reports and publications represent such objects, largely to meet the needs of typological analysis. This form of distortion ignores the potential that objects may have been intentionally broken, however. Broken pots reassembled to study profiles, rims, bases, or decoration, or metal objects placed alongside one another for comparative study, ultimately obscure any intentionality behind the act of deposition, including the choice to break up objects prior to burial.

Only recently have scholars inquired more deeply into the mechanisms by which grave-goods circulated and appeared in burial contexts (see Halsall, Chapter 8; Perez, Chapter 9; and Theuws, Chapter 38, this volume). More typically, scholars have assumed the process of circulation to be relatively straightforward: objects found in funerary contexts belonged to the people buried in the graves, reflecting the appearance of the deceased in life (Périn and Kazanski 2011, pp. 315–316). Objects of daily use such as pottery revealed traditional manufacturing techniques, and objects of personal adornment represented the specific ethnic costume of the inhumed (Zeller 1996, p. 672). These conclusions derived from general assumptions about the nature of the archaeological record, which held that objects recovered through archaeological excavation represented the remnants of now-dead cultural processes or traditions (Patrik 1986, pp. 34–35). Considering the circulation and treatment of objects prior to burial, however, permits a view of material culture as more dynamic and culture change as not beholden to the movement of peoples.

THE CONTEXT OF FURNISHED BURIALS

Furnished inhumation was neither the only nor even the most popular means of burying the dead in late-antique and early medieval southern Gaul. In an article on the funerary practices of southern Gaul, Didier Paya has argued that the myriad rites observed across the region indicated that people used whatever resources were handy to memorialize their dead (Paya 2003, p. 165; see also Corrochano 2011, p. 61). The differences range from the location of the site to the construction and layout of graves and to the furnishings, if any, included in the burial. While the stereotypical "barbarian" cemeteries of the fifth and sixth centuries were apparently located well beyond human settlements and often appeared on hillsides, suburban and even urban cemeteries have also been observed across the southwest, such as those found around Toulouse (Wild 1999; Paya 2009; Ollivier 2010). Likewise, burial sites have been located in rural settlements, such as at Isle-Jourdain (Gers), where a large cemetery appears to have developed around an old *mutatio*, or Roman waystation along the Toulouse-Auch road (Bach and Boudartchouk 1998, p. 213). Indeed, villa sites, possibly abandoned, were frequent locations for late-antique and early medieval cemeteries, exemplified by the site of Beaucaire-sur-Baïse "La Turraque" (Gers) (Larrieu, et al. 1985; on villas, see Chavarría Arnau, Chapter 29, this volume). The reuse of old features is perhaps most striking in the departments around the Massif Central, where several burial sites reused prehistoric burial mounds or dolmens (Delbos 1966; Azemar 1998).[5]

The graves themselves appeared in a wide variety of forms. Perhaps the most well known were the sarcophagus burials, in use from the late Roman period through early Middle Ages. However, cemeteries also featured graves lined in stone, wood (both nailed coffins and wooden planks supported by stones), tile, or simply dug into the earth. In some cases, multiple types can be observed at the same site. Unfortunately, art historical interest in sarcophagi, in particular, meant that archaeologists largely focused their attention on these objects. The site of La Turraque, excavated in the 1960s, contained a number of graves in simple trenches, but the excavators chose not to record these graves in favor of focusing on the area in which the sarcophagi were concentrated (Larrieu et al. 1985, p. 27).

While furnished burials seem to date back to at least the fourth century in southwestern Gaul, the metal grave deposits and large, rural cemeteries so common in northern Gaul appeared relatively late in the southwest and by and large cannot be dated any earlier than perhaps the second quarter of the sixth century.[6] While those examples from the southwest do generally follow the form of row grave cemeteries in the north, with ordered rows of graves usually oriented east-west, in other cemeteries, different considerations may have influenced the orientation and layout of the burials. For instance, graves dug in and around extant structures or ruins, such as at La Turraque, La Gravette, or Jau-Dignac-et-Loirac "La Chapelle" (Gironde), often followed the orientation of the pre-existing buildings.

The late appearance of furnished row graves like those seen in northern Gaul, in addition to the wide variety of rites observed in southern Gallic cemeteries, have confounded attempts to interpret the mortuary archaeology as evidence of barbarian migrations (Young 2012; although see Greene 1987). The intersection of objects and cultural practice is much more complicated than the simple mapping of ethnic identity onto artifacts, a point that scholars committed to ethnic ascription models rightly recognize. In addressing the complexities revealed in the myriad material culture practices uncovered through mortuary archaeology, scholars revising ethnic ascription models have argued for two significant modifications: a focus on the individual rather than on the collective, and a more flexible concept of ethnic dress. Variations in grave deposits within cemeteries or unique finds of items of personal adornment are to be seen as evidence of the "multicultural" nature of the barbarian confederations that settled in Gaul and Spain (Kazanski and Périn 2009, p. 161; Périn and Kazanski 2011, p. 305; Pinar 2013). These scholars explain the appearance of objects with typological connections to objects found along the Danube frontier in northern Gaul, rather than southern Gaul, by the spread of an "international" barbarian-*cum*-aristocratic style (Kazanski 1989, p. 66; Périn and Kazanski 2011, pp. 308–310; Pinar and Ripoll 2007; Young 2012). From this perspective, the absence of this style in the regions of Visigothic settlement south of the Loire is evidence of "acculturation" (Kazanski and Périn 2009, p. 151; Périn and Kazanski 2011, pp. 305–308).

Indeed, while scholars still maintain the belief that *Tracht*, that is, ethnic costume, was a wholly traditional method of (primarily female) self-identification (Werner 1970; for belts as *Tracht*, see Martin 1991; critiques of the concept: Brather 2007; von Rummel 2007), more recent scholarship admits that such sartorial conservatism likely did not extend beyond one or two generations (Kazanski and Périn 2009, p. 151). Thus, the more time that "foreigners" spent in Roman territory, the more Roman they tended to look.

The plate buckles of southwestern Gaul are no exception to the trend, common in early medieval archaeology, to associate new forms with incoming populations. In the late nineteenth century, the lawyer and amateur archaeologist Casimir Barrière-Flavy argued that the plate buckles of southwestern Gaul were material evidence of the Visigothic settlement on Gallic soil in the fifth century (Barrière-Flavy 1893, p. 60; 1901, p. 170; on Barrière-Flavy, see Effros 2012). Writing some fifty years later, Édouard Salin argued that the carved bronze buckles showed Steppic influences, likely due to the presence of Alans in southern Gaul. This approach modified the earlier view but maintained the underlying assumptions of population change (Salin 1952, pp. 312–313).

Roughly six years prior to Salin's work, however, Nils Åberg had proposed that the Aquitanian plate buckles represented an indigenous material tradition in southwestern Gaul, although he also maintained that there must have been foreign influence in the design, if the objects did not necessarily belong to barbarian settlers (1947, p. 46). Edward James pursued this line of thought and argued on stylistic and typological grounds that the bronze plate buckles formed a unified type. He suggested that they represented an indigenous southern Gallic tradition descended in design from the late Roman *cingulum militiae*, a belt denoting office and rank in the Roman military and civilian bureaucracy (James 1977, p. 100). James argued that the carved designs, particularly the geometric patterns frequently adorning Aquitanian buckles, shared many characteristics with the patterns of late-Roman mosaics (James 1977, pp. 142–144). Furthermore, he argued against the prevailing opinion that stylistic and material influences moved north to south in the post-Roman period. Rather, James hypothesized that the Aquitanian plate buckles, specifically those of the middle Garonne, were some of the earliest post-Roman examples and that these types spawned those buckles found along the Loire and points north and east, notably the Merovingian kingdoms in northern Gaul and Burgundy (James 1977, pp. 150–151).

Critics of James's work maintained the influence of "Frankish" material culture on southern Gaul (Périn 1978; Lerenter 1991, p. 122) and noted that items of personal adornment only circulated when borne by the people whose identity these objects expressed (Stutz 1999, pp. 39–41). Sophie Lerenter argued that those instances of Aquitanian buckles found north of the Loire provided evidence of "migrations ponctuelles" of Aquitanians through the Frankish kingdoms (Lerenter 1991, p. 161). Likewise, Françoise Stutz and Claude Lorren both argued that the spread of such forms represented the movement of peoples in their works, which focused on "northern" objects in southwestern Gaul and Normandy, respectively (Lorren 2001; Stutz 2003). In particular, Françoise Stutz argued that, although mortuary archaeology reveals a much more complicated picture than one in which Franks from the north conquered the Visigothic south of Gaul, she nevertheless linked the variety of material types to the movement of different barbarian groups into the region (2003, p. 235).

There have been theoretical challenges to these positions, which maintain a close connection between objects and ethnic identity (for recent examples, see Halsall 2011 and Becker 2014). The data also suggest an alternative approach, one that, overall, questions these assumptions about the nature of personal adornment in funerary contexts. The treatment of buckle sets prior to their inclusion in the grave assemblage presents a challenge to the assumption that objects of personal adornment only circulated with the people who bore them and whose identity they expressed. On the one hand, breaking up objects such as belt sets would suggest that these items were not "sacral," as the concept of *Tracht* holds. Moreover, the act of fragmentation opened up many more possibilities for the circulation of objects. Pieces could have been exchanged, as in the anecdote about Eberulf above, but they could also have been deposited in graves, or kept among the living as heirlooms, or used to replace lost or broken pieces of other belt sets.

INCOMPLETE BELT SETS AND INTENTIONAL FRAGMENTATION

Belt sets, as with many objects recovered during archaeological excavation, were often fragmented, broken, or incomplete in some way, and only the context of the finds can reveal if this was the result of human action. In many cases, natural processes or disturbances exacerbated the objects' material degradation over time. In those instances where disturbance can be ruled out, however, it is possible that the people responsible for creating the grave deposit included incomplete belt sets, or indeed fragments of belt fittings. This is most likely the case in instances when belt fragments appear alongside complete sets, or when incomplete sets are found in contexts that show no other sign of disturbance.

Given that, apparently by choice, those responsible for burying the dead would deposit pieces from a belt set, it is possible that grave furnishings related to dress need not have dressed the corpse. These objects were not simply part of a costume, or *Tracht*, but they were chosen for inclusion in the burial and need not have been buried intact. At the same time, such items could still be personal, indicating some aspect of the deceased or his or her family that those responsible for burying the dead wished to highlight. That is not to say, however, that belt fittings, or indeed any grave furnishings, need have belonged to the deceased, but rather that such objects were capable of transmitting messages about the living and the dead.

The existence of incomplete buckle sets in significant numbers over a wide geographic area strongly suggests that fragmentation was an intentional practice. Of course, taphonomic processes (decomposition or material degradation due to burial), use wear or accidental breakage, and intentional or unintentional disturbance such as grave robbery could all explain incomplete belt sets. To account for cases of unintentional fragmentation, this analysis has excluded graves displaying obvious signs of robbery, including badly disturbed skeletal remains in combination with lost or broken sarcophagus lids, or additional signs of disturbance such as ditches or pits cut through the graves (Klevnäs 2013, p. 6). Clear evidence of postdepositional destruction was also reason to exclude fragmented buckles from the analysis.[7] The remaining examples form a secure and significant group of graves on which to base the analysis. Of the graves surveyed from cemeteries in France between the Loire and Pyrenees dated between the sixth and seventh centuries, just under 25 percent of those furnished with plate buckles contained buckles that were fragmented in some way (Fig. 39.2).

Incomplete belt sets, deprived of their functionality as items of clothing, attest to the possibility of alternative meanings, particularly when these objects appeared alongside otherwise complete belt sets. At Venerque "Rivel" (Haute-Garonne), grave 54, a plain earth burial dated to the first half of the seventh century, contained a tinned bronze plate buckle with five rivets, as well as a piece of a bronze plate with ten rivets (Vidal 1982, pp. 6–8; Vidal 1991, p. 196). The two items did not belong to the same set, and no apparent connection exists between them save for their inclusion in the same assemblage. Unfortunately, the skeletal remains were not preserved well enough to permit an analysis of either age or sex. Grave 735 of Luxé "Les Sablons" (Charente), likewise dated to the early seventh century, featured a similar assemblage: excavators uncovered the body of a child between seven and eleven years of age interred with a buckle and chatelaine, as well as the plate from an unarticulated plate buckle (Maury 2013, p. 420).[8] Again, the items were not in any coherent relationship with one another, further suggesting that they were included in the assemblage as individual objects rather than as a set.

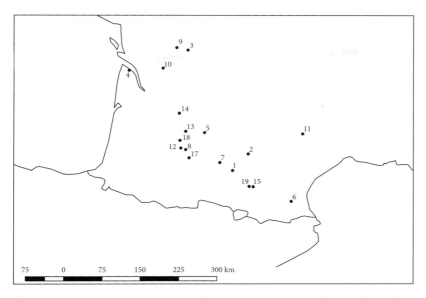

FIGURE 39.2. Sites surveyed: 1. Venerque "Rivel"; 2. Giroussens "Martels"; 3. Chasseneuil-sur-Bonnieure "Saint-Saturnin"; 4. Jau-Dignac-et-Loirac "La Chapelle"; 5. Puymirol "Touron"; 6. Estagel "Las Tombas"; 7. Isle-Jourdain "La Gravette"; 8. Beaucaire-sur-Baïse "La Turraque"; 9. Luxé "Les Sablons"; 10. Barbezieux "Font-Pinette"; 11. Millau "Aire de Repos-Brocuejouls"; 12. Mouchan "Gelleneuve"; 13. Bruch "Saint-Martin"; 14. Lachapelle "Saint-Cloud"; 15. Mirepoix "Les Olivettes"; 16. Poitiers "Les Hospitaliers"; 17. Ordan-Laroque "Saint-Brice-de-Cassan"; 18. Saint-Laurent-des-Hommes "Belou-Nord"; 19. Teilhet "Tabariane."

This possibility is further suggested by the fragmentation of items within the assemblage, in which buckle sets appear to have been intentionally spread around the inhumed rather than deposited whole and adorning the body. Teilhet "Tabariane" (Gers) grave 82, a plain earth burial, contained two skeletons, one of which was in reduction below the feet of a whole skeleton.[9] The complete skeleton, supine with its arms crossed over the pelvis, was buried with a large tinned bronze plate buckle and counterplate (Portet 2003, p. 17). The plate and buckle were placed between the femurs, just above the knees. A large scutiform tongue was located just above the left elbow, opposite the counterplate, which was located between the right elbow and spine (Portet 2003, Fig. 11). The excavators noted no disturbances to the grave outside of the possibility that the body decomposed in an empty space, allowing for the movement of objects. The remarkable symmetry of the set in the grave, however, indicates that the objects were placed there intentionally and did not move due to natural processes.

In this case, as with those cases discussed earlier in this chapter featuring buckle pieces alongside complete sets, the possible implication is that buckles served some purpose other than simply as a corpse's dress accessories. Similarly, single items from belt sets, when found in otherwise undisturbed graves, suggest that the purpose of belt fittings was something other than adornment. At Estagel, grave 32 contained a single inhumation and featured two ansated fibulae with bird-head protuberances as well as a silver plate fragment from a plate buckle, located at waist level (Lantier 1943, p. 162). At Les Sablons, a triangular belt ornament adorned the skeleton of an adolescent (over 14 years of age, per the report), located roughly in the middle of the pelvis (Maury 2013, p. 410). A belt set fragment found in La Turraque grave 119, a sarcophagus burial dated to the seventh century, is noteworthy for the way those responsible for creating the grave treated the belt. The grave featured two small bronze plate buckles associated with the inhumed, one under the left thigh and the other under the left arm, as well as several bronze fragments, a bone comb, and an iron nail. Finally, a plate and counter-plate from a buckle set were placed on the thorax. The items were still riveted together and sandwiched a scrap of leather. As the lid was intact and the sarcophagus contained only a single inhumation, there is no evidence whatsoever to suggest postdepositional disturbance. In the absence of any other belt fittings, it seems quite possible that the section was cut from a whole belt at some point prior to deposition (Larrieu et al. 1985, pp. 117–118).

Belt fittings deposited in such a way as to suggest that they were keepsakes, or per-haps heirlooms, indicate that such items could possess personal significance to either the deceased or the surviving kin responsible for his or her burial. Examples of this practice include a fourth-century silver buckle, possibly a northern object and at any rate an antique, included in a seventh-century burial, grave 12 at La Chapelle, along-side a complete plate-buckle set composed of a plate, counterplate, and back plate (Cartron and Castex 2010, p. 196). A pouch clasp indicating the presence of a leather or cloth bag at the time of burial suggests the possibility that the older buckle was included as a keepsake rather than as a dress accessory (Young 1992, p. 138; on heir-looms, see Kars 2012). An example from Estagel "Las Tombas," found in grave 201, pro-vides a particularly clear example of this practice (Lantier 1949, p. 69). A stone sarcophagus, the lid of which had collapsed due to the weight of the fill layer above, contained a double inhumation, sexed rather unscientifically by Robert Lantier as male and female.[10] The "male" skeleton was associated with a pouch clasp, iron knife fragments, and an iron buckle tongue from a plate buckle. Unlike the example from La Chapelle, there is no indication of chronological disjunction between the buckle tongue and the other grave deposits. However, the association with a pouch clasp indi-cates that the tongue was likely deposited inside a bag of keepsakes or other items of personal significance.[11]

The examples presented in this chapter demonstrate the possibility that individual belt fittings could circulate independently of the entire set, possibly because these items held meaning for their bearers that was not strictly speaking associated with dress. Other instances featuring examples of composite buckles, made up of replaced or repaired parts, reveal a more functional reason for the circulation of individual belt pieces. The late sixth- or early seventh-century grave 50 at Venerque featured a single skeleton, the age and sex of which were not recorded, in a supine position with arms crossed over the abdomen (Vidal 1982, p. 8, 1991, pp. 194–195). Included with the skele-ton was a semicircular plate buckle of tinned bronze, decorated with three rivets on the plate. The iron tongue and possibly the buckle do not appear to be original to the plate, and Michel Vidal has argued that this combination indicates the repair or replacement of some portion of the buckle (Vidal 1982, p. 8).

The presence of buckle components of different styles is provocative: evidence of repair indicates that while breakage due to accident or use wear may have occurred, such instances could be fixed, further suggesting that incomplete sets or pieces deposited in graves were intentionally broken. It is also possible that such mismatched objects were the result of personal touches or modifications made to the belt fittings, as seen in La Turraque grave 105, dated to the sixth century, which included a plate buckle, a large oval buckle, and an iron dagger (Larrieu et al. 1985, pp. 109–110, 147). The bronze plate buckle featured a narrow oval buckle and large scutiform tongue decorated with three eyelets. The plate to which both buckle and tongue were attached appears to have been clipped or cut just past the base of the tongue. The reasons behind such a modification are unclear, but the lack of any additional fragments in the grave suggests that the modification of the plate buckle was both intentional and occurred before the deposition of the item. The entire assemblage was placed in a limestone sarcophagus, the lid of which consisted of a partial sarcophagus lid and roof tiles firmly mortared to the base (Larrieu et al. 1985, p. 109), indicating possible reuse of the container. Nevertheless, the use of mortar to seal the sarcophagus suggests that the grave remained undisturbed from the time of deposition. At Isle-Jourdain, a heavily disturbed grave featured a buckle that had been clipped just after the two distal rivets, and at Giroussens "Martels" (Tarn), an openwork trapezoidal plate buckle was recovered from grave 31 that featured a plate cut close to the buckle (Lassure 1988, p. 61; Duhamel 1995, p. 419). It is not clear what purpose these modifications served—whether aesthetic, or to remove damaged portions, or indeed to fulfill some other, unknown requirement or desire on the part of the owner. What is apparent is that buckles could record the personal touch of those who possessed them.

Buckles do appear to have conveyed messages about the people who bore them, or with whom they were buried in mortuary contexts. Recent research has highlighted the role that such objects played in expressions of personal piety, from secret compartments for relics, which turned buckles into portable reliquaries, to decoration and inscriptions proclaiming eschatological expectations (Treffort 2002; Gaillard de Sémainville 2011; see also Poulain 2004). One such example, from Bruch "Saint-Martin" (Lot-et-Garonne) featured a carved decoration identified as a representation of the adoration of the Magi (Cartron, Castex, and Sachau-Carcel 2013, pp. 97–98). Elsewhere, at Gelleneuve, grave 40 included a triangular plate and buckle tongue, the latter item adorned with a human face framed by a double-headed dragon or serpent (Boube and Fouet 1956, pp. 18–19, 41). Some scholars have suggested that this *masque humaine* motif, which developed in the La Tène period and reappeared on plate buckles in the sixth century, may have taken on Christian overtones by the Merovingian era (Young 2016, pp. 342–343). Yet despite the confessional nature of certain buckle decoration, it does not follow that the buckles recovered from graves must have belonged to the deceased. Such objects just as easily may have expressed the mourners' hopes for the deceased's salvation.

The Social Significance of Belts

Belt sets had a social function that was as visible, if not more so, than the vestimentary role they played, particularly as physical manifestations of personal allegiance. From the late Roman Empire, the *cingulum militiae* served to mark out holders of office, both military and civil, from the rest of the population (Hoss 2012, p. 30; see also Sarti, Chapter 12, this volume). The belt had also long served as an embodiment of the soldier's individual oath to the emperor. In the fourth-century *acta* of the martyr Marcellus, for example, the saint rejected his service to the emperor in favor of dedicating his life to Christ by "[throwing] down his *cingulum* in the presence of the legionary standards" in defiance of the order to sacrifice in honor of the emperor's birthday (*Les actes de S. Marcel*, p. 261; for the fourth-century date, see Lanata 1972). While the term for the military belt of the late Roman Empire was *cingulum*, by about the third century another piece of equipment, the sword belt or baldric (*balteus*) also became part of the soldier's kit (Hoss 2012, p. 30). Whereas the word *balteus* seems to have retained a general meaning of belt or sword belt, *cingulum* came to refer to everything from the badge of rank or honor that was the military belt to the office itself (civil or military, but also eventually ecclesiastical in Gaul; see Sommer 1984, p. 83).

In general, legal texts from Late Antiquity and the early Middle Ages used the term to refer more broadly to office, such as in the *Edictum Theodorici* (LXXIII.18) or in the *Breviarium Alarici* (II.X.3).[12] More specifically, a reference to the *militiae cingulum* in canon 13 of the Council of Clermont (535) most likely refers to the ecclesiastical office (*Concilia Antiqua Galliae*, pp. 243–244). By contrast, the literary output of both Gregory, bishop of Tours, and Venantius Fortunatus, peripatetic, poet, and eventual bishop of Poitiers, was less restrained by the technical language of later Roman law and offered more fluid meanings of the terms. This fluidity permitted both authors to engage in the combination of categories through metonymy. The representations of belts in these authors' works offer good evidence suggesting that the exchange of belt sets specifically retained significance regarding the political alliances in the late sixth and early seventh centuries. Both authors maintained connections with the royalty and nobility of the Merovingian kingdoms, and they often wrote about and for the society in which belt sets circulated (George 1992, p. 28; Murray 2008, p. 166 n. 26).

Critically, the metonymic relationships found in the works of the two authors largely focused on the intersection of belts, status, and allegiance. To appreciate those connections more fully, a brief survey of the uses of belts in contemporary sources is necessary. In some instances, for example, Gregory of Tours seems to have used *cingulum* to refer to the waist, such as in *Historiae* IV.33.24 and VII.29.18, although Gregory may have been referring specifically to a belt in those contexts of an item kept in or hanging from it. Thus, Eberulf, defending himself against an agent of the king, drew his sword "from [his] *cingulum*" (*Historiae* VII.29.18). Gregory also described keys as hanging from a *cingulum* (*Liber in Gloria Martyrum* 33.16), as well as a dagger (*Historiae* X.10.12).

It could be reasonably inferred that here, too, Gregory meant waist, although he also used the same construction with *balteus*, a term that does not appear to have had the same double meaning as *cingulum*. Generally, Gregory seems to have preferred the term *balteus* to refer to the ostentatious belt sets favored by those possessing office and rank. Thus, for example, he spoke of a "golden *balteus* adorned with precious stones" accompanied by a bejeweled sword (*Historiae* X.21.4).

Venantius Fortunatus used *cingulum* more frequently than Gregory did, although it was not always clear from the context whether he was referring specifically to a physical object rather than office. In his panegyric to Conda, *domesticus* under several Neustrian kings, he celebrated the lowborn official's rise in prominence and status by proclaiming that the king had given him "*cingula* worthy of his service" (*Carmina* VII.XVI.19). It is possible to interpret *cingula* as meaning either the offices worthy of the service Conda rendered to his king, or the material rewards in the belts with which the king would invest such an officer (see Murray 2016, p. 212). Similarly, in another panegyric dedicated to Duke Lupus, Fortunatus praised the nobleman's evenhandedness in court cases, claiming that the *cingula* all sought him out to hear their cases (*Carmina* VII.VII.39). Again, from the immediate context it is unclear if Fortunatus is using *cingulum* metonymically, that is, the belts as representing their bearers, or if he simply meant to refer to the officeholders and magnates of the kingdom. Fortunatus clearly meant to refer to an object in the *Vita Sancti Radegundis*, where he described the noblewoman and saint adorning an altar with her finery, including a "heavy and costly golden *cingulum*" donated for the benefit of the poor (I.13.3). At the very least, the term appears to have been sufficiently malleable to permit the connection between the concepts of belt and nobility. The audience must have been aware of this ambiguity of meaning for the metonym to work. The implications of the close association between a person, his or her social standing, and objects of personal adornment such as belts help make a very clear case that belts were central to the public role of the aristocratic retainer.

Both authors' works clearly demonstrate the role that elaborate belts played in the formation of alliances and the maintenance of bonds between people. Gregory recounted an episode in which the Merovingian king Clovis attempted to win over some of a rival king's retainers through bribery (*Historiae* II.42.7). Offering them gilt belt buckles and armbands, Clovis swayed their loyalties, and they soon betrayed Ragnachar, the king of Cambrai. The exchange of buckles to seal an agreement points to the social role such objects played. The loss or rejection of a belt set could likewise signal a broken alliance. When Queen Fredegund stripped her servant Leonard of his belt and robes while in a rage at the treatment of her daughter, his disgrace was marked by the loss of his status, including those objects that he had received in royal service (*Historiae* VII.15.24). Elsewhere, at the end of Gundovald's insurgency in southern Gaul, when his allies betrayed him to Guntram Boso, they asked that he return his golden belt and sword. Gundovald, aware of his betrayal and that this act represented his abandonment by his allies, lamented that those things "which he had used in friendship" were being taken away from him (VII.38.3; see also Sarti 2013, pp. 240-241). In all cases, the transfer of a belt set signaled a relationship of dependence (Curta 2006, p. 698), manifesting both service and allegiance. It is significant, for instance, that Fortunatus referred to Conda's *obsequium* to the Theudebert in his panegyric, a term implying servitude or service in the capacity of a social inferior, as the low-born Conda would have been.

Belts were therefore highly personal items, revealing alliances, status, office, and even a person's true nature. The sets themselves were of course quite elaborate, and the sources tend to focus on the ostentation of both their raw materials and their elaboration through the addition of gemstones or cloisonné. Whether precious metals adorned all official belts is less clear. Certainly, few buckles recovered through mortuary excavations are made of gold or silver, although in some cases silver plate, and more frequently tinned bronze, gave the impression of solid silver objects.[13] The true value of the belt sets, however, derived from their roles as manifestations of the alliances finalized by their exchange. In the case of Ragnachar's treacherous retainers (*leudes*) above, Gregory linked the buckles' true nature—that of gilded bronze, rather than solid gold—to the value of a traitor's allegiance (Curta 2006, p. 682).

THE CIRCULATION OF BELT FRAGMENTS: A HYPOTHESIS

Although contemporary authors drew clear connections between social bonds and belts, archaeological excavation only ever reveals belt fittings. There are no direct correlations between metal belt adornments, buckles, and whole *cingula*, or between the mechanisms of exchange among the living and those involved in the creation of the grave deposit. However, considering early medieval mental categories and the ways in which people formed conceptual relationships suggests that it is possible to draw connections between ornate belt buckles recovered from mortuary contexts and the *cingula* and *baltei* of the works of Gregory and Fortunatus.

Principally, the rhetorical techniques of metonymy and synecdoche help to establish the possibilities for connecting the dots. Authors and scholars in the early Middle Ages would have been familiar with both techniques, which handbooks of rhetoric largely derived from Ciceronian tradition had preserved (Murphy 1974). Indeed, Giselle de Nie has argued that Gregory's use of metaphor to demonstrate Christian truth in his works hinged on a worldview in which "all formally analogous phenomena and acts were thought to cohere and participate in each other" (2002, p. 263). The principle of *pars pro toto* would have been central to such a view.

The ambiguity of meaning for the term *cingulum* permitted one to draw mental associations between belts, rank, and people, inviting the use of belts as metonyms. It is quite possible that, in a similar fashion, synecdoche was a material strategy meant to accomplish the same goal. The exchange of buckle sets between people in life established the social meaning of belt sets. Transferred in the establishment of relationships of political dependence, belt sets were the material expression of having powerful friends. While anecdotal evidence suggests that such objects were gifts given as part of the process of confirming or creating alliances or as part of a rise in station, the practice of fragmentation could have drawn such relationships to the fore. As David Rosand argued with respect to fragmentation in the visual arts, "information withheld simultaneously frustrates and implicates; it forces active engagement" (Rosand 1981, p. 27). By this logic, belt fittings would have been potent resources for families wishing to advertise their political connections, as fragmented sets might have drawn the viewers' minds to the complete set and the relationships bound up in it. This perspective may give some sense of the meaning of fragmented belt sets as part of the grave assemblage.

The connection that made the belt and fragment possible was itself a resource drawn on by the living to commemorate the dead and to establish their status in his or her absence. Such memories were on the one hand a means of helping the surviving kin to grieve. At the same time, the expense of such objects and their symbolic power also proclaimed the status of the surviving family. In the south, more so than in the north, not every grave was adorned with grave deposits. The relative scarcity of grave furnishings in southern Gaul further speaks to the inclusion of fragmented buckle sets as part of one material strategy among many available for burying the dead. The creation of memory through the resources at hand was at the very least an attempt to ensure social reproduction in the absence of the persons whose role that was.

The process by which buckle fragments enchained the living and the dead to extended networks of allegiance could take numerous forms, and it is difficult to state with certainty precisely how and when buckle sets were divided. While any attempted reconstruction is entirely hypothetical, such an exercise permits us to explore some of the possibilities as revealed through the context of the grave. La Turraque grave 119, noted above, potentially demonstrates the results of a buckle set broken up possibly at the grave site. The plate and back plate, which protected a scrap of leather from the original belt, could have been cut from the belt just prior to deposition in the grave. This scenario reveals the further possibility that surviving kin kept some or all of the remaining belt set, creating at once an heirloom and a memorable link between the deceased and the living through the now-incomplete belt set. The retained pieces could then be further divided among family members or make their way into other graves, a possibility raised by the case of the buckle tongue in Estagel 201. Alternatively, single pieces could themselves have been gifts or rewards for service, and included as prized possessions in the grave assemblage as a sign of the family's continued allegiances. The belt plate uncovered next to the inhumation of grave 1505 at Les Sablons might have served this purpose. Located just below the pelvis, between the femurs, the plate was not associated with any other belt fittings whatsoever. The only other object recovered from the grave, a scramasax, was located along the skeleton's left side, nestled between the arm and what would have been the rib cage (the remains of which did not survive intact). Excavators estimated that the skeleton belonged to an adolescent around fourteen years of age, around the time that a child would receive the trappings of adulthood, potentially including any social obligations of which a belt set and a weapon would have been part.[14] Once again, this is not to suggest that the belt piece or the scramasax belonged to the deceased of

Les Sablons 1505, but rather that the people who buried him or her, and who constructed the grave tableau, wished to maintain those relationships through the burial of their deceased, whose role it would have been to continue them in life.

We must also consider the role that belt sets, complete or otherwise, played in the burial as a *ritual*, which is to say as a practice that had importance in both a social and cosmological sense (see Theuws and Alkemade 2000, p. 414; Halsall 2010, pp. 207–208). This meaning seems to have derived from the belt's social function. As material expressions of social bonds, oaths of service, and status, belts defined social personas. This function of the belt could have been expressed by using it to adorn the corpse, as was often the case, or certainly by encircling the body with its constituent parts, as seen in Tabariane grave 82. There is yet another example, from La Gravette, in which a belt buckle appears to have functioned as a kind of seal for the grave itself. Grave 180, located beneath the nave of an early church, featured a sarcophagus that was largely empty save for two skeletons, both in reduction, one of which was sexed as male, and both of which belonged to younger adults (Duhamel 1995, p. 417).[15] The remains were contained in a small box made of *tegulae* (ceramic roof tiles) placed at one end of the sarcophagus. On top of the tile forming the box's lid, the excavators found an iron and bronze plate buckle. Although this is the only example of a plate buckle placed on top of a grave from any of the nineteen cemeteries surveyed, it is also one of only a handful of burials protected by extant structures. Indeed, several buckle fragments found at Rivel and La Turraque appeared as stray finds (Vidal 1984, pp. 19–21; Larrieu et al. 1985, pp. 120–121). It is possible that such items were placed on top of closed graves and displaced due to later activity. The use of belt fragments to complete the burial rite increased the visibility of these objects and emphasized the social weight borne by buckles in the Merovingian world. A chief defining quality of a person was whom one knew and how one could prove it, and plate buckles provided an immediate and indelible badge of associations.

Conclusions

The question of allegiance and legacy brings us back to Eberulf and his unnamed accomplice. Gregory does not explain Eberulf's gift of a piece of his belt. One may object that, given Gregory's mention of precious material, we should simply read this interaction as a commercial exchange in which a golden trinket was payment for services rendered. Golden belt fittings were certainly prized for their precious metal contents elsewhere in Gregory's *oeuvre*, such as in the tale of Count Britto's death after pilfering a belt and its golden fittings from a church altar. In this instance, however, Gregory seemed to suggest that avarice blinded Britto to the actual value of the belt set, which was as a donation to the church. Based on the context of the *Historiae*, however, it should be clear that for Gregory, belts, particularly those that were richly adorned, were manifestations of specific forms of social obligations and political associations. These objects were inseparable from the relationships that brought them into being: one could be raised up or brought low by the bestowal or removal of a belt, a mark of rank and status as evidenced by the centrality of belts as metonyms for important and powerful people.

It is similarly a mistake to claim that anything could be mere exchange, as though the circulation of objects did not carry with it the potential to create social bonds. Indeed, economic exchange, particularly in rare or precious items, often played a central role in the formation of extended human networks (Chapman 2008, p. 336). Even if this were not the case, however, it is still significant that Eberulf chose a piece of his belt to give to his co-conspirator. Why was this object selected, when Eberulf had so many other riches at his disposal? After all, Gregory made it clear that Eberulf, thanks to his plundering of church property, was quite wealthy. Gregory's special mention of the sort of precious item Eberulf offered, a piece of his belt, highlights the complex web of associations that the movement of belts invoked.

Of course, Gregory may have been making a joke at Eberulf's expense and the "insignificant person" (*quondam levem*) with whom he associated by offering an image of two loathsome creatures forming a partnership through the exchange of only a piece of a belt set, a mockery of the process by which the elite created and reinforced rank and privilege (on Gregory's sense of humor, see Goffart 1988).[16] The fuller context of the chapter, however, heightens the irony of this exchange. Gregory began book VII, chapter 22, by describing how Eberulf, having fallen out of favor with the king, lost all his possessions: his wealth was seized and distributed, and his houses, which were full of the goods he had stolen from the church, were ransacked. Eberulf thereby lost his ability to use his wealth to create a legacy and to contract alliances with others (Hardt 2004, pp. 236–248). It was at this point that the disgraced official, dispossessed and without friends, slunk back to the church of Saint Martin, which he had so often plundered. Gregory, for all his anger, offered pity. However, in ending the chapter with the story of Eberulf's belt, he reminded his audience of one important point: the only lasting connection that Eberulf made, sealed by the exchange of a golden ornament from his belt, was with a worthless person.

NOTES

1. I wish to thank Bonnie Effros, Edward James, and Isabel Moreira for their comments on early drafts of this chapter. In addition, Laurent Cases, Rebecca Devlin, Michael Gennaro, Christopher Patrello, and Christopher Woolley provided invaluable feedback, for which I am sincerely grateful. The research represented here would not have been possible without funding provided by the University of Florida's Center for European Studies, the Center for the Humanities and the Public Sphere, the Rothman Dissertation Research Grant, and the Society for French Historical Studies' Wolf Travel Grant.

2. Nineteen cemeteries from the modern administrative regions of Nouvelle-Aquitaine and Occitanie were chosen based on the date of excavation, the presence of descriptions of the individual graves uncovered, and the existence of site plans. Of these sites, fifteen featured burials containing plate buckles.

3. John Chapman's work in fragmentation studies has offered the approach as a means of understanding the active role of objects in social formation. Chapman accepts a perspective on human–object relations in which both people and things mutually constitute one

another (2000b, p. 171) and as such cannot be divorced from one another entirely. Items created from (and that create) people are "inalienable," a term Chapman borrows from Annette Weiner, who argued that such objects were special due to their "exclusive and cumulative identity with a particular set of owners through time" (Weiner 1992, p. 33; see also Chapman 2000a, p. 37). In essence, the value of inalienable objects derives from the vital role they play in the creation of a person's social identity. When exchanged (as gifts since inalienable objects cannot be commodified), such items create and reinforce social networks through enchainment, a process in which objects connect people through their circulation due to the objects' connections with the social identities of their various owners (2000a, p. 28). This form of object biography is most clearly expressed in the medieval world through the genealogy of named objects in heroic epics, such as weapons in *Beowulf* (Theuws and Alkemade 2000, p. 426). Arguably, a similar process occurred through the exchange of belts.

4. Mirjam Kars has noted that many belt sets were incomplete in Merovingian-era cemeteries around Maastricht (Kars 2011, p. 225).

5. Such sites have also been located in the British Isles (for examples and an outline of the interpretive problems these sites present, see Halsall 2010, pp. 72–77).

6. In some cases, however, dating is based on circular argument. In the case of La Gravette, the well-furnished "Frankish" burial ground was dated on the basis of the assumption that the graves contained the remains of Frankish soldiers and their families who participated in the conquest or garrisoning of the southwest following Clovis's war against the Visigoths in 507. The post–507 date, therefore, was proof that the graves contained the remains of a Frankish garrison, and the nature of the graves as "Frankish" meant that they could only have appeared after 507.

7. For instance, the plate buckle in Chasseneuil-sur-Bonnieure "Saint-Saturnin" grave 72, which was missing its tongue, is not among those considered here because the object was highly oxidized and contained in a grave very badly damaged by later construction on the site (Poignant 2004). A similar example from Luxé "Les Sablons" grave 374 likewise appears to have simply degraded over time (Maury 2013. p. 417).

8. The buckle portion appears to have been removed.

9. Although initially excavated in the early twentieth century by Robert Roger (1908), the results of those excavations were, by modern standards, very poorly published. A series of excavations led by Nicholas Portet have provided much more detailed descriptions of the cemetery's graves and overall plan, and any reference to Tabariane depends on the twenty-first-century excavations. A study of some of the plate buckles uncovered during Roger's initial excavations was published by Françoise Vallet (1978).

10. In addition to assuming skeletal sex based on grave deposits, Robert Lantier, who led the excavations at Estagel, sexed every double inhumation as male and female, evidently assuming all interred pairs to be husband and wife. Such assumptions, however, have been thrown into question by recent genetic testing on skeletons from Jau-Dignac-et-Loirac, in the Gironde department. Studies of the mitochondrial DNA preserved in the remains located in graves 169 and 170 revealed that the two individuals were related through their maternal line (Deguilloux et al. 2010, pp. 245–246).

11. Buckle tongues are often absent in graves, such as in "La Turraque" 34 or "Les Sablons" 374.

12. Notably, the *interpretatio* provided for *CTh* 2.10.3 by the compilers of the *Breviarium* (see Matthews 2001) replaced references to the *cingulum* with more general references to arms.

13. Childeric's grave is a notable exception (see, for instance, Kazanski and Périn 1988).

14. Guy Halsall has demonstrated, for northern Gaul, that although legal adulthood was reached for both males and females at some point between twelve and fifteen years of age, "male" grave goods such as weapons and belt sets do not appear in graves until around age twenty (1995, pp. 72, 84). If the same patterns hold true for southern Gaul, and if the remains in Les Sablons 1505 have been aged and sexed correctly, then this example would appear to be an outlier, although the mid-seventh-century date of the grave could likewise explain this discrepancy.

15. Isabelle Barthélémy, who performed extensive skeletal analysis, aged one individual between fifteen and twenty-one years, and the other as younger than thirty years (1999, p. 248).

16. Gregory's use of *levis* was likely meant as a play on the usual description of important people as *gravis*. I thank Laurent Cases for this observation.

Works Cited

Ancient Sources

"Les actes de S. Marcel le centurion." H. Delehaye (ed.). (1923). *Analecta Bollandiana* 41: 257–287.

Breviarium Alarici. G. Haenel (ed.). (1848). *Lex Romana Visigothorum*. Leipzig: Teubner.

Concilia Antiqua Galliae. Jacques Sirmond (ed.). (1970). Aalen: Scientia Verlag.

Edictum Theodorici. F. Bluhme (ed.). (1889). *Edictum Theoderici regis*. MGH Leges nationem Germanicarum 5. Hanover: Hahn.

Gregory of Tours, *Liber in Gloria Martyrum*. B. Krusch (ed.). (1885). *Gregorii episcopi Turonensis Miracula et Opera Minora*. MGH SRM 1.2 (pp. 484–562). Hanover: Hahn.

Gregory of Tours, *Historiae*. B. Krusch and W. Levison (eds.). (1951). *Gregorii episcopi Turonensis Libri Historiarum X*. MGH SRM 1.1. 2nd ed. Hanover: Hahn.

Venantius Fortunatus, *Carmina*. F. Leo (ed.). (1881) *Venanti Honori Clementi Fortunati presbyteri Italici Opera poetica*. MGH AA 4.1. Berlin: Weidmann.

Venantius Fortunatus, *Vita Sancti Radegundis*. B. Krusch (ed.). (1988). *Fredegarii et aliorum Chronica. Vita Sanctorum*. MGH SRM 2. Hanover: Hahn.

Modern Sources

Åberg, N. (1947). *The Occident and Orient in the Art of the Seventh Century, Part III: The Merovingian Empire*. Stockholm: Wahlström and Widstrand.

Azemar, R. (1998). "Place et traitement des morts sur les causses sud-aveyronnais au haut moyen âge." In P. Gruat (ed.), *Croyances et rites en Rouergue des origines à l'an mil* (pp. 217–238). Espalion: Musée du Rouergue.

Bach, S., and Boudartchouk, J.-L. (1998). "La nécropole franque de l'Isle-Jourdain." In X. Delestre and P. Périn (eds.), *La datation des structures et des objets du haut moyen âge: méthodes et résultats* (pp. 213–232). Saint-Germain-en-Laye: Association française d'archéologie mérovingienne.

Barrière-Flavy, C. (1893). *Études sur les sépultures barbares du Midi et de l'Ouest de la France— Industrie wisigothique*. Toulouse: Privat.

Barrière-Flavy, C. (1901). *Les arts industriels des peuples barbares de la Gaule du Ve au VIIIe siècle*. Toulouse: Privat.

Barthélemy, I. (1999). "Morphologie et évolution: le peuplement du sud ouest de la France entre le VIe et le XIe siècles." PhD Thesis. Université de Toulouse III—Paul Sabatier.

Becker, A. (2014). "Ethnicité, identité ethnique. Quelques remarques pour l'Antiquité tardive." *Gerión* 32: 289–305.

Brather, S. (2007). "Von der 'Tracht' zur 'Kleidung': Neue Fragestellungen und Konzepte in der Archäologie des Mittelalters." *Zeitschrift für Archäologie des Mittelalters* 35: 185–206.

Chapman, J. (2000a). *Fragmentation in Archaeology: People, Places, and Broken Objects in the Prehistory of South Eastern Europe.* London: Routledge.

Chapman, J. (2000b). "Tension at Funerals: Social Practices and the Subversion of Community Structure in Later Hungarian Prehistory." In M.-A. Dobres and J. Robb (eds.), *Agency in Archaeology* (pp. 169–195). London: Routledge.

Chapman, J. (2008). "Approaches to Trade and Exchange In Earlier Prehistory (Late Mesolithic-Era–Early Bronze Age)." In A. Jones (ed.), *Prehistoric Europe: Theory and Practice* (pp. 333–355). Malden, MA: Wiley-Blackwell.

Corrochano, A. (2011). "Entre nécropoles et cimetières: tombes, lieux d'inhumation et mémoire funéraire à travers l'archéologie des VIIe–XIe siècles dans le sud de la France." *Les Cahiers de Saint-Michel de Cuxa* 42: 59–64.

Curta, F. (2006). "Merovingian and Carolingian Gift Giving." *Speculum* 81: 671–699.

De Nie, G. (2002). "History and Miracle: Gregory's Use of Metaphor." In K. Mitchell and I. Wood (eds.), *The World of Gregory of Tours* (pp. 261–279). Leiden: Brill.

Effros, B. (2002). *Caring for Body and Soul: Burial and the Afterlife in the Merovingian World.* State College: Pennsylvania State University Press.

Effros, B. (2012). "Casimir Barrière-Flavy and the (Re)Discovery of Visigoths in Southwestern France." In S. Patzold, A. Rathmann-Lutz, and V. Scior (eds.), *Geschichtsvorstellungen. Bilder, Texte und Begriffe aus dem Mittelalter. Festschrift für Hans-Werner Goetz* (pp. 559–576). Cologne: Böhlau.

Gaillard de Sémainville, H. (2011). "Décor chrétien des objets de parure: l'exemple des plaques-boucles mérovingiennes de Burgundia." *Antiquité Tardive* 19: 223–236.

George, J. (1992). *Venantius Fortunatus: A Latin Poet in Merovingian Gaul.* Oxford: Clarendon Press.

Goffart, W. (1988). *The Narrators of Barbarian History (A.D. 550–800): Jordanes, Gregory of Tours, Bede, and Paul the Deacon.* Notre Dame: University of Notre Dame Press.

Greene, K. (1987). "Gothic Material Culture." In I. Hodder (ed.), *Archaeology as Long-Term History* (pp. 117–131). Cambridge: Cambridge University Press.

Halsall, G. (1995). *Settlement and Social Organization: The Merovingian Region of Metz.* Cambridge: Cambridge University Press.

Halsall, G. (2010). *Cemeteries and Society in Merovingian Gaul: Selected Studies in History and Archaeology, 1992–2009.* Leiden: Brill.

Halsall, G. (2011). "Ethnicity and Early Medieval Cemeteries." *Arqueologia y Territorio Medieval* 18: 15–27.

Hardt, M. (2004). *Gold und Herrschaft: Die Schätze europäischer Könige und Fürsten im ersten Jahrtausend.* Berlin: Akademie.

Hoss, S. (2012). "The Roman Military Belt." In M.-L. Nosch and H. Koefoed (eds.), *Wearing the Cloak: Dressing the Soldier in Roman Times* (pp. 29–44). Oxford: Oxbow.

James, E. (1977). *The Merovingian Archaeology of Southwest Gaul.* British Archaeological Reports Supplementary Series, 25, 1–2. Oxford: British Archaeological Reports.

Kars, M. (2011). "A Cultural Perspective on Merovingian Burial Chronology and the Grave Goods from the Vrijthof and Pandhof Cemeteries in Maastricht." PhD Thesis, Universiteit van Amsterdam.

Kars, M. (2012). "(Re)considering the Pre-Burial Life of Grave Goods. Toward a Renewed Debate on Early Medieval Burial Chronology on the Continent." *Medieval and Modern Matters* 3: 107–134.

Kazanski, M. (1989). "La diffusion de la mode danubienne en Gaule (fin du IVe-début du VIe siècle): Essai d'interprétation historique." *Antiquités Nationales* 21: 59–73.

Kazanski, M., and Périn, P. (1988). "Le mobilier funéraire de la tombe de Childeric Ier: état de la question et perspectives." *Revue archéologique de Picardie* 3: 13–38.

Kazanski, M., and Périn, P. (2009). "'Foreign' Objects in the Merovingian Cemeteries of Northern Gaul." In D. Quast and H. W. Böhme (eds.), *Foreigners in Early Medieval Europe: Thirteen International Studies on Early Medieval Mobility* (pp. 149–167). Mainz: Römisch-Germanisches Zentralmuseums.

Klevnäs, A. (2013). *Whodunnit? Grave Robbery in Anglo-Saxon England and the Merovingian Kingdoms*. Oxford: Archaeopress.

Lanata, G. (1972). "Gli atti del processo contro il centurione Marcello." *Byzantion* 42: 509–522.

Lantier, R. (1943). "Le cimetière wisigothique d'Estagel." *Gallia* 1: 153–188.

Lantier, R. (1949). "Le cimetière wisigothique d'Estagel (Pyrénées-Orientales)." *Gallia* 7: 55–80.

Larrieu, M., Marty, B., Périn, P., and Crubézy, É. (1985). *La nécropole mérovingienne de la Turraque: Beaucaire-sur-Baïse (Gers)*. Soréze: Société de Recherche Spéléo-Archéologique du Sorezois et Revelois.

Lassure, J.-M. (1988). "La nécropole wisigothique des Martels à Giroussens (Tarn)." *Archéologie du Midi médiéval* 6: 51–64.

Lerenter, S. (1991). "Les plaques-boucles en bronze de style aquitain à l'époque mérovingienne." PhD Thesis, Université de Paris I—Sorbonne.

Lorren, C. (2001). *Fibules et plaque-boucles à l'époque mérovingienne en Normandie: contributions à l'étude du peuplement, des échanges et des influences, de la fin du Ve au début du VIIIe siècle*. Saint-Germain-en-Laye: Association française d'archéologie mérovingienne.

Martin, M. (1991). "Zur frühmittelalterlichen Gürteltracht der Frau in der Burgundia, Francia und Aquitania." In I. Bóna (ed.), *L'art des invasions en Hongrie et en Wallonie: Actes du colloque au Musée royal de Mariemont du 9 au 11 avril 1979*. Morlanwelz: Musée royal de Mariemont.

Matthews, J. (2001). "Interpreting the *Interpretationes* of the *Breviarium*." In R. W. Mathisen (ed.), *Law, Society, and Authority in Late Antiquity* (pp. 11–32). Oxford: Oxford University Press.

Moser, S. (2012). "Archaeological Visualization: Early Artifact Illustration and the Birth of The Archaeological Image." In I. Hodder (ed.), *Archaeological Theory Today*, 2nd ed. (pp. 292–322). Cambridge: Polity.

Murray, A. C. (2008). "Chronology and the Composition of the *Histories* of Gregory of Tours." *Journal of Late Antiquity* 1: 157–196.

Murray, A. C. (2016). "The Merovingian State and Administration in the Times of Gregory of Tours." In A. C. Murray (ed.), *A Companion to Gregory of Tours* (pp. 191–231). Leiden: Brill.

Murphy, J. (1974). *Rhetoric in the Middle Ages: A History of Rhetorical Theory from St. Augustine to the Renaissance*. Berkeley: University of California Press.

Olivier, L. (1999). "The Hochdorf 'Princely' Grave and the Question of the Nature of Archaeological Funerary Assemblages." In T. Murray (ed.), *Time and Archaeology* (pp. 109–138). London: Routledge.

Ollivier, J. (2010). "Les sépultures de l'ENSEEIHT à Toulouse (Haute-Garonne)." *Archéologie du Midi médiéval* 28: 335–341.

Patrik, L. (1986). "Is There an Archaeological Record?" *Advances in Archaeological Method and Theory* 8: 27–62.

Paya, D. (2009). "Aux portes de Toulouse, le cimetière mérovingien et carolingien du Mouraut (Vernet, Haute-Garonne)." *Gausac* 34–35: 273–291.

Périn, P. (1978). "Edward James, *The Merovingian Archaeology of Southwest Gaul* (British Archaeological Reports Supplementary Series, 25, 1–2)." *Bulletin Monumental* 136: 192–202.

Périn, P., and Kazanski, M. (2011). "Identity and Ethnicity during the Era of Migrations and Barbarian Kingdoms in the Light of Archaeology in Gaul." In R. Mathisen and D. Shanzer (eds.), *Romans, Barbarians, and the Transformation of the Roman World: Cultural Interactions and the Creation of Identity in Late Antiquity* (pp. 299–330). Farnham: Ashgate.

Pinar, J. (2013) "A Crossroads Of Cultures in a Mosaic of Regions? The Early Visigothic Regnum From the Perspective of Small Finds." *Archeologia Baltica* 18: 103–117.

Pinar, J., and Ripoll, G. (2007) "Männergräber in Aquitanien, Septimanien und Hispanien (ca. 450–520). Neue Überlegungen." *Acta Praehistorica et Archaeologica* 39: 65–92.

Poulain, R. (2004). "Les plaques-boucles de ceinture de bronze à figurations chrétiennes dans l'est de la Gaule mérovingienne (Bourgogne, Franche-Comté, Suisse romande): étude critique." PhD Thesis. Université de Paris I—Panthéon Sorbonne.

Roger, R. (1908). "Cimetière barbare de Tabariane, commune de Teilhet (Ariège)." *Bulletin de la Société ariégoise des sciences, lettres et arts*: 73–84.

Rosand, D. (1981). "Composition/Decomposition/Recomposition: Notes on the Fragmentary and the Artistic Process." In L. Kritzman (ed.), *Fragments: Incompletion and Discontinuity* (pp. 17–30). New York: New York Literary Forum.

Salin, É. (1952). *La civilisation mérovingienne: d'après les sépultures, les textes et le laboratoire 2.* Paris: Picard.

Sarti, Laury. (2013). *Perceiving War and the Military in Early Christian Gaul (ca. 400–700 A.D.).* Leiden: Brill.

Shanks, M. (1997). "Photography and Archaeology." In B. Molyneaux (ed.), *The Cultural Life of Images: Visual Representation in Archaeology* (pp. 73–107). London: Routledge.

Sommer, M. (1984). *Die Gürtel und Gürtelbeschläge des 4. und 5. Jahrhunderts in römischen Reich.* Bonn: Rheinische Friedrich-Wilhelms-Universität.

Stutz, F. (1999). "L'inhumation habillée à l'époque mérovingienne au sud de la Loire." *Mémoires de la Société Archéologique du Midi de la France* 60: 33–49.

Stutz, F. (2003). "Les objets mérovingiens de type septentrional dans la moitié sud de la Gaule." PhD Thesis, Université Aix-Marseille I.

Theuws, F., and M. Alkemade (2000). "A Kind of Mirror for Men: Sword Depositions in Late Antique Northern Gaul." In F. Theuws and J. Nelson (eds.), *Rituals of Power from Late Antiquity to the Early Middle Ages* (pp. 401–476). Leiden: Brill.

Treffort, C. (2002). "Vertus prophylactiques et sense eschatologique d'un dépot funéraire du haut Moyen Age: les plaques-boucles rectangulaires burgondes à l'inscription." *Archéologie médiévale* 32: 31–53.

Vallet, F. (1978). "Plaques-boucles de Tabariane (Ariège) au Musée des Antiquités Nationales." *Antiquités Nationales* 10: 65–73.

Vidal, M. (1991). "La nécropole mérovingienne de Rivel à Venerque (Haute-Garonne): Synthèse des résultats." In P. Périn (ed.), *Gallo-romains, wisigoths et francs en Aquitaine, Septimanie et Espagne* (pp. 189–204). Rouen: Association française d'archéologie mérovingienne.

von Rummel, P. (2007). *Habitus Barbarus: Kleidung und Repräsentation spätantiker Eliten im 4. und 5. Jahrhundert*. Berlin: Walter de Gruyter.

Weiner, A. (1992). *Inalienable Possessions: The Paradox of Keeping-While-Giving*. Berkeley: University of California Press.

Werner, J. (1970). "Zur Verbreitung frühmittelalterlicher Metallarbeiten (Werkstatt-Wanderhandwerk-Handel-Familienverbindung)." *Early Medieval Studies* 1: 65–81.

Wild, G. (1999). "La genèse du cimetière médiéval urbain: l'exemple de la topographie funéraire de Toulouse (vers 250–1350)." *Archéologie du Midi médiéval* 17: 1–24.

Williams, H. (2006). *Death And Memory in Early Medieval Britain*. Cambridge: Cambridge University Press.

Young, B. (1992). "Text Aided or Text Misled? Reflections on the Uses of Archaeology in Medieval History." In B. Little (ed.), *Text-Aided Archaeology* (pp. 135–148). Boca Raton, FL: CRC.

Young, B. (2012). "Has Anyone Seen the Barbarians? Remarks on the Missing Archaeology of the Visigoths in Gaul." In R. Mathisen and D. Shanzer (eds.), *The Battle of Vouillé, 507 CE: Where France Began* (pp. 183–202). Berlin: Walter de Gruyter.

Young, B. (2016). "The Imagery of Personal Objects: Hints of 'Do-It-Yourself' Christian Culture in Merovingian Gaul?" In A. Cain and N. Lenski (eds.), *The Power of Religion in Late Antiquity* (339–354). New York: Routledge.

Zeller, G. (1996). "Tracht der Frauen." In *Die Franken—Wegbereiter Europas* 2 (pp. 672–683). Mainz: Philipp von Zabern.

Archival Sources

Boube, J., and Fouet, G. (1956). *Le cimetière barbare de Gelleneuve (Gers)*. Toulouse. Service Régional de l'Archéologie.

Cartron, I., and Castex, D. (2010). *Du temple antique à la chapelle Saint-Simeon: L'occupation d'un ancien "îlot" du rivage de l'estuaire de la Gironde*. Bordeaux: Service Régional de l'Archéologie.

Cartron, I., Castex, D., and Sachau-Carcel, G. (2013) *Saint-Martin, Bruch (Lot-et-Garonne)*. Bordeaux: Service Régional de l'Archéologie, 47: 5834–5832.

Deguilloux, M.-F., Pemonge, M.-H., Thibon, D., and Castex, D. (2010). "Analyse de parenté par l'approche paléogénétique." In I. Cartron and D. Castex (eds.), *Du temple antique à la chapelle Saint-Simeon: L'occupation d'un ancien "îlot" du rivage de l'estuaire de la Gironde*. Bordeaux: Service Régional de l'Archéologie.

Delbos, G. (1966). *Rapport: Fouilles archéologiques de Faycelles, campagne 1966*. Toulouse: Service Régional de l'Archéologie.

Duhamel, C. (1995). *L'Isle-Jourdain "La Gravette" DFS de sauvetage urgent: 1ère operation* 1. Toulouse: Service Régional de l'Archéologie de Midi-Pyrénées.

Maury, M. (2013). *Luxé "Les Sablons": Rapport d'opération de fouilles archéologiques*. Bordeaux: Archéosphère.

Paya, D. (2003). "Analyse des pratiques funéraires en Midi-Pyrénées et en Languedoc durant les premiers temps chrétiens." In J.-L. Boudartchouk (ed.), *Projet Collectif de Recherche: L'époque mérovingienne en Midi-Pyrénées: État de la question et perspectives* (pp. 154–166). Toulouse: Service Régional d'Archéologie.

Poignant, S. (2004). *Document final de synthèse: Chasseneuil-sur-Bonnieure (Charente) Nécropole Saint-Saturnin*. Poitiers: Service Régional de l'Archéologie.

Portet, N. (2003). *Nécropole mérovingienne de Tabariane (commune de Teilhet, Ariège): fouille programmée, rapport intermédiaire*. Toulouse: Service Régional de l'Archéologie de Midi-Pyrénées. RAP 02650.

Vidal, M. (1982). *Haute-Garonne, nécropole mérovingienne de Rivel à Venerque*. Toulouse: Service Régional de l'Archéologie.

Vidal, M. (1984). *Venerque—Nécropole de Rivel (Haute-Garonne – 1984)*. Toulouse: Service Régional de l'Archéologie.

PART VIII

....

THE SUPERNATURAL AND THE AFTERLIFE

....

CHAPTER 40

···

AMULETS AND IDENTITY
IN THE MEROVINGIAN
WORLD

···

GENEVRA KORNBLUTH

AMULETS have a peculiar place in modern scholarship. They speak to beliefs about the intersection of material and invisible worlds, and so they might be part of a discourse about religion, but they generally lack the kind of overt theological underpinning and liturgical expression that easily lend themselves to discussion. Some could be classified as magical, but their owners often do not consider them as such (on magic, see Klingshirn, Chapter 41, this volume). Their use is widespread through most cultures and periods, so they can be ethnographically studied over the very longue durée. But while the appearance of the same materials in ancient Greek and nineteenth-century contexts suggests historical continuity of interest, it does not explain how such materials functioned in any one society. The Merovingian world was awash in amulets, from bear claws to pendants of gemstone and gold (accessible introduction: Meaney 1981; Merovingian: Dübner-Manthey 1985, Arends 1978). The objects are carefully recorded by archaeologists and exhibited in museum displays of grave assemblages, but their social functions have largely been ignored. Indeed, most current scholarship is either largely ahistorical or purely typological. This chapter introduces some of the dominant forms of early medieval amulets, focusing on one type—the bound pendant—to draw out insights into how these artifacts functioned in the construction of Merovingian identity.

At the most general level, amulets may be defined as objects carried or worn on the body to ward off injury or promote recovery from it. They are thought to act by means other than purely physical barriers to harm. In our own society, a rabbit's foot might be carried as an amulet, just as a cross or hand of Fatima might serve a similar purpose. It is of course impossible to be sure why any object is carried or worn without interrogating the wearer, so absolute certainty in historical interpretation is impossible. Scholars tend to identify as amulets the objects found in inhumation burials close to or on the body, for which no practical physical function is known. Many such objects are highly decorative and probably served as ornaments; but even the most beautiful jewelry has many functions beyond those that are purely aesthetic.

The Merovingian objects whose amuletic function is most clear are not, however, the most beautiful. They are natural objects only slightly modified for wear, mostly animal teeth, claws, antler segments, and shells. Such objects have little in common with those highly crafted items that demonstrate early medieval aesthetic preferences. Unlike the most common bead forms, they are not brightly colored (see Pion et al., Chapter 36, this volume), and unlike most jewelry and luxury items, they are not highly reflective. None received elaborate metalwork mounts. Instead they were simply pierced at one end, with a loop of wire or organic material passing through the hole. That loop allowed them to be suspended on the body, most often attached to the chains or long bands (usually now lost but frequently attested by surviving small plaques in neat rows) that descended from a woman's or child's waist or near it (Fig. 40.1) (on gender, see Halsall, Chapter 8, this volume; on children, see Perez, Chapter 9, this volume). It is precisely the difference from clearly decorative objects that most strongly suggests an artifact's amuletic value.

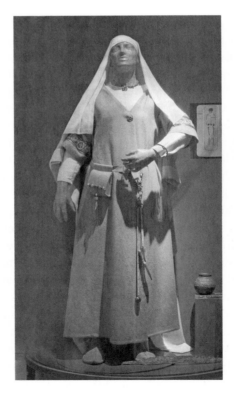

FIGURE 40.1. Amulet bands, material from Szentendre grave 56, ca. 550–570, displayed on reconstructed clothing. Budapest, Hungarian National Museum. Photo © Genevra Kornbluth.

NATURAL AMULETS

Bear teeth and claws (Fig. 40.2) are situated in a well-documented conceptual framework. Gregory of Tours listed bear claws and fat among the deceptive stock-in-trade of a would-be holy man (Gregory of Tours, *Libri Historiarum X*, p. 419). As a fierce proponent of exclusively saintly power, Gregory cast such items in a negative light, but his remarks reinforce the suggestion by archaeological evidence that they were valued and that contemporaries attributed some kind of power to them. In the first century BCE/CE along the Elbe and Rhine river systems, and continuing through the Viking era in Denmark and Scandinavia, full bear skins (without heads but with claws) were buried under or over both male and female bodies, perhaps as status markers (Wamers 2009). Individuals living in the Merovingian era, however, normally buried pierced claws and teeth (like the other objects discussed later in this chapter) with women or children, not with men. Under Carolingian rulers the ability to hunt for bears and other dangerous predators, long a hallmark of the elite, shifted from a communal to a purely masculine activity (Goldberg 2013; legal evidence: Jarnut 1985), and that association with masculinity became enshrined in later medieval literature (Oehrl 2013). The continuity of

FIGURE 40.2. Claw and tooth amulets from Schretzheim. Dillingen, Stadt- u. Hochstiftmuseum. Photo © Genevra Kornbluth.

interest in bears' teeth and claws—before, during, and after the Merovingian era—joins with Gregory's testimony to make their identification as amulets reasonable. There may have been some connection between bears and fertility, as suggested by broad anthropological and folkloric studies (Kivisalo 2008).[1] But the clear shifts in gender associations, from ungendered (pre-Merovingian) to feminine (Merovingian) to masculine (Carolingian) to ungendered (Viking Scandinavia), show that the significance of bears was nuanced. We cannot assume that a bear claw or tooth served the same social functions through the whole early medieval period.

Rarely do we have textual evidence to help interpret specific archaeologically attested amulets. Some appear to have been valued because of their own or their sources' anthropomorphism. The bear was plausible as the heroic opponent of a warrior in part because it fights standing on its back legs, grabbing and clawing with its forelegs (Wamers 2009; Isidore, *Etymologies* XII.ii.22, p. 253). Cowrie shells, more common than bear claws and teeth in Merovingian burials, visually resemble the human vulva when pierced at one end to hang vertically (Fig. 40.3). In prehistoric cultures, pharaonic Egypt, and modern Oceania, cowrie shells have been worn on aprons or otherwise suspended over the womb and genital areas, and have been thought to enhance fertility (Kóvacs and Radócz 2008).[2] The writings of the ninth-century bishop Hincmar of Reims may reflect such an

FIGURE 40.3. Cowrie shell amulet, unprovenanced. Cologne, Römisch-Germanisches Museum D708. Photo © Genevra Kornbluth.

association with reproduction, since he listed snail shells (though not specifically cowries: *clocleolis, cocleolis*) among the tools witches used to disturb marital relations (Hincmar of Reims, *De Divortio,* p. 206, 14). But their burial with very young children suggests that, like the phalluses omnipresent at Roman sites, they were principally apotropaic (Lennartz 2004). The shells were not locally available to the Merovingians, but had to be imported from the Red Sea and Indo-Pacific Ocean. The resources that went into their acquisition tell us how important they must have been to their owners.

CRAFTED AMULETS

Unlike the claws and shells that could be collected already formed and that humans needed only to pierce, other objects were completely crafted. Many objects were produced for different uses and were later transformed into amulets. Coins, minted both locally and in the Roman Empire (East and West), are among the most common of these (Bursche 2008; on Merovingian coins, see Strothmann, Chapter 35, this volume) (Fig. 40.4). Some coins probably retained a sense of their monetary value, especially when collected together and held in a purse, as famously done at Sutton Hoo in East Anglia. Single coins placed inside the mouth of the deceased, a practice that continued in Merovingian Gaul, seem to have reflected belief in something like Charon's obol, paying for passage to the afterlife. But a great many coins were, like teeth and shells, pierced and/or fitted with suspension loops (Codine-Trecourt 2014; Audy 2015), and hung on

FIGURE 40.4. Coin pendant, "third brass" antoninianus of Carus (deified 284–285), Mosel/Rhine region. London, British Museum 1902,1108.39. Photo © The Trustees of the British Museum.

long bands. The act of suspension lifted them out of the monetary context and placed them among amulets (Meaney 1981, pp. 213–222; Kemmers and Myrberg 2011). When pseudo-coin pendants were made in the Byzantine East, explicitly apotropaic inscriptions were added to them ("health," "use with good fortune"), documenting their protective functions (Maguire 1997, p. 1042). Even without such words, some owners may have worn them to benefit from an emperor's saving power, as in the East (Maguire 1997, pp. 1039–1040). But whether imperial or royal, coins' imagery and inscriptions probably evoked power just as surely as the teeth or claws of a large predator did. The same may be true of Roman glass or silver vessels, engraved ring stones, and the like. These high-prestige items (Ament 1991) could have served the same practical functions as the more common locally produced versions. But it appears that sometimes fragments of such items, fragments much too small to have been used for their original purposes—particularly, for some reason, shards of blue glass—were interred with the dead. These fragments could not contain food, drink, perfume, or any other perishable. Instead, their presence probably signaled their symbolic and/or amuletic function (Mehling 1998; Pion 2012).

Both natural and repurposed amulets have a certain complexity. I choose, however, to focus on a third category, whose complexity is both more overt and more directly subject to analysis: objects produced specifically for use as Merovingian amulets. Such production entailed considerable effort and expense, and many choices had to be made by both patrons and artisans. Not limited by components already formed, the objects reflect purposeful choices of materials and shapes. Among amulet types in this category are keys, miniature weapons and tools, spindle whorls, large beads, bracteates, and bound pendants. Many of these objects are physically quite practical, but their forms go far beyond physical necessity. Some are very decorative, and all appear to have had apotropaic functions. Practical iron keys have been found in many Merovingian burials. Such normal keys were gradually supplanted by pairs of key-like objects ("latch-lifters" or "girdle-hangers") in silver or bronze. Generally devoid of the abrasion marks that come from locking and unlocking, these objects ultimately developed forms that could not even fit inside contemporary locks (Steuer 1982). Usable weapons are among the best known features of Merovingian burials, though their significance is disputed. While key-like objects became very large, weapons sometimes became very small, miniaturized and buried with women (Schienerl 1984). All of these objects were probably amuletic, though they lack the helpful inscriptions of bracteates (single-sided coin-like pendants sometimes inscribed with the saying "I give luck") (Wicker 2010). Spindle whorls of course had practical physical usage, twisting and lengthening fibers in conjunction with a drop spindle, but many were considerably more elaborate than necessary for that use. There is a large corpus of green glass whorls with trailed and combed white designs (Willemsen 2014). In addition, over 250 elaborately faceted whorls survive, around 40 in opaque glass but most cut from rock crystal. Surface wear shows that while some were used in spinning, others were carried for long periods as pendants (Kornbluth 2015). Some were worn on necklaces or strings of beads across the chest, but many others were attached to the same long bands as claws and teeth, along with isolated large beads on suspension loops (Figs. 40.1 and 40.5). Also connected to those long bands were some of the most distinctive Merovingian amulets: bound pendants.

BOUND PENDANTS: FEATURES AND POWERS

Bound pendants from Merovingian Gaul consist of varied materials, usually stone, held in cages of metal straps (Figs. 40.5–40.12). They have (or had) suspension loops attached at the top, unlike stones mounted in rings or on larger objects. While they are closely related to other forms, they are distinguished by technical criteria: they are not primarily supported by wires or fibers running through a central hole. A bead may be strung, sometimes with a knot or knob below to stop it from falling off. A bound pendant, by contrast, is supported by the metal straps that surround it. And unlike regular necklace pendants that are normally framed by metalwork around the edges, leaving the central field of stone or other material clear, the settings of bound pendants usually cross over front and back as well.

Location within burials reveals how these and other objects were worn. Like most Merovingian artifacts, amulets are known almost entirely from funerary archaeology (see Theuws, Chapter 38, and Effros, Chapter 4, this volume; Kornbluth 2016b). Although each body was dressed by others for burial, and the items arrayed on it might not all have been worn every day or together, it seems reasonable to assume that objects were usually placed in their normal positions. A bracelet would probably not be put on an ear, nor an earring on a foot. Of the 211 bound pendants I have so far documented from known sites

FIGURE 40.5. Large beads and bound pendant (rock crystal and silver) from Giberville grave 27 on reconstructed band. Caen, Musée de Normandie, pendant: 79.4.80. Photo © Genevra Kornbluth.

of the Merovingian era in modern France, Germany, Belgium, the Netherlands, Italy, Switzerland, and Hungary, 84 can be localized within burials (Hinz 1966; Kornbluth forthcoming).[3] Of those, only 11 were placed at the neck or chest.[4] Sixty-four were found around the legs, most often between them (forty-five examples) but sometimes to one side (fourteen examples). So while bound pendants could be worn on a necklace or otherwise held at the upper body, it was more typical for them to hang at the legs. And counterintuitive though the observation is, it was not only the lighter pendants that were centered: unusually large examples were also found between the knees, for example, in Straubing-Bajuwarenstrasse grave 465 (weight 100 grams/3.5 ounces; Giesler 1998). Either these people did not walk much when wearing the pendants or enough cloth padded their legs to keep them from being bruised. In any case, we know that the objects were indeed worn and not newly made for burial, because most of them are abraded from wear, and some were repaired or altered before interment.[5]

Why, then, did people wear these pendants? Like other objects worn with them, they were probably apotropaic. Over half of the 211 pendants mentioned earlier hold rock crystal (naturally occurring quartz: 120 examples or 57 percent). Gemstones were thought to have invisible powers, considered natural by some and supernatural by others, that could ward off the evil eye and other harmful forces. Rock crystal was classified as such a precious gem. Gregory of Tours, for example, testified to its high value, though he praised its beauty rather than any other quality (Gregory of Tours *Glory of the Martyrs*, p. 68, chapter 45). Several early medieval texts refer to the helpful powers of crystal (Kornbluth 2016a), which they name either with variants of the Latin *cristallum* or with a color descriptor, white rather than transparent or colorless as in our day. St. Boniface (d. 754), for example, metaphorically described divine wisdom as more shining-white than crystal (*candidior crystallo*) (Boniface *Epistolae*, p. 250, letter no. 9). When the stone has many internal flaws or negative crystals, it does indeed look white even to a modern viewer (Fig. 40.6). But pendants were also made with darker stone (Fig. 40.7), sometimes termed smoky quartz or topaz in the older literature.[6] While there are some variations in the stones used in different regions (perhaps due to availability or preference), I have found no indication that their interpretation depended on their relative darkness or lightness (Kornbluth 2020).

The most explicit texts on the power of crystal use color terms. In the Insular Life of Columba written by St. Adamnan (628–704), several miracles were performed using such a stone taken from a river (*lapidem de flumine candidum*) (Adamnan *Life of Columba*, I i, 7a and II 33, 79b–81a, pp. 196–197 and 398–405). In a text written to celebrate the capabilities of a saint, healing power was of course attributed to the holy man rather than to the physical object. In a slightly later secular text, the Old English *Bald's Leechbook*, probably compiled in the ninth century, that power was attributed to the rock itself: "The white stone (*se hwita stan*) is good for stitch and flying venom, and for all strange mishaps. You must scrape it into water and drink a good deal and scrape a part of the red earth into it; and the stones are all very good to drink from against all unknown things." (Bald, *Leechbook* 2.64, pp. 290–291; Meaney 1978; Garrett 1909, pp. 63–64).[7]

FIGURE 40.6. Bound pendant from Maastricht St. Servaeskerk Pandhof grave 418, rock crystal and silver, third quarter of sixth- to seventh-century. City of Maastricht MST 418. Photo © Genevra Kornbluth.

The next most popular raw material, iron ore (50 of the 211 pendants studied here, or 24 percent), is more ambiguous (Herdick 2001). It was generally used in naturally occurring nodules of roughly spherical form, called in scholarly literature everything from "Bohnerz" to pyrite. But those nodules could be smooth and dark brown, black or bluish with pebbly surfaces, brown to yellow, or irregular in both texture and color (Figs. 40.8 and 40.9). Only a few are still lustrous. Without knowing how much the ores were polished and what color the surfaces formerly revealed, we cannot know how they would have been classified by their original users. Textual evidence is full of fine distinctions. Pliny the Elder (23–79 CE) and his successors differentiated between pyrites that were porous or gold or silver, hematites that were brownish-yellow, mottled "iron stone" and "mountain stone," and other variants, each of which had different helpful and healing properties (Pliny the Elder *Naturalis Historia*, 34.138–156, vol. 9, pp. 228–241). A circle drawn with iron could protect both adults and infants from noxious drugs. Rust healed wounds, and flakes from the wrought metal were good against bleeding, menstrual discharge, and hemorrhoids. Dioscorides (ca. 40–90 CE), known in Latin translation by the sixth century, prescribed liquid that had quenched hot iron for "colic, dysentery, spleen disease, cholera, and for a slackened stomach" (Dioscorides, *De materia medica*

FIGURE 40.7. Bound pendant from Cologne cathedral grave 808 found with coin dated 526–534, rock crystal and gold. Cologne Domschatzkammer, F536 1/11700. Photo © Genevra Kornbluth.

FIGURE 40.8. Bound pendant from Arcy-Sainte-Restitue grave 3047, iron ore and silver. St-Germain-en-Laye, Musée d'Archéologie Nationale 36301. Photo © Genevra Kornbluth.

FIGURE 40.9. Bound pendant from Cologne St-Severin grave V, 217, first third of the sixth century, iron ore in silver. Cologne, Römisch-Germanisches Museum 57,101. Photo © Genevra Kornbluth.

V, 80, pp. 366–367; Riddle 1980, pp. 20–23). Solinus's third-century reworking of Pliny mentioned that pyrite could burn the hand holding it too firmly (Solinus, *Collectanea rerum memorabilium* 30, 34, and 37, 16, pp. 136, 159), a characteristic also mentioned by Augustine in the early fifth century (Augustine, *City of God* 21.5, p. 456). The fifth- or sixth-century Latin version of the *Orphic Lapidary* claimed that spheroidal *orite* can heal all animal bites; when tied on the body, it relaxes tendons and is beneficial against all ills (*ligatus facit contra omnia maleficia et <ad> omnes dolores expellendos*) (*Orphic Lapidary*, pp. 253–255, 285). Isidore of Seville (ca. 560–636) both repeated material from Pliny and added information about hematite from Egypt, Bablyonia, and his native Spain: red only when ground (i.e., when the iron is exposed and rusts), "otherwise a dark bluish color, also purplish," it "preserves rather than corrodes the body" (Isidore, *Etymologies* 16.4.16, p. 320).

We cannot say whether the ores bound in pendants were thought to be hematite, pyrite, siderite, or some other particular variety. But most of them retain at least a slight metallic appearance even now, which doubtless was more pronounced originally, and they are noticeably heavy compared to other materials of comparable size. They were

FIGURE 40.10. Bound pendant from Picquigny, rock crystal in gold. Oxford, Ashmolean Museum 1909.661a. Photo © Genevra Kornbluth.

probably recognized as iron of some sort, and according to the textual evidence, all kinds of iron were thought to have useful powers. It is no stretch to read the pendants holding iron ores as medicinal and amuletic.

The remaining bound pendants under study here hold a variety of materials, mostly pebbles or smoothed stones (fourteen pendants, or 6.6 percent) and glass (thirteen to fifteen pendants, or 6.2–7.1 percent). Four contain game pieces, two hold glass spindle whorls, and two enclose fossilized sea urchins (Fig. 40.11). For each material, there is some evidence suggesting apotropaic value. Game pieces, for example, evoke the connection between the ludic and the amuletic, much like the fuzzy dice that still occasionally hang in cars (Kornbluth forthcoming; bound game piece from Mülhofen: Grunwald 1998, pp. 67, 206, plate 100/8). And in most cases, it appears that one such amulet per person was enough: it is very rare for two to be found in an individual burial. In the few graves with more than one bound pendant, the materials held are different. In various burials, crystal was paired with iron ore, with an engraved agate, with an organic material, or with millefiori glass. Iron ore accompanied green glass. One small black bound stone was worn at the neck, while a larger brown stone was carried on a band at the lower legs. Doubled pendants might have deployed the diverse invisible powers of various substances.

FIGURE 40.11. Bound pendant from Friedberg grave 8, fossil sea urchin in silver. Darmstadt, Hessisches Landesmuseum, Friedberg II.B.40. Photo © Genevra Kornbluth.

BOUND PENDANTS: GENDER AND AGE ASSOCIATIONS

So, who were the people who used these amulets? In every case where the sex of the individual buried with a bound pendant has been anthropologically determined (53 cases of the 211), the deceased was female. The bound pendants can therefore contribute to a discussion of gender (Arnold 2007; see Halsall, Chapter 8, this volume). Guy Halsall has defined masculine and feminine grave assemblages for the area around Metz: objects that were buried in coherent, nonoverlapping groups and that can be associated with two distinct sexes defined by anthropological examination of skeletons (Halsall 1995; Stoodley 1999; Dickinson 2002; problems with early sexing: Effros 2000). The groups vary from cemetery to cemetery but have enough in common to delineate gendered burial. The feminine kit usually included bracelets, necklaces, and earrings. Knives could accompany those items but in some locations were part of the masculine assemblage.

Spindle whorls, long bands or chains starting at the waist or near it, and shells could be included in the feminine assemblage. The masculine kit typically included weapons (swords, spears, axes, scramasaxes), buckles and belt fittings, purse fasteners, keys (though not latch lifters), and bronze needles. Most burials were not, in fact, given either gender assemblage: archaeologically ungendered graves greatly outnumber gendered ones. Apparently, it was not invariably thought necessary to express feminine or masculine gender in burial, but in the Metz region that option was always available.

The 113 bound pendants studied here come from 108 continental burials that were sufficiently complete for their assemblages to be evaluated (including 41 that could be anthropologically sexed).[8] The most numerous finds are jewelry and other items that call attention to the appearance of the body, in line with the feminine assemblage defined by Halsall. One hundred of these burials contained beads in glass and/or amber. Other such items include fibulae (98 graves: 29 with sets of four fibulae; 60 with bow fibulae, 51 with disk, saucer, or rosette fibulae, 13 with bird fibulae, 10 with S fibulae, 6 with quadruped fibulae, and 5 with various other forms); buckles (79 graves); strap or belt ends, plaques, and fittings (55); pins, including hair pins (41); finger rings (29); bracelets or arm rings (25); and earrings (19–21). Many finds are both decorative and probably amuletic: 20 graves held coins known to be pierced or provided with suspension loops (another 3–4 held unmodified coins, and 8 had coins of unknown configuration); 20 contained bracteates and other pendants; 14 held pierced disks; 10 included shells, in 8 cases cowries; 10 held keys or latch-lifters; 3–5 had animal teeth/claws/bone clubs; 2 had antler rings, and 2 had potsherds pierced or held in a pouch. Five graves contained additional stones of the types used in bound pendants, but not mounted: crystal, iron ore, and fossil sea urchins. Four graves held crosses. Textile equipment was often included: spindle whorls, mostly ceramic but also amber, bone, glass, and stone (18—20 graves); and other equipment including needles, scissors, weaving battens, and a loom or loom weights (21). Some items seem very utilitarian: knives or scrapers (72—76 graves); vessels in ceramic, glass, copper alloy, or wood (62—64 graves); combs (32), sometimes with cases; wide rings (48); and spoons (14–15, known to be perforated: 9).

While feminine assemblages have not been defined for all of the cemeteries involved, the bound pendants as such appear to be firmly gendered. They were buried with types of objects that call attention to the body and with textile-working equipment. Fiber- and cloth-making is, of course, stereotypically feminine activity, but some textual evidence suggests that the stereotype largely held true between the fifth and eighth centuries. A poem of Sidonius Apollinaris (461/462) made the ideal groom philosophize while the ideal bride produced cloth and clothing (Sidonius Apollinaris, *Carmen* 15). Bishop Martin of Braga in 573 worried about the deity invoked by women at their looms (*mulieres in tela sua*), and the Council of Braga in 579 admonished them to call on God during wool working (*mulieres… in suis lanificiis*) (Martin of Braga *De correctione rusticorum* 16, pp. 66–69, dated p. 11; Council chapter 75: Herlihy 1990, pp. 25, 34–35). And in 789, Charlemagne decreed that the Sabbath should be kept by avoiding customary labor in public:

men are not to engage in rural work by cultivating the vines, ploughing the fields, reaping. . . . Further, women are not to engage in cloth-working or to cut out clothes or to sew or to embroider; they are not to be allowed to card wool, to break flax, to launder in public or to shear sheep.

(Charlemagne *Admonitio generalis*, pp 218–219)

More of the pendants' graves lacked textile-working equipment than included it, but the number of such tools is still significant. So too is the number of other amulets buried with the bound pendants. Fifty-six graves (just over half) contained some amulets besides the pendants themselves, suggesting that the different amulets may have been intended to function in tandem. It has been proposed that perforated spoons were meant to work together with Anglo-Saxon crystal pendants in such a way, perhaps to strain wine that a crystal might cool, emphasizing a woman's role in hospitality (e.g., Meaney 1981, pp. 82–88). Since only nine Continental graves held such "sieve spoons" (with another four that may have been perforated), and in only four of those nine cases (and two possibles) did the pendants hold rock crystal, that function seems unlikely here. Nonetheless, the correlation with feminine-gendered objects is strong. Equally noteworthy is the very low number of pendant graves that appear to be gender neutral. Only eight burials (7.4 percent) lacked beads, and those are the same graves that contained very few fibulae or pins, no bracelets, finger rings, or strap ends, only one possible earring, and no textile working equipment.

If, as I argue, bound pendants were gendered as feminine, then, in addition to their amuletic functions, they must have helped to build and manifest the feminine identity of their wearers, in life and/or in death. The pendants were not, however, simply given to anyone born female (judging from their rarity in child burials), nor were they necessarily retained by older women. In sixty-one cases, it has been possible to estimate anthropologically the age of the person with whom the pendants were buried. Various archaeologists have defined the stages of the life cycle in different ways, so an individual described as an "adult" in one cemetery report may be slightly older or younger than the "adult" in another; but in most cases the variation is no more than a few years (Lohrke 2004; Stauch, 2008, 2012), so it is possible to draw at least rough conclusions.

In the Merovingian period, most bound pendants were buried with women of childbearing age. Among the sixty-one aged incumbents, thirteen were classed as young adults between eighteen and thirty years of age and thirty-eight as adults eighteen to forty years of age (mostly undifferentiated but including the "young adults": 62.3 percent). Another two incumbents might have been as old as sixty, and another one between twenty and sixty-nine. The biological age for burial with bound pendants closely corresponds to the socially constructed age of maturity and maximum "value." Girls were old enough to marry at the end of the twelfth year according to the *Leges Langobardorum* (Liutprand 12.6, 111 [112], pp. 410, 455; *The Lombard Laws* 1973, pp. 148–149, 192), and both girls and boys came to majority at twelve according to the *Lex Salica* (*Pactus Legis Salicae* 24.1, 24.4, 24.7, 65e.2, pp. 89–92, 235; *The Laws of the Salian Franks* 1991, pp. 86, 127) and at fifteen according to the *Lex Ribuaria* (*Lex Ribuaria*

84 [81], p. 130; *Laws of the Salian and Ripuarian Franks* 1986, p. 210). In the Mediterranean literature of the same period, such as Oribasius' *Institutes* of Justinian, the age of menarche was expected to be twelve or fourteen (Amundsen and Diers 1969). If the age span of "adults" is increased to begin at age twelve, rather than using the archaeologists' cutoff ages, the number of adults buried with bound pendants increases to forty-three, or 70.5 percent.

Unfortunately, however, we have no northern literature with a similar anatomical focus. The Ripuarian Law code foregrounded a period in a woman's life "from the time that she begins to have children until age forty" (*Lex Ribuaria* 7, 12–13 [13a], 55 [54], pp. 77–79; 103–104; *Laws of the Salian and Ripuarian Franks*, pp. 173, 175, 191). The Salic Law code privileged the woman who was "of mature age up to her sixtieth year, as long as she is able to bear children" (*Pactus Legis Salicae* 24.9, 41.15, and 17). Wherever that age distinction was made, its purpose was to define the period during which the highest sum had to be paid for a woman's injury or death. In both the *Lex Salica* and the *Lex Ribuaria*, free women were normally valued the same as free men, but during their fertile years that amount rose to the value of a count and three times the value of young girls or elderly women (*Pactus Legis Salicae* 24.8, 41.16; 54.1, pp. 90, 160–161, 203; *Laws of the Salian Franks*, p. 127 [65e]). The inclusion of bound pendants in feminine graves probably served in part to mark the special status of fertile women. During her lifetime, such a woman could have worn a pendant to construct and signal her comparatively high standing. And the death of a woman during her childbearing years could easily have merited special treatment because of the social disruption that it caused, upsetting marriage alliances, childrearing, and inheritance (or plans for those arrangements), which would have had to be renegotiated (Hadley and Morre 1999, p. 35).

By contrast, almost no bound pendants were buried with children (5 percent). One incumbent is classed a child, one aged four to eight, and one aged seven to fourteen (Hincker et al. 2011, grave 4005; Koch 2001, grave 94; Koch 1968, Straubing Wittelsbacherhöhe grave 5). Young children may not have been considered to have gender or to be sufficiently enmeshed in the social web to merit such pendants (see Perez, Chapter 9, this volume). Perhaps in recognition of high infant mortality, the *Lex Visigothorum* and the *Pactus Legis Salicae* both specified relatively low compensation for young children (Lohrke 2004, pp. 27–29).

The situation for older women is more complex, particularly since in absolute numbers there are fewer burials of the aged than of the merely mature in any Merovingian cemetery, and skeletons of older individuals are notoriously hard to age accurately. Eleven women (and these were indeed all female) buried with bound pendants were forty years of age or older (18 percent). Of those, eight were at least fifty years old and two at least fifty-five. These women may well have passed menopause. The presumed end of the fertile period is less narrowly defined than its beginning in Mediterranean texts, variously placed between thirty-five and sixty years (Wemple 1981, p. 255 n. 11; Clark 1993, pp. 76–81, 88–89), and we still have little reliable information on the actual biological facts. But if these were postmenopausal women, perhaps it is their changed status that was reflected in less strongly gendered burial. As Eva Stauch has demonstrated, in several south German cemeteries women over sixty were interred with comparatively few textile working tools (Wenigumstadt, Weingarten, Marktoberdorf, Altenerding: Stauch 2012, especially pp. 149–150),[9] a circumstance mirrored in the present corpus: only one spindle whorl (and no loom weights, weaving battens, etc.) was found in the grave of an older woman with a pendant. The burials of elder women still contained fibulae, beads (except for one grave), bracelets, finger rings, and pins, but in small quantities. Perhaps in the normal course of life, such items were passed along to the next generation (Kars 2013). And perhaps a woman who had passed through menopause had to be exceptional (perhaps with particularly strong economic or other power) to require the most elaborate community negotiations at her death.

Variations among the bound pendants probably could have been used to reinforce fine age distinctions, but those possibilities appear not to have been exploited. No one bound material, metal, or type of setting can be associated with any particular age group. But unfortunately, this and all such observations must be regarded as tentative, pending revision. Less than a third of the known bound pendants (28.9 percent) can be included in these age statistics, and, more seriously, relatively little secure information is available for areas outside Germany, Hungary, and Switzerland. Most problematic is France, where among twenty pendant graves with coherent assemblages, only three have been even roughly aged and only three anthropologically sexed (though another five without full assemblages have been aged and four sexed). There could easily be undocumented regional variations in practice.

BOUND PENDANTS: SOCIAL STATUS AND GEOGRAPHIC DISTRIBUTION

Along with age and gender, wealth is a part of identity constructed and manifested by means of bound pendants, though, again, one that can only be assessed through intact burial assemblages. There is no single objective measure of the richness of a grave, and of course there is no assurance that such wealth reflects the affluence of an individual or family, but it probably mirrors the complexity and ostentation of the burial ritual. Most systems for evaluating richness assess the quality and number of types of objects buried, the size and elaboration of the burial chamber, and the location of the grave relative to others in the same cemetery (Christlein 1973; Donat 1989). It has not been possible to take these different factors into account for all of the sites encompassed by this study. One can get a general idea of relative wealth, however, by comparing the numbers of different types of objects in the burials and the variations among fibulae and beads, the items most frequently found in all the graves. Beads could number up to 279, with an average of 52 and a median of 23, and there could be up to six fibulae, on average and median, two. A single burial could contain up to eighteen object types in addition to the pendant, with an average and median of eight. Given the luxury materials involved, the richness of the assemblages will be no revelation. What is perhaps more surprising is that graves containing crystal and iron ore pendants were equally rich, and the one full burial assemblage with a bound fossil was very rich indeed (Nieder-Erlenbach grave 31: Dohrn-Ihmig et al. 1999). This is true despite signs of hierarchy among settings: crystal regardless of size was set in gold, silver, or copper alloy; ores were bound in silver, copper alloy, or iron; glass, organic materials, and stones other than crystal (even engraved gems) were normally put in silver or copper alloy. Crystal was indeed precious, but the ore pendants were apparently not just cheaper substitutes, and neither were fossils. Burials with bound glass, stones other than fossils, and organic pendants appear to have been slightly less rich, so perhaps those materials represented a step down. But as a class, bound pendants were probably markers of high status as well as of feminine gender and adulthood.

Up to this point, I have discussed the pendants as a corpus, but there are of course many differences among them, and those variations are significant for another aspect of identity: geographical location. They help to differentiate one region's people from others, another kind of "us" versus "them." I am not arguing here for ethnic identity. Regional difference is not the same as ethnic difference. Historians have for a long time associated archaeological material with ethnic names, but the linkage between textually attested names and artifacts found in the ground is problematic (Pohl 1991; Jones 1999; Bartlett 2001; Geary 2001; Brather 2004). The evidence that I have assembled here does not, I think, support the paradigm of ethnic self-identification.

There are three major groups of pendant mounts, none of which correlate with burial richness or skeletal age. On the earliest group, appearing in the mid-fifth century and continuing in use through the seventh, the four ends of the supporting bands are bent over at the shoulder of the pendant (Figs. 40.8–40.10). The hooks so produced grasp either the edges of a disk or a thick wire ring that runs horizontally around the shoulder. On another group, the supporting bands continue beyond the shoulder to nearly meet at the top, then bend up to form a four-sided box (Figs. 40.6 and 40.7). That box may be horizontally encircled by another band, capped on top, and/or filled by organic material or metal. In all its variants, this setting is the most common from the first third of the sixth century to the second half of the seventh. On the last pendant group, only one of the major crossing bands actually carries the stone, its two ends usually bent up and pierced where they meet at the top (Fig. 40.12). The other major band does not directly support the bound material's weight, but may encircle it horizontally, or simply pass under the first band. Members of this group are datable from the first quarter of the sixth century to the late sixth/early seventh.

The distribution of pendants divides central Europe into four major regions: the land between the southern Rhine and the Danube, including the Neckar Valley (often termed "Alamannia"; for convenience and to avoid ethnic connotations, this region will be referred to here as the "southeast"); the central and northern Rhineland; the central and northern parts of modern-day France (again for convenience, northern Gaul); and Kent in southeastern England. Kent is outside the scope of this chapter, and will be discussed

FIGURE 40.12. Bound pendant from Saint-Martin-de-Fontenay grave 62, first quarter of the sixth century, iron ore in copper alloy. Caen, Musée de Normandie, D 87.9.62.1. Photo © Genevra Kornbluth.

only when necessary to clarify the situation on the Continent. Other locations have produced too few pendants to constitute clusters.

Judging by numbers, continuity, and longevity, the homeland of wire ring/disk mounts (the earliest form) is in the southeast. Although one mid-fifth-century example comes from northern Gaul, it is quite isolated (Arcy-Sainte-Restitue grave 1777: Wieczorek et al. 1996, p. 846, no. III.4.12.). A gap of a generation or more intervenes before the next dated examples, which then cluster in the first half of the sixth century; and only five undated pendants of this type have been found there. In the southeast, where bound pendants survive in an unbroken sequence from the second half of the fifth century, the earliest examples are also of this type, and it is there that nearly half of the thirty-six wire-ring/disk pendants with known provenance have been found. Only one example comes from the central to northern Rhineland (Cologne, St-Severin grave V, 217: Päffgen 1992), and none from Kent. Wire-ring and disk pendants are visually quite different from others. During the fifth century and possibly later, when a woman wore one in life or death, she proclaimed her residence in or links to the communities of the southeast.

It is impossible to pinpoint the location where box-top mounts first emerged. In most cases, the dating of graves containing them, sometimes spanning a full century, is insufficiently precise for chronological sequencing. Those whose possible dates lie entirely within the first half of the sixth century were found in all four major regions, and the form was popular everywhere. But the fashion for what might be called the classic Merovingian bound pendant, holding a crystal sphere—the type often described as Frankish—appears to have spread through Europe from two centers, one in eastern Kent and one along the Rhine and Neckar rivers.[10] The Kent group is notable for its homogeneity.

All seventeen of the box-top pendants there hold crystal, and only one of the stones is dark and one slightly so. This pattern does not, incidentally, reflect either a lack of the other materials used elsewhere or a dislike of them. Iron ore nodules have been found in many burials in England. They simply show no evidence of having been bound.

A larger group of eighty-nine box-top pendants has been found in the southeast and the areas to its north along the Rhine River (with a gap between the Main and the Mosel, modern Wiesbaden, and Koblenz). Crystal box-top pendants, first datable there around 525–570, constitute 66.3 percent of the total. Excluding dark stones brings that figure down to 48.3 percent, and excluding crystal left in its natural hexagonal prisms—which among provenanced pendants is found only in this region—brings it down to 43.8–44.9 percent. Clear spheroid crystal was not the only choice for box-top pendants in this large area. The materials bound already included one ivory game piece and several iron ore nodules in the sixth century. Materials in this group assumed even greater variety in the seventh century. The pendants hold dark and white stones, an ore nodule, black, green, and millefiori glass, sandstone, and a fossil sea urchin. There are also undated examples from this region with almost all of these materials, even another fossil, otherwise unknown in the Merovingian corpus. Noticeably dark crystal is far more common in this area than in others: of twenty-four dark box-top pendants overall, seventeen are from this area. While the box-top setting was popular in the southeast and on the Rhine to its north (which for this class of object form essentially one single territory), it was not there associated only with clear crystal balls, as in Kent.

West of the Rhine in northern Gaul is an additional cluster of box tops, though a cluster that was always much less dense than the others. The eight objects that can be narrowly dated begin in the mid-sixth century, after box-top pendants had become common elsewhere. The earliest ones were found directly on the Channel coast (La Caloterie: *Trésors Archéologiques du Nord de la France*, pp. 140–147, no. 192/12; Frénouville grave 603: Pilet 1980). Others nearby can be dated to the second half of the century, and in the seventh century more were buried further inland. These few closely datable pendants appear to have spread inland from the Channel, suggesting a possible link with Kent. That suggestion is reinforced when less-well-dated pendants are added in (for a total of twenty-six). The materials bound are less diverse than in the Rhine group. Twenty-one of the pendants hold crystal (80.8 percent, though 65.4 percent if one excludes dark stones); the others contain ore and, in one case, an unidentified opaque stone. While not dispositive, the choice of materials is closer to the Kent fashion than to the polyglot selection further east. The region of northern Gaul was probably a follower in pendant usage, not a leader. For at least part of its history, the stereotypical Merovingian bound crystal was more likely Kentish in flavor than Frankish. When fashion in northern Gaul changed around the middle of the sixth century, from iron ore bound in wire-ring/disk settings (as in the southeast) to shaped crystals with box-top mounts (as in Kent), it may well have signaled a changing sense of intercommunity and/or interpersonal connections. (If these objects were ethnic signifiers, we would have to think of a change in the population of northern Gaul around 550 and ask why the western Franks never showed any sense of kinship with the Franks of the northern Rhine.) When people started burying the crystal box tops in northern Gaul, they may well have been proclaiming strengthened social/political/economic ties across the water.[11] Once the new fashion was established, of course, it probably became an aspect of local culture. It must have been part of the "look" that told others from whence one came.

The regions that I have been discussing are quite large. Within each region there must have been many more local styles. Within the southeast, for example, glass was much more often bound in the southern Rhine Valley than elsewhere (Theune-Vogt 2002). And the area just west of the Rhine between the Main and the Neckar rivers is home to more than the usual sprinkling of crystal bound in copper alloy, as is another small area on the Rhine just north of the Mosel.

In northern Gaul, wire-ring and disk mounts (visually differentiated, though structurally closely related) were used in slightly different areas; and those areas appear to correlate with the roughly contemporary division of lands among the heirs of Clovis in 511 (Ewig 1952). Although the principles of that division are not fully understood, there may well have been some sense of cultural unity within the boundaries of each of the northern territorial segments. The wire-ring pendants were almost entirely a fashion of the territory allotted to Chlothar. Six of the nine examples from the region were found very close to Soissons, Chlothar's capital according to Gregory of Tours. Another two come from the area just to the north. Only one is certainly from another territory (Dieue-sur-Meuse "Thumelou" grave 14: Guillaume 1974/1975). The two or three disk mounts, on the other hand, have been found in the territory given to Childebert, and perhaps to Theuderic (Maule "Pousse-Motte" grave 807: *L'Île-de-France* 1993, pp. 221–222; 231–232, no. F23; Picquigny: MacGregor et al. 1997, p. 190, no. 82.1; Mézières-Manchester grave 35: Lamont 1968, pp. 9, 24). (Bound pendants of any kind are very rare in the territory allotted to Chlodomer; only one is certainly from there: Paley grave 757, Salin 1949–1959, 4 pp. 97–98, Fig. 17c.) The bound pendants could then have functioned as markers not of ethnicity, but of locational identity even more narrowly defined than by region.

CONCLUSION

Each bound pendant, like other amulets, offered valuable protection to a wearer. But when buried, it also told a story about the woman who wore and/or was interred with it. It named her an adult who was or could be a mother, who had a role in the economic life of her community, and who was linked to the community in a specific place. Whether we interpret the burial ritual as the commemoration of an individual, as the reification of a feminine ideal, as the transformation of a deceased person into an ancestor, or as part of the negotiation reconfiguring social networks to carry on without someone's physical presence, the amulet had a role to play in that process. It helped to create identity.

NOTES

1. To my knowledge, the forest symbolism of the Finnish pendants is not a feature of Merovingian thought, but the element of negotiation between community and wilderness could still be a factor.

2. Although Kóvacs's and Radócz's argument about meaning is dependent on quotations from earlier scholarship, it is supported by a large catalog of finds. See also, for example, African pubic aprons in the Brooklyn Museum: https://www.brooklynmuseum.org/opencollection/objects/161784/Pubic_Apron?referring-q=%22cowrie+shell%22+%22pubic+apron%22.

3. I know of another thirty-two such pendants from sites in England and sixteen unprovenanced.

4. Eight of the eleven hold iron ore or unidentified dark stones. While it is possible that a pendant was placed on the chest as a gift, rather than reflecting how it was worn, no bound pendant has been found away from the body (in a container or otherwise), only one was found by an arm, and only one at a hand.

5. For example, in Riedstadt-Leeheim grave 19, where a replacement pebble occupies only half of the length of the mount (Möller 1987, 112–113, plate 78/3). A recently excavated pendant from Dover preserves a repair in early medieval thread, suggesting that other pendants found broken might have had repairs in perishable materials. (Parfitt and Anderson et al. 2012).

6. There is no consensus on precise stone varieties, and the objects have only rarely been examined by geologists. To avoid false precision, I use the generic term *crystal* for all macrocrystalline quartz untinted by other elements (e.g., the iron in amethyst), as ancient and medieval writers did.

7. The identity of the stone is not certain. If the compiler of the text misunderstood his source and wrote of "striking" fire from the stone rather than "lighting" such a fire, the problem would be resolved in favor of rock crystal.

8. The difference between the numbers of pendants and of graves results from five burials, each of which contained two pendants.

9. Stauch also found that the types of jewelry buried changed as incumbent women advanced through their thirties, and again after they passed age sixty. My dataset cannot be checked for similar changes because of the way in which ages have been defined in the archaeological reports, and because only one woman certainly over sixty years old was buried with a bound pendant.

10. An example from L'Isle-Jourdain, Ictium grave 333, dated ca. 530, is geographically isolated, and there is no evidence to suggest that it was part of a larger regional group (Boudartchouk 1998, pp. 133–135, Fig. 6).

11. Tab-top settings do not form a distinctive group, but insofar as its structural configuration had a home, that home was probably in England.

WORKS CITED

Ancient Sources

Adamnan, *Life of Columba*. A. Anderson and M. Anderson (ed. and trans.). (1961). *Adamnan's Life of Columba*. London: Thomas Nelson and Sons.

Augustine, *City of God*. M. Dods (trans.). (1887). *St. Augustine's City of God and Christian Doctrine*. NPNF 2. Buffalo: Christian Literature Co.

Bald, *Leechbook*. T. Cockayne (ed. and trans.). (1864). *Leechdoms, Wortcunning, and Starcraft of Early England* (pp. 1–360). London: Longman, Green, Longman, Roberts, and Green.

Boniface, *Epistolae*. E. Dümmler (ed.). (1892). MGH Epistolae 3 (pp. 215–233). Epistolae Merowingici et Karolini Aevi 1. Berlin: Weidmann.

Charlemagne, *Admonitio generalis*. P. King (trans.). (1987). *Charlemagne: Translated Sources* (pp. 209–220). Lambrigg: King.

Dioscorides, *De materia medica*. L. Beck (trans.). (2005). *Dioscorides, De materia medica*. Altertumswissenschaftliche Texte und Studien 38. Hildesheimk: Olms-Weidmann.

Gregory of Tours, *Glory of the Martyrs*. R. Van Dam (trans.). (1988). *Gregory of Tours, Glory of the Martyrs*. Translated Texts for Historians. Liverpool: Liverpool University Press.

Gregory of Tours, *Libri Historiarum X*. B. Krusch and W. Levison (eds.). (1951). (MGH SRM 1.1. Hanover: Hahn.

Hincmar of Reims, *De Divortio Lotharii Regis et Theutbergae Reginae XV*. L. Böhringer (ed.). (1992). *Hinkmar von Reims. De Divortio Lotharii Regis et Theutbergae Reginae XV*. MGH: Concilia 4, suppl. 1. Hanover: Hahn.

Isidore, *Etymologies*. S. Barney et al. (ed. and trans.). (2006). *The Etymologies of Isidore of Seville*. Cambridge: Cambridge University Press.

Laws of the Salian and Ripuarian Franks. T. Rivers (trans.). (1986). New York: AMS Press.

The Laws of the Salian Franks. K. Drew (trans.). (1991). Philadelphia: University of Pennsylvania Press.

Leges Langobardorum. G. Pertz (ed.). (1868). MGH LL 4. Hanover: Hahn.

Lex Ribuaria. F. Beyerle and R. Buchner (eds.). (1954). MGH LL nat. Germ. 3.2. Hanover: Hahn.

The Lombard Laws. K. Drew (trans.). (1973). Philadelphia: University of Pennsylvania Press.

Martin of Braga, *De correctione rusticorum*. M. Naldini (ed.). (1991). *Martino di Braga, Contro le Superstizioni catechesi al popolo: De Correctione Rusticoru*. Florence: Nardini.

Orphic Lapidary. R. Halleux and J. Schamp (ed. and trans.). (1985) *Les Lapidaires Grecs*. Paris: Les Belles Lettres.

Pactus Legis Salicae. K. Eckhardt (ed.). (1962). MGH LL nat. Germ. 4.1. Hanover: Hahn.

Pliny the Elder, *Naturalis Historia Libri XXXVII*. D. Eichholz (ed. and trans.). (1962). *Pliny: Natural History*. Cambridge, MA: Harvard University Press.

Sidonius Apollinaris. *Carmen 15, Epithalamium*. W. Anderson (trans. and notes). (1936). *Sidonius Poems and Letters* (pp. 202–212). Cambridge, MA: Harvard University Press.

Solinus, *Collectanea rerum memorabilium*. T. Mommsen (ed.). (1958). *Collectanea rerum memorabilium*. Berlin: Weidmann.

Modern Sources

Ament, H. (1991). "Zur Wertschätzung antiker Gemmen in der Merowingerzeit." *Germania* 69(2): 401–424.

Amundsen, D., and C. Diers. (1969). "The Age of Menarche in Classical Greece and Rome." *Human Biology* 4(1): 125–132.

Arends, U. (1978). "Ausgewählte Gegenstände des Frühmittelalters mit Amulettcharakter." PhD diss. Ruprecht-Karl-Universität Heidelberg.

Arnold, B. (2007). "Gender and Archaeological Mortuary Analysis." In S. Nelson (ed.), *Women in Antiquity: Theoretical Approaches to Gender and Archaeology* (pp. 107–140). Lanham, MD: AltaMira Press.

Audy, F. (2015). "When Was the Loop Added? Dating the Transformation of Coins in the Viking Age." In T. Talvio and M. Wijk (eds.), *Myntstudier: festskrift till Kenneth Jonsson* (pp. 1–4). Stockholm: Svenske Numismatiska Föreningen.

Bartlett, R. (2001). "Medieval and Modern Concepts of Race and Ethnicity." *Journal of Medieval and Early Modern Studies* 31: 39–56.

Boudartchouk, J.-L. (1998). "La nécropole franque de Ictium à L'Isle-Jourdain (Gers, Midi-Pyrénées, France)." *Acta Praehistorica et Archaeologica* 30: 126–136.

Brather, S. (2004). *Ethnische Interpretationen in der frühgeschichtlichen Archäologie. Geschichte, Grundlagen und Alternativen.* Ergänzungsbände zum Reallexikon der Germanischen Altertumskunde 42. Berlin: Walter de Gruyter.

Bursche, A. (2008). "Functions of Roman Coins in Barbaricum of Later Antiquity. An Anthropological Essay." In A. Bursche et al. (ed.), *Roman Coins outside the Empire* (pp. 395–416). Wetteren: Moneta.

Christlein, R. (1973). "Besitzabstufungen zur Merowingerzeit im Spiegel reicher Grabfunde aus West- und Süddeutschland." *Jahrbuch des Römisch-Germanischen Zentralmuseums Mainz* 20: 147–180.

Clark, G. (1993). *Women in Late Antiquity: Pagan and Christian Life-styles.* Oxford: Clarendon Press.

Codine-Trecourt, F. (2014). "Les monnaies mérovingiennes modifiées à des fins non moné-taires." *Revue Numismatique* 171: 497–547.

Dickinson, T. (2002). "What's New in Early Medieval Burial Archaeology?" *Early Medieval Europe* 11: 71–87.

Dohrn-Ihmig, M., et al. (1999). *Das fränkische Gräberfeld von Nieder-Erlenbach, Stadt Frankfurt am Main.* Frankfurt-am-Main: Denkmalamt.

Donat, P. (1989). "Die Adelsgräber von Großorner und Stössen und das Problem der Qualitätsgruppe D merowingerzeitlicher Grabausstattungen." *Jahresschrift für mittel-deutsche Vorgeschichte* 72: 185–204.

Dübner-Manthey, B. (1985). "Die Gürtelgehänge als Träger von Kleingeräten, Amuletten und Anhängern symbolischer Bedeutung im Rahmen der frühmittelalterlichen Frauentracht: Archäologische Untersuchung zu einem charakteristischen Bestandteil der weiblichen Tracht." PhD diss., FU Berlin.

Effros, B. (2000). "Skeletal Sex and Gender in Merovingian Mortuary Archaeology," *Antiquity* 74: 632–639.

Ewig, E. (1952). *Die fränkischen Teilungen und Teilreiche (511–613).* Wiesbaden: F. Steiner.

Garrett, R.M. (1909). *Precious Stones in Old English Literature.* Leipzig: A. Deichert/Georg Böhme.

Geary, P. (2001). "Barbarians and Ethnicity." In G. Bowersock, P. Brown, and O. Grabar (eds.), *Interpreting Late Antiquity: Essays on the Postclassical World* (pp. 107–129). Cambridge, MA: Belknap Press of Harvard University Press.

Giesler, H. (1998). *Das Frühbairische Gräberfeld Straubing-Bajuwarenstraße I: Katalog der archäologischen Befunde und Funde.* Rahden/Westf.: Leidorf.

Goldberg, E. (2013). "Louis the Pious and the Hunt." *Speculum* 88, 613–643.

Grunwald, L. (1998). *Grabfunde des Neuwieder Beckens von der Völkerwanderungszeit bis zum frühen Mittelalter.* Rahden/Westf.: Leidorf.

Guillaume, J. (1974/5). "Les nécropoles mérovingiennes de Dieue/Meuse (France)." *Acta praehistorica et archaeologica* 5(6): 211–249.

Hadley, D., and Morre, J. (1999). " 'Death Makes the Man'? Burial Rite and the Construction of Masculinities in the Early Middle Ages." In D. Hadley (ed.), *Masculinity in Medieval Europe* (pp. 21–38). London: Longman.

Halsall, G. (1995). *Settlement and Social Organization: The Merovingian Region of Metz*. Cambridge: Cambridge University Press.

Herdick, M. (2001). "Mit Eisen gegen die Angst: Überlegungen zur Interpretation Vor- und Frühgeschichtlicher Mineralien-Amulette und Bemerkungen zu einer Gruppe Merowingerzeitlicher Kugelanhänger." *Concilium medii aevi* 4: 1–47.

Herlihy, D. (1990). *Opera Muliebria: Women and Work in Medieval Europe*. Philadelphia: Temple University Press.

Hincker, V., et al. (2011). "La courte histoire du cimetière mérovingien de Banneville-la-Campagne (Calvados, France)." *Archéologie médiévale* 41: 1–48.

Hinz, H. (1966). "Am langen Band getragene Bergkristallanhänger der Merowingerzeit." *Jahrbuch des Römisch-Germanischen Zentralmuseums Mainz* 13: 212–230.

L'Île-de-France de Clovis à Hugues Capet: du Vᵉ siècle au Xᵉ siècle (1993). Saint-Ouen-l'Aumône: Valhermeil.

Jarnut, J. (1985). "Die frühmittelalterliche Jagd unter rechts- und sozialgeschichtlichen Aspekten." In *L'Uomo di fronte al mondo animale nell'alto Medioevo: 7–13 aprile, 1983* (pp. 765–800). Spoleto: Presso la sede del Centro.

Jones, S. (1999). "Historical Categories and the Praxis of Identity: The Interpretation of Ethnicity in Historical Archaeology." In P. Funari et al. (ed.), *Historical Archaeology: Back from the Edge* (pp. 219–232). London: Routledge.

Kars, M. (2013). "The Early-Medieval Burial Evidence and Concepts of Possession: Questioning Individual Identities." In B. Ludowici (ed.), *Individual and Individuality? Approaches towards an Archaeology of Personhood in the First Millennium AD*. Neue Studien zur Sachsenforschung 4: 95–106.

Kemmers, F., and Myrberg, N. (2011). "Rethinking Numismatics. The Archaeology of Coins." *Archaeological Dialogues* 18(1): 87–108.

Kivisalo, N. (2008). "The Late Iron Age Bear-Tooth Pendants in Finland: Symbolic Mediators between Women, Bears, and Wilderness?" *Temenos* 44(2): 263–291.

Koch, U. (1968). *Die Grabfunde der Merowingerzeit aus dem Donautal um Regensburg*. Berlin: Walter de Gruyter.

Koch, U. (2001). *Das alamannisch-fränkische Gräberfeld bei Pleidelsheim*. Stuttgart: Konrad Theiss.

Kornbluth, G. (2015). "Merovingian Rock Crystal: Practical Tools and Status Markers," In A. Willemsen and H. Kik (ed.), *Golden Middle Ages in Europe: New Research into Early-Medieval Communities and Identities* (pp. 49–55; 88–90). Turnhout: Brepols.

Kornbluth, G. (2016a). "Early Medieval Crystal Amulets: Secular Instruments of Protection and Healing." In B. Bowers (ed.), *The Sacred and the Secular in Medieval Healing* (pp. 143–181). London: Routledge.

Kornbluth, G. (2016b). "Merovingian Period Art." *Oxford Bibliographies Online*. <https://www.oxfordbibliographies.com/view/document/obo-9780199920105/obo-9780199920105-0095.xml>

Kornbluth, G. (2020). "Transparent, Translucent, and Opaque: Merovingian and Anglo-Saxon Crystal Amulets." In C. Hahn and A. Shalem (eds.), *Seeking Transparency: The Medieval Rock Crystals* (pp. 67–77). Berlin: Reimer.

Kornbluth, G. (forthcoming). *Amulets, Power, and Identity in Early Medieval Europe*.

Kóvacs, L., and Radócz, G. (2008). *Vulvae, Eyes, Snake Heads: Archaeological Finds of Cowrie Amulets*. Oxford: Archaeopress/BAR.

Lamont, J-P. (1968). "Journal des fouilles." *Études ardennaises* 55: 20–28.

Lennartz, A. (2004). "Die Meeresschnecke Cypraea als Amulett im Frühen Mittelalter. Eine Neubewertung." *Bonner Jahrbücher* 204: 163–232.

Lohrke, B. (2004). *Kinder in der Merowingerzeit: Gräber von Mädchen und Jungen in der Alamannia*. Rahden/Westf.: Leidorf.

MacGregor, A., et al. (1997). *Ashmolean Museum. A Summary Catalogue of the Continental Archeological Collections (Roman Iron Age, Migration Period, Early Medieval)*. Oxford: Archaeopress/BAR.

Maguire, H. (1997). "Magic and Money in the Early Middle Ages." *Speculum* 72(4): 1037–1054.

Mehling, A. (1998). *Archaika als Grabbeigaben: Studien an merowingerzeitlichen Gräberfeldern*. Rahden/Westf.: Leidorf.

Meaney, A. (1978). "Alfred, the Patriarch and the White Stone." *Journal of the Australasian Universities Language and Literature Association* 49: 65–79.

Meaney, A. (1981). *Anglo-Saxon Amulets and Curing Stones*. Oxford: BAR.

Möller, J. (1987). *Katalog der Grabfunde aus Völkerwanderungs- und Merowingerzeit im südmainischen Hessen (Starkenburg)*. Stuttgart: Franz Steiner.

Oehrl, S. 2013. "Bear Hunting and Its Ideological Context." In O. Grimm and U. Schmölcke (eds.), *Hunting in Northern Europe Until 1500 AD. Old Traditions and Regional Developments, Continental Sources and Continental Influences* (pp. 297–332). Neumünster: Wachholtz.

Päffgen, B. (1992). *Die Ausgrabungen in St. Severin zu Köln*. Kölner Forschungen 5. 3 vols. Mainz am Rhein: Philipp von Zabern.

Parfitt, K., Anderson, T., et al. (2012). *Buckland Anglo-Saxon Cemetery, Dover: Excavations 1994*. Canterbury: Canterbury Archaeological Trust.

Pilet, C. (1980). *La Nécropole de Frénouville: Étude d'une population de la fin du IIIe à la fin du VIIe siècle*. 3 vols. Oxford: BAR.

Pion, C. (2012). "La pratique du remploi dans les sépultures mérovingiennes de Belgique. Entre recyclage, esthétique et symbolique." *Cahiers des Thèmes Transversaux ArScan* 10: 47–55.

Pohl, W. (1991). "Conceptions of Ethnicity in Early Medieval Studies." *Archaeologia Polona* 29: 39–49.

Riddle, J. (1980). "Dioscorides." In P. Kristeller (ed.), *Catalogus Translationum et Commentariorum: Mediaeval And Renaissance Latin Translations and Commentaries; Annotated Lists and Guides* 4 (pp. 1–143). Washington, DC: Catholic University of America Press.

Salin, E. (1949–1959). *La civilisation mérovingienne d'après les sépultures, les textes et le laboratoire*. 4 vols. Paris: Picard.

Schienerl, P. (1984). "Zur Amulettwertigkeit merowingerzeitlicher Waffennachbildungen," *Archäologisches Korrespondenzblatt* 14: 337–341.

Stauch, E. (2008). "Alter ist Silber, Jugend ist Gold! Zur altersdifferenzierten Analyse frühgeschichtlicher Bestattungen." In *Zwischen Spätantike und Frühmittelalter. Archäologie des 4. bis 7. Jahrhunderts im Westen* (pp. 275–296). Berlin: Walter de Gruyter.

Stauch, E. (2012). "Alt werden im Frühmittelalter." In B. Röder, B, W. de Jong, and K. Alt (eds.), *Alter(n) anders denken. Kulturelle und biologische Perspektiven* (pp. 133–160). Cologne: Böhlau.

Steuer, H. (1982). "Schlüsselpaare in frühgeschichtlichen Gräbern. Zur Deutung einer Amulett-Beigabe." *Studien zur Sachsenforschung* 3: 185–247.

Stoodley, S. (1999). *The Spindle and the Spear: A Critical Enquiry into the Construction and Meaning of Gender in the Early Anglo-Saxon Burial Rite*. Oxford: BAR.

Theune-Vogt, C. (2002). "Gemeinsamkeiten und Unterschiede auf Gräberfeldern der Alamannia im Frühmittelalter." In C. Bücker (ed.), *Regio Archaeologica. Archäologie und*

Geschichte am Ober- und Hochrhein. Festschrift für Gerhard Fingerlin zum 65. Geburtstag (pp. 351–361). Rahden/Westf.: Leidorf.

Trésors Archéologiques du Nord de la France (1997). Valenciennes: Musée des Beaux-Arts.

Wamers, E. (2009). "Von Bären und Männern: Berserker, Bärenkämpfer und Bärenführer im frühen Mittelalter." *Zeitschrift für Archäologie des Mittelalters* 37: 1–46.

Wemple, S. (1981). *Women in Frankish Society: Marriage and the Cloister 500 to 900.* Philadelphia: University of Pennsylvania Press.

Wicker, N. (2010). "Scandinavian Migration Period Gold Bracteates," *Oxford Bibliographies*, [http://www.oxfordbibliographies.com/view/document/obo-9780195396584/obo-9780195396584-0107.xml?rskey=VcN9Xu&result=1&q=bracteates#firstMatch]

Wieczorek, A., et al. (eds.). (1996). *Die Franken: Wegbereiter Europas.* 2 vols. Mainz: Reiss-Museum Mannheim.

Willemsen, A. (2014). "Merovingisch Glas." In A. Willemsen (ed.), *Gouden Middeleeuwen, Nederland in de Merovingische wereld, 400–700 na Chr.* (pp. 86–106). Zutphen: Walburg Pers.

CHAPTER 41

....

MAGIC AND DIVINATION IN THE MEROVINGIAN WORLD

....

WILLIAM E. KLINGSHIRN

THE study of Merovingian magic and divination has long been haunted by categories of "superstition," "sacrilege," and "idolatry" that continue to shape the historical literature. Embedded in the written sources, theologically potent, and deployed over the centuries for a variety of ecclesiastical and political purposes (Glatthaar 2004), these expressions of clerical ideology certainly merit the close attention they have received.[1] As analytical tools, however, their utility is doubtful. It is now clear, for instance, that a substantial portion of the evidence used to characterize large swaths of the Merovingian world and its margins as "pagan" derives from a fundamental misunderstanding of the meanings of magical, divinatory, and ritual practice generally.[2]

In an effort to move beyond such confining interpretations, this chapter situates practices of magic and divination within the framework of what we may conceptualize as a lived Merovingian religion. In so doing, it identifies magical and divinatory practices not as rejections of Christianity or expressions of residual paganism, but as strategies for accessing divine power and knowledge in a world of deep uncertainty and risk. Grounded in religion, but not requiring any particular metaphysics, pagan or otherwise, these ideas and techniques relied for success on the widespread belief, not diminished by Christianity, that divine assistance was readily available, either directly or mediated through nature. The tools they offered for facilitating access took different forms according to location and cultural tradition, but did not diverge fundamentally from, and indeed often had close links with, those in operation elsewhere in the Mediterranean world.

Divination and magic are themselves highly problematic terms, and the tendency to treat them together, though historically defensible, masks significant differences between them. This chapter distinguishes them by considering *magic* as a set of practices that aimed primarily at accessing occult power (through the use of spells, incantations, amulets, and natural and human substances for healing and protection) and *divination* as a set of practices that aimed primarily at accessing occult knowledge (through sortilege, dreams, astrology, and inspired prophecy). Even when these distinctions are blurred in practice, they can still, as ideal types, make sense of the evidence and offer a useful structure for explanation. Distinguishing these domains of practice from one another also discourages the definition of divination as a species of magic, a taxonomy that owes much of its influence in the Middle Ages and beyond to Isidore's *De Magis* (*Etym.* 8.9). Isidore's inclusion in the chapter not only of magicians, but of many other practitioners as well, has encouraged readers to assume from its title that diviners, healers, and makers of amulets were also magicians. A close reading of the chapter, however, suggests that Isidore used the term *magi* in its much broader Hellenistic sense to mean wise men of all sorts: we need not define every figure to whom he referred as a magician in any narrower sense of the term (Klingshirn 2003).

With such distinctions in mind, this chapter seeks to understand the wide variety of Merovingian cultural practices that can be labeled as magic or divination by examining them on their own terms, rather than focusing on the judgments applied to them in the texts. We are aided in this effort by the ubiquity of divination and magic across the world and the attention these practices have received from scholars specializing in all periods and regions. The interconnected worlds of Greek and Roman divination and magic offer a particularly rich set of comparanda, textual and material. At the same time, while it undeniably stood on a cultural continuum with classical Mediterranean practices (Dickie 2012), the Merovingian world also encompassed regions and traditions well beyond the frontiers of Roman Gaul and Germany. Particularly as our narrative approaches the eighth century, it will be important to take note of magical and divinatory practices across an increasingly extensive late Merovingian and early Carolingian cultural world.

UNCERTAINTY, RISK, AND PERSONAL AGENCY

As Esther Eidinow (2007) has recently demonstrated, divination and magic can be seen to constitute related responses to problems of risk and uncertainty in the ancient Mediterranean world, or what Peregrine Horden and Nicholas Purcell have termed its "chaotic variability" (2000, p. 175). Eidinow's study of the inscriptions from the sanctuary of Zeus at Dodona and curse tablets from the Greek world between the sixth and first centuries BCE argues for a "socially constructed" understanding of risk in ancient Greece (2007, p. 5) and demonstrates the usefulness of oracular consultation and binding spells, among other mechanisms, for identifying and managing it. The risks of most concern in the Merovingian world would have differed in some ways, of course, as would the specific divinatory and ritual means available for controlling them. However, the motivation to use such technologies in the first place would have rested on the same basic cultural assumption: the perceived value of supernatural assistance in a physical and social world that was rife with both danger and opportunity, but at the same time often lacked adequate information and tools either to protect against the one or take advantage of the other. Problems of agricultural subsistence, health, the prosperity and well-being of one's family, personal rivalry, and legal status are everywhere in Merovingian narrative and documentary sources. Only by giving due consideration to their importance can we give divinatory and magical practices the serious attention they deserve.

This approach also allows us to give full weight to the personal agency implicit in every act of divination and magic, as well as to the complex array of local conditions and cultural assumptions that went into the decision to employ not just any diviner or practitioner, but a particular type of professional or even (if the market was robust enough) a particular individual. Although he addresses mainly agricultural, fiscal, and social conditions, Cam Grey's treatment of risk, decision making, and personal agency in the late Roman countryside can be applied more broadly to the problems under investigation here (2011). The use of ritual mechanisms for resolving problems involved a complex interplay of structure and agency, tradition and improvisation, individual, family, and community at every social level (Grey 2011, pp. 98–105).

We can illuminate these late Roman realities with Merovingian evidence. According to Gregory of Tours, it was "the custom of peasants" (*mos rusticorum*) that motivated the parents of a son demonically possessed while out hunting with his father. Their solution was to obtain "bindings and potions for him" (*ligamenta ei et potiones*) from *sortilegi* and *harioli* (*VM* 1.26, 27). When the wife of one of his slaves collapsed after working in the fields, *harioli* diagnosed the problem as the attack of a midday demon and prescribed herbal bindings and incantations (*VM* 4.36). When another of Gregory's slaves contracted a serious intestinal illness while traveling with the bishop, his fellow slaves brought in a "certain *hariolus*" (*VJ* 46a). He "muttered incantations, cast lots, and hung amulets" from the patient's neck. But it was not only peasants who made use of such mechanisms: Duke Guntram Boso "frequently employed *harioli* and lots, desiring to know the future from them" (*Hist.* 9.10).

The Specialties of Practitioners

Although Gregory occasionally mentions more specialized practitioners, such as the inspired women (*pythonissae*) whose divinatory powers were thought to derive from direct revelation (*Hist.* 5.14, 7.44; see further Wiśniewski 2005), most of Gregory's diviners offered practical remedies in addition to hidden information. This was also true of the itinerant holy men whom he singles out as "false prophets" and "false Christs" (*Hist.* 9.6, 10.25). In 580, the cross-bearing man later discovered to be the runaway slave of Bishop Amelius of Bigorre was found with amulets made of plants and the inedible parts of wild animals: the teeth of a mole, mice bones, and bear claws and fat (*Hist.* 9.6).[3] These were probably to be used, along with the vials of holy oil that he carried, for healing the sick. Seven years later, Desiderius of Bordeaux attracted attention for his healing of paralytics (*Hist.* 9.6). In 591, a man whom Gregory believed to be from Bourges, accompanied by a woman named Mary, healed the sick and predicted "future things," including diseases, financial losses, and good health (*Hist.* 10.25).

The same diversity of skills applies to practitioners of magic in Gregory. The *maleficae* of Paris whom Queen Fredegund questioned about the death of her son Theuderic—from a case of dysentery allegedly caused by magic—confessed under torture that they had caused the death of many (*Hist.* 6.35; for more on Fredegund, see James, Chapter 11, this volume). But they also supplied to the prefect Mummolus *inunctiones* and *potiones* by which he could win the favor of the king and queen. They were probably also his source for the *herba* that he boasted would, when drunk, cure even a very bad case of dysentery.[4]

A wider array of practitioners with distinct specialties can be found in the sermons of Caesarius of Arles. This is not surprising in a city and region that at every point in the sixth century remained more economically and demographically complex and better connected to the resources of Mediterranean culture than Tours and its neighbors. Caesarius's sermons are not only important for what they say about his own time and place, but also for their reuse in homiletic, penitential, and canonical literature in Latin, Anglo-Saxon, and Old Norse-Icelandic (Klingshirn 1994, ch. 10). In a sermon preserved only in the eighth-century "Homiliary of Burchard" (Würzburg, Universitätsbibliothek, MS p. th. f. 28; Hen 2013), Caesarius depicts women with sick children seeking out individual practitioners with a variety of titles and skills: "Let us consult that *hariolus* or *divinus*, that *sortilegus* or *herbaria*; let us sacrifice the patient's clothing, his belt that should be examined and measured; let us offer some magical characters, let us affix some spells (*praecantationes*) to his neck" (*Serm.* 52.5). A similar passage can be found in his *Sermon* 184, preserved in a tenth-century patristic florilegium (Paris, BnF, MS lat. 2730):

> It sometimes happens, brethren, that a persecutor from the devil's party comes to a sick person and says, "If you had brought in that *praecantator*, you would now be healthy; if you had wanted to affix those *characteres* to yourself, you could be healed." … Perhaps another man comes and says, "Send to that *divinus*, hand over to him your belt or bandage, let it be measured or examined; and he will tell you what you will do, or whether you can escape." Someone else says, "That man really knows how to conduct a suffumigation (*ille bene novit suffumigare*),[5] for on behalf of whomever he did this, it immediately got better, and every trial departed from his house." … In this respect, the devil can even be expected to deceive unwary and lukewarm Christians to the extent that if someone has experienced a theft, that very cruel persecutor stirs up one of the man's friends who says to him, "Come in secret to that place, and I will summon up a person for you (*ego tibi excitabo personam*) to tell you who stole silver or money from you, but if you want to find this out, don't make the sign of the cross when you come to that place." … Some women even persuade one another that they should apply something to protect their sick children against a spell (*ad fascinum*, i.e. *adversus fascinum*[6]), which contravenes the Catholic faith.   (*Serm.* 184.4)

The practitioners whom Caesarius mentions in sermons 52, 184, and elsewhere in his preaching are for the most part familiar figures in the Latin literature of magic and divination. They include diviners in general (*divini*), specialists in lot divination (*sortilegi*), and those who had to do with spells: *praecantatores* (*Serm.* 12.4, 13.3, 5, 14.4, 19.5, 50.1), *incantatores* (*Serm.* 189.2, 197.2), and, in one recently discovered sermon, *incantatrices* (Étaix 1978, p. 274, line 87). These men and women recited spells over amulets, potions, and natural substances to activate their powers, and also directly over the sick. The *hariolus* in sermon 52 is the only one Caesarius mentions, but *haruspices*, the originally Etruscan diviners from whom *harioli* may have derived their name, are found in other passages (*Serm.* 13.3, 52.1, 54.1, 189.2, 197.2). By this time they had abandoned the practice for which they were best known—the divinatory examination of the entrails of sacrificed animals—in favor of more acceptable practices, such as the interpretation of lightning.[7] The necromancer darkly alluded to in sermon 184 is, of course, well known from classical literature, even if it is difficult to find believable historical examples.[8] Astrologers (*mathematici*) appear far less frequently in Caesarius (*Serm.* 18.4; 59.2) than in his Augustinian models (Dolbeau 2003). This may be because he did not consider them to be a pastoral problem, although he does complain of practices that point to the use of astrological almanacs, such as the observation of certain days (*Serm.* 54.1). Caesarius also does not mention dream interpreters, not because he did not consider dreams an important source of knowledge (*Vita Caesarii* 1.9; 2.36), but either because most people considered themselves adequate interpreters of their own dreams (as he himself did) or because he had no objection to those who offered dream interpretation for others (see further Moreira 2003).

A few practitioners are attested for the first time in Caesarius. The *herbaria*—a female specialist in medicinal, amuletic, or poisonous *herbae*—makes her first appearance in Latin in sermon 52 (Campetella 2006), and *filacterarii*, amulet-makers, in sermon 50 (for more on amulets, see Kornbluth, Chapter 40, this volume). A practitioner of unknown specialization is also mentioned for the first time by Caesarius: this is the *cara(g)ius*, whose frequent appearance in subsequent homiletic literature was largely due to Caesarius's influence (Filotas 2005, pp. 233–234). A number of scholars, following du Cange, have identified this figure with a writer of magical *c(h)aracteres*, supposing an etymological link (Campetella 2001, pp. 91–98). The contexts in which the word is used, however, suggest that the *caragius* was a diviner. This is especially clear from the Council of Narbonne (589, c. 14), which called for punishment "if any men and women are the diviners whom they say are *caragii* and casters of lots" (*si qui viri ac mulieres divinatores quos dicunt esse caragios atque sorticularios*).

MEROVINGIAN DIVINATORY TEXTS

Given the climate of uncertainty and risk in which they lived, it was important for the clientele of such figures to identify the exact nature of a problem before seeking a solution. This is why divination often appears in our sources not only as a problem-solving strategy of its own, but as the gateway to other ritual practices. We are fortunate to have divinatory texts from the Merovingian world that illuminate this process of consultation and diagnosis. All the extant texts are collections of lots (*sortes*) based on Greek models. They fall into three main categories, or families, distinguished by their method of organization and selection.[9]

> **Family A:** This category consists of lots grouped into groups of tens or twelves and accessed by a complicated algorithm. The best known example is the *Sortes Astrampsychi* in Greek (Naether 2010). The *Sortes Sangallenses* (ed. A. Dold), found in fragmentary form in a well-known palimpsest (Sankt Gallen, Stiftsbibliothek MS 908), is modeled on the *Sortes Astrampsychi*. Dating to the late sixth or early seventh century, it answers specific questions that, although no longer extant, can be reconstructed from the surviving responses (Klingshirn 2005).
>
> **Family B:** This category consists of collections of lots selected by throws of (four-sided) knucklebones or (six-sided) dice. Greek examples are found on a number of inscriptions in Asia Minor.[10] The best documented Latin example is the *Sortes Sanctorum* (ed. E. Montero Cartelle), first attested at the Council of Vannes in 462/468 (Klingshirn 2002). Latin copies are found in manuscripts dating from the early ninth to the fifteenth century, and there are also copies in Provençal and old French. This collection consists of fifty-six responses selected by three dice (thrown in any order). An earlier Greek version on papyrus has now been identified (Wilkinson 2015). A related collection, the *Sortes Monacenses*, found in a tenth- or eleventh-century manuscript (Munich, Bayerische Staatsbibliothek, clm 14846, fols. 106r–121v) includes fifty-one surviving responses of an original fifty-six.
>
> **Family C:** This category consists of lots organized in a sequentially numbered list and accessed by various methods. Related sayings, or "interpretations," are found in a wide number of manuscripts, written in Greek, Syriac, Coptic, Armenian, and Georgian. The best Latin example is the *Sortes Sangermanenses,* a collection of 182 (originally 316) responses written in a mid-ninth-century hand into the margins of a Latin copy of John's Gospel that dates to circa 800 (Paris, BnF, MS lat. 11553).[11]

There is little doubt that it was texts like these that lot diviners used in the divinatory consultations to which churchmen such as Caesarius and Gregory objected. But there is a significant difference in how we can apply them as historical evidence. The answers clients received from texts belonging to families B and C were of such a general nature—for example, *Sortes Sangermanenses* cxcvii (Harris 1901, p. 116): "What you want will happen" (*quod speres fiet*)—that they could only have been meaningful in the light of a client's specific circumstances. Interpretations of these responses would of course have been discussed in detail with the *sortilegus*, but none of that is available to us. Thus, while such texts can help us to understand the process of dialogue in which client and diviner engaged to decide upon a particular course of action, they cannot shed much light on the type of action or the type of problem it was meant to solve. Collections in family A, on the other hand, are rich in detail about the problems they were intended to solve. The fact that it is (in its surviving form) more securely datable to the Merovingian period than any other Latin lot collection makes the *Sortes Sangallenses* even more valuable as a source of evidence, not only for how the divination it offered might have operated, but also for the range of problems that diviners were called upon to solve. That many of its responses were copied from earlier texts need not pose a problem: in a living text, as we must assume divinatory manuals to be, responses that were no longer relevant could (up to a point) be adapted into a form that was.

The *Sortes Sangallenses* covers a wide range of problems—love, illness, enemies and friends, political office, business relations, legal troubles, bequests, captivity and freedom, exile, military action, and life expectancy, among others—and includes several that directly bear on the subjects of divination and magic. One group of responses addresses the utility and truth of dreams (9.5–12), while others cover poisoning (104.4, 113), curses placed on individuals (114), and protection for a house (109–112).

The problems raised in such inquiries may well have gone beyond what individuals could diagnose and do for themselves. "Your dream is not applicable (*utilis*),[12] but be careful not to fall into the trap set by your enemies" (9.5). In the face of such a warning, what could one do? Perhaps one's enemy would die soon (27.6, 7), or perhaps one could expect his destruction by the Lord (*Dominus per[d]it illum*, 37.4). By contrast, perhaps he would not die (27.12), for instance (27.5), "because the demons he worships stand guard around him" (*quia de[mo]nes [cir]cumcustodiunt quos colit*). Could the client do anything about this? According to one response, "You will have the occasion to do away with your enemy (*Habebis occa[sionem u]t interimas inimicum tuum*, 31.2), but according to another, it was best to do nothing: "I warn you not to do harm to your enemy, because he is nothing (*Moneo ne malefacias inimico tuo, quia nihil est*, 31.3). And how did one go about harming an enemy? Apart from overt violence, there were two obvious paths. The *Sortes* suggested one: "If you want to go to court, soon, soon you will destroy your enemy" (*Si adire volueris iudicia, mox mox interficies inimicum*, 31, 9). The other was to hire a specialist in spells and potions. Such figures are referred to in the law by their actions: killing or attempting to kill someone by *maleficia* or *herbae* (*Pactus Legis Salicae* 19.1–2), putting a spell (*maleficium*) on someone wherever he goes (19.3), or performing a *maleficium* that prevents a woman from having children (19.4).

The *Sortes Sangallenses* touches on the problems that could be caused by poisons. One fragmentary response suggests the use of water (presumably mixed with another substance) to deal with a poison that has been administered (104.4). Another response advises, "Get help for yourself, because you have been poisoned" (*succurre tibi, quia medicamentatus*, 113.9), or in a more detailed version, "because you have been poisoned by a woman" (*quia a muliere medicamentatus es*, 113.10). Once clients knew the cause of their troubles, it was important to know where help could be found. Although the text of the *Sortes Sangallenses* has nothing to offer on this subject, we can assume from the magical underworld described by Gregory of Tours that there were other specialists the *sortilegus* could recommend.

A related problem was presented by binding curses, a form of ancient magic by which practitioners sought to "bind" or control on behalf of clients the wishes or actions of their rivals, lovers, or enemies (Graf 1997, ch. 5). Such spells are the subject of two responses in the *Sortes Sangallenses*. One reassures the client that he has not been "bound" (*obligatus*), and that his condition will improve with time (114.8, reading *immutaris*).[13] The other informs him that while he has not been "cursed" (*maleficatus*), he has instead been "placed under subjection" (*subiectus*). What this distinction meant was no doubt to be explained in the consultation. Richard Meister (*Sortes Sangallenses* 1951, p. 34) suggests that the subjection was erotic in nature, in other words that it was a variety of binding spell. It is possible that the distinction is visible in the penitential included in the *Bobbio Missal*, datable to ca. 700.[14] For someone who produces a *maleficium* that destroys someone (or something), the penitential prescribes ten years of penance, with three on bread and water (*Bobbio Missal* 577.9). For someone, by comparison, who produces an erotic *veneficium* (*pro amore*) that does not destroy anyone, it prescribes a penance of three years, with one on bread and water (*Bobbio Missal* 577.10).

How one became cursed or bound in Merovingian times is not well known. Curse tablets of the classical variety were probably not the main vehicle. Michaël Martin (2012) reports on only two such tablets datable to the Merovingian period; neither, unfortunately, bears a readable text. One was excavated at a cemetery in Vouciennes (Marne) between 1928 and 1935 (Thiérot and Lantier 1940; Salin 1949–1959, vol. 2, pp. 348–349), and the other was discovered in a cemetery at Vindrac (Tarn) in the 1970s (Labrousse 1978, pp. 425–426). It is probable that most curses did not leave behind material traces. When Bishop Franco of Aix (mid-sixth century) wanted to curse the man who had improperly taken possession of a property belonging to his church, "he knelt in prayer before the tomb of Saint Mitrias, recited the verses of a psalm, and said, 'Most glorious saint, no more lights will be lit here, no more melodies of psalms will be sung, until you first ... restore to the holy church the properties that have been violently taken from you.' He wept as he said this. Then he threw briers with sharp thorns on top of the tomb; after he left, he shut the doors and put other briers likewise in the entrance. Immediately the man who had invaded [the church property] was struck with a fever" (*GM* 71, trans. Van Dam).

It is apparent from the *Sortes Sangallenses* that not only individuals, but also their houses could be cursed. "Get help for yourself, because your house has been cursed (*Sucurre tibi, quia obligata est domus tua*, 111.12; see also 111.10, 11). A house might also contain enemies by whom the inhabitant could be driven out. "In the house in which you are living, you have many enemies, and you should be afraid that they will drive you out" (*In domo qua m[or]a[r]is, multos inimicos habes, et vere[re] ne te effugent*, 112.9). Whether the enemies were internal or external, visible or invisible, it was important to be protected. The *Sortes* make two suggestions for ensuring this. To keep from being driven out, they suggest that "You must be protected by *remedia*, if you do not want to be driven from your house" (*Remediis tibi tuendum est, si vis non fugari de domo*, 112.10). They also suggest the importance of maintaining "effective protection" more generally: "The house in which you want to remain, remain, because the protection is effective" (*Domus, in qua vis manere, mane, quia utilis tutela est*, 110.11; see also 109. 12; 110.12).

The main threat, of course, was demonic, and Christians had many ways to protect their houses from attack: by prayer, righteous living, and material resources, including crosses, floor mosaics, textiles, relics, and other holy objects (Maguire et al. 1989). In addition, specialists were available to treat emergency conditions. One of the canons adapted from the Council of Ancyra (314) and translated into Latin by Martin, bishop of Braga (566–579), points directly to this practice:

> If anyone, observing pagan custom, brings diviners and *sortilegi* into his house for the purpose of driving out evil, discovering *maleficia*, or performing pagan purifications, he should do penance for five years.[15]

Such figures could provide the *remedia* needed to protect homes and banish demonic forces. The suffumigation mentioned by Caesarius (*Serm.* 184.4) falls into this category, as do, on the side of the church, the blessings found in liturgical manuscripts:

> Whatever this wave [of consecrated water] sprinkles in the houses of the faithful, may it be free of impurity and free from harm. May no malevolent spirit reside in that place, nor harmful air corrupt it. Let all traps of the lurking enemy depart, and all disturbances flee far away.   (*Bobbio Missal* 543)[16]

THE MEROVINGIAN CLERGY

Such prayers remind us of the role the clergy played not only in performing Christian rituals, but also in providing amulets and other forms of protection. The Greek canons translated by Martin of Braga include a prohibition against clerics serving as *incantatores* or making amulets.[17] Among the amulets noted by Caesarius were those that contained "holy things and divine readings" (*res sanctas et lectiones divinas*); sometimes (*aliquotiens*) these were offered by clergy or religious (*Serm.* 50.1). This was a normal practice. When Florentius, the father of Gregory of Tours, wanted saints' relics to protect him on a long journey,

> he asked a certain bishop to grant him something from these relics....He put the sacred ashes in a gold medallion (*in lupino aureo*) and carried it with him. Although he did not even know the names of the blessed men, he was accustomed to recount that he had been rescued from many dangers. He claimed that often, because of the powers of these relics, he had avoided the violence of bandits, the dangers of floods, the threats of turbulent men, and attacks from swords (*GM* 83, trans. adapt. Van Dam).

Gregory later used these relics himself. He also wore a golden cross that contained relics of the Virgin Mary, the holy apostles, and St. Martin. These exercised a remarkable power against fire (*GM* 10). Caesarius's own staff, when fashioned into a cross by a prominent landowner in Provence, defended his fields against the hailstorms that had previously beset the property (*Vita Caesarii* 2.27). Christian amulets could do the same by invoking, as in an eighth-century Visigothic example from Asturias, St. Christopher and a host of angels (Fernández Nieto 2010).

Clerics were also active providers of divinatory services. The council convened in Vannes between 462 and 468 by Bishop Perpetuus of Tours noted as much in a canon repeated, with minor variations, in three sixth-century councils (Agde 506, Orléans 511, Auxerre 561/605), and in the seventh-century in the *Bobbio Penitential* (577.26), and Isidore of Seville (*Etym.* 8.9). According to canon 16 at Vannes: "Some clergy are devoted to auguries, and under the label of what pretends to be religion—which they call *Lots of the Saints*—they profess a knowledge of divination, or by looking into any kind of writings whatever predict future events."[18] In addition to the *Sortes Sanctorum* and other divinatory manuals, clergy also found themselves in a position to consult the holy scriptures for divinatory advice, a practice to which no one could object. Gregory of Tours explains the logic of the practice in his narrative of a meeting with Merovech, the rebellious son of Chilperic:

> One day, I came to have dinner with him. While we sat together, he humbly asked that some things be read for the instruction of his soul. I opened the book of Solomon, and seized upon the verse that first came up. It read as follows: "The eye that mocketh at his father, let the ravens of the valleys pluck it out" [Prov. 30:17, trans. Douay-Rheims, adapt.]. Although he did not understand it, I considered this verse to have been chosen by the Lord.   (*Hist.* 5.14)[19]

In this and the other examples of biblical sortition cited by Gregory (*Hist.* 4.16, 5.49, and 8.4), the verses chosen by God are presented as obvious in their meanings and not requiring interpretation. But in the event that they did require interpretation, many clergy and religious would have been prepared by their training to do so. Caesarius required the deacons he ordained to have read the Old and New Testament books "four times in order" (*Vita Caesarii* 1.56), and he himself had a comprehensive knowledge of the scriptures. Indeed, his biographers describe his application of biblical teachings to the problems of his congregation in terms that closely resemble the actions of a diviner:

> And so, if circumstances demanded, he recited in succession countless *exempla* from the divine books (1.16).

> Like a good physician he provided different remedies (*medicamina*) for different ailments; he did not offer what would please the patient, but rather what would cure him (1.17).

> Through the Lord's inspiration he possessed this unique skill, that when he revealed details to individuals, he exposed to each person's eyes the course of his life (*vitae suae cursum*) (1.18).

In this case, as in others, the line between spiritual advice and Christian divination may be difficult to draw, but that in itself echoes the paramount preference in the Merovingian world for practical results over theological absolutes. The material record affirms this point at the same time as it reveals a wide diversity of practice and new problems of interpretation. We can illustrate this by a brief look at amulets (see also Kornbluth, Chapter 40, this volume).

Among its other accomplishments, Édouard Salin's *La civilisation mérovingienne* showed, particularly in Chapter 30 on amulets (1949–1959, vol. 4), how broad a category of material objects, both natural (animals, plants, and minerals) and human-made, could be at least considered, if not proven, to have amuletic purposes. In its pages, we find the kinds of amulets that Caesarius objected to, for instance, those made of amber (*Serm.* 13.5, 14.4, 51.1; cf. Salin, vol. 4: 78–80) or other natural material (*Serm.* 13.5, 14.4, 51.4; cf. Salin, vol. 4: 80–85). Salin also drew attention to the (luxury) articles the bishop himself wore for spiritual protection (vol. 4: 105–109): a carved ivory buckle depicting Christ's empty tomb (vol. 4: 410–411, fig. 186) and a leather belt bearing traces of a cross and the paired Greek letters that served as symbols of Christian power: Alpha-Omega and Chi-Rho (vol. 4: 350).[20]

We also find in Salin a wide range of other objects that may have served as amulets, including animal bones and teeth, pieces of flint, beads, small metal objects, and snail shells (vol. 4: 68–78), and some that more certainly did, such as containers of oil and dust (vol. 4: 85–87, 112–8) and the so-called *boules magiques* (vol. 4: 94–99). While the number of objects that can be confidently identified as amulets may have been overestimated in past decades (Effros 2003, pp. 138–139, 167–168), it is not unlikely that in their sheer multitude, some of these items, found far and wide among grave goods, were designed or could be used for protective or magical purposes.

The same caution applies to inscribed objects. A careful survey by Mindy MacLeod and Bernard Mees (2006) discusses numerous objects with runic writing that may have served magical or protective purposes. But identifying an inscription as amuletic is not always straightforward, as we can see in a fibula discovered in the 1830s near Charnay-lès-Chalon (Saône-et-Loire), now held in the Musée d'Archéologie Nationale in Saint-Germain-en-Laye (inv. no. 34722) (see Fig. 41.1, front and back). Dating to the sixth century, its writing contains several features that MacLeod and Mees identify as "amulet text-forming elements" (2006, p. 82): a letter sequence (in this case, an almost complete *futhark*), a naming expression (with what are almost certainly the names of a man, Idda or Iddo, and a woman, Liano), and less certainly, two rune complexes that MacLeod and Mees regard as abbreviations for charm words (Kr, Ïia). Not all experts, however, agree on the transcription of the text or the meaning of the inscription; even the language in which it is written, east or west Germanic, is uncertain. The translation by MacLeod and Mees—"May Liano discover Idda. Christ. Iao."—suggests that the inscription was meant as a "leading charm" (2006, p. 42), while Elmer Antonsen's more prosaic—"To (my) husband, Iddo, Liano."—leaves the purpose of the object in greater doubt (Antonsen 1975, pp. 77–78).

Yet, at the same time that such disagreements raise questions about the interpretation of particular objects, they also illustrate the diversity of expressive forms that personal agency could take in the Merovingian world. Appreciating the extent and depth of this

FIGURE 41.1. (front and back): Decorated silver bow fibula with runic inscription on the back, second half of the sixth century, discovered near Charnay-lès-Chalon (Saône-et-Loire). Saint-Germain-en-Laye: Musée d'Archéologie nationale, inv. 34722. The inscription begins with a *futhark* at the top of the headplate, and continues down the right side of the headplate and back up on the left. Three letters appear on the right side of the footplate and two more (almost illegible) below the pin holder (Findell 2012, pp. 383–385, cat. no. 15). Reproduced by permission of the Musée d'Archéologie nationale—Domaine national de Saint-Germain-en-Laye.

diversity, and in particular acknowledging the limits of our current understanding of it, is an essential step in our analysis of the role played by magic and divination in the lives of Merovingian people. It is particularly important to bear this in mind as we move toward the transition in the first half of the eighth century from a late Merovingian to an early Carolingian world, when opposition to magic and divination by Boniface of Mainz and other proponents of church reform brought renewed attention to suspect practices.

MAGIC AND DIVINATION IN THE EIGHTH CENTURY

Just as in other aspects of culture, language, and religion, so too in the practice of magic and divination, over time the Merovingian world was characterized by a high degree of geographical diversity and substantial change. Unfortunately, in the present state of scholarship, it is not possible to offer a full account of how magic or divination changed from one region or period of Merovingian history to another. What does seem clear is that by the eighth century, the rituals of magic and divination described in our texts appear to demonstrate a greater variety of methods and cultural settings than those described by sixth-century sources such as Caesarius of Arles and Gregory of Tours. The explanation could be that eighth-century churchmen chose to comment, for pastoral or political reasons, on a wider array of practices than their sixth-century counterparts, but it could equally (and simultaneously) be that the world they knew was larger and more diverse, culturally, linguistically, and religiously, than the worlds described by Caesarius or Gregory.

A good example of linguistic diversity may be found in the *Indiculus superstitionum et paganiarum* (Vatican, B.A.V., Pal. Lat. 577, fols. 7r–7v). Composed in the mid-eighth century, almost certainly in connection with Boniface's councils of the early 740s, it consists of thirty headings: three on magical subjects (10, 12, 22), three on divinatory ones (13, 14, 17), and the remainder on various forms of "paganism." Four of the headings in this last group are glossed with non-Latin words whose meanings and (Germanic or Celtic) etymologies are still the subject of discussion: *dadsisas* (2), *nimidas* (6), *nodfyr* (15), and *yrias* (24).[21] Although all of the words pertain to pagan rather than magical or divinatory practices, they can still be taken to represent the overall cultural richness of this short text. The headings on magic and divination are very general but contain some unexpected details. *Indiculus* 22, on weather magic (*De tempestatibus*), includes *cornua* (horns), attested elsewhere for protection against hail (*Homilia de sacrilegiis* 16), but also *cocleae* (snails), widely used as amulets but better known for their magical value in medicine (Marcellus, *medicam.* 12.34, 33.60) and agriculture (Palladius, *opus agr.* 1.35.8) than in managing the weather. *Indiculus* 13 lists some common varieties of auguries: those produced by birds and horses (*De auguriis vel avium vel equorum*) and the observation of sneezes (*sternutationes*), a type of twitch divination (Caesarius, *Serm.* 54.1), but also mentions the examination of cattle excrement (*bovum stercora*), for which early medieval parallels are difficult to find.[22]

The *Homilia de sacrilegiis* (Einsiedeln, Stiftsbibliothek MS 281, pp. 101–108, ed. C. P. Caspari) represents a different kind of diversity. Composed in the eighth century, perhaps in Alamannia or Raetia (Glatthaar 1999, pp. 74–76), it is divided into two parts. The first part (§§1–22) consists of a catalog of pagan customs (§§2–3), diviners and divinatory practices (§§4–13), and magicians and magical activities (§§14–22). Pagan practices are said to destroy one's faith and baptism, while divination and magic are said to be practiced not by Christians but by pagans. The second part consists of paraphrases of two sermons by Caesarius: sermon 192 on the Kalends of January (§§ 23–26) and sermon 54 on auguries (§27).

Many, perhaps most, of the divinatory subjects listed in the *Homilia de sacrilegiis* are familiar from Merovingian texts: *pythonissae* and other diviners (5), sortilege (6), the *Sortes Sanctorum* (7), the *sortes biblicae* (8), divination from domestic objects, involuntary sounds, and animal behavior (9, 10), astrology (4, 8, 10), and the observation of days of the week and phases of the moon to guide particular activities (10–13). The catalogue of magical subjects is even more extensive: spells written on lead or other materials (14, 15, 16, 19, 20), amulets inscribed with *characteres*, names of angels, and Solomonic writings (15, 19), bindings for healing wounds and eye pain, or driving away snakes (21), and much else, in far more detail than one usually sees in sermons, penitentials, or church councils. In a text that Dieter Harmening called "consistently well-informed" (*stets gut informierte*, Harmening 1979, p. 239), it is difficult to judge how much is founded on the observation of contemporary practice and how much on antiquarian research, but it would be a mistake to underestimate its value either as a record of past divination and magic or as a guide to current practice.[23]

As a demonstration of the possibilities that remain for future research, we end with a passage from the *Homilia de sacrilegiis* that describes the methods experts used to drive out demons:

> And those who perform a suffumigation on demoniacs by any means, and lead them to the monuments, that is the ancient sacred places which they also call "ancestral," to cure them, or who through spells and roots and herbal potions, and by carrying a ring and iron arm bracelets on his body, or who places in his home iron objects that demons fear, and who fix colored wands in the ground by driving them in, and iron nails under the bed of the demoniac, and believe that they can drive a demon out of someone through these magical rituals—these are not Christians, but practitioners of sacrilege (22).[24]

From suffumigation to iron nails, from martyrs' tombs to the manifold remedies of nature and the power of amulets, we see a parade of familiar scenes alongside less familiar practices.[25] The challenge for future research is not merely to better locate this and other texts in time and place, to use them more systematically as a commentary on past or contemporary behavior, or to define with further precision changing fashions in Christian standards of piety. It is also to continue the effort to animate this catalog of ritual practice and to restore to our narratives the Merovingian persons who invested time, effort, money, worry, and equal reserves of pragmatism and religious faith into their hopes for a decent life, for relief from suffering, and for some small measure of control over the uncertainty and risk that beset their world.

Notes

1. Among the most useful studies in this genre are the following, in chronological order: Boudriot 1928; Harmening 1979; Flint 1991; Nicoli 1992; Hen 1995; Pontal 1995–1996; Zeddies 2003; and Filotas 2005.
2. Couser 2010 is a model study. See also Wood 1995.
3. Identified by the bishop as instruments of magic (*maleficia*), these may be considered amulets of two very common types in Merovingian Gaul: one made of vegetal matter and the other of the inedible parts of wild animals (Lavarra 1982, pp. 38–39).

4. As Dickie (2012, p. 323) has pointed out, such substances could be used either to harm or to heal.

5. Caesarius's editor (Morin 1953) did not have access to the manuscript itself, and following a printed edition, read *fumigare*. The manuscript, however, clearly reads *suffumigare*, the technically more correct term, as *Homilia de sacrilegiis* 22 suggests. The verb refers to the use of smoke or vapor for purposes of purification, exorcism, or healing. On its use in the Latin medical tradition, see Montero Cartelle 2004. I am grateful to my colleague Frank A. C. Mantello for confirming the manuscript reading.

6. Morin (1936, p. 10) credits Samuel Cavallin with this observation.

7. A precedent was provided by the emperor Constantine himself, *Cod. Theod.* 16.10.1 (December 17, 320): *Si quid de palatio nostro aut ceteris operibus publicis degustatum fulgore esse constiterit, retento more veteris observantiae quid portendat, ab haruspicibus requiratur et diligentissime scriptura collecta ad nostram scientiam referatur, ceteris etiam usurpandae huius consuetudinis licentia tribuenda, dummodo sacrificiis domesticis abstineant, quae specialiter prohibita sunt.*

8. For a recent review of the question, see Bremmer 2015.

9. A fuller discussion of the literature of lot divination can be found in Luijendijk and Klingshirn 2018, pp. 27–55. Family A is included in Group 1, Family B in Group 2, and Family C in Group 3.

10. Studied by Graf 2005. The inscriptions are published, with an introduction and commentary, in Nollé 2007.

11. A study of this collection appears in Wilkinson 2018.

12. For this translation, see *Sortes Sangallenses* 1951, p. 35.

13. The reading, suggested by Vinzenz Bulhart, can be found in *Sortes Sangallenses* 1951, p. 125.

14. For the date, see McKitterick 2004.

15. *Si quis paganorum consuetudinem sequens divinos et sortilegos in domo sua introduxerit, quasi ut malum foras mittant aut maleficia inveniant vel lustrationes paganorum faciant, quinque annis poenitentiam agant.* (*Canones ex Orientalium Patrum Synodis* 71, ed. Barlow, p. 130). On Martin's reception in Merovingian Gaul, see Hen 2001.

16. *quicquid in domibus fidelium haec unda asparserit, cariat immundicia, liberitur a noxia. non illic resediat spiritus pestelens, non aura corrumpens. abscedant omnes latentis insidiae inimici omnesque inquietudines procul aufugiant.* See also *Bobbio Missal* 540–542, 544, 556, and further examples in Hen 2015, pp. 198–199.

17. *Canones ex orientalium patrum synodis* 59 (ed. Barlow, p. 138): "It is not permitted for clerics to be *incantatores* and to make amulets, which is a binding of souls. If anyone does these things, he should be ejected from the church" (*Non liceat clericis incantatores esse et ligaturas facere, quod est colligatio animarum. Si quis haec facit, de ecclesia proiciatur*).

18. *aliquanti clerici student auguriis et sub nomine confictae religionis quas sanctorum sortes uocant, diuinationis scientiam profitentur aut quarumcumque scripturarum inspectione futura promittunt*, Vannes (462/8), can. 16.

19. *Dum pariter sederemus, suppliciter petiit aliqua ad instructionem animae legi. Ego vero, reserato Salomonis libro, versiculum qui primus occurrit arripui, qui haec contenebat: Oculum, qui aversus aspexerit patrem, effodiant eum corvi de convallibus* (Prov. 30:17). *Illo quoque non intellegente, consideravi hunc versiculum ad Dominum praeparatum.*

20. Illustrated in Guyon and Heijmans 2013, p. 183.

21. For sharply different interpretations, see Haderlein 1992 and Homan 2000.

22. Bargheer 1933. For a Roman example, see Cicero, *De divinatione* 2.77, with commentary by Pease 1963, p. 477.

23. A point well made by Hen 2015, p. 156.

24. *Et quicumque demoniacos alicunde suffomigant et eos ad monumenta, id est sacratas [sarandas MS] antiquas, quae et maiores uocant, quasi pro remedio ducunt, uel qui per incantationes et radices et pociones herbarum et anolum et brachiales ferreos in corpore suo portando, aut in domo sua quecumque de ferro, propter ut demones timeant, ponit [MS] et uirgas colorias in terra fodendo et claues ferreos sub lecto demoniaci figent et demonem de homine per haec maleficia credunt expellere, isti non christiani, sed sagrilici sunt.* For the emendation of *sarandas* to *sacratas*, see Petersmann 1996, p. 146.

25. One might simply note Filotas's dry admission: "the meaning of coloured rods (*virgae coloriae*) escapes me" (Filotas 2005, p. 263).

Works Cited

Ancient Sources

Bobbio Missal. E. A. Lowe (ed.). (1920). *The Bobbio Missal: A Gallican Mass-Book (Ms. Paris. lat. 13246).* London: Henry Bradshaw Society.

Caesarius of Arles, *Sermones (Serm.).* G. Morin (ed.). (1953). *Sancti Caesarii Arelatensis Sermones.* CCSL 103–104. Turnhout: Brepols.

Canones ex Orientalium Patrum Synodis. C. W. Barlow (ed.). (1950). *Martini Episcopi Bracarensis Opera Omnia.* New Haven, CT: Yale University Press.

Cicero, *De divinatione.* A. S. Pease (ed. and comm.). (1963). *M. Tulli Ciceronis De divinatione.* Darmstadt: Wissenschaftliche Buchgesellschaft.

Codex Theodosianus (Cod. Theod.). T. Mommsen and P. M. Meyer (eds.). (1905). *Theodosiani Libri XVI.* 2 vols. in 3. Berlin: Weidmann.

Council of Narbonne (589). J. Vives (ed.). (1963). *Concilios visigóticos e hispano-romanos.* Barcelona: Consejo Superior de Investigaciones Científicas.

Council of Vannes (462/468). C. Munier (ed.). (1963). *Concilia Galliae a. 314–a. 506.* CCSL 148. Turnhout: Brepols.

Cyprianus of Toulon et al., *Vita Caesarii Arelatensis (Vita Caes.).* G. Morin (ed.). (1942). *Sancti Caesarii episcopi arelatensis Opera omnia nunc primum in unum collecta.* Vol. 2: *Opera varia.* Maredsous: Abbaye de Maredsous.

Gregory of Tours, *De passione et virtutibus sancti Juliani martyris (VJ).* B. Krusch (ed.). (1885). MGH SRM 1.2 (pp. 112–134). Hanover: Hahn.

Gregory of Tours, *De virtutibus sancti Martini episcopi (VM).* B. Krusch (ed.).(1885). MGH SRM 1.2 (pp. 134–211). Hanover: Hahn.

Gregory of Tours, *Historiae (Hist.).* B. Krusch and W. Levison (eds.). (1937–1951). *Decem Libri Historiarum.* MGH SRM 1.1. Hanover: Hahn.

Gregory of Tours, *In gloria martyrum (GM).* B. Krusch (ed.). (1885). MGH SRM 1.2 (pp. 34–111). Hanover: Hahn.

Gregory of Tours, *In gloria martyrum (GM).* R. Van Dam (trans.). (1988). *Glory of the Martyrs.* Liverpool: Liverpool University Press.

Homilia de sacrilegiis. C. P. Caspari (ed.).(1886). *Eine Augustin fälschlich beilegte Homilia de sacrilegiis.* Christiania: Jacob Dybwad.

Indiculus superstitionum et paganiarum. A. Boretius (ed.). (1883). MGH Capitularia 1 (pp. 222–223). Hanover: Hahn.

Isidore of Seville, *Etymologiae (Etym.).* W. M. Lindsay (ed.). (1911). *Isidori Hispalensis Episcopi Etymologiarum sive Originum.* 2 vols. Oxford: Clarendon Press.

Marcellus, *De Medicamentis (medicam.).* M. Niedermann and E. A. Liechtenhan (eds.). (1968). *Über Heilmittel.* 2nd ed. 2 vols. Corpus medicorum Latinorum 5. Berlin: Akademie Verlag.

Pactus Legis Salicae. K. A. Eckhardt, (ed.). (1962). MGH, LL nat. Germ. 4.1. Hanover: Hahn.

Palladius, *Opus agriculturae (opus agr.).* R. H. Rodgers (ed.). (1975). *Palladii Rutilii Tauri Aemiliani viri inlustris Opus agriculturae, De veterinaria medicina, De insitione* (pp. 1–240). Leipzig: Teubner.

Sortes Monacenses. H. Winnefeld (ed.).(1887). *Sortes Sangallenses. Adjecta sunt alearum oracula ex codice Monacensi primum edita* (pp. 53–60). Bonn: Cohen.

Sortes Sanctorum. E. Montero Cartelle (ed.) (2013). *Les Sortes sanctorum: étude, édition critique et traduction,* trans. A. Maillet. Paris: Classiques Garnier.

Sortes Sangermanenses. J. R. Harris (ed.). (1901). *The Annotators of the Codex Bezae (with some notes on Sortes Sanctorum)* (pp. 59–69). Cambridge: Cambridge University Press.

Sortes Sangallenses. A. Dold (ed.). (1948) *Die Orakelsprüche im St. Galler Palimpsestcodex 908 (die sogenannten 'Sortes Sangallenses').* Österreichische Akademie der Wissenschaften, Philosophisch-historische Klasse, Sitzungsberichte 225(4). Vienna: Österreichische Akademie der Wissenschaften.

Sortes Sangallenses. R. Meister (comm.). (1951). *Die Orakelsprüche im St. Galler Palimpsestcodex 908 (die sogenannten 'Sortes Sangallenses') Erläuterungen.* Österreichische Akademie der Wissenschaften, Philosophisch-historische Klasse, Sitzungsberichte, 225(5). Vienna: Österreichische Akademie der Wissenschaften.

Modern Sources

Antonsen, E. H. (1975). *A Concise Grammar of the Older Runic Inscriptions.* Tübingen: Max Niemayer Verlag.

Bargheer, E. (1933). "Kot-Mantik." *Handwörterbuch des deutschen Aberglaubens* 5, col. 332.

Boudriot, W. (1928). *Die altgermanische Religion in der amtlichen kirchlichen Literatur des Abendlandes vom 5. bis 11. Jahrhundert.* Bonn: Röhrscheid.

Bremmer, J. N. (2015). "Ancient Necromancy: Fact or Fiction?" In K. Bielawski (ed.), *Mantic Perspectives: Oracles, Prophecy and Performance* (pp. 119–140). Gardzienice and Lublin: Ośrodek Praktyk Teatralnych 'Gardzienice'; Warsaw: Wydzial Artes Liberales, Uniwersytetu Warszawskiego.

Campetella, M. (2001). " 'Sermo humilis' e comunicazione di massa nei 'Sermones' di Cesario di Arles." In I. Mazzini and L. Bacci (eds.), *Evangelizzazione dell'Occidente dal terzo all'ottavo secolo: Lingua e linguaggi. Dibattito teologico* (pp. 75–104). Rome: Herder.

Campetella, M. (2006). "Superstition et magie chez Cesaire d'Arles (470–542)." In C. Arias Abellán (ed.), Latin vulgaire, latin tardif VII: actes du VIIème Colloque international sur le latin vulgaire et tardif. Séville 2–6 septembre 2003 (pp. 179–188). Sevilla: Universidad de Sevilla.

Couser, J. (2010). "Inventing Paganism in Eighth-Century Bavaria." *Early Medieval Europe* 18(1): 26–42.

Dickie, M. W. (2012). "Magic in Merovingian Gaul: Continuity or Discontinuity?" In M. Piranomonte and F. M. Simón (eds.), *Contesti magici, contextos magicos: Atti del*

Convegno Internazionale, Roma, Palazzo Massimo, 4–6 novembre 2009 (pp. 313–325). Rome: De Luca Editori d'Arte.

Dolbeau, F. (2003). "Le combat pastoral d'Augustin contre les astrologues, les devins et les guérisseurs." In P.-Y. Fux, J.-M. Roessli, and O. Wermelinger (eds.), *Augustinus Afer. Saint Augustin: africanité et universalité. Actes du colloque international Alger-Annaba, 1–7 avril 2001*, 2 vols. (vol. 1, pp. 167–182). Fribourg: Éditions Universitaires.

Effros, B. (2003). *Merovingian Mortuary Archaeology and the Making of the Early Middle Ages*. Berkeley: University of California Press.

Eidinow, E. (2007). *Oracles, Curses, and Risk among the Ancient Greeks*. Oxford: Oxford University Press.

Étaix, R. (1978). "Les épreuves du juste: Nouveau sermon de saint Césaire d'Arles." *Revue des études augustiniennes* 24: 272–277.

Fernández Nieto, F. J. (2010). "A Visigothic Charm from Asturias and the Classical Tradition of Phylacteries against Hail." In R. L. Gordon and F. M. Simón (eds.), *Magical Practice in the Latin West: Papers from the International Conference held at the University of Zaragoza, 30 Sept. – 1st Oct. 2005* (pp. 551–600). Leiden: Brill.

Filotas, B. (2005). *Pagan Survivals, Superstitions and Popular Cultures in Early Medieval Pastoral Literature*. Toronto: Pontifical Institute of Mediaeval Studies.

Findell, M. (2012). *Phonological Evidence from the Continental Runic Inscriptions*. Berlin: Walter de Gruyter.

Flint, V. I. J. (1991). *The Rise of Magic in Early Medieval Europe*. Princeton, NJ: Princeton University Press.

Glatthaar, M. (1999). "Rätisches Recht des 8. Jahrhunderts in der Predigt *De signum Christi*." In T. M. Buck (ed.), *Quellen, Kritik, Interpretation: Festgabe zum 60. Geburtstag von Hubert Mordek* (pp. 57–88). Frankfurt-am-Main: Peter Lang.

Glatthaar, M. (2004). *Bonifatius und das Sakrileg: Zur politischen Dimension eines Rechtsbegriffs*. Frankfurt-am-Main: Peter Lang.

Graf, F. (1997). *Magic in the Ancient World*, trans. F. Philip. Cambridge, MA: Harvard University Press.

Graf, F. (2005). "Rolling the Dice for an Answer." In S. I. Johnston and P. T. Struck (eds.), *Mantikê: Studies in Ancient Divination* (pp. 51–97). Leiden: Brill.

Grey, C. (2011). *Constructing Communities in the Late Roman Countryside*. Cambridge: Cambridge University Press.

Guyon, J., and Heijmans, M. (eds.). (2013). *L'Antiquité tardive en Provence, IVᵉ–VIᵉ siècle: naissance d'une chrétienté*. Arles: Actes Sud/Aux sources chrétiennes de la Provence.

Haderlein, K. (1992). "Celtic Roots: Vernacular Terminology and Pagan Ritual in Carlomann's Draft Capitulary of A.D. 743, Codex Vat.Pal.Lat.577." *Canadian Journal of Irish Studies* 18(2): 1–30.

Harmening, D. (1979). *Superstitio: Überlieferungs- und theoriegeschichtliche Untersuchungen zur kirchlich-theologischen Aberglaubensliteratur des Mittelalters*. Berlin: E. Schmidt.

Hen, Y. (1995). *Culture and Religion in Merovingian Gaul: AD 481–751*. Leiden: Brill.

Hen, Y. (2001). "Martin of Braga's *De correctione rusticorum* and Its Uses in Frankish Gaul." In E. Cohen and M. De Jong (eds.), *Medieval Transformations: Texts, Power, and Gifts in Context* (pp. 35–49). Leiden: Brill.

Hen, Y. (2013). "The Content and Aims of the So-Called Homiliary of Burchard of Würzburg." In M. Diesenberger, Y. Hen, and M. Pollheimer (eds.), *Sermo Doctorum: Compilers, Preachers, and Their Audiences in the Early Medieval West* (pp. 127–152). Turnhout: Brepols.

Hen, Y. (2015). "The Early Medieval West." In D. J. Collins (ed.), *The Cambridge History of Magic and Witchcraft in the West: From Antiquity to the Present* (pp. 183–206). New York: Cambridge University Press.

Homan, H. (2000). "Indiculus superstitionum et paganiarum," *Reallexikon der germanischen Altertumskunde* 15: 369–379.

Horden, P., and Purcell, N. (2000). *The Corrupting Sea: A Study of Mediterranean History.* Oxford: Blackwell Publishing.

Klingshirn, W. E. (1994). *Caesarius of Arles: The Making of a Christian Community in Late Antique Gaul.* Cambridge: Cambridge University Press.

Klingshirn, W. E. (2002). "Defining the *Sortes Sanctorum*: Gibbon, Du Cange, and Early Christian Lot Divination." *Journal of Early Christian Studies* 10(1): 77–130.

Klingshirn, W. E. (2003). "Isidore of Seville's Taxonomy of Magicians and Diviners." *Traditio* 58: 59–90.

Klingshirn, W. E. (2005). "Christian Divination in Late Roman Gaul: The *Sortes Sangallenses*." In S. I. Johnston and P. T. Struck (eds.), *Mantikê: Studies in Ancient Divination* (pp. 99–128). Leiden: Brill.

Labrousse, M. (1978). "Circonscription de Midi-Pyrénées." *Gallia* 36(2): 389–430.

Lavarra, C. (1982). "Pseudochristi e pseudoprophetae nella Gallia merovingia." *Quaderni medievali* no. 1313: 6–43.

Luijendijk, A.-M. and Klingshirn, W. E. (2018). *My Lots are in Thy Hands: Sortilege and its Practitioners in Late Antiquity.* Leiden: Brill.

MacLeod, M., and Mees, B. (2006). *Runic Amulets and Magic Objects.* Woodbridge: Boydell.

Maguire, E. D., Maguire, H., and Duncan-Flowers, M. J. (eds.) (1989). *Art and Holy Powers in the Early Christian House.* Urbana-Champaign: University of Illinois Press.

Martin, M. (2012). "Les plombs magiques de la Gaule meridionale." *Ephesia Grammata* 5(2), no. 12. Online at http://www.etudesmagiques.info/index2.php?go=revues.

McKitterick, R. (2004). "The Scripts of the Bobbio Missal." In Y. Hen and R. Meens (eds.), *The Bobbio Missal: Liturgy and Religious Culture in Merovingian Gaul* (pp. 19–52). Cambridge: Cambridge University Press.

Montero Cartelle, E. (2004). "Nivel de lengua, connotaciones y léxico técnico: el campo de *suffumigare*," In M. Baldin, M. Cecere, and D. Crismani (eds.), *Testi medici latini antichi. Le parole della medicina: Lessico e Storia, Atti del VII Convegno Internazionale, Trieste, 11–13 ottobre 2001* (pp. 611–626). Bologna: Pàtron Editore.

Moreira, I. (2003). "Dreams and Divination in Early Medieval Canonical and Narrative Sources: The Question of Clerical Control." *Catholic Historical Review* 89(4): 621–642.

Morin, G. (1936). "Quelques raretés philologiques dans les écrits de Césaire d'Arles." *Bulletin du Cange* 11: 5–14.

Naether, F. (2010). *Die Sortes Astrampsychi: Problemlösungsstrategien durch Orakel im römischen Ägypten.* Tübingen: Mohr Siebeck.

Nicoli, F. (1992). *Cristianesimo, superstizione e magia nell'alto medioevo: Cesario di Arles, Martino di Braga, Isidoro di Siviglia.* Bagni di Lucca: Edizioni Maxmaur.

Nollé, J. (2007). *Kleinasiatische Losorakel: Astragal- und Alphabetchresmologien der hochkaiserzeitlichen Orakelrenaissance.* Munich: C. H. Beck.

Petersmann, H. (1996). "L'Homélie pseudo-augustinienne 'Sur le sacrilege.'" In J. Dion (ed.), *Culture antique et fanatisme* (pp. 141–149). Paris: De Boccard.

Pontal, O. (1995–1996). "Survivances païennes, superstitions et sorcellerie au Moyen Âge d'après les décrets des conciles et synodes." *Annuarium historiae conciliorum* 27(8): 129–136.

Salin, E. (1949–1959). *La civilisation mérovingienne d'après les sépultures, les textes et le laboratoire*, 4 vols. Paris: A. and J. Picard.

Thiérot, A., and Lantier, R. (1940). "Le cimetière mérovingien du Maltrat à Vouciennes." *Revue Archéologique* 6th ser. 15: 210–246.

Wilkinson, K. W. (2015). "A Greek Ancestor of the *Sortes Sanctorum*." *Zeitschrift für Papyrologie und Epigraphik* 196: 94–102.

Wilkinson, K. W. (2018). "*Hermēneiai* in Manuscripts of John's Gospel: An Aid to Bibliomancy." In A.-M. Luijendijk and W. E. Klingshirn (eds.), *My Lots are in Thy Hands: Sortilege and its Practitioners in Late Antiquity* (pp. 101–123). Leiden: Brill.

Wiśniewski, R. (2005). "La consultation des possédés dans l'antiquité tardive: pythones, engastrimythoi et arrepticii." *Revue d'études augustiniennes et patristiques* 51: 127–152.

Wood, I. N. (1995)."Pagan Religion and Superstitions East of the Rhine from the Fifth to the Ninth Century." In G. Ausenda (ed.), *After Empire: Towards an Ethnology of Europe's Barbarians* (pp. 253–279). Woodbridge: Boydell and Brewer.

Zeddies, N. (2003). *Religio et sacrilegium: Studien zur Inkriminierung von Magie, Häresie und Heidentum (4.–7. Jahrhundert)*. Frankfurt-am-Main: Peter Lang.

CHAPTER 42

....

VISIONS AND THE AFTERLIFE

....

ISABEL MOREIRA

As affirmed by the Nicene Creed, God was maker "of all things visible and invisible," and faith could be defined as "the demonstration of things not seen" (Augustine, *Enchiridion* 2 [8] drawing on Hebrews 11.1). Mostly, the invisible remained invisible, but sometimes, in exceptional circumstances, there were those who claimed to have been granted a sight of this normally invisible, God-created world. Church leaders took an active role in evaluating such claims, lending weight only to dreams and visions that supported Christian theology and practice. Stories of supernatural visitations have always been popular. Merovingian authors reveal a strong appetite for such stories, and they recorded them in substantial numbers.

Vision narratives are to be found in a variety of Merovingian sources. For example, healing visions were recorded at the public shrines of saints by individuals assigned to that task and some of these lists have survived either as independent documents or appended to hagiographies. Gregory of Tours included visions in his *Histories* and other writings. Still more visions of monks and nuns were recorded at their monastic institutions by confessors or others delegated by the abbot to the task. In at least one case we know that the visions of a mystic, Aldegund of Maubeuge, were recorded by a confessor with a long-term connection to his spiritual charge. Visions found their way into other kinds of literature, too. Poetic works imagined celestial realms and versified earlier accounts of visions, for example, Paulinus of Périgueux and Venantius Fortunatus versified Sulpicius Severus' *Life of St. Martin*. When included in histories (see Reimitz, Chapter 22, this volume), a vision could help explain human action and motivation, splicing God's will into a variety of human, environmental, and cosmic events. Finally, visions of otherworldly travel were the theological juggernauts of the medieval visionary world: epic in scope and larded with scriptural citations, these vision texts were composed, shaped, revised, and adapted to new audiences in Merovingian scriptoria. Viewed as a whole, visions, apparitions, and visions seen in dreams (Merovingian texts did not always make phenomenological or linguistic distinctions) are well documented in this era. Alongside other forms of cultural expression such as art, material crafts, architecture, poetry, and the liturgy, stories of visions evoked images of real and imagined worlds, contributing to a Merovingian spiritual and religious aesthetic.

Yet, vision stories are tricky things when removed from the context of the faith in which they were written, and consequently they comprise particularly opaque forms of historical evidence. We cannot know the extent to which any given account replicated a genuine experience, nor can we penetrate its full historical context. What we can say is that this form of religious documentation could not have been produced in such numbers, or given such approbation by the church, had not clerics, monks, and nuns, the primary authors of these texts, seen visions as evidence that divine power saturated their society and that this power legitimated the claims of the church to provide a path to salvation. This was an era that, primarily through the medium of cultic writings, saw the integration of vision narratives into the fabric of religious culture. Furthermore, since religious authors were apt to view political events as guided by divine agency, major political actors like kings and bishops were viewed as society's conduits of good and bad outcomes, and their affairs were regarded as being of public interest. In short, Merovingian sources reveal that many Christians in this time period were attentive to visions—both their own and those of others. They recorded these stories in quantity. As a result, vision texts illuminate many aspects of Merovingian religion and culture. However, the student of Merovingian visions should be cautioned that some nineteenth-century editors excised visions and miracles from their editions of Merovingian texts, judging such material to have limited historical worth. To remedy this deficit, modern scholars may have to consult earlier editions of hagiographic texts such as are found in the Acta Sanctorum and Patrologia Latina.

Merovingian Christians may have been geographically distant from the religious centers of Rome and Constantinople, but they were by no means insulated from religious ideas and events emanating from those centers. Religious leaders were aware of the great Christological debates that swayed the sixth- and seventh-century Mediterranean world (see Esders, Chapter 16, this volume), and for as long as they continued, church councils provided opportunities for debating beliefs and practices. However, it was when facing alien or suspect ideas such as Homoousian Christology (Arianism), Jewish practices, or new ideas about sin and the afterlife in the religious movements from the north, that the Merovingian clerisy flexed its theological muscles and showed itself most attuned to the dangers of religious error. Vision accounts could be the means both to introduce and resolve religious error. Visions that ostensibly "proved" the errors of Homoians, Jews, and superstitious "pagans" can be found in the writings of Gregory of Tours in the sixth century (Moreira 2000). In the seventh century, it was the danger of new ideas about the afterlife that placed some of the Merovingian clergy on guard.

For all their relevance to historical debates, visions can often be overlooked as sources for Merovingian history and culture. Visionary literature is generally discussed in specialized analyses of the genre.[1] This is a pity, as visionary narratives were integral to discourses of power. At their inception, at least, they were not simply "stories" gliding across political boundaries (although sometimes they became that); rather, vision narratives were rooted in historical interests and concerns, even if these are not always easy for us to reconstruct today. Merovingian authors used dream and vision stories to comment on many dimensions of life: on dynastic legitimacy, religious competition, the supernatural skills of a saint or specialization of a shrine, the optimal conduct of the religious life, an individual's spiritual reputation, the chance of healing in this life, and the expectation of life after death. The public airing of visionary "evidence" could elevate the stakes of a given issue, directing us to deep-seated desires and priorities (see the discussion on Praeiectus, below). When visionaries claimed personal knowledge of the afterlife, we are given insight into the hopes, fears, and crises of individual Christians and of the communities that sought to frame their experiences. It was through vision texts that new ideas about the afterlife came to be accepted. In this respect, Merovingian vision narratives were a continuation of ancient Christian visions that shaped expectations of death, judgment, and the afterlife. Finally, for the modern reader, vision narratives evoke an immersive aesthetic environment, replete with images, sounds, smells, and emotion. In these texts we enter the polychrome world of Merovingian churches, we learn of monastic boundary walls that offered a view of the stars, we encounter residents of cities and monasteries, the smell of incense and sulfur, the beauty of the psalms chanted in moments of community, joy, fear and grief, and the solitude of the darkened, tomblike cell. Above all, scriptural references and the poetic rhythms of the liturgy infused the language of these texts providing them with an internal religious authority.

In this chapter we will encounter some of the contexts in which visions were recorded in the Merovingian era and how they fit with religious concerns. The final section discusses the Merovingian afterlife through the example of the *Vision of Barontus*, a text that illuminates tensions within Merovingian theologies of the afterlife, and the challenge posed by new ideas, especially about the existence of immediate postmortem purgation (purgatory).

Affirming God's Presence

Everyone dreams. Theoretically, any Christian could experience a dream or vision that contained religious meaning, although ancient tradition held that the scope of the message was commensurate with the status or official sphere of the visionary. In fact, since the act of recording such events was limited to those who could write, primarily the religious elite, it is their perspective on visions that predominates.

From the earliest times, monks and nuns were closely associated with visions of the supernatural. This was to be expected since the monastic movement claimed spiritual descent from the prophets, and its traditions were forged from the example of the desert fathers and mothers. These penitential communities provided conditions in which revelations were taken seriously. St. Anthony of Egypt had gone into the wilderness in the expectation of encountering demons, since demons sensed spiritual weakness. As a result, monastic writings were at the forefront of the science of distinguishing true visions from false, claiming that through the intellectual illumination of prayer, their heroes could discern demons even when disguised as angels (Moreira 2000, pp. 39–75, especially 43–46). However, identifying what was demonic possession and what was divine inspiration was often very much in the eye of the beholder. Out in the world, clerics encountered stories related by individuals from all levels of society. This required that, as individuals and as members of a group, religious leaders develop a stance on visionary matters that allowed them to investigate and assess visions that came to their attention from a variety of directions (Moreira 2000, 2003). Clerics were not above scrutinizing the visions of monks and nuns, especially when they had the potential to compete with clerical authority and interests. At the same time, it was never a simple matter for clerics to ignore the claims of visions among their flocks. Nonetheless, some clerics did try to ignore them, particularly when the message was unappealing, or if the claims appeared fabricated. However, ignoring a "true" vision could result in further visions and a bad outcome for the skeptic. In short, there are more stories that promoted the veracity of visions in Merovingian sources than stories that dismissed them, which suggests that the literate elite were comfortable keeping visionary accounts in the public eye, and were willing to accept them as a legitimate vehicle for expressing divine will, especially in hindsight. A story of this kind follows.

Bishop Gregory of Tours relates a cautionary tale that spelled the danger in disparaging visions of holy men (*Histories* 2.1). He tells us that as a very young man (*primaevae aetatis iuvenis*), Bricius, who eventually succeeded St. Martin as bishop of Tours, had tried to discredit the visions of his episcopal predecessor as the ramblings of a demented old man who was always looking at the sky. This disparaging behavior continued even after Bricius had become a priest. On becoming bishop, Bricius devoted himself to the religious life until, thirty-three years after his ordination (that is, when he was in his sixties), he was accused of having impregnated a laundry woman who had taken on the religious habit. He was exiled by the city's infuriated inhabitants. Bricius headed to Rome to appeal his case to the pope, but, while he lingered abroad, the inhabitants of Tours set up first one, then another bishop in his place. Gregory tells us that during his time in exile, Bricius lamented his former disrespect of Martin's visions and miracles, and blamed his harsh words for his current predicament. Eventually, with fitting irony, Bricius discovered for himself the value of a very timely vision. With the pope's blessing, he set out again for Tours and, while resting at a village six miles outside the city, was informed in a vision that Armentarius, who had been set up as bishop of Tours, had died. This vision allowed Bricius to enter one gate of the city just as Armentarius's body was being taken out through the other. His perfectly synchronized entry presented the city with a fait accompli, and Bricius remained as bishop in the city happily (*feliciter*) until his death seven years later. In the end, Bricius's ridicule of St. Martin harmed no one but himself. With the support of the pope, and having learned the great value of a fortuitous vision, Bricius lived out his final years as bishop in a way that Gregory of Tours thought fitting, and he was eventually venerated alongside his predecessor.

A story in which a bishop could be converted to a belief in visions through personal experience was obviously a powerful statement of the value of visions to those in power. Timely visions were useful. A vision could help sort out true cults from false ones, especially when the memory of cultic traditions was confused or lacking.[2] A timely vision could offer a pragmatic explanation for a change in political direction or the forging of new alliances—a valuable tool for the clerical administrator. And since bishops were theoretically chosen by God through clerical election and visions could be used to sway electoral opinion, the very office of bishop was, in a sense, a potential hostage to visionary intervention. The seventh-century *Passion of Praeiectus* provides an example of this (ed. Krusch 1910; trans. Fouracre and Gerberding 1996). Praeiectus had hoped to be elected bishop of Clermont. When the time came, Praeiectus made public a vision his mother had experienced while pregnant with him. Evidently, her vision portended good things, while also suggesting to later readers that he had been destined to die a holy death as a martyr. When a rival claimant, Garivald, learned that Praeiectus was disseminating the story, he produced a written document recording an agreement among some of the clergy that he, Garivald, would be bishop next. "In opposition (*in contrarietatem*)" to the vision story, we are told, he "displayed the document openly in the church to be read out to everybody" (*Passion of Praeiectus* 13). According to Praeiectus's hagiographer, the story of the vision started to influence people so that in the end Garivald bribed the laity to support his candidacy. Although Garivald prevailed in the short term, Praeiectus succeeded him as bishop and came to the very bloody end predicted for him by his mother's vision. Evidently, the hagiographer was comfortable arguing (whether it was true or not) that the story of a vision and a signed document could carry comparable weight in the public sphere.

Once bishops held their office, visions might be seen to aid their activities. For example, in some dioceses, Merovingian bishops were grappling with errant beliefs among their flocks. As noted earlier, visions that helped correctly identify the disputed inhabitant of a tomb could aid in the process of Christianizing the countryside (de Nie 1987; Moreira 2000; van Egmond 2006; Keshiako 2015). In the sixth century in particular, bishops in cities with communities of Jews or Homoian "Arians" responded to religious friction by recalling visions that validated Christian theology (Moreira 2000, pp. 99–107). Finally, bishops could evoke the supernatural presence of their episcopal predecessors and their patron saints to add weight to tussles with secular powers, especially in protecting clerical prerogatives, revenues, and immunities.

We are well informed about visions in episcopal contexts because bishops were well positioned to record them. But it was also the clergy's responsibility to provide guidance to others. How the clergy did this in individual cases is mostly hidden from us, especially when a vision was deemed "empty," or devoid, of religious meaning, but how they did this in their writing is not. Clerics weighed in. They could interpret visions through a variety of means: through prayer, by reference to earlier examples, or by reference to theoretically informed works on dreams and visions such as Macrobius's *Commentary on the Dream of Scipio*, or Augustine of Hippo's tripartite vision theory, widely known through florilegia (Moreira 1996, 2000, pp. 5–8; Keshiako 2015). It is even possible that they consulted books on dream interpretation listing images and their meaning, although clear evidence for this is lacking at this time.[3] The terms used to reference dreams and visions in Merovingian texts were those that had been used for centuries to describe such phenomena, in Latin, *visio, apparitio, somnium, oraculum*, the false vision, *somnium vanum*, or rarely, in Greek, *fantasma*. In Merovingian narratives, the Latin terms were used loosely, sometimes interchangeably or in combination; dreams could be visions, and visions were seen in dreams. In other areas of Europe, greater care was taken to distinguish dreams from visions (Keskiaho 2015). In the later Merovingian era, readers also had recourse to Pope Gregory I's sixfold classification of dreams (*Dialogues*, 4.50).[4] However, when Pope Gregory explained to Augustine of Canterbury how illusions in dreams might arise (through overeating, bodily ill health, or impure thoughts), he was not stating anything radically new (Bede, *Ecclesiastical History* 1.27). Common sense and personal discretion must also have played a part in the way bishops assessed such phenomena. Through the privilege of literacy and their supervision of diocesan activities, bishops could shape Christian expectations of the supernatural in their regions. In some cases, clerics may have taken an interest in visions because they were, after all, in the business of navigating supernatural claims, or because such events spoke to their desire as individuals to believe that divine benevolence shaped their world. Consequently, however risky visionary claims might be, supernatural sights were attributed to a wide variety of people in texts of this era: monastic leaders, hermits, nuns, pregnant women, children, sinners, the sick, soldiers, and even, on one occasion, a horse.

Visions and the Cult of Saints

Whereas faith was "defined" as belief in things unseen, Christians were also taught to believe that God could intervene in temporal matters, performing miracles through his "servants." Sounding a characteristically cautious note, Augustine of Hippo had suggested that some miracles were performed by "methods which are quite beyond mortal comprehension" but that they nevertheless witnessed, as had the martyrs, to the "faith in which the resurrection to eternal life is proclaimed" (*City of God*, 22.9). But for most, the activity of the saints was explanation enough for the miracles that were reported at the shrines of the saints, and some of these miracles were effected through visions.

Christians of the Merovingian era were deeply devoted to the cult of the saints—both to individual patron saints and to the community of saints as a whole. In this regard, they reflected Christian interests that prevailed across the Mediterranean world at this time.[5] However, the nature of the saints' powers, especially with respect to ideas about intercession and the afterlife, changed over time (Moreira 2010a). This did not dim awe for the saints. The lives and exploits of saints recorded in hagiographies personalized religious ideas, and visions and other signs of supernatural activity were recorded in significant numbers in this literature.

Saints and martyrs were revered by Christians because their personal lives and public actions were constructed by their biographers to reflect values designed to inspire ordinary Christians to be better ones. Saints were also thought to be in close contact with, and attuned to, divine powers; they were the "friends of God" (Brown 1981). Indeed, Merovingian saints were commonly portrayed as having been predestined to sanctity, a concept that was aided by stories of saints' mothers who had visions in pregnancy (Moreira 2003; Keskiaho 2015), and childhood miracles. Hagiographers used visions to herald many aspects of the saint's biography: the saint's birth, the decision to convert to the religious life, the choice of ascetic retreat, the location of a monastic rule, the companionship of the deceased, the needy dead (ghosts) hoping for intercession, the time and circumstances of death, and the likelihood of a future heavenly abode. All these events could be supported by timely visions (Moreira 2000; on ghosts, see Moreira, in press). If the site of a saint's body was relocated, as often happened when a cult developed over centuries, a vision could help the saint's devotee find the new resting place. For example, in the ninth century, the Merovingian saint, Glodesind, miraculously appeared in a "vision" to a blind woman to lead her to the new location of her relics (*Life of Glodesind of Metz* 25, 26). Although visions were not required of a saint, they were nevertheless sufficiently accepted that such stories rarely raised concerns. A vision experienced by a solitary in her cell, or by an observer at the death bed, might give assurance of salvation. So powerful was this idea that some hagiographers who lacked information on a saint's visions hypothesized that such an event must indeed have occurred, but that the saint's own modesty and discretion had suppressed knowledge of it.

Shrine records are relatively abundant for this era and remain underused sources. They survive in part because shrines were supervised and cures were recorded, an activity that had been long in practice at pagan shrines. Augustine of Hippo's comment that he "desired that narratives might be written, judging that the multitude should not remain ignorant of these things," was likely a general expectation in Merovingian Gaul also (*City of God* 22.8). Recordkeeping promoted the reputation of a site, suggesting the saint's continued activity on behalf of devotees, attracting pilgrims, and ensuring revenue streams and other forms of patronage. We can suppose that miracle lists were common at shrines and that they were generated in greater numbers than the surviving evidence suggests. And, as visions were reported in the context of miracles, this is another place where we find vision stories. The miracles at the shrine of St. Martin in Tours in particular were well publicized because Gregory of Tours edited them for a wider audience. It took a substantial investment of time and energy to shape such lists into literary material (Van Dam 1993); most lists that remained in the form of raw data were probably lost or destroyed over time. However, miracle lists with visionary content sometimes survive because they were incorporated into hagiographies, often as addenda to the biographical portion of the works.[6] While it was not uncommon for two or three healing visions to be recorded at the end of a saint's *vita*, since such accounts served to verify the saint's status as an intercessor (e.g., Gregory of Tours, *Life of Monegund* 10), some hagiographic dossiers included longer lists that can be readily supposed to have originated in a separate document. Venantius Fortunatus's *Life of St. Germanus of Paris*, and the *Life of St. Austrigisilus of Bourges* are examples.

Where there is a strong cultural acceptance that saints have visions, or appear in visions to others, the historical value of any individual account may be suspect. Undoubtedly, some hagiographers embellished or even fabricated supernatural tales to adorn their works. However, hagiographers also provided context for these stories.

Deep prayer and meditation, fasting and other forms of deprivation, grave sickness, and deathbeds observed by family and friends, were among the occasions when visions reportedly occurred. Such contexts appeared authentic to their readers.

DYNASTIC VISIONS AND POLITICAL MEMORY

With the notable exception of King Chilperic I (d. 587), Merovingian kings did not feature directly in visions recorded in the Merovingian era. But Chilperic was a remarkable exception. He has the dubious distinction of being the first French king reported to have ended in the flames of hell (Gregory of Tours, *Histories* 8.5).[7] He was certainly not the last since consigning kings and queens to hell, and later to purgatory, became something of a cottage industry among the Anglo-Saxons and Carolingians in the centuries that followed. With three doom-laden visions having Chilperic as their subject, the king was clearly a magnet for bad publicity. However, in this case, all three stories were related by a single individual–Gregory of Tours—who had his own reasons for viewing the king as a threat.[8] Gregory of Tours, our source for some memorably unflattering portraits of Merovingian kings, did not hold back in condemning Chilperic as a persecutor of biblical proportions, calling him the "Nero and Herod of our time." It was Gregory who, at a dinner party, reported to the guests that he had seen a vision of Chilperic in a dream (*per visionem somnii inspexi*). Tonsured like a bishop and carried on a *cathedra* with torches and candles, the king appeared in a kind of infernal ordination ceremony. The dark tones of this imaginary procession reflected Gregory's condemnation of Chilperic for his interference in clerical matters (de Nie 1987, pp. 285–287; Moreira 2000, pp. 96–99). However, the *cathedra* on which he was carried may also have referenced Herod, seated on a chair, as he was described in the *Vision of Ezra*.[9] Gregory's account of his dream prompted a story from another dinner party guest—Chilperic's own brother, Guntram. In the past, King Guntram had been the target of Chilperic's machinations, as Gregory pointed out to him on this very occasion, yet Guntram reportedly wept when he saw his dead brother with his limbs broken and cast into a boiling cauldron where he dissolved and liquefied (*Histories* 8.5). Despite the very different images in these two visions, Gregory interpreted both as representing Chilperic's postmortem state. Furthermore, Chilperic's plight prompted no action by Gregory. He offered no prayers of intercession, or indeed any hope at all. The mechanisms of clerical intercession for deceased spirits were only developing in the sixth century, and Gregory was in any case unsympathetic to final acts of repentance (*Histories*, 6.28). Gregory saw his own hopes for salvation in a life of service to the church and the saints. By the time he was writing this story, Gregory judged Chilperic to be wicked beyond redemption: his vision of Chilperic, his characterization of the king as Nero and Herod, and his designation of his sins as *scelera*, signals this. He may even have wanted to evoke the idea that Chilperic was the anti-Christ (see Bernstein 2010). The visions relegated the king to an infernal place, and the stories invited no further comment from Gregory or, as far as we know, from Guntram.

Chilperic may have been a "Herod" incarnate, but he was also a Merovingian king and his progeny was expected to play a role in future political affairs. Gregory reported a prediction by Bishop Salvius of Albi that Chilperic's house was doomed—a dynastic *damnatio* that weighed heavily on medieval kings. As it happened, the prediction failed to take into account Fredegund's early-stage pregnancy at the time of her husband's death. The immediate dynastic crisis was averted, and indeed later Merovingian kings were his descendants. As far as we know, no other Merovingian king attracted a similar infernal reputation in the Merovingian period. In fact, Carolingian kings fared far worse, as kings in hell and purgatory became a more developed theme from the ninth century onward. Indeed, we learn in the *Gesta Dagoberti*, a Carolingian work attributed to Hincmar, that the Merovingian King Dagobert (d. 639) narrowly escaped being thrown into hell by some devils. Calling on St. Martin, St. Maurice, and St. Denis, he was rescued by the three saints (*Gesta Dagoberti* 3). Retrospective mythmaking associated with the abbey of Saint Denis to support claims to past legacies and royal prestige reached back in time to encompass a Merovingian king (Bernstein 2017, pp. 163–165), but Dagobert, although no saint, was not in peril of damnation in Merovingian sources and his dynasty was expected to survive (*Life of Eligius*, 2. 33).

It is not surprising that prominent men had visions or that a king like Chilperic was seen in them; as political leaders and public figures, their activities were significant beyond their individual person. A public figure dreaming of events in the public sphere represented one of Macrobius's categories.[10] Salvius' vision of Chilperic, and Eligius of Noyon's prophesies about the sons of Clovis II and Balthild in the next century, reflect the importance supernatural signs for the mystique of Merovingian dynasty.

WOMEN'S VISIONS

Merovingian queens attracted more cultic attention than kings (on queens, see James, Chapter 11, this volume). Merovingian queens bore the dynastic burden differently than kings, owing to the belief that royal status was determined by the king's blood, not the queen's. For queens, dynastic security was often tied to personal security (*Life of Eligius*, 2. 33). A fair number of queens ended their careers and lives in convents, some by choice, some not. Queens helped convents attract resources and patronage, and a saintly queen who had visions, or who could be imagined to have them, was well positioned to have them recorded for posterity. Two queens had notable visions: Radegund in the late sixth century and Balthild in the late seventh.[11] Both were promised a place in heaven, and both were the focus of long-lived royal cults. Two of Radegund's visions were of Christ-like figures. The first, in the year of her conversion to the religious life, had a penitential theme: a ship in the form of a man (Christ) had many people sitting on its limbs, and she herself was seated at the knees. The "man-ship" spoke to her: "Now, you are sitting on my knee, but in time you will find a place in my bosom" (Baudonivia, *Life of Radegund* 3). A year before her death, Radegund had another vision, which seemed to fulfill the promise of the first. A richly clad, sympathetic youth sought to console her and dry her tears. Interpreted as Christ, the boy promised her that she was the foremost jewel in his crown (Baudonivia, *Life of Radegund* 20; Moreira 2000). Balthild's vision was a delightful spectacle: a ladder set before the altar, with angels going up and down and Balthild herself ascending (*Life of Balthild* 13–14). We are told that she took it as a sign of her impending death. Her hagiographer took it as a sign of her sanctity.

Where queens trod, aristocrats followed. When they took up administrative roles at court, in cities, or in monasteries, it was recorded that officials were guided by supernatural signs. Merovingian saints, especially episcopal saints, arose largely (although not exclusively) from the upper echelons of Frankish society, appropriating in the seventh and eighth centuries the tradition of saintly bishops that had flourished among Gallo-Romans in the fifth and sixth centuries. Furthermore, in the mid-seventh century, when women may have had favorable opportunities for inheritance (see James, Chapter 11, this volume), women from landed families set up convents and made the religious life a highly valued pursuit. Noble women who joined royal convents were educated and thus well positioned to express and shape their spiritual lives for posterity.

Because each religious community had its own demographics, characteristics, and culture, and only some were provided an opportunity to have their activities recorded, we tend to see some visions in single-authored clusters. These clusters reflected a momentary interest in recording events in an ascetic community. Gregory of Tours penned a joyous cluster about the Sainte-Croix convent where his niece was prioress from 590. A second, more somber, set of stories was recorded by the monk Jonas in the seventh century.

Gregory, well informed about the Sainte-Croix (Holy Cross) convent in Poitiers (Vienne), situated the following events in 583. A nun, Disciola, was visited three times on the day of her death by an invisible messenger, and a possessed pilgrim saw her being taken directly to heaven by the archangel Michael (*Histories* 6.29). In another story, with some resonances of the visions of Perpetua, an unnamed nun was led to a fount of living water where she was invited to quench her thirst. Stripped naked by her abbess, the girl (*puella*) was dressed in a bejeweled royal robe, a gift from her celestial husband. Her response to this vision was to enclose herself in a walled-up cell (*Histories* 6.29). (Unless it was common to wall up nuns at this convent, it is possible that this was the same nun who escaped her walled-up cell during the revolt at the convent some years later [*Histories* 9.40]). Radegund herself was reported by her second hagiographer, the nun Baudonivia, to have experienced three visions; the first related to her relic collection (Baudonivia, *Life of St. Radegund* 13), the other visions, discussed above, commented on Radegund's religious status as first a penitent and then a bride (Baudonivia, *Life of St. Radegund* 3 and 20). These four visions indicate that, in this convent, meditation on Christ as a celestial husband was a fully developed theme in Poitiers in the sixth century, strengthened by the convent's possession of a relic of the True Cross; the nuns of the Sainte-Croix convent confidently appropriated the rich, jewel-like imagery associated with marriage to Christ.

The second cluster of visions is gloomier in tone (Jonas, *Life of Columbanus* 2: 11–22). At the convent of Faremoutiers (Seine-et-Oise) established by Burgundofara, a number of nuns reported having visions when they were sick or in their final hours. It is perhaps not surprising that we hear their voices at this time. With their waking hours dominated by the liturgy and the customs of the house, it was at night or on their sickbeds that their dreams and fears were their own. The broken sleep of nuns produced the most vivid visionary dreams. A common thread was that the nuns expected to be saved, although sometimes they needed (and were given) extra time to complete a course of penance (on penance, see Uhalde, Chapter 45, this volume). The nuns confessed their sins to the abbess Burgundofara three times a day, so the abbess and her nuns were deeply involved in the thoughts and acts of penitential atonement. The visions reveal that adequate time for penance was an important issue for the nuns as they faced death, and time was often granted by a celestial dispensation. But hunger, too, was an issue that brought nuns to confession. Two stories of nuns who surreptitiously ate the community's foodstuffs shows that they risked damnation for this infraction (Jonas, *Life of St. Columbanus* 2.22). Two different nuns who rejected confession escaped from the convent but were forcibly returned; their continuing recalcitrance resulted in their being snatched by demons. But for the nuns who had run their course, the overriding boon they sought was an angel to come to their immediate aid on leaving the body. This was the positive side of the idea of immediate judgment. The endangered soul might expect to see demons, but the saved soul would enjoy the immediate relief of salvation. But still, a journey was ahead. These nuns feared to traverse the terrifying ether alone. They hoped for an angel or a saint as an escort. They wanted not to be alone at death. Even those assured of salvation in their visions anticipated their immediate judgment with anxiety, it seems. As Peter Brown notes, some nuns only "scraped by" (Brown 2015, p. 200).

Finally, in the Merovingian era, as in other eras, there were rare individuals, mystics, whose lives were transfigured by their visionary experiences. One such was Aldegund of Maubeuge, exceptional for her visions even in her lifetime. She had the special attention of a confessor who was both receptive to the spiritual import of her visions and a conscientious transcriber of them. In this case, the confessor's name, Subnius, is also known, suggesting that being associated with Aldegund's gifts lent him status, also. It is not possible to do justice to Aldegund's visions here. Suffice it to say that Aldegund's visions were extraordinarily frequent and personal. Even if we accept some editing by Subnius and the later authors of her vita, her dictated visions provide a rare glimpse into self-authored female spirituality in this age (*Life of Aldegund*; Moreira 2000, pp. 198–223).

THE MEROVINGIAN AFTERLIFE

Christians in this period drew their ideas about God and the afterlife from the core texts of Mediterranean Christianity: scriptures, creeds, patristic works, and apocalypses. Such texts provided ready tools for describing and interpreting visions. In addition, Augustine's description of the last judgment, heaven, and hell in the final books of his *City of God* provided surprisingly concrete answers to questions about the nature of the human condition after death, answering such questions as: will women retain a female appearance? (yes); at what age do the saints appear in heaven? (30); and will eyes be needed to "see"? (unclear). Such details aided writers, and presumably artists, too, in their endeavor to represent these realms correctly.[12] Furthermore, speculations about the geography of the otherworld and the precise order of events at the last judgment solidified as a result of the circulation of Augustine's works, the writings of Pope Gregory (the *Moralia in Job*, and the *Dialogues*, in particular) in the seventh century, the works of Bede at the turn of the eighth, and the continuous circulation of older texts of cosmic travel such as the *Book of Ezra* (Bremmer 2018) and the *Vision of Paul*. Indeed, the more we know about the circulation of apocalyptic texts, the longer the shadow they seem to cast over the visions of the early Middle Ages.

While the Merovingian era has left no great theological monuments on the order of the works of Julian of Toledo or Bede, most bishops were at least conversant with theology. Indeed, some were interested in theological debates beyond Frankish borders. When evaluating the state of theological knowledge in the seventh century, it is important to recognize that, as realized eschatology, visions of the otherworld reflected theological ideas and were vehicles for theological exploration and dissemination.

At the most basic level, Merovingian Christians believed what Mediterranean Christians believed: that there would be a time in the future when Christ would return to judge the living and the dead, and that on this day of judgment the soul would be consigned to eternal torment in hell or to eternal bliss in heaven. Yet these centuries saw the beginning of changes that were to affect views of the afterlife for centuries to come. The question of what happened precisely between an individual's death and her "final" judgment was somewhat hazy. Some accounts imagined the body in the tomb, quietly awaiting the resurrection; other tales imagined an immediate judgment after which the soul would experience proleptically the torment or bliss that would be eventually confirmed. This view, of immediate judgment, represented an emerging trend in Christian belief about the afterlife and visions of the otherworld. However, some went even further, claiming that the probing, purifying fire of the last day was, in fact, a fire in the present existence, and that it could begin its work of purification immediately. In principle, this fire would purge only minor sins. However, the idea was abroad that this fire might even save some of the most sinful humans, provided that certain conditions were fulfilled (Bede, *Ecclesiastical History* 5.12). In the *Vision of Barontus* discussed in the next section, a major otherworld vision of the Merovingian era, we see a hybrid case. It is a work that embraced the idea of an immediate judgment and the effective intercession of St. Peter, while at the same time avoiding any notion of immediate postmortem purgation.

BARONTUS MEETS ST. PETER

Barontus will be our guide to the Merovingian afterlife (*Visio Baronti* [hereafter: *VB*]; Hillgarth 1986, pp. 195–204; Levison 1910, pp. 368–394). In an age dominated by accounts of saints, Barontus, a wealthy Frank, who had only recently joined the monastic community of St. Peter at Lonrey (Indre, in the diocese of Bourges) where his son was already a member, is an unusual specimen. Father to at least one son, husband to three wives (probably sequentially), monk, and sinner, his is the story of a soul only narrowly saved. His vision was recorded soon after it had taken place, in 678 or 679. At the text's core is Barontus's first-person account, but it is framed by a narrator–commentator well versed in scripture, especially the psalms, the liturgy, and earlier accounts of visionary travel, specifically the *Vision of Paul*. This well-informed scribe also knew Pope Gregory's writings on the afterlife and appealed to these writings in support of the veracity of Barontus's experience. Before addressing its theological position, here is a brief synopsis:

Barontus's vision occurred as death approached. Returning to his bed after early morning prayers, Barontus was struck by a fever so extreme that he called for the deacon to come to him. By the time he arrived, Barontus was almost dead and remained in this critical state for twenty-four hours until he suddenly awoke, crying out "Glory to Thee, God," three times. The assembled monks who had been chanting psalms were both relieved and curious, immediately asking Barontus what he had seen. Barontus's tale was such as would make those who heard it "greatly fearful of their sins" (*ut qui audiunt expavescunt de illorum vitia*) (*VB* 2).

Barontus's troubles began as soon as his soul left his body: two "foul" demons began to strangle him with the intent of dragging him down to hell (*VB* 3). Barontus struggled with them alone until suddenly the archangel Raphael appeared to help him, upbraiding the demons. The demons retorted that if God's glory would not help Barontus, then neither could he, at which point Raphael suggested that they all go together to God's throne of judgment. With the demons still clinging to their intended prey, the group climbed into the air, flying over woods and fields until they came to the monastery of Millebeccus 12 miles away, where Raphael had other business—comforting and healing its abbot, Leodaldus. By this time, four more demons had joined the assault, greatly terrifying Barontus, but then two angels also joined the fray, and the additional demons fell away (*VB* 7). Barontus, Raphael, and two of the demons continued on their aerial ascent until they reached the first gate of Paradise (*VB* 8). This was an assembly point where Barontus saw some of his deceased brethren. These monks were already saved, sheltered within heaven's protective walls, and awaiting the last day in the company of their brethren. They grieved at Barontus's danger, claiming that thus far no members of their monastery had been lost to hell. They prayed for him. The foursome moved on to the second gate where many children and virgins, like spectators at a procession, cried out, chanting "A soul is going to judgment" (*anima vadit ad iudicium*) and "Conquer, Warrior Christ, conquer, and let not the devil take him down to hell" (*Tu vince, bellator Christe, tu vince, et non diabolus ipsam ducat in tartarum*) (*VB* 9). At the third gate of heaven, "like glass" (*similitudinem vitri*), Barontus saw the saints seated on thrones and houses built from gold bricks, as had been described in Gregory's *Dialogues* (*VB* 10; Gregory, *Dialogues*, 4.36). This third area was a building site with houses being continually prepared for those who gave to the poor. Barontus saw the mansion of a certain Francardus (still living) being erected; his occupation of the mansion seemed imminent as he was being purified by long illness (*quem longa egritudo purgavit ad purum*) (*VB* 10). The martyrs, also in this area, called on Christ, as the virgins had done. At the fourth gate, Barontus recognized another monk from his monastery, Betolenus, who had been given a task by St. Peter of making sure that the lights stayed on in churches (*VB* 11). St. Peter was aware that the lights at Barontus's monastery of Lonrey went out at night (on use of lights, see Fouracre 2002). This was as far into paradise as Barontus was allowed to go—four gates in.[13] Even so, Barontus could hardly see because of the splendor and light.

The time for Barontus's judgment had come. Summoned by an angel, St. Peter swiftly appeared. The demons accused him of "major sins" (*principalia vitia*), recalling some from as far back as his childhood, but focused especially on his three wives and his "many" adulteries (*VB* 12). St. Peter asked Barontus if these accusations were true, and Barontus confirmed them. St. Peter began to defend his monk to the demons: Barontus had given alms, he had confessed his sins and done penance for them, he had been tonsured, he had entered the monastery, and he had "given up all his possessions for God" (*omnia propter Deum dereliquid*) (*VB* 12). The demons continued to insist until finally, St. Peter, losing his cool, tried to hit the demons over the head with his keys, at which point the demons took flight.

With the demons gone, it was Barontus's time of reckoning. Having defended Barontus so tenaciously, Peter now turned sternly to Barontus: "Ransom yourself, brother!" (*Redime te, frater!*) (*VB* 13). Barontus started to claim lack of resources, but St. Peter knew better: Barontus was to reveal to all the twelve *solidi* he had kept hidden. St. Peter then told him how to divest himself of the money—by giving one *solidus* a month to a priest to dispense to the poor. When an old man standing by asked whether Barontus would be saved if he did this, St. Peter affirmed that he would, stating somewhat bafflingly, "This is the price of the rich man and the poor, twelve *solidi*" (*Haec est praetium divitis et pauperis XII solidi*) (*VB* 13). Barontus's judgment was now over; he was to be returned to his brethren at the first gate, taken through hell by them, and thence to his monastery again. A certain Framnoaldus agreed to take him back to the monastery on condition that Barontus ensured that his grave was swept every day. Provisioned with a candle blessed by a certain Ebbo, a man of high birth who had done many good deeds and given alms, Barontus also benefited from Ebbo's advice to protect himself by saying, "Glory to Thee, O God" (*Gloria tibi Deus*) (*VB* 15). As Barontus and the monks traveled from heaven to hell, they passed an old man of beautiful appearance, with a long beard, sitting quietly on a high throne: this was Abraham. Barontus was instructed to ask to rest in the bosom of Abraham when next he was on the point of death.[14] They finally came to hell. Barontus and his companions were not allowed to enter, but through the dense smoke he saw thousands of souls in chains: the proud, the perjurers, the homicides, deceivers, lecherous priests, and sinners bound with like sinners, as described by Pope Gregory. They saw two bishops there, Vulfoleodus of Bourges and Bishop Dido of Poitiers, some relatives, and also foolish virgins. Those who had done some good were given manna from heaven, "like clouds" (*similitudinem nebulae habens*), each day at the sixth hour and they were refreshed (*VB* 17). This food was brought to them by white-clothed deacons.

At this point, Barontus and his guide joined a troupe of pilgrims on their way to the shrine of St. Hilary in Poitiers (Vienne) until they reached the monastery. Framnoaldus showed Barontus the site of his tomb that was to be swept, and then he left Barontus without his aerial body and without the candle. Finding himself at the arch of the church, Barontus dragged himself along the ground until a divine gust carried him to the roof of his cell where he could see the brethren and his son sitting by his bed. Barontus entered his body again through the mouth, still calling on the protective phrase taught to him by Ebbo: "Glory to Thee, O God" (*VB* 19). This first-person narrative ends at Chapter 19, and in the final paragraphs of the text (Chapters 20–23) the editor admonished the reader to attend to Pope Gregory's teachings: do not love the things of the world, and do good deeds.

Barontus's vision has attracted sustained interest among scholars of the Merovingian world. The work has been explored for its sources, audience, monastic context, its connections to the liturgy, and the value of almsgiving (Carozzi 1994; Hen 1996; Roper 1999; Moreira 2000, 2010; Effros 2002; Contreni 2003; Brown 2015), and for its manuscript tradition, illustrations, and cult (Nees 2003; Torrigiani and Porta 2013). However, keeping to its immediate Merovingian context, the *Vision of Barontus* text was positioned to contribute to two interrelated "conversations" about death and the afterlife that were active in the last quarter of the seventh century. One conversation was about the fate of the soul immediately after death and was basically theological in nature. The other conversation was about the role of the church and the sacraments provided by the clergy to control this fate. Clerics, bishops, and ultimately the pope, as representatives of St. Peter, offered remedies for sin and held out the promise of salvation. The prominence of St. Peter in Barontus's story and the text's appeal to Pope Gregory's writings indicate that a context for the vision lay in the clearer articulation of the authority of the papacy not only in the matter of salvation, but also in the definition of the afterlife.

St. Peter is a prominent figure in Barontus's vision. Although he occasionally appears in earlier visions alongside other saints, St. Peter's starring role in afterlife judgment was new. His prominence in this vision points to the papacy's claims to regulate access to the afterlife. In early Christianity, apocalyptic visions looked to a future end of the world (*eschaton*), while at the same time being anchored to past "events" such as the harrowing of hell. The scope of apocalypses were usually cosmic and concerned with the salvation history of all humankind. Interest in apocalyptic literature continued to thrive, but visions centered on the immediate fate of the dead were more personal and "relatable," and therefore were very interesting to medieval readers. Even though St. Peter's control of access to heaven was rooted in scripture (Matthew 16:19: "I will give you the keys of the kingdom of heaven, and whatever you bind on Earth shall be bound in heaven, and whatever you loose on Earth shall be loosed in heaven"), St. Peter did not have a particularly active role in earlier visionary literature, not even in the *Apocalypse of Peter* where he was depicted primarily as a curious observer of the fate of the dead (Elliot 2005). By contrast, in the new conceptions of the immediate fate of the soul after death, St. Peter, alongside the archangels Michael and Raphael (venerated as saints), assumed a more active and critical role.

Even so, Barontus's vision owes much to earlier apocalyptic literature. For example, as he was escorted to judgment, Barontus was cheered along with shouts of "Conquer,

O Warrior Christ," referencing Christ's conquest of "death" in the harrowing of hell.[15] As in the *Apocalypse of Peter* and *Vision of Paul,* in Barontus's vision, the damned were provided with refreshment—although every day at the sixth hour, rather than once a week, or once a year as was the case in earlier works (*Vision of Paul* 44; *VB* 17). The reference in Barontus's vision to the "bosom of Abraham" was a feature of earlier apocalyptic visions and prayers for the dead that endured into the Middle Ages (Trumbower 2001). These examples do not exhaust the work's debt to the earlier literature. However, the author of Barontus's vision nowhere claimed earlier apocalypses in support of the vision's veracity. It was the impact of new ideas from Rome that gave the text its immediate authority. The vision claimed that on leaving the body the soul could enjoy the rewards of paradise or the pains of hell, even though the last judgment was yet to come.[16] And between the body's death and its resurrection, St. Peter would adjudicate the soul's immediate fate.[17]

Two areas of afterlife belief caused anxiety and surprise among Barontus's listeners. First, there was the snatching of the soul at death. Pope Gregory's writings (*Dialogues* and *Homilies on the Gospels*) asserted that the soul could be snatched away by demons and dragged immediately to hell. Evidently, there were "many" who did not believe this (*multi non credunt*) (*Visio Baronti* 20). These skeptics may have been monks within the monastery. The idea that demons could snatch away the soul so quickly (*tam velociter rapiunt*), seemingly without a trial, may not have sat well with judicially minded Christians; it was patently a view that contradicted older ideas of the soul waiting until the last judgment to learn its fate. At the same time, the idea was not entirely new. It appears in the *Apocalypse of Zephaniah* (Bauckham 1998), in Origen's fifth Homily on the Psalms, and closer to home, St. Martin, on his deathbed, had seen the devil standing by (Sulpicius Severus, *Letter* 3.16). The journey through the ether to the world beyond had long been considered dangerous, with demons snatching at vulnerable souls, but the idea that a divinely sanctioned immediate judgment anticipated the eternal judgment of the last day may have felt new.

Second, St. Peter's role in the vision was displacing a traditional view among some Gallic writers that patron saints powerfully protected their suppliants at the moment of judgment. St. Augustine had decried such hopes in the *City of God*, but it was commonly believed in Gaul and elsewhere. Gregory of Tours expressed his hope that St. Martin would shield him, and others may have had like thoughts. In a situation in which demons could whisk the soul away to hellish torture and angels were the ones to come to the rescue, the formality of a trial in which patron saints would intercede became more distant. Still, in the figure of Peter as a saint, the vision offered a conceptual bridge of sorts. St. Peter represented both the office and the man: the rock on which the church was built, but also the fisherman, a former sinner, who might be appealed to by sinners. In the dramatic moments of Barontus's vision, it was not the distant binding and loosing Church of St. Peter that came to Barontus's rescue, but Peter himself as intercessor–saint. He was a shrewd replacement for St. Martin and other saints traditionally associated with chthonic powers. (On St. Martin as intercessor for the dead, see Moreira 2010b). Saints and martyrs continued to be invoked as intercessors but in ways that did not compete with the power of clerics and the authority of Rome.

Finally, recognition of papal authority in church matters had always been strong, but the seventh century was a time of religious reform, missionary fervor, and theological disagreements within Christendom. Support for, and loyalty to, the papacy was intensified in some quarters. Church dedications to St. Peter and other indications of cultic observance had existed as early as the fifth century (Beaujard 2000), but many monastic foundations and churches adopted the patronage of St. Peter in the seventh century and beyond. The claim of the papacy to control the afterlife through the apostolic tradition of St. Peter, a claim firmly pressed on the Anglo-Saxons, was likely a key feature in this trend (on contacts with England, see Fleming, Chapter 17, this volume). The rash of new dedications may also have been a symptom of support for orthodoxy in an era when the papacy was engaged in a protracted battle against the monothelete heresy and was a figurehead for Western orthodoxy against official pronouncements issuing from Constantinople at this time (see Esders, Chapter 16, this volume). At the time of Barontus's vision, Pope Agatho was engaged in this longstanding effort. Barontus's vision, with its focus on St. Peter, was embedded in the concerns of its time—a time of new ideas and intensified loyalties.

A CASE OF THEOLOGICAL RESISTANCE? PURGATORY

An important idea taking shape at this time was the concept of purgatory: a postmortem purification of the imperfect soul that occurred immediately after death and that, unless mitigated in some way, could potentially last until the final judgment. The roots of this idea were ancient; they were to be found in the religious cults and philosophies of the Mediterranean world. However, the rise of purgatory in the early Middle Ages represented a critical moment in the history of the idea (Carozzi 1994; Brown 2000, 2015; Moreira 2010a). What did Merovingian writers make of purgatory? The short answer is that while it is possible to show that ideas about purgatory were circulating in the sixth, seventh, and eighth centuries, Merovingian sources on purgatory are scant and challenging to interpret. The most significant developments in the early history of purgatory in the West were happening elsewhere: in Italy, Spain, Ireland, and England. In England, exposure to Greek thought was especially strong during the time when Theodore of Tarsus was archbishop of Canterbury (668–690), appointed by Rome. Merovingian texts that address ideas about a third place, and about protracted postmortem purgation, reveal caution, suspicion, even resistance (Moreira 2010a). For example, in the early sixth century, Bishop Caesarius of Arles, who accepted that light sins might be purged by the fire of judgment, even over a considerable amount of time, decried the notion of a dedicated third place in the afterlife, according to his hagiographer (*Life of Caesarius of Arles* 2.6). Caesarius continued to be an important authority for seventh-century Christians.

We have seen that Merovingian authors were aware of trends in afterlife thinking developed outside their borders. However, while the author of Barontus's vision in the late 670s viewed Gregory's *Dialogues* as an authoritative reference for immediate judgment, he did not adopt the idea of postmortem purgation for the sinful Barontus, nor did he describe such a place during the otherworldly tour. This was not for lack of a model. Twenty years earlier, a monk at the monastery of Péronne (Somme) in northern France penned an account of the youthful visions of the Irish saint Fursey. In setting down an account that appears to have circulated orally for some time, the anonymous author recorded how Fursey was purged by fire in the otherworld. However, one point of detail discomforted the author: the suggestion that penance might occur after death. Even Bede, a major figure in the development of purgatory, who provided an abbreviated account of Fursey's vision in his *Ecclesiastical History*, excised the suggestion of postmortem penance from it (3.19; Moreira 2010a). Evidently, both the Merovingian author of Fursey's *Life* and Bede were in agreement with Augustine that any form of purgation in the afterlife, whether immediate or on the last day, would proceed through punishment, not penance. Indeed, purgatory would not be viewed as a place of penitential activity until later in the Middle Ages.

Ideas about purgation and salvation were in the air in the seventh century. A minor scene in another Merovingian text, the *Life of Leudegar of Autun*, interweaves ideas about martyrdom, purification by fire, purified gold, and prayer for the dead. In this episode, a secular potentate named Hector was portrayed as purged through martyrdom, which was not a new idea. However, by conflating the cleansing fire with the liturgy's traditional image of cleansing water, the hagiographer forced a new reading of a traditional prayer for the dead. In restoring the reputation of a major public figure in the aftermath of a widely condemned dispute, the account of Hector's imagined purgation through martyrdom shows that, as in the account of Chilperic in hell, one's status in the afterlife was central to the political reputation of the Merovingian elite. Hector's purging restored his reputation, just as Fursey's purgation had restored his. The utility of the idea of postmortem purgation as a means of political rehabilitation had begun (Moreira 2012). As far as I can tell, this is the first recorded case of purgation imagery being used to restore the reputation of a secular leader in the West.

Creative politics aside, from the perspective of what would happen to ordinary sinners, Merovingian authors did not endorse new ideas about postmortem purgation. Two letters from the time when Anglo-Saxon missionaries were operating in Frisia and Germany (the *Vision of the Monk of Wenlock* in 716; the *Fragmentary Vision of 757*) attest that new ideas were circulating there. However, while ideas about postmortem purgation occasionally appear in Merovingian texts, such as in Fursey's vision, it was not until the Carolingian era that purgatory took a firmer hold on the Frankish afterlife.

Conclusion

The Merovingian elite gained international prestige from being orthodox Christians in an age of conversion in Europe. Alongside other supernatural signs, inspired visions were endorsements of the religious culture they fostered. Furthermore, visions helped explain historical events. They may not have created a master narrative for their dynasty (see Reimitz, Chapter 22, this volume), but through hagiography and other cultic writings,

Merovingian authors asserted their place in Christian history. Visions promised them a share of a Christian afterlife to whose imaginative and theological framework their own texts contributed. In this they were connected with their Christian neighbors in England, Ireland, Spain, Italy, and Byzantium, who likewise claimed such signs.

Yet, Merovingian-era authors were not undiscerning producers or consumers of the supernatural. We have seen that they were open to the influence of texts generated outside their borders but that individual authors selected, appropriated, and modified, these influences. The *Vision of Paul* and Pope Gregory's works informed the *Vision of Barontus,* but it did not dictate its concerns. The visions of the nuns of Faremoutiers show responsiveness to emerging trends in penitential culture. Merovingian writers may have been hesitant to adopt early developments in the rise of purgatory, but this may reveal their confidence in protecting theological boundaries. A reputation for orthodoxy was a high accolade. Wilfrid of Ripon's protracted stays in Merovingian Gaul and Rome were, in his hagiographer's view, evidence of his desire to be schooled and steeped in orthodoxy. Seen from outside, this was the Merovingian church's reputation in the late seventh century.

At the end of the day, visions made for good stories to tell and to read. The dedication of Merovingian writers to recording supernatural events has preserved such stories in greater number in Gaul than in surrounding communities. Their works reveal that people enjoyed talking about visions and that others listened. We learn from Gregory of Tours that visions could be the topic of dinner conversations or a casual conversation after a meeting. The visions of monks and nuns had a ready audience in their own communities and beyond. Visions associated with cures were the greatest marvel of all since they combined two things people liked to talk about—their ailments and their dreams. Near-death experiences, like Barontus's, must have been discussed widely in a variety of settings. Such stories were a medium for theology in the public domain. Indeed, it was in city streets and in private and public conversations that many of the stories of visions must have been told. Although we have them as written texts, we hear of dreams and visions being spoken about to others. Inevitably, such conversations would have crossed political boundaries. The trade of goods and movement of people, especially the vigorous movement of the elite (bishops, priests, monks, nuns, pilgrims, royal exiles) crisscrossing the Channel and the Irish Sea, or people who sojourned in Merovingian lands on their way to and from Rome, ensured this. Merovingian authors preserved these stories for us. They did not ignore them, and therefore, neither should we.

Notes

1. Scholarship on visions in this period includes de Nie (1987), Carozzi (1983, 1994), Moreira (2000 and 2010), Effros (2002), Keskiaho (2015), Brown (2015), and Bernstein (2017). For the early Christian tradition and Byzantium, see: Amat (1985), Bauckham (1998), Trumbower (2001), Bremmer (2002), Baun (2007) and Angelidi and Calofonos (2014), who provide useful starting points. Gardiner (1989) provides a translation of some of the major medieval visionary texts.

2. A particularly elaborate example is the *Revelatio Corcodemi*, one of the cultic writings included in the hagiographic dossier of St. Germanus of Auxerre (Duru 1850; van Egmond 2006).

3. Macrobius's *Commentary on the Dream of Scipio*, and its classification of dreams (Book 1 chapter 3) in particular, was widely known in the Middle Ages. It transmitted dream classifications, language, and ideas from a variety of ancient sources, including Artemidorus (Stahl 1990, pp. 87–92, especially p. 87, n. 1.). Augustine outlined three types of vision in his *De Genesi ad litteram* 12.6: *visio corporalis* (a vision seen through the bodily faculty of sight); *visio spiritualis* (spiritual vision seen through the imagination); and *visio intellectualis* (the vision of the mind, without image; it was through such a vision that divine powers might be seen). We cannot be sure which specific oneirological or oneiromantic works existed in Gallo-Roman libraries, or how they circulated (Moreira 1996). The *Somnia Danielis*, an important medieval dream book, is known only through later manuscripts.

4. "They are generated either by a full stomach or by an empty one, or by illusions, or by our thoughts combined with illusions, or by our thoughts combined with revelations." Some dreams were prompted by diabolic illusions, yet others were genuine revelations. "Seeing, then, that dreams may arise from such a variety of causes, one ought to be very reluctant to put one's faith in them, since it is hard to tell from what source they come." Trans. Zimmerman, pp. 261–262.

5. On the cult of the saints, see Brown (1981), Van Dam (1993), and Beaujard (2000).

6. The Bollandists' *Acta Sanctorum* (AASS) published more of these miracle lists than appeared in the *Monumenta Germaniae Historica*.

7. King Theoderic of Italy (d. 526) was reportedly there earlier, but as an "Arian" heretic, his damnation was assumed. Pope Gregory reports the story in *Dialogues* 4.31.

8. Chilperic and his queen, Fredegund, had accused Gregory of treason, and, as de Nie (1987) notes, Gregory's purpose was also to deflect Guntram's threat against his friend, Theodore of Marseille (de Nie, pp. 285–287; Moreira, pp. 96–99). Halsall (2002) reassesses the chronology of Gregory's attitude towards Chilperic arguing that a writing strategy rather than his trial lay behind Gregory's changed attitude to Chilperic.

9. Herod appears seated on a chair (*cathedra*) in the Greek and Latin versions of the *Vision of Ezra* (Bremmer 2018, 174–175). Bremmer argues a mid-sixth century date for the Latin translation of the *Vision of Ezra*. Herod's figure would be apt inspiration for Chilperic's infernal situation.

10. Macrobius distinguished five types of dream (*Commentary on the Dream of Scipio*, 1.3). Three of the five could be prophetic and were thus worth interpreting: enigmatic (requiring interpretation); prophetic (a dream that comes true); and oracular (revelation by a pious figure, parent, priest, or a god). Two dream types were thought to have no prophetic meaning: the nightmare and apparition. There were five types of enigmatic dream: the personal (relating to the dreamer herself); alien (a dream pertaining to someone else); social (concerning the dreamer and others); public (concerning the city and public matters); and universal (relating to the cosmos). These categories were not mutually exclusive.

11. The Lives of queens Clothild, Radegund, and Balthild are available in English translation in McNamara, Halborg, and Whatley, *Sainted Women of the Dark Ages*.

12. Augustine, *City of God*, Book 22: 17 and 29. See also Bynum (1995).

13. Visions of the afterlife suggested a variety of numbers of gates in the heavens. (See Moreira 2000, p. 161, n. 98 for bibliography).

14. The prayerful hope that the soul resides in the "bosom of Abraham" is a traditional form of prayer for the dead based on Luke 16: 22. It was recalled in liturgies for the dead in the early Middle Ages based on Gen 22:18 and Gal 3:16. For examples, see Sicard 1978.

15. Earlier, apocalyptic visions focused on the drama of Christ's descent into hell, his conquest of death, his release of the souls captured by death (personified), and the disruption of the infernal kingdom in what is termed the "harrowing" of hell. These visions focused on the future judgment, shaped by the events of the last day when Christ would judge souls.

16. It should be noted that Barontus's vision was not the first to focus on the immediate fate of the dead: the *Apocalypse of Zephaniah* (Bauckham 1998) was a very early and, for its time, anomalous text to depict an immediate judgement. The Latin *Vision of Paul* handled the fate of the dead, set within an apocalyptic time frame.

17. In Gregory's *Dialogues* 4.14, St. Peter appeared to a nun to assure her that her sins were forgiven before her death. In the same work (4.18), another story told how the Virgin Mary appeared to a little girl named Musa, predicting the day of her death and inviting her to join her court of little girls. Both Peter and Mary were considered arbiters and protectors of souls after death. St. Peter appeared to the visionary Aldegund to assure her of his power to bind and loose (*Life of Aldegund* 1.10).

Works Cited

Ancient Sources

Apocalypse of Peter. J. K. Elliott (ed.). (2005). *Apocalypse of Peter*. In *The Apocryphal New Testament: A Collection of Christian Literature in English Translation* (pp. 593–512). Oxford: Oxford University Press.

Audoin, *Life of St. Eligius*. J. A. McNamara (trans.). (2001). In T. Head (ed.), *Medieval Hagiography: An Anthology* (pp. 137–168). New York: Routledge.

Audoin, *Life of St. Eligius*. J.-P. Migne (ed.). (1863). *Vita S. Eligii*. PL 87 (pp. 473–594). Paris: J.-P. Migne Editorem.

Augustine of Hippo, *City of God*. D. Bombart and A. Kalb (eds.). (1954–1955). *Augustine of Hippo, City of God*. 2 vols. CCSL 47–48. Turnhout: Brepols.

Augustine of Hippo, *City of God*. H. Bettenson (trans.). (1984). *Augustine of Hippo, City of God*. London: Penguin Books.

Augustine of Hippo, *De Genesi ad litteram libri XII*. J. Zycha (ed.). (1894). CSEL 28. Vienna: F. Tempsky.

Augustine of Hippo, *Enchiridion*. E. Evans (ed.). (1969). CCSL 46. Turnhout: Brepols.

Baudonivia, *Life of St. Radegund*. B. Krusch (ed.). (1888). *De vitae s. Radegundis II* (pp. 377–395). MGH SRM 2. Hanover: Hahn.

Baudonivia, *Life of St. Radegund*. J. A. McNamara, J. E. Halborg with E. G. Whatley, (trans.) (1992). *Sainted Women of the Dark Ages* (pp. 86–105). Durham, NC: Duke University Press.

Bede, *Historia Ecclesiastica gentis Anglorum*. B. Colgrave and R.A.B. Mynors (trans.). (1969). *Ecclesiastical History of the English People*. Oxford: Clarendon Press.

Gregory I, Pope, *Dialogues*. U. Moricca (ed.). (1924). *Gregorii Magni Dialogi*. Rome: Istituto Storico Italiano.

Gregory I, Pope, *Dialogues*. O. J. Zimmerman (trans.). (1959). *Saint Gregory the Great: Dialogues. The Fathers of the Church*, vol. 39. New York: Fathers of the Church.

Gregory I, Pope, *Dialogues*. A. de Vogüé (ed. and trans.). (1978–1980). *Grégoire le Grand: Dialogues*. 3 vols. SC 251, 260, 265. Paris: Editions du Cerf.

Gregory I, Pope, *Moralia in Job*. M. Adriaen (ed.). (1979–1985). CCSL 143, 143A, 143B. Turnhout: Brepols.

Gregory of Tours, *Histories*. B. Krusch and W. Levison (eds.). (1951). *Historiae libri decem*. MGH SRM 1.1. Hanover: Hahn.

Gregory of Tours, *Histories*. L. Thorpe (trans.). (1974). *Gregory of Tours: History of the Franks*. Harmondsworth: Penguin.

Gregory of Tours, *Life of Monegund*. E. James (trans.) (1991). *Gregory of Tours: Life of the Fathers* (pp. 118-125). Liverpool: Liverpool University Press.

Hincmar (attributed), *Gesta Dagoberti regis*. B. Krusch (ed.). (1888). MGH SRM 2 (pp. 396–425). Hanover: Hahn.

Jonas, *Life of Columbanus*. B. Krusch (ed.). (1902). *Vita Columbani*. MGH SRM 4 (pp.64–108). Hanover: Hahn.

Jonas. *Life of Columbanus*. A. O'Hara and I. Wood (trans.). (2017). *Jonas of Bobbio, Life of Columbanus, Life of John of Réomé, and Life of Vedast*. Liverpool: Liverpool University Press.

Life of Aldegund of Maubeuge. J. Bollandus (ed.). (1643). *Vita s. Aldegundis*. AASS Ianuarii 3 (pp. 649–662). Paris: Victor Palmé.

Life of St. Austrigisilus of Bourges. B. Krusch (ed.). (1902). *Vita et miracula s. Austrigisili ep. Bituricensis* (pp. 188–208). MGH SRM 4. Hanover: Hahn.

Life of Caesarius of Arles. W. E. Klingshirn (trans.). (1994). *Caesarius of Arles: Life, Testament, Letters*. Liverpool: Liverpool University Press.

Life of Glodesind. J. A. McNamara, J. E. Halborg, with E. G. Whatley (trans.). (1992). *Sainted Women of the Dark Ages* (pp. 86–105). Durham, NC: Duke University Press.

Macrobius, *Commentary on the Dream of Scipio*. W. H. Stahl (trans.). (1990). *Macrobius, Commentary on the Dream of Scipio*. New York: University of Columbia Press.

Origen, Homily 5.7. E. Prinzivalli (trans.). (1995). *Origène. Homélies sur les Psaumes 36 à 38*. SC 411. Paris: Editions du Cerf.

Passion of Praeiectus. B. Krusch (ed.). (1910). *Passio Praeiecti episcopi et martyris Arverni*. MGH SRM 5 (pp. 212–248). Hanover: Hahn.

Passion of Praeiectus. P. Fouracre and R. Gerberding (ed and trans.). (1996). *Late Merovingian France: History and Hagiography*, (pp. 640–720). Manchester: Manchester University Press.

Revelatio Corcodemi. L. M. Duru (ed.). (1850). "Libellus de mirabili revelatione s. Corcodemi m. et conversion s. Mamertini ab idololatria." In *Bibliothèque historique de l'Yonne ou collection de légends chroniques et documents divers* (pp. 57–66). Vol. 1. Auxerre and Paris. Auxerre: Imprimerie de Perriquet.

Somnia Danielis. S. Fisher (ed.). (1982). *The Complete Medieval Dreambook: A Multilingual Alphabetical Somnia Danielis Collation*. Bern: Peter Lang.

Sulpicius Severus, *Letter 3*. J. Fontaine (ed.). (1967). *Sulpice Sévère, Vie de Saint Martin*, vol 1. (pp. 334–345). Paris: Éditions du Cerf.

Venantius Fortunatus, *Life of St. Germanus of Paris*. B. Krusch (ed.). (1885). *Vita S. Germani*. MGH AA 4.2. Berlin: Weidmann.

Vision of Barontus. W. Levison (ed.). (1910). *Visio Baronti monachi Longoretensis*. MGH SRM 5 (pp. 368–394). Hanover: Hahn.

Vision of Barontus. J. N. Hillgarth (trans.). (1986). *Christianity and Paganism, 350–750: The Conversion of Western Europe* (pp. 195–204). Philadelphia: University of Pennsylvania Press.

Vision of Fursey. M. P. Ciccarese. (trans.) (1984–1985). "Le Visioni di S. Fursa." *Romanobarbarica* 8: 231–303.

Vision of Paul (Apocalypse of Paul). T. Silverstein and A. Hilhorst. (eds.). (1997). *Apocalypse of Paul: A New Critical Edition of Three Long Latin Versions with Fifty-Four Plates.* Geneva: Patrick Cramer.

Vision of Paul. L. Jiroušková (ed.). (2006). *Die Visio Pauli. Wege und Wandlungen einer Orientalischen Apokryphe im Lateinsischen Mittelalter.* Leiden: Brill.

Modern Sources

Amat, J. (1985). *Songes et visions. L'au-delà dans la littérature latine tardive.* Paris: Études Augustiniennes.

Angelidi, C., and Calofonos, G. T. (2014) (eds.). *Dreaming in Byzantium and Beyond.* London: Routledge.

Bauckham, R. (1998). *The Fate of the Dead: Studies on the Jewish and Christian Apocalypses.* Leiden: E. J. Brill.

Baun, J. (2007). *Tales from Another Byzantium: Celestial Journey and Local Community in the Medieval Greek Apocrypha.* Cambridge: Cambridge University Press.

Beaujard, B. (2000). *Le culte des saints en Gaule. Les premiers temps: D'Hilaire de Poitiers à la fin du VIᵉ siècle.* Paris: Editions du Cerf.

Bernstein, A. (2010). "Named Others and Named Places: Stigmatization in the Early Medieval Afterlife." In I. Moreira and M. Toscano (eds.), *Hell and Its Afterlife: Historical and Contemporary Perspectives* (pp. 53–71). Farnham: Ashgate.

Bernstein, A. (2017). *Hell and Its Rivals. Death and Retribution among Christians, Jews, and Muslims in the Early Middle Ages.* Ithaca, NY: Cornell University Press.

Bremmer, J. N. (2002). *The Rise and the Fall of the Afterlife.* London: Routledge.

Bremmer, J. N. (2018). "The Long Latin Version of the Vision of Ezra: Date, Place and Tour of Hell." In J. N. Bremmer, V. Hirschberger, and T. Nicklas (eds.), *Figures of Ezra* (pp. 162–184). Leuven: Peeters.

Brown, P. (1981). *The Cult of the Saints: Its Rise and Function in Late Antiquity.* Chicago: Chicago University Press.

Brown, P. (2000). "The Decline of the Empire of God: Amnesty and Penance, and the Afterlife from Late Antiquity to the Early Middle Ages." In C. W. Bynum and P. Freeman (eds.), *Last Things: Death and the Apocalypse in the Middle Ages* (pp. 41–59). Philadelphia: University of Pennsylvania Press.

Brown, P. (2015). *Ransom for the Soul. Afterlife and Wealth in Early Western Christianity.* Cambridge, MA: Harvard University Press.

Bynum, C. W. (1995). *The Resurrection of the Body in Western Christianity, 200–1336.* New York: Columbia University Press.

Carozzi, C. (1983). "La géographie de l'au-delà et sa signification pendant le haut moyen âge." Settimane di Studio 19. Popoli et paesi nella cultura altomedievale 1981, vol. 2 (pp. 423–481). Spoleto: Presso la Sede del Centro.

Carozzi, C. (1994). *Le voyage de l'âme dans l'au-delà d'après le littérature latine (Vᵉ-XIIIᵉ siècle).* Palais Farnèse: École Français de Rome,

Contreni, J. (2003). "Building Mansions in Heaven. The *Visio Baronti*, Archangel Raphael, and a Carolingian King." *Speculum* 78(3): 673–706.

De Nie, G. (1987). *Views from a Many-Windowed Tower: Studies of Imagination in the Works of Gregory of Tours.* Studies in Classical Antiquity 7. Amsterdam: Editions Rodopi B. V.

Effros, B. (2002). *Caring for Body and Soul: Burial and the Afterlife in the Merovingian World*. University Park: Pennsylvania University Press.

Fouracre, P. (2002). "Eternal Light and Earthly Needs: Practical Aspects of the Development of Frankish Immunities." In W. Davies and P. Fouracre (eds.), *Property and Power in the Early Middle Ages* (pp. 53–81). Cambridge: Cambridge University Press.

Gardiner, E. (1989). *Visions of Heaven and Hell before Dante*. New York: Italica Press.

Halsall, G. (2002). "Nero and Herod? The Death of Chilperic and Gregory's Writing of History." In K. Mitchell and I. Wood (eds.) *The World of Gregory of Tours* (pp. 337–51). Leiden: Brill.

Hen, Y. (1996). "The Structure and Aims of the 'Visio Baronti.'" *Journal of Theological Studies* n.s. 47: 477–497.

Keskiaho, J. (2015). *Dreams and Visions in the Early Middle Ages: The Reception and Use of Patristic Ideas, 400–900*. Cambridge: Cambridge University Press.

McNamara, J. A., Halborg, J. E., with Whatley, E. G. (1992). *Sainted Women of the Dark Ages*. Durham, NC: Duke University Press.

Moreira, I. (1996). "St. Augustine's Three Visions and Three Heavens in Some Early Medieval Florilegia." *Vivarium* 34: 1–14.

Moreira, I. (2000). *Dreams, Visions, and Spiritual Authority in Merovingian Gaul*. Ithaca, NY: Cornell University Press.

Moreira, I. (2003). "Dreams and Divination in Early Medieval Canonical and Narrative Sources: The Question of Clerical Control." *Catholic Historical Review* 89: 607–628.

Moreira, I. (2010a). *Heaven's Purge: Purgatory in Late Antiquity*. Oxford: Oxford University Press.

Moreira, I. (2010b). "Plucking Sinners Out of Hell: Saint Martin of Tours' Resurrection Miracle." In I. Moreira and M. Toscano (eds.), *Hell and its Afterlife: Historical and Contemporary Perspectives* (pp. 39–52). Farnham: Ashgate.

Moreira, I. (2012). "Hector of Marseilles Is Purged: Political Rehabilitation and Guilt by Association in the 7th century *Passion of Saint Leudegar of Autun*." *Quaestiones Medii Aevi Novae* 17: 191–209.

Moreira, I. (in press). "Purgatory's Intercessors and the Communion of Saints: Bishops, Ghosts, and Angry Wives." In R. Pollard (ed.), *Imagining the Medieval Afterlife*. Cambridge: Cambridge University Press.

Nees, L. (2003). "The Illustrated Manuscript of the *Visio Baronti* [*Revelatio Baronti*] in St Petersburg (Russian National Library, cod. Oct.v.I.5)." In C. Cubitt (ed.), *Court Culture in the Early Middle Ages: The Proceedings of the First Alcuin Conference* (pp. 91–128). Turnhout: Brepols.

Roper, M. (1999). "Uniting the Community of the Living with the Dead: The Use of Other-World Visions in the Early Middle Ages." In D. Mowbray, R. Purdie, and I. Wei (eds.), *Authority and Community in the Middle Ages*. Stroud: Sutton Publishing.

Sicard, D. (1978). *La liturgie de la mort dans l'église latine des origins à la réforme carolingienne*. Munster, Westfalen: Aschendorff.

Torrigiani, I., and M. V. Porta. (2013). *La vita e la visio sancti Baronti: Monaco, eremita, santo*. Pistoia: GF Press.

Trumbower, J. A. (2001). *Rescue for the Dead: The Posthumous Salvation of Non-Christians in Early Christianity*. Oxford: Oxford University Press.

Van Dam, R. (1993). *Saints and Their Miracles in Late Antique Gaul*. Princeton, NJ: Princeton University Press.

Van Egmond, W. S. (2006). *Conversing with the Saints. Communication in Pre-Carolingian Hagiography from Auxerre*. Turnhout: Brepols.

CHAPTER 43

....

INSCRIBED IN THE BOOK OF LIFE

Liturgical Commemoration in Merovingian Gaul

....

ELS ROSE

THE past decades have witnessed important shifts in the scholarly approach to medieval public worship, or liturgy.[1] The traditional focus on liturgical texts of the early medieval West as evidence of the development of Christian theology and doctrine, often chosen by scholars with a confessional background, has made way to a contextualized study of texts that takes into account their social, cultural, and political context (Palazzo 2008). An increasing awareness of the fragmentary character of the transmitted texts, which often lack any indication of performance and practice (Symes 2016), has incited the inclusion of related sources, both textual and material, in order to win insight into the nature of the communities that produced and used these texts. Thus, liturgical evidence has become more and more an instrument to study the complex societies of the early Middle Ages.

In a recent article, Yitzhak Hen characterizes the church in sixth-century Gaul as "perhaps the most secure and stable institution in an ever changing political, social and cultural reality." Hen ascribes the qualities of the church, as well as the strength of Merovingian culture in general, to the tendency in this period to provide cultural institutions inherited from Antiquity with new meaning (Hen 2016, pp. 233–234). In the present chapter, I examine how the Merovingian church reused terms and terminology rooted in ancient concepts of cultural institutions in order to answer the needs of new social, political, and religious circumstances.

One of the most important means the church had available to redefine existing and inherited concepts was through its public worship, or liturgy (see also Bailey, Chapter 44, this volume). To the liturgical community of the Christian Church belonged those men and women who were baptized as well as those who prepared for the initiation rite of baptism or were interested in becoming a Christian through membership of the church. Although the latter group had only partial access to the celebration of mass as the core element of Christian worship,[2] liturgy was not a purely clerical concern in which only the "ritual experts" would play a role. During the celebration of mass, both laypeople and the clergy contributed in their own way to the fulfillment of the religious rituals (Rose 2019).

During liturgical gatherings in the early medieval period, the character of the celebrating community was expressed through rituals and was particularly conveyed in texts. Christianity, as a "religion of the book," is a text-oriented religion, and each ritual performed in the early medieval liturgy was accompanied by texts of chants and prayers. Although the written documents that give evidence of liturgical practices are relatively scarce for the Merovingian period, the sources that have been preserved give us the possibility to form an idea about the way the church "infused" new meanings into inherited concepts and institutions, as Hen phrases it (2016).

One such process of reuse involving inherited concepts in a new social, cultural, and religious setting is the issue of membership: of belonging to and participating in a public community. This chapter concentrates on the way Christians defined their membership of the Christian community, more specifically of the liturgical assembly that gathered around the celebration of the sacrament of the eucharist (or mass). The focus is on the role of the public recitation of names of those participating in this celebration, a fixed part of the early Christian mass. The ritual recitation of the names was a characteristic element of the Merovingian liturgical tradition, the form of which became subject to change in the late eighth century. During the Merovingian period, the names of those participating were recited aloud in each mass celebrated on Sundays and feast days, and for every mass a proper prayer to accompany the ritual was composed. These prayers offer ample material giving evidence of the way membership of, and participation in, the community of faithful of the Merovingian world were characterized. As we will see, the prayers accompanying the recitation of the names illustrate the Christian community's efforts to create and strengthen ideas of belonging in this complex time of many changes. These texts reused ancient terminology defining membership of the community and infused this vocabulary with new, sometimes radically changed, meaning.

The Importance of Names in Christian Liturgy

Two early Christian and medieval liturgical rituals in particular involved the listing and public pronunciation of names: baptism and the eucharist. In a recent publication, Claudia Rapp has indicated baptism, the Christian ritual of initiation—during which the newborn or newly converted receives his or her Christian name—as a rite that brought about a transformation of people's identity and belonging. Rapp points to the fourth-century bishop of Antioch, John Chrysostom (349–407), who in his catechetical treatises impresses on his baptismal candidates the awareness that after they will have gone through the ritual of baptism, they will be inscribed as "citizens in heaven" (Rapp 2014, p. 160). The notion of baptism as changing one's "civic identity" is brought forward even more poignantly in a canon most likely connected to the third Council of Seville, which was probably held under the episcopacy of Isidore (560–636) in 624, as Wolfram Drews suggests (Drews 2002, p. 190). The canon defines the relationship between Christians, Jews, and "pagans," creating a chasm between the world of those baptized and those not. This division, according to Drews, coincides seamlessly with what is regarded as the "public" sphere and its counterpart, which is basically to be understood as a position of "illegality" (Drews 2002, p. 202; see Drews, Chapter 6, this volume). In this construction of a negative identity of those to be marked as nonmembers, baptism and membership of the Christian community would become a highly political issue (Drews 2002, p. 207).

The recitation of names in the context of the eucharist or mass has been evaluated in traditional scholarship as a spiritual membership of the heavenly afterlife rather than as an expression also of political and social relations in the here and now. Thus, Leo Koep links the ritual of the recitation of names in early Christian mass liturgy to similar customs to create lists of membership in the ancient world, referring to Greek and Roman as well as Jewish antecedents, and identifies the Christian lists of names as "heavenly citizen rolls" ("himmlische Bürgerliste"; Koep 1952, pp. 68–69). According to Koep, insertion in the Christian book of life was directed toward "eine konkrete, religiös-jenseitige Wirklichkeit" (Koep 1952, p. 69), a spiritual reality in the hereafter that had little to do with lists counting persons for practical administrative reasons in earthly society (Koep 1952, pp. 38–39). Even when Koep links the inscription of a Christian in the book of life to his or her deeds (Koep 1952, pp. 72–80), he discusses this relation from the perspective of the future salvation of the Christian's soul, rather than making it relevant to community life in the here and now.

In contrast to interpretation of the book of life as predominantly concerned with the life to come, more recent historiography on intercession connected to the listing and recitation of names in and outside the liturgy of the mass makes a deliberate effort to relate such practices to the sphere of human cohabitation in the here and now (Oexle 1976, 1983; Schmid and Wollasch 1984), and to matters of identity with regard to religious communities (Raaijmakers 2006, 2012). These studies focus mainly on the early Carolingian development of the *liber vitae* or confraternity books. In these documents, monastic houses listed the names of their members (both the living and those already deceased), as well as the names of inhabitants of related monastic houses and of their benefactors. The Merovingian practice of reciting names in public during the celebration of mass is seen, from this perspective, as a "preliminary stage" of the Carolingian *libri vitae* (Oexle 1976, p. 70).

The present chapter focuses on the ritual of reciting names in the public performance of the Merovingian mass as a phenomenon worth studying in itself because it informs us about issues of membership and belonging in this specific period. Studying the ritual from the perspective of the texts that accompanied it also grants us the opportunity to reevaluate previous interpretations based on a predominantly spiritual understanding or, conversely, an exclusive focus on communal life in this world. We shall see that the ritual of the names redefined the identity and belonging of the members of the eucharistic communities in Merovingian Gaul in a way that connected concerns about the future salvation of the faithful indelibly with their life in the community here and now.

The Ritual of Names in the Merovingian Mass

The recitation of the names of those participating in the eucharistic celebration is a distinctive feature of the Merovingian liturgy. The ritual was a fixed component of every mass. Numerous examples of the prayer that accompanied it, indicated as "collect (prayer of gathering) after the names" (*collectio post nomina*), were transmitted by service books known as sacramentaries. These books provided the prayers for mass to be recited by the celebrant (i.e., the priest or bishop).[3] Only later, as a consequence of Carolingian liturgical reforms, did this practice come to an end. It was then stipulated that the public recitation of names should be replaced by the insertion of a commemorative ritual in the eucharistic prayer (*canon missae*), as this chapter will describe.

Most eastern liturgies and the Roman rite inserted the recitation of names in the eucharistic prayer itself (Taft 1991, p. 24), once the gifts of bread and wine were brought in during the offertory ritual. The liturgical tradition as it developed in late-antique and Merovingian Gaul, however, situated the recitation of names during the offertory ritual, as was also the custom in early medieval Spain (Taft 1991, p. 24). This positioning expresses the close connection that was assumed between those who offered the gifts to be consecrated (the faithful) and those to whom the sacrifice of the mass and the related intercession was dedicated: the beloved dead.[4] In Merovingian Gaul, it was still the practice for lay members of the community to contribute to the eucharist with the material gifts needed to celebrate this liturgy: bread and wine. The faithful prepared their bread at home and took it with them to hand over to the deacon, who collected the gifts in the appointed space (McKitterick 1977, p. 144; Foley 1997, p. 210; Smyth 2003, pp. 348–349). Once the liturgy of the word, comprising the readings from the scriptures and its accompanying chants, and the general prayers of intercession were completed, a solemn offertory procession was formed to bring the gifts to the altar where, through the words of the eucharistic prayer, they were presented, thanked for, and consecrated by the celebrant. During the offertory, the deacon recited the list of names, at least as far as time would allow,[5] after which the celebrant recited the "collect after the names." The custom of including the recitation of names as part of the offertory ritual, in which the people had an important role, changed during the Carolingian period. Two issues seem to have stimulated this alteration: the first related to the internal logic of the ritual, and the second to implications for religious practice.

First, the Carolingians took up an old discussion that questioned the relevance of associating a public recitation of names with those who bring in their gifts. Jerome sharply condemned the custom (Jerome, *In Hieremiam* II.11 and *In Hiezechielem*, VI.18,5–9; cf. Taft 1991, pp. 38–39). He considered the ritual to be an act of self-glorification by those who participated in it while being oblivious of the parable of the widow who had nothing but a penny to throw into the box (Lk. 21, 1–4). Pope Innocent I (401–417) also criticized the custom, which he knew was observed in several regions outside Rome, but his objection was for different reasons. He considered a public recitation of names to a God to whom nothing is unknown (*quamvis illi incognitum sit nihil*) to be superfluous (*superfluum sit*), as he wrote in a letter to Bishop Decentius of Gubbio (dated March 19, 416).[6] To mention the names of the offerers before the offering itself was to put events in the wrong order. Rather, according to Innocent, the names should be included in the prayers that gave thanks for the gifts and that asked for their transformation into Christ's gift of salvation (*sacra mysteria*), "in order to open through the consecration the way to the subsequent intercession" (…*ut ipsis mysteriis viam futuris precibus aperiamus*). Rather than serving a purely informative function, the recitation of the names should have a performative role in such a way that the intercession of, and for, those involved in the eucharist would be heard. Whether Charlemagne and his liturgical advisors agreed with Innocent that the names should be encapsulated in a performative context of intercession, or whether they just wanted to copy the Roman practice that they deemed authoritative, the fact is that, in reference to Innocent's statement, they repeatedly called for the abandonment of the old practice connecting the names to the offertory and promoted its replacement with the new practice of including the names within the eucharistic prayer itself.[7]

The second issue that might have played a role in replacing the recitation of the names is related to changing ideas about the role of the people in the offertory ritual in general, in particular the increasing emphasis on the purity not only of those who celebrated the eucharist, but also of the gifts that were offered. This development changed the entire outlook of the oblation of the gifts. A letter written by Alcuin and dated 798 (Alcuin, *Epistula* 137) stresses the importance of the most pure state (*mundissimus*) of the eucharistic bread, which was preferably unleavened bread (*absque fermento*). Purity requirements would eventually exclude the laity from preparation of the bread, although the role of the people in the offertory and the gifts seems not to have ended before the tenth or even eleventh century (Bishop 1909/1967, p. 101; McKitterick 1977, p. 144).

Whatever the rationale for transferring the recitation of names to the eucharistic prayer proper, the Carolingians adopted Innocent I's preference to incorporate the people involved in the eucharistic offering into what was increasingly experienced as the most holy of prayers.[8] The Carolingians copied this practice in their effort to model the Frankish custom on the Roman example. This adaptation did not, however, mean that the solemn recitation of names came to an end—far from it. One could argue that it brought the names of the participants even closer to the heart of the eucharistic ritual.

In the Merovingian liturgical sources *stricto sensu* there are no explicit indications of the ritual of reciting the names. The sacramentaries, preserving the prayers recited by the priest, only provide the "collects after the names" which would have followed the recitation. These collects enable us to retrieve the meaning behind the so-called "ritual of the diptychs"[9] as it developed in the Merovingian liturgy. How do these prayers reflect the relevance of the recitation of names? How do they characterize the eucharistic community and the participation of both living and dead members? And how does the expression of membership of, and the sense of belonging to, this eucharistic community make use of ancient concepts and terms by granting them a new meaning? To answer these questions, the "collects after the names" will now be discussed.

Source Material: The "Collects After the Names"

Collects that accompany the recitation of the names are found in masses in a number of service books dating to the late seventh and early eighth centuries, most importantly the *Gothic Missal*, the *Bobbio Missal*, the *Missale Gallicanum Vetus*, the *Missale Francorum*, the *Irish Palimpsest Sacramentary*, and the set of seven masses known as Mone Masses.[10] Of these, the *Bobbio Missal* and particularly the *Gothic Missal* are the most detailed sources. The analysis of prayers in the following sections is based primarily on material offered by the *Gothic Missal*, or *Missale Gothicum* (Vat. Reg. lat. 317), a sacramentary made in Burgundy in the final decades of the seventh century most probably for use in an urban cathedral community, most likely Autun (*Gothic Missal*, 2017, pp. 14–15).

A sacramentary, as is the case with all early medieval liturgical service books, gives only a fragmentary view of what the liturgy of the mass actually looked like. This is because the sacramentary is a book of texts, leaving out practically all indications of the performance of the ritual. Moreover, in the *Gothic Missal*, as in other sacramentaries, not all mass orders include the same prayers. Some orders are longer than others, and high feasts are given different prayers than feasts of minor importance.[11] The "collect after the names" is, however, a constant feature: no feast or Sunday mass in the *Gothic Missal* lacks this particular prayer. This yields a sum total of sixty-nine collects after the names in this sacramentary alone, with few repeats.[12]

Collects after the names focus on the names of those seen as participants in the eucharistic celebration, both living and dead. They also have an intercessory function, formulating a prayer or request and asking for God's benevolence toward the oblations offered by the people and toward those who benefit from this sacrifice. In that sense, many examples of "collects after the names" in the *Gothic Missal* could also be considered as "prayer over the gifts" (*oratio super oblata*), as service books from other Western liturgical families label the prayer that closes the offertory ritual:[13] praying that God graciously accept the offering and procure the salutary *effectus* of the sacrifice for both living and dead.[14] As both the living and the dead are included, the intercessory part of the collects *post nomina* is essentially twofold (Rose 2017, pp. 4–10). Moreover, the large number of unique collects after the names in the *Gothic Missal* reveals the proper (*proprium*) character of these prayers. Instead of being one unchanging text for all occasions, each mass has its own variant, often dealing with the theme of the Sunday or feast celebrated, particularly in the case of saints' feasts. The element that primarily interests us here is the part of the collect that expresses the membership of the people involved in the eucharistic ritual: the living who offer their oblation and the dead for whom the oblation is brought in. However, the three main elements (recitation of names, offertory intercession, and theme of the feast) are intrinsically related as we shall see in the following.

SAINTS AND THEIR CO-CITIZENS

What, then, lies behind the mention of names in the Merovingian liturgy of the mass? How, and in what terms, does the ritual of the recitation of names define the character of the eucharistic assembly or, more broadly, the Christian community? A first answer to these questions lies in the way the ritual of the names and the accompanying collects express the intrinsic quality of the liturgical community. Even though much of recent scholarship studies the ritual of the names from the perspective of the commemoration of the dead,[15] the essential quality of the community that gathers in the celebration of the mass is its inclusion of all members of the eucharistic assembly, both the living and the dead, as we have seen. This is made clear by the frequent reference to recitation of the names of both groups alike: those who bring the offer and the beloved dead. An important role in linking these two categories of members is played by the saints, which comes to the fore particularly (though not exclusively) in "collects after the names" for masses in commemoration of saints in the *Gothic Missal*.

A fitting example is from the mass for the feast day of the Burgundian saints Ferreolus and Ferrucio (June 16), martyrs of Besançon. The collect in this mass mentions both the living (*fratrum*) and the deceased (*carorumque nostrorum*)[16] when it invokes the help of the saints to make the faithful inhabitants of the heavenly Jerusalem:

> 365 AFTER THE NAMES. Now that the names of our brothers and beloved (*fratrum carorumque nostorum*) have been enumerated, let us pray for the mercy of the Lord, that he will bring about that in the middle of Jerusalem, in the congregation of the saints, these names will be enumerated to him by the angel of sanctification, to the beatitude of eternal joy, and that through his power he will sanctify this offering of ours after the prefiguration of Melchisedek. And that he will also mercifully grant the prayers of those who offer in this oblation, that through the commemoration of the blessed martyrs Ferreolus and Ferruccio and all the saints, and assisted by their prayers, they are deemed worthy to obtain not only protection for the living but also rest for our beloved deceased.[17]

The first part of the text is a remarkable patchwork using elements taken from three prayers that are part of the *canon missae*. This fixed series of collects became the regular eucharistic prayer from the ninth century onward and is often referred to as "the Roman canon," although it is found first in Merovingian sacramentaries (Hen 2004, pp. 150–152). Yet the "collect after the names" in the mass for the martyrs of Besançon in the *Gothic Missal* does not cut and paste without further interference (*Missale Gothicum*, ed. Rose 2005, p. 302). Instead, the author (or compiler) of this prayer changed the texts of the *canon*, which he must have known, in a significant way. In the prayer *Supplices* of the *canon missae*, it is the angel of God who is asked to carry the gifts from the altar to the heavenly altar to expose them to God's countenance:

> We humbly ask you, almighty God: grant these [gifts] to be carried through the hand of your holy angel to your exalted altar in the countenance of your divine majesty so that every time we have obtained by our participation in this altar the most sacred body and blood of your son, we may be filled with celestial blessing and with your mercy.[18]

In the "collect after the names" for Ferreolus and Ferrucio, however, it is not the gifts that are asked to be carried up on high and transformed into the body and blood of Christ, as the *Supplices* formulates. Rather, it is the names of those participating in the eucharistic ritual. And they are not just asked to be read before God's countenance, but instead "in the middle of Jerusalem, in the congregation of the saints (*in medio Hierusalem in congregacione sanctorum*)." Thus, the names of the faithful, be they the living members of the community on earth or those who have passed away, are not only to be recited during the celebration of mass in the earthly liturgy, but are also believed to resound in the congregation living together in the heavenly city, where "the saints" receive and carry on the names of the faithful living on earth.

The image of the inhabitants of the heavenly city who receive the earthlings as "co-citizens" is expressed in an even more pronounced way in a prayer that is not a "collect after the names", but one of the collects in the great Easter intercession in the *Gothic Missal*:

> 239 COLLECT FOLLOWS. Return, O Lord, to the travellers the ground of the fatherland which they long for, so that through the contemplation of your mercy, while for this life they give thanks for your benefits, they eagerly desire to be "fellow citizens of the saints (*ciues sanctorum*) and members of your household" (Eph. 2, 19).[19]

The preceding *oratio* (238), or exhortation to pray, formulates the intercession for "all our brothers and sisters who are subjected to the necessities of travels."[20] The nature of these travels remains ambiguous in the collect itself, suggesting with the word "return" (*restitue*) that the travelers are homebound, yet at the same time changing the *peregrinatio* into a spiritual journey, of which the goal is the heavenly city where the saints await their co-citizens (*Gothic Missal*, 2017, p. 214). Similar "co-citizenship" is granted to the members of the eucharistic assembly gathered in commemoration of Ferreolus and

Ferrucio. Their "civic identity" is redefined through their participation in the ritual of mass, in particular the ritual of the names.

MEMBERSHIP AND EXCLUSION

The examples discussed so far express the identity of the eucharistic assembly as a community in which the living and the dead are held together, and as a bond that unites as co-citizens those dwelling on earth with the saints who live in the heavenly city above. The following example, the "collect after the names" in the second Sunday mass (490) in the *Gothic Missal*, explicitly employs the terminology the ancient Roman authors used to distinguish between those who were full members of the civic community and those who were strangers or outsiders to it. The context of the eucharist infuses new meaning in the terminology inherited from the ancient world. The collect phrases the prayer that none of those for whom the eucharist is celebrated (*pro quibus holocausta franguntur*) be excluded (*muneris sui exterum esse paciatur*), and that the sins and merits of both living and dead are regarded in the light of grace (for the living) and forgiveness (for the dead):

> 490 AFTER THE NAMES. Now that we have heard the enumeration of the names, most beloved brothers, let us pray to the God of love and mercy, that he graciously receives what has been offered, [and that] he does not allow that one of those for whom the offerings are broken is ever excluded (*exterum*) from his gift, and that as he considers the merits as well as the sins of the living and the dead, he commands that the last pertain to grace, the first to forgiveness.[21]

The prayer is important because of the word *exterum*, a term Suetonius and Cicero used to denote, as a synonym of *alienus* and *peregrinus*, foreigners and foreign cities in contrast to citizens.[22] The word is not frequently used in the Bible, but it occurs in patristic writings, most relevantly in a letter by Bishop Cyprian of Carthage († 258) discussing the possibility for lapsed bishops to do penance and the impossibility that they will regain clerical ordination (Cyprian, *Epistula* 67.6.2; see Blaise 1954 and Souter 1949, s.v. *exterus*). The words *exterarum gentium* (foreign peoples) are used here not to distinguish between "citizens" and "strangers" in the way Roman authors would understand these two (legal) categories in the context of defining citizenship, but, rather, to evoke the unbridgeable distance between members of the church and those "outside." The term emphasizes notions of religious inclusion and exclusion with the help of terms used in ancient Rome that denote the boundaries between those who were part of the civic community as citizens and those who were not. Thus, ancient citizenship vocabulary is reused in a radically new semantic context. In the context of the collect in the second Sunday mass, the word *exterus* is used positively to pray for the inclusion of all members of the eucharistic community, which holds the world of the living and the dead together so that nobody becomes a "foreigner."

Ancient Terminology Obtains
New Meanings

The collects quoted above make clear that the Merovingian practice of reading and listing names displayed strong interest in the coherence and unity of the Christian assembly, including living and deceased members. The word *exterus* in the final collect in the previous section echoed citizenship vocabulary by implying that those included in the ritual and its salutary effect are the opposite: insiders, members. The present section explores how this "membership" is further articulated.

The most central image of membership and being registered as a member in the "collects after the names" is the prayer for inscription in the heavenly register. This central notion occurs in twelve of the sixty-nine collects *post nomina*. The heavenly register referred to in these prayers is indicated in the *Gothic Missal* by use of different terms: "book of life" (*liber vitae*: 177, 182), "heavenly book" (*caelestis pagina*, also plural: 172), "eternal book" (*aeternalibus pagines*:[23] 294), "heavenly register" (*litterae caelestes* 1). Although these indications echo various ancient religions (Koep 1952), they reflect biblical usage as well (Koep 1954, pp. 726–728). The "collect after the names" in the sixth Lenten mass (193) does not mention the book or register itself, but speaks of a *titulo aeternitatis*: the label of eternity. The combination of words has a ring of heavenly bookkeeping all the same, given Cassiodorus's use of *titulus* to refer to "an item in an account book" (Souter 1949, s.v. *titulus*).

Apart from the noun that denotes the heavenly register or book, the relevant verbs to describe the act of inscription are also significant. There are many variants of *scribere*. It is used only once as a simple verb (in collect no. 15). Compound alternatives are more frequent, mainly *adscribere* (177, 182), *inscribere* (in *inscriptio* 188), and, particularly, *conscribere* (1, 172, 427). These forms evoke the association of the Christian book of life with the *patres conscripti*, a term referring to the senatorial register in the Roman Empire (Koep 1952, pp. 120–123).[24] Other verbs make clear that the inscription of names was experienced as a public event. Not only were the names read aloud (*recitare* 172, 177, 182, 376, 391, 427, 438; *patefacta sunt* 427) in church, they were also thought to be "made public" in heaven, as the verb *intimare* ("to make public," "to announce" 391, 439, both in the context of "to be announced in the heavenly Book") suggests. Both in heaven and on earth the Christian community expresses itself as a public body with a "controllable registration."[25]

Finally, the reference to the public recitation of names with the verb *recensiri* ("enumerate" 365) stands out. This word, which also occurs in the stock *incipit offerentium nominibus recensitis* or *auditis nominibus recensitis* (160, 490, 501, and 534: "Now that the names of those who offer have been enumerated" or "Now that we have heard the enumeration of the names") echoes the task and activity of the Roman censor, the official responsible for the assessment of citizens and their properties (Lewis and Short 1951, s.v. *recensio*). The verb occurs twice in the "collect after the names" in the mass for Ferreolus and Ferrucio (365). In this collect, no mention is made of a book or list, but the verb *recensiri* is used both with regard to the earthly ritual of public recitation and in the context of the public recitation of the same names in the heavenly Jerusalem. The idiom of imperial taxation and census is even more present in the verb phrase *ut…censeas deputare* in the "collect after the names" in the mass for Peter and Paul (376): "…that you consider the names of those that have been recited worthy to be counted in the Book of Life."[26] In this prayer, God is depicted as the heavenly censor who is implored to open his register to those who are publicly announced as members in the earthly ritual.

Although the word *civis* or *civitas* is not mentioned explicitly in the collects that speak of the heavenly book of life, terminology used by ancient Roman authors to mark the boundaries of citizenship is reused in a new semantic context. In particular, terms that resonate with the ancient Roman practice of enumerating citizens (*recensiri*) and their properties (*census*) imply that the members of the Christian community, the living and the dead, were all counted as belonging to the same "city," involved as they were in the one ritual of the eucharistic offering. While their names were enumerated publicly in the mass ritual of the church community on earth, the image of a similar enumeration in the heavenly city in the assembly of saints was evoked.

A close reading of the "collects after the names" in the *Gothic Missal*, as one of the service books that best represents the Merovingian liturgical world, shows how the ritual of a public proclamation of the members of the eucharistic community literally "intertwines" (*texuit*, a word used in "collects after the names," nos 78 and 84) the living and the dead to one common destiny: to be counted among the elect (*inter electos iubeas adgregare* 78, 84). At the same time, the collects in the *Gothic Missal* make clear that the implication of membership of the Christian community is not simply a longing for an otherworldly celestial city, but a genuine concern for the commonwealth of the living. Being enrolled in the "citizen lists" of the heavenly city is not only a privilege but also assumes the conversion to a Christian way of life that such membership implies. This will be the topic of the final section of this chapter.

Rest for the Deceased, "Correction" for the Living

Thus far, we have seen that the "collects after the names" in the *Gothic Missal* link the ritual practice of the recitation of names to the inscription of the members of the eucharistic community in the heavenly record, including the names of living and dead alike. Yet even if the living and the dead were brought and held together in this particular ritual and through the inscription in one register, they did not have the same position in the assembly, for the simple reason that the dead are dead and the living are still alive. In the following, we shall see that the inscription of all Christians in the book of life, making the living and the dead equal members of one community, was not purely spiritual, nor something the dead enjoyed already as inhabitants of the heavenly Jerusalem. It was something for which the living still had to wait to become real.

The differentiation of the two categories of members of the eucharistic community comes forward in the twofold intercession phrased in the "collects after the names" as we find them in the *Gothic Missal* (*Gothic Missal*, 2017, pp. 11–17). While rest and eternal consolation were invoked for the deceased, different "blessings" were requested for the living. In a number of collects, the intercession on behalf of the members of the community living on earth comes down to "correction" or "conversion" (*emendatio*) (Rose 2017, pp. 16–17). The word is present in the collects after the names for the mass for Our Lord's Circumcision in the *Gothic Missal* (collect no. 53) and in the mass in commemoration of the martyr Leudegar in the same sacramentary (collect no. 427). Both collects ask, in the intercessory part, for correction (*emendatio*) for the living: "that these offers are as beneficial to the correction (*ad emendationem*) of the living as they help the dying to find rest" (53)[27]; "that [the Lord] deigns to grant that the oblation of this sacred [feast] which is offered obtains correction (*emendationem*) for the living and remission of sins for the dead" (427).[28]

The word *emendatio* had a special ring in the Carolingian period as a frequently used synonym of *correctio*, the *Stichwort* indicating the royal reform program that emphatically included the betterment of the laity (McKitterick 2008, p. 304). Yet the Merovingian world was just as well characterized by the efforts of the rulers to create a Christian people and improve its morals through *emendatio*. This point was emphasized by Giles Brown more than twenty years ago in an article in which he related the Frankish concern for moral improvement of the people to similar tendencies in Anglo-Saxon England (Bede) and Visigothic Spain (Isidore of Seville), and firmly rooted it in ancient Roman, early Christian, and biblical culture (Brown 1994). With regard to Merovingian Gaul, Brown points to a number of capitularies issued by the Merovingian kings of the sixth and seventh centuries to eradicate from the populace practices that the ecclesiastical point of view condemned as superstition and misbehavior (Brown 1994, pp. 6–8). At the same time, these royal capitularies instructed the clergy and made them responsible for the proper execution of a program of *emendatio* and *correctio* of the people. This correction should lead to a way of life (*conversatio*) coming forth from "love of righteousness" and leading to "peace in this life and salvation of the people," as an edict issued by King Guntram and dated November 10, 585 phrases it.[29]

Conversatio, emendatio: these terms refer to a way of life that was considered to be fitting or even typical of Christians on earth. As Guntram's edict clearly expresses, this language was thought to contribute to the salvation of the people. Life in the here and now and life hereafter were indissolubly connected, both in the rhetoric of reform employed by the Merovingian kings and in the "collects after the names" in the Merovingian service books for the mass.

LITURGY AS EXPRESSION AND IMPRESSION OF A THOUGHT WORLD

The ritual of mentioning names is almost as old as the Christian cult and is rooted in ancient religious practices. Although the "ritual of the diptychs" in the context of mass as we know it from the Merovingian sources died out, it was transformed into other customs that identified members of the Christian community. Listing names had dangerous potential as well. From early Christian times, deletion from the diptychs was an equally impressive reality. Apart from creating membership, the listing of names was a powerful instrument in Christian excommunication practices (Koep 1952, pp. 110–111). This could be applied to clergy, as in Augustine's sermon 356.14 (ed. Lambot 1950, pp. 141–142) where he discusses the case of a *clericus* who was to be excluded from the *tabula clericorum* because of his way of life that was not in accordance with Augustine's standards for ecclesiastics. The sermon was reiterated in the Council of Aachen of 816 (ed. Werminghoff 1906, p. 393). Application of this practice of deletion to laypeople is also attested as, for example, in the Council of Elvira held ca. 305, at which it was forbidden to include possessed people (*energumenoi*) in the recitation of names (Laeuchli 1972, p. 129). Thus, excluding names from recitation affects both the living and the dead. Likewise, excommunication affected not only the living but could also affect the dead, as is illustrated by an example from the Greek Acts of Melania, where it was considered wrong to include the name of a dead woman whose orthodoxy had been questioned (ed. Delehaye 1903, p. 23).

In both its negative (excluding) and its confirmative (including) application, the public recitation of names in Christian rituals during the early Middle Ages was linked more directly to community life in the here and now than previous studies suggest. If we consider the "ritual of the diptychs" in the wider context of late-antique and early medieval culture, it comes to the fore as an integral and important element in the transformative processes that took place in this age of transition from the hegemonic Roman Empire to the patchwork of the new political communities that took over in the early medieval West. In this period, not all ancient models of community life were abandoned overnight. Instead they were gradually adapted to the new situation, while the ancient Roman terminology to indicate these models received new meanings in changed cultural and religious contexts. One of the ancient models preserved through this transformation made belonging and membership explicit. The ritual of the names in the context of the mass was a specific *locus* where issues of belonging were expressed in terms referring to ancient and biblical citizenship discourse, which overrode the division between categories of spiritual (hereafter) and mundane (here and now).

In his latest study, *Ransom of the Soul*, Peter Brown gives a harmonious picture of Christian community life in the early, pre-Constantinian period. The way Christians depicted their beloved dead, in a pastoral idyll where later notions of purgatory and anxiety were still far away, is in his eyes a reflection of their own tranquil life in the still small and familiar Christian community (2015, pp. 36–37). Brown's impression that the conversation of the living with the dead indicates a close, "almost symbiotic" bond between the two categories (2015, p. 41), is highly relevant for the study of later ritual practices that focused on bridging the boundaries of life and death (on the afterlife, see also Moreira, Chapter 42, this volume). With the post-Constantinian and later postimperial changes in Western Christianity, the bond between living and dead remained strong, as the continuity of ritual practices that brought them together proves.

To what extent can we, following Peter Brown, claim that the "collects after the names" in the *Gothic Missal* mirrored the world-view and beliefs of the inhabitants of, presumably, Autun in the late seventh century? Here two questions merge that are the subjects of ongoing debates. First, there is the matter of the "topicality" of liturgical prayers, which were often age-old compositions by the time they were either first codified, or codified in the way that they are transmitted to the twenty-first century (Bradshaw 2002, pp. 4–6). Indeed, the *Gothic Missal* includes prayers composed by known figures such as Eucherius of Lyon (380–449) and his fifth-century contemporaries—how "topical" were these texts in the late seventh century? The question seems to be less relevant when we reverse it. Liturgical texts do not necessarily express the mindset of the people that pray them or hear them recited. Rather, they impress this mindset and help to form the religious frame of reference of the community that uses them.

The second question concerns the accessibility of highly stylized prayers recited in the presence of a diverse group of laypeople in a language that gradually ceased to be a mother tongue for all, including the members of the clergy who performed the recitation. The *Gothic Missal* is an important source of spoken Latin and linguistic developments, testifying to the ongoing process in which the pronunciation of Latin performative texts adapted to regional usage (*Missale Gothicum*, ed. Rose 2005, pp. 23–187). Whatever the outcome of the debate with regard to the accessibility of Latin texts in a performative public ritual, the recitation of the names and the subsequent "collect after the names" must have been a ritual that was very close to the lay members of the eucharistic community. The capitulary by Guntram (585), mentioned above, summons all faithful (*universae plebis coniunctio devotionis congregatur studio*) to come to church on Sundays and for all other solemnities (ed. Boretius 1883, p. 11). If the king's authority was taken seriously, the people would have been present during the celebration of mass, to which they brought their offerings of bread and wine, and where they would hear the names of the community pronounced at the altar where the sacred oblations were collected. At the altar, clerics sounded their names and defined their membership in a community that was proudly envisaged as the heavenly city, yet firmly rooted in the earthly here and now.

NOTES

1. On the nature and history of the term *liturgy*, see Symes 2016, pp. 239–241. A first draft of this article was written during my stay at the Institute for Advanced Study, Princeton, where I was a member of the School of Historical Studies during the autumn term of 2015–2016. I thank the Institute, its director, staff, and library staff for their hospitality and support, and the Herodotus Fund for its financial assistance. For inspiration and critical comments, I am particularly grateful to Patrick Geary and the members of the medieval seminar of that term: Courtney Booker, Giles Constable, Albrecht Diem, Eric Goldberg, Michael Kulikowski, Jason Moralee, Eric Ramirez-Weaver, and Maria de Lurdes Rosa. In addition, I thank Janneke Raaijmakers for her helpful remarks. This article is published within the framework of the project NWO VICI-Rose 277-30-002 *Citizenship Discourses in*

the Early Middle Ages, 400-1100, funded by the Netherlands Organisation for Scientific Research (NWO).

2. On the difficulty of establishing whether or not the demarcation of the eucharistic rite only for those baptized was still regular practice in the Merovingian period, see Bernard 2008, pp. 148–149; 153–156.

3. On the liturgical books of the early medieval period, see Palazzo 1993, 1998.

4. On the close connection between the living and the dead members of the eucharistic community as expressed particularly in the ritual of the names, see Rose 2017, pp. 4–10.

5. On this practical issue, see Oexle 1976, 77–79.

6. The text of Innocent's letter is published in Cabié 1973, pp. 44–52, and included in Cabrol 1920, p. 1051. See also Bishop 1909/1967, p. 109; Taft 1991, pp. 28–29; Bernard 2008, p. 236.

7. *Admonitio generalis* 54: *Sacerdotibus.* Item *eiusdem, ut nomina publice non recitentur ante precem sacerdotalem.* Ed. Mordek et al. 2013, p. 206. In this passage, *eiusdem* refers to Innocent, whose *decretales* are mentioned in the preceding canon 53 concerning the kiss of peace; the use of *precem* (*sacerdotalem*) for the eucharistic prayer *stricto sensu* occurs already in the work of Augustine, Innocent I, and Gregory the Great: Blaise 1954, s.v. *prex.* The second admonition concerning the names is found in the Synod of Frankfurt (794), c. 51: *De non recitandis nominibus, antequam oblatio offeratur,* ed. Werminghoff 1906, p. 171.

8. For an example of the awe and reverence with which the *canon missae* was surrounded in the late eighth and ninth centuries, see the lavish decoration of the prayers in the *Sacramentary of Gellone*: Paris, BnF lat. 12048, f. 143v, now accessible through http://gallica.bnf.fr/ark:/12148/btv1b60000317 (last accessed November 9, 2015).

9. Although the material form in which the names were presented to the deacon for recitation was only exceptionally the ivory diptychs that resemble the consular diptychs of the classical world, and of which only a small number of Christian reuses have been preserved (Bernard 2008, pp. 226–232), the ritual recitation of the names was still called the "ritual of the diptychs" in the tenth century: see, for example, Folcuin of Lobbes, *Gesta abbatum Lobiensium* 7, pp. 58–59 (*quae super diptica dicitur*).

10. The Mone Masses derive their name from their nineteenth-century discoverer, Franz Joseph Mone (Mohlberg 1958, p. 62). The *Missale Francorum* is an exception with examples of a collect *ante* instead of *post nomina* (no. 123, 141, 150). On the liturgical sources of late-antique and Merovingian Gaul in general, see Vogel 1986, p. 108.

11. For an overview of the prayers that occur throughout the book and their functions, see *Gothic Missal,* 2017, pp. 44–74.

12. See the table of concordance in *Missale Gothicum,* ed. by E. Rose, pp. 553–569. In the following, the numbering of prayers is according to the most recent edition: *Missale Gothicum,* ed. Rose.

13. Particularly the books that follow the tradition referred to as "the Gregorian sacramentaries," of which the sacramentary sent to Charlemagne by Pope Hadrian I in the late eighth century is the most famous example. Cf. Vogel 1986, p. 79.

14. On *effectus* in a liturgical context, see Diezinger 1961; Rose 2016.

15. For a summary of recent scholarship and its main directions, see Rose 2017, pp. 1–2.

16. It is difficult to establish a definite interpretation of *fratrum carorumque nostrorum.* I consider *fratrum* to be a reference to the living and *carorumque nostrorum* an indication of the deceased, although other "collects after the names" distinguish between the living and

the dead by indicating the living as "our beloved" (*cari nostri*) and the dead with "the souls of our beloved." See Rose 2017, pp. 7–8, with regard to *Missale Gothicum* 268.

17. 365 POST NOMINA. *Recensitis nominibus fratrum carorumque nostrorum oremus dominicam misericordiam ut in medio Hierusalem in congregacione sanctorum haec nomina sibi faciat ab angelo sanctificacionis in beatitudinem aeterni gaudii recensiri sacrificiumque hoc nostrum sicut in praeformacionem Melchisedech in uirtute sanctificet. Praeces quoque offerencium in hac oblacionem propiciatus exaudiat, commemoracionem beatissimorum martyrum Ferreoli et Ferrucionis omniumque sanctorum, ut eorum praecibus adiuti, non solum uiuentibus praesidia, uerum etiam defunctis caris nostris requiem obtenere mereantur.* Missale Gothicum, ed. Rose 2005, p. 489; trans. *Gothic Missal*, 2017, pp. 257-258.

18. *Supplices te rogamus, omnipotens Deus, iube haec perferri per manus sancti angeli tui in suplimi altario tuo in conspectu diuine maiestates tuae ut quotquod ex hoc altari participacionis sacrosanctum filii tui corpus et sanguenem sumpserimus omni benedictione celesti et gracia repleamur.* Text according to *The Bobbio Missal*, ed. Lowe, p. 12. I leave the orthographic characteristics of this manuscript without comment here.

19. 239 COLLECCIO SEQVITVR. *Restitue, domine, peregrinis desideratum patriae solum, ut contemplacionem misericordiae tuae, dum ad praesens agunt beneficiis tuis gracias, ciues esse sanctorum ac tui domestici concupiscant.* Missale Gothicum, ed. Rose 2005, p. 443; trans. *Gothic Missal*, 2017, p. 214.

20. *...fratres nostros ac sorores quicumque peregrinacionum necessitatibus subiacent.* Missale Gothicum, ed. Rose 2005, p. 443; trans. *Gothic Missal*, 2017, p. 214.

21. 490 POST NOMINA. *Auditis nominibus recensitis, dilectissimi fratres, deum pietatis et misericordiae dipraecimor, ut haec quae oblata sunt, benignus adsumat. Nullum umquam ex his, pro quibus holocausta franguntur, muneris sui exterum esse paciatur, tam uiuencium quam defunctorum uel ad merita uel ad peccata respiciens alios iubeat ad graciam, alios ad ueniam pertinere.* Missale Gothicum, ed. Rose 2005, p. 531; trans. *Gothic Missal*, 2017, pp. 295–296.

22. Lewis and Short (1951), s.v. *exterus* refer to Suetonius, *De vita caesarum*, 84: *non modo vestris civibus, verum etiam exteris nationibus* and to Cicero in various works to indicate *exterae civitates* or *exterae nationes*; note the similar use in Acts 26, 11: *exteras civitates* (foreign cities).

23. For *paginis*.

24. The image of the apostles as a heavenly senate also occurs in an eleventh-century poem in honor of the apostle Matthew composed by archbishop Alfanus of Salerno, who in the same poem refers to the citizens of Salerno as *cives Matthaei*: Alfanus of Salerno, *Apostolorum nobili victoria*, ed. Lentini and Avagliano, p. 85. On this hymn, see Rose 2009, pp. 198–206 and Rose 2013.

25. The self-representation of the early medieval church as dominating the public sphere in contrast with pagan or heretic milieus as "private groupings" is demonstrated by Drews 2002, pp. 197, 201–202.

26. *censeas*: "to assess, to tax, to esteem." The word signals the relevance of the *census* and identifies the task of the *censor* as the person who keeps records of the "registering and rating of Roman citizens, property, etc.": Lewis and Short 1951, s.v. *censeo* I.A.1 and 2. *census*; see also Koep 1952, p. 71.

27. *...ut haec sacrificia sic uiuentibus proficient ad emendationem, ut defunctis opitulentur ad requiem;* Missale Gothicum, ed. Rose 2005, p. 371; trans. *Gothic Missal*, 2017, p. 136.

28. ...*ut concidere dignetur ut sacrae praesentis oblatio, quae offertur, uiuentibus emendation*?*m et defunctis remissionem obteneant peccatorum. Missale Gothicum*, ed. Rose 2005, p. 513; trans. *Gothic Missal*, 2017, p. 279.

29. *Guntchramni regis edictum* (dated November 10, 585): *Guntchramni regis edictum* (dated November 10, 585): *Ad vos ergo, sacrosancti pontifices, quibus divina clementia potestatis paternae concessit officium, imprimis nostrae serenitatis sermo dirigitur, sperantes quod ita populum vobis providentia divina comissum frequenti praedicatione studeatis corrigere et pastorali studio gubernare, quatenus, dum universi diligendo iustitiam conversatione praecipua cum omni honestate studuerint vivere, melius, cuncta rerum adversitate remota, coelesti beneficio concedatur tranquillitas temporum et congrua salvatio populorum.* Boretius (ed.) 1883, pp. 11–12.

Works Cited

Ancient Sources

Acta graeca Melaniae H. Delehaye (ed.). (1903). *Analecta Bollandiana* 22: 5–50.

Admonitio generalis. H. Mordek, K. Zechiel-Eckes, and M. Glatthaar (eds.). (2013). *Die Admonitio generalis Karls des Großen.* MGH Fontes iuris germanici antiqui in usum scholarum separatim editi 16. Wiesbaden: Harrasowitz.

Alcuin, *Epistula* 137. E. Dümmler (ed.). (1892–1999). *Epistolae karolini aevi* 2. MGH Epistolae 4 (pp. 210–216). Berlin: Weidmann.

Alfanus of Salerno, *Apostolorum nobili victoria.* A. Lentini and F. Avagliano (eds.). (1974). *I carmi di Alfano I, arcivescovo di Salerno.* Montecassino: Badia di Montecassino.

Augustine, *Sermo* 356. C. Lambot (ed.). (1950). *Sancti Aurelii Augustini Sermones selecti duodeviginti* (pp. 132–143). Utrecht: Spectrum.

Capitularia. A. Boretius (ed.). (1883). MGH Capitularia 1. Hanover: Hahn.

Concilia. A. Werminghoff (ed.). (1906). MGH Concilia aevi Karolini 1. Hanover-Leipzig: Hahn.

Cyprian, *Epistulae.* G. F. Diercks (ed.). (1994–1999). *Sancti Cypriani episcopi epistularium.* CCSL 3C. Turnhout: Brepols.

Folcuin of Lobbes, *Gesta abbatum Lobiensium.* G. H. Pertz (ed.). (1841). MGH SS 4 (pp. 52–74). Hanover: Hahn.

The Gothic Missal. E. Rose (ed.). (2017). *The Gothic Missal: Introduction, Translation and Notes.* Corpus Christianorum in Translation 27. Turnhout: Brepols.

Innocent, *Epistula ad Decentium.* R. Cabié (ed.). (1973). *La lettre du pape Innocent Ier à Décentius de Gubbio (19 mars 416)* (pp. 44–52). Bibliothèque de la *Revue d'histoire ecclésiastique* 58. Louvain: Publications universitaires de Louvain.

Irish Palimpsest Sacramentary A. Dold and L. Eizenhöfer (eds.). (1964). *Das irische Palimpsestsakramentar im CLM 14429 der Staatsbibliothek München.* Beuron: Beuroner Kunstverlag.

Jerome, *In Hieremiam.* S. Reiter (ed.). (1960). *In Hieremiam libri VI.* CCSL 74. Turnhout: Brepols.

Jerome, *In Hiezechielem.* F. Glorie (ed.). (1964). *Commentariorum in Hiezechielem libri XIV.* CCSL 75. Turnhout: Brepols.

Missale Bobbiense E. A. Lowe (ed.). (1917–1924). *The Bobbio Missal: A Gallican Mass-Book (MS Paris lat. 13246).* HBS 53, 58, 61. London: Henry Bradshaw Society.

Missale Francorum. L. C. Mohlberg (ed.). (1957). *Missale Francorum*. Rerum ecclesiasticarum documenta, series maior, fontes II. Rome: Herder.

Missale Gallicanum Vetus. L. C. Mohlberg (ed.). (1958). *Missale Gallicanum Vetus*. Rerum ecclesiasticarum documenta, series maior, fontes III. Rome: Herder.

Missale Gothicum. E. Rose (ed.). (2005). *Missale Gothicum e codice Vaticano reginensi latino 317 editum*. CCSL 159D. Turnhout: Brepols.

Mone Masses L. C. Mohlberg (ed.). (1958). *Missale Gallicanum Vetus*. Rerum ecclesiasticarum documenta, series maior, fontes III (pp. 61–91). Rome: Herder.

Modern Sources

Bernard, P. (2008). *Transitions liturgiques en Gaule carolingienne. Une traduction commentée des deux « lettres » faussement attribuées à l'évêque Germain de Paris*. Paris: Hora decima.

Bishop, E. (1909/1967). "Appendix. Observations on the Liturgy of Narsai." In R. H. Connolly (ed.), *The Liturgical Homilies of Narsai* (pp. 85–163). Cambridge: Cambridge University Press.

Blaise, A. (1954). *Dictionnaire latin-français des auteurs chrétiens*. Turnhout: Brepols.

Bradshaw, P. (2002). *The Search for the Origins of Christian Worship. Sources and Methods for the Study of Early Liturgy*, second edition. New York: Oxford University Press.

Brown, G. (1994). "Introduction: The Carolingian Renaissance." In R. McKitterick (ed.), *Carolingian Culture: Emulation and Innovation* (pp. 1–51). Cambridge: Cambridge University Press.

Brown, P. (2015). *The Ransom of the Soul. Afterlife and Wealth in Early Western Christianity*. Cambridge, MA: Harvard University Press.

Cabrol, F. (1920). "Diptyques (liturgiques)." In F. Cabrol and H. Leclercq (eds.), *Dictionnaire d'archéologie chrétienne et de liturgie* 4.1 (col. 1045–1094). Paris: Letouzey.

Diezinger, W. (1961). *Effectus in der römischen Liturgie*. Bonn: P. Hanstein.

Drews, W. (2002). "Jews as Pagans? Polemical Definitions of Identity in Visigothic Spain." *Early Medieval Europe* 11: 189–207.

Foley, E. (1997). "The Song of the Assembly." In L. Larson-Miller (ed.), *Medieval Liturgy. A Book of Essays* (pp. 203–234). New York: Garland Publishing.

Hen, Y. (2004). "The Liturgy of the Bobbio Missal." In Y. Hen and R. Meens (eds.), *The Bobbio Missal. Liturgy and Religious Culture in Merovingian Gaul* (pp. 140–153). Cambridge: Cambridge University Press.

Hen, Y. (2016). "The Church in Sixth-Century Gaul." In A. Murray (ed.), *A Companion to Gregory of Tours* (pp. 232–255). Leiden: Brill.

Lewis, C., and Short, C. (1951). *A Latin Dictionary*. Oxford: Clarendon Press.

McKitterick, R. (1977). *The Frankish Church and the Carolingian Reforms, 789–895*. London: Royal Historical Society.

McKitterick, R. (2008). *Charlemagne: The Formation of a Christian Identity* Cambridge: Cambridge University Press.

Koep, L. (1952). *Das himmlische Buch in Antike und Christentum. Eine religionsgeschichtliche Untersuchung zur altchristlichen Bildersprache*. Bonn: Peter Hanstein Verlag.

Koep, L. (1954). "Buch IV (himmlisch)." In Theodor Klauser (ed.), *Reallexikon für Antike und Christentum* 2 (col. 725–731). Stuttgart: Hiersemann.

Laeuchli, S. (1972). *Power and Sexuality: The Emergence of Canon Law at the Synod of Elvira*. Philadelphia: Temple University Press.

Oexle, O. G. (1976). "Memoria und Memorialüberlieferung im früheren Mittelalter." *Frühmittelalterliche Studien* 10: 70–95.

Oexle, O. G. (1983). "Die Gegenwart der Toten." In H. Braet and W. Verbeke (eds.), *Death in the Middle Ages* (pp. 19–77). Leuven: Leuven University Press.

Palazzo, É. (1993). *Histoire des livres liturgiques. Le Moyen Âge. Des origines au XIIIᵉ siècle.* Paris: Beauchesne.

Palazzo, É. (1998). *A History of Liturgical Books. From the Beginning to the Thirteenth Century,* trans. M. Beaumont. Collegeville, MN: Liturgical Press.

Palazzo, É. (2008). "The Peformance of the Liturgy." In Th. Noble et al. (eds.), *The Cambridge History of Christianity Volume 3: Early Medieval Christianities, c.600–c.1100* (pp. 472–488). Cambridge: Cambridge University Press.

Raaijmakers, J. (2006). "Memory and Identity: The Annales Necrologici of Fulda." In R. Corradini et al. (eds.), *Texts and Identities in the Early Middle Ages* (pp. 303–321). Forschungen zur Geschichte des Mittelalters, 13. Vienna: Verlag der Österreichischen Akademie der Wissenschaften.

Raaijmakers, J. (2012). *The Making of the Monastic Community of Fulda.* Cambridge: Cambridge University Press.

Rapp, C. (2014). "City and Citizenship as Christian Concepts of Community." In C. Rapp and H. A. Drake (eds.), *The City in the Classical and Post-Classical World. Changing Contexts of Power and Identity* (pp. 153–166). Cambridge: Cambridge University Press.

Rose, E. (2009). *Ritual Memory: Apocryphal Acts and Liturgical Commemoration in the Early Medieval West, c. 500–1215.* Leiden: Brill.

Rose, E. (2013). "Reinventing the Apostolic Tradition: Transition and Appropriation in the Medieval Commemoration of the Apostles." In B. Boute and T. Småberg (eds.), *Devising Order: Socio-Religious Models, Rituals, and the Performativity of Practice* (pp. 123–144). Leiden: Brill.

Rose, E. (2016). "*Emendatio* and *effectus* in Frankish Prayer Traditions." In R. Meens et al. (eds.), *Religious Franks: Religion and Power in the Frankish Kingdoms. Studies in Honour of Mayke de Jong* (pp. 128–147). Manchester: Manchester University Press.

Rose, E. (2017). "The Ritual of the Names: A Practice of Intercession in Early Medieval Gaul." *Frühmittelalterliche Studien* 51: 1–18.

Rose, E. (2019). "*Plebs sancta ideo meminere debet.* The Role of the People in the Early Medieval Liturgy of Mass." In U. Heil (ed.), *Das Christentum im frühen Europa. Diskurse – Tendenzen – Entscheidungen* (pp. 459–476). Berlin: De Gruyter.

Schmid, K., and Wollasch, J. (eds.). (1984). *Memoria. Der geschichtliche Zeugniswert des liturgischen Gedenkens im Mittelalter.* Munich: Wilhelm Fink Verlag.

Smyth, M. (2003). *La liturgie oubliée. La prière eucharistique en Gaule antique et dans l'Occident non romain.* Paris: Cerf.

Souter, A. (1949). *A Glossary of Later Latin to 600 A.D.* Oxford: Oxford University Press.

Symes, C. (2016). "Liturgical Texts and Performance Practices." In H. Gittos et al. (eds.), *Understanding Medieval Liturgy. Essays in Interpretation* (pp. 239–267). Burlington: Ashgate.

Taft, R. F. (1991). *A History of the Liturgy of St. John Chrysostom, vol. 4: The Diptychs.* Orientalia christiana analecta 238. Rome: Pontificium institutum studiorum orientalium.

Vogel, C. (1986). *Medieval Liturgy. An Introduction to the Sources,* trans. W. G. Storey and N. K. Rasmussen. Washington, DC: Pastoral Press.

CHAPTER 44

··

LITURGY AND THE LAITY

··

LISA KAAREN BAILEY

> Prolonging the nocturnal vigil until daybreak
> The reverent crowd form an angelic choir
> Persisting with deliberate steps in the venerable task
> It strengthens and stirs to arms the heavens with its chants
> …
> Responding to the urging of the pontiff
> Clergy, populace and children sing praises to the Lord
> Whence through this brief and worthy labour
> Will come their reward
>
> (Venantius Fortunatus, *Carmen* 2.9.49–52, 67–68)[1]

THIS poem, by the sixth-century author Venantius Fortunatus, expressed the clerical ideal of how liturgy should work and what it should do. Venantius depicted a Christian community united, but led by their bishop, reverent and engaged in ritualized action, set apart from the normal, laboring in the here and now. But the community was focused on the world to come and engaged in an act that drew their attention to heaven and therefore to the rewards for piety and obedience. These themes of commonality and idealization of the liturgy in Merovingian Gaul helped to determine the ways in which lay congregations experienced and reacted to the central ritual of their faith community. However, it only gave one part of the story: lay Christians had many opportunities to engage with liturgy on their own terms, or to appropriate it to their own ends. As far as possible, this chapter explores Merovingian liturgy from the perspectives of those taking part in it. This is a difficult task, given the evidence we have. It is, however, essential. Liturgy was not words on a page. Rather it was an experience in which a variety of words, spoken, sung, and chanted, were combined with ritualized acts in a ceremony that was central to Christian interactions with God. The experiential element was therefore definitional of liturgy and so is at the heart of our analysis.

I have focused in this chapter on liturgical forms that involved both clergy and laity, especially, but not exclusively, the eucharistic liturgy in a community church. There were many other kinds of liturgical services in Merovingian Gaul: clerics conducting rituals without lay presence, monks engaged in the regular singing of the hours, baptisms, deathbed masses, and liturgical responses to crises. The range and variety is so wide that it would not be possible to offer here a coherent discussion of all of them. The eucharistic liturgy, however, was the liturgical form that would have been most familiar to the largest number of Merovingian Christians. Along with baptism, the eucharistic offering was one of the primary liturgical acts of the Christian community, one with which all the faithful were expected to engage on a regular basis. It therefore provides a useful starting point for discussion, and other liturgical forms can be brought into the analysis as appropriate.

Scholars who have examined the role of liturgy in Christian communities have offered some radically different interpretations of how it operated and therefore how it would have been experienced. Liturgy often appears in scholarship as a force for unity and the basis for a Christian sense of community (see Rose, Chapter 43, this volume). Irénée-Henri Dalmais (1992), for example, made its communal character central to the definition of liturgy, describing it as an act of worship with a public character, involving the whole ecclesial community rather than just a particular group of religious ministers. Gregory Dix has argued, likewise, that eucharistic worship was "of necessity and by intention a *corporate action*" (1954, pp. 1–2). Frank C. Senn (2006, p. 10) describes the eucharistic ritual as the "social glue of the Middle Ages," and Brigitte Beaujard (2000) presents it as an idealized expression of the consensus and fellowship of the Christian community. Robin M. Jensen has argued that liturgy was one of the great mechanisms of inclusion by which ordinary believers were integrated into the church and was fundamental to lay religious experiences. "Christian identity," she insists, "is claimed, developed, and reinforced through ritual practice as much as—or perhaps more than—by the doctrines articulated by theologians. Both day-to-day communal experiences of worship and seasonal rites and festivals are essential to the way ordinary believers understand their place in the social and cosmic orders" (2005, p. 117). Richard D. McCall is blunter: "The church is differentiated according to class and gender, but it is one in its enactment of the sacrament" (2007, p. 133).

This optimistic view of the place and importance of liturgy as an expression of Christian unity, however, runs alongside another scholarly tradition that sees early medieval liturgy as becoming the property of clergy, a ritual from which the laity were increasingly excluded, alienated, and distanced. Ramsay MacMullen (2009) has argued that even in earlier periods very few Christians attended church services and that, when they did, they were screened from the altar, pushed to the back of the church, and denied any substantial role in the proceedings. Megan McLaughlin (1991) has a similar view of late-antique and Merovingian Gaul, with laypeople being presented in texts as a polluting risk to an essentially clerical mystery. Karen Jo Torjesen (2008) has argued that the sacralization of the eucharistic ceremony, and the exclusion of the laity from it, was one of the key elements of lay differentiation and subordination by the clergy. In this view, liturgy was not a force for unity but, rather, was symbolic of increasing division within the Christian community, especially between religious professionals and the ordinary faithful.

These perspectives seem far apart, but in fact both express some part of the truth. Liturgy was meant to be an act of community, but it was also, and simultaneously, a ritual that inscribed difference and hierarchy within that community. The eucharistic mass was the moment when the difference between the layperson and cleric most mattered and when that difference was publicly enacted: one side offered and one side received. It was therefore integral to the process by which the clergy sought to identify themselves as a distinct group and describe particular spaces (over which they had primary control) as sacred zones that should not be subject to secular pollution. The community, unified by liturgy, was supposed to be unified *behind* the clergy. This was the point made in Venantius's poem: the other clergy, people, and children respond to the urging of their bishop in a clear hierarchy. But this set of clerical intentions, complicated though they are in themselves are not the full story. As Frank Senn puts it: "The clergy did come to the point of dominating the performance of the liturgy. The hierarchy did find ways of controlling the liturgy in order to fence it off from false doctrine or excessive piety. But the more interesting story is how the people found ways of claiming their rightful place in the assembly and participating according to their inclinations and means of expression" (2006, p. 7). In other words, the lay experience of the liturgy involved commonality, exclusion, *and* opportunity.

In order to understand the intentions and experiences of those engaged with the liturgy, however, we need first to reconstruct it. Here, the scholar of the Merovingian liturgy is at a disadvantage. With the relative wealth of sources available on Byzantine rituals, scholars in that field have produced important work on how the liturgy was designed as an experience and how it operated as part of the formation of the self in religious terms (Frank 2006; Krueger 2014; Gador-Whyte 2016). The task in the West has proved far more difficult. The fundamental problem is that very few written sources describe the Merovingian liturgy before the Carolingian period, and those sources we do have are fragmentary or difficult to date (Spinks 2007, p. 610; Doig 2008, p. 102). The *Expositio antiquae liturgicae Gallicanae* (*Explanation of the ancient Gallic liturgy*) provides a detailed commentary on the mass and has been attributed to the sixth-century bishop Germanus of Paris, but it survives only in a ninth-century manuscript, and a number of scholars have denied that it is Merovingian at all.[2] There are several eighth-century sacramentaries and lectionaries that can be traced back to Merovingian originals (Hen 1995; Smyth 2003; Bernard 2016). None of them, however, can answer all the questions scholars have about the shape and structure of the liturgy. Even if we had the complete written texts we desire, we would still not have a full picture of the liturgical experience, for it was about so much more than the words spoken. To understand them fully, we would have to place them in the context of the places, persons, objects, music, aromas, lights, and images that were so much a part of the experience (Heffernan and Matter 2001, p. 5; Palazzo 2014). Liturgy, as Thomas F. Mathews points out, is "an enormously complex symbol whose message is carried in gesture, motion and display as much as in words" (1971, p. 8).

Furthermore, as Yitzhak Hen (1996) points out, the Merovingian liturgy was highly diverse and eclectic. It drew on influences from many directions and was celebrated in different ways in different parts of Gaul (Griffe 1951). Each of the liturgical manuscripts that survives contains a different number of masses, commemorates different saints, and lists different reading passages and prayers for the same occasions (Hen 2001, pp. 28–33). Bishops were in a position to be quite creative in their construction of some elements of the service (Scheibelreiter 2005, p. 700). Priests in smaller churches, often at great distance from their bishops, could become quite independent (Senn 2006, p. 109). It was even possible for laypeople to contribute. King Chilperic, for example, was reported to have composed hymns and masses of his own accord (Gregory of Tours, *Libri historiarum decem* 6.46). There were numerous outside influences on liturgy and very few attempts to impose any kind of uniformity (Hen 2001).[3] The result was the "fruitful confusion so characteristic of Frankish liturgy" (Wallace-Hadrill 1983, p. 118). As Hen puts it, "there is no real basis for the claim that in the west a single, uniform way of celebrating the Eucharist existed, nor that a standard text was available" (2004, p. 152). Indeed, he objects to the entire premise of looking for a "pure" Merovingian liturgy (2004, p. 150).

There are, therefore, important limitations on what we can know about the Merovingian liturgy. Some recent scholarship has demonstrated that we can make much more out of what we do have than has been done to date. The recent volume on the Bobbio Missal, for example, seeks to place this manuscript into its cultural context and uses it as a way to understand the place of the liturgy in the Merovingian world (Hen and Meens 2004). This particular missal, the authors conclude, was copied perhaps as early as the late seventh century and was designed for use by a bishop or priest who had to travel between different communities to offer services to secular, clerical, and monastic congregations. The Bobbio Missal would facilitate all of a cleric's most important liturgical tasks: saying mass on Sundays and feast days, baptizing at Easter, taking care of the sick and dying, or performing blessings at important occasions (Meens 2004, p. 154). The missal confirms the importance of liturgical action among clerical duties and the efforts made to ensure that this was possible. This kind of careful situating of specific liturgical texts represents an exciting way forward for liturgical scholarship.

Moreover, church councils did seek to standardize the acts and gestures that constituted the structure of the eucharistic mass, so that although there may have been perfectly acceptable diversity of texts used and words spoken, "no part of the essential rite would be neglected or even missed out by the celebrant" (Hen 1996, p. 27). Furthermore, the doubts earlier expressed over the Merovingian provenance of the *Expositio* have been largely put to rest by Hen (2001, pp. 5–7). This means that we can use this text as an outline at least of a liturgical model. According to this text and the reconstructions offered by Hen (1995, 2001), the celebrant would enter while an antiphon was sung, greet the members of the congregation, and they would reply. Canticles would then be sung and the celebrant would say a prayer. This would be followed by readings that were usually from the scriptures, although they may have also included readings from the biographies of saints on their particular festivals. These readings were interspersed with singing by the choir, and the books might also be brought in with a solemn procession. All of this would be followed by the sermon, which was often based on the reading, but might also be an unrelated moral exhortation. There were then some prayers, uttered by the faithful and by the celebrant, which seemingly could vary widely in character. If catechumens, public penitents, or excommunicants were present, they would be dismissed. The elements of the offering were brought in and placed on the altar, accompanied by prayers and possibly singing. This would be followed by the recital of the names of the dead, as well as prayers for them, and the kiss of peace. There was then a sequence of eucharistic prayers and responses, the fraction of the host, its mixing with the wine, and the actual communion. The congregation sang the Pater Noster (Our Father) during the final preparations for this act. During the taking of communion, there would have been further singing by the choir. Afterward, the celebrant thanked God, gave the benediction, and dismissed the congregation. This process may have taken between one and two hours, depending on the occasion and degree of elaboration (Beck 1950, pp. 130, 136; Hen 1995, p. 67).

Each element of the liturgy had a particular role in shaping the experience of those present and participating. The liturgy was marked, for example, by extensive use of song. There was singing at key points, including during the entry of the celebrants, the conveyance and return of the Gospel books, the procession of the offerings, and the fraction of the Host. These were supplemented by numerous chanted prayers and blessings from the clergy, congregants, and dedicated singers (Wright 1989, pp. 42–43). This singing could involve lay congregants. The *Vita Caesarii* claimed that the bishop of Arles sought to keep the laity occupied in church by getting them to sing psalms and hymns, sequences, and antiphons, "in a loud and measured voice, like the clergy, some in Greek and some in Latin" (1.19). Caesarius may have had especially high expectations, but Hen (1995, p. 74) argues that this active role was inherent to Merovingian liturgical practice. Indeed, as Senn notes, the very structure of Hebrew poetry lent itself to "antiphonal and responsive recitation in which two groups or a leader and a group recite the two parts of each verse" (2006, p. 127). Singing was also a key feature of vigils, some of which may have been very popular. Certainly singing was the central feature of Venantius's poem cited at the start of this chapter, with special emphasis on the involvement of *all* members of the community. However, the Merovingian period seems also to have seen some use of professional or dedicated singers, especially when the singing required particular expertise (Senn 2006, p. 124). This singing worked to elevate the solemnity of a particular liturgical moment (Hen 1995, p. 78). For clergy, liturgical singing therefore offered a number of opportunities. It was a way to build community identity and communal action within an appropriately controlled and hierarchical context: the people united but were led by a cleric. It also acted to sacralize a moment by rendering it out of the ordinary: this singing was ritualized, not spontaneous; respectful, not turbulent. Caesarius explicitly contrasted it with lay singing and its problematic secular subject matter, as Lucy Grig (2013) has demonstrated (*Sermo* 6.3). Song was therefore integral to the clerical perspective on the liturgy and undoubtedly was important in the lay experience of the liturgy.

The liturgy was also punctuated by regular, organized prayers, although this was an aspect that seems to have offered wide opportunities for variation: a celebrant could choose which prayers to use or could even compose his own (Hen 1995, p. 71). The Merovingian liturgy was especially noted for the "long-winded, bombastic and effusive" style of its prayers, which could be very prolonged, and which Hen has described as "a unique and most eloquent witness to the liturgical vitality and creativity of Merovingian Gaul" (2004, p. 143). Prayers and responses could also be moments for congregational participation. Caesarius made clear that he expected congregants not only to utter these prayers, but to take them to heart and act upon their meaning. "If those who remain in church do not dismiss the debts of their debtors, they speak the Lord's prayer more to their judgement than to their remedy" (*Sermo* 73.2). However, prayers could also be a moment for teaching. Louise Batstone has observed that the prayers used in the Bobbio Missal suggest either a powerful tradition or continuing need for anti-Arian instruction. Batstone also notes some prayers that are anti-Pelagian in their emphasis on God's grace. "In all the prayers of the Bobbio Missal," she remarks, "we see clear doctrinal assertions and easily memorised doctrinal formulae" (2004, p. 186). As Senn puts it, "Liturgy has been used to promote confessional identity because liturgy encodes meaning" (2006, p. 238). Prayers helped to articulate as well as enact a sense of what it meant to be part of a Christian community.

Prayers were offered by all members of the Christian community, but blessings were only offered by the clergy. Blessings could work to raise events, objects, or people to an elevated position, separating them from ordinary secularity (Rivard 2009). However, many blessings, as Derek Rivard notes, were "composed to meet the expressed needs and desires of the laity in their daily lives" (2009, p. 9). Those in the Old Gelasian sacramentary include blessing of houses; against pestilence, drought, and storm; for trees and fruit; for peace; and for kings in time of war (Rivard 2009, p. 31; Hen 2010, pp. 47–48). Indeed, Mary Garrison argues that this last example—of blessings for secular leaders—would once have been "extremely commonplace" (2004, p. 188) and that the *missa pro principe* (*Mass for the Prince*) in the Bobbio Missal was an extension of this practice. Meanwhile, the Frankish-Gelasian sacramentary contains a number of apotropaic blessings designed to protect congregants from the Devil and his minions (Rivard 2009, p. 32). These blessings show how liturgy could be responsive, but also how clergy sought to keep lay needs and desires under appropriate control and to channel petitions and intercessions into forms they directed.

An additional spoken element of the liturgy were the readings. On festival occasions these could involve passages from a saint's *vita*, but eucharistic masses typically involved more than one reading from different parts of the scriptures. These readings were important moments of lay exposure to the Bible: although Caesarius urged his congregants to read the words of the texts themselves, most undoubtedly learned what they said from the recitations in church. These were not ordinary acts of reading, however. The texts were conveyed to specially appointed readers in ritual processions and were accompanied by singing, as already mentioned. The readings came from texts that claimed to impart not just divine truths but the very word of God himself. As Caesarius of Arles put it, "the divine scriptures have been transmitted to us like letters from our homeland" (*Sermo* 7.2). We have to assume that they were therefore read in a reverential tone.

Prayers, songs, readings, and blessings all created an atmosphere of solemnity and ritualization: this was not normal speech, but a series of elevated and formalized speech acts. Very often, the readings would have been the springboard for a sermon that would expand on the meaning of the passages or use them as opportunities for moral instruction. Sermons were a standard part of the Merovingian liturgy. They were listed in the *Expositio* as coming after the readings but before the eucharistic offering, at a point of high drama in the service. The late seventh-century Council of Saint-Jean de Losne prescribed that all bishops should preach on Sundays and feast days (canon 18). This was an ideal not necessarily observed in reality, and lay exposure to regular preaching undoubtedly depended on where they resided. Nonetheless, preaching aids were available even for ill-educated or unconfident clergy, and these seem to have circulated widely (Bailey 2010). Sermons were a less ritualized form of speech, but in Merovingian Gaul they were probably seldom spontaneous or informal. They therefore worked in tandem with the other spoken elements of the liturgy in shaping the experiences of those attending and participating in the service.

Merovingian preaching built on a strong late-Roman Gallic tradition, represented in the surviving works of bishops Valerian of Cimiez, Hilary of Arles, Faustus of Riez, Caesarius of Arles, Avitus of Vienne, and the Eusebius Gallicanus collection. These sermons continued to be copied and circulated in the Merovingian period, along with sermons from preachers outside Gaul, especially bishops Ambrose of Milan, Augustine of Hippo, and Maximus of Turin. These sermons formed the basis of homiliary collections that were designed as preaching handbooks, and they often focused on the specific needs of a community or congregation. The opportunity for copying and preservation means that most of the Merovingian homiliaries that survive were produced in monasteries and designed for use within these communities.[4] Many sermons from this period, however, were aimed at lay audiences and would have been preached and read in community churches. These homiliaries were a vital aid to the continuation of preaching in Merovingian Gaul. They effectively facilitated preaching on the days of highest expected church attendance, so that even clergy without a rhetorical education could read out appropriate, orthodox, and sanctioned words to their lay congregations.

Some clergy, however, continued to compose their own sermons. Gregory of Tours tells us that Nicetius of Trier "preached to the people every day," uncovering their vices and praying for their remission (*Liber vitae patrum* 17.2). He also mentions that Praetextatus of Rouen was known for his orations, although their style did not always please his fellow bishops (Gregory of Tours, *Libri historiarum decem* 8.20). A selection of the sermons given by Columbanus have survived, while hagiography informs us of the preaching efforts of Audoin of Rouen, Eligius of Noyon, Eucherius of Orléans, and Amandus of Maastricht-Liège (Fouracre, 1979). The *Vita* of Audoin described him as a distinguished and effective preacher (*Vita Audoini* 4), while Eucherius was depicted preaching diligently to the people to correct their errors (*Vita Eucherii* 6;

Amos, 1983, pp. 69–73). Although some of this preaching took place in nonliturgical contexts, the majority of sermons experienced by lay Christians were probably delivered in a church in the course of a service.

Sermons were less formal and less ritualized than other elements of the service. There was much less emphasis on display, but also less evident opportunity for lay participation. Nonetheless, many sermons demonstrate the considerable effort that preachers put into communicating with lay Christians. Caesarius of Arles repeatedly urged his fellow preachers to undertake what he considered to be a religious duty: "all priests of the Lord, entering the church, should not cease to make a noise, that is preach, about the last things, that is about the end of the world and the future judgement" (*Sermo* 1.5). He also stressed that they had to make their words accessible to a wide audience: "my priests of the Lord should preach to the people in simple and plain language which all the people can grasp" (*Sermo* 1.20). This accessibility was also emphasized in the *Expositio*, which stated that the sermon ought to be neither so rustic that it offended the learned nor so loquacious that it was obscure to the rustic (*Expositio* 13). Preachers also took great care to explain difficult passages in scripture and important theological points (Bailey 2010, 2016). Although these sermons were a part of the liturgy, they were not "intoned…over an uncomprehending laity" (McLaughlin 1991, p. 78). Instead, these texts were highly engaged and responsive to lay concerns.

The sermons that survive demonstrate that lay Christians in Merovingian Gaul could have been exposed to a wide variety of preaching styles. However, the use of model collections did not mean uniformity, since these could differ in both substance and emphasis. The sermons of Caesarius of Arles, for example, which made their way into a number of collections, focused on attacking problematic lay behaviors, providing a thorough and wide-ranging exegesis of the scriptures, and giving appropriate words for the major feast days of the liturgical calendar. Their style was confrontational and blunt, drawing clear lines around acceptable behavior within the Christian community. The sermons of the Eusebius Gallicanus collection, on the other hand, which were also very popular and widely copied, gave priority to the liturgical calendar and included a number of sermons for local Gallic saints. The works in this compilation tended to adopt an encouraging rather than hectoring tone and placed great emphasis on the importance of individual responsibility for ensuring salvation. The collection displays little interest in exegesis, although there are sermons explaining important theological concepts (Bailey 2010). Missionary preaching must have had quite different goals again, and although few examples now survive, the sixth-century *Instructiones* of the Irish monk Columbanus give a taste of the ascetic and penitential elements that he would have particularly stressed.

These speech acts took place in a context of ritualized movement. The liturgy in Merovingian Gaul was marked by dramatic solemn movement as the celebrants, gospels, and offerings processed into the church. Processions also marked a number of other liturgical events and provided a way for liturgy to extend beyond the church walls and incorporate more people than could fit at a single service (Palazzo 2008, p. 45). As John Francis Baldovin puts it: "This form of procession enabled not only the participation of many people and an expression of their piety, but also the expression of the religious faith of Christians as the 'common-sense' foundation of the life of the city"(1987, p. 251). These were ritualized acts, clearly distinguished from ordinary walking by means of a slowed pace, special dress, musical accompaniment, and the solemnity of the participants (Smith 1987; Bell 1992). McCall argues that action and enaction were at the heart of the liturgy and that processions were key to this expression of religiosity (2007, p. 2). The rituals drew attention to particular players because they were necessarily hierarchical; to particular spaces as end points; and to particular objects as the items "processed." They therefore acted to set these people, spaces, and things apart from secularity, even as they provided opportunities for lay participation.

The key ceremony in a eucharistic mass, the one to which all of the earlier elements of the service served as dramatic build-up, was the transformation of the bread and wine into the body and blood of Christ, and its consumption by the faithful as a sign of their unity with him and as a way of commemorating his sacrifice. This was fundamentally a moment of remembrance through reenactment. A series of actions were performed over and around the eucharistic host: it was processed, sung over, placed on special dishes, revealed, consecrated, broken, mixed, distributed, and consumed (Hen 1995, pp. 68–69). Congregants exchanged the kiss of peace, responded when called on, and prayed at the appropriate moments. This was the peak of the liturgy, and it ended soon after, with perhaps only a benediction and dismissal to send the congregation on their way.

Many of these elements of the liturgy worked to support the clerical goal of communal unity. This goal required, however, that the laity attend liturgical services, which is why the obligation to come to church on Sundays was emphasized in church councils, in secular law codes, and in miracle stories that described punishments for those who worked when they should have been at church (see Halfond, Chapter 13, and Kreiner, Chapter 24, this volume).[5] Regular attendance was expected for city dwellers, even if the reiterated penalties in legal texts suggest this was not always observed in practice. There were also many other, small-scale services going on throughout the day and week, which the laity could attend, and they were indeed sometimes encouraged to do so. Caesarius instituted daily observance of the canonical hours in Arles in the hope of attracting lay attendance and encouraged laypeople to join in the singing of this daily office (*Sermo* 75.1). He also urged his congregation during Lent to attend not only the vigils, but also terce, sext, and none (*Vita Caesarii* 1.15; Caesarius of Arles, *Sermo* 196.2).[6] Beck argues that there was a night office every week to prepare for the Sunday, that there were solemn vigils before the feasts of Epiphany and Pentecost, and that "the daily observance of the Divine Office was the normal practice" in the south of France at least (1950, pp. 110–111, 119), although Hen (1995, p. 71) has disagreed with him on this. Certainly, such daily offices were not always or even regularly attended by laypeople; although some did, this would have been unusual.[7] More standard, perhaps, was attendance at the office during Lent. Caesarius emphasized this as part of ideal lay pious practice (*Sermones* 86.5, 196.2). By the end of the sixth century, it had also become the custom to offer public masses in the afternoons several days a week during Advent (Beck, 1950, 130). Arnold Angenendt (1983) has demonstrated that anniversary masses were offered on a variety of occasions. These Christian markers of time therefore could, at least potentially, provide the rhythm of the days and weeks in a layperson's life, especially if he or she chose to attend services on a regular basis.

Moreover, these services could act to bind people to the Christian community and provide opportunities for lay religious engagement. As our discussion has already made clear, the laity could participate in the service in a number of ways. Lay members had to exchange the kiss of peace. They had to respond and sing at various points during the service, an element of dialogue between clergy and laity that served as a defining feature of the service. They were also addressed, engaged, and exhorted directly during the sermon. Indeed, Hen has argued that the mass "required the full attention, cooperation and participation of the congregation" (1995, p. 75). Given the many clerical complaints about lay inattention, this may be optimistic, but certainly it reflects the ideal. A sermon in the Eusebius Gallicanus collection makes clear that the laity was expected both to participate and listen quietly at the appropriate moments: "It is a serious sin both of lukewarmness and infidelity, standing in the holy place before the presence of majesty, either not to respond, when the psalm is sung, or, not to be silent when the reading is poured into your ears" (64.8). McCall (2007) has recently emphasized the dramatic and performative elements of the mass and the intended impact of these on participants and spectators alike. The singing that accompanied all of the important moments would have been a central part of this experience, working both to impress and to incorporate the laity at various points. Add in the other elements of the experience—movement in processions, elaborate dress, incense, light, and ritualized action—and the impact on the laity potentially was profound (Hen, 1995, p. 80). These could indeed be moments in which the Christian community was bound together by a compelling shared experience.

At the same time, however, the liturgy was also a mechanism for establishing a hierarchy within the church and for setting apart the clergy and their associated places and acts as sacred and special. It designated as holiest those places where the most important ritual acts took place, and those sites were at their most sacred at the moments when those rites were enacted. Liturgy sometimes resulted in or required a physical separation of spaces (see Chevalier, Chapter 30, this volume). In a sermon on the dedication of a church, Avitus of Vienne spoke of an altar "discretely separated from the nave by a slightly elevated platform" (*Sermo* 24). Gregory of Tours mentioned railings marking out an area where the clergy stood to sing psalms (*Liber in gloria martyrum* 38). A canon from the Council of Tours in 567 decreed that "the laity should not at all dare to stand at the altar, where the sacred mysteries are celebrated interiorly among the clergy either at vigils or at masses, but that part, which is divided by the chancel facing the altar, should be accessible only to the choirs of clerics singing psalms" (canon 4). This restriction was not absolute, however. The canon went on to state that "for prayer and communication the holy of holies should be accessible to laity and to women, as is the custom." In other words, the spatial restriction was particularly strict only when the rituals were underway, and it was the rituals, and the clergy who enacted them, that had to be kept apart from secularity most of all.[8]

A number of scholars have argued that the laity was in fact excluded from parts of the liturgy and that their view of key moments was deliberately blocked. Although internal arrangements could vary, lay worshippers generally watched the eucharistic rites from a distance, and were separated from the altar by some kind of marker or barrier (Frank 2007, p. 537; Michel 2008, p. 583). William H. C. Frend has insisted that all over the Mediterranean provinces in Late Antiquity "a substantial screen of stone or marble divided the nave, or *quadratum populi*, from the altar and apse whither only the clergy might approach" (1963, p. 59). Robert Austin Markus (1978) argues that there may have been some kind of iconostasis screen in Gaul, although his case is largely based on a questionable reading of canon three of the Council of Tours in 567.[9] Allan Doig (2008, p. 68) raises the possibility that curtains between columns screened lay observers in ways that are not documentable in the archaeological record. However, literary accounts of church services in this period do not make any reference to or invoke such screening, and we only start to get references to it in later periods (Hamilton and Spicer 2005, p. 15; Hamilton 2013, p. 166). Joan Rebekah Branham (1992) and Richard Kieckhefer (2009) see some archaeological evidence for screens, but emphasize that these were symbolic demarcations of space, rather than obstacles to vision. Kieckhefer argues that even where screens did exist, "they did not necessarily separate the lay congregations very effectively from the priests celebrating Mass" (2009, p. 111), while Branham maintains that seeing over such screens was the point— they marked out an audience who viewed from those who enacted. Sible De Blaauw (1991) stresses the openness of church design and the visibility of liturgical activities from the nave. It would be misleading to project into the Merovingian period the far more elaborate screening of later ages, in both the East and West.[10] Moreover, even in times and places where elaborate screening did exist, it did not necessarily serve as a mechanism of exclusion. In the East in this period, Mathews emphasizes the "extraordinary openness" of church design (1971, p. 105), while Jacqueline E. Jung (2000) has argued that in the Gothic churches of the high and late Middle Ages, screens were highly permeable to laypeople. Nonetheless, it was important to those building and using a church that the most sacred area around the altar be symbolically marked by some kind of barrier. This was part of the physical and rhetorical separation of the laity and their secular world from the clergy and their sacred one.

It also seems that fewer laypeople took communion when they attended church in Merovingian Gaul than had been the case in earlier periods. As Dix (1954) points out, to be present at the eucharist had virtually meant being a communicant in the first three centuries. This had changed due to a combination of factors, including the enormous increase in the numbers of the faithful, the practice of child baptism, and increasing reverence for the Host, with subsequent emphasis on needing to be pure and worthy in order to consume it. This ensured that communion had become relatively infrequent for many laity (McLaughlin 1994; Caesarius of Arles, *Sermones* 62, 229.4). The Council of Agde in 506 had to dictate that communion be taken at least three times a year (canon 18). Otherwise, receiving communion was not an act of lay piety that clergy especially emphasized or promoted (Smith 1995; Chélini 1968). In the sixth century, Venantius Fortunatus still urged Christians to receive the eucharist every day if they were able (*Carmen* 10.1.55). Beck argues that this would indeed have been possible in some areas (1950, p. 132). In many Gallic cities, however, it would have been difficult to accommodate the entire baptized community if they had all communicated every Sunday (Chélini 1968, pp. 165–166; Senn 2006, p. 106; MacMullen 2009, p. 101). This gradual development changed the nature of the eucharistic liturgy and the experience of laypeople attending it. Many came to church as spectators rather than participants, and by the sixth century the ceremony began to be something done by the clergy rather than something shared with the whole Christian community.[11]

The eucharistic liturgy could therefore represent and articulate both the divisions within the Christian community and its unity. These qualities coexisted in an interesting tension. However, the liturgy was not wholly under clerical control. Our sense of the restrictions on lay access and vision therefore needs to be balanced against an awareness that the laity could access the liturgy and its associated meanings outside churches. One of the most obvious ways this happened was through eucharistic reservation, the practice of setting aside some of the consecrated eucharist for use outside the mass. This was permitted for the sick, who could therefore consume the eucharist at home, and in some areas it may have been more widespread (Paxton 1990; Bowes 2008). This practice took control of the eucharist out of the hands of the clergy and made it available for use in private rituals and domestic expressions of piety (King 1964). Liturgy could thus take place in private households. An episcopal letter from the early sixth century condemns two Breton priests for using a portable altar to conduct masses in private homes and allowing women to take part in the ceremonies (Bailey 2012). The letter makes clear that this practice had been going on for some time, despite episcopal censure, demonstrating how little control bishops actually exercised over the liturgy in some regions of Gaul. Such practices fundamentally threatened the division of sacred from secular space and sacred from secular people. As the letter makes clear, the bishops feared that heresy and pollution could result.

However, many wealthy lay Christians had chapels in their own homes, where they took communion from clergy effectively in their employ, a practice that can be documented in both the archaeological and literary evidence. Gregory of Tours mentioned in passing an oratory in his mother's house and noted that it contained relics (*Liber in gloria confessorum* 3). The home of Nicetius of Lyon's mother also contained an oratory where the saint performed the divine office (Gregory of Tours, *Liber vitae patrum* 7.2). The virgin Gibitrude, who later became a nun, first asked her parents to build an oratory for her in their home so that she could show her devotion (Jonas of Bobbio, *Vita Columbani* 12). Kimberly Bowes has documented the considerable evidence for private chapels on rural estates and suggests that at least some of these villa-churches could have accommodated processions and "a surprising degree of ritual sophistication" (2008, p. 133). Some complexes included baptisteries (Bowes 2008, p. 150). These churches can be considered "private" in the sense that they were built and paid for by lay individuals and were designed for the use of their own family, friends, and dependents (Bowes 2008, p. 5). Such arrangements were not necessarily antagonistic to the institutional church and clerical hierarchy; they simply existed quite separately from them and were often out of their practical power (Bowes 2008, pp. 168–169).

Clerics tried to keep private chapels under some kind of supervision, but it is unclear how successful they were. At the Council of Épaone in 517, the assembled clerics determined that "the relics of saints shall not be placed in villa oratories, unless perhaps a cleric of some parish happens to be near, who can serve the sacred ashes with frequent psalm-singing" (canon 25). Church councils also insisted on the right of bishops to supervise clerical appointments in such chapels. In practice, however, any clergy serving at such establishments did so at the pleasure of the building's owners and would have considered themselves under their patronage, perhaps even as part of the family's retinue (Council of Orléans 511, canon 25; Bowes 2008, pp. 150, 158). In the mid-seventh century, clerics at the Council of Chalons complained about the independence of villa churches (on villas, see Chavarría Arnau, Chapter 29, this volume). In particular, they noted that the powerful laypeople who controlled these oratories treated them as their own private concerns: "they oppose the bishops and already do not permit those clerics that served at that oratory to be controlled by the archdeacon" (canon 14). The assembled clergy insisted that the ordination of clerics in such places, the structure of the divine office, and the dispensation of resources should all be in the purview of the local bishop, but the canon made clear that landowners did not agree. Beyond villas, Gregory of Tours's *miracle* collections suggest that the rural landscape was filled with oratories for saints, where laypeople could pay reverence to relics, attend services, or seek cures.[12] One oratory was built by Patroclus, for example, in the village of Néris, which he furnished with appropriate relics (*Liber vitae patrum* 9.2). The church councils confirmed the legitimacy of these establishments but tried to make sure that they did not become permanent alternatives to the episcopal church. The Council of Agde in 506 decreed:

> If anyone, even outside the parish, in which the assembly is legitimate and regular, should want to have an oratory in a field, by a just ruling we permit on other festivals that they may hold masses there on account of the weariness of the family, but truly they must have Easter, Christmas Day, Epiphany, Ascension, Pentecost, and the feast of St John the Baptist nowhere else but in the city or the parish, or if many days of festival are held. Indeed, if any clerics should want to hold or perform masses in oratories on the festivals mentioned above without the order and permission of their bishop, they should be expelled from communion.   (canon 21)

For many rural dwellers, the churches of the city were distant monuments, both physically and psychologically. Their religious worlds may have centered on an estate church where they attended services, a monastery down the road, or an oratory marking the site of a saint's former dwelling, depending on their local circumstances. These religious spaces were much more amenable than urban churches to lay influence and authority.

The laity also took the models of the eucharistic mass and of the daily office, and appropriated them in their own personal devotions, imitating clergy and implicitly undermining some of the category distinctions that lay at the heart of the formalized church ceremony (Hamilton 2013, p. 226). The *Life of Radegund*, for example, described her as a child carrying a wooden cross and leading a procession of fellow children into a private oratory (*Vita Radegundis* 2). The *Life of Genovefa*, meanwhile, depicted her organizing vigils along with the laywomen of Paris to ward off the threat posed by Attila the Hun (*Vita Genovefae* 10). Therefore, although the liturgy was a potential expression of both unity in the Christian community and of hierarchical division between clergy and laity, the laity could appropriate it in ways that undermined both of these goals, and it could become a site of contest for power and control.

Sometimes, however, the laity did not appropriate—they rejected. Our best examples are those related to preaching. Several times Caesarius of Arles mentioned that his sermons made some people angry (*Sermones* 42.6, 46.6, 57.1), and his *Vita* noted that he saw himself as a doctor dispensing unpleasant medicine in his preaching, who was "offering not what would please each one, but rather what would cure them, not considering the desires of the sick man, but quite properly striving for the health of the patient" (*Vita Caesarii* 1.17).

Perhaps this is why some of his congregation preferred to leave church before the sermon:

> Although there are many people about whose faith and devotion we rejoice, there are, however, many others thinking less about the salvation of their souls, who leave the church immediately after the divine lessons are read, some even while those readings are being read, while some are so occupied with idle things and worldly tales that they neither hear the readings, not permit others to hear them.   (*Sermo* 73.1)

Caesarius's *Vita* records that the preacher often locked the doors of the church to keep them inside (*Vita Caesarii* 1.27). Caesarius was probably unusual in his vehemence and his confrontational style. We only hear about the lay resistance, however, because he (and his hagiographers) reveled in it as a sign of his status as a prophet. More mellow and inclusive homiliaries such as the Eusebius Gallicanus may have been designed to avoid such confrontations or to accommodate lay preferences on preaching style (Bailey 2010).

These struggles helped to define and determine the place of liturgy in Gallic society. As Catherine Bell (1992) has argued, ritualization creates a power relationship between the primary enactors and the rest of the community, but neither group has absolute control over the other. Instead the relationship "simultaneously involves both consent and resistance, misunderstanding and appropriation" (p. 8). Our sources make clear that clergy struggled to maintain control over the rituals of the faith and that there were many spaces and opportunities for the laity to claim them as their own. The clergy might have been aiming at consensus and unity, two of the goals often claimed for ritual acts, but ritual was an *argument* for such consensus, not an enactment of it (Smith 1987, p. 54). Although the liturgical experiences of Merovingian Christians therefore remain necessarily indistinct, the evidence we have affirms both the importance of liturgy as a part of the Merovingian Christian world, and the roles of both clergy *and* laity in shaping and using it.[13]

Notes

1. Translations from Latin are my own, with the exception of this poem, the translation for which was taken from Wright 1989, p. 41. This chapter expands on some material discussed in Bailey 2016.

2. See discussion of the dating and provenance of this text in Duchesne 1912, pp. 189–226; van der Mensbrugghe 1962; Cabié 1972; Beck 1950; Hen 2001, pp. 5–7; Bernard 2007.

3. For attempts by Gallic church councils to impose some standardization on the mass, see Vannes 461/491, c. 15; Épaone 517, c. 27; Vaison 529, c. 3; Auxerre 561/605, c. 11.

4. For discussion of examples, see Amos 1983, pp. 62–63; Bailey 2010, pp. 135–137.

5. Auxerre 561–605 c. 16; Orléans 538 c. 31; Mâcon 585 c. 1; Chalon 647–655, c. 18; *Decretio Childeberti, Capitulary* 6, 3.7 (an addition to the *Pactus legis Salicae*); Gregory of Tours, *Libri de virtutibus Martini episcopi* 3.29; Gregory of Tours, *Liber vitae patrum* 15.3. [5] Caesarius of Arles, *Sermo* 75.1.

6. These were fixed hours of prayer used especially for the recitation of psalms in the daily Divine Office.

7. Such attendance was described in examples of particular piety by laypeople in Gregory of Tours—*Liber in gloria confessorum* 64; *Liber vitae patrum* 7.2.

8. When the liturgy was not in progress, laypeople seemed to have been able to access the apse and tombs located behind or below the altar. See, for example, Gregory of Tours, *Liber in gloria confessorum* 94; Gregory of Tours, *Libri de virtutibus Martini episcopi* 2.47.

9. An iconostasis screen physically separated the nave from the sanctuary. Canon three of the Council of Tours 567 reads: "*Vt corpus Domini in altari non imaginario ordine, sed sub crucis titulo componatur.*" Jean Gaudemet and Brigitte Basdevant, in their edition and translation of the text, interpret this as an injunction that the eucharist should be placed on the altar not in the shape of a human body, but in the shape of a cross. Markus prefers to translate it as an injunction that the eucharist be placed "not amid an arrangement of images, but under the sign of the cross" (p. 154). He goes on to comment: "I am inclined to think that what the bishops were trying to control by this canon was something like the development of the monumental *cancelli* in churches in the later and fully fledged iconostasis" (p. 155). There is also a third possible reading, which Markus acknowledges, and which I prefer, which sees the injunction as being to place the bread on the altar in the shape of a cross rather than any other arrangement.

10. On the development of the iconostasis in the East, see Krueger 2006, p. 12; Frank 2007, p. 539; Doig 2008, pp. 78–80. On the West, see Brooke 1971, pp. 162–182 and Kieckhefer 2009, pp. 109–111.

11. See discussion of this shift in Chélini 1968, p. 173; Senn 2006, p. 7. Dix (1954) sees this change as beginning in the fourth to fifth century in the East and gradually spreading to the West, p. 13. Gregory of Tours gives an example of a woman who gave some expensive Gaza wine to be used in masses in honor of her deceased husband, but although she attended these regularly, she did not drink the wine herself and so did not notice that the priest had substituted a less costly substitute, *Liber in gloria confessorum* 64.

12. See, for example, Gregory of Tours's examples in *Liber in gloria confessorum* 9, 11, 79, 103; *Liber vitae patrum* 12.2, 15.1; *Libri de virtutibus Martini episcopi* 1.14, 1.18, 4.12; *Libri historiarum decem* 5.7, 6.11.

13. I am grateful to Bonnie Effros and Isabel Moreira for their assistance in preparing this chapter and especially to Yitzhak Hen, who read a draft and offered many helpful

suggestions. Thank you also to audiences who posed questions and discussed ideas at the International Medieval Congress in Leeds and at the University of Auckland.

WORKS CITED

Ancient Sources

Avitus of Vienne, *Sermones*. R. Peiper (ed.). (1983). MGH AA 6.2. Berlin: Weidmann.

Caesarius of Arles, *Sermones*. G. Morin (ed.). (1953). CCSL 103 and 104. Turnhout: Brepols.

Columbanus, *Instructiones*. G. S. M. Walker (ed.). (1957). Dublin: Institute for Advanced Studies.

Councils of Saint Jean de Losne (673–675) and Tours (567). J. Gaudement and B. Basdevant (eds. and trans.). (1989). *Les canons des conciles mérovingiens (VIe–VIIe siècles)*. SC 354. Paris: Éditions du CERF.

Eusebius Gallicanus. F. Glorie (ed.). (1970). *Collectio Homiliarum*. CCSL 101, 101A, 101B. Turnhout: Brepols.

Expositio antiquae liturgicae Gallicanae P. Bernard (ed.). (2007). *Epistulae de ordine sacrae oblationis et de diversis charismatibus ecclesiae Germano Parisiensi episcopo adscriptae*. CCCM 187. Turnhout: Brepols.

Gregory of Tours, *Liber in gloria confessorum*. B. Krusch (ed.). (1969). MGH SRM 1.2 (pp. 294–370). Hanover: Hahn.

Gregory of Tours, *Liber in gloria martyrum*. B. Krusch (ed.). (1969). MGH SRM 1.2 (pp. 34–111). Hanover: Hahn.

Gregory of Tours, *Liber vitae patrum*. B. Krusch (ed.). (1969). MGH SRM 1.2. (pp. 211–294). Hanover: Hahn.

Gregory of Tours, *Libri de virtutibus Martini episcopi*. B. Krusch (ed.). (1969).MGH SRM 1.2 (pp. 584–661). Hanover: Hahn.

Gregory of Tours, *Libri historiarum decem*. B. Krusch and W. Levison (eds.). (1951). MGH SRM 1.1. Hanover: Hahn.

Jonas of Bobbio, *Vita Columbani*. B. Krusch (ed.). (1902). MGH SRM 4 (pp. 1–152). Hanover: Hahn.

Pactus legis Salicae. K. A. Eckhardt (ed.). (1962). MGH Leges 4.1. Hanover: Hahn.

Venantius Fortunatus, *Opera poetica*. F. Leo (ed.) (1881). MGH AA 4.1. Berlin: Weidmann.

Vita Audoini. W. Levison (ed.). (1910). MGH SRM 5 (pp. 536–567). Hanover: Hahn.

Vita Caesarii. B. Krusch (ed.). (1977). MGH SRM 3 (pp. 433–501). Hanover: Hahn.

Vita Eucherii. B. Krusch and W. Levison (eds.). (1920). MGH SRM 7 (pp. 41–53). Hanover: Hahn.

Vita Genovefae. B. Krusch and W. Levison (eds.). (1977). MGH SRM 3 (pp. 204–238). Hanover: Hahn.

Vita Radegundis. B. Krusch (ed.). (1888). MGH: SRM 2 (pp. 364–395). Hanover: Hahn.

Modern Sources

Amos, T. L. (1983). *The Origin and Nature of the Carolingian Sermon* (Doctoral dissertation). Michigan State University.

Angenendt, A. (1983). "Missa specialis: Zugleich ein Beitrag zur Entstehung der Privat-Messen." *Frühmittelalterliche Studien* 17: 153–221.

Bailey, L. K. (2010). *Christianity's Quiet Success: The Eusebius Gallicanus Sermon Collection and the Power of the Church in Late Antique Gaul.* Notre Dame, IN: University of Notre Dame Press.

Bailey, L. K. (2012). "The Strange Case of the Portable Altar: Liturgy and the Limits of Episcopal Authority in Early Medieval Gaul." *Journal of the Australian Early Medieval Association* 8: 31–51.

Bailey, L. K. (2016). *The Religious Worlds of the Laity in Late Antique Gaul.* London: Bloomsbury.

Baldovin, J. F. (1987). *The Urban Character of Christian Worship: The Origins, Development and Meaning of Stational Liturgy.* Rome: Pont. Institutum Studiorum Orientalium.

Batstone, L. (2004). "Doctrinal and Theological Themes in the Prayers of the Bobbio Missal." In Y. Hen and R. Meens (eds.), *The Bobbio Missal: Liturgy and Religious Culture in Merovingian Gaul* (pp. 168–186). Cambridge: Cambridge University Press.

Beaujard, B. (2000). *Le culte des saints en Gaule: Les premiers temps, d'Hilaire de Poitiers à la fin du VIᵉ siècle.* Paris: Éditions du Cerf.

Beck, H. G. J. (1950). *The Pastoral Care of Souls in South-East France during the Sixth Century.* Rome: Apud Aedes Universitatis Gregorianae.

Bell, C. (1992). *Ritual Theory, Ritual Practice.* New York: Oxford University Press.

Bernard, P. (2007). *Epistulae de ordine sacrae oblationis et de diversis charismatibus ecclesiae Germano Parisiensi episcopo adscriptae.* Turnhout: Brepols.

Bernard, P. (2016). *Du chant romain au chant grégorien.* Paris: Éditions du Cerf.

Bowes, K. (2008). *Private Worship, Public Values and Religious Change in Late Antiquity.* Cambridge: Cambridge University Press.

Branham, J. R. (1992). "Sacred Space under Erasure in Ancient Synagogues and Early Churches." *The Art Bulletin* 74: 375–394.

Brooke, C. N. L. (1971). "Religious Sentiment and Church Design in the Late Middle Ages." In *Medieval Church and Society* (pp. 162–182). London: Sidgwick and Jackson.

Cabié, R. (1972). "Les lettres attribuées à Saint Germain de Paris et les origines de la liturgie gallicane." *Bulletin de littérature ecclésiastique* 73: 13–57.

Chélini, J. (1968). "Les laïcs dans la société ecclésiastique carolingienne." In *I laici nella «societas christiana» dei secoli XI e XII* (pp. 23–50). Milan: Società Editrice Vita e Pensiero.

Dalmais, I.-H. (1992). "Liturgy." In *Encyclopedia of Early Christianity* (Vol. 1, p. 494). New York: Oxford University Press.

de Blaauw, S. (1991). "Architecture and Liturgy in Late Antiquity and the Middle Ages: Traditions and Trends in Modern Scholarship." *Archiv für Liturgiewissenshaft* 33: 1–34.

Dix, G. (1954). *The Shape of the Liturgy.* Westminster: Dacre Press.

Doig, A. (2008). *Liturgy and Architecture from the Early Church to the Middle Ages.* Aldershot: Ashgate.

Duchesne, L. (1912). *Christian Worship: Its Origin and Evolution. A Study of the Latin Liturgy up to the Time of Charlemagne,* trans. M. L. McClure. New York: S.P.C.K.

Fouracre, P. (1979). "The Work of Audoenus of Rouen and Eligius of Noyon in Extending Episcopal Influence from the Town to the Country in Seventh-Century Neustria." In D. Baker (ed.), *The Church in Town and Countryside* (pp. 77–91). Oxford: Basil Blackwell.

Frank, G. (2006). "Romanos and the Night Vigils in the Sixth Century." In D. Krueger (ed.), *Byzantine Christianity: A People's History of Christianity 3* (pp. 59–78). Minneapolis, MN: Fortress Press.

Frank, G. (2007). "From Antioch to Arles: Lay Devotion in Context." In A. Casiday and F. W. Norris (eds.), *The Cambridge History of Christianity 2* (pp. 531–547). Cambridge: Cambridge University Press.

Frend, W. (1963). "The Church of the Roman Empire." In S. C. Neill and H.-R. Weber (eds.), *The Layman in Christian History* (pp. 57–87). London: SCM Press.

Gador-Whyte, S. (2016). *Theology and Poetry in Early Byzantium: The Kontakia of Romanos the Melodist*. Cambridge: Cambridge University Press.

Garrison, M. (2004). "The *missa pro principe* in the Bobbio Missal." In Y. Hen and R. Meens (eds.), *The Bobbio Missal: Liturgy and Religious Culture in Merovingian Gaul* (pp. 187–205). Cambridge: Cambridge University Press.

Griffe, É. (1951). "Aux origines de la liturgie gallicane." *Bulletin de littérature ecclésiastique* 52: 17–43.

Grig, L. (2013). "Approaching Popular Culture: Singing in the Sermons of Caesarius of Arles." *Studia Patristica* 69: 197–204.

Hamilton, S. (2013). *Church and People in the Medieval West, 900–1200*. London: Routledge.

Hamilton, S., and Spicer, A. (2005). "Defining the Holy: The Delineation of Sacred Space." In S. Hamilton and A. Spicer (eds.), *Defining the Holy: Sacred Space in Medieval and Early Modern Europe* (pp. 1–23). Burlington, VT: Ashgate.

Heffernan, T. J., and Matter, E. A. (eds.). (2001). *The Liturgy of the Medieval Church*. Kalamazoo, MI: Medieval Institute Publications.

Hen, Y. (1995). *Culture and Religion in Merovingian Gaul A. D. 481–751*. Leiden: Brill.

Hen, Y. (1996). "Unity in Diversity: The Liturgy of Frankish Gaul before the Carolingians." In R. N. Swanson (ed.), *Unity and Diversity in the Church* (pp. 19–30). Oxford: Blackwell.

Hen, Y. (2001). *The Royal Patronage of Liturgy in Frankish Gaul to the Death of Charles the Bald (877)*. London: Henry Bradshaw Society.

Hen, Y. (2004). "The Liturgy of the Bobbio Missal." In Y. Hen and R. Meens (eds.), *The Bobbio Missal: Liturgy and Religious Culture in Merovingian Gaul* (pp. 140–153). Cambridge: Cambridge University Press.

Hen, Y. (2010). "Converting the Barbarian West." In D. E. Bornstein (ed.), *Medieval Christianity: A People's History of Christianity* 4 (pp. 29–52). Minneapolis, MN: Fortress Press.

Hen, Y., and Meens, R. (eds.). (2004). *The Bobbio Missal: Liturgy and Religious Culture in Merovingian Gaul*. Cambridge: Cambridge University Press.

Jensen, R. M. (2005). "Baptismal Rites and Architecture." In V. Burrus (ed.), *Late Ancient Christianity: A People's History of Christianity* 2 (pp. 117–144). Minneapolis, MN: Fortress Press.

Jung, J. E. (2000). "Beyond the Barrier: The Unifying Role of the Choir Screen in Gothic Churches." *The Art Bulletin* 82: 622–657.

Kieckhefer, R. (2009). "The Impact of Architecture." In D. E. Bornstein (ed.), *Medieval Christianity: A People's History of Christianity* 4 (pp. 109–146). Minneapolis, MN: Fortress Press.

King, A. (1964). *Eucharistic Reservation in the Western Church*. New York: Sheed and Ward.

Krueger, D. (2006). "The Practice of Christianity in Byzantium." In D. Krueger (ed.) *Byzantine Christianity: A People's History of Christianity* 4 (pp. 1–15). Minneapolis, MN: Fortress Press.

Krueger, D. (2014). *Liturgical Subjects: Christian Ritual, Biblical Narrative, and the Formation of the Self in Byzantium*. Philadelphia: University of Pennsylvania Press.

MacMullen, R. (2009). *The Second Church: Popular Christianity A. D. 200–400*. Leiden: Brill.

Markus, R. A. (1978). "The Cult of Icons in Sixth-Century Gaul." *Journal of Theological Studies* 29: 151–157.

Mathews, T. F. (1971). *The Early Churches of Constantinople: Architecture and Liturgy*. University Park: Pennsylvania State University Press.

McCall, R. D. (2007). *Do This: Liturgy as Performance*. Notre Dame, IN: University of Notre Dame Press.

McLaughlin, M. (1994). *Consorting with Saints: Prayer for the Dead in Early Medieval France*. Ithaca, NY and London: Cornell University Press.

McLaughlin, R. E. (1991). "The Word Eclipsed? Preaching in the Early Middle Ages." *Traditio* 46: 77–122.

Meens, R. (2004). "Reforming the Clergy: A Context for the Use of the Bobbio Missal." In Y. Hen and R. Meens (eds.), *The Bobbio Missal: Liturgy and Religious Culture in Merovingian Gaul* (pp. 154–167). Cambridge: Cambridge University Press.

Michel, V. (2008). "Furniture, Fixtures and Fittings in Churches: Archaeological Evidence from Palestine (4th–8th C.) and the Role of the *Diakonikon*." L. Lavan, E. Swift, and T. Putzeys (eds.), *Objects in Context, Objects in Use: Material Spatiality in Late Antiquity* (pp. 581–606). Leiden: Brill.

Palazzo, É. (2008). *L'espace rituel et le sacré dans le Christianisme: La liturgie de l'autel portatif dans l'antiquité et an Moyen Âge*. Turnhout: Brepols.

Palazzo, É. (2014). *L'invention chrétienne des 5 sens dans la liturgie et l'art au Moyen Age*. Paris: Éditions du Cerf.

Paxton, F. (1990). *Christianizing Death: The Creation of a Ritual Process in Early Medieval Europe*. Ithaca, NY: Cornell University Press.

Rivard, D. A. (2009). *Blessing the World: Ritual and Lay Piety in Medieval Religion*. Washington, DC: Catholic University of America Press.

Scheibelreiter, G. (2005). "Church Structure and Organization." In P. Fouracre (ed.), *The New Cambridge Medieval History* 1 (pp. 675–709). Cambridge: Cambridge University Press.

Senn, F. C. (2006). *The People's Work: A Social History of the Liturgy*. Minneapolis, MN: Fortress Press.

Smith, J. M. H. (1995). "Religion and Lay Society." In R. McKitterick (ed.), *The New Cambridge Medieval History* 2 (pp. 654–678). Cambridge: Cambridge University Press.

Smith, J. Z. (1987). *To Take Place: Toward Theory in Ritual*. Chicago: University of Chicago Press.

Smyth, M. (2003). *La liturgie oubliée*. Paris: Éditions du Cerf.

Spinks, B. D. (2007). "The Growth of Liturgy and the Church Year." In A. Casiday and F. W. Norris (eds.), *The Cambridge History of Christianity* 2 (pp. 601–617). Cambridge: Cambridge University Press.

Torjesen, K. J. (2008). "Clergy and Laity." In D. G. Hunter and S. A. Harvey (eds.), *The Oxford Handbook of Early Christian Studies* (pp. 389–405). Oxford: Oxford University Press.

van der Mensbrugghe, A. (1962). "Pseudo-Germanus Reconsidered." *Studia Patristica* 5: 172–184.

Wallace-Hadrill, J. M. (1983). *The Frankish Church*. Oxford: Clarendon Press.

Wright, Cr. (1989). *Music and Ceremony at Notre Dame of Paris 500–1500*. Cambridge: Cambridge University Press.

CHAPTER 45

···

THE LIFE OF PENANCE

···

KEVIN UHALDE

MEROVINGIAN authors knew well how to tell a penance story. The funniest one, written soon after 676, began with three penitents showing up at a crowded dinner party (*Passio Praeiecti* 8, pp. 229–230). Their host was a deacon named Praeiectus, later called St. Prix. At that time, he was assigned to the village of Issoire, about twenty miles to the south. But he kept a house in Clermont, the episcopal see of the Auvergne. He and other clergy from the diocese were in town to celebrate Easter with their bishop. Because only bishops were allowed to perform Easter mass (Kreiner 2014, p. 183), this was an annual event. Accustomed to a good turnout, Praeiectus prepared a banquet in the upper-floor solarium. His guests reclined, as their Gallo-Roman ancestors would have done, and the plates were sent around. Some of the banqueters began to joke, jibe, and jeer at the penitents, even going so far as to deride the very idea of penance. Their host's modest plea for civility was lost in the rising laughter. Suddenly, joists cracked, split apart, and half the floor gave way. Those hurling insults a moment earlier suddenly fell through, crashing below in a pile of rubble. The deacon and penitents, still seated upstairs at the table, rejoiced. Downstairs, their fallen companions were pulled from the wreckage and made their way home. They would not again dare to insult penitents, the servants of the Lord (Fouracre and Gerberding 1996, pp. 277–278; cf. Effros 2002, pp. 27–28).

Christians in the Merovingian kingdoms knew penance when they saw it. But what was it that they saw? Could it have been something Ambrose of Milan long ago described seeing in the pale, emaciated faces of penitents he had known: the image of death in a living, breathing body (*De paenitentia* 1.16.91, p. 126)?[1] Along with sexual continence, almsgiving, and vigilant prayer, penance traditionally required fasting, which might include abstaining from meat, at least when there were vegetarian options (Caesarius, *Sermo* 67.3, pp. 132–134; de Jong 2000, p. 205). Might three penitents stand out because they declined to eat meat?[2] Were they not eating or drinking at all or were they simply not being gluttons (Effros 2002, pp. 9–37)? Fasting did not make one a penitent any more than did humble attire or a shaved head, although those, too, were sometimes required. An elderly woman dressed in black and hanging around the church, for instance, might be fulfilling a penitential vow. She also might be a beggar. Or she might be the bishop's wife, an *episcopa*, living a religious life of her own. Such a case of mistaken identity once happened to the wife of Namatius, a bishop of Clermont (446–462). A poor man, struck more by her dark clothes than by the book in her lap, gave her some of his own bread (Gregory of Tours, *Historiae* 2.17, pp. 64–65). Long before Praeiectus's time, the story had become part of local "Auvergnian legend" (Brennan 1985, pp. 317–318).

Similarly, penitents were expected to weep, their tears springing up from heartfelt remorse and staining cheeks that were pallid from sleeplessness and hollow from fasting. Yet, of course, early medieval Christians also wept out of joy, in grief for the death of loved ones, and with laughter (Effros 2002, pp. 179–180; Rosenwein 2006, pp. 49–50).[3] Whatever it was that made the penitents at this dinner party stand out from a roomful of priests, deacons, and monks, Merovingian readers evidently did not need to be told. They knew why "among the diners, three penitents were dining" made for a good joke. The author was careful, however, to make sure they also knew where the joke went too far. Those who fell were the ones mocking penance. Only God's grace saved them from a fall that should have killed them.

The story of the penitents at supper worked because the story of penance itself was so familiar. It was part of what Peter Brown calls a "long span of penitential piety" (2015, p. 143) forged in texts, some of them originating in the eastern Mediterranean from as early as the second century. Much of the literature that shaped Merovingian penance was translated, copied, or written in southern Gaul during the fifth and early sixth centuries (Diem 2007, p. 556 n. 199; Diem 2005, pp. 339–393), in the midst of political unrest. While the Merovingians were still wrestling for control over the Auvergne, sermons, letters, and treatises concerning penance were circulating as far away as Bangor in County Down, Ireland (Bullough 1997, pp. 5–7; Stancliffe 1997, 2011). There Columbanus discovered the "medicines of penance," which he brought with him when he arrived in Francia around 591. Penitential piety was not exclusive to clergy, monks, or saints. Instead, it was devotion's highest common denominator, whether penitents submitted to a monastic rule or sought forgiveness within the church through ecclesiastical penance (also called public or canonical penance). Still in the seventh century, even in the remote monasteries Columbanus and his disciples favored, the laity might stop by to share a meal and express their common interest in a life of penance (Raga 2014). This chapter begins with how the story of penance itself came to encompass the diverse forms of devotion and atonement found in Gallo-Roman and Merovingian sources.

THE STORY OF PENANCE

Christian penance formed over the course of several centuries. Its liturgical roots were in Jewish tradition, which advocated daily prayers for divine forgiveness; annual confession of wrongs; and sacrifice at the Temple of Jerusalem on behalf of all of Israel. The language and even the look of Christian penance were Jewish, too, inspired especially by Job's mourning (Job 2:8), Nineveh's sorrow (Jon 3:5–6), and David's supplication in

2 Samuel 12 and the so-called penitential Psalms (although a different verse—"I rebuke you and make your indictment plain" (Ps. 49:21)—was on the lips of the penitents who survived the deacon's dinner party). In his book *How Repentance Became Biblical* (2015), David Lambert argues that those ancient rituals and gestures were formed into a new, personal understanding of penance within rabbinical Judaism and early Christianity, more or less simultaneously. It made for a powerful story in which individuals turned away from sin and found the power to persevere, through a life full of temptation, in hope of ultimate salvation. According to Lambert (2015), "repentance became biblical" when generations of Jews and Christians began reading the Bible in light of this story.

By the time Merovingians took control of Clermont and the rest of Gaul in the first decades of the sixth century (Wood 1994, pp. 51–54), the story of penance had become familiar, resilient, and pliable. It was tailored and retold in ways intended to inspire atonement within diverse communities of laity, clergy, and monks. The deacon Praeiectus, for example, was eventually chosen as bishop of Clermont. Now responsible for rescuing laymen and women throughout the Auvergne from "the snares of the ancient snake," he partnered with Evodius, a monk expert in administering *poenitentie salubri antidotum*—"the antidote of salubrious penance" (*Passio Praeiecti* 15, p. 234). It was not the first time penance brought clergy, monks, and laity together around common cause. Among the so-called Eusebius Gallicanus sermons, written by various authors in the fifth century and circulating widely from the sixth onward, Homily 45 identified the serpent's snares more precisely: perjury, fornication, and murder, of course, but also consultation with "augurers, diviners, and enchanters." When such serious sins as these led Christians into "captivity," they must seek "weightier, more severe, and public cures" in the form of ecclesiastical penance. By accepting the remedy and publicly seeking forgiveness, those penitents then became, in effect, preachers of penance through their actions, "redeeming" themselves through the "edification of many."[4] As Lisa Kaaren Bailey demonstrates in a series of studies on the Eusebius Gallicanus sermons and other sources, such calls to penance were heard and answered by laity, clergy and monks (Bailey 2009, 2010, ch. 5).

The story of penance also worked in retrospect, giving coherence to individual lives that crossed between lay, clerical, and monastic communities, sometimes in contradiction of rules pertaining to penance itself. The church, for example, prohibited laymen who had done penance from joining the clergy, and clergy from doing penance (Godding 2005, pp. 75–77, 310). Yet, as Mayke de Jong points out, the "most complex and extensive narratives" in Gregory of Tours's *Histories* turned around bishops doing penance (2000, pp. 209–215). Some of these "tales of episcopal penance" involved public scandal, ecclesiastical censure, and unsavory characters—the bishops Salonius of Embrun and Sagittarius of Gap most notoriously of all, thanks to Gregory's partial telling of events (Geltner 2008, p. 96; Brown 2011, pp. 34–37). However, as a native of the Auvergne (Wood, 1994, pp. 28–29; Heinzelmann, 2001, pp. 23–28), Gregory also knew the relatively benign story of Urbicus, second bishop of Clermont, who succumbed to his passionate wife—no mistaking that *episcopa* for a devout old beggar (Brennan 1985, p. 315). Having broken their mandatory vows of continence, Urbicus eventually secluded himself inside a monastery for the purpose of doing penance (*acturus paenitentiam*). "With lamentation and tears he atoned for his misdeeds, and finally came back to his own town," which later venerated him as a saint (*Historiae* 1.44, pp. 28–29, trans. Thorpe, pp. 93–94). Penance that Urbicus undertook for a serious offense became, in Gregory's tale, proof of his holiness. Like other Merovingian authors, he used the story of penance to smooth the contingencies and contradictions of ordinary life into a pious whole.

TIME, JUDGMENT, AND AWARENESS

Early Christian authors developed this story of penance around three essential elements, which underpinned the various forms in which laity, clergy, and monastic men and women atoned for their sins in Merovingian Gaul. The first element was temporal. Penance had a clear starting point—a pang of conscience, for example, which medieval authors, following Cassian and Gregory the Great, called compunction (Stewart 1998, pp. 25, 122–129). In this sense, conversion and penance overlapped. All penitents converted from sin, but not all converts were penitents. Unlike conversion, penance was a continuous process. Whereas converts might put their past firmly behind them, penitents stayed on the straight and narrow by remembering the past, including the pain of conversion.

The second, judicial element was similarly ongoing. It involved rigorous self-scrutiny, which was often described metaphorically in terms of torture and punishment. Moreover, the prospect of facing the divine tribunal after death gave penance urgency. Merovingians were often reminded of the final judgment in sermons, histories, visions, and miracle literature (Brown 2015, pp. 141, 155–157, 164–167). Whether or not the dangerous times in which they lived made them more mindful than other Christians of their ultimate reckoning is debatable (cf. Palmer 2014, pp. 50–54, 59–61, 76–78). In any case, fear was playing a salubrious role in penance from the beginning. "Go and meditate like the criminals in prison," Abba Ammon told a monk in one of the sayings of the desert fathers. His advice is from the section on compunction in the "massively influential" sixth-century Latin translation known as the *Verba seniorum* (Ward 2003, p. xxxi). Ammon's analogy with guilty prisoners continues: "They keep asking, where is the judge, when will he come? and because they are waiting for him they dread their punishment. The monk should always be waiting for his trial, chiding his soul," and in that way find salvation through repentance (*Verba seniorum* 3.2, col. 860, trans. Ward, p. 12).

Remembering the past, keeping vigilant in the present, and anticipating the future all entailed the third and final element of penance: awareness. Bishop Urbicus of Clermont resolved to do penance for sleeping with his wife at the point where he "recovered his wits"—literally, when he returned to himself (*ad se reversus*), "and grieved for the sin which he had committed" (Gregory of Tours, *Historiae* 1.44, trans. Thorpe, pp. 93–94). Hundreds of years earlier, in the second century *Shepherd of Hermas*, the Greek word for repentance and penance (*metanoia*) was defined as *megalê sunesis*, "great awareness" (Commandments 30 (IV.2).2, p. 248). Despite being repeatedly condemned by church authorities, the *Shepherd* circulated widely in a variety of versions, including multiple Latin translations (Tornau and Cecconi, 2014, pp. 4–12). One of these versions was referred to by name in the Merovingian *Life of Genovefa* from around 540 (*Vita Genovefae* 16, p. 221) and is believed to have originated in Gaul sometime within the previous century (Mazzini and Lorenzini 1981; Vezzoni 1994). "I am in charge of repentance and grant discretion (*prudentiam*) to all who are changing themselves for the better," the eponymous Shepherd explains in this Latin version. "Or do you think this is not the same thing, that when someone does penance for his prior life, this is awareness (*sapientiam*)?" Weaving together the three defining elements of penance, the Shepherd describes what it means for a penitent to understand (*intellegit*) and repent: "For the memory of his deed rises in that one's heart, causes him to repent, and he does not any further do what is bad but hands himself over to what is good and works copious good and his soul he makes humble and tortures on account of the sins that came before. So you see," the Shepherd summarizes, "repentance is the greatest discretion" (Palatine *Shepherd of Hermas*, Commandments 30 (IV.2).2, ed. Vezzoni, p. 92).

Conversations about penance revolved around these same temporal, judicial, and intellectual elements for centuries to come. "Here is the full and perfect definition of repentance," according to Abba Pinufius in Cassian's *Conferences*, "that we should never again commit the sins for which we do penance and on account of which our conscience is pricked" (20.5.1, trans. Ramsey, p. 696). Cassian, who read and quoted from what he called "the book of the Shepherd" (*Coll.* 8.17.2, p. 233), was a well-traveled monk from Scythia Minor. He died in Marseille around 435. Only a few texts were as commonly read and copied in Merovingian monastic libraries as the *Conferences*, in which he recalled his conversations with Egyptian ascetics. The discussion with Pinufius sought to reassure anchorites and cenobitic monks despairing over the long path to perfection (Cassian, *Coll. praefatio* 3.2, p. 503). From his initial moment of conversion, the penitent remained a penitent for "as long as the image of the things that he did or of similar misdeeds dances before his eyes while he is giving himself over to reparation and groaning." Because awareness was both a means and an end—The End—to penance, "the truest judge of repentance" was therefore the penitent's own conscience, "which reveals to us who are still living in the flesh the absolution of our sinfulness before the day of recognition and judgement" (*Coll.* 20.5.2–3, p. 558, trans. Ramsey, p. 696). Forgiveness felt like "forgetfulness," when the "recollection" of wrongdoing "faded away." Getting there required work. "As we repent, then, and are still bitten by the memory of our wrongdoing, the torrent of our tears which has arisen from the confession of our sins will certainly put out the fire of our conscience" (*Coll.* 20.7.1–2, p. 560; trans. Ramsey, pp. 697–698).

FORMS OF PENANCE

These temporal, judicial, and intellectual elements defined the contours of penance in early Christian literature. This is not to suggest either that they constituted a rigid definition of penance or that virtues and behaviors associated with penance became exclusively penitential. The "copious good," for example, that the Shepherd expected from anyone doing penance included prayer, fasting, alms for the poor, and other acts of humility (Brox 1991, pp. 512–523)—the same, most common forms of atonement known and practiced by Merovingian Christians. Hermas himself, though, still fasted and kept vigil for other reasons, including his desire to continue receiving visions (Palatine *Shepherd of Hermas*, Visions 9 (III.1).2, ed. Vezzoni, p. 62; Moreira 2000, p. 21). Late-antique authors therefore found it helpful to explain, even to enumerate, the various "remedies" or "fruits" of penance (Torrance 2013, pp. 53–54, 84–85). Origen informed laypeople in third-century Palestine of seven "remissions of sins" found in the Gospels, beginning with baptism. Along with martyrdom and conversion from error, there were almsgiving, forgiveness of others, and charity. Finally came ecclesiastical penance, administered by a priest and carried out with tears, fasting, and abstinence (Origen, *Homily on Leviticus* 2.4, pp. 106–112). Deeply influenced by Origen (Stewart 1998, p. 36 and 2015, p. 376), Cassian offered a less tidy inventory of the "many fruits of repentance by which the expiation of sins is achieved." Most were among Origen's seven—baptism, martyrdom, almsgiving, forgiveness of others—or else included within his description of ecclesiastical penance—tears, fasting, and confessing and seeking forgiveness. Another of Cassian's fruits was inspiring others to turn from sin, either through preaching or by fraternal rebuke (*Coll.* 20.8, pp. 561–565, trans. Ramsey, pp. 698–770; Stewart 1998, p. 129). Although Cassian had in mind a monastic context, this reciprocal form of repentance was similar to the compound redemption of ecclesiastical penance extolled in the Eusebius Gallicanus sermon for lay penitents and those who witnessed their penance.

Christian penance was a "multi-layered concept" (Torrance 2013, p. 67), an explanatory framework for emotions and behaviors that together could lead Christians to salvation. Tertullian, an older contemporary of Origen, said as much in his influential sermon, *On Penance*. He argued that a transcendent "reason" or "logic" (*ratio*) distinguished Christian penance from other, mundane experiences of regret (*De paenitentia* 1.1–2, p. 144), and he described an ongoing process: "a penance that must be taken hold of once and perpetually preserved," marked at its beginning by conversion to truth and reason (*De paenitentia* 6.1, p. 164). "Penance," he wrote, "is life" (*De paenitentia* 4.2, p. 156). In an influential metaphor gleaned from earlier authors, Tertullian pictured penance as a plank for clinging to across the stormy seas of human existence.[5] Christians who lost their grip on penance could have recourse to ecclesiastical penance, which Tertullian called "exomologesis." He used the unusual term deliberately, seeking to circumscribe ecclesiastical penance as one possible variation within the larger process of penance. His depiction of exomologesis, however, was as vivid as his vocabulary was precise: how penitents must dress in mourning clothes (*sacco et cineri*—cf. Dan 9:3; Jon 3:5–6), let their spirits sink deep into sorrow, subsist on austere diets, and pray for days on end. Exomologesis culminated in the penitent "groaning, weeping, crying out day and night to the Lord your God, prostrating yourself at the feet of the priests, kneeling before God's altars, joining all the faithful together" in one common appeal for forgiveness (*De paenitentia* 9.4, p. 180).

Ecclesiastical penance brought to life the story of penance with all its temporal, judicial, and intellectual elements. Tertullian's portrait was drawn just as vividly in his later treatise, *On Modesty*, where he denied that bishops could reconcile and absolve adulterers, any more than they could murderers and idolaters. All the same, he encouraged such sinners to submit themselves to the rigors of exomologesis. "For adulterers and fornicators we fix the very same limit at the threshold, where they shall pour forth tears that thirst for peace and receive nothing from the church beyond the publication of their shame" (*De pudicitia* 1.21, p. 152). "The heartless cruelty of this sentence is unparalleled," a modern translator comments, "even in a work conspicuous for intolerance and severity" (Le Saint 1959, p. 197 n. 39).[6] Anticipating precisely this reaction, however, Tertullian defended the value of penance without priestly absolution. The true end of Christian penance was divine, not human, forgiveness. When penitents appealed directly to God, they were more likely to find pardon. Meanwhile, their penance amplified the reciprocal effect later commended by Cassian and the Eusebius Gallicanus, as it "stands before the doors" of the church, "admonishes others by its stigmatic example, summons the brethren's tears on its behalf, and returns more enriched by compassion than it would by communion"—than if reconciliation had been granted. "Penance of this sort is not in vain," Tertullian concluded, "and discipline of this sort is not cruel. Both honor God" (*De pudicitia* 3.4–6, p. 160).

PENANCE IN PERSPECTIVE

The prospect of penance with no end in sight did not disturb Gallo-Roman and Frankish authors, who conveyed the story of penance in its most "drastic" and "dramatic form" to a range of potential penitents (Brown 2015, pp. 126–127), whether or not liturgical reconciliation within the church was the intended outcome. Tertullian's evocative images supplied the *mise-en-scène* for generations of writers and preachers of penance, from Eusebius Gallicanus and Caesarius of Arles to Jonas of Orléans (cf. de Jong 2000, pp. 194–196). "Like the long span of a great bridge," writes Peter Brown, "penitential piety...joined the last days of the [Roman] empire to the first centuries of the postimperial kingdoms of the West" (2015, p. 143). His book, *The Ransom of the Soul: Afterlife and Wealth in Early Western Christianity*, focuses on death and what came next. Penance mattered for measuring piety against the weight of sin that every Christian should expect. Gradually, among many "low-profile continuities" affecting how Gallo-Romans and Merovingians imagined their postmortem souls, space opened up for intercession to take place: first, through the particular power of saints venerated at urban shrines throughout Gaul and later, through the industrial power of prayer generated in rural monasteries. As the screen lowered between this world and the next, penitential piety reached beyond the grave, extending the life of penance but also prolonging uncertainty, as a "democracy of souls" awaited the final judgment (Brown 2015, pp. 204, 208–210).

The spiritual landscape Brown describes is very different from the desolation evoked by the twentieth century's most important historians of penance. "Precisely in the years when sins importuned men most strongly," between the sixth and eighth centuries, penance "fell into complete oblivion," leaving only a "penitential void."[7] This bleak prospect derived from two faulty premises and one misread text. First, that penance strictly speaking can be only ecclesiastical penance, whose severe, lifelong demands amounted to *mort civile et sociale*, "civil and social death" (Vogel 1952, p. 117).[8] Second, that ecclesiastical penance, being "too rigorous" for Merovingian laity, "dwindled into a deathbed ritual"—a widespread notion implying statistical knowledge that does not exist for Gregory of Tours's any more than for Tertullian's time.[9] Only from the late eighth century does the evidence begin to support claims about the frequency of penance (Meens 1998). Third, that Jonas of Bobbio was talking about ecclesiastical penance when he described the scarcity of "the medicines of penance and love of mortification" in Gaul around the time Columbanus arrived (*Vita Columbani* 1.5, p. 161). Clearly, he was not.[10] Writing half a century later, nearly thirty years after Columbanus founded a monastery at Bobbio and just before becoming abbot of that monastery, Jonas had his own reasons to imagine a landscape devoid, not of ecclesiastical penance, but of rivals in ascetic discipline. The practice of repeated confession and use of penitentials that Columbanus and his followers helped spread were part of a watershed, not a crisis, in the history of penance.

The rich and diverse evidence for penitential piety in Gallo-Roman and Merovingian sources flatly contradicts *ex silentio* arguments for the decline of penance. "Penance was a major theme in ecclesiastical life in the fifth and sixth centuries," Rob Meens observes, "while the bishops at the close of the sixth century could hardly be accused of negligence" (2014, pp. 71–73). His *Penance in Medieval Europe, 600–1200*, along with earlier essays by Meens, Mayke de Jong, and others, lays to rest the myth that Merovingians only did penance on their deathbeds. Just as importantly, Lisa Kaaren Bailey's work, especially in *The Religious Worlds of the Laity in Late Antique Gaul* (2016), expands the demographic profile of Christian devotion and thereby expands our scope for understanding penitential piety in its many, diverse forms. "The penitential landscape has appeared to flatten out," Marilyn Dunn remarks, "as the consensus of opinion moves towards the idea that the decline of an older type of penance was less steep and the rise of a new [i.e., Columbanus's] less sharp and distinctive than we had been led to accept" (2012, pp. 18–19). Even so, flatter does not mean simple or uniform. Christians found a variety of ways to "honor God" and atone for their sins. Penance was as important in life as in death, not least because it made a good story.

PENANCE BY ANY OTHER NAME

The usual familiarity of penance and penitents in Gallic society informs some unusual tales of mistaken or ambiguous identity. There was the woman mistaken for a beggar who actually was married to Bishop Namatius. A more revealing tale comes from one of his famous successors, Sidonius Apollinaris. Two centuries before penitents showed up at Praeiectus's dinner party, Sidonius attended a dinner hosted by an apparent penitent. In a letter, he describes stopping on his way to Toulouse at an old friend's country villa in the Aquitaine. Sidonius's own career, both before and after becoming bishop of Clermont in 470/472, was as varied and unpredictable as it was distinguished (Mathisen 1993, pp. 89–96). Yet even he was taken aback when Maximus came out to greet him. Once bursting with energy and charm, the man's appearance was changed completely. "His dress, his step, his modest air, his colour and his talk, all had a religious suggestion." Maximus had cut his hair short and grown out his beard. His home furnishings were minimal and threadbare, as was the meal laid out for Sidonius and other guests: meat was scarce, and the host contented himself with vegetables. Obviously he had undertaken a life of penance but under what circumstances? Sidonius turned to the person sitting beside him and asked, "what way of life from among the three orders (*ordines*) had he suddenly adopted? Was he a monk or clergyman or penitent?" (*Letter* 4.24.3–4, pp. 158–161, translation slightly changed). Which "order" Maximus had joined apparently did not affect his present condition, but it might affect his future.

We might be tempted to recognize in Sidonius's question a scholarly affection for categories (Rebillard 2012, 2016; Sessa 2015). The answer would explain not only in what form but more importantly to what end Maximus had chosen to do penance. It turned out to be clergyman because his local community had chosen him to become their priest. Sidonius now could understand his penance as an expression of clerical devotion, in the same way that a monk would have implied monastic devotion. Had the answer been penitent, however, Maximus's future would have been less predictable, for he would still have been part of the laity. His penance might lead to formal absolution by his bishop. In that case, without the possibility of further absolution, a prudent Christian could avoid the dangers of public life and accept "civil and social death" as the price of forgiveness. Death, however, seems too strong a word for the lifestyle Maximus appears to have accepted voluntarily, whatever the circumstances or direction of his penitential piety. In such cases, some scholars take "penitent" and "penance" to be misnomers for "convert" and "conversion," implying that what Sidonius called "penitent" represented membership in a "third-order monastic" category.[11]

Such an "institution," invented with modern lay tertiaries in mind, is thought to have provided motivated Christians all the rigors and rewards of penance in a "less shameful" form than ecclesiastical penance (Poschmann 1928, pp. 136, 141). If converts who were called penitents shied away from the temporary shame of exomologesis, however, it seems odd that they be willing to be commemorated as penitents on their tombstones. Among more than two dozen inscriptions that describe the deceased doing penance, receiving penance, or being penitent, seven are from southeastern Gaul (Vogel 1966; Handley 2003, 10 n. 26). Historians sometimes refer to them as a group for demonstrating the "prestigious preparation" deathbed penance provided (Tentler 1977, p. 7 n. 5; Jong 2000, p. 198 n. 38; Carroll 2006, p. 260). Yet it is always possible and in some cases clear that penance was no last-minute ritual. Carusa, who died in 520 and was buried in

Lyon, is described as a woman "of good memory and religious, who did penance twenty-two years and lived in peace sixty-five years" (Le Blant 1999, pp. 549–550 no. 663). Should we conclude from this and similar inscriptions "that in daily life the faithful distinguished poorly between a *paenitens*, a *conversus*, and a *religiosus*," and understand convert wherever we read penitent, even though no Gallo-Roman or Merovingian inscription calls anyone convert (Vogel 1966, p. 325)? A simpler deduction is that different sorts of people did penance in a "wide variety of forms" (Meens 2014, pp. 77–78), all of which were forms of penance.

Penance and penitents conjured strong associations. Just as being invited to a dinner party raised certain expectations of hospitality, sociability, and indulgence, there also was a generally familiar way of being a penitent. The three penitents who showed up to dinner in the *Passion of Praeiectus* evidently looked and acted like penitents, although we are not told how. While their penance was left to speak to readers for itself, the author did provide some personal information about those collectively referred to four times as penitents (*paenitentes*) and twice as servants (*servi*). The first was named "Venerianus, servant (*famulus*) of God, who fulfilled his name's meaning in his work." Next was Gosoaldus, called a witness of Christ (*testis Christi*). This seems to be the same Gosoald who later settled as a hermit near Limoges in Aquitaine, where he would be remembered as Saint Goussaud (Aubrun 1981, pp. 108–109). The third penitent, Marialdus, was identified simply as "monk" (*Passio Praeiecti* 8, pp. 229–230). What mattered more to the story than their lay, clerical, or monastic statuses was their condition as penitents.

Later in the *Passion*, the *vir vit[a]e venerabilis* Venerianus is found at "his work," helping to inventory and transfer church property (*Passio Praeiecti* 35–36, pp. 245–246). The epithet *famulus*, "servant," might simply have been meant to signal his humility, especially if he was a priest: the more prestigious the "servant," the greater the humility (Carroll 2006, p. 275).[12] Yet the title also "intersected with the large group of lay people" who performed real service—"cleaning, providing food, washing linen, lighting lamps and so forth"—at churches, clerical residences, and saints' shrines (Bailey 2016, pp. 44–45). Venerianus was unlikely to have scrubbed floors for a living, but he may well have been a lay penitent who donated his accounting skills as service to the church. Drawing on a wide array of literary and epigraphic evidence, Lisa Bailey makes it clear that titles of divine service (e.g., *famulus/famula*, *servus/serva*, *ancilla*) were commonly attributed not only to prestigious clergy, monks, or nuns, but to laymen and women, as well as to people identified as penitents on their tombstones. At least a half-dozen contemporary epitaphs from Visigothic Spain identify the deceased with penance and as God's *famulus* or *famula* (Vives 1969, nos. 42, 44, 57, 66, 142; Mateos Cruz 1999, p. 141; Handley 2003, p. 43).

"The concept of service," like the life of penance, "cut across the categories of lay, clerical and ascetic and offered a means for understanding and representing a range of quite different relationships with religious institutions" (Bailey 2016, pp. 43–51 with bibliography at n. 173). Being called *famulus Dei* did not make Venerianus a cleric or monk, any more than being called *paenitens* made him anything other than a penitent. Sometimes penance turned out to be a layperson's first step on a path leading to clerical ordination, monastic vows, or even sainthood. The role penance played in a penitent's life remained uncertain—and negotiable—until the end.

PENITENTIAL LIVES

The *Life of Eligius of Noyon* is one of the few lives of native Gallic saints that appear to have been genuinely popular among Frankish scribes (Heinzelmann, 2012, pp. 39–41)—the "jewel in the crown of Carolingian hagiography" (Hen 1995, pp. 196–197; on hagiography, see Kreiner, Chapter 24, this volume). Although claiming to be from the pen of Eligius's close friend, Audoin of Rouen (609–686), whose own *Life* also survives (Fouracre and Gerberding 1996, pp. 133–152), the text was extensively revised and embellished by at least one author, probably a monk in Noyon (Krusch 1902, pp. 634–663; Moreira 2010, p. 123 n. 43). A remarkable penance story, however, appears to be original because it is quoted directly in another seventh-century *vita*.[13] The story is in Book I of the *Life of Eligius*, which describes the successful career of a Gallo-Roman who served the Merovingian kings of Neustria as goldsmith, advisor, and diplomat before becoming bishop of Noyon from 642 until his death in 660 (Wood 1994, pp. 150–151; Meens 2014, p. 84).

Like Audoin, his companion at court who also was ordained bishop of Rouen on the same day, Eligius was arguably "not important because he was bishop; he was bishop because he was important" (Fouracre and Gerberding 1996, p. 148). That was of course not quite how the *Life* remembered him. Rather than a saint whose kingdom was not truly of this earth, Eligius was said to have found grace equally "before the Lord and before the kings of the Franks" (*Vita Eligii* 1.9, p. 676; Helvétius 2012, p. 66; Heinzelmann 2012, pp. 56–57). Royal grace brought wealth, allowing Eligius to leverage divine grace with pious donations. In 632, for example, King Dagobert awarded him an estate at Solignac, not far from Limoges and his own birthplace (Mathisen 1999, p. 18; see also Strothmann, Chapter 35, this volume). Eligius decided to establish a monastery there according to the model he knew from visiting Luxeuil, the oldest of Columbanus's monasteries. "[W]hatever the king gave him, whatever he could buy, whatever he was paid in gratuities by the powerful, he sent to that place." The author depicts these gifts arriving at Solignac: "There you would see loaded carts, vessels for every use of both copper and wood, vestments and lectuaries and linens and volumes of sacred Scripture and all things needful for the use of a monastery in such profusion that it kindled the envy of many depraved great folk" (*Vita Eligii* 1.15, trans. McNamara, pp. 146–147).

By then, other monasteries and convents were flourishing in the countryside of the Frankish kingdoms, supported by other royalty, nobles, and servants like Eligius (Fox 2014; see Diem, Chapter 15, this volume). These "powerhouses of prayer" caused a shift in not only the physical topography but the temporal boundaries of penitential piety. As Peter Brown demonstrates in *Ransom of the Soul*, the watershed many historians of penance have long located in the seventh century was real, even if the decline of penance was not as we imagined. Not only does evidence then begin to emerge of laity repeatedly confessing and repenting individual sins similar to the way Cassian had and Columbanus now recommended for ascetics. But traditional acts of penance, especially almsgiving, were made to work for salvation even after death. Brown finds the "stupendous imagined results" of such acts epitomized in "the words of one wealthy courtier: 'I cede…small things for great, earthly things for things celestial, what is on earth for what abides forever.'" The courtier is Eligius, and the words are from Solignac's foundation charter (*Eligii charta cessionis Solemniacensis*). Brown may not name Eligius here because his focus is on donors who expected their extravagant gifts to insulate them from the "raw sacrality" of the monastic foundations they helped build. They belonged to "a laity that remained impenitently profane" (cf. Fouracre and Gerberding 1996, p. 141; Brown 2015, pp. 196–197). Eligius moved in those circles, shared the same charitable habits, but could in no way be called impenitent. Audoin recalled in the *Life of Eligius* that his friend had intended originally to join the monastery he established at Solignac, "except that the dispensation of God obligated him to something else" (*Vita Eligii* 1.15, trans. McNamara, p. 147). In hindsight, something else was obviously the episcopate. At the time, however, ordination may have seemed neither obvious nor possible to someone who already had done penance.

When he turned twenty-five years old and reached the age of virility, Eligius "confessed his adolescent deeds before a priest (*coram sacerdotem*)."[14] The sins he feared "might stain his breast" were probably sexual, to judge from the timing and nature of his repentance (Diem 2005, p. 290). "Imposing a severe penance upon himself," Eligius began to mortify his flesh with vigils and fasting. Fear, memory, and the prospect of divine punishment helped him resist succumbing again to lust. His awareness of life's end and God's judgment grew sharper as his physical form withered. Like Tertullian's penitents, prostrating themselves in church and weeping for mercy, Eligius spent nights on his back, "beating his breast with his hands and dripping tears." Just as Pinufius assured Cassian that penitents would be the first to know they were forgiven, Eligius became the truest judge of his own repentance (*Vita Eligii* 1.7, pp. 673–675, partial trans. McNamara, p. 143). Alone in his bedchamber, beneath his collection of hanging reliquaries, Eligius kept vigil by prostrating himself on a haircloth until he could stay awake no longer. The moment he fell asleep, a figure appeared before him saying, "'Behold Eligius! Your prayers have been heard and the sign you asked for in the past will now be given to you.' As soon as he heard this, he sensed a sweet odor, and the softest drops from the chrism of the reliquaries flowed smoothly upon his head" (*Vita Eligii* 1.8, p. 675, trans. McNamara, p. 143).[15]

O felix penitentia—"Oh happy penance," the *Life's* author exclaimed, "that so swiftly attracts the mercy of Christ to itself." The temporal, judicial, and intellectual elements of penance emerge repeatedly in this description of a process that begins with sacerdotal confession, ends in ritual absolution, and in most respects looks enough like ecclesiastical penance to worry modern scholars. The absence of a congregation as witnesses or a priest to reconcile the penitent has been interpreted as evidence for penance "breaking down" (Waldron 1976, pp. 142–143). Oscar Watkins, who called Eligius "one of the most interesting and attractive personalities of the Merovingian period," found "no hint of public penance, of public reconciliation, or of [consequent] disabilities. It is the striving of an earnest soul after the more perfect way. It is the private system of Luxeuil" (Watkins 1920, pp. 574–578, 625). If that were so, we would expect more than a single confession. More importantly, though not "public," Eligius's penance had what mattered most according to preachers of penance. First, shame: "the more he humiliated himself, the humbler he became" (*Vita Eligii* 1.7, p. 674). Second, reciprocity: Eligius told Audoin the story in confidence, whereupon his friend "began experiencing heartfelt compunction" and started emulating Eligius (*Vita Eligii* 1.8, p. 675). Cyrille Vogel, similarly commenting on the "absence of any context," suggesting ecclesiastical penance, explained that penance "obviously means penance in the broad sense (*œuvres de mortifications*)" (1956, pp. 11–12). This does not explain the confession, the miracle that gives the episode obvious closure, or the difference between this penance and what followed.

For at least a decade, until their ordination, Eligius and Audoin did adhere to penance "in the broad sense." Along with others, they lived as courtiers by day and penitents by night. Whether Eligius was observing the "disabilities" entailed by ecclesiatical penance even after reconciliation or joining a fashionable wave of Columbanian spirituality would be indiscernible to anyone who did not know his story.[16] Whether it was Audoin the bishop or even a monk who told the story of Eligius's confession, penance, and absolution, the author surely knew the difference between penitents, converts, and religious. On the one hand, the story would assure credulous readers that Eligius had atoned fully for whatever sins were weighing on him. On the other hand, the greater part of the *Life* concerned Eligius's career as a bishop, which he began by opposing any improprieties with regard to the episcopal office (*Vita Eligii* 2.1–2, pp. 694–695). As important as it may have been to cleanse Eligius of prior indiscretions, it would have been just as important not to discredit his eligibility for serving as bishop and a preacher of penance himself. Later readers certainly associated Eligius with penance: one or more Carolingian authors attributed to him a series of penitential sermons, employing all the elements and images of penance most important to earlier authors, whose work "Pseudo-Eligius" freely copied (McCune 2008; Moreira 2010, p. 97). As a saint, Eligius was exceptional by definition. But he was typical in the way penitential piety gave his life shape in both prospect and retrospect.

Conclusion

The *Life of Eligius* demonstrates the story of penance at work, shaping life's real inconsistencies into a pious whole. By way of contrast as well as conclusion, let us return once more to the *Passion of Praeiectus*. Praeiectus is unusual, especially for a saint. Not from one of those families who sent their children to great monasteries to be educated, he was brought up almost entirely within the clerical community. His network seems limited to Clermont and the Auvergne, "not exactly a peer of the great elites we usually meet in Merovingian hagiography" (Kreiner 2014, p. 166). And compared to contemporary saints' lives, the story of Praeiectus's life is remarkably devoid of penitential piety up until the end. Although penitents were on his guest list, no personal connection between them was implied in the dinner party episode. When it came to saving souls, Praeiectus relied on someone else to preach penance. He is once described as keeping vigil, but not out of any sense of atonement: part of a night was spent praying for God to reveal where a stolen vessel was buried. When revealed, like a good bishop, Praeiectus assigned his thieving servant penance to perform in front of the entire household (*Passio Praeiecti* 19, p. 237, and, similarly. 17, p. 236). His life appears to have been one the other bishops envisioned in their canons, raised for the office and free from scandal, avoiding the contingencies and contradictions that penance helped resolve in other, more conventional lives. Or else the *Passion*'s author scrubbed the story clean of any penitential activity on Praeiectus's part, in the process of producing a life that would appease diverse audiences in troubled times. For Praeiectus had made powerful enemies over a disputed bequest. Some of them wanted him dead.[17]

On a winter's day in 676, Praeiectus and a companion, Abbot Amarinus, found themselves trapped in a house, abandoned by their retinue, with an armed band outside blowing war horns. Twenty of them forced their way inside. Amarinus suggested trying to escape, but Praeiectus prayed instead that this chance at martyrdom would not pass them by. As the assassins entered, "the man of God lay on his bed and drenched his couch with his tears." For the first time in his life—this version of his life, anyway—Praeiectus acted like a penitent, and not just any penitent: he was King David in Psalm 6:7, the first penitential Psalm. Meanwhile, mistaking abbot for bishop, the assassins cornered Amarinus and slit his throat. About to be defrauded of his martyr's crown, Praeiectus had to insist that someone kill him. A Saxon named Radbert finally obliged; in return, Radbert was later devoured by worms (*Passio Praeiecti* 30, p. 243). Two senators who helped orchestrate the attack, however, were saved by seeing three stars pass over where Amarinus and Praeiectus were slain. The miracle not only revealed their deaths to have been a glorious martyrdom, as the *Passion*'s author explained. It also turned the senators to penance (*revocare ad poenitentiam*), "for no one placed in this life needs to despair of forgiveness, so long as they are willing to be converted" (*Passio Praeiecti* 31, pp. 243–244).

Unlike the three guests whose appearance once threw his dinner party into disarray, Praeiectus did not go through life looking or acting like a penitent. There is little in his *Passion* to suggest that his reputation or career was helped in any way by his penitential piety. Yet the end of his life was portrayed as an act of penance. For those who conspired against him, meanwhile, conversion was the beginning of their lives as penitents (cf. Fouracre and Gerberding 1996, pp. 265–267). The senators were laymen whose need to repent was tied to serious crimes rather than spontaneous piety. Even so, by accepting penance and sharing their story with others, they joined the martyred abbot and bishop in the larger story of penance. This story was taking shape centuries earlier around temporal, judicial, and intellectual elements that distinguished it from other forms of piety and conversion. Otherwise it remained a flexible narrative, encompassing diverse forms of devotion and atonement within lay, clerical, and monastic communities. Penitents accepted a condition that visibly distinguished them from ordinary society but was not entirely exclusive. The life of penance that is reflected in Gallo-Roman and Merovingian sources was also inclusive across boundaries of social and religious status, of time and space, and of life and death.

Notes

1. Labriolle 1928, p. 286, wrongly identifies the passage as II.i.5; followed by McNeill and Gamer 1990, p. 22 and Kidder 2010, p. 25.
2. As Vogel claimed (1956, p. 4). Vogel proved his inference by interpolating the telling phrase (*qui esum carnis sumere recusabant*) from a later version of the story into text he cited as that of Bruno Krusch's critical edition; cf. Krusch's recension B, ed. d'Achery and Mabillon, p. 647. For other historians of penance using hagiographical evidence, see Waldron 1976, pp. 3–8, as well as p. 128, where he noticed Vogel's textual change.
3. *Vita Audoini* 5, p. 577: *Quem ita esuries corpore illius tenuaverat, ut caro adtrita et matie pallore subfusa, maxillae eius lacrimarum imbrem madefactae*; Cassian, *Coll.* 9.29, pp. 274–276: *Non omnis lacrimarum profusio uno adfectu uel una uirtute depromitur*; cf. Kreiner, 2014, pp. 112–114, on "tearful remembrance" as *imitatio*.
4. *Eusebius Gallicanus* 45.3, p. 537, with references to relevant conciliar canons: *sed graues causae grauiores et acriores et publicas curas requirunt, ut, qui cum plurimorum destructione se perdidit, simili modo cum plurimorum aedificatione se redimat*; Bailey 2010, pp. 88–89.
5. Tertullian, *De paenitentia* 7.5, p. 129, and 12.9, p. 190; cf. Ez 33:11; Philo, *The Posterity and Exile of Cain* 178, p. 434; Plutarch, *On Compliancy* 19, pp. 86–88.
6. For similar rebukes, see, for example, Poschmann 1964, p. 49; Torrance 2013, pp. 77–78; cf. Burns and Jensen, 2014, pp. 300, 309.
7. Gaudemet 1953, pp. 237–238; Poschmann 1964, p. 123; Vogel 1992; cf. Price 2004, p. 34 ("fallen largely into disuse by the sixth century").
8. "Penitential void" is often repeated, for example, Gaudemet 1953, p. 236; Vogel 1966, p. 318; Treffort 1996, p. 43; Guyon 1999, p. 96.
9. de Jong 1992, p. 43, corrected by de Jong, 2000, p. 187 n. 6. Gaudemet, Vogel, and Poschmann all connected the decline of penance with reliance on deathbed penance, for example, Vogel, 1952, p. 152: "la pénitence canonique qui rebutait les Francs, trop violents et trop frustes…après une vie de péchés, les pires barbares n'aient accueilli avec reconnaissance la *penitentia* [*sic*] *in extremis* dont ils attendaient le salut éternel."
10. See Helvétius 2012, p. 63; Meens 2014, pp. 70–71, 76–78; Fox 2014, p. 16; Brown 2013 [1996], p. 252; Stancliffe, 2011; Wood 1981, 1982; cf. Dunn, 2012, p. 18.
11. Vogel 1966, pp. 320, 322–323: "La *conversio* correspondrait assez bien à un tiers-ordre religieux des temps modernes"; Poschmann 1928, pp. 128–142; Mortimer 1939, p. 2; more influentially, Galtier 1934, followed by, for example, Dallen 1986, pp. 82–86, though he wonders whether such an "undoubtedly attractive" alternative was "really penance"; Waldron 1976 surveys the scholarship and offers a useful study of conversion and penance, but his analysis is affected by assuming the "decline of canonical public penance" (e.g., pp. 137, 142, 148). Cf. Alciati 2012, 486: "*resta ancora argomento di dibattito.*"
12. Cf. Fouracre and Gerberding 1996, p. 70 ("the phrase *vir venerabilis* usually means simply 'monk'"), p. 124 n. 171, and p. 397, *s.v.* "Veneranius, priest in Clermont"; Godding 2001 does not include Venerianus in his prosopography (but for Praeiectus, see pp. 193–194); Handley 2003, p. 42 (with bibliography) decides the meaning of *vir venerabilis* is

"uncertain": "some scholars have seen the title as largely referring to bishops. The example of Modoaldus, a 16-year-old *vir venerabilis* from Trier, makes this unlikely."

13. *Vita Eligii* 1.7–8, ed. Krusch, pp. 673–676; *Vita Aridii*, 1.6–7, pp. 583–584. The *Life of Aredius* is Merovingian and seventh-century (Hen 1995, pp. 191 n. 219 and 196). Krusch singled it out as the most useful of the earliest witnesses to *Vita Eligii*, whose exemplar must have been available to its author. Cf. James 1991 p. 104 n. 1, who calls it a Carolingian life; Heinzelmann 2001 pp. 84–85; Dailey 2015, pp. 22–23. Note that McNamara's translation in Head (Ed.) 2001, pp. 137–167, omits some of the passages discussed here; an earlier, more complete version of her translation is available online, retrieved June 7, 2016 from http://legacy.fordham.edu/halsall/basis/eligius.asp.

14. One of the two major alterations to the story, which is otherwise copied almost verbatim, occurs at this point in *Vita Aridii* 6, p. 583. Two long sentences are inserted here, which identify Nicetius of Trier as the confessor. He successfully urges Aredius to abandon secular society, decline the "*regalis palatii vanas superstitiones et indisciplinatas sociorum fabulas*," and submit to a monastic rule—precisely what Eligius did not do!

15. This is the other major departure from the original story in *Vita Aridii* 6–7, pp. 583–585: Aredius never asks for a sign, only that his penance be accepted in God's eyes. He gets one anyway—not oil on his head but instead a dove, which returns daily for thirty more days. Gregory of Tours, *Historiae* 10.29 is the source of the dove story, but he describes it taking place publicly in the church as a sign of Aredius being special. Like Eligius's experience, the *Vita Aridii* version takes place in his private chamber, known only because Aredius told about it in secret and is clearly tied to his confession to Nicetius.

16. While there is no doubt that Columbanian spirituality had an effect on Eligius, it is not clear at what point, or how much, tariffed penance and frequent confession were what influenced him. Later in the *Life*, in a digression from allegedly describing his own visit to Solignac, the author recalls Eligius visiting Luxeuil, where "you would see him" entering dejected and humble like a penitent, prostrating himself with great seriousness before each of the monks he encountered (*Vita Eligii* 1.21, p. 685; McNamara does not translate the passage). Similarly, Eligius once threw himself in front of the king, accused himself of lying because of an error in land assessment, and begged for either pardon or death (*Vita Eligii* 1.17, pp. 682–684).

17. On these enemies and Praeiectus's part in the larger politics surrounding "the regicide of 675," see Kreiner 2014, pp. 77–82; Fouracre and Gerberding 1994, pp. 254–270; Wood 1994, pp. 224–229. Praeiectus's episcopal career did not get off to an ideal start: see Fouracre and Gerberding 1994, p. 268.

Works Cited

Ancient Sources

Ambrose, *De paenitentia*. R. Gryson (ed. and trans.). (1971). *La pénitence*. SC 179. Paris: Les Éditions du CERF.

Caesarius of Arles, *Sermones*. M-J. Delage (ed. and trans.). (1986). *Sermons au peuple 3*. SC 330. Paris: Les Éditions du CERF.

Cassian, *Collationes*. M. Petschenig (ed.). (2004).CSEL 13. 2nd ed. Vienna: Österreichischen Akademie der Wissenschaften.

Cassian, *The Conferences*. B. Ramsey (trans.). (1997). *John Cassian: The Conferences*. Ancient Christian Writers 57. New York: Newman Press.

Eligii charta cessionis Solemniacensis. B. Krusch (ed.). (1902). MGH SRM 4 (pp. 743–749). Hanover: Hahn.

Eusebius Gallicanus, *Collectio homiliarum*. F. Glorie (ed.). (1970–1971). CCSL 101, 101A, 101B. Turnhout: Brepols.

Gregory of Tours, *Historiae*. B. Krusch and W. Levison (eds.). (1951). MGH SRM 1.1, rev. ed. Hanover: Hahn.

Gregory of Tours, *The History of the Franks*. L. Thorpe (trans.). (1974). *Gregory of Tours: The History of the Franks*. Baltimore: Penguin.

Head, T. (ed.). (2001). *Medieval Hagiography: An Anthology*. New York: Routledge.

James, E. (trans.). (1991). *Gregory of Tours: Life of the Fathers*. Liverpool: Liverpool University Press.

Jonas of Bobbio, *Vita Columbani*. B. Krusch (ed.). (1905). MGH SRG 37 (pp. 1–294). Hanover: Hahn.

Le Blant, E. (ed.). (1999). *Inscriptions chrétiennes de la Gaule antérieures au VIIIe siècle*, repr. ed. 2 vols. Hildesheim: Georg Olms.

The Life of Audoin, Bishop of Rouen. P. Fouracre and R. Gerberding (trans.). (1996). *Late Merovingian France: History and Hagiography, 640–720* (pp. 133–165). Manchester: Manchester University Press.

Life of St. Eligius of Noyon. J. A. McNamara (trans). (2001). In T. Head (ed.), *Medieval Hagiography: An Anthology* (pp. 137–167). New York: Routledge.

Mathisen, R. W. (trans.). (1999). *Ruricius of Limoges and Friends: A Collection of Letters from Visigothic Gaul*. Liverpool: Liverpool University Press.

McNeill, J. T., and Gamer, H. M. (trans.). (1990). *Medieval Handbooks of Penance: A Translation of the Principal "Libri Poenitentiales" and Selections from Related Documents*, repr. ed. New York: Columbia University Press.

Origen, *Homily on Leviticus* 2. M. Borret (ed. and trans.). (1981). *Homélies sur le Lévitique, Tome I (Homélies I–VII)*. SC 286. Paris: Les Éditions du CERF.

Palatine, Shepherd of Hermas. A. Vezzoni (trans.). (1994). *Il pastore di Erma: Versione Palatina con testo a fronte*. Il Nuovo melograno 13. Florence: Le lettere.

Passio Praeiecti, Recension B. L. d'Achery and J. Mabillon (eds.). (1669). *Acta sanctorum ordinis S. Benedicti in saeculorum classes distributa, Saeculum II* (pp. 645–651). Paris: Billaine.

Passio Praeiecti. B. Krusch (ed.). (1910). MGH SRM 5 (pp. 212–248). Hanover: Hahn.

Philo, *The Posterity and Exile of Cain*. F. H. Colson and G. H. Whitaker (trans.). (1929). *Philo II* (pp. 321–340). Loeb Classical Library 227. Cambridge, MA: Harvard University Press.

Plutarch, *On Compliancy*. P. H. De Lacy and B. Einarson (trans.). (1959). *Plutarch's Moralia VII* (pp. 42–89). Loeb Classical Library 405. Cambridge, MA: Harvard University Press.

Shepherd of Hermas. B. D. Ehrman (ed. and trans.). (2003). *The Apostolic Fathers II* (pp. 162–173). Loeb Classical Library 25. Cambridge, MA, London: Harvard University Press.

Sidonius Apollinaris, *Letters*. W. B. Anderson (ed. and trans.). (1965). *Sidonius Apollinaris, Letters 3–9*. Loeb Classical Library 420. Cambridge, MA: Harvard University Press.

The Suffering of Praejectus. P. Fouracre and R. Gerberding (trans.). (1996). *Late Merovingian France: History and Hagiography, 640–720* (pp. 254–300). Manchester: Manchester University Press.

Tertullian, *De paenitentia*. C. Munier (ed. and trans.). (1993). *La pénitence*. SC 394. Paris: Les Éditions du CERF.

Tertullian, *De pudicitia*. C. Munier (ed. and trans.). (1971). *La pudicité*. SC 179. Paris: Les Éditions du CERF.

Verba seniorum. J.-P. Migne (ed.). (1849). PL 73. Paris: Garnier.

Vita Aridii. B. Krusch (ed.). (1896). MGH SRM 3 (pp. 576–609). Hanover: Hahn.

Vita Audoini. W. Levison (ed.). (1910). MGH SRM 5 (pp. 536–567). Hanover: Hahn.

Vita Eligii. B. Krusch (ed.). (1902). MGH SRM 4 (pp. 663–741). Hanover: Hahn.

Vita Genovefae. B. Krusch (ed.). (1977). MGH SRM 3 (pp. 204–238). Hanover: Hahn.

Ward, B. (trans.). (2003). *The Desert Fathers: Sayings of the Early Christian Monks*. London: Penguin Books.

Modern Sources

Alciati, R. (2012). [Review of the book *Ruricio di Limoges: Lettere*, ed. M. Neri]. *Rivista di storia del cristianesimo* 9: 485–487.

Aubrun. (1981). *L'ancien diocèse de Limoges des origines au milieu du XIᵉ siècle*. Clermont-Ferrand: Institut d'études du Massif central.

Bailey, L. K. (2009). "'Our Own Most Severe Judges': The Power of Penance in the Eusebius Gallicanus Sermons." In A. Cain and N. Lenski (eds.), *The Power of Religion in Late Antiquity* (pp. 201–211). Farnham: Ashgate.

Bailey, L. K. (2010). *Christianity's Quiet Success: The Eusebius Gallicanus Sermon Collection and the Power of the Church in Late Antique Gaul*. Notre Dame, IN: University of Notre Dame Press.

Bailey, L. K. (2016). *The Religious Worlds of the Laity in Late Antique Gaul*. London: Bloomsbury.

Brennan, B. (1985). "'Episcopae': Bishops' Wives Viewed in Sixth-Century Gaul." *Church History* 54: 311–323.

Brown, P. (2013). *The Rise of Western Christendom: Triumph and Diversity, A.D. 200–1000*, rev. ed. Malden, MA: Wiley-Blackwell.

Brown, P. (2015). *The Ransom of the Soul: Afterlife and Wealth in Early Western Christianity*. Cambridge, MA: Harvard University Press.

Brown, W. C. (2011). *Violence in Medieval Europe*. Harlow: Longman.

Brox, N. (1991). *Der Hirt Des Hermas*. Göttingen: Vandenhoeck and Ruprecht, 1991.

Bullough, D. (1997). "The Career of Columbanus." In M. Lapidge (ed.), *Columbanus: Studies on the Latin Writings* (pp. 1–28). Studies in Celtic History 17. Woodbridge: Boydell .

Burns, J. and Jensen, R. (2014). *Christianity in Roman Africa: The Development of its Practices and Beliefs*. Grand Rapids, MI: Eerdmans.

Carroll, M. (2006). *Spirits of the Dead: Roman Funerary Commemoration in Western Europe*. Oxford: Oxford University Press.

Dailey, E. T. (2015). *Queens, Consorts, Concubines: Gregory of Tours and Women of the Merovingian Elite*. Leiden: Brill.

Dallen, J. (1986). *The Reconciling Community: The Rite of Penance*. New York: Pueblo.

de Jong, M. de. (1992). "Power and Humility in Carolingian Society: The Public Penance of Louis the Pious." *Early Medieval Europe* 1: 29–52.

de Jong, M. de. (2000). "Transformations of Penance." In F. Theuws and J. L. Nelson (eds.), *Rituals of Power: From Late Antiquity to the Early Middle Ages* (pp. 185–224). Leiden: Brill.

Diem, A. (2005). *Das monastische Experiment: die Rolle der Keuschheit bei der Entstehung des westlichen Klosterwesens*. Munster: LIT-Verlag.

Diem, A. (2007). "Monks, Kings, and the Transformation of Sanctity: Jonas of Bobbio and the End of the Holy Man." *Speculum* 82: 521–539.

Dunn, M. (2012). "Paradigms of Penance." *Journal of Medieval Monastic Studies* 1: 17–39.

Effros, B. (2002). *Creating Community with Food and Drink in Merovingian Gaul*. New York: Palgrave Macmillan.

Fouracre, P., and Gerberding, R. (1996). *Late Merovingian France: History and Hagiography, 640–720*. Manchester: Manchester University Press.

Fox, Y. (2014). *Power and Religion in Merovingian Gaul: Columbanian Monasticism and the Frankish Elites*. Cambridge, UK: Cambridge University Press.

Gaudemet, J. (1953). "La discipline pénitentielle en Gaule du IVe au VIIe siècle." *Revue de droit canonique* 3: 233–238.

Geltner, G. (2008). "*Detrusio*: Penal Cloistering in the Middle Ages." *Revue Bénédictine* 118, 89–108.

Godding, R. (2005). *Prêtres en Gaule mérovingienne*. Brussels: Société des Bollandistes.

Guyon, G. (1999). "L'héritage religieux du pardon dans la justice pénale de l'Ancien Droit." In J. Joreau-Dodinau, X. Rousseaux, and P. Texier (eds.), *Le pardon* (pp. 87–115). Limoges: Presses de l'Université de Limoges.

Handley, M. A. (2003). *Death, Society and Culture: Inscriptions and Epitaphs in Gaul and Spain, AD 300–750*. Oxford: Archaeopress.

Heinzelmann, M. (2001). *Gregory of Tours: History and Society in the Sixth Century*, trans. C. Carroll. Cambridge, UK: Cambridge University Press.

Heinzelmann, M. (2012). "Pouvoir et idéologie dans l'hagiographie mérovingienne." In E. Bozóky (ed.) *Hagiographie, idéologie et politique au Moyen Âge en Occident*, (pp. 37–58). Hagiologia 8. Turnhout: Brepols.

Helvétius, A.-M. (2012). "Hagiographie et formation politique des aristocrates dans le monde franc (VIIe–VIIIe siècles)." In E. Bozóky (ed.), *Hagiographie, idéologie et politique au Moyen Âge en Occident* (pp. 59–80). Hagiologia 8. Turnhout: Brepols.

Hen, Y. (1995). *Culture and Religion in Merovingian Gaul, A. D. 481–751*. Leiden: Brill.

Kidder, A. S. (2010). *Making Confession, Hearing Confession: A History of the Cure of Souls*. Collegeville, MN: Liturgical Press.

Kreiner, J. (2014). *The Social Life of Hagiography in the Merovingian Kingdom*. Cambridge: Cambridge University Press.

Labriolle, P. de. (1928). *The Life and Times of St. Ambrose*, trans. H. Wilson. St. Louis, MO: Herder.

Lambert, D. A. (2015). *How Repentance Became Biblical: Judaism, Christianity, and the Interpretation of Scripture*. New York: Oxford University Press.

Le Saint, W. P. (1959). *Treatises on Penance: On Penitence and on Purity*. Ancient Christian Writers 28. Westminster, MD: Newman Press.

Mathisen, R. W. (1993). *Roman Aristocrats in Barbarian Gaul: Strategies for Survival in an Age of Transition*. Austin: University of Texas Press.

Mateos Cruz, P. (1999). *La basílica de Santa Eulalia de Mérida: Arqueología y Urbanismo*. Madrid: Consejo Superior de Investigaciones Científicas.

Mazzini, I., and Lorenzini, E. (1981). "Il pastore di Erma: Due versioni o due antologie di versioni?" *Civiltà Classica e Cristiana* 2: 45–86.

McCune, J. (2008). "Rethinking the Pseudo-Eligius Sermon Collection." *Early Medieval Europe* 16: 445–476.

Meens, R. (1998). "The Frequency and Nature of Early Medieval Penance." In P. Biller and A. J. Minnis (eds.), *Handling Sin: Confession in the Middle Ages* (pp. 35–61). York: York Medieval Press.

Meens, R. (2014). *Penance in Medieval Europe, 600–1200.* Cambridge: Cambridge University Press.

Moreira, I. (2000). *Dreams, Visions, and Spiritual Authority in Merovingian Gaul.* Ithaca, NY: Cornell University Press.

Moreira, I. (2010). *Heaven's Purge: Purgatory in Late Antiquity.* New York: Oxford University Press.

Mortimer, R. C. (1939). *The Origins of Private Penance in the Western Church.* Oxford: Clarendon Press.

Palmer, J. T. (2014). *The Apocalypse in the Early Middle Ages.* Cambridge, UK: Cambridge University Press.

Poschmann, B. (1928). *Die abendländische Kirchenbusse im Ausgang des christlichen Altertums.* Munich: Kösel and Pustet.

Poschmann, B. (1964). *Penance and the Anointing of the Sick*, trans. F. Courtney. New York: Herder and Herder.

Price, R. (2004). "Informal Penance in Early Medieval Christendom." In K. Cooper and J. Gregory (eds.), *Retribution, Repentance, and Reconciliation* (pp. 29–38). Studies in Church History 40. Woodbridge: Boydell.

Raga, E. (2014). "L'influence chrétienne sur le modèle alimentaire classique: la question de l'alternance entre banquets, nutrition et jeûne." In M. Gaillard (ed.), *L'empreinte chrétienne en Gaule du IVᵉ au IXᵉ siècle* (pp. 61–87). Turnhout: Brepols.

Ramsey, B. (1997). *John Cassian: The Confessions.* Ancient Christian Writers 57. New York: Newman Press.

Rebillard, É. (2012). *Christians and Their Many Identities in Late Antiquity: North Africa, 200–450 CE.* Ithaca, NY: Cornell University Press.

Rebillard, É. (2016). "Everyday Christianity in Carthage at the Time of Tertullian." *Religion in the Roman Empire* 2: 91–102.

Rosenwein, B. (2006). *Emotional Communities in the Early Middle Ages.* Ithaca, NY: Cornell University Press.

Sessa, K. (2015). "Cleric." In C. M. Chin and M. Vidas (eds.), *Late Ancient Knowing: Explorations in Intellectual History* (pp. 218–239). Berkeley: University of California Press.

Stancliffe, C. (1997). "The Thirteen Sermons Attributed to Columbanus and the Question of Their Authorship." In M. Lapidge (ed.), *Columbanus: Studies on the Latin Writings* (pp. 93–202). Studies in Celtic History 17. Woodbridge: Boydell.

Stancliffe, C. (2011). "Columbanus's Monasticism and the Sources of His Inspiration: From Basil to the Master?" In F. Edmonds and P. Russell (eds.), *Tome: Studies in Medieval Celtic History and Law in Honour of Thomas Charles-Edwards* (pp. 17–28). Woodbridge: Boydell.

Stewart, C. (1998). *Cassian the Monk.* New York: Oxford University Press.

Stewart, C. (2015). "Another Cassian?" *Journal of Ecclesiastical History* 66: 372–376.

Tentler, T. N. (1977). *Sin and Confession on the Eve of the Reformation.* Princeton, NJ: Princeton University Press.

Tornau, C., and Cecconi, P. (2014). *The Shepherd of Hermas in Latin: Critical Edition of the Oldest Translation Vulgata.* Berlin: Walter de Gruyter.

Torrance, A. (2013). *Repentance in Late Antiquity: Eastern Asceticism and the Framing of the Christian Life, c. 400–650 CE*. Oxford: Oxford University Press.

Treffort, C. (1996). *L'Église carolingienne et la mort: christianisme, rites funéraires et pratiques commémoratives*. Lyon: Presses universitaires de Lyon.

Vives, D. J. (1969). *Inscripciones cristianas de la España romana y visigoda*. Barcelona: Consejo Superior de Investigaciones Científicas.

Vogel, C. (1952). *La discipline pénitentielle en Gaule des origines à la fin du VIIe siècle*. Paris: Letouzey et Ané.

Vogel, C. (1956). "La discipline pénitentielle en Gaule des origines au IXe siècle: Le dossier hagiographique." *Revue des Sciences Religieuses* 30: 1–26, 157–186.

Vogel, C. (1966). "La discipline pénitentielle dans les inscriptions paléochrétiennes." *Rivista di Archeologia Cristiana* 42: 317–325.

Vogel, C. (1992). "Penitence." In A. Di Berardino (ed.), *Encyclopedia of the Early Church* 2, trans. Adrian Walford (pp. 667–668). New York: Oxford University Press.

Waldron, H. N. (1976). *Expressions of Religious Conversion among Laymen Remaining within Secular Society in Gaul, 400–800 A.D.* (Unpublished doctoral dissertation). Columbus: Ohio State University.

Wood, I. (1981). "A Prelude to Columbanus: The Monastic Achievement in the Burgundian Territories." In H. B. Clarke and M. Brennan (eds.), *Columbanus and Merovingian Monasticism* (pp. 3–32). Oxford: BAR.

Wood, I. (1982). "The *Vita Columbani* and Merovingian Hagiography." *Peritia* 1: 63–80.

Wood, I. (1994). *The Merovingian Kingdoms, 450–751*. London: Longman.

CHAPTER 46

....

MEROVINGIAN
MEDITATIONS ON JESUS

....

LYNDA COON

Retrieving devotion to the human savior Jesus from the murky Merovingian past is a complex and seemingly impossible act of scholarly excavation. The stability imposed on the life of Jesus by the authoritative recounting of his earthly existence in the gospels exploded into extraordinary narrative and visual synapses in the Merovingian North. There, the divine intruded on the ordinary in spectacular ways. Nowhere is this spiritual invasion more apparent than in Merovingian understandings of the evangelical portrait of Jesus' passion, especially his torture, crucifixion, and resurrection. This final chapter of the *Oxford Handbook of the Merovingian World* explores the conversation on Jesus held between material and textual sources, where monumental works of sculpture extend salvific themes found in the lives of saints and the verses of poets. Merovingian meditations on Jesus are multivocal, reflecting the cross-cultural rhythms of a world open to and receptive of external influences, whether originating in classical or biblical texts, or hailing from Mediterranean or Northern lands, as the preceding essays have made abundantly clear.

This chapter posits that multimedia Merovingian sources played a game of theological "hide-and-seek," where Jesus' humanity had to be fished out of what at first glance might seem to be an ocean of divinity. In seamless fashion, the Merovingian cross metamorphosed into the human body, and human actors took on the attributes of the wood of salvation. These saintly players did so as part of an intricate dance between a remote, cosmological figure, Christ, and a suffering human savior, Jesus. Christian audiences interrogated the distance between the human and the divine in both works of art and hagiography, which themselves were influenced by innovations in Merovingian hymnody and liturgical poetry. As a part of this theological strategy of collapsing the chasm between humanity and the deity, Merovingian Christians were invited to meditate on the role of their own bodies in the march toward salvation. Rather than the distant deity depicted in much scholarship on Merovingian Christianity, Jesus was made accessible to his followers through meditation and ascetic acts; Christ was incorporeal but could be embodied again and again through contemplation and heroic self-denial.

In order to prove this hypothesis on the Merovingian body and the embodied savior, three works of sculpture produced during the early Middle Ages will serve as sounding boards for Jesus' earthly ministry as enacted by human players: the crucified savior featured on the seventh-century Moselkern Stele; the eighth-century Hypogée des Dunes's sculpted relief of the two thieves crucified along with Jesus; and the so-called Niederdollendorf "Christ," carved most likely in the seventh century.[1] Saintly actors, such as Radegund of Poitiers (d. 587), whose provocative story appears earlier (see James, Chapter 11, this volume), will animate three themes expressed in the sculpted sources, respectively: (1) absence, (2) torture, and (3) light. These three subjects, light, torture, and absence, all point to strategies of integrating the realm of humanity within the celestial spheres, and each motif tracks different styles of meditating on Merovingian Jesus.

Jesus the Absent Deity

While well known in academic circles dedicated to the archaeology of the Merovingian world, the Moselkern Stele (Fig. 46.1) exists outside of the canon of art history and even to one side of the history of Christianity (on stone epigraphy, see Handley, Chapter 26, this volume). The stele originated in a Rhineland sector of Merovingian lands where Christian funerary art found its place alongside Roman tombs, baths, aqueducts, and urban fortifications (on architecture, see Chevalier, Chapter 30, this volume). The sculpture's imagery channels classical reliefs and their attention to the human form, albeit in a rudimentary way, as well as the monumental Christian carvings of early medieval Ireland (Elbern 1955, p. 191). Originally, the verticality of this tapered stone would have been enhanced by a no longer extant base (Ristow 2007, p. 177). Carved out of basalt lava rock, this singular artifact of the Merovingian world presents its viewers with a striking recreation of the crucifixion of Jesus. The lava stone is divided into two parts. In the lower zone, a diagonal cross framed by a square is decorated with incised lines. These lines draw the eye toward a smaller cross uniting the four arms of the larger, diagonal cross in the center of the lower register. This central, smaller cross is anthropomorphic in the sense that a human body casts a ghostly presence on its contours because the vertical and horizontal arms bring to mind the physical frame of the dying savior. In the second, higher zone, an amazing representation of Merovingian Jesus emerges out of hewed stone, his body replicating the silhouette of the smaller, anthropomorphic cross situated at the center of the diagonal cross below. Jesus' humanity clearly can be seen in the Moselkern Stele: imposing head, thick hair and beard, eyes, nose, mouth, arms, and outsized hands. In comparison to Jesus' hands, his legs are truncated with feet set at impossibly perpendicular angles. The savior stands on an incised line forming the top layer of the foursquare frame below. The sculptor(s) emphasized Jesus' physicality by electing not to render a background to the cross. Instead, the artist(s) chose to eliminate

FIGURE 46.1. Front side, Moselkern Stele (seventh century), Rheinisches LandesMuseum, Bonn, Germany. Courtesy of photographer Jürgen Vogel, LVR-LandesMuseum Bonn.

the rock surrounding the savior's torso and legs, thereby giving the audience a more intense view of the sacred body. At the same time, body and cross collapse into one in front of the viewers' eyes.

On the reverse side of the stele (Fig. 46.2), Jesus' body vanishes altogether to give way to more crosses, a diagonal cross at the bottom of the sculpture corresponding to the one on the other side, mounted by a cross with equidistant arms similar to the cross supporting Jesus' crucified body on the flip-side (Berg 2005, p. 151). Instead of a human head at the top, the reverse side of the stele sports a small cross inside of a circle, an engraving nevertheless reminiscent of the savior's head on the other side. On the flanks of the monument, more crosses appear matching the shape of the cross of the crucifixion, and hence the human body (Peers 2004, p. 13), which is at center stage in the stele. Human physicality reverberates throughout the stone by means of these anthropomorphic crosses, which are undoubtedly apotropaic in nature and serve to protect the savior's body. In a similar fashion, Merovingian corpses found solace in the crosses placed in their mouths or on their foreheads or even sewn into their funerary garments (Effros 2002a, p. 158; Schutz 2001, pp. 148–149). Tomb slabs often had multiple carved crosses at the level of the skull of the corpse, just as the Moselkern Jesus wears defensive crosses around his head (Effros 2002a, p. 107).

FIGURE 46.2. Reverse side, Moselkern Stele (seventh century), Rheinisches LandesMuseum, Bonn, Germany. Courtesy of photographer Jürgen Vogel, LVR-LandesMuseum Bonn.

In the Moselkern Stele, Jesus' body is there but not there. Visible and yet incompletely rendered, as if the savior is struggling to pull his human form out of the funerary rock, or perhaps the cross itself is dangerously swallowing up his humanity. Conversely, the godhead commands this monument because Christ's head exists on a cosmic scale, dominating the rockwork and projecting a stony stare at the passerby. Moreover, crosses pop out from the body of the crucified god, protruding from the top of his cranium and bursting out of his ears, an effect directing the viewers' attention to the mysteries of the Trinity. With their sharp angles, Jesus' shoulders and arms unnaturally shape the top register of the foursquare form. Both tiers, the lower and upper, are made transparent through excising the stone to produce eight empty spaces. In later illuminated manuscripts, angels and human spectators of the crucifixion take up residence in the stonework's vacant zones: the top register being reserved for celestial beings, such as angels; the bottom register housing spectators of the crucifixion, including the Virgin Mary and the evangelist John. Jesus' squared-off, rigid upper-body attracts the viewers' gaze to his enormous hands with their elongated fingers grasping at either cross issuing out of the savior's mid-zone or cross-shaped hilts of daggers guarding the numinous body. On his chest, the faint trace of yet another cross can be detected.

The Moselkern Stele presents a human figure overwhelmed by the stark geometry of the cross and by the cosmic proportions of a disembodied god. At the same time, the stele demonstrates how the human body can easily transmute into the cross and vice-versa. Therefore, what may not at first seem to be a body is actually a subtle rendering of the human form. Much of the scholarship on this perplexing monument of the Merovingian age resists seeing the human side of Jesus in the stone, favoring instead reading the cosmological godhead onto the carved rock. For archaeologists and histori-ans, the Moselkern figure is Christ—triumphant, militaristic, distant, emotionless, upright, and heroic. The strong geometry of the sculpture sets a celestial backdrop for this deity: the four cardinal directions speak to the four-cornered nature of the universe moored to a precise spot in a Christian cemetery in the Rhineland-Palatinate region of modern-day Germany. There is no room in the stele for religious intimacy between the crucified god of the Moselkern and his spectators, or so scholars have speculated. According to this line of scholarly thinking, the god depicted here is not a suffering savior exhibiting a wounded, human body nailed to a cross.

Reading the Moselkern Christ within the context of a more famous work of early medieval art, the figure of John the Evangelist from the *Book of Kells* (ca. 800), helps to extract a subtle Merovingian devotion to the human Jesus. While the two works of art are separated by time and place, their ability to spark spiritual intimacy through an incompletely rendered human form of Jesus is analogous. In the Kells visualization of John, the evangelist's body is the focal point of a luxurious manuscript page resplendent with geometrical forms and vivid hues (Fig. 46.3). John is depicted as a scribe wielding his gospel book in his left hand and grasping a stylus in his right while occupying a throne-like structure. His legs are awkwardly spread apart so that his body emulates the throne and his feet appear pedestal-like. John's garments are provocatively ren-dered, swirling about his thighs and forming a womb-like opening into the interior spaces of the body. Startlingly, this uterine gap into the male body sits above a small orifice situated in between the apostle's two splayed feet. In this fine example of a "world-womb mandala," that is, a map-like space inviting its observer to enter into its frame and meditate on the wounded body of Jesus, John serves as a conduit for the savior's story, which is written onto the pages of the gospel book the evangelist holds out to entice the viewer's eye. John's humanity operates as a portal to the savior-body, which is itself hidden behind the barrier created by the elaborate—and distracting—border surrounding the evangelist. Meditating on the evangelist's body sharpens the contemplative focus of the spectator thereby granting access to the mysteries of the crucifixion.

This exquisite frame attracts the human eye while concealing the crucified Jesus, whose feet, hands, and head pop out from the four stunted arms of the cross, which are delineated by the four beautiful crosses decorated with geometric designs. Importantly, the choice, fleshly parts of the savior-body are left for the evangelist to occupy. Jesus' feet echo those of John above—they shoot out from underneath the intricate cross which is pushing the eye up toward the orifice-like decoration situated in between the apostle's

FIGURE 46.3. Evangelist John, *Book of Kells*, fol. 291v (early ninth century), Trinity College Dublin. Courtesy of The Board of Trinity College Dublin. Image(s) may not be further reproduced from software.

spread legs. Jesus' hands with their clenched fingers obscure the puncture wounds of the crucifixion, and his head, now damaged beyond recognition, lodges in the top, heavenly register. The right hand displays faint traces of a red rod. John's head is encircled by one of the most spectacular halos in early medieval art—perhaps representing a cosmic map of the Holy Sepulcher in Jerusalem (Meehan 2012, p. 131). By hiding Jesus' body, apart from his feet, hands, and head, the artist is actually training the audience to zoom in more on what is invisible to the eye. Thus, the crucified torso is absent here only to be regained through the art of meditation, prompting Christian viewers to be active spectators of the crucifixion and puncture the divide between early medieval time and biblical time, and to do so through the medium of the human body of the gospel writer, who pens the story of the passion.

In a number of ways, the Moselkern Stele (Fig. 46.1) anticipates this tension in insular art between visibility and invisibility, bounded and porous, artistic object and human observer, disembodied god and embodied worshipper. The Kells manuscript induces its observer to move through the parchment page by means of the gateway formed in the evangelist's body. Similarly, the Moselkern Stele invites the pious to peer through its rocky frame to an unseen reality beyond indicated by the light streaming through the voids in the stone. In the stele, the body of Jesus is emergent, yet strained, yoked to the strong geometry of the cross, which itself is evocative of the human form as the little, anthropomorphic crosses scattered throughout the front, the sides, and the back of the monument clarify. The Moselkern Jesus is slippery—sliding back and forth between assuming the guise of the cross and taking on human flesh. Because this fascinating example of Merovingian Jesus exists in the realm of freestanding, three-dimensional art, the audience of the stele could assume the role of biblical spectators of the crucifixion, filling in for the missing Apostle John, the Virgin Mary, or the two Roman soldiers at the foot of the cross. Merovingian Christians were given privileged access to the body of the human savior carved into the top register, thereby telescoping the distance between the biblical world and the Frankish age. Seventh-century spectators would have seen each other through the stele, their bodies appearing in the geometrical cutouts, not as whole bodies but as bodies in parts on account of the rocky frame.

In the Moselkern Stele, the human Jesus is a savior of absence, whose embodiment in the rock must be puzzled out by the meditative viewer, who is also expected to be an active participant in the saving agency of the cross and a bearer of the second person of the Trinity. Merovingian churchman and hagiographer, Gregory of Tours (d. 594), understood well the role of the Christian body in the promulgation of the culture of the cross. In his little book on the ascetic fathers, Gregory advises his audience to channel continuously the wisdom of the apostle Paul and to think about how they themselves must "bear about in the body the dying of the Lord Jesus, that the life also of Jesus might be made manifest in your mortal body" (2 Corinthians 4.10).[2] The Rhineland stele represents a triangulation among cosmic deity (Christ), suffering savior (Jesus), and Merovingian spectator, whose contemplation of the human form carved into the rock would serve as a reminder of the role of their own bodies as material witnesses to the passion of Jesus. This interactive artifact from the Merovingian age gestures toward a narrative-like rendition of the crucifixion but never fills in the details according to the text. The meaning remains open-ended, operating somewhere between art as a system of symbolic signs and art as a tool for the contemporary viewers to transcend the material world.

JESUS THE TORTURED DEITY

The eighth-century Hypogée des Dunes in Poitiers (Vienne) has survived into the present day (McClendon 2005, p. 46; Crook 2000, p. 61; see Chevalier, Chapter 30, this volume). This crypt finds its inspiration in the Mediterranean world of saints' tombs and is similar to the Merovingian "funerary caves" described by Gregory of Tours (Sapin 2003, pp. 303–304). Its subterranean spaces preserve part of a sculpted Merovingian crucifixion (Heitz 1975, pp. 396–398; Grabar 1974, p. 10). Unfortunately, the top section of the sculpture, which most likely exhibited the body of the crucified Jesus, is absent. Yet the two men described in the gospels as being executed along with the savior (Mark 15.27; Matthew 27.38; Luke 23.32; John 19.18) can still be seen occupying what appears to have been the base of a monumental cross (Fig. 46.4). Whereas the Moselkern Stele was probably intended to be an outdoor memorial located in a public cemetery in the Rhineland, the sculpted crucifixion now graces the cave-like crypt built for Abbot Mellobaudes in the Gallo-Roman region of the Merovingian world. At Poitiers, Merovingian Jesus has moved from the Rhineland sphere of the collective dead and the apotropaic powers of the cross to become part of the funerary ambitions of one elite churchman. Mellobaudes may have envisioned his final resting place as a Merovingian equivalent to Christ's Holy Sepulcher in Jerusalem, making the imagery of the passion and the crucifixion even more salient here (Morris 2005, p. 120; Wood 1999, p. 39). How precisely the two thieves came to join Mellobaudes's funerary splendor is not certain, however. Given that the thieves were once part of a larger, monumental cross of the crucifixion, the scale of the full sculpture seems unlikely for such a small crypt. Yet formal stylistic analysis of the iconography securely dates the base—and its thieves—to the eighth century. It may be the case that the two thieves were originally part of Mellobaudes's sepulchral ensemble, but their location was not in the tomb, and they were moved into the Hypogée at a later date (Grabar 1974, pp. 12, 15).

The sculpted figures of the two thieves intensify this study of Merovingian Jesus because they offer a narrative space, albeit an idiosyncratic one, from which to evaluate the human savior. Unlike the crucifixion portrayed in the Moselkern Stele, which is largely free-floating and lacks the presence of witnesses to Jesus' suffering, the Hypogée des Dunes features two biblical figures tethered to crosses with their hands bound behind their backs and exhibited like trophies of war from ancient statuary. Perhaps they were imagined as *spolia* exhibited in the savior's triumphant march into the heavens through the highway of the cross. In between the two captives is a classical column in all probability referencing the pillar associated with Jesus' scourging in the gospels.

FIGURE 46.4. Two Thieves Crucified along with Christ, Hypogée des Dunes (8th century), collection des Musées de la Ville de Poitiers et de la Société des Antiquaires de l'Ouest; Musées de Poitiers/Christian Vignaud.

Here, the body of Jesus is absent too. Beholders did not see Jesus' beaten body tethered to the column; the flagellation is a very rare subject for art before the Carolingian period. From the sides of each criminal emerges the arms of his cross, thereby visually stressing the torsos of the bound men. These cross-arms find their terminus in the column of Jesus' flogging, hence yoking the two thieves to this instrument of the passion. The bottom part of each cross can be seen surrounding the feet of the two victims. The height of the cross springs from the top of the men's heads but does so without betraying the remainder of its vertical arm. In fact, the apex of these two crosses resembles the column base of the pillar of scourging, which is positioned in between the feet of the two men. This visual strategy accentuates the thieves' function as Atlas figures holding up the crucified body above (now missing). As such, their position in the sculpture mimics that of the central column, especially considering that columns often function as analogues for the human body, in this instance, the tortured body of Jesus.

The crosses the two thieves inhabit are akin to the anthropomorphic ones displayed on the Moselkern Stele. In contrast to the Jesus of the Moselkern, whose body struggles to free itself from the rock, the two thieves of Poitiers have clearly defined torsos, limbs, and heads. Both are girded with short loincloths. Their bellybuttons are prominent, reminding viewers of the mystery of human birth and its accompanying mortality. The awkward position of their feet, thrusting outwards and pointing down, calls attention to the holes made by the nails of crucifixion now offered up for the viewers' meditation and presumably echoed in the crucified body of Jesus above. Their bondage-like pose recalls the penal systems of the Merovingian world with their public display of shackled prisoners.[3] The brigands' elongated faces and striated apparel resonate with other works of early medieval art, most notably the sculpted figures decorating the eighth-century Ratchis's altar at Cividale (Grabar 1974, pp. 12–13). These Atlas figures holding up the dying victim above them anticipate manuscript illuminations of the Carolingian era (Fig. 46.5), where the two thieves turn their gazes upward toward the body of Jesus as if to take in the spectacle of the crucifixion while they themselves are being crucified (Kupfer 2011, pp. 134–135; Elbern 1961, pp. 153, 158–159).

The sculpture's emphasis on the pillar of Jesus' passion is unexpected. The bodies of the two thieves serve to frame the column, which then functions as the focal point of the ensemble. The column is the most unswerving support for the cross directly above it; the two Atlas-thieves only bear the ground overhead on which the crucifixion was staged. Because the classical column crosses over into the upper register, visually it would transform itself into the wood of the cross. The scourging pillar, which was reproduced in

FIGURE 46.5. Crucifixion of Christ, *Breton Gospel Book* (ninth or tenth century), Ms. Laud. Lat. 26, fol. 9v, Bodleian Library, Oxford, England. Courtesy of the Bodleian Library.

artistic and textual ways, was an object of meditation in the later Middle Ages, as scholars have noted. Less work, however, has been done on early medieval instruments of the passion (*arma Christi*), because the early Middle Ages is an epoch known more for its distant, terrifying Christ-figure than the bloody victim of a Roman-style execution (Edsall 2014).

Interest in the column can be found in Merovingian texts produced in the vicinity of the Hypogée des Dunes. A frequent pilgrim to Poitiers, Gregory of Tours, confirms this fact. In his Glory of the Martyrs, Gregory offers a verbal vision of the relics of the passion, the *arma Christi*: lance, column, crown of thorns, sponge, Jesus' loincloth. Two objects merit special attention here: the pillar and the crown of thorns. In terms of the pillar, Gregory informs his audience that the column is the site where Jesus was whipped in Jerusalem. Nowadays, Gregory adds, the faithful in that holy city commemorate the assault against the savior-body by tying cords that they themselves have woven around the pillar of the passion (note the rope molding below the capital on the column featured in the Hypogée crucifixion). These cords then miraculously soak up the power of Jesus' body and enact cures once they have been detached from the column. Similarly, the crown of thorns, a material reminder that Jesus' head was punctured in addition to his hands and feet, would die and then green up each day, an aid to memory for the verdant power of the passion (Peers 2012, pp. 980–981). Gregory also meditates on the holes drilled into Jesus' flesh by the nails of the crucifixion, paying special attention to the savior's feet, the manner of their piercing, and how precisely they were attached to the cross.[4] Merovingian poet Venantius Fortunatus (d. 609) put the wounded body of the human savior into Latin verse, asking his refined audience of secular and spiritual potentates, male and female, to contemplate the holes in Jesus' hands, the bloody nails, the penetrating spear, the pierced feet, and the fleshy, dying body hung on the cross (van Tongeren 2000, pp. 243–244, 247–248). The poetry itself was designed to conjure up vividly for Merovingian audiences the gore of the cross and to instill pathos in listeners of Fortunatus's verse. The now absent image of Merovingian Jesus on the cross at the Hypogée des Dunes came into being as a sculpted extension of these literary *arma Christi*, such as the ones authored by Gregory of Tours and Venantius Fortunatus, with their meditative focus on the objects of Jesus' torture and the savior's human body in pain.

CHRIST THE LIGHT-BEARING DEITY

The final sculpture under examination is perhaps the most perplexing of the three. Like the Moselkern monument, the late seventh-century Niederdollendorf Stele originates in the Rhineland in the vicinity of modern-day Bonn and in all probability was designed for a mass graveyard. The stele has been the object of much speculation by archaeologists and historians of Merovingian mortuary culture, especially in terms of its religious origins. The front and reverse of the stone present equally compelling images: on one

FIGURE 46.6. Front side, Niederdollendorf Stele (late seventh century), Rheinisches LandesMuseum, Bonn, Germany. Photograph courtesy A. Thünker DGPh, LVR-LandesMuseum Bonn.

side (Fig. 46.7), a bearded warrior, most likely the dead man in the tomb, is combing his hair, a symbol of virility and free status, while firmly grasping an intimidating sword with his left hand (Halsall 2010, p. 352; Sarti 2013, p. 256). Combs were common mortuary objects in the Merovingian world, and swords have been found scattered among the graves in Frankish lands (Effros 2002a, p. 129; Schutz 2001, pp. 155–168). The deceased's upper body is framed by two snapping serpentine creatures, one attacking his left shoulder and the other gnawing on the right hand holding the comb. A third snake bites at the hilt of the man's sword. The serpents direct the eye of the viewer toward the ritual objects found buried with the Merovingian dead—comb, sword, and maybe even the armor decorating the upper-body. The curved body of the two-headed serpent creates an unusual reptilian halo for the deceased. More snakes adorn the flanks of the stele, mirroring the apotropaic crosses on the Moselkern stele. Archaeologists have identified the flask positioned to the warrior's right as an eastern type carried by Christian pilgrims, possibly another mortuary piece (Schutz 2001, p. 179). On the reverse side of the stele is a splendid rendition of a light-bearing figure, presumably Christ (Fig. 46.6). As a product of multivocal cultures along the Rhine and extending down to Rome, the Niederdollendorf "Christ" can be interpreted in a number of ways, including

FIGURE 46.7. Reverse side, Niederdollendorf Stele (late seventh century), Rheinisches LandesMuseum, Bonn, Germany. Courtesy of photographer A. Thünker DGPh, LVR-LandesMuseum Bonn.

identifying the figure as a solar Christ indebted to classicizing Mediterranean artistic forms but strongly embedded in the material culture of the Merovingian grave.

The representation of Christ as a solar deity has been the subject of much scholarly debate in art history circles. Most famously, the third-century mosaic located in the mausoleum of the Julii family in the Vatican necropolis in Rome contains a brilliant depiction of an Apollo-like figure with rays of sunlight streaming from his head while riding a cosmic chariot drawn by impressive horses (Fig. 46.8). Art historians and archaeologists have identified this celestial charioteer as Christ because of the mosaic's location in a Christian mausoleum and on account of a longstanding iconography linking the circuit run by the chariot in the games to the cosmic course of the universe with charioteer as celestial driver, a motif deployed in late ancient Christian circles (Dunbabin 1982; Bergmann 2008; Latham 2016). The cosmological associations with chariot-racing and charioteers were known in Germania (Fig. 46.9), as the floor mosaic from a Roman villa at Bingen (circa 300 CE) and the so-called Cologne Circus Bowl (circa 340–360 CE; Fig. 46.10/46.10A) indicate (Fraser 1964). Here, charioteers assume the guise of sun gods and horse-drawn chariots run the cosmic race, such as the one detailed by Christian writer Tertullian of Carthage (d. 240). Tertullian mapped onto the universe

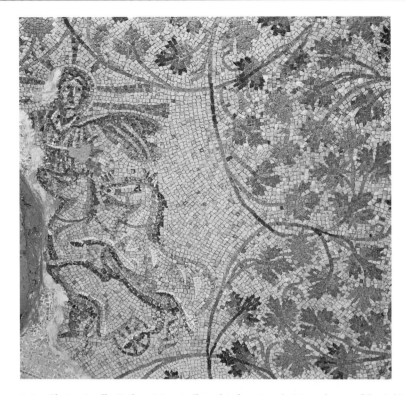

FIGURE 46.8. *Christ-Apollo* Ceiling Mosaic (late third century), Mausoleum of the Julii, Vatican Necropolis, Rome. Courtesy of Scala/Art Resource.

the attributes of the Roman circus, from the number of starting gates, horses pulling the chariots, laps run, and so forth. Running the circuit in a cosmic race signaled life eternal and fame following resurrection.[5]

The Niederdollendorf Christ is not running the race or commanding a cosmic chariot, but he shows attributes of the late ancient sun deity, *Sol Invictus*, or the "Unconquerable Sun." In fact, this solar "Christ" flamboyantly bursts onto the funerary slab. His head emits sunrays creating a solar nimbus (Heitz 1987, p. 120); his right hand grasps a spear in keeping with the militarism of the imperial sun cult, with its emphasis on celestial conquest, and creating a bellicose dialogue with the warrior figure on the reserve side of the stone. Christ's chest boasts a sun disk as a pectoral, heightening the stele's association with the solar deity. Rays of sunlight emanate from Christ's upper torso where the sun disk can clearly be discerned; their diagonal nature points back to this circular object lodged in Christ's breast. Like the crucified figure on the Moselkern Stele, the Niederdollendorf Christ has unnaturally squared-off shoulders and enormous hands. Rudimentarily engraved into the rock are the savior's eyes, nose, and a mouth. The Sol-Christ figure appears to be standing between two mountains, where he takes up a threshold position between the land of the living and the land of the dead, with the rising sun glowing behind him. The edges of the mountains form part of a bi-fold

FIGURE 46.9. Floor mosaic from a Roman villa at Bingen (fourth century), Rheinisches LandesMuseum, Bonn, Germany. Courtesy of photographer Jürgen Vogel, LVR-LandesMuseum Bonn.

mandorla, or a diamond-shaped aureole of light surrounding this cosmic figure and marking him off as a salvific force.[6] The bi-fold mandorla was a signature Merovingian artistic style, one exhibited in Carolingian copies of no longer extant manuscripts (Fig. 46.11). For example, in Venantius Fortunatus's figural poems on the cross (Ernst 1991, pp. 149–157), the vertical and horizontal bars of the cross are surrounded by a bi-fold mandorla very much like the one framing the Niederdollendorf Christ (Kessler 2007,

FIGURE 46.10/46.10A. Cologne Circus Bowl (late fourth century), Römisch-Germanisches Museum, Köln. Courtesy of the Römisch-Germanisches Museum, Köln, photographer Mario Carrieri.

pp. 145–146). In the stele, the strips of woven earth beneath Christ's feet are similar to Merovingian sarcophagus covers, which in certain parts of the kingdoms were decorated with sunbursts. The strigilated lines on certain slabs call to mind the sun-god Jesus in the linearity of their design but the patterns are curvilinear, not straight (Fig. 46.12). Underneath the slab-like strips are chevrons—geometric forms also inscribed on Merovingian gravestones. The slab-like strips may also form a serpentine figure directly underneath Sol-Christ, a theme also in keeping with apocalyptic imagery. With the presence of the shining corona, the paradisal horizon, and the ruptured earth's crust, this stele may well depict judgment day with a triumphantly resurrected, militaristic Christ bursting open the earth surrounding the graves of the righteous, such as the one inhabited by the upper-class soldier depicted on the other side. Like the flagellation, the last judgment is an extremely rare Western iconography before the high Middle Ages (e.g., Romanesque tympana) but is slightly more common in Byzantine art.

FIGURE 46.10A. Artistic rendering of the iconography of the Cologne Circus Bowl, Römisch-Germanisches Museum, Köln. Artist Helga Stöcker.

Comparing the sculptured figures from Moselkern and Poitiers with the Niederdollendorf Christ forces viewers to confront the Dark Age deity as he moved across different social and cultural settings, from the Rhineland to the Gallo-Roman heartland. These sculptures highlight the importance of sanctifying a variety of spaces with Jesus imagery, whether the savior inhabited a public cemetery or a private memorial. While the first two artistic works surveyed above stress the crucifixion and its evangelical

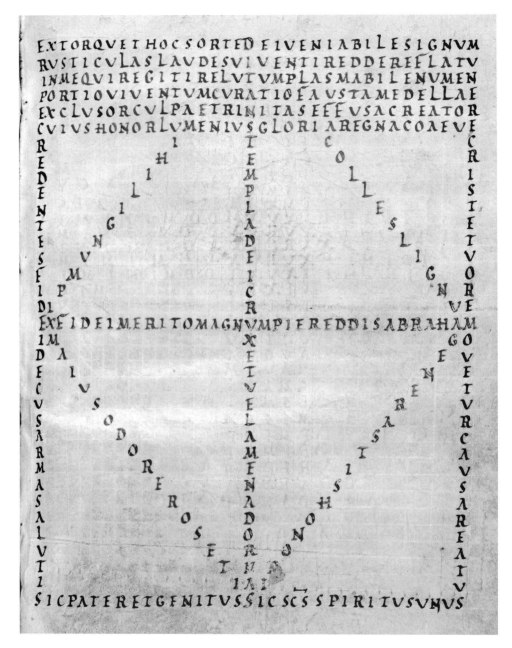

FIGURE 46.11. Venantius Fortunatus, *Carmen* 2.5 (tenth century), Stiftsbibliothek, Saint Gall, Switzerland, Cod. Sang. 196, p. 39. Courtesy of the Stiftsbibliothek.

FIGURE 46.12. Merovingian Sarcophagi, Baptistery of Saint-Jean, Poitiers, France. Courtesy of photographer Kim Sexton, Fay Jones School of Architecture and Design, University of Arkansas.

roots, the third sculpture takes the audience far away from the narrative rhythms of the gospels and allows the Niederdollendorf Christ to stand alone without a secure biblical tether. Hence, it is extremely difficult to interpret the religious setting of this singular artwork that has come down to us from the seventh century.

Scholars often highlight the militarism of the Niederdollendorf Stele, with its armed warrior on one side and spear-bearing cosmic figure on the other. While the martial reading of this stele is convincing, equally important is the monument's emphasis on light. Sunbursts were related to the cross of the crucifixion in the funerary world of the Merovingians (Schutz 2001, p. 149). The rays of light emanating from the Niederdollendorf Christ, as well as the sun disk bedecking his chest, may very well point to both the resurrection, which seems obvious, and the crucifixion, a less evident interpretation. The attention to the savior's chest is shared in Venantius Fortunatus's acrostic poem on the little sign (*signaculum*) of the cross, in which later Carolingian manuscript copies, most likely following the Merovingian originals, draw the viewer's eye toward the chest zone by setting it off in a different color (Fig. 46.13). Textual sources from the Merovingian era also help elucidate this mysterious image of the solar Christ. In his *Glory of the Confessors*, Gregory of Tours bequeaths to posterity a saint's life in which Merovingian tombs are the stars of the narrative rather than human actors. In fact, these theatrical tombs play out a scene from the gospel of Matthew (27.52–53), where Jesus breathes his last breath on the cross, causing the earth to shake and the ground to split wide open, a theophany liberating the Christian dead from the grave. Matthew adds that after Jesus' resurrection, revived corpses walked the earth, entered Jerusalem, and were seen by the

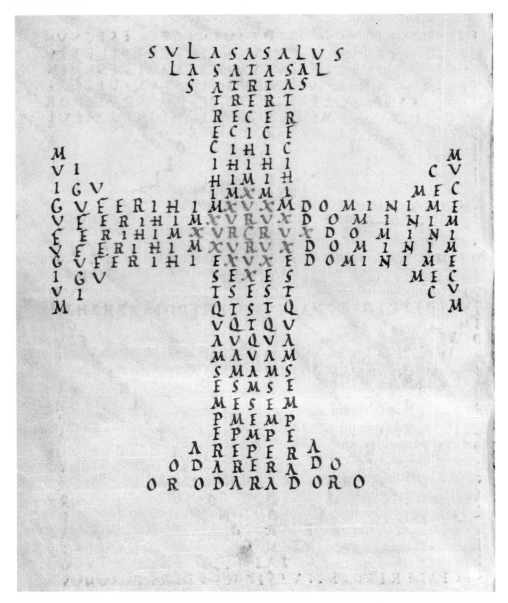

FIGURE 46.13. Venantius Fortunatus, *Carmen* 2.4 (10th century), Stiftsbibliothek, Saint Gall, Switzerland, Cod. Sang. 196, p. 40. Courtesy of the Stiftsbibliothek.

inhabitants of the holy city. In Gregory of Tours's retelling of this arresting and visually lush passage from the gospels, Merovingian lands transmute into biblical time and space, and this metamorphosis hinges on the presence of an unseen crucified savior. Gregory reports that in the vicinity of the village of Aire-sur-l'Adour in the Aquitaine, an extraordinary incident occurred. One after another, tombs began to thrust themselves up from the subterranean world of the crypt, bursting through the hard pavement until they came into full view of the congregation above ground. Gregory's comment on these kinetic tombs is straightforward: the parade of sepulchers erupting onto the ground from below reminds the faithful of the inevitability of the resurrection of the pure body, which "must not be given to the worm or to dying, but who must be made equal to the bright light of the sun and who must be glorified by their resemblance to the body of the Lord."[7]

Gregory of Tours's text animates for his audience the crucifixion/resurrection passages from the gospel of Matthew. In so doing, the bishop of Tours offers a perfect verbal platform from which to reconsider the meaning of the Niederdollendorf Christ. All the actors in the gospel account and Gregory's rendition of it are inscribed on the funerary rock: the tombs (chevrons), the worms (the prophylactic serpents), the dead (nobleman), the reactivation of corpses represented by the resurrected Christ, and the "bright light of the sun," itself a circumlocution for the cross of the crucifixion. Jesus' crucified body haunts the triumphant image of the solar Christ carved on the stele. It is the power of his cross—and by extension the human savior's final cry out from it—that activates the tombs of the Merovingian dead. And yet this activation occurs at the crossroads of multiple cultures and religions, for Christ as solar deity had the power to appeal to the liminal spaces occupied by the mixed-religious identities of the early medieval North.

SAINTLY ANIMATIONS

The second half of this chapter moves the reader from the realm of the dead to human actors who also embody the cross through their saintly performances. Three themes have thus far united this study of Merovingian Jesus: absence (the crucifixion of the Moselkern Stele); torture (the two thieves of the Hypogée des Dunes); and light (the Christ of the Niederdollendorf Stele). A saintly performer, Radegund of Poitiers, will further animate the three sculpted works discussed above. This animation will be centered on the motifs of light, torture, and absence, and on how they reverberate from artistic monuments to hagiographical narratives. Radegund's disturbing biography has been dealt with earlier in this volume.[8] A few details from her life suffice to set the stage for how the saint *performs* the second person of the Trinity by slipping back and forth between being a human player in the story of salvation and assuming the nature of the cross of the crucifixion in provocative ways.

Radegund's life exists as a series of theatrical vignettes, crafted by male and female voices, and put into writing through hagiographical and poetic styles. She was an aristocratic figure of Thuringian ancestry who became part of the plunder of battle after a major defeat of her royal house by Merovingian warlords. A captive-bride to a Merovingian king, Chlotar, Radegund fled her royal marriage to take up the life of self-abnegation, eventually founding an important women's monastery in Poitiers devoted to the *Rule* written by Gallo-Roman churchman, Caesarius of Arles (Klingshirn 1994). The saintly story comes down to us in two hagiographical accounts, one written by Radegund's male confidant, the poet Venantius Fortunatus (circa 587), and the other by a member of her own ascetic community at Poitiers, the nun Baudonivia (circa 600). The male-authored text foregrounds the human body in voyeuristic ways; its female-counterpart pinpoints Radegund's saintly story on the ancient desert theme of the "focused mind" (*mens intenta*), an asomatic state of spellbound contemplation in which the most disciplined ascetics transcend the body and exert absolute control over it (Kreiner 2014, p. 117).

For modern-day scholars, the differences between the two saints' lives have often been stressed, especially from the perspective of gender history (on gender, see Halsall, Chapter 8, this volume). The emphasis on the dissimilarities between the two texts makes sense because of the rarity from this time period of having a male and female hagiographer fashion the account of the same saint and the logical conclusion that a nun's interests in representing a religious woman's life would be different from that of a churchman. Yet together, these sacred biographies have a strategic cultural logic. Both hagiographers delineate the structure of their *vitae*. For Fortunatus, Radegund's spiritual journey begins with fasting and ends with torment.[9] Her spiritual practice is all about embodiment. Baudonivia's Radegund runs through her numinous paces, from the virtue of patience to the "incessant meditating on the law of God by night and by day."[10] Her religious style is that of disembodiment or moving away from the immersion in the body to becoming an empty receptacle only to be filled with sacred speech. In the first *Life*, the body is the vehicle for ascetic transformation, resulting in an assimilation to the cross of the crucifixion. In the second text, the *mens*, the rational element of the soul, bridles the body through the saint's metamorphosis into a vessel of liturgical language. The conversation between *corpus* and *mens* is logically thought out and imagined as a balance between embodiment and its counterbalance disembodiment rather than an antagonistic duality.

Like the visual representation of Merovingian Jesus, which fluctuated depending on where the savior resided spatially and theologically, Radegund's story reverberated from the luxurious spaces of Merovingian feasting halls only to bounce back to the penitential ground of a private oratory. Her royal biography unfolded in a frigid bed at the center of a loveless marriage to a violent Merovingian king, who was responsible for the murder of her male relatives, only then to shift direction to the cold, hard floor of a palace latrine, where the prostrate queen set her soul on fire through mental contemplation of the celestial bridegroom. The ascetic imagery in the sacred biography jolts the reader to this day: the aristocratic saint carried with aplomb basins full of human dung or red-hot coals that scorched her bare hands. Her self-denial was an asceticism of the "guts," a spirituality centered on the deep innards (*viscera*) of the human body where Jesus was hidden from view or could be located in the foul flux erupting out of the bodies of demoniacs, after they had confronted the invisible power of the saint (Moreira 2010, p. 80). Radegund's spiritual prowess was so intense that she could free prisoners from their bondage by miraculously fracturing their chains and do so at a distance or order even the Devil himself to lay prostrate on the ground. He obeyed.[11]

The geographical range of the royal holy woman is as impressive as her wonderworking abilities. Radegund possessed political, spiritual, and economic authority around Tours and Poitiers, occupying both ascetic space and the urbane world of the late Roman villa. She had connections in the Byzantine court at Constantinople. She used her alliances to influence sacred affairs in the Holy Land and Jerusalem, the site of Jesus' passion and crucifixion, to which the holy woman had a strong, theatrical attachment (Schulenburg 1998, p. 394). She was a consummate collector of Christian antiquities, whether in the form of the body parts of Gallo-Roman confessors or late-Roman martyrs. The female hagiographer Baudonivia informs her audience that Radegund's command over the cult of the holy dead encompassed the globe, East, West, North, and South. A case in point is her success in obtaining the right little finger of the Cappadocian martyr, Mammes, from Jerusalem, a relic empowering the right hand of the female saint. Radegund protected the inviolability of her monastery at Poitiers by making the sign of the cross with her right hand, thereby vanquishing 1,000 demons standing on the wall surrounding her community and threatening the chaste women inside.[12]

Radegund also hunted down the instruments of the passion, including a fragment of the Holy Cross (Hahn 2006). As previous chapters have shown, the queen is most famous for her ability to deploy her political network in the Byzantine East to extract a fragment of the relic of the cross for her monastic community in Poitiers, an ascetic fortress built right into the ancient fabric of the old Roman fortified walls of the city with their attached towers (Brennan 1985, p. 343; Moreira 1993, p. 286). During key ceremonial events, the queen's nuns stood watch atop the Roman battlements and inhabited their towers, a public enactment of the female community's commitment to defending their bodies' margins from assault and maintaining their virginity.[13] Radegund's sister ascetics were not unlike the Levites in scripture who kept the night watch on the Temple walls. Radegund set a model for all of the women in her community of being the jailors of their own bodies and keeping the watch over their flesh through long night vigils, a key feature of Merovingian religious practice during high holy days (Hen 1995, pp. 64–65). In spite of all these amazing deeds and far-reaching fame, Radegund was, according to a poem written by Venantius Fortunatus, a "woman not known in any place" (*nullis femina nota locis*) chasing an absent spouse, whom she will never hold in her arms (Smith 2009, p. 315).[14]

RADEGUND AND THE ABSENT JESUS

Radegund's relationship with Jesus was based on a series of absences. She strove to be absent from the embrace of an earthly husband but burned with desire for an invisible savior. She mourned for an absent homeland and the faraway dead body of an assassinated brother, whose freezing bowels could not be warmed by his sister's hot tears (George 1992, pp. 164–165).[15] Absent the ability to live in biblical time, Radegund peopled her table with Jesus' preferred company in the gospels' convivial scenes: the poor, the diseased, women, and lepers, thereby setting intensely visual tableaux (Effros 2002b, pp. 47–52). Continuing the historical trajectory, Radegund was a martyr in an age absent martyrdom.[16] The goal of her intense brand of asceticism, characterized by burning the flesh in order to cool the fever of her spirit, was to erase the "self," the ultimate form of absence, in preparation for receiving her celestial bridegroom. Her life in the monastery at Poitiers fluctuated between her visible presence in full view of her ascetic sisters and her Lenten retreats to a private cell where her body and its spiritual practices would be scrutinized by the panoptic deity alone (Brooks Hedstrom 2009). Absence, too, framed the hagiographical conversation about religious authority in the holy woman's *vitae*. Barred from being a priest, though reportedly consecrated as a deacon, the powerful holy woman adopted liturgical or paraliturgical activities as a personal style, a number of which echo Christly, priestly, and episcopal actions: anointing, preaching, blessing, exorcizing, relic-collecting, and organizing public processions. These actions challenged the authority of the bishop of Poitiers, Maroveus, who is largely an absent and ineffectual figure in Radegund's hagiographical corpus. Absence as a central hagiographical theme enables the holy woman to foreground her access to biblical power.

Absence haunted by Jesus is also a central theme in the literary triangulation among the poet Fortunatus, the ascetic Radegund, and the abbess of the monastery at Poitiers, Agnes. The three Christians exchanged multiple letters, lines of verse, and gifts, and did so within the recondite form of late-Roman epistolary culture closely associated with the opulent world of the rural villa (on letters, see Gillett, Chapter 25, this volume). And yet, these epistles were letters of distance, substitutions for the absent body of the sender, such as the male author, Fortunatus, whose ability to infiltrate the bounded precincts of the ascetic women's urban compound was limited, but whose virtual presence was made manifest through the nuns reading aloud his works or meditating on their meaning in private (Roberts 2009, pp. 284–285). Poetry in particular was an excellent substitution for the male body, even that of the human savior. During excruciating bouts of penance in a narrow cell, an exhausted Radegund dropped to the hard floor fast asleep only to receive an unexpected visitor, Jesus, who laid down beside her to provide comfort in an intimate way.[17] The poet Fortunatus unpredictably scripted Radegund in this mode and did so as a spiritual voyeur who, like the panoptic deity, was then given full access to the most hidden moments of the female ascetic's life. The religious intimacy shared between Radegund and her embodied savior, and, by extension, the male poet, is also a feature of the holy woman's hagiography (Moreira 2000, p. 193). This intimacy takes on multiple forms, all of which play off of this theme of absence. Jesus may be the "invisible or deathless bridegroom" inhabiting the cosmological spaces of the heavens, but Radegund brings the savior down to earth: Jesus inhabits her bowels; Jesus lives in her breast; Jesus is the food filling up her belly withered by fasting; Jesus is the object of her focused mind; Jesus' body dwells within her.[18] At one point, Radegund clings to Jesus' feet as if her savior were physically present.[19] Radegund's entry into Poitiers where she would go on to establish her monastery is presented in Baudonivia's life as a wedding scene in which the earthbound bride opened her body up to a heavenly spouse, who then dwelt within her. Absent the physical body of Jesus, Radegund brought to her nuns a relic of the saving wood made precious by the touch of his holy flesh.

The attention paid in these poetic and hagiographical texts to imagining an invisible Jesus as being physically present or even embodied within the interior spaces of the pious offers another way to analyze the works under consideration here. What is incompletely etched into the stone of the Moselkern Stele—that is, the possibility of religious intimacy with a human savior—is made manifest in Radegund's life and in her relic of the True Cross. In a manner of speaking, Radegund is a saintly action figure, who bridges the divide between a distant deity, such as the cosmological Christ depicted on the Moselkern Stele, and the human votary, who takes Jesus into the body. Radegund's ascetic story, penned in verse and in hagiographical prose, demands spectators—a reading audience, a hearing audience, and even a visual audience considering the dramatically staged scenes in her *vitae* which could be conjured up through the art of meditation. Radegund's corporeal acts instruct audiences in how to embody the second person of the Trinity through a life of expunging the self. Similarly, the evangelist John in the *Book of Kells* visually induces viewers to move through his body to access the hidden Crucified One. As Baudonivia sees it, once Radegund had entered her monastery in Poitiers, "she felt that Christ had come to dwell within her."[20] And even as a creature of this earth, Radegund's "flesh remained in the world. Her spirit was already in heaven,"[21] a transcendent condition highlighting the porous nature of the boundary separating the Merovingians and their seemingly remote deity.

RADEGUND AND THE TORTURED JESUS

Radegund's experiments with the flesh are notorious among scholarly circles devoted to the study of Christian asceticism. Indeed, her self-mortification is off the charts within the larger context of Merovingian hagiography (Kitchen 1998, p. 117). At one point during her Lenten ascetic rituals, Radegund fettered her head and arms with an iron yoke complete with chains that could be tightened to intensify the pain. After her fast had ended and the iron was taken off, the saint's bleeding upper torso was cut on the back and front sides.[22] In some ways, Fortunatus was a pioneer in writing the history of asceticism, coining the term *self-torturer*, or *tortrix*, a feminine noun derived from the classical Latin verb *torqueo*, "to torture."

The most spectacular ascetic event in the life of Radegund appears in Fortunatus's *vita* and is part of the male hagiographer's prurient interest in the female body, whether that body be vexed by foul fluxes, made unclean through leprosy, or scarred and burnt through ascetic practice. During Lent, Fortunatus writes, Radegund absented herself from her community and occupied a small cell (*cellula*), where she engaged in desert-like penances, long vigils, fasts, and chants. The ascetic climax of Fortunatus's sacred biography occurs when Radegund retreats to her cell presumably during Lent and brands herself with the cross. The description is graphic and designed to shock. The saint commands unnamed attendants to fashion a brass plate (*lamina oricalca*) in Christ's sign (*in signo Christi*). Radegund alone performs the role of a pagan torturer of Christian martyr. Persecutors used fire to brutalize nubile bodies, such as that of the girl-martyr Agnes, the namesake of Radegund's spiritual daughter and abbess. (Trout 2015, pp. 149–152; Smith 2009, pp. 316–317). In the privacy of her little cell, Radegund heated the brass, pressed the plate directly onto her skin, especially in two spots, with her flesh totally melting (*tota carne decocta*).[23] Fortunatus is vague about the precise location of this wounding, telling his audience that Radegund applied the metal to the higher regions of her body. In so doing, the male hagiographer opens a meditative space to his audience to muse on the upper torso of the suffering female body and its nude flesh. The intimacy of the private ascetic cell grants Fortunatus's audience the godlike power of seeing the saint in action as she maps the history of Christian martyrdom onto her tortured flesh.

The fire imagery is as gripping as the sacred voyeurism. The hagiographer discloses the religious logic behind burning: the saint consumes her flesh to temper her fiery spirit, thereby restoring the balance between these two key parts of a Christian identity. The verb used for the ascetic practice of cooling the spirit, *refrigero*, is an ancient Christian martyr's term associated with paradise. Burning the flesh in this world leads to celestial cooling in the next. The fleshly details in Fortunatus's life are unembellished. Radegund roasts her flesh through and through, imposing stiff penances on the body to scrape it raw as if she were a piece of fresh vellum awaiting the scribal razor to strip her clean of imperfections (Carruthers 1998, pp. 127—128). To intensify the sensation of being scraped clean, Radegund dons a hair shirt over her battered limbs, bruised and blistering from the fiery assault and violated yet again by the bristles of the animal hair. Another ascetic rationale follows: the saint torments her body to brace her quivering flesh for worse pain to follow, echoing the scourging of the passion in advance of the crucifixion. The hagiographer again fetishizes the female body in pain. Radegund exposes her tortures to the audience's gaze, who are expected to summon up before their eyes the brutality being conducted in the little cell and the damage done to the saint's sizzling skin: furrows (*fossae*) carved into the queen's flesh accompanied by two holes (*foramina*).[24] Radegund tries to conceal the holes, but the fact that they oozed blood made them possible to detect. According to Fortunatus, Radegund's voice divulges no hint of the suffering she had inflicted on her flesh; yet the body betrays her with its bloody eruptions from the two holes.

Once the saint ends this Lenten ritual, she immediately goes on to heal a blind woman with the sign of the cross. The timing is not coincidental. Through self-torture, Radegund metamorphoses into the cross, which now is burned into her skin. Fortunatus reads the history of the church and its missionary movement onto Radegund's tortured flesh, from the crucifixion of Jesus on the cross to the execution of martyrs in the arena. As the hagiographer remarks, Radegund's anguish is only a precursor to the greater pain to come. Her body assimilates itself to that of the crucified Jesus. As with the sculptured image of the two thieves in the Hypogée des Dunes, who display their pierced feet to their audience as a memory prompt of Jesus' human suffering on earth, the bored holes into Radegund's upper-torso remind Merovingian Christians of the human body's ability to carry the story of the passion within its carnal frame and to serve as the conduit for Jesus' humanity here on earth. Embodiment negates absence and the "remoteness" of the deity.

Additionally, Radegund animates the story of the cross as recounted by Fortunatus in his liturgical hymn, *Crux benedicta* (van Tongeren 2000, pp. 246–248). A number of the verses in this poem stress Jesus' physicality, his bleeding, his suffering, and his humanity. Fortunatus pays particular attention to the bloody nails of the crucifixion and their ability to pierce the savior-body. Similarly, Fortunatus hones in on Radegund's bleeding *foramina*, "holes," somewhat hidden but also open to the viewer's gaze. Their location is obscure; their inscription onto the human body is different because they are the result of branding with the cross and not being nailed to its wood. Radegund's "holes" are objects of meditation, sites on her holy body singled out for Christians to contemplate. These holes are also circumlocutions for the wounds of the crucifixion, part of a larger Merovingian strategy of "hide-and-seek" theology, in which the audience must tease out the invisible human savior through literary clues encoded into texts and engraved onto the bodies of human actors. In his *Life* of Radegund of Poitiers, the poet Venantius Fortunatus confronts his Merovingian audience with a female protagonist perilously close to *becoming* the crucified Jesus.

RADEGUND AND THE LIGHT-BEARING JESUS

Radegund's life sets a context for the light imagery in the fascinating Niederdollendorf Stele. As noted earlier, the cosmic figure carved into the stone has clear associations with the imperial sun cult of late antiquity, a religious phenomenon known in Germania. In addition to exhibiting the wounded body of the human savior analyzed earlier, Radegund's life also embodies the late ancient Christian chant, the *Exultet*. The *Exultet* was performed by deacons during the ritual of lighting the paschal candle, a climax of the Easter vigil and a liturgical ritual known in Merovingian lands (Palazzo 2008, p. 483; Kelly 1996, pp. 50–53). The *Exultet* centers its elegant verses on a series of dualities: hot/cold, day/night, sin/innocence, defeat/triumph, death/resurrection. In the *Exultet*, Christ appears as a candle, a liturgical object, and as the fiery pillar lighting the way through the darkness for the children of Israel as they make their pilgrimage back to the promised land (Exodus 13.21). Scholars of eastern hagiography have noted the ability of ascetic bodies to transmute into liturgical objects, such as a Syrian stylite metamorphosing into a censor emitting the sweet smells of paradise (Harvey 2006, p. 203). In Radegund's life, the royal ascetic becomes the paschal candle, a liturgical lantern, featured in the *Exultet*, a fitting role considering her (reported) status as a deacon.

Fortunatus's *Life* of Radegund contains a passage in which the saint makes candles with her own hands. She intends these candles to adorn oratories and sacred places where they would burn all night long, clear substitutions for Radegund's own body in perpetual prayer. Moving further into the *vita*, the reader discovers a fascinating little history of the Merovingian candle. In order to cure a young nun (*monacha*) who was suffering from chills and who could find no relief from the numerous medicines dispensed to her, a candle measuring the same height as the sick girl takes the place of a doctor. At the hour when the feverish chills typically overcame her, the nun lit the candle and grasped it—the candle's heat dispelled the disease from her body. This ritual was carried out in Radegund's name. Moreover, Christians suffering from ailments would bring candles to the saint's residence, depositing them with her servants. Once these candles were lit, they killed the diseases afflicting the pious. Impressively, Radegund's connection with candles intensifies to the degree where simply lighting a candle in her name could eradicate pustules and drive out fevers. A final candle narrative appears in Baudonivia's account of Radegund's funeral.[25] As in Gregory of Tours's story of the kinetic tombs miraculously projecting themselves out of the ground and onto the space of the living, candles surrounding Radegund's open grave take an active part in her burial. One of the candles leaps out of the hand of a servant and lies down obediently at the foot of Radegund's tomb. This particular candle solved a ritual dispute occurring above ground about whether candles should go outside the tomb or reside for eternity inside with the dead saint. Clearly, candles function as ritual substitutions for the bodies of the semi-free domestics who metaphorically will be buried with their *domina*. Equally true is the ability of a candle to stand in for the body of the saint during the healing process and, by extension, the body of Christ.

Radegund is a light-bearing saint; her austerities usher in brightness, sight, Easter, fertility, and resurrection. In Fortunatus's verse, Radegund's claustration in her narrow cell during Lent ends at Easter, when the saint reappears among her cohort of female ascetics as a "double-light" returning after a dark period of self-torture and metaphorical crucifixion (Roberts 2009, p. 289). In this sense, Radegund's cell, like the crypt of Abbot Mellobaudes, is a symbolic re-creation of Christ's tomb. The returning Radegund brings light, fertility, and the promise of resurrection with her, powers captured in one hagiographical vignette where she "greens up" a dying laurel tree outside of her cell parallel to the way Gregory of Tours describes the "greening up" of the crown of thorns in Jerusalem each day (Squatriti 2013, p. 38). The connection between light and Easter is made equally clear in Gregory's *Glory of the Martyrs*, where the hagiographer recounts an incident that occurred during Eastertime in Radegund's monastery at Poitiers. On Good Friday, the most solemn day of the liturgical year, the nuns were keeping the night vigil in the dark. Suddenly a spark of light stood before the altar of the gloomy oratory. The ember began to engulf the space, shooting off rays of light in multiple directions, raising itself up to the height of the sacred space, and offering solace to the nuns during the darkest day of the liturgical year.[26] Clearly this beacon of light was the resurrected body of Jesus welcomed into Radegund's space through the agency of the relic of the Holy Cross she had successfully brought back to Poitiers from the Holy Land.

This scene in Gregory of Tours's hagiographical text builds on imagery from the ancient Christian prayer, the *Exultet*.[27] The spark entering the oratory of the monastery at Poitiers is the "column of fire" that "purged the shadows of sin."[28] As the *Exultet* clarifies: "The flame which though it may be divided into parts, yet knows no diminution of the divided flame."[29] According to the *Exultet*, the night of Good Friday is as dazzling as the day, a formerly ominous time now possessing sanctifying power. The *Exultet* connects the events of Easter to the delivery of Israelites from bondage in Egypt, led through the Red Sea by the pillar of light to emerge on the other side dry and unharmed. The light also releases Christians from the misery of sin and is witness to Christ's triumph over death and his ascent from the underworld (on the afterlife, see Moreira, Chapter 42, this volume). In the *Exultet*, Christ is the candle, the pillar of fire. He is the Morning Star (*lucifer matutinus*) that never sets. The candle, a metonymy for Christ's body, is a sacrifice, an offering to the godhead. The salvific candle is "nourished by the melting waxes which mother bee fashioned into the substance of this precious lamp."[30] In her hagiographical and poetic portrait, Radegund is the mother bee who builds the torch (Christ). Wax itself is a metaphor for the purity of the female body. The *Exultet* offers testimony: "O truly marvelous bee, whose sex is not violated by the male, nor shattered by childbearing, neither do children destroy her chastity."[31] Radegund is the chaste, learned bee who draws honey from the *florilegia* of scripture and the church fathers (Brennan 1985, p. 342).[32] She is the fashioner of liturgical candles who herself symbolically transmutes into one. Like Christ, she is the victim of (self-) torture and the bearer of Easter light. Her corporeal purity is signified by fire and the wax of the candle. The imaginative ways in which Fortunatus builds on the liturgy to create an image of Radegund as a liturgical object demonstrates the dynamic nature of Merovingian hagiography (Kreiner 2014, p. 17).

The incorporation of the *Exultet* into the life of Radegund unveils yet another context for reading the Christ of the Niederdollendorf Stele. As in the ancient prayer *Exultet*, the cosmic figure incised into the funerary rock squares with the hymn's imagery of the "Morning Star," "column of fire," "fire divided into many flames," "lights of heaven," and "torch so precious." This spectacular sculpture captures the power of the light-bearing deity to dispel the dominion of darkness and to thwart the sinister shadows of the night. And yet his cosmic figure does so through the agency of the hidden cross, the sacrifice imagined in the *Exultet* as the "solemn offering" of a candle, fashioned by the pure hands of the pious servant (Radegund) and existing as a metonymy for the crucified body, which remains invisible in the Niederdollendorf Stele but haunts its imagery of militant triumph over the realm of death.

MEDITATING ON MEROVINGIAN JESUS

The Moselkern Stele offers the perfect way to close these meditations on Merovingian Jesus. The monument captivates (Fig. 46.1). In fact, the organic quality of the artwork is so intricate that only a brief glance at its contours may cause any spectator, early medieval or contemporary, to miss a great deal of the meaning. The artist(s) who sculpted the memorial expected the audience to be an active one because the stele

FIGURE 46.14. Detail, "Little Christ," Moselkern Stele (seventh century), Rheinisches LandesMuseum, Bonn, Germany. Courtesy of photographer Jürgen Vogel, LVR-LandesMuseum Bonn.

compels its viewers to circle around it even to this day. Perhaps Merovingian Christians circumambulated the stonework during festival occasions. The three-dimensional quality of the funerary *memoria,* coupled with the transparency of its design, intensify the feeling that the deity at the top sporting a cross-nimbus is about to project himself out at the viewer. His stance is somewhat threatening. More importantly, there appears to be yet another crucified figure on the monument in addition to the Christ featured at the top. Archaeologist Sebastian Ristow has theorized that the lower half of the Christ figure, with its stunted legs, is actually the body of a smaller crucified man carved in low relief and signposted by the huge hands of the larger male image, almost as if the big Christ is holding up little Christ (Fig. 46.14). Rather than hilts of swords adorned with crosses and pointing inwards toward the productive center of the deity, it is possible that these crosses are extensions of the spread-out arms of the little Christ (Ristow 2007, p. 177).

Both readings are fascinating and underscore the difficulty of interpreting this grainy rock. The first scheme accords with a great deal of scholarship on the Moselkern Stele—the sculpture promotes a militaristic, heroic, remote, and cosmic figure of Christ; the second supports the hypothesis of this chapter. Jesus' humanity is something to be seined from an ocean of divinity, and his body operates a portal to the next world. The stele confronts its observer with the cosmological godhead at the top. At the level of human guts, however, a second victim of the cross, smaller in scale and certainly less in control of the iconography, is spread out, his arms and legs stretching to their maximum capacity. The ensemble together creates a Trinity of images—an anthropomorphic cross (bottom); Jesus crucified (center); and the godhead (top). The three crosses surrounding Christ's head and forming a nimbus accentuate this Trinitarian reading. Is this a Merovingian version of the Book of Kells's "embodied savior" (Fig. 46.3)? If there is indeed a second crucified figure being held up and framed by the larger, more cosmo-logical image, then the stele is an excellent example of Merovingian Christianity as a religion of embodiment in which human actors, including the savior, function as entry-ways to the divine. Like Radegund of Poitiers, who carries Jesus within her womb (Brown 2003, p. 230), the Moselkern Stele visualizes the embodied savior. If we imagine Radegund as a spectator of the Moselkern Stele, then we have captured the thesis of this chapter. Merovingian Christianity was built upon a triangulation among godhead, embodied savior, and human actor, whose spiritual fluidity vacillated between heights of divinity and depths of tortured humanity. The latter was always present in the former, just as it is in the Moselkern Stele, but as this chapter has shown, the human side of the Dark Age deity was a tough, interactive puzzle to be solved by the pious (Coon 2016).

NOTES

1. The three Merovingian sculpted works featured in this chapter are as follows: (1) Hypogée des Dunes = Frankish funerary crypt, second quarter of the eighth century; Poitiers. (2) Moselkern Stele = Frankish memorial, late seventh century; Bonn, LVR_Rheinisches LandesMuseum. (3) Niederdollendorf Stele = Frankish memorial, late seventh cen-tury; Bonn, LVR-Rheinisches LandesMuseum. McClendon 2005, Morris 2005, Sapin 2003, Crook 2000, Wood 1999, Heitz 1975, Grabar 1974, and Elbern 1961, have analyzed the archi-tecture and iconography of the Hypogée des Dunes. Sarti 2013, Halsall 2010, Ristow 2007, Berg 2005, Effros 2002a, Schutz 2001, and Elbern 1955, have discussed the religious and social contexts of the Moselkern Stele. For the funerary and martial culture of the Niederdollendorf Stele, see Sarti 2013, Halsall 2010, Effros 2002a, Schutz 2001, and Heitz 1987.
2. Gregory of Tours, *Life of the Fathers* 2. Translation in James 1988, p. 35.
3. Fortunatus, *Life of Radegund* 11. Translation in McNamara, Halborg, and Whatley 1992, p. 74.
4. Gregory of Tours, *Glory of the Martyrs* 5–6. Translation in Van Dam 1988, pp. 22–27.
5. Tertullian, *De spectaculis* 8, 29. Translation in Glover 1931, pp. 251–255, 295.–297.
6. The mandorla most likely originated in the *imago clipeata*, an ancient Roman iconography centered on surrounding the figures of emperors with circular, diamond, or oval-like frames. Mandorlas are associated with light imagery and cosmic forces. For a history of this iconographic style, see Andreopoulos 2005, pp. 83–96.
7. Gregory of Tours, *Glory of the Confessors* 51. Translation in Van Dam 1988, p. 60.
8. For more on Radegund's life, see James, Chapter 11; Gillett, Chapter 25; Diem, Chapter 15; Bailey, Chapter 44; Sarti, Chapter 12; Halsall, Chapter 8; and Moreira, Chapter 42, this volume.
9. Fortunatus, *Life of Radegund* 21.
10. Baudonivia, *Life of Radegund* 8. Translation in McNamara, Halborg, and Whatley 1992, p. 91.
11. Fortunatus, *Life of Radegund* 11, 30.
12. Baudonivia, *Life of Radegund* 18.
13. Baudonivia, *Life of Radegund* 24.
14. Fortunatus, *Carmen* 8.232: "nullis femina nota locis"; *Carmen* 8.229–230: "Sponso absente manens tam dura cubilia servo/nec mea quem cupiunt membra tenere queunt"; French translation in Reydellet 1998, 2, p. 139.
15. Fortunatus, *On the Thuringian War* 137–138. Translation in McNamara, Halborg, and Whatley 1992, p. 69.

16. Fortunatus, *Life of Radegund* 2.
17. Fortunatus, *Carmen* 8.253–254.
18. Fortunatus, *Life of Radegund* 1 ("in quarum visceribus"); Baudonivia, *Life of Radegund* 2 ("Christum in pectore gestans"); Fortunatus, *Life of Radegund* 6 ("Christus tota refectio et tota fames erat in Christo"); Baudonivia, *Life of Radegund* 2 ("mens intenta ad Christum"); Baudonivia, *Life of Radegund*, 5 ("Christum in se habitatorem esse sentiret").
19. Fortunatus, *Life of Radegund* 6.
20. Baudonivia, *Life of Radegund* 5; Translation in McNamara, Halborg, and Whatley 1992, p. 89.
21. Fortunatus, *Life of Radegund* 36; Translation in McNamara, Halborg, and Whatley 1992, p. 84.
22. Fortunatus, *Life of Radegund* 25.
23. Fortunatus, *Life of Radegund* 26.
24. Fortunatus, *Life of Radegund* 26.
25. Baudonivia, *Life of Radegund* 25.
26. Gregory of Tours, *Glory of the Martyrs* 5.
27. For the Latin text of the Franco-Roman version of the *Exultet* with an English translation, see Kelly 1996, pp. 36–40.
28. "Hec igitur nox est que peccatorum tenebras/columne illuminatione purgavit." Latin text and English translation in Kelly, p. 36.
29. "Qui licet sit divisus in partes/mutuati tamen luminis detrimenta non novit." Latin text and English translation in Kelly, p. 37.
30. "Alitur liquantibus ceris/quam in substantiam pretiose huius lampadis apes mater eduxit." Latin text and English translation in Kelly, p. 38.
31. "O vere mirabilis apis cuius nec sexum masculi violant/fetus non quassat nec filii destruunt castitatem." Latin text and English translation in Kelly, p. 38.
32. Baudonivia, *Life of Radegund* 9.

WORKS CITED

Ancient Sources

Baudonivia, *Life of Radegund*. B. Krusch (ed.). (1888). *Fredegarii et aliorum chronica. Vitae sanctorum* (pp. 377–395). MGH SRM 2. Hanover: Impensis Bibliopolii Hahniani.

Baudonivia, *Life of Radegund*. J. A. McNamara, J. E. Halborg, and E. G. Whatley (trans.).(1992). *Sainted Women of the Dark Ages* (pp. 86–105). Durham, NC: Duke University Press.

Damasus, *Epigrams*. A. Ferrua (ed.). (1942). *Epigrammata damasiana*. Vatican City: Pontificio Istituto di Archeologia Cristiana.

Damasus, *Epigrams*. D. Trout (trans.). (2015). *Damasus of Rome: The Epigraphic Poetry*. Oxford: Oxford University Press.

Exultet. T. F. Kelly (ed. and trans.). (1996). *The Exultet in Southern Italy* (pp. 32–40). Oxford: Oxford University Press.

Gregory of Tours, *Glory of the Confessors*. B. Krusch (ed.). (1885). *Gregorii episcopi Turonensis Miracula et Opera minora* (pp. 297–370). MGH SRM 1.2. Hanover: Impensis Bibliopolii Hahniani.

Gregory of Tours, *Glory of the Confessors*. R. Van Dam (trans.). (1988). *Gregory of Tours: Glory of the Confessors*. Translated Texts for Historians 4. Liverpool: Liverpool University Press.

Gregory of Tours, *Glory of the Martyrs*. B. Krusch (ed.). (1885). *Gregorii episcopi Turonensis Miracula et Opera minora* (pp. 37–111). MGH SRM 1.2. Hanover: Impensis Bibliopolii Hahniani.

Gregory of Tours, *Glory of the Martyrs*. R. Van Dam (trans.). (1988). *Gregory of Tours: Glory of the Martyrs*. Translated Texts for Historians 2. Liverpool: Liverpool University Press.

Gregory of Tours, *Life of the Fathers*. B. Krusch (ed.). (1885). *Gregorii episcopi Turonensis Miracula et Opera minora* (pp. 211–294). MGH SRM 1.2. Hanover: Impensis Bibliopolii Hahniani.

Gregory of Tours, *Life of the Fathers*. E. James (ed.). (1988). *Gregory of Tours: Life of the Fathers*. Translated Texts for Historians 1. Liverpool: Liverpool University Press.

Tertullian, *On Spectacles*. T. R. Glover (ed. and trans.). (1931). *Apology. De Spectaculis. Minucius Felix: Octavius* (pp. 230–301). Loeb Classical Library 250. Cambridge, MA: Harvard University Press.

Venantius Fortunatus, *Life of Radegund*. B. Krusch (ed.). (1888). *Fredegarii et aliorum chronica. Vitae sanctorum* (pp. 364–377). MGH SRM 2. Hanover: Impensis Bibliopolii Hahniani.

Venantius Fortunatus, *Life of Radegund*. J. A. McNamara, J. E. Halborg, and E. G. Whatley (trans.). (1992). *Sainted Women of the Dark Ages* (pp. 70–86). Durham, NC: Duke University Press.

Venantius Fortunatus, *On the Thuringian War*. F. Leo (ed.) (1881). *Venanti Honori Clementiani Fortunati presbyteri Italici opera poetica* (pp. 271–275). MGH AA 4.1. Berlin: Weidmann.

Venantius Fortunatus, *On the Thuringian War*. J. A. McNamara, J. E. Halborg, and E. G. Whatley (eds.). (1992). *Sainted Women of the Dark Ages* (pp. 65–70). Durham, NC: Duke University Press.

Venantius Fortunatus, *Poems*. M. Reydellet and M. (ed. and trans.) (1998[1994]). *Venance Fortunat Poèmes*, 2 vols. Paris: Les Belles Lettres.

Modern Sources

Andreopoulos, A. (2005). *Metamorphosis: The Transfiguration in Byzantine Theology and Iconography*. Crestwood, NY: St. Vladimir's Seminary Press.

Bergmann, B. (2008). "Pictorial Narratives of the Roman Circus." In J. Nelis-Clément and J. Roddaz (eds.), *Le cirque romain et son image* (pp. 361–391). Bordeaux: Ausonius.

Brennan, B. (1985). "St. Radegund and the Early Development of Her Cult at Poitiers." *Journal of Religious History* 13: 340–354.

Brooks Hedstrom, D. L. (2009). "The Geography of the Monastic Cell in Early Egyptian Monastic Literature." *Church History* 78: 756–791.

Brown, P. (2003). *Rise of Western Christendom: Triumph and Diversity*. Rev. ed. Oxford: Blackwell.

Carruthers, M. (1998). *The Craft of Thought: Meditation, Rhetoric, and the Making of Images 400–1200*. Cambridge: Cambridge University Press.

Coon, L. (2016). "Gendering Dark Age Jesus." *Gender and History* 28: 8–33.

Crook, J. (2000). *The Architectural Setting of the Cult of the Saints in the Early Christian West c. 300–c. 1200*. Oxford: Oxford University Press.

Dunbabin, K. M. D. (1982). "The Victorious Charioteer on Mosaics and Related Monuments." *American Journal of Archaeology* 86: 65–89.

Edsall, M. A. (2014). "The *Arma Christi* before the *Arma Christi*: Rhetorics of the Passion in Late Antiquity and the Early Middle Ages." In L. H. Cooper and A. Denny-Brown (eds.), *The Arma Christi in Medieval and Early Modern Material Culture* (pp. 21–51). Farnham: Ashgate.

Effros, B. (2002a). *Caring for Body and Soul: Burial and the Afterlife in the Merovingian World*. University Park: Pennsylvania State University Press.

Effros, B. (2002b). *Creating Community with Food and Drink in Merovingian Gaul*. New York: Palgrave.

Elbern, V. H. (1955). "Die Stele von Moselkern und die Ikonographie des frühen Mittelalters." *Bonner Jahrbücher des Rheinischen Landesmuseums in Bonn und des Vereins von Altertumsfreunden im Rheinlande* 1: 184–914.

Elbern, V. H. (1961). "Das Relief der Gekreuzigten in der Mellebaudis-Memorie zu Poitiers: Über eine vorkarolingische Nachbildung des heiligen Grabes zu Jerusalem." *Jahrbuch der Berliner Museen* 3: 148–189.

Ernst, U. (1991). *Carmen Figuratum: Geschichte des Figurengedichts von den antiken Ursprüngen bis zum Ausgang des Mittelalters*. Cologne: Böhlau.

Fraser, A. (1964). "The Cologne Circus Bowl: Basileus Helios and the Cosmic Hippodrome." In L. F. Sandler (ed.), *Essays in Memory of Karl Lehmann* (pp.105–113). New York: Institute of Fine Arts.

George, J. W. (1992). *Venantius Fortunatus: A Latin Poet in Merovingian Gaul*. Oxford: Oxford University Press.

Grabar, A. (1974). "Recherches sur les sculptures de l'Hypogée des Dunes, à Poitiers, et de la crypte Saint-Paul de Jouarre." *Journal des savants* 1: 3–43.

Hahn, C. J. (2006). "Collector and Saint: Queen Radegund and Devotion to the Relic of the True Cross." *Word and Image* 22: 268–274.

Halsall, G. (2010). *Cemeteries and Society in Merovingian Gaul*. Leiden: Brill.

Harvey, S. (2006). *Scenting Salvation: Ancient Christianity and the Olfactory Imagination*. Berkeley: University of California Press.

Heitz, C. (1975). "*Adoratio Crucis*: Remarques sur quelques crucifixions préromanes en Poitou." In *Études de civilization médiévale IXe–XIIe siècles: Mélanges offerts à Edmond-René Labande* (pp. 395–405). Poitiers: Centre d'études supérieures de civilisation médiévale.

Heitz, C. (1987). *La France Pré-Romane: Archéologie et architecture religieuse du Haut Moyen Âge IVe siècle—An Mille*. Paris: Éditions Errance.

Hen, Y. (1995). *Culture and Religion in Merovingian Gaul A.D. 481–751*. Leiden: Brill.

Kelly, T. F. (1996). *The Exultet in Southern Italy*. Oxford: Oxford University Press.

Kessler, H. L. (2007). "The Word Made Flesh in Early Decorated Bibles. In J. Spier (ed.), *Picturing the Bible: The Earliest Christian Art* (pp. 141–168). New Haven, CT: Yale University Press.

Kitchen, J. (1998). *Saints' Lives and the Rhetoric of Gender*. Oxford: Oxford University Press.

Klingshirn, W. E. (1994). *Caesarius of Arles: The Making of a Christian Community in Late Antique Gaul*. Cambridge: Cambridge University Press.

Kreiner, J. (2014). *The Social Life of Hagiography in the Merovingian Kingdom*. Cambridge: Cambridge University Press.

Kupfer, M. (2011). "The Cult of Images in Light of Pictorial Graffiti at Doué-la-Fontaine." *Early Medieval Europe* 19: 125–152.

Latham, J. A. (2016). *Performance, Memory, and Processions in Ancient Rome: The Pompa Circensis from the Late Republic to Late Antiquity*. Cambridge: Cambridge University Press.

McClendon, C. B. (2005). *The Origins of Medieval Architecture: Building in Europe, A.D. 600–900*. New Haven, CT: Yale University Press.

Meehan, B. (2012). *The Book of Kells*. London: Thames and Hudson.

Moreira, I. (1993). "Provisatrix optima: St. Radegund of Poitiers' Relic Petitions to the East." *Journal of Medieval History* 19: 285–305.

Moreira, I. (2000). *Dreams, Visions, and Spiritual Authority in Merovingian Gaul.* Ithaca, NY: Cornell University Press.

Moreira, I. (2010). *Heaven's Purge: Purgatory in Late Antiquity.* Oxford: Oxford University Press.

Morris, C. (2005). *The Sepulchre of Christ and the Medieval West: From the Beginning to 1600.* Oxford: Oxford University Press.

Palazzo, É. (2008). "Performing the Liturgy." In T. F. X. Noble and J. M. H. Smith (eds.), *The Cambridge History of Christianity: Early Medieval Christianities c. 600–c. 1100* (pp. 472–488). Cambridge: Cambridge University Press.

Peers, G. (2004). *Sacred Shock: Framing Visual Experience in Byzantium.* University Park: Pennsylvania State University Press.

Peers, G. (2012). "Object Relations: Theorizing the Late Antique Viewer." In S. F. Johnson (ed.), *The Oxford Handbook of Late Antiquity* (pp. 970–993). Oxford: Oxford University Press.

Ristow, S. (2007). *Frühes Christentum im Rheinland: Die Zeugnisse der archäologischen und historischen Quellen an Rhein, Maas, und Mosel.* Cologne: Rheinischer Verein für Denkmalpflege und Landschaftsschutz.

Roberts, M. (2009). *The Humblest Sparrow: The Poetry of Venantius Fortunatus.* Ann Arbor: University of Michigan Press.

Sapin, C. (2003). "Archéologie des premières cryptes du haut moyen âge en France." *Hortus Artium Medievalium* 9: 303–313.

Sarti, L. (2013). *Perceiving War and the Military in Early Christian Gaul, ca. 400–700 A.D.* Leiden: Brill.

Schulenburg, J. T. (1998). *Forgetful of Their Sex: Female Sanctity and Society, ca. 500–1100.* Chicago: University of Chicago Press.

Schutz, H. (2001). *Tools, Weapons and Ornaments: Germanic Material Culture in Pre-Carolingian Europe, 400–750.* Leiden: Brill.

Smith, J. M. H. (2009). "Radegundis peccatrix: Authorizations of Virginity in Late Antique Gaul." In P. Rousseau and M. Papoutsakis (eds.), *Transformations of Late Antiquity: Essays for Peter Brown* (pp. 303–326). Farnham: Ashgate.

Squatriti, P. (2013). *Landscape and Change in Early Medieval Italy: Chestnuts, Economy, and Culture.* Cambridge: Cambridge University Press.

Trout, D. (2015). *Damasus of Rome: The Epigraphic Poetry.* Oxford: Oxford University Press.

van Tongeren, L. (2000). *Exaltation of the Cross: Toward the Origins of the Feast of the Cross and the Meaning of the Cross in Early Medieval Liturgy.* Liturgia condenda 11. Louvain: Peeters.

von Berg, A. (2005). *Cochem-Zell: Landschaft an der Mosel.* Führer zu archäologischen Denkmälern in Deutschland 46. Stuttgart: Theiss.

Wood, I. (1999). "Images as a Substitution for Writing: A Reply." In E. Chrysos and I. Wood (eds.), *East and West: Modes of Communication. Proceedings of the First Plenary Conference at Merida* (pp. 35–46). Leiden: Brill.

Index